ISBN 978-1-5284-5560-2
PIBN 10924744

English
Français
Deutsche
Italiano
Español
Português

www.forgottenbooks.com

Mythology Photography **Fiction**
Fishing Christianity **Art** Cooking
Essays Buddhism Freemasonry
Medicine **Biology** Music **Ancient
Egypt** Evolution Carpentry Physics
Dance Geology **Mathematics** Fitness
Shakespeare **Folklore** Yoga Marketing
Confidence Immortality Biographies
Poetry **Psychology** Witchcraft
Electronics Chemistry History **Law**
Accounting **Philosophy** Anthropology
Alchemy Drama Quantum Mechanics
Atheism Sexual Health **Ancient History**
Entrepreneurship Languages Sport
Paleontology Needlework Islam
Metaphysics Investment Archaeology
Parenting Statistics Criminology
Motivational

THESE VOLUMES ARE INSCRIBED

TO THE MEMORY OF

NATHANIEL BACON

1802-1869

A PIONEER LAWYER AND JUDGE WHOSE LIFE AND INFLUENCE
COUNTED FOR MUCH IN THE SETTLEMENT OF
SOUTHWESTERN MICHIGAN

F. H. B.

PREFACE.

The first edition of "Benefit Societies and Life Insurance" was published in 1888. The beneficiary societies at that time were new and the courts were called upon to decide many questions for which few precedents could be found. The book received a flattering reception from the profession and the courts. The second edition appeared in 1894 in an enlarged form and a chapter on accident insurance was added. The third edition was in 1904 and all the cases up to that time were referred to.

While it was the aim of the author to make these various editions full and complete discussions of the law of life and accident insurance, an impression seemed to prevail, because of its title, that the book was devoted to a consideration only of the cases relating to the beneficiary societies, while the fact was that it was intended to cover that subject and life and accident insurance as well.

Twelve years have passed and the volume of litigation in this branch of the law has greatly increased. It has been deemed best in the new edition to make the title more indicative of its scope, and for that reason it is called "The Law of Life and Accident Insurance." The matter of the last edition of Benefit Societies has been retained, but the arrangement is different. Many new features, have been added and all the cases, both relating to life and accident insurance, as well as to beneficiary societies and voluntary associations, have been cited, bringing the discussion down to date.

The plan adopted in former editions of giving full extracts from the opinions of the courts has been adhered to and it is hoped that they will prove of service. The cases are cited with reference to the official reports, the National Reporter System, the Lawyers' Reports Annotated and Annotated Cases.

The author is grateful for the kind reception his work has received and trusts that this favor will be continued and that the profession will find this new edition both reliable and helpful.

FREDERICK H. BACON.

December 1, 1916.

PREFACE TO THIRD EDITION.

Ten years have passed since the publication of the second edition of this work. During this period more than three thousand cases, relating to principles herein considered, have been decided by appellate courts. These adjudications have not so much changed the law as they have added to it. It was necessary, therefore, that a new edition be prepared, incorporating all these cases. This has been done to the best of the ability of the author, who has given much time and thought to the work.

Where new features have been considered, free quotations have been made from the opinions, on the same general plan of previous editions, which seems to have met with the favor of the profession. An effort has been made to make all references accurate, having alone in view the practical use of the book by active practitioners. A large number of new sections have been added which have made clearer many of the principles of this branch of the law.

In addition to the law of voluntary and fraternal beneficiary associations the subjects of regular life and accident insurance have been carefully and exhaustively reviewed in all particulars, even more so than in former editions, so that in this respect the work will, it is believed, be found satisfactory.

The author is grateful for the kind appreciation his work has received from bench and bar, and trusts that this new edition will meet with continued confidence and favor.

FREDERICK H. BACON.

St. Louis, October, 1904.

PREFACE TO SECOND EDITION. ·

When the first edition of this work appeared the law of beneficiary insurance was in its infancy. During the six years that have elapsed since it publication numerous new decisions have been rendered, sometimes modifying or changing, but more frequently adding to, the principles there laid down. The importance of these new cases, as well in regard to life insurance proper, as beneficiary indemnity, or questions arising in cases involving the acts of voluntary associations, or clubs, imperatively demanded their incorporation in a new edition.

The text has therefore been carefully revised, incorporating all the cases bearing on the subjects herein treated of up to October 1, 1894. In this work of revision five hundred pages of new matter and twelve hundred cases not cited in the first edition have been added.

A chapter on accident insurance in all its phases has been included, as that branch of business has increased enormously during the last ten years.

The subject of regular life insurance was fully treated in the first edition and is now still more carefully and thoroughly considered. It is believed that all the cases on this subject decided by courts of last resort have been cited.

In the revision the plan of quoting liberally from the opinions of the courts has been adhered to because in this way the reasons for conclusions are shown, and the work gains an added value to those who either have not access to full law libraries, or wish to be relieved from the necessity of consulting the authorities cited. The conscientious effort has been made to be fair in all respects, giving the law as it is found in the adjudications of the courts, and to avoid, as far as possible, the expression of personal views. If the question has been decided differently by different courts the reasoning on both sides has been given, leaving the reader to decide which is most sound.

(ix)

The author desires to express his gratitude for the flattering and generous reception given his work by the profession and the many kind words spoken in its behalf. He hopes that the new edition will merit continued favor and success.

FREDERICK H. BACON.

St. Louis, October, 1894.

PREFACE TO FIRST EDITION.

The secret benevolent and beneficiary orders, or beneficiary societies, which are both social clubs and life insurance companies, have multiplied amazingly during the last twenty years. Branches of these organizations are now found in nearly every village in the land and in the larger cities lodges are numbered by scores and even hundreds. They have characteristics in common with ordinary clubs and the familiar fraternities, the Masons and Odd Fellows.

The litigation connected with these societies is novel and important. It embraces two classes of cases; the first involving the discipline of members and their personal liability for the community debts; the second includes the still more important questions relating to the rights of beneficiaries, the decision of which often requires an application of the principles of the law of life insurance. The numerous cases, decided during the last ten years, by the courts of last resort of the several States and the Federal courts, are not collected or discussed in any legal textbook, consequently they are unfamiliar to most lawyers, who do not realize their extent and value.

Cases that have arisen in my own practice have convinced me of the need of a treatise on the subject, one in which the rights and liabilities of members of the beneficiary orders and of their beneficiaries should be considered in close connection with the law of life insurance proper. This need I have tried to supply. The work covers the entire subject of life insurance and includes all cases decided up to date.

The extent to which I have succeeded must be determined by the profession. Although I make public the results of my labors with diffidence, I am content to do so without apology other than this brief explanation. My work must speak for itself—its value must be measured by the merit its use may develop, its faults could not be lessened or excused by anything I here might say.

I have generally cited the cases, in addition to a reference to the regular reports, by the volume or page of the American Decisions,

American Reports and the National and Co-operative Systems of Reporters, if re-reported. I have not, however, given all of these references each time the case is referred to. The full citations may be found by consulting the table of cases which follows the text.

I wish to here acknowledge my obligations to P. Wm. Provenchere, Esq., of the St. Louis Bar, who carefully read the work in manuscript and materially aided me with valuable suggestions.

• FREDERICK H. BACON.

St. Louis, October, 1888.

TABLE OF CONTENTS

[REFERENCES ARE TO PAGES]

CHAPTER I.

INTRODUCTORY.

SCOPE OF WORK, CLASSES OF LIFE AND ACCIDENT INSURANCE ORGANIZATIONS—
HISTORY AND GROWTH OF FRATERNAL BENEFICIARY SOCIETIES—
LIFE AND ACCIDENT COMPANIES—DEFINITIONS.

LIFE AND ACCIDENT INSURANCE.

xiv

CHAPTER III.

GOVERNMENT AND MEMBERSHIP, BY-LAWS.

CHAPTER IV.

OFFICERS AND AGENTS.

CHAPTER V.

NATURE AND SUBJECT-MATTER OF CONTRACT—AFTER ENACTED LAWS OF
BENEFIT SOCIETIES.

CHAPTER VI.

Application, Warranty, Representation and Concealment.

· CHAPTER VII.

INSURABLE INTEREST—DESIGNATION OF BENEFICIARY.

CHAPTER VIII.

CONSUMMATION OF CONTRACT—INCOMPLETE CONTRACTS—JURISDICTION OF EQUITY TO REFORM OR CANCEL.

CHAPTER IX.

ASSIGNMENT—CHANGE OF BENEFICIARY.

CHAPTER X.

CONDITIONS WHICH AVOID THE RIGHT—SUICIDE—INTEMPERANCE, ETC.

LIFE AND ACCIDENT INSURANCE.

CHAPTER XI.

PREMIUM, ASSESSMENTS AND DUES.

xxvi

CHAPTER XII.

ACCIDENT INSURANCE.

CHARACTERISTICS OF CONTRACT—DEFINITION OF ACCIDENT—LIMITATIONS—
PROXIMATE CAUSE—EXCEPTED RISKS.

CHAPTER XIII.

Accident Insurance—Continued.

Excepted Risks—Suicide—Intentional Injuries—Disability—Conditions to Be Performed After Loss.

CHAPTER XIV.

Maturity of Contract—Proofs of Loss.

THE LAW

OF

LIFE AND ACCIDENT INSURANCE

Benefit Societies and Voluntary Associations

CHAPTER I.

INTRODUCTORY.

SCOPE OF WORK, CLASSES OF LIFE AND ACCIDENT INSURANCE ORGANIZATIONS
—HISTORY AND GROWTH OF FRATERNAL BENEFICIARY SOCIETIES
—LIFE AND ACCIDENT COMPANIES—DEFINITIONS.

have a supreme value. The direct contribution of insurance to civilization is made not in visible wealth but in the intangible and immeasurable forces of character upon which civilization itself is founded. It is pre-eminently a modern institution. 'It has done more than all gifts of impulsive charity to foster a sense of human brotherhood and of common interests.' "

§ 4. **Definitions of Life Insurance.**—The definitions of life insurance are numerous, but they do not differ except in the form of expression. Without attempting to coin a new one we will refer to some given by the English courts and then state that which now is most approved in the United States. In the great case of Dalby v. India and London Life Assurance Company,[2] in explaining the difference between the contract of life assurance and that of fire or marine insurance, holding that the former is not like the latter, a contract of indemnity, Baron Parke, said: "The contract, commonly called life assurance, when properly considered, is a mere contract to pay a certain sum of money on the death of a person, in consideration of the due payment of a certain annuity for his life—the amount of the annuity being calculated, in the first instance, according to the probable duration of the life; and, when once fixed, it is constant and invariable. The stipulated amount of annuity is to be uniformly paid on one side, and the sum to be paid in the event of death is always (except when bonuses have been given by prosperous offices) the same, on the other. This species of insurance in no way resembles a contract of indemnity."

Bunyon, the English insurance writer, after quoting the definition of Chief Justice Tindal, [3] that it is a contract in which a sum of money is paid as a premium in consideration of the insurers incurring the risk of paying a larger sum upon a given contingency, adds: "The contract of life insurance may be further defined to be that in which one party agrees to pay a given sum, upon the happening of a particular event, contingent upon the duration of human life, in consideration of the immediate payment of a smaller sum, or certain equivalent periodical payments by another."[4] The American definition most generally approved is

[2] 15 C. B. 365; C. L. R. 61; 24 L. J. C. P..2; 18 Jur. (Ex. Ch.) 1024.
[3] Patterson v. Powell, 9 Bing. 320.
[4] Bunyon on Ins. 1.

that of Justice Gray of the Supreme Court of Massachusetts, as follows:"[5]

"A contract of insurance is an agreement, by which one party, for a consideration (which is usually paid in money, either in one sum, or at different times during the continuance of the risk), promises to make a certain payment of money upon the destruction or injury of something in which the other party has an interest. In fire insurance and marine insurance, the thing insured is property; in life or accident insurance, it is the life or health of a person. In either case neither the times and amounts of payments by the assured, nor the modes of estimating or securing the payment of the sum to be paid by the insurer, affect the question whether the agreement between them is a contract of insurance. All that is requisite to constitute such a contract is the payment of the consideration by the one, and the promise of the other to pay the amount of the insurance upon the happening of injury to the subject by a contingency contemplated in the contract."[6]

§ 5. **Assurance and Insurance.**—The words "insurance" and "assurance" are synonymous[7] and are used indiscriminately. One of the earliest English writers,[8] however, says: "The terms *insurance* and *assurance* have been used indiscriminately for contracts relative to life, fire and shipping. As custom has rather more frequently employed the latter term for those relative to life, I have in this volume entirely restricted the word *assurance* to that sense. If this distinction be admitted, *assurance* will signify a contract dependent on the duration of life, which must either happen or fail, and *insurance* will mean a contract relating to any other uncertain event, which may partly happen or partly fail. Thus, in adjusting the price for insurance on houses and ships, regard is always had to the chance of salvage arising from partial destruction." Other writers have sought to establish fanciful distinctions, as that a person *insures* his life, his house or his ship, and the company *assures* to him in each of these cases a sum of money payable upon their injury or destruction. Another is that *assurance* represents the principle, and insurance the practice.

---

[5] Commonwealth v. Wetherbee, 105 Mass. 149. See also State v. Beardsley, 88 Minn. 20; 92 N. W. 472.

[6] See *post,* § 48; New York L. Ins. Co. v. Statham, 93 U. S. 24.

[7] Bouvier L. Dic.

[8] Babbage on Assurance of Lives (1826).

The Supreme Court of Iowa has said[9] that "assured" means the party procuring the insurance, "insured" designates the person whose life is covered, though ordinarily the words are synonymous. Another State court has said[10] that where a third party procures insurance on another's life such third person is spoken of as the assured.

Were we to discriminate we would say that, in life insurance contracts, if the policy is payable to the person whose life is covered, or his legal representatives, he is the *insured,* while if it is payable to some one else, such person is the *assured.* In other words, the party whose death determines the contract is the *insured,* while he for whose benefit it is made and to whom it is payable is the *assured.* Strictly speaking, however, there is no difference in the meaning of the two words.[11]

Where a policy of life insurance shows upon its face that it was applied for and the premium paid by another person and that it was issued for his benefit, the words "the assured" in the policy apply to the person for whose benefit the policy was effected, and not to the party whose life was insured.[12]

§ 6. **The First Insurers.**—The organizations of which the English Friendly Societies were the successors may well be called the first insurers. Their plans were crude, the benefits paid were small, the membership was confined to the poorer classes, but the protection given by them in the nature of sick or burial benefits was practically a form of life insurance. Later when the business of fire insurance began to be conducted by individual underwriters, they soon undertook to issue policies of insurance on life. For quite a long period these underwriters had a monopoly, but the advantages of co-operation became evident and corporations were formed which in time became practically the only life insurers, although there are still in England individual underwriters. Lloyds is an association of individuals who either singly

9 Thompson v. Northwestern Mutual Life Ins. Co., 161 Ia. 446, 143 N. W. 518.

10 Chandler v. Traub, 159 Ala. 519; 49 Sou. 240.

11 For a discussion of these terms see Rowe v. Brooklyn Life Ins. Co., 38 N. Y. Supp. 621; 16 Misc. 323; Boston M. I. Co. v. Scales, 101 Tenn. 628; 49 S. W. 743.

12 Conn. Mut. L. Ins. Co. v. Luchs, 108 U. S. 498; Cyrenius v. Mut. L. Ins. Co., 26 N. Y. Supp. 248.

or in groups engage in all kinds of insurance. The first life insurance case reported in America is Lord v. Dall, decided in 1815 by the Supreme Court of Massachusetts,[13] and shows that the policy was written by individual underwriters, the defendant having underwritten the sum of five hundred dollars out of the five thousand dollars, the whole amount of the policy. The term of insurance was seven months and the premium was seven per cent. A very early English case is Whittingham v. Thornburgh,[14] where suit was brought by the individual underwriters to cancel a policy of life insurance alleged to have been obtained by fraud.

§ 7. **History of Life Insurance.**—Protection against certain hazards afforded by societies and clubs, of which we will hereafter speak, is in effect insurance and while we are told that marine insurance practically dates from the beginning of the sixteenth century, burial and sick benefit societies undoubtedly existed as long ago as the palmy days of the Roman Empire. The business of life, as well as that of marine and fire insurance, was originally carried on by individual underwriters who in conjunction, or alone, underwrote specified amounts on acceptable risks. No definite rules existed for the calculation of premium and rates were made according to the judgment of the insurers. The first life insurance policy of which we have any knowledge was issued June 18, 1583, on the life of William Gibbons. It was for the sum of three hundred and eighty-three pounds, six shillings and eight pence and was for the term of twelve months and the premium was eight per cent. The policy was issued by individual underwriters and when Gibbons died in 1584, they refused to pay on the ground that twelve months meant lunar months and not calendar months. Suit was brought on the policies and the insurers were held liable.

The first regular life insurance company was probably ''The Amicable Society for a Perpetual Assurance Office,'' founded in London in 1706 by royal charter. The scheme was simply to raise a fixed contribution from each member, and from the proceeds to distribute a certain sum each year among the representatives of those who died during the year. None could be admitted under the age of twelve nor above fifty-five (afterwards altered to forty-five) and all paid the same rate of contribution. In 1734 arrange-

13 12 Mass. 115; 7 Am. Dec. 38.
14 2 Vern 206; 24 Eng. Reprints 11.

ments were made by the society for guaranteeing that the dividend for each deceased member should not be less than £100. In 1807 the company began to rate members according to their age and received a new charter. Soon afterwards charters were granted to the Royal Exchange and the London Assurance companies, which included life insurance among their schemes and have continued in business until now. The latter part of the eighteenth century saw the development of the theory of life contingencies, and the Northampton tables supplied what was believed to be a sound basis for calculations on the duration of life. In 1762 "The Society for Equitable Assurances on Lives and Survivorships" began business and its success further encouraged the new enterprise. The nineteenth century began with eight life assurance offices in existence in Great Britain, one of which, the Pelican, founded in 1797, is still in a flourishing condition. In 1844 the first insurance law was passed by Parliament, and after various amendments was succeeded in 1870 by the Life Assurance Companies Act, by the terms of which a deposit with the Court of Chancery was required and frequent reports were to be made to the Board of Trade.

The business of life insurance in Great Britain has attained enormous proportions, and at present nearly one hundred companies are doing business in that country, all apparently prosperous.[15]

The first life insurance organization in America was organized in 1769, in Pennsylvania, under the name of "Corporation for the Relief of the Widows and Children of Clergymen of the Communion of the Church of England and America," although that society was intended more to provide for an annuity than for a fixed amount payable at death. In 1812 the Pennsylvania Company was organized for the insurance of life exclusively, with a capital of $500,000. The Massachusetts Hospital Life Insurance Company was organized in 1818. The first of the present great life insurance corporations of the United States, the Mutual Life Insurance Company of New York, was incorporated in 1842, as a purely mutual company, and has, owing to good management, met with continued success.

[15] See article Insurance of Life in eleventh edition Encyc. Brit. and "Les Assurance" by Chaufton, Paris, 1884.

8

About the same time other of the present great life insurance companies were organized, among which we name the New England Mutual of Boston, finally organized in 1843; the State Mutual Life in 1849, which afterwards became the New York Life Insurance Company; the Mutual Benefit of Newark, organized in 1845; the Connecticut Mutual of Hartford, Connecticut, in 1846; the Penn Mutual Life in 1847, and the Equitable, organized in 1859. Of these companies the Mutual Life, the New York Life and the Equitable are the largest, and their operations extend throughout the world. All are subject to a rigid State supervision, and their experience has been such as to create confidence on the part of the people, has resulted in definite knowledge as to what may be expected in the way of mortality, and has demonstrated the necessity of life insurance.[16]

§ 8. **Accident Insurance.**—Accident insurance is of comparatively recent origin. The first company, known as the Railway Passengers' Assurance Co., was organized in England in 1849. It was many years later that the business extended to the United States. The Travelers' Insurance Company of Hartford, Conn., was organized in 1863. Within the last thirty or forty years it has assumed large proportions and numerous corporations are engaged in insuring people against injuries and death resulting from accident. In effect accident insurance is life insurance because it agrees to pay a specified amount in event of death from specified causes. It is more comprehensive in that it undertakes to also indemnify the insured against loss of time because of injuries from accident. For this reason it has been held that an accident insurance policy is a contract of indemnity. It has been said:[17] "Looking at this contract as a whole, construing it as a whole, it is very apparent that the main idea of it is indemnity, and the main feature in it is indemnity for loss of time in consequence of injury."[18]

[16] Reliable compilations show that in 1916 the life insurance companies of the United States, nearly two hundred in number, had 9,877,050 policies in force, amounting to $18,023,511,201. In addition, the industrial companies had 32,133,561 policies outstanding, amounting to $4,378,951,-675. The life companies in 1916 had assets amounting to $5,269,256,380.

[17] Lemaitre v. National Cas. Co. (Mo. App.), 186 S. W. 964.

[18] See *post*, Ch. XII.

§ 9. **Life and Accident Insurance as Now Conducted in the United States.**—Life and accident insurance in practically all the States is regulated by statute. These not only provide that this business shall only be conducted by corporations, or associations, which have obtained authority by conforming to certain specified requirements. Limitations are also imposed on the power to contract. In many States the form of policy must be approved by the Superintendent of the Insurance Department, and in some it is provided that certain conditions in policies shall be void, and absolute forfeitures on account of non-payment of premium are forbidden, but extended, or paid-up, insurance must be given to the extent of the reserve taken as a single premium. The statutes generally provide for two great classes of life insurance organizations, namely, regular, or "old line," life insurance companies and fraternal beneficiary societies, whether corporations, or voluntary associations. The regular or "old line" companies are divided into those that are purely mutual, in the management and profits of which the policy holders alone participate; those which are owned and controlled entirely by the stockholders, and in neither the management nor the profits of which the policyholders participate; and stock and mutual companies, in the management or in the profits of which, or in both, the policyholders, or any class, or classes, of policyholders are, or may become, entitled to participate.[19] The business conducted by all these classes of organizations is life insurance and, while the same rules and principles of law often apply to each class, in construing and enforcing their contracts, a broad distinction is made between regular, or old line, and fraternal beneficiary insurance. We shall later consider these distinctions and differences, which are year by year becoming fewer.

§ 10. **Nature of Benefit Societies.**—The modern mutual benefit life insurance organizations, now known as "Fraternal Beneficiary Societies," have come prominently into public view only during the last fifty years. From this fact we are not to conclude that they are wholly a modern institution; on the contrary, they are the composite results of the experience of many generations, and even centuries, they represent what is best and most useful

[19] R. S. Mo. 1909, § 6896.

of the multitude of social associations of all kinds that have existed in all times in every land. They seem to have sprung suddenly into the strength of mature life, yet, in fact, they have been developing for hundreds of years. Their powers are now in most of the States regulated by laws which define what they are and contain provisions and restrictions intended to secure their solvency and perpetuity. Benefit societies have a dual nature and in determining their responsibilities, powers and rights and those of their members this fact must never be lost sight of. Very different conclusions will be reached as we consider one class of characteristics or the other.[20]

[20] Mulroy v. Knights of Honor, 28 Mo. App. 463; Wist v. Grand Lodge, etc., 22 Ore. 271; 39 Pac. 610. The statutes of many of the States define what a fraternal beneficiary society is. The definition given by the statutes of Missouri, Laws of 1911, p. 284, which is similar to that found in the laws of other States, is as follows: A fraternal beneficiary association is declared to be "a corporation, society or voluntary association without capital stock, organized and carried on solely for the mutual benefit of its members and their beneficiaries, and not for profit, having a lodge system, with ritualistic form of work and representative form of government, and which shall make provision for the payment of benefits in accordance with section 6 of this act."

The section referred to (6) and that succeeding, are as follows:

Sec. 6. Benefits.—Subsection 1.—Every society transacting business under this act shall provide for the payment of death benefits, and may provide for the payment of benefits in case of temporary or permanent physical disability, either as the result of disease, accident or old age: Provided, the period of life at which the payment of benefits for disability on account of old age shall commence, shall not be under seventy years, and may provide for monuments or tombstones to the memory of its deceased members and for the payment of funeral benefits. Such society shall have the power to give a member, when permanently disabled or attaining the age of seventy, all or such portion of the face value of his certificate as the laws of the society may provide: Provided, that nothing in this act contained shall be so construed as to prevent the issuing of benefit certificates for a term of years less than the whole of life which are payable upon the death or disability of the member occurring within the term for which the benefit certificate may be issued. Such society shall, upon written application of the member, have the power to accept a part of the periodical contributions in cash, and charge the remainder, not exceeding one-half of the periodical contribution against the certificate with interest payable or compounded annually at a rate not lower than four per cent per annum: Provided, that this privilege shall not be granted

11

§ 11. **They are Social Clubs.**—They are, in the first place, social organizations, or clubs of congenial associates, bound together by secret obligations, mystic signs and fraternal pledges. They have generally initiatory rites and ceremonials and a more or less elaborate ritual; their members are pledged to fraternity and mutual assistance in times of distress and need. Usually the organization is made up of local lodges, or societies, with higher, grand or supreme lodges, the latter being fountains of law for the whole association and the corporate entities of the confederations.[21]

Considered as clubs, questions may arise as to their power over their members, or, if unincorporated, the personal liability of the latter to creditors of the association. In settling these external and internal controversies the principles of the law of agency apply;[22] or *mandamus* is resorted to for the restoration of members wrongfully expelled,[23] or courts of equity interfere to wind

except to societies which have readjusted or may hereafter readjust their rates of contributions and to contracts affected by such readjustment.

Subsection 2.—Any society which shall show by the annual valuation hereinafter provided for that it is accumulating and maintaining the reserve necessary to enable it to do so, under a table of mortality not lower than the American experience table and four per cent interest may grant to its members, extended and paid-up protection or such withdrawal equities as its constitution and laws may provide: Provided, that such grants shall in no case exceed in value the portion of the reserve to the credit of such members to whom they are made.

Sec. 7. Beneficiaries.—The payment of death benefits shall be confined to wife, husband, relatives by blood to the fourth degree ascending or descending, father-in-law, mother-in-law, son-in-law, daughter-in-law, stepfather, stepmother, stepchildren, children, by legal adoption, or to a person or persons dependent upon the member: Provided, that if after the issuance of the original certificate the member shall become dependent upon an incorporated charitable institution, he shall have the privilege with the consent of the society to make such institution his beneficiary. Within the above restrictions each member shall have the right to designate his beneficiary, and, from time to time, have the same changed in accordance with the laws, rules or regulations of the society, and no beneficiary shall have or obtain any vested interest in the said benefit until the same has become due and payable upon the death of the said member: Provided, that any society may, by its laws, limit the scope of beneficiaries within the above class.

[21] See *post*, § 20.
[22] *Post*, Ch. IV.
[23] *Post*, Ch. XVI.

12

up the societies and distribute their assets, or exercise other supervisory powers.[24]

§ 12. **They are Business Organizations.**—They are also business corporations and derive their name of benefit societies from this fact. All of them collect, monthly or oftener, from their members certain contributions or assessments, in consideration of which they agree to pay to the member, if sick or disabled, an agreed amount, or upon his death to pay to his designated beneficiary a specified sum, or an amount equal to the aggregate of one assessment not exceeding a certain sum. In most cases these beneficiaries must be of the family of the deceased or those dependent upon him in some way for support. In token of these rights certificates of membership are generally issued.

These societies are the poor man's life insurance companies, for they furnish to those of moderate incomes a cheap and simple substitute for life insurance. The assessments are comparatively small, are called as occasion requires,-but as a rule every month, and the benefit paid is from five hundred to five thousand dollars.

Litigation often arises over these contracts, and, as we shall see,[25] involves the application of the principles of the law of life insurance. Disputes are also frequent concerning the rights of living members. This litigation is increasing in volume and often presents complicated and interesting questions of law.

§ 13. **Kindred Societies.**—There are also organizations which are benefit societies only in name, but are similar to them in having their insurance feature. Such are the associations collateral to the great secret societies, the Freemasons, Odd Fellows and Knights of Pythias. While their membership is drawn from the orders, whose names they respectively bear, the insurance feature is the one object of the organizations and they are practically mutual life insurance companies, having a different plan from the older regular life insurance companies. Of these societies we shall speak later.[26]

§ 14. **Ancient Origin of Benefit Societies.**—Benefit societies, as now known, are the legitimate successors of the clubs and guilds

[24] *Post*, Ch. XVI.
[25] *Post*, Ch. II.
[26] *Post*, § 21.

that have existed from ancient times in all countries. By the processes of increasing and extending civilization with its new needs and greater knowledge, each succeeding generation has improved upon the customs and resources of its predecessors, and, so, through the centuries, we can trace the gregarious habit and co-operative idea, until from the numerous sodalities and secret societies of remote periods it leads to the formation of the social and industrial associations of the present century—to the friendly societies of Great Britain and the co-operative life insurance and fraternal bodies of the last half century in this country.

§ 15. **History of Guilds.**—Men are social beings and their instincts and needs have, from the earliest times, caused them to unite with each other for the pleasures of mutual enjoyment or for the attainment of a common purpose. They have sought the power of numbers for resisting oppression, or mutual assistance in times of need, and again, their affinities for those having similar occupations and interest have led to the formation of societies or guilds.

The Eranoi of Greece and the Collegia of Rome were the earliest of these associations and they continued in various forms through the decline of the empire, reviving and gaining new vigor as the guilds of the Middle Ages. "The essential principle of the guild is the banding together for mutual help, mutual enjoyment and mutual encouragement in good endeavor." These societies were numerous in the palmy days of Rome, when most of them were trade corporations devoted to the interests of their crafts, while some were formed for good fellowship, to promote religion and to provide for burial of members. Persons of the highest rank were often glad to belong to them and many were exceedingly rich and influential. The plan of organization was simple; they chose their own officers, made rules for self-government, collected contributions for a common fund and met and feasted together at stated times.

In the middle ages social guilds sprang up all over Europe, but chiefly in England and Germany and one or more was found in every village. Their objects, says an authority,[27] included "not only devotions and orisons, but also every exercise of Christian

[27] Brentano; History and Development of Guilds.

14

charity, and, therefore, above all things, mutual assistance of the guild brothers in every exigency—especially in old age, in sickness, and in cases of impoverishment—if not brought on by their own folly—and of wrongful imprisonment, in losses by fire, water or shipwreck, aid by loans, provision of work, and lastly the burial of the dead. It included further the assistance of the poor and sick, and the visitation and comfort of prisoners not belonging to the guild.''

In England many of these guilds numbered among their members men and women of all ranks and were rich and powerful, so that kings and princes did not disdain to become guild brethren. Henry IV and Henry VI were members of one organization and Henry VIII of another. The work done by these societies was humane and charitable; they furthered public and benevolent objects and founded schools and colleges; they assisted in the construction of municipal works and were a valued adjunct in the proceedings of the important cities. Their social features were popular and highly appreciated in their communities. When the Reformation came the guilds in most Protestant countries were abolished under pretense of their being superstitious foundations.

In contradistinction from the social were the trade guilds, or merchant guilds, craft guilds, which attracted more attention because of their wealth and importance. Returns of all guilds were made into chancery in 1389, and the borough records of England and Scotland show the influence and power of the trade associations. ''The guild merchant arose in this way: the same men who, in the growth of towns became citizens by reason of possessing town lands, frequently were also traders; the uncertain state of society in early times naturally caused them to unite for protection of their trade interests in a *gilda mercatoria*, which made internal laws akin to those of other guilds; the success of these private interests enlarged their importance; and when the towns and boroughs obtained confirmation of their municipal life by charter, they took care to have it included that the men of the place should also have their guild merchant. Thus these guilds obtained the recognition of the State; in their origin they had been as other guilds, partaking especially of the character of peace guilds, but now the citizens and the guild became identical and what was guild law often became the law of the town. In great cities, such as London

15

and Florence, we do not hear of merchant guilds;[27a] there the separate occupations or crafts early asserted their associating power
and independence, and the craft guilds gradually took a place in
the organization of the town government. Many craft guilds, the
heads of which were concerned in the government of the commune,
are found in Italy between the ninth and twelfth centuries.[28] But
in England and the north of Europe the guild merchants during
this period, having grown rich and tyrannical, excluded the land-
less men of the handicrafts; these then uniting among themselves,
there arose everywhere by the side of the guilds merchant the
craft guilds, which gained the upper hand on the Continent in the
struggle for liberty in the thirteenth and fourteenth centuries. In
England these companies usually existed side by side with the old
town or merchant guild, until at length their increasing importance caused the decay of the old guilds, and the adoption of these
crafts as part of the constitution of the towns (thirteenth to fifteenth century). The separation of the richer, and perhaps the
older, from the poorer of the companies occurred, and thus arose
the paramount influence of a few—as the twelve great companies
of London, the *Arti Majori* of Florence, and others.

"The constitution of the trade guilds was formed on the model
of other guilds: they appointed a master, or alderman, and other
officers, made ordinances, including provisions for religious ob-
servances, mutual help and burial; the town ordinances yet remaining of many places, as of Berwick, Southampton and Worcester, show traces of the trade laws of the old guild merchant. As
their principal objects, 'the craft guildmen provided for the maintenance of the customs of their craft, framed further ordinances
for its regulations (including care against fraudulent workman-
ship), saw these ordinances properly executed, and punished the
guild brothers who infringed them. Though the craft guilds, as
voluntary associations, did not need confirmation by the authorities at their birth, yet this confirmation became afterwards of the
greatest importance, when these guilds wanted to be recognized
as special and independent associations, which were thenceforth
to regulate the trade instead of the authorities of the town.'[29] Hence

[27a] Norton's Commentaries on the History of London.
[28] Perren's Hist. de Florence.
[29] Brentano; History and Development of Guilds.

obtained the practice of procuring a charter in confirmation and recognition of their laws, in return for which certain taxes were paid to the king or other authority. It is therefore erroneous to state, as is sometimes done, that these companies owe their origin to royal charter, or that they required a license.''[30]

§ 16. **Decay of Guilds, their Successors.**—Under the influence of the refinements of civilization and the new necessities of commerce, as well as the strong arm of the Reformation and changing human taste and recreations, the social, merchant and craft guilds practically lost their popularity and power, even their very being, though a few of the latter may yet be in existence. The social guilds were succeeded by the modern friendly societies, and social and literary clubs, and probably also in part by the great secret fraternities like the Freemasons and Odd Fellows. The merchant guilds gradually disappeared, although some still survive, and our present Boards of Trade and Chambers of Commerce grew up. The craft guilds may be looked upon as in one sense the parents of the trade unions of today. Of these clubs, secret fraternities and the English friendly societies, we shall speak in the order named.

§ 17. **History of Clubs.**—Clubs have been said to be the natural and necessary offshoot of men's gregarious and social nature, and the records of nations show that they have flourished in all countries from the beginnings of history. They were particularly numerous in the prosperous days of Greece and Rome, and interesting statements are made of their workings and influence. They were religious, commercial, political or merely social, according to the class of people who were members, though the most of them were either a species of craft guilds, or formed for religious purposes. All, undoubtedly, combined pleasure with business, or worship, and frequently met for social relaxation.

In ancient times the State did not always countenance the worship of strange gods, so that the devotees of new deities associated together in clubs and met in secret. Little, however, is known of their rites or ceremonies. The great secret organizations, like the Pythagoreans, Essenes, Carmathites and Fedavi, or the grosser Bacchanalians are described in history, and their philosophical

---

[30] L. Toulmin Smith in 9th Ed. Encyc. Brit., Art. "Guild."

teachings have been the subject for multitudes of essays and pon-
derous tomes. It is not to our purpose to enter into a prolonged
discussion of the work of these dead and buried institutions, we
can merely refer to them.

There were, in the early days before the Christian era, or shortly
afterwards, many clubs organized for private advantage. ''There
was nothing in the functions of these clubs to obtain for them a
place in the page of history. The evidence, therefore, of their
existence and constitution is but scanty. Monumental inscriptions,
however, tell us of clubs of Roman citizens in some of the cities of
Spain, of a club of strangers from Asia resident in Malaga, of
Phœnician residents at Pozzuoli, and of other strangers elsewhere.
These all were probably devised as remedies against that sense of
ennui and isolation which is apt to come over a number of for-
eigners residing at a distance from their native country. Something of the same kind of feeling may have led to the toleration
of a club consisting of old soldiers who had been in the armies
of Augustus; these were allowed to meet and fight their battles
over again spite of the legal prohibition of military clubs. Another military club of a different kind existed among the officers
of a regiment engaged in the foreign service in Africa. Its existence can have been no secret, for its rules were engraved on pil-
lars which were set up near the headquarters of the general, where
they have lately been found in the ruins of the camp. The contribution of each member on admission scarcely fell short of £25,
and two-thirds of this sum were to be paid to an heir or representative on the occasion of his death, or he might himself recover
this proportion of his original subscription on retirement from
military service. The peculiarity, however, of this aristocratic
collegium was this, that it provided that a portion of the funds
might also be spent for other useful purposes, *e. g.*, for foreign
traveling. It is to be presumed that a member who had availed
himself of this privilege thereby forfeited all claim to be buried
at the expense of his club.''[31]

The extent of the clubs of the Middle Ages is not accurately
known, for the difference in those countries between these clubs
and the guilds of various kinds was slight. In the early part of

[31] Canon J. S. Northcote in 9th Ed. Encyc. Brit.

the eighteenth century the lodges of Odd Fellows and Freemasons appeared, tracing their ancestry back to the remote ages of antiquity, and perpetuating to some extent the ancient rituals of very old secret organizations. The true precursors of the Masons were probably the mediæval building organizations, for example, the stonemasons of Germany, who had religious ceremonies, oaths, benefits, burial funds and registers, and officers by whom they were instructed in secret. Such associations existed in Gaul and Britain for centuries and as early as the twelfth century the Bauhutten had a general association, secret signs and ritual, and graded divisions or degrees. The word lodge first occurs in 1491 in a statute governing the Masons of Edinburgh.[32]

The Freemasons and Odd Fellows, and later the Knights of Pythias, had their mystic signs of recognition, secret initiatory rites and ceremonies, various grades of dignity and honor, and performed extensive social and benevolent work. They now number their members by millions.[33]

The modern clubs of Europe, organized for literary and political, as well as for social objects, are numerous and wealthy and in London especially some are flourishing whose names are known throughout the world. The courts were at an early period called upon to adjudicate concerning the individual liability of the members of these clubs for the debts of the association as well as the remedies of members unjustly expelled.[34] In America clubs are increasing rapidly, hold large amounts of property and are constantly gaining in membership and influence, and few cities of any size can be found where they do not exist, while lodges of the great secret fraternities are in every village, and have been and are immensely popular.

§ 18. **Analogies Between Ancient and Modern Clubs.**—Many analogies can be traced between ancient and modern clubs and the ecclesiastical, political and secret societies of recent times. Viewed from a legal standpoint, they are all formed upon essentially the

---

[32] 9th Ed. Encyc. Brit., Art. "Freemasons."

[33] In 1881 in Great Britain there were 10,000 lodges of Freemasons with 1,000,000 members or more, and over 500,000 Odd Fellows. In 1881 the British Odd Fellows had a capital of over five million pounds sterling. Encyc. Brit.

[34] *Post*, Ch. III.

same principles. Generally, they are unincorporated voluntary associations, but in probably every State they may incoroporate under acts of the legislatures regulating the formations of corporations for benevolent, charitable and educational purposes. By the provisions of these statutes they are allowed special privileges, while in most States churches are further recognized and given exemption from taxation, because of their conserving and helpful influence over the people, and the absence of any objects of pecuniary advantage to their members.

In many, if not a majority, of States, statutes exist authorizing the incorporation of "Fraternal Beneficiary Associations" and regulating the business which they can do. Under these statutes the societies are required to annually report to the insurance department the details of their business and are under State supervision although exempted from the laws governing the regular life insurance companies.[34a]

Although numerous cases are found in the courts relating to the

[34a] Such codes exist in the District of Columbia and twenty-five different States as follows: District of Columbia, Code, Subchapter 12, Secs. 749-765. Arizona, Rev. State., Tit. 24, Secs. 3493, 3494. (Law, 1913, Ch. 94, Secs. 100, 101.) Alabama, General Acts of 1911, pp. 713, ff. Act of April 24, 1911, Secs. 23, 23a. California, General Laws, Ch. 49, Act., 440, Secs. 23, 23a. (Act of May 1, 1911.) Colorado, Mills Stats., Ch. 65, Secs. 3042, 3043. (Act of June 2, 1911.) Connecticut, Public Acts of 1913, Ch. 185, Secs. 33-42. (Act of June 7, 1913.) Idaho, Session Laws, 1911, Ch. 225, Secs. 23, 23a. (Also Session Laws, 1913, Ch. 184. Louisiana, Act No. 256 of 1912, Sec. 23; Act No. 287 of 1914, Secs. 1, 3. Maryland, Laws 1912, Ch. 824, Sec. 12a (applying only to new societies). Massachusetts, St. 1911, Ch. 628, Secs. 22, 23; St. 1913, Ch. 617, Sec. 3. Michigan, Public Acts 1913, No. 169, Secs. 23, 23a, 23b. Missouri, Laws 1911, p. 293, Act of March 30, 1911, Secs. 25, 26. Montana, Session Laws, 1911, Ch. 140, Secs. 23, 23a. New Hampshire, St. 1913, Ch. 122, Secs. 23, 23a, 23b. New York, L. 1911, Ch. 198, Sec. 242. North Carolina, Public Laws, 1913, Ch. 89, Secs. 20, 20a, 20b. North Dakota, Laws, 1913, Ch. 191, Secs. 23, 23a, 23b. Ohio, Laws, 1911, pp. 542-544, Act of May 31, Secs. 23, 23a, 24, Code, Secs. 9484, 9485. Oregon, General Laws, 1911, Ch. 217, Secs. 23, 23a. Rhode Island, Public Laws, 1912, Ch. 803, Sec. 23, Public Laws of 1913, Ch. 958, Sec. 2. Tennessee, Acts of 1909, Ch. 99 (Permissive). Texas, Laws of 1913, Ch. 113, Secs. 23, 23a, 23b, 23c. Utah, Laws of 1911, Ch. 148, Secs. 23, 23a. Washington, Laws of 1911, pp. 290-2, Ch. 49, Secs. 228, 229; Code 6059, 228, 229. Wisconsin, 1913, Ch. 251. Wyoming, Session Laws, 1913, Ch. 127, Secs. 23, 23a, 23b.

rights, privileges and responsibilities of ecclesiastical organizations and their members, we shall not refer to them, except incidentally and by way of illustration, for ecclesiastical law is a subject worthy of its own individual treatises, and learned authors have considered its authorities and principles with great research and ability.

§ 19. **The English Friendly Societies.**—In the law which now regulates Friendly Societies in Great Britain,[35] they are defined as "societies established to provide by voluntary subscriptions of the members thereof, with or without the aid of donations, for the relief of maintenance of the members, their husbands, wives, children, fathers, mothers, brothers or sisters, nephews or nieces, or wards being orphans, during sickness or other infirmity, whether bodily or mental, in old age or in widowhood, or for the relief or maintenance of the orphan children of members during minority; for insuring money to be paid on the birth of a member's child, or on the death of a member, or for the funeral expenses of the husband, wife, or child of a member, or of the widow of a deceased member; or, as respects persons of the Jewish persuasion, for the payment of a sum of money during the period of confined mourning; for the relief or maintenance of the members when on travel in search of employment, or when in distressed circumstances, or in case of shipwreck, or loss or damage of or to boats or nets; for the endowment of members or nominees of members at any age; for the insurance against fire to any amount not exceeding £15 of the tools or implements of the trade or calling of the members." They are limited in their contracts for assurance of annuities to £50, and for insurance of a gross sum to £200.

These organizations have been more briefly defined to be "the mutual assurance societies of the poorer classes, by which they seek to aid each other in the emergencies arising from sickness and death and other cause of distress."

The friendly societies of the present time are in one sense the successors of the ancient guilds and some of them are very old, tracing their foundation back as early as 1634. They are supposed by some to have their origin in the burial clubs of early English

[35] 33 and 39 Vic., Ch. 60, amended 39 and 40 Vic., Ch. 32. These acts and amendments were consolidated in 1887. 50 and 51 Vic., Ch. 56, and later in 1896 and 1908.

21

history, when the desire of the poor to have respectable burial led
to the formation of associations, whereby through the co-operation and periodical contributions of many, a fund was established
for the purpose of burying their deceased members.   The organization of these societies is more complex than that of any of the
associations which they have succeeded, and they proceed on a different principle, though the modern may be the natural results
of the improvements of each successive generation over the methods
of that preceding.   In all there is the common provision for a contingent event by a joint contribution; but the friendly society has
attempted "to define with precision what is the risk against which
it intends to provide, and what should be the contributions of the
members to meet that risk."

In the eighteenth century these societies were numerous, and
in 1793 their existence was recognized by what is known as Sir
George Rose's Act, by which they were styled "societies of good
fellowship" and given encouragement by special privileges.   The
benefits offered by this statute were eagerly received and in the
county of Middlesex alone nearly a thousand societies were en-
rolled in a few years after the passage of this act.   This prosperity
was succeeded by depression and failure of many societies and
general mistrust.   For the purpose of encouraging greater confidence in these organizations and affording "further facilities
and additional security to persons who may be willing to unite in
appropriating small sums from time to time to a common fund,"
the act of 1819[36] was passed.

By this statute a friendly society was defined as "an institution, whereby it is intended to provide, by contribution, on the
principle of mutual insurance, for the maintenance or assistance
of the contributors thereto, their wives or children, in sickness, infancy, advanced age, widowhood, or any other natural state or
contingency, whereof the occurrence is susceptible of calculation
by way of average."   The act of 1829[37] was a great improvement
over the one it displaced and by it the law relating to these organizations was entirely reconstructed.   The various acts of 1834[38]

[36] 59 George III., Ch. 128.
[37] 10 George IV., Ch. 56.
[38] 4 and 5 William IV., Ch. 40.

and 1846[39] were still further improvements, and by the latter the present office of "Registrar of Friendly Societies" was established. In 1850[40] and 1855[41] the law was again changed and this was succeeded by the law passed in 1875,[42] amended in 1876[43] and again in 1887,[44] 1896 and 1908.

It will be seen, therefore, that the English Friendly Societies have long been recognized by the government as organizations beneficial to society and deserving the support and encouragement of the community. They are now under a careful supervision, as much so as the more pretentious life insurance companies, and they are required to make regular returns to the chief registrar; special provisions are also made by the laws for the restraining power of the courts and the winding up of the societies when insolvent.[45]

[39] 9 and 10 Vic., Ch. 27.
[40] 13 and 14 Vic., Ch. 115.
[41] 18 and 19 Vic., Ch. 63.
[42] 38 and 39 Vic., Ch. 60.
[43] 39 and 40 Vic., Ch. 32.
[44] 50 and 51 Vic., Ch. 56.

[45] For most of these facts we are indebted to a very full and carefully prepared article in the eleventh edition of the Encyclopædia Britannica by E. W. Brabrook. From that essay it seems that these societies are divided by the registrar into thirteen classes, ranging from the affiliated societies, or "orders," such as The Manchester Unity of Odd Fellows, Ancient Order of Foresters, Rechabites, Druids, etc., to cattle insurance societies. There are also "general societies," of which 8 in London have 60,000 members; county societies with 30,000 members; local town societies; "collecting societies," of which 329 have over 680,000 members and £203,777 of funds; "annuity societies;" female societies; workingmen's clubs, etc. In the period between 1793 and 1855 it is stated that 26,034 societies registered under the various acts. In 1905, 29,588 furnished returns, though more were in existence, and these had 13,978,790 members and £50,459,060 funds. Twenty-two returned over 10,000 members each, and 9 over 30,000 members. From the report of the Registrar of Friendly Societies, etc., it appears that the Friendly Societies proper, collecting societies, various miscellaneous societies, including industrial and provident societies, building societies, loan societies, trades unions and railway savings banks are all under the charge of one bureau. These so-called Friendly Societies are divided into two classes, what are called affiliated orders, or societies having subordinate branches, and the independent societies, composed of various lodges, or branches, which contribute a certain amount annually for the purpose of keeping up a central organization yet are really inde-

§ 20. **The American Beneficiary Orders.**—The American benefit societies or orders resemble in many respects the English friendly societies, although they have many of the characteristic features of the great secret orders like the Freemasons and Odd

pendent organizations. The affiliated orders are centralized bodies having various subordinate lodges, for whose dealings they are in a measure responsible. In the statistics of the number of societies, subordinate lodges are included. The two largest of the affiliated orders are the Ancient Order of Foresters with 830,720 members and the Independent Order of Odd Fellows, Manchester Unity, with 769,503 members. The registrar estimates the annual contributions of the members of the independent societies at £1,707,000 and the other receipts at £1,410,-000, making a total of £2,117,000. The affiliated orders are estimated to annually receive £3,024,000 in contributions. The total income of the two classes, that is of the independent societies and the affiliated orders with branches, is estimated to be: contributions, £4,731,-000; other receipts, £941,000; or a total annual income of £5,672,000. The yearly benefits paid are estimated at £4,277,000; expenses, £644,000, leaving as an accumulated saving, £751,000. These figures exclude the collecting societies, the various provident societies, workingmen's clubs and trades unions, as well as savings banks.

The benefits of registration are stated to be as follows:

"Power to hold land and vesting of property in trustees by mere appointment; remedy against misapplication of funds; priority in bankruptcy or on death of officer; exemption from stamp duties; membership of minors; certificates of birth and death at reduced cost; investment with National Debt Commissioners; reduction of fines on admission to copy holds; discharge of mortgages by mere receipt; obligation on officers to render accounts; settlement of disputes; insurance of funeral expenses for wives and children without insurable interest; nomination at death; payment without administration; services of public auditors and valuers; registry of documents of which copies may be put in evidence."

In his testimony before a parliamentary committee the registrar estimated that the unregistered societies are nearly as numerous as the registered societies and with as large a membership. This would give the Friendly Societies of Great Britain, not including the collecting societies and the other numerous industrial and provident societies, a membership of over 16,000,000 and accumulated funds on hand of about £65,000,000 sterling.

This report also gives statistics of the societies in the colonies and in France and Switzerland. For example, in Australia are more than 100 societies with, in round numbers, 100,000 members, and accumulated funds of nearly £2,000,000. They are valued actuarily every five years.

24

Fellows. Most of them have a secret organization and ritual, with mystic signs and passwords, are oathbound and have grades or degrees of honor. The local lodges are generally under the supervision of grand lodges, composed of delegates from the local bodies, and these in turn acknowledge the supremacy of a supreme lodge, made up of representatives from the grand lodges.

The benefits paid are of two kinds, those to sick members for which the local lodges are responsible, and a specific sum to be paid on the decease of a member to his beneficiary, designated as such in accordance with the rules of the order. This death benefit is paid by the highest body in the order, which is usually incorporated, and, in evidence of the right of the member to have this benefit paid, a certificate is issued to him by this supreme or grand lodge. The amount thus paid in each case ranges from $500 to $5,000, and the fund from which it is disbursed is collected by assessments, generally of a definite sum, from one or more dollars, called monthly, or oftener as occasion requires, or as needed when a death occurs. The local lodges act as agents of the grand or supreme lodge, in receiving new members, and, to some extent, unless otherwise provided, in collecting assessments.

The local lodges are supported by monthly or quarterly calls or dues, which are levied and collected by the lodge direct and used as prescribed by the by-laws of each body. The sick benefits are paid out of this lodge fund. These local lodges enroll the new members, or receive them by a secret ceremonial, but before initiation the applicants must pass a medical examination, the report of which must be usually approved by a supervising medical authority, after which they are initiated in due form and become full-fledged members.[46]

[46] The oldest fraternal beneficiary society in the United States, "The Ancient Order of United Workmen," was founded in 1868. Its growth was very slow for several years when the plan quickly became popular and soon a multitude of similar societies were organized. The protection in the nature of life insurance, at first incidental to the fraternal feature, soon became the dominant purpose. The early plans were crude and the advancing age of the members with a consequent increase in mortality proved the inadequacy of the rates. A reliable compilation, "The Fraternal Monitor Chart," shows that in 1916, 182 of these organizations showed 8,128,908 certificates or policies outstanding, amounting to $9,-443,671,501, and possessed assets of $264,068,045. The largest society is

§ 21. **The Secret Fraternities.**—Closely allied to the beneficiary or mutual aid life insurance organizations, are the secret ritualistic societies and charitable fraternities, whose characteristic features are good-fellowship, social enjoyment and benevolence. The Freemasons, Odd Fellows and Knights of Pythias are examples. These numerous societies are secret in their organization and work, use a ritual and have initiatory ceremonies and their members are pledged to secrecy. They are organized on the plan of local assemblies or lodges under the government and control of grand or supreme lodges. Some, like the Masons, make no promise of financial aid to members, but are charitable, only donating when necessity requires. Others, such as the Odd Fellows, expressly agree to pay stated amounts to the members in sickness or disability and at death a certain sum for funeral expenses, and also to look after the widow and orphan. These societies have no life insurance feature.[47] It is not often that legal complications arise

the "Modern Woodmen of America" with a million members. The "Royal Arcanum" has 250,000 members. Some of the older societies have failed, owing to inadequate rates, and others are facing the problem of how to secure solvency under the adverse conditions of a high average age of the members and reluctance on their part to pay the necessary largely increased contributions. Nearly all the societies in the beginning adopted either an inadequate level rate or the impracticable natural premium plan of advancing premiums with advancing age, instead of an adequate level premium providing for a reserve to be accumulated at compound interest to meet the deficit in advanced age. The uniform fraternal beneficiary law, which has been adopted in nearly forty states, places the societies under the supervision of the insurance department and requires them to gradually become actuarily solvent by readjustment of rates with adequate reserves, or discontinue business. These societies have done wonderful work in the past and have paid out hundreds of millions of dollars to dependents of deceased members. With more scientific methods of doing business they ought to have greater prosperity in the future.

[47] The Independent Order of Odd Fellows was the first fraternal society in America to guarantee to its members a certain amount of money in event of sickness and for a funeral benefit. It was founded in this country in 1819, and now has about 17,500 lodges and 1,630,000 members, and during its existence has disbursed to its beneficiaries upwards of $100,-000,000. The largest secret fraternal society is the Masonic order, which now has in this country about 15,316 lodges, with a membership of nearly 1,700,000 members, and has expended millions of dollars in unostentatious charity. The Knights of Pythias, which was originated within the last

in these bodies, necessitating a resort to the courts, though some cases are found to which they are parties.

§ 22. **Allied Organizations.**—In connection with the Masonic, Pythian and Odd Fellows' orders are in many States associations formed for mutual life insurance, whose membership is drawn exclusively from the societies in aid of which they are organized. These organizations are distinct and separate from the orders, are strict business companies and are life insurance companies, operating on the assessment plan instead of on the principles underlying the scientific theory of life insurance.

There are also in this country a number of regular corporations, formed for the conduct of the business of life insurance on the plain of the benefit societies—the collection of frequent periodical assessments as required to meet death losses. The business of these companies is regular life insurance conducted upon a new theory, for, except in this respect, they do not differ from the regular life insurance companies with which all are familiar. These organizations are known as assessment companies, or life insurance companies doing business on the assessment plan and in some States the business is regulated by statute.[48] Most of them operated on the natural premium, or increasing scale of contributions with advancing age, which experience has shown to be impracticable. Very few of these assessment companies have survived.

§ 23. **Trades Union.**—In Great Britain trades unions are required to report to the Registrar of Friendly Societies and are under the superintendence of that bureau.[49] In America they are usually unincorporated voluntary associations and partake of the

half century, has a membership of probably 500,000 and the Elks, organized still later, about the same.

On principle, a distinction should be made between the mutual aid or beneficiary orders proper, having a life insurance feature, and the purely charitable and fraternal societies, whose donations are more strictly charities, but this cannot always be done. In nearly every large city there are local orders not known away from the vicinity, and throughout the United States are numerous Hebrew, Scottish, English and other organizations deriving their membership from some one nationality, creed or religious sect. These societies are too numerous to mention and the number is constantly increasing.

48 R. S. Mo. 1899, § 7901, *et seq.*

49 *Ante,* § 19.

nature both of clubs and benefit societies, often paying the members stimpulated or arbitrary sums for relief in times of sickness, although it is probable that a majority of such associations are organized more for social advantages and purpose of profit to the members of the association in times of differences with employers. In treating of voluntary associations, both clubs and benefit societies, it will be necessary to consider many cases where different branches of trades unions have been interested, and no distinction can be made between trades unions and other clubs or associations, whether corporate or incorporate, so far the governing principles of law are concerned. It has been said that "Labor organizations are lawful and generally laudable associations, but they have no legal status or authority, and stand before men and the law on no better footing than other social organizations, and it is preposterous that they should attempt to issue orders that free men are bound to obey; and no man can stand in a court of justice and shelter himself behind any such organization from the consequences of his own unlawful acts."[50] And it is not unlawful for the members of an association to combine together for the purpose of securing the control of the work connected with their trade and endeavor to affect such purpose by peaceable means.[51] There is no reason why trades unions should not be incorporated under general incorporation laws if their purposes fall within their purview. In one State, at least, associations of farmers are specially authorized to become corporations by adoption of the act of the legislature conferring the authority.[52] Statutes also exist authorizing the formation of trades unions, but such law does not sanction the making of war on the nonunion laboring man, or illegally interfering with his rights and privileges.[53] In order to prove the character of a club as a voluntary association a witness can testify that he had been elected president and had acted in such capacity.[54]

[50] In re Higgins (C. C.), 27 Fed. 443.

[51] Mayer v. Journeymen Stonecutters' Ass'n, 47 N. J. Eq. 519; 20 Atl. 492; Longshore Printing, etc., Co. v. Howell, 26 Ore. 527; 38 Pac. 547; 28 L. R. A. 464, and note.

[52] Durham Fertilizer Co. v. Clute, 112 N. C. 440; 17 S. E. 419.

[53] Lucke v. Clothingcutters, etc., Assembly, 77 Md. 396; 26 Atl. 505; 19 L. R. A. 408.

[54] Lavretta v. Holcombe, 98 Ala. 503; 12 Sou. 789.

Like other associations, the members of trades unions are bound
by the constitution or articles of association.[55] A union may prescribe qualifications for its membership. It may make it as exclusive as it sees fit. It may make the restriction on the line of
citizenship, nationality, age, creed, or profession, as well as numbers. This power is incident to its character as a voluntary association, and cannot be inquired into, except on behalf of some
person who has acquired some right in the organization, and to
protect such right.[56] But a by-law of a trade union, providing for
the expulsion of a member for taking the place of a brother member who has been discharged for upholding the laws of a society,
is void against public policy.[57] A person who has secured membership in a trades union by feigning qualifications which did
not exist, and persists in retaining membership after such disqualifications have been established, can be expelled, and where
no by-laws or regulations appear in the record and the proceedings appear to have been reasonably fair the Court will not interfere.[58] But a court of equity has no jurisdiction to compel the
admission to an association of a person not elected to membership
in such union according to its rules and by-laws.[59] Where a labor
organization refused to admit a nonunion man to membership
and informed his employers that in case he was any longer retained by them it would be compelled to notitfy the other organizations in the city that their house was a nonunion house, in consequence of which act such nonunion man was discharged, it was
held[60] that the association was guilty of a wrongful act and such
a nonunion man could maintain an action against it for damages
that he had suffered in consequence of such discharge.[61] The prom-

55 Coniff v. Jamour, 65 N. Y. Supp. 317; 31 Misc. 729.
56 Mayer v. Journeymen Stonecutters' Ass'n, 47 N. J. Eq. 519; 20 Atl.
492.
57 People v. N. Y. Ben. Soc,. 3 Hun. 361; 6 Thomp. and C. 85.
58 Beesley v. Chicago Journeymen Plumbers, etc., Ass'n, 44 Ill. App. 278.
59 Mayer v. Journeymen Stonecutters' Ass'n, 47 N. J. Eq. 519; 20 Atl.
492. See also McKane v. Democratic General Committee, 123 N. Y. 609;
25 N. E. 1057.
60 Lucke v. Clothingcutters, etc., Assembly, 77 Md. 396; 26 Atl. 505; 19
L. R. A. 408.
61 See also Bowen v. Hall, 6 Q. B. Div. 338; Chipley v. Atkinson, 23 Fla.
206; 1 Sou. 934. In this latter case the cases bearing upon the liability of

ıse to reinstate an expelled member, if a claim for damages is released, is without consideration.[62]   But the union is liable for damages for a wrongful expulsion of a member.[63]   The member, on withdrawal from his union, is not entitled to share in its funds.[64]

A provision of the constitution and by-laws of the Knights of Labor providing that on suspension of a local assembly its property shall be forfeited to the general assembly is void,[65] and after revocation by the general executive board of the charter of the local assembly such assembly still has the right to sue for and collect debts due to it.[66]

Where several local lodges purchased a hall to be used for their joint benefit, the title to which was taken in the name of a committee in trust for such lodge, and subsequently the lodges organized themselves into a corporation to administer the property, it was held that the committee would be compelled to transfer the property to such corporation and account for the rents and profits, although the different local lodges never formally requested the committee to make the transfer.[67]

While it would be interesting to consider the numerous cases involving the principles of law applicable to trade unions, it is not within the province of this work to do more than refer to them as a class of organizations having many of the characteristics of clubs or lodges and hence governed by the general rules applicable in such cases.

§ 24. **Characteristics in Common.**—In the consideration of these social, benevolent and mutual aid societies, as well as other organizations for the mutual assistance of their members in their particular field of work, we find that while the fraternal associa-

persons for procuring the discharge of an employe are exhaustively reviewed.

[62] Connell v. Stalker, 48 N. Y. Supp. 77; 21 Misc. 609.

[63] Connell v. Stalker, 21 Misc. 423; 45 N. Y. Supp. 1048.

[64] Local Union v. Barrett, 19 R. I. 663; 36 Atl. 5.

[65] Wicks v. Monihan, 130 N. Y. 232; 29 N. E. 139; 14 L. R. A. 243. See also *post*, Ch. III.

[66] Wells v. Monihan, 129 N. Y. 161; 29 N. E. 232.

[67] Organized Labor Hall v. Gebert, 48 N. J. Eq. 393; 22 Atl. 578. See, as to fines, Meurer v. Detroit Musicians, etc., Ass'n, 95 Mich. 451; 54 N. W. 954. As to assignment of funds by members in good standing, Brown v. Stoerkel, 74 Mich. 269; 41 N. W. 921; 3 L. R. A. 430.

tions have the characteristic features of ordinary clubs which have often figured in the courts, many have the additional feature of agreeing to pay a specified sum on the death of a member to his designated beneficiaries or to himself in case of his disability. This fact gives them the dual nature, of which we spoke at first, and makes them practically life insurance companies, as well as social organizations. The business, therefore, is, legally speaking, life insurance in form and substance, although from reasons of public policy, as we shall see later, the legislatures have considered that it is not technical and scientific life insurance. The courts, however, while distinguishing the contracts of "old line," or regular, life insurance companies from those of the fraternal beneficiary societies, are disposed more and more to apply the same general rules to both. It is therefore necessary in considering the law of life and accident insurance to also consider the peculiar characteristics of the fraternal beneficiary societies which constitute such a large class of the organizations which carry on such business.

§ 25. **State Supervision.**—The Supreme Court of New Hampshire has said, stating the principle now universally admitted:[68] "The business of insurance is no longer a private right but a matter of public concern and subject to regulation by the State for the public good." This regulation was made necessary by the enormous growth of the business of insurance and the peculiar nature of the contracts, especially those of life insurance, which often do not mature for possibly more than half a century. Public policy requires that insurers be prohibited from inserting in their contracts onerous or unreasonable conditions; that they be required to make annual reports of their business and submit to expert examination as to their financial condition. We shall in due time consider in detail the power of the State in this respect and the rules which have been laid down by the courts governing State regulation of life and accident and fraternal beneficiary insurance.[69]

§ 26. **Method of Conducting Business.**—The common practice of life insurance companies is to only issue policies upon

68 Boston Ice Co. v. Boston & Maine R. R. Co., 86 Atl. 356.
69 See *post*, § 54.

healthy lives and, before the policy is issued, the applicant is required to answer numerous questions in regard to his family, health, business, age, condition and personal history, and undergo a physical examination by a physician.   If these preliminaries are satisfactory to the company the contract is consummated.   The basis of life insurance is the doctrine of average and the theory of probability; that is the average rate of mortality or probable number of deaths out of a certain number and the rate of interest on excess contributions or investments that the company expects to receive.   The consideration is the payment of certain sums periodically during the term of the insurance, as annually, semi-annually or quarterly; or the consideration may be paid at one time or in a certain number of payments.   This consideration, or premium, varies according to the age of the applicant and is based upon the accumulating power of compound interest and the probable duration of human life, ascertained by experience and shown in certain tables or compilations of statistics.   There are many of these compilations, of which the best known are the Northampton, Carlisle, Actuaries, and the American Experience Tables of Mortality.[70]

[70] Several very old tables exist which are now obsolete, such as those of Halley, De Parcieux and others. The first reliable compilation was the Northampton Table. This was constructed by Dr. Thomas Price from the registers kept in the parish of All Saints, Northampton, for the forty-six years, 1735 to 1780. It is said that this table gives the chances of death too high at the younger ages and too low at later ages, but for many years it was the basis of all life contingency calculations and even now is still in use. The Carlisle Table was constructed by Joshua Milne from materials furnished by Dr. John Heysham. These materials comprised two enumerations of the population of the parishes of St. Mary and St. Cuthbert Carlisle, in 1780 and 1787 (the numbers being in the former year 7,677 and in the latter 8,677) and the abridged bills of mortality of these two parishes for the nine years, 1779 to 1787, during which period the total number of deaths was 1,840. The care and dexterity with which these tables were compiled made them popular and the figures there given have generally agreed with the experience of the life companies. These two tables are of all lives in a certain district and the mortality in the earlier ages is consequently greater than that of selected lives.

Other tables are in use by life insurance companies in England, such as the Equitable Experience, the Seventeen Offices experience, which were made from statistics, covering 83,905 policies, and the English Life Ta.

§ 27. **Analogies Between Benefit Societies and Life Insurance Companies.**—From what has been said it already appears that the modern benefit societies are engaged in furnishing to their members substantially life insurance. Like the first life insurance corporations, some of them in the beginning had a fixed and uniform payment, or assessment, for all ages, while others had graded assessments for different ages. All have now adopted a more scientific method to comply with the laws, which are aimed to make them actuarily solvent; that is, the present value of liabilities must not exceed the present value of resources. The predominating feature of both benefit societies and life insurance companies is the payment of a specific sum on the death of the person who is a member of the organization or whose life is insured. In the societies the fund is obtained by a periodical tax upon the members, at stated intervals, or as required, sufficient to meet the demand. In the companies the principle is based upon the probable duration of human life and the estimate that a certain number of men can, by a comparatively speaking small periodical contribution, which is carefully improved at compound interest, pay in, during their aggregate lives, enough to give a specified amount to the beneficiaries of each upon his death.

Both companies and societies have the same careful medical examination and certificates, and the contracts of both are avoided by the violation of certain agreed conditions, or by misrepresentations prior to entering into the contract. As we continue with the discussion these analogies will become clearer.

Numerous life insurance companies operating on the assessment plan of the benefit societies, although they are mere business cor-

bles. In America the table generally used, and the one frequently prescribed by law for use by the State insurance departments, is the American Experience Tables, compiled by Mr. Sheppard Homans from the statistics of the Mutual Life Insurance Company of New York City. A still later table and one which is supplanting others is the Actuaries or Combined Experience table. We give in the Appendix these tables of mortality.

It is not germane to this work to examine into the science of life insurance or its processes, except as adjudicated by the courts. For a full and interesting review and explanation of the business the reader is referred to the artitcle, Insurance, in the last edition of the Encyclopædia Britannica, an authority generally accessible.

porations, have at various times been organized and for a time been popular, but few have stood the test of time, and those that have survived have modified their plans.

§ 28. **Various Classes of Life Insurance.**—There are two principal classes of life insurance, each consisting of several varieties. The first class are those in which the sum insured is certain to become payable, provided only the insurance in duly kept in force; the second are those which are of a temporary or contingent character, so that the sum insured may or may not become payable, according to circumstances.

To the first class belong the great bulk of the transactions of life insurance companies, namely:

(*a*) *Whole Term Assurances on Single Lives.*—These are contracts to simply pay a certain sum, with or without dividends, on the death of the person named in the policy whenever that may occur. Usually the premium, or consideration for the policy, is an annual sum payable during the whole continuance of the policy. It may, however, be arranged differently, as by a single payment at the beginning of the transaction; or a limited number of contributions, each larger than the annual premium for the whole of life; or by a modified rate during a limited period and thereafter a correspondingly higher rate.

(*b*) *Endowment Assurances.*—In these the sum insured is payable to the assured if he should survive a certain period, or attain a specified age, or to his representatives at his death, if that should occur before such period has expired.

(*c*) *Insurance on Joint Lives.*—Here two or more lives are included in the policy and the sum insured is payable when either or any one of them dies.

(*d*) *Longest Life Assurances or Insurance on Last Survivor.*— These cover two or more lives, but mature on the death of the last survivor instead of upon the death of any one of the parties.

There are two varieties of the second class named above:

(*a*) *Temporary or Short Period Insurances.*—These are affected for short periods to cover special contingencies, the sum insured becoming payable only if death should occur during the time specified in the policy, just as policies of fire insurance. These

34

may be upon one or more lives, payable on the·end of one, or of both, or if one should fail before the other, as in the next variety.

(b) *Survivorship Insurances, or on One Life Against Another.* —In these the sum insured is payable at the death of A if that should happen in the lifetime of B, but not otherwise. Should B die before A, the transaction fails.[71]

§ 29. **An Early English Case.**—One of the earliest life insurance cases in England was the famous one of Godsall v. Boldero,[72] decided in 1807, where an assurance had been effected by the plaintiffs on the life of Hon. William Pitt. 'In this case, Lord Ellenborough held that a contract of life insurance was one of indemnity and, though a creditor may insure the life of his debtor to the extent of his debt, yet if, after the death of the debtor, his executors pay the debt to the creditor, the latter cannot afterwards recover upon the policy, although the debtor died insolvent and the executors were furnished the means of payment by a third party. The doctrine of this case was afterwards overruled.[73]

§ 29a. **First American Case.**—The first life insurance case in the United States was that of Lord v. Dall,[74] decided in 1815 by the Supreme Court of Massachusetts. Here an insurance for $5,000 had been effected for seven months on the life of one Jabez Lord, who was bound on a voyage to South America. Of this amount the defendant had underwritten five hundred dollars, or one-tenth, thus showing that the business was carried on by individual underwriters. Three defenses were interposed to the action, want of insurable interest, concealment of· material facts, and the illegality of the transaction, the insured being bound on a voyage for the purpose of procuring slaves.

[71] G. M. Low, Actuary, in 9th Ed. Encyc. Brit., Art. "Insurance—Life." A popular form of life insurance at the present time is tontine endowment, or where the profits from lapses and dividends are allowed to accumulate for a specified period and at the end of such period divided among the holders of the policies then in force. These profits are large because none inure to the benefit of the policies terminated by death or lapse during the tontine period. For a discussion of tontine insurance see *post*, Ch. V.

[72] 9 East. 72.

[73] Dalby v. India & London Life Assurance Co., 15 C. B. 365.

[74] 12 Mass. 115; 7 Am. Dec. 38.

In deciding the case on all points in favor of plaintiff the Court referred to the newness of the business and the doubts of its legality, but held that it was legal, using this language: "It is true that no precedent has been produced from our own records of an action upon a policy of this nature. But whether this has happened from the infrequency of disputes which have arisen, it being a subject of much less doubt and difficulty than marine insurances; or from the infrequency of such contracts, it is not possible for us to decide. By the common principles of law, however, all contracts fairly made, upon a valuable consideration, which infringe no law, and are not repugnant to the general policy of the laws, or to good morals, are valid and may be enforced, or damages recovered for the breach of them. It seems that these insurances are not favored in any of the commercial nations of Europe except England; several of them having expressly forbidden them, for what reasons, however, does not appear, unless the reason given in France is the prevailing one, viz.: 'That it is indecorous to set a price upon the life of man, and especially a freeman, which, they say, is above all price.' It is not a little singular that such a reason should be advanced for prohibiting these policies in France, where freedom has never known to exist, and that it never should have been thought of in England, which, for several centuries, has been the country of established and regulated liberty. This is a contract fairly made; the premium is a sufficient consideration; there is nothing on the face of it which leads to the violation of law; nor anything objectionable on the score of policy or morals. It must then be valid to support an action until something is shown by the party refusing to perform it, in excuse of his non-performance."

§ 30. **Early Beneficiary Life Insurance Cases in the United States.**—Probably the earliest case in the United States involving questions of benefit society life insurance was that of Wetmore v. Mutual Aid and Benevolent Association of Louisiana, decided in 1871.[75] This was an action on a policy, issued by defendant, and the defense was breach of a condition, relating to the payment of an assessment. The contract was that certain assessments were

75 23 La. Ann. 770.

to be paid by the assured within thirty days after being notified thereof by publication in one daily newspaper for five consecutive days. The company contended that the thirty days began to run from the day of the first publication, but the Court held that it began to run from the last day of publication.

The next case was that of Maryland Mutual Benevolent Society, etc., v. Clendinen, in 1875,[76] where the Court of Appeals of Maryland held that the rights of a member of a benefit society in the sum to be paid upon his death was a mere power to designate the beneficiary, which lapsed if not exercised, and that the benefit was not assets recoverable by his administrator. In 1876 came the case of Arthur v. Odd Fellows' Beneficial Association,[77] in which the Supreme Court of Ohio decided that the laws and regulations of the society determined the rights of its members, and also that the rights of the members in the benefit was only a power to designate a beneficiary in accordance with such laws.[78] Since these cases the number relating to benefit societies has steadily increased each year, and bids fair to become still larger as time passes. The newness of the business and doubts as to the proper construction of the contract have caused frequent questions to be submitted to the courts and these questions are still constantly arising. The courts have taken the position that the beneficiary societies are to be encouraged because of their kindly and helpful influence and have construed their laws liberally so as to further these purposes.

§ 31. **Definition of Terms Used in Insurance.**—The terms ordinarily used in insurance law are thus defined by Phillips:[79] "The party undertaking to make the indemnity is called the insurer or underwriter; the party to be indemnified, the assured or insured. The agreed consideration is called a premium; the instrument by which the contract is made, a policy; the events and causes of loss insured against, risks or perils; and the property or rights of the assured, in respect to which he is liable to loss, the subject or insurable interest." In respect to the terms applicable to the contracts of benefit societies the organizations are the insurers, and

[76] 44 Md. 429; 22 Am. Rep. 52.
[77] 29 Ohio St. 557.
[78] *Post*, Ch. VII.
[79] Phillips on Insurance, § 2.

the power to designate recipients of the benefits is in the members. These recipients are called the beneficiaries; the consideration, assessment, or assessments and dues;[80] and the instrument evidencing the contract, the certificate.

[80] *Post*, Ch. XI.

CHAPTER II.

ORGANIZATION, POWERS AND LIABILITIES; DISSOLUTION.

§ 32. **Life and Accident Insurance in the United States and Canada.**—As at present conducted in the United States and Canada the business of life and accident insurance is divided between regular life insurance corporations which for a certain consideration or premium, paid at one time, or annually, or oftener, agree to pay a specified amount at an agreed time, or sooner in case of the death of the party insured, or simply upon the death of the assured, or indemnity in the case of accidental injury; other corporations which promise to pay a definite amount, or the proceeds of certain assessments not to exceed a certain amount, upon a specified contingency, either death, disability or expiration of a certain period, the consideration of which agreement is the promise of the assured to pay certain assessments as called by the company; and fraternal beneficiary societies consisting of lodges, or sections, governed by a grand or supreme lodge, or both, composed of representatives elected from such lodges. All these various organizations have much in common and are all doing, either directly, or incidentally to other purposes, an insurance business; the same principles also often apply to all three classes. We shall treat of the relative dependence and government of the subordinate, grand and supreme lodges under the title "Government and Membership."[1]

§ 33. **Incorporating Under General Laws.**—Under the general corporation laws all persons who comply with the prescribed conditions may become a corporation. A substantial

[1] See succeeding chapter.

compliance with all the terms of the law is a prerequisite and, though in the first instance the Secretary of State, or other person charged with the duty of filing articles of incorporation and issuing a certificate thereof, may decide whether the provisions of the statute have been complied with, the ultimate decision rests always with the courts.[2] A recent able writer on the subject has so concisely stated the law of organization of corporations under the general law that we cannot do better than to quote his words: "A substantial compliance with all the terms of a general incorporation law is a prerequisite of the right of forming a corporation under it. Thus, where it is provided that a certificate, or articles of association, setting forth the purposes of the corporation about to be formed, the amount of its capital and other details, shall be filed with some public officer, a performance of this requirement is essential; and until it has been performed, the association will have no right whatever to assume corporate franchises. So, under some statutes, a license or certificate must be issued by a specified public officer before the corporation can be legally formed. The articles of incorporation must contain everything in substance that the laws under which the corporation is organized prescribe. Thus, if it is prescribed that the number or the names of the first directors of the corporation shall be set forth, a compliance with this provision is essential. A provision requiring the articles of incorporation to set forth that a majority of the members of the asso-

---

[2] Morawetz on Corp., §§ 15, 27. Thompson on Corp. (2nd. Ed.), §§ 178-179, *et seq.* As to what must be stated in articles of association see Moore v. Union Frat. Acc. Ass'n, 103 Ia. 424; 72 N. W. 645. As to powers of such corporation see International Frat. Alliance v. State, 86 Md. 550; 39 Atl. 512; 40 L. R. A. 187. In People v. Golden Gate Lodge, etc., 128 Cal. 257; 60 Pac. 865, the law of California relative to organization of fraternal corporations is discussed. As to reincorporation see People v. Payn, 59 N. Y. Supp. 851; 28 Misc. 275, where the right to reincorporate under the laws of New York is discussed. It is not enough to set forth the general objects of the corporation but the means by which these objects are to be accomplished must also be set forth. *In re* Right Worthy Grand Court, etc., 8 Pa. Dist. R. 127. Or where the society is formed for "social enjoyment," the character of the social enjoyment must be particularly stated; *In re* Burger's Military Band Ass'n, 19 Pa. Co. Ct. 651; *In re* Americus Club, 20 Pa. Co. Ct. 237; 9 Pa. Dist. 760.

ciation voted at the first election of directors is obligatory; and if the articles omit the required statement, proof cannot be admitted to show that a majority were in fact present and voted. Under a law requiring a certificate to be filed showing the manner of carrying on the business of the association, it is not sufficient to state merely that the manner of carrying on the business shall be such as the association may, from time to time, prescribe by rules, regulations and by-laws. Any other conditions precedent imposed by the express terms of the law must, of course, be complied with before the corporators can lawfully form a corporation. Upon the same general principle it follows that a corporation cannot lawfully act in a foreign State and carry on business there until all conditions precedent, prescribed by the laws of such State, have been performed."[3] Life and accident insurance companies and fraternal beneficiary societies are not considered in law as ordinary corporations, but their incorporation is regulated by statutes specially applicable to such organizations. These statutes generally provide how such corporations may be formed and require certain formalities to be observed, among which is the approval of the Superintendent of the Insurance Department, and also that a deposit shall be made with the Department for the security of policyholders and in the case of mutual companies that a certain number of policies shall have been applied for. It is not possible to particularize the various statutes on this subject, but reference must be had to those of each state. The legislature has not only power to enact laws governing the formation of such corporations, but the statutes are always subject to amendment.[4] The Supreme Court of Ohio[5] held that where the certificate provided that the manner of carrying on the business should be such as the association should, "from time to time, prescribe by its rules

---

[3] Morawetz on Corp., §§ 27, 28; also §§ 641, 645, 939; Cook on Corp. (7th Ed.), §§ 696-700.

[4] See next section. For a construction as to what is compliance with the Illinois statute; see Crawford v. Northwestern Traveling Men's Ass'n, 226 Ill. 57; 80 N. E. 736; 126 Ill. App. 468. For a construction of the incorporation laws of Oklahoma, see King v. Howeth & Co., 42 Okla. 178; 140 Pac. 1182.

[5] State v. Central Ohio Relief Ass'n, 29 Ohio St. 407.

and by-laws," not inconsistent with the State laws, it did not sufficiently comply with the statute requiring the certificate to specify "the manner of carrying on the business." Where the statute provides that a sworn statement shall be filed showing that at least 200 persons have made application in writing for membership in the association and subscribed in writing to be beneficiary members the latter requirement is as necessary as the first.[6] A general incorporation act can never be extended by construction to cases not reasonably within its terms. Upon this point the Supreme Court of Michigan has said:[7] "The present association was probably incorporated under the act in question, not as being precisely applicable, but as coming nearer to the purposes sought than any other statute. But it must always be remembered that no act for creating corporations can ever be extended by construction to cases not reasonably covered by its terms. It can never be assumed that incorporation will be allowed until the attention of the legislature has been given to each subject meant to be covered. The determination of the powers and conditions of corporate existence is peculiarly a matter of policy and not of law and requires legislative judgment. There are many lawful purposes for which no corporate powers have been granted, and there is much difference between the terms of such corporation laws as have been enacted." The duties of the superintendent of insurance in determining whether the requirements of a statute have been complied with are judicial in their nature and a decision that membership was not entered into in good faith will not be interfered with and mandamus will not lie.[8] Where the charter has been improvidently granted by the court under a statute and the scheme is found fraudulent such charter can be revoked by the same court, since having been granted without authority it is void *ab initio*.[9] A statute enlarging the powers of a beneficiary association takes

---

[6] *In re* Schmitt, 57 Hun. 590; 10 N. Y. Supp. 583.

[7] Stewart v. Father Matthew Soc., 41 Mich. 67.

[8] *In re* Schmitt, *supra;* citing People v. Chapin, 104 N. Y. 369; 11 N. E. 383; People v. Barnes, 114 N. Y. 317; 20 N. E. 609, and 21 N. E. 739; People v. Common Council, 78 N. Y. 33.

[9] *In re* National Indemnity and Endowment Co., 142 Pa. St. 450; 21 Atl. 879.

effect without formal adoption by the association and when, after such legislation, an application for membership is accepted, it cannot be said, in the absence of any express determination on the part of the association, that it was exercising the more limited powers under the earlier statute.[10]

§ 34. **Special Charters.**—Many of the older life insurance companies are doing business under special charters granted by legislative authority. While the general incorporation acts may limit the duration of the existence of corporations, it has been held that the courts will look at the nature of the corporation to ascertain the intent of the legislature, and while ordinarily the word continuous, or perpetual, succession, so far as business corporations are concerned, does not confer unlimited duration of life, yet where it is evident from the nature of the business that in order to insure its success the duration must continue for an unlimited period, it will be held that the legislature so intended. The Supreme Court of Missouri has said:[11] "It may be truly said that life insurance companies are not founded with a view of being maintained for a brief period only, or for any limited time. Their nature and purpose denote perpetuity, and without which it would not be reasonable to suppose men of affairs would organize such companies or invest their money in the same as a protection for their families if they thought such companies might, and in all probability would, be dissolved long prior to the time when their policies would mature and become payable. These observations are supported by the cases of State ex rel v. Lesueur,[12] and State ex rel v. Trustees of Westminster College.[13] So viewing this case in the light of both reason and authority, we are clearly of the opinion that the intention of the Legislature was to make this charter perpetual—that

[10] Mass. Catholic Order, etc., v. Callahan, 146 Mass. 391; 16 N. E. 14; Marsh v. Supreme Council A. L. H., 144 Mass. 512; 21 N. E. 1070; 4 L. R. A. 382 and note; Grand Lodge A. O. U. W. v. McKinstry, 67 Mo. App. 82.

[11] State ex rel Major v. German Mut. Life Ins. Co., 224 Mo. 84; 123 S. W. 19; 19 Ann. Cas. 1210.

[12] 141 Mo. 29; 41 S. W. 904.

[13] 175 Mo. 52; 74 S. W. 1116.

is, everlasting.''[14] The same Court has held:[15] "It would be preposterous to assume that men would enter into the work of founding a college, erecting buildings, and gathering the necessary appliances for the conduct of such an institution, to be dissolved at the end of twenty years. Therefore, although this charter contains no express words declaring that there is to be no period to its duration, yet it is impossible to read it without perceiving that it was the design of the legislature to make it perpetual." The general rule, of course, applies that in construing the charter of a corporation, whether created under a general act relating to all corporations, or under a special charter, the intent of the legislature must be ascertained and the language will be liberally construed to enable the corporation to carry out the purposes of its creation.[16]

§ 35. **The Modern Idea of Corporations.**—The modern and most approved doctrine concerning the nature of a corporation is that it is simply a voluntary association of persons, endowed by the law with certain special privileges, conferred by the general acts concerning corporations or the special charter, chief among which is always that of a distinct entity, by which it is known and in which the personalities of its members or stockholders are merged. Often the law goes behind this artificial entity and deals with the corporators or members as an association of individuals, or partnership. A corporation is nothing more or less than a peculiar kind of partnership. The corporate entity, as an association, or partnership, acts through and by its agents. The charter and articles of association are supposed to be known to all persons dealing with a corporation and the authority of the agents is determined by this source of authority. The laws of agency are constantly referred to in testing the validity of corporate acts. While acts in excess of corporate authority are generally void, as being what is tech-

---

[14] See also State *ex rel* v. Ladies of Sacred Heart, 99 Mo. 533; 12 N. W. 293.

[15] State v. Westminster College, 175 Mo. 52; 74 S. W. 990.

[16] Farmers' L. & T. Co. v. Perry, 3 Sandf. Ch. 371; Farmers' L. & T. Co. v. Clowes, 3 N. Y. 470.

nically known as *ultra vires*, it must always be remembered that what may be beyond the powers of a corporation under some circumstances will not be so considered under different circumstances. When a contract of a corporation has not been executed it will not be enforced specifically if in excess of corporate authority, but if executed a different rule is generally applied and the corporation is not allowed to take advantage of its own wrong. This subject of the validity of corporate acts, or *ultra vires*, is one of the most perplexing, complicated and least understood in the domain of corporate law and from the mass of conflicting decisions we cannot attempt to deduce specific rules. Of all modern writers, Mr. Morawetz has most understandingly collated the authorities and evolved the governing principles, and to his work we must refer, for, when incorporated, neither life insurance companies nor benefit societies are different in law from other corporations so far as general legal principles are concerned.[17]

§ 36. **Rights of Policyholders.**—Life insurance companies, as we have seen, are either stock, where the capital is like that of any other corporation owned by individual stockholders, or a mutual company, where, so to speak, the policyholders are also stockholders, or they partake of the nature of both by reserving to the stockholders a certain return on their investment and providing that the policyholders shall be given the benefit of any surplus over the amount required to pay the dividend on the stock. One of the latter is the Equitable Life Assurance Society of New York.

In the case of Polk v. Mutual Reserve Fund Life Ass'n,[18] the Court said: "That the rights of the policyholders and the insurer must be ascertained and determined in connection with the constitution and by-laws of the company and the certificates of insurance, which constitute the contract between the par-

---

[17] Morawitz on Corp., Ch. VII, §§ 577-725; Cook on Corp. (7th Ed.), Ch. XL.

[18] 137 Fed. 273. See also Benjamin v. Mut. Reserve Fund Life Ass'n, 146 Cal. 34; 70 Pac. 517.

ties, will not admit of serious dispute.[19] The decisions of the highest courts of the state upon this question are of controlling authority.[20] The contract determines the rights and liabilities of the members thereof, and the fact of membership in a mutual insurance corporation does not alter the relations thus created.[21] The question involved in that case was whether or not the contract obligations between an association insuring lives upon the co-operative plan, were not unconstitutionally impaired by the reorganization of such association as a mutual level premium company. The case was finally determined by the Supreme Court,[22] in which the Court held, citing Wright v. Minn. Mutual Life Ins. Co.,[23] that no constitutional right was impaired by such a reorganization. In the case of Lord v. Equitable Life Assur. Soc.,[24] it was held that the power to amend a general law of incorporation involves the power to amend the charter taken out under such law; that the stockholders of a corporation, as such, have no direct power of management, but they have the right to vote for directors and thereby protect the property from loss and make it effective in earning dividends, and depriving a stockholder of the right to vote for directors is depriving him of an essential attribute of his property. The Court held under the peculiar provisions of the charter of that company that the law did not require that the net surplus should be divided among all the policyholders, but they became the equitable owners of an equitable share therein, and a division must be made on some equitable basis consistent with the safety

19 Matter of Equitable Reserve Fund Life Ass'n, 131 N. Y. 354; 30 N. E. 114; C. H. Venner Co. v. United States Steel Corp. et al. (C. C.) 116 Fed. 1012; Uhlman v. N. Y. Life Ins. Co., 109 N. Y. 421, 17 N. E. 363, 4 Am. St. 482; Everson v. Equitable Life Assur. Soc., 71 Fed. 570; 18 C. C. A. 251; Hunton v. Equitable Life Assur. Soc. of the U. S. (C. C.) 45 Fed. 661; Cohen v. N. Y. Mut. Life Ins. Co., 50 N. Y. 610; 10 Am. 522.

20 Schurz v. Cook, 148 U. S. 397, 13 Sup. Ct. 645, 37 L. Ed. 498.

21 People ex rel Meyers v. M. G. & B. Ass'n, 126 N. Y. 615; 27 N. E. 1037.

22 Polk v. Mut. Reserve Life Ass'n, 207 U. S. 310.

23 193 U. S. 657.

24 194 N. Y. 212; 87 N. E. 443; reversing 110 N. Y. Supp. 1135; 126 App. Div. 937.

and prosperity of the company. The State alone has power to inquire into the right of an insurance company to invest in stock of a bank.[25]

A policyholder cannot bring a suit in equity for an accounting as to distribution of surplus and for the appointment of a receiver.[26] The Court, citing Uhlman v. New York Life Ins. Co.,[27] said "that it cannot be said that the defendant is, in any sense, a trustee of any particular fund for the plaintiff, or that it acts as to him and in relation to any such fund in a fiduciary capacity." It has been said that the holder of a policy in a mutual company is in no sense a partner of the corporation which issued the policy and that the relation between the policyholder and the company is one of contract, measured by the terms of the policy.[28]

A policyholder in a mutual company entitled to a vote at the elections of trustees and to a credit at the end of each five years to his equitable part of the profits, has the right to inspect the books of the company.[29]

It has been decided[30] that "a policyholder of a stock life insurance corporation, conducted on the mutual plan above a limited dividend to the stockholders, cannot sue to restrain a transfer of the assets of the corporation to a foreign stock insurance corporation pursuant to a contract for the merger of the two corporations."

In the case of St. John v. American Mut. Life Ins. Co.,[31] the Court said: "I am not aware of any principle of law that distinguishes contracts of insurance upon lives from other ordi-

[25] Hyde v. Equitable Life Assur. Soc., 116 N. Y. Supp. 219; 61 Misc. Rep. 518.

[26] Equitable Life Assur. Soc. v. Brown, 213 U. S. 25; reversing 151 Fed. 1, 81 C. C. A. 1.

[27] 109 N. Y. 421; 17 N. E. 363; 4 Am. St. Rep. 482.

[28] See also Greeff v. Equitable Life Assur. Soc., 160 N. Y. 19; 54 N. E. 712; 46 L. R. A. 288.

[29] State v. Germania Mut. Life Ins. Co., 169 Mo. App. 354; 152 S. W. 618.

[30] Russell v. Pittsburgh L. & T. Co., 116 N. Y. Supp. 841; 132 App. Div. 217, reversing 115 N. Y. Supp. 950

[31] 13 N. Y. 31; 64 Am. Dec. 529.

nary contracts, or that takes them out of the operation of the same legal rules which are applied to and govern such contracts.'' A society has no power to ratify a contract with a promoter, agreeing to pay plaintiff a commission for obtaining contracts of insurance before the association is organized.[32]

Nor can incorporators control the internal affairs of a corporation after organization without statutory authority.[33]

Under the Missouri statute the issuance of a certified copy of the articles of association makes it a body corporate and a fraternal beneficiary association does not become a corporation, with power to issue benefit certificates, until the Secretary of State issues a certified copy of the articles of agreement.[34]

In the case of Huber v. Martin,[35] it was held that the interest of policyholders in a mutual insurance company are two-fold—they are both insurers and insured. In respect to the former they are entitled to share in the losses and profits of the business on the basis of a partnership, except so far as the charter, or policy contract, provides otherwise. An extract from the opinion is as follows: ''The principle which lies at the foundation of mutual insurance, and gives it its name, is mutuality; in other words, the intervention of each person insured in the management of the affairs of the company, and the participation of each member in the profits and losses of the business in proportion to his interest.''[36] ''Each person insured becomes a member of the body corporate, clothed with the rights, and subject to the liabilities, of a stockholder.''[37] ''Although the members of a mutual company are not usually denominated stockholders, and are not stockholders in the usual sense of the

[32] First National Bank v. Church Federation of America, 129 Ia. 268; 105 N. W. 578.

[33] Eminent Household Co. v. Thornton, 134 Ga. 405; 67 S. E. 849.

[34] Sloan v. Fraternal Home Ass'n, 139 Mo. App. 443; 123 S. W. 57. As to the right of participation in profits see Anderson v. Buckley, 147 Ala. 415; 41 Sou. 748; Jenkins v. Sun Life Ins. Co., 120 Ky. 790; 87 S. W. 1143.

[35] 127 Wis. 412; 105 N. W. 1031; 3 L. R. A. (N. S.) 653.

[36] 2 May, Ins. 4th Ed. Sec. 548.

[37] Id. Sec. 548; 21 Am. & Eng. Enc. Law, 2nd Ed., p. 267; Korn v. Mut. Assur. Soc., 6 Cranch, 192, 3 L. Ed. 195.

word, yet they are in point of fact stockholders.''[38] ''The property of the corporation belongs to its members.''[39] ''There is nothing to prevent a mutual company from carrying on its operations with a view to profits and dividends.[40] In Riddell v. Harmony Fire Ins. Co.[41] the distribution of the assets, not surplus, of a mutual organization was enjoined at the suit of a member on the ground that such distribution was improper, except on surrender of the charter or dissolution of the corporation. The case proceeds upon the ground that the property of a non-stock corporation, not public, needed for its business, belongs to the members, but not recoverable, of course, in possession, so long as the corporation is a going concern. The title to the property in any corporation—the substantial, beneficial ownership—is in its members.[42]

§ 37. **Corporate Powers.**—It is a well-settled principle that a corporation has no other powers than such as are specifically granted; or such as are necessary for the purpose of carrying into effect the powers expressly granted.[43] ''A corporation and an individual,'' says a standard authority,[44] ''stand upon a very different footing. The latter, existing for the good of society, may do all acts, and make all contracts which are not in the eye of the law inconsistent with this great purpose of his creation; whereas, the former, having been created for a specific purpose, not only can make no contract forbidden by its charter, which is, as it were, the law of its nature, but in general can make no contract which is not necessary either directly or incidentally, to enable it to answer that purpose.'' A corporation cannot by combining one purpose with others, if any one is forbidden by statute, destroy or subvert the conditions and limitations attaching by law, and where the statute limited the amount of a policy to be issued by a co-operative assessment asso-

---

[38] 2 May, Ins. 4th Ed. Sec. 549.

[39] Opinion of District Judge in Temperance Mut. Benev. Ass'n v. Home Friendly Soc., 187 Pa. 38-44, 40 Atl. 1100.

[40] Mygatt v. New York Protective Ins. Co., 21 N. Y. 52-66.

[41] 8 Phila. 310.

[42] Clark & M. Priv. Corp., p. 23.

[43] Ang. & Ames on Corp., § 111.

[44] Ang. & Ames on Corp., § 256.

ciation to $1,000, it could not issue policies for larger amounts because its charter provided not only for insurance but also for social and fraternal beneficial purposes.[45] An incorporated society is not liable for policies issued before incorporation.[46] Nor can the directors, in the absence of legislative authority, and without any previous action of the members, transfer the entire property and membership of the association to another corporation.[47]

§ 38. **The Charter the Source of Corporate Powers.** — The charter, therefore, or the articles of association, is the fountain of authority for the corporation. It contains the agreement and contract on the part of the corporators and the State which specifies the terms of association, and the limits and bounds in which the associated body can act.[48] And it is a settled rule that a person who deals with a corporation must, at his peril, take notice of its charter or articles of association. The rule applies to both foreign and domestic corporations and rests on the necessities of the case. All persons having transactions with corporate bodies must not only notice the terms of their charters, but also all the general legislation of the State creating them, by which business with corporations is affected.[49] Members of an incorporated society must also take notice that the charter is subject to amendment.[50] Charters of corporations and articles of association of unincorporated societies are construed like other written instruments. The object is to discover the intention of the parties, and to this end, and to carry out the objects of the organization, a liberal policy has been generally adopted.[51] A corporation chartered for "benevolent or pro-

[45] International Fraternal Alliance v. State, 86 Md. 550; 39 Atl. 572; 40 L. R. A. 187. See § 265 for discussion of question of *ultra vires*.

[46] Montgomery v. Whitbeck, 12 N. D. 385; 96 N. W. 327.

[47] Temperance Mut. Benev. Ass'n, v. Home Friendly Soc., 187 Pa. St. 38; 40 Atl. 1100.

[48] Morawetz on Corp., §§ 642, 318, and cases cited. Cook on Corp. (7th Ed.), § 2.

[49] Montgomery v. Whitbeck, 12 N. D. 385; 96 N. W. 327; Morawetz on Corp., §§ 591, 592.

[50] Park v. Modern Woodmen, 181 Ill. 214; 54 N. E. 932.

[51] Morawetz on Corp., §§ 316-388 inc.

tective purposes to its members from funds collected therein" cannot extend its operations by means of agents and so-called "subordinate lodges" throughout a State for the pecuniary advantage of its officers and managers of the concern, assessing members of subordinate lodges who are excluded from membership in the central corporation.[52] But the fact that some of the rules of a society are illegal does not make the society such.[53]

§ 39. **Right to Corporate Name.**—In a well considered case,[54] the Court said: "It seems to be well settled that the name of a corporation, while not a part of its franchise, is, to a certain extent, property; and that it will be protected in a proper case on principles somewhat analogous to those which are applied to trade-marks."[55] It has also been said,[56] that "When there are no statute provisions as to the choice of name, and parties organize a corporation under general laws, it may be that they choose a name at their peril; and that, if they take one so like that of an existing corporation as to be misleading and thereby to injure its business, they may be enjoined, if there is no language in the statute to the contrary." Where a faction of an Order of the Knights or Pythias separated from the main body and adopted the name of "Improved Order of Knights of Pythias, "

[52] Commonwealth v. Order of Vesta (Pa. Com. P.), 12 Pa. Co. Ct. R. 481; 2 Pa. Dist. R. 254. See also Fogg v. Sup. L. Order Golden Lion, 156 Mass. 431; 31 N. E. 289.

[53] Swaine v. Wilson, L. R. 26 Q. B. Div. 252; 31 Am. & Eng. Corp. Cas. 164; Collins v. Locke, 4 App. Cas. 674. In the case of Park v. Modern Woodmen, 181 Ill. 215; 54 N. E. 932, it was held that the legislature may validate corporate acts, that a corporation is not liable on a contract made by its promoters before incorporation unless it ratifies it and that the head office can be changed by amending its constitution. This case distinguishes Bastian v. Modern Woodmen, 166 Ill. 595; 46 N. E. 1090.

[54] Grand Lodge A. O. U. W. v. Graham, 96 Ia. 592; 65 N. W. 837; 31 L. R. A. 133.

[55] Newby v. Oregon Central R. R., 18 Fed. Cas. 38; Deady, 609; Am. & Eng. Enc. of Law, 268 (old ed.).

[56] American Order of Scottish Clans v. Merrill, 151 Mass. 558; 24 N. E. 918; 8 L. R. A. 320, and a case in point in St. Patrick's Alliance v. Byrne, 59 N. J. Eq. 26; 44 Atl. 716.

it was held,[57] that the test is whether by the use of the name by the new corporation the order will be damaged by depriving it of members who would otherwise join it. The right to enjoin a rival concern may be lost by laches.[58] It has been held[59] that, under the statute, a State officer may be invested with the power of determining whether the name of a proposed corporation conflicts with any other, in which case his decision is final; but it has also been held that the certificate of the State officer as to the right of a corporation to a name is not binding upon another body claiming the right to such name.[60] The right of a corporation to use its name is a part of its franchise and cannot be annulled or taken away at the suit of the members of a voluntary association who claim adversely.[61] If the statute does not require the name of the corporation to be in English a charter cannot be refused because the name is in a foreign language.[62]

§ 40. **The Same Subject—Remedies.**—The New York Court of Appeals has held,[63] that the right to injunctive relief against the unfair and misleading use of a corporate name is not limited to trading, industrial, or financial, business corporations, but extends as well to benevolent, or fraternal, corporations not engaged in business. The Connecticut Supreme Court of Errors

[57] Supreme Lodge K. of P. v. Improved Order K. of P., 113 Mich. 140; 71 N. W. 473; 38 L. R. A. 658.

[58] Grand Lodge A. O. U. W. v. Graham, *supra.* Great Hive L. O. M. v. Supreme Hive L. O. M., 129 Mich. 324; 97 N. W. 779; 99 N. W. 26. See also Same v. Same, 129 Mich. 324; 88 N. W. 882.

[59] American Order Scottish Clans v. Merrill, *supra.*

[60] Grand Lodge A. O. U. W. v. Graham, 96 Ia. 592; 31 L. R. A. 133. Exhaustive briefs on the subject of this section will be found in 31 L. R. A. 133 and 38 L. R. A. 658.

[61] Paulino v. Portuguese Benev. Ass'n, 18 R. I. 165; 26 Atl. 36; 20 L. R. A. 272. See also High Court of Wisconsin, etc., v. Commissioner of Insurance, 98 Wis. 94; 73 N. W. 326.

[62] *In re* Deutch Amerikanischer, etc., Verein, 200 Pa. St. 143; 149 Atl. 949.

[63] Benevolent & Protective Order of Elks v. Improved & Benevolent Order of Elks of the World, 205 N. Y. 450; 98 N. E. 756; Ann. Cas. 1913 E. 639.

has said:[64] "The defendants endeavor to establish a distinction between cases where the corporations involved are created for the purpose of financial profit, and membership corporations whose sole purposes are the literary and social advancement of the members and the payment of a death benefit at their decease. It is claimed that an injunction should not lie in the latter class of cases, although it lies in the former. No sufficient reason is suggested for a distinction. It will be more difficult to show that the use of the name is injurious and a fraud upon the public in the latter than in the former, but there is no difference in principle between the two. A corporation has such a property in its name, whether organized for pecuniary profit or not, that equity will protect it by enjoining another corporation from the use of the same name or one so similar to it as to mislead the public."[65]

The principle upon which courts of equity act in restraining similarity of names is not that there is property acquired in the name, but to prevent fraud and deception.[66] The name must not be calculated to deceive, and if the name of a corporation is calculated to deceive the use of the name will be enjoined.[67] But where a society had existed as an unincorporated body for several years and afterwards a controversy arose between it and the Supreme Lodge, and some members were attempting to transfer its corporate rights to another fraternal organization by applying for an amendment of its charter, changing its name, such petition for change of name must be refused.[68] A

---

[64] Daughters of Isabella, etc., v. National Order Daughters of Isabella, 83 Conn. 679; 78 Atl. 333; Ann. Cas. 1912 A. 822. In a later case in the Federal Court, National Council, Daughters of I. v. National Order Daughters of I., 232 Fed. 907, it was held that the case in Connecticut had no extra-territorial effect and an injunction was refused.

[65] People v. Rose, 225 Ill. 496; 80 N. E. 293; International Committee of Young Women's Christian Ass'n v. Young Women's Christian Ass'n, 194 Ill. 194; 62 N. E. 551; 56 L. R. A. 888.

[66] Most Worshipful Grand Lodge F. A. & F. M. v. Grimshaw, 34 App. D. C. 383.

[67] Von Thodorovich v. Franz-Josef Benev. Ass'n, 154 Fed. 911.

[68] In re Liberty Bell Lodge, etc., 231 Pa. 112; 80 Atl. 532; State Council Jr. O. U. A. M. v. National Council, etc., 71 N. J. E. 433; 64 Atl. 561.

mere addition to the name of other words does not affect the right for an injunction.[69] A charter has been refused for a negro lodge of the Elks on the ground of similarity of name.[70]

The right, however, to have another fraternal order enjoined from using a similar name may be lost by laches in asserting the right.[71] It has also been held that where a branch of a fraternal order, although organized by the parent order is incorporated under the laws of another state, it cannot be enjoined from using the name of the order after secession from the parent order.[72] And wherever the use of the name of a new company will tend to confusion such use will be enjoined.[73] Where seceding members of a voluntary association procured a charter under the name of the voluntary association, it was held that the latter could not sue to enjoin the use of its name, because the act of incorporation fixed the name of the corporation and its right to use that name is part of its franchise, conferred on it by law, which can no more be annulled at the suit of private persons than can its franchise to be such corporation.[74]

§ 41. **Regular, or "Old Line," Insurance Companies.** — Deferring the discussion of what constitutes a contract of insurance for the present, and remembering that life insurance companies have been roughly classified as "regular," or "old line," and fraternal beneficial, corporations, it is necessary to refer to some cases where this classification has been considered. In the case of Filley v. Illinois L. Ins. Co. et al.,[74a] the Court said: "An 'old line life insurance company' is generally a corporation which insures any applicant who passes the medical examina-

[69] Creswell v. Grand Lodge K. P., 133 Ga. 837; 67 S. E. 188.

[70] In re Charter Iron City Lodge, Improved B. & P. O. of Elks, 39 Pa. Super. Ct. 365; Grand Lodge K. P., etc., v. Grand Lodge K. P., 174 Ala. 395; 56 Sou. 963; Benev., etc., Order of Elks v. Improved Benev. Order, etc., 122 Tenn. 141; 118 S. W. 389.

[71] Creswell v. Grand Lodge K. P., 225 U. S. 246; reversing 133 Ga. 837; 18 Ann. Cas. 453; 67 S. E. 188.

[72] Council of Jewish Women v. Boston Soc., etc., 212 Mass. 219; 98 N. E. 862.

[73] Knights of Maccabees v. Searle, 75 Neb. 285; 106 N. W. 448.

[74] Paulino v. Portuguese Benev. Ass'n, 18 R. I. 165; 26 Atl. 36; 20 L. R. A. 272. See also Perham v. Richman, 158 Fed. 546

[74a] 93 Kan. 193; 144 Pac. 257; affirming 91 Kan. 220; 137 Pac. 793.

tion and otherwise can meet the rules of the company, and the insured does not thereby become a member of the company. Yet, as in this case, the consent of the policyholder would be necessary to substitute another corporation in place of the insurer and to relieve the insurer from liability. On the other hand, the individual member of a strictly mutual life insurance association or fraternal benefit association is at once an insurer as to his fellow members and, in turn, is insured by them.'' So an association of railway mail clerks has been held to be an accident insurance company.[75] And an association whose contracts were not such as the law relating to fraternal beneficiary societies authorized, has been held to be an old line insurance company.[76]

§ 42. **Classification of Insurance Companies.**—With the enactment of laws regulating the business of insurance and providing certain arbitrary conditions, as, for example, that suicide shall be no defense,[77] or that a misrepresentation in the application shall not avoid the policy, unless it shall have contributed to the event upon the happening of which the policy becomes payable,[78] and providing that certain organizations shall be exempt from either of these conditions, or other provisions of the insurance laws of the State, the courts have often been called upon to determine the classification of insurance organizations. In construing the statute of Missouri providing for the exemption from certain requirements of insurance laws of companies doing business on the assessment plan, the Court said :[79] ''It is immaterial what name a company may adopt, its liability is determined by the character of its contracts of in-

---

[75] Young v. Ry. Mail Ass'n, 126 Mo. App. 325; 103 S. W. 557.

[76] Wilson v. General Assembly Am. Benev. Ass'n, 125 Mo. App. 597; 103 S. W. 109. See also Schmidt v. Mut. Reserve Fund Life Ass'n, 128 Mo. App. 497; 106 S. W. 1082; Smoot v. Bankers' Life Ass'n, 138 Mo. App. 438; 120 S. W. 719.

[77] *Post*, § 441.

[78] *Post*, § 240.

[79] Toomey v. Supreme Lodge K. of P., 147 Mo. 129; 48 S. W. 936; affirming 74 M. A. 507. See also McDonald v. Life Ass'n, 154 Mo. 618; 55 N. W. 999; Westerman v. Knights of Pythias, 196 Mo. 670; 94 S. W. 470.

surance and the law then places the company in its proper class.'' The fact that an insurance company is licensed to do business in the State as an assessment company does not make it such, nor in any way, nor any wise change its character or status.[80] And the same Court has also said :[81] ''The calling of a contract of insurance, an accident, tontine or regular life policy, or, for that matter by any other appellation that may be adopted for business or conventional uses or classification, cannot make a policy containing an agreement to pay to another a sum of money designated upon the happening of an unknown or contingent event depending upon the existence of life, less a policy of insurance on life.'' So, a society in issuing a contract providing for extended or paid up insurance, a fraternal society has been held to be an ''old line'' company.[82] To constitute a life policy on the assessment plan, there must be a provision for an assessment and a personal liability on the members to pay it, as well as a right given to a beneficiary to have the assessment made.[83] In a case in Ohio, although there was a provision in the contract for extra assessments in case of emergency, but a fixed schedule of rates was provided for, the Supreme Court said : ''The ordinary, regular, and chief source of revenue open to the relator is the fixed periodical payments named in the policy, and, in our opinion, for the purpose of admission into the State, they characterize the method of insurance which the company pursues. The possibility that some grave and unforeseen calamity may call into operation an authority vested in the trustees to call for an additional and uncertain sum should not be regarded as sufficient to assign the company to that class which transacts the business of insurance on the assessment plan.''[84] A policy

[80] Aloe v. Fidelity Mut. Life Ass'n, 164 Mo. 675; 55 S. W. 993.

[81] Logan v. Fidelity & Casual Co., 146 Mo. 114; 47 S. W. 948.

[82] McPike v. Sup. Ruling Fraternal Mystic Circle, 187 Mo. App. 679; 173 S. W. 71.

[83] Folkens v. N. W. National L. Ins. Co., 98 M. A. 480; 72 S. W. 720.

[84] State v. Mathews, 58 Ohio St. 1; 49 N. E. 1034; 40 L. R. A. 418. See also Morton v. Royal Tribe of Joseph, 93 Mo. App. 78. Other cases, where the nature and privileges of assessment companies are considered, are: Aloe v. Mut. Reserve L. Ass'n, 147 Mo. 561; 49 S. W. 553; Hanford v. Mass. Benev. Ass'n, 122 Mo. 50; 26 S. W. 680; Haynie v.

providing for the payment of a fixed sum but authorizing an assessment if necessary is a contract of insurance on the assessment plan.[85] The question whether a given society is a fraternal benefit association is to be determined alone by its charter and the law under which it is operated.[86]

§ 43. **General Incorporation Laws for Insurance Organizations.**—The policy of the various States of the Union has been to encourage the formation of corporations and to this end, and to avoid any appearance of discrimination, general laws exist, by compliance with the terms of which corporations may be organized for almost every imaginable purpose.[87] Practically all the regular, or old line, life insurance companies are corporations, either organized under general laws, or by special charters granted by legislative authority. Benefit societies in nearly all the states are not regarded as strictly charitable and benevolent organizations, although they may become incorporated under special provisions of statutes relating to the incorporation of such societies. It is essential, however, that they have no capital stock and be not formed for pecuniary profit to the members. At the present time uniform acts of the legislatures of the various states regulate the organization of fraternal beneficiary societies and the business to be conducted by them. The Cali-

Knights Templars and Masons Indem., 139 Mo. 416; 41 S. W. 461; Elliott v. Des Moines L. Ass'n, 163 Mo. 132; 63 S. W. 400; Jacobs v. Omaha L. Ass'n, 142 Mo. 49; 43 S. W. 275; Grimes v. N. W. L. of H., 97 Iowa, 315; 64 N. W. 806; People v. Industrial, etc., Ass'n, 92 Hun, 31; 36 N. Y. Supp. 963; Shotliff v. Mod. Woodmen, 100 Mo. App. 138; 73 S. W. 326.

[85] Moran v. Franklin Life Ins. Co., 160 Mo. App. 407; 140 S. W. 955; McCoy v. Bankers' Life Ass'n, 134 Mo. App. 35; 114 S. W. 551.

[86] Baltzell v. Mod. Woodmen, 98 Mo. App. 153; 71 S. W. 1071. But see Morton v. Royal Tribe of Joseph, 93 Mo. App. 78; and Shotliff v. Modern Woodmen, *supra*. The Supreme Court of Missouri, in Franta v. Bohemian, etc., Union, 164 Mo. 304; 63 S. W. 1100; 54 L. R. A. 723; considers also the characteristics and definition of a fraternal beneficiary association, which views are somewhat opposed to those expressed in National Union v. Marlow, 21 C. C. A. 89; 74 Fed. 775. The question is also considered in Kern v. Supreme Council A. L. of H., 167 Mo. 471; 67 S. W. 252. See also *post*, § 48.

[87] 1 Morawitz on Corp., §§ 8, 9 and 10. Cook on Corp. (7th Ed.), § 2

fornia statute as to religious, etc., corporations does not apply to a lodge of Elks.[88]

§ 44. **Benefit Societies Incorporated Under Special Charters.** —Benefit societies are often incorporated under special acts of the legislature, the charters in such cases forming contracts between them and their members to be construed like other contracts. Unless expressly forbidden by the constitution State legislatures can create corporations for any purpose.[89] Corporate powers, however, cannot be created by implication or extended by construction.[90]

§45. **Benefit Societies as Charities.**—The extent to which these associations are to be regarded as charities has often been discussed. The Supreme Court of Indiana,[91] has said "a corporation which promises to pay a certain sum as benefits during a member's illness in consideration of his payment of dues, is not a purely benevolent organization; it may be and doubtless is benevolent and charitable in a great degree, but it is not a benevolent organization in the sense of dispensing benefits without consideration." In California, the Supreme Court[92] held, in a suit brought to dissolve the "Riggers and Stevedore's Union Association," as follows: "This is a voluntary association, formed for the benefit of the members of it. It partakes of the nature of a partnership. We do not see why a number of persons, capable of contracting, may not associate and agree, as the basis and consideration of the association, that the funds raised by voluntary contribution, or otherwise, through the by-laws of the company, shall be appropriated absolutely or in a given contingency, to the benefit of the individual members. This is such an agreement. A number of the members of a particular avoca-

---

[88] People v. Golden State Lodge, 128 Calif. 257; 60 Pac. R. 825.

[89] United States Trust Co. v. Brady, 20 Barb. 119; Bishop v. Brainerd, 28 Conn. 289; Franklin Bridge Co. v. Wood, 14 Ga. 80; Aurora v. West, 9 Ind. 74. Some of the oldest benefit societies are incorporated under special acts. This was true of the Knights of Honor, now defunct, incorporated in Kentucky.

[90] Pennsylvania R. Co. v. Canal Commissioners, 21 Pa. St. 9; Stewart v. Father Matthew Soc., 41 Mich. 67.

[91] Bauer v. Sampson Lodge, 102 Ind. 262.

[92] Gorman v. Russell, 14 Cal. 535.

tion meet for mutual benefit and protection, and prescribe rules for the government of the society thus organized. They agree that each shall contribute a certain fixed sum to the common treasury, and that this sum shall be applied in a certain event, as in sickness, etc., to the relief of the necessities or wants of the individual members or of their families. This is not a charity any more than an assurance society against fire, or upon life, is a charity. It is simply a fair and reciprocal contract among the members to pay certain amounts, in certain contingencies, to each other, out of a common fund."[93] Masonic lodges have been held to be charities, and as such exempted from taxation,[94] though as to this latter point the contrary has been held.[95] In Alabama[96] the Supreme Court held that it would take judicial notice that the grand and subordinate lodges of the Masonic society within that State constituted a charitable or eleemosynary corporation. In a New Hampshire case,[97] the plaintiff sued to recover his share of the funds of a Masonic lodge whose members had voted its dissolution and division of its property, and the Court held that the action could not be maintained, as the society was for charitable purposes and the funds were in the custody of the lodge for charitable uses.[98] As bearing on this question, whether benefit societies are to be considered charities, we may cite the test laid down by the Supreme Court of Pennsylvania:[99] "Private or individual gain, in a pecuniary sense, is not the sole test. 'The true test is to be found in the objects of the institution.' Where these are to advance the interest of a party, of an association, of a private corporation, of a religious denomination, and the like, however beneficial to the public their

[93] See Goodman v. Jedidjah Lodge, 67 Md. 117; 9 Atl. 13; Miner v. Mich. Mut. Benev. Ass'n, 63 Mich. 338; 29 N. W. 852; dissenting opinion Sperry's Appeal, 116 Pa. St. 391; 9 Atl. 478; Bauer v. Sampson Lodge, 102 Ind. 262.

[94] Indianapolis v. Grand Master, 25 Ind. 518; Mayor, etc., v. Solomon's Lodge, 53 Ga. 93; State v. Addison, 2 S. C. 499.

[95] Morning Star, etc., v. Hayslip, 23 Ohio St. 144; Bangor v. Masonic Lodge, 73 Maine, 429.

[96] Burdine v. Grand Lodge, 37 Ala. 478.

[97] Duke v. Fuller, 9 N. H. 536; 32 Am. Dec. 392.

[98] See also Spiller v. Maude, 10 Jur. (N. S.) 1089; 13 W. R. 69.

[99] Burd Orphan Asylum v. School District, etc., 90 Pa. St. 29.

growth and success may be, there is a private object to gain; the institution is not unqualifiedly public. In such case the purpose is wholly private or the private blends with the public.'' In the same case on rehearing the Court thus construed the word "purely" as used by statutes in reference to benevolent and charitable organizations: "As to the meaning of the word "purely" when used in this connection, we concur in the construction which was given by the Supreme Court of Ohio in the case of Gerke v. Purcell,[100] that 'when the charity is public, the exclusion of all idea of private gain or profit is equivalent in effect to the force of 'purely,' as applied to public charity in the constitution.' ''[101] We shall refer to this subject again in discussing the relations of benefit societies to the insurance laws of the several states.[102] But it may be here said that "a charitable corporation is not an association of shareholders, like a business corporation or joint-stock company; but is merely an agent or trustee for the administration of trust funds, and the beneficiaries of the trust or the donees of the charity, and not the members of the corporation."[103] This definition sheds light on the subject for, tried by this test as well as others, benefit societies are seldom, if ever, "charities" in the strict sense of the word. As the Supreme Court of Iowa said:[104] "But counsel for defendant insists that the system of insurance, to which the policy involved in this suit belongs, is 'purely benevolent,' and therefore ought not to be subject to the legislation applicable to other classes of insurance. We think the 'benevolence' in the case is purchased for, at least, a fair, if not a liberal consideration, and rests upon a contract which must be regarded and enforced by the law as any other contract." In Franta v. Bohemian, etc., Union,[105] the Court said: "These societies are sometimes referred to as organized for charitable purposes, but

[100] 25 Ohio St. 229.

[101] See note to Hennepin v. Brotherhood of Gethsemane, in 38 Am. 298 (same case 27 Minn. 460) and cases there cited.

[102] Post, §§ 47, 48.

[103] Morawetz on Corp., § 34.

[104] McConnell v. Iowa Mut. Aid Ass'n, 79 Ia. 757; 43 N. W. 188. See also McCarty v. Cavanaugh, Mass. 113 N. E. 271.

[105] 164 Mo. 304; 63 S. W. 1100; 54 L. R. A. 723.

death losses on such benefit certificates are not to be classed under that head, for they are enforced according to the terms of the contract, and even sick benefits do not fill the legal meaning of the word 'charity,' because they are limited to the members of the society. An act to be charitable in a legal sense must be designed for 'some public benefit open to an indefinite and vague number; that is, the persons to be benefited must be vague, uncertain and indefinite, until they are selected or appointed to be the particular beneficiaries of the trust for the time being.' 'Money contributed by the members of a club to a common fund, to be applied to the relief and assistance of the particular members of the club when in sickness, want of employment, or other disability is not a charitable fund to be controlled by a court of equity.'[106] It is not charity to give to your friend because of friendship, nor to your associate in a society because of your duty imposed by the laws of that society. Charity in the legal sense has been illustrated by reference to the custom of the ancient Jews, to leave at random a sheaf of corn here and there in the field for the poor gleaners who followed the harvesters, it being unknown who would get it. Therefore, there is nothing in the idea of charitable trust to influence the decision in this case. If the plaintiffs are entitled to recover it must be upon the theory that their father held a contractual relation with the defendant corporation at the time of his death which entitled him to membership therein and the benefits incident to such membership.''

§ **46. English Friendly Societies Not Charities, Nor Assurance Companies.**—The English friendly societies are not regarded by the courts of that country as charitable institutions, and it has been held that where a bequest is made to such a society and the society is wound up, the doctrine of *cy pres* will not apply.[107] Neither is such a friendly society an assurance company, within the meaning of a covenant contained in a marriage settlement, whereby the husband agreed that he would forthwith effect a policy of assurance upon his life with some respectable assurance company for a certain sum and assign the policy to trustees. A policy of assurance effected with a friendly

[106] Perry on Trusts, § 710.
[107] *Re* Clark, 1 L. R. Ch. D. 497; L. J. Ch. 194; 24 W. R. 233.

society, if it be not assignable, or if it be less beneficial than a policy effected with an ordinary assurance company, it was said,[108] is not within the meaning of such covenant.

§ 47. Exemption of Benefit Societies From General Insurance Laws.—In practically all of the United States life and accident insurance companies, either home or foreign, are only allowed to do business upon compliance with specified conditions, the principals of which are the deposit with the Insurance Department of approved securities, or money, to a certain amount, and the furnishing annually reports and statements in prescribed form, the object being to protect policyholders by means of the security of supervision and deposit of securities, and incidentally to obtain revenue for the State. In order, however, to encourage the formation of fraternal beneficiary societies, the advantages of which seem to be valued by legislatures, there is an express provision in most of the States for the organization of benevolent, charitable and educational corporations. In the earlier statutes a further provision was made that they might provide in their laws for the payment upon the death of a member to a designated person, within certain prescribed classes of relationship, or dependency, of an agreed amount and that such corporations should be exempt from the general insurance laws of the State. From these earlier statutes evolved general laws enacted in most of the States, providing for the organization of the regular fraternal beneficiary corporations. These laws provide how they may be organized, what powers they shall have, limiting the classes of beneficiaries to be provided for, and practically making them life insurance companies. Doing business through the agency of subordinate lodges, which are voluntary associations, their methods are entirely different from those of the regular life and accident companies and different principles are applied to them. A review of the adjudications of the courts show this evolution and the questions that have arisen considering the functions of these corporations and finally determining their status.[109]

[108] Courtenay v. Courtenay, 3 Jones & La. T. 519.

[109] Barbaro v. Occidental, etc., 4 Mo. App. 429; Sup. Council v. Fairman, 62 How. Pr. 386; 10 Abb. N. C. 162; Commonwealth v. Keystone Ben. Ass'n, 171 Pa. St. 465; 32 Atl. 1027. See ante, § 20.

In order to avail itself of the exemption from the general insurance laws of the State a society must have not only the characteristics of such associations as defined by law, but do business in the manner specified by law. Thus a commercial travelers' association, although duly incorporated, which has no lodge system, or ritualistic form of work, is not a fraternal benefit association within the meaning of the Missouri statute.[110] Defining what is a representative form of government and where a benefit society has not complied with the law requiring a representative form of government, a voluntary body is without power to adopt a constitution, or by-laws, or to amend the same changing the terms of the contract with one of its members.[111]

And an association which has no ritual for initiation of members is not a fraternal beneficiary society but an ordinary insurance company.[112] And the exact amount to be paid must be stated in the benefit certificate.[113] The question whether an insurance company is a fraternal beneficiary association is to be determined in part from the certificate of incorporation, or of authority to do business, and in part from facts showing its business as conducted in the manner prescribed by the statute, and if the company does not have a lodge system, or ritualistic form of work, and a representative form of government and does not pay benefits entirely from assessments, it is not a fraternal beneficiary association entitled to exemption from the insurance laws.[114]

[110] Western Commercial Travelers' Ass'n v. Tennent, 128 Mo. App. 541; 106 S. W. 1073. See also Griggs v. Royal Highlanders, 84 Neb. 834; 122 N. W. 69; 85 Neb. 830; 124 N. W. 911; 126 N. W. 141

[111] Johnson v. Bankers' Union of the World, 83 Neb. 48; 118 N. W. 1104. Also defining what constitutes a representative form of government is Lange v. Royal Highlanders, 75 Neb. 188; 110 N. W. 1110; 10 L. R. A. N. S. 666.

[112] Heralds of Liberty v. Bowen, 8 Ga. App. 325; 68 S. E. 1008.

[113] Easter v. Brotherhood of American Yeoman, 154 Mo. App. 456; 135 S. W. 964.

[114] Thompson v. Royal Neighbors of America, 154 Mo. App. 109; 133 S. W. 146. See also Almond v. M. W. A., 133 Mo. App. 382; 113 S. W. 695; Clover v. W. of the W., 152 Mo. App. 155; 133 S. W. 153; Ogle v. Barron, 247 Pa. 19; 92 Atl. 1071.

§ 48. **The Status of Benefit Societies Considered by the Courts.**—The courts in many of the earlier cases were frequently called upon to determine whether or not certain acting corporations were subject to the supervision of the State Insurance Departments; or required to comply with provisions of laws regulating companies doing a life insurance business; or whether the corporation was excepted as a benevolent organization within the meaning of the law. They in many cases also considered the nature of benefit societies and in what respects they are to be considered life insurance companies and wherein they are different and *sui generis*. The questions have generally arisen in considering whether the associations were subject to the laws of the State regulating life insurance companies; in determining the powers of persons or bodies acting for them, and in defining what is included in the term, "other insurance," used in application forms. We will consider some of the authorities here and others elsewhere.[115] It was held by the Supreme Court of Minnesota,[116] that an association, the purpose of which was to endow the wife of each member with a sum of money equal to as many dollars as there are members of the association, to be raised by assessments on them, was not a "benevolent society" within the meaning of the laws of that State, because "it is clear from the plan of the association," says the Court, "it was not intended to bestow any benefit or help without what was thought to be an equivalent."[117] The Supreme Court of Massachusetts early applied this rule when it declared:[118] "The contract made between the Connecticut Mutual Benefit Company and each of

[115] As to powers of agents, see *post*, Ch. 4. In matters relating to applications, *post*, Ch. 6. An elaborate and valuable discussion of this subject will be found in a note (38 L. R. A. 1) to the case of Penn. Mut. L. Ins. Co. v. Mechanics' Savings Bank, etc., 37 U. S. App. 692; 43 U. S. App. 73; 72 Fed. 413. See also 40 L. R. A. 187, 408, 418; 41 L. R. A. 194; 45 L. R. A. 264.

[116] State v. Critchett, 37 Minn. 13; 32 N. W. 787; following Foster v. Moulton, 35 Minn. 458; 29 N. W. 155; and being followed in turn by State v. Trubey, 37 Minn. 97; 33 N. W. 554.

[117] Somewhat of the same nature was the organization considered in Rockhold v. Canton Masonic, etc., Ass'n, 129 Ill. 440; 19 N. E. 710; 21 N. E. 710.

[118] Commonwealth v. Wetherbee, 105 Mass. 149.

its members, by the certificates of membership issued according
to its charter, does not differ in any essential particular of form
or substance from any ordinary policy of mutual life insurance.
The subject insured is the life of the member. The risk insured
is death from any cause not excepted by the terms of the contract. The assured pays a sum fixed by the directors and not
exceeding ten dollars, at the inception of the contract, and
assessments of two dollars each annually, and of one dollar each
upon the death of any member of the division to which he belongs during the continuance of the risk. In case of the death
of the assured by a peril insured against, the company absolutely promises to pay to his representatives, in sixty days after
receiving notice and proof of his death, 'as many dollars as
there are members in the same division, the number of which is
limited to five thousand.' The payment of this sum is subject
to no contingency but the insolvency of the corporation. The
means of paying it are derived from the assessments collected
upon his death from other members; from the money received
upon issuing other certificates of membership, which the by-
laws declare may, after payment of expenses, be 'used to cover
losses caused by the delinquencies of members,' and from the
guaranty fund of one hundred thousand dollars, established by
the corporation under its charter. This is not the less a contract
of mutual insurance upon the life of the assured, because the
amount to be paid by the corporation is not a gross sum, but a
sum graduated by the number of members holding similar con
tracts; nor because a portion of the premiums is to be paid upon
the uncertain periods of the deaths of such members; nor because, in case of non-payments of assessments by any member,
the contract provides no means of enforcing payment thereof,
but merely declares the contract to be at an end, and all moneys
previously paid by the assured, and all dividends and credits
accrued to him, to be forfeited to the company. The fact offered to be proved by defendant, that the object of the organization was benevolent and not speculative, has no bearing upon
the nature and effect of the business conducted and the contracts made by the corporation.'' The same court gives this
general definition: ''A contract by which one party promises

to make a certain payment upon the destruction or injury of something in which the other party has an interest, is a contract for insurance, whatever may be the terms of payment of the consideration, or the mode of estimating or securing payment of the sum to be insured in case of loss.'"[119]. This is a leading case on the subject and has been generally followed and approved.[120] The St. Louis Court of Appeals in a somewhat similar case[121] shed additional light upon the subject stating the difference between mutual life insurance organizations and benefit societies. It said: "If, as we think, the contract of defendant with its members is a contract of insurance, then it would appear that the main, and indeed the only, object of its existence is to do an insurance business. It is not a society bound together by any other common object, men of all races, creeds, professions and classes may belong to it, and it can in no respect be assimilated to organizations formed for religious, benevolent or literary purposes. Its one feature is life insurance; its active officers are paid; and it offers a premium for bringing in new risks. The only condition of membership is a certain condition of health and probability of duration of life. The case presented is not that of an organization whose primary object is social, literary, or benevolent, and to which a feature of mutual insurance is added for mutual aid. Such associations may exist which cannot be said to be carrying on the business of insurance, and with which we suppose it was not the intention

[119] *Ante*, § 4.

[120] State v. Farmers', etc., Benev. Ass'n, 18 Neb. 276; 25 N. W. 81; State ex rel., etc., v. Merchants' Exchange Benevolent, etc., 72 Mo. 146; State v. Vigilant Ins. Co., 30 Kan. 585; State v. Citizens' Ben. Ass'n, 6 Mo. App. 163; Golden Rule v. People, 118 Ill. 492; 9 N. E. 342; State v. Bankers', etc., Ass'n, 23 Kan. 499; Bolton v. Bolton, 73 Me. 299; State v. Standard Life Ass'n, 38 Ohio St. 281; Farmer v. State, 69 Tex. 561; 7 S. W. 220; State v. National Ass'n, etc., 35 Kan. 51; 9 Pac. 956; Rensenhouse v. Seely, 72 Mich. 603; 40 N. W. 765; Daniher v. Grand Lodge, 10 Utah, 110; 37 Pac. 245; Supreme Lodge K. of H. v. Davis, 26 Colo. 252; 58 Pac. 595.

[121] State v. Citizens' Ben. Ass'n, 6 Mo. App. 163. To the same effect is the case of National Union v. Marlow, 21 C. C. A. 89; 74 Fed. 775. Also Thassler v. German American, etc., Ass'n, 67 Mo. App. 505.

of the legislature to interfere." The Supreme Court of Iowa,[122] in passing directly on the question whether an organization, fraternal in its nature yet affording indemnity in the nature of life insurance, was subject to the provisions of the Iowa statutes relative to life insurance companies, said: "The association has assumed the characteristics of a fraternal organization, and also of a life insurance company. The former, however, possibly predominate; for it is true, we think, that many, if not all, fraternal associations dispense in some form pecuniary benefits, and that purely life insurance companies do not have what is called secret work, a pass-word, or anything of a moral or scientific character, which in any manner affects the organization. Nor do purely fraternal organizations require that the member should be insurable. It is evident that the declared objects of the association should not alone be the controlling consideration, for they may be a mere pretense. To ascertain the primary purpose of this association, reference must be had to the business conducted, the manner of conducting it, and what provisions have been adopted for carrying into effect the several avowed objects of the organization. Doing this we find that the certificate of membership provides that upon the death of each member there shall be paid to such person as he may designate the sum of $2,000 and that thereunder he or his beneficiary is entitled to nothing more. Elaborate and stringent provisions are made in relation to the beneficiary fund payable on the death of a member and for collecting and enforcing the payment of such amounts as are assessed on each member; but we have been unable to discover any provision for enforcing any of the other declared objects of the association stated in the preamble to the constitution of the Supreme Lodge, including 'sick benefits.' If the provisions of a fraternal character be eliminated from the association, its primary and only purpose is that of a life insurance organization.[123] We are satisfied, from an exam-

[122] State v. Miller, 66 Ia. 26, followed and approved in State v. Nichols, 78 Ia. 747; 41 N. W. 4.

[123] State v. Bankers and Merchants' Mut. B. A., 23 Kan. 499; Folmer's Appeal, 87 Pa. St. 133; Ill. Masons' B. Soc. v. Winthrop, 85 Ill. 537; Same v. Baldwin, 86 Ill. 479; State v. Cit. Ben. Ass'n, 6 Mo. App. 163; Bolton v. Bolton, 73 Me. 299.

ination of the record, that the primary purpose of the association of the Ancient Order of United Workmen is to provide a
beneficiary fund to be paid upon the death of each member, and
that the avowed fraternal character of the association is merely
incidental thereto. In fact, we go farther than this, and from
the record find that one of two things is true; that is to say,
either the fraternal objects of the association as avowed have
been abandoned, or they never were intended to be enforced.
We find no evidence of their enforcement, or that they ever
were regarded as material by the members of the association;
while, on the other hand, the provisions in relation to the beneficiary fund have been enforced, and the accumulation and payment of such fund has been regarded as the object and purpose
of the association. Therefore, it must be regarded as a life insurance organization, and within the provisions of the statute,
which provides that no foreign life insurance company, aid
society, or association for the insurance of the lives of its members, and doing business on the assessment plan, shall be allowed to do business in this State unless it has a guaranteed
capital of not less than $100,000 in the State in which it is or-
ganized.' ''[124] The Supreme Court of Texas has also considered
the question whether a corporation, the Masonic Mutual Benevolent Association of Texas, organized to provide for its members
during life and their families after death, and providing for the
payment, to the beneficiaries of the member at his death, of a certain sum in consideration of a membership fee and certain future
assessments, was an insurance company and subject to the insurance laws of the State. In its opinion the Court says:[125] ''What,
then, are the purposes of the body under consideration? Its charter
makes its object to provide for its members during life, and their

[124] Code, § 1160.
[125] Farmer v. State, 69 Tex. 561; 7 S. W. 220. This case was approved
in the subsequent case of Supreme Council, etc., v. Larmour, 81 Tex. 71;
16 S. W. 633, in which the American Legion of Honor is held to be an
insurance company and the certificate issued by it a valid insurance
policy yet exempted from certain requirements under the statute. In
the case of Order of the International Alliance, etc., v. State, 77 Md.
547; 26 Atl. 1040, the association was held to be doing an insurance
business within the statutes of that State.

families after death. This is apparently a benevolent object; but how is this to be accomplished? The association makes a contract with each member when he joins it, that for the consideration of a certain sum of money paid in cash, and other sums to be paid in future, which he agrees to do, that they will, ninety days after proper proof of his death, pay to certain beneficiaries a certain sum, graduated in amount, according to the length of time he lives, and, of course, according to the amount of assessments he has paid into the treasury. Before any one can enter into such a contract, he must undergo a regular examination as to his health, habits, occupation, and as to his family, and how much insurance upon his life, etc. A physician must make an examination as to his bodily condition, and according as he is sufficiently sound and of a certain age, is he accepted into the fraternity. This contract has all the features of a life insurance policy. It is a contract by which one party, for a consideration, promises to make a certain payment of money upon the death of the other; and it is well settled that whatever may be the terms of payment of the consideration by the assured, or the mode of estimating or securing payment of the insurance money, it is still a contract of insurance, no matter by what name it may be called.[126]   It is in effect the ordinary contract made by insurance companies with the assured, differing from it in no important respect. The terms of payment are somewhat different, the amount being greater or less, according as the member lives long or dies early; still it is a payment to be made at his death. The assured cannot be forced by suit to pay future premiums; but he loses his membership if he defaults in this respect. It is a common provision in insurance policies that if the assured fails to perform some of the conditions of his contract, that his policy may be canceled, and the premiums paid shall, in that event, become forfeited to the company. The provision that membership may be forfeited for non-payment of assessments is in effect the same thing; for the assessments serve the purposes of premiums in an ordinary life policy. The examination, too, which precedes admission into membership is the same as that which occurs before the issuance of a policy, and is intended to secure the society against fraud or imposition; to prevent an unsound person from

[126] Commonwealth v. Wetherbee, 105 Mass. 149; State v. Benev. Ass'n, etc., 18 Neb. 281; 25 N. W. 81.

becoming insured, and to reduce its risks of loss, and increase its chances of profit. It matters not that the member was entitled to benefits in case of sickness. Insurance can be effected upon the health as well as the life of an individual. These benefits, too, are incidental to the main object of the institution, and the certificates issued by it are none the less policies of insurance, though the insured derive sums of money from the contract other than those for which he has specially bargained. We are of the opinion, therefore, that the appellants constituted an insurance company within the spirit and true meaning of that term, and not an association conducted in the interest of benevolence, as contemplated by title 20 of our Revised Statutes." And the Supreme Court of Illinois says:[127] "But it is urged that the defendant in the present case is not an insurance company, within the meaning of the statute above mentioned and cannot, therefore, be affected by its provisions. The object and purpose for which the defendant was incorporated, as the bill alleges, and as the plea must be deemed to admit, was to furnish pecuniary aid to the widows, heirs, devisees, and representatives of the deceased members of the association; and it is further alleged, by way of showing the mode in which the proposed aid was to be furnished, that it was provided by the constitution and by-laws of the association that in case of the death of a member, on proof of such death, the association should assess and collect from each surviving member the sum of $2.50 for the benefit of the heirs or devisees of the deceased member, the same to be paid to him or them, to the amount of not exceeding $2,500, within 30 days after the collection of the assessment. There can be no doubt, we think, that the benefits provided for by the constitution and by-laws of the association are in the nature of life insurance, and that the contract between the association and the member, evidenced by the constitution, by-laws and membership certificate, is, in substance, a policy of insurance upon the life of the member. See Rockhold v. Society,[128] and cases cited. It is true the membership certificate bears upon its face no promise of indemnity, but it entitles the holder to membership in the association, and to all rights that appertain thereto, and it

[127] Railway Passenger, etc., Ass'n v. Robinson, 147 Ill. 138; 35 N. E. 168.
[128] 129 Ill. 440; 21 N. E. 794.

is to be construed in connection with the constitution and by-laws, the same as if all of those documents were combined in one. Taken together, they constitute an undertaking on the part of the association, subject, it is true,. to certain conditions which will be hereafter noticed, in case of the death of a member, on proper proof of his death to levy and collect an assessment of $2.50 on each surviving member, and to pay the same over, to an amount not exceeding $2,500 to a certain designated beneficiary or beneficiaries. This is clearly, in substance and effect, a contract of insurance, and an association organized for the purpose of entering into and performing contracts of that character is in reality an insurance company. But it is said that the defendant is not an insurance company within the meaning of the act in relation to suits against such corporations, because the statute under which the defendant was organized declares that such associations and societies shall not be deemed insurance companies. Section 31 of the act concerning corporations, approved April 18, 1872—that section being a part of the subdivision of the act relating to corporations not for pecuniary profit—as amended May 22, 1883, provides that 'associations and societies which are intended to benefit the widows, orphans, heirs and devisees of deceased members thereof, and members who have received a permanent disability, and where no annual dues or premiums are required, and where the members shall receive no money as profit or otherwise, except for permanent disability, shall not be deemed insurance companies.' It may be noticed that the plea in this case fails, by proper averments, to bring the defendant within the provisions of this statute. There is no averment that no annual dues or premiums were required of its members, or that its members received no money as profit or otherwise, except for permanent disability. It is difficult to see how, without such averments, the defendant can be held to be exempted by this statute from the character and status of an insurance company." The Supreme Court of Kansas[129] has held that a contract by an association to pay at stated periods of time certain sums of money as endowments to living members, or, in case of their death, to pay certain other sums of money as benefits to their beneficiaries, is life

[129] Endowment & Benev. Ass'n v. State, 35 Kan. 253. See also State v. Natioanl Ass'n, 35 Kan. 51.

insurance both as to the endowments and the benefits. The Supreme Court of Illinois[130] has decided that, where a corporation establishes a relief fund, to be raised and kept up by voluntary contributions of its members, from which it agrees, upon the death of a member, to pay a sum, not exceeding a certain amount, to a beneficiary named by such deceased member, and a sum not to exceed another certain amount, to the members holding certificates next in number above and below that of the deceased, and upon the death of a member, notice is given to all other members, who are expected to contribute to the relief fund, such corporation will be liable to the charge of engaging in the business of life insurance and in addition its business is illegal because in the nature of wagering. It also held that, under the Illinois act of 1872, a corporation could be organized for any lawful purpose except (among others named) that of insurance. The Court said: "By the last clause of section 31 of the act, it is provided that societies intended to benefit the widows, orphans, heirs and devisees of deceased members thereof, and members who have received a permanent disability, and where no annual dues or premiums are required, and where the members shall receive no money, as profit or otherwise, except for permanent disability, shall not be deemed insurance companies. Here is the strongest implication that a society doing such a business as the pleas present, is doing an insurance business, and that it is to be deemed an insurance company. Not to be deemed an insurance company under the act, it must be intended to benefit the widows, or orphans, heirs and devisees of deceased members, and members who have received a permanent disability, and where the members shall receive no money as profit or otherwise, except for permanent disability. But here the declared object is the benefit of members, and the pecuniary benefits are enjoyed, not by the widows, etc., of deceased members, and by members who have received a permanent disability, but by the appointees of deceased members, the beneficiary named in the application, and by certain of the members generally and not members who had received a permanent disability."[131] In another case it was said: "It is

130 Golden Rule v. Swigert, 118 Ill. 492.

131 But in New York (Supreme Council, etc., v. Fairman, 10 Abb. N. C. 162; 62 How. Pr. 386) it has been held that an association formed to

further objected that the contract sued on is a contract of life
insurance and *ultra vires* because expressly prohibited by the
charter of the Grand Grove, and not necessary to carry into effect
the objects of the corporation.[132] The charter of the Grand Grove
names as one of the main objects of the corporation, 'aiding the
families of deceased members.' The payment of a small stipend
to the helpless children of a deceased member seems to be a very
reasonable way of carrying out this provision; and though the last
clause of section 1 of the charter provides that the powers hereby
granted shall not be used for banking or insurance purposes, it is
clearly not the intent of that provision to prohibit the payment of
money by the corporation to the surviving representatives of deceased members. The corporation is not to carry on an insurance business in the usual acceptation of the term in the commercial world.[133]

furnish aid to members in cases of physical disability was not an insurance company within the statute of that State. In Fawcett v. Supreme Sitting Order of Iron Hall, 64 Conn. 170, 29 Atl. 614; 24 L. R. A.
815, a concern whose scheme was obviously impracticable was held entitled to the exemption given fraternal associations by the laws of
Maryland. To the contrary is Supreme Sitting Order Iron Hall v.
Griggsby, 178 Ill. 57; 52 N. E. 956.

[132] Barbaro v. Occidental Lodge, 4 Mo. App. 429.

[133] See also Commonwealth v. National Mut. Aid. Ass'n, 94 Pa. St.
481; State v. Mut. Protective Soc., 26 Ohio St. 19; White v. Madison, 26
N. Y. 117. For other questions arising under statutes of the several
States see Railway Passenger, etc., Ass'n v. Robinson, 147 Ill. 138; 35 N.
E. 168, affg. 38 Ill. App. 111; State v. Whitmore, 75 Wis. 332; 43 N.
W. 1133; State v. Taylor, 56 N. J. L. 49; 27 Atl. 797; Whitmore v.
Supreme Lodge, etc., 100 Mo. 36; 13 N. W. 495; McConnell v. Iowa
Mut. Aid Ass'n, 79 Iowa 757; 43 N. W. 188; Rensenhouse v. Seeley, 72
Mich. 603; 40 N. W. 765; Rockhold v. Canton Masonic, etc., 129 Ill.
440; 19 N. E. 710; 21 N. E. 794; State v. Root, 83 Wis. 667; 54 N. W.
33; Dunlevy v. Supreme Lodge, etc., 49 Legal Intel. 145. The nature
and privileges of such associations has also been considered in the fol-
lowing cases which held that the business is practically life insurance:
Home Forum Ben. Order v. Jones, 5 Okla. 598; 60 Pac. 165; Modern
Woodmen v. Colman, 64 Neb. 162; 89 N. W. 641; on rehearing 64 Neb.
162; 94 N. W. 814, and 96 N. W. 154; Supreme Assembly Royal Soc.
Good Fellows v. McDonald, 59 N. J. L. 248; 35 Atl. 1061. A valuable
note with a full review of the authorities is found in 38 L. R. A. 1.

§ 49. Difference Between a Fraternal Benefit Society and a Life Insurance Company.—The Supreme Court of Pennsylvania in a well-considered case[134] thus points out the distinction between a fraternal society for "beneficial and protective purposes" and the regular life insurance companies: "The general object or purpose of an insurance company is to afford indemnity or security against loss. Its engagement is not founded in any philanthropic, benevolent, or charitable principle. It is a merely business venture, in which one, for a stipulated consideration, or premium per cent, engages to make up, or in a certain agreed amount, any specific loss which another may sustain; and it may apply to loss of property, to personal injury, or to the loss of life. To grant indemnity or security against loss for a consideration is not only the design and purpose of an insurance company, but is also the dominant and characteristic feature, of the contract of insurance. What is known as a 'beneficial association,' however, has a wholly different object and purpose in view. The great underlying purpose of the organization is not to indemnify or secure against loss. Its design is to accumulate a fund from the contributions of its members 'for beneficial or protective purposes,' to be used in their own aid or relief in the misfortunes of sickness, injury or death. The benefits, although secured by contract, and for that reason to a limited extent-assimilated to the proceeds of insurance, are not so considered. Such societies are rather of a philanthropic or benevolent character. Their beneficial features may be of a narrow or restricted character. The motives of the members may be to some extent selfish, but the principle upon which they rest is founded in the considerations mentioned. These benefits by the rule of their organization are payable to their own unfortunate, out of funds which the members have themselves contributed for the purpose, not as an indemnity or security against loss, but as a protective relief in case of sickness or injury, or to provide the means of a decent burial in the event of death. Such societies have no capital stock. They yield no profit, and their contracts, although beneficial and protective, altogether exclude the idea of

---

[134] Commonwealth v. Equitable Beneficial Ass'n, 137 Pa. St. 412; 18 Atl. 1112.

insurance, or of indemnity, or of security against loss.''[135] The subject has also been treated in another leading case,[136] where Judge Caldwell said: ''There are corporations in which the element of insurance is so mingled with benevolent, charitable, social or other ends that it is difficult to tell whether they should be classed as insurance companies or benevolent societies. But that difficulty does not arise in this case. It is apparent from an examination of its charter, and its methods of doing business, that the defendant is a mutual life insurance company on the assessment plan. Its business is insurance and nothing else. There is not a social, charitable or benevolent feature in its organization or the conduct of its business. It has no lodges, pays no sick dues and distributes no aid, and gives no attention to members in distress or poverty. It deals with its members on the strictest business principles. . . . A popular or captivating name often performs a useful office as a business advertisement, but it goes for nothing in determining the legal character of the company adopting it.'' The fact that an association, paying a benefit in case of death, restricts its membership to certain persons, as for example, Masons, does not make it a secret benevolent or fraternal society.[137] An association organized by a railroad company for its employes, which agrees to pay stated sums to its members or their beneficiaries in case a member is killed or injured in its service, the company paying operating expenses and making good deficiencies after assessments have been collected, is not an ''insurance company.''[138] Nor is the Grand Lodge I. O. O. F., which is organized mainly for relief and benefits, other than financial.[139]

§ 50. **Conclusion: Benefit Societies are Insurance Organizations.**—It follows from the foregoing adjudications, that all benefit societies, whether corporations or mere voluntary associations,

[135] See also State v. Citizens' Ben. Ass'n, 6 Mo. App. 163; Knights of Honor v. Oeters, 95 Va. 610; 29 S. E. 322; ante, § 47.

[136] Berry v. Knights Templars, etc., 46 Fed. 439; affd. 1 C. C. A. 561; 50 Fed. 311.

[137] Masonic Aid Ass'n v. Taylor, 2 S. Dak. 324; 50 N. W. 93. Also Berry v. Knights Templars, etc., supra; but see State v. Whitmore, 75 Wis. 332; 43 N. W. 1133.

[138] Donald v. C. B. & Q. Ry. Co., 93 Ia. 284; 33 L. R. A. 492; 61 N. W. 971; Johnson v. R. R. Co., 163 Pa. St. 127; 29 Atl. 854.

[139] Anthony v. Carl, 58 N. Y. Supp. 1084; 28 Misc. 200.

are, strictly speaking, insurance organizations whenever, in consideration of periodical contributions, they engage to pay the member, or his designated beneficiary, a benefit upon the happening of a specified contingency. Although they may also partake of the nature of clubs or fraternal societies, and although they are often technically not called insurance companies, we must admit that, whether the benefit be paid for sickness, or to provide burial, or to accumulate a fund out of which payments are to be made to beneficiaries of deceased members, the contract falls within the definition of an insurance contract, viz.: "An agreement, by which one party for a consideration (which is usually paid in money, either in one sum, or at different times during the continuance of the risk), promises to make a certain payment of money upon the destruction or injury of something in which the other party has an interest."[140] It has been said, however,[141] that the contract of a society which pays sick and funeral benefits is not one of insurance. It may also be asserted as a general principle that wherever or whenever a benefit society, paying a benefit to the beneficiaries of its deceased members, claims to be exempt from the operation of certain laws applicable to persons or companies doing a life insurance business, it can only safely base such claim upon express provisions of its charter or of the statutes exempting similar organizations from such liability. The association may be benevolent and charitable, and only incidentally provide benefits for its members or their beneficiaries, but nevertheless, when it contracts to pay a certain sum to the appointees of its members upon their decease, while in good standing, in consideration of certain contributions made by such members while living, it is doing a life insurance business. We shall find, as we proceed further to discuss the questions concerning the contracts and liabilities of benefit societies, that many of the principles of the law of life insurance are applied to these societies because they are in some respects simply life insurance companies doing business on a plan only partially different from that of regular life insurance organizations.

In Colorado it has been held that a benefit certificate is a life

140 Commonwealth v. Wetherbee, 105 Mass. 149; Franklin Ben. Ass'n v. Commonwealth, 10 Pa. St. 357; *ante*, § 48.

141 Piries v. First Russian Slavonic Soc., 83 N. J. Eq. 29; 89 Atl. 1036.

insurance policy, subject to the law of that State providing that
suicide shall be no defense.[142] And a policy of a fraternal society, non-forfeitable after the specified number of assessments
have been paid, and providing for extended insurance is an old
line policy.[143] The power to accumulate a reserve fund authorized by the Missouri statute does not mean a technical reserve
but a fund for emergency.[144] A fraternal benefit society is not
deprived of its character by a provision of its by-laws authorizing
the payment of benefits to a class not provided for by the Missouri
statute.[145] A fraternal beneficiary society authorized to do business on a certain plan cannot make contracts on any other plan.[146]
It has therefore been held that a policy· on any other plan than
that authorized by the charter is void.[147]

§ 51. **The Same Subject—Limitations.**—Fraternal beneficiary societies can only do business as provided by law. In the
case of State *ex rel* v. Vandiver,[148] the Court in discussing the
powers of a fraternal beneficiary society says: "The character of
relator is an essential fact to be shown in this case, because unless
it is a fraternal society, as defined by the statute, it has no right
to do even the limited kind of life insurance that the statute
authorizes; but the fact that it does entirely fill that definition
does not authorize it to go beyond the limit prescribed by the
statute. If the relator while issuing only such life insurance policies as the statute authorizes and holding a license from the Insurance Department should be called into court to answer by what

---

[142] Head Camp Pac. Juris. W. of the W. v. Sloss, 49 Colo. 177; 112
Pac. 49; Modern Brotherhood of America v. Lock, 22 Colo. App. 409;
125 Pac. 556.

[143] McPike v. Supreme Ruling Fraternal Mystic Circle, 187 Mo. App.
679; 173 S. W. 71.

[144] State *ex rel* v. Vandiver, 213 Mo. 187; 111 S. W. 911.

[145] Armstrong v. Modern Brotherhood of America, 245 Mo. 183; 149
S. W. 459; Ordelheide v. Modern Brotherhood of America, 158 Mo. App.
677; 139 S. W. 269. But see Kroge v. Modern Brotherhood of America,
126 Mo. App. 693; 105 S. W. 685.

[146] Missey v. Supreme Lodge K. & L. of H., 147 Mo. App. 137; 126
S. W. 539.

[147] Smoot v. Bankers' Life Ass'n, 138 Mo. App. 438; 120 S. W. 719.

[148] 213 Mo. 187; 111 S. W. 911. See also McCartney v. Supreme Tent
K. O. T. M., 132 Ill. App. 15.

authority it is issuing such policies it would be sufficient to say: We are a fraternal society, with our lodge system, our ritual, our representative form of government and we are not doing this for profit. But if it is issuing policies of a character not authorized by the statute, then its fraternal character, its lodge system, its ritual, its form of government, and its no-profit plan, would be no answer or justification of its conduct. . . . If fraternal societies have authority to issue twenty-year paid-up policies and policies non-forfeitable, there is no reason why they may not issue any kind of life insurance policies that a regular life insurance company may issue, and, if so, then they are in the arena of life insurance as competitors of the old line companies with none of the restrictions that come from supervision of the Insurance Department and investigation of their affairs, none of the deposits that the law requires of the old line companies for security for policyholders, and no obligation to pay the tax of two per cent per annum on premiums. A statute conferring such authority would not only be vicious class legislation, but it would sanction a course of business obnoxious to the public policy of the State in reference to life insurance, as set forth in our general statutes on that subject.''

§ 52. **Liberality of Exemption in Certain States.**—In some States the field is practically unlimited, as in New York, where the Court of Appeals[149] held that there was no restriction in the act of 1875 providing ''for the incorporation of societies or clubs for certain lawful purposes,'' which requires, where a society is organized under it for ''mutual benefit'' or ''benevolent'' purposes, that the benefits or benevolence be confined to members or the families of members. ''There is nothing,'' said the Court, ''in the by-laws which requires that the beneficiaries named in the certificate should be members of the family of the deceased member, and if no beneficiaries are designated the payment is to be made to his legal representatives. The power of the company to create a fund for the insurance of the lives of its members is not questioned on this appeal, and we do not, therefore, discuss it. The act of 1875 authorizes the incorporation of societies for purposes of 'mutual benefit,' and it must be under this head that the power

[149] Massey v. Mut. Relief Soc., 102 N. Y. 523.

is claimed, to contract for the application of the joint contributions of the members to the payment of a gross sum to the legal representatitves of each member, or to such beneficiary as he may designate to receive it upon his death. "There is nothing in the act which restricts the objects of the societies formed under it to the relief of families of their members. They may be formed for general purposes of benevolence and for many other objects, such as social, political, athletic, sporting, etc. Neither does the certificate of association of the defendant restrict the application of its funds to the relief of a member or his family except where such relief is to be extended during the life of the member." The statutes of Illinois are almost as broad. The Supreme Court of that State says:[150] "The first section of the act under which the defendant is organized, in express terms authorizes the organization of such associations for the purpose of furnishing life indemnity or pecuniary benefits to devisees or legatees. If, as is plain from the language of the statute, a person may take out a policy on his own life, and devise such policy to a stranger, what principle of public policy would be violated by a provision in the policy making it payable to a stranger, in lieu of doing the same thing by will? If the policy may be made payable to a stranger who has no insurable interest in the life of the assured, as it may be by statute, we perceive no reason which will prevent the same thing being done by a clause the insured may have inserted in the policy at the time the insurance is procured . . . We now come to the second question. Section 1, of the act under which the defendant is incorporated, is as follows: 'That corporations, associations, or societies, for the purpose of furnishing life indemnity or pecuniary benefits to the widows, orphans, heirs or relatives, by consanguinity or affinity, devisees or legatees, of deceased members, or accident or permanent disability indemnity to members thereof, and where members shall receive no money as profit, and where funds for the payment of such benefits shall be secured, in whole or in part, by assessment upon the surviving members, may be organized, subject to the conditions hereinafter provided.' It is contended that all persons not named in the act are prohibited from becoming beneficiaries. It will be observed that the contract involved is not absolutely prohibited by statute. All that can prop-

150 Bloomington Mut. Ben. Ass'n v. Blue, 120 Ill. 121.

erly be claimed is, that it was not expressly authorized by the statute.''[151]

§ 53. Benefit Societies Can Exercise Only the Powers Given by Statute.—The rule seems to be, as is said in a well-considered case:[152] ''Incorporated associations, or societies of the class to which the defendant order belongs, are creations of the statute, incapable of exercising any power which is not therein either expressed or clearly implied.'' A fraternal beneficiary association cannot do an endowment insurance business.[153] The Supreme Court of Ohio has repeatedly held[154] that the corporate powers of mutual relief associations, incorporated and organized under the statute of that State authorizing the formation of such societies ''for the mutual protection and relief of their members, and for the payment of stipulated sums of money to the families or heirs of the deceased members of such associations,'' are limited to the carrying into effect of the purposes thus declared. ''The only beneficiaries for whom it has power to provide are 'families or heirs of deceased members.' '' In that State foreign benefit societies cannot do business if they issue certificates payable to other persons than those of the families or heirs of the deceased members. The Court says:[155] ''The law of comity which the relator invokes in support of his application, is fully satisfied where foreign companies are permitted to do business in this State upon the terms prescribed for domestic companies.'' The Massachu-

---

[151] Lamont v. Hotel Men's Mut. Ben. Ass'n, 30 Fed. 817; Lamont v. Iowa Legion of Honor, 31 Fed. 177; Maneely v. Knights Birmingham, 115 Pa. St. 305; 9 Atl. 41. See also Walter v. Odd Fellows M. B. Soc., 42 Minn. 204; 44 N. W. 57, and State v. Whitmore, 75 Wis. 332; 43 N. W. 1133.

[152] Ferbrache v. Grand Lodge A. O. U. W., 81 Mo. App. 268. In this case the Missouri cases are all cited and reviewed.

[153] Walker v. Giddings, 103 Mich. 344; 61 N. W. 512; Dishong v. Iowa Life and End. Ass'n, 92 Ia. 163; 60 N. W. 505; State ex rel, etc., v. Orear, 144 Mo. 167; Preferred Mas. Mut. L. Ins. Co. v. Giddings, 112 Mich. 401; 70 N. W. 1026; National Legion v. O'Brien, 102 Minn. 15; 112 N. W. 1050.

[154] State v. Mutual Protection Ass'n, etc., 26 Ohio St. 19; State v. Central Ohio Mut. Relief Ass'n, etc., 29 Ohio St. 399; State v. Standard Life Ass'n, 38 Ohio St. 281; State v. People's Ben. Ass'n, 42 Ohio St. 579; National Mut. Aid Ass'n v. Gonser, 43 Ohio St. 1; 1 N. E. 11.

[155] State v. Moore, 38 Ohio St. 7.

81

setts statute[156] provides that certain benevolent associations may "for the purpose of assisting the widows, orphans or other persons dependent upon deceased members, provide in its by-laws for the payment by each member of a fixed sum to be held by such association until the death of a member occurs, and then to be forthwith paid to the person or persons entitled thereto." In construing this statute the Supreme Court of that State[157] has held that associations organized under its provisions have no power to create a fund for other persons than of the classes named.[158] The contract made by a benevolent corporation in conformity with its charter will be enforced through comity in another State where such contract would have been contrary to the statutes of such State.[159] In the case cited the Court says: "It is a part of the common law that a corporation may carry on business in foreign jurisdictions, and it is under this law of comity, which is also a part of the common law, that foreign courts lend their aid to the enforcement of its contracts, provided the contract itself is not expressly prohibited by a local statute and is not repugnant to the settled adjudications of the courts of the State or to the general policy of its laws. The statute of this State which confines the beneficiaries in such societies to the members of the family of the member, or to some person or persons dependent upon him, has reference solely to domestic corporations. We think it would be a wrong and improper application of the law of comity to say that, by reason of this statute, the courts of this State ought not to enforce the collection of the amount due under this certificate on the ground that such a contract is repugnant to the general policy of the law of the State."[160]

[156] Stat. 1874, Ch. 375; Amended Stat. 1877, Ch. 204, re-enacted Pub. Stat. 1882, Ch. 115; amended 1882, Ch. 175, § 2.

[157] American Legion of Honor v. Perry, 140 Mass. 580.

[158] Elsey v. Odd Fellows' Ass'n, 142 Mass. 244; Mass. Catholic Order Foresters v. Callahan, 146 Mass. 413; 16 N. E. 14; Commercial League v. The People, 90 Ill. 166; Ben. Soc. v. Dugre, 11 Revue Legale (Queb.) 344. See, for further discussion of this subject, post, § 319.

[159] Hysinger v. Supreme Lodge K. & L. of H., 42 Mo. App. 627.

[160] The following cases will be found instructive: As to exemption in California, Marshall v. Grand Lodge A. O. U. W., 133 Cal. 686; 66 Pac. 25; in New Hampshire, Brotherhood Acc. Co. v. Linehan, 71 N. H. 7; 51 Atl. 266; in South Dakota, Ancient Order, etc., v. Shober, 16 S. D.

§ 54. **State Regulation of the Business of Insurance.**—In most, if not all, of the States the business of insurance is regulated by statute. The reasons have been well stated, as follows:[161] "Insurance in its early existence, when the nature of the risks were few and the amount of business small, was done chiefly, if not entirely by individuals. But in more recent times it has been extended until it embraces almost every kind of a risk and has grown to such proportions that it enters into every department of business and affects all classes of people and their property; and has in consequence everywhere become the subject of legislative regulation and control. The several States have enacted laws designed to place the business within their limits on such substantial basis as will afford adequate protection to the citizens and their property. There can be no doubt of the power of the State to do so nor that the power extends to the enactment of such laws as its legislative body may deem wise and proper for the purpose, not in conflict with the fundamental law, and, therefore, within the legitimate exercise of that power, foreign companies may be excluded altogether from doing business in the State or admitted on their compliance with such terms and conditions as its legislature chooses to impose." If individuals attempt to do an insurance business which the statute provides shall be done only by corporations they will be enjoined.[162] If the statute does not forbid in express terms the transaction of such business by individuals, they are free to engage in it, and the same rule applies to corporations.[163] Only the State is concerned in the right of a corporation to do business and no suit lies on the part of third parties to determine whether such corporation shall be licensed.[164] The real character of the contract and the acts to be performed under

513; 94 N. W. 405; in Missouri, Kern v. American Legion of Honor, 167 Mo. 471; 67 S. W. 252; Toomey v. Knights of Pythias, 74 M. A. 507; affirmed 147 Mo. 129; 48 S. W. 936.

[161] State v. Ackerman, 51 Ohio St. 163; 37 N. E. 828; 24 L. R. A. 298 and note.

[162] State v. Ackerman, *supra;* State v. Stone, 118 Mo. 388; 24 S. W. 164; 25 L. R. A. 243.

[163] Fort v. State, 92 Ga. 8; 18 S. E. 14; 23 L. R. A. 86; Hoadley v. Purifoy, 107 Ala. 276; 18 Sou. 220; 30 L. R. A. 351; People v. Fidelity, etc., Co., 153 Ill. 25; 38 N. E. 752; 26 L. R. A. 295.

[164] High Court, etc., v. Commissioner, 98 Wis. 94; 73 N. W. 326.

it cannot be concealed or changed by the use or absence of words in the contract itself. It is immaterial that such a contract does not on its face purport to be one of insurance.[165]   The right of a State to regulate the business of insurance is undoubted.[166]   In New York Life Ins. Co. v. Hardison,[167] it was said that the State has power to regulate insurance corporations either under its police power for the protection of the public, or as a creator and controller of corporations, domestic and foreign.   It may regulate the business and provide what kind of contracts can be made.[168]   A foreign corporation can only transact the business in a State authorized by its charter,[169] nor can it do business unless licensed to do so.[170]   The companies are usually required to file with the insurance department certain reports and submit, if required, to an examination by the superintendent of the department, or as he is generally styled, insurance commissioner.   What the powers of such officers are of course depends upon the language of the statute.   He may have almost unlimited powers.[171]   In the two cases of Metropolitan L. Ins. Co. v. McNall,[172] and Mutual Life Ins. Co. v. Boyle,[173] it was held that while the duties of an insurance commissioner were not of an entirely ministerial nature, but were largely discretionary, it was not to be inferred that there was no limit to discretionary powers.   The commissioner

[165] State v. Beardsley, 88 Minn. 20; 92 N. W. 472; Missouri, K. & T. Co. v. Krumsag, 23 C. C. A. 1; 77 Fed. 32; M. K. & T. Co. v. McLachlan, 59 Minn 468; 61 N. W. 560.

[166] Orient Insurance Co. v. Daggs, 172 U. S. 557; affirming 136 Mo. 282; New York Life Ins. Co. v. Cravens, 178 U. S. 380. Practically all the authorities cited in this chapter sustain this view. See also notes in 24 L. R. A. 298 and 26 L. R. A. 295.

[167] 199 Mass. 190; 85 N. E. 410.

[168] General Accident Ins. Co. v. Walker, 99 Miss. 404; 55 Sou. 51.

[169] State v. Union Central Life Ins. Co., 8 Idaho 240; 67 Pac. 647.

[170] People v. Howard, 50 Mich. 239; 15 N. W. 101; as to doing business by comity see State v. Aetna Life Ins. Co., 69 Ohio State 317; 69 N. E. 608. As to investments, Union Pacific L. Ins. Co. v. Ferguson, 64 Ore. 395; 129 Pac. 529; 130 Pac. 978; 43 L. R. A. (U. S.) 958. What are liabilities, In re Empire State Surety Co., 214 N. Y. 553, 108 N. E. 825; affg. 150 N. Y. Supp. 567; 165 App. Div. 135.

[171] Spruance v. Farmers', etc., Ins. Co., 9 Colo. 73; 10 Pac. 285.

[172] 81 Fed. 888.

[173] 82 Fed. 705.

could not therefore revoke a license and deprive a company of its right to do business merely because it disputed a claim and "to say that it must either forego its rights in that respect (to resort to the courts) and submit to pay all claims made against it or quit business in the State is arbitrary, unreasonable and dictatorial."[174] A corporation is subject to the prescribed penalties for abuse of its franchise or for wrongful acts.[175] An insurance company, authorized by its charter to do an employers' liability insurance business, may engage in that business in another State by comity although similar companies organized in such State may not have such power.[176] When a company does business in a State it is subject to the laws of the State whether it applied for the privilege of doing business therein or not.[177] The statutes in force at the time of the making of a contract enter into and become a part thereof, as if copied therein.[178] If any company claims to have immunity from any provisions of the insurance laws, "it

[174] See also State v. Vorys, 69 Ohio, 56; 68 N. E. 580, where it was held that under the statute the commissioner had no discretion but to grant a license when the statutory requirements had been complied with. In addition to those cited the following deal with incidental questions relating to the powers of the commissioner and compliance with the laws of the State: State v. Mathews, 58 Ohio St. 1; 49 N. E. 1034; 40 L. R. A. 418 (defining what is an assessment company); Travelers' Ins. Co. v. Fricke, 99 Wis. 367; 74 N. W. 372; 41 L. R. A. 557; State v. Fricke, 102 Wis. 117; 77 N. W. 734; People v. Payne, 161 N. Y. 229; 55 N. E. 49, affirming 60 N. Y. Supp. 1146; Rand v. Mass. B. L. Ass'n, 42 N. Y. Supp. 26; 18 Misc. 336; Hayne v. Metropolitan Trust Co., 67 Minn. 245; 69 N. W. 916; Sparks v. National Masonic Acc. Ass'n, 100 Ia. 458; 69 N. W. 678; People v. Payne, 50 N. Y. Supp. 234; 26 App. Div. 584.

[175] International Fraternal Alliance v. State, 86 Med. 550; 39 Atl. 512; 40 L. R. A. 187; Knowlton v. Bay State Ben. Ass'n, 171 Mass. 455; 50 N. E. 929; State v. Mathews, 58 Ohio St. 1; 40 L. R. A. 418; Continental Ins. Co. v. Riggen, 31 Ore. 336; 48 Pac. 476.

[176] State v. Aetna Life Ins. Co., 69 Ohio St. 317; 69 N. E. 608.

[177] Corley v. Travelers' Prot. Ass'n, 105 Fed. 854; Sparks v. National Masonic Acc. Ass'n, 73 Fed. 277.

[178] New York Life Ins. Co. v. Cravens, 178 U. S. 389; affirming Cravens v. N. Y. Life Ins. Co., 148 Mo. 503; 53 L. R. A. 305; Knights Templar and Masons Life Indem. Co. v. Jarman, 187 U. S. 197, approving same case 44 C. C. A., 93; 104 Fed. 638; McCracken v. Hayward, 2 How. 608; Smith v. Mut. Ben. L. Acc. Ass'n, 173 Mo. 329; 73 S. W. 935.

must put its finger upon the law granting such immunity, otherwise that law applies."[179]   And the State has a right to require fraternal beneficiary societies to have a schedule of assessments not lower than one incorporated in the law.[180]   Certain other matters which might be considered here will be reviewed later.[181]

§ 55. **Powers of Insurance Commissioner.**—The laws of the different States of course vary as to the authority and powers of the officer variously styled insurance commissioner, or superintendent of the insurance department. He is invested with a *quasi* judicial authority and has power to refuse to issue a license,[182] but he cannot refuse arbitrarily to grant a license to a company which has complied with the requirements of the law.[183]   The Kentucky statute authorizing the issuance of a license to insurance companies does not authorize the revocation of a license unless it has violated some statute of the State.[184]   It has been held that a foreign insurance company doing business in New York under a license is a citizen of New York, so far as litigation is concerned.[185]

---

[179] Kern v. Supreme Council A. L. of H., 167 Mo. 471; 67 S. W. 262; Nielsen v. Provident Savings L. Ass'n Soc., 139 Cal. 332; 73 Pac. 168.

[180] State v. Fraternal Knights and Ladies, 35 Wash. 338; 77 Pac. 500.

[181] As to computing reserve, Bankers' Life. Ins. Co. v. FleetWood, 76 Vt. 297; 57 Atl. 239, and *post*, Ch. 11. As to tax on premiums see Northwestern, etc., Ass'n v. Waddell, 138 Mo. 628; 40 S. W. 648. As to power to make loans, Key v. National Ins. Co., 107 Ia. 446; 78 N. W. 68. As to discrimination and rebates, see *post* Ch. 11. As to non-forfeiture laws, see *post*, § 478, *et seq.* As to service of process on commissioner, see *post*, § 627.

[182] Mut. Life Ins. Co. v. Boyle, 82 Fed. 705; Seamans v. The Temple Co., 105 Mich. 400; 63 Mo. 408; 28 L. R. A. 430; Citizens' Life Insurance Co. v. Commissioner, 128 Mich. 85; 87 N. W. 126.

[183] Bankers' Life Ins. Co. v. Holland, 73 Vt. 1; 48 Atl. 435; 57 L. R. A. 374; Bankers' Life v. Fleetwood, 76 Vt. 297; 57 Atl. 239; Equitable Life Assur. Soc. v. Host, 124 Wis. 651; 102 N. W. 579.

[184] Mut. Life Ins. Co. v. Prewitt, 127 Ky. 399; 105 S. W. 463.

[185] Webster v. Columbian National Life Ins. Co., 196 N. Y. Supp. 1114; affirming 116 N. Y. Supp. 404; 131 App. Div. 837. See also Owen v. Bankers' Life Ins. Co., 84 S. C. 253; 66 S. E. 290. As to powers of commissioner under the laws of New York, see Travelers' Insurance Co. v. Kelsey, 118 N. Y. Supp. 873; 134 App. Div. 80; affirmed, Travelers' Ins. Co. v. Hotchkiss, 197 N. Y. 585; 91 N. E. 1121.

It has been held,[186] that the Superintendent of the Insurance Department properly refused a license to an assessment company whose contracts did not plainly state that the liability of members was not limited by a fixed premium. The commissioner has power to revoke a license and an injunction will not lie against him to prevent such revocation.[187]   He has, however, no power to determine whether the proposed name of a society too closely resembles that of another, that power residing in the courts alone.[188]   The courts will enjoin the action of the commissioner of insurance in going through the books of a company to make public a list of policyholders who had the right to cash surrender value on lapsed policies under the Kentucky non-forfeiture law.[189]   Where a company is required to appoint an attorney to receive service of process, such authority cannot be canceled so long as its obligations remain outstanding.[190]   And the authority exists so long as the necessity to sue the company may continue.[191]   The withdrawal of the company from the State does not revoke the authority of the commissioner to accept service of process.[192]   Where a company has built up business in a State by establishing agencies, etc., it may challenge the validity of statutes subsequently enacted.[193] While a company which has not complied with the State law cannot recover the premium,[194] such failure to comply with the law

186 State ex. rel Reserve Life Ins. Co. v. Revelle, 260 Mo. 112; 168 S. W. 697.

187 North British, etc., Co. v. Craige, 106 Tenn. 1021; 62 S. W. 155.

188 Modern Woodmen of America v. Hatfield, 199 Fed. 270.

189 Metropolitan Life Ins. Co. v. Clay, 158 Ky. 192; 104 S. W. 968.

190 Birsch v. Mut. Reserve Life Ins. Co,. 181 N. Y. 538; 174 N. E. 1115; affirmed 200 U. S. 612; Collier v. Mut. Reserve Fund Life Ass'n, 119 Fed. 617.

191 Equity Life Ass'n v. Gammon, 119 Ga. 271; Magoffin v. Mut. Reserve Fund Life Ass'n, 87 Minn. 260; 91 N. W. 1115; Biggs v. Mut. Reserve Fund Life Ass'n, 128 N. C. 5; 37 S. E. 955.

192 Hunter v. Mut. Reserve Life Ins. Co., 103 N. Y. Supp. 71; 118 App. Div. 94.

193 Niagara Ins. Co. v. Cornell, 110 Fed. 816.

194 Wieslling v. Warthin, 1 Ind. App. 217; 27 N. E. 576; Barker v. Lamb, 99 Ia. 686; 68 N. W. 686; 34 L. R. A. 704; Seamans v. Christian & Bros., 68 N. W. 1065; Presbyterian Ministers' Fund v. Thomas, 126 Wis. 281; 105 N. W. 801.

does not prevent recovery on policies.[195] The legislature has power to inflict penalties on an insurance company for violation of the statute.[196] And benefit societies also are subject to State regulation.[197] Under the Georgia law the commissioner may apply to the Court to take charge of a life insurance company and have a receiver.[198] The North Carolina statute prohibiting the issue of a policy for less than five hundred dollars until the form has been approved by the insurance commissioner, does not invalidate the contract of insurance for less than five hundred dollars.[199]

A deliberate attempt by a corporation to evade the insurance law of the State in one of its most important provisions is ground for forfeiting the charter, and the insurance of a policy for an amount exceeding that which is allowed by law for such policies is forfeiture of the franchise.[200] A company which has surrendered its license, withdrawn its agencies, and only does such business as is necessary to collect premiums on outstanding business, is not doing business in the State under the insurance law requiring statements to be made annually.[201]

§ 56. **Defective Organization of Corporation.**—The same rule applies to the members of an acting corporation, the organization of which, however, is defective, as to parties who have contracted with a corporation as such, and, after having received the benefit of the contract, seek to avoid it on the ground that it had no authority to contract in a corporate capacity; the right of a member to pecuniary benefit from the association by virtue of his membership must stand upon the basis that it is a corpo-

---

[195] Hartford Live Stock Ins. Co. v. Matthews, 102 Mass. 221; Continental Ins. Co. v. Riggen, 31 Ore. 336; 48 Pac. 476.

[196] Boswell v. Sec. Mut. Life Ins. Co., 193 N. Y. 465; 86 N. E. 532.

[197] State v. Arlington, 157 N. C. 640; 73 S. E. 122.

[198] Wright v. State Mut. Life Ins. Co., 142 Ga. 764; 83 S. E. 666.

[199] Blount v. Royal Fraternal Ass'n, 163 N. C. 167; 79 S. E. 299.

[200] International Fraternal Alliance v. State, 86 Md. 550; 39 Atl. 512; 40 L. R. A. 187; State v. Equitable Indemnity Ass'n, 18 Wash. 514; 52 Pac. 234. As to appeal from rulings of insurance commissioner, see State v. McMaster, 94 S. C. 379-382; 77 S. E. 401. As to procedure see Yates v. Prudential Ins. Co., 207 Ill. 512; 69 N. E. 779.

[201] State v. Columbian National Life Ins. Co., 141 Wis. 557; 124 N. W. 502.

ration *de facto*.[202] Whether or not, in cases where the organization of the corporation is defective and the requirements of law have not been met, so that there is no legal corporation, the members are liable as partners, is one of those questions upon which there is an almost equal division of opinion, and the decisions are conflicting. A leading writer[203] has collected the various cases bearing on the subject and concludes that the weight of authority is in the favor of a rule that "if an association assumes to enter into a contract in a corporate capacity, and the party dealing with the association contracts with it as if it were a corporation, the individual members of such association cannot be charged as parties to the contract, either severally or jointly, as partners.[204] Where the incorporation of a former association is illegal, because the provisions of the constitution are not followed, the incorporated association cannot compel allegiance to it from the subordinate lodges.[205]

The Supreme Court of Illinois has held[206] that the members of an association are liable as partners to outsiders for a debt contracted before the defective incorporation of the association.

§ 57. **Fraternal Beneficiary Societies, and Subordinate Bodies of the Same, May be Voluntary Associations.**—A fraternal beneficiary association, or society, under the statutes relating to such organizations may be incorporated or unincorporated. The subordinate bodies of the same, lodges, councils, or by whatsoever other name they be called, are almost always voluntary associations, partaking of the nature of clubs. The society itself, if not incorpor-

---

202 Foster v. Moulton, 35 Minn. 458; 29 N. W. 155; Independent Order Mut. Aid v. Paine, 122 Ill. 625; 14 N. E. 42; Morawetz on Corp., § 750; Railroad Co. v. Cary, 26 N. Y. 75; Chubb. v. Upton, 95 U. S. 665.

203 Morawetz on Corp., § 748. Cook on Corp. (7th Ed.), §§ 233-234.

204 Blanchard v. Kaull, 44 Cal. 440. See also Hudson v. Spalding, 6 N. Y. Supp. 877.

205 National Grand Lodge, etc., v. Good Samaritan Lodge, etc., 175 Pa. St. 241; 34 Atl. 602. As to question of identity see Adams v. Northwestern Endowment, etc., Ass'n, 63 Minn. 184; 65 N. W. 360. As to recovery of money contributed for the purpose of incorporating, Meyer v. Bishop, 129 Cal. 204; 61 Pac. 919. In Moore v. Union Frat. Acc. Ass'n, 103 Ia. 424; 72 N. W. 645, where it was sought to hold individual members of an association the subject is also discussed.

206 Hossack v. Ottawa Development Ass'n, 244 Ill. 274; 91 N. E. 439.

ated, is still subject to the statutes of the State of its domicile relating to such organizations. It is necessary in any discussion of the law of life and accident insurance to consider the nature of voluntary associations and clubs; the effect of their articles of association; the liabilities of the members to each other and to third parties; and the right to expel a member and the procedure in such cases, and the legal remedies for unjust expulsion as well as the powers of the courts over the affairs of these associations. This we shall endeavor to do, although the subjects may on first thought seem foreign to such a treatise.

§ 58. **Legal Status of Voluntary Associations Uncertain.**—The legal *status* of unincorporated societies, whether formed for religious, social, benevolent or benefit purposes, has never been satisfactorily determined. The adjudicated cases are not in harmony and the courts have differed in their declarations. As a learned writer[207] has said: "The language of many authorities (particularly those where the peculiar rules applicable to voluntary associations do not seem to have been brought to the attention of the court), proceeds upon the idea that every organization must be either a corporation or a partnership. Many of the cases in the books have been decided upon this principle: Is this society a corporation? No. Then it must be a partnership. But this is not the only alternative. There may be a joint or a common tenancy in property—there may be a mutual or reciprocal agency in transactions for a specified purpose—and there may be a well-defined organization of the owners of such property, or the actors in such transactions, or both—an organization even having articles (like a partnership) or having a constitution and by-laws (like the charter and by-laws of a corporation), yet the organization may be in the eye of the law, neither a partnership nor a corporation." The question is not so much one of definition as of application of well-known principles of law to determine the jurisdiction of courts and liabilities of members. As in other cases, more depends upon the nature of the liability sought to be enforced and the varying facts of the different cases than upon mere abstract doctrines. Under certain conditions the members of a voluntary association may be considered partners, while in a different forum and

[207] Abbott's note to Ebbinghausen v. Worth Club, 4 Abb. N. C. 300.

under other circumstances the same organization will be deemed something else.[208]

§ 59. **Members of Voluntary Associations Sometimes Not Partners.**—In many cases it has been held that if a number of persons associate themselves together for purposes of charity, benevolence, pleasure, or any other lawful object not trade, or business, or profits, they are generally not to be regarded as among themselves, as partners.[209] In a case in Michigan[210] the members in good standing of a lodge of the Knights of Labor voted an assignment of the funds to plaintiff. In holding that he was entled to recover in an action against the persons in possession of the money the Court said: ''The parties who originally joined the Local Assembly No. 8104, might in a certain sense be said to be 'interested' in the funds belonging to the assembly, because it is provided by the rules of the order that they can at any time, by paying their arrearages of dues, resume their rights as members. This would reinvest them with the rights in the funds of the association, and. in the moneys sought to be collected in this suit, but until they pay their dues, and while they were in arrears and suspended, they had no rights or legal interest in the moneys of the assembly. They had perhaps while suspended a contingent interest, depending upon their retaining their rights, but not such an interest as made them necessary parties to the assignment. The jury must have had reference to this contingent interest in their answer to the second question. But the defendants claim that the judgment of the court is right, because, under all evidence, the plaintiff was not entitled to recover, and the jury should have

[208] For discussion of the status of voluntary associations, see 1 Beach on Priv. Corp., § 169 et seq. Daly's Club Law: Club Law, 27 Alb. L. J. 326; Leache's Club Cases.

[209] Thomas v. Ellmaker, 1 Pars. Sel. Cases, 98; White v. Brownell, 3 Abb. Pr. (N. S.) 325; 4 Abb. Pr. (N. S.) 162; McMahon v. Rauhr, 47 N. Y. 67; Lafond et al. v. Deems, 81 N. Y. 514; Leech v. Harris, 2 Brewst. 571; Tyrell v. Washburn, 6 Allen, 466; Smith v. Virgin, 33 Me. 148; Kuhl v. Meyer, 35 Mo. App. 206; Richmond v. Judy, 6 Mo. App. 465; Burt v. Lathrop, 52 Mich. 106; Edgerly v. Gardner, 9 Neb. 109; and as to members of mutual insurance companies, Krug v. Lycoming F. Ins. Co., 77 Pa. St. 15.

[210] Brown v. Stoerkel, 74 Mich. 269; 41 N. W. 921; see also note to this case in 3 L. R. A. 430.

been so instructed in the first place. This claim is based upon the proposition that this voluntary unincorporated association, consisting of many members contributing to a fund for the joint benefit of all, is a co-partnership, and therefore the respective rights and duties of the members with regard to their common property, can only be settled in a court of equity; that the rights of the individual members are entitled to as much respect in the courts as are the rights of any number of associates less than the whole; and it would be manifestly improper for the court to permit 38 members, out of any great number, to recover for themselves that which belongs to all the members. This association was in no sense a copartnership. There was no business carried on by it, and nothing involving loss or profit in a business sense.[211] It was purely a benevolent and social organization having also in view the protection, benefit and welfare of its members in their various employments. It must now be considered as well settled that persons have a right to enter into such associations, and to bind themselves as to their membership and rights in such societies, and the funds of the same by the constitution and by-laws of the association which they adopt, or subscribe to after adoption. Such an organization may be neither a partnership nor a corporation. The articles of agreement of such an association whether called a 'constitution,' 'charter,' 'by-laws,' or any other name, constitute a contract between the members which the courts will enforce, if not immoral or contrary to public policy or the law of the land.[212] The only persons having control of these funds were the members in good standing in the local assembly, by the agreement of all the members, as shown by the constitution and by-laws of the Knights of Labor, which constitution and by-laws in this respect were known to all the members when they paid in their money, as found by the jury under the charge of the court. Not only did the assembly in regular lodge meeting vote this assignment to plaintiff, but in pursuance of that vote, all the members of the assembly in good standing executed an assignment to plaintiff of their right, title and interest in this money to plaintiff. He was thereby under the law of the order and of the land, entitled to

[211] Burt v. Lathrop, 52 Mich. 106; 17 N. W. 716.
[212] Hyde v. Woods, 94 U. S. 523; 2 Sawy. 655; Subd. 1 Austin Abbott's note to Ebbinghausen v. Worth Club, 4 Abb. N. C. 300, 301.

sue and recover the money in the hands of the defendants, if it belonged to the assembly, as the jury found it did. The defendants divided this money up between themselves and Hemison relying upon difficulties and technicalities in the law as they supposed it to be to keep it. It is not to be regretted that they were mistaken in the law, and therefore deprived of the fruits of at least an attempted moral larceny.''

§ 60. **When Societies Are Partnerships.**—But in the settlement of disputes among the members, in the division of property, in determining the liabilities of members to creditors, in winding up the societies, and generally in all equitable proceedings, the courts will generally treat the members as ordinary partners, and the associations as partnerships, yet as far as possible giving effect to the articles of association of the members.[213] No liability attaches to members from the mere fact of membership but must be determined by the principles of the law of agency.[214] It has been said,[215] that while the courts will generally treat members of voluntary associations as partners, they will so far as possible, give effect to the articles of association when the members are the only ones interested, and if such association is organized for pecuniary profit so far as the rights of third persons are concerned the association will be regarded as a partnership. And in other

[213] Gorman v. Russell, 14 Cal. 537; Protchett v. Schaefer et al. 11 Phila. 166; Bullard v. Kinney, 10 Cal. 60; Butterfield v. Beardsley, 28 Mich. 412; Beaumont v. Meredith, 3 V. & B. 180; Pearce v. Piper, 17 Ves. 15; Carlton v. Southern Mut. Ins. Co., 72 Ga. 371; Reeve v. Parkins, 2 Jac. & W. 390; Ellison v. Reynolds, 2 Jac. & W. 511; Cockburn v. Thompson, 16 Vt. 321; Wallworth v. Holt, 4 Myl. & Cr. 619; Adkyns v. Hunt, 14 N. H. 205; Womersley v. Merritt, L. R. 4 Eq. Cas. 695; Richardson v. Hastings, 7 Beav. 323; Whitman v. Porter, 107 Mass. 522; Taft v. Ward, 106 Mass. 518; Harper v. Raymond, 3 Bos. 29; Mann v. Butler, 2 Barb. Ch. 362; Townsend v. Goewey, 19 Wend. 424; Burgan v. Lyell, 2 Mich. 102; Claggett v. Kilbourne, 1 Black, 346; Brown v. Curtis, 5 Mason, 421; Brown v. Gilman, 4 Wheat. 255; Brown v. Dale, L. R. 9 Ch. D. 78; Adams' Eq. 247-239-240; Story Eq. Jur. §§ 1243, 1535, 1256.

[214] In re St. James Club, 16 Jur. 1075; Volger v. Ray, 131 Mass. 439; Flemyng v. Hector, 2 Mees. & W. 172; 1 Beach on Priv. Corp., § 169.

[215] Hassack v. Ottawa Development Ass'n, 244 Ill. 274; 91 N. E. 439.

cases[216] it has been held that associations organized for business purposes are partnerships in all things not defined and governed by the articles of association or by-laws. These differences will more fully appear from the examination of some of the authorities bearing upon the subject.

§ 61. **Cases Where No Partnership Was Held to Exist.**—The Court of Appeals of New York, in passing upon a case where several members of an unincorporated lodge of a benevolent society, called "The Independent Order of Rechabites," brought suit against the others, alleging mismanagement, and seeking to dissolve the lodge and wind up its affairs and distribute its property among the members, said:[217] "Associations of this description are not usually partnerships. There is no power to compel payment of dues, and the right of the member ceases when he fails to meet his annual subscription. This, certainly, is not a partnership, and the rights of the copartners as such are not fully recognized. The purpose is not business, trade or profit, but the benefit and protection of its members, as provided for in its constitution and by-laws. In accordance with well established rules, no partnership exists under such circumstances." In Caldicott v. Griffiths,[218] the Court said: "The rules do not create a partnership between the members of the society. The question is, whether this is a scheme where certain persons enter into a partnership or *quasi*-partnership, or whether they are like members to a hospital or club. The solution of the question is not to be found by examining the cases with reference to the liability of committeemen or shareholders, but by looking at the rules of the society to see what liabilities they create." In Flemyng v. Hector,[219] an action brought by a tradesman against one of the members of a club, the Court said: "This is an action brought against the defendant on a contract, and the plaintiff must prove that the defendant, either by himself or his agent, has entered into that contract. That should always be borne in mind in cases of this class, for on most questions of this

216 Engvall v. Buchie, 73 Wash. 594; 132 Pac. 231; Crowley v. American Soc. of Equity, 153 Wis. 13, 139 N. W. 734; Slaughter v. American Baptist Pub. Soc. Tex. Civ. A., 150 S. W. 224.
217 Lafond et al. v. Deems et al., 81 N. Y. 514.
218 22 Eng. L. & E. 529; 8 Ex. 898; 1 C. L. R. 715; 23 L. J. Ex. 54.
219 2 M. & W. 171.

kind the real ground of liability is very apt to be lost sight of. As the defendant did not enter into the contract personally, it is quite clear that the plaintiff cannot recover against the defendant, unless he shows that the person making the contract was the agent of the defendant, and by him authorized to enter into the contract on his behalf. . . . It is said in this case that the order was given by the committee, and that they were the agents of the members generally; but the question is, whether there was any sufficient evidence to go to the jury that they were authorized by the defendants to enter into and make these particular contracts in their behalf. . . . These cases resolve themselves into questions of construction as to the meaning of the original rules of the club.'' In this case the members were held, under the rules, not to be liable for debts contracted by the managing committee.

§ 62. **The Case of Ash v. Guie.**—In Ash v. Guie,[220] a case where creditors sought to charge the members of a Masonic lodge for debts incurred in erecting a building, the Court said: ''A benevolent and social society has rarely, if ever, been considered a partnership. In Lloyd v. Loring,[221] the point was not made, but Lord Elden thought the bill would lie on the ground of joint ownership of the personal property in the members of a Masonic lodge; there was no intimation that they were partners. Where a society of Odd Fellows, an association of persons for purposes of mutual benevolence, erected a building, which was afterwards sold at sheriff's sale in satisfaction of mechanics' liens, in distribution of the proceeds. it was said that, as respects third persons, the members were partners, and that lien creditors, who were not members, were entitled to preference as against the liens of members.[222] Had the members been called joint tenants of the real estate the same principle in the distribution would have applied. . . . A mutual beneficial society partakes more of the character of a club than a trading association. Every partner is agent for the partnership, and as concerns himself he is a principal, and he may bind the other by contract, though it be against an agreement between himself and his partners. A joint tenant has not the same power,

---

[220] 97 Pa. St. 493; 39 Am. 818. See also Wood v. Finch, 2 Fos. & Fin. 447.

[221] 6 Ves. 773.

[222] Babb v. Reed, 5 Rawle, 151; 28 Am. Dec. 650.

by virtue of the relation, to bind his co-tenant. Thus one of several co-adventurers in a mine has not, as such, any authority to pledge the credit of the general body for the purposes of the concern. And the fact of his having the general management of the mine makes no difference, in the absence of evidence from which an implied authority for that purpose can be inferred.[223] "Here there is no evidence to warrant an inference that when a person joined the lodge he bound himself as a partner in the business of purchasing real estate and erecting buildings, or as a partner so that the other members could borrow money on his credit. The proof fails to show that the officers, or committee, or any number of the members, had a right to contract debts for the building of a temple, which would be valid against every member from the mere fact that he was a member of the lodge. But those who engaged in the enterprise are liable for the debts they contracted, and all are included in such liability who assented to the undertaking or subsequently ratified it. Those who participated in the erection of the building, by voting for and advising it, are bound the same as the committee who had it in charge, and so with reference to borrowing money. A member who subsequently approved the erection or borrowing could be held on the ground of ratification of the agent's acts. We are of the opinion that all the members so assenting were liable as partners in their relation to third persons in the same manner as individuals associated for the purpose of carrying on a trade."

§ 63. **Cases Where Members of Associations Were Held to be Partners.**—In Park v. Spaulding,[224] also an action brought by a creditor to charge as individuals certain members of a voluntary association called "The Worth Club," the Court said: "Its members remained at all times in that nebulous and inchoate condition in which an aggregation of individuals, assuming a name under which they incur liability, are held personally liable for the benefit of creditors by the application of common law principles. . . . Where such a body of gentlemen join themselves together for social intercourse and pleasure, and assume a name under which they commence to incur liabilities, by opening an account, they

---

[223] Ricketts v. Bennett, 4 M. G. & S. 686; 56 E. C. L.
[224] 10 Hun, 128.

become jointly liable for any indebtedness thus incurred; and if either of them wishes to avoid his personal responsibility by withdrawal from the body, it is his duty to notify the creditors of such withdrawal.'' The Supreme Court of New York[225] lays down this rule: _ ''Personal responsibility to the full extent of the indebtedness to third parties can only be avoided by persons constituting any association where they become a corporation or *quasi-corporation*. Companies or societies, which are not sanctioned expressly by the legislature, pursuant to some general or special law, are nothing more than ordinary partnerships and the laws respecting them are the same.'' The principle has been well stated as follows:[226] Where parties unite in a voluntary unincorporated association and for convenience contract under an associate name, the acts of the association, it not being a legally responsible body, are the acts of the members who instigate and sanction the same.''[227] Generally it may be said that members of a voluntary association are liable as partners for indebtedness incurred in the business for which it was organized.[228]

§ 64. **The Declaration of Collyer on Partnership.**—The following strong declaration is from Collyer on Partnership:[229] ''Societies and clubs, the object of which is not to share profits, are not partnerships·in any sense. . . . It is a mere abuse of words to

225 Wells v. Gates, 18 Barb. 554. The question also arose in the following cases where a member of the association was held liable for its debt. Murray v. Walker, 83 Ia. 202; 48 N. W. 1075; McFadden v. Leeka, 48 Ohio St. 513; 28 N. E. 874. The principles were also fully discussed in Burt v. Oneida Community, 61 Hun, 626; 16 N. Y. Supp. 289, where among others the following cases were cited: Hyde v. Woods, 94 U. S. 523; Belton v. Hatch, 109 N. Y. 593; 17 N. E. 225.

226 Winona Lumber Co. v. Church, 6 S. Dak. 498; 62 N. W. 107.

227 So of a member of a college class which sanctioned a publication. Wilcox v. Arnold, 162 Mass. 577; 39 N. E. 414. Of a press association, United Press v. Abell, 84 N. Y. Supp. 425. Of an exposition, Jenne v. Matlack, 19 Ky. 503; 41 S. W. 11. But see Hornberger v. Orchard, 39 Neb. 639; 58 N. W. 425; and Midwood v. Wholesale Grocers, 20 R. I. 152; 37 Atl. 946. The subject is discussed in Cheney v. Goodwin, 88 Me. 563; 34 Atl. 420. See also McKenney v. Bowie, 94 Me. 397; 47 Atl. 918.

228 Schumacher v. Sumner Teleph. Co., 161 Ia. 326; 142 N. W. 1034; Hardy v. Carter, Tex. Civ. A., 163 S. W. 1003.

229 Wood's edition, 1878, § 29.

call such associations partnerships; and if liabilities are to be fastened on any of their members it must be by reason of the acts of those members themselves, or by reason of the acts of their agents; and the agency must be made out by him who relies on it, for none is implied by the mere act of association.''

§ 65. **The Principle Stated by Another Writer.** — A careful writer thus states the result of his investigation:[230] ''The true principle is, and upon this view the apparent discordance in the cases may be nearly reconciled, that the law allows associates to imitate the organization and methods of corporations *so far as their rights between themselves is involved,* and will enforce their articles of agreement (nothing illegal or unconscientious appearing) as between the parties to them. But the public and creditors have a right to invoke the application of the law of partnership to the dealings of any trading association, unless such association has the shield of incorporation. Thus, if the controversy is between members of the association, and relates to such objects as the mode of acquiring membership, tenure of the property, division of the profits, transfer of shares, voting, expulsion, dissolution, or the like; the courts may deal with the association by analogy to the law of corporations, so far as the compact between the members contemplates. But if the question is between the association, or its members, and third parties, and relates to such points as in what name the association may sue, whether members are individually liable to the creditors for debts, etc., a mere compact of association cannot vary the rights of strangers to it, but the associates must submit to the general rules of law applicable to the questions raised.''

§ 66. **A General Rule.**—The general rule seems to be that the articles of association, or rules, or if there are no such articles of association or rules, then the customs and usages of the members, are to be looked to in order to determine whether the associated individuals are a partnership or not, and to adjust the rights of these individuals among themselves.[231] The questions involved are of construction and of fact. So far as creditors are concerned

---

[230] Abbott Digest of Corp., tit., Associations.
[231] Brown v. Stoerkel, 74 Mich. 269, and *ante,* § 59.

and outsiders generally their rights are governed by the law of agency, and in each case it will be necessary to ask whether the agents of the association were authorized to contract the obligation, and if so, whether it was contracted in behalf of all the members of the association, or some of them only.[232] Necessarily the facts in each particular case will decide whether any liability attaches and also its extent.[233]

An unincorporated beneficial society not organized for trade, or profit, which continues its existence, regardless of changes in its membership, is not as between its own members a partnership, though at the suit of others it may be held to be one,[234] and it has been said,[235] that clubs whose objects are social, or political, are not partnerships and pecuniary liability can be fastened upon individuals thereof only by reason of their acts or the acts of their agents, and agency cannot be implied from the mere fact of association.

[232] McCabe v. Goodfellow, 133 N. Y. 89; 30 N. E. 728; 17 L. R. A. 204; cited in Hosman v. Kinneally, 86 N. Y. Supp. 263; Winona Lumber Co. v. Church, 6 S. D. 498; 62 N. W. 107; Bennett v. Lathrop, 71 Conn. 613; 42 Atl. 635; Pelton v. Place, 71 Vt. 430; 46 Atl. 63.

[233] Ash v. Guie, 97 Pa. St. 493; Flemyng v. Hector, 2 M. & W. 171; Caldicott v. Griffiths, 22 Eng. L. & E. 529; Cutler v. Thomas, 25 Vt. 73; Hill v. Beach, 12 N. J. Eq. 31; Carlew v. Drury, 1 Ves. & B. 157; Keasly v. Codd, 2 Car. & P. 408; Harrison v. Heathorne, 6 M. & G. 81; Pipe v. Bateman, 1 Ia. 369; Babb v. Reed, 5 Rawle, 151; Carlton v. Southern M. Ins. Co., 72 Ga. 371; Waller v. Thomas, 42 How. Pr. 337; Foley v. Tovey, 54 Pa. St. 190; Payne v. Snow, 12 Cush. 443; Gorman v. Russell, 14 Cal. 533; Hess v. Wertz, 4 Serg. & R. 356; Pearce v. Piper, 17 Ves. 15; Fuller v. Rowe, 57 N. Y. 23; Protchett v. Schaefer, 11 Phila. 166; Leech v. Harris, 2 Brewst. 571; Koehler v. Brown, 2 Daly, 78; Richmond v. Judy, 6 Mo. App. 465; Ferris v. Thaw, 5 Mo. App. 279; s. c. 72 Mo. 450; De Voss v. Gray, 22 Ohio St. 159; Heath v. Goslin, 80 Mo. 310; Sproat v. Porter, 9 Mass. 300; Kuhl v. Meyer, *supra,* and 1 Beach on Priv. Corp., § 168 *et seq.* Some recent cases illustrating this principle are: Castner v. Rinne, 31 Colo. 256; 72 Pac. 1052; McKinnie v. Postles 4 Penn (Del.) 16; 54 Atl. 798; Associazione, etc,. v. Gobbi, 82 App. D. 635; 81 N. Y. Supp. 354; Comfort v. Graham, 87 Ia. 295; 54 N. W. 242. As to evidence of membership, Lanheim v. Green, 54 N. Y. Supp. 145; 25 Misc. 757, and Bennett v. Lathrop, *supra.* See also as to liabilities of members, *post,* 138, *et seq.*

[234] Rohde v. U. S., 34 D. C. 249.

[235] Meriwether v. Atkin, 137 Mo. App. 32; 119 S. W. 36; O'Rourke v. Kelly, The Printer, Corp. 156 Mo. App. 91; 135 S. W. 1011.

§ 67. **Liability and Status of Members.**—If one or more members order work done or supplies furnished he or they are personally liable unless credit was given to the association.[236] If an officer of a voluntary association signs a note in his official capacity for money lent the association he binds all his associates, including himself.[237] The liability of members attaches when they sign the articles of association,[238] although such signing is not a prerequisite of membership,[239] and continues until notice of withdrawal is given;[240] and the law of the place where the association was formed and did business determines such liability.[241] All the members are liable where the obligation arises in the following out of the business for which the association was created, as for publishing a class book.[242] If the relation of partnership exists one member cannot sue the others at law;[243] nor can a member sue

[236] Wells v. Turner, 16 Md. 133; Heath v. Goslin, 80 Mo. 310; Lewis v. Tilton, 64 Ia. 220; s. c. 52 Am. 436; Hutchinson v. Wheeler, 3 Allen, 557; McKenney v. Bowie, 94 Me. 397; 47 Atl. 918; Detroit Light Guard etc., v. First Mich. Inftry., 134 Mich. 598; 96 N. W. 934.

[237] Kierstead v. Bennett, 93 Me. 328; 45 Atl. 42. And so of directors. Pelton v. Place, 71 Vt. 430; 46 Atl. 63. See also Detroit, etc., Band v. First Michigan Ind. Infantry, 134 Mich. 598; 96 N. W. 934; Evans v. M. C. Lilly & Co., 95 Miss. 58; 48 Sou. 612; Rankin v. Proby, 115 N. Y. Supp. 832; 131 App. Div. 328; Bennett v. Lathrop, 71 Conn. 613; 42 Atl. 634; 71 Am. St. 202; Jenne v. Matlack, 19 Ky. L. R. 503; 41 S. W. 11.

[238] Dennis v. Kennedy, 19 Barb. 517.

[239] United Hebrew, etc., v. Benshimol, 130 Mass. 325; Tyrell v. Washburn, 6 Allen, 466.

[240] Tenney v. N. E. Protective Union, 37 Vt. 64; Park v. Spaulding, 10 Hun, 128. A member is not liable if he withdraws before the transaction. Rhoads v. Fitz Gibbon (Central, etc., Ass'n), 166 Pa. St. 294; 31 Atl. 79.

[241] Cutler v. Thomas, 22 Vt. 73; Knights of Honor v. Nairn, 60 Mich. 44; 26 N. W. 826. But see Taft v. Ward, 106 Mass 518, where it is held that members of a joint stock company under the laws of New York are liable to third parties as partners.

[242] Wilcox v. Arnold, 162 Mass. 577; 39 N. E. 414.

[243] Bullard v. Kinney, 10 Cal. 60; McMahon v. Rauhr, 47 N. Y. 67; Holms v. Higgins, 1 B. & C. 74. But see Boston Base Ball Ass'n v. Brooklyn, etc., Club, 75 N. Y. Supp. 1076; 37 Misc. 521, and Simpson v. Ritchie, 110 Me. 299; 86 Atl. 124; Rowell v. Seneborn, 76 N. H. 620; 85 Atl. 665.

an unincorporated association for negligence;[244] nor can the majority bind the minority except by consent, or by acting under the articles of association.[245] If the Court is satisfied that the association is a bubble and cannot answer the purpose of its creation it will wind it up;[246] and, if necessary, restrain operations by injunction.[247] `Where an "unauthorized corporation" or "private society" was organized for the purpose of providing a common fund and erecting tombs for its members, and the latter by its rules are to receive, in return for dues and fees, relief and medical treatment during illness, burial at death, and certain specified assistance to their widows and orphans when left in necessitous circumstances; it was held that the death of any member does not dissolve the association; that the interest in the assets of a member of the association does not pass to his heirs but lapses in favor of his associates.[247e] It was held that where under a statute a certain amount was deducted from the pay of police officers to create a special fund the discharge of an officer forfeited his rights to any part of the fund, he having no vested rights in the matter.[248] The authority of a committee to borrow money is not to be implied from the existence of a general power to borrow money.[249]

§ 68. **The Effect of Articles of Association.**—We shall discuss this question of *status* of unincorporated voluntary associations further when we come to consider the rights and liabilities of members to each other. It is always true, however, as said in Protchett v. Schaefer et al.,[250] that "the articles of association are doubtless to be considered in the light of an agreement, between the members, extending or limiting any general obligation, which binds

[244] Martin v. Northern Pacific & Ass'n, 68 Minn. 521; 71 N. W. 701.

[245] Livingston v. Lynch, 4 Johns. Ch. 594; Torrey v. Baker, 1 Allen, 120.

[246] Buckley v. Cater, stated 17 Ves. 15; Pearce v. Piper, 17 Ves. 1; Ellison v. Bignold, 2 Jac. & Walk. 511. But see *post*, §§ 72, 73.

[247] Reeve v. Parkins, 2 Jac. & Walk. 390; Gorman v. Russell, 14 Cal. 538.

[247e] Sociedad Union Espanola v. Docurro, 1 McGloin (La.), 218. See also Mason v. Atlanta Fire Co., 70 Ga. 604; 48 Am. 585; Social Union No. 1 v. Barrett, 19 R. I. 663; 36 Atl. 5.

[248] Clarke v. Reis, 87 Cal. 543; 25 Pac. 759, citing Pennie v. Reis, 80 Cal. 269; 22 Pac. 176; 132 U. S. 471; 10 S. C. 149.

[249] Siff v. Forbes, 119 N. Y. Supp. 773; 135 App. Div. 39, reversing 117 N. Y. Supp. 143.

[250] 11 Phila. 166.

them to each other as members of the partnership.'' ''The members have established a law to themselves.''[251] This fundamental compact is generally called the constitution and is analogous to the charter of a corporation.[252] The constitution, or articles of association, constitute a contract to which the members are parties.[253] It is admissible in evidence as part of the record, although not recorded in its books,[254] and will be liberally construed.[255] Where the constitution was printed iñ Russian and English, the English translation after 20 years cannot be questioned.[256] It is not required by law to possess a seal.[257] The society has no power except such as is given in the articles of association.[258] The benefits to be received constitute a consideration for the obligation on the part of the members to pay dues[259] and the obligation to pay dues exists so long as the membership continues. The dues when assessed can be assigned[260] and the amount of dues can be increased[261] The incorporation of an unincorporated benefit association is an amendment of its constitution and is not binding on the subordinate lodges unless the provisions of its constitution in regard to amendments thereof are followed.[262]

[251] Leech v. Harris, 2 Brewst. 571; Tyrrell v. Washburn, 6 Allen, 466; Hyde v. Woods, 2 Sawyer, 655, affd. 94 U. S. 523; Liederkranz Singing Soc. v. Germania Turn Verein, 163 Pa. St. 265; 29 Atl. 918; Dingwall v. Amalgamated Ass'n, 4 Cal. App. 565; 88 Pac. 597.

[252] Bray v. Farrell, 81 N. Y. 660; Hyde v. Woods, 94 U. S. 523; 2 Sawy. 655; Bergman v. St. Paul Mut., etc., 29 Minn. 275, also cases cited next section.

[253] McLaughlin v. Wall, 86 Kans. 45; 119 Pac. 541; Boston Club v. Potter, 212 Mass. 23; 98 N. E. 614; Willoughby v. Hildreth, 182 Mo. App. 80; 167 S. W. 639.

[254] Tarbell et al. v. Gifford, 82 Vt. 222; 72 Atl. 921.

[255] Starnes v. Atlanta Police Relief Ass'n, 2 Ga. App. 237; 58 S. E. 481. Appeal of Baylor, 93 S. C. 414; 77 S. E. 59.

[256] Piries v. First Russian Slavonic, etc., Soc., 83 N. J. Eq. 29; 89 Atl. 1036.

[257] White v. Hartman, 26 Colo. App. 475; 145 Pac. 716.

[258] Kerr v. Hicks, 154 N. C. 285; 70 S. E. 468.

[259] Taplin v. Webster, 76 Ohio St. 590; 81 N. E. 1196.

[260] Anderson v. Amidon, 114 Minn. 202; 130 N. W. 1002.

[261] Thompson v. Wiandauck Club, 127 N. Y. Supp. 195; 70 Misc. Rep. 299.

[262] National Grand Lodge, etc., v. Good Samaritan Lodge, etc., 175 Pa. St. 241; 34 Atl. 602. See also post, § 115.

§ 69.   **Powers of Voluntary Associations and of the Members.**
—An unincorporated voluntary association may do any legal act within the scope of its articles of association or constitution and by-laws, which articles, constitution and by-laws form the contract of the members and fix the powers of their agents, the officers. There can, however, be no judgment against such an association as such unless some statute permits.[263]   A mutual aid association authorized by its charter to pay sick and death benefits has no power to issue policies under which assessments are to be returned at the expiration of a certain time.[264]   Nor has a fraternal beneficiary association, organized under a charter which does not confer power to issue notes, the implied power to do so when such authority is unnecessary to enable the association to exercise the powers expressly given.[265]   Nor can a fraternal beneficiary association under the laws of Nebraska possess any authority to purchase the business and assume the liabilities to another similar concern.[266]   The principles and rules of partnership and agency determine the right and liabilities of these associations and their members and the questions which arise concerning them are to be adjusted accordingly. [267]   An unincorporated voluntary association is at common law incapable of taking as a beneficiary in a trust[268] unless charged with a use, and the specific performance of a trust by which a fund was transferred will be enforced.[269]   Members of voluntary association can hold property in no other way than

[263] O'Connell v. Lamb, 63 Ill. App. 652; Hajek v. Bohemian, etc., Soc. 66 Mo. App. 565.

[264] Boyd v. Mut. Aid Ass'n, 145 Ala. 167; 41 Sou. 164.

[265] Scott v. Bankers' Union, 73 Kan. 575; 85 Pac. 604.

[266] Starr v. Bankers' Union, 81 Neb. 377; 116 N. W. 61.

[267] Bullard v. Kinnea, 10 Cal. 60; Gorman v. Russell, 14 Cal. 537; White v. Brownell, 3 Abb. Pr. (N. S.) 318; Leech v. Harris, 2 Brewst. 571; Ridgley v. Dobson, 3 Watts & S. 118; Wells v. Gates, 18 Barb. 554; Protchett v. Schaefer et al., 11 Phila, 166; Robinson v. Robinson, 10 Me. 240; Dow v. Moore, 47 N. H. 419; Flemyng v. Hector, 2 M. & W. 171; Rosenberger v. Washington Mut., etc., 87 Pa. St. 207.

[268] White v. Rice, 112 Mich. 403; 70 N. W. 1024; In re Winchester's Est., 133 Cal. 271; 65 Pac. 475; Lounsbury Trustees Square Lake, etc., Mich. 129 N. W. 36.   A deed to a voluntary association as such is void. Miller v. Oliver, 65 Mo. App. 435.

[269] Associate Alumni, etc., v. General Theological Seminary, etc., 163 N. Y. 417; 57 N. E. 626.

through trustees. Each beneficiary is a joint owner.[270] A conveyance of land to the trustees of a Masonic lodge will be held to have placed the legal title in them and their successors for the benefit not of the individual members but for the lodge itself.[271] The interest of a member in the property of a Masonic lodge is an incident of his membership and ceases on withdrawal.[272] And the association can dispose of the property, his interest being only the right to enjoy its privileges as of a club.[273] A lease to an unincorporated association does not for that reason fail, as the title vests in the members.[274] If the members knowingly acquiesce in or consent to a departure from the requirements of the laws of the society, evidence of this fact is admissible to determine the liability.[275] The association cannot change the purposes for which it was organized, as specified in its articles of association, without the consent of all the members;[275] nor does the withdrawal of two-thirds of the membership destroy the identity of the association,[276] and although a minority, present at a meeting where money is disposed of for a purpose different from that prescribed in the articles of association, are bound unless they then and there dissent, the vote does not bind those not present.[277] A part of the members cannot bind the others without their consent before the act which it is claimed binds them is done, or they, with knowledge of the facts, ratify and adopt it; although, if the act is clearly in furtherance of the object for which the association is organized,

[270] Clark v. Brown, 48 Tex. Civ. App. 212; 108 S. W. 421.

[271] Minor v. St. John's Union Grand Lodge, etc., 62 Tex. Civ. App. 100; 130 S. W. 893.

[272] Lawson v. Hewell, 118 Cal. 613; 50 Pac. 763; 49 L. R. A. 400.

[273] Manning v. Canon City, 45 Colo. 571; 101 Pac. 525.

[274] Edwards v. Old Settlers' Ass'n, Tex. Civ. App. 106 S. W. 423.

[275] Henry v. Jackson, 37 Vt. 431; Dow v. Moore, 47 N. H. 419.

[275] Morton v. Smith, 5 Bush, 467; Zabriskie v. Hackensack, etc., 18 N. J. Eq. 178; Marston v. Durgin, 54 N. H. 347; Hochreiter's Appeal, 93 Pa. St. 479; Torrey v. Baker, 1 Allen, 120; Kalbitzer v. Goodhue, 52 W. Va. 435; 44 S. E. 264. See as to incorporation of voluntary association, National Grand Lodge, etc., v. Good Samaritan Lodge, etc., 175 Pa. St. 241; 34 Atl. 602.

[276] Schiller Commandery v. Jaennichen, 116 Mich. 129; 74 N. W. 458.

[277] Abels v. McKeen, 16 N. J. Eq. 462; Ray v. Powell, 134 Mass. 22; Keen v. Johnson, 9 N. J. Eq. 401.

all will be presumptively bound by it.[278] The executive board of a voluntary association cannot convert it into a corporation unless the power is conferred upon it by the constitution and by-laws or an express resolution of the association,[279] nor can the dissatisfied members of an association by incorporating themselves deprive the voluntary association of the right of using its own name.[280] The Supreme Court of Michigan has held[281] that a Masonic lodge which was in existence before the organization of a corporation of the same name, and which had never by any action authorized or recognized the corporation as formed in the same behalf, and where each had been distinct in meetings, officers, property and other incidents, and not even identical in membership, was not merged in the corporation. The Court said: "There is nothing but unanimous consent which can bind any member of an unincorporated company by any action not within the terms of the association. In joint enterprises, matters within the proposed scheme are usually left to be determined by such agencies or such votes as are agreed upon. Outside of the agreement, no one can be bound without his assent."[282] But where an unincorporated mutual benefit society procures a charter and its members are continued as members of the corporation it is a mere continuation of the original contract and a contract entered into by it which is invalid under the original articles of association remains so,[283] and it has been held that the fact that officers and members of an unincorporated society as individuals unite with an association of a similar character does not vacate their offices nor forfeit their membership in the absence of a provision of the constitution of the first society to the contrary, although the constitution of the second society forbids its

[278] Sizer v. Daniels et el., 66 Barb. 426; Richmond v. Judy, 6 Mo. App. 465; Carter v. Stratford Savings Bank, 70 N. H. 456; 48 Atl. 1083.

[279] Rudolph v. Southern Ben. League, 7 N. Y. Supp. 135. As to action necessary on incorporation of a voluntary association to vest its property in the corporation. Kopruki v. Wojciehowski, 130 N. Y. Supp. 736; 73 Misc. R. 46.

[280] Association v. Munday, 21 App. D. C. 99.

[281] Mason v. Finch, 28 Mich. 282.

[282] Mears v. Moulton, 30 Md. 142.

[283] Swett v. Citizens' M. Relief Soc., 78 Me. 541; 7 Atl. 394.

members to join any other similar organization.[284] A voluntary association cannot hold real estate as such;[285] nor take a bequest, unless coupled with a use.[286] It has been held, however, that a legacy bequeathed to an unincorporated society by name but ·not impressed with any trust, is payable to the persons composing the society. Such association may receive and hold the property in common as individuals.[287] The members must exercise good faith towards each other;[288] and they have the right to insist upon a literal carrying out of the provisions of the articles of association in regard to property, though it may not be for the interests of the concern or may be against the will of the majority.[289] If the decision of a committee of a voluntary association transferring property and affecting pecuniary interests operates injuriously as to any members the enforcement of the decision will be enjoined.[290] And an action lies on behalf of an unincorporated association to enjoin part of its members from procuring the incorporation of a society under the same name.[291] While an associa-

[284] Farrell v. Cook, 5 N. Y. Supp. 727; Farrell v. Dalzell, 5 N. Y. Supp. 729. See also National Grand Lodge, etc., v. Good Samaritan Lodge, etc., 175 Pa. St. 241; 34 Atl. 602.

[285] Baptist Ass'n v. Hart, 4 Wheat. 1; Kain v. Gibboney, 101 U. S. 362; Douthitt v. Stinson, 73 Mo. 199; East Haddam, etc., v. East Haddam, etc., 44 Conn. 259; Miller Lumber Co. v. Oliver, 65 Mo. App. 435. But see Byan v. Bickford, 140 Mass. 31; Inglis v. Sailors' Snug Harbor, 3 Pet. 99; Vidal v. Girard, 2 How. 127; Perin v. Carey, 24 How. 465; Ould v. Washington Foundling Hosp., 95 U. S. 303; Russell v. Allen, 107 U. S. 163. A discussion of the rights of members of an unincorporated association to hold real estate will be found in Crawford v. Cross, 140 Pa. St. 297; 21 Atl. 356. See also 1 Beach on Priv. Corp., § 379.

[286] Sherwood v. Am. Bible Soc., 4 Abb. App. Dec. 227; Betts v. Betts, 4 Abb. N. Cas. 317. Also authorities last cited. See also Swift's Executors v. Eastern Ben. Soc., 73 Pa. St. 362; Blenon's Estate, Brightly, 338; Miller v. Oliver, 65 Mo. App. 435; Fralick v. Lyford, 95 N. Y. Supp. 433; 107 App. Div. 543; affd. 187 N. Y. 524; 79 N. E. 1105.

[287] Guild v. Allen, 28 R. I. 430; 67 Atl. 855.

[288] Densmore Oil Co. v. Densmore, 64 Pa. St. 43; Getty v. Devlin, 54 N. Y. 403; Sizer v. Daniels, 66 Barb. 426.

[289] Mann v. Butler, 2 Barb. Ch. 362; Torrey v. Baker, 1 Allen 120.

[290] Rudolph v. Southern Ben. League, *supra.* See also National Grand Lodge v. Good Samaritan Lodge, *supra.*

[291] McGlynn v. Post, 31 Abb. N. C. 97.

106

tion can dispose of its property to pay its debts such disposal must be fair and not give a part of the members an undue advantage.[292]

§ 70. **The Same Subject Continued, Rights of Members in Property and Funds of Society.**—Where property belongs to an association organized for purposes other than profit and the possession of such property is a mere incident to the social or other purposes of the organization, a member has neither any proprietary interest in it nor right to any proportional part of it, either during his continuance in membership or upon his withdrawal. He has merely the use and enjoyment of it while a member, the property belonging to and remaining with the society. But when the society ceases to exist, those who may then be members may become entitled to their share of the assets[293] It has been held,[294] that the rights of members of an association in a building on land donated by the defendant were not forfeited by abandonment of the undertaking, and any members of the association, after defendant took possession of the building, could maintain an action against him for an accounting. Where a benefit society has transferred its entire assets in good faith to another similar association for a valuable consideration, they cannot be recovered, though such transfer was a breach of duty toward the beneficiaries of the association.[295] Where an association has decided to transfer its immovable property in a certain manner, the executive board is without authority to transfer it in a different manner.[296] The contributors to a fund raised and placed in the hands of trustees for a specific purpose have the right to compel repayment to them proportionately of any surplus not needed for the object,[297] and to require the fund to be applied to the objects for which it was

[292] Blais v. Brazeau, 25 R. I. 417; 56 Atl. 186.
[293] White v. Brownell, 3 Daly, 329; Brown v. Stoerkel, 74 Mich. 269; 41 N. W. 921; *In re* St. James Club, 13 Eng. L. & Eq. 592. As to real estate, Brown v. Dale, 25 Moak Eng. 776; Crawford v. Gross, 140 Pa. St. 297; 21 Atl. 356; Local Union No. 1 v. Barrett, 19 R. I. 663; 36 Atl. 5; Sommers v. Reynolds, 103 Mich. 307; 61 N. W. 501; O'Brien v. Musical, etc., Union, 64 N. J. Eq. 525; 54 Atl. 150.
[294] Rowell v. Sandborn, 76 N. H. 520; 85 Atl. 605.
[295] Harvey v. Wasson, 74 Kan. 489; 87 Pac. 720.
[296] North Louisiana Baptist Ass'n v. Milliken, 110 La. 1002; 35 Sou. 264.
[297] Abels v. McKeen, 18 N. J. Eq. 462.

raised,[298] or to recover a contribution where the funds are still on hand and the objects and purposes for which the contribution were made have failed.[299] But seceding members cannot maintain a suit for the recovery of a debt due the society from which they have seceded,[300] and where members of a lodge withdrew from the jurisdiction of the grand lodge and surrendered the charter but certain other members remained true in their allegiance the latter are entitled to the charter and property of the original lodge.[301] Even if practically all the members unite in the act of severance, so long as a quorum remains loyal they can continue the organization and can claim to be the society[302] The funds of a subordinate circle accumulated for sick benefits belong to the subordinate body and is impressed with a trust and a vote to withdraw from the association confers no authority to devote the fund to a different organization, and the members who withdraw lose their interest in the accumulated funds.[303] Title to the property of a mutual insurance corporation is in the company, but the equitable interests are vested in the membership, while the corporation owns the property, the members own the corporation.[304] The fact that certain members of an association organized a corporation under the same name and were treated thereafter by the other members as having withdrawn from membership did not deprive the members who incorporated of their interest in the property of the voluntary asso-

[298] Morton v. Smith, 5 Bush (Ky.), 467; Ostrom v. Greene, 161 N. Y. 353; 55 N. E. 919; Bachman v. Hoffman, 104 Ill. App. 159; Gorman v. O'Connor, 155 Pa. St. 239; Schiller Commandery v. Jaennichen, 116 Mich. 129; 74 N. W. 458.

[299] Kuehler v. Brown, 2 Daly, 78.

[300] Smith v. Smith, 3 Desau (S. C.), 557.

[301] Altman v. Benz, 27 N. J. Eq. 331. See also Goodman v. Jedidjah Lodge, 67 Md. 117; 9 Atl. 13; Thomas v. Ellmaker, 1 Par. Sel. Cas. 98; Livingston v. Lynch, 4 Johns. Ch. 573; Stadler v. District Gr. L. I. O. B. B., 3 Am. L. Rec. 589; Red Jacket Tribe, etc., v. Gibson, 70 Cal. 128; Schiller Commandery v. Jaennichen, 116 Mich. 120; 74 N. W. 458.

[302] Union Benev. Soc. etc., v. Martin, 113 Ky. 25; 76 S. W. 1098; 25 Ky. L. Rep. 1039.

[303] National Circle Daughters of Isabella v. Hines, 88 Conn. 676; 92 Atl. 401.

[304] Huber v. Martin, 127 Wis. 412; 105 N. W. 103; 3 L. R. A. (N. S.) 653.

ciation.[305] Certain societies or communities of a *quasi*-religious character exist where, upon joining, a member surrenders his property and receives certain rights as to support. Interesting questions have often arisen concerning the rights of the members of these associations.[306] One of these cases is Burt v. Oneida Community,[307] where a member of the Oneida Community, voluntarily and against the rules, left the community and afterwards brought an action to recover compensation for his services and to share in the community property. In the course of the discussion the Court said: "Plaintiff, having assented to the practices, customs, agreements and covenants existing among the members of the community, may reasonably be held bound by the tenor and terms thereof. The United States Supreme Court in Goessele v. Bimeler,[308] had occasion to examine an organization not wholly unlike the one now before us. In that case, 'the articles of association or constitutions of 1819 and 1824 contained a renunciation of individual property,' and it was held 'the heirs of one of the members who signed these conditions, and died in 1827 cannot maintain a bill of partition.' Also it was further held, viz.: 'The ancestor of these heirs renounced all right of individual property when he signed the articles, and did so upon the consideration that the society would support him in sickness and in health; and this was deemed by him an adequate compensation for his labor and property, contributed to the common stock. The principles of the association were that land and other property were to be acquired by the members but they were not to be vested with the fee of the land. Hence, at the death of one of them, no right of property descended to his heirs. There is no legal objection to such a partnership; nor can it be considered a forfeiture of individual rights for the community to succeed to his share, because it was a matter of voluntary contract. Nor do the articles of association

305 Strong v. Los Nietos Ass'n, 137 Cal. 607; 70 Pac. 734.

306 Grosvenor v. United Society, 118 Mass. 78 (right of expelled Shaker); Waite v. Merrill, 4 Me. 102; Burt v. Oneida Community, 61 Hun, 626; 16 N. Y. Supp. 298; Goessele v. Bimeler, 14 How. 589; Nachtrieb v. Harmony, etc., 3 Wall. Jr. 66; Lennix v. same, 3 Wall. Jr. 87.

307 61 Hun, 626; 16 N. Y. Supp. 289; affirmed 137 N. Y. 346; 33 N. E. 307; 19 L. R. A. 297.

308 14 How. 589.

constitute a perpetuity. The society exists at the will of its members, a majority of whom may, at any time, order a sale of the property, and break up the association.' In the course of the opinion of Judge McLean it is said of the plaintiff's ancestor, viz.: 'He then signed the first articles, which, like the amended articles, renounced individual ownership of property, and an agreement was made to labor for the community, in common with others for their comfortable maintenance. All individual right of property became merged in the general right of the association. He had no individual right and could transmit none to his heirs. It is strange that the complainants should ask a partition through their ancestor, when, by the terms of his contract, he could have no divisible interest. They who now enjoy the property enjoy it under his express contract.' And again he says: 'As a general rule, chancery may not enforce a forfeiture; but will it relieve an individual from his contract, entered into fairly and for a valuable consideration? What is there in either of these articles that is contrary to good morals, or that is opposed to the policy of the laws? An association of individuals is formed under a religious influence, who are in a destitute condition, having little to rely on for their support but their industry; and they agree to labor in common for the good of the society, and a comfortable maintenance for each individual; and whatever shall be acquired beyond this shall go to the common stock. This contract provides for every member of the community, in sickness and in health, and under whatsoever misfortune may occur; and this is equal to the independence and comforts ordinarily enjoyed. The ancestor of the complainants entered into the contract fairly and with a full understanding of its conditions. The consideration of his comfortable maintenance, under all circumstances, was deemed by him an adequate compensation for his labor and property contributed to the common stock.' Again he says: 'If members separate themselves from the society, their interest in the property ceases and new members that may be admitted, under the articles, enjoy the advantages common to all.' In that case the bill in equity was denied 'on a deliberate consideration of all the facts in the case,' the opinion concluding that 'there is no ground to authorize the relief prayed for by the complainants.' In Hyde v. Woods,[309] the

[309] 94 U. S. 523.

question arose as to the property rights of a member of the San Francisco Stock and Exchange Board, which was a voluntary association for business purposes, and it was held that a rule of the association was binding upon a member, and the Court observed: 'Though we have said it is property, it is incumbered with conditions, when purchased, without which it could not be obtained. It never was free from the conditions of article 15, neither when Fenn bought nor at any time before or since. That rule entered into and become an incident of the property when it was created and remains a part of it into whose hands soever it may come.' In Belton v. Hatch,[310] a question arose as to the relation to each of the other members composing the association of the New York Stock Exchange, and the extent and the validity of the powers reserved by its constitution and by-laws. That was a voluntary association of individuals united without a charter in an organization for the purpose of affording to the members thereof certain facilities for the transaction of their business, and in the course of the opinion delivered it was said, viz.: 'It cannot be said to be strictly a copartnership, for its objects do not come within the definition of one,' and it was further said that 'whatever a member acquires is subject to the self-imposed condition that his title and the rights which accrue from his membership are regulated by, and are dependent upon, the laws adopted by the association, and expressly consented to by him when he joined.' A similar case was expressed to the Court in White v. Brownell,[311] and in that case it was held that the 'open board of brokers in the city of New York is not a corporation, nor is it a joint-stock association; nor is it, as respects questions relating to the continuance or termination of membership in it, a partnership. That board is a voluntary association of persons who, for convenience, have associated to provide, at the common expense, a common place for the transaction of their individual business as brokers. The agreement which the members of such an association have made upon the subject of membership and what shall be the terms on which it shall be acquired, and the grounds and proceedings upon which it shall be terminated, must determine the rights of parties on that subject. A court of justice must recognize and enforce

[310] 109 N. Y. 593; 17 N. E. 225.
[311] 3 Abb. Pr. (N. S.) 318.

these provisions of the compact. It cannot substitute another contract for the one which the parties have made.' In that case an injunction was dissolved which restrained the board from interfering with the privileges of a member of the board, and the decision made at general term was affirmed.[313] Daly, F. J., said in the course of an elaborate opinion, viz.: 'Individuals who form themselves together into a voluntary association for a common object may. agree to be governed by such rules as they think proper to adopt, if there is nothing in them to conflict with the law of the land; and those who become members of the body are presumed to know them, to have assented to them, and they are bound by them.' ''[314] The heirs of a founder of a community association cannot claim dissolution and its property on the theory of a resulting trust.[315] Similar questions often arise in regard to religious associations, but it is not germane to the subject to here discuss the principles involved, and reference must be made to works on religious societies.[316]

§ 71. Voluntary Association May be Estopped from Showing Its True Nature.—A voluntary association may, by holding itself out as a corporation, be estopped from denying its corporate capacity and thus, so far as third parties are concerned, be deemed a corporation.[317] If a partnership association, whose members are partners as between themselves, does business in a corporate name, any person dealing with the association in that name may hold the

---

[313] 4 Abb. Pr. (N. S.) 162.

[314] Innes v. Wylie, 1 Car. & K. 262; Brancker v. Roberts, 7 Jur. (N. S.) 1185; Hopkinson v. Marquis of Exeter (London Times, Dec. 31, 1867), L. R. 5 Eq. 63.

[315] Everett v. Duss, 197 Fed. 401; affg. 206 Fed. 590.

[316] In 20 Am. & Eng. Encyc. of Law, p. 773, will be found a carefully prepared article on Religious Societies. A recent case, Schwartz v. Duss, 187 U. S. 8, affirming 103 Fed. 561, 43 C. C. A. 323, contains a full discussion of the nature and powers of such associations and what amounts to a dissolution.

[317] Tarbell v. Page, 24 Ill. 46; Baker v. Backus, 32 Ill. 79; Independent Order Mut. Aid v. Paine, 122 Ill. 625; 14 N. E. 42; Grand Lodge Brotherhood Locomotive Firemen v. Cramer, 60 Ill. App. 212. And so one who conveys by warranty deed property to a company is estopped to deny the capacity of such grantee to take. Reinhard v. Va. Lead Mining Co. 107 Mo. 616; Morawetz on Corp., § 752.

members liable as partners, although he did not know the real character of the association at the time. The liability of the members of the association under these circumstances arises from the fact that they are actually partners as between themselves.[318]

§ 72. **Dissolution of Voluntary Associations.**—Benefit societies, if incorporated, may be dissolved and ended by consent of the members, but the procedure in such case must be that prescribed by statute if provisions are made for such cases. While it has been said that a voluntary association can be dissolved only in the manner provided by its articles of association,[319] it is undoubtedly the law that a voluntary association can be dissolved by the action of the members.[320] In some States the method of winding up voluntary associations is prescribed by statute. Of course in such cases the procedure is governed by law.[321] And it has been said that members in good standing of a voluntary association organizing a club for taking a lease of a hall do not lose their joint property in the lease by the dissolution.[322] On dissolution, generally speaking, the property of a voluntary association belongs to the members.[323] The question of disposition of property of a subordinate lodge, when a voluntary association, is more difficult to answer. It has been held,[324] that the legal title to a reserve fund held by the different local branches was in the supreme body and not in such local branches, and was held in trust for all the holders of benefit certificates and on appointment of a receiver he is entitled to the funds held by the local bodies, which after deduction of expenses, must be paid to the foreign receiver

---

318 Cook on Corp. (7th Ed.), §§ 231-234 and cases cited, page 663.

319 Koerner v. Lodge No. 6, etc., 146 Ind. 639; 45 N. E. 1103. See also B. & O. R. Co. v. Flaherty, 87 Md. 102; 39 Atl. 524; Hopkins v. Crossly, 138 Mich. 561; 108 N. W. 822; Atnip v. Tenn. etc., Co. (Tenn.); 52 S. W. 1093.

320 Summer Lodge, etc., v. Odd Fellows' Home, 77 N. J. Eq. 386; 77 Atl. 36; Primm v. White, 162 Mo. App. 594; 142 S. W. 802.

321 Henry v. Simanton, 67 N. J. Eq. 606; 61 Atl. 1065; reversing 64 N. J. Eq. 572; 54 Atl. 153.

322 Sommers v. Reynolds, 103 Mich. 307; 61 N. W. 501.

323 Parks v. Knickerbocker Trust Co., 122 N. Y. Supp. 521; 137 App. Div. 719; Pierson v. Gardner, 81 N. J. Eq. 505; 86 Atl. 443.

324 Buswell v. Supreme Sitting, etc., 161 Mass. 224; 36 N. E. 1065; 23 L. R. A. 846.

if there is one, and a by-law of a superior body that no lodge shall be dissolved if. five members wish to continue, is valid.[325]   In the case of Engvall v. Buchie,[326] it was held that in the absence of anything in the articles of association, or by-laws, the members are liable for contributions among themselves for the payment of the association's debts on its dissolution, the liability of the members being determined by the law of partnership.   Generally speaking, the right to property on dissolution is determined by the articles of association.[327]   The Supreme Court of the United States has said in regard to the interest of the members in a communistic society,[328] where the property was claimed by the last survivor, that the adoption by the members of a communistic society of a plan by which all property contributed to the use and benefit of the community was to be "joint and indivisible stock," and all contributions were to be irrevocable, was not the creation by the members of a trust in the property for the benefit of the society, as such, which, on the doctrine of resulting trusts, conferred on the descendants of members who contributed no property to the society any such proprietary right of interest as entitled them on the dissolution of the society to share in its property or assets, or to have an accounting.   In this case, however, there was a strong dissent by Chief Justice Fuller, with whom Justice Brewer concurred.   He says: "Joint tenancy with survivorship, or tontine, excluding all but living members and casting - accumulations on the survivor, are neither of them to be presumed.   They are the result of express agreement, and there is none such in these documents.   On the contrary, this property was held in trust for the use and benefit of the society, as a society, and not for the individual members.   The trust was for the use and benefit of the society in the maintenance of its principles as declared by its constitution and laws.   When the purposes of the society were abandoned or could not be accomplished, or the

---

[325] Freundschaft Lodge, etc., v. Alehenburger, 235 Ill. 438; 85 N. E. 653; affirming 138 Ill. App. 204.

[326] 73 Wash. 534; 132 Pac. 231.

[327] Nichols v. Bardwell Lodge, 105 Ky. 168; 48 S. W. 426; Union Benev. Soc. v. Martin, 113 Ky. 25; 67 S. W. 38.

[328] Schwartz v. Duss, 187 U. S. 8; affirming 103 Fed. 563; 43 C. C. A. 323.

society ceased to exist, the trust failed, and the property reverted, by way of resulting trust, to the owners who subjected it to the trust, living, and to the heirs and legal representatives of those of them who are dead. " The existence of a voluntary association may also be terminated by implied abandonment because of failure to hold meetings for a protracted period.[329] Where a voluntary association ceased to do business for eight years, after which some of the shareholders organized a new association in the name of the old, it was held that such new association was a distinct organization from the old and did not succeed to the property of the latter and a conveyance of such property by the new association was void.[330] Generally where the objects of an association have been abandoned or when it appears that the power to resume business does not exist, a legal dissolution will be decreed.[331] It has been held,[332] that a voluntary association cannot go out of business while its contracts or obligations are outstanding so as to prevent the service of process on an "officer" of such society. But where by unanimous consent the society decides to incorporate, the former organization is dissolved.[333] A society cannot, however, be dissolved on account of loss of members if enough remain to fill vacancies and continue the succession.[334] It has been held[335] that a court will not enjoin a society from dissolving itself where a great majority of the members agree to such dissolution, notwithstanding a rule that "if three agree to hold the society it shall not be dissolved." A court will not, however, in these cases make mere declarations of right,[336] nor interfere in the contentions and quarrels of an association where the

329 Strickland v. Pritchard, 37 Vt. 324; Penfield v. Skinner, 11 Vt. 296.
330 Allen v. Long, 80 Tex. 261; 16 S. W. 43. A contrary view under the facts is held in Monroe County, Alliance v. Owens, 75 Miss. 500; 25 Sou. 876, and see also Marcoux v. Society, etc., 91 Me. 250; 39 Atl. 1027, as to reorganization.
331 Kuehl v. Meyer, 50 Mo. App. 648; s. c. 42 M. A. 474.
332 Camden, etc., Co. v. Guarantors of Pa., 59 N. J. L. 328; 35 Atl. 796.
333 Red Polled Cattle Club v. Red Polled Cattle Club, 108 Ia. 105; 78 N. W. 803.
334 St. Mary's Ben. Ass'n v. Lynch, 64 N. H. 213; 9 Atl. 98; see also State v. Society Republicaine, 9 Mo. App. 114.
335 Waterhouse v. Murgatroyd, 9 L. J. Ch. 272.
336 Clough v. Ratliff, 1 DeG. & Sm. 164; 16 L. J. Ch. 476.

government is fairly and honestly administered.[337] Whenever the objects of the society are impracticable, or the organization is in the nature of a fraud, it will be dissolved and the fund distributed as. on the winding up of a partnership,[338] and wrongful exclusion of a member is cause for dissolution.[339] It is safe to assume that courts of equity will always interfere with all voluntary associations wherever necessary in the interests of their members, or society, or to prevent injustice, imposition or fraud, and will act on the same general principles invoked and practiced in partnership cases.[340] Where the funds on an attempted dissolution have been misappropriated a court of equity will compel a restoration and a member may institute proceedings for that purpose without demand on the trustees.[341] Where a committee was formed to erect a monument and abandoned the project, but afterwards a member of the committee completed the monument, using for the purpose in part what had previously been collected, it was held that the other members of the committee who subsequently undertook to carry out the project could not call him to account.[342] The same rules apply in such cases so far as practicable as in the case

[337] Lafond v. Deems, 81 N. Y. 508.

[338] Beaumont v. Meredith, 3 Ves. & Bea. 181; Reeve v. Parkins, 2 Jac. & Walk, 390; Ellison v. Bignold, Id. 511; Pearce v. Piper, 17 Ves. 1.

[339] Gorman v. Russell, 14 Cal. 537.

[340] Lowry et al. v. Stotzer et al., 7 Phila. 397; Toram v. Howard Ass'n, 4 Barr, 519. Calkins v. Bump, 120 Mich. 335; 79 N. W. 491, is in point.

[341] Ashton v. Dashaway Ass'n, 84 Cal. 61; 22 Pac. 660; State Council, etc., v. Sharp, 38 N. J. Eq. 24. In many other cases courts have exercised supervision over societies for the purpose of justice to prevent misappropriation and compel restoration. Stadler v. District Grand Lodge, etc., 3 Am. L. Rec. 589; Red Jacket Tribe, etc., v. Gibson, 70 Cal. 188; Bailey v. Lewis, 3 Day (Conn.), 450; Munn v. Burgess, 70 Ill. 604; Miller v. Lebanon Lodge, 88 Ind. 286; Brown v. Griffin, 14 W. N. C. 358; Bush v. Sherman, 80 Ill. 160; Birmingham v. Gallagher, etc., 112 Mass. 190. See also Blais v. Brazeau, 25 R. I. 417; 56 Atl. 186. The members cannot sue the treasurer of an association for money paid in in pursuance of an agreement, although the money was disbursed by such treasurer without obtaining the desired results. Meyer v. Bishop, 129 Cal. 204; 61 Pac. 919.

[342] Doyle v. Reid, 33 App. Div. 631; 53 N. Y. Supp. 365.

116

of corporations.[343]   A society, however, cannot be administered by a court in perpetuity by continued collection of dues, but the funds must be distributed and the society wound up.[344]   In like manner, wherever a trust, express or implied, is violated, equity will interfere.   The general rules of equity jurisprudence and partnership apply.[345]   It is unnecessary to enter more into detail at this place or refer to the well-known works of eminent writers on the subject.

§ 73.   **Jurisdiction of Equity in Regard to Voluntary Associations.**—It is the settled doctrine that civil courts will not interfere with the internal operations of a voluntary unincorporated association of individuals· for benevolent and fraternal objects, or review their failure to conduct their business affairs according to their laws and rules, except to protect some civil or property right of the complaining party.[346] And in controversies between individual members of secret fraternal organizations, where rights are purely fraternal, civil courts have no jurisdiction.[347]   Equity will interfere to require a voluntary association to pay over a fund to a charity when created for its benefit, and the association has no power to devote the fund to some other charity.   In a recent case, the Court says:[348]   ''The money that the society accumulated prior to the amendment of its by-laws was raised for a specific purpose by its officers and members, and donated for that purpose by its contributors within and without the society.   It is therefore im-

<hr />

[343] Kuhl v. Meyer, 50 M. A. 648.   For a case where an action at law by the assignee of the members was allowed, see Brown v. Stoerkel, 74 Mich. 269; 41 N. W. 269.

[344] Collier v. Steamboat Captains, etc., Ass'n, 1 Cin. L. B. 18.

[345] Gorman v. Russell, 14 Cal. 531.   All the trustees of an unincorporated association must be served in an action to wind it up.   Wall v. Thomas, 41 Fed. 620, citing Barney v. Baltimore City, 6 Wall. 280-285. Where under an impracticable scheme of an association which afterwards failed, a member received a sum grossly disproportionate to what he had paid in, but nevertheless in accordance with his contract, he is not liable as 'for a trust fund to a receiver of such concern.   Calkins v. Green, 130 Mich. 57; 89 N. W. 587.

[346] Gaines, *et al.* v. Farmer, *et al.*, 55 Tex. Civ. App. 601, 119 S. W. 874; Lone Star, etc., v. Cole, 62 Tex. Civ. App. 500, 131 S. W. 1180.

[347] National Grand Lodge, etc., v. United Brothers of Friendship, 36 Okla. 738, 129 Pac. 724.

[348] Leatherman ·v. Wolf, 240 Pa. 557, 88 Atl. 17.

117

pressed with and held upon the trust that it shall be so applied. The society holds it as a trustee and can no more divert the fund from the use for which it was raised than any other trustee could. If, as has happened, the members of the society undertake to divert the fund to some other purpose, equity will raise up another trustee to administer it, and apply it according to the original donors or subscribers.''[349]   Courts will take jurisdiction in the case of voluntary associations where property rights are involved, but the member must exhaust his remedies in the association before applying for relief.[350]   The property of a voluntary association represented by certificates. and held by trustees may be reached and sold by proper proceedings in a court of equity.[351]   The Supreme Court of Vermont has thus laid down the general rule as to the basis upon which a court of equity will act if it entertains jurisdiction over these societies:[352]   ''If jurisdiction is entertained over them (voluntary associations) by a court of chancery, it appears to me that it will become necessary to examine their constitution or by-laws, or articles of association, in order to discover the object for which they were formed; and every member contributing, and every one receiving donations, whether styled officer or not, must be considered as having regard to the articles of association, whether they are called constitution or by-laws, and must proceed accordingly.   And if it is so provided, the majority may control the minority by a vote, if such vote is for the purposes of the association and within its provisions.   The court of chancery has power to see that such associations are faithful trustees in the disposition of the charitable fund, and will see that it is appropriated to the object designed, and will not suffer it to be diverted, unless with the consent of the contributors.   If the object should entirely fail, probably each contributor would be entitled to have his money refunded, and might, or might not, according to the circumstances of the case, have a remedy therefor, either at law or in chancery.[353]   Generally equity will exercise its powers to prevent diversion of funds. protect the rights of members of the associations,

349 Schnorr's App., 67 Pa. 138, 5 Am. Rep. 415.

350 Crutcher v. Eastern Division, etc., 151 Mo. App. 622, 132 S. W. 307.

351 Frost v. Thompson, 219 Mass. 360, 106 N. E. 1009.

352 Penfield v. Skinner, 11 Vt. 296.

353 Duke v. Fuller, 9 N. H. 536; 32 Am. Dec. 392. See *ante*, § 70.

118

declaring and enforcing such rights, and will to that end even compel the delivery of a specific chattel,[354] or place the property in the custody of a receiver,[355] or order a sale of the property,[356] but it will not exercise this power unless the interests of justice so require.[357] A court of equity will enforce an equitable lien against an unincorporated association upon a note in order to avoid a multitude of actions.[358]

§ 74. **Jurisdiction of Equity in Regard to Corporations.**— Upon sufficient cause shown a court of equity will always interfere to prevent a misuse of corporate franchises or abuse of the rights of members and will wind up the association if it is manifest that it cannot accomplish the purposes of its organization. The comprehensive and flexible rules of equitable jurisprudence apply to all kinds of corporations and courts of equity are always open to those who are wronged or aggrieved by the tortious acts or the mismanagement of the officers or members of these associations. Where the scheme of a beneficiary organization is unjust and fraudulent in its workings, and where the officers have been guilty of illegal conduct, an injunction will be granted to protect the assets from further illegal management. In a case of this kind the New Jersey Court of Chancery says:[359] "Unquestionably the act of the legislature should be liberally construed. Nothing can be clearer than that its purpose is to enable numbers of citizens to unite in order that they may support and maintain those of their number who perchance become unfortunate; and yet the answer expressly admits, that upon the basis upon which this union is formed, it cannot be at all successful, unless a very large proportion of its members forfeit their right to membership by failing and refusing to comply with all the terms or conditions of the

354 Fello v. Read, 3 Ves. Jr. 70, where a silver tobacco box was ordered to be delivered. ·

355 Hinkley v. Blethen, 78 Me. 221; 3 Atl. 655; State v. Peoples, etc., 42 Ohio St. 579; McCarthy's App., 17 W. N. C. 182.

356 Clerks Investment Co. v. Sydnor, 19 App. D. C. 89.

357 Robbins v. Waldo Lodge, 78 Me. 565; 7 Atl. 540; Hinkley v. Blethen, *supra.*

358 Soc. of Shakers v. Watson, *et al.*, 15 C. C. A. 632; 68 Fed. 730; see also Schwartz v. Duss, 187 U. S. 8; affg. 43 C. C. A. 323; 103 Fed. 561.

359 Pelz v. Supreme Chamber Order of Financial Union (N. J), 19 Atl. 668.

constitution and by-laws. It will be observed, therefore, that in
all probability the great majority of those who need the protection
of such an institution are not only deprived of its benefits, but by
forfeiting the right, contribute to the benefit of those who are not
in such need, and who have not been unfortunate. It is admitted
that at least 33⅓% of the members of such institutions forfeit
their membership by failing to comply with all the conditions;
and during the progress of the cause I became convinced that there
was every probability that this union if continued for any length
of time, would show a much larger percentage of forfeitures. I
was not a little surprised at what seemed to be the boast of the
officers of the defendant company, that the very foundation of
their scheme rested upon the unsuccessful efforts of such large
numbers to continue their membership. I find it very difficult to
conclude that a scheme based upon such acknowledged weakness,
misfortune, or disability of large numbers of citizens is at all
within the true spirit or meaning of the act. A calculation based
upon the theory of these officers shows that instead of the possibility of a member in full standing ever receiving $1,000 for
$260 paid in, he can only receive about $450, and this only after
making allowance for the immense numbers of forfeitures above
spoken of. How can it be said that the legislature ever intended
to allow the learned and skillful and financially able to make profit
under the guise of benevolence and charity out of the unlearned,
unskilled, and those who are so unfortunate as to suffer from financial disability? After the fullest and most careful reflection, I
am unable to discover any method or principle of law by which
this scheme can be sustained under the act. With all due respect
for the learned counsel who presented the case for the defendant,
it seems to me that the scheme presented by the constitution and
by-laws in this case has more the appearance of a lottery than of
a charity. It is not necessary for me to say that any such result
was intended, it being enough to find that the scheme has culmi-
nated in disaster. The cases which support the jurisdiction of the
court, and also show the extent to which courts of equity have
gone in winding up such institutions, are hereby referred to in
part.''[360] Where an association departs from the business author-

[360] Pearce v. Piper, 17 Ves. 1, 16, 19 and notes; St. Louis, etc., Min Co.
v. Sandoval, etc., Min. Co., 116 Ill. 170; 5 N. E. 370; Bac. Ben. Soc., §§ 51.

ized by its charter, as by employing paid agents and paying endowments, the Court will appoint a receiver. The members may also sue to recover back assessments paid.[361] In a recent case,[362] the Supreme Court of Michigan said: "Although a court of equity may not decree a dissolution of the corporation, yet in virtue of its general jurisdiction over trusts, and to afford remedies in cases where courts of law are inadequate to grant relief, it has jurisdiction to grant relief against a corporation upon the same terms it might against an individual under similar circumstances."[363] Equity will not interfere at the suit of a minority stockholder to restrain the sale of the corporate assets made upon reasonable grounds and without fraud,[364] nor will a forfeiture be enforced in equity against a subordinate lodge incorporated under the State laws, where the enforcement of the forfeiture will incapacitate the corporation from performing the very duty for which it was organized.[365] And a corporation which by its articles of association is to continue a certain number of years cannot dissolve itself until that period has expired unless all the shareholders consent.[366]

§ 75. **Dissolution of Incorporated Societies.**—Like other corporations, benefit societies, if incorporated, may be dissolved and their existence wholly terminated by either of the following contingencies:—

First. By expiration of charter.

54, 57-59; Stamm v. Association, 65 Mich. 317; 32 N. W. 710; Slee v. Bloom, 19 Johns. 456.

[361] Fogg v. Order Golden Lion, 156 Mass. 431; 31 N. E. 289; Chicago Mut., etc., Ass'n v. Hunt, 127 Ill. 257; 20 N. E. 55, where numerous questions of what constitutes mismanagement are discussed.

[362] Stamm v. Northwestern Mut. Ben. Ass'n, 65 Mich. 317; 32 N. W. 710.

[363] Cramer v. Bird, L. R. 6 Eq. 143; *Re* Suburban Hotel Co., L. R. 2 Ch. App. 737-743-750; Marr v. Union Bank, 4 Coldw. 484; Bradt v. Benedict, 17 N. Y. 93; Slee v. Bloom, 19 Johns. 456; 10 Am. Dec. 273. But see State v. Equitable Indemnity Ass'n, 18 Wash. 514; 52 Pac. 234.

[364] Beidenkopf v. Des Moines Life Ins. Co., 160 Ia. 629; 142 N. W. 434.

[365] Grand Court Foresters of America v. Court Cavour, etc., 82 N. J. Eq. 89; 88 Atl. 191.

[366] Barton v. Enterprise B. & L. Ass'n, 114 Ind. 226; 16 N. E. 486; Von Schmidt v. Huntington, 1 Cal. 55, 73.

Second. By dissolution and surrender of the franchises with the consent of the State.

Third. By legislative enactment, if no constitutional provision be violated.

Fourth. By forfeiture of the franchises and judgment of dissolution obtained in a proper judicial proceeding.[368]

The rule is laid down by the standard writers on the subject that there is a broad and fundamental distinction between the dissolution of a corporation and the loss of its franchise or legal right to exist. An association may still be a corporation *de facto* though not *de jure,* and *vice versa.*[369]

§ 76. Forfeiture of Corporate Franchises.—Only the State can claim the forfeiture of corporate franchises for wrongful acts of omission or commission.[370] The Supreme Court of California[371] has thus laid down the general rule: "There is a broad and obvious distinction between such acts as are declared necessary steps in the process of incorporation, and such as are required of the individuals seeking to become incorporated, but which are not made prerequisites to the assumption of corporate powers. In respect to the former any material omission will be fatal to the existence of the corporation, and may be taken advantage of collaterally in any form in which the fact of incorporation can properly be called in question. In respect to the latter, the corporation is responsible only to the government, and in a direct proceeding to forfeit its charter.[372]

[368] Morawetz on Corp., § 1004. Cook on Corp. (7th Ed.), § 628.

[369] The subject of dissolution of corporations is fully considered in a note to Chicago Mut. L. Ind. Co. v. Hunt (127 Ill. 257), in 2 L. R .A. 5490; Morawetz on Corp., § 1002.   See also Cook on Corp. (7th Ed.), § 628, *et seq.*

[370] Morawetz on Corp., § 1015. Cook on Corp. (7th Ed.), §§ 632, 637.

[371] Mokelumne Mining Co. v. Woodbury, 14 Cal. 424, 426; 23 Am. Dec. 658.

[372] Morawetz on Corp., § 31 and cases cited.

CHAPTER III.

123

§ 77. Benefit Societies Doing a Life Insurance Business Are Like Other Life Insurance Corporations.

—So far as corporations,

carrying on a life insurance business, either on the plan of annual, semi-annual or quarterly premiums and the accumulation of a reserve fund or upon the assessment plan where calls are made as necessity requires, monthly, or less or more frequently, are concerned, it may be said that it is hard to conceive of any reason why such organizations should be governed by any rules different from those regulating other corporations. The contracts of all alike must be judged by the laws applicable to all similar contracts of other corporations. The fundamental agreement of the members is contained in the charter, and their affairs are administered and contracts made under the rules and restrictions there and in the by-laws contained, subject to the usual qualifications arising out of the application of the law of agency and estoppel.[1] In the application, however, of the laws of agency, a substantial difference is found to exist between the practical workings of benefit societies and those of the regular life insurance corporations, which will more fully appear when we come to discuss the agency of lodges.

§ 78. **Plan of Organization of Benefit Societies.**—A majority of benefit societies are fraternal and social in their organization and have secret meetings and rituals. Frequently the organization is composed of several distinct, but not entirely disconnected, judicatories or assemblies. The subordinate lodges or associations, most numerous, are first; above these are State, or district, societies, or grand lodges, made up of representatives from the local lodges, and over all is sometimes a supreme or national governing body, composed of delegates from the State or district grand lodges. These various organizations are sometimes incorporated, often mere voluntary associations, and frequently the subordinate lodges or grand lodges are corporations while the governing authority, to which they acknowledge subjection, is a voluntary association. This complex situation gives rise to different rules applicable to the varying circumstances and at times renders it difficult to apply the proper legal principles to the various cases.

§ 79. **Element of Property Rights of Members.** — The law under some circumstances distinguishes between the soci-

[1] Morawetz on Corp., Ch. 7.

125

eties which are incorporated and those that are mere voluntary associations, and again between questions involving the property rights of members and those concerning discipline only or
policy of government. In regard to the latter the Supreme Court
of Indiana[2] has said: "Claims for money due by virtue of an
agreement are unlike mere matters of discipline, questions of doctrine, or of policy, and are not governed by the same rules. . . .
One who asserts a claim to money due on a contract, occupies an
essentially different position from one who presents a question of
discipline of policy, or of doctrine of the order or fraternity to
which he belongs." Questions of discipline of members where
the membership involves, or has connected with it property rights,
are differently regarded from disputes concerning membership in
mere social clubs when such membership has no element of property connected with it. These differences will appear as the subject is further discussed.[3]

§ 80. **Common Characteristics of Corporations and Voluntary
Associations.**—Remembering that a corporation is simply a voluntary association of persons for an agreed and lawful purpose,
endowed by the State with an artificial entity or individuality, and
also that "the real nature of a corporation, in every case, depends
upon the charter under which it is formed and must be determined by reference thereto,"[4] it follows that voluntary associations of all kinds, whether partnerships, charities, corporations
or mere clubs or societies, have many characteristics and rules in
common, the principal of which is that all rights of the members
and their powers, as well as of the association or corporation, are
derived from the original compact between them which is contained in the articles of association or charter.[5] The constitution,
rules and by-laws of a voluntary association is a contract between
the members.[6]

[2] Bauer v. Sampson Lodge, etc., 102 Ind. 262; see also Wist v. Grand
Lodge A. O. U. W., 22 Ore. 271; 29 Pac. 610; Hogan v. Pacific Endowment
L., 99 Cal. 248; 33 Pac. 924.
[3] *Post*, §§ 81, 94.
[4] Morawetz on Corp., §§ 6, 7, 316, 580.
[5] Leech v. Harris, 2 Brewst. 571; Commonwealth v. St. Patrick's Soc.,
2 Binn. 441; 4 Am. Dec. 453; *post*, § 81.
[6] Dingwall v. Amalgamated Ass'n, etc., 4 Cal. App. 565; 88 Pac. 597. *

§ 81. **Membership Governed by Articles of Association or Charter.**—The articles of association, or charter, regulate the admission of members of societies and define their qualifications. The rule is applicable to all associations, incorporated or voluntary, and if wrongfully admitted the member can be expelled; nor is the society bound by the acts of its officers in admitting a person ineligible under its constitution so as to become liable to him for benefits.[7] Charter members of a fraternal society have no rights not common to other members.[8] If the charter limits the age of members the admission of one over that age is void. If the prohibition is contained in a by-law it can be waived.[9] It has been held that where a member of an association by statute has a voice in its management only adult persons are eligible to membership,[10] but in the absence of statutory prohibition it has also been held that minors are eligible.[11] The Supreme Court of Pennsylvania[12] has said: "It is true, the power of admitting new members being incidental to a corporation aggregate, it is not necessary that such power be expressly conferred by the statute. Yet when the statute does limit and restrict the power, it erects a barrier beyond which no by-laws can pass." Where the statute required all practicing physicians to become members of the county medical society, and a physician so applying was rejected because of alleged unprofessional acts in violation of the society's by-laws, the New York Court of Appeals held[13] that the code of medical ethics adopted by such a society was binding on members alone and its non-observance previous to membership furnishes no legal cause for either exclusion or expulsion. But in this case the party excluded had a clear presumptive title for admission to the exer-

7 Fitzgerald v. Burden Benev. Ass'n, 69 Hun, 532; 23 N. Y. Supp. 647; Burbank v. Boston, etc., R. Ass'n, 144 Mass. 434, 11 N. E. 691.

8 Pond v. Royal League, 127 Ill. App. 476.

9 Sherry v. Catholic Order of Foresters, 166 Ill. App. 254.

10 *In re* Globe Ben. Ass'n, 135 N. Y. 280; 32 N. E. 122; 17 L. R. A. 547; affg. 17 N. Y. Supp. 852; State v. Central Ohio, etc., Ass'n, 29 Ohio St. 407.

11 Chicago Mut. L., etc., v. Hunt, 127 Ill. 257; 20 N. E. 55; 2 L. R. A. 549. See, as to insurance of minors and their powers to make insurance contracts, *post*, § 193.

12 Diligent Fire Co. v. Commonwealth, 75 Pa. St. 291; Alsatian Ben. Soc., 35 Pa. St. 79.

13 People v. Erie Medical Soc., 32 N. Y. 187.

cise of a corporate franchise.[14] Where, however, the membership
is recruited from a certain class, as Masons or Odd Fellows, and
the association is not for pecuniary gain, no person can compel
the society to admit him. As has been said:[15] "Where the condition of membership is that the members shall all be of some particular religious denomination, or of some widespread and well-
known society, such as the Masons, the courts would not undertake
to determine as to this member or that—whether he is in fact a
Baptist, a Methodist, a Presbyterian, or a Freemason—but would
leave that to be determined by the peculiar rules and the judicial
action of the proper members of such society, entirely regardless
whether the charter of the particular religious society or the particular Masonic lodge gave, in express terms, such judicial power
to these officers. . . . When men once associate themselves with
others as organized bands, professing certain religious views, or
holding themselves out as having certain ethical and social objects, and subject thus to a common discipline, they have voluntarily submitted themselves to the disciplinary body of which they
are members, and it is for that society to know its own."[16] Membership is a personal right.[17] Where the membership is restricted
to certain occupations false representation as to occupation avoids
the membership.[18]

§ 82. **The Articles of Association, or Charter, Forms a Contract Between the Society and the Members.**—The rights of
members of all societies, incorporated or not, depend upon the
articles of association or charter to which the member assents upon
becoming such. Practically, all the cases which relate to societies
or corporations and which are cited in this work, recognize this
fact and declare the doctrine. The Supreme Court of Pennsylvania says:[19] "Each member pledges himself to obey these laws

[14] *Ex parte* Paine, 1 Hill 66; People v. Medical Soc. of Erie, 24 Barb. 577;
Fawcett v. Charles, 13 Wend. 473; Bagg's Case, 11 Coke 99.

[15] State v. Odd Fellows' Grand Lodge, 8 Mo. App. 148.

[16] See also Franta v. Bohemian, etc., Union, 164 Mo. 304; 63 S. W. 1100;
54 L. R. A. 723.

[17] Dingwall v. Amalgamated Ass'n, 4 Cal. App. 565; 88 Pac. 597.

[18] Holland v. Supreme Council Chosen Friends, 54 N. J. L. 490; 25 Atl.
367.

[19] St. Mary's Ben. Soc. v. Burford's Admr., 70 Pa. St. 321; Kalbitzer v.
Goodhue, 52 W. Va. 435; 44 S. E. 264. See also *ante*, § 28, and, as to imposition of fines, Leahy v. Mooney, 39 Misc. 829; 81 N. Y. Supp. 360.

as a condition of his membership, by an express undertaking in signing the constitution, and his promise to support the constitution and by-laws as a brotherly member. Nor is this pledge executed under the by-laws until he shall have answered· on his word of truth that he is acquainted with the constitution and by-laws. . . . The association having the right under its charter to make the by-law for the well-being of the society and the proper regulation of its affairs, the regulation being a reasonable and proper one, contributing to the value of membership, and the association, and the member having accepted the by-law in express terms in his entry into membership, the by-law constitutes a part of the terms of the contract.'' In construing the nature of an unincorporated voluntary organization, such as the St. Louis Stock Exchange, the Supreme Court of Missouri says:[20] ''The constitution, rules and by-laws constitute the contract of membership, and no person can invoke the benefits of a contract or incur any liability thereunder unless he assents to such contract; and it has been repeatedly held that before such constitution and by-laws can have any binding force whatever upon a member of an unincorporated association which will be recognized and enforced by the courts, it must appear that such member personally assented to their provisions. The evidence in this case not only shows that Mr. Konta did not assent to the constitution, rules and by-laws of the St. Louis Stock Exchange, but that he did not, either by word or action, assent to its organization, and I am satisfied from the evidence, not only that he did not become a member of the new organization, but also that he never intended to join the St. Louis Stock Exchange.'' In Texas the Supreme Court of the State has said:[21] ''When membership in certain societies confers upon the individual important benefits, as in aid societies, benev. olent societies, etc., or peculiar advantages in trade and business, as in chambers of commerce, these are important valuable rights which are protected by the law of the land, and are generally se. cured in some way by the charter of incorporation. . . . But we think it has been generally held that clubs or societies, whether

<hr />

[20] Konta v. St. Louis Stock Exchange, 189 Mo. 26; 87 S. W. 969.

[21] Manning v. San Antonio Club, 63 Tex. 166; s. c. 51 Am. Rep. 639. To the same' effect are McLaughlin v. Wall, 86 Kan. 45; 119 S. W. 541; Greer Mills Co. v. Stoller, 77 Fed. 1; Tauffer v. Brotherhood, etc., 122 N. Y. Supp. 527; 137 App. Div. 838; Montano v. Missenelli, etc., Soc., 130 N. Y. Supp. 455; 72 Misc. 515.

religious, literary or social, have the right to make their own rules upon the subject of the admission or exclusion of members, and these rules may be considered as articles of agreement to which all who become members are parties. . . . The fact that a club or society is incorporated would not, we think, in any way affect its right to make its own rules, unless there was something in the charter or in the general law under which it was incorporated which controlled it in this respect.''[22] *

§ 83. **Admission to Membership, Formalities Required.** — If the charter or articles of association prescribe the manner of electing and admitting new members, these requirements must be observed or the election is invalid. If no form be prescribed for the election each candidate must be proposed singly and voted on as such. If a list of several be proposed the election will be void, although the names were read several times and all consented, for it may be presumed that the members, instead of using their individual judgment on each candidate, compromised their opinion as to some in order to secure the admission of others.[23] - The election must be at a regular meeting or one legally called. Where the by-laws of a society provided that new members must be approved by a vote of the society and that the object of a special meeting should be stated in the call, a warrant simply for a special meeting to ''transact any other business that may legally come before said meeting'' is not sufficient to make the meeting a legal one for the admission of members and the election of such persons is invalid.[24] Ordinarily an agreement by the members of a volun-

---

[22] Van Poucke v. Netherland Soc., 63 Mich. 378; 29 N. W. 863; Sperry's Appeal, 116 Pa. St. 391; 9 Atl. 478; McCabe v. Father Mathew, etc., 24 Hun, 149; Gooch v. Ass'n Aged Females, 109 Mass. 558; Skelly v. Private Coachmen's Ben. Soc., 13 Daly 2; Bauer v. Sampson Lodge K. of P., 102 Ind. 262; Harrington v. Workingmen's Ass'n, 70 Ga. 340; Black & Whitesmith's Soc. v. Vandyke, 2 Whart. 312; Osceola Tribe v. Schmidt, 57 Md. 98; Flemyng v. Hector, 2 M. & W. 171; Innes v. Wylie, 1 Car. & K. 262; Brancker v. Roberts, 7 Jur. (N. S.) 1185; Hopkinson v. Marquis of Exeter, L. R. 5 Eq. 63; Thompson v. Adams, 7 W. N. C. 281; Moxey's Appeal, 9 W. N. C. 441; Protchett v. Schaefer, 11 Phila. 166; Heath v. N. Y. Gold Exch., 38 How. Pr. 168; 7 Abb. Pr. (N. S.) 251; Kuhl v. Meyer, 42 M. A. 628.

[23] Angell & Ames on Corp., § 126.

[24] Gray v. Christian Soc., 137 Mass. 329.

tary association to receive a person as a member and his acceptance constitutes him a member.[25] Where a ceremony of initiation is required by the laws of a society a person though duly elected is not entitled to benefits unless regularly initiated, and it is immaterial that the ceremony is secret, such secrecy not being considered against public policy.[26] In the case last cited[27] the Court says: ''The objects of this order, as stated in the constitution, are not merely to establish a fund for purposes of insurance of members, 'who have complied with all lawful requirements,' as stated in the constitution, but, as also declared in the same article and section, 'to unite fraternally all acceptable white men of every profession, business and occupation,' and 'to give all possible moral and material aid in its power, to its members, and those depending on its members, by holding moral, instructive and scientific lectures, by encouraging each other in business, and by assisting each other in obtaining employment.' With these and other beneficial objects in view, it is not difficult to see why there should not be a regular initiation into the order, and why members only can participate in its benefits. That the ceremony of initiation is secret does not affect it; it is doubtless intended to bind the members to a performance of their duties in respect to the objects to be accomplished. We could not say that it is a useless and unreasonable requirement. The affiliation is close and confidential for good purposes so far as can be seen from the testimony. Were the ceremonies open, they could not be said to be unreasonable; because they are secret does not make them so. The entire system, its existence and objects, are based upon initiation. We think there can be no membership without it, and no benefit, pecuniary or otherwise, without it. Matkin specially contracted in his application for membership, with reference to the initiation, that the payment of the 'proposition fee' should not entitle him to any benefit, or constitute him a member, unless he was duly 'initiated according to the ritual and laws of the order.' . . . The stipulation in Matkin's contract making initiation necessary to membership, and the enjoyment of benefits attaching thereto, is not against law, or public policy, unreasonable,

25 Bennett v. Lathrop, 71 Conn. 613; 42 Atl. 634.
26 Matkin v. Supreme Lodge K. of H., 82 Tex. 301; 18 S. W. 306.
27 Matkin v. Supreme Lodge K. of H., *supra.*

131

nor opposed to the good government and objects of the society. On the contrary, it is reasonable and calculated to promote the objects and welfare of the órder.' Where the statute requires fraternal beneficiary associations to have a lodge system, it intends that no one can become a member without being initiated into one of the lodges, and until one has been initiated the association cannot rightfully issue a benefit certificate to him.[28] The Missouri Court of Appeals has said:[29] "Section 7109, Revised Statutes 1909, which was then in force, governed this case, and provided that such an association is carried on for the 'sole benefit of its members.' The only source of revenue is the assessments paid by members. The payment of benefits must be to those sustaining certain relations to members. It is imperative that each association doing business under this law have a lodge system with ritualistic form of work and representative form of government. The whole scheme of such an association contemplates a course of dealing in regard to levying assessments and paying benefits only among members. Regular initiation is the birth of a member. Until such event occurs, the association is dealing with an outsider, a nonmember, and an assessment paid by such a person or a benefit paid to him is a course of dealing beyond the power given by law to such associations. It is a condition precedent that is necessary to give life to the beneficiary certificate. The following cases hold that there must be an initiation to create liability."[29a] The delivery of a certificate by an officer of the local

[28] Hiatt v. Fraternal Home, 99 Mo. App. 105; 72 S. W. 463.

[29] Porter v. Loyal Americans, etc., 180 Mo. Ap. 538; 167 S. W. 578. To the same effect are the following: McWilliams v. Modern Woodmen of America, .. Tex. Civ. App. ..; 142 S. W. 641; Arrison v. Supreme Council Mystic Toilers, 129 Ia. 303; 105 N. W. 580; Loyal Mystic Legion, etc., v. Richardson, 76 Neb. 562; 107 N. W. 795; Bruner v. Modern Brotherhood of American Yeomen, 136 Ia. 612; 111 N. W. 977; Supreme Lodge K. & L. of H. v. Johnson, 81 Ark. 512; 99 S. W. 834; Schworm v. Fraternal Bankers' Reserve Soc., 168 Ia. 579; 150 N. W. 714; Lloyd v. Modern Woodmen, 113 Mo. App. 19; 87 S. W. 530; Gilmore v. Modern Brotherhood, 186 Mo. App. 445; 171 S. W. 629; Norman v. Order of United Commercial Travelers, 163 Mo. App. 175; 145 S. W. 853; Shartle v. Modern Brotherhood of America, 139 Mo. App. 433; 122 S. W. 1113.

[29a] See cases *supra*.

lodge does not excuse failure to be initiated,[30] nor does the receipt of dues waive the lack of initiation. The Grand Medical Examiner, however, has no power to reject an application solely on the ground that the applicant was not initiated within the time prescribed by the by-laws.[31] It has been held, however,[32] that a fraternal order, after receipt of assessments from a person, and delivery to him of a benefit certificate, cannot question his membership though he were not initiated. The delivery of a benefit certificate is not essential if other requirements for admission have been complied with unless there is a provision in the laws of the order to the contrary.[33] Where the society has two classes of members, social and beneficial, one who qualified as a social, but paid dues as a beneficial member, with the understanding that he was to pass an examination, which he did not do, is not entitled to the benefits of the beneficiary class.[34] The requirements of the by-laws as to formalities for admission of new members do not apply to charter members.[35]

§ 84. **Liability for Injuries Received During Initiation.**—It has been held[36] that rules of discipline for all voluntary associations must conform with the laws; and, when a member of such an association refused to submit to the ceremony of expulsion established by the same, which ceremony involved a battery, it could not lawfully be inflicted, and those who participated were liable criminally for assault. In a case in Canada,[37] it was held that a

30 Kolosinski v. Modern Brotherhood of America, 175 Mich. 684; 141 N. W. 589.

31 Brotherhood of Locomotive Firemen, etc., v. Corder, 52 Ind. App. 214; 97 N. E. 125.

32 Supreme Ruling Frat. Mystic Circle v. Crawford, 32 Tex. Civ. App. 603; 75 S. W. 845.

33 Pledger v. Sovereign Camp Woodmen, etc., 17 Tex. Civ. A. 18; 42 S. W. 653; Supreme Council O. C. F. v. Bailey, 21 Ky. 1627; 55 S. W. 889. The delivery of the certificate was held essential in McLendon v. Woodmen of the World, 106 Tenn. 695; 64 S. W. 36; 52 L. R. A. 444; Logsden v. Supreme Lodge Frat. Union, 34 Wash. 666; 76 Pac. 292; Wilcox v. Sovereign Camp Woodmen of the World, 76 Mo. App. 573. See also *post*, § 355 as to when the contract of a benefit society is complete.

34 Asselto v. Supreme Tent K. O. T. M., 192 Pa. St. 5; 43 Atl. 400.

35 Shackelford v. Supreme Conclave, etc., 98 Ga. 295; 26 S. E. 746.

36 State v. Williams, 75 N. C. 134.

37 Kinver v. Phoenix Lodge I. O. O. F., 7 Ont. 377.

lodge was liable to plaintiff for injuries, because of the rough usage of some of the members, received during his initiation as a member of the lodge, in the presence of its principal officers and a number of members, the meeting being considered a full and perfect one. It appeared that this and other proceedings were taken with the knowledge of all those who were present, and that somewhat similar proceedings had happened on the occasion of other initiations, and that they were allowed and not checked, and it was considered that they must be taken to have been inflicted with the consent of the corporate body. It has also been held[38] that, where a fraternal order, which issues insurance certificates to its members of a local camp, and having a sovereign camp which has been incorporated, such incorporation bearing relation to the business or insurance features of the order, and having also local camps which are authorized to initiate members into the order in accordance with the ritual prescribed by the sovereign camp, that, in the absence of evidence showing further the relation between the sovereign and subordinate camps, the latter cannot be considered the servants or agents of the former in such sense as to hold it liable in its corporate capacity for a personal injury inflicted on an accepted candidate for membership by the members of a local camp during the ceremonies of initiation, the part of the ceremony which resulted in the injury not being prescribed by the ritual. On principle, it seems that a distinction should be made between injuries received as a result of the negligence of the officers of the lodge conducting the initiation, according to a ritual prescribed by the superior body, and the torts of the individual members in inflicting injuries upon a candidate by doing something not prescribed by the ritual of the order. It might be held that, where a ritual is prescribed by a supreme body, and, in observing that ritual, the lodge, which is authorized to conduct the ceremony, is guilty of so negligently performing the duties enjoined upon them that injuries result to the candidate, the supreme body could, under possible conditions, be liable; but, clearly, if the members of a lodge, on their own responsibility, indulge in horse play, or do some act not prescribed in the ritual, which results in injury, neither the supreme, nor

[38] Jumper v. Sovereign Camp Woodmen of the World, 62 C. C. A. 361; 127 Fed. 635. *Contra*, Mitchell v. Leech, 69 S. C. 413; 48 S. E. 290.

subordinate lodges, as such, would be liable for such injury, but only the members who participate in their individual capacity, either as actors or spectators.[39] In the case of Thompson v. Supreme Tent K. O. T. M.,[40] it was held that the Supreme Lodge of a fraternal association organized as a corporation, possessing exclusive jurisdiction and control over all subordinate tents, or lodges, and having by-laws requiring the officers' of such subordinate tents to carry out, in initiation of members, the ritual established and promulgated by the Supreme Tent, is liable in damages for injuries sustained by a person while undergoing initiation in a subordinate tent in accordance with such ritual, as the officers and members of the subordinate tent conducting the initiation and following the directions of the ritual are the lawfully constituted agents of the Supreme Tent. The Court says: ''It doubtless did not occur to the officers of the Supreme Tent, in adopting the ritual, that the act authorized by them might in some instances produce harm, or that some of its subordinate officers might execute the command of the ritual with more force than others. But it is apparent that they intended that the applicant should be taken unawares and frightened.'' And in Mitchell v. Leech,[41] it was held that the Sovereign Camp of the Woodmen of the World was liable for damages sustained by the plaintiff in consequence of the use of a mechanical goat during his initiation into a subordinate camp, although there was nothing in the ritual of the order authorizing the use of the goat as a part of the initiation proceedings. The Court said: ''In order to accomplish the objects for which the Sovereign Camp was organized it was necessary from the very nature of the business to call to its assistance the services of persons through whom it might act, in transacting the affairs of the order in various localities. It selected and organized local lodges for the purpose of meeting this necessity. Not only the subordinate camps, but the members as well, were under the complete direction and control of the parent camp, in whose

---

[39] Kendrick v. Modern Woodmen of Am., 131 Mo. App. 31; 109 S. W. 805; Grand Temple, etc., v. Johnson, .. Tex. Çiv. App. ..; 135 S. W. 173; Kaminski v. Great Camp K. O. T. M., 146 Mich. 16; 109 N. W. 33.

[40] 189 N. Y. 294; 82 N. E. 141; 12 Ann. Cas. 552; 13 L. R. A. (N. S.) 314.

[41] 69 S. C. 413; 48 S. E. 290; 66 L. R. A. 723; 104 Am. St. Rep. 811.

name the benefit certificates were required by the constitution to be issued; and when a member died payment of the benefit certificate was to be made by the Sovereign Camp. These facts show that when a person was initiated in a local lodge, he became, to all intents and purposes, a member of the Sovereign Camp.''

§ 85. **Majority Can Bind Minority.**—Another fundamental rule applicable to all associations, partnerships and corporations is that, within the express or implied terms of the charter or partnership agreement, the majority has power to bind the entire membership.[42] The rule laid down in regard to partnerships and companies by Lindley,[43] is: ''A corporation acts by a majority; the will of the majority is the will of the corporation; and whatever it is competent for the corporation to do can be done by a majority of its members against the will of the minority. . . . It appears: (1) That within the limits set by the original constitution of a partnership or company, the voice of a majority must prevail. (2) That it is not competent for any number of partners or shareholders, less than all, to pass beyond those limits. (3) That it is competent for all to do so, unless they are bound together not only by agreement amongst themselves, but by some charter, letters-patent, or act of parliament.'' The general rule is also thus expressed: ''The fundamental principle of every association for self-government is, that no one shall be bound except with his own consent expressed by himself or his representatives; but actual assent is immaterial, the assent of the majority being the assent of all; for this is not only constructively true, but actually true; for that the will of the majority shall in all cases be taken as the will of the whole, is an implied, but essential stipulation in all associations of this sort.''[44] It has been held, however,[45] that a voluntary association having adopted a constitution, or rules and by-laws, the same are to be considered in the light of a contract,

[42] Morawetz on Corp., § 641.

[43] 2 Lindley on Part. 608.

[44] *In re* St. Mary's Church, 7 Serg. & R. 517; New Orleans v. Harris, 27 Miss. 537; Morawetz on Corp., §§ 641, 474. But see Livingston v. Lynch, 4 Johns. Ch. 594, and Torrey v. Baker, 1 Allen 120.

[45] Kalbitzer v. Goodhue, 52 W. Va. 435; 44 S. E. 264.

and the "majority rule" in the government of the association does not obtain unless it is so provided in the contract.[46]

§ 86. **Limitations on Action of Majority.**—The majority in order to bind the minority by its acts must comply with every formality which is prescribed by the company's, or association's, charter or articles of association, or by custom; must act within the objects of the articles of association or charter, and is bound in all transactions to the utmost fairness and good faith to the minority.[47] A majority of the members of a subordinate lodge have no power to secede from the organization, taking with them the money and property of a subordinate lodge, against the wishes of the minority.[48] And the objecting members of the society can maintain a suit to set aside an unlawful merger with another association, having appealed in vain to the corporation's officers to bring a suit.[49] Nor can a by-law authorize a society by a majority vote to transfer its members to another society, especially when a quorum of the first society seeks to maintain its existence, nor can the property be transferred by such a proceeding;[50] nor can the majority divert the property from the objects specified in the articles of association.[51] The majority cannot incorporate against the will of the minority.[52]

§ 87. **Rights of Minority.**—It has been held, that, before the aid of the civil courts can be invoked by aggrieved members of a

46 See Union Benev. Soc. v. Martin (Ky.), 76 S. W. 1098; 25 Ky. L. 1037; Koerner Lodge K. of P. v. Grand Lodge, 146 Ind. 639; 45 N. E. 1103; Schiller Commandery, etc., v. Jaennichen, 116 Mich. 129; 74 N. W. 458.

47 State v. Ancker, 2 Rich. (S. C.) 245; Morawetz on Corp., §§ 475, 477. See also Industrial Trust Co. v. Green, 17 R. I. 586; 23 Atl. 914; 17 L. R. A. 202, where the powers of officers and members of a volunteer association are considered. Kane v. Shields, 167 Mass. 392; 45 N. E. 758, is also in point.

48 Grand Court Foresters of America v. Hodel, 74 Wash. 314; 133 Pac. 436.

49 Knapp v. Supreme Commandery, etc., 121 Tenn. 212; 118 S. W. 390.

50 Hill v. Rauhan Arre, 200 Mass. 438; 86 N. E. 924; Sabourin v. Lippe, 195 Mass. 470; 81 N. E. 282.

51 Bachman v. Hofman, 104 Ill. App. 159; Kalbitzer v. Goodhue, 52 W. Va. 135; 44 S. E. 264.

52 Strong v. Los Nietos, etc., 137 Cal. 607; 70 Pac. 734.

society, they must have exhausted the remedies prescribed by the constitution and laws of such society and its superior governing bodies. A minority of an unincorporated society, formed for social and benevolent purposes, cannot maintain an action to have the property divided or sold, or to compel the majority to purchase their interest, while the property is being used for the purposes for which it was procured, although occupied or used by a different lodge.[53] But a minority can generally insist upon a carrying out of the purposes of the society, at least so far as property is concerned.[54] The withdrawal of two-thirds of the members does not destroy the identity of a society and the minority will be entitled to the funds of the society.[55] In a recent case in Pennsylvania[56] these principles were fully discussed. The report of the Master was approved by the Court and applied the law as follows: "The position, therefore, is that of a majority of the number of members present at the meeting constituting but a fraction of the entire membership, attempting to carry the whole body into secession against the will of the minority. The Master is unable to perceive any distinction in principle between this and the cases, whereof many precedents occur in the reports, of members of a congregation forming part of a general conference or synod, professing a certain form of religious belief, attempting against the will of a minority, to secede from the synod and carry the property of the congregation with them. The leading case in Pennsylvania on the subject is McGinnis v. Watson,[57] followed by Sutter v. Trustees,[58] Winebrenner v. Colder,[59] Schnorr's Appeal[60] and others—wherein the right is persistently and emphatically denied.

[53] Robbins v. Waldo Lodge, 78 Me. 565; 7 Atl. 540; Hinkley v. Blethen, 78 Me. 221; 3 Atl. 655.

[54] Mann v. Butler, 2 Barb. Ch. 362; Torrey v. Baker, 1 Allen 120; Mc Fadden v. Murphy, 149 Mass. 341; 21 N. E. 868; Ashton v. Dashaway Ass'n, 84 Cal. 61; 22 Pac. 660; Grand Court Foresters, etc., v. Hodel, 74 Wash. 314; 133 Pac. 438; Kayler v. McCourt, 235 Pa. 304; 83 Atl. 830; Hill v. Rauhan Arre, 200 Mass. 438; 81 N. E. 924; Freundschaft Loge v. Alchenburger, 235 Ill. 438; 85 N. E. 653; affg. 138 Ill. App. 204; Minor v. St. John's Lodge, .. Tex. Civ. A. ..; 130 S. W. 893.

[55] Schiller Commandery, etc., v. Jaennichen, 116 Mich. 129; 74 N. W. 458.

[56] Gorman v. O'Connor, 155 Pa. St. 239; 26 Atl. 379.

[57] 41 Pa. St. 9.   [59] 43 Pa. St. 244.

[58] 42 Pa. St. 503.   [60] 67 Pa. St. 138.

'People join such associations,' says Judge Lowrie, in Sutter v. Trustees (page 511), 'for the sake of their benefits, and from faith that they will be conducted according to known principles, and not by mere whims of majorities. It is therefore of no sort of importance what may be the majority in such matters; it cannot weigh a feather in well-known law in affecting the rights of the minority. Before civil authority the question is not which party has the majority, but which is right according to the law by which the party has hitherto consented to be governed.' And in the appeal of First Methodist Protestant Church,[61] the Court, in the language of McGinnis v. Watson, says the 'title to church property adheres to that party which is in harmony with its own laws; and the ecclesiastical laws, usages, customs and principles which were accepted before the dispute arose are the standards for determining which party is right.' The act of the majority at the meeting, therefore, in severing allegiance to the parent organization, cannot be interpreted as the act of the division, but only as the act of separate individuals composing the majority. Had the entire body seceded, the organization would have become extinct. What before existed as an organization would then have become a new organization pertaining to another body. The opposition of those who refused to follow the lead of the seceding body served to keep the organization alive, and the funds remained with them. In McFadden v. Murphy,[62] where the facts were almost identical with those shown by the evidence, except that it directly appeared that a large majority of the members sought to transfer the division of an organized body to the new organization, and took possession of the property of an old association as a division of the new society, the Court held that the majority ceased to be members of the (old) association, and that the proceedings of the minority who remained members were regular, and that the action of the majority in joining the new division was an evidence of their intention to withdraw from the old, and that by such action they ceased to be members of the society and division under the old constitution. The Master holds that the principles laid down in that case fully applied to the case presented here for his determination, and confirm the conclusions at which he has arrived.

61 16 Wkly. Notes Cas. 245.
62 149 Mass. 341; 21 N. E. 868.

"If it be asserted that the proceedings by which the minority sought to continue the organization were in themselves irregular in violation of the provisions of the constitution, to use the words of the Court in Schnorr's Appeal,[63] 'it does not lie in the mouth of the defendants (plaintiffs here) to object in any way in this proceeding to the regularity of the election of the plaintiffs (defendants here). The defendants are strangers. They made themselves so by their solemn act, throwing off their connection with the church. That they then seceded and withdrew from the church cannot be doubted.' Judge Williams, in concurring, clearly sets forth the state of the law when he says that 'those who adhere and submit to the regular order of the church, local and general, though a minority, are the true congregation and corporation, if incorporated.[64] But it is a fact that the constitution was violated by the minority in their subsequent proceedings. Their first step subsequent to the meeting of January 7, was the issue of a call of a special meeting of the organization, signed by the regular secretary and the four members who claimed allegiance to the old organization, which for convenience the Master has termed the 'Cleveland Body.' The fact of this meeting being called, and its object, were known to all the members on both sides of the controversy. It was the only thing that the adherents of the Cleveland party could do, in order to preserve the entity of the division under the old order of things. The by-laws, it is true, do not specifically provide for a special meeting or for any method by which the body may be convened, but these by-laws were framed by the State convention, and by the terms of the constitution a division can frame its own laws, so far as consistent with the constitution. By the terms of the by-laws, also, a quorum of the division consists of five members, with the officers or their representatives. Now, the officers who sided with the New York party were the new president and the financial secretary. They refused or neglected to attend the meeting, and there is no intimation that a quorum of the old division did not assemble at the special meeting. Everything was done that could be done to sustain the life of the organization. If any subsequent action of this organization can, under any view, be construed as a departure from its organic law

[63] 67 Pa. St. 138.
[64] Citing Winebrenner v. Colder, *supra*.

so far as the filling of vacant offices is concerned, the defect was certainly cured at the next annual election; and inasmuch as no voice was raised against the illegality of any such subsequent action under the constitution, and the division was always recognized in the national and State conventions as the only division No. 4, in rights seemed to be prejudiced by such action.'' The provisions of the articles of association must govern in all cases involving the rights of the members.[65]

§ 88. **Must Act at Properly Called Meeting.**—The majority can act only at a meeting called together in a proper manner.[66] It is essential that every member be notified of a meeting before it is held. If notice to any one was omitted, those present at the meeting have no authority to act for the whole body of members, and the transactions at the meeting will not be binding as corporate acts. If the charter or by-laws of an association or company fix the time and place at which regular meetings shall be held, this is itself sufficient notice to all the members and no further notice is necessary. The general rule has been well stated by a standard authority, as follows:[67] ''The members of a corporation, public or private, can do no corporate act of a constituent character, such as must be done at a general meeting of all the members or of a quorum of them, unless the meeting is duly assembled, in conformity with the law of its organization. It has been well said that the act of a majority of the corporators does not bind the minority, if it has not been expressed in the form pointed out by law; and accordingly, that the act of a majority, expressed elsewhere than at a meeting of the shareholders, is not binding on the corporation, as where the assent of each one is given separately and at different times. The reason is that each member has the right of consultation with the others, and that the minority have the right to be heard. In the line of authority establishing the foregoing principles no break has been discovered, although it should be added that an election or other proceeding had at a meeting irregularly assembled may be valid if all attend and act or assent. This leads to the conclusion that

[65] Penfield v. Skinner, 11 Vt. 296; St. Mary's Ben. Ass'n v. Lynch, 64 N. H. 213; 9 Atl. 98.
[66] Kuehl v. Meyer, 42 Mo. App. 474.
[67] 10 Cyc. 323.

141

corporate meetings are invalid, and that the business transacted thereat is voidable, unless the members have been duly notified of the meeting in accordance with the governing statute or by-laws, except in the case of stated-meetings, of which every member is bound to take notice." Every reasonable presumption is made in favor of the regularity of all meetings and the giving of proper notice will be presumed until the contrary appears.[68] It has been held that members attending an illegal meeting are not estopped from setting up such illegality.[69]

§ 89. **Meetings of Association or Corporation, Notice of.**— Meetings of the members of an association or corporation are not binding unless called by competent authority, as where the meeting was called by a deposed president,[70] or unless all the members entitled to vote are present. It has been held, however,[71] that where the secretary refused to act the notice might be given by the president. If the by-laws or articles of association prescribe by whom meetings shall be called, these requirements must be observed and if the officers wrongfully refuse to call a meeting they may generally be compelled to do their duty by *mandamus* proceedings. In the absence of by-laws and constitution custom will be considered as governing the association so far as meetings are concerned.[72] In the absence of by-laws the acts of a majority of the members of a society present at a meeting are binding upon all.[73] A distinction is made between regular and special meetings. The former are those that are held at stated times according to the charter or rules of the association, while the latter are called at irregular or unusual times under authority given by the charter or laws of the association. Notice of a meeting of the members of an association or corporation must be given in the manner prescribed by the charter, if no way is laid down then such notice must fix the exact time and place of the meeting and generally

[68] Morawetz on Corp., § 479 and note; Sargent v. Webster, 13 Metc. 497.

[69] Kuehl v. Meyer, *supra*; but see to the contrary Abels v. McKeen, 18 N. J. Eq. 401, and Fisher v. Raab, 57 How. Pr. 87.

[70] Industrial Trust Co. v. Greene, 17 R. I. 586; 23 Atl. 914.

[71] Whipple v. Christie, 122 Minn. 73; 141 N. W. 1107.

[72] Ostrome v. Greene, 20 Misc. 177; 45 N. Y. Supp. 852; Goller v. Stubenhaus, 134 N. Y. Supp. 1043; 77 Misc. 29.

[73] Francis v. Perry, 144 N. Y. Supp. 167; 82 Misc. 274.

indicate the nature of the business to be transacted.[74] "The time of meeting must be stated precisely; if a meeting is called to order, and business is transacted before the time set, the proceedings will not be valid. If the time of meeting is prescribed by the charter or a by-law, that is sufficient notice; and it has been held, that if the time of meeting has been fixed by usage, or the tacit consent of the members or shareholders, no other notice is required. The meeting should be opened within a reasonable time after the hour indicated in the notice. The place of meeting must also be fixed. And if a meeting is held at a different place from that prescribed, it will not be valid. In case of an extraordinary or special meeting, the notice must indicate the nature of the business to be brought before it; but this is not necessary in case of a regular meeting for the transaction of ordinary business. The notice must be served upon each shareholder in person unless otherwise provided by the charter or a by-law and if the charter does not prescribe how long before a meeting notice must be served, a reasonable time is required."[75] It seems that meetings of a beneficiary society may lawfully be held on Sunday.[76] While ordinarily meetings of a corporation outside of the territorial limits of the State in which it was incorporated are invalid,[77] yet it has been said[78] that, where the corporation constitutes the supreme legislative department of a benevolent order to be established by it, with power to organize subordinate bodies throughout the United States and Canada, authority to hold its meetings outside the State of incorporation arises by implication, because the general rule of public policy as to holding such meetings does not prevail and because

74 St. Mary's Ben. Ass'n v. Lynch, 64 N. H. 213; 9 Atl. 98; as to what is sufficient notice under the Texas statute, see Hackler v. International Travelers' Ass'n, .. Tex. Civ. App. ..; 165 S. W. 44.

75 Morawetz on Corp., §§ 478-483. As to proxies see Chicago, etc., Ass'n v. Hunt, 127 Ill. 257; 20 N. E. 55. In the case of Appeal of Woolford, 126 Pa. St. 47; 17 Atl. 524, will be found a full consideration of the questions of legality of consolidation of lodges and the meetings held therefor.

76 McCabe v. Father Matthew, etc., 24 Hun. 149; Robinson v. Yates City Lodge, 86 Ill. 598; People v. Young Men's, etc., Soc., 65 Barb. 357; see also Society, etc., v. Commonwealth, 52 Pa. St. 125.

77 Angell & Ames on Corp., § 498.

78 Sovereign Camp W. O. W. v. Fraley, 94 Tex. 200; 59 S. W. 879; 51 L. R. A. 898; Head Camp, etc., v. Woods, 34 Colo. 1; 81 Pac. 261.

it is contemplated that the greater part of the business will be transacted beyond the territory of the State where it has its origin.[79] Usually the laws of the States now provide for meetings of fraternal beneficiary corporations outside the State in which they are incorporated.

§ 90. **Quorum.**—The rule of the common law is said to be,[80] that where a body is composed of an indefinite number of persons, a quorum, for the purposes of elections and voting upon other questions which require the sanction of the members, consists of those who assemble at any meeting regularly called and warned, although such number may be a minority of the whole, in which case a majority of those who assemble may elect, unless a different rule is established by statute, or by a valid by-law. In all cases where an act is to be done by a corporate body, and the number is definite, it has been held that a majority of the whole number is necessary to constitute a legal meeting, and that if the actual number is reduced from any cause, the number necessary to constitute a quorum remains the same, but that at a legal meeting a majority of those present may act. It has been held, however, that in the absence of statute, or by-law provision, a number less than one-half of the members do not constitute a quorum.[81] Where there was no quorum present at the meeting of an executive board, the action taken was ineffective.[82] It is not necessary that the record of the meeting of a lodge should show that a quorum was present.[83] Where a by-law provided that an assessment might be made by a majority of the executive committee consisting of twenty members, and another by-law that five members of the executive committee should constitute a quorum, it was held[84] that an assessment could not be made by a majority of the quorum, but that it must be made by a majority vote of the entire committee.

§ 91. **Special Meetings.**—The notice of a special meeting must always state the purpose of the meeting and the subjects to

[79] See also Derry Council, etc., v. State Council J. O. U. Am. M., 197 Pa. St. 413; 47 Atl. 208.

[80] 10 Cyc. 329.

[81] Farmers' L. & T. Co. v. Aberle, 41 N. Y. Supp. 638; 18 Misc. 257.

[82] North La. Baptist Ass'n v. Milliken, 110 La. 1002; 35 So. 264.

[83] Coombs v. Hartford, 99 Me. 426; 59 Atl. 529.

[84] Rogers v. Boston Club, 205 Mass. 261; 91 N. E. 321.

be considered and no other business than that specified in the notice can be transacted. This is an elementary rule applicable both to corporations and voluntary associations.[85] In a recent case,[86] the Court reviews the law governing special meetings of corporations or voluntary associations, considering incidentally the rights of the majority. The court through Judge Seymour D. Thompson said: "It is a long settled principle in the law of corporations that, in order to give validity to acts done at a special meeting, all the members must be notified.[87] And it is a further principle equally well settled, that where the time or manner of giving notice is prescribed by statute, by charter, or by-laws of the corporation, it is essential to the validity of the acts done, at the meeting, that the notice should be given as thus prescribed.[88] But the prescribed notice may be dispensed with by unanimous consent. If, therefore, notwithstanding that the meeting has not been properly notified, all the members appear and participate in its proceedings without objection, this will be a waiver by each member of any objection to the notice.[89] But, if a single member having a right to be present and vote, is absent or refuses his assent to the acts done at the meeting, its proceedings will be illegal and void.[90] In the case of unincorporated voluntary associations like the present, the rights affixed by their constitution and by-laws rest in contract; but for reasons equally strong the mode of acting pointed out by those instruments must be pursued.[91] For the majority cannot break the contract which they have made, any more than a minority could do it. They have raised a fund for certain purposes of mutual benefit, and placed it under the control of trustees for the purposes of the trust declared in their constating instruments. The

[85] State v. Seattle Base Ball Ass'n, 61 Wash. 79; 111 Pac. 1053.

[86] Kuhl v. Meyer, 42 Mo. App. 474.

[87] Smyth v. Darley, 2 House of Lords' Cases 789; Commonwealth v. Guardians, 6 Serg. & R. 469, 474; Knyaston v. Mayor of Shrewsbury, 2 Strange 1051; Rex v. Liverpool, 2 Burr. 734.

[88] Hunt v. School Dist., 14 Vt. 300; s. c. 39 Am. Dec. 99; Stockholders, etc., v. Railroad, 12 Bush (Ky.) 62.

[89] Judah v. Ins. Co., 4 Ind. 333; Jones v. Milton, etc., Co., 7 Ind. 547.

[90] Angell and Ames on Corp., 495; Rex v. Theodorick, 8 East. 543; Rex v. Gaborian, 11 East. 77.

[91] Coleman v. Knights of Honor, 18 Mo. App. 189; Grand Lodge v. Elsner, 26 Mo. App. 108; Mulroy v. Knights of Honor, 28 Mo. App. 471.

majority cannot, by their irregular. action, contrary to the rules by which all have agreed to abide, divert this fund from the purposes of the trust and distribute it among such of the members as may be willing to receive their proportionate shares of it.''

§ 92. **Jurisdiction of Grand and Supreme Lodges.**—The jurisdiction of Supreme and Grand lodges over those that are subordinate is in many respects analogous to that of certain ecclesiastical bodies over the churches in a certain territory. Upon this subject the Supreme Court of the United States has said:[92] ''The right to organize voluntary religious associations to assist in the expression and dissemination of any religious doctrine and to create tribunals for the decision of controverted questions of faith within the association and for the ecclesiastical government of all the individual members, congregations and officers within the general association, is unquestioned. All who unite themselves to such a body do so with an implied consent to this government, and are bound to submit to it. But it would be a vain consent and would lead to the total subversion of such religious bodies, if any one aggrieved by one of their decisions could appeal to the secular courts and have them reversed. It is of the essence of these religious unions and of their right to establish tribunals for the decisions of questions arising among themselves, that those decisions should be binding in all cases of ecclesiastical cognizance, subject only to such appeals as the organism itself provides for.''[93] The preponderance of authority is in favor of the doctrine that as to all questions of policy, discipline, internal government and custom the legal tribunals must accept as binding the decision of the regularly constituted judicatories of the church, fraternity, association or society. The rule is different when property rights are involved. In such cases the civil courts are strict in asserting their powers to protect the property rights of members.[94] A voluntary association is responsible for the acts of a branch organized by it.[95]

[92] Watson v. Jones, 13 Wall. 679.

[93] This opinion reviews all the cases bearing on the subject, but they are here omitted because they relate to ecclesiastical organizations only.

[94] See also *post*, § 131, *et seq.*

[95] Spaulding v. Evensen, 149 Fed. 913; affirmed 82 C. C. A. 263; 150 Fed. 517; 9 L. R. A. (N. S.) 904.

§ 93. **The Same Subject—Property Rights.**—It has been said,[96] that the property owned by a subordinate lodge of a fraternal insurance order is subject to the constitution and laws of such order and the right of the members of a subordinate lodge is. simply the right to use the property and when the lodge is dissolved the right ceases, but the revocation of the charter of a subordinate body does not vest its property in the supreme body, nor give a portion of the members, to whom the charter was reissued, the right of possession.[97] It has also been held that the assets of a subordinate lodge are not only held in trust but the Grand Lodge can maintain an action for the funds appropriated among the members when dissolved.[98] The constitution and laws of a subordinate lodge acknowledging allegiance to the supreme body, if the lodge is incorporated, have only the effect of a by-law.[99] The incorporation of the supreme body without the knowledge of the local body, changing the character of the relations existing between the supreme and subordinate bodies, relieves the latter from allegiance to the supreme body.[100] The dissolution of a subordinate lodge on insufficient charges is void.[101] Where the Grand Lodge has suspended the charter of a local lodge, to which plaintiff belonged, and the charter was restored on condition that plaintiff be excluded from membership and he was forced to withdraw without a trial, it was held in an action for damages that the expulsion was illegal and the Grand Lodge was liable for damages. It was further held that on an illegal expulsion, the member was not bound to appeal but might resort to the courts at once.[102] It is no ground for the revocation of a charter of a subordinate lodge by the Grand Lodge, that it failed to convict a member charged with defrauding such Grand Lodge.[103] The governing body of a fraternal society which has not a representative form of govern-

[96] Lone Star Lodge K. & L. of H. v. Cole, 62 Tex. Civ. App. 500; 131 S. W. 1180.
[97] Wolfe v. Limestone Council, etc., 233 Pa. 357; 82 Atl. 499.
[98] Die Gross Loge, etc., v. Wolfer, 42 Colo. 393; 94 Pac. 329.
[99] Grand Court Foresters of America v. Court Cavour, etc., 82 N. J. Eq. 89; 91 Atl. 1068; affg. 82 N. J. Eq. 89; 88 Atl. 191.
[100] Pierson v. Gardner, 81 N. J. Eq. 505; 86 Atl. 442.
[101] Grand Grove, etc., v. Garivaldi Grove, 130 Colo. 116; 62 Pac. 486.
[102] Malmstead v. Minn. Aerie, etc., 111 Minn. 119; 126 N. W. 486.
[103] Golden Star Lodge v. Watterson, 158 Mich. 696; 123 N. W. 610.

ment as required by statute, is without power to adopt a by-law changing the terms and obligations of a benefit certificate.[104] The national body has authority to decide a dispute between rival claimants for office in the subordinate body, and the incorporation of such subordinate body does not render it independent of the order.[105] The courts will not inquire into the regularity of the procedure of the members of a Grand Lodge separating from it and organizing an independent order.[106] Where a lodge was transferred from an old to a new grand lodge the member was bound to comply with the by-laws of the new grand lodge.[107]

§ 94. **Articles of Association, or Constitution and By-Laws, Regulate Rights and Powers of Officers and Members.**—The rights and powers of the officers and members of the association or lodges, superior or subordinate, are regulated by their articles of associations, or constitution and by-laws, which constitute the contract of the members with each other and by the provisions of which they undertake to be bound.[108] The right to impose a fine on a member depends upon whether it is given by the Articles of Association or it is void.[109] In all cases of dispute as to rights or duties of the various bodies, their officers or members, the origi-compact is the measure by which a decision is to be reached.[110] The opinions of the officers of the society, or its custom and usage in respect to the interpretation of terms used in the contract, are not admissible evidence in actions on the contract if the language

104 Briggs v. Royal Highlanders, 84 Neb. 834; 122 N. W. 69.

105 Commonwealth v. Heilman, 241 Pa. 374; 88 Atl. 666.

106 Grand Lodge A. O. U. W. of Conn. v. Grand Lodge A. O. U. W. of Mass., 83 Conn. 241; 76 Atl. 533. See also Servian Soc. v. Douglas Camp, 3 Alaska 5.

107 Grand Lodge A. O. U. W. v. Burns, 84 Conn. 356; 80 Atl. 157.

108 Ante, §§ 82, 94.

109 McCord v. Thompson, etc., Co., 198 N. Y. 587; affg. 113 N. Y. Supp. 383.

110 Lowry v. Stotzer, 7 Phila. 397; Austin v. Searing, 16 N. Y. 112; Chamberlain v. Lincoln, 129 Mass. 70; Leech v. Harris, 2 Brews. 587; Grosvenor v. United Soc., etc., 118 Mass. 78; White v. Brownell, 3 Abb. Pr. (N. S.) 318; Kuhl v. Meyer, 42 M. A. 628; Correia v. Sup. Lodge, etc., 218 Mass. 305; 105 N. E. 977; American Council, etc., v. National Council, etc., 63 N. J. L. 52; 43 Atl. 2; Holloman v. National Slavonic Soc., 51 N. Y. Supp. 720; 39 App. Div. 573.

used be not ambiguous.[111] Courts will not undertake to direct or control the internal policy of societies nor to decide questions relating to the discipline of its members but will leave the society free to carry out any lawful purpose in its own way in accordance with its own rules, but will protect property rights by injunction if necessary.[112] If the property of either a superior, or inferior body under its jurisdiction, is in the nature of a trust fund, or from necessity impressed with a trust the courts will protect it from being diverted to other uses or on dissolution of the local body being appropriated by the members or confiscated by the supreme body.[113]

§ 95. **Supreme, Grand and Subordinate Lodges a Single Organization.**—The various lodges, subordinate, superior and supreme, form, so far as most rights are concerned, but one organization or society, although each individual lodge or association has its own individuality and distinctive rights and liabilities.[114] A subordinate organization may often have a dual existence; first, as a corporation under the laws of the State of its residence, and second, under its conventional charter granted by its fraternal or

[111] Manson v. Grand Lodge, 30 Minn. 509; Davidson v. Knights of Pythias, 22 Mo. App. 263; Wiggin v. Knights of Pythias, 31 Fed. 122.

[112] Reno Lodge I. O. O. F. v. Grand Lodge, etc., 54 Kan. 73; 37 Pac. 1003; 26 L. R. A. 98; Supreme Lodge Order Golden Chain v. Simering, 88 Md. 276; 40 Atl. 723; 41 L. R. A. 720.

[113] State Council J. O. U. A. M. v. Emery, 219 Pa. 461, 68 Atl. 1023; 15 L. R. A. (N. S.) 336; Grand Lodge United Brothers, etc., v. Williams, .. Tex. Civ. A. .., 108 S. W. 195; Gross Loge, etc,. v. Brausch, 256 Ill. 185; 99 N. E. 908, reversing 167 Ill. App. 13; Die Gross Loge, etc., v. Wolfer, 42 Colo. 393, 94 Pac. 329; Grand Court Foresters, etc., v. Court Cavour, 82 N. J. Eq. 89, 91 Atl. 1068; affg. 82 N. J. Eq. 89; 88 Atl. 191; State Council J. O. U. A. M. v. Enterprise Council, etc., 75 N. J. Eq. 245; 72 Atl. 19, reversing 67 Atl. 432. An important case considering the relative powers of grand and supreme lodges is Grand Lodge A. O. U. W. of Conn. v. Grand Lodge of Mass., 81 Conn. 189; 70 Atl. 617, and as to being a trustee and not a guarantor, see McKemy v. Supreme Lodge, etc., 180 Fed. 961.

[114] Watson v. Jones, 13 Wall. 679; Smith v. Smith, 3 Dessau. 557; Austin v. Searing, 16 N. Y. 113; Poultney v. Bachmann, 62 How. Pr. 466; Lafond v. Deems, 81 N. Y. 507; Polish R. C. Union v. Warczak, 182 Ill. 27; 55 N. E. 64; Baldwin v. Hosmer, 101 Mich. 119; 59 N. W. 432; 25 L. R. A. 739.

agreed superior body, and either of these charters may be lost, surrendered or forfeited without affecting the other.[115] In a recent case[116] where the incorporated supreme governing body had issued an obligation to a member of one of the inferior, or subordinate, associations and the claim was made that such member was not a member of the corporation because it was made up of representatives from the grand lodge, which in turn was composed of representatives from the subordinate lodges, of one of which the obligee was a member, the Court said: "There is, it must be admitted, a certain confusion resulting from the fact that the supreme council is sometimes treated in the certificate of incorporation, constitution and by-laws, as the corporation, and sometimes as only its governing body who directs its operations. It is to the body acting in the latter capacity, that the article in question refers. The section quoted contemplates distinctly, by the use of terms referring to them, that there are other members of the order. An examination of the whole system will show that the association was established, among other things, for the purpose of affording mutual aid to its members, and also for the purpose of establishing what was termed a widows and orphans' benefit fund, for the payment of specific sums to the widows, orphans and other dependents of deceased members. It transacted its business mainly through the agency of grand councils composed from the subordinate councils in each State, and through the agency of their subordinate councils; both of which councils operated under charters granted by the supreme council, and in accordance with rules prescribed in such charters. As Robinson became a member of a subordinate council, he was entitled to a voice in its representation in the supreme council as the governing body. When, in the certificate of incorporation, members of the supreme council of the Royal Arcanum are referred to as those for whose benefit the association is intended, those who constitute the body which administers its affairs are not alone included, but all who, through the subordinate councils, become members of the organization, or order,

---

[115] Goodman v. Jedidjah Lodge, 67 Md. 117; 9 Atl. 13; Mason v. Finch, 28 Mich. 282; Smith v. Smith, 3 Dessau. 557; State v. Miller, 66 Iowa 26; Gorman v. O'Connor, 155 Pa. St. 239; 26 Atl. 379; Wells v. Monihan, 129 N. Y. 161; 29 N. E. 232; Morawetz on Corp., § 1002.

[116] Saunders v. Robinson, 144 Mass. 306; 10 N. E. 815.

as it is termed."[117] If the constitution of a grand lodge provides
for the suspension of a subordinate lodge for non-payment of an
assessment without notice, a member of the latter is not entitled
to notice of such suspension,[118] and if the laws of the order justify
the power a grand lodge may reverse the action of a subordinate
lodge suspending one of its members, although no appeal has been
prosecuted and the member is dead,[119] and the supreme lodge may,
where it appears to have unrestricted authority under its constitution, expel a member,[120] and can adopt any method of trial it
pleases, provided it be fair. In this case the Court said:[121] "By
the constitution of the Supreme Council, this body had the power
to make its own constitutions, rules of discipline and laws for the
government of the order. It was the body to which all appeals
were to be made on all matters of importance emanating from
grand and subordinate councils. It had power to alter or amend
the constitutions of grand or subordinate councils, and the laws
of the supreme council. It was, in short, a body of the highest,
and apparently unrestricted, authority. The trial of members or
officers of grand or subordinate councils might be had before a
special committee of one or more members of the order named by
the supreme leader. This committee need not consist of members
of the supreme council. The supreme council was a body whose
will was a law unto itself. It was to have original jurisdiction in
all cases of its own officers and members, but no mode of procedure
was specified for their trial. It would seem, therefore, that it
might adopt such mode of trial as it pleased, subject only to the
implied limitation that it must be fair.[122] In the present case there
is no reason to doubt that plaintiff's trial was conducted with such
substantial fairness as the nature of the case would admit of.
Charges in writing were preferred against him and he had an
opportunity to be heard upon them. No inference of unfairness
can be drawn from the report of the committee, nor from its rec-

[117] See also Scheu v. Grand Lodge, etc., 17 Fed. 214.
[118] Peet v. Great Camp K. of T. M., 83 Mich. 92; 47 N. W. 119.
[119] Vivar v. Supreme Lodge K. of P., 52 N. J. L. 455; 20 Atl. 36.
[120] Spillman v. Supreme Council Home Circle, 151 Mass. 128; 31 N. E.
776.
[121] Spillman v. Sup. Counc., *supra.*
[122] Gray v. Christian Society, 137 Mass. 329.

ommendations of expulsion. Assuming plaintiff's guilt, these were not unreasonable, though naturally distasteful to himself. The plaintiff, however, contends that the charges against him were insufficient in form. But it was expressly provided in section 5 of law 11 that the charges shall be sufficient if they state clearly the accusation, although not in technical terms. Taking the charges and specifications together, they appear to have been sufficiently minute and specific to give him notice of the ground of complaint against him. On the whole, the expulsion of the plaintiff appears to have been regular and valid according to the laws and usages to which he had voluntarily submitted himself.'' As a general rule, the constitutions and by-laws of grand and supreme lodges of the various orders or societies are binding upon the members of subordinate lodges, because by reference and adoption they are made parts of the laws of the subordinate bodies,[123] and this, too, whether they are incorporated or not, except, possibly, when a property right is involved.[124]

§ 96. **Rights of Subordinate Lodges and Members.**—The scheme of organization of fraternal beneficiary societies contemplates that there shall be a head body, which is, so to speak, the corporate entity of the society, generally incorporated, which is styled Supreme Lodge, or Council, State bodies called Grand Lodges, or Councils, and subordinate councils, the last two receiving their charters from the Supreme Body. The laws of the Supreme, or legal entity of the societies, regulate the organization of these various bodies and prescribe their powers and duties. Differences, however, often arise and part or all of the members of a subordinate body attempt to secede, or separate, themselves from the head organization so that the courts are called upon to decide the rights of ownership in the property. While the law is not as

[123] Chamberlain v. Lincoln, 129 Mass. 70; Altman v. Benz, 27 N. J. Eq. 331; Osceola Tribe v. Schmidt, 57 Md. 98; Hall v. Supreme Lodge, 24 Fed. 450. A corporation cannot amend its laws or articles of association so as to allow a foreign body to participate in making laws for its guidance. *In re* Grand Lodge, etc., 110 Pa. St. 613; 1 Atl. 582; Lamphere v. Grand Lodge, 47 Mich. 429; Messer v. Ancient Order, etc., 180 Mass. 321; 62 N. E. 252.

[124] Oliver v. Hopkins, 144 Mass. 175; 10 N. E. 776. See also Chamberlain v. Lincoln, 129 Mass. 70; Grosvenor v. Society, etc., 118 Mass. 78.

well settled as it might be, the general principles may be stated as follows: A benefit fund contributed by members of a subordinate lodge for their own use belongs to them and cannot, upon the revocation of its charter, be taken by the parent body under charter provisions which require the property of the former to be turned over to the latter, but in which no mention is made of money. In the leading case of State Council Jr. Order, etc., v. Emery,[125] it is said: "It does not appear that the State council had any plan or arrangement for the collection or payment of any sick or funeral benefits. All the beneficial features of that nature were left to the care of the local councils. This fund in question was made up entirely from the voluntary contributions of the members of the local council, placed in the hands of its trustees, to be disbursed by them for the benefit of the sick and the families of the dead of its members. With the control and administration of this fund the State council does not seem to have had anything to do. The authorities amply sustain the contention that funds raised by the members of subordinate bodies of this character for sick and funeral benefits belong to the subordinate association, and are to be distributed by them to the parties for whose use and benefit they were contributed. It is held that the revocation of the charter of a subordinate body by the supreme body cannot have the effect of confiscating the property owned absolutely by the local body." It has also been held that the majority of a subordinate lodge of a benevolent society cannot authorize a secession of the lodge from the parent organization and take with them the property of the order, if the general laws of the order provide that all property and funds of a lodge shall be held exclusively as a trust fund for carrying on the fraternal and benevolent features of the order and shall not be expended for any other purpose, and that no part of the property shall ever be divided among the members, and if any lodge for any reason shall cease to exist, all its property shall immediately and *ipso facto* revert to the superior lodge.[126] In this case the Court says: "The principal contention made by the appellants is that a subordinate lodge

125 219 Pa. 461; 68 Atl. 1023; 15 L. R. A. (N. S.) 336; 12 Ann. Cas. 870.
126 Grand Court Foresters of America v. Hodel, 74 Wash. 314; 133 Pac. 438; 47 L. R. A. (N. S.) 927. This case has an elaborate note concerning the rights of a subordinate lodge.

in an order such as the one in consideration here may secede from the parent organization, if the majority of such lodge wills it, and may take with them the money and property of the subordinate lodge. But such is not the rule. All of the property which this branch of the order, as a fraternal and benevolent organization, had gathered together, was trust funds, in the sense that they were collected for particular uses. They were held in trust for the purposes designated by the constitution and laws of the order, and every member of the order has an interest in the fund to the extent of seeing that it is appropriated to the uses for which it was collected. No number of the members of the order less than the whole could therefore divert the funds to other uses than the uses defined in the constitution and laws of the order. The majority of any subordinate court can undoubtedly direct the use of the funds of the order for purposes of the order, and when there are two or more purposes for which the funds can be lawfully used, may select between them, but the majority cannot, against the will of the minority, lawfully divert such funds for uses other than those permitted by the constitution and laws of the order. This, as we understand the authorities, is the universal rule.'' If the constitution and by-laws of an order provide that in no event can a subordinate lodge withdraw from the parent society except for specified causes, an attempt by a subordinate body to withdraw for a reason not mentioned in the by-law, was invalid.[127] It has been held[128] that in the absence of charter or constitutional provision to the contrary, a local lodge of a fraternal benefit association has the right to secede from the Grand Lodge without forfeiting its funds. It has been held in Canada, that the incorporation of a subordinate lodge does not constitute it an independent body, but it still remains a constituent part of the association and the surrender of its charter was a dissolution, so that its property on such dissolution became vested in the grand council in accordance with the provisions of its laws providing for

---

[127] Saborin v. Leppe, 195 Mass. 470; 81 N. E. 282; see also De Gross Loge, etc., v. Wolfer, 42 Colo. 393; 94 Pac. 329; Ahlendorf v. Barkons, 20 Ind. App. 657; 50 N. E. 887; McFadden v. Murphy, 149 Mass. 341; 21 N. E. 868; Schubert Lodge, etc., v. Schubert Kranken Intersturzen Verein, 56 N. J. Eq. 78; 38 Atl. 347.

[128] McCarty v. Cavanaugh, Mass., 113 N. E. 271.

such result.[129] In the case of Kennett v. Kidd,[129a] the Supreme Court of Kansas in holding that the subordinate lodge of a fraternal beneficiary society is not competent to take and hold property given to it by will, said: ''The legislature having twice taken pains to prescribe the only source of income to the parent order itself, we must conclude that it was not the intention to permit a local camp to be the beneficiary in a will. Neither organization is for profit, but each is for the mutual benefit of its members, and especially for the survivors of its members who have contributed to the general fund in accordance with the rules prescribed by the association itself. There is no restriction on using for the purpose of providing necessary buildings a portion of the income received in the manner pointed out by statute. But the case is not one of an ordinary corporation which all agree may take by will unless expressly precluded. It is the case of a local fraternal beneficiary body which the legislature has confined within a narrow zone of activity, dealing out its powers with a sparing hand. If a man in advanced years can be induced to devote the bulk of his estate to a local camp, as was the testator in this case, then there is no reason why other benefactors might not add their gifts until a local organization of a few neighbors could become the holder of property of great value far beyond any real or imaginary needs for the transaction of its business.''[129b]

§ 97. **An Early Masonic Case.**—One of the earliest cases. involving the rights of grand and subordinate lodges in respect to each other and the property of either was that of Smith *et al.* v. Smith *et al.* in 1813.[130] It involved the right to a certain fund belonging to the incorporated Grand Lodge of Ancient York Masons and was brought by the plaintiffs in behalf of a voluntary association claiming to be the successor of the corporation under the name of Grand Lodge of South Carolina. Incidentally the distinction between certain Masonic bodies and doctrines was

[129] McPherson v. Grand Council Provincial Workmen's Ass'n, 50 Can. Sup. Court R. 157.
[129a] 87 Kan. 652, 125 Pac. 36; 44 L. R. A. (N. S.) 544.
[129b] See also *post,* §§ 98, 99.
[130] 3 Dessau 557. Another case somewhat similar is Appeal of Woolford, 126 Pa. St. 47; 17 Atl. 524. The rules of Masonic authority are considered in Bayliss v. Grand Lodge A. F. & A. M., 131 La. 579; 59 Sou. 996.

discussed. The general rule laid down was that the Grand Lodge
of Freemasons cannot make new regulations subversive of fundamental principles and landmarks without the clear consent of
· the subordinate lodges; nor can the officers of a corporation composed of several integral parts, dissolve the corporation without
the full assent of the great body of the society. The dereliction
of the charter by the heads of a corporation does not dissolve
the corporate body, especially if the remaining members have
the power of renovating the head. The seceding members of
a chartered society, forming a new voluntary association, cannot
sustain a suit for the recovery of debts due to the corporation.[131]

§ 98. **The Odd Fellows' Case, Austin v. Searing: Power of
Grand Lodge of Voluntary Association Over Subordinate Lodges.**
—The Court of Appeals of New York was early called upon to
determine rights under the complex organization of the Odd Fellows' fraternity, where all the constituent bodies were unincorporated. In that case[132] Judge Selden said: ''The complaint,
upon which the questions in which this case arise, sets out what
appears to be a regular governmental organization, with its constitution and laws and powers legislative and judicial. The head
of this organization is a congress of representatives, called the
Grand Lodge of the United States, which not only legislates for
all lodges in the several States, but also exercises judicial powers
over them, for the complaint states that the grand lodges of the
several States are subject at all times to the resolves, orders and
decrees of the congress of representatives and are amenable to its
constitutional authority. The grand lodges of the several States
and districts exercise similar powers. They grant, revoke and
renew charters, make by-laws, and pass judicially upon charges
presented against subordinate lodges, expelling or reinstating
them at pleasure. These powers extend to the confiscation of the
entire property of a subordinate lodge, whenever, in the opinion

[131] Goodman v. Jedidjah Lodge, etc., 67 Md. 117; 9 Atl. 13; District
Grand Lodge v. Jedidjah Lodge, 65 Md. 236; Court Mount Royal v. Boul-
ton, Q. B. (Quebec) 1881; cited 2 Stephen's Digest, 106. But see Altmann
v. Benz, 27 N. J. Eq. 331.

[132] Austin v. Searing, 16 N. Y. 112; s. c. 69 Am. Dec. 665, where valuable note is appended.

of the grand lodge, upon a case brought regularly before it, it shall satisfactorily appear that such subordinate lodge is guilty of insubordination. Now, all this is very well, so long as the lodges neither violate nor ask any aid from the laws; but it may, with propriety, be doubted whether the judicial power of the State is to be invoked to uphold and enforce the decrees of these self-constituted judicatories. It is to be remarked that these lodges are charitable institutions, whose objects commend them extensively to public favor, and that there are nearly four hundred of them in northern New York alone, and, being purely voluntary associations, there is, of course, no limit to the amount of property which they may acquire. If this suit can be maintained, then all this property, however vast, is ultimately controlled, not by any power within the State, but by the Grand Lodge of the United States; for, by the constitution of these lodges, as given in the complaint, it will be seen that on the expulsion of any subordinate lodge (which is a matter resting entirely in the will of the grand lodge of the State or district), the whole property of the lodge expelled is, *ipso facto,* vested in the grand lodge, which is under no obligation to reinstate the lodge or restore the property; and, as the grand lodge of the State is bound to obey the decrees of the national lodge, the whole property is thus brought under the control of the latter. This is entirely unobjectionable, so long as submission to these decrees is merely voluntary; but the question is whether that submission is to be legally and judicially enforced. Let us see what a chancellor of England said about a case very similar to this. I refer to the case of Lloyd v. Loaring.[133] That was a bill filed by Evan Lloyd and two other persons to get possession of the dresses, decorations, books, papers, etc., of a lodge of Freemasons, called the Caledonian Chapter, No. 2. The plaintiff stated that this lodge was regularly organized under a charter from the grand or head chapter of Royal Arch Masons; that they were its chief officers, and as such were entitled, by virtue of the rules of the society, to the charge and custody of the property, etc., which the defendants had forcibly removed. The defendants demurred there, as here, to the bill. The opinion of Lord Chancellor Eldon, in that case, is so precisely applicable to this that I will make

[133] 6 Ves. 773.

one or two extracts from it. He said: 'A bill might be filed for
a chattel, the plaintiffs stating themselves to be jointly interested
in it with several other persons; but, it would be very dangerous
to take notice of them as a society having anything of a constitution in it. In this bill there is a great affectation of a corporate
character. They speak of their laws and constitution, and the
original charter by which they were constituted. In Cullen v.
The Duke of Queensbury,[134] Lord Thûrlow said he would con-
vince the parties that they had no laws and constitution.' And
again: 'That this court will hold jurisdiction to have a chattel
delivered up, I have no doubt; but I am alarmed at the notion
that these voluntary societies are to be permitted to state all
their laws, forms and constitutions upon the record, and then to
tell the court they are individuals, etc. The bill states that they
subsist under a charter granted by persons who are now dead;
and therefore, if this charter cannot be produced, the society is
gone. Upon principles of policy, the courts of this country do
not sit to determine upon charters granted by persons who have
not the prerogative to grant charters.' This appears to me to
be apt and sensible language in the case in which it was used,
where the charter, constitution, etc., were barely referred to;
but with what increased force does it apply to the case before
us, in which we have spread upon the record two formal constitutions, one of which contains fifteen distinct articles, the other
eleven, each article being subdivided into a variety of sections,
and altogether embracing a complete system of governmental
polity. There is, however, no objection to all this, provided we
apply to these articles the same rules as to ordinary agreements
inter partes, and give to them no peculiar force as the constitution and laws of an organized body. Admitting then the action
to be well brought, in the name of the treasurer, under the act
of April 7, 1849, about which I will not stop to inquire, it is
clear that the plaintiff can only recover by showing either a legal
or equitable title to the property in question in the lodge which
he represents, that is in the associated members of that lodge.
How does he show this? It is conceded by the complaint that the
property originally belonged to the lodge expelled, of which the

[134] 1 Bro. C. C. 101.

defendants were members. The defendants, therefore, were tenants in common, with the plaintiff and his associates, of the property, and had an equal right with them to its custody. It is incumbent on the plaintiff to show a legal transfer of this title. This he assumes to do by showing the expulsion by the grand lodge of the old Cayuga lodge, and the restoration of the new. The effect is supposed to be wrought through the operation of the 'constitutions of the two lodges. But it is obvious that these constitutions can have no binding force whatever, except what they derive from the assent of each individual member. That is, any member to be bound by them, must have personally assented to their provisions. It is only as contracts that these constitutions are in the least obligatory. The counsel for the plaintiff takes this view of the case in his printed argument. He says: 'The court is sitting to judge between individuals as to rights acquired by the contracts between them. It is immaterial whether such contracts are made in the form of subscriptions to general constitutions and by-laws, or to separate articles of agreement.' Viewed, then, as contracts, these constitutions must be subject to the same rules with all other contracts. It must be clearly shown that the defendants have assented to the written constitutions of these lodges. The complaint avers that the members of the present Cayuga lodge, 'have each and every one of them, in conformity with the usages and requirements of the order, subscribed to an article of association, denominated a constitution, a copy of which is hereunto annexed,' etc. There is also a general averment that the grand lodges in the several States have constitutions to which their members are obligated to subscribe, and do subscribe, and that one of these grand lodges is denominated the Grand Lodge of Northern New York, and that this lodge has public and printed articles of association, styled a constitution, a copy of which is thereunto annexed. But there is no averment that this constitution was ever in fact subscribed by anybody, nor does the complaint contain any direct averment that the defendants ever subscribed the constitution of any lodge, either grand or subordinate. The averment relied upon by the plaintiff upon the subject is this: after stating the existence of the original Cayuga lodge, and that the plaintiff and his associates and the defendants were all members of that lodge, the complaint proceeds thus: 'that, as such

159

members and associates, they had, each and every one of them,
covenanted with each other to observe, obey, conform to and
abide by the constitution, by-laws, rules and regulations of the
said lodge, and of said Grand Lodge of Northern New York.'
Covenanted? How? Under their hands and seals? It is not so
averred. There is neither profert nor offer to produce the covenant. Will this do in a legal pleading? I apprehend not. It
is altogether too vague. Again what constitution did they covenant to observe? The averment says: 'the constitution, by-laws,
etc., of the Cayuga lodge and of said Grand Lodge of Northern
New York,' but does not set forth the constitutions in this connection, nor give any reference by which they can be identified
or their provisions ascertained. We may conjecture that the
plaintiff means the same constitutions which are referred to elsewhere in the complaint, but it is not so averred. If we look at
the whole complaint we shall see that it is not intended to be
averred that the defendants ever subscribed the constitution of
the grand lodge itself. It is difficult to see, therefore, how the
provisions of that instrument are to be made obligatory on the
defendants as a contract. There is nothing in the constitution
of the expelled lodge (which probably was subscribed by the defendants, although that is not in terms averred) which adopts
the constitution of the grand lodge. It is this latter constitution
alone which confers the power by which the property in question
is claimed to have been transferred. But were it distinctly
averred that the defendants had subscribed the constitution of the.
grand as well as of the subordinate lodge, I should still be of the
opinion that public policy would not admit of parties binding
themselves by such engagements. The effect of some of the provisions of these constitutions is to create a tribunal having power
to adjudicate upon the rights of property of all the members of
the subordinate lodges, and to transfer that property to others;
the members of this tribunal being liable to constant fluctuations,
and not subject in any case to the selection or control of the parties upon whose rights they sit in judgment. To create a judicial
tribunal is one of the functions of the sovereign power; and although parties may always make such tribunal for themselves,
in any specific case, by a submission to arbitration, yet the power
is guarded by the most cautious rules. A contract that the parties

160

will submit, confers no power upon the arbitrator; and even where there is an actual submission, it may be revoked at any time. The law allows the party up to the last moment to ascertain whether there is not some covert bias or prejudice on the part of the arbitrator chosen. It would hardly accord with this scrupulous care to secure fairness, in such cases, that parties should be held legally bound by the sort of engagement that exists here, by which the most extensive judicial powers are conferred upon bodies of men whose individual members are subject to continual fluctuation." In the same case in a concurring opinion Judge Brown said: "The by-laws and regulations of these voluntary associations may be all very well in their place and sphere and may command generally the obedience and submission of those upon whom they are designed to act; they cannot, however, have the force of law, nor impair or effect the rights of property against the will of its real owners. So long as the members of these bodies yield their assent or concurrence, it is all very well; the law interposes no obstacle or objection. But when orders and decrees of the character of those referred to, are resisted, and the owners of property refuse to be deprived of it, then it will be found that property has rights, and the courts of justice have duties, of which the plaintiff in this action has an indifferent conception. The courts of justice cannot be called upon to aid in enforcing the decrees of these self-created judicatories. The confiscation and forfeiture of property is an act of sovereign power; and the aid of this or any other court will not be rendered to enforce such proceedings, or to recognize legal, or supposed legal, rights founded upon them."[135]

§ 99. **Other Cases Involving Same Question: the Element of Incorporation.**—In a somewhat similar case in Maryland the Court of Appeals held[136] that, when the charter granted by the State to a lodge is still in force the lodge has the right to hold its substantial property or pecuniary rights under the corporate powers conferred by that charter, unaffected by the forfeiture

---

[135] In Bauer v. Sampson Lodge, etc., 102 Ind. 262, and also in Wicks v. Monihan, 130 N. Y. 232; 14 L. R. A. 243, this case of Austin v. Searing was cited and approved, see *post*, § 99.

[136] Goodman v. Jedidjah Lodge, etc., 67 Md. 117; 9 Atl. 13.

of its conventional charter by the grand lodge. That "whatever powers the higher lodges in such an organization as this may have to make rules or laws for the government of the subordinate lodges and the discipline of their members, we think it is quite certain that the courts can never recognize as valid any rule or law so made, the effect of which is to confiscate property, or to arbitrarily take away property rights from one set of members and give them to another set; nor will the courts allow or recognize the enforcement of any such rule when its enforcement will accomplish and is designed to accomplish such a result." Where the subordinate lodge was incorporated it was held by the Supreme Court of California,[137] that an injunction would issue to protect its property although it was suspended by the grand lodge, although the laws of the order provided for a forfeiture of property in such cases to the grand lodge. The Court says: "The ownership of the property draws to itself the right of possession and control. And since the plaintiff is a corporation it can only be dissolved in the manner prescribed by the laws of California. The provision in the constitution of the grand lodge, that in certain contingencies the subordinate lodge 'shall be deemed an extinct lodge, and its charter shall be forfeited,' and the 'suspension' by the grand lodge and the action taken by the grand chief templar, have not the slightest effect upon the legal existence of the corporation; and as long as it exists its affairs must be managed by its duly elected officers as provided by law. If they misconduct themselves, appropriate proceedings to remove them must be resorted to. But the propriety of their conduct will not be inquired into in a suit by the corporation to protect its property."[138] The powers of a superior body are only such as the compact provides and the court will strictly scrutinize all disciplinary measures and hold the superior body to an accurate observance of all formalities.[139] In a recent case just cited the

[137] Merrill Lodge v. Ellsworth, 78 Cal. 166; 20 Pac. 399; 2 L. R. A. 841.

[138] To the same effect are: Wells v. Monihan, 129 N. Y. 161; 29 N. E. 232; affg. 13 N. Y. Supp. 156; Wicks v. Monihan, 130 N. Y. 232; 29 N. E. 139; affg. 8 N. Y. Supp. 121.

[139] Grand Grove U. A. O. D. v. Garibaldi Grove, etc., 130 Cal. 116; 62 Pac. 486. In this case the method of procedure is discussed. See also National Council, etc., v. State Council, etc. (N. J.), 43 Atl. 1082; Swain

New York Court of Appeals says, in regard to the property of a
voluntary association:[140] "Excelsior Assembly 4120 was composed
of women. Their charter was revoked for 'insubordination,' of
which, very likely, they were guilty. The offense and its punishment ended their powers and privileges so far, and so far only,
as they were derived from the rules and regulations of the Knights
of Labor; but could not destroy their rights as individuals, or as
an unincorporated association, derived from the law of the State.
Under that law they could, as they did, associate for a common
purpose, and choose officers, in whose name they could sue. These
powers they had when their charter from the Knights was given,
and retained when it was taken away. That event broke off
their relations with the order, but not with their own treasury.
That treasury they could control in their collective capacity until
some superior power took it away or it disappeared in a final
distribution among the members. The defendants have nothing
to do with that question. They owe their debt to the association,
of whom they borrowed the money, and which through its treasurer, seeks to recover it. It may be true that by their 'insubordination' and consequent expulsion from the society, and protection of the Knights, the members of the association have no
longer the common purpose which brought them together. That
may prove to be a reason for dissolving the association, but until
dissolved it can exist to collect its debts and pay its creditors,
and make distribution of its surplus. Even where the State
destroys a corporation for violation of its charter, it does not free
the debtors from the payment of their honest debts. What shall
be done with the money when restored is sometimes a serious
question, but it must first be collected. It does not belong to
the debtors, in any event, and no rule of the Knights or law of
the State allows them to confiscate it. The defendants do not
assert any conflicting claim to the money. If they did they would
still be obliged to pay to the true owner, and could not escape liability. That true owner is the association, which the Knights

v. Miller, 72 Mo. App. 446; St. Patrick's Alliance v. Byrne, 59 N. J. Eq.
26; 44 Atl. 716. So a subordinate lodge cannot be suspended by the act
of the secretary. Circus v. Independent Order, etc., 55 App. Div. 534; 67
N. Y. Supp. 342.
[140] Wells v. Monihan, *supra.*

have not utterly destroyed. There has been a divorce but that is quite different from death.'' The superior body cannot recover on a bond executed by the treasurer of a subordinate lodge money which belongs to the latter.[141] In Michigan, in a case involving the right of an incorporated grand lodge to suspend a member for not paying an assessment ordered by the supreme lodge, superior in authority, but incorporated in a different State, the Supreme Court said:[142] "The relator is not liable to pay the assessment. It is not competent for the respondent to subject itself or its members to a foreign authority in this way. There is no law of the State permitting it, nor could there be any law of this State which would subject a corporation created and existing under the laws of this State to the jurisdiction and control of a body existing in another State and in no manner under the control of our law. The attempt of the respondent to do this is an attempt to set aside and ignore the very law of its being.''[143] But in New Jersey the Court of Chancery held[144] that, where certain members of a subordinate lodge of the order withdrew from the jurisdiction of the grand lodge of the State and surrendered their charter, forming a new lodge under the same name, and the minority of the members continued steadfast in their allegiance and the surrendered charter was redelivered to them as the lodge, the body which continued true in its allegiance was entitled to the property of the society and was the true original lodge. In this case the analogy to religious associations was clearly considered, for the court refers to a decision of its own in a church dispute,[145] and members of a voluntary association who have withdrawn and incorporated themselves under the name of the association cannot thereby deprive the latter of the right

141 Independent Order Foresters v. Donahue, 91 Ill. App. 585. Detroit Savings Bank v. Haines, 128 Mich. 38; 87 N. W. 66' is also in point.

142 Lamphere v. Grand Lodge, 47 Mich. 429.

143 State ex rel., etc., v. Miller et al., 66 Ia. 26; Grand Lodge v. Stepp, 14 Pittsb. Leg. J. 164; 3 Penny 45; Bauer v. Sampson Lodge, 102 Ind. 262; Alnutt v. High Court of Foresters, 62 Mich. 110; 28 N. W. 802.

144 Altmann v. Benz et al., 27 N. J. Eq. 331; see also Koerner v. Grand Lodge K. of P., 146 Ind. 639; 45 N. E. 1103.

145 Hendrickson v. Shotwell, 1 N. J. Eq. 577; Yeates v. Roberts, 3 Drew 170; 1 Jur. (N. S.) 319; affd. 7 De G., M. & G. 227.

to the name,[146] and an injunction will lie to prevent such incorporation until the disputed question of authority can be determined.[147] Other cases fully support these principles.[148] And in a case in Missouri,[149] it was held that an incorporated lodge of Odd Fellows has the right, through its proper officers and in accordance with its established rules, to determine who are not members thereof, and the courts will leave that question to be determined by the lodge itself, through the judicial action of its proper officers, regardless of whether the charter of the lodge in which membership is claimed gives, in express terms, such power to these officers. But in this case no property right was involved. The subordinate lodge, whose charter had been arrested and then restored, had, in voting for the members to whom such charter was to be restored, excluded the plaintiffs, who sought to be reinstated by *mandamus*. The court places its decision on the ground of the assent of relators to what was done, and their further consent that they could have no vested right in what was called the property of the lodge. In this case also the analogy of fraternal societies to religious associations was admitted.[150] Mere breach of duty on the part of the officers will not justify the secession of a part of the members.[151]

§ 100. **Distinction Between Social Organizations and Those Furnishing Insurance Indemnity.**—Late decisions show an inclination to distinguish between purely social or benevolent organizations and those which provide for a benefit in the nature of life insurance, and the case quoted from[152] expressly declare that if

---

146 Black Rabbit Ass'n v. Munday, 21 Abb. N. C. 99.

147 McGlynn v. Post, 21 Abb. N. C. 97.

148 Gorman v. O'Connor, 155 Pa. St. 239; 26 Atl. 379; McFadden v. Murphy, 149 Mass. 341; 21 N. E. 868. Another case involving the rights of subordinate bodies is Pfeifer v. Supreme Lodge Bohemian, etc., 37 Misc. 71; 74 N. Y. Supp. 720.

149 State v. Odd Fellows' Grand Lodge, 8 Mo. App. 148.

150 See *post*, § 101.

151 McCallion v. Hibernia, etc., Soc., 12 Pac. 114; 70 Cal. 163.

152 Goodman v. Jedidjah Lodge, etc., 67 Md. 117; 9 Atl. 13; District Grand Lodge, etc., v. Jedidjah Lodge, 65 Md. 236; Supreme Council, etc., v. Garrigus, 104 Ind. 133; State v. Miller, 66 Ia. 26; Bauer v. Sampson Lodge, 102 Ind. 262; Mulroy v. Sup. L. Knights of Honor, 28 Mo. App. 463; Lamphere v. Grand Lodge, 47 Mich. 429; Alnutt v. High Court of Foresters, 62 Mich. 110; 28 N. W. 802.

such organizations "choose to go into that kind of business, they must expect courts to deal with and adjudicate the rights of the policyholders, upon the same principles of equity and justice that they apply in the usual and ordinary cases of life insurance contracts."[153] The further distinction is made, when the subordinate organization is incorporated, that "a cause of forfeiture cannot be taken advantage of or enforced against a corporation collaterally, or incidentally, or in any other mode than by a direct proceeding for that purpose against the corporation; and the government creating the corporation can alone institute the proceeding; and it can waive a forfeiture, and this it can do expressly, or by legislative acts recognizing the continued existence of the corporation.[154]

§ 101. **Analogy Between Lodges and Churches.**—It is not unreasonable to expect that in future, as in past, adjudications, the courts will to a greater or less extent adopt as applicable to fraternal, social, benevolent or benefit societies the rules laid down and now well settled by a long line of decisions in the United States, governing ecclesiastical organizations, subject to the qualifications already established concerning attempts to forfeit the rights of one class of members and transfer them to another, and the forfeiture of the property rights of members.[155] These rules have been declared by the Supreme Court of the United States[156] substantially as follows:—

§ 102. **Property Rights of Members of Religious Societies; How Determined.**—Controversies in the civil courts concerning property rights of religious societies are generally to be decided by a reference to one or more of three propositions: (1) Was the property or fund which is in question devoted by the express terms of the gift, grant or sale by which it was acquired, to the support of any specific religious doctrine or belief, or was it ac-

[153] Goodman v. Jedidjah Lodge, etc., 67 Md. 117; 9 Atl. 13.

[154] In re N. Y. Elevated R. R. Co., 70 N. Y. 337; Morawetz on Corp., § 1015.

[155] State v. Odd Fellows,' etc., 8 Mo. App. 148; Gorman v. O'Connor, supra.

[156] Watson v. Jones, 13 Wall. 679.

quired for the general use of the society for religious purposes, with no other limitation? (2) Is the society which owned it of the strictly congregational or independent form of church government, owing no submission to any organization outside of the congregation? (3) Or is it one of a number of such societies, united to form a more general body of churches, with ecclesiastical control in the general association over the members and societies of which it is composed? In the first class of cases the court will, when necessary to protect the trust to which the property has been devoted, inquire into the religious faith or practice of the parties claiming its use or control, and will see that it shall not be diverted from that trust. If the property was acquired in the ordinary way of purchase or gift, for the use of a religious society, the court will inquire who constitute that society, or its legitimate successors, and award to them the use of the property. In case of the independent order of the congregation, this is to be determined by the majority of the society, or by such organization of the society, as by its own rules constitute its government. In the class of cases in which property has been acquired in the same way by a society which constitutes a subordinate part of a general religious organization, with established tribunals for ecclesiastical government, these tribunals must decide all questions of faith, discipline, rule, custom, or ecclesiastical government. In such cases where the right of property in the civil court is dependent on the question of doctrine, discipline, ecclesiastical law, rule or custom or church government, and that has been decided by the highest tribunal within the organization to which it has been carried, the civil court will accept that decision as conclusive and be governed by it in its application to the case before it.[157]

The law of religious societies has recently been exhaustively considered by the courts in the cases involving the merger of two

[157] Opinion cites: Miller v. Gable, 2 Denio, 492; Shannon v. Frost, 3 B. Mon. 253; Smith v. Nelson, 18 Vt. 511; Gibson v. Armstrong, 7 B. Mon. 481; Harmon v. Dreher, 1 Speer's Eq. 87; Watson v. Avery, 2 Bush. 332; John's Island Church Case, 2 Rich. Eq. 215; Ferraria v. Vasconcelles, 23 Ill. 456; Chase v. Cheney, 58 Ill. 509; Watson v. Farris, 45 Mo. 183; German Ref. Ch. v. Seibert, 3 Barr. 291; McGinnis v. Watson, 41 Pa. St. 21. *Contra*, as to jurisdiction: Watson v. Avery, 2 Bush. 332; Watson v. Avery, 3 Bush. 635. See also Altmann v. Benz, 27 N. J. Eq. 331; Hendrickson v. Shotwell, 1 N. J. Eq. 577.

Presbyterian bodies, and the rights of members and different factions in the church property. The principles laid down in Watson v. Jones have been adhered to, but in applying the principles different courts have reached different conclusions.[158]   The Supreme Court of Missouri has said:[159]   "Of these pure ecclesiastical questions of creed, faith, or church discipline, we should wash our hands unless an investigation thereof is required to determine property rights.   If for that purpose it should be required, our constitutional duty is to so investigate."   The Supreme Court of Tennessee says:[160].   "The civil court in deciding a property right should honor the deliverances of the ecclesiastical court with the greatest attention and respect, but should not follow them unquestioningly in every case."

§ 103. **By-Laws: Definition of: How Proved.**—By-laws, according to all the authorities[161] are merely rules prescribed by the majority of the members of an association or corporation, under authority of the other members, for the regulation and management of their joint affairs.   In both voluntary and incorporated associations the power depends upon the articles of association, or charter, which is the fundamental law.[162]   In the case of a corporation the law "tacitly annexes to it the power of making by-laws or private statutes, for its government and support,"[163] and it is implied in every charter that the majority shall have power to make needful by-laws for the regulation of the affairs of the corporation.   Rules adopted for the government of an association which is incorporated are all by-laws, and that whether some of them are called such or not; what is often termed the "constitution" of a benefit society is merely a code of by-laws under an inappropriate name.[164]   By-laws properly adopted are

---

[158] Ramsey v. Hicks, 174 Ind. 428; 91 N. E. 344; 92 N. E. 164; 30 L. R. A. (N. S.) 665, where valuable note is appended. First Presbyterian Church et al. v. First Cumberland Presbyterian et al., 245 Ill. 74, 91 N. E. 761; 19 Ann. Cas. 275, and note.

[159] Boyles v. Roberts, 222 Mo. 613; 121 S. W. 805.

[160] Landrith v. Hudgins, 121 Tenn. 556; 120 S. W. 783.

[161] Morawetz on Corp., § 491; Ang. & Ames on Corp., § 327; 1 Beach on Priv. Corp., § 308 et seq.

[162] St. Mary's, etc., v. Burford's Admr., 70 Pa. St. 321.

[163] Ang. & Ames on Corp., § 325.

[164] Supreme Lodge K. of P., etc., v. Knight, 117 Ind. 489; 20 N. E. 479, p. 483; 3 L. R. A. 409; Mulroy v. Knights of Honor, 28 M. A. 463; Su.

as **bi**nding upon all the members of the association as a provision contained in the charter itself.[165] By-laws, when properly adopted, measure the duties, rights and liabilities of the members.[166] By-laws may be proved by officers or members who were present and saw them adopted,[167] or by production of the records or properly certified copies thereof. It has been said,[168] that the constitution and by-laws purporting to be published by the Supreme Council of the order and furnished the local lodge and used by it are admissible in evidence without further proof of their adoption. A resolution may have the force of a by-law.[169] The journal of the proceedings of a voluntary association is presumed to be correct,[170] and the presumption is in favor of the regularity of the proceedings.[171]

§ 104. **By Whom and How Made.**—The authority to make by-laws has been said to be incident to a grant of corporate existence, and associations, clubs and societies though not incorporated have the same power.[172] Unless delegated to a select body by the articles of association or charter, the power to make by-laws resides in the body of members themselves and is to be exercised by the majority.[173] This power cannot be delegated.[174] If the

preme Lodge, etc., v, Adams, 68 N. H. 236; 48 Atl. 380; Dòrnes v. Knights of Pythias, 75 Miss. 466; 23 Sou. 171; Toomey v. Supreme Lodge K. of P., 74 Mo. App. 507.

165 Morawetz on Corp., § 491.

166 Mo. Bottlers' Ass'n v. Fennerty, 81 Mo. Opp. 525.

167 Masonic Mut. Ben. Ass'n v. Severson, 71 Conn. 719; 43 Atl. 192; but see Lloyd v. Supreme Lodge K. of P., 98 Fed. 66; 38 C. C. A. 654.

168 Home Circle Soc. v. Skelton (Tex. Civ. A.), 81 S. W. 84.

169 Flaherty v. Longshoremen's Ben. Soc., 99 Me. 253; 59 Atl. 58.

170 National Council Junior Order, etc., v. State Council, etc., 27 D. C. 1.

171 Maxwell v. Theatrical, etc., 104 N. Y. Supp. 85; 54 Misc. 619.

172 *In re* Long Island R. Co., 19 Wend. 37; 32 Am. Dec. 429; Hodginson v. Exeter, L. R. 5 Eq. 63; Lyttleton v. Blackburn, 33 L. T. 641. This principle seems to be generally conceded, as appears in all the cases relating to enforcement of by-laws.

173 Morawetz on Corp., § 491; Ang. & Ames on Corp., § 327; 1 Beach on Priv. Corp., § 311.

174 Toomey v. Supreme Lodge K. of P., 74 Mo. App. 507; Supreme Lodge K. of H. v. Kutscher, 179 Ill. 340; 53 N. E. 620; reversing 72 Ill. App. 462; Supreme Lodge K. P. v. Stein, 75 Miss. 107; 21 Sou. 559; 37 L. R. A. 775.

charter, or the fundamental agreement of the members, prescribe the mode in which the by-laws shall be made and adopted, in order to insure their validity, that mode must be strictly pursued,[175] but if the charter is silent on this subject, the association may adopt by-laws "by its own acts and conduct, and the acts and conduct of its officers, as by an express vote, or an adoption manifested in writing."[176] The rule has been thus stated:[177] "While the governing body of a corporation has no power to delegate the exercise of its judicial functions, it, itself, can exercise such powers in a plenary way, except as limited by the charter of the corporation, and when not thus restricted may adopt or enact a by-law in disregard of the procedure for so doing, contained in previous by-laws, and this too by a majority vote." And this rule is abundantly sustained by other authority.[178] In Dornes v. Supreme Lodge K. of P.[179] it is said: "Any meeting could by a majority vote, modify or repeal the law of a previous meeting, and no meeting could bind a subsequent one by irrepealable acts or rules of procedure. The power to enact is a power to repeal; and a by-law requiring a two-thirds vote of members present to alter or amend the laws of the society may itself be altered, amended or repealed by the same power which enacted it."[180] It has, however, been held[181] that where a society has expressly adopted a code of by-laws other by-laws will not be implied from custom or usage. Still lodges often adopt resolutions in regard to matters which, if not, should be, covered by by-laws. Such

[175] Dunston v. Imperial Gas Co., 3 B. & Ad. 125. Statutory requirements must of course be observed. Knights of Maccabees v. Nitsch, 69 Neb. 312; 95 N. W. 626; Froelich v. Musicians' Ben. Ass'n, 93 Mo. App. 383.

[176] Ang. & Ames on Corp., § 328; Union Bank v. Ridgely, 1 Harr. & G. 324.

[177] Toomey v. Supreme Lodge K. of P., supra.

[178] Supreme Council A. L. H. v. Adams, 68 N. H. 236; 44 Atl. 380; Goulding v. Standish, 182 Mass. 401; 65 N. E. 803.

[179] 75 Miss. 466; 23 Sou. 191.

[180] But to the contrary see Deuble v. Grand Lodge A. O. U. W., 72 N. Y. Supp. 755; 66 App. Div. 323; affd. 172 N. Y. 665; 65 N. E. 1116; Cowan v. New York Caledonia Club, 61 N. Y. Supp. 714; 46 App. Div. 288. And also see as to burden of proof: United Brotherhood, etc., v. Forten, 107 Ill. App. 306.

[181] District Grand Lodge v. Cohn, 20 Ill. App. 335.

resolutions, especially if brought to the knowledge of the members, might, on principle, have the effect of by-laws if legal otherwise.[182] Eleemosynary corporations as such have no incidental power to make by-laws.[183] A committee appointed to revise the constitution has no power to originate amendments.[184]

§ 105. **Binding Upon all Members: All are Presumed to
· Know Them.**—The by-laws of a society are binding upon all the members and all are conclusively presumed to know them. They are in the nature of a contract to which all have assented. The Supreme Court of Indiana says:[185] "One who becomes a member of such an organization is chargeable with knowledge of its laws and rules and is bound by them. He cannot be ignorant of them, nor can he refuse obedience to them, unless, indeed, they are illegal, or require the performance of acts which the law forbids. By-laws not in themselves illegal and not requiring the performance of acts contrary to law, must, therefore, be deemed binding upon all persons who become members."[186] The reason of this rule is, that by becoming a member, one impliedly agrees to be bound by all legal acts of the majority under the compact of the articles of association.[187] And a member cannot question the validity of the by-laws under which he became a member. A

[182] Miller v. Hillsborough, etc., Ass'n, 42 N. J. Eq. 459; Pfister v. Gerwick, 122 Ind. 567; 23 N. E. 1041; Dornes v. Supreme Lodge K. of P., *supra*. It has been held that a decision interpreting the law made by the head officer if approved by the Grand Lodge and acted upon may have the effect of a by-law. State *ex rel.* v. Grand Lodge A. O. U. W., 70 Mo. App. 456.   ·

[183] Ang. & Ames on Corp., § 330.

[184] National Council Junior Order, etc., v. State Council, etc., 27 D. C. 1.

[185] Bauer v. Sampson Lodge, 102 Ind. 262.

[186] Fugure v. Mut. Soc. St. Joseph, 46 Vt. 368; Cimeral v. Dubuque Mut. F. Ins. Co., 18 Ia. 319; Coles v. Ia. State Mut. F. Ins. Co., 18 Ia. 425; Coleman v. Knights of Honor, 18 Mo. App. 189; Mitchell v. Lycoming Mut. F. Ins. Co., 51 Pa. St. 402; People v. St. George Soc., 28 Mich. 261; Osceola Tribe v. Schmidt, 57 Md. 98; Sperry's Appeal, 116 Pa. St. 391; 9 Atl. 478; Harvey v. Grand Lodge, 50 M. A. 472; Emmons v. Hope Lodge, etc., 1 Del. 187; 40 Atl. 956; Home Forum Ben. Order v. Jones, 5 Okla. 598; 50 Pac. 165; Gaines v. Farmer, 55 Tex. Civ. App. 601; 119 S. W. 874; Louisville Board, etc., v. Johnson, 133 Ky. 797; 119 S. W. 153; Bones v. Supreme Lodge K. & L. of H., 231 Ill. 134; 83 N. E. 127.

[187] Morawetz on Corp., § 500a; Ang. & Ames on Corp., § 359.

member of a foreign fraternal society is bound by the by-laws though the certificate is delivered in another State.[188]   In a recent case[189] the Supreme Court of Indiana said: ''A person who becomes a member of a mutual insurance company, assents to the by-laws under which he acquires a membership, and he cannot afterwards successfully assail their validity on the ground that they were not regularly adopted.   Or, as Mr. Waterman states the rule: 'A person who has voluntarily become a· member of a corporate body cannot object that the corporation had no power to make a by-law.'[190]   There is an essential difference between strangers and the members and stockholders of a corporation; for strangers are not always precluded from questioning the validity of by-laws, nor always bound to take notice of them, although there are instances in which they cannot question them, and wherein they are chargeable with notice of them.[191]   One of the duties of a person who becomes a member of a mutual insurance company is to inform himself of its by-laws, and he cannot escape their force although he may have had no actual knowledge of them.   A very strong application of this rule was made in a mutual insurance company case in which Chief Justice Gibson declared that without such a rule mutual companies could not exist.[192]   In the case of Miller v. Hillsborough Mutual Fire Assurance Company,[193] the general doctrine was carried very far, the Court saying: 'But it is clear that a member of the company is chargeable with notice of all the by-laws of the company and of the conditions of insurance adopted by the company, whether contained in the by-laws or in resolutions.' ''

§ 106. **Requisites of Valid By-Laws.**—All by-laws, to be valid, must have three essential and vital qualifications: (1) they must be consistent with the charter or articles of association; (2) they must not be in conflict with any provisions of statute or common

---

[188] Supreme Lodge New England Order, etc., v. Hine, 82 Conn. 315; 73 Atl. 791.

[189] Pfister v. Gerwig, 122 Ind. 567; 23 N. E. 1041.

[190] 1 Wat. Corp. 235.

[191] *Id.* 273.

[192] Insurance Co. v. Perrine, 7 Watts & S. 348.

[193] 42 N. J. Eq. 459; 7 Atl. 895.

law, and lastly (3) they must be reasonable. This principle is universally accepted and has never been questioned. In the case of Kent v. Quicksilver Mining Co.,[194] the New York Court of Appeals said: "All by-laws must be reasonable and consistent with the general principles of the law of the land, which are to be determined by the courts when a case is properly before them. A by-law may regulate or modify the constitution of a corporation, but cannot alter it. The alteration of a by-law is but the making of another, on the same subject. If the first must be reasonable, and in accord with the principles of law, so must that be which alters it. If, then, the power is reserved to alter, amend, or repeal, and that reservation enters into a contract, the power reserved is to pass reasonable by-laws agreeable to law."[195]

§ 107. Must be Consistent with Charter.—The prime essential of a valid by-law is that it be consistent with the charter or articles of association. Upon this subject the Supreme Court of Minnesota has said:[196] "These articles (of association) are its charter, and, subject to the constitution and general laws of the State, its fundamental and organic law. Among other things they fix the rights of stockholders. They are in the nature of a fundamental contract, in form between the corporators—a contract which, as in other cases, neither party is at liberty to violate. This can no more be done through the form of by-laws and resolutions of the stockholders adopted and acted upon, than it can in any other way. The authority to pass by-laws is, as a matter of course, authority to pass such as are consistent with the articles of incorporation, and not a power to subvert the law of corporate existence. The by-laws of a corporation are only rules and regulations as to the manner in which the corporate powers shall be exercised. Any attempt on the part of defendant, by by-laws or otherwise, to deprive an unconsenting stockholder of a right secured to him by the corporate articles, is in excess of corporate authority, or, in legal parlance, *ultra vires*."[197] In the same line

[194] 78 N. Y. 159.
[195] Morawetz on Corp., §§ 494, 495, 496. As to after enacted laws see *post*, § 228.
[196] Bergman v. St. Paul Mut. Bldg. Ass'n, 29 Minn. 278.
[197] Ang. & Ames on Corp., § 345.

is the declaration of the Supreme Court of Pennsylvania[198] that
"no corporation can make any valid by-law in conflict with its
charter. That would enable the corporation to make a new constitution for itself and thereby wholly defeat the object of the
law which gave it birth." Upon analogy it follows that voluntary
associations cannot pass beyond the limitations of their articles
of association so as to bind members not thereto consenting, except
by unanimous consent of all their members. By-laws in contravention of the provisions of a charter are void.[199] In a case in
New York[200] where the general purposes of the society as declared
in the articles of association were declared to be the welfare of
themselves and others, and particularly the mutual relief of the
members in times of sickness and distress, it was held that "the
society could extend its benefits to the families of its members,
and that such provision in favor of the widows of deceased members, was not only highly meritorious, but fairly within the scope
of the general purposes of the organization. The constitution and
laws should have a liberal interpretation, for the purpose of pro-
moting the general objects of the society, and, as such a provision
for the benefit of the families of the members is in no way hostile
or opposed to the general plan of the organization, I am of the
opinion it should be upheld as a proper exercise of the powers
conferred upon the association."[201]

§ 108. **Must Not be Contrary to Common or Statute Law.**—
The by-laws of all associations and corporations must not be contrary to either statute or common law. In the quaint language of
Chief Justice Hobart:[202] "For, as reason is given to the natural
body for the governing of it, so the body corporate must have

[198] Diligent Fire Co. v. Commonwealth, 75 Pa. St. 291. To the same ef-
fect are Supreme Royal Circle v. Morrison, 105 Ark. 140; 150 S. W. 561;
Roulo v. Schiller Bund, 172 Mich. 557; 138 N. W. 244; Carney v. Jedudta
Casky Dam, 146 Ill. App. 518.

[199] Presb. Mut. Ass'n Fund v. Allen, 106 Ind. 593; Raub v. Masonic Mut.
Rel. Ass'n, 3 Mackey, 68 People ex rel. Stewart v. Father Matthew, etc.,
Soc., 41 Mich. 67; Ang. & Ames on Corp., § 345 and cases cited; Mora-
wetz on Corp., § 494 and cases cited.

[200] Gundlach v. Germania Mech. Ass'n, 4 Hun. 339; 49 How. Pr. 190.

[201] Sup. Council, etc., v. Fairman, 10 Abb. N. C. 162; 62 How. Pr. 386;
Barbaro v. Occidental Lodge, 4 Mo. App. 429.

[202] Norris v. Staps, Hob. 211.

laws, as a politic reason to govern it; but those laws must ever be subject to the general law of the realm, as subordinate to it." "If a corporation undertakes to make by-laws in contravention of the statute they are *ultra vires* and of no effect."[203]   In State v. Williams[204] the Supreme Court of North Carolina, in passing upon a case where the ceremony of expulsion from a benevolent society involved a battery, held that it could not be lawfully inflicted. "It is not the less a battery because they were all members."[205]   So a by-law of a society compelling members to join in a "strike" is void,[206] as is the by-law of a labor organization requiring a war on "non-union" men[207] and a by-law of a voluntary association of fire underwriters prohibiting the employment of solicitors except under certain restrictions,[208] and a by-law of a superior providing for forfeiture of property of a subordinate organization.[209]   By-laws in restraint of trade are void.[210]   The Supreme Court of Massachusetts has said concerning the construction of by-laws:[211] "The by-law should be construed with reference to the statute, and, if practicable, such a meaning should be given to it as will make the two consistent, for it is not to be assumed that the by-law is intended to go beyond the scope of the statute, and thus violate its provisions."[212]

[203] Am. Legion of Honor v. Perry, 140 Mass. 580; Diligent Fire Co. v. Commonwealth, 75 Pa. St. 291; Briggs v. Earl, 139 Mass. 473; Kent v. Quicksilver Mining Co., 78 N. Y. 159; Nelson v. Gibson, 92 Ill. App. 595; Brower v. Supreme Lodge Nat. Res. Ass'n, 74 Mo. App. 490.

[204] 75 N. C. 134.

[205] Bell v. Hansley, 3 Jones 131.

[206] People v. N. Y. Ben. Soc., 3 Hun. 361; Farrer v. Close, L. R. 4 Q. B. 602; Doyle v. Benev. Soc., 6 Thompson & C. 88. But see Snow v. Wheeler, 113 Mass. 179.

[207] Lucke v. Clothingcutters, etc., Assembly, 77 Md. 396; 26 Atl. 505.

[208] Huston v. Reutlinger, 91 Ky. 333; 15 S. W. 867.

[209] Wicks v. Monahan, 130 N. Y. 232; 29 N. E. 139; affg. 8 N. Y. Supp. 121; Austin v. Searing, 16 N. Y. 112; Wells v. Monahan, 130 N. Y. 232; 29 N. E. 232; affg. 13 N. Y. Supp. 232.

[210] Soc. of Gunmakers v. Fell, Willis' R. 384.

[211] Elsey v. Odd Fellows' Mut. Relief Ass'n, 142 Mass. 224.

[212] See cases collected in Ang. & Ames on Corp., §§ 333, 334, 335 *et seq.*, specifying particular by-laws which are against statute or common law and therefore void. See for further discussion following section.

§ 109. **Must be Reasonable.**—A third essential of all by-laws of every association is that they be reasonable. The power to make by-laws is upon the implied condition that it be exercised with discretion; it follows that all rules which are unequal, vexatious, oppressive, or manifestly detrimental to the interests of the society are void.[213] A prime essential to by-laws is that they be uniform, applying to all members alike.[214] What are to be deemed reasonable by-laws depends upon the objects and purpose of the society, and what might be proper in the case of a social club would be unreasonable if adopted by a benevolent organization.[215] Where the purpose of the society was to afford relief in sickness, and to provide for expenses of the funerals of deceased members and their families, it was held by the Supreme Court of Pennsylvania,[216] that a by-law providing that a widow of a member should not be entitled to benefits if the deceased came to his death because of intemperance was a reasonable regulation. In this case the Court said: "An association of this kind is formed for the benefit of its members. Being a purely voluntary association, it may adopt such reasonable regulations as are conducive to their interests. Now, unless we deny that temperance and regularity of habits have much to do with health and long life, we must concede that the value of the benefits to be derived from such an association depends greatly on the good conduct of its members. Then clearly the members have not only a right to choose their associates, but to stipulate also for the power to prohibit their indulgence in those vices and crimes which multiply disease and death among them and thus diminish the general fund. It is not the purpose of the charter to regulate conduct, and that must be left to divine and human laws. But this law strikes only at those acts which are the causes of disease and death. . . . The by-law therefore appears to be reasonable and to promote the well-being of all the associates collectively and individually." It has been held that a by-law restricting

[213] Ang. & Ames on Corp., § 347; Gosling v. Veley, 12 Q. B. 347; People v. Father Matthew, etc., 41 Mich. 67; Cartan v. Father Matthew, etc., 3 Daly 21.

[214] Supreme Council R. A. v. Brashears, 89 Md. 624; 43 Atl. 866.

[215] Commonwealth v. St. Patrick's Benev. Soc., 2 Binn. 441.

[216] St. Mary's Ben. Soc. v. Burford's Admr., 70 Pa. St. 321.

176

membership in a sick benefit society to those who should not belong to any other society is valid.[217] A by-law of a benevolent society providing that a member in arrears for three months' dues "shall not be entitled to benefits until three months after such arrearages shall have been paid" is unreasonable and inoperative.[218] Such by-laws · have, however, been upheld and the weight of authority is the other way.[219]   In Pennsylvania it was held,[220] that where a society was formed for mutual assistance in time of sickness or inability to labor, a by-law that "no soldier of a standing army, seaman or mariner shall be capable of admission" was held good, and also the further provision that if a member should enlist as a soldier or become a mariner he should forfeit his membership. By-laws compelling members to do what is absurd, or of no benefit to themselves or the society, are unreasonable,[221] and all by-laws conflicting with express statute law or public policy are void as unreasonable. A by-law, to be reasonable, must be adapted to the purposes of the society.[222] A by-law to expel a member for villifying another member is void.[223]   In

[217] Bretzlaff v. Evangelical Lutheran, etc., Soc. 125 Mich. 39; 83 N. W. 1000.   In Screwmen's Benev. Ass'n v. O'Donohoe, 25 Tex. Civ. A. 254; 60 S. W. 683, a by-law was considered which provided that members should join in "labor day" parade but its validity was not expressly passed on.

[218] Brady v. Coachmen's, etc., Ass'n, 39 N. Y. St. 181; 14 N. Y. Supp. 272; citing Cartan v. Soc., 3 Daly 21; Nelligan v. Typographical Union, 2 City Ct. R. 263.   See also Kennedy v. Carpenters', etc., Union, 75 App. Div. 243; 78 N. Y. Supp. 85; Skelly v. Society, etc., 13 Daly 2.

[219] Littleton v. Wells, etc., Council, 98 Md. 453; 56 Atl. 798; Alters v. Journeymen's, etc., Ass'n, 43 W. N. C. 336; Jennings v. Chelsea Div., etc., 59 N. Y. Supp. 862; 28 Misc. 556; Dabura v. Sociedad de la Union (Tex. Civ. A.), 59 S. W. 835; Hart v. Adams, etc., Ass'n, 69 App. Div. 578; 75 N. Y. Supp. 110; Boyd v. Gerant, 82 App. Div. 456; 81 N. Y. Supp. 835; Stanton v. Eccentric Ass'n, 114 N. Y. Supp. 480; 130 App. Div. 125.

[220] Franklin v. Commonwealth, 10 Pa. St. 359; see also *In re* David Mulholland Soc., 10 Phila. 19. ·

[221] Ang. & Ames on Corp., § 348.

[222] People v. Med. Soc. of Erie, 24 Barb. 570; Commonwealth v. German Soc., 15 Pa. St. 251; People v. Med. Soc., etc., 32 N. Y. 189; Dickenson v. Chamber of Commerce, etc., 29 Wis. 49; Ellerbe v. Faust, 119 Mo. 653; 25 S. W. 390; Lysaght v. St. Louis Stonemasons, etc., 55 Mo. App. 538.

[223] Commonwealth v. St. Patrick's Benev. Soc., 2 Binn. 441.

the case just cited, Chief Justice Tilghman said: "The offense of villifying a member, or a private quarrel, is totally unconnected with the affairs of the society and therefore its punishment cannot be necessary for the good government of the corporation."[224] But villifying the officers of the association has been held to be good ground for expulsion.[224a] A by-law must be equal in its operation and apply to all members alike; it cannot exempt certain members from its operations.[225] A by-law which provides for the expulsion of a member without notice is void, because unreasonable;[226] and so are provisions for forfeitures without notice or opportunity to be heard;[227] and by-laws having a retroactive, or *ex post facto* effect.[228] A by-law providing that the trustees first elected shall hold office during life is void.[229] So is a by-law of a beneficiary society making an appeal of a member to the civil courts a cause for expulsion.[230] Or, limiting the time for bring-

[224] Schmidt v. Abraham Lincoln Lodge, 84 Ky. 490; 2 S. W. 156; Mulroy v. Supreme Lodge Knights of Honor, 28 Mo. App. 463; Commonwealth v. German Soc., 15 Pa. St. 251; Evans v. Phila. Club, 50 Pa. St. 107; Erd v. Bavarian, etc., Ass'n, 67 Mich. 233; 34 N. W. 555; Alnutt v. High Court of Foresters, 62 Mich. 110; 28 N. W. 802.

[224a] Del Ponte v. Societa, etc., 27 R. I. 1; 60 Atl. 237.

[225] People v. Father Matthew, etc., 41 Mich. 67; Taylor v. Griswold, 14 N. J. L. 223.

[226] Pulford v. Fire Department, etc., 31 Mich. 458; Fritz v. Muck, 62 How. Pr. 72; Wachtel v. Noah Widows', etc., 84 N. Y. 28; Commonwealth v. Penn. Ben. Ass'n, 2 Serg. & R. 141; Erd v. Bavarian, etc., Ass'n, 67 Mich. 233; 34 N. W. 555; Thibert v. Supreme Lodge K. of H., 78 Minn. 448; 81 N. W. 220; 47 L. R. A. 136.

[227] Roehler v. Mechanics' Aid Soc., 22 Mich. 89; Commonwealth v. Germ. Soc., 15 Pa. St. 251; Queen v. Saddlers' Co., 10 H. of L. Cas. 404; Pulford v. Fire Dept., 31 Mich. 458; Butchers' Ben. Ass'n, Matter of, 38 Pa. St. 298; Green v. African, etc., Soc., 1 Serg. & R. 254.

[228] Pulford v. Fire Dept., 31 Mich. 458; Taylor v. Griswold, 14 N. J. L. 223; Phillips v. Wickham, 1 Paige 590; Howard v. Savannah, etc., Charlt. (Ga.) 173; Kent v. Quicksilver M. Co., 78 N. Y. 159; Graftstrom v. Frost Council, 43 N. Y. Supp. 266; 19 Misc. 180; Berlin v. Eureka Lodge, etc., 132 Cal. 294; 64 Pac. 254.

[229] State v. Standard L. Ass'n, 38 Ohio St. 281.

[230] Sweeney v. Rev. Hugh McLaughlin Ben. Soc., 14 W. N. C. 466. See also State v. Merchants' Exch., 2 Mo. App. 96; State v. Chamber of Commerce, 20 Wis. 63; Supreme Council, etc., v. Forsinger, 125 Ind. 52; 25 N. E. 129.

ing suit, to six months after the right accrued.[231] A by-law authorizing the board of directors to impose fines for specified offenses but prescribing no limit as to the amount of such fines is void.[232] It has been held that a by-law providing that no length of absence or disappearance on the part of the member without proof of actual death shall entitle his beneficiary to recover is not repugnant to law or against public policy though setting aside a rule of evidence.[233] So also is a by-law making suicide a defense to recovery on a benefit certificate.[234] The Supreme Court of Illinois has held[235] that a by-law of a fraternal beneficiary society that a member shall stand suspended after disappearance for a year is not unreasonable as to a certificate issued before its enactment authorizing changes in by-laws. The Court said: "We are of opinion the by-law (section 9) was not invalid as being unreasonable. By-laws of a similar nature have been sustained in Kelly v. Catholic Mutual Benefit Association,[236] and in McGovern v. Brotherhood of Firemen and Engineers.[237] The by-law was no more unreasonable than by-laws passed subsequent to issuing the benefit certificate forfeiting the benefit when the insured changed his employment to certain prohibited occupations or committed suicide, and such by-laws have been sustained."[238] A religious society may make its membership dependent upon good standing in some religious body or upon the member observing the sacraments of the church. As was said by the Supreme Court

[231] Wagner v. Mut. Life Ass'n, 17 App. Div. 13; 44 N. Y. Supp. 862.

[232] Albers v. Merchants' Exchange, 39 Mo. App. 583; Huntsville v. Phelps, 27 Ala. 58; Piper v. Chappell, 14 Mees. & W. 624; Master Stevedores' Ass'n v. Walsh, 2 Daly 14.

[233] Kelly v. Supreme Council, etc., 46 App. Div. 79; 61 N. Y. Supp. 394; Porter v. Home F. Soc., 114 Ga. 937; 41 S. E. 45. But see Sovereign Camp W. O. W. v. Robinson, .. Tex. Civ. A. ..; 187 S. W. 215, where it was held that a by-law providing that a member's disappearance should not be any evidence of his death was invalid as in contradiction of statutory law. See *post*, § 648.

[234] Tisch v. Protected Home Circle, 72 Ohio St. 233; 74 N. E. 188.

[235] Apitz v. Supreme Lodge Knights and Ladies of Honor, .. Ill. ..; 113 N. E. 63.

[236] 46 App. Div. 79; 61 N. Y. Supp. 394.

[237] 21 O. C. D. 243, affirmed without an opinion in 85 Ohio St. 460; 98 N. E. 1128.

[238] See *post*, § 648.

179

of Missouri:[239] "He (the member) expressly represented as a
condition to his admission that he was a member of the Roman
Catholic church, and that he observed its laws and would continue to do so while he remained a member of the corporation,
and that if he should cease to conform to the laws of the church
in the particular mentioned in the answer, he expressly agreed
that the corporation might suspend or expel him and thereby
exclude him from its benefits. Under the constitution and laws
of this State a man cannot be coerced into observing the sacraments of any church, and even if he should enter into a solemn
contract to do so, he is free to break the contract and for breaking
it, he cannot be deprived of any right that he has independent
of it. But, if by contract a special benefit is created for him,
he cannot break the contract and have the benefit too." A by-law
providing for expulsion if the member joins any society not approved by the Catholic church is valid.[240] A benefit certificate
providing that it shall be void if the member belonged to a secret
non-Catholic aid association, is not forfeited by his membership
in a secret aid association open to Roman Catholics and not dis-
approved by that Church.[241] The following by-laws have been
held to be reasonable: that a member should not belong to any
other society;[242] that members in order to entitle them to receive
benefits must provide themselves with uniforms;[243] that non-payment of an assessment shall *ipso facto* operate as expulsion;[244]

[239] Franta v. Bohemian R. C. Cent. Union, 164 Mo. 304; 63 S. W. 1100;
54 L. R. A. 723, and to the same effect is Hitter v. St. Aloysius Soc., 4
Ky. Law 871; 27 Alb. L. Jour. 401. The Supreme Court of Iowa in Matt.
v. Roman Cath. M. P. Soc., 70 Ia. 455, doubted whether a by-law providing that if a member should neglect his "Easter duties" he should
thereby forfeit all his rights and interest in the society was valid. See
post, § 580.

[240] Mazurkiewicz v. St. Adelbertus Aid Soc., 137 Mich. 145; 86 N. W.
543; 54 L. R. A. 727.

[241] Geronime v. German Roman Catholic Aid Ass'n, 127 Minn. 247; 149
N. W. 291.

[242] Bretzlaff v. Evangelical, etc., Lutheran Soc., 135 Mich. 39; 83 N. W.
1000; Neto v. Conselho, etc., 18 Cal. App. 234; 122 Pac. 973.

[243] Solari v. Italian Soc. of Col., 211 Mass. 382; 97 N. E. 765. .

[244] Nelson v. Modern Brotherhood of America, 78 Neb. 429; 110 N. W.
1008.

that notice of an assessment may be given by mail;[245] that misstatement of age should be ground for expulsion and the decision of the trial committee shall be final;[246] that the members shall be obedient to the mandate of the superior body;[247] that a relief assessment may be levied and payment of the same shall be compulsory.[248] Where the object of an association is to elevate the moral and social standing of its members and give aid in case of reverses, a by-law providing for a wedding present is not *ultra vires*,[249] but a by-law denying the right to resort to the civil courts until the remedies are exhausted in the order, is invalid where the highest tribunal does not meet for three years.[250] A by-law of a railroad relief society which precludes representatives of the deceased member from benefits unless her claim for damages is released, is unreasonable.[251']

§ 110. Construction of By-Laws Question for the Court.— The construction of by-laws, when the facts are undisputed, is in all cases a question for the court.[251a] In construing by-laws courts will interpret them reasonably; not scrutinizing their terms for the purpose of making them void, nor holding them invalid for slight or trivial reasons; the unreasonableness should clearly appear.[252] While the courts have no visitorial power to determine whether the by-laws of a voluntary association are reasonable, they may determine whether they have been adopted by the rule

[245] Duffy v. Fidelity Mut. Life Ins. Co., 142 N. C. 103; 55 S. E. 79; 143 N. C. 697; 55 S. E. 1047; 77 L. R. A. (N. S.) 238.

[246] Marcus v. National Council K. & L. of S., 123 Minn. 145; 143 N. W. 265.

[247] Commonwealth v. Heilman, 241 Pa. 374; 88 Atl. 666.

[248] Ward v. David, etc., Lodge, 90 Miss. 116; 43 Sou. 302.

[249] Merim v. Minsker, Young Men's, etc., Ass'n, 147 N. Y. Supp. 440.

[250] Lindahl Sup. Court I. O. F., 100 Minn. 87; 110 N. W. 358; see also Markham v. Supreme Court I. O. F., 78 Neb. 295; 110 N. W. 638.

[251] Chicago, B. & Q. Ry. Co. v. Hendricks, 125 Ill. App. 580.

[251a] Clarkson v. Supreme Lodge K. P., 99 S. C. 134; 82 S. E. 1043.

[252] Genest v. L. Union, etc., 141 Mass. 417; Paxon v. Sweet, 1 Green, 196; State v. Overton, 24 N. J. L. 440; Queen v. Saddlers' Co., 10 H. of L. Cas. 404; People v. Sailors' Snug Harbor, 5 Abb. Pr. (N. S.) 119; Butchers' Ben. Ass'n, 38 Pa. St. 298; People v. Med. Soc. Erie, 32 N. Y. 187; Fritz v. Muck, 62 How. Pr. 72; Commonwealth v. Worcester, 3 Pick. 462; St. Mary's Ben. Soc. v. Burford's Admr., 70 Pa. St. 321; People v. Father

agreed upon by the members.[253] If associations are organized for benevolent purposes, courts will not construe their constitutions and by-laws so as to favor the forfeiture of the rights of the members or those dependent on them.[254] By-laws will be construed in reference to the statutes so as to give them effect if possible.[255] In the absence of express provisions showing an intention to the contrary by-laws will be construed to operate prospectively only. As the Supreme Court of Iowa said:[256] "The articles and by-laws as amended cannot be treated as retrospective in their operation. Mere silence as to the effect of revision and amendment of the constitution and by-laws will not warrant the inference that any change wrought will limit or extend the obligation heretofore created by the issuance of certificates of membership. Statutes are construed so as to give them a prospective operation, unless the intention that they operate retrospectively is clear and undoubted, and it is not perceived why the same canon of construction should not be applied to the rules adopted by a mutual insurance association for the transaction of its business and the government of its members." The same principle is laid down in other cases.[257] A court will, as a rule, construe the by-laws as the members and officers or authorities of the

Matthew, etc., 41 Mich. 67; Poultney v. Bachman, 62 How. Pr. 466; Pulford v. Fire Dept., 31 Mich. 458; Supreme Lodge K. of P. v. Knight, 117 Ind. 489; 20 N. E. 479; Ang. & Ames on Corp., § 357; Roxbury Lodge v. Hecking, 60 N. J. L. 439; 38 Atl. 693; 64 Am. St. R. 596.

[253] Green v. Felton, 42 Ind. App. 675; 84 N. E. 166.

[254] Schunck v. Gegenzeiten, etc., 44 Wis. 369; Erdmann v. Mut. Ins. Co., etc., 44 Wis. 376; Ballou v. Gile, 50 Wis. 614; Schillinger v. Boes, 9 Ky. L. 18. Indeed this principle is laid down in all cases bearing upon the validity of assessments and forfeiture for their non-payment. See post, § 484, et seq.

[255] Elsey v. Odd Fellows, 142 Mass. 224; Am. Legion of Honor v. Perry, 140 Mass. 580.

[256] Carnes v. Iowa Traveling Men's Ass'n, 108 Ia. 281; 76 N. W. 683.

[257] Knights Templars v. Masons, etc., Co. v. Jarman, 187 U. S. 197; Spencer v. Grand Lodge, 22 Misc. 147; 48 N. Y. Supp. 590; affd. 65 N. Y. Supp. 1146; Grand Lodge, etc., v. Stumpf, 24 Tex. Civ. App. 309; 58 S. W. 840; Hobbs v. Ass'n, 82 Ia. 107; 47 N. W. 983; 11 L. R. A. 299; Sieverts v. Ass'n, 95 Ia. 710; 64 N. W. 671; Benton v. Brotherhood, etc., 146 Ill. 590; 34 N. E. 939; Guthrie v. Supreme Tent K. O. T. M., 4 Cal. App. 184; 87

order construe them.[258] The by-laws will be considered as an entirety and a claim cannot be based on one section to the exclusion of another.[259] The construction of by-laws relating to sick benefits may be a mixed one of law and fact.[260]

§ 111. **What is Bad as a By-Law May be Good as a Contract: Exception.**—What is bad as a by-law, as against common right, may, however, be good as a contract, since, as a learned writer expresses it:[261] ''A man may part with a common right voluntarily, of which it would be impolitic and unjust to deprive him by a by-law passed without his assent, or perhaps knowledge, by those who would not consult his individual interests.''[262] The unanimity of the vote of those present at a meeting will not bind or affect the rights of those absent where the vote is unauthorized.[263] A by-law may be invalid only in part, as, for example, one which provides for the expulsion of a member, without giving him the opportunity of defending himself against the charge upon which his expulsion is based, is not altogether null and void but only so to the extent that it deprives the member of a hearing from which he might derive a benefit possibly, and where it conclusively appears that no such result has followed its enforcement the existence of such a provision in it will not invalidate the proceedings taken under it.[264] Yet certain rights are esteemed so sacred that they cannot even be parted with by contract, because to permit such action would be against public policy. It has accordingly been held that a by-law prohibiting members

Pac. 405; Hayes v. Grand Ben. Union, 55 Pa. Super. Ct., 142; Grant v. Independent Order, etc., 97 Miss. 182; 52 Sou. 698; Kaemmerer v. Kaemmerer, 23 Ill. 154; 83 N. E. 133.

[258] Kalinski v. Supreme Lodge, 57 Fed. 348; Supreme Lodge K. of P. v. Kalinski, 163 U. S. 289.

[259] Badesch v. Congregation, etc., 23 Misc. 160; 50 N. Y. Supp. 958; Thomas v. Societa Italiana, etc., 10 Misc. 746; 31 N. Y. Supp. 815.

[260] Montano v. Missanellese Soc., 130 N. Y. Supp: 455; 72 Misc. 515.

[261] Ang. & Ames on Corp., § 342.

[262] Austin v. Searing, 16 N. Y. 112; Goodard v. Merchants' Exchange, 79 Mo. 609; 9 Mo. App. 290; Purdy v. Bankers' Life Ass'n, 101 Mo. App. 91; 74 S. W. 486.

[263] Stetson v. Kempton, 13 Mass. 282.

[264] Berkhout v. Supreme Council Royal Arcanum, 62 N. J. L. 103; 43 Atl. 1.

from resorting to the courts, especially where a property right is involved, is void;[265] and a by-law of a mutual beneficial society cannot oust the courts of jurisdiction to determine whether a member of it has been expelled for sufficient cause. Neither can it make an appeal to the civil courts a cause of expulsion.[266]

§ 112. **Enforcement of By-Laws—Penalties for Violation— Fines.**—The power to make by-laws implies the right to enforce them by appropriate penalties. No general rule can be laid down as to what is a reasonable penalty; this must be determined by the nature of the offense. The courts in each case will determine the reasonableness of the penalty. Without going extensively into the subject, it may be said the penalty must be a sum certain; the specification in the charter of one method of enforcing by-laws is an exclusion of other methods; the offender cannot be imprisoned or his property forfeited for any violation of rules, nor can the offender be disfranchised. The penalty can only be given to the society whose regulations are infringed. In a Michigan case[267] the Supreme Court of that State discussed the doctrines of the law on this subject somewhat elaborately and in the discussion said: "It is well settled that the right to levy burdens on the members is governed, to some extent, at least, by the occasion for them.[268] As the original constitution contained no authority to forfeit membership, the power must be derived elsewhere. The charter contains no such power. It is held in Matter of Long Island R. R. Co.[269] that there can be no power to impose forfeitures unless granted by clear legislative enactment. No such power is consistent with ancient right and it cannot be obtained from anything but the sovereignty.[270] The only implied means

---

[265] Supreme Council, etc., v. Garrigus, 104 Ind. 133; Bauer v. Sampson Lodge, 102 Ind. 262; Mulroy v. K. of H., 28 Mo. App. 463; Scott v. Avery, 5 H. of L. Cas. 811; Ins. Co. v. Morse, 20 Wall. 445; Austin v. Searing, 16 N. Y. 112; Supreme Council, etc., v. Forsinger, 125 Ind. 52; 25 N. E. 129.

[266] Sweeney v. Rev. Hugh McLaughlin Ben. Soc., 14 W. N. C. 466.

[267] Pulford v. Fire Dept., 31 Mich. 458.

[268] London Pipe Co. v. Woodroffe, 7 B. & C. 838.

[269] 19 Wend. 37.

[270] Westcott v. Minnesota Mining Co., 23 Mich. 145; Kyd on Corp., 109; Ang. & Ames on Corp., §§ 360, 340.

for the enforcement of corporate charges and penalties is by action. Summary means and methods unknown to the common law must be authorized by express authority. And it would not be reasonable to enforce a pecuniary obligation or penalty by means disproportionate to its importance. The law of the land is made the test for analogies in cases where it affords analogies, as is recognized in the case cited and elsewhere. It is equally abhorrent to all reason to allow a forfeiture to be enforced on an alleged default, without notice and hearing, or an opportunity to be heard.[271] If any expulsion could be had for such a cause the by-laws themselves expressly require that there shall be a trial before the trustees, who for this purpose act as a corporate tribunal. But inasmuch as our general corporation law has always limited the penalties for violations of by-laws, expulsion cannot be allowed for any mere infraction of a by-law."[272] A new constitution repeals the old and the penalties imposed by the latter fall with it if omitted from the new.[273]

§ 113. **Distinction Between Voluntary Associations Where No Property Right is Involved, and Corporations in Regard to By-Laws.**—If no property right be involved a distinction is made, in respect to by-laws and regulations between incorporated societies and those which are voluntary associations. In the former the by-laws must be reasonable, but in the latter the members are bound by their duly adopted by-laws and regulations, whether they be reasonable or not; provided, however, they are not in conflict with the law of the land, or public policy, and the courts will only examine whether they have been adopted in the way agreed on by the members.[274] In Kehlenbeck v. Logeman,[275] the Court said: "It has been held in this court upon more than one

[271] Roehler v. Mechanics' Aid Soc., 22 Mich. 89; Commonwealth v. Germ. Soc., 15 Pa. St. 251; Queen v. Saddler's Co., 10 H. of L. Cas. 404; Com. v. Penn. Benev. Ass'n, 2 Serg. & R. 141.

[272] Ang. & Ames on Corp., § 360; Erd v. Bavarian, etc., Ass'n, 67 Mich. 233; 34 N. W. 555; Otto v. Journeymen Tailors', etc., Union, 75 Cal. 308; 17 Pac. 217.

[273] Bachman v. Harrington, 102 N. Y. Supp. 406; 52 Misc. 26.

[274] Elsas v. Alford, 1 City Ct. Rep. 123; Manning v. San Antonio Club, 63 Tex. 166; McDonald v. Ross-Lewin, 29 Hun. 87.

[275] 10 Daly 447.

occasion in respect to the by-laws of a voluntary association the court has no visitorial power and cannot determine whether they are reasonable or unreasonable, and the only question which it can examine is whether they have been adopted in the way which' has been agreed upon by the members of the association. . . . The association being a voluntary one, as has above been stated, this court has no power to pass upon the question as to whether such rules and regulations as they choose to adopt for the guidance of their own affairs are reasonable or unreasonable.''[276] It is doubtful, however, if this rule applies in all cases, especially those in which property rights are involved or principles of public policy are violated. Agreements to refer any controversy to arbitrators have not always been upheld,[277] especially when harsh or involving forfeitures.[278]

§ 114. **Societies Have a Right to the Service of Their Members.**—It is a general rule that all societies have the right to the service of all their members subject to the contract of the articles of association and the modifying circumstances of the case. The principle applies to corporations, and is thus laid down by an admitted authority:[279] ''A corporation has a right to the service of all its members, and may make by-laws to enforce it. It may thus impose a penalty on members eligible to an office, who refuse to accept it; or who refuse to take the oath appointed by law, as a necessary qualification for holding it; and on members who refuse to attend the corporate meetings. Nor, it would seem, is a by-law of this nature less valid, though it require that the person accepting the office shall pay a fee on his admission; and the court will not scrutinize the reasonableness of the fee, since the members of the corporation have assented to the reasonableness of the

---

[276] White v. Brownell, 2 Daly 329; Hyde v. Woods, 2 Saw. 655; Innes v. Wylie, 1 Car. & K. 262; Fritz v. Muck, 62 How. Pr. 74.

[277] Heath v. N. Y. Gold Exch., 7 Abb. Pr. (N. S.) 251; 38 How. Pr. 168; Savannah Cotton Exchange v. State, 51 Ga. 668. See *post*, § 622.

[278] Bauer v. Sampson Lodge, 102 Ind. 262; Supreme Council v. Garrigus, 104 Ind. 133; Austin v. Searing, 16 N. Y. 112; Mulroy v. Supreme Lodge K. of H., 28 Mo. App. 463; Goodman v. Jedidjah Lodge, 67 Md. 117; Gray v. Christian Soc., 137 Mass. 329; s. c. 50 Am. Rep. 310. See *post*, § 622.

[279] Ang. & Ames on Corp., § 352.

amount; which raises a presumption that under their peculiar circumstances it is reasonable, or, at least, that they deem it so.''

§ 115. **Amendment or Repeal of By-Laws.**—Generally speaking the same body which can make by-laws has the power to amend or repeal them, subject to the additional restrictions and limitations of the by-laws themselves, as well as those of the articles of association or charter, and the implied conditions of being reasonable and not contrary to law.[280] The general rule as to amendment of by-laws has been well stated by the Supreme Court of Mississippi[281] as follows: ''Now, these constitutions are of no higher dignity than by-laws. All are, alike, the creations of the corporation, and the power which creates can alter or repeal. So far, therefore, as the mere mode of enacting the law—the suicide amendment—is concerned, it must necessarily follow that the adoption of the suicide amendment by the resolution was a repeal of the stringent provisions of the supreme constitution referred to, since the power which first enacted them was competent to repeal them by the passage of any law in a different mode. The valid passage of a law by the Supreme Lodge, in any mode not prohibited by its charter or the general law of the land, is necessarily a repeal of any other mode previously prescribed by the same Supreme Lodge,—the same source of power. The authorities make this perfectly clear. In Supreme Lodge v. Knight,[282] it is said: 'Charters are not created by the act of the corporation or association, but are granted by the sovereign power of the State. A constitution of a voluntary association or a corporation is nothing more than a by-law under an inappropriate name. The power that can enact a by-law, whether called a constitution or not, can alter or abrogate it, unless some higher rule restrains or prohibits a change or repeal. When the authorities speak of a charter they mean an essentially different thing from a law or constitution of the association's own creation. What counsel call a charter is nothing more than a code of laws established,

280 Morawetz on Corp., § 499; Ang. and Ames on Corp., § 329; Dick v. General Assembly, Order of Amaranth, 130 Mich. 215; 113 N. W. 1125.

281 Dornes v. Supreme Lodge, K. P., 75 Misc. 466; 23 Sou. 191. See also Supreme Lodge, etc., v. Adams, 68 N. H. 236; 48 Atl. 380; Toomey v. Supreme Lodge, K. P., 74 Mo. App. 507.

282 117 Ind. at page 495, 20 N. E. 483.

187

not by the sovereign power of the government, but by the creature
of that power, the corporation or association. The most that can
justly be said is that the later by-laws are in conflict with the
earlier. There is therefore no clashing between corporate utter-
ances and charter·provisions.' And this was said by Elliot, C. J.,
speaking of provisions of the supreme constitution of the order
itself. In Richardson v. Society,[283] the Court said: '.Complaint
is made that the amendment of By-law 13, requiring a two-thirds ·
vote for the admission of new members, was not properly and
legally enacted, because its passage was not obtained by a vote
of two-thirds of those present, according to By-law 12,. requiring
a vote of two-thirds of the members present to alter or amend the
by-laws of the society. . . . By-law 12 was no part of the charter
or constitution of the society, and not a law for the guidance of
its officers and agents. It was an enactment made by one meeting of the society to govern the proceedings of future meetings,
and was inoperative beyond the pleasure of the society acting
by a majority vote at any regular meeting. The power of the
society, derived from its charter and the laws under which it
was organized, to enact by-laws, is continuous, residing in all
regular meetings of the society so long as it exists. Any meeting
could, by a majority vote, modify or repeal the law of a previous
meeting, and no meeting could bind a subsequent one by irrepealable acts or rules of procedure. The power to enact is a power
to repeal; and a by-law requiring a two-thirds vote of members
present to alter or amend the laws of the society may itself be
altered, amended or repealed by the same power which enacted
it.[284] The society, by a majority vote, might amend or repeal
By-law 12. By a like vote they might adopt any mode for the
admission of members. This is directly in point. Mr. Thompson,
in Commentaries on the Law of Corporations (Vol. 1, Sec. 943)
lays down the same rule, saying: 'If the charter is silent as to
the formalities to be observed, a by-law may be adopted by acts
as well as by words.' '[285] The adoption of a new constitution

[283] 58 N. H., at page 188.

[284] Ang. & A. Corp 459; Com. v. Mayor, etc., 5 Watts, 152; 155; Christ
Church v. Pope, 8 Gray 140, 142.

[285] To the same effect is Mr. Freeman in his learned note to Sayre v.
Ass'n, 85 Am. Dec., at page 618.

differing from the old is a repeal of the old.[286]   The simultaneous. repeal and re-enactment in terms, or in substance, of parts of a by-law of a fraternal association preserve without interruption the re-enacted provisions of the original by-law.[287]   It has been said, however,[288] that an amendment made without notice to the members is unreasonable.   The by-laws of an association not being regularly amended, the adoption of a by-law providing for a new governing body does not change the existing order of things.[289] Where the by-laws contained no provision for amendment it was held that a majority of the members could amend and the others by silence might acquiesce.[290]   The body of members at an annual meeting may adopt a rule in the nature of a by-law, which under the delegated power to the directors to make by-laws the latter would not have, even though it seems to impair vested rights.[291] Where the charter of a corporation expired in 1890 and was renewed in 1896 it was held that by-laws adopted in the interim were void.[292]   A by-law of an unincorporated society is not repealed by the adoption of a new constitution making no reference to the by-law.[293]   A by-law cannot be repealed by non-user.[294] In order to be valid amendments must be adopted at a legal meeting of the association.[295]   The question of vested rights often arises in determining the validity of changes in by-laws; while this question will be considered later on,[296] yet we may here say that although generally speaking it is true that no by-law can be amended or repealed so as to affect an existing cause of action or impair vested rights, and although a by-law that will disturb

[286] Supreme Tent K. O. T. M. v. Altman, 134 Mo. App. 363; 114 S. W. 1107; Bachman v. Harrington, 102 N. Y. Supp. 406; 52 Misc. 26.

[287] Quick v. M. W. A., 91 Neb. 106; 135 N. W. 433.

[288] Lewin v. Koerner Ben. Ass'n, 112 N. Y. Supp. 508; 6 Misc. 576.

[289] Moore v. Hillsdale Co. Tel. Co., 171 Mich. 388; 137 N. W. 241.

[290] Kehlenbeck v. Norddeutcher Bund, 10 Del. 447.

[291] Borgards v. Farmers' Mut. Ins. Co., 79 Mich. 440; 44 N. W. 856.

[292] Supreme Lodge K. of P. v. Weller, 93 Va. 605; 25 S. E. 891.

[293] Herman v. Plummer, 20 Wash. 363; 55 Pac. 315.

[294] Yeaton v. Somersworth Grange, etc., 77 N. H. 332; 91 Atl. 868.

[295] Metropolitan, etc., Ass'n v. Windover, 137 Ill. 417; 27 N. E. 538.

[296] *Post*, § 228 *et seq.*

vested rights is unreasonable,[297] yet where the member agrees to obey and conform to subsequently enacted laws, as well as those existing at the time, or the by-laws themselves contain provision for their alteration, a change regularly made and not unfair of itself will be valid and binding although it may seem to impair vested rights.[298]   Of course a member may expressly consent to be bound by the amendment, in which case he is estopped to dispute it.[299]

§ 116.   **By-Laws Relating to Sick Benefits.**—Many benefit societies provide in their by-laws for a certain sum to be paid to a member in case of his sickness. The question has sometimes arisen as to the respective rights and liabilities of the member and the society in regard to these benefits. In all these cases it has been held that the làws of the society are to be considered in determining the right, and they are to govern unless contrary to municipal law. Where no definite amount is fixed for the benefit, but it is in the nature of a donation, the member has no right of action against the lodge.[300]   In St. Patrick's Male Society v. McVey,[301] the Supreme Court of Pennsylvania held that a member of a beneficial society does not stand in the relation of a creditor

[297] Kent v. Quicksilver Mining Co., 78 N. Y. 159; Morrison v. Wisconsin Odd Fellows, etc., 59 Wis. 162; Gundlach v. Germania Mech. Ass'n, 4 Hun. 339; 49 How. Pr. 190; Pellazino v. Germ. Catholic, etc., Soc., 16 Cin. L. B. 27; Becker v. Berlin Ben. Soc., 144 Pa. St. 232; 22 Atl. 699; Hobbs v. Iowa Ben. Ass'n, 82 Ia. 107; 47 N. W. 983; Wist v. Grand Lodge A. O. U. W., 22 Ore. 271; 29 Pac. 610; Thibert v. Supreme Lodge K. of H., 78 Minn. 448; 81 N. W. 220; 47 L. R. A. 136; Brotherhood of Painters, etc., v. Moore, 36 Ind. App. 580; 76 N. E. 262; Van Alten v. Modern Brotherhood, 132 Ia. 232; 108 N. W. 313; Johnson v. Grand Fountain, etc., 135 N. C. 385; 47 S. E. 463.

[298] Poultney v. Bachman, 31 Hun. 49; reversing 62 How. Pr. 466; Stohr v. San Francisco Mus. F. Soc., 82 Cal. 557; 22 Pac. 425; Pepe v. City, etc., Soc., 3 R. Ch. 47; Davis v. Second Chatham, etc., Soc., 61 L. T. R. 80; Supreme Lodge, etc., v. Knight, 117 Ind. 489; 20 N. E. 483; Ellerbe v. Faust, 119 Mo. 653; 25 S. W. 390; 25 I. R. A. 149; see post, § 227. As to notice see Warnehold v. Grand Lodge A. O. U. W., 83 Ia. 23; 48 N. W. 1067. As to proof of by-laws, Greenspan v. American Star Order, 20 N. Y. Supp. 945; and ante, § 103.

[299] Penachio v. Saati Soc., 67 N. Y. Supp. 146; 33 Misc. 751.

[300] Daburn v. Sociedad, etc., Tex., 59 S. W. 835.

[301] 92 Pa. St. 510.

to it, and can only claim such benefits as are prescribed by the by-laws existing at the time he applies for relief; that it is wrong to treat the by-law, in existence when the plaintiff became a member, as part of a contract unalterable except with his consent. "It is manifest," said the Court, "that the plaintiff ought not to have been allowed to recover under a by-law which had been repealed before he fell sick." In a case in New York,[302] it was held that in these societies the rights of the members may be taken away by an alteration of the constitution without notice unless the constitution provides for it. In this case the Court said: "The plaintiff was bound by these changes. The charter gave no right of action. The constitution and by-laws were liable to change. The changes were made in the way pointed out by the constitution and laws. . . . No notice was required to be given to plaintiff. The by-laws provide for none, and they do provide for a change by resolution proposed one week before it could be passed. It was doubtless designed that this delay would operate to give notice to all persons interested. A notice to all the members would be a great burden." In the same case it was said that whatever contract there was between the parties arose under the charter, constitution and by-laws of the society.

In a well-considered case[303] the Supreme Court of California held that where both the laws of the State and the by-laws of the society, which was incorporated, gave the right to repeal, alter or amend the by-laws, it was not a breach of the contract to amend a by-law, which provided that a member in case of sickness should receive ten dollars per week by limiting such allowance to a certain number of weeks thereafter though a member was sick at the time of such an amendment. In discussing the phrase "vested rights" the Court says: "In view of this power to alter the contract, it cannot be said that the defendant could not alter its by-laws in any respect. The respondent argues, however, that it

[302] McCabe v. Father Matthew, etc., Soc., 24 Hun. 149. See also Poultney v. Bachman, 31 Hun. 49, reversing 62 How. Pr. 466.

[303] Stohr v. San Francisco Mus. Fund Soc., 82 Cal. 557; 22 Pac. 1125. Also Bowie v. Grand Lodge, etc., 99 Cal. 392; 34 Pac. 103. See also Ellerbe v. Faust, 119 Mo. 653; 25 S. W. 390; 25 L. R. A. 149; Berg v. Badenser, etc., Verein, 90 App. Div. 474; 86 N. Y. Supp. 429; Pain v. Societe St. Jean Baptiste, 172 Mass. 319; 52 N. E. 502.

had no power to alter them so as to impair a vested right.   This
must be conceded, but we do not think that the new by-law pur-
ported to impair a vested right.   The term 'vested right' is often
loosely used.   In one sense every right is vested.   If a man has
a right at all, it must be vested in him; otherwise how could it
be a right?   The moment a contract is made a right is vested in
each party to have it remain unaltered, and to have it performed.
The term, however, is frequently used to designate a right which
has become so fixed that it is not subject to be divested without
the consent of the owner, as contradistinguished from rights which
are subject to be divested without his consent.   Now a right,
whether it be of such a fixed character or not, must be a right
to something; and when a man talks vaguely of his vested right,
it conduces to clearness to ask: 'A vested right to what?'   In
the present case the plaintiff can have no right to have the contract remain unchanged, because, as we have seen, the contract
itself provided that it may be changed.   Nor has he a right to
remain unaffected by any change that may be made; for, if such
right be common to all the members, it is merely another way of
saying that no change can be made; and, if the right be not
common to the other members, it would be to assert a privilege
or superiority over them, of which there is no pretense.   If the
plaintiff has any right which is so fixed that it is not subject to
change, we think it can only be to the fruits which ripened before
the change was made; in other words, to such sums as became
due before the new by-law was adopted.   To express it differently,
the change could not be retroactive.   This is all that we think can
be meant by 'vested right' in a case like the present.   Now, under
the contract, nothing was due before the sickness actually took
place.   Benefits do not accrue for future sickness.   The right of
the plaintiff to benefits for future sickness is not different in its
nature from the right of the well members to benefits for future
sickness.   In the one case the members have a right to future
payment in case they become sick; in the other the plaintiff has
a right to future payments in case he continues sick.   And if
there was no power to change the by-law in the one case, there
was no power to change it in the other, which is equivalent to
saying that there was no power to change it at all.   The cases
where a specific sum becomes due upon the happening of a certain

event, as upon death, are not like the present. In such cases an alteration in the contract cannot be made after the fact; for that would be to make that not due which had already become due. We are inclined to think that the foregoing would apply if the by-law under consideration had specified that the weekly payments were to continue as long as the sickness continued. But it does not so specify. The time during which the payments were to continue is left indefinite. The substance of the contract is, in our opinion, that, in case of sickness, the member is to receive weekly payments for an indefinite period of sickness, subject to the power of the defendant to change the provision authorizing such payments so far as future payments are concerned.'' But these views have not always been followed.[304]

§ 117. **Construction of Same.**—Like other by-laws, those relating to benefits must have a reasonable construction and, if possible, harmonize with the constitution of the society.[305] Thus, is was held[306] that where the by-laws provided that a member who "became incapable of working, in consequence of sickness or accident," should receive from the society a certain sum per week, the member by trying to resume work and working two days during the period of sickness did not debar himself from receiving benefits during the time, as it could not be said as a matter of law that he was not "incapable of working" within the meaning of the by-law. The word, "year" refers to the period of a year, not a calendar year.[307] If possible the language of the by-laws will be construed so as to avoid a forfeiture.[308] The by-laws relating to sick benefits will have a liberal construction, thus a provision releasing the society from liability in case

[304] Pellazzino v. Germ. Cath. Soc., 16 Cin. L. Bul. 27; Gundlach v. Germania Mech. Ass'n, 4 Hun. 339; Bauer v. Sampson Lodge, 102 Ind. 262; Kent v. Quicksilver Mining Co., 78 N. Y. 159; Becker v. Berlin Soc., 144 Pa. St. 232; 22 Atl. 699; Hobbs v. Ia. Ben. Ass'n, 82 Ia. 107; 47 N. W. 983; Wist v. Grand Lodge A. O. U. W., 22 Ore. 271; 29 Pac. 610; State v. Monti (N. J.), 36 Atl. 666. For definition of paralysis see Yarborough v. National Ben. Soc., 88 Mo. App. 465.

[305] Leahy v. Ancient Order, etc., 54 Ill. App. 108.

[306] Genest v. L'Union St. Joseph, 141 Mass. 417.

[307] Thibault v. St. Jean, etc., Ass'n, 21 R. I. 157; 42 Atl. 518.

[308] Connelly v. Shamrock Benev. Soc., 43 Mo. App. 283. See also *post,* § 554.

of paralysis does not apply where the paralysis is a sequence of a disease,[309] and the society will be liable for sick benefits although the illness is caused by the indiscretion of a member, if there is no provision in the constitution, or by-laws, releasing the society from liability for any such cause.[310] A lodge cannot make an unreasonable regulation in regard to benefits, for example, that a member receiving benefits should forfeit them if absent from his home after eight o'clock in the evening.[311] A society cannot deprive a member of benefits by expelling him.[312] A provision that the member should not be entitled to funeral benefits unless the society conducts the funeral is valid,[313] and the property of the lodge is a trust fund against which claims for benefits are to be allowed.[314] A benefit society is not liable for interest until the claim is rejected.[315] The right to sick benefits is one which survives and in case of the member's death the administrator may sue for the amount.[316]

If under the by-laws a member is entitled to the service of a physician and such service is denied, he may employ a physician, selected by himself, and recover for his services.[317] A member cannot become entitled to benefits while in arrears by paying up.[318] By-laws providing that members in arrears will not be entitled to benefits until after a certain time has elapsed after the payment are reasonable and valid.[319] A beneficial certificate insuring against sickness, and not extending to surgical

---

[309] Yarborough v. National Ben. Soc., 88 Mo. App. 465.

[310] Wuerthner v. Workingmen's Ben. Soc., 121 Mich. 90; 79 N. W. 921.

[311] Wuerthner v. Workingmen's Ben. Soc., *supra.*

[312] Royal Fraternal Union v. Stahl, Tex. Civ. App. 126 S. W. 920; Strauss v. Thoman, 111 N. Y. Supp. 745; 60 Misc. 72. See also Richardson v. Brotherhood, etc., 70 Wash. 76; 126 Pac. 82; 41 L. R. A. (N. S.) 320; Westfall v. Bedford Lodge, etc., 156 Iowa 615; 137 N. W. 931.

[313] Weisher v. Erste Bornslawer, etc., 132 N. Y. Supp. 430.

[314] Piries v. First Russian, etc., Soc., 83 N. J. Eq. 29; 89 Atl. 1036.

[315] Dary v. Providence, etc., 27 R. I. 377; 62 Atl. 53.

[316] Pearson v. Anderburg, 28 Utah 495; 80 Pac. 307.

[317] Geraci v. Italian, etc., 107 N. Y. Supp. 557; 56 Misc. 653.

[318] Page v. National Council, etc., 153 N. C. 404; 69 S. E. 414.

[319] Jennings v. Chelsea, etc., 59 N. Y. Supp. 862; 28 Misc. 556; Hess v. Johnson, 58 N. Y. Supp. 983; 41 App. Div. 465; Kennedy v. Carpenters' Local Union, 78 N. Y. Supp. 85; 75 App. Div. 243; Burns v. Manhattan, etc., 92 N. Y. Supp. 846; 102 App. Div. 467.

treatment not necessitated by injury, does not exempt the association from liability for benefits accruing after a surgical operation which was necessitated as a means of curing the sickness . and which did not cause any sickness distinct from that existing previously. Provisions for benefits in case of ''sickness'' do not extend to a case of bodily injury not affecting the general health of the person injured.[320] But insanity has been held to be sickness and disease.[321] And so with blindness produced as the result of injuries.[322] And so with a surgical operation.[323] But a bite of a dog is not sickness.[323a]

§ 118. Proceedings to Obtain Sick Benefits: Rights of Members to Resort to Civil Courts.—A member of a benefit society must, in applying for benefits under its by-laws, follow the procedure therein prescribed.[324] He is not excused from such compliance because of insanity.[325] A local lodge cannot impose conditions in addition to those imposed by the general association.[326] It is a well-established rule that before resorting to the civil courts for redress a member must exhaust all the remedies provided by the society by appeal or otherwise.[327] It has been held,

[320] Kelly v. Ancient Order of Hibernians, 9 Daly 289.

[321] Burton v. Eyden, 8 Q. B. 295; Kelly v. Ancient Order Hibernians, supra; McCullough v. Expressmen's M. B. Ass'n, 133 Pa. St. 142; 19 Atl. 355; Robillard v. Society St. Jean, etc., 21 R. I. 348; and 142 (Part II) 43 Atl. 635; 45 L. R. A. 559.

[322] Moge v. Societe, etc., 167 Mass. 298; 45 N. E. 749; 35 L. R. A. 736.

[323] Lord v. National Prot. Soc., 129 Mich. 335; 88 N. W. 876.

[323a] Villone v. Guardia Perticare, 114 N. Y. Supp. 801; 62 Misc. 257.

[324] Field v. National Council K. & L. of S., 64 Neb. 226; 89 N. W. 773; Smith v. Sovereign Camp, etc., 179 Mo. 119; 77 S. W. 286. To the same effect are the other cases cited to this section.

[325] Walsh v. Consumnes Tribe, etc., 108 Cal. 496; 41 Pac. 418; Noel v. Modern Woodmen, 61 Ill. App. 596.

[326] Taylor v. Pettee, 70 N. H. 38; 47 Atl. 733.

[327] Poultney v. Bachman, 31 Hun. 49; Robinson v. Irish, etc., Soc., 67 Cal. 135; Supreme Council v. Forsinger, 125 Ind. 52; 25 N. E. 129; Burns v. Bricklayers' Union, 10 N. Y. Supp. 916; 14 N. Y. Supp. 361; Blumenfeldt v. Korschuck, 43 Ill. App. 434; Breneman v. Franklin Ben. Ass'n, 3 W. & S. 218; McMahon v. Supt. Counc. O. C. F., 54 M. A. 468; Brautenstein v. Accident Death Co., 1 Best & Smith, 182; Cin. Lodge v. Littlebury, 6 Cin. L. B. 237; Peyre v. Mut. Relief Ass'n, 90 Cal. 240; 27 Pac. 191.

however, that this rule does not apply to a death claim.[328] And by affirming the action of its officers in rejecting a claim the right to require an appeal is waived.[329] In a case in Georgia the Supreme Court of that State, in passing upon the question whether a member could bring an action for his benefits said:[330] "Among the objects of the organization of this benevolent association, it is evident that the mutual aid to be rendered to the members thereof by the observance of self-imposed duties and obligations was among the most important. It was to be a brotherhood of workingmen; governed, managed and controlled by its own membership, under its own laws, without extrinsic compulsion. Its operations for the execution of its benevolent designs were to be internal, and by persons of its own appointment; provision was made to accomplish all the ends in view; there was nothing in any of its laws prohibited by statute or constitution; hence, whosoever became a member could only avail himself of the rights to be enjoyed in that way and manner provided by its own rules." In an early case,[331] the Supreme Court of Pennsylvania held in a similar case that, when the committee or tribunal created by the lodge or society had passed on the matter, the civil courts had no jurisdiction to inquire into the regularity of the proceedings. The Court said: "The matter here, however, depends not merely on presumption of assent to a by-law, but on the charter to which the plaintiff expressly assented at his initiation; and he is consequently bound by everything done in accordance with it." In a very recent case,[332] the Supreme Court of Michi-

---

[328] Bukofzer v. U. S. Grand Lodge, 15 N. Y. Supp. 922; Railway Passenger, etc., Ass'n v. Robinson, 147 Ill. 138; 35 N. E. 168; affg. 38 Ill. App. 111.

[329] McMahon v. Sup. Counc. O. C. F., 54 M. A. 468.

[330] Harrington v. Workingmen's Benev. etc., 70 Ga. 340. See also Mullen v. Order of Foresters, 70 N. H. 327; 47 Atl. 257.

[331] Black and Whitesmith's Soc. v. Vandyke, 2 Whart. 309; 30 Am. Dec. 263.

[332] Van Poucke v. Netherland, etc., Soc., 63 Mich. 378; 29 N. W. 863; followed in Canfield v. Great Camp of the Maccabees, 87 Mich. 626; 49 N. W. 875; Hemhean v. Great Camp of the Maccabees, 101 Mich. 161; 59 N. W. 417; Grand Lodge Brotherhood, etc., v. Orrell, 97 Ill. App. 246, and Grand Central Lodge v. Grogan, 44 Ill. App. 111. See post, § 564, where extracts from the opinions in these cases are given; but see to the contrary Kinney v. B. & O. Employes' R. Ass'n, 35 W. Va. 385; 14 S. E. 8, and post, § 624.

gan held that if the by-law of a mutual benefit and co-operative insurance society was reasonable and valid, not oppressive nor against public policy, it forms part of the contract entered into between each member and his fellow-members constituting the society; and all are bound by its terms. It is not unreasonable that the sick committee of such a society should be invested with authority to determine whether a member, claiming to be sick, is entitled to sick benefits, and when such benefits should cease. And further that a party can only recover sick benefits according to the terms prescribed in the by-laws; and if they provide for a committee to determine the question for him, and he has referred it to a committee, he has made it a tribunal to determine the question, and the decision of such committee is final.   In Maryland the Court of Appeals has held[333] that one by becoming a member "assented to be governed by the tribe and council according to the regulations, it follows that he was bound by their application and construction in his own case. It is provided that the tribe shall determine matters of this kind, and the decision, on appeal, was final.   These are private beneficial institutions operating on the members only, who for reasons of policy and convenience, affecting their welfare and, perhaps, their existence, adopt laws for their government, to be administered by themselves, to which every person who joins them assents. They require the surrender of no right that a man may not waive, and are obligatory on him only so long as he chooses to recognize their authority.   In the present instance the party appears to have been subjected to the general laws and by-laws according to the usual course, and if the tribunal of his own choice has decided against him he ought not to complain." In all the cases it has been held that the same principles govern as those applying to arbitrations, and when the prescribed forms have been observed without fraud and in good faith, the decision of the committee or society is final.[334] If the by-law is unequal or vexatious then

333 Anacosta Tribe v. Murbach, 13 Md. 91; 71 Am. Dec. 625.

334 Sperry's Appeal, 116 Pa. St. 391; 9 Atl. 478; McAlees v. Supreme Sitting, etc. (Pa.), 13 Atl. 755; Woolsey v. Odd Fellows, etc., 61 Ia. 429; Harrison v. Hoyle, 24 Ohio St. 254; Toram v. Howard Ben. Soc., 4 Pa. St. 519; Osceola Tribe v. Schmidt, 57 Md. 98; Reg. v. Evans, 3 El. & Bl. 363; 23 L. J. M. C. 100; Grinham v. Card, 7 Ex. 833; 21 L. J. Ex. 321; also Matron v. Wentworth, 4 Cin. L. B. 513.

the court will not be bound by it.[335] Where the officer of the local
body of the association refuses to certify to the claim, the member of that body is not bound to submit it to the physician of the
association who under the laws of the latter can only act when
the claim is so certified.[336] Nor can a member sue the physician
for wrongfully refusing to certify to the bill of another physician
for attendance during a member's illness as required by the by-
laws.[337] Where a member invokes the tribunals of the society and
they decide against him he is bound as by an award of arbitrators,
although the laws contain no provision as to submission.[338] In
the case first cited the Supreme Court of California says:[339] "It
is not alleged that the defendant here has any provision in its
by-laws, to the effect that the benefits which it agrees to pay to
its members in case of sickness shall not be payable except upon
the favorable report or recommendation of some committee of the
order specially authorized by its constitution or by-laws to investigate such claims for benefits. But on the contrary it will be
noticed that by the terms of the contract between plaintiff and
defendant, as stated in the complaint, the plaintiff was under no
obligation to resort in the first instance to the tribunals established by the laws of the order under which defendant was organized, or even to make any demand upon defendant for the
benefits claimed, other than by the commencement of an action
therefor in some court of competent jurisdiction. It is, however,

[335] Cartan v. The Father Matthew, etc., 3 Daly 20; Ruecking v. Robert
Blum City Lodge, 1 City Ct. 51. ·

[336] Supreme Sitting Iron Hall v. Stein, 120 Ind. 270; 22 N. E. 136;
Ramell v. Duffy, 82 App. Div. 496; 81 N. Y. Supp. 600. But in Audette
v. L'Union St. Joseph, 178 Mass. 113; 59 N. E. 668, it was held that
the refusal of the physician to give the sworn certificate required by the
by-laws did not excuse compliance. And see also McVoy v. Keller, 36
Misc. R. 803; 74 N. Y. Supp. 842.

[337] Gleavy v. Walker, 22 R. I. 70; 46 Atl. 180.

[338] Robinson v. Templar Lodge, etc., 97 Cal. 62; 31 Pac. 609; Valentine v. Valentine, 2 Barb. Ch. 430; Grand Central Lodge A. O. U. W. v.
Grogan, 44 Ill. App. 111. But see Wuerthner v. Workingmen's Benev.
Soc., 121 Mich. 90; 79 N. W. 921, where it is held that if the constitution and by-laws do not make the decision final the member can resort
to the civil courts.

[339] Robinson v. Templar Lodge, etc., *supra.*

alleged in the complaint, as we construe it, that plaintiff did voluntarily submit his claim against defendant to the decision of the
tribunals of the order of which he became a member when he
joined the defendant lodge, and that such tribunals 'adjudged
and determined' that he was not entitled to the payment of the
benefits now claimed, or to any part thereof. The question, therefore, is, what effect has this determination upon the right of
plaintiff to maintain the action? It does not appear that plaintiff
made any express agreement to be bound by the determination of
the tribunals referred to, but we think that, when he voluntarily
submitted to them for decision the differences which existed between himself and defendant, there was an implied agreement
upon his part to be bound by their judgment or award, in the
absence of any fraud or mistake or other cause which in equity
would entitle him to avoid the same. 'Where a matter is submitted to arbitrators, it is not necessary that there should be
any express agreement to abide by the award when made; for
the law implies such an agreement from the very fact of submission.'[340] It would seem from the allegations of the complaint
that the tribunals whose jurisdiction plaintiff invoked, are established for the purpose of settling all matters of difference which
may arise between a subordinate lodge and any of its members,
growing out of a refusal upon the part of the lodge to pay benefits
claimed, if the member consents to submit such matter to them
for settlement; and it seems clear to us that plaintiff's voluntary
submission of his claim for benefits to their decision was in the
nature of a submission to arbitration, and their decision in the
nature of an award and should be considered equally conclusive.
It is not alleged that there was any misconduct upon the part
of those to whom he submitted the justice of his claims, or that
there was any fraud or mistake in the award itself, or that, for
any reason, the matters in difference between himself and defendant were not fully and fairly tried.'' If the by-laws provide
for no tribunal to test the right to benefits, the member may have
an immediate right of action,[341] and of course an action lies to

[340] Valentine v. Valentine, 2 Barb. Ch. 430.
[341] Dolan v. Court Good Samaritan, 128 Mass. 477; Smith v. Soc., etc.,
12 Phila. 380; Harrington v. Workingmen's, etc., 70 Ga. 340; Wuerthner
v. Workingmen's Benev. Ass'n, 121 Mich. 90; 79 N. R. 921; Gray v.
Chapter, etc., 70 App. Div. 155; 75 N. Y. Supp. 267.

enforce the award of the lodge or society tribunal. The courts latterly incline to adopt the rule that where a society agrees, in consideration of the payment of dues, to pay a certain sum as benefits during a member's illness, it may not deprive the member of his right to resort to the courts in the first instance.[342] the theory being that "agreements to submit a matter to arbitraion are valid when made after the specific controversy has actually arisen, and not where made in advance, certainly not when the agreement provides that one of the interested parties shall be sole arbitrator. The weight of authority is very decidedly against the power of parties to bind themselves in advance that a controversy that may possibly arise shall be conclusively settled by an individual or a corporation."[343]   But a by-law is valid providing that what shall be a total disability shall be determined by a tribunal of the society.[344]   A member cannot recover for benefits accruing after suit brought.[345]

§ 119. **Expulsion of Members.**—One of the most vital questions that arises in relation to the rights of members of societies and associations, whether incorporated or not, is that concerning the power of expulsion, and it becomes most important to inquire when and under what circumstances a member can be expelled and what procedure must be observed in the exercise by a society of this power. At the beginning of the discussion we

[342] Bauer v. Sampson Lodge, 102 Ind. 262; Supreme Council, etc., v. Garrigus, 104 Ind. 133; Harrington v. Workingmen's, etc., 70 Ga. 340; Rigby v. Connol, 24 L. R. Ch. D. 482; Myers v. Jenkins, 63 Ohio St. 101; 57 N. E. 1089; Pepin v. Societe St. Jean Baptiste, 23 R. I. 81; 49 Atl. 387; 60 L. R. A. 626. And where the question is solely one of law the courts take jurisdiction in the first instance. Brown v. Supreme Court I. O. F., 34 Misc. 556; 70 N. Y. Supp. 396; Voluntary Relief Dept. Pa. Lines v. Spencer, 17 Ind. App. 123; 46 N. E. 477.

[343] Bauer v. Sampson Lodge, 102 Ind. 262, citing Kistler v. Indianapolis etc., R. R. Co., 88 Ind. 460; Insurance Co. v. Morse, 20 Wall. 445; Mentz v. Armenia F. Ins. Co., 79 Pa. St. 478; Wood v. Humphrey, 114 Mass. 185; Austin v. Searing, 16 N. Y. 112. See also Railway Passenger, etc., Ass'n v. Robinson, 147 Ill. 138; 35 N. E. 168, and *post*, § 623 and 564.

[344] Sanderson v. Brotherhood R. R. Trainmen, 204 Pa. St. 182; 53 Atl. 767.

[345] B. & O. Employe's Ass'n v. Post, 122 Pa. St. 579; 15 Atl. 885.

must remember that benefit societies have a dual existence; they are social and fraternal in their nature, yet provide for their members, or their beneficiaries, certain pecuniary benefits, consequently, while expulsion in the case of a member of a church or club, or fraternity purely social, might be well enough, if the proceedings were regular, the same offenses in the case of a member of a benefit society could not be punished by expulsion having the consequences of a forfeiture of pecuniary rights. This distinction will appear more clearly as we proceed with the diccussion of the subject.[346] The power to expel a member of a beneficial association can be conferred only by charter and not by by-law.[347]

§ 120. **Same Rules Apply to Incorporated and Unincorporated Societies.**—The same rules apply to voluntary, unincorporated associations as to incorporated societies. Upon this subject the court in a Pennsylvania case[348] says: ''These associations have some elements in common with corporations, joint-stock companies and partnerships; such as association and being governed by regulations, adopted by themselves for that purpose, . . . I have very little doubt, therefore, that the same rules of law and equity, so far as regards the control of them and the adjudication of their reserved and inherent powers to regulate the conduct and to expel their members, apply to them as to corporations and joint-stock companies.''[349] After the expiration of the charter of a corporation the right to expel a member is lost.[350]

§ 121. **Power of Corporation to Expel Members When Charter is Silent: Grounds for Expulsion.**—''When a corporation is

[346] A valuable article on the expulsion of members of corporations and voluntary associations, from the pen of Hon. Seymour D. Thompson, will be found in 24 American Law Review, p. 537. A valuable note is appended in 49 L. R. A. 353 to Ryan v. Cudahy, 157 Ill. 108; 41 N. E. 760, in which the authorities are exhaustively reviewed.

[347] Macavicza v. Workingmen's Club, 246 Pa. 136; 92 Atl. 41.

[348] Leech v. Harris, 2 Brewst. 571.

[349] Gorman v. Russell, 14 Cal. 531; Loubat v. Leory, 15 Abb. N. C. 1; Babb v. Reed, 5 Rawle, 158; 28 Am. Dec. 650; Otto v. Journeymen Tailors' etc., Union; 75 Cal. 308; 17 Pac. 217; Beaumont v. Meredith, 3 Ves. & B. 180; Lindley on Par. 56; Kuehl v. Meyer, 42 M. A. 474; Lawson v. Hemell, 118 Cal. 613; 50 Pac. 763; 49 L. R. A. 400.

[350] United Brothers, etc., v. Williams, 126 Ga. 19; 54 S. E. 907.

duly organized,'' says the Supreme Court of Wisconsin,[351] ''it
has power to make by-laws and expel members, though the charter
is silent upon the subject. If the power is expressly granted in
general terms, it is conferred to enable the corporation to accomplish the objects of its creation, and is limited to such objects
or purposes. It appears to be well settled that where the charter
of a corporation is either silent upon the subject of expulsion,
or grants the power in general terms, there are but three legal
causes of disfranchisement.'' These three causes were stated by
Lord Mansfield,[352] and are again recited by the Supreme Court
of Pennsylvania[353] as follows: ''There is a tacit condition annexed to the franchise of a member, which, if he breaks, he may
be disfranchised. The cases in which this inherent power may
be exercised are of three kinds: 1. When an offense is committed, which has no immediate relation to a member's corporate
duty, but is of so infamous a nature as renders him unfit for
the society of honest men. Such are the offenses of perjury,
forgery, etc. But before an expulsion is made for a cause of this
kind it is necessary that there should be a previous conviction
by a jury, according to the law of the land. 2. When the offense
is against his *duty as a corporator,* and in that case he may be
expelled on trial and conviction by the corporation. 3. The
third is an offense of a mixed nature, against the member's duty
as a corporator, and also indictable by the law of the land''[354]
An unincorporated association not organized for profit may lawfully expel a member, though it may own property and the membership be of pecuniary value; if he is charged with conduct for
which expulsion is a proper remedy, if he has notice of the
charges and be given a fair hearing.[355]

[351] State v. Chamber of Commerce, 20 Wis. 71.
[352] Rex v. Town of Liverpool, 2 Burr. 732.
[353] Commonwealth v. St. Patrick's Benev. Soc., 2 Binney, 441; 4 Am.
Dec. 453.
[354] People v. Medical Soc., etc., 32 N. Y. 187; Dickenson v. Chamber of Commerce, etc., 29 Wis. 49; People v. Medical Soc., 24 Barb. 577;
Leech v. Harris, 2 Brewst. 571; Society v. Commonwealth, 52 Pa. St.
125; Loubat v. Leroy, 15 Abb. N. C. 1; Weiss v. Musical Prot. Union,
189 Pa. St. 446; 42 Atl. 118. See *post,* § 127.
[355] Harris v. Aiken, 76 Kan. 516; 97 Pac. 537; Fritz v. Knaub, 108 N.
Y. Supp. 1133; affg. 103 N. Y. Supp. 1003.

§ 122. **English Rule as to Voluntary Associations.**—In England, however, it has been held that in the absence of any provision in the constitution or by-laws of an incorporated voluntary association giving power of expulsion, there is no inherent power to expel a member, since it forms no part of the written contract by which the members are associated together.[356]

§ 123. **When No Power to Expel Exists.**—This power to disfranchise or expel members is incident to every corporation or society, except where formed primarily or exclusively for the purpose of gain, in which latter case such power cannot be exercised unless expressly granted by charter.[357] And where the corporation or society owns property, a member cannot be expelled or deprived of his interest in the stock and general funds unless this power is contained in the charter.[358] But where the interest of a member in the property of the association is only incidental to his membership it will not prevent his expulsion.[359] And when expelled and therefore not a member all rights in the property of the association are lost.[360]

§ 124. **Power to Expel Belongs to Body Generally: Cannot be Delegated.**—The power of expulsion of members of a society, club or corporation belongs to the body at large,[361] and, in the

[356] Dawkins v. Antrobus, L. R. 17 Ch. D. 615; affd. 44 L. T. Rep. (N. S.) 557.

[357] *In re* Long Island R. R. Co., 19 Wend. 37; 32 Am. Dec. 429; Evans v. Philadelphia Club, 50 Pa. St. 107; Purdy v. Bankers' Life Ass'n, 101 Mo. App. 91; 74 S. W. 486.

[358] Bagg's Case, 11 Co. 99; Davis v. Bank of England, 2 Bing. 393; Hopkinson v. Marquis of Exeter, L. R. 5 Eq. 63; State v. Tudor, 5 Day, 329; Roehler v. Mechanics' Aid Soc., 22 Mich. 86; Evans v. Philadelphia Club, 50 Pa. St. 107; Society v. Commonwealth, 52 Pa. St. 125. See also note in 63 Am. Dec. 772, to Hiss v. Bartlett, 3 Gray, 468.

[359] Lawson v. Hewell, 118 Cal. 613; 50 Pac. 763; 49 L. R. A. 400. See also Kopp v. White, 65 N. Y. Supp. 1017; 30 Civ. Proc. R. 362; Franklin v. Burnham, 82 N. Y. Supp. 882; 40 Misc. 566.

[360] Missouri Bottlers' Ass'n v. Fennerty, 81 Mo. App. 526. See *ante*, § 70.

[361] Hassler v. Phila. Mus. Ass'n, 14 Phila. 233; Green v. African, etc., Soc., 1 Serg. & R. 254; Commonwealth v. Pennsylvania Ben. Ass'n, 2 Serg. & R. 141; Med. & Surg. Soc. v. Weatherly, 75 Ala. 248; Gray v. Christian Soc., 137 Mass. 329; s. c. 50 Am. Rep. 310.

absence of the clearest authority in the constitution and by-laws, cannot be delegated to a committee or officer. Says one case :[362] "The transfer from the body of the society, where it properly belongs, to a small fraction of its members, of so large and dangerous a power as that of expulsion, must appear, if it be claimed to exist, by the plainest language. It cannot be established by inference, or presumption, for no such presumption is to be made in derogation of the rights of the whole body, nor is it to be supposed, unless it appears by the most express and unambiguous language, that the members of the society have consented to hold their rights and membership by so frail a tenure as the judgment of a small portion of their own number.'' But when the charter provides for expulsion and authorizes the regulation of the proceedings by by-laws the board of directors may expel a member in conformity with such by-laws.[363] It has been held[364] that the power to expel a member of a beneficial association can be conferred only by the charter and not by a by-law. The power to expel does not include the power to suspend.[365] In a case in Texas it was held that, where the by-laws provided for suspension for non-payment of assessments, the dictator or presiding officer of a lodge could not without a vote of the members declare a member suspended.[366] It has been held that the revision of mem-.

---

[362] Hassler v. Phila. Mus. Ass'n, 14 Phila. 233. And see Leahy v. Mooney, 39 Misc. 829; 81 N. Y. Supp. 360; and People v. Alpha Lodge, etc., 13 Misc. 677; 35 N. Y. Supp. 214. In this case last cited the Court refers with disapproval to Spillman v. Supreme Council, etc., 157 Mass. 128; 31 N. E. 778, and Green v. Board of Trade, 174 Ill. 585; 51 N. E. 599; 49 L. R. A. 365.

[363] Commonwealth v. Union League Club, 135 Pa. St. 301; 19 Atl. 1030; Society v. Commonwealth, 52 Pa. St. 125; Pitcher v. Board, etc., 20 Ill. App. 319; Corrigan v. Coney Island Jockey Club, 20 N. Y. Supp. 437; Green v. Board of Trade, 174 Ill. 585; 51 N. E. 599; 49 L. R. A. 365; Brandenberger v. Jefferson Club, 88 Mo. App. 148; State v. St. Louis Med. Soc., 91 Mo. App. 76.

[364] Macavicza v. Workingmen's Ben. Club, 246 Pa. 136; 92 Atl. 41.

[365] Schassberger v. Staendel, 9 W. N. C. 379.

[366] Knights of Honor v. Wickser, 72 Tex. 257; 12 S. W. 175. This is evidently a case where the Court confused the provisions of the laws of the order relative to suspension under the penal provisions of the laws

bership lists by dropping certain names from the roll is equivalent to the expulsion of the members whose names are thus stricken off. "The revision," says the Supreme Court of Alabama,[367] "of the roll of members must, in our judgment, be the act of the· society itself, transacted, as any other order of corporate busi- ness, by the recorded vote of the body in its corporate capacity, showing the fact that the roll was revised by at least a majority of the members present and constituting a quorum, voting in the affirmative," and further, "the clerical work of revision is, in one sense, the act of the secretary, inasmuch as the duty of striking off names and the preparation of a revised list are de- volved upon him. But the corporate act of revision, which is a legal ratification of the act of the secretary, is an order of busi- ness judicial in its character, and of great importance in its nature and results, and for these reasons, as we have said, must be transacted by a vote of the members in their corporate capacity."[368] There may be a provision for *ipso facto* expul- sion, or forfeiture of rights by non-payment of assessments, or engaging in a forbidden occupation. Such provisions have been upheld by the courts.[369] The members of a trial committee ap- pointed to try a member on charges that have been preferred are not liable in a suit for damages brought by the accused.[370] Where the by-laws of the society provided for a trial before a committee and an appeal afterwards, a judgment by the com- mittee is conclusive if not appealed from.[371]

with those of suspension *ipso facto* by the non-payment of assessments. So it is not sufficient simply to make an entry in the secretary's book. Tourville v. Brotherhood, etc., 54 Ill. App. 71. This subject, however, is further treated in *post*, § 492.

[367] Medical & Surgical Soc. v. Weatherly, 75 Ala. 248.

[368] Gray v. Christian Soc., 137 Mass. 329; s. c. 50 Am. Rep. 310; State *ex rel.* Sibley v. Carteret Club, 40 N. J. L. 295; Delacy v. Neuse River Navigation Co., 1 Hawks, 274; 9 Am. Dec. 636; People v. American In- stitute, 44 How. Pr. 468; Loubat v. Leroy, 40 Hun. 546; People v. Mechanics' Aid Soc., 22 Mich. 86; Pulford v. Fire Dept., etc., 31 Mich. 458.

[369] Moerschbaecher v. Supreme Council R. L., 188 Ill. 9; 59 N. E. 17; 52 L. R. A. 281; Langnecker v. Trustees Grand Lodge, etc., 111 Wis. 279; 87 N. W. 293; 55 L. R. A. 185. See also *post*, § 419.

[370] Moon v. Flack, 74 N. H. 140; 65 Atl. 829.

[371] Rigler v. National Council K. & L. of S., 128 Minn. 51; 150 N. W. 178.

§ 125. **Procedure for Expulsion: Notice.**—All proceedings in the expulsion of members must be in substantial accordance with the letter of its rules.[372] While it has been held that if the by-laws of the society provide for no notice, the member is not entitled to any notice, no property right being involved,[373] yet even in such case the proceedings must be had at a regular meeting, for of only such is the member supposed to have knowledge.[374] It has often, however, been held that by-laws which provide for expulsion of a member without notice are void as being unreasonable.[375] And it has also been held that where no notice is given the proceedings are void.[376] Expulsion, if a property right is involved, must always be on notice, and, if no other method of notice is prescribed by the by-laws, it must be served personally, and failure on the part of the member to give notice of a change of address as required by the laws of the society will not change the rule.[377] Mere posting in the corporate premises

[372] Labouchere v. Earl of Wharncliff, .L. R. 13 Ch. Div. 346; Commonwealth v. German Soc., 15 Pa. St. 251; Wachtel v. Noah Widows' and Orphans', etc., 84 N. Y. 28; People v. Am. Institute, 44 How. Pr. 468; Foster v. Harrison, cited 72 Law Times, 185; 15 Abb. N. C. 45; Roehler v. Mechanics' Aid Soc., 22 Mich. 87; White v. Brownell, 4 Abb. Pr. (N. S.) 162; Med. & Surg. Soc. v. Weatherly, 75 Ala. 248; Supreme Lodge K. of P. v. Eskholme, 59 N. J. L. 255; 35 Atl. 1055.

[373] Manning v. San Antonio Club, 63 Tex. 166; s. c. 51 Am. Rep. 639; McDonald v. Ross-Lewin, 29 Hun. 87; People v. St. Franciscus, etc., 24 How. Pr. 216.

[374] Medical & Surgical Soc. v. Weatherly, 75 Ala. 248.

[375] Pulford v. Fire Dept., 31 Mich. 458; Fritz v. Muck, 62 How. Pr. 72; Erd v. Bavarian, etc., Ass'n, 67 Mich. 233; 34 N. W. 555.

[376] Slater v. Supreme Lodge K. & L. of H., 76 Mo. App. 387; Seehorn v. Supreme Council Catholic Knights, etc., 95 Mo. App. 233; 68 S. W. 949; Women's Cath. Order v. Haley, 86 Ill. App. 330.

[377] Wachtel v. Noah Widows' and Orphans', etc., 84 N. Y. 28; People v. Medical Soc., 32 N. Y. 187; Commonwealth v. Penn. Ben. Ass'n, etc., 2 Serg. & R. 141; Innis v. Wylie, 1 C. & K. 257; Downing v. St. Columbia's, etc., 10 Daly 262; Pulford v. Fire Department, 31 Mich. 458; Commonwealth v. German Soc., 15 Pa. St. 251; People v. Musical, etc., Union, 1 N. Y. S. R. 770; 47 Hun. 273; People v. Hoboken Turtle Club, 14 N. Y. Supp. 76 Zangen v. Krakauer, etc., Ass'n, 26 Misc. 332; 56 N. Y. Supp. 1052; Dubach v. Grand Lodge, etc., 33 Wash. 651; 74 Pac. 832. The following cases support the principle that expulsion without

is not a sufficient notice.[378] Service of notice is not excused by a change of residence.[379] Nor by insanity of the member.[380] Nor by appearing without notice and objecting to the hearing of the case in the absence of the prosecutor.[381] This notice must contain a statement of the charges against the member.[382] The member need not request a hearing,[383] nor does he waive notice by appearing and entering on his defense;[384] nor is notice waived by the member appearing at the time fixed for the hearing, and denying the right of the directors to proceed against him and refusing to answer the charges.[385] It is not necessary that the accused be actually present at the trial.[386] In Fisher v. Keane,[387] it was held that in proceedings to expel a member the committee or society is a *quasi*-judicial tribunal and are bound in proceeding under their rules against a member for alleged misconduct, to act according to the ordinary principles of justice and are not to convict him of an offense warranting his expulsion without giving him due notice of the intention to proceed against him and affording

notice is void. Horgan v. Metropolitan Aid Ass'n, 202 Mass. 524; 88 N. E. 890; Wallace .v. Fraternal Mystic Circle, 127 Mich. 387; 86 N. W. 353; Byrne v. Sup. Circle, etc., 74 N. J. L. 258; 65 Atl. 839; Federal Life Ins. Co. v. Risinger, Ind. App. 61 N. E. 533.

[378] State *ex rel.* Sibley v. Carteret Club, 40 N. J. 295. But it has been said that posting under a by-law may take the place of other notice. Ruhle v. Diamond, etc., Ass'n, 5 Lack. Leg. N. 101.

[379] Wachtel v. Noah Widows', etc., Soc., 84 N. Y. 28; Harmstead v. Washington Fire Co., 8 Phila. 331.

[380] Supreme Lodge A. O. U. W. v. Zuhlke, 129 Ill. 298; 21 N. E. 789; Dubach v. Grand Lodge, etc., 33 Wash. 651; 74 Pac. 832.

[381] People v. Musical Protective Union, 118 N. Y. 680; 23 N. E. 129; affg. 42 Hun. 656.

[382] Murdock's Case, 7 Pick. 303; Murdock v. Phillips' Acad., 12 Pick. 244; People v. Musical Mut. Protective Union, 47 Hun. 273; Sleeper v. Franklin Lyceum, 7 R. I. 523.

[383] Loubat v. Leroy, 40 Hun. 546; Delacy v. Neuse Nav. Co., 1 Hawks (N. C.) 274; 9 Am. Dec. 636; Loubat v. Leroy, 65 How. Pr. 138.

[384] Downing v. St. Columbia's, etc., 10 Daly 265. But see Commonwealth v. Penn. Ben. Soc., 2 Serg. & R. 141; and § 102. The better rule is that appearance generally is a waiver of irregularities in the notice. Fritz v. Knaub, 103 N. Y. Supp. 1003.

[385] People v. Musical & Protective Union, 47 Hun. 273.

[386] Byram v. Sovereign Camp, etc., 108 Ia. 430; 79 N. W. 144.

[387] 11 L. R. Ch. D. 353; 49 L. J. Ch. 11; 41 L. T. 335.

him an opportunity of defending or palliating his conduct.[388]
The power to expel must be exercised *bona fide* and not capri-
ciously or arbitrarily, or maliciously.[389]   The trial will be upheld
if the accused has opportunity to be heard and present all his
evidence.[390]

§ 126.   **Procedure Continued: Charges: Trial.**—The methods of procedure prescribed by the by-laws of the association must
be followed and all their requirements observed.[391]   And a member can be expelled at a meeting held on Sunday if that is the
regularly appointed day for the meetings of the association.[392]
He cannot be expelled at a special meeting.[392a]   If the by-laws so
require, the charges against a member must be in writing and
signed as required by the accuser, and the notice must specify
the time of hearing,[393] but by appearing generally the member
waives objections as to notice and the regularity of the appointment of the tribunal.[394]   The record should show the procedure.[395]

---

[388] Loubat v. Leroy, 40 Hun. 546; Gray v. Christ. Soc., 137 Mass. 329;
50 Am. Rep. 310; Med. & Surg. Soc. v. Weatherly, 75 Ala. 248.

[389] Otto v. Journeymen Tailors', etc., Ass'n, 75 Cal. 308; 17 Pac. 217;
Hopkinson v. Marquis of Exeter, 37 L. J. Ch. 173; 5 L. R. Eq. 63; 16 W. R.
266; Lyttleton v. Blackburne, 45 L. J. Ch. 219; 33 L. T. (N. S.) 641;
Dawkins v. Antrobus, 17 L. R. Ch. D. 615; 44 L. T. 557; 29 W. R. 511.

[390] Harris v. Aitken, 76 Kan. 516; 90 Pac. 537.

[391] Green v. Board of Trade, 174 Ill. 585; 51 N. E. 599; 49 L. R. A.
365 and note; Woodmen of the World v. Gillilland, 11 Okla. 384; 67 Pac.
485; Supreme Lodge, etc., v. Eskholme, 59 N. J. L. 255; 35 Atl. 1055.

[392] Pepin v. Societe Jean Baptiste, 24 R. I. 550; 54 Atl. 47; 60 L. R. A.
626; People v. Carrigan, 65 Barb. 357; McCabe v. Father Matthew Soc., 24
Hun. 149. As to various questions of procedure see Doljanin v. Austrian
Benev. Soc., 137 Cal. 165; 69 Pac. 908.

[392a] Lahiff v. St. Joseph's, etc., Soc., 76 Conn. 648; 57 Atl. 692; 65 L. R.
A. 92.

[393] Society, etc., v. Commonwealth, 52 Pa. St. 125; People v. Musical, etc.,
Union, 47 Hun. 273; People v. American Institute, etc., 44 How. Pr. 468.

[394] Sperry's Appeal, 116 Pa. St. 391; 9 Atl. 478; Burton v. St. George's
Soc., 28 Mich. 261; Commonwealth v. Penn. Ben. Soc., 2 Serg. & R. 141;
Austin v. Dutcher, 56 App. Div. 393; 67 N. Y. Supp. 819; Moore v. Na-
tional Council, etc., 65 Kan. 452; 70 Pac. 352; Durel v. Perseverance F.
Co., 47 La. Ann. 1101; 17 Sou. 591; Moore v. National Cermalic, 65 Kan.
452; 70 Pac. 352. See § 101, *ante.*

[395] Seehorn v. Supreme Council, 95 Mo. App. 233; 68 S. W. 944.

The association must act fairly and in good faith and it will be held to a fair and honest administration of its rules. The accused must be allowed to be present to confront his accusers and cross-examine them, for "ordinary principles of justice and of right" require this to be done.[395]   But if after being regularly cited the member fail to appear he may be expelled as being in contempt if the by-laws so provide.[396]   In the case first cited[397] it was said, after a review of the authorities, that "the principle to be deduced from all these cases is, that in every proceeding before a club, society or association having for its object the expulsion of a member, the member is entitled to be fully and fairly informed of the charge and to be fully and fairly heard." The Court further said: "Again, while these proceedings are not to be governed by the strict rules which apply to actions at law or suits in equity, or even, perhaps, by the rules which obtain in regard to arbitrations, there is, I think, a strong analogy between the principles which govern in arbitrations and those which relate to proceedings of this character. In the case of Sharpe v. Bickerdyke,[398] Lord Eldon said that, by the 'great principle of eternal justice which was prior to all these acts of *sederunt* regulations and proceedings of court, it was impossible an award could stand where the arbitrator heard one party and refused to hear the other; and on this great principle, and on the fact that the arbitrator had not acted according to the principles upon which he himself thought he ought to have acted, even if he decided rightly he had not decided justly, and therefore the award could not stand.' In the matter of Plews v. Middleton[399] an award was set aside, because the three arbitrators, after having determined within a small amount the sum to be paid, agreed to examine a witness separately, and did so. Coleridge, J., in that case, says: 'To uphold this award would be to authorize a proceeding contrary to the first principles of justice. The arbitrators here carried on examinations apart from each other and

[395] Hutchinson v. Lawrence, 67 How. Pr. 47; Otto v. Journeymen Tailors' Ass'n, 75 Cal. 308; 17 Pac. 217.
[396] Levy v. Magnolia Lodge, etc., 110 Cal. 297; 42 Pac. 887.
[397] Hutchinson v. Lawrence, *supra*.
[398] 3 Dow's 102.
[399] 6 A. & E. (N. S.) 845; 14 L. J. Q. B. 139; 9 Jur. 160.

from the parties to the reference, whereas it ought to have been conducted by the arbitrators and umpire jointly in the presence of the parties.' In Oswald v. Earl Grey,[400] it was held that no usage can justify the arbitrators in hearing one party and his witnesses only, in the absence of and without notice of the other party.[401] In Walker v. Frobisher,[402] an award was set aside, the arbitrator having received evidence after notice to the parties that he would receive no more, in which they acquiesced. In this case Lord Eldon says: 'A judge must not take it upon himself to say whether evidence improperly admitted had or had not an effect upon his mind. The award may have done perfect justice, but upon general principles it cannot be supported.' . . . In Drew v. Leburn,[403] it was held 'that an arbitrator greatly errs, if he, in any of the minutest particulars, takes upon himself to listen to evidence behind the back of any of the parties to the submission.' ''[404] "Hearing" means a right to have counsel and opportunity to question witnesses and offer evidence;[405] "evidence" means legal evidence,[406] and the trying must be unprejudiced.[407] If the method of procedure is prescribed, an expulsion on motion is insufficient.[408] In a recent case[409] the Supreme Court of California thus reviewed the general principles applicable to these proceedings: "The right of expulsion from associations of this character may be based and upheld upon two grounds: *First,* a violation of such of the established rules of the association as have been subscribed or assented to by the members, and as pro-

---

[400] 24 L. J. Q. B. 69.

[401] See *In re* Brook, 15 C. B. (N. S.) 403; 33 L. J. C. P. 246; 10 L. T. 378.

[402] 6 Ves. 69.

[403] 2 Macq. H. of L. Cas. 1.

[404] Fisher v. Keane, 11 L. R. Ch. D. 353; Dean v. Bennett, L. R. 6 Ch. 489; Innes v. Wylie, 1 Car. & K. 257, 263; Queen v. Saddlers' Co:, 10 H. L. Cas. 404; State v. Adams, 44 Mo. 570; Wood v. Wood, L. R. 9 Exch. 190; Fuller v. Plainfield Academy, 6 Conn. 532; Gray v. Christ. Soc. 137 Mass. 329.

[405] Murdock v. Phillips Academy, 12 Pick. 244.

[406] Modern Woodmen v. Deters, 65 Ill. App. 368.

[407] Smith v. Nelson, 18 Vt. 511.

[408] Byram v. Sovereign Camp, etc., 108 Ia. 430; 79 N. W. 144; Weiss v. Musicians' Union, 189 Pa. St. 446; 42 Atl. 118.

[409] Otto v. Journeymen Tailors', etc., Union, 75 Cal. 308; 17 Pac. 217.

vide expulsion for such violation; *second*, for such conduct as clearly violates the fundamental objects of the association, and, if persisted in and allowed, would thwart those objects or bring the association into disrepute. We content ourselves with stating the propositions thus broadly, and, for the purposes of this case, need not refer to the numerous authorities defining and limiting the power. In the matter of expulsion the society acts in a *quasi*-judicial character, and, so far as it confines itself to the exercise of the powers vested in it, and in good faith pursues the methods prescribed by its laws, such laws not being in violation of the laws of the land, or any inalienable right of the member, its sentence is conclusive, like that of a judicial tribunal.[410] The courts will, however, decide whether the ground for expulsion is well taken.[411] It has been held in reference to the expulsion of members from societies of this character, that the courts have no right to interfere with the decisions of the societies, except in the following cases: *First.* If the decision arrived at was contrary to natural justice, such as the member complained of not having an opportunity to explain misconduct. *Secondly.* If the rules of the club have not been observed. *Thirdly.* If the action of the club was malicious and not *bona fide*.[412] Article 25 of the appellant's constitution provides as follows: 'If any member defrauds this union, he shall be dealt with as the central body may decide.' Beyond this no specific provision appears in the constitution or by-laws under which members may be expelled. The contention of appellants is that the power of expulsion is inherent in every society, and that the offense of which plaintiff was found guilty was sufficient ground for expulsion, as matter of law, irrespective of any provision of the constitution or by-laws. We subscribe to that portion of the proposition which asserts the inherent right of expulsion, subject, however, to the limitations hereinbefore expressed. For the purposes of this case

---

410 Commonwealth v. Society, 8 Watts & S. 250; Burt v. Grand Lodge, 44 Mich. 208; 33 N. W. 13; Robinson v. Yates City Lodge, 86 Ill. 598; People v. Women's Catholic Order Foresters, 162 Ill. 78; 44 N. E. 401; Murray v. Supreme Hive Ladies, etc., 112 Tenn. 664; 80 S. W. 827.

411 Cotton Exchange v. State, 54 Ga. 668.

412 Dawkins v. Antrobus, 17 L. R. Ch. D. 615; 44 L. T. 557; 29 W. R. 511; Lambert v. Addison, 46 L. T. 20.

we assume, also, without deciding.—*First*, that the charges and specifications against plaintiff were sufficient, upon being proven, to warrant his expulsion under the inherent right so to do mentioned; *Second*, that the 'central body'—that is to say, the board of delegates of shop societies, as contradistinguished from the entire body of members—may exercise the power of expulsion. Conceding these propositions, however (so far as the latter is concerned, we doubt if it can be maintained), the facts as found by the court still remain, that the plaintiff was really and in fact found guilty for no other offense than that for which he was expelled in the first instance, viz.: for working for parties against whom a strike had been ordered; that the expulsion was not in good faith, was not fair, and was contrary to natural justice; that the charge of 'conspiracy to injure and destroy the union' was in substance but a pretext to punish him for an offense only subjecting him to a fine, in a manner wholly different from the imposition of the penalty provided therefor, etc. We think, as before stated, that there was evidence from which the facts as found were fairly deducible. These facts raise the inevitable conclusion, that the trial and conviction of plaintiff was a travesty upon justice, and lacking in the essential elements of fairness, good faith and candor, which should characterize the action of men in passing upon the rights of their fellowmen. We are referred to the provision of appellant's constitution which provides that 'any member having a grievance, shall have the right to lay his case before the central body, who shall take action thereon, and whose decision shall be final.' No doubt when action is properly taken in the manner indicated, it is final, and the courts will not interfere, but when, under the guise of remedying the grievance of a member, the central body acts in bad faith, and maliciously makes the subject of the grievance a pretext for oppression and wrong, its action may, however, to that extent, be the subject of review." It would seem from analogy at least that a record should be kept of the proceedings of the society or committee in acting upon accusations against a member, that the charges be specific and that the proof must correspond and be sufficient. "The facts must be stated as found after a formal investigation and not rest upon inference alone," and the find-

ings must support the charge.[413] Although there may be irregu-.
larities in the procedure the accused by submitting his case and
afterwards taking an appeal acknowledges the jurisdiction and
cannot afterwards sue the association for wrongful expulsion.[414]
It has also been held[415] that where a member has been wrongfully
expelled from a propriety club where the members have no right
of property, he must obtain relief by a suit for damages not by
injunction. In a proceeding to expel a member a brother of
the person who preferred the charges cannot sit on the trial committee.[416]

§ 127. Charges Must be Sufficient.—The Charges must not
be trivial in their nature or trifling. They must be definite and
certain.[417] The following accusations have been held to be insufficient to justify expulsion or suspension: "Slander against the
society;"[418] "talking against the society;"[419] "illegally drawing
aid in time of sickness;"[420] "defrauding the society out of 50
cents;"[421] "villifying a member;"[422] although a member can be
expelled for slandering the society;[423] "doing business at less
than the established tariff of the society;"[424] "unprofessional con-

[413] Schweiger v. Society, 13 Phila.-113; Commonwealth v. St. Patrick's
Benev. Soc., 2 Binn. 441; Roehler v. Mechanic's Aid Soc., 22 Mich. 86;
State v. Adams. 44 Mo. 570.
[414] Peyre v. Mut. Relief Soc., 90 Cal. 240; 27 Pac. 191.
[415] Baird v. Wells, L. R. 44 Ch. D. 661; 31 Am. & Eng. Corp. Cas. 240;
post, § 134.
[416] People v. Alpha Lodge, etc., 13 Misc. 677; 35 N. Y. Supp. 214.
[417] Zangen v. Krakauer, etc., Ass'n, 26 Misc. 332; 56 N. Y. Supp. 1052.
[418] Roehler v. Mechanics' Aid Soc., 22 Mich. 86. In this case, although
the charge was held insufficient, and the member restored, it was said
that if a member of a society can be expelled for "slander against the
society," the offense must be analogous to the common law offense of
slander, as applicable to individuals. See Allnutt v. High Court of Foresters, 61 Mich. 110; 28 N. W. 802.
[419] Radice v. Italian, etc., Soc., 67 N. J. L. 196; 50 Atl. 691.
[420] Schweiger v. Society, 13 Phila. 113.
[421] Commonwealth v. German Soc., 15 Pa. St. 251.
[422] Commonwealth v. St. Patrick's Soc., 2 Binn. 441; 4 Am. Dec. 453;
Mulroy v. Knights of Honor, 28 Mo. App. 463.
[423] People v. Alpha Lodge, etc., 13 Misc. 677; 35 N. Y. Supp. 214.
[424] People v. Med. Soc., 24 Barb. 570.

duct in advertising;"[425] "disrespectful and contemptuous language to associates;"[426] stating that the lodge would not pay and never intended to pay.[427] Guilty of "actions that may injure the association;"[428] "offense against law;"[429] "ungentlemanly conduct," which consisted of a member of a medical society becoming surety on the bonds of colored citizens charged with disorderly conduct and riot.[430] It is sufficient cause for expulsion from a trades union that membership was obtained by feigning a qualification which did not exist and such member persisted in remaining after such disqualification was established.[431] Defamation by a member of the character of another member is, by common law, no cause of discipline.[432] Nor the exercise of a statutory right, as to file a lien.[433] Fraud, such as representing himself in good health, when in fact he had an incurable disease, is a ground of expulsion,[434] and generally it may be said that violations of reasonable by-laws are sufficient to justify infliction of the penalty prescribed, whether it be suspension or expulsion.[435] Opening a letter addressed to the president authorizes expulsion from a club.[436] The courts will look at the facts in each case and, construing the by-laws to be reasonable when they are calculated to carry out the objects of the association, and are not unjust under the circumstances, will sustain regular proceedings thereunder.[437] If the by-laws so provide expulsion can be

[425] People v. Med. Soc., etc., 32 N. Y. 187.

[426] Fuller v. Plainfield Academy, 6 Conn. 532.

[427] Erd v. Bavarian, etc., Ass'n, 67 Mich. 233; 34 N. W. 555.

[428] Butchers' Ben. Ass'n, 38 Pa. St. 298.

[429] Beneficial Ass'n, 38 Pa. St. 299.

[430] State v. Georgia Medical Soc., 38 Ga. 608.

[431] Beesley v. Chicago Journeymen Plumbers', etc., Ass'n, 44 Ill. App. 478.

[432] Allnut v. High Court of Foresters, 61 Mich. 110; 28 N. W. 802.

[433] Miller v. Building League, etc., 53 N. Y. Supp. 1016.

[434] Durantaye v. Soc. St. Ignace, 13 L. C. J. 1; 1869.

[435] See, however, Pulford v. Fire Department, 31 Mich. 458; and also following section.

[436] People v. Manhattan Club, 23 Misc. 500; 52 N. Y. Supp. 726.

[437] Dickenson v. Chamber of Commerce, etc., 29 Wis. 45; People v. Board of Trade, 45 Ill. 112; State v. Chamber of Commerce, 20 Wis. 63; Savannah Cotton Exchange v. State, 54 Ga. 668; People v. St. George's Soc., 28 Mich. 261; People v. Board of Trade, 80 Ill. 134; Sperry's Appeal,

made for non-payment of a fine;[438] and for failure to pay funeral assessments.[439] Expulsion can be had for non-observance of religious duties required by the by-laws,[440] In Slater v. Supreme Lodge, etc.,[441] it is said: "The offense charged was that he had feigned illness and thereby fraudulently obtained sick benefits from the lodge. This was ground for expulsion, if true—ground by an express provision of the constitution of the order—ground according to law and justice." A member may be expelled for calling the other members "a lot of dogs"[442] and for publishing scurrilous accusations against the members.[443] There may be expulsion for insubordination, but the specific acts must appear.[444] A member cannot be expelled for testifying against the society.[445] A charge for embezzling money is insufficient where the right of the accused to the money was established by a judgment of the court.[446] If the charges are insufficient the suspension is a nullity and can be collaterally attacked.[447]

§ 128. **Expulsion of Members of Subordinate Lodges of a Beneficiary Order.**—The subordinate lodges of a benefit society are not only social clubs, generally unincorporated, but are also constituent parts of the society of which the entity and head is an incorporated superior governing body. In considering the rights of such subordinate lodges and those of the society itself,

116 Pa. St. 391; 9 Atl. 478. As to revoking charter of a subordinate chapter of a college secret fraternity, see Heaton v. Hull, 64 N. Y. Supp. 279; 51 App. Div. 126; affg. 59 N. Y. Supp. 281; 28 Misc. 97.

[438] Sinek v. Lodge No. 80, etc., 118 Mich. 81; 76 N. W. 1124; Albrecht v. Peoples Life, etc., Ass'n, 129 Mich. 444; 89 N. W. 44.

[439] Reynolds v. Fidelis Lodge, etc., 14 Pa. Super. Ct. 515.

[440] Hitter v. German, etc., Soc., 4 Ky. Law Rpts. 728.

[441] 88 Mo. App. 177.

[442] Josich v. Austrian, etc., Soc., 119 Cal. 74; 51 Pac. 18.

[443] Barry v. Players, 130 N. Y. Supp. 701; 73 Misc. 10.

[444] Crow v. Capital City Council, etc., 26 Pa. Super. Ct. 411; Del Ponte v. Societa, etc., 27 R. I. 1; 60 Atl. 337; 114 Am. St. Rep. 17.

[445] Radice v. Italian Am. Soc., 67 N. J. Law, 196; 50 Atl. 691; St. Louis, S. W. Ry. of Texas v. Thompson, Tex. Civ. App. 108 S. W. 453. The judgment in this case, however, was reversed by the Supreme Court on other grounds, 102 Tex. 89; 113 S. W. 144; 19 Ann. Cas. 1250.

[446] Spier v. Douglas, etc., 144 Ill. App. 195.

[447] Pepin v. Societe St. John, etc., 24 R. I. 1; 54 Atl. 47; 60 L. R. A. 626; Plattdeutsche, etc., v. Ross, 117 Ill. App. 247.

in regard to the expulsion of members, this fact must be remembered. There may be an expulsion from membership in the subordinate lodge for violation of the penal provisions of its laws, which generally carries expulsion from the society itself with it,. and there may be a conditional expulsion, or suspension, for nonpayment at the prescribed time of an assessment called by the superior incorporated body. In the first case the lodge may act as an independent body, in the latter as agent of the superior body, if any affirmative act is required to perfect the expulsion. Generally, if an assessment is not paid at the fixed time, the nonpayment, by the laws of the order, works, *ipso facto,* a suspension, which, in fact, is an expulsion, although the member may be restored to membership by compliance with certain requirements of the laws of the order.[448]   The rights of the members of these associations rest in contract and such rights therein secured can only be divested in the manner provided in the contract.[449]   The directors cannot expel a member of an assessment company, although the by-laws provide for such expulsion.[450]   A member cannot be expelled while insane when no notice has been given and the expulsion is based on his admissions.[451]   Nor can an insane member waive anything.[452]   Nor can liability for such benefits be avoided by expulsion.[453]   The supreme governing body may expel a member although the by-laws only provide for expulsion of members of subordinate lodges.[454]   A suspended member must still pay dues.[455]   In a case in the St. Louis Court of Appeals,[456]

[448] *Post,* § 492.

[449] McDonald v. Supreme Council Chosen Friends, 78 Cal. 49; 20 Pac. 41; Knights of Honor v. Wickser, 72 Tex. 257; 12 S. W. 175; High Court of Foresters v. Zak, 35 Ill. App. 613; Hoeffner v. Grand Lodge, etc., 41 M. A. 45, and indeed all cases involving rights of members.

[450] Purdy v. Bankers' Life Ass'n, 101 Mo. App. 91; 74 S. W. 486.

[451] Supreme Lodge A. O. U. W. v. Zuhlke, 129 Ill. 298; 21 N. E. 789.

[452] Hoeffner v. Grand Lodge Harugari, 41 Mo. App. 359.

[453] Wuerthner v. Workingmen's Benev. Soc., 121 Mich. 90; 79 N. W. 921.

[454] Spillman v. Supreme Council Home Circle, 157 Mass. 128; 31 N. E. 776.

[455] Palmetto Lodge v. Hubbell, 24 S. C. (2 Strob.) 457.

[456] Mulroy v. Supreme Lodge Knights of Honor, 28 Mo. App. 463. See also Slater v. Supreme Lodge K. and L. of H., 76 Mo. App. 387; 88 Mo. App. 177.

Judge Seymour D. Thompson considered the subject of the expulsion of members of a subordinate lodge of a benefit society in a remarkably clear opinion. The lodge in that suit was a local lodge of the order of the Knights of Honor and under the control of a Supreme Lodge, by which assessments were levied, which the local lodge collected and remitted. The action was brought by the beneficiary of a deceased member, who had been expelled by the local lodge, to recover the amount named in his certificate of membership. The other facts sufficiently appear in the opinion from which we take the following extract, although it is to some extent a repetition of what we have already said: ''The turning point in the case, therefore, is, whether James Mulroy was lawfully expelled from the order on the tenth of November, 1884. In determining this question, we must also lay out of view a number of considerations which have been pressed upon us in argument, which either have no bearing upon it, or which it is not necessary to consider. In the first place, we concede that there is a great array of judicial authority in favor of the proposition, that where members are expelled from religious societies, social clubs, benevolent societies, and other voluntary organizations, incorporated or unincorporated, the judicial courts will not interfere to reinstate them or to revise the judgment of expulsion, until the expelled member has exhausted all the remedies available to him within the organization itself, by appealing to a higher judicatory, provided by the rules of the society or otherwise.[457] But all the cases which so hold, either expressly state or tacitly assume, that, in the action which the society took, and against which relief was sought, it acted within the scope of its powers, and in prosecuting their inquiries into the propriety of the action of such societies in the expulsion of members, or in the disposition of property or otherwise, courts have in general proceeded no further than to inquire whether the judicatory provided by the laws of the society, which acted, had jurisdiction in

[457] Karcher v. Supreme Lodge, 137 Mass. 368; Chamberlain v. Lincoln 129 Mass. 70; La Fond v. Deems, 81 N. Y. 507; White v. Brownell, 2 Daly 329; Harrington v. Workingmen's Benev. Soc., 70 Ga. 340; Loubat v. Leroy, 15 Abb. N. C. 1.

LIFE AND ACCIDENT INSURANCE.

the particular case.[458] It is true that the English courts and the Supreme Judicial Court of Massachusetts have, in dealing with social clubs, and even with mutual benefit and other societies, gone beyond this, and have said that there must not only be a power to expel the member, but that the power must be exercised in good faith—in other words, these courts will interfere either in the case of a want of jurisdiction, or of fraud in its exercise.[459] It follows from the preceding statements that the -judicial courts will not, on the one hand, declare the expulsion of a member to be invalid because of mere irregularities in the steps which have led up to it;[460] and that they will, on the other hand, set aside or disregard the expulsion of a member which has been had without notice to him and an opportunity to defend against the charges preferred;[461] or for offenses for which the society has no express power to expel, and which are not injurious to the society or contrary to law.[462] In early cases the doctrine has been announced that corporations have the same inherent power to expel members for reasonable causes, which they have to make by-laws, and that it is not necessary that the power should be found in the express language of their charters.[463] The offenses for which cor-

[458] State v. Farris, 45 Mo. 483; Commonwealth v. Green, 4 Whart. 531; Gibson v. Armstrong, 7 B. Mon. 481; Shannon v. Frost, 3 B. Mon. 253; Robertson v. Bullions, 9 Barb. 134; Harmon v. Dreher, 1 Speer Eq. 87; German Reformed Church v. Seibert, 3 Pa. St. 282; Den v. Pilling, 4 Zab. (24 N. J. L.) 653; Commonwealth v. Pike Ben. Soc., 8 Watts & S. 247; Black & Whitesmith's Soc. v. Van Dyke, 2 Whart. 309.

[459] Karcher v. Supreme Lodge, 137 Mass. 368; Hopkins v. Marquis of Exeter, L. R. 5 Eq. 63; Dawkins v. Antrobus, 17 Ch. D. 615; Inderwick v. Snell, 2 Mac. & G. 216, 221; Lambert v. Addison, 46 L. T. (N. S.) 20; Manby v. Life Ins. Soc., 29 Beavan, 439; 31 L. J. Ch. 94; Drummer v. Corp of Chippenham, 14 Ves. 245, 252; Blisset v. Daniel, 10 Hare, 493.

[460] Bouldin v. Alexander, 15 Wall. 131; Shannon v. Frost, 3 B. Mon. 253; German Ref. Ch. v. Seibert, 3 Pa. St. 282; State v. Farris, 45 Mo. 183.

[461] Com. v. Germ. Soc., 15 Pa. 251; Dawkins v. Antrobus, 17 Ch. D. 615; Labouchere v. Earl of Wharncliff, 13 Ch. Div. 353; Wachtel v. Noah Widows', etc., Soc., 84 N. Y. 28; Rex v. Town of Liverpool, 2 Burr. 732.

[462] People v. Medical Soc., 32 N. Y. 187; Com. v. St. Patrick's Ben. Soc., 2 Binn. 441; Com. v. Germ. Soc., 15 Pa. St. 251; Green v. African Soc., 1 Serg. & R. 254.

[463] Bruce's Case, 2 Strange, 819; Rex v. Richardson, 1 Burr. 519; Com. v. St. Patrick's Ben. Soc., 2 Binn. 441.

porations possess the inherent power of removing an officer or corporator were thus classified by Lord Mansfield: '1· Such as have no immediate relation to his office, but are in themselves of so infamous a nature as to render the offender unfit to execute any public franchise. 2. Such as are only against his oath and the duty of his office as a corporator, and amount to a breach of the tacit conditions annexed to his franchise or office. 3. The third sort of offenses for which an officer or corporator may be displaced is of a mixed nature; as being an offense not only against the duty of an office, but also a matter indictable at common law.'[464] Mutual benefit societies, such as the one under consideration, are of a two-fold character: 1. They are social organizations resembling religious societies and social clubs. 2. They are also mutual insurance companies. If the courts could deal with them in their character of mere social organizations, most of the foregoing principles would be applicable. In such a case it might be that the courts of the present day, following the doctrine laid down by Lord Mansfield and others, would hold that they possess an inherent power to expel members for offenses which injuriously affect the society, although such a power is not granted by their charter, or by the statute under which they are organized. It is not necessary for us, in this case, to express a definite opinion whether a court ought so to hold or not. We may say, for the purposes of this case, that, assuming the inherent power of expelling a member to exist, it cannot be exercised upon the mere ground that the member has uttered false and malicious charges against another member. It has been held, in a case where this inherent power of expulsion was conceded, that a by-law providing for the expulsion of a member for villifying another member of the society was void.[465] But in determining whether the expulsion of Mulroy was valid, so as to revoke his benefit certificate, we had to deal with this society primarily in its character of a mutual insurance association. In societies such as this, the members to whom benefit certificates are issued acquire property rights in the society of a very important character; and in dealing with these rights it is highly essential that the courts should

[464] Rex v. Richardson, 1 Burr. 519; Rex. v. Town of Liverpool, 2 Burr. 732.
[465] Commonwealth v. St. Patrick's Ben. Soc., 2 Binn. 441.

confine themselves strictly to the terms of the contract which the members have made among themselves.[466] It would be a very dangerous doctrine to apply to societies which, in addition to the character of social clubs, possess also the character of life insurance companies, and which undertake to insure the lives of their members for the benefit of their families, paying them a large sum in the event of the death of the member, the rule that they can expel their members, and thereby deprive their families of the benefits of this insurance, it may be, after the member has paid assessments for many years, and when, by reason of age or bad health, he has passed into such a state that new insurance upon his life cannot be procured—for causes not named in their constating instruments, or in the public statutes, but such as the members of the subordinate lodge may, in the excitement of the hour, deem a good ground of expulsion. We hold in this case, as we have held in other cases of this kind, that the rights of the beneficiary in such a certificate are strictly a matter of contract; that this contract is to be found in the terms of the certificate itself, in the statutes of the society, and in the case of a society incorporated under the laws of this State, in the statutes of this State relating to such societies. Looking at these instruments we find no authority in them for the expulsion of a member of this society for the cause for which the lodge to which James Mulroy belonged undertook to expel him. The cause for which he was tried and expelled was, according to the record which was read in evidence, 'making false and malicious charges against a member of this lodge,' and in another place, 'making false and malicious charges against Brother Tobin,' without specifying *to whom* the false and malicious charges were made. The constitution, and statutes of the society, which were put in evidence, contain no grant of authority to a subordinate lodge to expel a member for such a cause. Article X of the 'constitution governing subordinate lodges' enumerates eleven distinct offenses for which a member may be suspended or expelled, but none of them resemble the charge upon which James Mulroy was expelled in this case. The one which comes nearest to it is section 6, which recites that 'a

---

[466] Grand Lodge v. Elsner, 26 Mo. App. 108; Coleman v. Knights of Honor, 18 Mo. App. 189.

member who shall be guilty of immoral conduct shall, on conviction thereof, be suspended or expelled, as the lodge may determine.' But it would plainly be a misinterpretation of this provision to hold that it refers to the case of a member making false and malicious charges against another member. It manifestly refers to conduct involving the personal morals of the member, to such an extent as to render him unfit for fellowship with the other members. The succeeding article XI relates entirely to trials and punishment. Then follows article XII, under which it would seem this prosecution and expulsion were had. Section 1 of this article reads: 'If a member shall make *to this lodge* or *to its dictator,* any accusation against a member which shall prove to be false and malicious, he shall be suspended or expelled.' It is perceived that this section is a grant of authority to subordinate lodges to expel only in the case where a member shall make false and malicious accusations against another member, either to its lodge or to its dictator. It is not necessary for us to say whether or not such a regulation would be declared void as unreasonable. Although it is found in what is called the 'constitution governing subordinate lodges,' it is in the nature of a by-law; for the statute of this State under which this society is incorporated is its charter. But it nowhere appears in this record that James Mulroy was ever tried by his lodge, or expelled therefrom, for making false or malicious charges against a member, either to the lodge or its dictator. So far as the record discloses, he was tried and expelled for the mere offense of slandering a member, it may have been, for aught that appears, in another State, or even in a foreign country. It may have been while testifying as a witness in a court of justice, while making a communication as a client to his counsel, or upon some other occasion which in law rendered it absolutely privileged. To allow the rights of a member in a society, which is in the nature of a mutual life insurance company, to be forfeited for such a cause, by such of his associates as happen to compose a subordinate lodge or branch of the general society, would, we apprehend, be going further than any court has yet gone. It follows from these premises that the lodge to which James Mulroy belonged had no jurisdiction whatever to try or expel him upon the charge above named; that his expulsion was consequently null and void; that, being merely void,

221

it was not incumbent upon him to take steps to have it reversed in a higher judicatory of the society; but that it left him clothed with the rights of membership, at least in respect of the mutual benefit fund of the society to the same extent as though it had not taken place." In a subsequent case, however,[467] the same court, while generally approving the Mulroy case, qualified it to a decided degree. The court, after referring to the nature of beneficiary organizations and the duty of a member to his co-contributors, and referring to the injustice of placing a suspended or expelled member in a better position than those paying, says: "We take the just rule to be that, even in the case of a void expulsion or suspension, the expelled or suspended member is under a duty to his co-contributors to affirm or disaffirm the act of expulsion or suspension within a reasonable time, and in some distinct manner under the circumstances; and that where he takes no steps of any kind to secure his reinstatement, allows dues which had accrued and were payable *prior* to the date of his expulsion to remain unpaid, and neither tenders such dues nor any subsequently accruing dues, he must be taken to have acquiesced in and consented to the sentence of expulsion or suspension." By appealing to a higher judicatory in a society a member acknowledges jurisdiction.[468] A member of a fraternal beneficiary association unjustly expelled can recover the assessments he has paid in.[469]

§ 129. **The Same Subject: Trial Committee.**—While under the authorities, as we have seen, a fraternal beneficiary society may, either through the Superior Lodge or local bodies, expel a member for a sufficient cause and on sufficient notice and after a fair trial the right must be exercised in strict accordance with the requirements of the constitution and by-laws, and the trial committee, or tribunal, must be unprejudiced. In a recent case,[470] in holding that the validity of the expulsion of a member of a benefit society by a prejudiced committee might be collaterally attacked in an action on his benefit certificate, where there is

[467] Glardon v. Supreme Lodge Knights of Pythias, 50 Mo. App. 45.
[468] Peyre v. Mut. Relief Soc., 90 Cal. 240; 27 Pac. 191.
[469] Slater v. Supreme Lodge K. & L. of H., 76 Mo. App. 387.
[470] Wilcox v. Supreme Council R. A., 210 N. Y. 370; 104 N. E. 624; 52 L. R. A. (N. S.) 806.

no method of directly reviewing such expulsion, it was said, in regard to the necessity for fairness in the tribunal: "Moreover, the general charge was of improper conduct, violative of his duties or of his obligation and unbecoming his profession as a member of the order. Undoubtedly it would injure the order, temporarily at least, to accuse its officers of being 'grafters,' but if the charge were well founded, an impartial judge might conclude that it was made in the discharge of the highest duty to the order, and that the temporary injury resulting from the expose of wrongdoing was more than offset by the permanent good. It is no longer the law that the greater the truth the greater the libel. At any rate, one of the issues presented by the pleadings was the truth of the defamatory charges against the members of the Supreme Council, and, of course, the question of jurisdiction must be determined by the issues framed for trial, not by the evidence produced on the trial. It would seem plain that the trial committee had a direct interest in the determination of the question whether they themselves were grafters, unless the law places property above reputation. It is as though a judge defamed were to try the defamer for a criminal libel. . . . It is shocking to one's sense of fair play that persons defamed should be selected to try the defamatory charge, and it is sufficient, for the purposes of this case, to hold that they are disqualified by a direct interest in the subject-matter of the controversy. . . . The rule of necessity cannot apply in this case, as the trial committee could have been composed of members of the order who were not members of the Supreme Council. Certainly, if all the latter were disqualified, it would not be practicable to appoint a committee from among their members."

§ 130. **Acquittal: Appeal.**—If a member of a society is once acquitted on a trial upon charges preferred against him, as, for example, by the failure of a resolution or motion for expulsion to pass, by reason of its not receiving the majority of votes required by the charter, or by-laws, he cannot be tried again for the same offense. A subsequent passage of the same resolution, or motion, by the requisite majority of votes, is a nullity.[471] An appeal of a member of a subordinate lodge from a vote of ex-

471 Commonwealth v. Guardians of the Poor, 6 Serg. & R. 469.

pulsion does not abate by the death of such member during the pendency of the appeal;[472] if on such appeal the judgment of the lodge is reversed the beneficiary of the member is entitled to recover the benefit agreed to be paid upon the death.[473] An appeal is not necessary if the proceedings are void.[474]

§ 131. **Courts Will Not Interfere if No Property Right is Involved.**—Unless a property right is involved, the courts will not interfere in the affairs of a voluntary association,[475] and even if a property right is involved the remedies within the order must first be exhausted.[476] This subject of exhausting remedies within the order will be discussed later.[477] A distinction is to be made between cases in which the expulsion of members is for violation of the rules of the society, no property right being involved, in which case the courts decline jurisdiction, leaving the expelled member to bring a suit at law for damages,[478] and cases in which the expulsion is virtually a forfeiture of property rights.[479]

[472] Marck v. Supreme Lodge, K. of H., 29 Fed. 896; Green v. Watkins, 6 Wheat. 260; Berlin v. Eureka Lodge, etc., 132 Cal. 294; 64 Pac. 254.

[473] Marck v. Supreme Lodge, etc., *supra*. To the same effect is Connolly v. Masonic Ben. Ass'n, 58 Conn. 552; 20 Atl. 671.

[474] Longnecker v. Trustees Grand Lodge, etc., 111 Wis. 279; 87 N. W. 293; 55 L. R. A. 185.

[475] Wallace v. Grand Lodge United Brothers, etc., 32 Ky. L. 1013; 107 S. W. 724; State v. Covgiat, 50 Wash. 95; 96 Pac. 689; Wellenvoss v. Grand Lodge, etc., 103 Ky. 415; 45 S. W. 360; 40 L. R. A. 488.

[476] Crutcher v. Eastern Div. Order Ry. Conductors, 151 Mo. App. 622; 132 S. W. 307.

[477] *Post*, § 624.

[478] People v. Board of Trade, 80 Ill. 134; State v. Odd Fellows, etc., 8 Mo. App. 148; Dawkins v. Antrobus, 17 L. R. Ch. D. 615; 44 L. T. 557; Rigby v. Connol, 14 L. R. Ch. D. 482; Hopkinson v. Marquis of Exeter, 37 L. J. Ch. 173; 5 L. R. Eq. 63; Baird v. Wells, L. R. 44 Ch. Div. 661; 31 Am. & Eng. Corp. Cas. 240; McKane v. Democratic General Comm., 123 N. Y. 609; 25 N. E. 1057, affg. 4 N. Y. Supp. 401; Herschhiser v. Williams (Ohio Com. Pl.), 24 Weekly L. B. 314. Also authorities next cited.

[479] Pulford v. Fire Department, 31 Mich. 458; Otto v. Journeymen Tailors', etc., Union, 75 Cal. 308; 17 Pac. 217; Mulroy v. K. of H. Supreme Lodge, 28 Mo. App. 463; Thompson v. Soc. Tammany, 17 Hun. 305; Bauer v. Sampson Lodge, 102 Ind. 262; White v. Brownell, 2 Daly 329; Austin v. Searing, 16 N. Y. 112; Olery v. Brown, 51 How. Pr. 92; Supreme Council v. Garrigus, 104 Ind. 133; Schmidt v. A. Lincoln Lodge 84 Ky. 490; 2 S. W. 156. See *post*, § 134.

Where a member of the Masonic order was expelled for slandering the Grand Master the Court refused to interfere.[480] A distinction is also always to be made between a formal expulsion for an offense on the one hand and on the other an *ipso facto*, or conditional suspension, for non-compliance with the terms of the contract of membership, *e. g.*, for non-payment at the agreed specified times of assessments or dues.[481]

§ 132. Courts Will Not Inquire into Merits of Expulsion.— One of the earliest cases in the United States in which the right of a member of a society to resort to the courts after expulsion was considered is that of Black and Whitesmiths' Society v. Van Dyke,[482] where the Court said: "Into the regularity of these proceedings, it is not permitted us to look. The sentence of the society, acting in a judicial capacity and with undoubted jurisdiction of the subject-matter, is not to be questioned collaterally, while it remains unreversed by superior authority. If the plaintiff has been expelled irregularly he has a remedy by *mandamus* to restore him; but neither by *mandamus* nor action, can the merits of his expulsion be re-examined. He stands convicted by the sentence of a tribunal of his own choice; which, like an award of arbitrators, concludes him." In a later case in the Supreme Court of the same State,[483] it was further said: "The charter to the defendants below provides for the offense, directs the mode of proceeding and authorizes the society, on conviction of the member, to expel him. This has been done, after a hearing and trial, according to the mode prescribed; at least there is no allegation of the irregularity of the proceeding. Under these circumstances the sentence is conclusive on the merits, and cannot be inquired into collaterally either by *mandamus* or action, or in any other mode. It is like an award made by a tribunal of the party's own choosing; for he became a member under and

[480] Kopp. v. White, 30 Civ. Prac. R. 352; 65 N. Y. Supp. 1017. See also Franklin v. Burnham, 40 Misc. 566; 82 N. Y. Supp. 882.
[481] Palmetto Lodge v. Hubbell, 24 S. C. (2 Strob.) 457. See Ch. 11, § 492, and *ante*, § 119.
[482] 2 Whart. 309; 30 Am. Dec. 263. See also Murray v. Supreme Hive L. M. of W., 112 Tenn. 664; 80 S. W. 827; Josich v. Austrian, etc., Soc., 119 Cal. 74; 51 Pac. 18.
[483] Commonwealth v. Pike Beneficial Soc., 8 Watts & S. 247.

225

subject to the articles and conditions of the charter, and, of course, to the provisions on this subject as well as others. The society acted judicially, and its sentence is conclusive, like that of any other judicial tribunal. The courts entertain a jurisdiction to preserve these tribunals in the line of order and to correct abuses, but they do not inquire into the merits of what has passed *in rem judicatam* in a regular course of proceedings.'' The action of the society if regular is final.[484] This doctrine has received general approval in this country and in England, as appears by a long list of adjudications, subject however to some important modifications, if not exceptions, where property rights are involved, which we will consider in course.[485] The court, if a property right is involved, will, however, look so far into the case as to satisfy itself that there was not a capricious or arbitrary exercise of the power.[486]

§ 133. **When Injured Members Can Resort to the Courts.**—It has been held in many cases that before the member can resort to the courts he must first exhaust the remedies provided by the society of which he is a member,[487] as, for example, if he has been

[484] Spillman v. Supreme Council, etc., 159 Mass. 128; 31 N. E. 776; Froelich v. Musicians', etc., Ass'n, 93 Mo. App. 383.

[485] Osceola Tribe v. Schmidt, 57 Md. 98; Sperry's Appeal, 116 Pa. St. 391; 9 Atl. 468; Anacosta Tribe v. Murbach, 13 Md. 91; Farnsworth v. Storrs, 5 Cush. 412; Burton v. St. George's Soc., 28 Mich. 261; Grosvenor v. United Soc., etc., 118 Mass. 78; Woolsey v. Independent Order, etc., 61 Ia. 492; Karcher v. Supreme Lodge, 137 Mass. 368; Loubat v. Leroy, 15 Abb. N. C. 1; White v. Brownell, 4 Abb. Pr. (N. S.) 162; s. c. 2 Daly 329; Dolan v. Court Good Samaritan, 128 Mass. 437; Olery v. Brown, 51 How. Pr. 92; Lafond v. Deems, 8 Abb. N. C. 388; s. c. 81 N. Y. 507; Hutchinson v. Lawrence, 67 How. Pr. 38; Jones v. National, etc., Ass'n, 8 Ky. L. 599; 2 S. W. 447; Hopkinson v. Marquis of Exeter, L. R. 5 Eq. 63; Dawkins v. Antrobus, L. R. 17 Ch. D. 615, affd. 44 L. T. Rep. (N. S.) 557.

[486] Hopkinson v. Marquis of Exeter, 37 L. J. Ch. 173; 5 L. R. Eq. 63; Richardson-Gardner v. Freemantle, 24 L. T. (N. S.) 81; 19 W. R. 256; Dawkins v. Antrobus, 17 L. R. Ch. D. 615; 44 L. T. 557; 29 W. R. 511; Otto v. Journeymen Tailors', etc., Union, 75 Cal. 308; 17 Pac. 217.

[487] Karcher v. Supreme Lodge, etc., 137 Mass. 368; Chamberlain v. Lincoln, 129 Mass. 70; Dolan v. Court Good Samaritan, 128 Mass. 437; Grosvenor v. United Soc., etc., 118 Mass. 78; White v. Brownell, 4 Abb. Pr. (N. S.) 162; s. c. 2 Daly 329; Lafond v. Deems, 8 Abb. N. C. 388; s. c.

cited to appear before a committee to show cause why he should not be expelled he must appear before such committee before he can resort to the courts;[488] but a different rule prevails where property rights are involved. The courts are loath to adopt the rule that societies doing a life insurance business can expel a member for some infraction of a by-law regulating personal conduct and thereby cause him to forfeit his insurance for which he has perhaps paid for a long period, at a time, too, when possibly from ill health or other reasons he may not be able to replace the indemnity;[489] and, as was said by the Supreme Court of California:[490] "Court will interfere for the purpose of protecting property rights of members of unincorporated associations in all proper cases, and, when they take jurisdiction, will follow and enforce, as far as applicable, the rules applying to incorporated bodies of the same character." The Supreme Court of Mississippi has held[491] that one wrongfully expelled from a fraternal beneficiary society is not bound to exhaust his remedy within the order before suing for damages. The Court says: "The courts will take hold of and protect personal and property rights in whatever way it may be sought to disregard them. When it comes to

81 N. Y. 508; Poultney v. Bachmann, 31 Hun. 49; Carlen v. Drury, 1 Ves. & B. 154; Harrington v. Workingmen's Ass'n, 70 Ga. 340; Lewis v. Wilson, 2 N. Y. St. R. 806; Screwmen's Ass'n v. Benson, 76 Tex. 552; 13 S. W. 379; Supreme Council, etc., v. Forsinger, 125 Ind. 52; 25 N. E. 129; Robinson v. Irish-American, etc., Soc., 67 Cal. 135; Canfield v. Great Camp, etc., 86 Mich. 626; 48 N. W. 875; Levy v. Magnolia Lodge, etc., 110 Cal. 297; 47 Pac. 887; Moore v. National Council, etc., 65 Kan. 452; 70 Pac. 352; Jeane v. Grand Lodge A. O. U. W., 86 Me. 434; 30 Atl. 70; People v. Med. Soc., 84 Hun. 448; 32 N. Y. Supp. 445; McGinness v. Court Elm City, etc., 78 Conn. 43; 60 Atl. 1023; Whilty v. McCarthy, 20 R. I. 792; 36 Atl. 129; Wood v. What Cheer Lodge, etc., R. I. 35 Atl. 1045; Camp No. 6, etc,. v. Arrington, Md. 68 Atl. 548; Donnelly v. Sup. Council, etc., Md. 67 Atl. 276; Reno Lodge v. Grand Lodge, etc., 54 Kan. 73; 37 Pac. 1003; 26 L. R. A. 98; *post*, § 624.

488 Whiteside v. Noyac Cottage Ass'n, 68 Hun. 565; 23 N. Y. Supp. 63.

489 Austin v. Searing, 16 N. Y. 112; Bauer v. Sampson Lodge, 102 Ind. 262; Supreme Council v. Garrigus, 104 Ind. 133; Pulford v. Fire Dept., 31 Mich. 457; Olery v. Brown, 51 How. Pr. 92; Mulroy v. Knights of Honor, 28 Mo. App. 463.

490 Otto v. Journeymen Tailors', etc., Union, 75 Cal. 308; 17 Pac. 217.

491 Independent Order of Sons and Daughters of Jacob v. Wilkes, 98 Miss. 179; 53 Sou. 493; 52 L. R. A. (N. S.) 817.

a matter of insurance, or the doing of any willful wrong, a so-called benevolent, mutual, fraternal, or any other insurance organization, is entitled to no immunity from its wrongdoing by virtue of the cloak it wears. Rights are more sacred than names, and in modern days the so-called mutual and benevolent associations engaged in effecting life insurance are regarded as what they in truth are, mere insurance companies adopting that plan of insurance which best suits their ideas, but insurance associations at last. It is true that some courts have held that even in a suit for damages by a person unlawfully expelled from a society or order, of which he is a member, such person must first exhaust his remedies in the order. One of these cases is the case of Lavelle v. Society, St. Jean Baptiste[492] But the large majority of cases hold the reverse of this, and, in our judgment, announce the more correct and just rule. In the case of St. Louis Southwestern R. Co. v. Thompson,[493] in part of opinion found on page 147, the Court said, in speaking of the contention that one must exhaust the remedies provided by a society of which he was a member before suing for damages: 'This is not a proceeding to restore him to his membership. It is a suit for damages occasioned by his expulsion, and one in which his property rights, as well as personal rights, are involved. We are of the opinion that it was not necessary for him to have prosecuted his appeal further than he did before instituting his suit for damages.[494] On application for *mandamus* to restore plaintiff to membership, the court would not take jurisdiction until the applicant had exhausted his remedies under the laws of the brotherhood. The same reason does not apply in a suit for damages. The right to apply to the courts for redress of such injuries as in this case exist in favor of all citizens, and could not be abridged by any association, except by the consent of the member. The defendants have no ground upon which to stand in demanding that the remedy of appeal should be exhausted before they are called upon to repair the injury they have inflicted upon Thompson. The continuance of his member-

492 17 R. I. 680; 16 L. R. A. 392; 24 Atl. 467.

493 102 Tex. 89, 99; 113 S. W. 144; 19 Ann. Cas. 1250.

494 Benson v. Screwmen's Benev. Ass'n, 2 Tex. Civ. App. 66; 21 S. W. 562; Bauer v. Samson Lodge, K. P., 102 Ind. 262; 1 N. E. 571.

ship in the brotherhood does not concern the defendants."[405] If the lodge tribunal had no jurisdiction its sentence is a nullity. Although the action of such a tribunal according to its rules, on a question which it had authority to decide, honestly taken, after the requisite notice to the members, cannot be collaterally reviewed by the courts,[496] yet, if the action of the lodge be a usurpation, or without notice or authority, it cannot affect the legal rights or change the legal status of any one. "The obligation to appeal is not imposed when the judgment is void for want of jurisdiction. It may be likened to a judgment rendered by a court which has no jurisdiction of the subject-matter or the person. No appeal or writ of error is necessary to get rid of such a judgment; it is void in all courts and places."[497] And the duty of an expelled member to exhaust, by appeals or otherwise, all the remedies within the organization, arises only where the association is acting strictly within the scope of its powers.[498] Yet, by acquiescense in a wrongful expulsion the member may be considered as waiving his rights.[499] A member is not bound to resort to the tribunals of the order if it would be useless.[500].

§ 134. **The Jurisdiction of Equity.**—In controversies between members where the rights of the members are merely fraternal, neither courts of law or equity will take jurisdiction.[501] And so a court of equity will not interfere in disputes in an unincorporated society as to the election of officers.[502] In a case before the Master of

[495] See also Lahiff v. St. Joseph's Total Abstinence & Benev. Soc., 76 Conn. 648; 65 L. R. A. 92; 100 Am. St. Rep. 1012; 57 Atl. 692; Fort v. Iowa, L. H. 146 Iowa, 183; 123 N. W. 224; Benson v. Screwmen's Benev. Ass'n, *supra*, and Thompson v. Grand International Brotherhood, L. E. 41 Tex. Civ. App. 176; 91 S. W. 834.

[496] Karcher v. Supreme Lodge, etc., 137 Mass. 368.

[497] Hall v. Supreme Lodge Knights of Honor, U. S. Cir. Ct. E. D. Ark., 24 Fed. 450.

[498] Mulroy v. Supreme Lodge Knights of Honor, 28 Mo. App. 463; Blumenfeldt v. Korschuch, 43 Ill. App. 434; Hoeffner v. Grand Lodge, etc., 41 M. A. 45.

[499] Glardon v. Supreme Lodge K. of P., 50 M. A. 45; Lavin v. Grand Lodge Comm., 104 Mo. App. 1; 78 S. W. 325.

[500] State v. Grand Lodge, A. O. U. W., 70 Mo. App. 456.

[501] National Grand Lodge, etc., v. United Brothers, etc., 36 Okla. 738; 129 Pac. 724.

[502] Bennett v. Kearns, R. I. 88 Atl. 806.

the Rolls in the Chancery Division,[503] the grounds of the interference of court of equity in matters of this kind were thus discussed: "The first question that I will consider is, what is the
jurisdiction of a court of equity as regards interfering at the
instance of a member of a society to prevent his being improperly
expelled therefrom. I have no doubt whatever that the foundation
of the jurisdiction is the right of property vested in the member
of the society and of which he is unjustly deprived by such unlawful expulsion. There is no such jurisdiction that I am aware
of reposed, in this country at least, in any of the Queen's courts
to decide upon the rights of persons to associate together when the
association possesses no property. Persons, and many persons,
do associate together without any property in common at all. A
dozen people may agree to meet and play whist at each other's
houses for a certain period, and if eleven of them refuse to associate with the twelfth any longer, I am not aware that there is
any jurisdiction in any court of justice in this country to interfere. Or a dozen or a hundred scientific men may agree with each
other in the same way to meet alternately at each other's houses,
or at any place where there is a possibility of their meeting each
other; but if the association has no property, and takes no subscriptions from its members, I cannot imagine that any court of
justice could interfere with such an association, if some of the
members declined to associate with some of the others. That is
to say, the courts, as such, have never dreamt of enforcing agreements strictly personal in their nature, whether they are agreements of hiring and service, being the common relation of master
and servant, or whether they are agreements for the purpose of
pleasure, or for the purpose of scientific pursuits, or for the purpose of charity or philanthropy—in such cases no court of justice
can interfere so long as there is no property the right to which
is taken away from the person complaining. If that is the foundation of the jurisdiction, the plaintiff, if he can succeed at all,
must succeed on the ground that some right of property to which
he is entitled has been taken away from him. That this is the
foundation of the interference of the courts as regards clubs I
think is quite clear. If we look at the Lord Chancellor's judg-

[503] Rigby v. Connol, 14 L. R. Ch. D. 482.

ment in the case of *In re* St. James' Club,[504] he says this: 'What, then, were the interests and liabilities of a member? He had an interest in the general assets as long as he remained a member, and if the club was broken up while he was a member, he might file a bill to have its assets administered in this court, and he would be entitled to share in the furniture and effects of the club.' So he puts it that the member has an interest in the assets. In the case of Hopkinson v. Marquis of Exeter,[505] Lord Romilly says this: 'This is an application by the plaintiff asking a declaration that he is entitled to the enjoyment of the property and effects of the Conservative Club, and to participate in its rights, privileges, and benefits, and also that the defendants, the committee of the club, may be restrained by injunction from excluding him therefrom.' So that he starts with the enjoyment of property, and the subsequent cases have gone on the same ground.''[506] In a recent case,[507] the complainant had been expelled from a proprietary club and sought remedy by injunction. In holding that equity had no jurisdiction the Court said: ''In all the cases of this nature in which up to the present time an injunction has been granted, the club has been one of the ordinary kind, *i. e.*, it has been possessed of property (such as a freehold or leasehold house, furniture, books, pictures and money at a bank) which was vested in trustees upon trust to permit the members for the time being to have the personal use and enjoyment of the club house and effects in and about it. But the interest of the members is not confined to that purely personal right. The members might, if they all agree, put an end to the club; and in that case they would be entitled, after the debts and liabilities of the club were satisfied, to have the assets divided among them. In the present case the club, as such, has no property. The club-house and furniture belong to the defendant Wells, and by him the subscriptions are taken. He is not a trustee but the owner of the property. If the club were dissolved at any moment there would be nothing whatever to divide among the members. Now the interference of the court in the cases which

504 2 D. M. & G. 383; 16 Jur. 1075.
505 L. R. 5 Eq. 63.
506 Van Houten v. Pine, 36 N. J. Eq. 133 and note; *post*, § 613.
507 Baird v. Wells, L. R. 44 Ch. D. 661; 31 Am. & Eng. Corp. Cas. 240-246.

have hitherto occurred has been based on the rights of property of which the member had been improperly deprived. The general principle was laid down by Lord Cranworth in the case of Forbes v. Eden,[508] where he said:[509] 'Save for the due disposal and administration of property there is no authority in the courts of either England or Scotland to take cognizance of the rules of a voluntary society entered into merely for the regulation of its own affairs.' And the same principle was stated at great length by the late Master of the Rolls (Sir George Jessel) in the case of Rigby v. Connol.[510] In that case the plaintiff sought to restrain the defendant from excluding him from the benefits of a trades union of which he was a member. Sir George Jessel said:[511] 'The first question that I will consider is, what is the jurisdiction of a court of equity as regards interfering at the instance of a member of a society to prevent his being improperly expelled therefrom? I have no doubt whatever that the foundation of the jurisdiction is the right of property vested in the member of the society and of which he is unjustly deprived by such unlawful expulsion. There is no such jurisdiction that I am aware of reposed, in this country at least, in any of the Queen's courts to decide upon the rights of persons to associate together when the association possesses no property . . . I cannot imagine that any court of justice could interfere with such an association if some of the members declined to associate with some of the others. That is to say, the courts as such have never dreamt of enforcing agreements strictly personal in their nature . . . in such cases no court of justice can interfere so long as there is no property the right to which is taken away from the person complaining. If that is the foundation of the jurisdiction, the plaintiff, if he can succeed at all, must succeed on the ground that some right of property to which he is entitled has been taken away from him. That this is the foundation of the interference of the courts as regards clubs I think is quite clear.' Then his lordship referred to certain cases and came to the conclusion that the plaintiff was not entitled to any relief. Here, as I have pointed out, there are

508 Law Rep. 1 H. L. 568.
509 L. R. 1 H. L. 568.
510 14 Ch. D. 482.
511 14 Ch. D. 487, 488.

no funds vested in trustees, or settled to be disposed of by the members of the Pelican Club in accordance with the rules of that association and the question is whether the plaintiff, as a member of that club, has any right of property for the protection of which the court will interfere by way of injunction, and in my judgment he has not. The position appears to me to be this: each member is entitled by contract with the defendant Wells to have the personal use and enjoyment of the club, in common with the other members, so long as he pays his subscription and is not excluded from the club under rule 17. That right is, as it seems to me, of a personal nature such as, if infringed, may give rise to a claim for damages, but not such as the court will enforce by way of specific performance or injunction. The contract in its legal nature closely resembles contracts for providing board and lodging in a particular house, as when the head of a household admits a boarder into his family for a fixed period, or the proprietor of a private boarding house agrees to provide for a term, board and lodging for one boarder in common with others; as to which Wright v. Stavert,[512] may be referred to. The contracts in these cases fall, in my opinion, under the head of agreements strictly personal in their nature, and consequently in neither of them would the court interfere by way of injunction at the instance of the boarder. So, also, in my judgment, is it in the present case. It was contended that damages might be an insufficient remedy by reason of a decision being given which affects the character and position in society of the plaintiff and does not satisfy the requirements of the law. In no case, so far as I am aware, has the existence of such circumstances been treated as affording ground for the granting of an injunction to restrain the proceedings of a voluntary society, and indeed upon the principle laid down in the case of Forbes v. Eden,[513] it might well happen that decisions which gravely affect some members of a voluntary society and do not satisfy the requirements of the law, might be arrived at by the committee or other like body without being open to be questioned in any civil court or giving rise to any right of action whatever."

[512] 2 E. & E. 721.
[513] L. R. 1 H. L., § 568.

§ 135. **The Remedy of Mandamus: What the Court Will Consider.**—As a general rule, a member wrongfully expelled from a society, or when the proceedings are irregular, may be restored by *mandamus,* and this is the proper remedy.[514] However, the courts, in these actions or in applications to enjoin interference, will only examine to see if the proceedings were in accordance with the rules of the society, and not inherently against the principles of justice. The rule is thus laid down by the High Court of Appeal:[515] ''The only question which a court can properly consider is whether the members of the club, under such circumstances, have acted *ultra vires* or not, and it seems to me the only questions which a court can properly entertain for that purpose are, whether anything has been done which is contrary to natural justice, although it is within the rules of the club—in other words, whether the rules of the club are contrary to natural justice; secondly, whether a person who has not condoned the departure from them has been acted against contrary to the rules of the club; and thirdly, whether the decision of the club has been come to *bona fide* or not. Unless one of those charges can be made out by those who come before the court, the court has no power to interfere with what has been done.''[516]

§ 136. **Presumption of Regularity of Expulsion Proceedings.** —While ordinarily there is a presumption that there is fairness on the part of the fellow-members of a society in proceedings for expulsion of another,[517] and, while if jurisdiction be shown, courts will also presume that the proceedings were regular, and will look at justice rather than form,[518] yet there are to be no presump-

---

[514] See *post,* § 613.

[515] Dawkins v. Antrobus, 17 L. R. Ch. D. 630.

[516] Society v. Commonwealth, 52 Pa. St. 125; Commonwealth v. German Soc., etc., 15 Pa. St. 251; Otto v. Journeymen Tailors', etc., Union, 75 Cal. 308; 17 Pac. 217; Schweiger v. Society, etc., 13 Phila. 113; Sibley v. Carteret Club, 40 N. J. L. 295; People v. N. Y. Ben. Ass'n, 3 Hun. 362; People v. St. Franciscus, etc., 24 How. Pr. 216; People v. St. George, etc., 28 Mich. 261; Commonwealth v. Guardians of Poor, etc., 6 Serg. & R. 469; Pulford v. Fire Dept., 31 Mich. 458; People v. Medical Soc., Erie, 24 Barb. 570. See *ante,* § 132.

[517] Bachmann v. N. Y. Arbeiter, etc., 64 How. Pr. 442; Harman v. Dreher, 1 Speer Eq. 87; Shannon v. Frost, 3 B. Mon. 253.

[518] Burton v. St. George Soc., 28 Mich. 261.

tions in the case of forfeiture of property, or other important rights,[519] because the law is opposed to sharp, summary proceedings involving forfeitures.[520]

§ 137. **Withdrawal of Member of Voluntary Association.**— Unless the compact between the members of a voluntary association provide to the contrary, a member may withdraw from it at any time. ''The entering into it, the remaining in it, the performance of duties incumbent upon the member, by reason of his membership, are purely voluntary.'' Consequently the member may withdraw when he pleases without the consent of the association. But by so doing he cannot avoid any obligations incurred by him to the association, nor can it, after such withdrawal, impose any new obligations upon him.[521] It has been said[522] that a member of a fraternal society may with or without cause terminate his membership. A notice of withdrawal by a member is a bar to an action for benefits although the society had not assented or dissented thereto or erased his name.[523] The court in the case last cited says: ''It will be observed that this right of withdrawal on the part of the insured is absolute and in no way dependent upon the assent or dissent of the company. Its omission to erase his name or accept his withdrawal in no way restricts or limits the absolute right of withdrawal under the contract. . . . The insured, therefore, by his own act, during his lifetime, availed himself of his right under the contract, and ceased to be a member, which effectually bars a recovery.'' Nor is the association estopped from asserting that the member has voluntarily withdrawn from membership, although it has denied his right to voluntarily withdraw, unless, in so doing, it has led the member to believe, to his prejudice, that he is still a mem-

519 Pulford v. Fire Department, 31 Mich. 458.

520 People v. Medical Soc., 32 N. Y. 187.

521 Ellerbe, etc., v. Barney, 119 Mo. 632; 25 S. W. 384; Borgraefe v. Knights & Ladies of Honor, 26 M. A. 218; 22 Mo. App. 127; Stewart v. Supreme Council A. L. H., 36 M. A. 319; Springmeyer v. Benev. Ass'n, 5 Cin. L. B. 516; Cramer v. Masonic L. Ass'n, 9 N. Y. Supp. 356; Gray v. Daly, 40 App. Div. 41; 57 N. Y. Supp. 527. The question is also considered in Patrons' Mut. Aid Soc. v. Hall, 19 Ind. App. 118; 49 N. E. 279.

522 Cholcupka v. Bohemian Roman Catholic, etc., 111 Ill. App. 585.

523 Cramer v. Masonic L. Ass'n, *supra.*

ber.[524] It is not necessary that a resignation be accepted or be acted upon by the society.[525] By a voluntary withdrawal the member loses any interest in the property or funds of the association,[526] an intention to withdraw may be shown by conduct as well as words and is a waiver of any informalities in manner of suspension,[527] and a member of a fraternal beneficiary association may abandon his membership and thereby lose all rights to benefits.[528] It has been held, however,[529] that where the rights of a beneficiary have attached the withdrawal is not complete unless the benefit certificate is surrendered, the society having notice of the facts. The question is one of intention.[530]

§ 138. **Personal Liability of Members of Unincorporated Society.**—As to the personal liability of members of a voluntary association, for, if incorporated, the identity of the members of the society is for general purposes merged in the entity of the corporation, a distinction is made between differences arising between members themselves, or internal controversy, and questions between a creditor on the one hand and the body, or one or more members, on the other, or external controversies. ''The courts have always distinguished between the principles applicable to the two cases of controversies, and have, in the absence of a better guide, leaned in the one class of cases toward the-rules offered by corporations, and often in the other class of cases, towards those offered by the law of partnership or agency.''[531] It is no

---

[524] Borgraefe v. Knights, etc., of Honor, 26 Mo. App. 218; Stewart v. Sup. Council Am. Leg. of H., 36 M. A. 319.

[525] Kelly v. Knights of Father Mathew, 170 Mo. App. 608; 162 S. W. 682; Ewald v. Medical Soc., 128 N. Y. Supp. 886.

[526] Burt v. Oneida Community, 137 N. Y. 346; 33 N. E. 307; 19 L. R. A. 297; Missouri Bottlers' Ass'n v. Fennerty, 81 Mo. App. 525.

[527] Railway Passenger, etc., Ass'n v. Leonard, 82 Ill. App. 214; Lavin v. Grand Lodge A. O. U. W., 112 Mo. App. 5; 78 S. W. 325.

[528] Lavin v. Grand Lodge, *supra;* Hansen v. Supreme Lodge K. of H., 140 Ill. 310; Van Frank v. U. S. Ben. Ass'n, 158 Ill. 560.

[529] Conselyea v. Supreme Counc. A. L. H., 3 App. Div. 464; 38 N. Y. Supp. 248; affd. 157 N. Y. 719; 53 N. E. 1124.

[530] Wanek v. Supreme Lodge Bohemian, etc., Soc., 84 Mo. App. 185; Ryan v. Mut. Reserve F. L. Ass'n, 96 Fed. 796; Foxheyer v. Order Red Cross, 24 Ohio Cir. Ct. R. 56.

[531] Ebbinghousen v. Worth Club, 4 App. N. C. 300 (See note by reporter).

defense to an action against the member that a creditor agreed to look to the lodge for payment..[352] The general principle has thus been laid down :[533] "Certain societies, as clubs, which are not constituted for any purpose of profit, are exposed to liabilities similar in many respects to those of a partnership. All parties who take an active part in working out a project, who attend meetings. at which resolutions are made or orders given for the supply of goods, in furtherance of a joint undertaking, are, in general, jointly responsible. The act of a secretary of a voluntary association will not bind the board, if not authorized; but it will bind any members who were present at a meeting, and concurred in giving authority to the secretary. Where members of a voluntary association authorize its officers to engage in a particular transaction in the name of the society, as they do not bind the society as a body, or give to persons interested a tangible third party against whom they can proceed, they are themselves the only persons that can be sued, and are, in fact, principals in the transaction.[534] If the appellant's members of an organized club or association of gentlemen, expressly authorized the presiding officer of the association to execute a note in the name of the club, or in any other name whatever, expressive of an association of men, and to use this note when made, for the purpose of purchasing bonds to be owned by and used for the club of which they were members, and these bonds were purchased and the note executed in the name of the club, whatever may be said as to the liability of the other members of the association, we cannot see on what principle it can be denied that those expressly sanctioning or ratifying this use of the club's name are liable upon the note to the person who advanced the money. It is not necessary to invoke the doctrine of partnership, perhaps; yet as to this particular transaction these men became partners, though not

[532] McClellan v. Rohe, 93 Ind. 298.

[533] Ferris v. Thaw, 5 Mo. App. 279; affd. 72 Mo. 446.

[534] Heath v. Goslin, 80 Mo. 310; Lewis v. Tilton, 64 Ia. 220; s. c. 52 Am. Rep. 436; Ray v. Powell, 134 Mass. 22; Newell v. Borden, 128 Mass. 31; Doubleday v. Muskett, 7 Bing. 110; Blakeley v. Bennecke, 59 Mo. 193; Horseley v. Bell, 1 Brown Ch. 101; Cullen v. Duke Queensbury, I Brown Ch. 101. See also Murray v. Walker, 83 Ia. 202; 48 N. W. 1075 and Hornberger v. Orchard, 39 Neb. 639; 58 N. W. 425.

partners in trade, and however distinct as to other matters. And if they choose to assume a common name, under that name they will, each and every one, be liable as if the name signed to the note was the individual name of each man; and if they employ an agent's hand to write that name, it is as if each man himself had held the pen. If, on the maturity of this note, it was by express authorization or sanctioning of these several men, renewed by another note, executed in the name of the club by its presiding officer, this note also would be the note, not of the agent, but of all those who had sanctioned this use of the club name, and for the purposes of this transaction adopted it as their own. The mere name is nothing; its only office is that of identification. If Smith choose to call himself Snooks, and to make a contract by the name of Snooks, he binds himself as effectually as if he had signed the name of Smith.[535] If the appellants authorized Thaw to execute a promissory note, to be used to purchase property for their purposes, and told him to execute it in the name of the lodge, it is manifest that they intended to enter into a contract by that name. They did not mean that Thaw alone should be bound, for Thaw could bind himself without any authority from them, and in his own proper name; they could not by their act bind the lodge, for it was not a corporate body; nor could they bind the individual members of the lodge, for whom they were not authorized to act. They were themselves the principals in the transactions, if they directed or sanctioned the making and renewal of the note; and if the money was obtained on this note, and received by the lodge of which they were members, they are personally liable on the just principles of the common law." In another case, where an action had been brought to charge the members of a campaign committee[536] the Court said: "Associations and clubs, the objects of which are social or political and not for purposes of trade or profit, are not partnerships, and pecuniary liability can be fastened upon the individual members of such associations only by reason of the acts of such individuals or of their agents; and the agency must be made out—none is implied

[535] Snooks' Petition, 2 Hilt. 575.
[536] Richmond v. Judy, 6 Mo. App. 467.

from the mere fact of association.[537] . . . If the work was done with the previous concurrence or subsequent approbation of defendants, they and all the members of the club who stood in the same situation were liable to pay for the goods if the credit was given to the members of the club. . . . If the plaintiff had trusted solely to the state of the funds, and this had been shown, the members of the committee could not have been liable unless the funds were collected; but if the credit was given to the members of the committee, such members as were aware of the dealing and authorized or sanctioned it are undoubtedly liable. So far as the evidence of agency goes, a course of dealing may amount to proof of original authority. The fact that defendants, when the bill was presented to them, recognized it as correct, together with the publicity of the work, go to show that defendants knew that the work was being ordered in the name of the committee of which they were members, especially as the work done was so clearly in furtherance of the object for which the committee was organized. The evidence of ratification, even though doubtful and susceptible of different interpretation, is properly submitted to a jury; and slight circumstances and small matters are sometimes sufficient to raise a presumption of ratification. It may further be said that though a part of the members of a voluntary organization cannot, as a general rule, bind the others without their consent before the act which it is claimed binds them is done, or they have ratified it and adopted it with full knowledge of all the facts, yet there are cases, as is said in Sizer v. Daniels,[538] in which the objects for which the association is organized are so clear, and the acts done so essentially necessary to the furtherance of that object, that all will be presumptively bound by them without evidence of consent or ratification. . . . The question is purely one of agency.[539] And

[537] Bailey v. Macauley, 19 L. J. Q. B. 73; Wood v. Finch, 2 Fost. & Fin. 447; Delaunay v. Strickland, 2 Stark. 416; Sizer v. Daniels, 66 Barb. 426; Luckombe v. Ashton, 2 Fost & Fin. 707; Flemyng v. Hector, 2 M. & W. 172.

[538] 66 Barb. 426.

[539] Ridgeley v. Dobson, 3 Watts & S. 118; Sproat v. Porter, 9 Mass. 300; Flemyng v. Hector, 2 M. & W. 172; s. c. 2 Gale, 180; McMahon v. Rauhr, 47 N. Y. 67; Devoss v. Gray, 22 Ohio St. 159; Beaumont v. Meredith, 3 Ves. & B. 180; Todd v. Emly, 7 M. & W. 427; In re St. James

the Supreme Court of Nebraska has said:[540] "The plaintiffs in error were entitled to an instruction to the effect that their liability did not attach for any debts of the society prior to the date of their becoming members of it, and nowhere in the record was there any such instruction given; and, as before observed, Orchard based his right to hold the plaintiffs in error liable on the theory that they were members of the society when the goods were purchased. The charges of the court and the instructions given by him at the request of the plaintiff left room for the jury to infer that if the plaintiffs in error became members after the debt was contracted, and then attended meetings of the society, at which the debt was spoken of, acknowledged to be unpaid, and promise made to pay it, the plaintiffs in error thereby ratified and became liable to pay for what the society had done before they joined it. No member of a voluntary, unincorporated association is liable for any debt contracted by such society unless at the time the debt was incurred he was a member thereof, except by an express contract, based on a good consideration, all which must be alleged and proved." The Supreme Court of Iowa said,[541] that the power of a member of an unincorporated association to bind another is confined to transactions within the natural and proper scope of the business in which they are associated and a non-trading association has no power to borrow money or to make negotiable paper. A member of a voluntary association is liable for the obligations within the scope of the society, although he did not consent to them. Loss, before the record had been made up, of the informal minutes of a meeting of a voluntary association, where an act was authorized, does not preclude the plaintiff, in an action against the members of the society for work and materials furnished in fitting up its meeting room, from showing by oral evi-

Club, 2 D. G. M. & G. 383; Caldicott v. Griffiths, 8 Exch. 898; Babb v. Reed, 5 Rawle, 151; Leech v. Harris, 2 Brewst. 571; Ebbinghausen v. Worth Club, 4 Abb. N. C. 300 and note; Gorman v. Russell, 14 Cal. 537; Heath v. Goslin, 80 Mo. 310; Volger v. Ray, 131 Mass. 439; Newell v. Borden, 128 Mass. 31; Ehrmantraut v. Robinson, 52 Minn. 333; 54 N. W. 188; Nelson Distilling Co. v. Loe, 47 Mo. App. 31; McCabe v. Goodfellow, 133 N. Y. 89; 30 N. E. 728. See ante, § 58, et seq.

[540] Hornberger v. Orchard, 39 Neb. 639; 58 N. W. 425.

[541] Schumacher v. Sumner Tel. Co., 161 Iowa 326; 142 N. W. 1034.

dence that such a vote was passed.[542] Members of a voluntary as- ·
sociation may pay notes, or renewals of notes, given in behalf of
a loan made to the association and enforce contributions from their
fellow members.[543]

§ 139. **Personal Liability of Members, How Avoided.**—If a
member of an unincorporated society wishes to avoid responsibility for debts which it is likely to incur by withdrawal he should
give notice to the public;[544] but if obligations have already been ·
incurred he cannot avoid any liability by withdrawing from membership.[545]

§ 140. **Individual Liability for Sick or Funeral Benefits.**—
It has often been attempted to hold the members of a lodge liable
personally for the promised benefit in time of sickness. It may
be a question of construction in each particular case whether the
members are personally liable or not. In at least one case, that
of a lodge of the order of Chosen Friends,[546] the members were
held personally liable; but the better rule seems generally to be
that laid down by the Supreme Court of Massachusetts, where it
was sought to personally charge the members of a lodge of Odd
Fellows for a death benefit. The Court held in that case,[547] that
under the constitution and the laws of the lodge, the credit was
given to the fund created by the joint contributions of the members who only agreed to pay these certain and stated contributions or dues. In the case of Cochran v. Boleman,[548] the Court
says: "When Asa S. Cochran, appellant's husband, now deceased,
became a member of said mutual benefit department of said order,
he consented and agreed to the by-laws of said department and
the application and certificate issued to said Cochran, in which
appellant is named as the beneficiary, as the contract which was

542 Newell v. Borden, 128 Mass. 31.

543 Hardy v. Carter, Tex. Civ. A., 163 S. W. 1003.

544 Park v. Spaulding, 10 Hun. 128.

545 *Ante*, § 137, *et seq.*

546 Pritchett v. Schafer, 2 W. N. C. 317.

547 Payne v. Snow, 12 Cush. 443; 59 Am. Dec. 203. See also Foster v.
Moulton, 35 Minn. 458. To the same effect is Myers v. Jenkins, 63 Ohio
St. 101; 57 N. E. 1089.

548 162 Ind. 659; 71 N. E. 47; 1 Ann. Cas. 388; 65 L. R. A. 516.

to govern him and the other members of said department in adjusting their rights and obligations among themselves.[549] According to this contract there was no promise to each member by all the other members that in the event of his death they would pay his beneficiary anything. The only provision made to compel the payment of the assessments to said department is the penalty of forfeiture of membership in said department and of all rights under said contract. In such a case the assessments cannot be collected by a suit against the member refusing to pay the same.[550] Under this kind of a contract, the members of said department are not personally liable to a beneficiary for a death claim."[551]

§ 141. **Liability of Persons Contracting in Name of Voluntary Association.**—Generally, whenever any person, or persons, contract in the name of an unincorporated organization, he or they are personally liable for the obligations so incurred. In such a case the Supreme Court of Iowa said:[552] "It is said these defendants did not contract. They certainly represented that they had a principal for whom they had authority to contract. They, for or on behalf of an alleged principal, contracted that such principal would do and perform certain things. As we have said, there is no principal, and it seems to us that the defendants should be held liable, and that it is immaterial whether they be so held because they held themselves out as agents for a principal that had no existence, or on the ground that they must, under the contract, be regarded as principals, for the simple reason that there is no other principal in existence."[553] The question, however, would seem to be in all cases an inquiry of to whom credit was given.[554]

[549] Bacon Ben. Soc., §§ 37, 38, 39; St. Mary's Beneficial Soc. v. Burford, 70 Pa. 321.

[550] Gibson v. Megrew, 154 Ind. 273; 48 L. R. A. 362; 56 N. E. 674; Lehman v. Clark, 174 Ill. 294; 43 L. R. A. 648; 51 N. E. 222; Clark v. Schromeyer, 23 Ind. App. 565; 55 N. E. 785.

[551] Hammerstein v. Parsons, 38 Mo. App. 332; Payne v. Snow, 12 Cush. 443; 59 Am. Dec. 203; Bryden v. Hinds (Cal.) 55 Alb. L. J. 327.

[552] Lewis v. Tilton, 64 Ia. 220; 52 Am. Rep. 436.

[553] Ash v. Guie, 97 Pa. St. 493; Fredendall v. Taylor, 26 Wis. 286; *ante*, § 35.

[554] *Ante*, § 62, *et seq.*

§ 142. **Summary of Principles Stated in This Chapter.**—From the cases hereinbefore cited we deduce the following general rules:

1. Members of all associations, incorporated or voluntary, are bound by the charter or articles of association and by-laws, lawfully adopted in accordance therewith, provided such by-laws do not contravene the charter, or common or statute law and are not unreasonable. This reasonableness will be determined by the courts, they being governed by considerations growing out of the nature of the society and by the fact whether or not property rights are involved.

2. In seeking to obtain rights under the by-laws or rules of a society the member must proceed as therein required and generally exhaust the remedies established by the by-laws and rules before applying to the courts for relief. If no tribunal is established by the rules he may at once resort to the courts. In the case, however, of property rights, it has been held that he may or may not leave the determination to the tribunals of the order; he may sue at once or he may consent to an adjudication by the society, in which latter case, he is bound as by an arbitration, provided no principles of natural justice have been violated by the tribunal and the proceedings are regular.

3. All voluntary associations or incorporated societies may expel a member as provided in their rules, or for violation of his duty as a corporator, or if he becomes infamous, but, if property rights are involved, or if the society be incorporated, the courts will judge of the reasonableness and validity of such rules and will be reluctant to enforce or permit forfeiture of important rights. In any event the proceedings by the society must be in accordance with its rules; notice must be given to the accused and he afforded an opportunity to explain his conduct and defend himself, and then if the proceedings are regular and fair or if no property right is involved, the court will not interfere; if, however, the rules are illegal or unreasonable or the proceedings irregular, the court will enjoin the procedure, or any interference with the rights of the members, or, if he has been wrongfully expelled, restore him by mandamus, provided some property rights attaches to membership, or he may have his action for damages.

4. In regard to the jurisdiction of superior over inferior bodies

243

in an order, or society, the courts will not enforce a forfeiture of
the property rights of the latter, but may even interfere to prevent it. In such cases considerations of public policy will always
prevail. In mere matters of discipline, where no property right is
involved, the decision of the superior organization, if regularly
rendered and not inherently unjust, will be regarded as final.

5. Where subordinate organizations have a conventional as well
as a State charter either may be forfeited or taken away without
affecting the other. But in no case can a State charter be impaired or taken away except by direct action of the State. Forfeiture of the conventional charter of a society incorporated by
the State will not divest its property, nor can the property be
affected by a secession of part of its members. Even if unincorporated, the majority of a society have generally the right to cut
loose from a superior governing body, and the minority have no
redress if the property is used for the general purposes for which
it was acquired.

6. In regard to personal liability of the member for the debts
or obligations of the society, the rule is that liabilities can only
be fastened on him by reason of his own acts, or by reason of the
acts of his agents; and the agency must be made out by the person
who relies on it, for none is implied by the mere fact of association.

CHAPTER IV.

§ 143. **Associations and Corporations Act Through Agents.**
—It stands to reason that all associations of individuals, whether endowed with corporate powers and privileges, or unincorporated, must of necessity do most acts through the intervention of agents, for the members can act as a body upon comparatively few occasions. The liability of the associated persons, either as an association or individuals, must usually, if not always, be determined by an application of the general principles of the law of agency, modified sometimes by the circumstances of each particular case.[1] Life and accident insurance companies are corporations which must act through agents, so that it is important to know by what rules their liability is determined. Benefit societies have certain peculiar and individual characteristics: in some cases, their undertakings resemble the contracts of life insurance companies, at other times their engagements are only such as arise in the ordinary business of clubs or associations for social or commercial objects. The one class of contracts are those of life insurance and are similar in many respects to those of ordinary life insurance companies, they are consequent to and generally arise out

[1] *Ante,* § 35.

246

of the membership and as incident thereto; the second class may be made up of all other undertakings and agreements and are not different from those of individuals or of other corporations. We propose, therefore, in this chapter to consider the law applicable to the acts of officers and agents of both classes of companies, and also of voluntary associations. The necessity of this discussion will appear more plainly as we proceed.

§ 144. **When General Engagements of Clubs are Binding on Their Members.**—In regard to the general engagements of associations or clubs, which are contracted through agents, the rule is that they are binding upon all the members if the rules and constitution of the organization either expressly or impliedly authorize the acts, or if the objects of the association are so clear and the acts done so essentially necessary to the furtherance of that object that all the members will be presumptively bound by such acts without evidence of consent or ratification.[2] Otherwise only those members who have either authorized the act or ratified it when done will be bound.[3]

§ 145. **General Principles of Law of Agency.**—To determine the rights and liabilities of these corporations, or associations, their members or their agents, involves a consideration of the whole law of agency. It is not necessary, however, to here undertake so arduous a task nor would it be to the advantage of the reader. There are, it is true, peculiar contingencies and circumstances which we may consider with profit, but it must always be remembered that the contracts of all individuals, corporations or associations entered into through agents are to be construed and the liability determined by an application of the general principles of the law of agency. The extent of the authority of an agent is a question of fact to be determined by the circumstances of each case, and it is difficult if not impossible to devise a code of rules applicable universally. In some States statutes have been enacted on the subject.[4]

---

[2] *Ante,* § 139, *et seq.*

[3] *Ante,* § 142.

[4] Iowa Ann. Code 1897, § 1749, *et seq.* Similar statutes have been enacted in thirty-five other States.

§ 146.   General Rules of Agency Apply to Agents of all Kinds of Companies.—It must not be thought that the established rules of the law of agency do not apply to the transactions of life insurance companies. There is no particular sanctity about the business of life or any other kind of insurance. The companies engaged in it have the right to employ agents and to give to them such authority as they please; whatever limitations are imposed upon such agents, if communicated to those dealing with them, will be binding, and if this authority is exceeded, the act will not hold the principal. On the other hand, if the agents are held out to the public as possessing certain powers, their acts within the apparent scope of their authority will bind their principals. While the business of life insurance has its recognized peculiarities, the courts have constantly endeavored to apply to all the transactions of the agents of fire or life insurance organizations, or mutual benefit societies engaged in doing a life insurance business, the general doctrines of the law of agency. The inquiry always is: What was the contract entered into by the parties? If made through an agent what was the authority of the agent, and had the party dealing with him any notice of limitations or restrictions upon such authority, or were there sufficient circumstances to put him on his guard and to require him to acquaint himself with this actual authority? The principles of the law of waiver and estoppel are also involved to a great extent.[5] Of course, in these, as in other cases, much depends upon the special circumstances of each case, but the same rules must be applied to all. It is reasonable, on principle, to distinguish between the acts of agents of mutual organizations, where the assured is supposed to acquaint himself with the laws of the society and the limitations, if any there be contained in them, upon the powers of such agents, and cases where the agent represents a corporation dealing with all as a stranger. As we inquire further into the subject we shall find that the cases are not always consistent, though these inconsistencies become fewer as we study them. It is not that the courts are in doubt as to what is the principle of the law of agency which is to be applied, but because other legal principles are invoked to modify the hardships of a vigorous application of the

[5] See *post*, § 589, *et seq.*

strict rules of agency, that the difficulties in reconciling the cases exist.

§ 147. **Officers and Committees are Special Agents.**—The officers and committees of an unincorporated society, as well as those of an incorporated organization, are the agents of the body of members for certain specific purposes and are therefore to be deemed special agents, whose commission and authority is to be found in the rules and articles of association or in the special orders appointing them. As is said in Flemyng v. Hector:[6] "It is therefore a question here how far the committee, who are to conduct the affairs of this club as agents, are authorized to enter into such contracts as that upon which the plaintiffs now seek to bind the members of the club at large; and that depends upon the constitution of the club, which is to be found in its own rules." In another case,[7] it is said that the constitution of the society and its laws agreed upon by the members, which contain all the stipulations of the parties, form the law which should govern. The members have established a law themselves.[8] So the executive board cannot turn a voluntary association into a corporation in the absence of express authority in the constitution and laws of association.[9] The officers and agents of the regular insurance companies are subject to the same rules, although frequently they have the powers of general agents with almost unlimited powers.

§ 148. **Presumptions of Law Concerning Members.**—The presumption is that each person upon becoming a member of an association consents that it shall be represented by such officers and agents as are reasonably necessary for the transaction of its business, and that in the absence of express provisions in the charter limiting their powers, they shall possess the powers and perform the duties ordinarily possessed and performed by such officers and agents; and such member is bound by the rules of the company which he is presumed to know.[10]

[6] 2 Mees. & W. 179.

[7] Leech v. Harris, 2 Brewst. 571.

[8] Cockrell v. Aucompte, 26 L. J. C. P. 194; 2 C. B. (N. S.) 440; 3 Jur. (N. S.) 844; White v. Brownell, 2 Daly 329.

[9] Randolph v. Southern Ben. L., 7 N. Y. Supp. 135.

[10] Protection Life Ins. Co. v. Foote, 79 Ill. 361.

§ 149. **Charter or Articles of Association Fountain of Author-ity of Officers, Agents and Committees.**—The affairs of all cor-porations and societies must be managed by agents through whom all their business is transacted and, whether these agents be called officers, directors or committees, they are, nevertheless, agents, and the general rules of agency apply. The articles of associa-tion, or charter, taken generally in connection with the by-laws, is the fountain of authority defining and limiting their duties and powers,[11] and beyond these definite powers they cannot go, although in the case of executed contracts, the company is, upon principles analogous to those of estoppel, sometimes debarred from asserting this defense, when this authority has been exceeded. The society is bound by acts done within the apparent scope of the agent's authority and such as are usually performed by agents of a similar class in that particular course of business.[12] It fol-lows that officers, directors and committees may do all such acts as are within the scope of their apparent authority and usually incident to their offices. This rule, however, must be taken with some degree of allowance, for much will depend upon the special circumstances of each case.[13]

§ 150. **When Judicial Powers Cannot be Conferred.**—But an association cannot, by its constitution or by-laws, confer judicial powers upon its officers or committees so as to enable such officers, or committees (without voluntary submission to their authority on the part of lodges or members), to adjudge a forfeiture of property rights, or to deprive lodges or members of their prop-erty, or to arbitrarily take property away from one set of members and give it to another set. This is on the ground that the creation of judicial tribunals is one of the functions of sovereign power and because to allow such powers to be conferred would be contrary to public policy, just as agreements to refer future controversies to arbitration cannot be enforced. An adjudication of these offi-cers, or committees, which has this effect of forfeiture of prop-erty, or property rights, is not good either as an award or as

11 Herndon v. Triple Alliance, 45 M. A. 426; *ante,* § 144.
12 Morawetz on Corp., § 587, *et seq.*
13 *Ante,* § 146.

a judgment.[14] But this must not be understood to mean that the officers of Grand or Supreme Lodges cannot (if no property rights are involved and the inferior lodge is not incorporated in a different State), acting in accordance with the laws of the association, and by way of discipline, deprive local or subordinate lodges of their fraternal charters;[15] or that subordinate lodges cannot provide in their laws that no member shall be entitled to benefits for sickness or otherwise, unless certain officers, or a committee, shall determine the amount and extent of the same,[16] or, possibly, the right.[17] Or that lodges may not, by their laws, provide that if a member does not pay an assessment, or his dues, within a specified time, he shall by such failure, forfeit his membership, or be subject to expulsion;[18] or that lodges may not, by their laws, and under the restrictions and limitations hereinbefore stated, provide for tribunals or committees by which members charged with certain offenses may be tried and, if found guilty, expelled from membership.[19]

§ 151. **Election of Officers.**—It is not within the scope of this work to enter into a discussion of the law of corporate elections, or the election of officers of a voluntary association, other than to say that the requirements of the charter, by-laws or articles of association must be substantially followed and that the election must be at a regular, or stated, or annual meeting of the body, unless there is a provision in the charter or articles of association providing for an election at a special meeting.[20] However, as

[14] Austin v. Searing, 16 N. Y. 112; 69 Am. Dec. 665; Bauer v. Sampson Lodge, 102 Ind. 262; Supreme Council v. Garrigus, 104 Ind. 133; Schmidt v. A. Lincoln Lodge, 84 Ky. 490; 2 S. W. 156. See Bouvier L. D., tit. Submission; also *ante*, § 116 and *post*, § 564 where the subject is fully considered.

[15] State v. Odd Fellows' Grand Lodge, 8 Mo. App. 148.

[16] *Ante*, § 116, *et seq.*

[17] Rood v. Railway, etc., Mut. Ben. Ass'n, 31 Fed. 62. This case, however has been severely criticised and a contrary doctrine laid down by the Supreme Court of Illinois in Railway Passenger, etc., Ass'n v. Robinson, 147 Ill. 138; 35 N. E. 168; see *post*, § 564.

[18] *Post*, § 492. *Ante*, § 119, *et seq.*

[19] *Ante*, § 119, *et seq.*

[20] Thompson on Corp., Ch. 15. Illustration of invalid election. *In re* Empire State Supreme Lodge, etc., 103 N. Y. Supp. 1124.

was said by the Supreme Court of Rhode Island:[21] "It is matter of common knowledge that both corporations and voluntary associations often disregard, to some extent, the strict rules of procedure prescribed in their charters or by-laws in transacting their internal affairs; but, so far as we are aware, the courts have not held that such technical variation from prescribed forms relieved them from liability to outside parties doing business with them in good faith upon the strength of what appeared by their own records to have been regularly and properly done;" and the same court has said:[22] "Many things may be done improperly by an association; but if its members acquiesce in them and go on as if they were right, they will be bound by them." Where no term of office is fixed the tenure is at the pleasure of the association.[23] The trustees of a mutual life insurance company need not necessarily be policyholders.[24]

§ 152. **The Same Subject.**—Disputes concerning the election of officers often arise in the case of fraternal beneficiary societies, whether voluntary associations or corporations. The general rule regarding the jurisdiction of the courts has been considered by the Court of Civil Appeals of Texas,[25] in which the Court said: "When one seeks to recover an office, it is essential that he should allege its pecuniary value, and it must also affirmatively appear that this value is within the jurisdiction of the court where the suit is filed. We do not think the right to hold an office or position in a purely benevolent society, carrying with it no salary or emolument, is such a right as can be made the basis of a civil suit in the district court. The person deprived of it loses no valuable civil or property right. He is deprived of nothing for which he could claim damages. But even if it be shown that a salary, or some emoluments were attached to the position of National Grand Master of this society, it does not follow that the mere fact that Farmer received a majority of the votes actually cast would vest him with such a right as could be made the basis of a civil action.

21 McDermott v. St. Wilhelmina Ben. A. Soc., 24 R. I. 527; 54 Atl. 59.
22 Industrial Trust Co. v. Green, 17 R. I. 586; 23 Atl. 914; 17 L. R. A. 202; St. Patrick's Alliance v. Byrne, 59 N. J. Eq. 26; 44 Atl. 716.
23 Ostrom v. Greene, 20 Misc. 177; 45 N. Y. Supp. 852.
24 In re Mut. Life Ins. Co., 133 N. Y. Supp. 326; 73 Misc. 536.
25 Gaines et al. v. Farmer, 55 Tex. Civ. App. 601; 119 S. W. 874.

The distinction between the effect of receiving a majority of the votes cast in such an election and one held under the provisions of the statute to fill a public office is manifest. In the latter case the law provides that the one receiving the most legal votes shall fill the office, and hence that fact alone confers the right to the office; while in this society it was shown to be merely the duty of the National Grand Lodge to select the national officers, and presumably this might be done in any manner it saw fit to adopt. Hence the mere receipt by one of a majority of the ballots cast did not *ipso facto* vest in him any right to the position. The lodge, should it see proper to do so, might reconsider the vote, or adopt a different method of making the selection. The fact that Gaines was declared elected, was regularly installed according to the forms of the order, and had held the position for nearly one-third of the term, is sufficient to justify the conclusion that his selection, if not regular, was at least acquiesced in by the membership of the National Grand Lodge in such a manner as to negative the claim of election by Farmer. Neither the original petition nor the petition of intervention presents any cause of action.[26] The Supreme Court of Georgia has also considered the question.[27] In that case a construction of the statute requiring fraternal beneficiary associations to have a representative form of government was involved. The Court said: "But it is also insisted by the petitioners, who contest the right of the Eminent Council to elect the ritual officers in question and to confer upon them the power to vote in the Eminent Household, that if there is provision made for this in the constitution and by-laws, such a provision is null and void as contrary to the policy of the law, because, under the law relative to the fraternal beneficiary orders similiar to this, the government should have a representative form, and that, if these ritual officers and the other officers of the order are permitted to vote at the meeting of the Eminent Household, self-elected and self-selected officers will be in the majority, and can control the action of the Eminent Household, and override the

26 Wellenvess v. Grand Lodge, 103 Ky. 415; 45 S. W. 360; St. Patrick's Alliance v. Byrne, 59 N. J. Eq. 26; 44 Atl. 717; Ryan v. Cudahy, 157 Ill. 108; 41 N. E. 760; 49 L. R. A. 353; 48 Am. St. Rep. 305, and cases cited in notes.

27 Graham v. Eminent Household of Columbian Woodmen, 135 Ga. 777; 70 S. E. 649.

will of the elected delegates, and that to carry out the provisions of the law relative to these fraternal beneficiary orders the control of the order should devolve upon the elected delegates solely, or at least that the Eminent Household should be so constituted that the elected delegates would be in the majority. In one or more of the States having laws relative to the formation and control of fraternal beneficiary societies the statutes do expressly make provision that the elected delegates to the Supreme Body of the order shall be in the majority. Our statute on the subject does not contain this express provision, but defines a fraternal beneficiary order to be a corporation, society, or voluntary association, which has no capital stock, . . . and having a representative form of government and a lodge system,[28] etc. The act then provides: 'Such grand or supreme bodies may be composed of its officers, incorporators, representatives elected by local, district or grand bodies, past officers and standing committees. Such orders or associations may make a constitution, by-laws, rules and regulations consistent with the existing laws of the State, for the government of all under its authority, for the management of its properties and the due and orderly conduct of its affairs. In view of the provision that the 'supreme bodies' of these orders may be composed of its officers, past officers and standing committees, as well as representatives elected by local bodies, and that such orders may make a constitution and by-laws consistent with the existing laws of the State, for the government of the order, and that no limitation is put upon the number of officers, or of the past officers and standing committees, who may thus become members of the supreme legislative and judicial bodies within the order, we do not think, because the elected delegates to the Eminent Household are not equal in number to the number of Eminent Officers attending the meeting as constituent members, that such a body fails to conform to the provisions of the statute. Nor do we think that changes in the constitution and by-laws with reference to the constituent elements of the supreme legislative body of the order, such as the creation of ritual officers and giving to the officers a vote in the meetings of the supreme body, violate any of the stipulations in the policies of the members of the order or affect the vested interests of such policyholders.''

[28] Acts 1900, p. 71.

254

When an association has adopted no constitution, or by-laws, the manner of the election of officers and their tenure, is to be determined from the resolutions and usages of the association and as a general rule a majority of the members of an association possess authority to control its action within the scope of its objects.[29] An election in a Supreme Council of a beneficiary order is not invalidated by unauthorized votes where the qualified delegates voted unanimously for the officers elected.[30] Generally before resorting to the courts remedies in the society must be exhausted.[31] Where, however, proceedings for the removal of the officers of a society are void, resort may be had to the courts without application for relief within the organization.[32] If necessary, equity will decide which of two sets of officers is legal.[33] And a society may be estopped from claiming the non-election of an officer in a suit for compensation.[34]

§ 153. **Power of Amotion of Officers, Who Has.**—The power of removing or suspending officers of an association or corporation, resides in the body at large and cannot be exercised by other officers unless the articles of association expressly confer the power.[35] Where the constitution of a society gives one of the officers power to remove other officers for cause and on notice, an attempt to remove such officers without notice is void.[36]

§ 154. **Agents of Corporations.**—The rule in regard to corporations is not different from that applied to persons: "The

[29] Goller v. Stubenhaus, 134 N. Y. Supp. 1043; 77 Misc. 29.

[30] *In re* Triennial Election Catholic Relief, etc., Ass'n, 127 N. Y. Supp. 143; 142 App. Div. 307.

[31] Hickey v. Baine, 195 Mass. 446; 81 N. E. 201.

[32] State v. Board of Officers of Gegenseitige, etc., 144 Wis. 516; 129 N. W. 630.

[33] St. Patrick's Alliance v. Byrne, 59 N. J. Eq. 26; 44 Atl. 716. See also as to *de jure* and *de facto* officers. *In re* Hetra Hased v. Emet, 7th Hun. 333.

[34] McDermott v. St. Wilhelmina, etc., Soc., 24 R. I. 527; 54 Atl. 58.

[35] Potter v. Search, 7 Phila. 443; Lowry v. Stotzer, 7 Phila. 397; Neall v. Hill, 16 Cal. 145.

[36] Caine v. Benev. etc., Order, 88 Hun. 154; 34 N. Y. Supp. 528. For procedure in suspending subordinate councils or lodges, see Grand Grove, etc., v. Garibaldi Grove, etc., 105 Cal. 219; 38 Pac. 947. *Ante,* § 96. *Post,* § 493.

powers possessed by the various agents of a corporation may be limited by the terms of their appointment, or by custom; but the ultimate source of their authority is always the agreement of the shareholders expressed in their charter or articles of association. It follows, therefore, that if an act is in excess of the chartered purposes of a corporation it will always be outside of the powers delegated to the company's agents, as well as in excess of the corporate powers which the company is authorized by law to exercise. The general rule, that a contract made by an agent of a corporation in excess of his powers does not bind the company, applies with peculiar force to a contract which is in excess of the charter itself. For a person dealing with a corporation must, at his peril, take notice of the terms of its charter, and of the fact that acts in excess of the charter are necessarily in excess of the authority of the agent performing them. . . . It is a settled rule, that a person who deals with a corporation must, at his peril, take notice of its charter or articles of association. It follows, therefore, that so far as the authority of an agent of a corporation is defined by its charter or articles of association, the scope of the agent's powers must always be considered as disclosed."[37]

§ 155. **Officers of Corporation are Special Agents.**—Officers of a corporation are special and not general agents; they have no power to bind a corporation except within the limits prescribed by the charter and by-laws. The principle, that persons dealing with the officers of a corporation are charged with notice of the authority conferred upon them, and of the limitations and restrictions upon such authority contained in the charter, is too well established to require to be supported by a citation of authorities.[38] But this rule is qualified by the statement that if a corporation either elects an officer or appoints an agent of a class, which, according to general custom, have certain functions and powers,

---

[37] Morawetz on Corp., §§ 580, 591; *ante,* § 149. This rule applies to beneficiary associations to its full extent and, as the members are conclusively presumed to know the laws of the association, they must know if acts done by officers are in excess of the powers conferred by the by-laws.

[38] Adriance v. Roome, 52 Barb. 399; Alexander v. Cauldwell, 83 N. Y. 480; De Bost v. Albert Palmer Co., 35 Hun. 386; Rice v. Peninsula Club, 52 Mich. 87.

it will be bound by his acts within the scope of authority usually exercised by such class, although his powers are limited by the by-laws.[39] The scope of the agent's or officer's authority may be established by "proofs of the course of business between the parties themselves; by the usages and practice which the company has permitted to grow up in its business, and by the knowledge which the board, charged with the duty of controlling and conducting the transactions and property of the corporation, had, or must be presumed to have had, of the acts and doings of its subordinates in and about the affairs of the corporation."[40] There is no inference that a general agent of a life insurance company for one State, who has permission from the company to solicit business in another State, has in such latter State any authority greater than that usually possessed by insurance agents.[41]

§ 156. **Authority of Officers and Agents.**—The authority of officers and directors of both voluntary associations and corporations is derived, either expressly or impliedly, from the articles of association or charter, as we have seen.[42] Where the officers or directors of an association had no power to do an act, and such act was done by the president, it was held that the directors could not ratify it.[43] A course of dealing may be sufficient to authorize an inference of authority, although the officer had not in fact any real authority;[44] and authority may be inferred from facts and circumstances;[45] for usage often interprets authority;[46] and ratification also may be implied from apparent consent, acqui-

[39] Minor v. Mechanics' Bank, 1 Pet. 46; Fay v. Noble, 12 Cush. 1; Merchants' Bank v. State Bank, 10 Wall. 604; Commercial Ins. Co. v. Union Ins. Co., 19 How. 318; Smith v. Smith, 62 Ill. 493; Union Mut. Life Ins. Co. v. White, 106 Ill. 67.

[40] Mining Co. v. Anglo-Californian Bank, 104 U. S. 192; Lee v. Pittsburg Coal, etc,. Co., 56 How. Pr. 376; Phillips v. Campbell, 43 N. Y. 271; Morawetz on Corp., § 509.

[41] Baldwin v. Conn. Mut. L. Ins. Co., 182 Mass. 389; 65 N. E. 837.

[42] *Ante*, § 149; Herndon v. Triple Alliance, 45 Mo. App. 426.

[43] Crum's Appeal, 66 Pa. St. 474.

[44] Union, etc., Mining Co. v. Rocky Mt. Nat. Bk., 2 Colo. 248; Fayles v. National Ins. Co., 49 Mo. 380; Richmond v. Judy, 6 Mo. App. 465.

[45] Dougherty v. Hunter, 54 Pa. St. 380; Northern Cent. R. Co. v. Bastian, 15 Md. 494; Olcott v. Tioga R. Co., 40 Barb. 179.

[46] Whart. on Ag., § 134; Story on Ag., § 95, *et seq.*

escence or acts and circumstances.[47]   In general, a party dealing
with any kind of an agent is bound to ascertain his authority;
as has been said:[48]   "He is put on inquiry by the very fact that
he is negotiating with an agent and is bound to ascertain whether
he can bind his principal in the transaction which he purports
to carry on in his behalf."[49]   For whatever purpose an agent is
constituted, it is always understood that he shall have authority
to do all necessary and usual acts incident to the nature of the
business which he is constituted to transact.[50]   "The principle,
which pervades all cases of agency, whether it be a general or a
special agency, is this," says Story:[51]   "The principal is bound
by all acts of his agent, within the scope of the authority which he
holds him out to the world to possess; although he may have
given him more limited private instruction, unknown to the persons
dealing with him.   And this is founded on the doctrine, that where
one of two persons must suffer by the act of a third person, he
who has held that person out as worthy of trust and confidence,
and having authority in that matter, shall be bound by it.   It
will at once be perceived, this doctrine is equally applicable to
all cases of agency, whether it be the case of a general or of a
special agency.   When I hold out to the public a person as my
agent in all my business and employment, he is deemed my general agent; and all acts done within the scope of that business
bind me, notwithstanding I have privately limited his authority
by special instructions.   Why?   Because he is externally clothed
with an unlimited authority over the subject-matter, and third
persons might otherwise be defrauded by his acts.   In such a case,
he is not less a general agent as to third persons, than if he
had received no private limitations of his authority.   As between
himself and his principal, his authority is not general, but *quoad*
hoc is limited.   In the same case, if the principal had privately
revoked his whole authority he would still be bound.   So, if he
had privately limited the authority to a single act in the same

[47] Story on Ag., § 253, *et seq.*
[48] Harrison v. City Fire Ins. Co., 9 Allen 233.
[49] Story on Ag., § 58 and note.
[50] Story on Ag., Ch. 6, § 57, *et seq.*
[51] Agency, § 127, note.   See also Modern Woodmen of America v. Lawson, 110 Va. 81; 65 S. E. 509.

business (and he would accordingly be, between himself and his principal, a special agent), still the principal would be bound. Precisely the same rule applies to a special agency. . . . In the case of a general agency, the principal holds out the agent to the public as having unlimited authority as to all its business. In the case of a special agency, like that above stated, the principal holds out the agent to the public, as having unlimited authority as to a particular act, subject or purchase. In each case, therefore, the same general principle applies.'' The same author continues:[52] ''But where the agency is not held out by the principal, by any acts or declarations, or implications, to be general in regard to the particular act or business, it must from necessity be construed according to its real nature and extent; and the other party must act at his own peril, and is bound to inquire into the nature and extent of the authority actually conferred.''

The general principle has been stated by the Supreme Court of Mississippi,[3] where in holding that an insurance company can stipulate in its policy that its provisions shall not be varied by notice, or representations, not brought home to the actual knowledge of the company's principal officers, and that no waiver was authorized by any other agent and that no agent should have power to modify the terms of the contract, or waive its conditions, that such provisions contained in the policy is notice to the insured of the limited authority of the agent in such respect, so that the insured may not rely on any conduct of the agent as constituting a modification of the contract, or waiver, said: ''The burden of proof is upon him who asserts it to show either a direct authorization of the agent, or by proving such facts or circumstances, or such a course of conduct, as by implication it can be presumed that the agent was acting within the real or apparent scope of his authority. If one invests another with real authority, he is bound by reason of the actual power conferred. If, however, he clothes him with apparent authority, he is bound, because he has induced others to deal with him as an agent. The one rests upon a fact; the other upon a supposed fact. But before the alleged principal is precluded from deny-

[52] Story on Ag., § 133.
[53] New York Life Ins. Co. v. O'Dom, 100 Miss. 219; 56 Sou. 379; Ann. Cas. 1914-A 583.

ing the existence of the supposed fact, it is necessary that the other party should show that he was misled, not by the alleged agent, but by the principal. An analytical examination of the adjudged cases will show that such is the predicate upon which such conclusions are drawn. Another principle is that, although one person has apparent, as contradistinguished from real, authority to act for another, yet if third persons dealing with an agent know, or in contemplation of law are charged with knowledge, that such person was not authorized to do or to perform the particular act, then such third persons cannot be heard to say that such agent was acting within the scope of his authority.''

One who acts for an insurance company with its consent in soliciting or procuring insurance, is an agent though not formally appointed.[54] But one not in fact the agent of an insurance company cannot make himself such agent by his own act so as to bind the company.[55] Notwithstanding the limitations in the policy of the authority of a soliciting agent, one may be estopped by his knowledge, because such agent was bound to communicate his knowledge,[56] and the representations of a soliciting agent furnished with blank applications in explaining the plans of policies, are within the scope of his authority.[57] The question seems to be what power did the company hold the agent out to the public as possessing, rather than what power the agent in fact possessed.[58] Still it has been said[59] that the apparent scope of authority of a soliciting insurance agent does not extend beyond the solicitation and delivery of the contract and receiving the premium required to bring it into being.

§ 157. **Agents Contracting in Name of Irresponsible Principal.**—Generally, an agent, contracting in the name of a foreign or irresponsible principal, or one incapable of contracting, is held personally, because the law presumes that he intended to bind himself or that credit was given to him. So, if an agent contracts in the name of a voluntary association having no legal entity, he

54 Wortham v. Illinois Life Ins. Co., 32 Ky. L. 827; 107 S. W. 276.
55 Monast v. Manhattan Life Ins. Co., 35 R. I. 294; 86 Atl. 728.
56 Rearden v. St. Mut. L. Ins. Co., 79 S. C. 526; 60 S. E. 1106.
57 Mut. Life Ins. Co. v. Summers, 19 Wyo. 441; 120 Pac. 185.
58 Coles v. Jefferson Ins. Co., 41 W. Va. 261; 23 S. E. 732.
59 Lauze v. New York Life Ins. Co., 74 N. H. 334; 68 Atl. 31.

is bound, although all the members who have consented to the act or ratified it afterwards are also bound.[60] "But," as Mr. Story in his commentaries on agency[61] says, "although it is thus true that persons, contracting as agents, are ordinarily held personally responsible, where there is no other responsible principal to whom resort can be had; yet, the doctrine is not without some qualifications and exceptions, as indeed the words, 'ordinarily held,' would lead one naturally to infer. For, independent of the cases already suggested, where the contract is, or may be treated as a nullity, on account of its inherent infirmity or defective mode of execution, other cases may exist, in which it is well known to both of the contracting parties, that there exists no authority in the agent to bind other persons for whom he is acting, or that there is no other responsible principal; and yet, the other contracting party may be content to deal with the agent, not upon his personal credit, or personal responsibility, but in the perfect faith and confidence that such contracting party will be repaid and indemnified by the persons who feel the same interest in the subject-matter of the contract, even though there may be no legal obligation in the case." The question generally is, "to whom is the credit knowingly given, according to the understanding of both parties?" "The law in all these cases, pronounces the same decision; that he to whom the credit is knowingly and exclusively given, is the proper person who incurs liability whether he be the principal or the agent.'"[62]

§ 158. **Agent Acting in Excess of His Authority.**—Whenever an agent who contracts for another party, whether a corporation or natural person, exceeds his authority, he is personally liable, unless his acts be afterwards adopted or ratified by the supposed principal;[63] and he may be sued either for breach of warranty

[60] Doubleday v. Muskett, 7 Bing. 110; Blakely v. Bennecke, 59 Mo. 195; Heath v. Goslin, 80 Mo. 310; Horsley v. Bell, 1 Brown Ch. 101; Lewis v. Tilton, 64 Ia. 220; 42 Am. Rep. 436; Burls v. Smith, 7 Bing. 704; Ridgley v. Dobson, 3 Watts & S. 118; Cullen v. Duke of Queensbury, 1 Brown Ch. 101; Gray v. Raper, L. R. 1 C. P. 694.

[61] § 287.

[62] Story on Ag., § 288; Whart. on Ag., §§ 507, 508, 509; ante, § 156.

[63] Ang. & Ames on Corp., § 303; Whart. on Ag., § 524.

or deceit,[64] but the agent will not be liable if the other contracting party have the same opportunities for knowledge as the agent.[65] Officers are liable if loans are made in violation of statute.[66]

§ 159. **Fiduciary Relation of Officers and Directors.**—The general rules must also be held to apply, in all cases, that, while directors and other officers have a wide range of discretionary authority, each one sustains a fiduciary relation to the members of the organization, and the utmost good faith is required of him. "He falls, therefore, within the great rule by which equity requires that confidence shall not be abused by the party in whom it is reposed, and which it enforces by imposing a disability, either partial or complete, upon the party intrusted to deal, on his own behalf, in respect to any matter involved in such confidence."[67] The powers conferred upon an agent must be exercised to advance the interests of the principal, and for no other purpose. He must not use either the assets or the credit of the principal, or any of the powers of his own office, except to advance the interests of the company irrespective of his own advantages or desires.[68] And it is the duty of the trustees to resist all invalid claims and protect its members and the funds in their hands.[69] So, the trustees of a benefit society cannot vote themselves back pay.[70] An officer of a corporation is liable to it for damages, or loss, occasioned by his breach of duty in investing in worthless securities.[71]

§ 160. **Discretionary Powers Cannot be Delegated.**—It is also the rule that discretionary powers, if conferred upon the agent,

[64] Whart. on Ag., § 524.

[65] Whart. on Ag., § 531.

[66] New Haven Trust Co. v. Boerthey, 74 Conn. 468; 51 Atl. 130.

[67] Hoyle v. Plattsburg, etc., R. R. Co., 54 N. Y. 314; 13 Am. Rep. 595; Cumberland Coal Co. v. Sherman, 30 Barb. 562; Michoud v. Girod, 4 How. 554.

[68] York, etc., R. Co. v. Hudson, 16 Beav. 485; Gallery v. Nat. Exch. Bank, 41 Mich. 169; Koehler v. Black River Falls Iron Co., 2 Black. 715; Wardell v. Union Pac. R. Co., 103 U. S. 561.

[69] Mayer v. Equitable Reserve F. L. Ass'n, 42 Hun. 237.

[70] State v. People's, etc., Ass'n, 42 Ohio St. 579.

[71] Supreme Lodge K. of P. v. Hinsey, 241 Ill. 384; 80 N. E. 728, affg. 138 Ill. App. 248.

cannot be delegated.[72] But this rule also cannot be said to be invariable, as the power depends in each case upon the intention of the principal. A leading writer says upon this point:[73] "It has sometimes been laid down as a rule, that powers involving the exercise of discretion and judgment cannot be delegated, except under an express grant of authority; but this statement of the rule is not strictly accurate. The authority of an agent to delegate powers to another agent depends always upon the intention of the principal. The appointment of an agent with powers requiring the exercise of judgment and discretion. is, in many cases, an indication that the principal intended the judgment and discretion to be exercised by the particular agent whom he selected, but this is not always so. Thus, the directors of a corporation have, undoubtedly, implied -authority to appoint various agents, the performance of whose duties involves the exercise of a high degree of judgment and discretionary power. Directors of a railroad company may, without express authority, appoint engineers, superintendents, freight and passenger agents, and any other officers that may be required for the proper construction and management of the railroad. The directors of banking, insurance and commercial corporations have implied authority to employ financial agents. The employment of attorneys to manage the legal affairs of a corporation, and to institute or defend suits, is clearly within the implied authority of the directors or general managing agents. The board of directors have also implied authority to appoint a committee of their number with authority to execute the resolutions of the board, and to exercise general control over the affairs of the corporation during the recess of the board. The extent of the powers which may thus be conferred by the board of directors upon a committee, depends upon the character of the corporation, the frequency with which the board is required to meet, the nature of its duties and upon established custom. No more definite rule can be, formulated."

§ 161. **Powers and Authority of Directors**.—Directors of a a corporation cannot make important changes in its business or in any respect modify or change the constitution, their authority

[72] Farmers' Fire Ins. Co., etc., v. Chase, 56 N. H. 341.
[73] Morawetz on Corp., § 535.

only extending to the supervision. and management of the company's ordinary or regular business.[74] Nor can the directors depart from the general purposes of the corporation as defined in the charter.[75] In the leading case upon this subject[76] the vicechancellor said: "The principle of jurisprudence which I am asked here to apply is, that the governing body of a corporation, that is in fact a trading partnership, cannot, in general, use the funds of the community for any purpose other than those for which they were contributed. By the governing body I do not, of course, mean exclusively either directors or a general council; but the ultimate authority within the society itself, which would ordinarily be a majority at a general meeting According to the principle in question, the special powers, given either to the directors or to a majority by the statutes or other constituent documents of the association, however absolute in terms, are always to be construed as subject to a paramount and inherent restriction that they are to be exercised in subjection to the special purposes of the original bond of association. This is not a mere canon of English municipal law, but a great and broad principle, which must be taken, in absence of proof to the contrary, as part of any given system of jurisprudence."[77] Directors of a mutual life insurance company have no authority to transfer its property to another association, the consideration to go to members who connect themselves with the new association,[78] and are personally liable for the amount a beneficiary should' have received where they wrongfully withheld payment and paid it on other account.[79] In the absence of express authority the executive committee of an accident insurance company have no authority to adopt a classification of risks.[80] They are liable for transferring assets of the association with claims unpaid.[81]

---

[74] Railway Co. v. Allerton, 18 Wall. 233.

[75] Minor v. Mechanics' Bank, 1 Pet. 71.

[76] Pickering v. Stephenson, L. R. 14 Eq. Cas.. 322.

[77] *Ante*, § 149.

[78] Temperance Mut. Ben. Ass'n v. Home Friendly Soc., 187 Pa. St. 38; 40 Atl. 1100.

[79] Home Ben., etc., Ass'n v. Wester, Tex. Civ. App.; 146 S. W. 1022.

[80] Kenny v. Bankers' Accident Ins. Co., 136 Ia. 140; 113 N. W. 366.

[81] Harvey v. Wasson, 74 Kan. 489; 87 Pac. 720.

§ 162. **Formalities to be Observed by Agents.**—If the charter or by-laws prescribe any formalities for the orderly transaction of business these ordinarily must be observed. The rule has thus been laid down:[82] "The agents of a corporation must observe all formalities which are required by the company's charter in the corporate transactions. Even the majority are not at liberty to disregard the forms prescribed by the charter, for they constitute a part of the fundamental agreement between the shareholders. And if any agent of a corporation acts in a manner which is not authorized by the company's charter, his acts will not be binding. Thus, it has been held that where the charter of a company requires contracts of a particular description to be in writing, and signed by specified officers, or approved in a specified manner, no agent can bind the company by a contract of that description unless it was executed in the manner prescribed. And if the constitution of a company requires the concurrence of a certain number of directors in the making of a contract, or the doing of any other corporate act, a less number cannot bind the company."

§ 163. **Distinction as to Matters Relating to Internal Management.**—A different rule sometimes prevails where certain formalities are prescribed for the internal management of the business of corporations. The same writer above quoted[83] says: "A party dealing with an agent of a corporation has usually no means of ascertaining whether formalities prescribed in the management of the internal affairs of the company have been complied with, and matters of this kind are peculiarly within the knowledge of the company's agents. It has therefore been held, that, if a person deals with an agent of a corporation within the scope of his apparent authority, and without notice of the non-performance of any formality prescribed by the charter or by-laws as a condition precedent to the agent's authority to act, he will be entitled to assume that the formality has been complied with, and the corporation will be estopped from showing that the agent had no authority to bind it, by reason of a failure to comply with the prescribed condition." It has also been said:[84] "A stranger must

---

[82] Morawetz on Corp., § 582.
[83] Morawetz on Corp., § 610.
[84] *In re* County Life Ass. Co., L. R. 5 Ch. App. 293.

be taken to have read the general act-under which the company is incorporated, and also to have read the articles of association; but he is not to be taken to have read anything more, and, if he knows nothing to the contrary, he has a right to assume as against the company that all matters of internal management have been duly complied with.''

§ 164. **Execution of Insurance Contracts.**—In an early case[85] it was held that, where the charter required that "all policies of assurance and other instruments" in order to be effectual and bind the company, should be "made and signed by the president of said company or any other officer thereof, according to the ordinances, by-laws and regulations of said company, or of their board of directors," the contract to cancel a policy is as solemn an act as a contract to make one; and, to become the act of the company, must be executed according to the forms in which by law they were enabled to make the contract, but in another court[86] it was held that, where the charter of an insurance company required all policies to be signed by the president, it was not necessary that a consent to an assignment of the policy should be signed by him.[87] Where the by-laws of a beneficiary society required an initiation in accordance with a secret ceremony it was held that the contract of membership was not complete until after initiation.[88]

§ 165. **Acts and Meetings of Directors and Committee.**— "When, by charter, a board are constituted the agent of a corporation for particular purposes, and the number necessary to be present at the doing of an act is therein specified, an act done or a contract made by less than, or others than, those specified, will not bind the company. If the charter specify no particular number of the board of directors as requisite to bind the corporation, that power resides either in the number specified in a by-law or in a majority, as a quorum, a majority of which have power to decide any question upon which they can act, and it

[85] Head v. Providence Ins. Co., 2 Cranch 166.
[86] New England Ins. Co. v. DeWolf, 8 Pick. 56.
[87] *Post*, § 596.
[88] Matkin v. Supreme Lodge K. of H., 82 Tex. 301; 18 S. W. 307.

is very clear that a contract made by a minority of a committee appointed for the purpose of making it, not assented to by a majority, nor by the corporation, does not bind the latter. A majority of a committee authorized to sell lands by legislative resolve, or to do business of a public nature, have power to execute the commission; but in case of *quasi*-corporations, where a certain number, as three persons, are appointed or authorized to do a particular act, as to choose a chaplain, or to contract for the building of a meeting-house, in general they must concur in the act or contract to render it binding, though perhaps direct proof that all assented would not be required."[89] A majority of the directors, in the absence of any regulation in the charter, is a quorum, and a majority of such quorum when convened, can do any act within the power of the directors.[90] It will be presumed that the meeting was legally called unless the contrary be shown.[91] Meetings can be held at any place,[92] and a member who is present at a meeting and makes no opposition to a resolution is presumed to assent to its adoption.[93] A formal meeting of the directors of a corporation is not necessary in order to enable them to do any act which is within their corporate powers[94] unless notice of a meeting is required by the by-laws,[95] but, where the clauses of a statute enact that the directors of companies incorporated under the act are to hold meetings, at which the prescribed quorum must be present, and that questions at such meetings are to be determined by a majority of votes, it is essential that the directors act together, and as a board, though a fixed place of meeting is unnecessary.[96] Still it has been deemed sufficient presumptive proof, for a stranger, of the concurrence of a quorum of a board of directors of a corporation, to show that

[89] Ang. & Ames on Corp., § 291.

[90] Wells v. Rahway White Rubber Co., 19 N. J. Eq. 402.

[91] Lane v. Brainerd, 30 Conn. 577; Sargent v. Webster, 13 Metc. 497.

[92] Ohio & Miss. R. Co. v. McPherson, 35 Mo. 13; Arms v. Conant, 36 Vt. 744; State v. Smith, 48 Vt. 266; Bellows v. Todd, 39 Ia. 209.

[93] Mowrey v. Indianapolis, etc., R. Co., 4 Biss. 78.

[94] Waite v. Windham Co. Mining Co., 37 Vt. 608.

[95] Edgerly v. Emerson, 23 N. H. 555.

[96] D'Arcy v. Tamar, etc., R. Co., 2 L. R. Exch. 158; 36 L. J. Exch. 37; 4 Hurl. & C. 463. See also Masonic Temple Ass'n v. Smith, 177 Ill. App. 161.

they assented separately.[97] It has been held[98] that where the
charter and by-laws provided that meetings of the directors should
be held on the call of the president and the latter refused to call
any meetings, whereupon the trustees convened without such
call, but after giving notice of the time and place of such meeting
to the president, the acts done at such meeting were irregular
and void.

§ 166. **Record of Proceedings of Meetings of Directors Need
Not be Kept.**—In the absence of directions to the contrary, a
board of directors, or agents, or a committee, are not bound to
keep a record or minutes of their proceedings.[99] The general
rule has been thus laid down:[100] "If, indeed, the charter or
creating and enabling act of a corporation, expressly make the
recording of the acts of its board of directors essential to their
validity, or a condition precedent thereto; or if it make a record
taken by a prescribed officer the only mode by which such acts
can be legally proven; it is very obvious that to render the acts
of the board obligatory, whether for or against the corporation,
the charter requisite must be complied with in the one case, and
that the charter mode of proof is the only one that can be resorted to in the other. The books, however, furnish us with no
such provision in the charter of any corporation; and without it
there seems to be nothing in principle or authority to distinguish
in this particular the acts of a board of agents, existing within
a corporation, from the acts of agents constituted by natural persons. It is usual, indeed, by way of notice, and to facilitate
proof, for the charter and by-laws to provide that a fair and
regular record of the proceedings of the managing board of a
corporation, should be made by some designated officer, as the
cashier of a bank, or the clerk or secretary of an insurance company. Such provisions are, in common, merely directory to the
corporation, its officers or agents; and the breach or neglect of
them, though it may render the directors or their scribe responsible in case of consequential damage for violation of duty, is a

[97] Tenney v. East Warren, etc., Co., 43 N. H. 343.
[98] State v. Ancker, 2 Rich. (S. C.) 245.
[99] Hutchins v. Byrnes, 9 Gray 367.
[100] Ang. & Ames on Corp. § 291a.

matter wholly between themselves and the stockholders, and between the latter and the government, as a violation of the charter and by-laws, and by no means affects the validity of the unrecorded acts.'' ''It is not necessary,'' said Chancellor Zabriskie,[101] ''that the minutes of a corporation should be written up by the secretary in his own handwriting, or that they should be approved by the board. And, in fact, if it was shown that the resolution had been passed by the board when lawfully assembled, it would be valid, although never entered upon the minutes.''

§ 167. **Powers of President.**—The president of a corporation is its chief executive officer, charged with the duty of a general superintendence of the company's affairs and of seeing that the directions of the board of directors are carried out. In some respects he is like an ordinary director and so in many companies their affairs are managed by an officer styled ''managing director'' instead of president. The powers of the president, or other chief officer, extend only to matters arising in the ordinary course of business,[102] and he may perform acts of an ordinary nature, which by usage or necessity are incident to his office, without special authority.[103] These powers may be inferred from facts and circumstances,[104] and from his habits of acting as business agent with the knowledge and without the objection of the company.[105] In the absence of any by-law showing that the president of a company had not the usual authority of the office he will be presumed to have the customary powers of such an officer.[106] If his acts be shown to be within the scope of his authority they are binding upon the company.[107] The Grand Master of a fraternal beneficiary association cannot by his order tem-

[101] Wells v. Rahway White Rubber Co,. 19 N. J. E. 402.

[102] Blen v. Bear River, etc., 20 Cal. 602; St. Nicholas Ins. Co. v. Howe, 7 Bosso. 450.

[103] Chicago, B. & Q. R. Co. v. Coleman, 18 Ill. 297.

[104] Northern Central R. Co. v. Bastian, 15 Md. 494.

[105] Martin v. Webb, 110 U. S. 7; Dougherty v. Hunter, 54 Pa. St. 380; Olcott v. Tioga R. R. Co., 40 Barb. 179.

[106] Traders' Mut. L. Ins. Co. v. Johnson, 200 Ill. 359; 65 N. E. 634.

[107] Farmers' Bank v. McKee, 2 Pa. St. 318; Bacon v. Mississippi Ins. Co., 31 Miss. 119.

porarily abrogate provisions of the constitution of the society.[108]
The president of a corporation can employ counsel;[109] but cannot
confess judgment;[110] nor sell the land of the corporation;[111] nor
dispose of the company's property generally;[112] nor act usually
for the company in matters not in the ordinary administration
of business.[113] The president of a mutual insurance company cannot waive the conditions of an insurance policy prescribed by the
by-laws of the company which are of the essence of the contract,
nor make a contract different from that prescribed by such
laws.[114] Nor can the president of a company make an oral contract with a general agent binding the company to pay him a
certain sum annually sufficient for his support.[115] There is no
objection to the president acting as secretary of a meeting of
the board of directors if so desired.[116] A meeting, called by a
deposed president, is illegal, and all acts done thereat are void.[117]
A contract of a life insurance company to pay a pension to a retiring president, the real consideration appearing to have been
past services, is invalid.[118]

§ 168. **Of Vice-President.**—In regard to the duties of vice-
president it has been said:[119] "As a general rule, in the absence
of the president, or where a vacancy occurs in the office, the vice-
president may act in his stead and perform the duties which devolve upon the president. And such being the case, it must be

[108] Champion v. Hannahan, 138 Ill. App. 387.
[109] Colman v. West Va. Oil Co., 25 W. Va. 148; Savings Bank v. Benton, 2 Metc. (Ky.) 240; Oakley v. Workingmen's Ben. Soc., 2 Hilt. 487.
[110] Stokes v. N. J. Pottery Co., 46 N. J. L. 237.
[111] Bliss v. Kaweah C. & I. Co., 65 Cal. 502.
[112] Walworth Co. Bank v. Farmers', etc., Co., 14 Wis. 325.
[113] Bright v. Metaire Cem. Ass'n, 33 La. Ann. 58.
[114] Priest v. Citizens' Ins. Co., 3 Allen, 602; McEvers v. Lawrence, Hoff.
Ch. 172; Brewer v. Chelsea F. Ins. Co., 14 Gray 203. But see *post*, § 596.
[115] Rennie v. Mut. Life Ins. Co., 99 C. C. A. 556; 176 Fed. 202.
[116] Budd v. Walla Walla, etc., Co., 2 Wash. T. 347.
[117] Industrial Trust Co. v. Greene, 17 R. I. 586; 23 Atl. 914.
[118] Beers v. N. Y. Life Ins. Co., 20 N. Y. Supp. 789. This is an interesting case dealing with the powers of trustees under the by-laws and
the passage of a resolution contracting with the president who presided
at the meeting at which action was held.
[119] Smith v. Smith *et al.*, 62 Ill. 496.

270

held that, as Rose refused to act as president of the company, Brough, the vice-president, could not only act as president, but it became his duty to do so in the transaction of the business of the company. Nor does it matter that the act under which the body was organized does not enumerate a vice-president as one of the officers of the company; but after providing that there shall be a president and other officers named, it authorizes the company to create other officers. And this company, by their by-laws, declared there should be a vice-president, and imposed the duty on him of assisting the president in the performance of such duties as he might require. In organizing such a body, such an office is, if not essential, usually created, and this organization, having provided for and elected such an officer, we must hold that he may perform the duties imposed upon the president in the same cases and under the same circumstances that such an officer may act when the office is created by the charter of the company. We see no objection to the deed because it was signed by Brough, as there was no president of the company.'' The second vice-president, who presided at a meeting of a society,[120] it was held, could after the adjournment of the meeting, appoint a committee of investigation, called for by a resolution adopted at such meeting, and the first vice-president could fill the vacancies in the committee caused by the declination of certain of the appointees. As in the case of other officers, the charter must be looked to for the enumeration of the powers of the vice-president and if the constitution is silent, then the by-laws or the custom of the society or of similar societies.

§ 169. **Of Secretary.**—The secretary of a corporation is its officer to keep its records, books and seal and to act generally under the directions of the directors and president. His powers and duties are usually prescribed by the by-laws, but if they are not he has the powers ordinarily exercised by the corresponding officer of companies in the same line of business, or those which the customs and habits of his company have conferred upon him. There is no reason why the secretary of an insurance

[120] Burton v. St. George's Soc., 28 Mich. 261.

company, or benefit society should have any other or different power than those of the corresponding officer of other organizations, or his authority be determined by any different rules. The secretary of the corporation is the proper person to have possession of, and prove, the books of the company;[121] and the directors are presumed to have control over him;[122] he can make minutes of a meeting of the directors after the meeting has been held and they will relate back to the time of the transaction.[123] He may impose fines on members for non-payment of contributions, if it be so provided by the by-laws,[124] but he cannot affix the corporate seal to a company obligation upon the consent of directors given as they are met separately on the street, if the law of the body or statutes require a formal meeting.[125] The secretary of a corporation remains, like other officers, in office until a successor is chosen.[126] The statement of the secretary of a mutual benefit association to the insured that he need not pay his dues until certain charges then pending against him which, if true, made the policy forfeitable, were disposed of, is not out of the scope of his duties, but binds the company.[127] A deed, though not attested by him, will be valid if the charter does not require such attestation, although it may be (unknown to the grantees) required by the by-laws.[128] Unless there is some provision in the charter of a society for a single secretary, the society may direct any of its officers or agents to perform any of the appropriate duties of the secretary, and in such case such agent so designated is made secretary for that purpose.[129]

§ 170. **Of Treasurer.**—The treasurer of a corporation is its officer charged by law with the custody of its funds, and responsible for their safe-keeping. So, where the by-laws provided that

---

[121] Smith v. Natchez Steamboat Co., 1 How. (Miss.) 479.

[122] Elmes v. Ogle, 2 Eng. L. & Eq. 379; 15 Jur. 180.

[123] Commercial Bank, etc., v. Bonner, 13 Smed. & M. 649.

[124] Parker v. Butcher, L. R. 3 Eq. Cas. 762.

[125] D'Arcy v. Tamar, etc., R. Co., L. R. 2 Exch. 158.

[126] South Bay, etc., v. Gray, 30. Me. 547.

[127] Jones v. National Mut. Ben. Ass'n, 599 Ky. L. 8; 2 S. W. 447.

[128] Smith v. Smith, 62 Ill. 496.

[129] Peck v. New London, etc., Ins. Co., 22 Conn. 575.

the treasurer should have custody of the moneys of a corporation and give bond for their safe-keeping, it was held[130] that the directors could not lawfully deprive the corporation of the benefit of this responsibility by depositing the funds with others, or causing such disposition to be made, and that they might be restrained by injunction from so doing at the suit of any stockholder, a proper case being made. It has been said[131] that a corporation by conferring upon a person the appointment of treasurer, holds him out to the world as its proper agent to receive funds paid to it; and such officer is the only proper person to whom, when payment is made, notice of the purpose to which the payment is to be applied should be given. The treasurer of a corporation must keep its moneys distinct from his own, unless it is otherwise agreed, and pay any balance due on demand,[132] and he only has power to bind the company by acts in the usual course of business; for unusual acts some special authority must be shown;[133] he cannot sell or assign, without such special authority, the securities of his company.[134] Without formal order, if the by-laws so provide, he must deposit all funds to the credit of the society.[135] In a case[136] where the treasurer purchased a claim against the company, it was held that he could not maintain a suit upon it against the corporation, because such purchase extinguished the debt. But upon principle he could recover what money he advanced to buy the claim, because he was acting as a trustee for its benefit and it should repay his advances. The treasurer of a voluntary association will be directed to account for moneys in his hands and pay over according to the interest of the association.[137] When by a resolution of an association, the treasurer was directed under certain con-

---

[130] Pearson v. Tower, 55 N. H. 215.

[131] N. E. Car Spring Co. v. Union Indian Rubber Co., 4 Blatchf. 1.

[132] Second Ave. R. R. Co. v. Coleman, 24 Barb. 300.

[133] Stark Bank v. U. S. Pottery Co., 34 Vt. 144; Dedham Inst., etc., v. Slack, 6 Cush. 408.

[134] Jackson v. Campbell, 5 Wend. 572.

[135] Scandanavian, etc., Soc. v. Eggan, 59 Mich. 65; 26 N. W. 282.

[136] Hill v. Frazier, 22 Pa. St. 320.

[137] Penfield v. Skinner, 11 Vt. 297; Piggott v. Thompson, 3 Bos. & Pul. 146.

tingencies to return to each member the amount contributed by him to the common fund, it was held that he was liable to an action brought against him by a member to recover his share, the agreed contingency having occurred.[138] So, if an unincorporated body, through its treasurer, has received on deposit, certain money, a suit by the owner will lie against the treasurer in his individual capacity to recover such money;[139] but it has also been held,[140] that no action can be maintained by the treasurer of an unincorporated association against one upon his promise in writing to pay money—the same being payable to the "treasurer" of such association alone. In that case the Court said: "To maintain that the plaintiff has a right to the action would be to put him upon the same ground he would occupy, if the association had been incorporated, and made capable by its charter, of suing in the name of whoever might be the treasurer of the club, upon instruments made payable to the treasurer. Such a capacity to maintain an action can be conferred by a charter only. If the money had been payable to the plaintiff by his individual name, the right to the action would belong to him, and the description of him as treasurer of the club would not affect the right. The only effect the description would have, would be to make him a trustee for the members of the association. If the treasurer of the club could maintain the action, the right to the action might belong to different individuals at different times. The club may remove from office a person who was the treasurer when such a promise was made, and appoint a successor. In such a case the right which once belong to one person as treasurer, would be exercised by another, without an assignment from him who was first entitled; for an assignment would be without effect, as the promise is made to no one individually." An action cannot be maintained by trustees of an association against a treasurer to recover the funds of the society, no provision being made therefor in the by-laws and no warrant on such treasurer having been drawn for the funds.[141] One who has been

138 Koehler v. Brown, 2 Daly 78.

139 Bennett v. Wheeler, 11 La. Ann. 763.

140 Ewing v. Medlock, 5 Port. (Ala.) 82.

141 Smith v. Pinney, 86 Mich. 484; 49 N. W. 305.

elected treasurer of a society holds the funds in trust for it and as such trustee is subject to the jurisdiction of a court of equity.[142] The society is not liable on a note given by the treasurer of a Masonic organization for money borrowed to cover his defalcation.[143]

§ 171. **Trustees.**—It is usual for voluntary associations of all kinds, especially lodges and clubs which are unincorporated, to provide for the election of one or more trustees at the same time that other officers are elected, who are charged with duties of holding the funds and property of such organization. What are the duties and powers of such trustees is a new and interesting question. If it be true that the articles of association constitute a contract both between the society and its members, and among the members themselves, as has generally been held,[144] it would naturally result that the trustees are governed by the articles of association and by-laws in the same way and to the same extent as general trustees are by the instrument creating the trust. The generally accepted doctrine has been,[145] that a mere voluntary association, unincorporated, has no legal capacity to take or hold real estate as such, and the fact that a deed was made to three grantees in trust for an association, there being no intimation as to who were the persons associated, has been held not to save it from being void;[146] but it has also been held[147] that a deed of land to a voluntary unincorporated society, not empowered to take and hold land, but the members of which are ascertainable, may be considered to convey to such members as tenants in common. The same court has also held,[148] that the conveyance of land to the trustees of an unincorporated religious society, and their successors in trust for the use and benefit of the society, does not vest the title in the new trustees, who may be elected from time to time, but it remains in the grantees named in the deed or the sur-

[142] Weld v. May, 9 Cush. 181.
[143] Bateman v. Sarbach, 89 Kan. 488; 132 Pac. 169.
[144] See *ante*, § 95, *et seq.*
[145] Beach on Corp., § 379.
[146] See cases cited in Beach on Corp., *supra.*
[147] Byam v. Bickford, 140 Mass. 31.
[148] Peabody v. Eastern Methodist Soc., 87 Mass. 540.

vivor of them. In a case in Missouri,[149] it is said: "If the laws of this association provide for trustees in whom its property vests, or who are to enforce obligations incurred to the society. such persons may sue as trustees of an express trust. In such event the contract, in contemplation of law, may be considered to be made with them for the benefit of all the members and other members of the association are not necessarily parties plaintiff." And the Court adds: "While members of these voluntary associations in many instances may become individually responsible to outside persons to the full extent of obligations incurred by the association, it has never been held that they are liable to each other beyond the limits fixed by their own agreement, nor that their responsibility within such limits is incapable of enforcement without the taking of a complete account and final winding up of the association." On a subsequent appeal of the same case,[150] the Court says: "The question of the right of the plaintiffs to sue as trustees of the society lies at the foundation of the action and ought to be first considered. The power of the members of an unincorporated society to confer on one or more of their number the care and custody of the common property and the right to maintain suit in reference to the same is not questioned." In this case the court also held that the funds of the society in the hands of the treasurer at the time of his removal from office, under the articles of association in this case, became surplus funds and belonged to the trustees as the financial agents of the society. And where a member of a society made his benefit payable to the trustees of his lodge for his burial and improvement of his cemetery lot without naming the trustees, it was held,[151] that the trustees for the time being of the lodge might maintain an action to recover the amount due under the certificate. The Court says: "Lastly the defendant says that the judgment must be affirmed for the reason that the plaintiffs are the trustees of one of its subordinate lodges and that they have not the legal capacity to accept and execute the trust imposed, and, therefore, can maintain no action for its enforcement. No authority is cited on either side of the question.

[149] Kuhl v. Meyer, 35 Mo. App. 206; citing Miles v. Davis, 19 Mo. 414.
[150] Kuhl v. Meyer, 50 M. A. 648.
[151] Hysinger v. Supreme Lodge K. & L. of H., 42 M. A. 627.

The plaintiffs are only members of the corporation, and their status is not different from that of other members, merely by reason of the fact that they are trustees of a subordinate lodge. It would certainly be permissible for an ordinary member of the ,defendant society to act as a trustee for a beneficiary in one of its certificates, and there would be nothing in the law prohibiting him as such trustee from suing his corporation to enforce the trust. It seems to us that there is no merit in this objection.'' It appears from the cases heretofore cited[152] that courts of equity treat the funds of voluntary associations and societies as trust funds placed in the hands of the trustees for a specific purpose, and consequently will exercise jurisdiction over the fund to prevent their diversion, and the trustees are subject to the jurisdiction the same as other trustees. Where an officer of an unincorporated association has custody and control of the funds of the society he is the only necessary party to a suit to establish a lien on the funds for a claim against it.[153] Recurring to the subject whether, where the funds of a society are vested in trustees, they pass without any conveyance to the new trustees upon their election and qualification, it must be said that such question is not altogether clear. As we have seen, where land has been conveyed to trustees for the benefit of a society the title does not pass to new trustees elected from time to time, but remains in the first trustees and the survivor of them.[154] But it is easy to see how the principle laid down in that case may be right, and yet, where the by-laws of a society provide that the property shall vest in the trustees elected from time to time and pass to their successors without formal conveyance, that such a provision might be held effective, although, if a conveyance of property was made merely to persons in trust for a voluntary association, it would remain in them until divested by their own act. It has been held that where, under a resolution of the majority, the surplus funds passed to the hands of the new trustees between whom and the original contributors there is no privity, such trustees are not accountable to them for the funds; the remedy being against the

[152] See *ante*, § 69, *et seq.* and *post*, § 612.
[153] Colley v. Wilson, 86 Mo. App. 396.
[154] Peabody v. Eastern Methodist Soc., *supra*.

original trustees only.[155] Nor can contributors to a fund to create a trust for religious and charitable purposes, as such, call the trustees to account.[156] But the court will always see that trust funds are applied to the object for which they were raised.[157] And where the funds of an association were deposited for its use in the names of its four trustees, and afterwards the name of the association was changed and one of the trustees refused to join with his cotrustees in an assignment of the funds to their successors, upon bill filed, the recalcitrant trustee was ordered to join in the assignment. And, generally, the trustees of a society will be compelled to transfer the trust estate to new trustees duly chosen.[158] In a case in Michigan,[159] the laws of the association provided that the funds should be placed in the hands of the treasurer and that no money should be drawn, except by an order of the executive council, signed by a chief officer and at least two trustees, without providing any manner of turning over the funds by the treasurer to his successor. In holding that an action to recover the funds could not be maintained against the treasurer merely becaused he refused to pay the money in accordance with the resolution of the executive council, when no order was drawn and signed as provided, the Court said: "It appears in evidence that the defendant was and still is a member of the association. Unless there is some warrant of authority for one or more members of an unincoporated society, no member or number of members can maintain a suit for the benefit of the society to enforce a contract made in its name or for its benefit, or recover property belonging to such society; and the question here presented is whether under the general law introduced in evidence, the plaintiffs, as trustees for the subsidiary high court are authorized to maintain this action. It must be confessed that the general laws are crude and lamentably wanting in matters of detail. The duties of the officers of the executive council, and of the trustees, are prescribed in the most general terms. There is no provision stating what the outgoing treasurer shall do with the funds on hand,

[155] Abels v. McKeen, 18 N. J. E. 462.
[156] Morton v. Smith, 5 Bush. 467; Penfield v. Skinner, 11 Vt. 296.
[157] Birmingham v. Gallagher, etc., Savings Bank, 112 Mass. 190.
[158] Brown v. Griffen, 14 W. N. C. 358.
[159] Smith v. Pinney, 86 Mich. 484.

nor to whom he shall hand over the books and papers in his custody. He is not required to deliver them to his successor, nor in express terms that he shall deliver the books and money to the executive council, which is the managing body, when the subsidiary high court is not in session. The only ways provided for withdrawing money from the custody and control are contained in section 2 of article 12 and section 12 of article 33, which have been both quoted. If the money is in the endowment fund it is presumably true that it was deposited in some bank specified or selected by the executive council and trustees, in which case it cannot be withdrawn except by drafts or checks upon the same, as provided for in section 17 of article 33. And if it is in such bank, there is no testimony in this case which shows that the proper officers could not have withdrawn the money from such bank. There is no direct testimony in this case that any bank was selected. It may, however, perhaps be inferred from the testimony of Edmund T. Mack, who testifies that he was cashier of the Citizens' Savings Bank of Detroit, and that it paid out for the benefit of the order, at the Chicago meeting, $15,600. The testimony of Mr. Greening is to the effect that when the accounts were audited in the usual way in August, 1887, just previous to the Chicago meeting, the amount then in defendant's hands, was $20,499.69. If any money was in the defendant's hands, and not in the bank and subject to draft or check, as provided for by section 17 or article 33, then it was subject to be drawn out of defendant's hands by virtue of section 2 of article 12. There is no testimony in this regard, showing that the defendant refused to pay any money in his hands, drawn in pursuance of section 2 of article 12. The only evidence that he refused to pay the money pursuant to any authority was his refusal to pay Mr. McMurtry when he called upon him in pursuance of the resolution passed by the executive council, but it does not appear that he was presented with any order signed by the subsidiary high chief ranger and two trustees, or the subsidiary high sub-chief ranger and two trustees countersigned by the permanent secretary; and until the proper order is drawn and presented to him it is difficult to see how he is liable to suit for not paying it over. The trustees themselves have no authority to draw the money from his hands, and the subsidiary high court has not directed this suit to be brought by them to obtain the money from Mr. Pinney in this manner. There is no testimony in the case tending to show any recognized custom with reference to the payment over by the retiring treasurer of the moneys in his hands to his successor in office. The general laws of the order have been introduced as containing the only method by which the moneys in his hands as treasurer are withdrawn. We think it was incumbent upon the plaintiffs to have shown some breach of duty on the part of defendant prescribed by the general laws of the society of which he was a member, before he can be compelled in a suit of this kind to pay over money in his hands. All the members of the association are bound by these general laws. The executive council cannot draw money from his hands simply by resolution. It requires an order, signed as provided for in section 2 of article 12, or by section 17 of article 33.'' We conclude that the articles of association constitute the fountain of authority for the trustees and are to be looked to to ascertain their powers, and, if such articles or association provide that property shall be vested in the trustees elected from time to time, such property vests in the new trustees without formal action on the part of the old trustees, at least so far as personal property is concerned. While this might be true also in regard to real estate, the safe way is for the trustees to make a conveyance to their successors of the real estate held in trust unless the deed of such property expressly provides that no such conveyance shall be necessary. In respect to general contracts and acts by trustees, the articles of association are to be looked to for their powers, they being, as are the other officers of corporations or voluntary associations, agents, whose authority is to be measured by the articles of association, and, probably so far as dealings with outside parties are concerned, by the authority which they are held out to the world as possessing.[160]

§ 172. **Authority of Life Insurance Agents.**—We shall gain a clearer idea of the difficulties that have arisen in construing the authority of the agents of insurance companies if we consider the methods of transacting the business in common use. The

[160] Deller v. Staten Island Athletic Club, 56 Hun. 647; 9 N. Y. Supp. 876. See *ante*, § 95.

companies seek customers throughout a wide extent of territory;
· they have their agents in every town of every State who devote
their time to securing business. These agents, particularly those
of life insurance companies, for the representatives of fire companies are generally now intrusted with blank policies which they
can countersign and issue, are not authorized to conclude contracts or to issue policies, but only to take the proposal of the
applicant, which is submitted to the principal and by it accepted
or rejected. The companies for their protection in dealing with
so many strangers make the form of these proposals, or applications, comprehensive, and in them are a large number of questions
to be answered by the person to be insured. By the terms of the
application the truth of the answers to these questions is warranted and the proposal is made a part of the policy, which is to
be void if any of the answers to these questions are found to be
untrue. It was found that frequently, though the applicant had
answered the questions truthfully, the agent of the company,
who had prepared the application and written down the answers,
had, through accident or design, incorrectly reported them, so
when the applicant signed the paper, supposing it contained what
he had stated, he warranted something to be true which was false
and when a loss occurred he discovered that he had stipulated
away his right of recovery. Naturally he sought to lay the blame
on the agent, for whose mistakes and faults, while acting in the
apparent scope of his authority, he claimed the principal was
responsible. On the other side the company claimed the protection of the express contract and invoked the aid of the rule
that parol testimony was not admissible to explain or modify the
terms of this written contract. The insured asked to have the
doctrine of equitable estoppel applied and insisted that, if the
answers were correct but were not truly written down by the agent
of the company the latter was precluded from insisting upon the
defense. Here was the first difficulty which presented itself and
often the companies lost through the inclination of the courts to
apply the principles of the law of estoppel. Then came up a new
complication. To avoid the effect of these decisions, and for the
purpose of taking away the right to invoke them, a clause was inserted in the contract whereby the insured agreed that any person, other than such insured, acting in preparing the application

281

or effecting the insurance (the agent of the company being thereby meant), should for all intents and purposes be taken and deemed to be the agent of the insured and not of the company. From this stipulation arose the much debated question of dual agency in insurance contracts,[161] which question has caused much of the apparent conflict in the cases. In dealing with this subject the rule has been applied that insurance contracts are to be liberally construed in favor of the insured and most strongly against the insurer. The disposition of the courts has also been to ignore the suggestion that an agent can represent both parties to a contract, but to require of insurance agents an undivided allegiance to a single principal and a faithful observance of all duties towards him, and in the determination of controversies as to the powers of agents the companies have been held responsible for all the acts of their agents within the apparent scope of their employment in carrying out the business intrusted to them.

In the case of Germania Life Ins. Co. v. Bouldin,[162] the Court fairly stated the general rule which applies to the transaction of agents of insurance companies, as follows: "The powers possessed by agents of insurance companies, like those of any other corporation or of an individual principal, are to be interpreted in accordance with the general law of agencies. No other or different rule is to be applied to a contract of insurance than is applied to other contracts. The agent of an insurance company possesses such powers only as have been conferred verbally or by the instrument of authorization, or such as third persons had a right to assume that he possesses under the circumstances of each particular case. Cases frequently arise where the principal is estopped from denying the authority of his agent, and this is especially true where the agent, with the knowledge and consent of the principal, holds himself out to the world as having certain powers. The essence of estoppel is that the party asserting the agency was deceived by the conduct of the party against whom it is asserted, and, though fraud may be an ingredient of the case, it is not essential. The principal need not authorize the agent to practice a

[161] This subject is exhaustively discussed in 6 South. L. Rev. 367, by J. O. Pierce, and in 10 Am. L. Reg. 680 (note to Von Bories v. United, etc., Ins. Co., 8 Bush 133), by W. W. Wiltbank.
[162] 100 Miss. 660; 56 Sou. 609.

fraud on third parties, yet if he authorize his agent to transact the business with a third party, and in so doing the agent practices the fraud on the party, the principal is liable. The estoppel may be allowed on the score of negligent fault of the principal. Where one or two innocent persons must suffer loss, the loss will be visited on him whose conduct brought about the situation.''

§ 173. **The Modern Doctrine.**—It follows, therefore, that the general rule may be thus stated: Agents of life insurance companies are like those of other corporations; in doing the business of their employers they can represent them alone, and not first one party to the contract and then the other. The principals are bound by all acts within the apparent scope of the authority of the agents while engaged in transacting the business, but all limitations upon the agent's powers, which are brought to the knowledge of the persons dealing with them, must be respected.[163] The difficulty is in the application of this rule, for, while the principles of the law are inflexible and always the same, the facts of no two cases are alike. It is hard to apply the proper principle to these varying facts. We may illustrate this modern doctrine by some free quotations from leading cases. The first of these,[164] while it relates primarily to a fire insurance contract, is applicable generally, for its summary of the law is undoubtedly correct. ''On principle, as well as for considerations of public policy, agents of insurance companies authorized to procure applications for insurance and to forward them to the companies for. acceptance, must be deemed the agents of the insurers and not of the insured in all that they do in preparing the application, or in representations they may make to the insured as to the character or effect of the statements therein contained. This rule is rendered necessary by the manner in which business is now usually done by the insurers. They supply these agents with printed blanks, stimulate them by the promise of liberal commis-

163 *Post*, §§ 274 and 594.

164 Kausal v. Minnesota Farmers', etc., Ass'n, 31 Minn. 17; 47 Am. Rep. 776. Also Whitney v. National, etc., Ass'n, 57 Minn. 472; 59 N. W. 943; Robinson v. Aetna Ins. Co., 128 Ala. 477; 30 Sou. 665; Van Werden v. Equitable Life Assur. Soc., 99 Ia. 621; 68 N. W. 892; Despain v. Mut. Life Ins. Co., 81 Kan. 722; 106 Pac. 1027; Pacific Mut. L. Ins. Co. v. Carter, 92 Ark. 372; 123 S. W. 584; 124 S. W. 704.

sions, and then send them abroad in the community to solicit in-- surance. The companies employ them for that purpose, and the public regard them as the agents of the companies in the matter of preparing and filling up the applications—a fact which the companies perfectly understand. The parties who are induced by these agents to make applications for insurance rarely know anything about the general officers of the company, or its constitution and by-laws, but look to the agent as its full and complete representative in all that is said or done in regard to the application. And in view of the apparent authority with which the companies clothe these solicitors, they have a perfect right to consider them such. Hence, where an agent to procure and forward applications for insurance, either by his direction or direct act, makes out an application incorrectly, notwithstanding all the facts are correctly stated to him by the applicant, the error is chargeable to the insurer and not to the assured.[165] After the courts had generally established this doctrine, many of the insurance companies, in order to obviate it, adopted the ingenious device of inserting a provision in the policy that the application, by whomsoever made, whether by the agent of the company or any other person, shall be deemed the act of the insured and not of the insurer. But, as has been well remarked

[165] Insurance Co. v. Mahone, 21 Wall. 152; Insurance Co. v. Wilkinson, 13 Wall. 222; Malleable Iron Works v. Phoenix Ins. Co., 25 Conn. 465; Hough v. City Fire Ins. Co., 29 Conn. 10; 76 Am. Dec. 581; Woodbury Savings Bank v. Charter Oak Ins. Co., 31 Conn. 517; Miner v. Phoenix Ins. Co., 27 Wis. 693; 9 Am. Rep. 479; Winans v. Allemania Fire Ins. Co., 38 Wis. 342; Rowley v. Empire Ins. Co., 36 N. Y. 550; Brandup v. St. Paul F. & M. Ins. Co., 27 Minn. 393. See also Mullin v. Vermont Mut. F. Ins. Co., 58 Vt. 113; Continental Ins. Co. v. Pierce, 39 Kan. 396; 18 Pac. 291; Eggleston v. Council Bluffs Ins. Co., 65 Ia. 308; Menk v. Home Ins. Co., 76 Cal. 50; 14 Pac. 837; 18 *Id.* 117; McGraw v. Germania Fire Ins. Co., 54 Mich. 145; Langdon v. Union M. L. Ins. Co., 14 Fed. 272; Lueders v. Hartford L. & A. Ins. Co., 12 Fed. 465; Dunbar v. Phoenix Ins. Co., 72 Wis. 492; 40 N. W. 386; Temminck v. Metropolitan L. Ins. Co., 72 Mich. 388; 40 N. W. 469; Ins. Co. v. Brodie, 52 Ark. 11; 11 S. W. 1016; Kan. Prot. Union v. Gardner, 41 Kan. 397; 21 Pac. 233; Ames v. Manhattan L. Ins. Co., 58 N. Y. Supp. 244; 40 App. D. 465; Robinson v. Metropolitan L. I. Co., 157 N. Y. 711; 53 N. E. 1131; La Marche v. New York Life Ins. Co., 126 Cal. 498; 58 Pac. 1053.

by another Court, 'there is no magic in mere words to change the real into the unreal. A device of words cannot be imposed upon a court in place of an actuality of facts.' If corporations are astute in contriving such provisions, courts will take care that they shall not be used as instruments of frauds or injustice. It would be a stretch of legal principles to hold that a person dealing with an agent, apparently clothed with authority to act for his principal in the matter in hand, could be affected by notice, given after the negotiations were completed, that the party with whom he had dealt should be deemed transformed from the agent of one party into the agent of the other. To be efficacious, such notice should be given before the negotiations are completed. The application precedes the policy and the insured cannot be presumed to know that any such provision will be inserted in the latter. To hold that by a stipulation unknown to the insured at the time he made the application, and when he relied upon the fact that the agent was acting for the company, he could be held responsible for the mistakes of such agent, would be to impose burdens upon the insured which he never anticipated. Hence, we think that if the agent was the agent of the company in the matter of making out and receiving the application, he cannot be converted into the agent of the insured by merely calling him such in the policy subsequently issued. Neither can any mere form of words wipe out the fact that the insured truthfully informed the insurer, through his agent, of all matters pertaining to the application at the time it was made. We are aware that in so holding we are placing ourselves in conflict with the views of some eminent courts. But the conclusion we have reached is not without authority to sustain it, and is, as we believe, sound in principle and in accordance with public policy.[166] It is con-

[166] Commercial Ins. Co. v. Ives, 56 Ill. 402; Gans v. St. Paul F. & M. Ins. Co., 43 Wis. 108; 28 Am. Rep. 535; Columbia Ins. Co. v. Cooper, 50 Pa. St. 331. See also Planters Ins. Co. v. Myers, 55 Miss. 479; 30 Am. Rep. 521; Piedmont & A. L. Ins. Co. v. Young, 58 Ala. 476; Delancey v. Ins. Co., 52 N. H. 581; Commercial Union Ass. Co. v. Elliott (Pa.), 13 Atl. 970; Baker v. Ohio Farmers' Ins. Co., 70 Mich. 199; 38 N. W. 216; McArthur v. Ins. Co., 73 Iowa, 336; 33 N. W. 430 and note; Sullivan v. Phenix Ins. Co., 34 Kan. 170; Ellenberger v. Protective, etc., Ins. Co., 89 Pa. St. 464; Dietz v. Providence, etc., Ins. Co., 31 W. Va. 851; 8 S. E. 616.

tended by respondent that there is a distinction in this regard between 'stock' and 'mutual' insurance companies; that the difference in the character of the companies makes a difference in the relative duties of the applicant and the company, and in the authority of the agents employed; that in the case of a mutual company, the application is in effect not merely for insurance, but for admission to membership—the applicant himself becoming a member of the company upon the issue of the policy. By some courts a distinction in this respect is made between the two classes of companies. This distinction is usually based upon the ground that the stipulations held binding upon the insured are contained in the charter, or by-laws of the company, and that a person applying for membership is conclusively bound by the terms of such charter and by-laws. Such is not this case, for the stipulations claimed to bind the insured are only in the policy. But so far as concerns the question now under consideration, we fail to see any distinction between the two kinds of companies, and we feel confident that the average applicant for insurance is rarely aware of any. It is true that in the case of a mutual company the insured becomes in theory a member of the company upon the issue of the policy. But in applying and contracting for insurance, the applicant and the company are as much two distinct persons as in the case of a stock company, and we see no reason for holding the agent who takes the application any less the agent of the insurer in the one case than in the other. The membership does not begin until the policy is issued. As to all previous negotiations the agent acts only for the company.''[167] The Supreme Court of the United States also has said :[168] ''The powers of the agent are, *prima facie*, co-extensive

[167] Columbia Ins. Co. v. Cooper, 50 Pa. St. 331. See also Ellenberger v. Protective, etc., Ins. Co., 89 Pa. St. 464; Whited v. Germania Ins. Co., 76 N. Y. 415; Lycoming Fire Ins. Co. v. Woodworth, 83 Pa. St. 223; Thompson v. Ins. Co., 104 U. S. 252, and Lycoming Fire Ins. Co. v. Langley, 62 Md. 196.

[168] Ins. Co. v. Wilkinson, 13 Wall. 235. See also Manhattan L. Ins. Co. v. Carder, 27 C. C. A. 344; 82 Fed. 986; Mut. L. Ins. Co. v. Logan, 31 C. C. A. 172; 87 Fed. 637; Kendrick v. Mut. Ben. L. Ins. Co., 124 N. C. 315; 32 S. E. 728; Back v. Employers' Liab. A. C., 93 Fed. 930; Knarston

with the business intrusted to his care, and will not be narrowed
by limitations not communicated to the person with whom he
deals. An insurance company, establishing a local agency, must
be held responsible to the parties with whom they transact business for the acts and declarations of the agent, within the scope
of his employment, as if they proceeded from the principal. In
the fifth edition of American Leading Cases,[169] after a full consideration of the authorities, it is said: 'By the interested or
officious zeal of the agents employed by the insurance companies
in the wish to outbid each other and procure customers, they not
unfrequently mislead the insured, by a false or erroneous statement of what the application should contain, or taking the
preparation of it into their own hands, procure his signature by
an assurance that it is properly drawn and will meet the requirements of the policy. The better opinion seems to be that, when
this course is pursued, the description of the risk should, though
nominally proceeding from the insured, be regarded as the act of
the insurers.' The modern decisions fully sustain this proposition, and they seem to us founded in reason and justice, and meet
our entire approval. This principle does not admit oral testimony to vary or contradict that which is in writing, but it goes
upon the idea that the writing offered in evidence was not the
instrument of the party whose name is signed to it, that it was
procured under such circumstances by the other side as estops
that side from using it or relying on its contents; not that it may
be contradicted by oral testimony, but that it may be shown by
such testimony that it cannot be lawfully used against the party
whose name is signed to it.'[170] But where "it is known to the
assured that the agent is only authorized to solicit insurance and
receive applications, which are to be forwarded to the company
for its aceptance or rejection, the agent has no implied authority

v. Manhattan L. Ins. Co., 124 Cal. 74; 56 Pac. 773; Metropolitan L. Ins.
Co. v. Larson, 85 Ill. App. 143; Mut. L. Ins. Co. v. Herron, 79 Miss. 381; 30
Sou. 691. New York Life Ins. Co. v. People, 195 Ill. 430; 63 N. E. 264; affg.
95 Ill. App. 136; Hallex v. New York L. Ins. Co., 22 Ky. L. 740; 58 S. W.
822; Robinson v. U. S. Ben. Soc., 132 Mich. 695; 94 N. W. 211; Bigger v.
Rock L. Ass. Co., 71 J. K. B. 79; 1 K. B. 516; 85 L. T. R. 636.

[169] Vol. 2, p. 817.

[170] Insurance Company v. Mahone, 21 Wall. 152; post, § 221 and § 428.

to bind the company by a contract for insurance and the company is not estopped from showing the restricted character of such authority."[171]   A life insurance agent taking out a policy on his own life in the company he represents, must act in good faith in the observance of the rules of the company as to delivery.[172]   A general agent for one State acting in another has no authority greater than that of an ordinary agent,[173] and a local agent with authority to take applications has no authority to appoint another agent, that being the exclusive province of the general agent.[174]

The Court will take judicial notice of the fact that applications for insurance are usually made with agents as representatives of the company and it is the duty of the company to bring any restrictions, or limitations, on their powers to the knowledge of the applicant.[175]   So a stipulation for return of premium if the risk is not accepted signed by. the solicitor, binds the company,[176] and agreements with an agent as to what the application shall contain are in legal effect made with the company.[177]   But it is also held that statements made by a local agent are not admissible to contradict the provisions of the application.[178]   An agent with authority to solicit life insurance, collect the premiums and deliver policies which may be sent to him for that purpose by the company, but who does not issue or countersign the policies, is not authorized to conclude contracts of life insurance.[179]

[171] U. S. Mut. Acc. Ass'n v. Kittenring, 22 Colo. 257; 44 Pac. 595; Rhodus v. Kansas City Life Ins. Co., 156 Mo. App. 281; 137 S. W. 907.

[172] Howell v. Missouri State Life Ins. Co., 153 N. C. 124; 69 S. E. 12.

[173] Baldwin v. Conn. Life Ins. Co., 182 Mass. 380; 85 N. E. 837; Otte v. Hartford Life Ins. Co., 88 Minn. 423; 93 N. W. 608.

[174] Mut. Life Ins. Co. v. Reynolds, 81 Ark. 202; 98 S. W. 963.

[175] Howe v. Provident Fund Soc., 7 Ind. App. 586; 34 N. E. 830; Travelers' Ins. Co. v. Ebert, 20 Ky. L. 1008; 47 S. W. 865; Halle v. New York Life Ins. Co., 22 Ky. L. 740; 58 Ky. 822.

[176] Mut. Life Ins. Co. v. Herron, 79 Miss. 381; 30 Sou. 691; Bowen v. Mut. Life Ins. Co., 20 S. D. 103; 104 N. W. 1040.

[177] Pfiester v. Mo. State Life Ins. Co., 85 Kan. 97; 116 Pac. 245.

[178] Allen v. Massachusetts Mut. Accident Ass'n, 167 Mass. 18; 44 N. E. 1055.

[179] Rhodus v. Kansas City Life Ins. Co., 156 Mo. App. 281; 137 S. W. 907.

§ 174. **The Contrary View.**—The views expressed in the foregoing cases have not always been received with approval, but have been criticised with great force and reason. The Supreme Court of New Jersey furnishes perhaps the leading authority[180] on the other side, and argues that the doctrine of Insurance Company v. Wilkinson,[181] strikes at the foundation of the recognized principle that parol evidence is not admissible to explain or modify the terms of a written contract. "To except policies of insurance out of the class of contracts to which they belong," says the Court, "and deny them the protection of the rule of law that a contract which is put in writing shall not be altered or varied by parol evidence of the contract the parties intended to make, as distinguished from what appears, by the written contract, to be that which they have in fact made, is a violation of principle that will open the door to the grossest frauds."[182]

§ 175. **The General Rule Unimpaired.**—The general rule must be taken to be unimpaired by these modern decisions, which apply the principle that where a written contract is entered into all previous preliminary agreements and negotiations are merged in it, and an insurance policy, together with the application, if incorporated therein or properly referred to, govern all matters covered by it.[183] If the contract, whether contained in the policy and application, or the constitution and by-laws of a mutual organization, provides that the insurers are not to be bound by any agreements or statements of the agent, unless the same be incorporated or referred to in the contract, then such provision of

180 Franklin F. Ins. Co. v. Martin, 40 N. J. L. 568; 8 Ins. L. J. 134.

181 13 Wall. 222, *supra*.

182 Van Schoick v. Niagara F. Ins. Co., 68 N. Y. 438; Jennings v. Chenango Co. Mut. Ins. Co., 2 Denio, 75; Sheldon v. Hartford F. Ins. Co., 22 Conn. 235; 58 Am. Dec. 420; Barrett v. Union Mut. Ins. Co., 7 Cush. 175; Dewees v. Manhattan Ins. Co., 6 Vroom (35 N. J. L.), 366; Lewis v. Phoenix M. L. Ins. Co., 39 Conn. 100; Ryan v. World M. L. Ins. Co., 41 Conn. 168; 19 Am. Rep. 490; *post*, § 221 and § 428.

183 Ins. Co. v. Mowry, 96 U. S. 544; Lycoming F. Ins. Co. v. Langley, 62 Md. 196; Thompson v. Ins. Co., 104 U. S. 252; New York L. Ins. Co. v. Fletcher, 117 U. S. 519; Am. Ins. Co. v. Neiberger, 74 Mo. 167.

the parties will be enforced.[184] The rule has well been stated as follows: "A principal may limit the authority of his agent, and when he does so the agent cannot bind his principal beyond the limits of his authority by contract, estoppel or waiver, to those who knew the limitations of his power."[185] The limitations in the policy as to the authority of agents do not apply to the preparation of the application.[186] The company is not bound by the statements of a mere local agent.[187] Under the facts an agent soliciting insurance may be agent of the insured and his knowledge will not prevent the company setting up a breach of warranty.[188] A local agent can bind his principal by acts within the ordinary authority of such agents unless his authority was limited and third persons had knowledge of the limitation. The company may be bound by the acts of the clerk of such agent.[189]

§ 176. **The Same Subject.**—The later cases, while recognizing the principle which we have heretofore stated that a person cannot at the same time be agent of the company and of the insured although so stipulated in the application, generally hold that there is a difference between the acts of the agent before the issuance of the policy and those afterwards. The limitations expressed in the policy of the authority of the agent, or a prohibition of his authority to waive conditions, have no application to those conditions which relate to the making or inception of the contract but only to conditions inserted in the contract as actually

[184] Enos v. Sun Ins. Co., 67 Cal. 621; Leonard v. Am. Ins. Co., 97 Ind. 299; Lycoming Ins. Co. v. Langley, 62 Md. 196; Loehner v. Home M. Ins. Co., 17 Mo. 247.

[185] Modern Woodmen v. Tevis, 54 C. C. A. 293; 117 Fed. 113; overruling s. c. 49 C. C. A. 256; 111 Fed. 113; Travelers' Ins. Co. v. Myers, 62 Ohio St. 529; 57 N. E. 458; 49 L. R. A. 760; Conway v. Phoenix M. L. I. Co., 140 N. Y. 79; 35 N. E. 420. See *post*, 600, *et seq.*

[186] Mut. Ben. L. Ins. Co. v. Robison, 7 C. C. A. 444; 58 Fed. 723; 22 L. R. A. 325; Mut. Reserve F. L. A. v. Farmer, 65 Ark. 581; 47 S. W. 850; Ward v. Metropolitan L. Ins. Co., 66 Conn. 227; 33 Atl. 902; Mut. L. Ins. Co. v. Herron, 79 Miss. 381; 30 Sou. 691.

[187] Allen v. Mass. Mut. Acc. Ass'n, 167 Mass. 18; 44 N. E. 1053.

[188] Travelers' Ins. Co. v. Thorne, 180 Fed. 82; 103 C. C. A. 436.

[189] Thompson v. Michigan Mut. Life Ins. Co., 56 Ind. App. 502; 105 N. E. 780.

made and to be thereafter observed.[190] Thus where the agent attached a rider to the policy it is binding though unauthorized.[191] So it has been held.that notwithstanding the application contains a restriction upon the authority of the agent, yet if he induces the applicant to sign the application without reading it, the company will be presumed to have knowledge of facts communicated to the agent,[192] or if the application was written by the agent without consulting the insured, the company is charged with the knowledge of its agent[193] or where the agent wrote in false answers the insured giving true information.[194] A private physician who, in the absence of the regular examiner, examined the applicant is not the agent of the insurer when he was procured by a friend of the applicant.[195] Where a statement contained in the application for insurance on the life of the daughter was prepared by her father, who was agent of the company, and she did not know that such statement was in the application, it was a mere expression of opinion and its falsity will not prevent recovery.[196] The cashier of defendant's branch office in New Mexico was held to have authority to bind the defendant by information concerning the value of the policy and amount of the premiums thereon,[197] but it has also been held[198] that the statement of an agent contradicting the terms of the policy does not affect it.

Most of the cases involving inquiry as to the authority or powers of an agent arise in questions relating to waiver, or setoppel, by the acts of such agent.[199]

[190] Maupin v. Scottish Union, etc., Ins. Co., 53 W. Va. 557; 45 S. E. 1003; Farwood v. Prudential Ins. Co., 117 Md. 254; 83 Atl. 169.

[191] Germania Life Ins. Co. v. Bouldin, 100 Miss. 660; 56 Sou. 609.

[192] Despain v. Pacific Mut. Life Ins. Co., 81 Kan. 722; 103 Pac. 1027.

[193] Maloney v. Maryland Cas. Co., 113 Ark. 174; 167 S. W. 845.

[194] Pacific Mut. Life Ins. Co. v. Van Fleet, 47 Colo. 401; 107 Pac. 1087; Suravitz v. Prudential Ins. Co., 244 Pa. 582; 91 Atl. 495. But see Silcox v. Grand Fraternity (N. J.), 76 Atl. 1018.

[195] Sovereign Camp Woodmen of the World v. Lilland, Tex. Civ. App. 174 S. W. 619.

[196] Home Circle Society v. Shelton, Tex. Civ. App. 85 S. W. 320.

[197] Lange v. New York Life Ins. Co., 254 Mo. 488; 162 S. W. 589.

[198] La Rue v. Provident Savings Life Assur. Soc., 138 Ky. 776; 129 S. W. 104·

[199] See post, § 600.

§ 177. **Dealings with Agents of Mutual Companies.**—A distinction has sometimes been made between policies issued by a stock company and those issued by a mutual company, but this distinction is without any substance. The insured, in a mutual company, by taking out a policy, becomes a member of it. But nevertheless a member of a corporation, and even a director, in dealing with the corporation, stand, in respect to their contracts, just the same as a stranger,[200] and the Supreme Court of Pennsylvania says:[201] "Too much is attempted to be made of the relation of co-corporator, in which the insured stands, in mutual insurance companies. In the act of insurance he is not so, but a stranger; and he becomes a corporator only by the consummation of that fact; and this does not convert the previous act of examination and description, by the agent of the company, into his act and change it into a representation by him."[202]

§ 178. **The Correct Doctrine as to the Authority of Insurance Agents Stated in Certain Cases.**—The correct doctrine in regard to the authority of insurance agents is laid down in a decision of the Court of Appeals of Maryland,[203] taken in connection with the modifications stated by the Supreme Court of Pennsylvania.[204] In the former the following was cited with approval from a standard work on insurance:[205] "In all cases where the assured has notice of any limitation upon the agent's power, or where there is anything about the transaction to put him on inquiry as to the actual authority of the agent, acts done by him in excess of his authority are not binding, as where it is generally known that limitations are imposed in certain respects. So, where direct notice, or any notice which the assured as a prudent man is bound to regard, is brought home to the assured, limiting the powers of the agent, he relies upon any act in excess of such limited authority at his peril. That an insurance company has the right to limit the

200 Franklin F. Ins. Co. v. Martin, 40 N. J. L. 579; Stratton v. Allen, 16 N. J. Eq. 229.

201 Cumberland Valley Ins. Co. v. Schell, 29 Pa. St. 31.

202 Kausal v. Minnesota Farmers', etc., Ins. Co., 31 Minn. 17; 47 Am. Rep. 776; *post*, 247, *et seq.*

203 Lycoming Fire Ins. Co. v. Langley, 63 Md. 196.

204 Ellenberger v. Protective, etc., Ins. Co. 89 Pa. St. 464.

205 Wood on Ins., § 387.

powers of its agents must be conceded, and when it does impose such limitations upon his authority, in a way that no prudent man ought to be mistaken in reference thereto, it is not bound by an act done by its agent in contravention of such notice.'' In the Pennsylvania case the Court said that no case ''declares that the fraud or mistaken of a knavish or blundering agent, done within the scope of the powers given him by the company, will enable the latter to avoid a policy to the injury of the assured, who innocently became a party to the contract. The authorities go far, very likely not too far, in holding the assured responsible for his warranty, and in excluding oral evidence to contradict or vary it; but they do not establish that where an agent of the assurer has cheated the assured into signing the warranty and paying the premium and the policy was issued upon the false statements of the agent himself, the assured shall not prove the fact and hold the principal to the contract, as if he had committed the wrong. The defendant is a mutual company, and holders of its policies are members. Membership dates from consummation of the contract, and not before. During negotiations for insurance, a mutual company occupies no other or better position than one organized on the stock plan, and cannot profit by a contract induced by the fraud of its agent; for the membership arises from, but does not precede the contract.[206] As to all preliminary negotiations, the agent acts only on behalf of the company. A stipulation in a policy that if the agent of the company, in the transaction of their business, should violate the conditions, the violation shall be construed to be the act of the insured, and shall avoid the policy, will not render the insured responsible for the mistakes of the agent.[207] This was said where the mistake was of representations, and does not qualify the rule which holds the assured upon his covenants or warranties. But it shows that a company contracting by its agent will not always escape the consequences of the fraud or mistake of its agent, by inserting a stipulation in the policy that such agent shall be deemed the agent of the insured, who, at the time of applying for the policy, was ignorant of the insurer's intention to so stipulate.'' We can see no reason why this rule should

206 Lycoming F. Ins. Co. v. Woodworth, 82 Pa. St. 223.
207 Columbia Ins. Co. v. Cooper, 50 Pa. St. 331.

not apply to mutual benefit societies wherever the facts are analogous.[208]

§ 179. How Far Knowledge of Agent Binds Principal—Fraud of Agent.—It is also an important inquiry how far the knowledge of the agent of an insurer is to be deemed that of his principal. The subject is necessarily closely connected with that of the application and the powers of agents generally to waive conditions and by their conduct to estop the company or society. It is sufficient to state briefly what is considered the true principle. In the absence of a written application, containing representations or warranties, where an agent upon his own knowledge or investigation, reports a certain state of facts upon which the policy or certificate is issued, then, in the absence of any attempt to mislead on the part of the insured, the principal is bound by the acts of the agent.[209] Again, material errors committed by the agent, or omissions of the agent in stating material facts, in the absence of fault upon the part of the insured, would affect the principal with the knowledge of the agent.[210] So, where the agent knew of the habits of applicant as to use of liquor,[211] or his having vertigo,[212] or his business which was falsely stated,[213] or where applicant did not know his age and the agent inserted an untrue age,[214] and generally where true answers are given and the agent writes false answers,[215] or where by advice of the agent a state-

208 *Post*, 190, *et seq.*

209 Cumberland Valley, etc., Ins. Co. v. Schell, 29 Pa. St. 31; Meadowcraft v. Standard F. Ins. Co., 61 Pa. St. 91; Caston v. Monmouth Mut. F. Ins. Co., 54 Me. 170; Comml. Ins. Co. v. Ives, 56 Ill. 402; Brink v. Merchants', etc., Ins. Co., 49 Vt. 442.

210 Campbell v. Merchants', etc., Ins. Co., 37 N. H. 65; 72 Am. Dec. 324; Behler v. German Ins. Co., 68 Ind. 353; Beebe v. Hartford, etc., Ins. Co., 25 Conn. 51; 65 Am. Dec. 553; Commercial Fire Ins. Co. v. Allen, 80 Ala. 571; 1 Sou. 202; Howard Ins. Co. v. Bruner, 23 Pa. St. 50; May on Ins., § 132.

211 Newman v. Covenant M. B. Ass'n, 76 Ia. 56; 40 N. W. 87.

212 Mut. L. Ins. Co. v. Daviess, 87 Ky. 541; 9 S. W. 812.

213 McGurk v. Metropolitan L. Ins. Co., 56 Conn. 528; 16 Atl. 263.

214 Keystone M. B. Ass'n v. Jones, 72 Md. 363; 20 Atl. 195.

215 Mut. Ben. L. Ins. Co. v. Robison, 7 C. C. A. 444; 58 Fed. 773; affg. 54 Fed. 580; O'Brien v. Home Ben. Soc., 117 N. Y. 310; 22 N. E. 954; Pudridzky v. Knights of Honor, 76 Mich. 428; 43 N. W. 373.

ment of an applicant is omitted.[216] The knowledge that the applicant must sign the application,, which was not done, binds the principal,[217] and where insured sued to recover premiums paid on a policy void for want of insurable interest, it was held that knowledge of the agent was that of the company.[218] Where the agent has a custom which ought to be known to the company the jury is justified in finding knowledge.[219] And where an accident policy was issued to a woman by an agent in violation of the rule of the company the latter was held liable.[220] The ignorance of assured to be availing must have been in ignorance of the falsity of the answers written for him by the agent.[221] Or, if a mutual mistake was made, on general principles equity would relieve the insured, either before or after loss, if he had acted in good faith,[222] as it certainly would in case of fraud on the part of the agent, if circumstances existed from which the authority of the agent could reasonably be inferred.[223] If, however, the agent and the insured, both knowing material facts, agree to conceal or omit them from the application, then their acts amount to fraud and the principal

[216] Kansas Protective Union v. Gardner, 41 Kan. 397; 21 Pac. 233.

[217] Fulton v. Metropolitan L. Ins. Co., 21 N. Y. Supp. 470.

[218] Fulton v. Metropolitan L. Ins. Co., 19 N. Y. Supp. 660. In the following cases the knowledge of the agent was held to be that of the company: Lewis v. Mut. Reserve F. L. Ass'n (Miss.), 27 Sou. 649; German-American Mut. L. Ass'n v. Farley, 102 Ga. 720; 29 S. E. 615; Germania L. Ins. Co. v. Koehler, 168 Ill. 293; 48 N. E. 297; Security Trust Co. v. Tarpey, 182 Ill. 52; 54 N. E. 1041, affg. 80 Ill. App. 378; Sun L. Ins. Co. v. Phillips (Tex. Civ. A.), 70 S. W. 603; Provident Savings L. Ass. Co. v. Cannon, 201 Ill. 260; 66 N. E. 388; Otte v. Hartford L. Ins. Co., 88 Minn. 423; 93 N. W. 608; Rogers v. Farmers, etc., Co., 106 Ky. 371; 50 S. W. 543; North Western M. L. A. Co. v. Bodurtha, 23 Ind. App. 121; 53 N. E. 787; Dewitt v. Home Forum Ben. Ord., 95 Wis. 305; 70 N. W. 476. As to knowledge of medical examiner see post, § 276. Generally also see post, § 274.

[219] Aetna L. Ins. Co. v. Smith, 31 C. C. A. 575; 88 Fed. 440.

[220] Travelers' Ins. Co. v. Ebert, 20 Ky. L. 1008; 47 S. W. 865.

[221] Globe R., etc., Co. v. Duffy, 76 Md. 293; 25 Atl. 227.

[222] Franklin F. Ins. Co. v. Martin, 40 N. J. 568; 8 Ins. L. J. 134; May on Ins., § 145; In re Universal Non-Tariff Ins. Co., L. R. 19 Eq. 385; post, § 365.

[223] McLean v. Equitable L. A. Soc., 100 Ind. 127; Union Mut. Ins. Co. v. Slee, 110 Ill. 35.

is not bound. As was said by the Supreme Court of Pennsylvania:[224] "Smith's case[225] rests upon a doctrine..that ought to prevail everywhere, to-wit: 'The principal is bound by the acts of his agent whilst he acts within the scope of the deputed authority; but if, departing from that sphere, or continuing in it, he commits a fraud upon his principal, *particeps criminis* .shall not profit by the fraud.' "[226] The Supreme Court of Wisconsin has also declared itself on this subject, saying,[227] "If there is a case in the books which holds that a principal is bound by the unauthorized and fraudulent acts of his agent done and performed pursuant to a corrupt conspiracy between such agent and the person who seeks to obtain the benefit of the fraud, we have not found it."[228] It has been said[229] that the law of estoppel is .a shield, not a sword, and the knowledge of an agent is not binding on his principal if to so hold would operate as a fraud. Where a wife, with her husband's knowledge, and consent, procures an insurance on his life for his benefit, he paying the premiums, he is bound by her statements in the application though ignorant of them, and if the agent enters into a conspiracy with her to insert false statements in the application he ceases to be the agent of the company and becomes the agent of the applicant and the company is not charged with notice of the facts known to the agent.[230]

In the case of Iverson y. Metropolitan Life Insurance Co.[231] the

224 Ellenberger v. Protective, etc., Ins. Co., 89 Pa. St. 464.

225 Smith v. Insurance Co., 24 Pa. St. 320.

226 New York L. Ins. Co. v. Fletcher, 117 U. 519; Ryan v. World Mut. L. Ins. Co., 41 Conn. 168.

227 Hanf. v. N. W. Mut. Aid Ass'n, 76 Wis. 450; 45 N. W. 315.

228 To the same effect are: Sprinkle v. Knights Templar, etc., Co., 124 N. C. 405; 32 S. E. 734; Speiser v. Phoenix M. L. I. Co., 119 Wis. 530; 97 N. W. 207; Mahon v. Royal Union Mut. L. Ins. Co., 67 C. C. A. 636;·134 Fed. 732; Wilhelm v. Order of Columbian Knights, 149 Wis. 583, 136 N. W. 160. But a company may be liable for the wrongful act or fraud of the agent. New York L. Ins. Co. v. Baese (Tex. Civ. A.), 31 S. W. 824.

229 Mudge v. Supreme Court, etc., 149 Mich. 467, 112 N. W. 1130.

230 Centennial Mut. L. Ass'n v. Parham, 80 Tex. 518; 16 S. W. 316; citing Insurance Co. v. Minch 53 N. Y. 150, and Smith v. Ins. Co., *supra*. For further discussion of this subject see *post*, § 594.

231 151 Cal. 746; 91 Pac. 609; 13 L. R. A. (N. S.) 866, see also New York Life Ins. Co. v. O'Dom, 100 Miss. 219; 56 Sou. 379;· Powell v. Prudential

Court said: "The position taken here by appellant simply is that, because the agent had information that a statement the assured warranted to be true was false, the mere possession of this knowledge bound the company and relieved the assured from his warranty, notwithstanding it was expressly provided in the application, and the insured knew, that the company could not be so bound, and could only be bound by having such information imparted in writing to the home officers, who were authorized to act upon it. This position could only be sustained by holding that it was not competent for the company to limit the authority of its agents, and that the insured is not bound by the knowledge of such limitations. If course, it cannot be so held. In the case at bar there is no question of fraud, deception, or misrepresentation practiced by the agent. The sole question is one of contract. The application contained a limitation on the authority of the agent expressly providing against the company being bound by any information possessed by him not disclosed in the application, and declaring the only way it could be bound, namely, by written statements furnished the officers at the home office for their action upon them. The assured knew all this and agreed to it. It was the contract of the parties upon the subject of the agent's authority, and prescribed the only method in which the company could be bound, which it is not pretended was followed; and we know no reason why the assured should not be controlled by the terms of the contract and the limitations on the authority of the agent, imposed thereby.[232]

A stipulation in a contract of a mutual benefit society that the local secretary should be agent of the insurer in the remittance of past due premiums is valid.[233] Where before the statutes

Ins. Co., 153 Ala. 611; 45 Sou. 208; Crook v. New York Life Ins. Co., 112 Md. 268; 75 Atl. 388; M. W. A. v. International Trust Co., 25 Colo App. 26; 136 Pac. 806.

[232] New York Life Ins. Co. v. Fletcher, 117 U. S. 519, 29 L. Ed. 934; 6 Sup. Ct. Rep. 837; Northern Assur. Co. v. Grand View Bldg. Ass'n, 183 U. S. 308; 46 L. Ed. 213, 22 Sup. Ct. Rep. 133; McCoy v. Metropolitan L. Ins. Co., 133 Mass. 82; Clemens v. Supreme Assembly, R. S. G. F., 131 N. Y. 485; 16 L. R. A. 33, 30 N. E. 496; Dimick v. Metropolitan L. Ins. Co., 69 N. J. L. 384, 62 L. R. A. 774, 55 Atl. 291.

[233] U. S. Ben. Soc. v. Watson, 41 Ind. App. 452; 84 N. E. 29.

against rebating of premiums was enacted the agent gave the insured a rebate on his first premium and the policy was delivered as if the premium had been paid in full, it was held that the company could not defeat the contract to show that it prohibited rebating by agents.[234] Where the organizers of an insurance society requested a person to procure applications and he used the blanks furnished by the society and wrote the answers of an applicant contrary to the answers given by him, which he knew to be true, and such application was received and acted upon by the insurer, such person in taking the application was the insurer's agent and his knowledge was the knowledge of the insurer so as to preclude resistance to a suit on the certificate on the ground of breach of warranty and it was held to be immaterial that a copy of the application was attached to the certificate with a request that insured read it and notify the insurer if any of the answers were incorrect.[235]

§ 180. **Notice to Agent.**—Often, under the provisions of the contracts of insurance companies and benefit societies, notice is required to be given of certain facts under specified contingencies. The general rule is that if the notice be given to the board of directors, or to any officer or agent of the company, whose duty by the by-laws, resolutions and usages of the company, is to communicate it to the directors or managing officials of the company, it is sufficient. "Notice of facts to an agent is constructive notice thereof to the principal himself, when it arises from, or is at the time connected with, the subject-matter of his agency; for, upon general principles of public policy, it is presumed that the agent has communicated such facts to the principal, and if he has not, still the principal, having intrusted the agent with the particular business, the other party has a right to deem his acts and knowledge obligatory upon the principal; otherwise the neglect of the agent, whether designed or undesigned, might operate most injuriously to the rights and interests of such party."[236] This rule

[234] Commercial Life Ins. Co. v. McGinnis, 50 Ind. App. 630; 97 N. E. 1018.

[235] Johnson v. Royal Neighbors of America, 253 Ill. 570; 97 N. E. 1084.

[236] Story on Ag., § 140. But when the policy limits the authority of the agent there is no presumption that such agent communicated his knowledge to the company. Ward v. Metropolitan L. Ins. Co., 66 Conn. 227; 33 Atl. 902.

has been applied to insurance companies, as for example, to cases where true answers have been given to the agent in filling up an application for life insurance but the agent has not correctly stated the answer,[237] and as to notice of prior or other insurance, or of an incumbrance.[238] In one case it was said:[239] "The notion that a corporation can only act under their corporate seal and by their president and secretary, has become obsolete. Unless they may be bound by the acts and admissions of their officers and agents acting in the ordinary affairs of the corporation, so far as relates to the business usually transacted by such officers and agents, they would enjoy an immunity incompatible with the rights of individuals and destructive of the object of their creation." Where there is nothing but a provision in general terms for a notice, without prescribing, either in terms, or by necessary implication, the mode in which it should be given, a verbal notice is good, unless the notice be in a legal proceeding, in which case it should be in writing.[240] For the protection of the assured and to prevent fraud, authority of an agent to do a particular act will often be presumed, although the requirements of the charter or by-laws as to matters of form have not been strictly complied with.[241] Notice to an agent is not notice to the company if the agent only had authority to take applications.[242]

[237] Insurance Co. v. Wilkinson, 13 Wall. 222; Miller v. Mut. Ben. Life Ins. Co., 31 Ia. 216; 7 Am. Rep. 122. Contra, Vose v. The Eagle L. & H. Ins. Co,. 6 Cush. 42. See also *ante*, § 179.

[238] New England F. & M. Ins. Co. v. Schettler, 38 Ill. 166; Rowley v. Empire Ins. Co., 36 N. Y. 550; Peck v. New London Mut. Ins. Co., 22 Conn. 575.

[239] N. E. Fire & M. Ins. Co. v. Schettler, 38 Ill. 171.

[240] McEwen v. Montgomery County, etc., Ins. Co., 5 Hill. 101; Sexton v. Montgomery County, etc., Ins. Co., 9 Barb. 191; Gilbert v. Columbia Turnpike Co., 3 Johns. Cas. 107; Miller v. Mut. Ben. L. Ins. Co., 31 Ia. 216; 7 Am. Rep. 124.

[241] Masters v. Madison, etc., Ins. Co., 11 Barb. 624; New Eng. F. & M. Ins. Co. v. Schettler, 38 Ill. 166; Miller v. Mut. Ben L. Ins. Co., 31 Ia. 216. The subject of the powers and authority of agents of insurance companies is further considered in treating of matters relating to the application, § 274, *et seq.;* those concerning payment of premiums, § 463, *et seq.;* those involving questions of notice, etc., in proofs of loss, § 571, and in discussing the subjects of waiver and estoppel, § 600, *et seq.*

[242] Bonewell v. North Am. Acc. Ins. Co., 167 Mich. 274; 132 N. W. 1067, affg. 160 Mich. 157, 125 N. W. 59.

§ 181. **Officers and Agents of Benefit Societies.**—The affairs of benefit societies are partly managed by superior governing bodies, sometimes styled grand or supreme lodges, which have, in addition to officers corresponding to president, secretary and treasurer, certain committees whose duties are defined in the constitution or articles of association. These committees have many of the characteristics of boards of directors of corporations. In their particular lines of duty they may be general agents with almost unlimited powers, or special agents restricted by provisions of the society's laws. In all cases the rules of the organization will govern unless the officer or committee is held out to the world as having the authority that the designation and name would imply, although in the case of dealings between members or between members and officers there can be no such implied authority held out. Modified by usage or habits of dealing, or restrictions of the articles of association and by-laws, their transactions would be governed by the same general principles appicable to the directors of corporations and, by analogy, at least, the same rules would determine the powers and liability of such committees and officers.

§ 182. **Members of Mutual Benefit Societies Must Know Limitations on Powers of Officers.**—It would seem reasonable that the doctrine ought to generally prevail that every person wishing to become a member of a mutual benefit society should be supposed to make himself acquainted with the charter and regulations of the society, and, where these are specific in their requirements, or limitations upon the powers of agents, or lodges, then that all such requirements and limitations should be presumed to be known to the agent and the applicant alike and must be complied with by both.[243] A distinction, however, is to be made between the requirements of the charter and those of the by-laws and between provisions that go to the essence of the contract and those that are directory merely.[244]

[243] Susquehanna Ins. Co., v. Perrine, 7 W. & S. 348; Eilenberger v. Protective, etc., Ins. Co., 89 Pa. St. 464; Leonard v. American Ins. Co., 97 Ind. 299; Belleville Mut., etc., Ins. Co. v. Van Winkle, 1 Beas. (N. J.)' 333; Hellenberg v. District No. 1, etc., 94 N. Y. 580; Eastman v. Providence, etc,. Ass'n, 62 N. H. 555; 20 Cent. L. J. 580.

[244] Cumberland, etc, Ins. Co. v. Schell, 29 Pa. St. 31; Priest v. Citizens',

§ 183. **Dual Capacity of Subordinate Lodges of an Order.**—
We have seen[245] that benefit societies generally have a complex
organization; first are the local and subordinate lodges under the
control of a grand lodge, next is the grand lodge made up of representatives from the local lodges, and lastly may be a supreme
lodge composed of delegates from the grand lodges. The certificate or policy of insurance is issued by the supreme or grand
lodge to the member through the local lodge, making the latter
an agent for this purpose; and then there may be a collateral
benefit to be paid by the local lodge in case of sickness, in the contract for payment of which the local lodge is a principal. The
contract in the former case is the constitution and by-laws of the
grand or supreme lodge, in the latter the constitution and by-laws
of the local lodge, which usually, however, refer to the constitutions and by-laws of the grand and supreme lodges and make them
also a part of the agreement. To these contracts the member assents when he becomes such and consequently is presumed to know
their terms.[246] The subordinate lodges, therefore, and sometimes
the grand lodges, are principals in certain transactions and agents
in others, and so are governed by different rules as they act in one
capacity or the other, and under the constitutions and laws of the
several bodies both supreme and subordinate lodges may be jointly
liable with the grand lodge.[247] These distinctions clearly appear
in the cases involving their transactions. Where the subordinate
body acts as the instrumentality of a superior body, the latter is
liable for the acts of the former.[248]

etc., Ins. Co., 3 Allen 602; Hale v. Mech., etc., Ins. Co., 6 Gray 169, s. c.
66 Am. Rep. 410; Brewer v. Chelsea Ins. Co., 14 Gray 203; Leonard v.
American Ins. Co,. 97 Ind. 299. For further discussion of this subject
see *post*, § 603.

[245] *Ante*, § 20, *et seq.*

[246] Hellenberg v. District No. 1, 94 N. Y. 580; St. Patrick's Soc. v.
McVey, 92 Pa. St. 510; Dolan v. Court Good Samaritan, 128 Mass. 439;
Coleman v. Supreme Lodge, etc., 18 Mo. App. 189; Leech v. Harris, 2
Brewst. 571.

[247] Supreme Lodge A. O. U. W. v. Zuhlke, 129 Ill. 298; 21 N. E. 789.

[248] Everson v. Spaulding, 82 C. C. A. 263; 150 Fed. 517; 9 L. R. A.
(N. S.) 904.

§ 184. **Officers and Committees of Benefit Societies are Special Agents.**—The affairs of the constituent parts of a benefit society, as local, grand and supreme lodges, are managed by officers, corresponding to president, secretary, treasurer, etc., the same as in other associations or corporations, and by standing, or regular, committees. The latter are generally provided for in the constitution, articles of association and by-laws, and have charge of certain matters, as finance, appeals from subordinate lodges or special branches of the business. They are like directors in many respects, and the members of each committee act together as one body upon the questions coming before them. They are special agents, whose powers and duties are prescribed by the fundamental law of the organization, but on principle can perform all things within the usual and ordinary scope of their employment. Their unauthorized acts are not binding on the principal.[249] The general rules of agency apply to them and also the principles which determine the authority of boards of directors. There may also be special committees, created at any time for special purposes, or to do certain things, in which case they will be authorized to employ such means as are necessary and usual to accomplish the objects of their appointment. The authority of many of these committees is so extensive as to really constitute them general agents in particular directions and bind their principals by whatever they do relating to such matters.[250]

§ 185. **Benefit Societies in Law are Mutual Life Insurance Companies.**—The disposition of the courts has been to hold that benefit societies paying a specified sum to the beneficiaries of a deceased member are to be treated as mutual life assurance organizations. The Supreme Court of Wisconsin in a case involving the liability of a benevolent mutual aid society for a death loss,[251] said: ''We suppose the company is subject to the application of those legal principles applicable to other mutual life in-

---

[249] Hiatt v. Fraternal Home, 99 Mo. App. 105; 72 S. W. 463. As to powers of W. M. of a Masonic Lodge see Halcyon Lodge v. Watson, 7 Kan. App. 661; 53 Pac. 879. See also *post*, 186, *et seq.*
[250] *Ante*, § 147.
[251] Erdmann v. Mut. Ins. Co., etc., 44 Wis. 376.

surance companies.'' In this case the defendant was the incorporated superior, governing a number of subordinate lodges of a social and benevolent organization, known as the ''Order of Hermann's Sons.'' The Supreme Court of Maine, in a case where the benefit promised by a Masonic relief association was in question, said :[252] ''If the prevalent purpose and nature of an association, of whatever name, be that of insurance, the benevolent or charitable results to its beneficiaries would not change its legal character. And that this association, et id omne genus are mutual life insurance companies, we entertain no doubt whatever.[253]

§ 186. **Authority of Subordinate Lodges When Acting for Grand or Supreme Lodge.**—That subordinate lodges are in many transactions agents of the superior, grand or supreme lodges is too clear for argument; the courts have often acted on this assumption.[254] In the case first cited the controversy was over a death benefit promised by the society and it was claimed by the plaintiff that the local lodge had waived the requirement of prompt payment of an assessment. The Court said :[255] ''The constitution and by-laws certainly contain the contract which was entered into by the parties. The grove surely acts for and represents the defendant in making the contract with the member unless we adopt as correct the idea or conclusion resulting from the counsel's position, namely, that the member by some one-sided arrangement makes a contract with himself through his own agent. It seems to us that any such position as that the grove is the sole agent of the member in effecting the insurance or collecting the assess-

[252] Bolton v. Bolton, 73 Me. 299.

[253] *Ante*, § 50. For a very complete review of the authorities see note in 38 L. R. A. 1 to Penn. Mut. L. Ins. Co. v. Mechanics' Savings Bank, etc., 37 U. S. App. 692; 72 Fed. 413; 38 L. R. A. 33.

[254] Schunck v. Gegenzeiter, 44 Wis. 369; Erdmann v. Mut. Ins. Co., etc., 44 Wis. 376; Scheu v. Grand Lodge, etc., 17 Fed. 214; Barbaro v. Occidental Grove, etc., 4 Mo. App. 429; Grand Lodge A. O. U. W. v. Lachmann, 199 Ill. 140; 64 N. E. 1022. As to power of officers of subordinate lodges to waive requirements of law or by their acts to estop their superior, see *post*, § 603.

[255] Schunck v. Gegenzeiter, etc., *supra*.

ments is untenable.''[256]   In a case in Missouri[257] the subject of the authority of local lodges, subordinate to a supreme lodge in matters relating to the benefit promised by the latter, was considered considerably at length.   In this case Judge Thompson delivered the opinion of the court, in the course of which he said: ''The subordinate lodges are no doubt the agents of the supreme lodge in dealings with the members for many purposes, and in those cases where the subordinate lodges act through their ministerial officers, and where the latter act in conformity with the rules governing the lodges and the order, these officers may become *pro hac vice* the agents of the subordinate lodges.   But it is not shown to us that these officers are anywhere endowed with power to set aside the rules of the order, or that the subordinate lodges are endowed with such a faculty.   On the other hand, it is perceived by the provisions of the laws of the order above quoted, that no grand' lodge has power even to alter or amend the laws governing the subordinate lodges.   The doctrine of waiver, which is often appealed to to prevent forfeitures in the case of policies of insurance, has no application to the forfeitures of memberships in these orders.   The laws and rules governing the different branches of such an order, are in the nature of contracts among all the members, and considering the widespread extent of these organizations and the very great extent to which these schemes of benevolence have taken the place of life insurance, especially among the working classes, it is highly important as a principle of public policy, that in cases of this kind, their rules and regulations should be substantially upheld by the judicial courts.[258]   Although the by-laws of an order may declare that the officers of subordinate-

[256] Supreme Lodge v. Abbott, 82 Ind. 1; Hall v. Supreme Lodge, 24 Fed. 450.

[257] Borgrafe v. Knights of Honor, 22 Mo. App. 127.   See also State v. Temperance, etc., Soc., 42 M. A. 485.

[258] Karcher v. Supreme Lodge, 137 Mass. 368; Hall v. Supreme Lodge, 24 Fed. 450.   Chamberlain v. Lincoln, 129 Mass. 70; Rood v. Railway, etc., Ass'n, 31 Fed. 62; Kempe v. Woodmen of the World (Tex. Civ. App.), 44 S. W. 688; Lavin v. Grand Lodge A. O. U. W. 104 Mo. App. 1; 78 S. W. 325; Supreme Lodge K. of H. v. Jones, 35 Ind. App. 121; 69 N. E. 718. But see Railway Passenger, etc., Ass'n v. Robinson, 147 Ill. 138; 35 N. E. 168.   See also *post*, § 590.

lodges are the agents of the members and not of the association, such declaration is not conclusive. "The law will determine whose agent one is, not from the mere declaration that he is the agent of the one or the other, but from the source of his appointment and the nature of the duties he is appointed to perform."[259]

Where the money due for a benefit was by the by-laws to be paid to a subordinate branch, and by it to claimant, and the money was so paid to the presiding officer of such lodge and by him embezzled, it was held that the lodge was liable for the funds.[260]

§ 187. **To What Extent Can Local or Subordinate Lodges Bind the Superior Body.**—Usually the agents of life insurance companies do not have authority to conclude absolutely a contract of insurance, but only to procure and receive applications, which they forward to the company to be acted upon by the immediate officers of the corporation, who alone have the power to issue the policy.[261] If, as in the case of fire insurance companies, the agents were intrusted with blank policies their powers would be very much greater and different rules would apply in determining the liability of their principals for their acts. The subordinate lodges of a great beneficiary order may have either a very limited or a very wide authority: if they have blank certificates which they can issue to whom they please they can bind their superior by almost anything they do in the line of issuing them. Generally, however, the local lodges are like the agents of life insurance companies in that they can only solicit applications which are referred to the superior body to be acepted or declined as its officers

259 McMahon v. Supreme Tent K. O. T. M., 151 Mo. 522; 52 S. W. 384; Godwin v. National Council K. & L. of S., 166 Mo. App. 229; 148 S. W. 980. Schunck v. Gegenzeitiger, 44 Wis. 369; Supreme Lodge K. of H. v. Davis, 26 Colo. 252; 58 Pac. 595; Schlosser v. Grand Lodge Brotherhood R. R. T., 94 Md. 362; 50 Atl. 1048; Grand Lodge A. O. U. W. v. Lachmann, 199 Ill. 140; 64 N. E. 1022; Modern Woodmen v. Tevis, 54 C. C. A. 293; 117 Fed. 369; Andre v. Modern Woodmen, 102 Mo. App. 377; 76 S. W. 710; Reed v. Ancient Order Red Cross, 8 Idaho 409; 69 Pac. 127; Boward v. Bankers' Union, 94 Mo. App. 442; 68 S. W. 369. For discussion of position of medical examiner see *post*, § 223.

260 Fisher v. Olive Branch Lodge, etc., 152 Pa. St. 441; 25 Atl. 869.

261 Bliss on Life Ins., § 283.

may elect. The subordinate lodges are tied down by instructions which they cannot violate even if they were so inclined. The law of benefit societies is not fully settled and many important questions are still to be determined in regard to the authority of the local lodges when acting as agents of the responsible corporation. For example, the courts must further consider to what extent knowledge of the local lodge is that of the superior; whether notice to the former binds the latter; and how far the principal is liable for the misfeasance or neglect of the agent. Of course, the rule applies to these societies as to mutual insurance companies, that the members are supposed to have knowledge of all limitations upon the powers of the lodge officers, or the lodge itself, contained in the charter and by-laws; but, as we shall see, the tendency of the courts is to ignore whenever possible the differences between purely mutual and the ordinary stock companies. The probabilities are that future decisions will trace stronger resemblances between benefit societies and life insurance companies, and, as their methods of business become more alike, so it will be easier to apply the same rules to the contracts of both and emphasize the distinctions because of difference in the methods of doing business. The society and regular company alike issue certificates or policies which are sent to the local agent, or lodge, who countersigns and delivers them, and afterwards collects and remits the assessments or premiums. Though the society has a fraternal and charitable feature that the company has not, the principal business of both is the sale of life insurance for a consideration. The reasonable inference is that the same principles of agency determine in each case the liability of the principal for the acts of the agent.[262]

§ 188. **Same Subject Continued.**—It is difficult, if not impossible, to deduce from the opinions of the Court in the numerous cases where the subject has been considered a general rule. It will be sufficient, however, to give a few extracts from cases bearing on the subject. In the case of Rasicot v. Royal Neighbors of America,[263] the Court said: ''The local camp of which the in-

---

[262] For further discussion of this subject, see *post*, § 594, *et. seq.* and § 274, *et seq.*

[263] 18 Idaho 85; 108 Pac. 1048.

sured was a member collected and received the dues and assessments from its members, and was charged with the duty of looking after the health and conduct of its members and of expelling or suspending its members for any violation of the laws of the order or breach of their duties as members of the society. The local lodge was therefore the agent of the society which issued the benefit certificate, and the appellant, after the lapse of more than four years, is chargeable with notice of the existence of the condition on the part of the insured which would have avoided the risk and prevented the contract from becoming effective and operative.[264] Under these facts and circumstances the doctrine of waiver should be applied to the society. In Supreme Lodge K. of H. v. Davis,[265] the Court said: 'In a mutual benevolent order, composed of a supreme lodge and subordinate lodges, an officer of a subordinate lodge charged with the duty of notifying the members of assessments made by the Supreme Lodge for the purpose of paying insurance certificates of deceased members, and of collecting and forwarding to the Supreme Lodge such assessments, is an agent of the Supreme Lodge, notwithstanding a rule or by-law of the order recites that such officer in collecting and forwarding assessments shall be the agent of the members of the subordinate lodge, and the Supreme Lodge is charged with all knowledge possessed by the agent in making the collection.' In Trotter v. Grand Lodge Legion of Honor,[266] the Court said: 'The rule that courts will give effect to any act or circumstance from which it may fairly be argued that the insurer has waived the right to strict and literal performance by the insured, or upon which an estoppel against forfeiture may be founded, applies to fraternal or lodge insurance. And whether a waiver of forfeiture of a certi-

[264] Modern Woodmen v. Breckenridge, 75 Kan. 373; 89 Pac. 661; 10 L. R. A. (N. S.) 136; 12 Am. & Eng. Ann. Cas. 638; Order of Foresters v. Schweitzer, 171 Ill. 325; 49 N. E. 506; 7 L. R. A. 262; Supreme Lodge K. of H. v. Davis, 26 Colo. 252; 58 Pac. 595; Modern Woodmen of America v. Lane, 62 Neb. 89; 86 N. W. 943; Modern Woodmen of America v. Coleman, 68 Neb. 660; 94 N. W. 814; 96 N. W. 154; Supreme Lodge K. of P. v. Wellenvoss, 119 Fed. 671; 56 C. C. A. 287; Pringle v. Modern Woodmen of America, 76 Neb. 384; 107 N. W. 756.

[265] Supra.

[266] 132 Iowa 513; 109 N. W. 1099; 7 L. R. A. (N. S.) 569.

ficate of insurance will be found in any particular case, depends, not on the intention of the insurer, against whom it is asserted, but on the effect which its conduct or course of business has had upon the insured, and this rule is applicable where the insurer acts under a mistake.' In Pringle v. Modern Woodmen of America,[267] Pringle held a benefit certificate which contained a clause to the effect that it should become null and void if the insured should at any time be convicted of a felony. While holding the certificate, the insured was convicted of felony and sentenced to the State penitentiary, where he was confined for about six months and died. The beneficiary sued on the contract to recover the amount of the policy. It appeared that the insured had continuously kept up the payment of his dues and assessments. The Supreme Court of Nebraska, in speaking through Mr. Justice Barnes, said: 'The local camp and its clerk being the agents of the association, the conclusive presumption, in the absence of fraud, is that they seasonably communicated the fact of Pringle's conviction to the head camp. Indeed, the clerk testified that the governing body knew of the fact, and his statement stands unchallenged, except by the evidence of one C. W. Hawes, the head clerk of the association. A like state of facts has often been held to amount to waiver of a similar forfeiture clause.'

"The State is vitally interested in the thrift and frugality of its citizens, and in encouraging the citizen in providing for his family and looking to their protection and comfort in the event of his demise. To allow him when acting honestly and from the most laudable motive to be led on under the belief that he is devoting his savings to the purchase of a legacy for his dependent ones, and then, when the beneficiary comes to make demand for that paltry recompense, to tell him that the court, the final arbiters of his rights, will not listen to the equity of the case, would be doing violence to the principles of fair dealing, and would be likewise contrary to the best interests of the public at large, which we term 'public policy.' Had the insured been in any manner advised that her policy was not in force, she would perhaps have procured one that would have been valid, and this would have been to the benefit of her family and in the interest of society as

[267] 76 Neb. 384; 113 N. W. 231.

well, and the State itself must feel an interest in having her take such precautions, and in that sense the construction of such contracts becomes a matter of public policy. The insurer cannot suffer half so much from such a policy and such a construction as the individuals interested, and society at large must in the end of necessity suffer from the cold-blooded, technical rule that seems to prevail in so many jurisdictions. This ought to be the rule in order to prevent organizations soliciting membership, receiving insurance applications, and accepting dues and assessments for years, and then, after the applicant is perhaps too old to procure insurance elsewhere, tell the insured that he made a false answer in some one of the numerous questions propounded by the society, and that consequently his policy has never been in force. Such a contract is clearly violative of the interests of society at large and of the welfare of its citizens and ought to be discouraged.''

Many other cases substantially support this view.[268]

In the case of Leland v. Modern Samaritans,[269] the Court said: ''It is further contended that the provisions of the by-laws to the effect that 'no act of any subordinate council or any officer thereof' during the time a member is under suspension shall have 'the effect to reinstate such member, nor waive non-payment of assess-

[268] Frank v. Switchman's Union, 87 Wash. 634; 152 Pac. 512; Crumley v. Sovereign Camp W. O. H., 102 S. C. 386; 86 S. E. 954; Knights of the Maccabees of the World v. Pelton, 21 Colo. App. 185; 121 Pac. 949; Collver v. M. W. A., 154 Ia. 615; 135 N. W. 67; Johnson v. Grand Lodge A. O. U. W., 31 Utah 45; 86 Pac. 494; Shultice v. M. W. A., 67 Wash. 65; 120 Pac. 531; Henton v. Sovereign Camp Woodmen of the World, 87 Neb. 552; 127 N. W. 869; Jones v. Supreme Lodge Knights of Honor, 236 Ill. 113; 86 N. E. 191; Henton v. Sovereign Camp Woodmen of the World, 87 Neb. 552; 127 N. W. 869; Thomas v. Modern Brotherhood of America, 25 S. D. 632; 127 N. W. 572; Leland v. Modern Samaritans, 111 Minn. 207; 126 N. W. 728; Patton v. Women of Woodcraft, 65 Ore. 33; 131 Pac. 521; Independent Order of Foresters v. Cunningham, 127 Tenn. 521; 156 S. W. 192; Gilmore v. Modern Protective Ass'n, 171 Ill. App. 525; Kelly v. Ancient Order of Hibernians Insurance Fund, 113 Minn. 355; 129 N. W. 846; Supreme Lodge United Benev. Ass'n v. Lawson, Tex. Civ. App., 133 S. W. 907; Grand Temple, etc., v. Johnson, Tex. Civ. App. 171 S. W. 491; Hendrickson v. Grand Lodge A. O. U. W., 120 Minn. 36; 138 N. W. 946; Mosiac Templars of America v. Jones, 99 Ark. 204; 137 S. W. 812.

[269] 111 Minn. 207; 126 N. W. 728. See also Willmont v. Grand Grove U. A. O. D., 111 Minn. 201; 126 N. W. 730.

ments' except as expressly authorized, prevents a waiver on facts like those here presented, binding on the Imperial body. This contention is not sustained. This provision of the by-laws is an attempt on the part of the Imperial Council to disable itself from future action with reference to delinquent members, even by mutual consent, is invalid. The subordinate council is the agent of the Imperial Council, and as such is clothed with exclusive authority with reference to the admission of members, other than members at large, and with power and authority on the subject of their reinstatement when in default. It constitutes the agency through which the Imperial body collects assessment and dues from members, and it has sole charge, subject to constitutional regulations, of the affairs of the local council. In view of this situation, it is clear that the Imperial body could not in this manner impair its authority or capacity for future contract, express or implied, with its members.[270] The contention of counsel that these provisions were made valid and effectual by Section 21, Ch. 345, Laws 1907, is not sound. Whatever force or effect may be given that statute, it has no application to the case at bar. It does not appear that defendant has ever acted upon it. The by-law in question was a part of the laws of the society long before the enactment of the statute, and it could not be construed as intended to give force and effect to by-laws previously adopted by societies of the kind. Moreover, the rights of the parties to this action had become fixed prior to the passage of the statute, and it can be given no retroactive operation or effect. The custom of receiving overdue assessments from members had been established and acted upon by decedent before the statute came into existence, and rights accruing from that custom cannot thus be impaired or destroyed.''

§ 189. **The Same Subject—Contrary Views.**—In the case of Hartman v. National Council K. & L. of S.,[271] the Court, follow-

[270] Lamberton v. Insurance Co., 39 Minn. 129; 39 N. W. 76; 1 L. R. A. 222; Anderson v. Insurance Co., 59 Minn. 182; 60 N. W. 1095; 63 N. W. 241; 28 L. R. A. 609; 50 Am. St. Rep. 400; Nichols & Shepard v. Weidemann, 72 Minn. 344; 75 N. W. 208; 76 N. W. 41; Insurance Co. v. Parsons, 47 Minn. 352; 50 N. W. 240; Michaud v. MacGregor, 61 Minn. 198; 63 N. W. 479.

[271] 76 Oregon 153; 147 Pac. 931; L. R. A. 1915-E 152.

ing the principle laid down by the Supreme Court of the United
States in Northern Assurance Co. v. Grand View Building Association,[272] said: "It was lawfully competent for the defendant
to forbid the local officer to waive the conditions mentioned, for
Section 20 of the act of the legislative assembly of date February
23, 1911,[273] 'for the regulation and control of fraternal benefit
societies' reads thus: 'Waiver of the Provisions of the Laws.—
The constitution and laws of the society may provide that no
subordinate body, nor any of its subordinate officers or members,
shall have the power or authority to waive any of the provisions
of the laws and constitution of the society, and the same shall be
binding on the society, and each and every member thereof, and
on all beneficiaries of members.' In this case there is no evidence,
as stated, to show that the local officer who acepted the arrearages,
or any one, ever communicated to the prinicpal officers of the defendant anything concerning the sickness of the assured. On the
contrary, the only evidence on that subject is to the effect that
the first knowledge they had of it was derived from the proofs
of death, based upon which they immediately rejected the claim
and offered to repay the arrearages which had been advanced.
Moreover, controlled as she was by the terms of her certificate and
the laws of the order, which are made a part thereof, and to which
she was subject, having had her part in the enactment of the same
through her representatives, the assured was bound to take notice
of the limitations upon the authority of the local officer, although
for some purposes he might be held to be the agent of the defendant. The beneficiaries can take nothing by reason of the
agent's violation of his instructions.'"[274]

[272] 183 U. S. 308.
[273] Laws 1911, p. 363.
[274] The following precedents are illustrative of the conclusion above
set down: Woodmen of the World v. Jackson, 80 Ark. 419; 97 S. W. 673;
Supreme Commandery U. O. G. C. v. Bernard, 26 App. D. C. 169; 6 Ann.
Cas. 694; Sheridan v. Modern Woodmen, 44 Wash. 230; 7 L. R. A. (N. S.)
973; 120 Am. St. Rep. 987; 87 Pac. 127; Hay v. People's Mut. Benev.
Ass'n, 143 N. C. 256; 55 S. E. 623; Gifford v. Workmen's Ben. Ass'n, 105
Me. 17; 72 Atl. 680; 17 Ann. Cas. 1173; Showalter v. Modern Woodmen 156
Mich. 390; 120 N. W. 994; Bixler v. M. Woodmen, 112 Va. 678; 38 L. R.
A. (N. S.) 571; 72 S. E. 704; Royal Highlanders v. Scovill, 66 Neb. 213;

Many cases, however, hold that local lodge officers have no authority to waive the provisions of the by-laws of the society.[275] The clerk of a local camp after loss cannot by statements bind the Supreme Lodge.[276] It has been held[277] that notice given to a collector, or a protest to collector of the subordinate council, is not a notice to the corporation and a deputy has no authority to waive a by-law requiring initiation by accepting an application,[278] nor can a deputy instituting a lodge deliver a certificate in advance of the organization of the lodge,[279] and a certificate issued to a person beyond the age for admission fixed by the charter is void.[280] The medical examiner of a beneficial association is agent of such a society in spite of the stipulation in the benefit certificate to the contrary.[281] The order can ratify the act of an officer employing an organizer.[282] Specific directions for delivery of a draft given to the officer of a local lodge control.[283] A member of an association receiving a blank application for membership from a foreign

4 L. R. A. (N. S.) 421; 92 N. W. 206; Modern Woodmen v. Tevis, 54 C. C. A. 293; 117 Fed. 369; Clair v. Supreme Council, R. A. 172 Mo. App. 709; 155 S. W. 892; Jones v. Modern Brotherhood, 153 Wis. 223; 140 N. W. 1059; Knode v. Modern Woodmen, 171 Mo. App. 377; 157 S. W. 818; United Commercial Travelers' v. Young, 128 C. C. A. 648; 212 Fed. 132; Grand Lodge, etc., v. Taylor, 44 Colo. 373; 99 Pac. 570.

275 Modern Brotherhood of America v. Beshara, 42 Okla. 604; 142 Pac. 1014; Bennett v. Sovereign Camp Woodmen of the World, Tex. Civ. App. 168 S. W. 1023; Larkin v. M. W. A., 163 Mich. 670; 127 N. W. 786; Frain v. M. W. A., Colo; 155 Pac. 330; Crowley v. Anicent Order Hibernians W. & O. B. Fund, 222 Mass. 228; 110 N. E. 276.

276 Larkin v. M. W. A., 163 Mich. 670; 127 N. W. 786; Lessman v. Catholic Order of Foresters, 163 Mich. 111; 128 N. W. 201; Clair v. Supreme Council R. A., 172 Mo. App. 709; 155 S. W. 892.

277 Attorney General v. Supreme Council A. L. of H., 206 Mass. 175; 92 N. E. 143.

278 McWilliams v. M. W. A., Tex. Civ. App., 142 S. W. 641.

279 Loudon v. Modern Brotherhood of America, 107 Minn. 12; 119 N. W. 425.

280 Sowersby v. Royal League, 159 Ill. App. 626.

281 Masonic Life Ass'n v. Robinson, 149 Ky. 80; 147 S. W. 882.

282 Stevens v. Knights of Modern Maccabees, 153 Mo. App. 196; 132 S. W. 757.

283 Grand Lodge, etc., v. State Bank of Winfield, 93 Kan. 310; 144 Pac. 257, affg. 92 Kan. 876; 142 Pac. 974.

benefit society with the request to obtain new members is the agent of such company.[284]

§ 190. **Have Subordinate Lodges the Characteristics of Ordinary Insurance Agents.**—We have seen from the last sections that benefit societies are like life insurance companies in that they are engaged in the same kind of business. We have also seen that the subordinate lodges are the agents through which the grand or supreme lodges transact this business. The suggestion at once arises that, if this be true, the local lodges, when acting for these superior organizations in bringing in new members, taking their applications and consummating the contract, are doing just what the ordinary life insurance agent does. There are many points of dissimilarity between them in the methods of conducting the business and the contract is made in an entirely different way, but nevertheless the principles underlying the contract in both cases are very much the same. The officers of subordinate lodges, however, are special agents whose authority is defined in the laws of the society and as this authority is equally known to the member and the officer, acts beyond the power of the latter will ordinarily not bind the superior.[285] In many States which have adopted the uniform fraternal society act the statute provides that such societies may provide in their by-laws that no subordinate body, nor any of its subordinate officers or members shall have the power or authority to waive any of the provisions of the laws and constitution of the society, and the same shall be binding on the society and each and every member thereof and on all beneficiaries of members.''[286]

§ 191. **Difference Between Powers of Agents of Stock and Those of Mutual Insurance Companies.**—A distinction has been sought to be made between agents of stock and those of mutual

[284] Tomson v. Iowa State Traveling Men's Ass'n, 88 Neb. 399; 129 N. W. 529.

[285] Harvey v. Grand Lodge A. O. U. W., 50 M. A. 472; Supreme Lodge K. of H. v. Keener, 6 Tex. Civ. App. 267; 25 S. W. 1084. See, however, Hoffman v. Supreme Counc. A. L. H., 35 Fed. 252; McDonald v. Chosen Friends, 78 Cal. 49; 20 Pac. 41; O'Connell v. Supreme Conclave, etc., 102 Ga. 143; 28 S. E. 282.

[286] Missouri Laws 1911, p. 184.

companies, and generally it may be said that the representatives of the former have greater powers in settling the terms of the contract and in waiving compliance with its conditions than have the agents of mutual companies where the by-laws enter into the contract and prescribe that the stipulations shall be the same in all policies and shall regulate alike the rights of all. In Massachusetts, New Jersey and Rhode Island, the courts have ruled strictly on the power of the officers and agents of mutual companies to depart from the directions and regulations of their charters and by-laws, interpreted in the light of the purposes for which these companies were established, but these views have not met with favor in other States, where a more liberal construction has been adopted and the differences between stock and mutual companies have been looked upon as more nominal than real. In the first mentioned States the safety of the companies had been the chief consideration, in the latter the protection and safety of the public. The Massachusetts doctrine may be illustrated by a few extracts. In one case[287] the by-laws of the company provided that insurance subsequently obtained without the written consent of the president should avoid the policy and that the by-laws should in no case be altered except by a vote of two-thirds of the members of the company. In this case subsequent insurance was obtained with the oral consent of the president and the court held that the policy was avoided. It said: "It is clear, upon the facts in this case, that the policy was annulled under the fifteenth article of the by-laws, by reason of the subsequent insurance obtained by Stone and Perry on the property, without the assent of the president of the corporation in writing; unless the waiver of such written assent by the president, and his verbal consent to such subsequent insurance, as found by the jury, operate to set aside this provision in the by-laws as to this particular policy and render the contract valid, notwithstanding by its express terms, as well as by the clause in the by-laws, it would be otherwise void. But the difficulty in maintaining the plaintiff's position on this part of the

[287] Hale v. Mechanics' Mut. F. Ins. Co., 6 Gray 169; 66 Am. Dec. 410. And for a later application of the same rule see McCoy v. Roman Catholic, etc., 152 Mass. 272; 25 N. E. 289; Lyon v. Supreme Assembly, etc., 153 Mass. 83; 26 N. E. 236.

case is, not only that it attempts to substitute for the written agreement of the parties a verbal contract, but that there is an entire absence of any authority on the part of the president to make such waiver, or give such verbal assent. He was an agent with powers strictly limited and defined, and could not act so as to bind the defendants beyond the scope of his authority.[288] By article fifteen of the by-laws, his power to assent to subsequent insurance was expressly confined to giving such assent in writing. In order to guard against the danger of over insurance, the corporation might well require that any assent on their part to further insurance on property insured by them should be given by the deliberate and well considered act of their president in writing and not left to the vagueness and uncertainty of parol proof. The whole extent and limit of the president's authority in this respect were set forth in the by-laws attached to the policy in the present case and, as the evidence shows, were fully known to the assured.''[289] In a subsequent case[290] the same court held that in matters that did not relate to the substance of the contract, but only to the remedy, the requirements of the by-laws could be waived by the officers of the company. This doctrine, that officers of a mutual company cannot waive the by-laws of the company, has been approved in other cases on the ground that if the officers have discretionary powers as to the terms of the contract the principle of mutuality would be completely abrogated.[291] In a recent case already cited[292] the Court briefly reviewed the law, saying: "But even if the officers of the corporation had attempted to waive the by-laws in this particular, which was of the sub-

[288] Story on Ag., §§ 127, 133; Salem Bank v. Gloucester Bank, 17 Mass. 29; 9 Am. Dec. 111.

[289] Worcester Bank v. Hartford Fire Ins. Co., 11 Cush. 265; 59 Am. Dec. 145; Lee v. Howard Fire Ins. Co., 3 Gray 584.

[290] Brewer v. Chelsea, etc., Ins. Co., 14 Gray 203.

[291] Evans v. Trimountain M. F. Ins. Co., 9 Allen 329; Behler v. German, etc., Ins. Co., 68 Ind. 354; Westchester, etc., Ins. Co. v. Earle, 33 Mich. 150; Baxter v. Chelsea M. F. Ins. Co., 1 Allen 294; Belleville M. Ins. Co. v. Van Winkle, 1 Beas. (N. J.) 333; Wilson v. Conway M. F. Ins. Co., 4 R. I. 141; Supreme Council Catholic, etc., v. Boyle, 10 Ind. App. 301; 37 N. E. 1105.

[292] McCoy v. Roman Catholic, etc., Co., 152 Mass. 272; 25 N. E. 289.

stance of the contract; we are of the opinion that they had no authority so to do. This is a corporation which does not make contracts of life insurance with strangers, but arranges a system of payments for the benefit of the relatives of its deceased members. It adopts by-laws to determine the relations of the members to each other and fix their rights against the corporation. The principles which apply to ordinary mutual insurance companies in regard to the waiver of by-laws by officers are equally applicable to this corporation.[293] It is well settled that the officers of a mutual insurance company have no authority to waive its by-laws which relate to the substance of the contract between an individual member and his associates in their corporate capacity.[294] In regard to a by-law in relation to the proof of loss which does not touch the essence of the contract, but relates only to the mode in which the liability of the company is to be established to the satisfaction of the officers who are to act upon the matter, the rule is different.[295] The officers of the defendant were agents with a limited authority. The corporation, by the law which it laid down for its government, received into association with its members and to participation in its benefit, only persons of a particular class. John McCoy did not belong to that class and he could not become a member of the corporation without appropriate action by the corporation itself. The defendant concedes that he paid his money without consideration, and has offered to repay it to his representatives.'' It has been held that although there may be a power to waive the provisions of the by-laws, charter requirements cannot be waived.[296] Other courts have inclined to the view that there is no difference between agents of mutual and those of stock companies, especially in soliciting applications. As was said in one case:[297] ''Incorporated companies,

[293] Bolton v. Bolton, 73 Me. 299; Swett v. Soc., 78 Me. 541; 7 Atl. 394.

[294] Baxter v. Insurance Co., 1 Allen 294; Evans v. Insurance Co., 9 Allen, 329; Hale v. Insurance Co., 6 Gray 169; Mulrey v. Insurance Co., 4 Allen 116; Swett v. Soc., 78 Me. 541; 7 Atl. 394. See also Burbank v. Ass'n, 144 Mass. 434; 11 N. E. 691.

[295] Priest v. Insurance Co., 3 Allen 602.

[296] Weiberg v. Minnesota Scandinavian, etc., Ass'n, 73 Minn. 297; 76 N. W. 37.

[297] Conover v. Mut. Ins. Co., 1 Comst. 290.

whose business is necessarily conducted altogether by agents, should be required at their peril to see to it that the officers and agents whom they employ, not only know what their powers and duties are, but that they do not habitually, and as a part of their system of business, transcend their powers. How else are third persons to deal with them with any degree of safety?''[298] It may safely be said that the courts are becoming less and less inclined to distinguish between agents of the different classes of corporations engaged in the business of life and accident insurance, but seek to apply to the acts of all agents the general principles of the law of agency.

§ 192. **Dealings Between Agent and Company.**—Numerous cases are reported in which the contracts between life insurance companies and their agents are construed. The questions that have arisen in these cases chiefly relate to the construction of agency contracts, the compensation of agents, or the right to commissions and the responsibility of the company to sub-agents. In many cases this subject is in part covered by statutory provisions and it is not deemed within the scope of this work to do more than refer to some of the authorities relating to the rights of the agent as against his principal. There is no reason why these contracts should not be construed and governed by the same general rules which apply to all contracts whether of corporations, or individuals. A special agency contract creating the insured a member of a select body of policyholders and conferring upon them a property right in the funds of the company, by which premiums were to be reduced, is an illegal discrimination.[299] A company can without cause discharge an agent under contract, but without effect as to his right to commissions on renewal premiums.[300] The right of the agent to commissions ceases on termination of contract.[301] An action for commissions brought before the renewal

[298] *Ante*, § 186.
[299] Smathers v. Bankers' Life Ins. Co., 151 N. C. 98; 65 S. E. 746.
[300] Armstrong v. National Life Ins. Co,. Tex. Civ. App. 112 S. W. 227; Martin v. Fraternal Ass'n, 80 Neb. 224; 114 N. W. 159.
[301] Neelis v. MacFarland, 9 Cal. App. 534; 99 Pac. 980.

premiums have become due, cannot be maintained on the ground that the company has reinsured its risks.[302]

302 Moore v. Security Trust & Life Ins. Co., 168 Fed. 496. As to agency contracts, Penn. Mut. Life Ins. Co. v. Onauer, 39 Cal. 498; 90 Pac. 846; Aldrich v. New York Life Ins. Co., 105 N. Y. Supp. 493; 121 App. Div. 18; Michigan Mut. Life Ins. Co. v. Coleman, 118 Tenn. 215; 100 S. W. 122; Heyn v. New York Life Ins. Co., 103 N. Y. Supp. 20; 118 App Div. 194; Boswell v. Security Mut. Life Ins. Co., 104 N. Y. Supp. 130; 119 App. Div. 723; Wightman v. New York Life Ins. Co., 104 N. Y. Supp. 214; 119 App. Div. 496.

As to construction of contract and rights to commissions: Montgomery v. Aetna Life Ins. Co., 38 C. C. A. 553; 97 Fed. 913; Mut. Life Ins. Co. v. Lewis, 13 Colo. App. 528; 58 Pac. 787; Lee v. Huron Indemnity Union, 135 Mich. 291; 97 N. W. 709; Bankers' Life Ins. Co. v. Stephens, 53 Neb. 660; 74 N. W. 34; Currier v. Mut. Reserve Fund Life Ass'n, 47 C. C. A. 651; 108 Fed. 737; New York Life Ins. Co. v. Rilling, 219 Ill. 72; 76 N. E. 73; Leviness v. Kaplan, 99 Md. 683; 59 Atl. 127; New York Life Ins. Co. v. Goodrich, 74 Mo. App. 355; Montgomery v. Aetna Life Ins. Co., 38 C. C. A. 553; 97 Fed. 913; Arbaugh v. Shockney, 34 Ind. App. 268; 72 N. E. 668; Lane v. Raney, 131 N. C. 375; 42 S. E. 820; Kansas Unoin Life Ins. Co. v. Berman, 73 C. C. A. 69; 141 Fed. 835; Vail v. North-western Mut. Life Ins. Co., 192 Ill. 567; 61 N. E. 651.

As to percentage of renewal premiums: Aetna Life Ins. Co. v. Nexsen, 84 Ind. 347; Schrimplin v. Farmers' Life Ass'n, 123 Ia. 103; 98 N. W. 613; Chase v. New York Life Ins. Co., 138 Mass. 271; 74 N. E. 225; Scott v. Travelers' Ins. Co., 103 Md. 69; 63 Atl. 377. As to accounting by agent: American Life Ins. Co. v. Long, 65 Ill. App. 295; Schrimplin v. Farmers' Life Ass'n, 123 Ia. 102; 98 N. W. 613; Castleman v. Southern Mut. Life Ins. Co., 77 Ky. 197; National Life Ins. Co. v. Anderson, 122 Ky. 794; 92 S. W. 976; German-American Ins. Co. v. Tribble; 86 Mo. App. 546. As to duration and termination of agency: Magregor v. Union Life Ins. Co., 57 C. C. A. 613; 121 Fed. 493; Andrews v. Travelers' Ins. Co., 24 Ky. 844; 70 S. W. 43. As to appointment or employment of agent: Union Casualty etc., Co. v. Gray, 52 C. C. A. 224; 114 Fed. 422; Employers' Liability Assur. Co. v. Morris, 14 Colo. App. 354; 60 Pac. 21; Moore v. New York Life Ins. Co. (Tenn.) 51 S. W. 1021; Hergren v. Union Mut. Life Ins. Co., 141 Cal. 585; 75 Pac. 168; New York Life Ins. Co. v. Mills, 51 Fla. 256; 41 Sou. 603. As to estoppel to deny agency: Hartford Life, etc., Co. v. Hayden, 90 Ky. 39; 13 S. W. 585. Contracts between agents and companies construed: Citizens' Nat. Life Ins. Co. v. Witherspoon, 127 Tenn. 363; 155 S. W. 139; Aetna Life Ins. Co. v. Farrell (Tex. Civ. App.), 154 S. W. 1164. Construction of contract as to commissions on renewal premiums: Gooding v. Northwestern Mut. L. I. Co., 85 Atl. 391; Wash-ington Life Ins. Co. v. Reinhardt (Tex. Civ. App.), 142 S. W. 596. Agent held to forfeit commissions on renewals by placing business with another

company: Herrick v. New York Life Ins. Co., 202 Mass. 478; 88 N. E.
1092. Contracts of employment construed and measure of damages for
breach of contract stated: Texas Life Ins. Co. v. Roberts, 55 Tex. Civ.
App. 217; 119 S. W. 926; Richey v. Union Centralia Life Ins. Co., 140
Wis. 486; 122 N. W. 1030. Rights in action against fraternal society for
commissions as agent: Duford v. Parliament P. P. P,. 152 Mich. 151; 115
N. W. 1057. There may be an implied authority of a representative of
the company to hire agents: Gore v. Canada Life Assur. Co., 119 Mich.
136; 77 N. W. 650; Mut. Life Ins. Co. v. Lewis, 13 Colo. App. 528; 58
Pac. 787; Van Werden v. Equitable Life Assur. Soc., 99 Iowa 621; 68 N.
W. 892. As to illegal contract with agent, see Caldwell v. Mut Reserve
Fund Life Ass'n, 53 App. Div. 245; 65 N. Y. Supp. 826. The following
cases involve questions as to the rights of agents and sub-agents and
construction of agency contracts: Lane v. Raney, 139 N. C. 64; 39 N.
E. 728; Employers' etc.. Co. v. Morris, 14 Colo. App. 354; 60 Pac. 21;
Raipe v. Gorrell, 105 Wis. 636; 81 N. W. 1009; Reed v. Union Cent. L. I.
Co., 21 Utah 295; 61 Pac. 21; Frankel v. Mich. Mut. L. Ins. Co., 158 Ind.
304; 62 N. E. 703; Wells v. National Life Ins. Co., 39 C. C. A. 476; 99
Fed. 222; 53 L. R. A. 33; Shrimplin v. Farmers', etc., Co., 123 Ia. 102;
98 N. W. 613; Newcomb v. Ins. Co., 54 Fed. 725; Stier v. Imperial L. Ins.
Co., 58 Fed. 843; Brackett v. Metropolitan L. Ins. Co., 18 Misc. 239; 41
N. Y. Supp. 375; Ballard v. Travellers' Ins. Co., 119 N. C. 187; 25 S. E.
956; Vail v. N. W. Mut. L. Ins. Co., 92 Ill. App. 655, affd. 192 Ill. 567;
61 N. E. 651; Currier v. Mut. R. F. L. Ass'n, 47 C. C. A. 651; 108 Fed.
737; Arbaugh v. Shockney, 34 Ind. App. 268; 71 N. E. 232.

CHAPTER V.

320

§ 193. **Parties to Insurance Contracts—Minors.**—Upon principle it would seem that, so far as the parties are concerned, the same rules apply to insurance contracts as to other contracts, and that any person capable of entering into an obligation of any kind can become a party to a contract of insurance. The relation between an insurance company and holder of a policy of insurance on the mutual plan is not fiduciary, but contractual.[1] The question has arisen whether minors can become members of a fraternal beneficiary association, and there is a conflict of authority on this point. In a recent case[2] the Court of Appeals of New York said: "It is plain that the powers conferred upon members cannot be exercised by children of tender years, such as have been permitted to become members of the corporation defendant. The children insured by the defendant, whose ages are given in the schedule, were incapable of exercising any choice in becoming members, or of appointing a beneficiary, or of exercising the powers with which members are invested by the statute. They could take no part in the co-operative scheme upon which the corporation rests, and which implies the voluntary association of persons capable of acting in the administration of the affairs of the corporation. There is nothing in the statute which permits the inference that a child may be made a member of the corporation upon the application of the parent, or that a beneficiary may be designated or changed by any person except the member himself. It has been held that where a statute authorizes persons to form a cor-

[1] Brown v. Equitable Life Ass'n Soc., 151 Fed. 1, 81 C. C. C. A. 1; 213 U. S. 25.

[2] *In re* Globe Mut. Ben. Ass'n, 135 N. Y. 280; 32 N. E. 122; 17 L. R. A. 547. See also People v. Industrial Ben. Ass'n, 92 Hun. 311; 36 N. Y. Supp. 96; affd. 149 N. Y. 606; 44 N. E. 1127.

poration, it is implied that they shall be persons of full age.[3] Infants admitted as members by the defendant become members of the corporation, if legally entitled to admission, and may be elected trustees or directors, and it might happen that management of the affairs of the corporation would become vested in persons who could not have organized it. We place our assent to the judgment below on the ground that it appears from a consideration of the statute of 1883, and the nature and object of cooperative insurance companies, and the relation which members hold to the corporation, that adult persons only were contemplated as entitled to membership. The law fixes an arbitrary period when persons become clothed with general legal capacity, and while, in many cases, youths under 21 are capable of exercising an intelligent judgment, and might properly be admitted to the advantage of membership in a company like that of the defendant, in many others they would be wholly unfitted to act as members of such an organization.'' In Pennsylvania it has also been held,[4] that minors under 21 years of age were incapable of contracting, and could not qualify as members of a benefit association. In the same State it has also been held,[5] that ''infants cannot make the contract of membership for themselves, and it is not clear how the parents can make it for them.'' The contrary view has been advanced by the Supreme Court of Illinois,[6] where the Court says: ''The statute under which the association was organized is silent on the subject, nor do we find any statute which either expressly, or, so far as we can discover, by implication, either permits or forbids their admission to membership. If, then, minors are ineligible, such ineligibility arises from some principle growing out of the nature and objects of these associations, or the policy of the law applicable thereto. The contention is that the certificate of membership is a personal contract between the member and the as-

[3] Hamilton & F. R. Co. v. Townsend, 13 Ont. App. 534; 16 Am. & Eng. Corp. Cas. 645.

[4] Commonwealth v. People's Mut., etc., Ass'n, 6 Pa. Dist. 561.

[5] Commonwealth v. Keystone Ben. Ass'n, 171 Pa. St. 465; 32 Atl. 1027.

[6] Chicago Mut. L. Ind. Ass'n v. Hunt, 127 Ill. 257; 20 N. E. 55; 2 L. R. A. 549. Another case practically to the same effect is Clements v. London & N. W. R. Co., 2 Q. B. 482; 9 Reports, 223; 42 Week. R. 338; 58 J. P. 816.

sociation, and that as an infant is capable of making only a voidable contract, his admission to membership is a violation of those principles of mutuality which lie at the basis of mutual benefit societies. We may admit in the broadest sense that these societies are founded upon the principle of entire mutuality in relation to burdens as well as benefits; yet we are unable to see how that principle places the membership of infants upon any footing different from that of adults. While the certificate of membership is a contract, such contract in the absence of express stipulations to the contrary, is purely unilateral. It may be enforced against the association where the member has performed all the prescribed conditions, but none of its stipulations are enforcible against the member. If he fails to pay his assessments or dues, or does any act forbidden by the certificate of membership, the certificate becomes void and the membership ceases. But the making of an assessment or the maturing of dues does not make the member a debtor to the association so as to authorize it to bring a suit for its recovery in case of his neglect or refusal to pay. Payment is left wholly to his discretion. The contract, then, not being one which has the legal effect of binding him to the payment of any money or the performance of any condition, we cannot see how it can be at all important whether it is voidable or otherwise. Performance is not more left to the option of the member where the contract is made by an infant than when made by an adult. If an infant performs the conditions prescribed in the certificate, he, the same as an adult, becomes entitled to the benefits thereby secured. If he fails to perform, his membership ceases, and that is all. We do not assent to the view that, as a further consequence of his disability, he may recover back the dues and assessments he may have already paid. 'If an infant advances money on a voidable contract which he afterwards rescinds, he cannot recover this money back because it is lost to him by his own act, and the privilege of infancy does not extend so far as to restore this money unless it was obtained by fraud.' (1 Parsons, Contracts, 332.) Nor are we able to see any force in the suggestion that minors should not be admitted to membership because of the incapacity to act as trustees, or to perform the duties of members at corporate meetings, such as con-

323

sulting or giving advice for the mutual benefit of the members, voting for officers, and the like. We know of no reason why the capacity to act as trustee should be a necessary qualification for membership. If a sufficient number of members possess the requisite capacity, so as to afford the members a reasonable and proper range of choice in the selection of trustees, the admission of others who are not thus qualified can work no injury to anybody. It will not be claimed that the want of the requisite intelligence or business experience on the part of an adult to qualify him to act as trustee would render him ineligible to membership, but these are quite as essential to the proper discharge of the duties of trustee as mere legal capacity. There would seem to be no legal obstacle in the way of minors taking part in corporate meetings, consulting, advising, or éven voting. The only objection to their doing so grows out of their inexperience and the immaturity of their judgments, but these are disqualifications which are not necessarily confined to persons under age of twenty-one years; and no one would allege them as a legal bar to the admission of an adult to membership.'' The right of fraternal beneficiary societies to accept minors to membership is now generally conferred by the uniform fraternal beneficiary act in the States which have adopted it. The limit is generally sixteen years. In regard to policies of ordinary life insurance, it seems to be conceded that a policy of insurance taken out by a minor on his own life is a valid contract, voidable only at the instance of the minor; and, if not voidable by him during minority, the company will be held liable thereon.[7] In the case of Johnson v. N. Western Mut. L. Ins. Co.,[8] it was held that an infant can disaffirm a contract of insurance taken out by him during infancy; but, if the insurance is taken out in a solvent company, at the ordinary and usual rates, for an amount reasonably commensurate with the infant's estate, or his financial ability to carry it, the infant cannot recover the premiums he has paid in so far as they were intended to cover the

[7] Union Cent. L. Ins. Co. v. Hilliard, 63 Ohio St. 478; 59 N. E. 230; 53 L. R. A. 462; Metropolitan L. Ins. Co. v. Brubaker, 78 Kan. 146; 16 Am. & Eng. Ann. Cas. 267, where valuable note is appended.

[8] 56 Minn. 365; 59 N. W. 992; 26 L. R. A. 189. Also Link v. N. Y. Life Ins. Co., 107 Minn. 33; 119 N. W. 488.

current annual risk assumed by the company. The Supreme Court of Massachusetts has on this point taken just the opposite view.[9] It has also been held,[10] that the surrender by an infant of a policy on his life, for a cash value fairly made without undue influence, cannot be avoided by his administrator, and the insurance contract enforced, although the infant did not receive the whole amount to which the contract entitled him. In a case in New York,[11] it was decided that an assignment by an infant to his aunt, of an insurance policy, was valid, because, while the infant might have disaffirmed the policy on reaching majority, yet the insurance company could not avail itself of that fact as a defense against the person who is authorized by the insured to receive the money. An infant is not bound by his warranties in a contract for life insurance, and a breach of warranty will not prevent recovery by the beneficiary if such beneficiary did not obtain the policy with knowledge of such false warranties.[12] The Supreme Court of Massachusetts has held,[13] that a contract of life insurance is not a necessary or within the class of contracts which, as a matter of law, are beneficial to or binding on an infant.

§ 194. **Consent of Insured.**—An important inquiry is to what extent the consent of a person whose life is insured, is necessary as a condition for insurance thereon. Under the present method of doing business where no policy is issued by a life insurance company except upon medical examination of the insured, to which he must consent if a policy be issued, it does not seem probable that such a policy can be issued without in some way involving the consent of the insured. In England, however, it seems that policies are issued without the consent, or knowledge, of the insured, where some loss would occur by the death of the insured personally. Such policies were issued to tradesmen

[9] Simpson v. Prudential Ins. Co., 184 Mass. 348; 68 N. E. 673; 63 L. R. A. 741.

[10] Pippen v. Mut. Ben. L. Ins. Co., 130 N. C. 23; 40 S. E. 822; 57 L. R. A. 505.

[11] Grogan v. U. S. Industrial Ins. Co., 90 Hun. 521; 36 N. Y. Supp. 687.

[12] O'Rourke v. John Hancock Mut. L. Ins. Co., 23 R. I. 457; 50 Atl. 834; 57 L. R. A. 496, where a valuable note is appended.

[13] Simpson v. Prudential Ins. Co., 184 Mass. 348; 68 N. E. 673.

and theater proprietors on the life of Queen Victoria, and it is
said that policies also were issued upon the life of a man promi-
nent in financial circles, where loss would occur in case of his
death.[14]   It seems to be taken for granted that a creditor can
insure the life of his debtor, even without his consent, or that
anyone having an insurable interest in the life of another can
insure such person's life.[15]   The question has more frequently
arisen in actions to recover the premium paid on account of
fraud of the company, or the invalidity of the policy; and this
subject will be further considered later.[16]   Where a policy was
issued on the life of a husband and the premiums were paid
by wife with his money without his consent, recovery of the
premiums so paid has been permitted.[17]   In the cases cited it
is held that an insurance contract made without the consent
of the insured is void, and the insured may in such a case recover from the company premiums paid from his own funds
without his knowledge, and generally it has been held that life
insurance policies taken without the consent of the insured are
void.[18]   It would seem to be different where the statutes of the
State permit a wife to insure the life of her husband, or where
the creditor insures the life of his ·debtor.   Industrial policies
are issued on the lives of children where evidently no consent
can be obtained.   There seems to be no objection urged against
such policies.   In many States, however, the amount of such insurance is limited.[19]   It has been said,[20] that ''these statutes by
implication at least sustain the validity of insurance within those
limits and indicate that such insurance is not against public
policy.   Nevertheless, as the question of consent has not been

14 See note to Martin v. McAllister, 56 L. R. A. 585.

15 *Post*, § 295, *et seq.*   See also Hearing's succession, 26 La. Ann. 326.

16 *Post*, § 361.

17 Metropolitan Life Ins. Co. v. Reinke, 15 Ky. Law 125; Metropolitan
Life Ins. Co. v. Schilhorst, 21 Ky. Law 912; 53 S. W. 524; Metropolitan
Life Ins. Co. v. Trembe, 21 Ky. Law 909; 53 S. W. 412; Metropolitan
Life Ins. Co. v. Smith, 22 Ky. Law 863; 53 L. R. A. 817; 59 S. W. 24.

18 Griffin's Admr. v. Equitable Assur. Soc., 119 Ky. 856; 84 S. W. 1164;
Metropolitan Life Ins. Co. v. Felix, 73 Ohio 46; 75 N. E. 941.

19 O'Rourke v. John Hancock Mut. Life Ins. Co., 31 N. Y. Supp. 130; 10
Misc. 405.

20 See note 56 L. R. A. 592.

clearly discussed and passed upon, the weight of such authority is not very great. The general doctrine that the insured person's consent is necessary to the validity of a life insurance policy might be regarded as inapplicable to insurance by parents on the lives of children who were too young to consent because of the peculiarly close relation of parent and child with its presumption of great affection."[21] A husband may use community funds without consent of his wife in the procurement of insurance upon her life and the proceeds on her death will belong to him in his individual right.[22]

§ 195. **Insurance Contract Need not be in Writing.**—Although in a few early cases it was said that a contract of insurance must be in writing, the validity of a parol insurance has been so frequently and uniformly affirmed that it is now the undoubted American doctrine. The reason is that a contract of insurance is not different from any other, nor is it to be governed by any other rules than those which apply in individual transactions. It has been said that, by prescribing a manner of executing the policy, the charter does not exclude the oral engagement because the contract and the policy are not identical. While the doctrine of parol insurance has been most frequently applied to fire or marine contracts,[23] the same principle has been recognized as applying to life insurance.[24] In the case of Pacific Mutual Ins. Co. v. Schaffer,[25] it was held that a parol contract was valid where the agent had authority to represent

[21] See also Wakeman v. Metropolitan Life Ins. Co., 30 Ont. Rep. 705.

[22] Martin v. McAllister, 94 Tex. 567; 63 S. W. 624; 56 L. R. A. 585. For an elaborate discussion of the subject of insurance upon life without consent of the party insured, see note 56 L. R. A. 585, where this case is reported.

[23] Commercial Mut. Ins. Co. v. Union Mut. Ins. Co., 19 How. 318; First Baptist Church v. Brooklyn Fire Ins. Co., 19 N. Y. 305; Northwestern Iron Co. v. Ætna Ins. Co., 23 Wis. 160; 99 Am. Rec. 145; Emery v. Boston Marine Ins. Co., 138 Mass. 398; Relief F. Ins. Co. v. Shaw, 94 U. S. 574; Walker v. Metropolitan Ins. Co., 56 Me. 371.

[24] Sheldon v. Conn. Mut. Life Ins. Co., 25 Conn. 219; Cooper v. Pacific Mut. Life Ins. Co., 7 Nev. 121.

[25] 30 Tex. Civ. App. 313; 70 S. W. 566. The court cites Insurance Co. v. Kuessner, 164 Ill. 275; 45 N. E. 540; Cohen v. Insurance Co., 67 Tex. 328; 3 S. W. 296; Phoenix Ins. Co. v, Ireland, 9 Kan. App. 644; 58 Pac. 1024.

the company in effecting the insurance, including the issuance of the policy, and had to refer nothing to the company.[26] It has been said that, in view of the custom of life insurance companies, where no policy is issued there is a presumption of no contract.[27] There is no reason why this rule should not apply to the contracts of mutual benefit societies wherever the agreement has been entered into and completed, except as to the issuance of a certificate or policy. There is no question but that when a member has been received into a benefit society, where certain benefits are incident to membership, he would be entitled to the full benefit upon maturity of the right, although no certificate had been issued, or, if it had been issued, not delivered.[28] But necessarily much depends upon the laws of the particular society.[29]

§ 196. **What Constitutes Perfect Parol Contract of Insurance.**—It has been established that to constitute a perfect parol contract all the elements of a perfect contract must be present.[30] A mere verbal assurance to the assured by the agent that he is insured from the date of the application and the giving of the receipt do not constitute a contract of insurance upon which an action can be maintained.[31] An insurance contract, it has been said,[32] to be valid must contain five essential elements: the subject-matter, the risk, the amount, the duration and the premium. It is not necessary, however, that all these elements be settled by the express contract, for several may be settled by

[26] See also Alabama Gold L. I. Co. v. Mayes, 61 Ala. 163.

[27] Equitable L. Ass'n Soc. v. McElroy, 28 C. C. A. 365; 83 Fed. 631. See also McMaster v. New York Life Ins. Co., 40 C. C. A. 119; 99 Fed. 856, and 183 U. S. 25.

[28] Lorscher v. Supreme Lodge K. of H., 72 Mich. 316; 40 N. W. 545.

[29] In Bishop v. Empire Order Mut. Aid, 43 Hun. 472, it was held that under the circumstances of that case the designation of a beneficiary was a condition precedent to the society's liability. But this case was expressly overruled and reversed on appeal. 112 N. Y. 627; 20 N. E. 562.

[30] Hartford F. Ins. Co. v. Wilcox, 57 Ill. 180; Sanford v. Trust, etc., Ins. Co., 11 Paige Ch. 547.

[31] Fowler v. Preferred Acc. Ins. Co., 100 Ga. 330; 28 S. E. 398. But see Preferred Acc. Ins. Co. v. Stone, 61 Kan. 48; 58 Pac. 986; Hollin v. Essex Mut. Ben. Ass'n, 88 N. J. L. 204; 96 Atl. 71.

[32] Tyler v. N. A. Ins., 4 Robt. 151.

implication from the circumstances of the case, from habits of dealing, from the nature of the property and from previous arrangements.[33] So, if a member were received into a benefit society, such reception would justify the assumption that the understanding was that he sought the benefit promised by the society and agreed to pay the amounts paid by other persons of his age. An insurance made without issue of a policy is to be regarded as made upon the terms and subject to the conditions in the ordinary forms of policies used by the company at the time.[34] So, upon analogy, a member being received into a society, the certificate to be issued is understood to be one in the usual form and containing the usual agreements. It may even be the custom under the laws of the order not to issue certificates to the members, in which case only the laws of the order are to be looked at for the contract.[35]

§ 197. **Informal Execution.**—Want of a seal does not vitiate a policy unless by the charter of the company a seal is essential to its validity.[36] and where the articles of an insurance association direct that its policies be signed by its president and countersigned·by its secretary, the omission of the president to sign a policy otherwise valid, does not render the policy invalid.[37] So, in regard to the countersigning of a policy. On this point the Supreme Court of Pennsylvania[38] says: ''We incline also to the opinion that, notwithstanding the express terms of the policy, the countersigning by the agents. is not under all circumstances essential. On an equitable interpretation of the whole transaction, it may become the duty of the court to dispense with a portion of the forms of contract, if it can find any reliable substitute for them, on the principle that cures defective execution of powers, where the intention to execute is sufficiently

33 Audubon v. Excelsior Ins. Co., 27 N. Y. 216; Train v. Holland, etc., Ins. Co., 62 N. Y. 598; Eames v. Home Ins. Co., 94 U. S. 621; Cooke v. Ætna Ins. Co., 7 Daly 555; Walker v. Met. Ins. Co., 56 Me. 371; Baile v. St. Joseph, etc., Ins. Co., 68 Mo. 617; Stone v. Ins. Co., 78 Mo. 658.

34 Eureka Ins. Co. v. Robinson, 56 Pa. St. 256; 94 Am. Dec. 65.

35 Grand Lodge v. Elsner, 26 Mo. App. 108.

36 National Banking, etc., v. Knaup, 55 Mo. 154.

37 Union Ins. Co. v. Smart, 60 N. H. 458.

38 Myers v. Keystone, etc., Ins. Co., 27 Pa. St. 268; 67 Am. Dec. 462.

plain. This contract was to be complete when delivered by the agents of the defendants, and we regard the countersigning by the agents as the appointed evidence of its proper delivery. If we do not find this evidence, we must treat it as not delivered, unless we have other evidence, which we can regard as equivalent.'[39]   But it is otherwise where it is to be countersigned only npon the happening of a future event, as the payment of a premium.[40]   On general principles it is hard to see why, if no policy need be issued in order to make the contract valid, the omission of a merely formal matter, the contract being otherwise complete, or supposed to be so, should have any effect upon it. Equity, it is believed, would always relieve in such cases, though at law the contract might be deemed incomplete.   An insurance policy is not executed by attaching the insurer's' corporate seal when the names of the president and secretary, called for by the attestation clause, are not attached.[41]   It has been held[42] that a new benefit certificate, issued to change the beneficiary, upon application made in accordance with the by-laws of the union, and signed by the supreme president and secretary of the union, and sealed with the seal of the Supreme Union, is not invalid because not signed and sealed by the officers of the subordinate union.   The counter signature of the secretary of the local lodge if required in the certificate is necessary for complete execution.[43]

§ 198.   **Lex Loci and Lex Fori.**—It is undoubtedly true that agreements of insurance are not governed by different principles than those that apply to other engagements, for all alike are contracts to which in general the same rules are applicable.[44]   Two general laws may be here laid down which are often applied, the

---

[39] Norton v. Phoenix M. L. Ins. Co., 36 Conn. 503; Kantrener v. Penn., etc., Ins. Co., 5 Mo. App. 581.   But see Badger v. Am. Pop. Life Ins. Co., 103 Mass. 244; McCully v. Phoenix M. L. Ins. Co., 18 W. Va. 782.

[40] Hardie v. St. Louis M. L. Ins. Co., 26 La. Ann. 242; Ormond v. Mut. Life Ass'n, 96 N. C. 158; 1 S. E. 796.

[41] Globe Acc. Ins. Co. v. Reid, 19 Ind. App. 203; 47 N. E. 947; 49 N. E. 291.

[42] Fisk v. Equitable Aid Union, 7 Pa. Sup. Ct. (Sadler) 567; 11 Atl. 84.

[43] Caywood v. Supreme Lodge K. & L. of H., 171 Ind. 410; 86 N. E. 482.

[44] St. John v. American Mut. L. Ins. Co., 2 Duer. 419; 13 N. Y. 31; 64 Dec. 529.

one, that of *lex loci*, which has been thus tersely stated:[45]   "It is a general principle applying to contracts made, rights acquired or acts done relative to personal property, that the law of the place of making the contract, or doing the act, is to govern it and determine its validity or invalidity, as well as the rights of parties under it, in all matters touching the modes of execution and authentication of the form or instrument of contract; and also in relation to the use and meaning of the language in which it is expressed, the construction and interpretation of it, the legal duties and obligations imposed by it, and the legal rights and immunities acquired under it. This principle, though general, does not, however, apply where the parties at the time of entering into the contract had the law of another kingdom in view, or where the *lex loci* is in itself unjust, *contra bonos mores*, or contrary to the public law of the State, as regarding the interests of religion or morality, or the general well-being of society. The *lex loci* is presumed to be the same as that of the forum unless shown to be otherwise." The second general law is that of *lex fori*, which Bouvier thus defines:[46] "The form of remedies, modes of proceeding, and execution of judgments are to be regulated solely and exclusively by the laws of the place where the action is instituted." In summing up the doctrine of *lex loci* and *lex fori*, Bishop says:[47] "A judicial tribunal should, in the decision of every question, follow the laws prescribed for it by the sovereignty under which it sits. But there is a comity of nations, as the term is, whereby it has become customary for the various governmental powers to respect one another's laws; so that, if a contract made in one country is drawn in question in another, the tribunals of the latter will, in the absence of any domestic rule or policy restraining, accept the foreign law as the domestic, for ascertaining its validity. But this rule stops short at every point where it would become subversive of the domestic law. The interpretation and effect of the contract are determined by the law of the place of its intended performance, whether at home or abroad; its discharge when by operation of law, by any law moving thereto, and having a jurisdiction over it. In enforcing the contract, the

45 Bouvier L. D., *tit. Lex Loci.*
46 Bouvier L. D. *tit. Lex Fori.*
47 Bishop on Cont., § 1412.

foreign procedure is never employed.''[48]   In insurance contracts the wording of the policy, or certificate, generally determines the place where it is made. If an application is sent direct to the home office and the policy or certificate is there made out and delivered, or mailed, to the applicant, the home office is the place of the contract.[49]   Generally there is a provision in the policy or certificate that it shall not be binding until payment of premium, or countersigning by a local agent. In such case the place of countersigning and delivery is that of the contract.[50]   The Federal Court in Oregon happily stated the law on this point as follows:[51]   ''Generally speaking the validity of a contract is to be decided by the law of the place where it is mede; and if valid or void there, it is valid or void everywhere. The few exceptions to this rule need not be mentioned in the application of it to this case.[52]   Where, then, was this contract made? In Wisconsin or Oregon? The answer to this question involves the inquiry, where did the final act take place which made the transaction a contract binding upon the parties? The premium was paid to the agent of the plaintiff at Portland, who then and there countersigned and delivered the

48 Whitridge v. Barry, 42 Md. 140; Cannon v. N. W. Mut. L. Ins. Co., 29 Hun. 470; Bloomingdale v. Lisberger, 24 Hun. 355.

49 Lamb v. Bowser, 7 Biss. 315-372; Hermano v. Mildred, 9 Q. B. 530; Northampton M. L. S. Ins. Co. v. Tuttle, 40 N. J. L. 476; Wright v. Sun Mut. Ins. Co,. 6 Am. L. Reg. 485; Voorheis v. People's Mut. Ben. Soc., 91 Mich. 469; 51 N. W. 1109; Wood v. Cascade, etc., Ins. Co., 8 Wash. 427; 36 Pac. 267. The subject of law of place and conflict of laws, so far as insurance contracts is concerned, is exhaustively considered in a note to Johnson v. Mut. L. Ins. Co., 180 Mass. 407; 62 N. E. 733; 63 L. R. A. 833.

50 Wall v Equitable L. Assur. Soc., 32 Fed. 273; Continental L. Ins. Co. v. Webb, 54 Ala. 688; Adler v. Stoffel (Breitung, Estate of), 78 Wis. 33; 46 N. W. 891; 47 N. W. 17; Yore v. Bankers', etc., Ass'n, 88 Cal. 609; 26 Pac. 514; Mut. Ben. Life Ins. Co. v. Robison, 54 Fed. 580. See also N. W. Masonic, etc., Ass'n v. Jones (Appeal of Chance), 154 Pa. St. 99; 26 Atl. 253, and Equitable L. Ass'n Soc. v. Willing, 7 C. C. A. 359; 58 Fed. 541; Pratt v. Globe M. B. L. Ins. Co. (Tenn.), 17 S. W. 352; Knights Templar, etc,. Co. v. Berry, 1 C. C. A. 561; 50 Fed. 511; affg. 46 Fed. 439; Hicks v. National L. Ins. Co., 9 C. C. A. 215; 60 Fed. 690; Assurance Soc. v. Clements, 140 U. S. 226.

51 Northwestern M. L. Ins. Co. v. Elliott, 7 Sawy. 17; 5 Fed. 225.

52 Cox v. United States, 6 Pet. 203; Hyde v. Goodnow, 3 N. Y. 269; In re Clifford, 2 Sawy. 428.

policy. This was the consummation and completion of the contract. But to put this beyond a doubt, the policy itself declares that it shall not be binding on the company until these acts are performed. And until it was binding upon the company, it was not binding on the applicant—in short, it was not yet a contract, but only a proposition.[53] The case of Hyde v. Goodnow,[54] cited by counsel for plaintiff, is not contrary to this conclusion. There the assured, living in Ohio, applied to a company in New York, through its local agent and surveyor, for insurance, sending with his application a premium note and the report of the surveyor thereon. The company accepted the application in New York, and mailed the policy direct to the applicant in Ohio, which in accordance with its by-law, contained the stipulation that it should not be binding until the application and premium note were deposited in the office of the company and approved by its directors. The contract, if made in Ohio, was illegal and void, because the company was not authorized to transact business there, but in a suit upon the premium note against the maker in New York, the court held that the contract was made in the latter State, and therefore valid, because, when the application was approved and the policy deposited in the mail, at New York, addressed to the defendant, the contract was then and thereby executed, and became binding on the parties thereto.'' Ordinarily the place of performance will be deemed the place of the contract,[55] but where policies are sent to an agent to be delivered, or where statutes of the State where the insured resides regulate the business of life insurance, the rule is that the place of the contract is where the premium is paid and the policy delivered.[56] Where a policy issued in Rhode Island lapsed and was revived in Massachusetts

[53] Pomeroy v. Manhattan L. Ins. Co., 40 Ill. 400; Thwing v. Great Western Ins. Co., 111 Mass. 109; Wood F. Ins., 189 n. 2; Hardie v. St. Louis M. L. Ins. Co., 26 La. Ann. 242; St. Louis M. L. Ins. Co. v. Kennedy, 6 Bush. 450.

[54] 3 N. Y. 269.

[55] Bottomley v. Metropolitan L. Ins. Co., 170 Mass. 274; 49 N. E. 438; Fidelity, etc., Ass'n v. McDaniel, 25 Ind. App. 608; 57 N. E. 645 and cases *infra.*

[56] New York Life Ins. Co. v. Cravens, 178 U. S. 389; Cravens v. New York L. Ins. Co., 148 Mo. 583; 50 S. W. 519; 53 L. R. A. 305; Dolan v. Mut. Res. F., 173 Mass. 197; 53 N. E. 398.

that fact did not, the insured still residing in the former State, make it a contract of the latter State,[57] The question is important especially in view of the application of State statutes, especially those relating to notice of premiums.[58] An offer by mail to insure certain property and an acceptance by letter of the proposition, constitute a valid contract at and from the place and date of mailing such letter of acceptance.[59]

§ 199. **The Same Subject Continued—Conflict of Laws.**—The later cases all recognize the principle that the place of the contract of life, or accident, or fraternal beneficiary associations, is where the last act is done necessary to put it in force and the State where the contract is made is where it is delivered and the premiums paid.[60] It has, however, been held,[61] that the parties

[57] Bottomley v. Metropolitan Life Ins. Co., *supra*.

[58] See *post*, § 461. The following cases consider the subject of law of place. Mut. Life Ins. Co. v. Dingly, 40 C. C. A. 459; 100 Fed. 408; 49 L. R. A. 132; Millard v. Brayton, 177 Mass. 533; 59 N. E. 436; 52 L. R. A. 117; Seiders v. Merchants' L. Ass'n, 93 Tex. 194; 54 S. W. 753; reversing 51 S. W. 547; Mut. Life Ins. Co. v. Hill, 24 Sup. Ct. 538; reversing 55 C. C. A. 536; 118 Fed. 708; Fidelity, etc., Ass'n v. Harris (Tex. C. A.), 57 S. W. 635; Johnson v. N. Y. Life I. Co., 109 Ia. 708; 78 N. W. 905; 50 L. R. A. 99; Seely v. Manhattan Life Ins. Co., 72 N. H. 49; 53 Atl. 425; Roberts v. Winton, 100 Tenn. 484; 45 S. W. 673; Mut. Life Ins. Co. v. Bradley (Tex. C. A.), 79 S. W. 367; Expressmen's, etc., Ass'n v. Hurlock, 94 Md. 585; 46 Atl. 957; Provident, etc., Soc. v. Hadley, 43 C. C. A. 25; 102 Fed. 856.

[59] Tayloe v. The Merchants' F. Ins. Co., 9 How. 398. See also Northhampton Mut., etc., Ins. Co. v. Tuttle, 40 N. J. L. 476; Continental L. I. Ins. Co. v. Webb, 54 Ala. 688; Smith v. Mutual Life Ins. Co., 5 Fed. 582; Cromwell v. Royal Can. Ins. Co., 49 Md. 366; Todd v. State Ins. Co., 11 Phila. 355.

[60] Williams v. Mut. Reserve Fund Life Ass'n, 145 N. C. 128; 58 S. E. 802; Fidelity Mut. Life Ass'n v. Jeffords, 46 C. C. A. 377; 107 Fed. 402; Manhattan Life Ins. Co. v. Albro, 62 C. C. A. 213; 127 Fed. 281; Northwestern Mutual Life Ins. Co. v. McCue, 223 U. S. 234; reversing 167 Fed. 435; 93 C. C. A. 71; Mut. Life Ins. Co. v. Hilton-Green, 202 Fed. 113; 120 C. C. A. 267; Moore v. Northwestern Nat'l Life Ins. Co., 112 Mo. App. 696; 87 S. W. 988; Coscarella v. Metropolitan Life Ins. Co., 175 Mo. App. 130; 157 S. W. 873; Crohn v. United Commercial Travelers, 170 Mo. App. 273; 156 S. W. 472; Whittaker v. Mut. Life Ins. Co., 133 Mo. App. 664; 114 S. W. 53; Roberts v. Modern Woodmen of America, 133 Mo. App. 267; 113 S. W. 726; Kavanaugh v. Supreme Council Royal League, 158 Mo. App.

can agree to establish the place according to the laws of which the contract shall be construed.[62] Where the application was signed in Wisconsin and mailed to insurer's office in Pennsylvania where the policy was issued and mailed to the applicant, the contract is made in Pennsylvania.[63] A Canadian society authorized by the laws of that country to apportion a deficiency on policy holders, binds the member holding a certificate issued in New York, although a New York contract.[64] The character of the business of a foreign fraternal association transacted in a State will be determined by the law of the State where the business is transacted,[65] so a life policy on an application made in another State

234; 138 S. W. 359; Schuler v. Metropolitan Life Ins. Co., 191 Mo. App. 53; 176 S. W. 271; Umberger v. Modern Brotherhood of America, 162 Mo. App. 141; 144 S. W. 898; Crevenig v. Washington Life Ins. Co., 112 La. 879; 36 Sou. 790; Jefferson v. New York Life Ins. Co., 151 Ky. 609; 153 S. W. 780; Head v. New York Life Ins. Co., 241 Mo. 403; 147 S. W. 827; Davis v. New York Life Ins. Co., 212 Mass. 310; 98 N. E. 1043; Wilde v. Wilde, 209 Mass. 205; 95 N. E. 295; Ulman v. Supreme Commandery, etc., 220 Mass. 422; 107 N. E. 960; Haas v. Mut. Life Ins. Co., 90 Neb. 808; 134 N. W. 937; McElroy v. Mut. Life Ins. Co., 84 Neb. 866; 122 N. W. 27; Pringle v. Modern Woodmen of America, .. Neb. ..; 127 N. W. 876; Franklin Life Ins. Co. v. Morrell, 84 Ark. 541; 106 S. W. 680; Fidelity Mut. Life Ins. Co. v. Miazza, 93 Miss. 18; 46 Sou. 817; National Union v. Sawyer, 42 App. D. C. 475; Travelers' Protective Ass'n of America v. Smith, 59 Ind. 183; 107 N. E. 817; Hamilton v. Darley, 266 Ill. 542; 107 N. E. 798; affg. 188 Ill. App. 229.

61 Green v. Security Mut. Life Ins. Co., 159 Mo. App. 277; 140 S. W. 325.

62 Burns v. Burns, 190 N. Y. 211; 82 N. E. 1107; Grand Fraternity v. Keatley, 4 Del. (Boyce) 308; 88 Atl. 553; reversing 82 Atl. 294.

63 Presbyterian Ministers' Fund v. Thomas, 126 Wis. 281; 105 N. W. 801; Supreme Lodge K. P. v. Meyer, 198 U. S. 508; affg. 178 N. Y. 63; 64 L. R. A. 840; 70 N. E. 111; Travelers' Protective Ass'n v. Smith, 59 Ind. 183; 101 N. E. 817; Tuttle v. Iowa State Traveling Men's Ass'n, 132 Ia. 652; 104 N. W. 1131; 7 L. R. A. (N. S.) 223; Equitable Life Assur. Soc. v. Perkins, 41 Ind. App. 183; 80 N. E. 682. But see Continental Casualty Co. v. Owen, 131 Pac. 1084.

64 Stockwell v. Supreme Court I. O. F., 216 Fed. 205; DeGraw v. Supreme Court I. O. F,. 182 Mich. 366; 148 N. W. 703.

65 Marcus v. Heralds of Liberty, 241 Pa. 429; 88 Atl. 678; Supreme Ruling of the Fraternal Mystic Circle v. Turner, 105 Miss. 468; 62 Sou. 497.

to a New York company where insured has no post office address in New York is not subject to the laws of New York in regard to notice of premiums.[66] A certificate payable to the legal heirs is to be construed according to the laws of the State of the member's residence at the time of his death.[67] Where a life policy is made payable at the principal office of the company and provides that the contracts shall be subject to the laws of the State in which such office is located, the remedy of insured in case of breach of contract is governed by the laws of such State wherever suit may be brought.[68] And so it has been held[69] that citizens of Georgia will not be denied any rights under a policy of life insurance allowed citizens of the place where the contract was made, when the laws of that State were chosen at the place of performance and consequently such damages and attorney fees as would be recoverable by citizens of that State may likewise be recovered by citizens of Georgia, and a statute of a sister State providing that changes in by-laws shall not be effective unless attached to the certificate is controlling on the courts of the State where an action on the certificate is brought if the certificate was issued in such sister State.[70] The statute of New York in regard to the appointment of a receiver other than on the application of the Attorney General, is part of the contract of every policy holder of a New York insurance company.[71]

[66] Ross v. Mut. Life Ins. Co., 240 Ill. 445; 88 N. E. 204; McElroy v. Mut. Life Ins. Co., 64 Neb. 866; 122 N. W. 27; Mut. Life Ins. Co. v. Ensco, 145 Ky. 575; 140 S. W. 566

[67] Thomas v. Supreme Lodge, 126 Wis. 593.

[68] Michaelson v. Security Mut. Life Ins. Co., 150 Fed. 224

[69] Missouri State Life Ins. Co. v. Lovelace, 1 Ga. App. 446; 58 S. E. 93.

[70] Supreme Council Catholic Knights of America v. Logsdon, 183 Ind. 183; 108 N. E. 587; Johnson v. Mut. Life Ins. Co., 180 Mass. 407; 63 L. R. A. 833; Anderson v. Royal League, 130 Minn. 416; 153 N. W. 853; McClement v. Supreme Court I. O. F., 154 N. Y. Supp. 700;' 169 App. Div. 77; reversing 152 N. Y. Supp. 136.

[71] Equitable Life Assur. Soc. v. Brown, 213 U. S. 25; reversing 81 C. C. A. 1; 151 Fed. 1; 10 Ann. Cas. 402, and affg. 142 Fed. 835. The subject of conflict of laws as to contracts of insurance is very fully reviewed in a note in the Lawyers' Reports Annotated, 63 L. R. A. 833; Johnson v. Mut. Life Ins. Co., 180 Mass. 407.

§ 200. **Stipulation in Policy Cannot Avoid Operation of Statute.**—A corporation cannot by stipulations in its contract avoid or withdraw the operation of a statute of the place in which it does business. The rule and the facts to which it was applied are sufficiently stated by Judge Treat thus:[72] "Inasmuch as the policy sued on declared that it rests on the basis of answers made in the application, and that said policy was to be issued at the home office in New York on return thereto of the application, can the plaintiff avail himself of the force of the Missouri statute? The defendant company was doing business in Missouri, with the privileges granted to it here; when said insurance was effected. It may be that the formal acceptance of the proposed contract was, by the *letter* of the contract, to be consummated in New York. The broad proposition, however, remains, no artifice to avoid which can be upheld. The statutes of Missouri for salutary reasons, permit foreign corporations to do business in the State on prescribed conditions. If, despite such conditions, they can, by the insertion of clauses in their policy, withdraw themselves from, the limitations of the Missouri statutes while obtaining all the advantages of its license, then a foreign corporation can, by special contract, upset the statutes of the State and become exempt from the positive requirements of law. Such a proposition is not to be countenanced. The defendant corporation chose to embark in business within this State under the terms and conditions named in the statute. It could not by paper contrivances, however specious, withdraw itself from the operation of the laws, by the force of which it could alone do business within the State. To hold otherwise would be subversive of the right of a State to decide on what terms, by comity, a foreign corporation should be admitted to do business or be recognized therefor within the State jurisdiction. Each State can decide for itself whether a foreign corporation, shall be recognized by it, and on what terms. Primarily a corporation has no existence beyond the territorial limits of the State creating it, and when it undertakes business beyond it does so only by comity. The defendant corporation having been permitted to do business in Missouri under the statutes of the latter, was

[72] Fletcher v. New York Life Ins. Co., 4 McCrary, 440; 13 Fed. 528.

bound by all the provisions of those statutes and could not, by the insertion of any of the many clauses in its forms of application, etc., withdraw itself from the obligatory force of the statute.'"[73] It has been said:[74] that the company is subject to the laws of the place where the policy is issued regardless of whether it applied for permission to do business there or not. And a provision in a policy, issued in New York, but to be delivered in Missouri on payment of the premium there, requiring payment of·three full annual premiums before the assured was entitled to temporary insurance, is void if the statutes of Missouri provide that payment of two full annual premiums shall entitle the insured to such temporary insurance.[75] Generally a statutory provision as to nonforfeiture cannot be waived.[76]

Nor can the parties contract away the provisions of the statute for the benefit of the insured in a life policy.[77] A provision in a benefit certificate that the claimant shall not be entitled to recover interest is invalid as against public policy.[78]

[73] White v. Connecticut Life Ins. Co., 4 Dill. 177; Lowell v. Alliance Life Ins. Co., 3 Cent. L. J. 699.

[74] Corley v. Travelers', etc., Ass'n, 105 Fed. 854.

[75] Wall. v. Equitable L. Assur. Soc., 32 Fed. 273; affd. on appeal Equitable Life Assur. Soc. v. Pettus, 140 U. S. 226; 11 S. C. 822. See also Knights Templar, etc., Co., v. Berry, 1 C. C. A. 561; 50 Fed. 511; affg. 46 Fed. 439; Price v. Conn. Mut. L. Ins. Co., 48 M. A. 282; New York Life Ins. Co. v. Cravens, 178 U. S. 389; Cravens v. New York Life I. C., 148 Mo. 583; 53 L. R. A. 305; 50 S. W. 519; Knights Templar & Masons' L. Ind. Co. v. Jarman, 187 U. S. 197; affg. 44 C. C. A. 93; 104 Fed. 638; Equitable L. A. Soc. v. Nixon, 26 C. C. A. 220; 81 Fed. 796; Eq. L. Assur. Soc. v. Trimble, 27 C. C. A. 404; 83 Fed. 85; New York Life Ins. Co. v. Orlopp, 25 Tex. C. A. 284; 61 S. W. 336.

[76] Griffith v. New York L. Ins. Co., 101 Cal. 627; 36 Pac. 113. See, as to endowment insurance, Rockhold v. Canton Masonic, etc., Ass'n, 129 Ill. 440; 19 N. W. 710; 21 N. W. 794; and as to construction of statute requiring uniform treatment of all policyholders, State v. Scharzchild, 83 Me. 261; 22 Atl. 164.

[77] Chandler v. John Hancock Mut. L. Ins. Co., 180 Mo. App. 394; 667 S. W. 1162; International Travelers' Ass'n v. Branum, Tex. Civ. App., 169 S. W. 389.

[78] Modern Brotherhood of America v. Bailey (Okla.), 150 Pac. 673.

§ 201.   **A Life Insurance Contract Is Not Strictly One of Indemnity.**—A contract of insurance is ordinarily one of indemnity; that is, the insurer agrees that upon the damage, loss or destruction of something he will, in the agreed way, indemnify the insured.   It has been vigorously contended that a contract of life insurance is also one of indemnity, as much as fire or marine insurance.   Mr. May, for example, in his treatise on insurance,[79] says: "In the one case, the insurance is against the loss of capital, which produces income; in the other, it is against the loss of faculties, which produce income."   And again:[80] "It (the contract) can never, therefore, properly be entered into except for the purpose of security or indemnity; though the fact that the contract may, under certain circumstances, result as a profitable investment, does not vitiate it, if entered into in conformity to the principles which underlie it.   But so far as it seeks any other object than indemnity for loss it departs from the legitimate field of insurance, and engrafts upon the contract a purpose foreign to its nature."   And yet the same author has said[81] that life insurance "in some of its phases, is not merely a contract of indemnity, but includes that with a possibility of something more."   In Dalby v. The India and London Life Ass. Co.,[82] it was said of life insurance that it "in no way resembles a contract of indemnity," and Baron Parke again in referring to the fact that Lord Mansfield decided the case of Godsall v. Boldero[83] on the theory that a life insurance contract was like one of marine insurance, one for indemnity only, says: "But that is not of the nature of what is termed an assurance for life; it really is what it is on the face of it—a contract to pay a certain sum in the event of death!"   The Supreme Court of the United States[84] cites this case and approves its reasoning, saying: "In life insurance the loss can seldom be measured by pecuniary values."   We must conclude, therefore, that though

[79] § 7.
[80] § 117.
[81] May on Ins., § 117.
[82] 15 C. B. 365; 24 L. J. C. P. 2.
[83] 9 East. 72.
[84] Conn. Mut. Life Ins. Co. v. Schaefer, 94 U. S. 457; Warnock v. Davis, 104 U. S. 779.

sometimes, as where a creditor insures the life of his debtor, the contract is in the nature of an indemnity, still, strictly speaking, a life insurance contract is not generally one of indemnity.[85] Public policy, however, forbids a person to take out a policy of insurance upon the life of another from the continuance of which he has no expectation of advantage or pecuniary interest, because such policies are in the nature of wagers upon human life and are gambling transactions. Moreover they furnish a strong inducement to the person holding such insurance to hasten the termination of the life of the insured.[86]

§ 202. **Is Executory and Personal.**—This Contract is executory and personal in its nature. Of a fire insurance policy the Supreme Court of Ohio said:[87] "It is a mere personal indemnity against loss to the person with whom it is made, or those falling within the scope of its provisions. As soon as the interest of such persons ceases in the property the contract is at an end, from the impossibility of any loss happening to him afterwards. It is not assignable without the consent of the insurer."[88] So far as the principle of the foregoing statement just cited applies to life insurance policies it is incorrect. The question of personality is of great importance in cases of fire insurance where restraints on alienation are insisted on, but in life insurance contracts it is of less importance. It is settled doctrine that a life policy originally valid does not cease to be so by the cessation of the interest of the party assured in the life of the insured.[89] The contract, however, must be considered

[85] See Scott v. Dickson, 108 Pa. St. 6; Ferguson v. Mass. M. L. Ins. Co., 32 Hun. 306; 102 N. Y. 647; Mowry v. Home L. Ins. Co., 9 R. I. 346; De Rouge v. Elliott, 8 Green (N. J.), 486; Trenton M. L. & F. Ins. Co., 4 Zab. (N. J.) 576; Ritter v. Smith, 70 Ind. 261; 16 Atl. 890; Emrich v. Coakley, 35 Md. 193; Whiting v. Ins. Co., 15 Md. 326. To the same effect is Wayland v. Western Indemnity Co., 166 Mo. App. 221; 148 S. W. 626, and Reed v. Provident Savings L. Assur. Soc., 190 N. Y. 111; 82 N. E. 724.

[86] See post, § 295, et seq., for discussion of insurable interest.

[87] McDonald v. Black's Admr., 20 Ohio St. 185; 55 Am. Dec. 448.

[88] Glendale Woolen Co. v. Protection Ins. Co., 21 Conn. 19; 54 Am. Dec. 309; Morrison's Admr. v. Tennessee, etc., Ins. Co., 18 Mo. 262; 59 Am. Dec. 305 and note.

[89] Conn. Mut. L. Ins. Co. v. Schaefer, 94 U. S. 457; post, § 253.

personal, because generally not assignable without the consent of the insurer.[90] The contract falls strictly within the definition of those that are executory; on the one hand, certain assessments or premiums are to be paid, on the other side, it is to be executed by the payment of the sum insured when the contingency occurs.[91] The doctrine of the personal nature of a life insurance contract and its non-assignability has been much shaken by the more modern decisions which tend to the holding that a life insurance policy is like any other *chose en action*. We will consider the subject when we come to speak of the assignment of insurance policies.[91a]

§ 203. **Is Aleatory.**—Another characteristic of the contract is that it is what the French writers call *aleatory*, "or one in which the equivalent consists in the chances for gain or loss, to the respective parties, depending upon an uncertain event, in contradistinction from a commutative contract in which the thing given or act done by the party is regarded as the exact equivalent of the money paid or done by the other."[92] In other words the parties take chances as they do in throwing dice; if, as example in cases of life insurance for specified terms, the assured lives, the company makes the premium which the party paying it loses, but if the assured dies within the time specified then the company loses the amount contracted for. At common law a life insurance contract was valid though no insurable interest existed and hence was often a mere wager.[93]

§ 204. **Life Insurance Policies Are Valued Policies.**—Regarding the certificate of membership as a contract similar to a life

---

[90] For discussion of the assignability of life insurance policies and change of beneficiary, see Ch. IX.

[91] Mutual Life Ins. Co. v. Wager, 27 Barb. 354; Hellenberg v. District No. 1, I. O. O. B. B., 94 N. Y. 586; New York L. Ins. Co. v. Statham, 93 U. S. 24.

[91a] *Post*, Ch. IX.

[92] May on Ins., § 5.

[93] Dalby v. East India & London L. Assur. Co., 15 C. B. 365; Crawford v. Hunter, 8 T. R. 242; Lucena v. Crawford, 2 B. & P. N. R. 269; Cousins v. Nantes, 3 Taunt. 513. This was changed by statute, 14 G. III., c. 48, making an insurable interest necessary.

insurance policy, it is what is termed a "valued" policy, which the Supreme Court of Pennsylvania says :[94] "Is not understood to be one which estimates the value of the property insured merely, but which values the loss, and is equivalent to an assessment of damages in the event of a loss."[95]   In this sense all policies of life insurance, or benefit certificates, are valued policies, for all specify the amount which the insurer is to pay without question as to the money value of the interest destroyed.[96]   And the policy is not to be considered as open as to the amount because the amount payable is to be determined by the number of members of a certain class, or of the society.

§ 205. **Peculiar Nature of Life Insurance Contract.**—It has been said by a learned judge concerning life insurance :[97] "The business of life insurance is *sui generis*. It differs widely from fire insurance and is controlled by principles essentially variant from those which limit the latter. Briefly stated, it may be said to rest upon the operation of two distinct, yet closely connected, factors—the average expectation of life and the cumulative power of interest compounded. In other words, the two somewhat uncertain elements which life insurance seeks to reduce to the precision and certainty of a mathematical proposition are the average length of life accorded to a thoroughly well man, on the one hand, and the earning capacity, for a certain definite term of years, of a certain sum of money to be paid certainly on a fixed date during that life, on the other. It is by the skillful use of these two factors that life insurance corporations are enabled to fix and determine, as the very foundation of their business, the sum of money or premium which must be paid by the insured to them, as a just consideration for their contract of insurance ; to enable them, in fact, to fulfill, honestly and promptly their part of the contract. It is perfectly clear, therefore, that promptness of payment of such yearly premiums when fixed at the times designated for such payment, is necessary and absolutely essential to the honest conduct of life insurance. If there

[94] Lycoming Ins. Co. v. Mitchell, 48 Pa. St. 372.
[95] Chisholm v. Nat. Capitol L. Ins. Co., 52 Mo. 213; 14 Am. Rep. 414.
[96] Rockhold v. Canton Masonic, etc., Soc., 129 Ill. 440; 21 N. E. 794.
[97] Green, J., in Kellner v. Mut. L. Ins. Co., 43 Fed. 623.

be uncertainty as to such payment of premium, all calculations based upon its prompt and certain receipt must be seriously disturbed if not radically destroyed, resulting finally and surely in the disastrous collapse of the entire business scheme.''

§ 206.   **Effect of Charter Provisions.**—The contract of a regular life, or accident, insurance company consists of the. policy, together with the application or other papers referred to therein to be construed with reference to charter provisions.   In the case of Relfe v. Rundle,[98] it was said: ''Every corporation necessarily carries its charter wherever it goes, for that is the law of its existence.   It may be restricted in the use of some of its powers while doing business away from its corporate home, but every person who deals with it everywhere is bound to take notice of the provisions which have been made in its charter for the management and control of its affairs both in life and after dissolution.   In the case of Equitable Life Assurance Society v. Brown,[99] it was held that in construing the charter of a corporation the federal courts will follow that given by the highest court of the State of the domicile.   The Court says: ''The insurance policy owned by complainant appears on its face to have been executed in New York, and there is no averment to the contrary.   The decisions of the highest court of New York are therefore binding upon this court as to the meaning and effect of the charter of the defendant, and as it is a New York company, and the contract is a New York contract, executed and to be carried out therein, its meaning and construction, as held by the highest court of the State, will be of most persuasive influence, even if not of binding force, in the absence of any federal question arising in the case.   There is no such question here.[100]   This principle has been so frequently decided that further reference to adjudged cases need not be made.''   The same rule applies to charters of the fraternal societies.   In the case

[98] 103 U. S. 222.
[99] 213 U. S. 25, reversing 151 Fed. 1; 81 C. C. A. 1.
[100] Stone v. Wisconsin, 94 U. S. 181, 183, 24 L. Ed. 102, 103; National Park Bank v. Remsen, 158 U. S. 337-342, 39 L. Ed. 1008-1010, 15 Sup. Ct. Rep. 891; Sioux City Terminal R. & Warehouse Co. v. Trust Co., 173 U. S. 99, 43 L. Ed. 628, 19 Sup. Ct. Rep. 341.

of Supreme Council R. A. v. Green,[101] it was held that under the
Federal Constitution the New York courts were bound to follow
a judgment of the Massachusetts court which held that a mutual
benefit society incorporated in that State has the power under
its charter and by-laws to increase assessment rates. The Court
says: "It is not disputable that the corporation was exclusively
of a fraternal and beneficiary character, and that all the rights
of the complainant concerning the assessment to be paid to provide for the widows and orphans' benefit fund had their source
in the constitution and by-laws, and therefore their validity
could be alone ascertained by a consideration of the constitution
and by-laws. This being true, it necessarily follows that resort
to the constitution and by-laws was essential unless it can be
said that the rights in controversy were to be fixed by disregarding the source from which they arose, and by putting out
of view the only considerations by which their scope could be
ascertained. Moreover, as the charter was a Massachusetts
charter, and the constitution and by-laws were a part thereof,
adopted in Massachusetts, having no other sanction than the
laws of the State, it follows by the same token that those laws
were integrally and necessarily the criterion to be resorted to
for the purpose of ascertaining the significance of the constitution and by-laws. Indeed, the accuracy of this conclusion is irre-
sistibly manifested by considering the intrinsic relation between
each and all the members concerning their duty to pay assessments and the resulting indivisible unity between them in the
fund from which their rights were to be enjoyed. The contradiction in terms is apparent which would rise from holding, on
the one hand, that there was a collective and unified standard
of duty and obligation on the part of the members themselves
and the corporation, and saying, on the other hand, that the
duty of members was to be tested isolatedly and individually
by resorting not to one source of authority applicable to all, but
by applying many divergent, variable and conflicting criteria.

101 237 U. S. 531; L. R. A. 1916 A 771; reversing 100 N. E. 411; 206 N.
Y. 591; 129 N. Y. Supp. 791; 144 App. Div. 761.

In fact, their destructive effect has long since been recognized.[102] And from this it is certain that when reduced to their last analysis the contentions relied upon in effect destroy the rights which they are advanced to support, since an assessment which was one thing in one State and another in another, and a fund which was distributed by one rule in one State and by a different rule somewhere else, would in practical effect amount to no assessment and no substantial sum to be distributed. It was doubtless not only a recognition of the inherent unsoundness of the proposition here relied upon, but the manifest impossibility of its enforcement which has led courts of last resort of so many States in passing on questions involving the general authority of fraternal associations and their duties as to subjects of a general character concerning all their members to recognize the charter of the corporation and the laws of the State under which it was granted as the test and measure to be applied.[103]   In fact, while dealing with various forms of controversy, in substance all these cases come at last to the principle so admirably stated by Chief Justice Marshall more than a hundred years ago,[104] as follows: 'Without ascribing to this body, which, in its corporate capacity, is the mere creature of the act to which it owes its existence, all the qualities and disabilities annexed by the common law to ancient institutions of this sort, it may correctly be said to be precisely what the incorporating act has made it, to derive all its powers from that act, and to be capable of exert-

[102] Gaines v. Supreme Council R. A., 140 Fed. 978; Supreme Council R. A. v. Brashears, 89 Md. 624, 73 Am. St. 244, 43 Atl. 866.

[103] Supreme Lodge, N. E. O. P. v. Hines, 82 Conn. 315, 73 Atl. 791; Supreme Colony U. O. P. F. v. Towne, 87 Corn. 644, 89 Atl. 264; Palmer v. Welch, 132 Ill. 141, 23 N. E. 412; Grimme v. Grimme, 198 Ill. 265; 64 N. E. 1088; Supreme Council A. L. H. v. Green, 71 Md. 263, 17 Am. St. Rep. 527, 17 Atl. 1048; Supreme Council R. A. v. Brashears, 89 Md. 624, 73 Am. St. Rep. 244, 43 Atl. 866; United Order G. C. v. Merrick, 165 Mass. 421, 43 N. E. 127; Gibson v. Imperial Council O. U. F. 168 Mass. 391; 47 N. E. 101; Larkin v. Knights of Columbus, 188 Mass. 22, 73 N. E. 850; Supreme Lodge K. H. v. Nairn, 60 Mich. 44, 26 N. W. 826; Tepper v. Supreme Council R. A., 59 N. J. Eq. 321, 45 Atl. 111, s. c. 61 N. J. Eq. 638, 88 Am. St. Rep. 449, 47 Atl. 460; Bockover v. Life Ass'n of America, 77 Va. 85.

[104] Head v. Providence Ins. Co., 2 Cranch. 127, 167, 2 L. Ed. 229, 242.

ing its faculties only in the manner which that act authorizes. To this source of its being, then, we must recur to ascertain its powers.'

In addition it was by the application of the same principle that a line of decisions in this court came to establish: first, that the law of the State by which a corporation is created governs in enforcing the liability of a stockholder as a member of such corporation to pay the stock subscription which he agreed to make; second, that the State law and proceedings are binding as to the ascertaining of the fact of insolvency, and of the amount due the creditors entitled to be paid from the subscription when collected; and third, that putting out of view the right of the person against whom a liability for a stockholder's subscription is asserted to show that he is not a stockholder, or is not the holder of as many shares as is alleged, or has a claim against the corporation which at law or equity he is entitled to set off against the corporation, or has any other defense personal to himself, a decree against the corporation in a suit brought against it under the State law for the purpose of ascertaining its insolvency, compelling its liquidation, collecting sums due by stockholders for subscriptions to stock and paying the debts of the corporation, in so far as it determines these general matters, binds the stockholder, although he be not a party in a personal sense, because by virtue of his subscription to stock there was conferred on the corporation the authority to stand in judgment for the subscriber as to such general questions.[105]

That the doctrines thus established if applicable here are conclusive is beyond dispute. That they are applicable clearly results from the fact that although the issues here presented as to things which are accidental are different from those which were presented in the cases referred to, as to every essential consideration involved the cases are the same and the controversy here presented is and has been, therefore, long since foreclosed.

[105] Selig v. Hamilton, 234 U. S. 652, 58 L. Ed. 1518, 34 Sup. Ct. Rep. 926; Converse v. Hamilton, 224 U. S. 243, 56 L. Ed. 749, 32 Sup. Ct. Rep. 415; Bernheimer v. Converse, 206 U. S. 516; 51 L. Ed. 1163, 27 Sup. Ct. Rep. 755; Whitman v. National Bank, 176 U. S. 559, 44 L. Ed. 587, 20 Sup. Ct. Rep. 477; Hawkins v. Glenn, 131 U. S. 319, 33 L. Ed. 184, 9 Sup. Ct. Rep. 739.

The controlling effect of the law of Massachusetts being thus established and the error committed by the court below in declining to give effect to that law and in thereby disregarding the demands of the full faith and credit clause being determined, we come to consider whether the increase of assessment which was complained of was within the powers granted by the Massachusetts charter, or conflicted with the laws of that State. Before doing so, however, we observe that the settled principles which we have applied in determining whether the controversy was governed by the Massachusetts law clearly make manifest how inseparably what constitutes the giving of full faith and credit to the Massachusetts judgment is involved in the consideration of the application of the laws of that State, and therefore, as we have previously stated, how necessarily the express assertion of the existence of a right under the Constitution of the United States to full faith and credit as to the judgment was the exact equivalent of the assertion of a claim of right under the Constitution of the United States to the application of the laws of the State of Massachusetts. We say this because, if the laws of Massachusetts were not applicable, the full faith and credit due to the judgment would require only its enforcement to the extent that it constituted the thing adjudged as between the parties to the record in the ordinary sense, and on the other hand, if the Massachusetts law applies, the full faith and credit due to the judgment additionally exacts that the right of the corporation to stand in judgment as to all members as to controversies concerning the power and duty to levy assessments must be recognized, the duty to give effect to the judgment in such case being substantially the same as the duty to enforce the judgment.

Additionally, before coming to dispose of the final question it is necessary to say that, in considering it in view of the fact that the appellate division treated the Massachusetts judgment as in the record and considered it and that the court below made no reference to its technical inadmissibility, but, on the contrary, treated the question as being one not of admissibility, but of merits, we shall pursue the same course and treat the judgment as in the record upon the hypothesis that the action of the trial court did not amount to its technical exclusion, but only to a ruling that as it deemed the law of Massachusetts inapplicable, it so considered the judgment, and therefore held it merely irrelevant to the merits.

Coming, then, to give full faith and credit to the Massachusetts charter of the corporation and to the laws of that State to determine the powers of the corporation and the rights and duties of its members, there is no room for doubt that the amendment to the by-laws was valid if we accept, as we do, the significance of the charter and of the Massachusetts law applicable to it as announced by the supreme judicial court of Massachusetts in the Reynolds case. And this conclusion does not require us to consider whether the judgment *per se* as between the parties was not conclusive in view of the fact that the corporation, for the purposes of the controversy as to assessments, was the representative of the members.[106] Into that subject, therefore, we do not enter.''

§ 207. **Endowment Insurance Is Life Insurance.**—''The term, life insurance, is not alone applicable,'' says the Supreme Court of California,[107] ''to an insurance for the full term of one's life. On the contrary, it may be for a term of years, or until the assured shall arrive at a certain age. It is simply an undertaking on the part of the insurer that either at the death of the assured, whenever that event may occur, or on his death, if it shall happen within a specified term, or before attaining a certain age, as the case may me, there shall be paid a stipulated sum. In either form, it is, strictly speaking, an insurance on the life of the party. In this case the policy was to become payable on the death of McCullough, provided he died within ten years, and it is to that extent certainly an insurance on his life. It is an undertaking to pay the stipulated sum if he shall die within a specified term, which is of the very essence of life insurance. The fact that the company is to pay the agreed sum at the expiration of ten years, even though McCullough shall not have

[106] See Hartford L. Ins. Co. v. Ibs, 237 U. S. 662, L. R. A. 1916 A 765, 35 Sup. Ct. Rep. 692.

[107] Briggs v. McCullough, 36 Cal. 550. See also Gould v. Curtiss, 1 K. B. (Eng.) 635.

died in the meantime, does not divest it of its character of life insurance. It is only a new and additional element in the contract not inconsistent with its other, which is its chief constituent part, to-wit, the undertaking to pay on the death of the assured within the specified term.''[109] It cannot affect the rights of various parties under a life insurance policy that, instead of fixing the exact period when an endowment shall mature, the policy gives the holder the option to fix it at any time after 15 years.[110] A mutual benefit society organized under a statute authorizing the formation of societies to "give financial aid and benefit to the widows, orphans and heirs or devisees of deceased members'' has no power to contract to pay a benefit to a member himself on his arriving at the age of 70 years or after he has been a member twenty-five years, and such a contract is *ultra vires* and void.[111] Nor can a fraternal beneficiary corporation engage in the business of endowment insurance by issuing endowment policies.[112] A contract of pure endowment by which the defendant agreed to pay the testator a certain sum if living at a specified time thereafter, but to be void if the insured should die in the meantime, is not a contract of insurance within the definition of the Massachusetts statute, but not being prohibited by any law of the State is valid.[113]

§ 208. **Tontine Policies—Right of Policy Holders to Dividends or Profits.**—The name, tontine, has often been applied to a form

[109] Endowment & Benev. Ass'n v. The State, 35 Kan. 262; Carter v. John Hancock Mut. L. Ins. Co., 127 Mass. 153.

[110] Travelers' Ins. Co. v. Healy, 25 App. Div. 53; 49 N. Y. Supp. 29.

[111] Rockhold v. Canton Masonic Ben. Ass'n, 129 Ill. 440; 21 N. E. 794; also 19 N. W. 710. But such a provision in the certificate does not invalidate the certificate as one to pay the benefits to the widow. See case last cited.

[112] State ex rel. v. Orear, 144 Mo. 157; 45 S. W. 1081; Calkins v. Bump, 120 Mich. 335; 79 N. W. 491; Walker v. Commissioner, 103 Mich. 344; 61 N. W. 512; Wagner v. Keystone M. B. Ass'n, 8 Pa. Dist. R. 231; Preferred M. L. I. Co. v. Giddings, 112 Mich. 401; 70 N. W. 1026, 1031. See also Chicago Mut. L. Indemnity Co. v. Hunt, 127 Ill. 257, 30 N. E. 55, 2 L. R. A. 549.

[113] Curtis v. New York Life Ins. Co., 217 Mass. 47, 104 N. E. 553, Ann. Cas. 1915 C 945.

of life insurance policy as well as to a period, after the expiration of which dividends or profits are to be adjusted and paid. The name is derived from Lorenzo Tonti, a Neapolitan banker, who originated the scheme about 1653. The term, tontine, has been defined by the Century Dictionary as follows: "An annuity shared by subscribers to a loan with the benefit of survivorship, the share of each survivor being increased as the subscribers die, until at last the whole goes to the last survivor, the whole transaction ceasing with his death." The same authority gives this definition of a tontine policy: "A policy of insurance in which the policy holder agrees, in common with the other policy holders under the same plan, that no dividend, return premium or surrender value shall be received for a term of years called the tontine period, the entire surplus from all sources being allowed to accumulate to the end of that period, and then divided among all who have maintained their insurance in force. This modification of ordinary life insurance has been adopted as optional with the insured for the purpose of countervailing the tendency to burden long lived and persistent policy holders with a large amount of premiums in comparison with those whose lives fall in shortly after obtaining insurance. The effect is to reduce the sum payable on deaths after but few years payment of premiums and to increase the sum payable on deaths occurring after a given number of years." The Court of Appeals of Kentucky,[114] in a suit brought by a matured tontine policy holder for an accounting of the surplus, defines a tontine policy as follows: "A tontine contract of insurance is more than a policy of life insurance. In addition, it is an agreement on the part of the insurer to hold all the premiums collected on the policies forming that class for the specified period, which is called the tontine period or period of distribution, and, after paying death losses, expenses, and other losses out of the fund so accumulated, to divide the remainder among those who are alive at the end of the tontine period, and who have maintained their policies in force. The premiums include a sum which at interest at $4\frac{1}{2}$ per cent compounded will at the end of the expiration of the expectancy of the life of the insured pay to his

[114] Equitable Life Assur. Soc. v. Winn, 137 Ky. 641; 126 S. W. 153.

estate the principal sum insured, which is called the reserve of the policy. That is always provided for and always collected in each life insurance premium. In addition, another sum is included in the premium, called the 'Mortuary Fund,' which pays the death losses of that per cent who die before the expiration of their life expectancies. Their aggregate is the flat or level cost of insurance. Then there is added a sum to cover costs of conducting the business, and for such losses as may occur from other causes than death of policy holders. This 'loading' of the premium is more or less arbitrary. All excess above costs, expenses, losses, death claims, and the reserve constitute what is known as the 'surplus,' which may also include sums realized from interest received upon the reserves at a greater rate than that upon which it was calculated, as well as from the death rate in a given year being less than the experience justified as certainly expected. At any rate, this surplus is regarded as belonging equitably to those policy holders who contribute it. In tontine insurance all who contribute agree that, instead of apportioning it among them all, it may be apportioned among those who outlive the period of distribution. The insurer undertakes to handle the fund for the parties. Its pay is the costs and expenses which it charges as toll. The balance not only belongs equitably to those contributing to it, according to the terms of their contracts, but the insurance company agrees to so apportion it among them. Now, why should it not keep its contract? To keep it faithfully, and honestly, it is required to keep books of account. Otherwise its apportionment would be a mere guess, even if it rose to that dignity. It is a trustee, an agent of those for whom it has essayed to act. It will not be heard to say that it would be too troublesome to keep the accounts, or would cost too much to render the parties a true statement, or on that account be impracticable to show to a court of chancery in a suit for accounting the state of the books.'' Few, if any strictly tontine policies are now issued, as the non-forfeiture laws of most of the States forbid the forfeiture of life insurance policies after two or three annual premiums have been paid, but a favorite plan is a sort of semi-tontine policy by which the dividends, which ordinarily would be paid annually, are to accumulate during a period of ten or more years and then be divided among the policies in force at the end of that time. The persistent and surviving policy holders in this way receive the dividends that have been accumulated on policies that have lapsed or been terminated by death during the agreed period, and the uncertainty of the results is an attraction to those of speculative minds. The legality of the tontine plan has been questioned. In Fuller v. Metropolitan L. Ins. Co.[115] a suit brought by the holder of a policy, upon what was called the "reserve dividend plan," or one in the nature of a tontine, for an accounting and for damages, the majority opinion of the court says: "All that distinguishes ordinary life insurance from a wagering contract, is the theory of protection against damage that may be suffered through another's death. This protection may be purchased by the insured in behalf of his own family, or of those he sees fit to make his beneficiaries; it may be purchased by one on his own account where he may suffer damage from another's death by reason of kinship, the relation of creditor or other insurable interest. But when this element of protection is entirely eliminated the insurance is a wager and the contract is void.[116] In the present case the policy holders stipulate between themselves that the surrender value of each policy lapsing, which represents payments made in behalf of the beneficiary, shall go to benefit other policy holders living at a certain time, who are total strangers to the policy and the insured. This is a mutual wager upon the chances of life. There is no conceivable element of protection. The sole purpose of the bet is personal profit. It is the risk of what is due to each in the case of a lapse, for the chance of winning what is due to others. It is correctly described by the plaintiff's counsel as 'the chance to speculate on his chances of surviving the other members.' On this ground these policies were urged upon the public, by appeals to the gambling instinct, claiming, as stated in the Stewart pamphlet that, 'Risk is the condition of success.' The only way of evading the invalidity of such a contract is by the claim that the policy holders in fact wager nothing, that all payments of

[115] 70 Conn. 647; 41 Atl. 4.
[116] Cronin v. Vermont L. Ins. Co., 20 R. I. 570; 40 Atl. 497.

premiums belong to the company, including those applied to maintain a reserve, and the policy holders are not entitled to any particular sum, but only to an equitable proportion of the excess of assets over liabilities at the time of dividend. We do not pass upon the sufficiency of this claim. But if the claim of the plaintiffs be true; if upon each lapse a sum equal in amount to the reserve value of the policy lapsing becomes a liability of the company which it must pay to the surviving policy holders; then all doubt as to the gaming nature of the transaction vanishes. The pool thus created is composed of definite sums of money of which the company is stakeholder, under an agreement to divide these sums among the winners who are to be determined by the chances of life.'' Other courts, however, do not seem to have entertained the same doubts concerning the tontine principle. In a case in Pensylvania,[117] ten persons holding life insurance policies had made an assignment of the same to a financial agency, as trustee, to collect on the death of each person insured the amount of his policy, and distribute the proceeds to the survivors. The court referred to the fact that property might be held by joint tenants where, on the death of one, the survivor would take, but while not expressly deciding the legality of the arrangement, held it good so far as the company discharging its liability by payment to the trustee was concerned, provided the insured had himself paid the premiums. In another case,[118] the court inclined to the belief that the contract was not a gambling transaction. The New York Court of Appeals has decided[119] that a life insurance company issuing policies on the tontine, or ten-year dividend system, is in no sense a trustee of any particular fund for the holder of such a policy: their relation is simply that of debtor and creditor; and the policy holder, at the expiration of the ten years, is not entitled to an accounting in the absence of any evidence of misappropriation, wrong-doing or mistake on the part of the com-

---

[117] Hill v. United Life Ass'n, 154 Pa. St. 29; 25 Atl. 771 .

[118] Simons v. N. Y. Life Ins. Co., 38 Hun. 309. Cited and approved, Romer v. Equitable L. Assur. Soc., 102 Ill. App. 621.

[119] Uhlman v. N. Y. L. Ins. Co., 109 N. Y. 421; 17 N. E. 363.

pany. Other cases support this view.[120] The rights of tontine policyholders have been fully considered by the New York Court of Appeals, in Greef v. Equitable L. Assur. Society.[121] In that case the court held that the equitable share of the surplus of a mutual insurance company, with which the policy holder should be credited, is only such a share as may be credited, with due regard to the safety of the policy holders and the security of the business of the company. The determination by the officers and managers of the company of the amount that should be accumulated and retained for the security of the company and its members, is *prima facie* to be regarded as equitable in the absence of any allegation of wrong-doing or mistake by them. No title to any part of the surplus of a mutual insurance company, which will enable a policy holder to maintain an action at law for its recovery, exists until a distribution is made and the proportion of the surplus which should be credited to the policy holders has been ascertained and determined. It has also been said,[122] that the parties to a contract of life insurance do not contemplate that the policy holder is to be permitted to participate in the management of the company or to dictate the amount of the dividend which it shall declare, or question the result after the discretion of its managers has been exercised in this behalf. A tontine provision as to the division of accumulation in a policy issued by an assessment association has been held to be in violation of the State law of Illinois relating to such organizations.[123] In an action to determine the liability of the company contemporaneous literature is admissible.[124] And a life policy and a paper containing estimates of results at end of

[120] Pierce v. Equitable L. Assur. Soc., 145 Mass. 56; 12 N. E. 858; Gadd v. Equitable L. Assur. Soc., 97 Fed. 834; Bogardus v. N. Y. Life Ins. Co., 101 N. Y. 328; 4 N. E. 522; Hunton v. Equitable L. Assur. Soc., 45 Fed. 661.

[121] 160 N. Y. 19; 54 N. E. 712; 46 L. R. A. 288; reversing 40 App. Div. 180; 57 N. Y. Supp. 871.

[122] Fuller v. Knapp, 24 Fed. 100. See also Bain v. Aetna L. Ins. Co., 20 Ont. Rep. 6, citing Manby v. Gresham L. Ins. Co., 7 Jur. (N. S.) 383.

[123] Chicago Mut. L. Ass'n v. Hunt, 127 Ill. 257; 20 N. E. 55; 2 L. R. A. 549.

[124] Fuller v. Metropolitan L. Ins. Co., 37 Fed. 163.

tontine period attached to it are to be construed together.[125]   A company declaring a dividend out of the surplus earnings of the company cannot limit it to such policies as may be continued in force by the payment of the next premium due thereon, although the policy provides that the amount of surplus as determined by the directors shall be conclusive.[126]   Policy holders in a mutual life insurance company can maintain a bill in equity to enjoin the payment of fraudulent claims on policies, and an allegation in such a bill, that the company has accepted proofs of loss on a fraudulent policy and is about to pay the same from the funds of the company, though the officers know that the policy is fraudulent; that the officers have refused to contest such claim, though requested by plaintiffs, and will not defend suit thereon, sufficiently shows that plaintiffs have no adequate remedy at law.[127]   An estimate of the probable cash value of a policy at the end of the tontine period has been held not to amount to a misrepresentation, but a mere expression of opinion.[128]

§ 209.   **The Same Subject Continued.**—The relation between the holder of a matured tontine policy and the company is that of creditor and debtor and the former can maintain a bill in equity for an accounting.[129]   In the case of Townsend v. Equitable Life Assur. Society[130] it was held that tontine policies create the relation of debtor and creditor and not a trust relation which would support an action for an accounting, and that a holder of a policy may sue in equity for a discovery and accounting notwithstanding existence of a remedy at law.   Such a con-

[125] Timlin v. Equitable L. Assur. Soc., 141 Wis. 276; 124 N. W. 253.

[126] Aetna L. Ins. Co. v. Hartley, 24 Ky. L. 57; 67 S. W. 19; 68 S. W. 1081; Mut. Ben. L. Ins. Co. v. Davis, 73 S. W. 1020; 24 Ky. L. 2291. But apparently to the contrary is Petrie v. Mut. Ben. L. Ins. Co., 92 Minn. 489; 100 N. W. 236.

[127] Carmien v. Cornell, 148 Ind. 83; 47 N. E. 216.

[128] Avery v. Equitable L. Assur. Soc., 117 N. Y. 451; 23 N. E. 3; reversing 52 Hun. 392; Donoho v. Equitable L. Assur. Soc., 22 Tex. Civ. A. 192; 54 S. W. 645; O'Brien v. Equitable Life Assur. Soc., 173 Mich. 432; 138 N. W. 1086.

[129] Peters v. Equitable Life Assur. Soc., 200 Mass. 579; 86 N. E. 885; Timlin v. Equitable Life Assur. Sov., 141 Wis. 276; 124 N. W. 253.

[130] 263 Ill. 432; 105 N. E. 324.

troversy does not relate to the internal management.[131] A tontine policy issued by a New York company must be interpreted in accordance with the decisions of the New York courts.[132] Where the charter of a life insurance company provides that net profits shall be divided among the policy holders and a large surplus was accumulated, the directors are bound to pay over the equitable proportion of the surplus to the policy holders.[133] A provision in a contract allowing policy holders to share in the profits does not transform the company into a mutual company, or estop it from treating the surplus as belonging to the stockholders.[134] Under the statutes of the State authorizing mutual benefit societies to pay benefit certificates from the surplus, or reserve funds derived from assessments and the amended charter of the society authorized the creation and maintenance of reserve, or surplus funds, the society has power to create a mortuary reserve fund and a reserve death benefit fund to be used in the payment of death claims under specified circumstances, and the money so accumulated is a trust fund of which the society is trustee.[135]

A mutual insurance company may as against its policy holders change its methods of entries and computation of dividends provided the change relates merely to the modes of bookkeeping.[136] It is difficult to state general rules applicable to the contracts of insurance companies whereby the policy holder has some claim, or right, to and in the surplus, or earnings, of the company. We give in a note reference to some of the cases where these questions have been considered.[137]

[131] See also Equitable Life Assur. Soc. v. Weil, 103 Miss. 186; 60 Sou. 133.

[132] Equitable Life Assur. Soc. v. Weil, 103 Miss. 186; 60 Sou. 133; Ann. Cas. 1915 B 636.

[133] White v. Provident Life & Trust Co., 237 Pa. 375, 85 Atl. 463.

[134] State v. Union Central Life In. Co., 84 Ohio 459; 95 N. E. 1155.

[135] Kane v. Knights of Columbus, 84 Conn. 96, 79 Atl. 63.

[136] Fuller v. Metropolitan Life Ins. Co., 70 Conn. 647; 41 Atl. 4.

[137] Equitable Life Assur. Soc. v. Host, 124 Wis. 657; 102 N. W. 579; Hackett v. Equitable Life Assur. Soc., 63 N. Y. Supp. 847; 30 Misc. 523; affd. 63 N. Y. Supp. 1092; 50 App. Div. 266; Romer v. Equitable Life Assur. Soc., 102 Ill. App. 621; Aetna Life Ins. Co. v. Hartley, 24 Ky. L. 57; 67 S. W. 19; 68 S. W. 1081.

§ 210. **Reinsurance.**—In the case of Vial v. Norwich Fire Ins. Society,[138] it is said: "Reinsurance is defined to be a contract that one insurer makes with another to protect the first insurer from a risk he has already. assumed. It is not denied such contracts are lawful and valid. 'The ordinary contract of reinsurance operates solely between the insurer and the reinsurer, and creates no privity whatever between the reinsurer and the person originally insured. The contract of insurance and that of reinsurance remain totally distinct and unconnected, and the reinsurer is in no respect liable, either as surety or otherwise, to the person originally· insured.[139] In a note to this text will be found cited numerous decisions of courts of last resort sustaining it, and we do not understand it to be disputed by plaintiff in error that this is the rule where the reinsurance contract is strictly one of reinsurance. In Barnes v. Hekla F. Ins. Co.,[140] the Court said: 'Reinsurance is a mere contract of indemnity, in which an insurer reinsures risks in another company. In such a contract the policy holders have no concern, are not the parties for whose benefit the contract of reinsurance is made and they cannot, therefore, sue thereon.'' The rule thus stated is generally approved.[141] While under a strict reinsurance agreement there is no privity of contract between the reinsuring company and the policy holders of the company reinsured, a reinsuring company may by express agreement assume the liabilities of the reinsured and agree to pay them, in which case the contract is something more than one of reinsurance,[142] and there may be an oral contract of reinsurance which will be enforced.[143] A life insurance company, however cannot transfer its policy holders to another company without their

[138] 257 Ill. 355; 100 N. E. 929; 44 L. R. A. (N. S.) 317, Ann. Cas. 1914 A 1141.
[139] 24 Am. & Eng. Enc. Law, 2nd Ed. 249.
[140] 56 Minn. 38, 45 Am. St. 438, 57 N. W. 314.
[141] Weil v. Federal Life Ins. Co., 264 Ill. 425; 106 N. E. 246; affg. 182 Ill. App. 322; Ann. Cas. 1915 D 974.
[142] Vial v. Norwich Fire Ins. Co., *supra*.
[143] McIntyre v. Federal Life Ins. Co., 142 Mo. App. 256; 126 S. W. 266; Morgan v. Royal Society, 170 N. C. 75; 86 S. E. 975; Federal Life Ins. Co. v. Risinger, 46 Ind. App. 146; 91 N. E. 533.

consent, but if a transfer is attempted a policy holder must elect whether he will treat it as an abandonment and then sue to recover the amount due, or continue to pay premiums under protest and keep alive his claim against the original insurer, or acquiesce in the transfer. If he continues to pay without objection he cannot repudiate the new contract[144] and it has also been said that an agreement for reinsurance is not binding upon policy holders in whose favor a right of action at once arises against their own company for breach of contract, such company having disqualified itself from performance.[145] The offer of an insurance company to issue new policies to policy holders of an insolvent company, is limited to such holders personally and could not be accepted for an insane policy holder by his guardian.[146] A reinsurance agreement will not affect policy holders' rights to extended insurance as against the reinsuring company[147] and the reinsuring agreement cannot make policies contestable that by their terms have become incontestable.[148] A reinsuring company, however, which issues its own policies to the policy holders of an insolvent company is bound only by the stipulations in its own policy.[149] An attempted consolidation not complying with statutory requirements is void.[150] Although a reinsurance contract may be void, a recovery can be had on a certificate where the association had received assessments.[151] but a reinsuring company is bound by the provisions of the contract of the company reinsured,[152] and cannot require a medical

[144] Watson v. National Life & T. Co., 189 Fed. 872; 111 C. C. A. 134.

[145] Northwestern National Life Ins. Co. v. Gray, 161 Fed. 488; Washington Life Ins. Co. v. Lovejoy (Tex. Civ. App.), 149 S. W. 398.

[146] Robinson v. Postal Life Ins. Co., 134 C. C. A. 155; 218 Fed. 347.

[147] Federal Life Ins. Co. v. Arnold, 46 Ind. App. 114, 90 N. E. 493; 91 N. E. 357.

[148] Federal Life Ins. Co. v. Kerr, 173 Ind. 613, 89 N. E. 398; affg. 82 N. E. 943.

[149] Brown v. U. S. Casualty Co., 88 Fed. 38; see also Franklin Life Ins. Co. v. Hickson, 197 Ill. 117; 64 N. E. 248.

[150] Conseil, etc., v. LaFleur, 215 Mass. 347; 102 N. E. 412.

[151] Timberlake v. Supreme Commandery U. O. G. C., 208 Mass. 411; 94 N. E. 685.

[152] National Annuity Ass'n v. Carter, 96 Ark. 495; 132 S. W. 633; Hatcher v. National Annuity Ass'n, 153 Mo. App. 538; 134 S. W. 1.

examination of a member who had paid his dues in good faith.[153] It has been held that a benefit society has no authority to reinsure and agree to pay benefits contracted to be paid by another society- and that such a contract is void and receipt of premiums does not estop the society.[154] The reinsuring society has, however, often been held liable for the contracts of the reinsured corporation.[155] A consolidated society is not estopped from relying upon the illegality of the consolidation.[156] The construction and effect of a contract of reinsurance, like any other, depends upon its terms and such a contract will be construed by the ordinary rules applicable in such cases.[157] A reinsuring company taking the assets of another is liable for damages for breach of contract with the agent of the latter company.[158] The right of a mutual life insurance company to reinsure does not carry with it power to sell or transfer all its property against the will of a minority of the policy holders and a contract to so sell or transfer is as against dissenting policy holders *ultra vires* and void.[159] The Supreme Court of Kansas has said:[160] that, unless the authority exists in the statute under which the fra-

---

[153] Cox v. Kansas City Life Ins. Co., 154 Mo. App. 464; 135 S. W. 1013.

[154] Alexander v. Bankers' Union, 187 Ill. App. 469. See also Knapp v. Supreme Commandery, 121 Tenn. 212; 118 N. W. 390, where merger was held unlawful.

[155] Supreme Lodge K. P. v. Mims (Tex. Civ. App.), 167 S. W. 385; Freemeyer v. Industrial Mut. Ind. Co., 101 Ark. 61; 141 S. W. 508; Grand Fraternity v. Cliff, 24 Colo. App. 480; 135 Pac. 125; Maloney v. North American Union, 177 Ill. App. 658.

[156] Gordon v. American Patriots (Tex. Civ. App.), 141 S. W. 331.

[157] National Life Ins. Co. v. Metropolitan Life Ins. Co., 226 Ill. 102; 80 N. E. 747; affg. 127 Ill. App. 605; Federal Life Ins. Co. v. Kerr (Ind. App.), 82 N. E. 943; Parvin v. Mut. Reserve Life Ins. Co., 125 Ia. 95; 100 N. W. 39; Kansas Mut. Life Ins. Co, v. Whitehead, 123 Ky. 21; 93 S. W. 605; Hayden v. Franklin Life Ins. Co., 69 C. C. A. 423; 136 Fed. 285; Bowles v. Mut. Reserve Fund Life Ass'n, 220 Ill. 400; 77 N. E. 198; reversing 120 Ill. App. 242, 251; Cosmopolitan Life Ass'n v. Koegel, 104 Va. 619; 52 S. E. 166.

[158] Israel v. Northwestern National Life Ins. Co., 111 Minn. 404; 127 N. W. 187.

[159] Barden v. St. Louis L. Ins. Co., 3 Mo. App. 248; Smith v. St. Louis Mut. L. Ins. Co., 2 Tenn. Ch. 727.

[160] Bankers' Union, etc., v. Crawford, 67 Kan. 449; 73 Pac. 79.

ternal beneficiary association is organized, one such association cannot be consolidated with another, and a contract by one such association to pay a death loss of another life association, already approved, in consideration of the transfer to it of the membership and offices of such another association, if unauthorized by the statutes of the State, is *ultra vires* and void, and the society is not estopped to set up such power. Such transfer, however, has been upheld.[161] A plan by the directors of an insurance company to exchange majority holdings of stock to a trust company, involving an expenditure of over eight million dollars, in order that they and those whom they may select from time to time, may forever dominate the appointment of directors of each corporation, is as a whole *ultra vires*.[162] One holding a policy in a company which has been absorbed by another, if he accepts a condition imposed to his becoming insured in the latter, instead of standing on his rights under his original contract, is bound thereby; though he did not understand it.[163] A contract of reinsurance by a company includes only the contracts in force at the time of the reinsurance.[164] Ordinarily a mere contract of reinsurance creates no privity between the original insured and the insurer, unless the loss or risk is expressly assumed by another company; in which case the original insured may sue upon such contract as having been made for his benefit.[165] The original insurer's liability, however, is not affected by the contract of reinsurance, and its liability remains the same.[166] Where the defendant company was consolidated with another which offered to assume plaintiff's policy which he re-

---

[161] Cathcart v. Equitable Mut. L. Ass'n, 111 Ia. 471; 82 N. W. 964.

[162] Robotham v. Prudential L. Ins. Co., 64 N. J. Eq. 673; 53 Atl. 842. See also Southern Mut. Aid Soc. v. Blount, 112 Va. 214, 70 S. E. 457. See as to *ultra vires*, *post*, § 342.

[163] Davitt v. National Life Ass'n, 36 App. Div. 632; 56 N. Y. Supp. 839.

[164] Parvin v. Mut. Reserve L. Ins. Co., 125 Ia. 95, 100 N. W. 39.

[165] Travelers' Ins. Co. v. Cal. Ins. Co., 1 N. D. 151; 45 N. W. 703; 8 L. R. A. 769n; Fisher v. Hope L. Ins. Co., 69 N. Y. 163.

[166] Glen v. Hope Mut. L. Ins. Co., 1 Thomp. & C. 463; 56 N. Y. 379; Fisher v. Hope Mut. L. Ins. Co., 69 N. Y. 161. As to reinsurance in general see note in 10 L. R. A. 423 to Faneuil Hall Ins. Co. v. Liverpool, etc., Ins. Co., 153 Mass. 63.

fused, the latter is not liable to plaintiff for defendant's alleged breach of contract.[167]

§ 211. **Contract of Benefit Society With Members, Where Found.**—The principal object of all benefit societies is to confer certain advantages upon their members and pay to them, or their beneficiaries, specified benefits. The understanding between the association and the individuals who compose it, as to the membership, the duties imposed on members and the benefits to be bestowed on them is a contract. The earlier authorities did not all agree as to where this contract is to be found in cases where a certificate is issued to the member, whether in such certificate, in the laws of the society, or in both. All conditions of the contract wherever found are binding on the beneficiary and such beneficiary is bound by the acts of the member.[168] The Court of Appeals of New York, in a case involving the right to recover a death benefit, said :[169] "The charter and by-laws of the defendant corporation constituted the terms of an executory contract to which the testator assented when he accepted admission into the order." In a similar case the Supreme Court of Wisconsin said :[170] "The constitution and by-laws certainly contain the contract which was entered into by the parties." On the other hand, it is asserted in some cases, that the certificate of membership contains the contract. In a case in the Federal court in Iowa[171] it was said: "The contract is contained in the certificates;" the Supreme Court of Indiana also says, in a case where the benefit of a beneficiary society was in dispute :[172] "The certificate, although issued by a mutual benefit association, is, in legal contemplation, a policy of insurance, and is in most respects governed by the general rules of law

[167] Provident Savings Life Assur. Soc. v. Ellinger (Tex. Civ. App.), 164 S. W. 1024.
[168] Montour v. Grand Lodge A. O. U. W., 38 Ore. 47; 62 Pac. 524; Cotter v. Grand Lodge A. O. U. W., 23 Mont. 82; 57 Pac. 650; Ebert v. Mut. R. F. L. Ass'n, 81 Minn. 116; 83 N. W. 506; 84 N. W. 457.
[169] Hellenberg v. District No. 1, I. O. O. B., 94 N. Y. 580.
[170] Schunck v. Gegenzeiten, etc., 44 Wis. 375.
[171] Worley v. Northwestern Masonic Aid Ass'n, 10 Fed. 228.
[172] Presbyterian, etc., Fund v. Allen, 106 Ind. 593.

which apply to insurance contracts.''[173]   In another case[174] the same court says: ''The essential difference between a certificate in a beneficiary association and an ordinary life policy is, that in the latter the rights of the beneficiary are fixed by the terms of the policy, while in the former they depend upon the certificate and the rights of the member under the constitution and by-laws of the society.'' In an action to recover a sick benefit, no certificate having been issued, the Supreme Court of Massachusetts said:[175] ''The corporation is not a mere charitable society, but is rather in the nature of an association for the mutual insurance of its members against sickness or accident. If it refuses to perform its contract, contained in the by-laws, the member who is injured may have recourse to the proper courts to enforce the contract.'' And it is possible that under certain circumstances the application may contain the contract.[176] Of course it is understood that the charter must be considered as part of the contract with the by-laws.[177] There is still another view. In a case, where the promised benefit of a beneficiary society was involved, the Supreme Court of New Hampshire said:[178] ''The charter, by-laws and certificate of membership, taken together, show what was the understanding of the parties.'' To the same effect is the statement in a similar case in Kentucky,[179] wherein the Court of Appeals said: ''The certificate of membership constitutes the contract; but it is to be construed and governed by the company's charter. In fact, it may be said that the charter is a part of the contract; and if it declares who, in a certain event, shall be the

[173] Bauer v. Sampson Lodge, 102 Ind. 262; Elkhart M. Aid Ass'n v. Houghton, 98 Ind. 149; Sup. Commandery, etc., v. Ainsworth, 71 Ala. 443; Supreme Lodge v. Schmidt, 98 Ind. 374.

[174] Masonic, etc., Ben. Soc. v. Burkhart, 110 Ind. 192.

[175] Dolan v. Court of Good Samaritan, 128 Mass. 437; and to the same effect are the cases Grand Lodge v. Elsner, 26 M. A. 108; Baldwin v. Golden Star Fraternity, 47 N. J. L. 111.

[176] Robinson v. U. S. Ben. Soc., 132 Mich. 695; 94 S. W. 211.

[177] Grand Lodge v. Elsner, and Baldwin v. Golden Star Fraternity, supra. See also Fricke v. Hartford Life Ins. Co· (Ia.), 159 N. W. 247.

[178] Eastman v. Provident M. Relief Ass'n, 62 N. H. 555; 20 Cent. L. J. 266 (1883).

[179] Van Bibber v. Van Bibber, 82 Ky. 350.

beneficiary, the parties cannot alter this legislative direction, because neither the company nor the insured can do anything in violation of it.'' In many other cases[180] this view is also taken. The document issued to the members of a benefit society must be such as its laws prescribe; it is usually a certificate which recites that the person named therein is a member of the society and ''entitled to all the rights and privileges of membership'' and to participate in its beneficiary fund to a specified amount, which shall be paid at his death, if then a member in good standing, to a named person, on condition that such member shall, in every particular, while a member of the society, comply with its laws, rules and requirements. This certificate, although not strictly speaking an insurance policy,[181] is in the nature of an insurance policy issued by a mutual company.[182] If the certificate refers to the laws of the order in such a way as to make them a part of it, then, of course, they are to be considered as a part of the contract, but if the charter is in general terms and simply provides that the society may conduct the business of paying benefits to its members, and, if the by-laws contain no restrictions or limitations, then the whole of the contract would be in the certificate. It has been held, however, that the by-laws form part of the contract although not referred to in the certificate,[183] and the constitution may

[180] Splawn v. Chew, 60 Tex. 535; Supreme Lodge K. of P. v. Stein, 75 Miss. 107; 21 Sou. 559; 37 L. R. A. 775; Zimmerman v. Masonic Aid Ass'n, 75 Fed. 236; Condon v. Mut. Reserve F. L. A., 89 Md. 99; 42 Atl. 944; 44 L. R. A. 149.

[181] Morton v. Royal Tribe of Joseph, 93 Mo. App. 78.

[182] In the following cases full copies of the certificates sued on are given: Grand Lodge A. O. U. W. v. Child, 70 Mich. 163; 38 N. W. 1; Wendt v. Iowa Legion of Honor, 72 Ia. 682; 34 N. W. 470; Supreme Lodge Knights of Honor v. Johnson, 78 Ind. 110; Richmond v. Johnson, 28 Minn. 447; Supreme Lodge Knights of Pythias v. Schmidt, 98 Ind. 374; Royal Templars of Temperance v. Curd, 111 Ill. 286; Holland v. Taylor, 111 Ind. 121; 12 N. E. 116; · Supreme Commandery, etc., v. Ainsworth, 71 Ala. 437.

[183] Gray v. Supreme Lodge K. of H., 118 Ind. 293; 20 N. E. 833; Hesinger v. Home Ben. Ass'n, 41 Minn. 516; 43 N. W. 481; Davidson v. Old People Soc., 39 Minn. 303; 39 N. W. 803; Supreme Lodge, etc., v. Knight, 117 Ind. 489; 20 N. E. 479; In re Globe Mut. B. Ass'n, 32 N. E. 122; 135

become part of the contract by express agreement in the application.[184] The conclusion, from an examination of all the cases, is that the contract is found in the certificate, if one is issued, taken in connection with the application if one is referred to,[185] but is to be construed and governed by the charter and by-laws of the society, and the statutes of the State of the domicile of the corporation.[186] It has been well said :[187] "The statute under which the corporation is organized, the articles of incorporation and the by-laws are made to contain the whole plan of insurance, its limitations, extent and the obligations imposed. They embrace the terms of the contract. Whatever vitality the policy of insurance possesses is derived from these sources. The statute authorizing and controlling the organization and business of this society, became as much part of the contract for insurance and membership as if its terms were incorporated into the printed certificate, and every person becoming a member was

N. Y. 280; affg. 17 N. Y. Supp. 852; Moore v. Union, etc., Ass'n, 103 Ia. 424; 72 N. W. 645; Galvin v. Knights of Father Mathew, 169 Mo. App. 496, 155 S. W. 45; Gibbs v. Knights of Pythias, etc., 173 Mo. App. 34; 156 S. W. 11; Benes v. Supreme Lodge, etc., 231 Ill. 134, 83 N. E. 127; affg. 135 Ill. App. 314. To the contrary is Goodson v. Mut. Masonic Acc. Soc., 91 Mo. App. 339.

[184] Hutchinson v. Supreme Tent K. O. T. M,. 22 N. Y. Supp. 801.

[185] Robson v. Ancient Order Foresters, 93 Minn. 24; 100 N. W. 381.

[186] Miner v. Mich. Mut. Ben. Ass'n, 63 Mich. 338; 29 N. W. 852; Mulroy v. Knights of Honor, 28 Mo. App. 463; Maryland Mut. Ben. Ass'n v. Clendinen, 44 Md. 429; Burbank v. Rockingham Ins. Co., 24 N. H. 550; 57 Am. Dec. 300; Masonic Relief Ass'n v. McAuley, 2 Mackey 70; Simeral v. Dubuque, etc., Ins. Co., 18 Ia. 319; Mitchell v. Lycoming, etc., Ins. Co., 51 Pa. St. 402; Susquehanna, etc., Ins. Co. v. Perrine, 7 W. & S. 348; Grand Lodge, etc., v. Elsner, 26 Mo. App. 109; McMurry v. Supreme Lodge, etc., 20 Fed. 107; National Ben. Ass'n v. Bowman, 110 Ind. 355; Britton v. Supreme Counc. R. A., 46 N. J. Eq. 102; 18 Atl. 675; Lorscher v. Supreme Lodge K. of H., 72 Mich. 316; 40 N. W. 545; Grand Lodge v., Jesse, 50 Ill. App. 101; Drum v. Benton, 13 App. D. C. 245; Polish, etc., Soc. v. Werzek, 182 Ill. 27; 55 N. E. 64; Fee v. National Mas. A. Ass'n, 110 Ia. 271; 81 N. W. 483; Newton v. Northern Mut. R. Ass'n, 21 R. I. 476; 44 Atl. 690; Lithgow v. Supreme Tent K. O. T. M., 165 Pa. St. 292; 30 Atl. 830; Grand Lodge, etc., v. Gaudy, 63 N. J. Eq. 692; 53 Atl. 142; Seitzinger v. Modern Woodmen, 204 Ill. 58; 68 N. E. 478; affg. 106 Ill. App. 449. Also cases cited just previously.

[187] Montgomery v. Whitbeck, 12 N. D. 385; 96 N. W. 327.

bound to take notice of it." A limitation, in a certificate is good although not provided for by the by-laws,[188] and a provision in the certificate may prevail over the by-laws.[189] Unquestionably, however, under the later authorities, the contract consists of the certificate if one be issued, the application if referred to therein, the by-laws, and the statutes of the State of the domicile and also the statutes of the State where the contract is made.[190]

§ 212. **Societies Incorporated in Two States—Schism.**—It has sometimes appeared in actions brought against benefit societies that the same society has, for some reason, after its first incorporation under the laws of one State, become reincorporated under the laws of a second State. In one case[191] the society was incorporated under the laws of the State of Kentucky and subsequently reincorporated under the laws of the State of Missouri, and the designation in that case was held, under the Missouri charter, to have been illegal but allowable under the charter received in Kentucky and it was also held that the contract, out of comity, would be enforced in Missouri. In a case in Illinois,[192] against the same society it was held that an organization having a charter from two States is two separate corporations and can act at its will under either charter. This is in accordance with the general rule laid down in standard works on corporations and as expressly decided in one case.[193] In a later

[188] McCoy v. N. W. Mut. Relief Ass'n, 92 Wis. 577; 66 N. W. 691; 47 L. R. A. 681n.
[189] Failey v. Fee, 83 Md. 83; 32 L. R. A. 311; 34 Atl. 839; Courtney v. Fidelity Mut. Aid Ass'n, 120 Mo. App. 110; 94 S. W. 768; 101 S. W. 1098. To the contrary is Boward v. Bankers' Union, 94 Mo. App. 422; 68 S. W. 369.
[190] Finnell v. Franklin, 55 Colo. 156; 134 Pac. 122; Love v. Modern Woodmen of America, 259 Ill. 102; 102 N. E. 183; Sherry v. Catholic Order of Foresters, 166 Ill. App. 254; Newman v. Supreme Lodge K. of P. (Miss.) 70 Sou. 241; Daffron v. Modern Woodmen of Am., 190 Mo. App. 303; 176 S. W. 498; Slaughter v. Grand Lodge, etc. (Ala.) 68 Sou. 367; Supreme Lodge Fraternal Brotherhood v. Price, 27 Cal. App. 607; 150 Pac. 803; Steele v. Fraternal Tribunes, 215 Ill. 190; 74 N. E. 121.
[191] Hysinger v. Supreme Lodge K. & L. of H., 42 M.-A. 628.
[192] Bachmann v. Supreme Lodge K. & L. of H., 44 Ill. App. 188.
[193] Newport Co. v. Wooley, 78 Ky. 525. Morawetz on Corp., § 997.

case[194] the Court said: "It is a well-settled law, that a corporation, which in its essential sense is a mere association of persons, may acquire a franchise as such in different States and at different times, and that the organization of a later corporate entity in one State, does not *per se* involve the loss of a prior corporate being granted by another State, and that the corporation may act in one State under one charter and in another State which it desires to enter for business, under a mere license, or under articles of full incorporation, the latter method being often adopted by a foreign corporation in order to acquire specific power to act as a domestic corporation in a particular State, independent of the principle of comity which it would otherwise be compelled to invoke."[195] In a case in Texas where the same organization was defendant,[196] the Civil Court of Appeals of that State said: "The defendant, the Supreme Lodge Knights of Honor, is but one association or corporation, incorporated first under the laws of Kentucky, and afterwards under the laws of the State of Missouri, but that defendant having elected to abandon the Kentucky charter and to continue its work and organization under the Missouri charter, since June 18, 1884, and having so continued and acted under said Missouri charter since said date, and the grand lodge and subordinate lodges of Texas including said Travis Lodge, No. 1015, having for many years recognized the Supreme Lodge of the order and the said John Fleming having also recognized said Missouri corporation for many years prior to his death, and was so recognizing said Missouri corporation as the Supreme Lodge of the order at the time plaintiffs were designated as his devisees in his will and at the time of his death that the Missouri charter of defendant, and the constitution and by-laws enacted thereunder, by the defendant, must govern and control the rights of the parties under the benefit certificate here sued on. . . . That even if the Kentucky charter and laws enacted thereunder by defendant, were to control, that the incorporation under the Missouri laws

194 Martinez v. Supreme Lodge K. of H., 81 Mo. App. 59.
195 Morawetz on Corp., § 991, *et seq.;* Tourville v. Railway, 148 Mo. 614; 50 S. W. 300.
196 Bollman v. Supreme Lodge K. of H. (Tex. Civ. App.), 53 S. W. 722.

would be in the nature of an amendment to the original charter, and if the additional limitations as to who could participate in the benefit fund as made by the Missouri charter would have been valid and binding on the original members under the Kentucky charter if made by an amendment to defendant's charter by the legislature of Kentucky, then it is valid if made by the legislature of Missouri." Closely allied with the subject of dual incorporation is that of double insurance, which arises where there is a schism in an order, which divides into two bodies, each claiming to be the true one. In a case of this kind,[197] a society had separated into two parts each claiming to be legitimate and claiming the members of the former body as its own. The deceased held a certificate in one body, receiving no new certificate but retained his membership in the rival body and continued to pay assessments and dues in both. The certificate was paid by the rival and surrendered, claim was made against the defendant and assessment thereof made and collected but payment was refused because of plaintiff's inability to surrender the certificate. It was held that the deceased was not doubly insured and that the contract of the defendant did not amount to an estoppel and that it was discharged from liability. In a subsequent case arising in the same State and where the same factions were interested it was held that recovery could be had from both factions and that the officers of the new lodge having received dues and assessments from the member with notice that he had not severed his connection with the old body, it was estopped from insisting upon his failure to do so as a ground of forfeiture.[198]

§ 213. **Contract Is One of Insurance.**—This contract, whether found in the certificate alone, or gathered from the certificate, charter and by-laws, is one of insurance. The Supreme Court of Massachusetts has made this very clear in the leading case of Commonwealth v. Wetherbee,[199] in which it said: "A contract of insurance is an agreement by which one party, for a consideration (which is usually paid in money, either in one sum or at different times, during the continuance of the risk), promises to

197 Bock v. A. O. U. W., 75 Ia. 462.
198 Warnebold v. Grand Lodge A. O. U. W., 83 Ia. 23; 48 N. W. 1069.
199 105 Mass. 149.

make a certain payment of money upon the destruction or injury of something in which the other party has an interest. In fire and marine insurance, the thing insured is property; in life or accident insurance, it is the life or health of a person. In either case, neither the times and amounts of payment by the assured, nor the modes of estimating or securing the payment of the sum to be paid by the insurer, affect the question whether the agreement between them is a contract of insurance. All that is requisite to constitute such a contract is the payment of the consideration by one, and the promise of the other to pay the amount of the insurance upon the happening of injury to the subject by a contingency contemplated in the contract. The contract made between the Connecticut Mutual Benefit Company and each of its members by the certificates of membership issued according to its charter, does not differ in any essential particular form or substance from an ordinary policy of mutual life insurance. The subject insured is the life of the member. The risk insured is death from any cause not excepted in the terms of the contract. The assured pays a sum fixed by the directors and not exceeding ten dollars, at the inception of the contract, and assessments of two dollars each annually, and of one dollar each upon the death of any member of the division to which he belongs, during the continuance of the risk. In case of the death of the insured by a peril insured against, the company absolutely promises to pay to his representatives, in sixty days after receiving satisfactory notice and proof of his death, 'as many dollars as there are members in' the same division, the number of which is limited to five thousand. The payment of this sum is subject to no contingency but the insolvency of the corporation. The means of paying it are derived from the assessments collected upon his death from other members; from the money received upon issuing other certificates of membership, which the by-laws declare, may, after payment of expenses, be 'used to cover losses caused by the delinquencies of members;' and from the guaranty fund of one hundred thousand dollars, established by the corporation under its charter. This is not the less a contract of mutual insurance upon the life of the assured because the amount to be paid by the corporation is not a gross sum, but a sum graduated by the number of members holding similar contracts; nor because a portion of the premiums is to be paid upon the uncertain periods of the deaths of such members; nor because, in case of non-payment of assessments by any member, the contract provides no means of enforcing payment thereof, but merely declares the contract to be at an end, and all moneys previously paid by the assured, and all dividends and credits accrued to him, to be forfeited to the company. The fact offered to be proved by the defendant, that the object of the organization was benevolent and not speculative, has no bearing upon the nature and effect of the business conducted and the contracts made by the corporation." This definition and application have been generally cited with approval by the courts of other States which have practically without exception, held that the contracts of benefit societies whether the agreed sum is to be paid upon the sickness or disability of the member to him in person, or upon his death to his designated beneficiary, is one having all the characteristics of an insurance contract.[200] In an action brought to recover the benefit promised by a benefit society on the death of a member, the Supreme Court of Alabama said:[201] "The instrument in writing upon which this suit is founded, and which is set out in full in the complaint entitled a 'Knight's Benefit Certificate,' has the elements and characteristics of a contract of life insurance. It purports to have been issued by the Supreme Commandery of the Knights of the Golden Rule, which is averred to be a corporation, created and organized under a law of the State of Kentucky. The commandery thereby promises on the death of the husband of the appellee to pay her two thousand dollars, in consideration of the husband having become a member of the order, and having paid the fee for admission to membership and of his payment in the future of

---

[200] Endowment & Ben. Ass'n v. State, 35 Kan. 253; State v. Merchants' Exchange, etc., 72 Mo. 146; Bolton v. Bolton, 73 Me. 299; Folmers' Appeal, 87 Pa. St. 133; State v. Bankers', etc., 23 Kan. 499; Minor v. Mich. Mut. B. Assur., 63 Mich. 338; 29 N. W. 852; State v. Farmers' & Mech., etc., Ass'n, 18 Neb. 276; Supreme Commandery, etc., v. Ainsworth, 71 Ala. 443; Chartrand v. Brace, 16 Colo. 19; 26 Pac. 152; Supreme Council A. L. H. v. Larmour, 81 Tex. 71; 16 S. W. 633; Littleton v. Lain, 126 Tenn. 461; 150 S. W. 423; 41 L. R. A. (N. S.) 1118; *ante*, § 50, *et seq.*

[201] Supreme Commandery, etc., v. Ainsworth, 71 Ala. 443.

all assessments levied and required by the supreme commandery, upon the condition that he remained a member of the order, in good standing, and complied with all the laws then in force or subsequently enacted. These are the essential elements of a contract of life insurance, made by a mutual insurance company with one of its members. Life is the risk and death is the event upon which the insurance money is payable. There is not, as in ordinary contracts or policies, a stipulation for the payment of premiums fixed and certain in amount, at the inception of the risk, and at periods definitely appointed, during its continuance. The payment of the fee for admission to membership and of the assessments levied and required by the commandery, are the equivalent of premiums, and form the pecuniary consideration of the contract. The condition expressed, that the assured shall remain a member of the order in good standing, observing its laws, is the expression of that which is implied in all insurance of members by mutual companies. Where a purchaser is induced to buy a newspaper, or make a subscription, because of the offer to pay a certain sum of money on the happening of a certain contingency contained in such issue, all the elements of a contract of insurance are present.[202] And a contract, by the terms of which certain notes are to be given and those remaining unpaid at the death of the maker are to be canceled by such death, is one of insurance.[203] The members of such companies are presumed to know the charter and by-laws, and to contract in reference to them though they may not be recited or referred to in the contract.[204] Where the proprietors of a medical preparation agreed to pay a specified sum to any one who should contract influenza after using the remedy for a certain period and on the faith of this promise a person bought some but afterwards fell ill of the influenza, the court held, in an action by such person to recover the promised amount, that the contract was neither a wager nor a policy of

[202] Commonwealth v. Phila. Inquirer, 15 Pa. Co. Ct. 463.

[203] M. K. & T. Trust Co. v. Krumseig, 23 C. C. A. 1; 77 Fed. 23; affd. 172 U. S. 351; M. K. & T. Trust Co. v. McLachlan, 59 Minn. 468; 61 N. W. 560.

[204] Holland v. Taylor, 111 Ind. 121; 12 N. E. 116; Farmer v. State, 69 Tex. 561; 7 S. W. 220.

insurance.[205]   An association which contracts with its members, in consideration of a specified annual sum, to repair bicycles in case of accident and to replace those destroyed by accident or stolen, but not to pay any money, is not an insurance company.[206] An organization which agrees for a consideration to defend actions for damages is conducting an insurance business.[207]   A contract binding an undertaker to furnish a respectable funeral is one of insurance.[208]

§ 214.   **Benefit Societies Restricted As to Beneficiaries.**—Benefit societies differ from other mutual insurance organizations in that their charters generally impose restrictions upon the issue of certificates by limiting the persons who may be beneficiaries of the members to those who are heirs, relatives or dependents of such members.   Wherever these restrictions are imposed by statute, or contained in the charter of the society, it has no power to pass beyond them by issuing a certificate in which any one other than of the specified classes is beneficiary.   The Court of Appeals of Kentucky early established this doctrine when it said:[209] ''the charter prescribes who may become members of the company and their obligations, and who shall be the beneficiaries of the membership after the death of the member, and it is not in the power of the company or of the member, or of both, to alter the rights of those who by the charter are declared to be the beneficiaries, except in the mode and to the extent therein indicated.''   This rule was approved by the Supreme Court of Massachusetts,[210] which says: ''The statute under which the plaintiff corporation is organized gives it authority to provide for the widow, orphans, or other persons dependent upon deceased members, and further

[205] Carbill v. Carbolic Smoke Ball Co., 2 Q. B. 484.
[206] Commonwealth v. Provident Bicycle Ass'n, 178 Pa. St. 636; 36 Atl. 197; 36 L. R. A. 589.
[207] Physicians' Defense Co. v. O'Brien, 100 Minn. 490; 111 N. W. 396. In Illinois the contrary has been held, Vredenburgh v. Physicians' Defense Co., 126 Ill. App. 509.
[208] Renschler v. State, 90 Ohio St. 363; 107 N. E. 758; Ann. Cas. 1916 C 1014; State v. Globe Casket Co., 82 Wash. 124; 143 Pac. 878; L. R. A. 1915 B 976. -
[209] Kentucky Masonic, etc., Ins. Co. v. Miller's Admr., 13 Bush. 489.
[210] Amercian Legion of Honor v. Perry, 140 Mass. 589.

provides that such fund shall not be liable to attachment.   The classes of persons to be benefited are designated and the corporation has no authority to create a fund for other persons than of the classes named.   The corporation has power to raise a fund payable to one of the classes named in the statute, to set it apart to await the death of the member, and then to pay it over to the person or persons of the class named in the statute, selected and appointed by the member during his life, and if no one is selected, it is still payable to one of the classes named. . . . If the fund were subject to testamentary bequest, then, upon the decease of the member, it might go into the hands of the executor, or the administrator of his estate, and become assets thereof liable to be swallowed up by the creditors.   If there were no creditors, the member by his will could divert it from the three classes named in the statute.   In either case this would defeat the purpose for which the fund was raised and held, and would be in direct conflict with the object of the statute for which the association was formed, and would set aside the contract entered into between the member and the corporation.''   And the principle thus established has been generally approved and followed.[211]   Under the Massachusetts statute, relating to insurance on the assessment plan and defining it as ''a contract whereby a benefit is to accrue to a party or parties named therein upon the death of a person, which benefit is in any way conditioned upon persons holding similar contracts,'' a member can hold a certificate payable to himself and on his death it forms part of his estate in the absence of anything showing an intention to make his heirs the beneficiaries.[212]   If, however, no restrictions are imposed by charter or statute the society may constitute any one the beneficiary of the member.[213]

[211] Elsey v. Odd Fellows', etc., Ass'n, 142 Mass. 224; Presbyterian, etc., Fund v. Allen, 106 Ind. 593; National, etc., Ass'n v. Gonser, 43 Ohio St. 1; Ben. Soc. v. Dugre, 11 R. L. (Queb.) 344; State v. People's M. Ben. Ass'n, 42 Ohio St. 579; Knights of Honor v. Nairn, 60 Mich. 44; 26 N. W. 826; Leonard v. American Ins. Co., 97 Ind. 305; post, §§ 244, 245.

[212] Harding v. Littledale, 150 Mass. 100; 22 N. E. 703.

[213] Massey et al. v. Mut. Relief, etc., Soc., 102 N. Y. 523; Mitchell v. Grand Lodge, etc., 70 Ia. 360; 30 N. W. 865; Swift v. Railway, etc., Ass'n, 96 Ill. 309; post, § 323.

§ 215.   Liberality of Construction of Charter By Some Courts.

—In some cases the courts have not been disposed to adhere strictly to the letter of the constitution or charter, as where the Supreme Court of Pennsylvania said, in a case where the benefit was made payable to a creditor of the member:[214] "The learned court below was of opinion that there was a fatal conflict between the charter and the constitution in respect of the persons who may receive benefits from the defendant company, and for that reason alone refused judgment to the plaintiff. The second section of the charter upon which this conclusion is based is in the following words: 'The purposes of this corporation shall be the maintenance of a society for the purpose of benefiting and aiding the widows and orphans of deceased members.' Construing these words the learned Court below held that it was not within the power of the defendant to stipulate for the payment of the benefits to any person other than the widow and orphans, who might be designated as the recipient by the deceased under article 19 of the constitution. We think this is too narrow and strained a view to take of the second section of the charter quoted above. While it is true that the general purpose of the corporation is there stated to be the maintenance of a society for benefiting and aiding widows and orphans of deceased members, it must be observed that this is only the statement of a general purpose. It is only the recital of an object sought to be accomplished and which doubtless is accomplished in the great majority of cases, even though in exceptional cases the benefits may, by special contract, be paid to other persons than the widow or orphans."[215] This decision carries to its extreme limits the doctrine that the laws of benevolent societies must be construed liberally to carry out the kindly objects of their creation,[216] but this construction has not evi-

<hr />

[214] Maneely v. Knights of Birmingham, 115 Pa. St. 305; 9 Atl. 41.

[215] Supplee v. Knights of Birmingham, 18 W. N. C. 280; and as to a creditor obtaining an equitable right see Binkley v. Jarvis, 102 Ill. App. 59.   The subject is also considered *post*, § 245.

[216] Supreme Lodge K. of P. v. Schmide, 98 Ind. 381; Ballou v. Gile, 50 Wis. 614; Erdman v. Ins. Co., 44 Wis. 376; Covenant Mut. B. Ass'n v. Sears, 114 Ill. 108; American Legion of Honor v. Perry, 140 Mass. 580.

dently been received with favor in other courts where a stricter rule has been laid down.[217]

§ 216. **Where Contract Is Executed Society May Be Estopped.** —If, however, a contract with a member has become executed by the death of such member it has been held that, although the beneficiary was not of one of the prescribed classes that fact cannot be set up to defeat the claim.[218] The general rule has been well stated by Seymour D. Thompson[219] as follows: "The great mass of judicial authority seems to be to the effect that where a private corporation has entered into a contract in excess of its granted powers and has received the fruits or benefits of the contract and an action is brought against it to enforce the obligation on its part, it is estopped from setting up the defense that it has no power to make it."[220] A contract may be void only in part.[221] The subject of *ultra vires* will be considered later.[222]

§ 217. **Contracts of Mutual Companies Where a By-Law Has Been Violated.**—It is an important consideration where some requirement of the by-laws of a mutual organization, like a benefit society, has been disregarded in the contract, to what extent the validity of the contract is affected. The question has arisen in actions against mutual fire insurance companies where the provisions of the by-laws have been violated, as for example in regard to subsequent insurance, incumbrances on the property and classification of risks. The Supreme Court of Massachusetts has distinguished mutual from stock companies in this respect on the ground that members of mutual organizations are bound to know their laws, which were intended to regulate and fix by the same stipulations in every policy, the rights of all the assured alike, and the officers being special agents with powers limited and de-

[217] *Post*, § 319.

[218] Bloomington Mut., etc., Ass'n v. Blue, 120 Ill. 127; Lamont v. Grand Lodge, etc., 31 Fed. 177; *post*, § 342. But see Mut. Ben. Ass'n v. Hoyt, 46 Mich. 473. See *post*, § 314 as to Resulting Trust.

[219] 10 Cyc. 1156.

[220] See Knott v. Security Mut. Life Ins. Co., 161 Mo. App. 579, 144 S. W. 178.

[221] Wheeler v. Mut. Res. F. L. Ass'n, 102 Ill. App. 48.

[222] *Post*, § 342.

fined by these laws, cannot virtually suspend them when matters touching the substance or essence of the contract are involved. This doctrine has been followed in a large number of cases[223] But other authorities hold that not only is a distinction to be made between matters which go to the substance and those which affect the form of the contract, but also between those that are mandatory, and others which are only directory requirements. In a case in New Hampshire, where the charter vested all powers relating to contracts in the directors and directed them to divide property insured into classes, and after by-laws had been made establishing a rule for the division of risks, the directors knowingly insured property in one class which properly fell in another, the Supreme Court of that State said.[224] ''The by-law cannot be regarded as a limitation and restriction of a power which is lodged by the charter in the directors. It can have no higher effect than instructions, or a general regulation, adopted by the directors themselves, as a convenient guide in ordinary cases. The action of the directors is, in this case, the action of the corporation; the corporation could act on this subject in no other way than through the directors, and, as a general rule, mutual fire insurance companies have power to waive provisions of their by-laws which have been introduced for the benefit and protection of the company. In this case the action of the directors may have been irregular, contrary to the established usage and in violation of their own rules, and of the by-laws; but it was still within the scope of their authority, expressly conferred on them by the charter and therefore binding on the company.''[225] Two principles seem to govern where the requirements of the by-laws of a corporation have not been observed in making a contract; the

223 Brewer v. Chelsea, etc., Ins. Co, 14 Gray. 209; Evans v. Tri-Mountain Ins. Co., 9 Allen 329; Hale v. Mechanics', etc., Ins. Co., 6 Gray. 169; 66 Am. Dec. 410; Leonard v. Am. Ins. Co, 97 Ind. 305; Behler v. German, etc., Ins. Co., 68 Ind. 354; Westchester F. Ins. Co. v. Earle, 33 Mich. 150; Lyon v. Supreme Assembly, etc., 153 Mass. 83; 26 N. E. 236; State v. Temperance Ben. Ass'n, 42 M. A. 485; Hysinger v. Supreme Lodge K. & L. of H., 42 M. A. 628. Also see *ante*, § 191, *post*, § 342.

224 Union Mut. F. Ins. Co. v. Keyser, 32 N. H. 313; 64 Am. Dec. 377.

225 Fuller v. Boston, etc., Ins. Co., 4 Metc. 207; Williams v. N. E. Mut., etc., Ins. Co., 31 Me. 227; Cumberland Valley, etc., Co. v. Schell, 29 Pa. St. 37.

first is that where an act had been done within the apparent scope
of the authority of an agent the principal will not be heard to
say that specific instructions have been violated, unless knowledge
be brought home to the party.[226]   The second principle is that
where provisions in the by-laws of a corporation are for the benefit of the company they can be waived.[227]   To this may be added
the further doctrine that after a contract has been executed by
the other side a corporation will generally not be allowed to deny
its power to make such a contract or to contract by such an
agent.[228]

§ 218.   **Interpretation of Contracts of Insurance.**—Contracts
of insurance have no particular sanctity over other kinds of
agreements, and the same rules of interpretation apply to all
alike.[229]   As a matter of course statutes prescribing the requisites of insurance policies must be read with the policy in construing its terms.[230]   It was said in the early days that insurance
contracts required the utmost good faith, because the facts were
of necessity less known to one party than to the other, but this
may be said of many different agreements, and modern decisions
have inclined to greater liberality to the insured than to the insurer.   And it is now a general rule that a polcy of insurance will
be liberally construed in favor of the insured.[231]   As in the case

[226] Emery v. Boston Marine Ins. Co., 138 Mass. 410; Ins. Co. v. Wilkinson, 13 Wall. 222; Davenport v. Peoria, etc.; Ins. Co, 17 Ia. 276; New
England, etc., Ins. Co. v. Schettler, 38 Ill. 166.

[227] Cumberland Valley, etc., Ins. Co. v. Schell, 29 Pa. St. 31; Prince of
Wales, etc., Co. v. Harding, 1 E. B. & E. 183; Sheldon v. Conn. Mut. L.
Ins. Co., 25 Conn. 221; Splawn v. Chew, 60 Tex. 532; Manning v. Ancient
Order United Workmen, 84 Ky. 136; 5 S. W. 385; Sanborn v. Ins. Co.,
16 Gray. 448; 77 Am. Dec. 419.   But see *post*, § 406.

[228] New England, etc., Ins. Co. v. Schettler, 38 Ill. 166; Bloomington,
etc., Ass'n v. Blue, 120 Ill. 127; Lamont v. Grand Lodge, etc., 31 Fed.
177; Fuller v. Boston, etc., Ins. Co., 4 Metc. 206.

[229] Supreme Commandery, etc., v. Ainsworth, 71 Ala. 448.

[230] Archer v. Equitable Life Assur. Soc., 218 N. Y. 18, 112 N. E. 433.

[231] Mut. Ben. L. Ins. Co. v. Dunn, 106 Ky. 591; 51 S. W. 20; McMaster
v. New York Life Ins. Co., 183 U. S. 25, reversing 40 C. C. A. 119; 99 Fed.
856; Kendrick v. Mut. Ben. L. Ins. Co., 124 N. C. 315; 32 S. E. 728; Provident Life, etc., v. Cannon, 103 Ill. App. 531; affd. 201 Ill. 260; 66 N. E.
388; Behling v. N. W. Nat. L., 117 Wis. 24; 93 N. W. 800.

of statutes the principal consideration is the intent, so in contracts of insurance the courts endeavor to ascertain what the parties intended by their contract,[232] and this is, first of all, to be sought by taking the words in which the agreement is expressed in their ordinary meaning, only resorting to other rules where there is ambiguity or doubt. The construction must be reasonable; as was said by Judge Nelson, in a case[233] where the contract provided that in case of a loss that a certificate should be given by the nearest magistrate and the contention of the company was that this had not been done: "This clause of the contract is to receive a reasonable interpretation; its intent and substance, as derived from language used, should be regarded. There is no more reason for claiming a strict literal compliance with its terms than in ordinary contracts. Full legal effect should always be given to it, for the purpose of guarding the company against fraud or imposition. Beyond this one would be sacrificing substance to form—following words rather than ideas." To the same purpose the Supreme Court of Illinois has said [234] "The question here, as in other cases of contract, is to arrive at the intention of the parties, and we are not authorized, in striving to do so, to construe words otherwise than as conveying their plain, natural and obvious meaning, unless from a consideration of the entire evidence, it shall appear, this could not have been intended."[235] The Supreme Court of Missouri has also said:[236] "The construction of the language of the policy is to be determined, as in other contracts, by usage and common acceptation; and the stipulations, though being of a character of warranties and condition, are to be reasonably construed with reference to the whole subject-matter, and not captiously or literally."[237] The

[232] Goodrich v. Treat, 3 Colo. 408; Foot v. Aetna Life Ins. Co., 61 N. Y. 571; Travelers' Ins. Co. v. Myers, 62 Ohio St. 529; 57 N. E. 458; 49 L. R. A. 760.

[233] Turley v. North Am. Ins. Co., 25 Wend. 377.

[234] Royal Templars, etc., v. Curd, 111 Ill. 288.

[235] Peoria, etc., Ins. Co. v. Whitehill, 25 Ill. 466.

[236] Tesson v. Atlantic M. Ins. Co., 40 Mo. 33; 93 Am. Dec. 296.

[237] St. John v. American Mut. Life Ins. Co., 13 N. Y. 31; 64 Am. Dec. 529; Ins. Co. v. Slaughter, 12 Wall. 404; Mark v. Aetna Ins. Co., 29 Ind. 390; May on Ins., § 172.

modern decisions simply reiterate in substance the words of Lord Ellenborough :[238] "In the course of the argument it seems to have been -assumed that some peculiar rules of construction apply to the terms of a policy of assurance which are not equally applicable to the terms of other instruments and in all other cases; it is therefore proper to state upon this head, that the same rule of construction which applies to all other instruments applies equally to this instrument of a policy of insurance, viz., that it is to be construed according to its sense and meaning, as collected in the first place from the terms used in it, which terms are themselves to be understood in their plain, ordinary and popular sense, unless they have generally, in respect to the subject-matter, as by the known usage of trade, or the like, acquired a peculiar sense distinct from the popular sense of the same words ; or unless the context evidently points out that they must in the particular instance, and in order to effectuate the immediate intention of the parties to that contract, be understood in some other special and peculiar sense. The only difference between policies of assurance, and other instruments in this respect is, that the greater part of the printed language of them, being invariable and uniform, has acquired from use and practice a known and definite meaning, and that the words superadded in writing (subject, indeed, always to be governed in point of construction by the language and terms with which they are accompanied) are entitled nevertheless, if there should be any reasonable doubt upon the sense and meaning of the whole, to have a greater effect attributed to them than to the printed words, inasmuch as the written words are the immediate language and terms selected by the parties themselves for the expression of their meaning, and the printed words are a general formula adapted equally to their case and that of all other contracting parties upon similar occasions and subjects."[239] Contemporaneous literature may be looked to for explanation of terms used in a contract when otherwise not to be understood.[240] Where the policy referred to a schedule as for the

[238] Robertson v. French, 4 East. 135.
[239] Colt v. Commercial Ins. Co., 7 Johns. 385.
[240] Fuller v. Metropolitan L. Ins. Co., 37 Fed. 163. For peculiar contracts see McIntyre v. Cotton States L. Ins. Co., 82 Ga. 478; 9 S. E. C. 1124; and Palmer v. Commercial Travelers' Acc. Ins. Ass'n, 53 Hun. 601;

amount to be paid, and underneath this schedule was printed a condition that the company should not be liable if the death of the insured occurred within ninety days from the issue of the policy, it was held[241] that this clause was not repugnant to the main body of the policy. Violation of the statutes of a State as to rebates will not make a policy void unless the statute so declares.[242]

§ 219. **Examples of Construction.**—The application and policy together, if the latter refers to the former, form the contract and the policy may contain conditions not found in the application. The application includes the medical examination.[243] A provision in the policy prevails over that of the application.[244] Contracts of insurance are to be construed according to the meaning of the terms which the parties use. A rule of construction as to liability in favor of the insured is only invoked to resolve uncertainties or ambiguity.[245] The construction of a contract will be so far as possible to carry out the intent of the parties.[246] A policy of assessment life insurance company is testamentary in its character,[247] and the character of a life policy is determin-

6 N. Y. Supp. 870. In the first case a clause relating to interest on loans is construed, in the latter the certificate and not the resolution of the directors accepting the proposal was held to contain the contract.

[241] Bruton v. Metropolitan L. Ins., 48 Hun. 204.

[242] Meridian Life Ins. Co. v. Dean, 182 Ala. 127; 62 Sou. 90, 94.

[243] Paquette v. Prudential Ins. Co., 193 Mass. 215; 79 N. E. 250; Langdeau v. John Hancock Mut. Life Ins. Co., 194 Mass. 56; 80 N. E. 452.

[244] Burt v. Burt, 218 Pa. 198; 67 Atl. 210; Harr v. Highland Nobles, 78 Neb. 175; 110 N. W. 713; Courtney v. Fidelity Mut. Aid Ass'n, 120 Mo. App. 110; 94 S. W. 768; 101 S. W. 1098; Logan v. Provident Savings Life Assur. Soc., 57 W. Va. 384; 50 S. E. 529; Hudson v. Jenson, 110 Wis. 26; 85 N. W. 689.

[245] Standard Life & Accident Ins. Co. v. McNulty, 157 Fed. 224; Arnold v. Mut. Annuity, etc., Co., 3 Ga. App. 685; Furry v. General Accident Ins. Co., 80 Vt. 526; 68 Atl. 655.

[246] Goff v. Supreme Council Royal Achates, 90 Neb. 578; 134 N. W. 239; Supreme Lodge Fraternal Brotherhood v. Jones (Tex. Civ. App.), 143 S. W. 247; Binder v. Royal Masonic Accident Ass'n, 127 Ia. 25; 102 N. W. 190.

[247] Hall v. Ayer's Guardian, 32 Ky. L. 288; 105 S. W. 911.

able by the nature of the contract.[248] An insurance policy taken out in exchange for a former policy is the same contract.[249] A second policy issued in lieu of the former will relate back to the issue of the first policy because of an endorsement in the margin as to original date and age.[250] The rule is otherwise where a second policy is issued after the expiration of the first.[251] A policy may be dated back and the beneficiary is bound by the contract.[252] And an agreement that the amount of the benefit should be reduced and the assessment based on the real age of the member, is valid though no new certificate was issued,[253] and so is a stipulation that no obligation is assumed by the insurer unless on the date of the policy the insured is in sound health,[254] and so is a provision for reduction of a benefit if the insured dies during the first year.[255] Though a life policy provides that it should be construed according to the laws of New York, if no evidence of such laws has been introduced the provision will be disregarded.[256]

Where a renewal receipt for an accident insurance policy acknowledges the receipt of a certain sum as a renewal premium for accident insurance to a specified amount and for a specified weekly indemnity "according to the tenor" of a policy of a certain number, the contract is a new insurance and not merely a renewal of an old one, as it is not one kept on foot by payment of,

[248] Knott v. Security Mut. Life Ins. Co., 161 Mo. App. 579; 144 S. W. 178.

[249] Silliman v. International Life Ins. Co. (Tenn.), 174 S. W. 1131; Grant v. Independent Order, etc., 97 Miss. 182; 52 Sou. 698.

[250] State National Bank v. U. S. Life Ins. Co., 238 Ill. 148; 87 N. E. 396; affg. 142 Ill. App. 624.

[251] Gans v. Aetna Life Ins. Co., 214 N. Y. 326; 108 N. E. 443; affg. 146 N. Y. Supp. 453; 161 App. Div. 250.

[252] New York Life Ins. Co. v. Franklin, 118 Va. 418; 87 S. E. 584.

[253] Reiter v. National Council K. & L. of S., 131 Minn. 82; 154 N. W. 665.

[254] Stephens v. Metropolitan Life Ins. Co., 190 Mo. App. 674; 176 S. W. 253.

[255] Watkins v. Brotherhood of American Yeomen, 188 Mo. App. 626; 176 S. W. 516. For construction of policy providing both for endowment payment and payment at death, see Breard v. New York Life Ins. Co., 138 La. 774; 70 Sou. 799.

[256] New York Life Ins. Co. v. Smith, 139 Ala. 303; 35 Sou. 1004.

or by the performance of conditions with which the insured may comply without the consent of the insurer, and by reference it imports the policy and all contained therein so that the policy and the receipt together constitute the insurance contract.[257] A life policy to which was attached a sheet of paper containing estimates of results at end of tontine period are to be construed together and both make up the contract.[258] That a construction of a policy would involve hardship, or absurdity, or contradict its general purpose, is strong evidence that such a construction was not intended by the parties where it was open to a reasonable construction consonant with their general purpose.[259] Under the laws of New York a mutual insurance company may create a reserve fund in the nature of a trust immune against creditors.[260] Where insured exercised his option of exchanging a renewable term policy for an ordinary life policy, the second is not mere continuation of the first but a new contract,[261] Industrial life policies will be treated by the courts as highly benevolent and they will not be construed as intending to provide a fund for the benefit of creditors unless that is distinctly set out in the policy itself and consequently where such a policy was payable to the estate of the insured, parol evidence is admissible that the agent of the insurer at the time he procured the application informed the insured that the policy would be paid to her only child and such child is entitled to recover on the policy.[262]

§ 220. **Interpretation of Contracts of Benefit Societies.**—In the case of benefit societies the contract must be construed liberally in order to carry out the benevolent object of the creation of

[257] Youlden v. London Guarantee & Acc. Co., 28 Ont. L. Rep. 161, Ann. Cas. 1914 B 654. See also Jenkins v. Covenant Mut. Life Ins. Co., 171 Mo. 375; 71 S. W. 688; McGeehan v. Mut. Life Ins. Co., 131 Mo. App. 417; 111 S. W. 604; Sheets v. Iowa State Ins. Co., 153 Mo. App. 620; 135 S. W. 80.

[258] Timlin v. Equitable Life Assur. Soc., 141 Wis. 276; 124 M. W. 253.

[259] Anderson v. Aetna Life Ins. Co., 75 N. H. 375; 75 Atl. 1051.

[260] Robinson v. Mut. Reserve Life Ins. Co., 189 Fed. 347; affg. 175 Fed. 624; 182 Fed. 850.

[261] Gans v. Aetna Life Ins. Co., 146 N. Y. Supp. 453; 161 App. Div. 250.

[262] Renfro v. Metropolitan Life Ins. Co., 148 Mo. App. 258; 129 S. W. 444.

these organizations. It is to be construed with reference to the statutes of the place of its organization, and it will never be presumed that the society intended to violate the law; but, whenever a by-law seems to go beyond the statute restrictions, such meaning will be given to it, if possible, as will make the two consistent, and generally the courts have manifested a liberality to these institutions and have looked upon them with favor.[263]

The same rules generally apply to the construction of the contracts of benefit societies as to those of the regular life insurance companies. It is often questioned whether the society is entitled to be called a fraternal beneficiary society. In case of Westerman v. Supreme Lodge K. P.[264] it was held that where a society was organized for fraternal purposes with a lodge system, issuing death benefit certificates to those of its members desiring and those to whom the certificates are issued constituting what is known as the endowment rank, the certificates are to be regarded as those of a fraternal beneficiary association. Where the statutes of the State of the domicile are different from those of the State in which the contract is issued, the statutes of the State where the contract is made govern for the purpose of determining the character of the association.[265] A fraternal beneficiary society cannot blend the business of a stock insurance company with that of a beneficial society under the laws of Maryland.[266] Under the laws of Virginia a society issuing a certificate providing for the payment of a specified sum in case of death and the members paying fixed sums at fixed intervals, is not a fraternal beneficiary

[263] Elsey v. Odd Fellows', etc., Ass'n, 142 Mass. 224; American Legion of Honor v. Perry, 140 Mass. 580; Ballou v. Gile, 50 Wis. 614; Supreme Lodge, etc., v. Schmidt, 98 Ind. 374; Erdmann v. Ins. Co., 44 Wis. 376; Covenant Mut. B. A. v. Sears, 114 Ill. 108; Maneely v. Knights of Birmingham, 115 Pa. St. 305 (March, 1887); 9 Atl. 41; Splawn v. Chew, 60 Tex. 532; American Order Protection v. Stanley, 5 Neb. Unoff. 132; 97 N. W. 467; Golden Star Fraternity v. Martin, 59 N. J. L. 207; 35 Atl. 908; Brock v. Brotherhood, etc. (Vt.), 54 Atl. 176; *post*, § 324.

[264] 196 Mo. 670; 94 S. W. 470; 5 L. R. A. (N. S.) 1113.

[265] Herzberg v. Modern Brotherhood, 110 Mo. App. 828; 85 S. W. 986; Loyd v. M. W. A., 113 Mo. App. 19; 87 S. W. 530.

[266] International Fraternal Alliance v. State, 86 Md. 550; 39 Atl. 512; 40 L. R. A. 187.

society.[267] The fact that in most States fraternal beneficiary societies are exempt from the insurance laws often has a material bearing upon the construction of the contracts of the society.[268] The construction of the by-laws and the benefit certificates issued by a fraternal beneficiary association will be liberal,[269] and the courts may look to the home State of a foreign association for the effect to be given to its contracts.[270] The construction of the charter of a fraternal beneficiary society by the highest court of the domicile of the corporation is binding, on the members of the order outside of the State of the domicile and courts of other States under the Constitution of the United States are bound to give full faith and credit to the judgments of such courts of the domicile.[271] A mutual benefit certificate providing for benefits upon either death or disability upon the same consideration is not a severable contract.[272] In case of conflict between the terms of the certificate and the statutes of the State, the statutory regulations prevail and amount to an amendment of the original charter.[273]

§ 221. **Construction When Language Is Ambiguous.**—It is also a rule of construction that where the language used is ambiguous or inaccurate and susceptible of two interpretations, it shall be construed most favorably to the promisee in the obligation. The Court of Appeals of New York has stated this general principle very clearly in a case where the insurance com-

[267] Continental Life Ass'n v. Koegel, 104 Va. 619; 52 S. E. 166.

[268] Knapp v. Brotherhood of American Yeoman, 128 Ia. 566; 105 N. W. 63; Sovereign Camp Woodmen of the World v. Carrington, 41 Tex. Civ. App. 29; 90 S. W. 921; Supreme Lodge U. B. A. v. Johnson, 98 Tex. 1; 81 S. W. 18; reversing 77 S. W. 661.

[269] Modern Woodmen of America v. Vincent, 40 Ind. App. 711; 82 N. E. 475; Grand Lodge A. O. U. W. v. Smith, 76 Kan. 509; 92 Pac. 710; Gilroy v. Supreme Court I. O. F., 75 N. J. Eq. 584; 67 Atl. 1037; Morgan v. Independent Order, etc., 90 Miss. 864; 40 Sou. 791; Bange v. Supreme Council L. of H., 128 Mo. App. 461.

[270] Valleroy v. Knights of Columbus, 135 Mo. App. 574; 116 S. W. 1130.

[271] Supreme Council R. A. v. Green, 237 U. S. 537; reversing 100 N. E. 411; 206 N. Y. 591; 129 N. Y. Supp. 791; 144 App. Div. 761.

[272] Indiana Life Endowment Co. v. Carnithan (Ind. App.), 109 N. E. 851.

[273] Finnell v. Franklin, 55 Colo. 156; 134 Pac. 122.

pany contended, that by one partner in a firm selling out to
the others the condition in the policy, that if the property assured should be sold or conveyed, then the policy should be void,
had happened. In that case the court, in deciding in favor of
the assured, held as follows :[274] "The design of the provision
was, not to interdict all sales, but only sales of proprietary interests by parties insured to parties not insured. If the words were
taken literally, a renewal of the policy would be required at the
close of each day's sales. Indeterminate forms of expression, in
such a case, are to be understood in a sense subservient to the
general purposes of the contract. It is true that the language
of the proviso against sales, was not guarded by a special exclusion of changes of interest as between the assured, or of the
sales of merchandise in the usual course of their business, but
this was for the obvious reason that there was nothing in the
tenor of the instrument to denote, that the application of the
clause to such a case was within the contemplation of the underwriters. 'The matter in hand is always presumed to be in the
mind and thoughts of the speaker, though his words seem to
admit a larger sense; and therefore the generality of the words
used shall be restrained by the particular occasion.'[275] Thus, in
an action on a life policy, containing a proviso that it should be
void 'in case the assured should die by his own hands,' it was
held by this court, that though in terms it embraced all cases of
suicide, it could not properly be applied to self-destruction by a
lunatic, as there was no reason to .suppose that such a case was
within the purpose of the clause or the contemplation of the
parties.[276] 'All words,' says Lord Bacon, 'whether they be in
deeds or statutes, or otherwise, if they be general, and not express and precise, shall be restrained unto the fitness of the matter and the person.[277] Reading the proviso as it was read by the
parties, it is easy to discern the purpose of its insertion. It was
to protect the company from a continuing obligation to the assured, if the title and beneficial interest should pass to others,

274 Hoffman v. Aetna Fire Ins. Co., 32 N. Y. 412.
275 Powell on Cont. 389; Van Hagen v. Van Rensselaer, 18 Johns. 423.
276 Breasted v. Farmers' Loan and Trust Co., 4 Seld. 299.
277 Bacon's Law Maxims, Reg. 10.

whom they might not be equally willing to trust. Words should not be taken in their broadest import, when they are equally appropriate in a sense limited to the object the parties had in view. The terms of the policy were not such as would naturally suggest even a query in the minds of the assured, whether a transfer of interest as between themselves would work a forfeiture of the insurance, and relieve the company from its promise to indemnify both—the buyer as well as the seller—the premium being paid in advance, and the risk remaining unchanged. One of two joint payees of a non-negotiable note would hardly be more surprised to be met with a claim, that by buying the interest of his associate he had extinguished the obligation of the maker to both. It is a rule of law as well as of ethics, that where the language of a promisor may be understood in more senses than one, it is to be interpreted in the sense in which he had reason to suppose it was understood by the promisee.[278] It is also a familiar rule of law, that if it be left in doubt, in view of the general tenor of the instrument and the relations of the contracting parties, whether given words were used in an enlarged or restricted sense, other things being equal, that construction should be adopted which is most beneficial to the promisee.[279] This rule has been very uniformly applied to conditions and provisos in policies of insurance, on the ground that though they are inserted for the benefit of the underwriters, their office is to limit the force of the principal obligation.[280] In the case first cited[281] the action was for a marine loss, and one of the issues was, whether a recovery was barred by the entry of a ship into a blockaded port, such ports being excepted by the policy. The court held, that though the case was within the terms, it was not within the intent of the exception; and that as the risk contemplated in the clause was merely that of capture, the rule of liberal construction must be applied in favor of the promisee. The reason assigned by Chief Justice Marshall was

[278] Potter v. Ontario Ins. Co., 5 Hill. 149; Barlow v. Scott, 34 N. Y. 40.
[279] Co. Litt. 183; Bacon's Law Maxims, Reg. 3; Doe v. Dixon, 9 East. 16; Marvin v. Stone, 2 Cow. 806.
[280] Yeaton v. Fry, 5 Cranch. 341; Palmer v. Warren Ins. Co., 1 Story 364; Pelly v. Royal Exchange Ins. Co., 1 Bur. 349.
[281] Yeaton v. Fry, 5 Cranch. 341.

that 'the words are the words of the insurer, not of the insured; and they take a particular risk out of the policy, which but for the exception would be comprehended in the contract.' ''[282] Contracts of insurance, because they have indemnity for their object, are to be construed liberally so as to give them effect if possible.[283] If the policy contains two provisions, one favorable to the assured and one unfavorable, they being inconsistent and contradictory, that provision most favorable to the assured will be accepted and the other disregarded.[284] Only a stern legal necessity will induce such a construction as will nullify the contract.[285] The rule that an insurance contract shall be construed most strongly against the insurer, can only be resorted to when, after using such helps as are proper to arrive at the intent of the parties, some of the language used, or some phrase inserted in the policy, is of doubtful import, in which case the rule should be applied because the insurer wrote the contract.[286]

§ 222. Contracts of Mutual and Stock Companies Construed Alike.—No distinction is made, as regards construction, between the policies of mutual and those of other companies. The fact that the policy is one of a mutual company cannot modify the construction which is to be given to the terms of the contract. While the relations of the parties are always to be considered in seeking the true interpretation of their language, their words used for a definite purpose and applied to a transaction of well understood character, must be held to convey the meaning and

[282] Merrick v. Germania Fire Ins. Co., 54 Pa. St. 277; Atlantic Ins. Co. v. Manning, 3 Colo. 226; Allen v. St. Louis, etc., Ins. Co., 85 N. Y. 473; Piedmont & Arlington, etc., Ins. Co. v. Young, 58 Ala. 746; Metropolitan L. Ins. Co. v. Drach, 101 Pa. St. 278; Symonds v. Northwestern M. L. Ins. Co., 23 Minn. 491; Niagara F. Ins. Co. v. Scammon, 100 Ill. 644.

[283] State Ins. Co. v. Hughes, 10 Lea. 461; Brink v. Merchants', etc., Ins. Co., 49 Vt. 442; Miller v. Insurance Co., 12 W. Va. 116.

[284] Northwestern M. L. Ins. Co. v. Hazlett, 105 Ind. 212; 55 Am. Rep. 192; Moulor v. American Life Ins. Co., 111 U. S. 335; National Bank v. Insurance Co., 95 U. S. 673; Teutonia F. Ins. Co. v. Mund, 102 Pa. St. 89.

[285] Carson v. Jersey City Ins. Co., 14 Vroom (43 N. J. L.), 300; 39 Am. Rep. 584; Franklin L. Ins. Co. v. Wallace, 93 Ind. 7; Burkhard v. Travelers' Ins. Co., 102 Pa. St. 262; 48 Am. Rep. 205.

[286] Foot v. Aetna Life Ins. Co., 61 N. Y. 585; post, § 468.

force which is ordinarily attached to them. There is no reason why a contract of insurance between a mutual company and its members should be given ány significance different from what would be the fair construction of a similar contract entered into between any parties.[287] The stipulations of a written contract are no less binding in a contract between a corporation and one of its members than in a contract made with a stranger, in each case the rules of construction are the same.[288] On this point it has been said:[289] "These benevolent associations or fraternities, not more than other parties to contracts, cannot be allowed to contrue the words they' use in making agreements otherwise than according to their plain and unambiguous meaning, in the English language they employ, whether of the words of the contract itself or of the rules and regulations which become, by the principle they insist on, embodied in the contract as a part of it. They cannot be permitted to interpret the contract as they please and become their own judges of what they mean by the use of the words employed that have either a technical or a well defined signfication, known of all men who use the language. Legislatures and parliaments cannot do that, and even they are bound by the common meaning of the words they use in their statutes which become part of a contract."

§ 223. **Other Papers Part of Contract, When.**—It is not necessary that a written contract be wholly embrac~d in one document. Other papers may become part of such contracts by either being incorporated or being properly referred to therein. The question is one of intent and the intention is to be found in the contract, and a writing intended to be a part thereof may be incorporated in it by apt reference as well as by extended recital.[290] The principle becomes chiefly important where application has been made in writing for insurance, and the inquiry is whether or not the

287 Cluff v. Mut. Ben. Life Ins. Co., 99 Mass. 325.

288 Willcuts v. Northwestern Mut. Life Ins. Co., 81 Ind. 300.

289 Wiggins v. Knights of Pythias, 31 Fed. 124.

290 Sheldon v. Hartford Fire Ins. Co., 21 Conn. 235; 58 Am. Dec. 420; Anderson v. Fitzgerald, 4 H. of L. Cas. 474; Carson v. Jersey City Ins. Co., 43 N. J. L. 303; Robertson v. French, 4 East. 130; Kelly v. Life Ins. Clearing Co., 113 Ala. 453; 21 Sou. 361.

application, by the terms of the policy, has been made part thereof so that its statements have become warranties. The subject will be further discussed when we come to consider the matters of warranty and representation,[291] and at present it is enough to refer to it in a general way. It is not every reference in a contract to another writing that will make the latter a part of the contract; there must sufficiently appear the intention to unite the two writings and merge them into one by reference or recital. Thus, where an application, by a member of a benefit society for a certificate in the nature of a life insurance policy contained this clause, "I further agree, that should I, at any time, violate my pledge of total abstinence, or be suspended or expelled for a violation of any of the laws of the order, or for non-payment of dues, etc., then all rights which either myself, the person or persons named in the certificate, my heirs, etc., may have upon the beneficiary fund of the order, shall be forfeited," it was held that the application was a part of the contract of insurance, and obligatory upon the beneficiary named in the certificate, to whom payment was promised on the death of the member, and that the language was in the alternative, making either or any one of the causes named, a ground of forfeiture of all right of recovery upon the certificate.[292] So, where a policy of life insurance contained a stipulation that it should be void if a certain declaration made in the application by or for the person whose life was insured, "and upon the faith of which the agreement was made, shall be found in any respect untrue," it was held that such declaration constituted a portion of the contract, and was made material by the contract, and the only question of fact respecting the same was whether it was true or false.[293] The Supreme Court of Iowa, in a case where the policy stated that it was issued and accepted in consideration of the agreements made in the application of the assured, and it was provided in the application that a failure to

---

[291] *Post*, Ch. VI.

[292] Supreme Council, etc., v. Curd, 111 Ill. 284. See also State v. Temperance, etc., Soc., 42 M. A. 485.

[293] Day v. Mut. Ben. L. Ins. Co., 1 McArthur 41; 29 Am. Rep. 565; Kelsey v. Universal L. Ins. Co., 35 Conn. 225; Byers v. Insurance Co., 35 Ohio St. 606; Jeffries v. Life Ins. Co., 22 Wall. 47.

pay the annual dues should avoid the policy, said:[294] "The policy, as we have seen, was issued in consideration of the statements made in the application, and the application states that it forms the basis and consideration upon which the policy was issued and, that a neglect to pay the annual dues shall render the policy void. We think these two papers should be read together, in order to ascertain what the contract between the parties is. The policy is based on the application. But for the latter the policy would never have been issued. . . . As the application is a part of the policy, it makes no difference in what part of either paper the condition is found which renders the policy void. It may be found partly in one and partly in the other. The two papers, when read together, form the contract. The rights of the parties in no other way can be ascertained."[295] An application for membership in a benefit society is a part of the contract though not referred to in the certificate;[296] and, consequently, a stipulation in the application, as that the benefit shall not be paid in case of suicide, will be construed as forming a part of the certificate.[297] The medical examination, if referred to in the application, is part of the contract.[298] In many States statutes exist requiring a copy of the application to be attached to the policy. These statutes have been construed to mean that the copy must be exact and slight variances have been held to exclude the ap-

[294] Mandego v. Centennial, etc., Ass'n, 64 Ia. 134. See also Supreme Lodge, etc., v. Underwood (Neb.), 92 N. W. 1051; Parish v. Mut. Ben. L. Ins. Co., 19 Tex. C. A. 457; 49 S. W. 153.

[295] Foot v. Aetna Life Ins. Co., 61 N. Y. 575; Chrisman v. State Ins. Co., 16 Ore. 283; 18 Pac. 466; Treat v. Merchants' Life Ass'n, 198 Ill. 431; 64 N. E. 692; Fletcher v. Bankers' L. Ins. Co., 135 App. Div. 296; 119 N. Y. Supp. 801; Lee v. Prudential Ins. Co., 203 Mass. 299; 89 N. E. 529.

[296] McVey v. Grand Lodge A. O. U. W., 53 N. J. L. 17; 20 Atl. 873. See also Clapp v. Mass. Ben. Ass'n, 146 Mass. 519; 16 N. E. 433; Flynn v. Mass. Ben. Ass'n, 152 Mass. 288; 25 N. E. 716; Studwell v. Mut. Ben. L. Ass'n, 19 N. Y. Supp. 709. But see Goodson v. National Mas. Acc. Ass'n, 91 Mo. App. 399.

[297] Northwestern Benev., etc., Ass'n v. Hand. 29 Ill. App. 73.

[298] Northwestern Life Ass. Co. v. Bodurtha, 23 Ind. App. 121; 53 N. E. 787; Dinick v. Metropolitan L. Ins. Co., 69 N. J. L. 384; 55 Atl. 291; Paulhamus v. Security Life, etc., Co., 163 Fed. 554. But see Leonard v. New Eng. M. L. I. Co., 22 R. I. 519; 48 Atl. 808, and Johnson v. Des Moines Life Ins. Co., 105 Ia. 273; 75 N. W. 101.

application.[299]   The omission of the words "question" and "answer" in the copy of the application does not show compliance with the statute.[299a]   When the application is pasted to the policy it is endorsed thereon.[300]   Where the by-laws must be by statute attached to the policy amended by-laws are not binding, unless so attached.[301]   The Kentucky statute that the application shall not be received in evidence unless a copy is attached to the certificate is of the substance of the contract;[302] and so is the statute of Virginia as to the type in which the policy shall be printed;[303] and the statute applies to an accident policy.[304]   The statute applies to all companies doing business in the State, and the law may be complied with subsequently to the contract by tendering a copy within a reasonable time.[305]   The delivery of a copy of the by-laws to the insured at the time of the delivery of the certificate is insufficient;[306] the entire application must be delivered with the policy.[307]   Such a provision is not void as against public policy,[308] and it applies to fraternal societies.[309]   The application must be attached to the certificate;[310] reference to the application in the policy is not sufficient.[310a]   The statute applies to the contracts of fraternal societies issued prior to the subsequent act exempting such societies from the provisions of the statute.[311]   If

[299] Seiler v. Economical Life Ass'n, 105 Ia. 87; 74 N. W. 941; 43 L. R. A. 537; Johnson v. Des Moines L. Ins. Co., 105 Ia. 273; 75 N. W. 101; Mut. L. Ins. Co. v. Kelly, 52 C. C. A. 154; 114 Fed. 268.   See also *post*, § 240.

[299a] Knapp v. Brotherhood of American Yeomen, 139 Ia. 136; 117 N. W. 298.

[300] Reynolds v. Atlas Acc. Ins. Co., 69 Minn. 93; 71 N. W. 831.

[301] Boyden v. Mass. Masonic L. Ass'n, 167 Mass. 242; 45 N. E. 735; Mooney v. Ancient Order United Workmen, 114 Ky. 950; 72 S. W. 288; 24 Ky. L. 1787.

[302] American Guild v. Wyatt, 125 Ky. 44; 100 S. W. 266;

[303] Fraternities Accident Order v. Armstrong, 106 Va. 746; 56 S. E. 535.

[304] Continental Cas. Co. v. Harrod, 30 Ky. L. 1117; 100 S. W. 262.

[305] Supreme Lodge K. P. v. Hunziker, 120 Ky. 33; 87 S. W. 134.

[306] Bankers' Fraternal Union v. Donohue, 33 Ky. L. 196; 109 S. W. 878.

[307] Metropolitan Life Ins. Co. v. Hawkins, 311 App. D. C. 493.

[308] New York Life Ins. Co. v. Hamburger, 174 Mich. 254; 140 N. W. 510.

[309] Heralds of Liberty v. Bowen, 8 Ga. App. 325; 68 S. E. 1008.

[310] Grand Lodge A. O. U. W. v. Edwards, 27 Ky. L. 469; 85 S. W. 701.

[310a] Bowyer v. Continental Gas Co., 72 W. Va. 333; 78 S. E. 1000.

[311] American Patriots v. Cavanaugh, 154 Ky. 654; 157 S. W. 1099.

a copy of the application be not attached to the policy, the policy alone constitutes the contract;[312] the law, however, applies only to the original policy and not an application for revival.[313] The by-laws of a fraternal society are not admissible in evidence unless attached to the certificate.[314] Under such statute the application is admissible in evidence in an action by a widow to obtain possession of the policy;[315] and notwithstanding such a statute requiring the application to be attached to the policy the insurer can show that the policy was obtained by fraud.[316] A photographic copy reduced in size but legible is a compliance with the law.[317] The statute of Kentucky as to attaching application and by-laws, does not apply when it is necessary to resort to the by-laws to ascertain the engagements of one of the parties or an essential element of the supposed contract such as the insurer's agreement to pay.[318]

§ 224. **The Same Subject: Further Illustrations.**—A paper drawn up in lead pencil, and containing statements made by the assured, and signed by him has been held to be a part of the policy if referred to therein by a number, although it was addressed to another than the insuring company.[319] Words and figures in the margin of a policy denoting that part of the agreed premiums have been paid may be considered part of it.[320] So an *ad interim* receipt reciting that the insurance under it is subject to the condition of the company's policies makes the conditions part of the contract.[321] So, in a mutual company, the premium

312 Rauen v. Prudential Ins. Co., 219 Ia. 725; 106 N. W. 198.

313 Holden v. Metropolitan Life Ins. Co., 188 Mass. 212; 74 N. E. 337; Moore v. Northwestern Mut. Life Ins. Co., 192 Mass. 468; 78 N. E. 488. But see Metropolitan Life Ins. Co. v. Burch, 39 App. D. C. 397.

314 Masonic Life Ass'n v. Robinson, 149 Ky. 80; 147 S. W. 882.

315 Knowles v. Knowles, 205 Mass. 290; 91 N. E. 212.

316 Southern Life Ins. Co. v. Hill, 8 Ga. App. 857; 70 S. E. 186; Johnson v. American National Life Ins. Co., 134 Ga. 860; 68 S. E. 731.

317 Arter v. Northwestern Mut. Life Ins. Co., 65 C. C. A. 156; 130 Fed. 768.

318 Muetzel v. Travelers' Protective Ass'n (Ky.), 181 S. W. 499.

319 City Ins. Co. v. Bricker, 91 Pa. St. 488.

320 Pierce v. Charter Oak Life Ins. Co., 138 Mass. 151.

321 Goodwin v. Ins. Co., 16 Low. Can. Jur. 298.

note ordinarily forms a part of the contract,[322] but not so if the note is absolute on its face, only reciting that its consideration was a policy of insurance;[323] and it has been held that the application, policy and premium note are parts of the same transaction and should be construed together.[324] Indorsements on a policy are generally to be construed in connection with its provisions,[325] and where the body of the policy refers to the annexed conditions, these, though printed on the back of the policy and unsigned, form a part of the contract,[326] but the reference may be such as not to make the indorsement a part of the policy.[327] It has been held also that where conditions are indorsed in small type upon the back of a policy they are not parts of it unless the attention of the insured is distinctly called to them at the time the contract is made.[328] A notice on the back of a premium receipt is a part of it,[329] and a letter accompanying the application.[330] Statements printed on the back of a benefit certificate have the same effect as if incorporated in it,[331] and so a due bill attached to an insurance policy executed at the same time with it,[332] and so with words and figures on the margin of the policy.[333] An application for the policy and one for a special agent's contract executed by the applicant on the same day form part of the contract;[334] and so with a note given for the first premium.[335] An application though part of the policy may not confer any rights on the

[322] Schultz v. Hawkeye Ins. Co., 42 Ia. 239; Murdock v. Chenango Ins. Co., 2 N. Y. 221.

[323] American Ins. Co. v. Gallahan, 75 Ind. 168.

[324] American Ins. Co. v. Stoy, 41 Mich. 385.

[325] Alabama, etc., Ins. Co. y. Thomas, 74 Ala. 578.

[326] Kensington National Bank v. Yerkes, 86 Pa. St. 227.

[327] Mullaney v. National, etc., Ins. Co., 118 Mass. 393.

[328] Bassell v. American F. Ins. Co., 2 Hughes, 531.

[329] Iowa Life Ins. Co. v. Lewis, 187 U. S. 335; 23 Sup. Ct. 126.

[330] Aetna Life Ins. Co. v. Frierson, 51 C. C. A. 424; 114 Fed. 56.

[331] Bass v. Life & Annuity Ass'n, 96 Kan. 205, 398; 150 Pac. 588; affd. 151 Pac. 1117.

[332] Globe Mut. Life Ins. Co. v. Meyer, 118 Ill. App. 55.

[333] Pierce v. Charter Oak Life Ins. Co., 138 Mass. 151.

[334] Urwan v. Northwestern Nat. Life Ins. Co., 125 Wis. 349; 103 N. W. 1102.

[335] Fidelity Mut. Life Ins. Co. v. Bussell, 75 Ark. 25; 86 S. W. 814.

beneficiaries.[336]   An indorsement on the margin of the policy does not control a policy provision,[337] and an indorsement on the back of the policy not referred to therein, or in the application, is not part of it.[338]   An application is made a part of the policy by a clause therein that it is issued in consideration of the application,[339] but a recital in the policy that it is issued in consideration of the warranties in the application does not make the application a part of the policy.[340]

§ 225.   **Reference in Policy to Other Papers Must Be Plain.—** Where it is desired to make other papers, as in contracts of insurance, the application, a part of the policy, the reference thereto in the latter must be plain.   Where there are no words of reference to the application in the policy they form no part thereof. If the insurer wishes to make them so he must refer to them and cannot claim that by implication they are to be treated as a part thereof.[341]   In the latter of the cases cited as supporting the foregoing proposition, the policy, provided that an application or survey, if referred to therein, should be considered part of the agreement, but no other reference being made, the Court held that the application was not to be regarded as embodied in the policy.   So, where the policy contained no reference to the application, but the latter provided that it was part of the contract, it was held that this stipulation did not make it so.[342]   The application is not part of the contract unless it is referred to in the policy.[343]   In the same way, if an indorsement or direction on the back of a policy is not referred to in the policy or by-laws of the company, there is nothing to show that the parties meant the indorsement to be part of the contract and it will not be so re-

[336] Burt v. Burt, 218 Pa. 198; 67 Atl. 210.

[337] Deakan v. Union Mut. Life Ins. Co., 125 Mo. App. 451; 102 S. W. 634.

[338] Gibson v. State Mut. Life Ins. Co., 184 Mo. App. 656; 171 S. W. 979.

[339] Grell v. Sam Houston Life Ins. Co. (Tex. Civ. App.) 157 S. W. 757.

[340] Spence v. Central Accident Ins. Co., 236 Ill. 444; 86 N. E. 104.

[341] Merchants' Ins. Co. v. Dwyer, 1 Tex. Unrep. Cas. 445; Moore v. State Ins. Co., 72 Ia. 414; 34 N. W. 183; Weed v. Schenectady Ins. Co. 7 Lans. 452.

[342] Brogan v. Manufacturers', etc., Ins. Co., 29 Up. Can C. P. 414.

[343] Manhattan L. Ins. Co. v. Verneuille, 156 Ala. 592; 57 Sou. 72; Gill v. Manhattan L. Ins. Co., 11 Ariz. 232; 95 Pac. 39; Bonville v. John Hancock Mut. L. Ins. Co., 200 Mass. 197; 85 N. E. 1057.

garded.[343]   It has been held, where an application for a policy
of life insurance contained an agreement that the ·answers and
statements should "be the basis and form part of the contract or
policy, and if the same be not in all respects true and correctly
stated, the said policy shall be void' according to the terms thereof," and the policy declared that the insurance was "in consideration of the representations," etc., and that fraud and intentional misrepresentations should vitiate the policy, but did not
otherwise refer to the application, that the agreement and statements in the application did not become a part of the policy.[344]
In that case the Court said: "to hold that the statements of the
proposal and application, notwithstanding the agreement therein
above quoted, are not incorporated into the policy, and, therefore,
are not warranties or conditions of insurance, is but to apply the
rule that where the parties to an agreement have reduced their
contract to writing, that writing, at law, determines what the contract is, and evidence cannot be received to contradict, add to,
subtract from or vary the terms of the writing. The policy in this
case is the agreement for insurance, and it must be held to contain the agreement and all the agreement of the parties to it.
Though the proposal and application contain an agreement on the
part of the insured, that the answers to the questions annexed
to them and the accompanying statements, together with the
statements made to the examining physician, shall be the basis
and form part of the contract or policy between the insured and
the company, yet the policy does not, directly or indirectly, so
declare, and it will be assumed that all previous negotiations have
been superseded and that the policy alone expresses the contract
of the parties.[345]   Where the face of the benefit certificate showed
an acceptance by the member of "all the conditions therein named,"

[343] Planters', etc., Ins. Co. v. Rowland, 66 Md. 240; Stone v. U. S.
Casualty Co,. 34 N. J. L. 371; Kingsley v. New Eng. etc., Ins. Co.,
8 Cush. 393; Ferrer v. Home Mut. Ins. Co., 47 Cal. 416; Farmers', etc,.
Ins. Co. v. Snyder, 16 Wend. 481; Union Cent. L. Ins. Co. v. Fox, 102
Tenn. 347; 61 S. W. 62. As to application for original policy being part
of new policy, Nelson v. Equitable Life Ass'n Soc., 73 Ill. App. 133.

[344] American Popular, etc., Ins. Co. v. Day, 39 N. J. L. 89; 23 Am.
Rep. 198.

[345] Pawson v. Watson, 1 Cowp. 785; Ins. Co. v. Mowry, 96 U. S. 544.

such acceptance did not carry a reference to the matters on the back of the certificate and make them a' part thereof.[345a]

§ 226. **What Constitutes the Contract of Insurance.**—The conclusion from the preceding statements is that the policy of insurance, after it is issued, together with all other writings aptly referred to therein, constitutes the contract of the parties; or in the case of benefit societies the certificate, in connection with the laws of the order, contains such contract. It follows that all previous verbal stipulations not contained in the policy or certificate, nor referred to therein, are not to be considered in any way as modifying such a written contract.[346] And parol agreements as to future conduct, or subsequent promises resting on a new consideration, cannot constitute a part of the contract.[347]

§ 227. **The Same Subject Continued—Change in Contract.**— As we have seen the various divisions or bodies of a beneficiary organization, such as supreme, grand and subordinate lodges, constitute a single society. While this is generally true it does not follow that all are bound for the liabilities and contracts of each other, such liability depends upon the laws of the society. A grand lodge may not be liable for the benefit promised by the order and payable at the death of a member,[348] although the subordinate lodge may be liable with the superior,[349] and by novation the grand lodge may become bound for the contracts of the supreme lodge.[350] In the absence of a statute creating a distinction between an insurance company and a beneficiary or-

---

[345a] Page v. Knights and Ladies of America (Tenn.), 61 S. W. 1068.

[346] Ins. Co. v. Mowry, 96 U. S. 544.'

[347] Hartford F. Ins. Co. v. Davenport, 37 Mich. 609; Knickerbocker L. Ins. Co. v. Heidel, 8 Lea. 488; Hearn v. Equitable, etc., Ins. Co., 3 Cliff. 328.

[348] Grand Lodge etc., v. Weyrich, 47 M. A. 391.

[349] Supreme Lodge A. O. U. W. v. Zuhlke, 129 Ill. 298; 21 N. E. 789.

[350] Burns v. Grand Lodge A. O. U. W., 153 Mass. 173; 26 N. E. 443. Where, owing to a schism, a beneficiary order divided into two bodies it was held under the special facts that there was a dual contract and there could be recovery from both by the beneficiaries of a deceased member. Warnebold v. Grand Lodge A. O. U. W., 83 Ia. 23; 48 N. W. 1070. In another case under somewhat similar facts only one recovery was allowed. Bock v. Grand Lodge A. O. U. W., 75 Ia. 462; 39 N. W. 709.

ganization the rights of the beneficiary are determined by the terms of the contract.[351] A provision in the certificate will pre-vail over a clause of the by-laws, no charter restriction being violated.[352] Unless the articles of association and the laws of the State authorize such a transaction a mutual benefit society has no right to contract to pay the death losses of another in-surance company, such a contract being *ultra vires*.[353] Under the by-laws a recovery may be limited to a particular fund,[354] but it is no defense to an action on a foreign judgment that the con-tract provides for a partial payment of a judgment under cer-tain conditions.[355] Generally the contract between a society and its members cannot be varied or enlarged without the consent of both contracting parties,[356] and a provision in the certificate of membership is not affected by the subsequent reincorporation of the society.[357] We shall speak later more in detail concern-ing the effect of changes in the by-laws which have the effect of modifying the contract,[358] but at this time it is well to give the views of the Supreme Court of the United States on the subject

[351] Block v. Valley Mut. Ins. Ass'n, 52 Ark. 201; 12 S. W. 477. See also Dial v. Valley M. L. Ass'n, 29 S. C. 560; 8 S. E. 27.

[352] Fitzgerald v. Equitable R. F. Ass'n, 3 N. Y. Supp. 214; Failey v. Fee, 83 Md. 83; 34 Atl. 839; 32 L. R. A. 311. To the contrary is Boward v. Bankers' Union, 94 Mo. App. 442; 68 S. W. 369.

[353] Twiss v. Guaranty Life Ass'n, 87 Ia. 733; 55 N. W. 8. See *ante*, § 210. Reinsurance.

[354] Hesinber v. Home Ben. Ass'n, 41 Minn. 516; 43 N. W. 481; Kerr v. Ass'n, 39 Minn. 174; 39 N. W. 312.

[355] Peoples Mut. Ben. Soc. v. Werner, 6 Ind. App. 614; 34 N. E. 105. For further discussion of rights under contract see *post*, § 613. For law as to minors becoming members, see *ante*, § 193. For construction of peculiar contracts, see Wadsworth v. Jewelers', etc., Ass'n, 132 N. Y. 540; 29 N. E. 1103; affg. 9 N. Y. Supp. 771, and Emmeluth v. Home Ben. Ass'n, 122 N. Y. 130; 25 N. E. 234; affg. 46 Hun. 681; Seitzinger v. Modern Woodmen, 204 Ill. 58; 68 N. E. 478; Supreme Lodge, etc. v. Meister, 105 Ill. App. 471; affd. 204 Ill. 527; 68 N. E. 454.

[356] Supreme Council Am. L. of H. v. Smith, 45 N. J. E. 466; 17 Atl. 770.

[357] Hysinger v. Supreme Lodge K. and L. of H., 42 M. A. 628; Grand Lodge A. O. U. W. v. Sater, 44 M. A. 445; Courtney v. U. S. Masonic, etc., Ass'n, (Ia.), 53 N. W. 238.

[358] *Post*, § 228, *et seq.*

as expressed in a recent case where the Court says:[359] "It is not every change in the charter or articles of associations of a corporation that will work such a departure from the purposes of its creation as to forfeit obligations incurred to it or prevent the carrying on of the modified business. A radical departure affecting substantial rights may release those who had come into the corporation on the basis of its original charter. There is much discussion in the authorities as to when a charter amendment is of that fundamental character that a majority of the members or stockholders cannot bind the minority by agreeing to a change in the nature of the business to be carried on or the purposes and objects for which the corporation was created. Each case depends upon its own circumstances and how far the right of amendment has been impliedly or expressly reserved in the creation of corporate rights. It would be unreasonable and oppressive to require a member or stockholder to remain in a corporation whose fundamental purposes have been changed against his will. On the other hand, where the right of amendment is reserved in the statute or articles of association, it is because the right to make changes which the business may require is recognized, and the exercise of the privilege may be vested in the controlling body of the corporation. In such cases, where there is an exercise of the power in good faith, which does not change the essential character of the business, but authorizes its extension upon a modified plan, both reason and authority support the corporation in the exercise of the right.[360] In the present case we have, by express stipulation, the right to amend the articles, with the reservation noted as to article 10. Nor does it appear that the changes were arbitrarily made without good and substantial reason. The testimony in this record discloses that the experience of this assessment insurance company was not anomalous or unusual. It was a case of history repeating itself. Insurance payable from assessments upon mem-

[359] Wright v. Minnesota Mut. L. Ins. Co., 193 U. S. 657; 24 Sup. Ct. Rep. 549.

[360] Nugent v. Putnam County, 19 Wall. 241, 251; 22 L. Ed. 83, 89; Picard v. Hughey, 58 Ohio St. 577; 51 N. E. 133; Miller v. American Mut. Acci. Ins. Co., 92 Tenn. 167-185; 20 L. R. A. 765; 21 S. W. 39; Supreme Lodge K. of P. v. Knight, 117 Ind. 489; 3 L. R. A. 409; 20 N. E. 479.

bers may begin with fine prospects, but the lapse of time, resulting in the maturing of certificates, and the abandonment of
the plan for other insurance by the better class of risks, has not
infrequently resulted in so increasing assessments and diminishing indemnity as to result in failure. The testimony that such
was the history of this enterprise is ample. The changes of 1898
to a plan of issuing, in exchange for certificates and upon new
business, a policy having some of the features of .old line insurance, seems to have been fully justified by the state of the company's business. And the subsequent change to a policy with
straight premiums and fixed indemnity was approved by the majority of the members upon proceedings had under the Minnesota statute, and has resulted in a successful business and a considerable change of the members to the new and more stable
plan. It does not appear that any certificate has been unpaid,
nor is any failure shown to levy assessments required under the
original articles. It is doubtless true that the assessments have
increased owing to the lesser number, subject to assessment, and
the death of members. What would have been realized from
assessments had there been no change of plan is matter of conjecture. The business is still that of mutual insurance, notwithstanding changed methods of operation. The new plan has been
legally adopted and approved by the insurance commissioner of
the State. The argument for appellants is that having begun
as an assessment company, the plan can never be changed without the consent of all interested. But we have seen that the
right of amendment was given in the original articles of association. There was no contract that the plan of insurance should
never be changed. On the contrary, it was recognized that
amendments might be necessary. There was no vested right to
a continuation of a plan of, insurance which experience might
demonstrate would result disastrously to the company and its
members. We are cited to the statutes of many States authorizing similar changes and transfer of membership, but to no case
holding legislative authorization of a change of this character
to work the impairment by the State of the obligation of a contract. The courts are slow to interfere with the management
of societies, such as this mutual insurance company. While the

rights of members will be protected against arbitrary action, such organizations will ordinarily be left to their own methods of action and management. The changes under consideration were made in good faith and have been accepted by many of the old members as well as those who have taken policies since the changes in plan have been made. In our view of the case the law of Minnesota did not impair the obligation of any contract, nor were the changes in the method and plan of this company beyond its corporate powers.'' Where the directors of an association dissolved the corporation by consolidating it with another and the latter refused to issue a certificate to a member of the old organization because she was uninsurable, it was held, under a statute of the State, providing that intentional fraud by persons having the management of a corporation, such as the diversion of the assets from their proper uses whereby insufficient funds remain to meet its liabilities, will constitute a cause of action in favor of any person injured thereby, that such member had a right of action for her damages against the directors for their action, the measure of which is the amount paid in by her to the old association.[361] Where the superior forfeited the charter of a subordinate branch the former is not relieved from liability to a member of the latter.[362]

§ 228. **After-Enacted Laws of Benefit Society Generally Bind Its Members.**—It is often the case that after a person becomes a member of a benefit society the laws are changed and it then becomes a question to what extent the original contract is thereby affected. As the laws of every benefit society enter into the contract between it and its members, whether it be so stipulated or not in the certificate,[363] it follows that, when the laws provide for their amendment or repeal and changes are made in the prescribed manner, the alterations are equally binding upon all the members because this is the express agreement of such members and no exceptions can be made. This is the view of

[361] Grayson v. Willoughby, 78 Ia. 83; 42 N. W. 591. See also Court-ney v. U. S. Masonic, etc. (Ia.), 53 N. W. 238.
[362] Supreme Sitting Order Iron Hall v. Moore, 47 Ill. App. 251.
[363] *Ante*, § 211.

the Supreme Court of the United States.[364]   And even if the by-
laws contain no provision for amendment, under general principles changes made with notice to all members and by consent
of the majority would bind all.[365]   The rule must be understood
with the proviso or exception, which applies to all legislation
alike, that laws cannot be retroactive or be so construed as to
cut off rights already fixed.   This rule may be also further modified by the language of the contract in each particular case.   It
is a settled rule that amendments to by-laws will be held to have
a prospective operation only unless a contrary intention clearly
appears.   In an Illinois case[366] the Court says: "It would seem
that the construction of the act passed in June, 1893, giving it
the effect to destroy that right of appointing a beneficiary, or
naming another beneficiary, which existed in favor of the deceased under his contract prior to the passage of the act, would
be to give the act a retrospective effect, and destroy the obligation of the contract entered into between the deceased and the
complainant.   It is a recognized rule in the construction of statutes that they should be so construed as to give them a prospective operation only, and they should be allowed to operate
retrospectively only where the legistive intention to give them
such operation is clear and undoubted."[367]   In another case[368] the
Court said: "Nothing in it (the constitution) authorized the association to amend, and thereby bind a member to any change in the
contract without his assent, nor do the amended articles purport to

[364] Supreme Lodge K. of P. v. Mims, U. S. 36 Sup. Ct. Rep. 702.

[365] Poultney v. Bachman, 31 Hun. 49; Supreme Lodge K. of H. v.
Knight, 117 Ind. 489; 20 N. E. 479. See also Stoher v. San Francisco
Mus. Fund Soc., 82 Cal. 557; 22 Pac. 1125; State v. Grand Lodge A.
O. U. W., 70 Mo. App. 456; Supreme Council, etc., v. Adams, 68 N. H.
236; 44 Atl. 380; Robinson v. Templar Lodge, etc., 117 Cal. 370; 49 Pac.
170; ante, § 115.

[366] Voight v. Kersten, 164 Ill. 344; 45 N. E. 543.

[367] See, also, Moore v. Chicago, etc., Society, 178 Ill. 102; 52 N. E.
882; Knights Templar, etc., Ind. Co. v. Jarman, 44 C. C. A. 93; 104 Fed.
638; 187 U. S. 197; 23 Sup. Ct. 108; Morton v. Supreme Council R. L.,
100 Mo. App. 76; 73 S. W. 259; Grand Lodge A. O. U. W. v. Brown, 112
Ga. 545; 37 S. E. 890; Sovereign Camp, etc., v. Thornton, 115 Ga. 798; 42
S. E. 236.

[368] Carnes v. Iowa Traveling Men's Ass'n, 106 Iowa 281; 76 N. W. 683.

change existing contracts or to authorize any such change by the adoption of by-laws. In the absence of such provisions, the articles and by-laws as amended cannot be treated as retrospective in their operation. Mere silence as to the effect of revision and amendment of the constitution and by-laws will not warrant the inference that any change wrought will limit or extend the obligation heretofore created by the issuance of certificates of membership. Statutes are construed so as to give them a prospective operation, unless the intention that they operate retrospectively is clear and undoubted, and it is not perceived why the same canon of construction should not be applied to the rules adopted by a mutual insurance association for the transaction of its business and the government of its members."[369] It seems to be settled by the weight of authority, that, under the reserved power to amend the by-laws, the amount of the assessments to be paid by the members, can be increased; such change being reasonable and exercised for the good of the organization. In a leading case,[370] the Court said: "This association was organized for the mutual benefit and support of its members. It has no capital except what is paid by the members of the mutual benefit of all in case of sickness, or their beneficiaries in case of death. It was not organized for profit, but to furnish a cheap rate of insurance for its members. The contractual relation between the members for such association and the association should not be measured by the same standard or determined by the same legal principle applicable between an ordinary insurance company and the holder of one of its policies. The insured are members of the association; each has a voice in all proceedings pertaining to the business or general welfare of the association, and in some ways it assimilates a partnership. All money collected by its scheme of assessment is the common property of the members, to be paid out in such amounts and to such persons as are designated by the member in his certificate, upon the happening of a certain event. For the purpose of better carrying out

---

[369] See also Spencer v. Grand Lodge, 22 Misc. 147; 48 N. Y. Supp. 590; affd. 65 N. Y. Supp. 1146; Grand Lodge, etc., v. Stumpf, 24 Tex. Civ. App. 309; 58 S. W. 840; Hobbs v. Ass'n, 82 Ia. 107; 47 N. W. 983; Sieverts v. Ass'n, 95 Ia. 710; 64 N. W. 671; Benton v. Brotherhood, 146 Ill. 590; 34 N. E. 939.

[370] Miller v. National Council K. & L. of S., 69 Kan. 234; 76 Pac. 830.

the scheme, a national council was created, upon which was conferred the power to decide all matters pertaining to the order, and it was provided that its decisions were final. The condition in plaintiff's certificate, that he would in every particular, while a member of the order, comply with all the laws, rules and requirements of the association, was not only a consent on his part that he would comply with the laws then in force, but it was a consent that he would abide and comply with all reasonable rules and regulations thereafter made in the interest of the association. Every person joining an association obligates himself, without so expressing it, to conform and to comply with all the existing laws of the association, and, if the provision in the plaintiff's certificate means anything, it means that he agreed to comply with all laws then in force or subsequently enacted by the national council." Other cases sustain this view.[371] If so provided the by-laws of a mutual fire insurance company can be changed so as to modify the contract and exempt the company from certain losses,[372] and no notice of the change need be given.[373] Even after a member has given notice of withdrawal the laws may be changed so as to affect his rights.[374] Amendments must be made in the prescribed manner and at a regular meeting called as the constitution provides[375] A condition in the contract that the death benefit would only be paid if a member complied with all laws then existing, or thereafter enacted, does not give the Order power by an after-

[371] Fullenwider v. Supreme Council R. L., 180 Ill. 621; 54 N. E. 485; Messer v. Ancient Order United Workmen, 180 Mass. 321; 62 N. E. 252; Haydell v. Mut. Reserve Fund Life Ass'n, 44 C. C. A. 169; 104 Fed. 718; Mut. Reserve Fund L. Ass'n v. Taylor, 99 Va. 208; 37 S. E. 854; but see Covenant Mut. L. Ass'n v. Tuttle, 87 Ill. App. 309; Ebert v. Mut. Reserve Fund L. Ass'n, 81 Minn. 116; 83 N. W. 506; 84 N. W. 457; Strauss v. Mut. Reserve Fund L. Ass'n, 126 N. C. 971; 36 S. E. 352; 54 L. R. A. 605. The division line between proper and improper amendments and the authorities bearing thereon, are discussed in Parish v. N. Y. Produce Exchange, 169 N. Y. 34; 61 N. E. 97; 56 L. R. A. 149.

[372] Borgards v. Farmers', etc., Co., 79 Mich. 440; 44 N. W. 856.

[373] Montgomery, etc., Ins. Co. v. Milner (Mich.), 57 N. W. 612.

[374] Pepe v. City, etc., Bldg. Soc., 3 R. (Ch.) 47; citing Davies v. Second Chatham, etc., 61 L. T. R. 680.

[375] Metropolitan, etc., v. Windover, 137 Ill. 417; 29 N. E. 538; Hutchinson v. Supreme Tent K. O. T. M., 22 N. Y. Supp. 801; Bowie v. Grand Lodge, etc., 99 Cal. 392; 34 Pac. 103. See also *ante*, § 115.

enacted law to provide that no full benefit shall be paid where the member commits suicide, sane or insane, but does give it power to pass a law providing that no benefit will be paid ·if the member commits suicide while sane, as no sane person has a vested right to commit suicide.[376]

§ 229. **The Same Subject—Leading Cases.**—One of the earliest cases was decided by the Supreme Court of Vermont, where Judge Redfield said:[377] "At the time the husband became a member of the society in 1862, the by-laws provided that each member paying the regular assessment, should 'be entitled to twenty-five cents per day during their sickness;' and 'to the widow of each member deceased, so long as she shall remain a widow, and shall enjoy a good reputation, twenty-five cents per day.' It was further provided that, 'so long as there shall be twenty dollars in the treasury, the society cannot reduce its aid to the sick.' There is also a special provision for the matter of altering or changing the by-laws; and there is, also, a provision in the charter that the society may alter or change its by-laws. In August, 1869, the defendant corporation adopted a set of by-laws which provided that such widows shall receive twenty-five cents per day 'until she had received $200.' The plaintiff has received $200, in accordance with the latter by-law of the society. It is insisted that a right had become vested in the plaintiff (her husband died Jan. 5, 1869) to have and receive of the defendant twenty-five cents per day during her widowhood; and that it was not competent for the defendant to deny or diminish it. The means of making these contributions to the sick, and the widows of deceased members, were derived solely from voluntary assessments upon the members of the society and must be graduated by such assessments. And experience might prove that, without assessments greater than the members could bear, there must be a limitation to the stipend to widows. Prevailing sickness among the members may have so exhausted the

[376] Supreme Conclave, etc., v. Rehan, 119 Md. 92; 85 Atl. 1035; Ann. Cas. 1914-D 58. See also Shipman v. Protected Home Circle, 174 N. Y. 398; 67 N. E. 83; 63 L. R. A. 347; Plunkett v. Supreme Conclave, etc., 105 Va. 643; 55 S. E. 9; Olson v. Court of Honor, 100 Minn. 117; 110 N. W. 374; 10 Ann. Cas. 622; 8 L. R. A. (N. S.) 521.

[377] Fugure v. Soc. St. Joseph, 46 Vt. 369. To the same effect is Chambers v. Supreme Tent, etc., 200 Pa. St. 244; 49 Atl. 784.

means of the society, that the provision for widows, must, necessarily, be modified, or it could not discharge the duties for which
it was formed. It must be incident to the very nature and purpose of such an association, that it should have power to modify
and change its by-laws so as to graduate its charities as experience and necessity may require. It cannot, indeed, pervert its
contributions to subserve other ends and purposes; but the society may regulate the manner in which they shall carry out the
purposes for which they associated. They provided that care for
the sick should not be suspended or abridged while $20 remained
in the treasury; thus, by necessary implication, conceding that
other provisions might be made. Some sweeping disease might so
exhaust the resources of the society, that stipends to widows in
health must necessarily be suspended or much abridged; and this
could be regulated only by practice and experience. The regulation limiting the widow's share in this charity to $200, was made
by a general law, and applicable to all; and there is no suggestion
of fraud, or that the regulation was not wise and salutary. We
think that the society were competent to make this by-law; and,
having fully performed the duty imposed the plaintiff cannot recover. But in this case there was an express provision in the constitution of this society, that the by-laws might be changed, and the
manner of doing it was specifically pointed out; so that the husband voluntarily became party in an association, and contributed
his money with full knowledge of all the provisions in the articles
of association, and fully assented to the same. There is no good
reason, therefore, for claiming that the widow had a vested right
which the society would not modify." · The Supreme Court of
Indiana in a leading case,[378] has also carefully considered this question and states its conclusions as follows: "The provisions of the
established by-laws of an association such as that with which the
assured united, are, as appellee's counsel justly affirm, elements of
the contract of insurance. They are factors that cannot be disregarded. That they have this effect all who become members of
the association must know. A person who enters an association
must acquaint himself with its laws, for they contribute to the '

[378] Supreme Lodge Knights of Pythias v. Knight, 117 Ind. 289; 20 N.
E. 479; 3 L. R. A. 409.

admeasurement of his rights, his duties and his liabilities.[379] It is not one by-law or some by-laws of which the member must take notice, but he must take notice of all which affect his rights or interests.[380] Where, as here, there is an express and clear reservation of the right to amend, he is bound to take notice of the existence and effect of that reserved power. The power to enact by-laws is inherent in every corporation as an incident of its existence. The power is a continuous one. No one has a right to presume that by-laws will remain unchanged. Associations and corporations have a right to change their by-laws when the welfare of the corporation or association requires it, and it is not forbidden by the organic law. The power which enacts may alter or repeal.[381] The duly chosen and authorized representatives of the members alone are vested with the power of determining when a change is demanded, and with their discretion courts cannot interfere. Were it otherwise, courts would control all benevolent associations, all corporations and all fraternities. It is only when there is an abuse of discretion, and a clear, unreasonable and arbitrary invasion of private rights, that courts will assume jurisdiction over such societies or corporations. With questions of policy, doctrine or discipline courts will not interfere. Courts will compel adherence to the charter, and to the purpose for which the society was organized, but they will not do more.[382] The principle which rules here is strictly analogous to those which prevail in controversies between the officers and members of religious organizations and it is well settled that in such cases courts will not control the exercise of discretionary powers, or direct the course of an action in matters of expediency or polity.[383] To justify interference by the courts, and warrant the overthrow of by-laws enacted in the mode

[379] Bauer v. Sampson Lodge, 102 Ind. 262; 1 N. E. 571; Fugure v. Soc., 16 Vt. 368; Simeral v. Ins. Co., 18 Iowa, 319; Coles v. Ins. Co., *Id.* 425; Coleman v. Knights of Honor, 18 Mo. App. 189; Mitchell v. Ins. Co., 51 Pa. St. 402; People v. Soc., 28 Mich. 261; Osceola Tribe v. Schmidt, 57 Md. 98; Sperry's Appeal, 116 Pa. St. 391; 9 Atl. 478; Bac. Ben. Soc., § 81.

[380] Poultney v. Bachman, 31 Hun. 49.

[381] Richardson v. Soc., 58 N. H. 187; Com. v. Mayor, 5 Watts, 152; Soc. r. McVey, 92 Pa. St. 510.

[382] Stadler v. Grand Lodge, 3 Am. Law Rec. 589; Crossman v. Ass'n, 143 Mass. 435; 9 N. E. 753; Hussey v. Gallagher, 61 Ga. 86.

[383] Dwenger v. Geary, 113 Ind. 106; 14 N. E. 903.

prescribed by the by-laws, it must be shown that there was an abuse of power, or that the later by-law is unreasonable. It is not enough to show that a better or wiser course might have been pursued, for it must be shown that there was an abuse of discretion, or that the by-law is so unreasonable as to be void. We do not affirm that a benefit society may, by a change in its by-laws, arbitrarily repudiate an obligation created by a policy of insurance; but we do affirm that where a change is regularly made in its by-laws, and the motive which influences the change is an honest one to promote the welfare of the society, and the members are all given an opportunity to avail themselves of the change, no actionable wrong is done the members or their beneficiaries. It may sometimes happen that the interests of an individual, or of a few individuals, may be impaired; but it is the right and indeed it is the duty, of the society, to protect the interests of the many rather than of the few. Persons who become members of such societies must take notice of this; and one person cannot, therefore, demand that the welfare of the society and the interests of the many be sacrificed for his sole benefit.''[384]

§ 230.   **The Same Subject Continued—The Washington Case.** —The Supreme Court of Washington has elaborately reviewed the subject of the power of a fraternal beneficiary society to increase its rates,[385] and we make the following extracts from the opinion in that case: ''It is lamentably true that most, if not all, of the fraternal benefit associations with which courts have been called upon to deal in recent years were founded upon false assumptions

[384] The following cases sustain the right to make reasonable amendments: Gilmore v. Knights of Columbus, 77 Conn. 58; 58 Atl. 223; Dornes v. Supreme Lodge K. of P., 22 Sou. 191; Schmidt v. Supreme Tent, etc.; 97 Wis. 528; 73 N. W. 22; Hughes v. Wisconsin Odd Fellows', etc., Ass'n, 98 Wis. 292; 73 N. W. 1015; Loeffler v. Modern Woodmen, 100 Wis. 79; 75 N. W. 1012; Morton v. Royal Tribe of Joseph, 93 Mo. App. 78; Richmond v. Supreme Lodge, etc., 100 Mo. App. 8; 71 S. W. 736; Evans v. Southern Tier, etc., 76 App. Div. 151; 78 N. Y. Supp. 611 and 88 N. Y. Supp. 162; Eversbarg v. Supreme Tent, etc., 33 Tex. C. A. 549; 77 S. W, 246; Supreme Tent v. Stensland, 105 Ill. App. 267; Ross v. Modern Brotherhood, 120 Ia. 692; 95 N. W. 207; Hall v. Western Travelers', etc., Ass'n (Ia.), 96 N. W. 170.

[385] Thomas v. Knights of the Maccabees of the World, 83 Wash. 665; 149 Pac. 7; L. R. A. 1916-A 750.

and self-deceptions, a purpose to make something out of nothing; to have others do for us without doing our whole duty to ourselves and to them. And the pity of it all is that those who promoted and organized such associations as well as those of us who have joined them, were undoubtedly honest in our beliefs. We did not know the horse was blind until we took him out on the road. Insurance societies have been generally organized and built up among young men. Low death rates for the first few years made a show of prosperity. Time, the increasing age and mortality of the membership, has brought them face to face with the problem of paying those who die in age, as they have paid those who died in youth. It took nearly 50 years for the truth to rise to the surface of our infatuations and the consequent realization that a new member who in fact was not paying the cost of his own insurance was a liability and not an asset to assert itself. We were foolishly blind to the simple equation that if 10 men mutually promise to pay each other $1,000 at death, $10,000 must be gathered from the promisors if all of the contracting parties are to be paid. The membership of such societies speak in mutual conclave through selected representatives, whose voice is their voice and whose act is their act. 'Every member, in fact, stands in the peculiar situation of being party of both sides, insurer and insured'[386] The latest expression to this effect is found in Hartman v. National Council of Knights and Ladies of Security,[387] where it is said: 'The contract is not purely between the individual member and the corporate organization. It is in spirit and in truth a covenant, not only with the central body, but with every other individual participating in the benefits afforded by the project, for the concern is mutual, and the co-operation of every member is essential to its success as an insurance society. . . . Moreover (she was) controlled by the terms of her certificate and the laws of the order, which are made a part thereof, and to which she was subject, having had her part in the enactment of the same through her representatives.'

'Insurance on the mutual plan being different from insurance on the old-line plan, the members of the company are, so to speak, partners.[388] The contractual relations between the members and

[386] Korn v. Mut. Assur. Soc., 6 Cranch. 192, 3 L. Ed. 195.
[387] 147 Pac. 931, Ore.
[388] Haydel v. Mut. Reserve Fund Life Ass'n (C. C.), 98 Fed. 200.

the association should not be measured by the standard, or determined by the legal principles, which are applicable between an ordinary insurance company and the holder of one of its policies. The insured are members of the association; each has a voice in all proceedings pertaining to its business or general welfare, and in some way it assimilates a partnership.'[389]

'The fraternal plan, with mutuality and without profit, distinguishes the work of such an association from a commercial enterprise.[390] There being no contract in the commercial sense, but a mutual promise of every member to pay the certificate of every other member, there can be no vested right in any provision of the contract, either express or implied, that is not subject to and controlled by the duty of the member to pay the cost of his own insurance, for under no construction of a mutual contract can he demand more than he is willing to give. Each member participates in the business results, and as there are profits or losses, so is his insurance affected in its cost to him.[391] He cannot throw his brothers overboard under the guise of contract and vested right. He must share his life belt with all. If it is not strong enough to sustain him, he is in duty bound to sink to the same level with them; for whatever the word of his contract may imply, it is to be measured by the object of the society which he has bound himself to support. . . .

He became an insurer as well as an assured. He cannot get away from his associates if he would. He must meet his obligation to them, and all this legislation does is to call upon him to pay his own cost as a member. To this end he agreed to be bound by the laws and rules of the order and such changes as might thereafter be made.

'There is no vested right in having the contract in the certificate remain unchanged, because the recognition of the power to make new by-laws is necessarily a recognition of the right to alter or amend those theretofore made.'[392] In the same case we said: 'To destroy a vested right arising out of a contract is, in some way, to

[389] Miller v. National Council, 69 Kan. 234; 76 Pac. 830.

[390] Reynolds v. Royal Arcanum, 192 Mass. 150; 78 N. E. 129; 7 L. R. A. (N. S.) 1154; 7 Ann. Cas. 776.

[391] Swan v. Mut. Reserve Fund Life Ass'n, 155 N. Y. 9; 49 N. E. 258.

[392] Klein v. Knights and Ladies of Security, 79 Wash. 173; 140 Pac. 72.

impair or destroy the rights guaranteed by the contract, not to enforce them.' It seems idle to attemp to add to the force of this language. If we were to attempt it, we would say that there can be no vested right in any contract so long as a duty to the other contracting parties rests upon the one asserting it and his duty is unperformed.''

For these reasons it is held by the greater number of cases, and, as we think, by the greater weight of authority, that it is within the legislative power of these associations to increase rates to the plane of adequacy. As said by the Supreme Court of the United States: 'There is no vested right to a continuation of a plan of insurance which experience might demonstrate would result disastrously to the company and its members.'[393] The test of a vested right is thus defined in 3 Am. & Eng. Enc. of Law,[394]

'The true criterion appears to lie in the determination of the question whether or not an actionable property right has in fact accrued; if so, it cannot be divested; but it is otherwise in case such rights are only prospective or in process of accruing, when they may be changed or arrested by the association under the general governing power, provided the member, in his contract of membership has agreed to conform to after-enacted laws.'

This definition is sustained by practically all of the authorities. Respondent has no right to insist that the society shall carry his certificate at a loss because of the form of the by-law at the time he took out his certificate. His position is not tenable, for no member of a mutual insurance society has a right to insist that it continue to do business upon an unsound basis for his individual benefit. Respondent complains that in the plan proposed no attempt was made to meet the alleged deficiency in rates by a general increase upon all of the members; that the entire burden is cast upon those who attain the age of 50 years, thus forcing members of 55 years and over into a class to take care of themselves, as if there were no other members. Respondent overlooks the fact that the mortality tables show that at about the age of 55 the adequacy of the original system begins to break down. It is not an arbitrary age or date fixed by the society and producing a class distinction.

[393] Wright v. Minnesota Mut. Life Ins. Co., 193 U. S. 657; 24 Sup. Ct. 549, L. Ed. 832.
[394] P. 1065.

It is the working of the law of experience which has demonstrated that the danger of default to the members among these societies have increased under old plans in geometrical proportion after the member has reached an age, approximately 55 years. However, it would seem that in these days of understanding, born of experience, that the fallacy of the 'new blood' theory has been exploded, or if there had ever been anything in it, that no lodge could hope to succeed by loading the rate upon men still young enough to find insurance at cost. or upon men who have been paying their own way, to make up a deficiency for those who had not. 'The new blood theory is simply a method of selling obligations to mature in the future at less than their face, or cost, and using. the money thereby obtained to tempoprarily meet the maturing obligations of the institutions. It works out simply to the end of accumulating liabilities for which no provision has been made, and for which, under the cumulative force of increasing obligations maturing more and more rapidly, no provision can be made in the end, and thereby reseults in ultimate bankruptcy.'

"That these societies were organized and for many years have continued to do business upon a fundamentally unsound basis has been known to all who have had the interest or the courage to make a simple arithmetical calculation. It has been found that in so far as maturing certificates upon the lives of members are concerned, fraternity is not always a dependable factor. This condition became apparent to most of these societies a long time ago and some of them have attempted to meet the situation by their own efforts and by appropriate legislation within their governing bodies. Progress has been slow. Men are loath to lose faith in their ideals. Wherefore, to insure the future stability of societies then doing business and to prevent the organization by designing men of new societies with inadequate rates, and which could not be promoted in the light of the experience of other societies without practicing fraud upon prospective members, the State, in the exercise of its sovereign right to regulate insurance companies, has defined the status of fraternal benefit societies and provided the terms under which they may do or continue to do business in the State of Washington.''

§ 231. **After Enacted Laws Must Not Be Retroactive or Affect Vested Rights.**—Notwithstanding the foregoing views it still remains a conceded doctrine that amendments to by-laws, or subsequently enacted laws, must not be retroactive or affect vested rights. A case of this kind arose in Oregon,[395] where the contract provided that compliance by the member with all laws of the society, then existing or such as it should thereafter adopt, should be the condition upon which he should be entitled to benefits. At the time a member became such no restrictions were placed by the laws of the society upon the designation of beneficiary, but subsequently an amendment was adopted requiring beneficiaries in all cases to be members of the family, blood relatives or dependents. This member had designated as beneficiary a person not of these classes and when the new law was enacted refused to make the change because he was unmarried and had no living relatives or dependents. He soon afterwards died and the Court held that the new law had no retroactive effect, or in any event did not apply to a member who was unable to comply with its requirements. In its opinion the Court says: ''The law does not undertake by its terms to disturb what has been done; it does not nullify previous appointments; it only undertakes to limit to the classes specified the power to designate beneficiaries, whenever it shall be exercised by a member. It is a settled rule of construction that laws will not be interpreted to be retrospective unless by their terms it is clearly intended to be so. They are construed as operating only on cases or facts which come into existence after the laws were passed. 'Every statute,' it has been said, 'which takes away or impairs vested rights, acquired under existing laws, or creates a new obligation, or imposes a new duty, or attaches a new disability in respect of transactions or considerations already passed, must be presumed, out of respect to the legislature, to be intended not to have a retroactive operation.[396] Rights will not be interfered with unless there are express words to that effect. It is not enough that upon some principles of interpretation a retroactive construction could be given to the law, but the intent to make it retroactive must be so plain and demonstrable as to exclude its prospective operation. 'It is not enough that general terms are employed, broad enough to cover past transactions,' for laws 'are to be construed as

[395] Wist v. Grand Lodge A. O. U. W., 22 Ore. 271; 29 Pac. 610.
[396] End. Interp. St., § 273.

prospective only,' if possible.[397]   In fact, so great is the disfavor
in which such laws are held, and so generally are they condemned
by the courts, that they will not construe any law, no matter how
positive in its terms, as intended to interfere with existing contracts or vested rights, unless the intention that it shall so operate
is expressly declared or is to be necessarily implied. As the law
of the society is prospective in its operation, it did not affect Freeman's contract with the defendant. It did not by its terms nor
by implication require him to change his policy. It would only
have affected his contract in the event he should have revoked the
appointment of the plaintiff as his beneficiary and then only to the
extent of requiring him to appoint a beneficiary that should belong
to the specified classes. There is not a word in the law requiring
any member to make a change of his beneficiary, or in case of his
failure to do so, as contended for by the appellant, that his benefit certificate should revert to the society. It may be conceded that
Freeman was bound by all subsequent laws enacted, but as the
law in question is not retroactive it.does not affect his contract. It
only affects him or any other member of the society in the issue
of certificates after its passage. While there is no pretense that
this contract was a cover for speculation, or a wager policy, it may
be conceded that the object of the law was to discourage wager
policies. And it was said by counsel, unless it was held 'that the
society could amend its laws so as to discourage wager policies, it
will be involved in a maze of difficulties.' By giving this law a
prospective operation it will greatly cut off the opportunities for
such speculation in life insurance policies, and will in a great
measure remedy the evil it was designed to abate, without denying
the power of the society to amend its laws, or to enact others, for
the promotion of its interest and welfare. But we may go further
and admit that the law is retroactive; that it was intended, as
claimed by counsel, to affect certificates not of the classes enumerated and requiring the holders of such certificates to designate
others conformably to such law; otherwise, upon their failure to
do so, that the fund payable under their certificates to such beneficiaries as do not belong to any of such classes, would descend under
the laws of the society or revert to it, and still we do not think
such a law would be construed to affect the certificate of Freeman,

[397] Sedgw. St. & Const. Law, 161a.

or the class to which he belongs or their beneficiaries. It is only addressed retroactively to those who can comply with its terms: for while it might have the effect to modify or vary the contracts of all such it does not operate as a destruction of their power to appoint a beneficiary, or as a repudiation of the obligation of the society. They can comply with its terms and make the change of beneficiary and preserve the fund for his benefit. The case is different with Freeman, or those belonging to his class, who prior to the time the law was enacted, had appointed the plaintiff as his beneficiary and who from the time of such appointment, continuously up to his death, had no family, nor anyone related to him by blood, nor dependent upon him. It was not possible for him to comply with the terms of the law naming another beneficiary. To give the law such a construction as would include his class would operate as a complete deprivation of their rights, and an absolute repudiation by the society of its obligations. Such an injustice will never be tolerated, if by any construction it can be avoided. We are bound to construe a law, if we can, so as to make it operate without impairing the obligation of existing contracts, or divesting vested rights. We may therefore assume, for the purposes of the case, that the law was retroactive, and intended to require a change of beneficiaries limiting them to the class specified and still we would be bound to construe it so as to make it operative and valid, which can only be done by confining its operations to those members who could make the change. So averse are courts to giving a law a retroactive operation that even where the retroactive character of the law is clearly indicated on its face, they always subject it to the most circumscribing construction that can possibly be made, consistent with the intention of the legislature.'' And this view has been followed in other cases.[398] In another case[399] the articles of association provided that upon the death of one of its members, his widow should be entitled to receive four dollars 'monthly during widowhood. After the death of the plaintiff's husband, who was a member of the society, the article was amended

[398] Benton v. Brotherhood Railway Brakemen, 146 Ill. 570; 34 N. E. 939; Hysinger v. Supreme Lodge K. & L. of H., 42 Mo. App. 627; Northwestern, etc., Ass'n v. Wanner, 24 Ill. App. 357; Becker v. Berlin Ben Soc., 144 Pa. St. 232; 22 Atl. 699.

[399] Gundlach v. Germania, etc., Ass'n, 4 Hun. 341.

so as to entitle the widows to receive one dollar from each member of the society. Under these facts the court held that the new article was not retroactive and did not affect plaintiff's rights. In a somewhat similar case in Ohio[400] the facts were that the defendant was a benevolent society of which the plaintiff's insane husband was a member, she being his guardian. By one of its by-laws, sick members were entitled to receive three dollars per week while unable to pursue their usual business. In these by-laws the usual right to amend was reserved. Plaintiff's husband had been a member for many years, and in October, 1881, became unable to work. In October, 1882, the original by-laws were amended, limiting the right to benefits to thirteen weeks in the year. The wife sued for benefits under the old law, her husband never having agreed to the change. The Superior Court, in upholding the claim, said: "It is true, as argued by counsel for defendant, and held by the Court in Vermont,[401] that by the terms of the agreement between the members, which constitutes the society, and of that between the society and each member, which amounts to a policy of insurance the right to amend was reserved. But it was a right to amend the by-laws, not to repudiate a debt. A by-law provides what the rights of members shall be in certain events if they continue to pay their dues until such events happen; this, of course, by virtue of the reserved right, may be amended or repealed. But when the event happens, what was a contract depending upon a contingency, becomes in law a debt. The right to modify a contract does not include the right to repudiate a debt any more than the reserved right of a legislature to repeal the charter of a corporation gives it the right to confiscate its property.[402] In another case[403] the Court said: "The corporation has no capacity, as a legislative power from which it derived existence, has no competency, by laws of its own enactment to disturb or divest rights which it had

400 Pellazzino v. German, etc., Soc., 16 Cin. W. L. B. 27.

401 Fugure v. Soc. St. Joseph, 46 Vt. 362, *supra.*

402 St. Patrick's, etc., Soc. v. McVey, 92 Pa. St. 510; Byrne v. Casey, 70 Tex. 247; 8 S. W. 38; McCabe v. Father Matthew, etc., Soc., 24 Hun. 149; Morrison v. Wisconsin, etc., Ins. Co., 59 Wis. 162; Stewart v. Lee Mut. etc., Ass'n, 64 Miss. 499; 1 Sou. 743; *ante,* § 116.

403 Hobbs v. Iowa Ben. Ass'n, 82 Ia. 107; 47 N. Y. 983.

created, or to impair the obligation of its contracts or to change its responsibilities to its members, or to draw them into new and distinct relations.'' In holding that an amendment to the by-laws of a freternal beneficiary association, providing for forfeiture in event of suicide, was not retrospective, the New York Court of Appeals said:[404] ''This defendant cannot, by amendment to its rules, deprive persons already insured, or their beneficiaries, of their rights under contracts of insurance in the event that death shall result from specific causes necessarily insured against by the original contract.'' So a society cannot by amendment to its by-laws cut down the amount of its benefit certificate. The Supreme Court of Massachusetts said in a case of this kind:[405] ''But the plaintiff's rights do not stand upon the by-laws alone. They stand also upon express contract. The promise to pay five thousand dollars is conditioned by the by-laws only to the extent that has been stated. Even if the 'full compliance with all the by-laws,' which is mentioned as a consideration for the promise, is not interpreted and limited by the more specific provisions of the express conditions, 'compliance' in this connection means doing what the by-laws may require the member to do, not submission to seeing his only inducement to do it destroyed. The case is not like Daley v. Association,[406] and Moore v. Association,[407] where the promise to pay a fixed sum was qualified by reference to a fund from which the payment was to come and which might turn out inadequate from causes over which the defendant had no control.''[408] By-laws

[404] Weber v. Supreme Tent K. O. T. M., 172 N. Y. 490; 65 N. E. 258.
[405] Newhall v. Supreme Council American Legion of Honor, 181 Mass. 117; 63 N. E. 1.
[406] 172 Mass. 533; 52 N. E. 1090.
[407] 103 Ia. 424; 72 N. W. 645.
[408] To the same effect are Gant v. Supreme Council A. L. H., 107 Tenn. 603; 64 S. W. 1070; 55 L. R. A. 465; Supreme Council, etc., v. Orcutt, 119 Fed. 682; Supreme Council, etc., v. Jordan, 117 Ga. 808; 45 S. E. 33; Russ v. A. L. H,. 110 La. 588; 34 Sou. 697; Porter v. Sup. Council, 183 Mass. 326; 67 N. E. 238; Makely v. Sup. Cl., 133 N. C. 367; 45 S. E. 649; O'Neil v. Supreme Counc. (N. J.), 57 Atl. 463; Boettger v. Sup. Cl., 78 App. D. 546; 79 N. Y. Supp. 713; Supreme Counc. v. Storey (Tex. C. A.), 75 S. W. 901; Williams v. Supreme Counc. 80 App. Div. 402; 80 N. Y. Supp. 713.

should be construed so as to operate prospectively unless the intention to give them retrospective operation is clear and undoubted.[409]

§ 232. **The Subject Discussed By the Supreme Court of Alabama.**—The subject has also been fully discussed by the Supreme Court of Alabama,[410] where a benefit society had issued a certificate, promising to pay a certain benefit in event of the death of the member, and containing a condition that it should be "subject to the laws of the order now in force or which may hereafter be enacted by the supreme commandery." After the issue of the certificate the supreme commandery enacted a by-law providing that any member who should "take his own life, sane or insane," should thereby forfeit all rights under the certificate and it should become void. The member did take his own life and the plea of forfeiture under the by-law was set up by the society in an action brought by the beneficiary named in the certificate. In deciding the point the Court said: "With a view of excepting from the operation of the policy, any intended self-destruction, whether the assured is sane or insane at the time of its commission, insurance companies are in the habit of inserting in policies a provision, the equivalent of that expressed in the law of the association now under consideration. The exception as to the insane has been supported, and it is said to be as much the right of the insurer to stipulate for exemption from liability in the event of intentional self-destruction by the insane, as to stipulate for an exemption from liability because the hazard of loss is increased from the fact of the assured engaging in occupations perilous to life, or taking up residence in an unhealthy climate.[411] In this respect the law adds a new term to the contract, relieves the association from an existing liability, and lessens the value and security of the certificate

[409] Kaemmerer v. Kaemmerer, 231 Ill. 154; 437 Ill. App. 28.

[410] Supreme Commandery, etc., v. Ainsworth, 71 Ala. 449. This case has been followed in Supreme Lodge K. of P. v. La Malta, 95 Tenn. 157; 31 S. W. 493; 30 L. R. A. 838; Daughtry v. Supreme Lodge K. of P., 48 La. Ann. 1203; 20 Sou. 712; and United Moderns v. Colligan, 34 Tex. Civ. App. 173; 77 S. W. 1032. To the contrary are Weber v. Supreme Tent, etc., 172 N. Y. 490; 65 N. E. 258; Smith v. Supreme Lodge K. of P., 83 Mo. App. 512; Morton v. Supreme Council R. L., 100 Mo. App. 76; 73 S. W. 259.

[411] Bigelow v. Berkshire Life Ins. Co., 93 U. S. 284.

416

to the assured. It is not claimed that there is an inherent power in the association, by the adoption of a by-law, to work such radical changes in its existing contracts. The power is derived from, and depends upon the stipulations of the contract at the time it was made. The stipulations are expressed in varying terms and several of them import no more than would be implied—the observance by the insured of the requirements of the association, such requirements as were reasonable, and intended to promote the harmony of the association, and the purposes and objects for which it was formed. They import also obedience to the by-laws, so far as reasonable, consistent with the charter and law of the land. We do not construe them as reserving, or as intended to reserve, to the association the power to change or avoid its contracts, to lessen its responsibilities, or to divest its members of rights. This is not the proper office of a by-law; and from the general expressions to which we are referring, it cannot be fairly presumed or intended that it was contemplated to affect the members by other than such by-laws, as it was within the competency of the association to enact. But in addition to these, the averment of the plea is, that the certificate was accepted by the assured 'subject to the laws of the order now in force, or which may be hereafter enacted by the supreme commandery.' These are words of large signification, and clearly express that the assured consented that the contract should be subject to future, as well as existing by-laws. Parties may contract in reference to laws of future enactment—may agree to be bound and affected by them, as they would be bound and affected if such laws were existing. They may consent that such laws may enter into and form parts of their contracts, modifying or varying them. It is their voluntary agreement which relieves the application of such laws to their contracts and transactions from all imputations of injustice. .. . . The members of associations, created for purposes and objects like those which seem to be the purposes and objects of this organization, may very properly be required to assent that the contract conferring upon them rights shall be subject to, and depend upon the future, as well as the existing laws adopted by the governing power. The fundamental principle of such organizations is the mutuality of duty and equality of rights of the membership, without regard to time of admission. This cannot well be preserved, if the members stipulating for benefits were not required to consent that they would be subject to future as well as existing by-laws. Time and experience will develop a necessity for changes in the laws, and if the consent was not required, there would be a class of members bound by the changed laws, and a class exempt from their operation. The case before us is an illustration. Of the legality and propriety of the provision relieving the association from liability, if a member while insane deprived himself of life, there is no good reason to question. If no other reason could be given that it relieves the association from litigating with the representatives of a deceased member the distressing question of his sanity, would be sufficient. If the law was applied only to certificates issued subsequent to its enactment there would be a class of members having certificates of greater value than the certificates held by another class; yet each class would be subject to the same assessments and the same duties. There is but little room, if any, for the apprehension, that advantage will be taken by the governing body of the assent of the members to be bound and affected by subsequent laws, to impose upon him unjust burdens or to vary the contract, save so far as an alteration or modification of it may be promotive of the general good. Subsequent or existing by-laws are valid only when consistent with the charter and confined to the nature and objects of the association. While a subsequent law, because of the assent of the member, may add new terms or conditions to a certificate, terms or conditions reasonably calculated to promote the general good of the membership, and may be valid and binding, it does not follow that a law operating a destruction of a certificate, or a deprivation of all rights under it, would be of any force."[412]

§ 233. **A Contrary View—New York Cases.**—In the leading case of Wright v. Knights of the Maccabees of the World,[413] the Court, after referring to a number of cases previously decided, says: "All these cases, among others, were cited and relied upon in Ayers v. Grand Lodge, A. O. U. W.[414] In that case, power to amend was expressly reserved, and an amendment was provided that the certificate should become void if the insured should there-

[412] Korn v. Mut. Ass'n Soc., 6 Cranch. 396.
[413] 196 N. Y. 391; 89 N. E. 1078; 31 L. R. A. (N. S.) 422.
[414] 188 N. Y. 280; 80 N. E. 1020.

after 'enter into the business or occupation of selling, by retail, intoxicating liquor as a beverage.' All the judges who sat united in holding the amendment void, in the absence of a reservation of the specific right to so amend the by-laws as to restrict the occupation or business of the insured, upon the ground that it violated a vested right. Among other things it was said, 'An amendment of by-laws which form part of a contract is an amendment of the contract itself; and when such a power is reserved in general terms, the parties do not mean, as the courts hold, that the contract is subject to change in any essential particular at the election of the one in whose favor the reservation is made. It would be not reasonable, and hence not within their contemplation, at least, in the absence of stipulations clearly specifying the subjects to be affected, that one party should have the right to make a radical change in the contract, or one that would reduce its pecuniary value to the other. A contract which authorizes one party to change it in any respect that he chooses would in effect be binding upon the other party only, and would leave him at the mercy of the former; and we have said that human language is not strong enough to place a person in that situation.[415] While the defendant may doubtless so amend its by-laws, for instance, as to make reasonable changes in the methods of administration, the manner of conducting its business, and the like, no change can be made which will deprive a member of a substantial right conferred expressly or impliedly by the contract itself. That is beyond the power of the legislature as well as the association, for the obligation of every contract is protected from State interference by the Federal Constitution.[416]

These cases establish the rule that benefits cannot be reduced or new conditions forfeiting the benefits added by an amendment of the by-laws, even when the general right to amend is expressly reserved. They are controlling, therefore, so far as all the amendments now in question are concerned, except that providing for an increase in the rate of assessments. Following the authorities

---

[415] Industrial & G. Trust v. Tod, 180 N. Y. 215, 225; 73 N. E. 7.

[416] See also Parish v. N. Y. Produce Exch., 169 N. Y. 34; 56 L. R. A. 149; 61 N. E. 977; Langan v. Supreme Council, A. L. H., 174 N. Y. 266; 66 N. E. 932; Simons v. Supreme Council, A. L. H., 178 N. Y. 263; 70 N. E. 776; Dowdall v. Supreme Council, C. M. B. A., 196 N. Y. 405; 89 N. E. 1075.

cited. we hold that the amendments which assume to cut down the benefits to which the plaintiff became entitled by his contract with the defendant are void and of no effect. I am, personally, of the opinion that the amendment increasing the rate of assessment is also void, for I can see no difference in principle between reducing benefits and increasing the amount to be paid for benefits. The plaintiff entered into the contract on the faith of the promise by the association that he should 'pay at the same rate thereafter so long as he remains continually in good standing in the order,' which he had the right to assume, and the defendant knew that he would assume, was a covenant not to increase the rate. The certificate states that 'he is entitled to all the rights, benefits and privileges' provided by the laws of the order, which are thus made a part of the certificate. Hence the right to pay at the old rate was one of the rights provided for and that he contracted for. It was a vested right, immune from change by amendment, in the absence of a specific reservation of power to amend in that particular. On the average, such contracts would be impaired by doubling assessments to the same extent as by cutting off one-half of the benefit. The price to be paid by the plaintiff for insurance is as essential a part of his contract as the amount of insurance to be paid to him by the defendant on the maturity of the policy. Whether the one is increased or the other proportionately decreased, makes no difference in principle, or in the final result. By either method the pecuniary value of the contract, which is property, would be reduced one-half.''

§ 234. **Same Subject—Conclusion.**—It will be seen from the cases cited in the preceding sections, that the views of different courts are conflicting, and that it is almost, if not altogether, impossible to lay down a general rule that will apply to all cases. We may, however, say that the weight of authority is that in all matters of internal management, those relating to rates, or to conduct of members, laws enacted after the issue of the benefit certificate will be binding on the member, provided no new condition is injected into the contract materially affecting it. After a review of most of the authorities, the St. Louis Court of Appeals said :[417] "The foregoing cases were all decided on the theory that

[417] Morton v. Supreme Council R. L., 100 Mo. App. 76; 73 S. W. 259.

subsequent by-laws, despite the member's agreement to comply with them, cannot defeat or abridge the essential rights created by the policy, but affect only the member's duties as such; not his interests as a contracting party.- In all of them we find the same argument here advanced and accepted by some courts, that the business experience of companies shows them what regulations ought to prevail and that it is necessary that they be permitted to avail themselves of the teachings of experience by enacting new regulations, as needed, to bind all members and control all agreements. There is some merit in that argument and it is pertinent to any legislation respecting contracts. It has not been thought, however, sufficiently meritorious to permit State legislatures to impair obligations, and we think it not sufficiently so to permit insurance societies.'' The difficulties because of the conflicting authorities are to a great extent removed by the authoritative decision of the Supreme Court of the United States in the case of Supreme Council R. A. v. Green,[418] which holds that if the court of last resort of the domicile of the corporation has decided that under its charter the association has the power to modify the contract entered into by it, this adjudication will be binding upon the courts of other States under the requirements of the Federal Constitution, that full faith and credit shall be given in each State to the public acts, records and judicial proceedings of every other State. Article IV, Section 1, Constitution of United States. We give in a note a list of the cases in which the right to change the by-laws has been sustained and those in which the right has been denied, which must be examined in order to arrive at a just conclusion; and to this list must also be added the cases cited in the last four sections.[419]

[418] 237 U. S. 531; L. R. A. 1916-A 771, *supra*. See also Supreme Lodge K. P. v. Mims, 36 Sup. Ct. Reptr. 702.

[419] In the following cases in addition to those previously referred to, the members were held bound by a subsequent amendment to the by-laws:

U. S.—Supreme Lodge K. of P. v. Mims, U. S., 36 Sup. Ct. Rep. 702; Haydel v. Mut. Reserve Fund Life Ass'n, 44 C. C. A. 169; 104 Fed. 718; Smythe v. Supreme Lodge K. P., 198 Fed. 967; Order of Commercial Travelers v. Smith, 112 C. C. A. 442; 192 Fed. 102; Barrows v. Mut. Reserve L. Ins. Co., 81 C. C. A. 71; 167 Fed. 461; Supreme Lodge Fraternal

Union v. Light, 195 Fed. 903; Gaines v. Supreme Council R. A., 140 Fed. 978.

Alabama.—Fraternal Union of America v. Zeigler, 145 Ala. 287; 39 Sou. 751; Ellison v. District Grand Lodge, etc., 11 Ala. App. 442; 66 Sou. 872.

Arkansas.—Knights of Pythias v. Long (Ark.), 174 S. W. 1197.

California.—Caldwell v. Grand Lodge A. O. U. W., 148 Cal. 195; 82 . Pac. 781.

Colorado.—Head Camp, etc., v. Woods, 34 Colo. 1; 81 Pac. 261; Head Camp, etc., v. Irish, 23 Colo App. 85; 127 Pac. 918.

Connecticut.—Kane v. Knights of Columbus, 84 Conn. 96; 79 Atl. 63; Gilmore v. Knights of Columbus, 77 Conn. 58; 58 Atl. 223; Coughlin v. Knights of Columbus, 79 Conn. 218; 64 Atl. 223.

Georgia.—Fraternal Relief Ass'n v. Edwards, 9 Ga. App. 43; 70 S. E. 265; Union Fraternal League v. Johnston, 124 Ga. 902; 53 S. E. 241.

Illinois.—Supreme Tent, etc., v. Stensland, 105 Ill. App. 257; Fullenwider v. Supreme Council R. L., 180 Ill. 621; 54 N. E. 485; Supreme Council R. A. v. McKnight, 238 Ill. 349; 87 N. E. 299; Scon v. Supreme Council R. L., 223 Ill. 32; 79 N. E. 42; Murphy v. Nowak, 223 Ill. 301; 79 N. E. 112; 7 L. R. A. (N. S.) 393.

Indiana.—Supreme Lodge K. of H. v. Bieler (Ind.), 105 N. E. 244; Court of Honor v. Hutchens (Ind. App.), 79 N. E. 409.

Iowa.—Ross v. Modern Brotherhood, etc., 120 Iowa 692; 95 N. W. 207; Norton v. Catholic Order of Foresters, 138 Iowa 464; 114 N. W. 893; Ury v. Modern Woodmen of America, 149 Iowa 706; 127 N. W. 665; House v. Modern Woodmen of America, 165 Iowa 607; 146 N. W. 817.

Kansas.—Miller v. National Council, etc., 69 Kan. 234; 76 Pac. 830; Supreme Tent K. O. T. M. v. Nelson, 77 Kan. 629; 95 Pac. 1052; Moore v. Life & Annuity Ass'n, 93 Kan. 398; 148 Pac. 981; 95 Kan. 591; 151 Pac. 1107; Kirk v. Fraternal Aid Ass'n, 95 Kan. 707; 149 Pac. 400; Uhl v. Life & Annuity Ass'n, Kan., 155 Pac. 926.

Kentucky.—Union Ben. Soc. v. Martin, 23 Ky. Law Rep. 2276; 67 S. W. 38; LaRue v. Provident Savings Life Assur. Soc., 138 Ky. 776; 129 S. W. 104; Winterberg v. Brotherhood of Locomotive Firemen, 148 Ky. 501; 146 S. W. 1105.

Louisiana.—Daughty v. Supreme Lodge K. P., 48 La. 1203; 20 Sou. 712.

Massachusetts.—Reynolds v. Supreme Council R. A., 192 Mass. 150; 78 N. E. 129; 7 L. R. A. (N. S.) 1154; Messer v. A. O. U. W., 180 Mass. 321; 62 N. E. 252.

Maryland.—Mathieu v. Mathieu, 112 Md. 625; 77 Atl. 112; Arold v. Supreme Conclave, etc., 123 Md. 675; 91 Atl. 829.

Michigan.—Wineland v. Knights of the Maccabees, 148 Mich. 606; 112 N. W. 696; Dolan v. Supreme Council, etc., 152 Mich. 266; 112 N. W. 383; Williams v. Supreme Council, etc., 152 Mich. 1; 115 N. W. 1060; Brown v. Great Camp K. O. T. M., 167 Mich. 123; 132 N. W. 562.

Minnesota.—Ledy v. National Council K. & L. of S. (Minn.), 151 N. W. 905.

Missouri.—Dieterich v. Modern Woodmen of A., 161 Mo. App. 97; 142 S. W. 460; Claudy v. Royal League, 259 Mo. 92; 168 S. W. 593; Morton v. Royal Tribe of Joseph, 93 Mo. App. 78; Richmond v. Supreme Lodge, etc., 100 Mo. App. 8; 71 S. W. 36; Dessauer v. Supreme Tent K. O. T. M., 191 Mo. App. 76; 176 S. W. 461; Schmidt v. Mut. Reserve Fund Life Ass'n, 128 Mo. App. 497; 106 S. W. 1082.

Mississippi.—Dornes v. Supreme Lodge K. P., 75 Miss. 466; 23 Sou. 191; Ward v. David & Jonathan Lodge, 90 Miss. 116; 43 Sou. 302; Newman v. Supreme Lodge K. P. (Miss.), 70 Sou. 241; L. R. A. 1916 C 1051.

Nebraska.—Lange v. Royal Neighbors, 75 Neb. 188; 10 L. R. A. (N. S.) 666; 110 N. W. 224; affd. 110 N. W. 1110; Hall v. Western Travelers, etc., 69 Neb. 601; 96 N. W. 170; Shepperd v. Bankers' Union, 77 Neb. 85; 108 N. W. 188.

New York.—O'Brien v. Supreme Council Catholic Ben. Legion, 176 N. Y. 597; 68 N. E. 1120; affg. 81 App. Div. 1; 80 N. Y. Supp. 776; Evans v. Southern Tier, etc., 76 App. Div. 151; 78 N. Y. Supp. 611; Parish v. New York Produce Exchange, 169 N. Y. 34; 61 N. E. 977; 56 L. R. A. 149; Maxwell v. Theatrical, etc., Ass'n, 104 N. Y. Supp. 815; 54 Misc. 619.

North Carolina.—Faulk v. Fraternal Mystic Circle (N. C.), 88 S. E. 431.

Ohio.—Tisch v. Protected Home Circle, 72 Ohio St. 233; 74 N. E. 188.

Pennsylvania.—Chambers v. Supreme Tent, etc., 200 Pa. St. 244; 49 Atl. 784.

South Carolina.—Clarkson v. Supreme Lodge K. P., 99 S. C. 134; 82 S. E. 1043.

Tennessee.—Connor v. Supreme Commandery Golden Cross, 117 Tenn. 549; 97 S. W. 306; Supreme Lodge K. of P. v. LaMalta, 95 Tenn. 157; 31 S. W. 493; 30 L. R. A. 838.

Virginia.—Plunkett v. Supreme Conclave I. O. H., 105 Va. 643; 55 S. E. 9; Mut. Reserve Fund Life Ass'n v. Taylor, 99 Va. 208; 37 S. E. 854.

Washington.—Klein v. Knights & Ladies of Security, 79 Wash. 173; 140 Pac. 72; Thomas v. K. O. T. M., 85 Wash. 665; 149 Pac. 7.

Wisconsin.—Schmidt v. Supreme Tent, 97 Wis. 528; 73 N. W. 22; Loeffler v. M. W., 100 Wis. 79; 75 N. W. 1012; Curtis v. M. W. A., 159 Wis. 303; 150 N. W. 417.

Ontario.—Re Standard Life Assur. Co., 8 Ont. W. N. 559; 34 Ont. L. R. 235; Granger v. Order of Canadian Home Circles, 26 Ont. W. R. 373. But see to the contrary, Royal Guardians v. Schneider, 23 Quebec K. B. 461.

In the following cases, in addition to those previously referred to, the amendment was either held beyond the powers of the association, or unreasonable, or inoperative, so far as existing contracts were concerned because an attempt to affect vested rights:

U. S.—Smith v. Supreme Lodge K. P., 220 Fed. 438; affg. 198 Fed. 967.

California.—Bornstein v. District Grand Lodge, 2 Cal. App. 624; 84

Pac. 271; Richter v. Supreme Lodge K. of P., 137 Cal. 8; 69 Pac. 483; Shack v. Supreme Lodge Fraternal Brotherhood, 9 Cal. App. 584.

Colorado.—Sexton v. National Life Ins. Co., 40 Colo. 60; 90 Pac. 56; Pittinger v. Pittinger, 28 Colo. 308; 64 Pac. 195.

Illinois.—Voight v. Kersterns, 164 Ill. 314; 45 N. E. 543; Covenant Mut. Life Ass'n v. Kentner, 188 Ill. 431; 58 N. E. 966; Benton v. Brotherhood, etc., 146 Ill. 590; 34 N. E. 939.

Iowa.—Carnes v. Iowa Traveling Men's Ass'n, 106 Ia. 281; 76 N. W. 683; Hobbs v. Iowa Ben. Ass'n, 82 Iowa 107; 47 N. W. 983; Seiberts v. Ass'n, 95 Ia. 716; 84 N. W. 671; Wassen v. American Patriots, 148 Iowa 142; 126 N. W. 778.

Kansas.—Grand Lodge, etc., v. Haddock, 72 Kan. 35; 1 L. R. A. (N. S.) 1064; 82 Pac. 583; Taylor v. Modern Woodmen, 72 Kan. 443; 83 Pac. 1099; 5 L. R. A. (N. S.) 283; Hart v. Life & Annuity Ass'n, 86 Kan. 318; 120 Pac. 363; Boman v. Bankers' Union, etc., 76 Kan. 198; 91 Pac. 49.

Maryland.—Supreme Conclave I. O. H. v. Rehan, 1119 Md. 92; 85 Atl. 1035.

Massachusetts.—Atty. General v. Supreme Council A. L. of H,. 196 Mass. 151; 81 N. E. 966; Spear v. Boston Relief Ass'n, 195 Mass. 351; 81 N. E. 196.

Michigan.—Pokrefky v. Detroit, etc., Ass'n, 121 Mich. 456; 80 N. W. 240; Startling v. Supreme Council, etc., 108 Mich. 140; 66 N. W. 340.

Minnesota.—Ruder v. National Council K. & L. of S., 124 Minn. 431; 145 N. W. 118; Tebo v. Supreme Council R. A., 89 Minn. 3; 93 N. W. 513; Thibert v. Supreme Lodge K. of H., 78 Minn. 448; 81 N. W. 220; 47 L. R. A. 136; 79 Am. St. 412; Leland v. Modern Samaritans, 111 Minn. 207; 126 N. W. 728; Olson v. Court of Honor, 100 Minn. 117; 110 N. W. 374.

Missouri.—Pearson v. Knights Templar, etc., 114 Mo. App. 283; 89 S. W. 588; Sisson v. Supreme Court of Honor, 104 Mo. App. 54; 78 S. W. 297; Edwards v. American Patriots, 162 Mo. App. 231; 144 S. W. 1117; Young v. Railway Mail Ass'n, 126 Mo. App. 325; 103 S. W. 557; Zimmerman v. Supreme Tent K. O. T. M., 122 Mo. App. 591; 99 S. W. 817; Lewine v. Supreme Lodge K. of P., 122 Mo. App. 547; Wilcox v. Court of Honor, 134 Mo. App. 547; Smail v. Court of Honor, 136 Mo. App. 434; 117 S. W. 116; Umbarger v. Supreme Council Royal League (Mo. App.), 118 S. W. 1199; Smith v. Supreme Lodge K. of P. 83, Mo. App. 512; Morton v. Supreme Council R. L., 100 Mo. App. 76; 73 S. W. 259.

New York.—Beach v. Supreme Tent K. O. T. M., 177 N. Y. 100; 69 N. E. 281; affg. 77 N. Y. Supp. 770; 74 App. Div. 527; Shipman v. Protected Home Circle, 174 N. Y. 398; 67 N. E. 83; 63 L. R. A. 347; modifying 73 N. Y. Supp. 594; 66 App. Div. 448; Fargo v. Supreme Tent K. O. T. M., 185 N. Y. 578; 78 N. E. 1103; affg. 89 N. Y. Supp. 65; 96 App. Div. 491; Ayers v. Grand Lodge, etc., 188 N. Y. 280; 80 N. E. 1020; Wright v. Knights of the Maccabees, 196 N. Y. 391; 89 N. E. 1078; 91 N. E. 1122; Green v. Supreme Council R. A., 206 N. Y. 591; 100 N. E. 411; reverisng 129 N. Y. Supp. 791; 144 App. Div. 761; Weber v. Supreme Tent, etc., 172 N.

Y. 490; 65 N. E. 258; Deuble v. Grand Lodge, 172 N. Y. 665; 65 N. E. 1116; Langan v. Supreme Council, 174 N. Y. 266; 66 N. E. 932.

New Jersey.—Sautter v. Supreme Conclave, etc., 74 N. J. Law, 608; 71 Atl. 232; affg. 62 Atl. 529; 72 N. J. Law 325; Parks v. Supreme Circle Brotherhood of America, 83 N. J., Eq. 131; 89 Atl. 1042; Poole v. Supreme Circle, etc. (N. J.), 80 Atl. 821; affd. 80 N. J. Eq. 259; 87 Atl. 1118.

North Carolina.—Brograw v. Supreme Lodge, etc., 128 N. C. 354; 38 S. E. 905; 54 L. R. A. 602; Strauss v. Mut. Reserve Fund Life Ass'n, 128 N. C. 465; 39 S. E. 55; 54 L. R. A. 605.

Oklahoma.—Hines v. Modern Woodmen of America, 41 Okla. 135; 137 Pac. 675.

Pennsylvania.—Hale v. Equitable Aid Union, 168 Pa. St. 377; 31 Atl. 1066; Marshall v. Pilots' Ass'n, 206 Pa. St. 182; 55 Atl. 916; Palmer v. Protected Home Circle (Pa.), 97 Atl. 188.

Tennessee.—Hicks v. Northwestern Aid Ass'n, 117 Tenn. 203; 96 S. W. 962; Gaut v. Supreme Council, 107 Tenn. 603; 64 S. W. 1070; 55 L. R. A. 465.

Texas.—Ericson v. Supreme Ruling Fraternal Mystic Circle, 105 Tex. 170; 146 S. W. 160; reversing 131 S. W. 92; Supreme Lodge K. P. v. Mims, (Tex. Civ. App.), 167 S. W. 835; reversed 36 U. S. Sup. Ct. Rep. 702; Grand Lodge, etc., v. Stumpf, 24 Tex. Civ. App. 309; 58 S. W. 840; Eaton v. International Travelers' Ass'n, Tex. Civ. App. 136 S. W. 817.

Wisconsin.—Jaeger v. Grand Lodge, etc., 149 Wis. 354; 135 N. W. 869; Stirn v. Supreme Lodge, etc., 150 Wis. 13; 136 N. W. 164.

CHAPTER VI.

426

§ 235. **Insurance Contract Result of Proposal and Acceptance.**—The contract of insurance is the result of a proposal, or application, upon the part of the insured, and its acceptance by the insurer. Whether life insurance be effected with stock or mutual companies, or through membership in benefit societies, the process is much the same. First is the proposal, or application, and then the acceptance. When accepted the application is followed by the issuance of the policy, or, in the case of benefit societies, the reception into membership, after which the certificate is furnished. The application is usually composed of several parts: first are the answers by the applicant to certain questions relating to age, family history, etc.; then is the certificate of the examining physician as to the results of the phy-

sical examination of the applicant, and sometimes lastly the certificate of a friend of the insured who occupies the position of a
referee. In the case of beneficiary societies a report concerning the qualifications of the applicant by an investigating committee appointed by the lodge is usually required. From this
proposal or application, the insurer determines the value of the
risk and whether or not he will accept it.

§ 236. **Difficulties in Construing Language of the Policy Referring to the Application.**—The policy, issued upon acceptance
of this proposal, generally refers in some way to the application.
It is in construing the language used in such reference that some
of the greatest difficulties have been experienced by the courts.
The effort of the companies has been to incorporate the application in the contract and have the insured warrant the truth of
all his statements. When these statements were true no differences could well arise, but when the answers of the applicant to
questions in the application were untrue, or equivocal, or.par-
tial, the only escape from loss of the insurance was to have the
language of the policy so construed that it would be held that
the statements made in the application were not warranted to
be absolutely true, whether material or not. In the reported
cases, therefore, the controversy has often been over this reference in the policy to the application, and whether the statements
in the latter were warranties, which must be literally true, or
representations which must be substantially true. In this chapter we propose to treat of the classes of statements made in the
application which are sometimes mere representations and sometimes warranties. Also of what is called concealment, or the
withholding of information which should be disclosed.

§ 237. **The Proposal or Application.**—The proposal, or application, consists of the written statements concerning the physical condition, family history and antecedents of the subject
for insurance; it is supposed to contain the information upon
which the insurer can estimate the desirability of the risk. As
has been said, this application may consist of several papers, or
series of answers to questions, by the applicant or some person
referred to by him. The person to be insured also submits to a

physical examination by an agent of the insurer. If the applicant conceals information that should have been imparted the contract may or may not be avoided, and the law of concealment applies. Whether the statements are representations or warranties depends upon the language used. Nice questions of construction arise in construing the language used and some of the most elaborate opinions of the courts are devoted to this subject. The word statements, in an application includes a warranty, as to representations therein, and a waiver of the provisions of law relating to the disclosure by a physician of communications relating to the patient's physical condition.[1] The reference, however, in an application to different sets of questions or forms must be plain to make them part of the contract.[2] Although the application generally must be signed such signature may be made by an agent and the company may be estopped from disputing such signature made in the presence of its agent;[3] nor can the company set up the defense that the signature to the application was forged unless it offers to return the premiums paid.[4] The beneficiary suing on a policy adopts the application and is bound by it.[5] A society may be bound even though an application was never made.[6]

§ 238. **The Doctrine of Warranty, Representation and Concealment.**—In construing the language of the application a distinction has been made between what are called warranties and those styled representations. We shall see as we proceed further that if a statement is contained in the policy, or what is the

[1] Foley v. Royal Arcanum, 151 N. Y. 196; 45 N. E. 456.

[2] Northwestern L. Ass. Co. v. Tietze, 16 Colo. App. 205, 64 Pac. 773.

[3] Somers v. Kansas Protective Union, 42 Kan. 619; 22 Pac. 702; Bohninger v. Empire Mut. Co,. 2 T. & C. 610; Fulton v. Metropolitan L. Ins. Co., 19 N. Y. Supp. 470; Prudential Ins. Co. v. Cummins, etc., 19 Ky. L. 1770; 44 S. W. 431; see also Sullivan v. Industrial Ben. Ass'n, 73 Hun. 319; 26 N. Y. Súpp. 186; Pickett v. Metropolitan L. Ins. Co., 20 App. Div. 114; 46 N. Y. Supp. 693.

[4] Home Mut. R. Ass'n v. Riel, 1 Pa. (Monaghan) 615, 17 Atl. 36.

[5] Centennial Mut. L. Ass'n v. Parham, 80 Tex. 518; 16 S. W. 816; Prudential Ins. Co. v. Fredericks, 41 Ill. App. 419; Kelly v. Home Life Ins. Co., 95 Mo. App. 627; 69 S. W. 612.

[6] Wagner v. Supreme Lodge K. & L. of H., 128 Mich. 660; 87 N. W. 903.

same thing in the application, referred to in the policy and made part of the contract, and is warranted to be true, it is a condition precedent to liability, but if the statement is not by the contract clearly and expressly warranted to be true it is a representation. Very marked differences result in the conclusions that follow. If information, which should have been disclosed by the applicant to the insurer, is concealed, the contract may be avoided on the ground that in effect a fraud has been practiced upon the insurer. Hence the doctrine of ''concealment.'' By a multitude of decisions of the various courts, which are often conflicting, has been built up what is technically known as the law of ''warranty,'' ''representation'' and ''concealment.'' These subjects will now be considered.

§ 239. **Early Interpretation Contrasted With Modern Construction.**—In no branch of the law have the decisions been more numerous or conflicting than in cases relating to applications for insurance, and it is difficult, if not impossible, to lay down any general rules which will apply in all cases. Says a standard writer on this subject:[7] ''The cases would have presented fewer difficulties of construction if the early jurisprudence had been less open to the admission of forfeitures of the policy, and more easily satisfied with a compliance with written stipulations substantially equivalent to a literal one, when such construction was not inconsistent with the express provisions of the contract. The recent jurisprudence tends to greater liberality of construction in favor of maintaining the contract. Such a rule may as well be applied to stipulations and recitals in the policy as to representations preliminary and collateral to it; and it is more equitable after the policy has gone into effect and the underwriter has a right to retain the premium, that the contract should be continued in force as long as its being maintained is consistent with its express provisions, and the underwriter is not thereby prejudiced.'' The companies themselves forced the courts into this departure, because their policies were generally so intricate, in their wording, and their liability so hedged in and restricted by a multiplicity of covenants and conditions;

[7] Phillips on Ins., § 638.

430

the assured was tied down by so many warranties concerning immaterial matters, that in most cases, especially those involving fire insurance, the payment of the policy in event of loss was optional with the insurer, for an avenue of escape was generally open if he wished to avoid responsibility. Judicial sentiment, somewhat akin to popular sentiment, began to set in against this perversion of justice, and the absolute necessity for different reasoning appeared, for it was seen that it was unjust to absolve the insurer by a rigid adherence to forms of words rather than the intent of the parties, when the assured had been persuaded into a contract the terms of which he generally could not understand, and where, after he had paid in good faith, the premium asked, he discovered too late that he had stipulated away any probability of getting his insurance if a loss occurred. The courts, therefore, began to condemn this scrupulously technical construction and to seek to avoid it. In one of the first cases, where this necessity for change was referred to, the Supreme Court of Iowa said:[8] "The business of insurance is rapidly increasing in magnitude and importance, and it is essential to the companies themselves as to the assured that the rules of law declared applicable to them should be based upon just and equitable principles, and administered in a manner in harmony with the doctrines of an enlightened jurisprudence. It is quite time that the technical constructions which have pertained with reference to contracts of this kind, blocking the pathway to justice, and leading to decisions opposed to the general sense of mankind, should be abandoned, and that these corporations, grown opulent from the scanty savings of the indigent, should be held to the same measure of responsibility as is exacted of individuals." About the same time the Supreme Court of the United States practically adopted the same doctrine,[9] and this doctrine, which had even earlier been favorably considered by a few courts, was still more generally accepted and approved, so that from reading some of the decisions in these cases, one would be justified in the conclusion that in many localities insurance com-

[8] Miller v. Mut. Ben. Life. Ins. Co., 31 Ia. 226; 7 Am. Rep. 122.
[9] Ins. Co. v. Wilkinson, 13 Wall. 222.

panies as a class, had made themselves disreputable in judicial eyes.[10]

§ 240. **Statutes on the Subject.**—These judicial declarations and the influence of public sentiment have led to the enactment, in some States, of statutes which provide that no misrepresentation or false statement in an application for life insurance shall be deemed material, or render the policy void, unless the matter misrepresented shall have actually contributed to the happening of the contingency or event on which the policy was to become due and payable, and that whether it so contributed in any case shall be a question for the jury.[11] The power of the legislature to define the public policy of the State in respect to life insurance, and to impose conditions upon the transaction of such business within the State, is exercised without ·violation of the Federal Constitution when a statute provides that a false answer in an application shall not bar recovery on a policy unless clearly proved to be willfully false and fraudulently made, and also material, and that it induced the company to issue the policy, and that the agent of the insurer had no knowledge of the falsity or fraud of such answer.[12] Such a statute includes ˉwarranties as well as representations,[13] and, under the Missouri statute, that the matter misrepresented contributed to the death must

[10] American Central Ins. Co. v. Rothschild, 82 Ill. 166; New England, etc., Ins. Co. v. Schettler, 38 Ill. 166; Piedmont & Arlington L. Ins. Co. v. Young, 58 Ala. 476; Kausal v. Minnesota, etc., Ass'n, 31 Minn. 17; Rowley v. Empire Ins. Co., 36 N. Y. 550; Combs v. Hannibal, etc., Ins. Co., 43 Mo. 148; Insurance Co. v. Wilkinson, 13 Wall. 222; Miller v. Mut. Ben. L. Ins. Co., 31 Ia. 226.

[11] R. S. Mo. 1909, § 6937. Similar provisions are found in some States relating to fire insurance.

[12] John Hancock Mut. L. Ins. Co. v. Warren, 181 U. S. 73; 21 Sup. Ct. 535. See also Schuermann v. Union Cent. L. Ins. Co., 165 Mo. 641; 65 S. W. 723; Kern v. Supreme Council A. L. H., 167 Mo. 471; 67 S. W. 252; ·John Hancock, etc., Co. v. Warren, 59 Ohio St. 45; 51 N. E. 546.

[13] Kern v. Supreme Council, etc., *supra;* White v. Provident Savings, etc., Ass'n, 163 Mass. 108; 37 N. E. 771; 27 L. R. A. 398; Dean v. Life Ass'n, 84 Mo. App. 459; Dodt v. Prudential Ins. Co., 186 Mo. App. 168, 171 S. W. 655; Conner v. Life & Annuity Ass'n, 171 Mo. App. 364; 157 S. W. 814.

be pleaded.[14] Statutes also have been enacted in many States requiring a copy of the application to be attached to the policy, or providing that the company shall be bound by the knowledge of its agent. The cases construing these statutes, as well as those in regard to misrepresentation, are cited in the note.[15]

[14] Christian v. Conn. Mut. L. Ins. Co., 143 Mo. 460; 45 S. W. 268.

[15] Marston v. Kennebec Mut. L. Ins. Co., 89 Me. 266; 36 Atl. 389; Hartford L. Ins. Co. v. Stalling, 110 Tenn. 1, 72 S. W. 960; John Hancock L. Ins. Co. v. Warren, 59 O. St. 45; 51 N. E. 546; Metropolitan L. Ins. Co. v. Howle, 62 O. St. 204; 56 N. E. 908; Albert v. Mut. L. Ins. Co., 122 N. C. 92; 30 S. E. 327; Dolan v. Mut. Reserve F. L. Ass'n, 173 Mass. 197; 53 N. E. 398; Johnson v. Philadelphia, etc., Co., 163 Pa. St. 127; 29 Atl. 854; Lithgow v. Supreme Tent, etc., 165 Pa. St. 292; 30 Atl. 830; Stocker v. Boston Mut. L. Ass'n, 170 Mass. 224; 49 N. E. 116; Md. Casualty v. Gehrmann, 96 Md. 634; 54 Atl. 678; Supreme Commander, etc., v. Hughes, 114 Ky. 175; 70 S. W. 405; 24 Ky. L. 924; Hunziker v. Supreme Lodge K. of P. 117 Ky. 418; 78 S. W. 201; 25 Ky. L. 1510; Rice v. Rice (Ky.), 63 S. W. 586; 23 Ky. L. 635; North Western L. Ass'n v. Findley, 29 Tex. Civ. App. 494; 68 S. W. 695; Smith v. Supreme Lodge, etc., 123 Ia. 676, 99 N. W. 553; Collins v. Life Ass'n, 85 Mo. App. 242; Summers v. Metropolitan L. Ins. Co., 90 Mo. App. 691; Seiders v. Merchants', etc., Ass'n, 93 Tex. 194; 54 S. W. 753; Jenkins v. Covenant Mut. L. Co., 171 Mo. 375; 71 S. W. 688; Jacobs v. Omaha L. Ass'n, 142 Mo. 49; 43 S. W. 375; Jacobs v. Omaha L. Ass'n, 146 Mo. 523; 48 S. W. 462; Deane v. South Western, etc., Ass'n, 86 Mo. App. 459; Ashford v. Metropolitan L. Ins. Co., 98 Mo. App. 505; 72 S. W. 712; Aloe v. Fidelity, etc., Co., 164 Mo. 675; 55 S. W. 993; Kern v. American Legion of Honor, 167 Mo. 471; 67 S. W. 252; Toomey v. Knights of Pythias, 147 Mo. 129; 48 S. W. 936; affg. 74 Mo. App. 507; Logan v. Fidelity & Casualty Co., 146 Mo. 114; 47 S. W. R. 948; McDonald v. Bankers', etc., Ass'n, 154 Mo. 618; 55 S. W. 999; Penn. Mut. L. Ins. Co. v. Mechanics', etc., 19 C. C. A. 286; 72 Fed. 413; 37 U. S. App. 692; 38 L. R. A. 33; Albro v. Manhattan L. Ins. Co. (C. C. A.), 127 Fed. 281; affg. 119 Fed. 629; Corley v. Travelers', etc., Ass'n, 105 Fed. 854; 46 C. C. A. 278; Manhattan Ins. Co. v. Myers, 109 Ky. 372; 59 S. W. 30; 22 Ky. L. Rep. 875; Fisher v. Fidelity, etc., Ass'n, 188 Pa. St. 1; 41 Atl. 467; Burruss v. National L. Ins. Co., 96 Va. 543; 32 S. E. 49; National L. Ass'n v. Berkley, 97 Va. 574; 34 S. E. 469; Stork v. Supreme Lodge, etc., 113 Ia. 724; 84 N. W. 721; National Acc. Soc. v. Dolph, 94 Fed. 743, 38 C. C. A. 1; Goodwin v. Provident Savings L. A. Soc., 97 Ia. 226; 66 N. W. 157; 32 L. R. A. 473; Considine v. Metropolitan L. Ins. Co., 165 Mass. 462; 43 N. E. 201; Fitzgerald v. Metropolitan Acc. Ass'n, 106 Ia. 457; 76 N. W. 809; Mut. L. Ins. Co. v. Kelly, 52 C. C. A. 154; 114 Fed. 268. The subject is exhaustively discussed in a note in 63 L. R. A. 833 to Johnson v. Mut. Life Ins. Co., 180 Mass. 407; 62 N. E. 733.

These beneficial provisions of the statute it has been held cannot be waived by agreement in the application.[16]   This is true although the contract was made in another State than that in which it is sought to be enforced and where no similar statute exists.[17]   The effect of these laws has been to benefit the assured and prevent technical forfeitures.[18]

[16] Hermany v. Fidelity Mut. L. Ass'n, 151 Pa. St. 17; 24 Atl. 1064.   In this case the Court says: "It would be contrary to public policy to recognize the right of parties to circumvent the law by setting up a waiver such as was insisted on in this case."

[17] Fidelity Mut. L. Ass'n v. Ficklin, 74 Md. 172; 23 Atl. 197; affg. 21 Atl. 680.

[18] The state of things out of which this necessity for the protection of the assured, in cases of fire insurance especially, sprang, has been thus graphically portrayed (Delancey v. Rockingham, etc., Ins. Co., 52 N. H. 581): "Some companies chartered by the legislature as insurance companies, were organized for the purpose of providing one or two of their officers, at headquarters, with lucrative employment—large compensation for light work—not for the purpose of insuring property; for the payment of expenses, not of losses.   Whether a so-called insurance company was originally started for the purpose of insuring an easily earned income to one or two individuals, or whether it came to that end after a time, the ultimate evil was the same.   Names of men of high standing were necessary to represent directors.   The directorship, like the rest of the institution and its operations, except the collection of premiums and the division of the same among the collectors, was nominal.   Men of eminent respectability were induced to lend their names for the official benefit of a concern of which they knew and were expected to know nothing, but which was represented to them as highly advantageous to the public.   There was no stock, no investment of capital, no individual liability, no official responsibility—nothing but a formal organization for the collection of premiums, and their appropriation as compensation for the services of its operators.   The principal act of precaution was, to guard the company against liability for losses.   Forms of applications and policies of a most complicated and elaborate structure, were prepared and filled with covenants, exceptions, stipulations, provisos, rules, regulations and conditions rendering the policy void in a great number of contingencies.   These provisions were of such bulk and character that they would not be understood by men in general even if subjected to a careful and laborious study; by men in general they were sure not to be studied at all.   The study of them was rendered particularly unattractive, by a profuse intermixture of discourses on subjects in which a premium payer would have no interest.   The compound, if read by him, would, unless he were an extraordinary man, be an inexplicable riddle, a

434

§ 241. **The Same Subject Continued.**—We have heretofore considered the statutes of the different States requiring a copy of the application to be attached to the policy, or benefit certi-

mere flood of darkness and confusion. Some of the most material stipulations were concealed in a mass of rubbish, on the back side of the policy and the following page, where few would expect to find anything more than a dull appendix, and where scarcely any one would think of looking for information so important as that the company claimed a special exemption from the operation of the general law of the land relating to the only business in which the company professed to be engaged. As if it were feared that notwithstanding these discouraging circumstances, some extremely eccentric person might attempt to examine and understand the meaning of the involved and intricate net in which he was to be entangled, it was printed in such small type, and in lines so long and so crowded, that the perusal of it was made physically difficult, painful and injurious. Seldom has the art of typography been so successfully diverted from the diffusion of knowledge to the suppression of it. There was ground for the premium payer to argue that the print alone was evidence, competent to be submitted to a jury, of a fraudulent plot. It was not a little remarkable, that a method of doing business not designed to impose upon, mislead and deceive him by hiding the truth, practically concealing and misrepresenting the facts, and depriving him of all knowledge of what he was concerned to know, should happen to be so admirably adapted to that purpose. As a contrivance for keeping out of sight the dangers created by the agents of the nominal corporation, the system displayed a degree of cultivated ingenuity, which if it had been exercised in any useful calling, would have merited the strongest commendation. Traveling agents were necessary to apprise the people of their opportunities, and induce them to act as policy holders and premium payers, under the name of 'the insured.' Such emissaries were sent out: 'The soliciting agents of insurance companies swarm through the country, plying the inexperienced and unwary who are ignorant of the principles of insurance law, and unlearned in the distinctions that are drawn between legal and equitable estates' (Combs v. Hannibal, etc., Ins. Co., 43 Mo. 152). The agents made personal and ardent application to people to accept policies, and prevailed upon large numbers to sign papers (represented to be mere matters of form), falsifying an important fact by declaring that they made application for policies, reversing the first material step in the negotiation. An insurance company, by its agent, making assiduous application to an individual to make application to the company for a policy, was a sample of the crookedness so characteristic of the whole business. When a premium payer met with a loss, and called for the payment promised in the policy, which he had accepted upon the most zealous solicitation, he was surprised to find that the voluminous, unread and unexplained papers had been so printed

ficate.[19]   While it is not necessary to consider the subject further it is well to add reference to additional cases bearing on the subject. . Under the Missouri statute false representations as to good health only avoid the policy when such misrepresentation actually contributes to the death,[20] and under the same statute a misrepresentation as to age does not defeat the policy unless · it contributes to the risk and a condition contained in the policy for a readjustment in case of misstatement of age is void.[21]   A statute requiring warranties to be deemed representations, cannot be evaded by endorsing such statements on the policy and

at headquarters, and so filled out by the agents of the company, as to show that he had applied for the policy. This, however, was the least of his surprises. He was informed that he had not only obtained the policy of his own application, but had obtained it by a series of representations (of which he had not the slightest conception), and had solemnly bound himself by a general assortment of covenants and warranties (of which he was unconscious), the number of which was equaled only by their variety, and the variety of which was equaled only by their supposed capacity to defeat every claim that could be made upon the company for the performance of its part of the contract. He was further informed that he had succeeded in his application by the falsehood and fraud of his representations,—the omission and misstatement of facts which he had expressly covenanted truthfully to disclose. Knowing well that the application had been made to him, and that he had been cajoled by the skillful arts of an importunate agent into the acceptance of the policy and the signing of some paper or other, with as little understanding of their effect as if they had been printed in an unknown and untranslated tongue, he might well be astonished at the inverted application, and the strange multitude of fatal representations and ruinous covenants. But when he had time to realize his situation, had heard the evidence of his having beset the invisible company, and obtained the policy by just such means as those by which he knew he had been induced to accept it, and listened to the proof of his obtaining it by treachery and guilt, in pursuance of a premeditated scheme of fraud, with intent to swindle the company in regard to a lien for assessments of some other matter of theoretical materiality, he was measurably prepared for the next regular charge of having burned his own property."

19 See *ante*, §§ 283, 284.

20 Roedel v. John Hancock Mut. Life Ins. Co., 176 Mo. App. 584; 160 S. W. 44.

21 Burns v. Metropolitan Life Ins. Co., 141 Mo. App. 212; 124 S. W. 539; Metropolitan Life Ins. Co. v. Stiewing, 173 Mo. App. 108; 155 S. W. 900.

declaring them warranties.[22] Under the Missouri law the false statements must actually contribute to the death.[23] While the insurer cannot rely upon warranties in the application unless a copy be attached to the policy, nevertheless the court in an action on the policy may consider the question of fraud, since fraud is not within the statute of Alabama relating to the subject.[24] The statute as to the effect of false statements practically abolishes the rule that a warranty is part of the contract.[25] Under the Iowa statute the false statements in the application in order to avoid the policy must have misled the insurer.[26] The same is true of the Texas statute,[27] and the same is true as to the Tennessee statute which applies to all domestic, or foreign, companies authorized to do business in the State.[28] Under the law of Massachusetts no misrepresentation avoids the policy unless it was made with intent to deceive,[29] and the same is true as to Minnesota statute.[30] Under the Virginia statute requiring conditions of the policy to be printed in certain type, a condition not printed in such type is void.[31]

§ 242. **These Statutes Do Not Apply to Benefit Societies.**— The question arises whether these statutes, for the most part, if not always, adopted before the organization of the beneficiary

[22] Continental Casualty Co. v. Owen, 38 Okla. 107; 131 Pac. 1084; National Life Ass'n v. Hagelstein (Tex. Civ. App.), 156 S. W. 353.
[23] Welsh v. Metropolitan Life Ins. Co., 165 Mo. App. 233; 147 S. W. 147; Bensen v. Metropolitan Life Ins. Co., 161 Mo. App. 480; 144 S. W. 122; Herzberg v. Modern Brotherhood, 110 Mo. App. 328; 85 S. W. 986.
[24] Empire Life Ins. Co. v. Gee, 171 Ala. 435; 55 Sou. 166. See also *ante*, § 283.
[25] Aetna Life Ins. Co. v. Mullar, 113 Md. 686; 78 Atl. 483; Reagan v. Union Mut. Life Ins. Co., 207 Mass. 79; 92 N. E. 1025; Lynch v. Prudential Ins. Co., 150 Mo. App. 461; 131 S. W. 145.
[26] Roe v. National Life Ins. Ass'n, 137 Ia. 696; 115 N. W. 500.
[27] Supreme Lodge Knights & Ladies of Honor v. Payne (Tex. Civ. App.) 110 S. W. 523.
[28] Arnold v. New York Life Ins. Co., 131 Tenn. 720; 177 S. W. 78.
[29] Kidder v. Supreme Commandery, etc., 192 Mass. 326; 78 N. E. 469.
[30] Wheelock v. Home Life Ins. Co., 115 Minn. 177; 131 N. W. 1081 and North Dakota; Satterlee v. Modern Brotherhood of America, 15 N. D. 92; 106 N. W. 561.
[31] Equitable Life Assur. Soc. v. Wilson, 110 Va. 571; 66 S. E. 836.

orders, apply to them as well as to the regular life insurance corporations. It would reasonably seem that the question is one of construction and probable intent. Where a statute forbade the setting up of the defense of suicide unless it was shown that the assured contemplated suicide at the time the policy was applied for, it was held that it applied to a co-operative association on the assessment plan whose membership was confined to the Masonic fraternity.[32] It was intimated by the Supreme Court of Missouri that the provisions in the statute of that State relative to the application do not apply to the benevolent orders:[33] and the same court has expressly held[34] that such provisions, under a subsequent statute, do not apply to assessment life insurance companies. But this question has been settled by a later statute and fraternal beneficiary societies are now exempt from these provisions of the law.[35] The same is true in most States. The statute of Texas in regard to the effect of false statements in the application do not apply to fraternal beneficiary associations.[36] The exemption of fraternal orders under the Missouri statute does not apply to a foreign association not authorized to do business in the State.[37]

§ 243. **Warranty Defined.**—The definition of warranty given by Angell,[38] and approved by the Court of Appeals of New

[32] Berry v. Knights Templar, etc., Co., 46 Fed. 439; affd. 50 Fed. 511. See *ante*, § 47, *et seq.*

[33] Whitmore v. Supreme Lodge, Knights & L. of H., 100 Mo. 47; 13 S. W. 495.

[34] Hanford v. Mass. Ben. Ass'n, 122 Mo. 50; 26 S. W. 680.

[35] Shotliff v. Modern Woodmen, 100 Mo. App. 138; 73 S. W. 326; McDermott v. Modern Woodmen, 97 Mo. App. 636; 71 S. W. 833. Prior to the statute of 1897 of Missouri foreign fraternal associations were not so exempt. Kern v. Supreme Council, etc., 167 Mo. 471; 67 S. W. 252. As to attaching by-laws to certificate under a statute requiring a copy of the application to be attached, see Fitzgerald v. Metropolitan Acc. Ass'n, 106 Ia. 457; 76 N. W. 809; Johnson v. Phila. & R. Ry. Co., 163 Pa. St. 127; 39 Atl. 854; Lithgow v. Supreme Tent, etc., 165 Pa. St. 292; 30 Atl. 830; Corley v. Travelers', etc., 105 Fed. 854; 46 C. C. A. 278; Kundan v. Grand Council, etc., 7 S. D. 214; 63 N. W. 911. See *ante*, § 223.

[36] Modern Order Praetorians v. Hollwig, Tex. Civ. App., 105 S. W. 846.

[37] Francis v. Supreme Lodge A. O. U. W., 150 Mo. App. 347; 130 S. W. 500.

[38] Angell on Ins., § 140.

York,[39] is that it is "a stipulation inserted in writing on the face of the policy, on the literal truth or fulfillment of which the validity of the entire contract depends. The stipulation is considered to be on the face of the policy, although it may be written in the margin, or transversely, or on a subjoined paper referred to in the policy." Lord Mansfield has said,[40] that in order to make written instructions valid and binding as a warranty, they must undoubtedly be inserted in the policy. "It is," said Lord Ellenborough,[41] "a question of construction in every case, whether a policy is so worded as to make the accuracy of a *bona fide* statement a condition precedent, and the rules of construction are the same in policies as in other written contracts." And Bunyon adds:[42] "In order to make any statements binding as warranties, they must appear upon the face of the instrument itself by which the contract of insurance is effected; they must either be expressly set out or by inference incorporated in the policy. If they are not so they are not warranties but representations."[43] The word "guaranty" is not equivalent to "warranty.[44] The substance of the decisions relating to the subject of warranty in insurance contracts is that the truth of all statements warranted to be true is a condition precedent of the liability of the insurer; for, if the statements so warranted are untrue, there is no contract. Where the policy recited that the statements made in the application were warranted to be true and were the basis of the contract and that any misstatements in the application should make the policy void the answers in the application are warranties.[45] In the case of Pelican v. Mutual Life Ins. Co.,[46] the Court says: "The general rule is that a warranty must be a part and parcel of the contract—made so by express agreement of the parties upon the

[39] Ripley v. Aetna F. Ins. Co., 30 N. Y. 136.
[40] Pawson v. Watson, 1 Cowp. 785.
[41] Robertson v. French, 4 East 135.
[42] Bunyon on Life Assur., 34.
[43] American Popular L. Ins. Co. v. Day, 39 N. J. L. 89; 23 Am. Rep. 198.
[44] Masons Union L. Ins. Ass'n v. Brockman, 20 Ind. App. 206; 50 N. E. 493.
[45] Provident Sav. L. Ass. Soc. v. Reutlinger, 58 Ark. 528; 25 S. W. 835; Foley v. Royal Arcanum, 28 N. Y. Supp. 952.
[46] 44 Mont. 277; 119 Pac. 778.

face of the policy. It is in the nature of a condition precedent and must be strictly complied with or literally fulfilled to entitle the assured to recover on the policy. It need not be actually material to the risk; its falsity will bar recovery because by the express stipulation the statement is warranted to be true, and thus is made material.'' If no other controlling question intervenes, any statement in the application warranted to be true is a condition precedent to liability and avoids the contract even though the statement be made in good faith.[47]

§ 244. **Difficulty of Determining What Amounts to Warranty.**—Warranties are not favored in law and it is no error to so instruct the jury,[48] and statements in an application for a policy of insurance will not be construed as warranties unless the provisions of the application and policy, taken together, leave no room for any other construction.[49] ·It is not always easy to determine what language in an insurance contract amounts to a warranty. As was said by the Supreme Court of Massachusetts:[50] ''There is undoubtedly some difficulty in determining by any simple and certain test what propositions in a contract of insurance constitute warranties and what representations. One general rule is, that a warranty must be embraced in the policy itself. If, by any words of reference, the stipulation in another instrument, such as the proposal or application, can be construed a warranty, it must be such as make it in legal effect a part of the policy. In another case it was said that 'the proposal or declaration for insurance, when forming a part of the policy, has been held to amount to a condition or warranty, which must be strictly true or complied with, and upon the truth of which, whether a statement be intentional or not, the whole instrument depends.[51] But no rule is laid down in that case for determining how or in what mode such statements, contained in the application or answer to interrogatories,

[47] Pacific Mut. Life Ins. Co. v. O'Neil, 36 Okla. 792; 130 Pac. 270.
[48] Masons Union L. I. Co. v. Brodeman, 20 Ind. App. 206; 50 N. E. 493.
[49] Modern Woodmen Acc. Ass'n v. Shryock, 54 Neb. 250; 79 N. W. 607; 39 L. R. A. 826.
[50] Daniels v. Hudson R. F. Ins. Co., 12 Cush. 416; 59 Am. Dec. 192.
[51] Vose v. Eagle Life & Health Ins. Co., 6 Cush. 47.

shall be embraced or incorporated into the policy so as to form part thereof. The difference is most essential, as indicated in the definition of a warranty in the case last cited, and as stated by the counsel for the defendants in the prayer for instruction. If any statement of fact, however unimportant it may have been regarded by both parties to the contract, is a warranty, and it happens to be untrue, it avoids the policy; if it be construed a representation, and is untrue, it does not avoid the contract if not willful or if not material. To illustrate this, the application in answer to an interrogatory is this: 'Ashes are taken up and removed in iron hods;' whereas it should turn out in evidence that ashes were taken up and removed in copper hods—perhaps a set recently obtained, and unknown to the owner. If this was a warranty, the policy is gone; but if a representation, it would not, we presume, affect the policy, because not willful or designed to deceive, but more especially because it would be utterly immaterial, and would not have influenced the mind of either party in making the contract or in fixing its terms. Hence it is, we suppose, that the leaning of all courts is to hold such a stipulation to be a representation rather than a warranty, in all cases where there is any room for construction; because such construction will, in general, best carry into effect the real intent and purpose which the parties have in view in making their contract.'' The trouble is caused by the difficulty of ascertaining the intent of the contracting parties because of the ambiguous language often used by them. The insurer on the one hand wishes to have the terms of the contract seem liberal, and yet, in fact, admit of a strict construction favorable to him. The insured, on the other hand, generally gives little thought to the conditions of the contract until a loss has occurred. The terms, warranty and condition precedent, are used interchangeably.[52]

§ 245. **Breach of Warranty Avoids the Contract.**—If the contract of life insurance therefore declares that the statements made in the application touching the subject of insurance are warranted to be true, and that the policy shall be void if they are untrue, the falsity of such statements will defeat the insur-

[52] Salts v. Prudential Ins. Co., 140 Mo. App. 142; 120 S. W. 714.

ance. The parties having in their contract so agreed, and having been free to agree upon whatever terms and conditions they chose, the contract being a voluntary one,[53] the courts have no other alternative than to give effect to the contract of the parties. The truth of the fact warranted is a condition precedent to recovery.[54] It is immaterial that the applicant believed the statements to be true.[55] And that the statements are not material to the risk.[56] And that he was illiterate and did not un-

[53] Keim v. Home Mut. F. Ins. Co., 42 Mo. 38; 97 Am. Dec. 291; Fullum v. New York U. Ins. Co., 7 Gray 61; 66 Am. Dec. 462; Brown v. Roger Williams Ins. Co., 5 R. I. 394; Wilson v. Aetna Ins. Co,. 27 Vt. 99.

[54] Fowler v. Aetna F. Ins. Co., 6 Cow. 673; 16 Am. Dec. 460; Aetna L. Ins. Co. v. France, 91 U. S. 510; Burritt v. Saratoga, etc., Ins. Co., 5 Hill, 193; 40 Am. Dec. 345; American Popular L. Ins. Co. v. Day, 39 N. J. L. 89; 23 Am. Rep. 198; Fitch v. American Popular L. Ins. Co., 59 N. Y. 557; 17 Am. Rep. 372; Glutting v. Metropolitan L. Ins. Co., 50 N. J. L. 287; 13 Atl. 4; Jeffries v. Economical Mut. L. Ins. Co., 22 Wall. 47; Wilkins v. Mut. R. F. Life Ins. Ass'n, 7 N. Y. Supp. 589; Johnson v. Maine, etc., Ins. Co., 83 Me. 182; 22 Atl. 107; Clements v. Conn. Ind. Co., 51 N. Y. Supp. 442; Fell v. John Hancock M. L. Ins. Co. 76 Conn. 494; 57 Atl. 175; Leonard v. State Mut. L. Ins. Co., 24 R. I. 7; 51 Atl. 1049; Metropolitan L. Ins. Co. v. Rutherford, 98 Va. 195; 35 S. E. 361 and 36 S. E. 719; Hubbard v. Mut. Res. F. L. Ass'n, 40 C. C. A. 605; 100 Fed. 719; McClain v. Provident Life, etc., Soc., 105 Fed. 834; National Fraternity, etc., v. Karnes, 24 Tex. C. A. 607; 60 S. W. 576; Farrell v. Security Life, etc., 125 Fed. 684; McGowan v. Supreme Court, etc., 107 Wis. 462; 83 N. W. 775; Kansas Mut. L. A. v. Pinson, 94 Tex. 553; 63 S. W. 531; Selby v. Mut. L. Ins. Co., 67 Fed. 490; Kelly v. Life Ins. Cl. Co., 113 Ala. 453; 21 Sou. 361; Finn v. Metropolitan L. Ins. Co., 70 N. J. L. 255; 57 Atl. 438; Priestly v. Provident Savings Co., 112 Fed. 271; Demick v. Metropolitan L. Ins. Co., 67 N. J. L. 367; 51 Atl. 692; Dwyer v. Mut. Life Ins. Co., 72 N. H. 572; 58 Atl. 502; McManus v. Peerless Cas. Co., 114 Me. 98; 95 Atl. 510; Knapp v. Brotherhood Am. Yeomen, 128 Ia. 566; 105 N. W. 63.

[55] Elliott v. Mut. Ben. Ass'n, 27 N. Y. Supp. 696; Modern Woodmen of America v. Owens, Tex. Civ. App., 130 S. W. 858; National Annuity Ass'n v. McCall, 103 Ark. 201; 146 S. W. 125; Scofield v. Metropolitan L. Ins. Co., 79 Vt. 161; 64 Atl. 1107.

[56] Central Acc. Ins. Co. v. Spence, 176 Ill. App. 32; Pacific Mut. L. Ins. Co. v. O'Neil, 36 Okla. 792; 130 Pac. 270; Citizens' Natl. L. Ins. Co. v. Swords, 109 Miss. 635; 68 Sou. 920; Kribs v. United Order of Foresters, 191 Mo. App. 524; 177 S. W. 766; Floyd v. Modern Woodmen of America, 166 Mo. App. 166; 148 S. W. 178; Fidelity Mut. L. Ins. Co. v. Miazzi, 93 Miss. 18; 46 Sou. 817; Prudential Ins. Co. v. Hummer, 36 Colo. 208; 84 Pac. 61.

derstand what the warranty meant. Whether the applicant acted in good faith is immaterial.[57] If the statements are not true, the policy is avoided.[58] The company can defend on the ground of fraud without returning the consideration.[58a] Matters warranted must be strictly true.[59]

§ 246. **Warranties Not Favored at Law; Strict Construction.** —In determining whether or not the language of the contract imports a warranty, the courts will endeavor to discover the intent of the parties, and with a disposition, if possible, to avoid holding the statements to be warranties. The strict rule of construction as to warranties does not find favor with modern judges. Many years ago a learned jurist said:[60] "The construction that our own, as well as the English courts, have unfortunately given to a warranty, is exceedingly strict, but it is too well established to be now changed by any exercise of judicial discretion. It is not enough that a provision construed as a warranty in its spirit and substance is fulfilled; its terms must be literally complied with. Its breach is not excused by showing that it was the result, not of choice, but of accident or necessity; that it worked no prejudice to the insurer, and not only had no influence on the loss that is claimed, but had no tendency to increase, or even vary, the risks that were meant to be assumed. If a breach, however slight, and confessedly imma-

[57] Woehrle v. Metropolitan Life Ins. Co., 21 Misc. 88; 46 N. Y. Supp. 862; Standard L. & Acc. Ins. Co. v. Sale, 57 C. C. A. 418; 121 Fed. 664; 61 L. R. A. 337; Jennings v. Supreme Council, etc., 81 N. Y. Supp. 90; 81 App. Div. 76; Hoover v. Royal Neighbors, 65 Kan. 616; 70 Pac. 595; Standard L. & A. Co. v. Lauderdale, 94 Tenn. 635; 30 S. W. 732.

[58] Valleroy v. Knights of Columbus, 135 Mo. App. 574; 116 S. W. 1130; Sovereign Camp, etc., v. Latham, Ind. App.; 107 N. E. 749; Beard v. Royal Neighbors of America, 53 Ore. 102; 99 Pac. 83; 19 L. R. A. (N. S.) 798; Krause v. Modern Woodmen of America, 133 Ia. 199; 110 N. W. 452.

[58a] Taylor v. Grand Lodge, etc., 96 Minn. 441; 105 N. W. 408; 3 L. R. A. (N. S.) 114; Elliott v. Knights of Mod. Macc., 46 Wash. 320; 89 Pac. 929. But see Supreme Lodge, etc., v. Watkins, Ind. App., 110 N. E. 1008; Peterson v. Grand Lodge, etc., (S. D.), 156 N. W. 70.

[59] Claver v. Modern Woodmen of America, 152 Mo. App. 155; 133 S. W. 153; Evans v. Modern Woodmen of America, 147 Mo. App. 155; 129 S. W. 485; Silcox v. Grand Fraternity, 79 N. J. L. 502; 76 Atl. 1018.

[60] Westfall v. Hudson River F. Ins. Co., 2 Duer 495.

terial, is proved, the entire contract is at an end, the assured loses his indemnity, and the insurer retains his premium, and rejoices in his discharge. When the provision that is claimed to be a warranty is at all ambiguous, it seems to us it is a reasonable presumption that the assured never meant to bind himself by a stipulation thus rigidly construed, and we cannot but think that this presumption, unless the words used are such as plainly, if not necessarily, to exclude it, ought to prevail."[61] The Supreme Court of the United States, in a case where the application was made a part of the policy and the assured covenanted that he had made a full and just exposition of the material facts in regard to the condition, situation and value of the property, in concluding that an overestimate of the value of the property did not vitiate the policy, said:[62] "Two constructions of the contract may be suggested. One is to regard the warranty expressed in the policy as limited or qualified by the terms of the application. In that view, the assured would be held as only warranting that he had stated all material facts in regard to the condition, situation, value and risk of the property, so far as they were known to him. This is, perhaps, the construction most consistent with the literal import of the terms used in the application and the policy. The other construction is to regard the warranty as relating only to matters of which the assured had or should be presumed to have had, distinct, definite knowledge, and not to such matters as values, which depend upon mere opinion or probabilities. But without adopting either of these constructions, we rest the conclusion already indicated upon the broad ground that when a policy of insurance contains contradictory provisions, or has been so framed as to leave room for construction, rendering it doubtful whether the parties intended the exact truth of the applicant's state-

[61] Price v. Phoenix Mut. L. Ins. Co., 17 Minn. 497; 10 Am. Rep. 166; Miller v. Mut. Ben. Life Ins. Co., 31 Ia. 216; 7 Am. Rep. 122; Wheelton v. Hardnisty, 8 El. & B. 232; Stokes v. Cox, 1 H. & N. Exch. 320; Anderson v. Fitzgerald, 4 H. of L. Cas. 484; 17 Jur. 995; 24 E. L. & E. 1; Jennings v. Chenango, etc., Ins. Co., 2 Denio, 78; Jefferson Ins. Co. v. Cotheal, 7 Wend. 72; 22 Am. Dec. 571; Crosse v. Supreme Lodge K. L. of H., 254 Ill. 80; 98 N. E. 261.

[62] National Bank v. Ins. Co., 95 U. S. 678.

ments to be a condition precedent to any binding contract the court should lean against that construction which imposes upon the assured the obligations of a warranty. The company can- not justly complain of such a rule. Its attorneys, officers or agents prepared the policy for the purpose, we shall assume, both of protecting the company against fraud, and of securing the just rights of the assured under a valid contract of insur- ance. It is its language which the court is invited to interpret, and it is both reasonable and just that its own words should be construed most strongly against itself.''[63] A statement in a rider pasted on an accident policy headed ''Schedule of Warranties'' does not make it a condition precedent.[64]

§ 247. **Warranty Never Created by Construction.**—It follows that a warranty will never be created by construction. The courts will not construe language to mean a warranty unless it is so clear as to preclude any other construction,[65] the language must be clear and unambiguous.[66] As has been said in a leading case upon the subject of warranty:[67] ''The doctrine of war- ranty in the law of insurance is one of great rigor, and fre- quently operates very harshly upon the assured. A warranty is considered as a condition precedent, and whether material or immaterial, as it regards the risk, must be complied with before the assured can sustain an action against the underwriters. A warranty, therefore, is never created by construction. It must either appear in express terms, affirmative or promissory, or must necessarily result from the nature of the contract. It must, therefore, appear on the face of the policy, in order that there may be unequivocal evidence of a stipulation, the non- compliance with which is to have the effect of avoiding the con-

---

[63] Mut., etc., Ins. Co. v. Robertson, 59 Ill. 123; Kentucky, etc., Ins. Co. v. Southard, 8 B. Mon. 634; Gracelon v. Hampden F. Ins. Co., 50 Me. 580; Moulor v. American Life Ins. Co., 111 U. S. 335; Woodruff v. Im- perial F. Ins. Co., 83 N. Y. 133.

[64] Everson v. General Life Assur. Corp., 202 Mass. 169; 88 N. E. 652.

[65] Spence v. Central Acc. Ins. Co., 236 Ill. 444; 86 N. E. 104; Pru- dential Ins. Co. v. Lear, 31 App. D. C. 184; Paulhamus v. Security Life & Annuity Co., 163 Fed. 554.

[66] Metropolitan L.-Ins. Co. v. Johnson, 49 Ind. App. 233; 94 N. E. 785.

[67] Jefferson Ins. Co. v. Cotheal, 7 Wend. 72; 22 Am. Dec. 571.

tract. It was once doubted whether it must not be incorporated into the body of the policy; and it was contended that it was not sufficient for it to be written in the margin. But if it appears on the face of the policy, that is sufficient."[68] On this subject the Supreme Court of Alabama says:[69] "While warranties are not favored, and will neither be created or extended by construction, when a warranty is expressly and in terms declared, its stipulations and conditions must be strictly complied with; the question is disembarrassed of any consideration of materiality, the parties having made it material by their agreement."[70] "In considering the question," says the Supreme Court of Massachusetts,[71] "whether a statement forming a part of the contract is a warranty, it must be borne in mind, as an established maxim, that warranties are not to be created nor extended by construction. They must arise, if at all, from the fair interpretation and clear intendment of the words used by the parties.[72] Where, therefore, from the designation of such statements as 'statements' or as 'representations,' or from the form in which they are expressed, there appears to be no intention to give them the force and effect of warranties, they will not be so construed."[73] But where an application is referred to in the policy as the basis of the contract and it is agreed that it shall be deemed and taken as part of the policy and as a war-

[68] Higbie v. Guardian M. L. Ins. Co., 53 N. Y. 603; Hobby v. Dana, 17 Barb. 114; Burritt v. Saratoga, etc., Ins. Co., 5 Hill, 191; 40 Am. Dec. 345; Ripley v. Aetna Ins. Co., 30 N. Y. 157.

[69] Ala. Gold L. Ins. Co. v. Garner, 77 Ala. 215.

[70] Jeffries v. Life Ins. Co., 22 Wall. 47; Aetna Life Ins. Co. v. France Ins., 91 U. S. 510; American Popular L. Ins. Co. v. Day, 39 N. J. L. 89; 23 Am. Rep. 198.

[71] Campbell v. New England M. L. Ins. Co., 98 Mass. 391.

[72] Daniels v. Hudson R. Ins. Co., 12 Cush. 416; 59 Am. Dec. 192; Blood v. Howard Ins. Co., 12 Cush. 472; Forbush v. Western Mass. Ins. Co., 4 Gray 340.

[73] Houghton v. Manufacturers' Ins. Co., 8 Met. 114; Jones' Manufacturing Co. v. Manufacturers' Ins. Co., 8 Cush. 83; 54 Am. Dec. 742; Towne v. Fitchburg Ins. Co., 7 Allen 51; Price v. Phoenix M. L. Ins. Co., 17 Minn. 497; Fitch v. American Popular L. Ins. Co., 59 N. Y. 557; 17 Am. Rep. 372; Union Mut. L. Ins. Co. v. Link, 230 Ill. 273; 82 N. E. 637; Fidelity Mut. L. Ins. Co. v. Beck, 34 Ark. 57; 104 S. W. 533; Erickson v. Ladies of the Maccabees, 25 S. D. 183; 126 N. W. 259.

ranty on the part of the assured, both the application and policy are to be construed together as one entire contract. And it has been held that the statement in the policy, which makes an application part of it, and which contains various warranties on the part of the assured, and the further statement therein that any false or untrue answers or statements, material to the hazard of risk, shall render the policy void, does not defeat or limit the express warranties contained in the policy.[74]

§ 248. **Must Be Express.**—Warranties, therefore, never being implied, must be express. "The stipulations in policies," says Judge Savage,[75] "are considered express warranties; an express warranty is an agreement expressed in the policy whereby the assured stipulates that certain facts relating to the risk are, or shall be true, or certain acts relating to the same subject have been, or shall be done. It is not requisite that the circumstance or act warranted should be material to the risk; in this respect an express warranty is distinguished from a representation. Lord Eldon says: 'It is a first principle in the law of insurance, that if there is a warranty, it is a part of the contract, that the matter is such as it is represented to be. The materiality or immateriality signifies nothing. The only question is as to the mere fact.' "

§ 248a. **Affirmative and Promissory Warranties.**—Warranties may be either affirmative, that is, those which allege affirmatively that certain facts are true; or promissory, that is, those which undertake that certain things shall or shall not be done. Promissory warranties are often also called executory. The distinction is thus illustrated by the Supreme Court of Iowa:[76] "The policy in this case contains both affirmative and executory warranties: 1. The acceptance of the policy with the clause that the lower story of the building insured was, at the time the policy was effected, occupied for stores, was an affirmative or express warranty that the same was at the time so occupied. And

---

[74] Chrisman v. State Ins. Co., 16 Ore. 283; 18 Pac. 466.

[75] Duncan v. Sun F. Ins. Co., 6 Wend. 494.

[76] Stout v. City Fire Ins. Co., 12 Ia. 371; 79 Am. Dec. 539. See also Waters v. Supreme Conclave K. of D., 105 Ga. 151; 31 S. E. 155.

if the representation was false, in other words, if the lower story was not then so occupied, whether material to the risk or not, would avoid the policy. 2. The upper portion of this building insured, as set forth in the policy, was to remain unoccupied during the continuance of the policy. This portion is promissory or executory, and must be strictly complied with on the part of the assured, or the policy will be avoided, whether material to the risk or not. The distinction between the affirmative or express, and promissory, or executory, warranties is very perceptible in this case. The former represents that a certain fact did exist at the time the policy was effected; and the latter, that a certain thing should exist during the continuance of the policy—both made equally material by the parties themselves, and each fatal to the assured if false or not executed.'' The promise which is to be a warranty may frequently consist only of an expression of intention. Language in a policy which imports that the assured intends to do or not to do an act which materially affects the risk involves generally an engagement to perform or omit such act. If the assured would reserve a right to change such intention, he must employ explicit language to denote the reservation.[77] But this intent must always appear from the language used and the courts will not infer a warranty in promissory any more than in affirmative statements. As where the application stated that the premises insured were ''occupied by Goodhue as a private dwelling'' the New York Court of Appeals[78] held that ''here was an affirmative stipulation, that the house was then occupied by Goodhue, but not a promissory agreement that he should continue to occupy it. If it had been the intention of the parties to make it a condition that he should remain the occupant during the term of the insurance, it would have been easy to say so, and there is no good reason in this case for supposing the parties intended what they have not expressed.''[79]

[77] Bilbrough v. Metropolis F. Ins. Co., 5 Duer, 587.

[78] O'Neil v. Buffalo F. Ins. Co., 3 N. Y. 123.

[79] Benham v. United G. & L. Ass. Co., 7 Exch. 744; 14 E. L. & E. 524; 16 Jur. 691; 21 L. J. Ex. 317. See also Kansas City Life Ins. Co. v. Blackstone, Tex. Civ. App., 143 S. W. 702.

448

The Court of Appeals of Alabama[80] says: "In the law of insurance, as established and declared by judicial decision, a warranty is a statement of the contract with reference to the conditions on which it is predicated, the truth of which is made a condition to its validity; while a representation is a statement made as an inducement to a proposed contract of insurance and collateral to it. Warranties are of two kinds, affirmative and promissory. Affirmative warranties may be express or implied, and consist of representations in the policy of the existence of some fact or state of things at or previous to the time of making the policy. Promissory warranties may also be express or implied, but they usually have respect to the happening of some future event, or the performance of some act in the future. The distinction between affirmative and promissory or executory warranties is that the former represent the existence of certain facts or condition of things at the time when the policy is effected, and the latter represent that certain things shall exist during the continuance of the policy. An affirmative warranty is in the nature of a condition precedent, while a promissory warranty is in the nature of a condition subsequent, to the contract; and, whether affirmative or promissory, the effect of a breach thereof by the insured is to relieve the liability of the insurer, and this regardless, until the enaction of Section 4572 of the Code, of whether the matters warranted to be material or not to the risk, and regardless of whether the insured acted in good faith or not in making the warranty. On the other hand, in order to avoid a contract of insurance for false representations or misrepresentations not amounting to warranties, which, as seen, are a mere inducement to the making of the contract, it must appear, or be made to appear, not only that the matters and things so represented are false, but also that they were material to the risk. A false representation or misrepresentation renders the policy void on the ground of fraud on the part of the applicant in procuring it, while a non-compliance with a warranty by him operates as a breach of the conditions of the contract. Quite frequently it is a difficult question, even for the courts, to determine whether a clause in a contract of insurance amounts to a warranty or only a representation."

[80] Metropolitan Life Ins. Co. v. Goodman, 10 Ala. App. 446; 65 Sou. 449.

§ 249. **Construction of Warranties Must Be Reasonable.**—
The construction of all warranties must be reasonable. A distinction, according to the later authorities, must be observed between those descriptive particulars, which are inserted in the
contract merely for the purpose of identification, and those
which are designed to indicate the nature, extent and incidents
of the risk. These two classes of statements are to be construed
with reference to the purpose for 'which they are respectively
made. These distinctions necessarily oftener arise in cases of
fire and marine than in those of life insurance.[81] As in all other
matters of construction the object to be attained is to ascertain
the intent of the parties, and warranties will never be held to
exist except upon a fair interpretation and clear intendment of
the words of the parties. The construction will never be forced.[82]
And of late the courts seem inclined to relax former rules. We
may instance the case of Supreme Lodge K. of H. v. Dickson,[83]
where the Court said: "It is true that any statement made of
a material fact which forms the basis of the contract must be
considered as a warranty, and, if false, will vitiate the contract,
whether made in good faith, though ignorantly, or willfully, and
with knowledge of its falsity. But there is a difference between
statements of fact, as such, and statements of opinion on matters where only opinion can be expressed. Falsehood may be
predicated of a misstatement of fact, but not of a mistaken
opinion as to whether a man has a disease when it is latent, and
it can only be a matter of opinion. As to what a person may
have died of may be largely, if not altogether, a matter of
opinion, about which attending physicians often disagree, and
as to such matters their statements made can only be treated as
representations, and not as warranties, and if made in good faith
and on the best information had or obtainable, they will not
vitiate a policy, if incorrect and not willfully untrue." In an-

81 See note to Fowler v. Aetna F. Ins. Co., 6 Cow. 673; 16 Am. Dec.
466, and cases cited.

82 Conover v. Mass. Mut. L. Ins. Co., 3 Dill. 217; Campbell v. New
England L. Ins. Co., 98 Mass. 381; Provident Life, etc., Ass'n v. Reutlinger, 58 Ark. 528; 25 S. W. 835.

83 102 Tenn. 255; 52 S. W. 862.

other case[84] it was said: ''Whether statements which obviously cannot lie within the knowledge of the applicant, and which both parties know are to be given upon information and belief, must be taken to be warranties, is a question which we need not decide: but that the above provisions constitute a warranty of the truth of the statements in the application, so far as they rest upon the applicant's own knowledge, is beyond question.[85]

§ 250. **Review of Rules of Construction.**—The modern rules of construction of insurance contracts in regard to warranties and representations are thus summarized by the Supreme Court of Alabama, in a recent case:[86] ''In construing contracts of insurance, there are some settled rules of construction bearing on this subject which we may briefly formulate as follows: 1. The courts, being strongly inclined against forfeitures, will construe all the, conditions of the contract, and the obligations imposed, liberally in favor of the assured, and strictly against the insurer. 2. It requires the clearest and most unequivocal language to create a warranty, and every statement or engagement of the assured will be construed to be a representation, and not a warranty, if it be at all doubtful in meaning, or the contract contains contradictory provisions relating to the subject, or be otherwise reasonably susceptible of such construction. The court, in other words, will lean against that construction of the contract which will impose upon the assured the burdens of a warranty, and will neither create nor extend a warranty by construction. 3. Even though a warranty in name or form be created by the terms of the contract, its effects may be modified by other parts of the policy, or of the application, including the questions and answers, so that the answers of the assured, so often merely categorical, will be construed not to be a warranty of immaterial facts stated in such answers, but rather a warranty of the assured's honest belief in their truth; or in

[84] Sweeney v. Metropolitan L. Ins. Co., 19 R. I. 171; 36 Atl. 9.

[85] See also Provident Savings L. A. Soc. v. Oliver, 22 Tex. Civ. App. 8; 53 S. W. 594; McCarthy v. Catholic Knights, etc., 102 Tenn. 345; 52 S. W. 142; Thompson v. Family Protective Union, 66 S. C. 459; 45 S. E. 19; Aetna L. Ins. Co. v. King, 84 Ill. App. 171.

[86] Alabama Gold L. Ins. Co. v. Johnson, 80 Ala. 467; 2 Sou. 128.

other words, that they were stated in good faith. The strong inclination of the courts is thus to make these statements or answers binding only so far as they are material to the risk, where this can be done without doing violence to the clear intention of the parties expressed in unequivocal and unqualified language to the contrary. In support of these deductions we need not do more than refer to the following authorities.[87] Many early adjudications may be found, and not a few recent ones also, in which contracts of insurance, and especially of life insurance, have been construed in such a manner as to operate with great harshness and injustice to policyholders, who, acting with all proper prudence, as remarked by Lord St. Leonards in the case of Anderson v. Fitzgerald,[88] had been 'led to suppose that they had made a provision for their families by an insurance on their lives, when in point of fact the policy was not worth the paper on which it is written.' The rapid growth of the business of life insurance in the past quarter of a century, with the tendency of insurers to exact increasingly rigid and technical conditions, and the evils resulting from an abuse of the whole system, justify, if they do not necessitate a departure from the rigidity of our earlier jurisprudence on the subject of warranties. And such, as we have said, is the tendency of the more modern authorities. There are, it is true, in this case, some expressions in both the policy and the application (which, taken together, constitute the contract of insurance) that indicate an intention to make all statements by the assured absolute warranties. The application, consisting of a 'proposal' and a 'declaration,' is declared to 'form the basis of the contract' of insurance, and the policy is asserted to have been issued 'on the

[87] Moulor v. American Life Ins. Co., 111 U. S. 335; National Bank v. Ins. Co., 95 U. S. 673; Price v. Phoenix Mut. L. Ins. Co., 17 Minn. 497; 10 Am. Rep. 166; Southern Life Ins. Co. v. Booker, 9 Heisk. 606; 24 Am. Rep. 344; Bliss Ins., § 34; Campbell v. New England L. Ins. Co,. 98 Mass. 381; Fowler v. Aetna F. Ins. Co., 6 Cow. 673; 16 Am. Dec. (note) 463; Piedmont, etc., Ins. Co. v. Young, 58 Ala. 476; Pars. Cont. 465; Glendale Woolen Co. v. Protection Ins. Co., 21 Conn. 19; 24 Am. Dec. 309; Wilkinson v. Conn. Mut. L. Ins. Co., 30 Ia. 119; 6 Am. Rep. 657; 1 Phill. Ins., § 638; Ang. Ins,. §§ 147-147a.

[88] 4 H. L. Cas. 484; 17 Jur. 995; 24 E. L. & E. 1.

faith' of the application. It is further provided that if the declaration, or any part of it, made by the assured, shall be found 'in any respect untrue,' or 'any untrue or fraudulent answers' are made to the questions propounded, or facts suppressed, the policy shall be vitiated, and all payments of premiums made thereon shall be forfeited. . So, if there were nothing in the contract to rebut the implication, it might perhaps be held out that the parties had made each answer of the assured material to the risk by the mere fact of propounding the questions to which such answers were made and that this precluded all inquiry into the question of materiality.[89] On the contrary, the policy purports to be issued 'in consideration of the representations' made in the application, and of the annual premiums. The answers are no where expressly declared to be warranties; nor is the application, in so many words, made a part of the contract so as to clearly import the answers into the terms and conditions of the policy. Among numerous other questions the assured was asked whether he had been affected since childhood with any one of an enumerated list of complaints or diseases, including 'fits or convulsions,' and whether he had 'ever been seriously ill,' or had been affected with 'any serious disease.' To each of these questions he answered 'no.' The concluding question is as follows: 'Is the party aware that any untrue or fraudulent answers to the above queries, or any suppression of the facts in regard to the party's health, will vitiate the policy, and forfeit all payments made thereon?' To this was given the answer 'yes.' It is significant, as observed in a recent case before the New York Court of Appeals, that the assured 'is not asked whether he is aware that any unintentional mistake in answering any of the host of questions thrust at him, whether material to the risk or not, will be a breach of warranty, and vitiate his policy.'[90] Then follows a declaration that 'the assured is now in good health, and does ordinarily enjoy good health,' and that in the proposal of insurance he 'had not withheld any material circumstance or information touching the past or present state of health or habits of life' of the assured with

89 Price v. Phoenix L. Ins. Co., 17 Minn. 497.
90 Fitch v. American, etc., Ins. Co., 59 N. Y. 557; 17 Am. Rep. 372.

which the company 'should be made acquainted.' One part of
the contract thus tends to show an intention to constitute the
answers warranties, while the other describes and treats them
as representations. There is thus left ample room for construction. What is to be understood by 'untrue' answers, or 'any
suppression of facts?' Can they have reference to any disease
with which the assured was alleged to have been afflicted, of
which he knew nothing, and could not possibly have informed
himself by the exercise of proper diligence? Are they intended
as absolute warranties of the fact that he had never, since childhood, or during life, been afflicted with diseases of which neither
he nor the most skillful physician could have had any knowledge whatever? The case of Moulor v. American Life Ins. Co.[91]
is a direct and strong authority for the position that the word
'untrue' in the above connection, in its broader sense, means
knowingly or designedly untrue, or recklessly so—that it is the
opposite of sincere, honest, not fraudulent. As said in that case,
it is reasonably clear that, 'what the company required of the
applicant as a condition precedent to any binding contract was
that he would observe the utmost good faith towards it and
make full, direct, and honest answers to all questions, without
evasion or fraud, and without suppression, misrepresentation or
concealment of facts with which the company ought to be made
acquainted, and that by doing so, and only by doing so, would
he be deemed to have made fair and true answers.' The case of
Southern Life Insurance Company v. Booker,[92] sustains the same
view. There the policy, as here, was conditioned to be avoided
by any 'untrue or fraudulent answer' to the questions in the
application. The answers were not strictly true as to the birth-
place, residence and occupation of the assured. It was held that
none of these being material to the risk, they would be construed as representations, although expressly declared to be
'the basis of the contract' of insurance. The Court said: 'It
would seem to be gross injustice to allow this (meaning the
avoidance of the policy, and the forfeiture of all payments made
under it), in a case where the insured has acted in the utmost

[91] 111 U. S. 335.
[92] 9 Heisk. 606; 24 Am. Rep. 344.

good faith, and honestly disclosed every fact material to be known, because, merely by inadvertence or oversight, an error of fact has been inserted in his application—an error that is clearly immaterial, and that could not by any possibility have affected the contract.' 'It is true that the parties have a right,' the Court adds, 'to make their own contract and by its terms we must be governed, but before a court could hold a policy void, and all premiums paid thereon forfeited because statements of this character in the application turned out to be untrue, they should be fully satisfied that such terms were fully and distinctly agreed to by the parties.' These views, in our judgment, announce the sounder and more just doctrine, and they meet with our approval, being supported by reason, as well as by the more recent decisions in this country, on the subject of life insurance.[93] So, the declaration embodied in the application would seem to indicate that it is the inadvertent suppression or statement only of material circumstances or information with which the company should in good faith be made acquainted that will vitiate the policy and cause a forfeiture. It cannot be supposed that one who, for the purpose of procuring insurance, alleges himself to be in good health, shall be understood as warranting himself to be in perfect and absolute health; for this is seldom, if ever, the fortune of any human being: and 'we are all born,' as said by Lord Mansfield in Willis v. Poole,[94] 'with the seeds of mortality in us.' These inquiries as to symptoms of diseases as said by Mr. Parsons, therefore must mean whether they 'have ever appeared in such a way, or under such circumstances as to indicate a disease which would have a tendency to shorten life;' and he adds: 'It is with this meaning the question is left to the jury.[95] It has accordingly been held in an English case, cited and approved both by Mr. Parsons and Mr. Addison, that even a warranty that the person whose life is insured 'has not been afflicted with, nor is subject to vertigo, fits,' etc., would not be falsified by having had one fit. To forfeit the policy on this

[93] Add. Contr. (Morgan's Ed.), § 1123; Price v. Phoenix M. L. Ins. Co., 17 Minn. 497; Fitch v. American, etc,. Ins. Co., 59 N. Y. 557.
[94] 2 Parke Ins. 650.
[95] 2 Pars. Contr. 468, 471; 3 Add. Conts., § 1233.

ground he must have been habitually or constitutionally afflicted with fits. 'Even then,' adds Mr. Parsons, 'we apprehend the materiality of the fact would be taken into consideration; that is, for example, the policy would not be defeated by proof that the life insured, long years before, and when a teething child, had a fit.' . . . Our conclusion is that the following is a just and fair construction of the contract of insurance under consideration: 1. That the answers of the assured were not absolute warranties, but in the nature of representations; or, if warranties, they are so modified by other parts of the contract as to be warranties only of an honest belief of their truth. 2. That any untrue statement or suppression of fact material to the risk assured will vitiate the policy, and thus bar a recovery whether intentional or within the knowledge of the assured or not. 3. If immaterial, such statement, to avoid the policy, must have been untrue within the knowledge of the assured; that is, he must either have known it, or have been negligently ignorant. of it. 4. The terms of the contract rebut the implication that all symptoms of diseases inquired about were intended to be made absolutely material, unless they had once existed in such appreciable form as would affect soundness of health, or have a tendency to shorten life, and thus affect the risk.''[96] Where the application was filled out by the medical examiner there is nothing to show that the answers as written were those of the insured, and hence no warranty exists.[97]

§ 251. **The Same Subject Continued.**—The evident tendency of the later decisions is to modify the strict rules as to warranty so that a warranty as to the truth of the answer, which by its nature expresses only the opinion of the applicant, should not

[96] The authorities are also reviewed in Provident Savings L. A. Soc. v. Llewellyn, 7 C. C. A. 579; 58 Fed. 940; 16 U. S. App. 405. See also Fidelity M. L. Ass'n v. Jeffords, 107 Fed. 402; 46 C. C. A. 377; 53 L. R. A. 193, where a most thorough note is appended; Leonard v. New England Life Ins. Co., 22 R. I. 519; 48 Atl. 808; N. W. Mut. L. Ins. Co. v. Woods, 54 Kan. 663; 30 Pac. 189; Roehm v. Commercial Alliance L. Ins. Co., 9 Misc. 529; 30 N. Y. Supp. 660.

[97] Leonard v. New England Mut. L. Ins. Co., 22 R. I. 519; 48 Atl. 808. See also Sweeney v. Metropolitan L. Ins. Co., 19 R. I. 171; 36 Atl. 9; 38 L. R. A. 297.

extend further than to insure the honesty and good faith of the party answering.[98] In the case of Collins v. Catholic Order of Foresters,[99] it is said: "We think the correct rule of interpretation to be applied to the interrogatories and answers under consideration is that statements concerning matters of fact that are made in the application, and which are presumably within the knowledge of the applicant, are to be treated as warranting the existence of such fact; but declarations and statements contained in such application, of matters of fact concerning which the insurer should know that the applicant could not have certain knowledge of, and such also as are necessarily opinions of the applicant, are to be regarded as warranting only the applicant's honest belief in the truth of the statements which are made, and of his honest opinion, where an opinion is given."[100] A breach of warranty renders the policy voidable only and the insurer may be estopped by not proceeding to enforce a forfeiture.[101] The beneficiary of a reinstated policy cannot recover where there was a breach of warranty as to health and consultation of a physician.[102] The use of the word warranty does not necessarily render a statement made in the application a warranty, but all the language of the contract will be taken into consideration.[103]

In the case of Weisguth v. Supreme Tribe of Ben Hur, 272

[98] Rasicot v. Royal Neighbors of America, 18 Idaho 85; 108 Pac. 1048. See also Lakka v. Modern Brotherhood of America, 163 Iowa 159; 143 N. W. 513; Green v. National Annuity Ass'n, 90 Kan. 523; 135 Pac. 586; Farragher v. Knights and Ladies of S. (Kan.), 159 Pac. 3.

[99] 43 Ind. App. 549; 88 N. E. 87.

[100] Owen v. Metropolitan Life Ins. Co., 74 N. J. Law, 770; 67 Atl. 25; 122 Am. St. Rep. 413. See also Cunningham v. Modern Brotherhood of America, 96 Neb. 827; 148 N. W. 917; Bryant v. Modern Woodmen of America, 86 Neb. 372; 125 N. W. 621; 27 L. R. A. (N. S.) 326; 21 Ann. Cas. 365; Daniel v. M. W. A., 53 Tex. Civ. App. 570; 118 S. W. 211.

[101] Modern Woodmen of America v. Vincent, 40 Ind. App. 711; 80 N. E. 427.

[102] New York Life Ins. Co. v. Franklin, 118 Va. 418; 87 S. E. 584; Supreme Ruling Fraternal Mystic Circle v. Hansen (Tex. Civ. App), 161 S. W. 54.

[103] North American Accident Ins. Co. v. Rehacek, 123 Ill. App. 219; Court of Honor v. Clark; 125 Ill. App. 490; Reppond v. National Life Ins. Co., 100 Tex. 519; 101 S. W. 786; reversing 96 S. W. 778.

Ill. 541,[104] the application provided as follows: "I do hereby agree and warrant as follows: That the statements and answers contained in this application and medical examination are full, complete and true . . . and that any untrue or fraudulent answers made by me in this application . . . shall vitiate my beneficial certificate and forfeit all payments made thereon." In holding that the statements were representations and not .warranties the Supreme Court of Illinois said: "It is insisted, as a matter of law, that the answers of the deceased to the questions propounded by the medical examiner were warranties and not mere representations, and therefore, some of them having been found untrue, defendant in error is not entitled to recover. It is only in cases where the policy will admit of no other construction that a statement contained therein will be construed as a warranty. 'The doctrine of warranty, in the law of insurance, is one of great rigor, and frequently operates very harshly upon the assured, and courts will never construe a.statement as a warranty unless the language of the policy is so clear as to preclude any other construction.'[105] Under the holding in Continental Life Ins. Co. v. Rogers,[106] the statements made in this application must be held to be representations and.not warranties. In that case the policy provided that the answers, statements and declarations contained in or indorsed upon the application, which was made a part of the contract, were warranted by the assured to be true in all respects, and that if the policy was obtained by or through any fraud, misrepresentation or concealment, it should be absolutely null and void. In passing upon the question whether that constituted a warranty or a mere representation we said: 'It is clear, the fraud, concealment and misrepresentation here contemplated can have no application to anything other than the answers to the questions in the application. If true and full answers, there could be neither fraud, concealment nor .misrepresentation, and if not full and true, upon the hypothesis they were warranties, the assured would incur a forfeiture of the policy whether there was any intentional misrepresentation or suppression of the

[104] 112 N. E. 350.

[105] Spence v. Central Accident Ins. Co., 236 Ill. 444; 86 N. E. 104; 19 L. R. A. (N. S.) 88.

[106] 119 Ill. 474; 10 N. E. 242; 59 Am. Rep. 810.

truth or not. If the answers, however, are simply representations, as contradistinguished from warranties, in the technical sense of those terms, then such of the answers, not material to the risk, as were honestly made, in the belief they were true, would not be binding upon the assured or present any obstacle to a recovery. It is clear, therefore, the only way in which to give that provision of the policy relating to fraud, concealment and misrepresentation any effect at all is by treating the answers in the policy as mere representations, and not warranties!"[107]

§ 252. **Where Partial or no Answers are Made to Questions.** —It may happen that a question in an application for insurance is either partially answered or is not answered at all. In the latter case there is no warranty that there is nothing to answer.[108] "And so," says the Court of Appeals of New York,[109] "in the case of a partial answer, the warranty cannot be extended beyond the answer. Fraud may be predicated upon the suppression of truth, but breach of warranty must be based upon the affirmation of something not true." The question has most frequently come up where the applicant has stated the name of a single physician as his attendant where he has had others; in such cases the rule has been laid down that where the answer is full and complete so far as it goes and does not purport to cover all possible cases, the company should exact a fuller answer if it desired it. In one case the interrogatory was, "Name and residence of the family physician of the party, or of one whom the party has usually employed or consulted?" and the answer was "Refer to Dr. A. T. Mills, Corning, N. Y." The Court of Appeals of New York said in regard to this:[110] "The language of the answer is equivocal. It neither declares Dr. Mills to have been, or to be the family physician of the applicant, or that he was the physician

---

107 See also Fidelity Mut. Life Ins. Co. v. Elmore (Miss.), 71 Sou. 305.

108 Liberty Hall v. Ins. Co., 7 Gray 261; Mut. L. Ins. Co. v. Selby, 19 C. C. A. 331; 72 Fed. 980; Thies v. Mut. L. Ins. Co. of Ky., 13 Tex. C. A. 280; 35 S. W. 676; Fitzgerald v. Supreme Counc. Catholic, etc., 56 N. Y. Supp. 1005; 39 App. Div. 251; affd. 167 N. Y. 568; 60 N. E. 1110; Billings v. Metropolitan L. Ins. Co., 70 Vt. 477; 41 Atl. 516; Triple Link v. Froebe, 90 Ill. App. 299. See also Knights of the Modern Maccabees v. Gillespie (Ala. App.), 71 Sou. 67.

109 Dilleber v. Home Life Ins. Co,. 69 N. Y. 256; 25 Am. Rep. 182.

110 Higgins v. Phoenix Mut. L. Ins. Co., 74 N. Y. 9.

whom he had usually employed or consulted, or if he occupied either relation, which it was. It is only upon the ground that the statement constitutes an express warranty; and was untrue in fact that the defense can be sustained. The answer is not responsive in terms to the interrogatory, and does not profess to give the information asked. If it was not satisfactory to the defendant, a fuller and more explicit answer should have been required. A breach of warranty as upon the affirmance of an untruth cannot be alleged in respect of an answer which does not profess to state any fact. The words of the answer cannot be extended by implication in aid of a defense founded upon a technical breach of a warranty beyond the fair import of its language and the intent of the party as indicated by its terms. It is always within the power of the insurer to have an explicit and clear affirmation as to every fact material to the risk and if the answers to the interrogatories are not full, and do·not give the information called for, they cannot be treated as affirmations of facts not stated, although called for by the interrogatories.''[111] The subject is further elucidated by the Supreme Court of the United States, which says:[112] ''Where an answer of the applicant to a direct question of the insurers purports to be a complete answer to the question, any substantial misstatement or omission in the answer avoids a policy issued on the faith of the application.[113] But where, upon the face of the application, a question appears to be not answered at all, or to be imperfectly answered, and the insurers issue a policy without further inquiry, they waive the want or imperfection in the answer, and render the omission to answer more fully immaterial.[114] The distinction between an answer apparently complete, but in fact incomplete, and therefore

[111] Baker v. Home Life Ins. Co., 64 N. Y. 648; Eddington v. Mut. L. Ins. Co., 67 N. Y. 185; Fitch v. American Ins. Co., 59 N. Y. 557; Penn. Mut. L. Ins. Co. v. Wiler, 100 Ind. 92; American Ins. Co. v. Mahone, 56 Miss. 180. See also Paulhamus v. Security Life, etc., Co., 163 Fed. 554; O'Connor v. Modern Woodmen of America, 110 Minn. 18; 124 N. W. 454.

[112] Phoenix Mut. L. Ins. Co. v. Raddin, 120 U. S. 183; 7 Sup. Ct. Rep. 500.

[113] Cazenove v. British, etc., Ass. Co., 29 L. J. C. P. (N. S.), 160; 6 Jur. (N. S.) 826; 8 W. R. 243 Ex. Ch.

[114] Conn. Mut. L. Ins. Co. v. Luchs, 108 U. S. 498; Hall v. People's Ins. Co., 6 Gray 185; Lorillard Ins. Co. v. McCulloch, 21 Ohio St. 176; Ameri-

untrue, and an answer manifestly incomplete and as such accepted by the insurers, may be illustrated by two cases of fire insurance,. which are governed by the same rules in this respect as cases of life insurance. If one applying for insurance upon a building against fire is asked whether the property is incumbered, and for what amount, and in his answer discloses one mortgage when in fact there are two, the policy issued thereon is avoided.[115] But if to the same question he merely answers that the property is incumbered, without stating the amount of incumbrances, the issue of the policy without further inquiry is a waiver of the omission to state the amount."[116] The English doctrine in regard to incomplete answers is more favorable to the companies.[117] There is no warranty where a question is unanswered.[118] The ditto mark placed under an answer of "No," in response to a question immediately above will be construed to mean the same and, if the answer be false, the policy will be avoided whether the answer be regarded as an evasion or a falsity.[119] But a mere check mark placed opposite a question cannot be construed to mean a negative answer when check marks of the same kind are placed opposite questions not answered and deemed immaterial.[120]

§ 253. **When Answers Are Not Responsive.**—Where the answers to questions in the application are not responsive they will not be considered warranties although made so by the policy. This was held in a case in the Federal Court in Ohio,[121] where the

can Ins. Co. v. Mahone, 66 Miss. 180; Carson v. Jersey City Ins. Co., 43 N. J. L. 300; s. c. 44 N. J. L. 210; Lebanon Ins. Co. v. Kelper, 106 Pa. St. 28.

[115] Towne v. Fitchburg Ins. Co., 7 Allen 51. See also Wright v. Equitable Life, etc., Soc., 50 How. Pr. 367.

[116] Nichols v. Fayette Ins. Co., 1 Allen, 63; Dunbar v. Phenix Ins. Co., 72 Wis. 492; 40 N. W. 386.

[117] London Ass. v. Mansel, 11 Ch. D. 363; 48 L. J. Ch. 381; 41 L. T. 225; 27 W. R. 444.

[118] Brown v. Greenfield L. Ass'n, 172 Mass. 498; 53 N. E. 129; Mut. Res. F. L. A. v. Farmer, 65 Ark. 581; 47 S. W. 850.

[119] Fitzrandolph v. Mut. R. Soc., 21 Nova Scotia R. 274.

[120] Manhattan L. Ins. Co. v. P. J. Willis & Bro., 8 C. C. A. 594; 60 Fed. 236.

[121] Buell v. Conn. Mut. L. Ins. Co., 2 Flipp. 9; Triple Link, etc., v. Froebe, 90 Ill. App. 299.

question was whether the father or certain other relatives had been afflicted with certain diseases, and continued, "If so, state full particulars of each case?" The reply was: "No, father died from exposure in water, age 58." In fact the father died at the age of 30. The Court held the latter part of the answer not responsive and therefore a representation, stating the rule thus: "Where the answers are responsive to direct questions asked by the insurance company, they are to be regarded as warranties, and where they are not so responsive, but volunteered without being called for, they should be construed to be mere representations. The part of the answer in question in this case in reference to the age of the father at death, being a mere representation, does not constitute a defense unless it appears to have been material as well as false.[122] In a case in Minnesota,[123] the Court says: "The answer to a material question may be in itself wholly immaterial and of no effect. An answer so irresponsive as to leave the fact inquired of wholly undisclosed, the question unanswered, will not avoid the contract in the absence of fraud."

§ 254. **Qualified Answers.**—If the answers of the applicant to the questions in the application are limited or qualified by any particular or general expression, clearly showing an intention so to limit or qualify his statements, effect will be given to such intent. Thus, where the question was whether certain relatives of the applicant had been afflicted with any hereditary disease and he replied, "Not to my knowledge," it was held by the Supreme Court of the United States[124] that the affirmation was narrowed down to what the applicant himself personally knew touching the subject. And to make out the defense sought to be established, that the answer was false, the company must show that the disease existed, that it was hereditary, and that both of these things were known to the applicant when he answered the question. So,

---

[122] Protection Ins. Co. v. Harmer, 2 Ohio St. 473.

[123] Perine v. Grand Lodge, A. O. U. W., 51 Minn. 224; 53 N. W. 367; Smith v. Bankers' Life Ass'n, 123 Ill. App. 392; Keatley v. Grand Fraternity, 198 Fed. 264; Peterson v. Manhattan L. Ins. Co., 244 Ill. 329; 91 N. E. 466, reversing 115 Ill. App. 421; Hanrahan v. Metropolitan L. Ins. Co., 72 N. J. Law, 504; 63 Atl. 280.

[124] Insurance Co. v. Gridley, 100 U. S. 614.

where the answers in the application were qualified by the words at its foot: "The above is as near correct as I remember it," it was held[125] that, to defeat recovery on the policy, the applicant must have been consciously incorrect in some one of the answers. In another case[126] the applicant stated that the facts recited in his application were "true to the best of his knowledge and belief." It was held that it would not avail the company to show that such acts were false, unless it also showed that at the time the statements were made the applicant knew them to be false.[127] This is much more the case when the question requires the applicant to answer "so far as he knows,"[128] or where the question calls for an opinion or judgment.[129] Where answers as to use of liquor are conflicting, the policy will not be avoided.[130]

A warranty of the answer to the best of knowledge and belief in one only of the good faith of the applicant,[131] and where the question was as to the employment or consulting a physician, and the answer was "Have no," although insured had previously consulted a physician but had not employed one, it was held that

125 Aetna Ins. Co. v. France, 94 U. S. 561.

126 Clapp v. Mass. Ben. Ass'n, 146 Mass. 519; 16 N. E. 433.

127 See also Fisher v. Crescent Ins. Co., 33 Fed. 549; Anders v. Supreme L. K. of H., 51 N. J. L. 175; 17 Atl. 119; O'Connell v. Supreme Conclave K. of D., 102 Ga. 143; 28 S. E. 282; and generally see as to qualified answers: Mut. Reserve F. L. Ass'n v. Sullivan (Tex. Civ. A.), 29 S. W. 190; Mut. Reserve F. L. Ass'n v. Farmer, 65 Ark. 581; 47 S. W. 850; Egan v. Supreme Counc. Cath. Benev. L., 52 N. Y. Supp. 978; affd. 161 N. Y. 650; 57 N. E. 1109; Jennings v. Supreme Counc. Loyal Ben. Ass'n, 81 App. Div. 76; 81 N. Y. Supp. 90; Henn v. Metropolitan L. I. Co., 67 N. J. L. 310; 51 Atl. 689; Minnesota Mut. L. Ins. Co. v. Link, 230 Ill. 275; 82 N. E. 637; affd. 131 Ill. App. 89.

128 Fitzgerald v. Supreme Council Cath., etc., Ass'n, 39 App. Div. 251; 56 N. Y. Supp. 1005; affd. 167 N. Y. 568; 60 N. E. 1110.

129 Royal Neighbors v. Wallace, 73 Neb. 409; 99 N. W. 256, following Aetna L. Ins. Co. v. Rehlaender, 68 Neb. 284; 94 N. W. 129; Security Trust Co. v. Tarpey, 182 Ill. 52; 54 N. E. 1041.

130 Schon v. Modern Woodmen of America, 51 Wash. 482; 99 Pac. 25.

131 Iowa Life Ins. Co. v. Haughton (Ind. App.), 87 N. E. 702; reversing 85 N. E. 127; Kidder v. Supreme Assembly, etc., 154 Ill. App. 489; Raymer v. Modern Brotherhood of America, 151 Ill. App. 510; Yeoman of America v. Rott, 145 Ky. 604; 140 S. W. 1018; Berman v. Fraternities Health, etc., Co., 107 Me. 368; 78 Atl. 462.

there was no breach of warranty.[132]   An applicant is not guilty
of misrepresentation or concealment, when in answer to the question "What is the amount of your daily consumption of liquor,
beer, or wine," replies "None at all," when he does not drink
habitually every day and who sometimes does not drink during
a period of six months.[133]   Where the applicant answers that the
statements made are true to the best of his knowledge, information
and belief, such declaration did not constitute a warranty and the
insurer must prove that the applicant knew that the answer was
false, if such answer was in fact false.[134]

§ 255.   **Representations.**—In the course of the preceding discussion much has been said in regard to representation as contradistinguished from warranty, and in speaking of the latter many
characteristics of the former have been mentioned.   A representation has been defined to be a verbal or written statement made
before the issuance of the policy as to some fact, or state of facts,
tending to induce the insurer more readily to assume the risk,
or to assume it for a less premium, by diminishing the estimate
he would otherwise have formed of it.[135]   Another definition[136]
is, that it is "a statement of facts, circumstances or information,
tending to increase or diminish the risks, as they would otherwise
be considered, made prior to the execution of the policy by the
assured or his agent to the insurer, in order to guide his judgment in forming a just estimate of the risks he is desired to assume.   It is usually made by parol or by writing not inserted
in the policy, but when the intention as to the construction is
sufficiently declared, may be expressed in the policy."   It is
extrinsic, collateral and incidental to the contract, because a
presentation of the elements upon which to estimate the risk
and the basis of the undertaking to be entered into.[137]   The Su-

132 Haughton v. Aetna Life Ins. Co., 42 Ind. App. 527; 85 N. E. 125,
1050; Metropolitan Life Ins. Co. v. Brubaker, 178 Kan. 146; 96 Pac. 62.
133 Prudential Ins. Co. v. Carrier, 43 Quebec Sup. Court R. 97.
134 Sawyer v. Mut. Life Ins. Co,. 8 Dominion L. R. 2.
135 Arnold on Ins., § 182; Bliss on Life Ins., § 35.
136 Duer on Ins. 644.
137 Campbell v. New England Mut. L. Ins. Co., 98 Mass. 381; Daniels
v. Hudson River Ins. Co., 12 Cush. 416; 58 Am. Dec. 192.

preme Court of Alabama happily says:[138] "A representation is not, strictly speaking, a part of the contract of insurance, or of the essence of it, but rather something collateral or preliminary, and in the nature of an inducement to it. A false representation, unlike a false warranty, will not operate to vitiate the contract or avoid the policy, unless it relates to a fact actually material, or clearly intended to be made material by the agreement of the parties. It is sufficient, if representations be substantially true. They need not be strictly nor literally true. A misrepresentation renders the policy void on the ground of fraud, while non-compliance with a warranty operates as an express breach of the contract."[139] While a breach of warranty vitiates the policy, the language used may modify the warranty so as to make it a representation only.[140] In order to avoid the policy the representations must be those of the insured and not mistakes of the company.[141] The effect of misrepresentations is often determined by statute.[142]

§ 256. **Difference Between Warranty and Representation.**— The Supreme Court of Connecticut[143] states the difference between a representation and a warranty thus: "The former precedes and is no part of the contract of insurance, and need be only materially true; the latter is a part of the contract and

[138] Alabama Gold Life Ins. Co. v. Johnson, 80 Ala. 467; 2 Sou. 128.

[139] Price v. Phoenix Mut. Ins. Co., 17 Minn. 497; 10 Am. Rep. 166; Fisher v. Crescent Ins. Co., 33 Fed. 549; Moulor v. Am. Ins. Co., 111 U. S. 335; Phoenix Mut. L. Ins. Co. v. Raddin, 120 U. S. 183; Thompson v. Weems, 9 App. Cas. 671. See also Maine Ben. Ass'n v. Parks, 81 Me. 79; 16 Atl. 339. See also Aetna L. Ins. Co., v. Rehlaender, 68 Neb. 284; 94 N. W. 129; Royal Neighbors v. Wallace, 66 Neb. 543; 92 N. W. 897.

[140] Reppond v. National Ins. Co., 100 Tex. 519; 101 S. W. 786, reversing 96 S. W. 778.

[141] Hewey v. Metropolitan L. Ins. Co., 100 Me. 523; 62 Atl. 600, but see Bankers' Life Ins. Co. v. Miller, 100 Md. 1; 59 Atl. 116.

[142] See as to Missouri statute Keller v. Home Life Ins. Co., 198 Mo. 440; 95 S. W. 903; Massachusetts, Leonard v. State Mut. L. Assur. Co., 27 R. I. 121; 61 Atl. 52; Kentucky, Provident Savings L. A. Soc. v. Dees, 120 Ky. 285; 86 S. W. 522.

[143] Glendale Woolen Co. v. Protection Ins. Co., 21 Conn. 19; 54 Am. Dec. 309.

policy, and must be exactly and literally fulfilled, or else the contract is broken and the policy becomes void." "A warranty, in
insurance," says the Supreme Court of Massachusetts,[144] "enters
into and forms a part of the contract itself. It defines, by ways
of particular stipulation, description, condition, or otherwise, the
precise limits of the obligation which the insurers undertake to
assume. No liability can arise except within those limits. In
order to charge the insurers, therefore, every one of the terms
which define their obligation must be satisfied by the facts which
appear in proof. From the very nature of the case, the party
seeking his indemnity, or payment under the contract, must bring
his claim within the provisions of the instrument he is undertaking to enforce. The burden of proof is upon the plaintiff
to present a case in all respects conforming to the terms under
which the risk was assumed. It must be not merely a substantial
conformity, but exact and literal; not only in material particulars,
but in those that are immaterial as well. A representation is, on
the other hand, in its nature no part of the contract of insurance.
Its relation to the contract is usually described by the term 'collateral.' It may be proved, although existing only in parol and
preceding the written instrument. Unlike other verbal negotiations, it is not merged in nor waived by the subsequent writing.
This principle is in some respects peculiar to insurance, and rests
upon other considerations than the rule which admits proof of
verbal representations to impeach written contracts on the ground
of fraud. Representations to insurers, before or at the time of
making a contract, are a presentation of the elements upon which
to estimate the risk proposed to be assumed. They are the basis
of the contract; its foundation, on the faith of which it is entered
into. If wrongly presented, in any way material to the risk, the
policy that may be issued thereupon will not take effect. To
enforce it would be to apply the insurance to a risk that was never

[144] Campbell v. New England Mut. L. Ins. Co., 98 Mass. 389. See
also Weil v. New York Life Ins. Co., 47 La. Ann. 1405; 17 Sou. 853;
Aloe v. Mut. Res. L. Ass'n, 147 Mo. 561; 49 S. W. 553; Mut. Ben. L.
Ins. Co. v. Lehmán, 132 Ala. 640; 32 Sou. 733; Royal Neighbors, etc.,
v. Wallace, 64 Neb. 330; 89 N. W. 758; 99 N. W. 129; Welch v. Union
Central L. I. Co., 117 Ia. 394; 90 N. W. 828; Supreme Conclave, etc., v.
Wood, 120 Ga. 328; 47 S. E. 940.

presented.[145] . . . When statements or engagements on the part of the insured are inserted or referred to in the policy itself, it often becomes difficult to determine to which class they belong. If they appear on the face of the policy, they do not necessarily become warranties. Their character will depend upon the form of expression used, the apparent purpose of the insertion, and sometimes upon the connection or relation to other parts of the instrument. If they are contained in a separate paper, referred to in such a way as to make it a part of the contract, the same considerations of course will apply. But if the reference appears to be for -a special purpose, and not with a view to import the separate paper into the policy as a part of the contract, the statements it contains will not thereby be changed from representations into warranties. It is perhaps needless to add that verbal representations can never be converted into warranties otherwise than being afterwards written into the policy. . . . The application is, in itself, collateral merely to the contract of insurance. Its statements, whether of facts or agreements, belong to the class of 'representations.' They are to be so construed, unless converted into warranties by force of a reference to them in the policy, and a clear purpose, manifest in the papers thus connected, that the whole shall form one entire contract. When the reference to the application is expressed to be for another purpose, or when no purpose is indicated to make it a part of the policy, it will not be so treated.[146] In Daniels v. Hudson River Ins. Co.,[147] the Court says: 'If by any words of reference the stipulations in another instrument, such as the proposal or application, can be construed a warranty, it must be such as make it in legal effect a part of the policy.' '' The warranty must appear on the face of the policy or be aptly referred to therein, otherwise it is a representation only.[148]

[145] Kimball v. Aetna Ins. Co., 9 Allen 540.

[146] Jefferson Ins. Co. v. Cotheal, 7 Wend. 72; 22 Am. Dec. 567; Snyder v. Farmers', etc., Co., 13 Wend. 92.

[147] 12 Cush. 423; 59 Am. Dec. 192.

[148] Catholic Order of Foresters v. Collins, 51 Ind. App. 285; 99 N. E. 745. To the same effect are the cases cited, *ante*, § 243.

§ 257. **Material and Immaterial Representations.**—The natural division of representations is into those which are material and those which are immaterial, the former having a tendency to influence the insurer to make the contract, and the latter not having any influence upon him. These definitions become more clear as we discuss particular examples..

§ 258. **Affirmative and Promissory Representations.**—According to some authorities representations are divided, like warranties, into affirmative and promissory. It has, however, been denied that there is any such thing as a promissory representation, although the textbook writers have approved the division.[149] It has been said[150] that "Language in a policy which imports that it is intended to do or omit an act which materially affects the risk, its extent or nature, is to be treated as involving an engagement to do or omit such act." This statement has been approved by the Federal Court in at least one case[151] where the engagement was that the policy should be void "if any of the statements and declarations made in the application for this policy, upon the faith of which this policy is issued, shall be found in any respect untrue." In the application the language used was that the applicant "declares" that he does not now and will not practice any pernicious habit tending to shorten life. The Court held as follows: "In this policy such statement and declaration is, in substance, incorporated into and made part of the policy. The language in regard to future pernicious habits is far more than a declaration of intention. It is a positive representation of a future fact, and is not to be regarded as an expression of the expectation or belief of the insured. I am, therefore, led to the conclusion that the clause in the policy imports an agreement that future pernicious habits shall not be entered into, and that if the insured thereafter practices any pernicious habit that obviously tends to shorten life, the policy will be thereby avoided." The Supreme Court of Pennsylvania, upon the same state of facts, came to a different conclusion. The defendant in both cases was

[149] May on Ins., § 182. And see Zepp v. Grand Lodge A. O. U. W., 69 Mo. App. 487.
[150] Bilbrough v. Ins. Co., 5 Duer 587.
[151] Schultz v. Mut. Life Ins. Co., 6 Fed. 672.

468

the same and the language of the application and policy identical. In this case[152] the Court said: "It is unnecessary to discuss the question as to whether the declarations of the insured as to existing facts of his application constitute a warranty. The authorities are by no means uniform on this point. Our own case of the Washington Life Insurance Company v. Schaible,[153] holds that they do not constitute such warranty. Where, however, the policy has been issued upon faith of such representations, and they are false in point of fact, the better opinion seems to be that the policy is avoided. And this is so even where the false statement is to a matter not material to the risk.[154] In such case the agreement is that if the statements are false, there is no insurance; no policy is made by the company, and no policy is accepted by the insured. In the case in hand the policy attached. There was nothing to avoid it *ab initio*. Were the mere declarations by the insured in his application, as to his future intentions, and his failure to carry out his declarations, or to comply with his intentions as to his future conduct sufficient to work subsequent forfeiture of the policy? In no part of the application did the assured covenant that he would not practice any pernicious habit. Nor did he promise, agree or warrant not to do so. He declared that he would not. To declare, is to state; to assert; to publish; to utter; to announce; to announce clearly some opinion or resolution; while to promise is to agree; 'to pledge one's self; to engage; to assure or make sure; to pledge by contract.'[155] There is no clause in the policy which provides that if the assured shall practice any pernicious habit tending to shorten life, the policy shall *ipso facto* become void. There is only the stipulation that 'if any of the statements or declarations made in the application . . . shall be found in any respect untrue, the policy shall be null and void.' This evidently referred to a state of things existing at the time the policy was issued. As to such matters, as I have already said, there was no untrue statement. But the assured declared, as a matter of intention, that he would not practice any

152 Knecht v. Mut. Life Ins. Co., 90 Pa. St. 120; 35 Am. Rep. 641.
153 1 W. N. C. 369.
154 Jeffries v. Life Ins. Co., 22 Wall. 47.
155 Worcester.

pernicious habit. Was this declaration of future intention false? There is no allegation, much less proof, that it was so. The assured might well have intended to adhere to his declarations in the most perfect good faith, yet in a moment of temptation have been overcome by this insidious enemy (intemperance). In the absence of any clause in the policy avoiding it in case the assured should practice any such habit, and of any covenant or warranty on his part that he would not do so, we do not think his mere declaration to that effect in the application sufficient to avoid the policy." In a Massachusetts case,[156] the Supreme Court of that State said: "The word 'representations' has not always been confined in use to representations of facts existing at the time of making the policy; but has been sometimes extended to statements made by the assured concerning what is to happen during the term of the insurance; in other words, not to the present but to the future; not to facts which any human being knows or can know. but to matters of expectation or belief, or of promise and contract. Such statements (when not expressed in the form of a distinct and explicit warranty which must be strictly complied with), are sometimes called 'promissory representations,' to distinguish them from those relating to facts, or 'affirmative representations.' And these words express the distinction; the one is an affirmation of a fact existing when the contract begins; the other is a promise, to be performed after the contract has come into existence. Falsehood in the affirmation prevents the contract from ever having any life; breach of the promise could only bring it to a premature end. A promissory representation may be inserted in the policy itself; or it may be in the form of a written application for insurance, referred to in the policy in such a manner as to make it in law a part thereof; and in either case the whole instrument must be construed together. But this written instrument is the expression, and the only evidence, of the duties, obligations and promises to be performed by each party while the insurance continues. To make the continuance or termination of a written contract, which has once taken effect, dependent on the performance or breach of an earlier oral agree-

---

[156] Kimball v. Aetna Ins. Co., 9 Allen 542.

ment, would be to violate a fundamental rule of evidence. A representation that a fact now exists may be either oral or written; for if it does not exist, there is nothing to which the contract can apply. But an oral representation as to a future fact, honestly made, can have no effect; for if it is a mere statement of an expectation, subsequent disappointment will not prove that it was untrue; and if it is a promise that a certain state of facts shall exist, or continue during the term of the policy, it ought to be embodied in the written contract." This opinion goes on to state that if the oral promise be made *mala fide*, and with the intention to mislead and deceive, the fraud will have the same effect as the material falsity of an affirmative representation. But if made *bona fide*, and without intention to mislead, or deceive, it cannot be set up to avoid a contract. Only those promissory representations are available for such a purpose which are reduced to writing and made part of the contract, thus becoming substantially, if not formally, warranties.[157] It is eminently reasonable, as well as consistent with authority, that promissory representations, when false, should avoid the contract only when they are either made under such circumstances that their breach substantially amounts to a fraud upon the insurer, or else when they are incorporated into the policy in such way as to become virtually warranties.[158]

§ 259. **False Representations Avoid Contract Only When Material.**—We have seen that in case of warranties the question of materiality cannot arise because the truth of the facts is made material by the contract itself, but inasmuch as representations are collateral and form only an inducement to the contract, they avoid it only when material, or in other words have led the insurer into an engagement he would have been less likely to have entered into if the statement or representation had not been made or if he had known that the representations were untrue. The Supreme Court of Massachusetts says on this point:[159] "When the insurer seeks to defeat a policy upon this ground (false representations) his position in court is essentially different from that

[157] Prudential Assur. Soc. v. Aetna L. Ins. Co., 52 Conn. 579; 2 Blatchf. 223; 23 Fed. 438; May on Ins., § 182.

[158] See *post*, § 419.

[159] Campbell v. New England Mut. L. Ins. Co., 98 Mass. 390.

which he may hold upon a policy containing a like description of the risk as one of its terms. It is sufficient for the plaintiff to show fulfillment of all the conditions of recovery which are made such by the contract itself. The burden is then thrown upon the defendant to set forth and prove the collateral matters upon which he relies. There is also another distinction very important in its practical application. As this defense relates entirely to the substance and not to the letter of the contract, it can only prevail by proof of some representation material to the risk, and that it was untrue in some material particular. . . . The answers contained in the application being in the nature of representations only, the question is of their substantial and not their literal truth. To defeat the policy they must be shown to be materially untrue, or untrue in some particular material to the risk.''[160] A statement that the applicant had not been confined to the house by illness is material when he had so been confined by an attack of pneumonia.[161] So a misrepresentation as to habits is material,[162] or as to use of liquor.[163] Generally statements, if false and material, avoid the policy, whether made in good faith or not.[164] An intentional false answer prevents recovery,[165] as, for example, false answer as to rejection by another company,[166] and as to consultation of a physician,[167] and a false answer in an application for increased insurance prevents recovery.[168]

[160] Murphy v. Am. Mut. Acc. Ass'n, 90 Wis. 206; 62 N. W. 1057; Prudential Ins. Co. v. Leyden, 20 Ky. L. 881; 47 S. W. 767; Higgins v. Jno. Hancock M. L. I. Co., 20 Misc. 231; 45 N. Y. Supp. 414; German-American M. L. Ass'n v. Farley, 102 Ga. 720; 29 S. E. 615.

[161] National Council K. & L. of S. v. Wilson, 147 Ky. 293; 143 S. W. 1000.

[162] Mut. L. Ins. Co. v. Mullen, 107 Md. 457; 69 Atl. 385.

[163] Landeau v. John Hancock Mut. L. Ins. Co., 194 Mass. 56; 80 N. E. 452.

[164] Germania L. Ins. Co. v. Klein, 25 Colo. App. 326; 137 Pac. 73; Blanke v. Citizens' Mut. L. Ins. Co., 145 Ky. 332; 140 S. W. 561.

[165] Mudge v. Supreme Court I. O. O. F., 149 Mich. 467; 112 N. W. 1130.

[166] Genrow v. Modern Woodmen of America, 151 Mich. 250; 114 N. W. 1009.

[167] Modern Woodmen of America v. Angle, 127 Mo. App. 94; 104 S. W. 927.

[168] Knights of the Maccabees v. Shields, 156 Ky. 270; 160 S. W. 1045; 157 Ky. 35; 162 S. W. 778.

§ 260. **The Same Subject—Examples of Construction.—** False representations to be effective must be in regard to matters material to the risk.[169] A fact stated in an application is material to the risk when, if known to the insurer, it would have caused him to reject the application or demand a higher premium.[170] The words "material to the risk" mean any fact concerning the health, condition or physical history of the applicant which would naturally have influenced the insurer in determining whether to issue the policy.[171] It has been held proper to instruct the jury whether the answer was substantially untrue and, if so, whether according to the usual course of business the policy would have been issued if the truth had been told,[172] and misrepresentations are material if they affect the risk, whether they relate to the actual cause of a loss or not,[173] and misrepresentations in an application for reinstatement are binding although the policy provides that no misrepresentations, not expressed in the application, shall avoid the policy;[174] and where the policy provides that state-

[169] Supreme Lodge Modern American Fraternal Order v. Miller (Ind. App.), 110 N. E. 556; Prudential Ins. Co. v. Moore, 231 U. S. 560; Aetna Life Ins. Co. v. Moore, 231 U. S. 543; Atlas Life Ins. Co. v. Moman (Ala. App.), 69 Sou. 989; Western & Southern Life Ins. Co. v. Quinn, 130 Ky. 397; 113 S. W. 456; Mut. Life Ins. Co. v. Morgan, 39 Okla. 205; 135 Pac. 279; National Annuity Ass'n v. Carter, 96 Ark. 495; 132 S. W. 633; Supreme Lodge K. P. v. Bradley, 141 Ky. 334; 132 S. W. 547; reversing 117 S. W. 275.

[170] McCaffrey v. Knights & Ladies of Columbia, 213 Pa. 609; 63 Atl. 189; U. S. Casualty Co. v. Campbell, 148 Ky. 554; 146 S. W. 1121; Miller v. Maryland Cas. Co., 113 C. C. A. 267; 193 Fed. 343.

[171] Modern Brotherhood of America v. Jordan (Tex. Civ. App.), 167 S. W. 794; Johnson v. National Life Ins. Co., 123 Minn. 453; 144 N. W. 218; U. S. Health & Accident Ins. Co. v. Bennett, 32 Ky. L. 235; 105 S. W. 433; Equitable Life Assur. Co. v. Claypool (Ky.), 107 S. W. 325; Goff v. Mut. Life Ins. Co., 131 La. 98; 59 Sou. 28; Aetna Life Ins. Co. v. Conway, 11 Ga. App. 557; 75 S. E. 915; Hoke v. National Life & Accident Ins. Co., 103 Miss. 269; 60 Sou. 218; Home Life Ins. Co. v. Mullen, 107 Md. 457; 69 Atl. 385; Atlas Life Ins. Co. v. Moman (Ala. App.), 69 Sou. 989.

[172] Illinois Life Ins. Co. v. DeLang, 124 Ky. 569; 99 S. W. 616.

[173] Provident Savings Life Assur. Soc. v. Whayne's Admr., 29 Ky. L. 160; 93 S. W. 1049.

[174] Mut. Life Ins. Co. v. Allen, 166 Ala. 159; 51 Sou. 877; Hoeland v. Western Union Life Ins. Co., 58 Wash. 100; 107 Pac. 866.

ments in the absence of fraud shall be deemed representations
and not warranties, false representations do not avoid the policy
unless fraudulent, with actual or imputed knowledge of the falsity
and if material to the risk.[175] Where the policy provides that in
the absence of fraud statements shall be deemed representations
and not warranties, it is not enough to show misstatements, but
fraud in the making of such statements must also be shown.[176]

§ 261. **Immaterial Whether False Representation Is Intentional Or Accidental.**—It is immaterial whether the misrepresentation was intentional or accidental. "It is not necessary in
all cases," says the Court of Appeals of New York,[177] in order
to sustain a defense of misrepresentation in applying for the
policy to show that the misrepresentation was intentionally
fraudulent. A misrepresentation is defined by Phillips to be
where a party to the contract of insurance, either purposely, or
through negligence, mistake or inadvertence, or oversight, mis-
represents a fact which he is bound to represent truly[178] and he
lays down the doctrine that it is an implied condition of the
contract of insurance that it is free from misrepresentation or
concealment, whether fraudulent or through mistake. If the
misrepresentation induces the insurer to enter into a contract
which he would otherwise have declined, or to take a less premium than he would have demanded had he known the representation to be untrue, the effect as to him is the same if it was
made through mistake or inadvertence, as if it had been made
with a fraudulent intent, and it avoids the contract. An immaterial misrepresentation, unless in reply to a specific inquiry, or
made with a fraudulent intent and influencing the other party,
will not impair the contract. But if the risk is greater than it
would have been if the representation had been true, the preponderance of authority is to the effect that it avoids the policy,

---

[175] Mut. Life Ins. Co. v. Hilton-Green, 211 Fed. 31.

[176] Prudential Ins. Co. v. Sellers, 54 Ind. App. 326; 102 N. E. 894.

[177] Amour v. Transatlantic F. Ins. Co., 90 N. Y. 455; Provident Savings,
etc., Soc. v. Llewellyn, 58 Fed. 940; 7 C. C. A. 579; McGowan v. Supreme
Court I. O. O. F., 107 Wis. 462; 83 N. W. 775.

[178] Phill. on Ins., § 537.

even though the misrepresentation was honestly made.[179] A material misrepresentation by the agent for effecting the insurance will defeat it, though not known to the assured, and though made without any fraudulent intent on the part of the agent, to the same extent as though made by the assured himself.[180] In this case (which was a case of fire insurance) Story, J., says: 'A false representation of a material fact is, according to well settled principles, sufficient to avoid a policy of insurance underwritten on the faith thereof, whether the false representation be by mistake or design.' " The assured, having given an untrue answer, whether by accident, mistake or design, it matters not, to a direct, plain and practical question, he cannot afterwards be heard to say it was immaterial.[181]

.. § 262. **Materiality of Representation Question of Fact.**— Where any doubt exists as to the materiality of the misrepresentation, it is a question of fact for the jury.[182] Where, however, the questions and answers in an application are clearly material, it is the duty of the court to determine the materiality and not leave it to the jury.[183] The Supreme Court of Massachusetts

[179] Phill. on Ins., §§ 537-542; Wall v. Howard Ins. Co., 14 Barb. 383.•
[180] Carpenter v. Am. Ins. Co., 1 Story C. C. 57.
[181] Davenport v. New England Ins. Co., 6 Cush. 340; Day v. Mut. Ben. L. Ins. Co., 1 McArthur, 41; 29 Am. Rep. 571; Anderson v. Fitzgerald, 4 H. of L. Cas. 484; 2 Big. 341; McCoy v. Metropolitan Life Ins. Co., 133 Mass. 82; Aetna L. Ins. Co. v. France, 91 U. S. 510; Foot v. Aetna L. Ins. Co., 61 N. Y. 571; Baker v. Home Life Ins. Co., 64 N. Y. 648; Cushman v. United States Life Ins. Co., 63 N. Y. 404; Galbraith v. Arlington, etc., Ins. Co., 12 Bush 29; Powers v. N. E. Mut. Life Ass'n, 50 Vt. 630; Metropolitan L. Ins. Co. v. McTague, 49 N. J. L. 587; 9 Atl. 766; Cazenove v. British Equitable Ins. Co., 29 L. J. C. P. 160; 6 Jur. (N. S.) 826; 8 W. R. 243; Perine v. Grand Lodge A. O. U. W., 51 Minn. 224; 53 N. W. 367; Levie v. Metropolitan Life Ins. Co., 163 Mass. 117; 39 N. E. 792; McGowan v. Supreme Court I. O. O. F., 104 Wis. 173; 80 N. W. 603.
[182] Armour v. Transatlantic F. Ins. Co., 90 N. Y. 450; Mut. Ben. L. Ins. Co. v. Miller, 39 Ind. 475; Campbell v. New England M. L. Ins. Co., 98 Mass. 395; Washington Mut. L. Ins. Co. v. Haney, 10 Can. 525.
[183] Lutz v. Metropolitan L. Ins. Co., 186 Pa. St. 527; 40 Atl. 1104; March v. Metropolitan L. Ins. Co., 186 Pa. St. 629; 40 Atl. 1100; Fidelity M. L. Ass'n v. Miller, 34 C. C. A. 211; 92 Fed. 63.

says upon this subject:[184] "It is true that a representation need not, like a warranty, be strictly and literally complied with, but only substantially and in those particulars which are material to be disclosed to the insurers to enable them to determine whether they will enter into the contract; and that, where the question of materiality of such particulars depends upon circumstances, and not upon the construction of any writing, it is a question of fact to be determined by the jury. But where the representations upon which the contract of insurance is based are in writing, their interpretation, like that of other written instruments, belongs to the court, and the parties may, by the frame and contents of the papers, either by putting representations as to the quality, history or relations of the subject insured into the form of answers to specific questions, or by the mode of referring to them in the policy, settle for themselves that they shall be deemed material; and, when they have done so, the applicant for insurance cannot afterwards be permitted to show that a fact which the parties have thus declared material to be truly stated to the insurers, was in fact immaterial, and thereby escape from the consequences of making a false answer to such a question."[185] The test of materiality is whether the matter misrepresented influenced the action of the insurer.[186] The falsity of a statement in an application raises no presumption that it was made with intent to deceive.[187]

§ 263. **Answers to Specific Questions Always Material—** Where a specific question is asked and the applicant makes an untruthful answer, the policy is avoided whether the answers are warranties or representations, because "the parties may by their contract make material a fact that would otherwise be immaterial, or make immaterial a fact that would otherwise be material."[188] On this point the Supreme Court of Iowa said:[189]

184 Campbell v. N. E. Life Ins. Co., 98 Mass. 402.

185 Anderson v. Fitzgerald, 4 H. L. Cas. 484; 17 Jur. 995; Von Lindenan v. Desborough, 3 M. & Rob. 45; 8 B. & C. 586; 3 C. & P. 350.

186 Matson v. Modern Samaritans, 91 Minn. 434; 98 N. W. 330.

187 Dolan v. Mut. Reserve F. L. A., 173 Mass. 197; 53 N. E. 398.

188 Phoenix Mut. L. Ins. Co. v. Raddin, 120 U. S. 183; Brignac v. Pacific Mut. L. Ins. Co., 112 La. 574; 36 Sou. 595; Thomas v. Grand

"A misrepresentation by one party of a fact specifically inquired about by the other, though not material, will have the same effect in exonerating the latter from the contract as if the fact had been material, since, by making such inquiry, he implies that he considers it so. In all jurisprudence this distinction is recognized. It is particularly applicable to written inquiries referred to in a policy. The rule is so because a party, in making a contract, has a right to the advantage of his own judgment of what is material, and if by making specific inquiry, he implies that he considers a fact to be so, the other party is bound by it as such.[190] Representations of this kind differ from warranties in that a substantial compliance with them is sufficient to answer their terms. Whether there has been such substantial compliance, that is, whether the representation is, in every material respect, true, is a question of fact for the jury. But it is not for the jury to say that the representation, though substantially untrue, is, notwithstanding, immaterial. An illustration will make plain the view of the court. Suppose that, in answer to a specific question, the assured states that his age is a week or a month greater. The question would be a proper one for the jury to say whether the representation, though strictly and technically untrue, was not substantially and materially true. But suppose it appears, from the evidence, that the age of the assured is fifty, instead of thirty, years. It is not the province of the jury to say that the representation, though untrue, is immaterial." It is not within the province of the jury, under the guise of determining whether the statements of the applicant were substantially true or false to find that diseases and infirmities were not material to be disclosed when the parties had, by the form of the contract of insurance and of the contemporaneous written application, conclusively agreed to consider them material. That is, it is for the

Lodge A. O. U. W., 12 Wash. 500; 41 Pac. 882; Brignac v. Pacific Mut. L. Ins. Co., 112 La. 574; 36 Sou. 595; 65 L. R. A. 322; Gardner v. North State Mut. L. Ins. Co., 163 N. C. 367; 79 S. E. 806; American Temperance, etc., Ass'n v. Solomon, (C. C. A.), 233 Fed. 213.

[189] Miller v. Mut. Ben. L. Ins. Co., 31 Ia. 232; 7 Am. Rep. 122.

[190] 1 Phil. on Ins., § 342; Campbell v. New England Mut. L. Ins. Co., 98 Mass. 401.

court to rule whether or not a matter is material, and for the jury to determine whether the statements concerning such matters, ruled material, were substantially true.[191]   Yet it has been held that the answer given to a material question may be immaterial and of no effect, even though untrue (in the absence of fraud), e. g., where the fact stated is not of itself material and is so irresponsive to the question as to leave it wholly unanswered.[192]   On this subject the Supreme Court of New Jersey has said in a recent case:[193]   "Usually the materiality of a representation will be inferred from the fact that it was made pending the negotiations, in response to a specific inquiry by the insurer; but this rule is not universal; for the purpose of an inquiry must be considered to see whether the information is sought to aid the insurer in fixing the terms on which he will contract, or with an entirely different object.   Thus, if a mutual insurance company should require its premiums to be paid within a definite time after mailing of notice addressed to the residence of the insured, and with this rule in view should require every applicant for insurance to state his residence in his application, and an applicant should give as his residence, not the truth, but the place where he ordinarily received his mail, it would seem absurd that this circumstance could invalidate the contract."   And the court held that a misrepresentation as to the relationship of the payee did not affect the risk in that particular case, conceding that under other circumstances statements as to relationship of the payee would be material.[194]   Still, as we have seen, it has often been left to the jury to say whether certain statements in the application were material to the risk.

[191] Campbell v. New England, L. Ins. Co., 98 Mass. 401; Davenport v. New England Ins. Co., 6 Cush. 341; Miller v. Mut. Ben. L. Ins. Co., 31 Ia. 233; Phoenix M. L. Ins. Co. v. Raddin, 120 U. S. 183; Day v. Mut. Ben. L. Ins. Co., 1 McArthur, 41; 29 Am. Rep. 565; Anderson v. Fitzgerald, 4 H. L. Cas. 484; Jeffries v. Life Ins. Co., 22 Wall. 47; Cooperative, etc., Ass'n v. Leflore, 53 Miss. 4.

[192] Perine v. Grand Lodge A. O. U. W., 51 Minn. 224; 53 N. W. 367.

[193] Vivar v. Supreme Lodge K. of P., 42 N. J. L. 455; 20 Atl. 36.

[194] See Supreme Council, etc., v. Green, 71 Md. 263; 17 Atl. 1048; Sup. Council A. L. H. v. Smith, 45 N. J. Eq. 466; 17 Atl. 770, and ante, § 262.

§ 264. **Representations to Be Material Need Not Always Be of Facts Relating Directly to the Risk.**—In order to be material a representation need not necessarily be of facts relating directly to the risk. If the applicant makes false statements as to some incidental matters, as for example concerning his pecuniary means or his social or business relations, from which an inference can be drawn as to the propriety of accepting or declining the risk, they will avoid the policy, provided the jury, for it is a question of fact to be left to a jury, find that the insurer was influenced by them, or, in other words, that they were material elements in the making of the contract. This doctrine has been laid down by the textbooks,[195] and also in an old English case,[196] and it has been approved by the Court of Appeals of New York.[197] In that case the insured, Schumacher, was, it was claimed, represented to be a partner in the firm of Valton, Martin & Co., and the moneyed man of the concern, when, in fact, he was only the porter who worked in the store, and the false representation was made by Martin, who was with the insured and took an active part in effecting the insurance and was one of the payees of the policy. In this case the Court said: "The judge, among other things, charged the jury that if the insured untruly represented that he was a partner of the firm of Valton, Martin & Co., or that if he untruly represented that he was the moneyed man of the firm, and either or both such untrue representations were material to the risk, then the policy was avoided, and there could be no recovery. That if Schumacher was dead in September, 1850, and his occupation that of a merchant at the time the proposals were signed, and the representations of his being a partner, or the moneyed man of the firm, were either not untrue or not material to the risk, then the action was *prima facie* sustained. The defendant's counsel requested the court to charge the jury that if Schumacher himself, or by Martin in his behalf, represented to the agent of the defendants that Schumacher was a partner of the firm of Valton, Martin & Co., when in fact at that time he was not such a partner, and if the defendants

195 Arnould on Ins., p. 520; 2 Duer 692; 3 Kent Comm. 282.
196 Sibbald v. Hill, 2 Dow's Parl. 263.
197 Valton v. National, etc., Soc., 20 N. Y. 32.

would not have issued the policy if the representation had not
been made, then the policy was void and the plaintiffs could not
recover. The judge declined so to charge, and the defendant's
counsel excepted. The defendant's counsel also requested the
judge to charge the jury that if they found that Schumacher
himself, or by Martin in his behalf, represented to the agent of
the defendants that Schumacher was the moneyed man of the
concern of Valton, Martin & Co., when in fact at that time he
was not such, and that the defendants would not have issued
the policy if the representations had not been made, then the
policy is void and the plaintiffs cannot recover. The judge refused so to charge, and the defendant's counsel excepted. The
charge of the judge was correct as far as given. If the representations were made, and false, the falsity must have been
known to Schumacher and Martin. The facts were within their
knowledge, and the representations fraudulent. The requests
to charge, considered in connection with the charge given, present the question whether fraudulent representations made by
the assured to the insurer upon his application for a policy,
though not material to the risk, yet material in the judgment
of the insurer, and which induced him to take the risk, will
avoid the policy. This question has not been determined by any
adjudged case in this State, so far as I have been able to discover. The elementary writers hold that the policy may be
avoided. In Sibbald v. Hill[198] it was held that when the assured
fraudulently represented to the underwriter that a prior insurance by another underwriter upon the same risk had been made
at a less premium than it was in fact made, the policy was
vitiated. In this case it is obvious that the risk itself was not
affected by the representations. Lord Eldon, in his opinion,
says that it appeared to him settled law, that if a person meaning to effect an insurance exhibited a policy underwritten by a
person of skill and judgment, knowing that this would weigh
with the other party and disarm the ordinary prudence exercised in the common transactions of life, and it turned out that
this person had not in fact underwritten the policy or had done
so under such terms that he came under no obligation to pay, it

[198] 2 Dow's Parl. 263.

appeared to him settled law that this would vitiate the policy. The courts in this country would say that this was a fraud; not on the ground that the misrepresentation affected the nature of the risk, but because it induced a confidence without which the party would not have acted. The principle of this case, when applied to the one under consideration, shows that the judge committed an error in refusing to charge as requested. It is clear that the circumstance of a party being engaged in commercial business, possessed of large means, might induce an insurer to make an insurance upon his life for a large amount, while were he a mere porter, the risk would be rejected, although the chance of life would be as good in the latter situation as in the former.''[199] So, where the residence of the applicant was stated at Fishertown Anger and it appeared that she had been in jail there, it was left to the jury to say whether the fact was material and ought to have been communicated.[200]

§ 265. **Representations Need Only Be Substantially True: Good Faith of Applicant.**—It is enough, however, if representations be substantially true; in this respect being unlike warranties, which are always material, and which must be literally true. The authorities are not, however, perfectly clear on this point, for in some cases it has been held that the element of good faith enters so far into the construction of statements warranted to be true that it is enough if they are substantially true. ''Substantially true, does not mean partly true, on the one hand; nor does it mean true in every possible and immaterial respect, on the other. It means true, without qualification, in all respects material to the risk:''[201] An interesting case was decided by the Supreme Court of Minnesota,[202] where the insured had stated that he had not had rheumatism, when he, in fact, had had sub-acute rheumatism, which is not ordinarily con-

[199] Higbie v. Guardian Muf. L. Ins. Co., 53 N. Y. 603.

[200] Huguenin v. Rayley, 6 Taunt. 186; Rawlins v. Desborough, 2 M. & Rob. 328.

[201] Jeffrey v. United Order of the Golden Cross, 97 Me. 176; 53 Atl. 1102. See also note to case of Fidelity Mut. L. Ass'n v. Jeffords, 46 C. C. A. 377; 107 Fed. 402; 53 L. R. A. 193.

[202] Price v. Phoenix Mut. L. Ins. Co., 17 Minn. 518; 10 Am. Rep. 166.

sidered a disease. In this case the Court said: "The rheumatism referred to in the question is the disease of rheumatism.
Any rheumatic affection not amounting to the disease of rheumatism, is not comprehended in its terms, any more than the
spitting of blood occasioned by a wound of the tongue, or the
extracting of a tooth, is the disease of 'spitting of blood' mentioned in the same question. The life insured had the right to
answer the question upon the basis that its terms were used in
their ordinary signification. If there was any ambiguity in the
question, so that its language was capable of being construed in
an ordinary, as well as in a technical sense, the defendant can
take no advantage from such ambiguity."[203] So, the Supreme
Court of the United States has said:[204] "It is contended that
if the answers of the assured are to be deemed representations
only, the policy was, nevertheless, forfeited, if those representations were untrue in respect of any matters material to the risk.
The argument is, that if the insured was, at the time of his application, or had been at any former period of his life, seriously
or in an appreciable sense afflicted with scrofula, asthma, or
consumption, his answer, without qualification, that he had never
been so afflicted, being untrue, avoided the policy, without reference to any knowledge or belief he had upon the subject. The
soundness of this proposition could not be disputed if, as assumed, the knowledge or good faith of the insured, as to the existence of such diseases, was, under the terms of the contract in
suit, of no consequence whatever in determining the liability of
the company. But is that assumption authorized by a proper interpretation of the two instruments constituting the contract?
We think not. Looking into the application, upon the faith of
which the policy was issued and accepted we find much justifying the conclusion that the company did not require the insured
to do more, when applying for insurance, than observe the utmost good faith, and deal fairly and honestly with it, in respect
of all material facts about which inquiry is made, and as to
which he has or should be presumed to have knowledge or information. The applicant was required to answer yes or no as

203 Wilson v. Hampden F. Ins. Co., 4 R. I. 159.
204 Moulor v. American Life Ins. Co., 111 U. S. 335.

to whether he had been afflicted with certain diseases. In respect to some of those diseases, particularly consumption, and diseases of the lungs, heart, and other internal organs, common experience informs us that an individual may have them in active form, without at the time being conscious of the fact, and beyond the power of any one, however learned or skillful, to discover. Did the company expect, when requiring categorical answers as to the existence of diseases of that character, that the applicant should answer with absolute certainty about matters of which certainty could not possibly be predicated? Did it intend to put upon him the responsibility of knowing that which, perhaps, no one, however thoroughly trained in the study of human diseases, could possibly ascertain? We shall be aided in the solution of these inquiries by an examination of other questions propounded to the applicant. In that way we may ascertain what was in the minds of the parties. Beyond doubt, the phrase, 'other known causes,' in the fourteenth question, serves the double purpose of interpreting and qualifying all that precedes it in the same clause or section. For instance, the applicant was not required to state all the circumstances, within his recollection, of his family history, but those only which rendered the proposed insurance more than usually hazardous, and of which he had personal knowledge, or of which he had information fairly justifying a belief of their existence. If he omitted to state circumstances in his 'family history' of which he had no knowledge, nor any information deserving attention, that omission would not avoid the policy, although it subsequently appeared that those circumstances, if known to the company, would have shown that the proposed insurance was more than usually hazardous. Apart from other questions or clauses in the application, the tenth question would indicate that an incorrect or untrue answer as to whether the applicant's 'father, mother, brothers or sisters had been affected with consumption, or any other serious family disease, such as scrofula, insanity,' etc., would absolve the company from all liability. Yet in the fourteenth question, the insured, being asked as to his family history and as to 'hereditary predispositions'—an inquiry substantially covering some of the specific matters referred to in the

483

tenth question—was, as we have seen, only required to state such circumstances as were known to him, or of which he had information, and which rendered an insurance upon his life more than usually hazardous. So, in reference to that part of the fourteenth question relating to the then physical condition of the applicant. Suppose, at the time of his application, he had a disease of the lungs or heart, but was entirely unaware that he was so affected. In such a case he would have met all the requirements of that particular question, and acted in the utmost good faith, by answering no, thereby implying that he was aware of no circumstance in his then physical condition which rendered an insurance upon his life more than usually hazardous. And yet, according to the contention of the company, if he had, at any former period of his life, been afflicted with a disease of the heart or lungs, his positive answer to the seventh question, that he had not been so afflicted, was fatal to the contract; this, although the applicant had no knowledge or information of the existence at any time of such a disease in his system. So, also, in reference to the inquiry in the fourteenth question as to any 'constitutional infirmity' of the insured. If, in answering that question, he was required to disclose only such constitutional infirmities as were then known to him, or which he had reason to believe then existed, it would be unreasonable to infer that he was expected, in answer to a prior question in the same policy, to guarantee absolutely, and as a condition precedent to any binding contract, that he had never, at any time, been afflicted with diseases of which, perhaps, he never had, and could not have any knowledge whatever. The entire argument in behalf of the company proceeds upon a too literal interpretation of those clauses in the policy and application which declare the contract null and void if the answers of the insured to the questions propounded to him, were, in any respect, untrue. What was meant by 'true' and 'untrue' answers? In one sense, that only is true which is conformable to the actual state of things. In that sense a statement is untrue which does not express things exactly as they are. But in another and broader sense, the word 'true' is often used as a synonym of honest, sincere, not fraudulent. Looking at all the clauses of the application, in connection with the policy, it is reasonably clear—certainly the contrary cannot be confidently asserted—that what the company required of the applicant as a condition precedent to any binding contract, was, that he would observe the utmost good faith towards it, and make full, direct and honest answers to all questions, without evasion or fraud, and without suppression, misrepresentation or concealment of facts with which the company ought to be made acquainted; and that by so doing, and only by so doing, would he be deemed to have made 'fair and true answers.' If it be said that an individual could not be afflicted with the diseases specified in the application, without being cognizant of the fact, the answer is that the jury would, in that case, have no serious difficulty in finding that he had failed to communicate to the company what he knew or should have known was material to the risk, and that consequently, for the want of 'fair and true answers,' the policy was, by its terms, null and void. But, whether a disease is of such a character that its existence must have been known to the individual afflicted with it, and, therefore, whether an answer denying its existence was or not a fair and true answer, is a matter which should have been submitted to the jury.''[205] The general disposition of the courts in matters of construction of applications is thus stated by the Kentucky Court of Appeals:[206] ''Forfeitures are regarded by courts with but little favor, and while the non-payment of premiums or a

[205] Alabama Gold Life Ins. Co. v. Johnson, 80 Ala. 467; 2 Sou. 130; Miller v. Mut. Ben. Life Ins. Co., 31 Ia. 229; Langdon v. Union M. L. Ins. Co., 14 Fed. 272; Campbell v. New England Mut. Life Ins. Co., 98 Mass. 405; Phoenix Mut. Life Ins. Co. v. Raddin, 120 U. S. 183; Fowkes v. Manch. & Lond., etc., Ins. Co., 3 B. & S. 917; 32 L. J. Q. B. 153; 11 W. R. 622; 8 L. T. (N. S.) 309. See also Royal Neighbors v. Wallace, 73 Neb. 409; 102 N. W. 1026.

[206] Germania Ins. Co. v. Rudwig, 80 Ky. 235. See also on the question of intent and good faith, Fidelity, etc., Ass'n v. Ficklin, 74 Md. 172; 21 Atl. 680; 23a, 197; and Maine Ben. Ass'n v. Parks, 81 Me. 79; 16 Atl. 339; Bloomington, etc., Ass'n v. Cummings, 53 Ill. App. 530; Louis v. Connecticut Mut. L. Ins. Co., 58 App. Div. 137; 68 N. Y. Supp. 683; N. W. Mut. L. Ins. Co. v. Montgomery, 116 Ga. 799; 43 S. E. 79; Rainger v. Boston M. L. Ass'n, 167 Mass. 109; 44 N. E. 1088; Tarpey v. Security Trust Co., 80 Ill. App. 378.

representation of facts fraudulently or innocently made, if untrue and material to the risk, or such as would induce the insurer to enter into the contract, must prove fatal to the policy, when minute and trivial questions are propounded and answered, having no bearing or influence on the minds of those about entering into the contract, and not material to the risk, the parties cannot be affected by them. An honest belief in the truth of the statement made, when not material to the risk, should not avoid a policy if the statement should prove to be untrue, and to adjudge that it works a forfeiture is contrary to the intent and meaning of the parties, and subversive of that rule of good faith and fair dealing, that should enter into and form a part of every insurance contract." As further illustrative of the principle that the representations of the applicant in his answer to questions in the application need be only substantially true, we may cite an opinion of the Supreme Court of the United States. In this case the defense was that the applicant had falsely answered the question, "Have you ever had any of the following diseases, . . . affection of liver?" by saying, "No." The Court said:[207] "It seems to the court, however, that the company by its question sought to know whether the liver had been so affected that its ordinary operations were seriously disturbed, or its vital power materially weakened. It was not contemplated that the insured could recall, with such distinctness as to be able to answer categorically, every instance during his past life, or even during his manhood, of accidental disorder or ailment affecting the liver, which lasted only for a brief period, and was unattended by substantial injury, or inconvenience, or prolonged suffering. Unless he had an affection of the liver that amounted to disease—that is, of a character so well-defined and marked as to materially derange for a time the functions of that organ—the answer that he had never had the disease called affection of the liver was a 'fair and true' one; for such an answer involved neither fraud, misrepresentation, evasion, nor concealment, and withheld no information as to his

---

[207] Connecticut Mut. L. Ins. Co. v. Union Trust Co., 112 U. S. 250; 5 Sup. Ct. Rep. 119. See also Prudential Ins. Co. v. Sellers, 54 Ind. App. 326; 102 N. E. 894.

physical condition with which the company ought to have been made acquainted." This case was followed by the Federal court in Indiana where the applicant had answered "no," to the question whether he had ever had "spitting or raising of blood." The Court held,[208] that this answer was true although on one occasion the applicant had "spit blood," and that the only warranty implied by the terms of the question was not that he had never had spitting or raising of blood, but that he had never had the complaint of spitting or raising blood, or "had blood-spitting in such form as to be called a disease, disorder, or constitutional vice." The Court continues: "If the question put to the applicant for the insurance had been whether or not he had had any spitting of blood, or had had any symptom of disease, such as spitting or raising of blood, it would doubtless have required the disclosure of a single instance of blood-spitting."[209]

A misrepresentation innocently made and in the belief of its truth will not void the policy,[210] but where misstatements are made in bad faith they will avoid the policy though the fact inquired about is immaterial, but if the misstatement is made in good faith it will not avoid the policy though untrue unless material to the risk,[211] and a misrepresentation by a woman as to pregnancy makes the certificate invalid though there was no intention to deceive.[212] In a case where the issue was as to false representation in an application as to the good health and freedom from disease

[208] Dreier v. Continental Life Ins. Co., 24 Fed. 670.

[209] On this point the opinion cites: Geach v. Ingall, 14 M. & W. 95; 2 Big. L. & A. Ins. R. 306; Insurance Co. v. Miller, 39 Ind. 475; Vose v. Eagle, etc., Ins. Co., 6 Cush. 42; Cushman v. Ins. Co., 70 N. Y. 72. See also § 276, et seq., and Mut. Ben. Life Ins. Co. v. Davis, 87 Ky. 541; 9 S. W. 812; Hoffman v. Supreme C. A. L. H., 35 Fed. 252, where the word "essentially" in an instruction was held equivalent to "strictly;" and Anders v. Sup. Lodge K. of H., 51 N. J. L. 175; 17 Atl. 119.

[210] American National Ins. Co. v. Anderson (Tex. Civ. App.), 179 S. W. 66; New York Life Ins. Co. v. Moats, 125 C. C. A. 143; 207 Fed. 481; Brotherhood of Railroad Trainmen v. Swearingen, 161 Ky. 665; 171 S. W. 455.

[211] Kaiper v. Equitable Life Assur. Soc., 159 Fed. 206.

[212] Supreme Lodge Knights & Ladies of Honor v. Payne, 101 Tex. 449; 108 S. W. 1160; 15 L. R. A. (N. S.) 1277.

of the applicant, in holding that tuberculosis of the lungs or of the bones of the wrist is a material matter,[213] the Court said: "If the applicant had no knowledge of the fact that his lungs were afflicted with tuberculosis or that it was tubercular disease of the bones of the wrist that rendered necessary the amputation of his arm, and the answers to the questions in the application were not made as absolute statements of facts, but as matters of belief or opinion and as to which he might be honestly mistaken, then, under the former decisions of this Court, the answers were mere representations, and his beneficiary might recover if they were made honestly and in good faith.[214] If the evidence should prove, however, that he had consulted reputable physicians as to his condition, and that he had been told by them that he was suffering from such an insidious and dangerous disease as tuberculosis at a time so near the time of making the application as to rebut and repel the idea of forgetfulness or good faith on his part, the concealment of such a fact, so material to the risk, and one that, if known, his application would have been rejected, would avoid the contract."

§ 266. **Understanding of Applicant as to Effect of False Answers.**—In many applications for insurance a question is included asking what the understanding of the applicant is as to the effect of untrue .answers upon the contract, or oftener, if the applicant does not understand that the contract will be avoided under certain conditions. Such statements in the application cannot control the legal construction of the policy afterwards issued and accepted, although the application warrants the facts stated therein to be true, and the policy is expressed to be made in consideration of the warranties made in the application. "The state-

213 Bryant v. Modern Woodmen of America, 86 Neb. 372; 125 N. W. 621; 21 Ann. Cas. 365.

214 Kettenbach v. Omaha L. Ass'n, 49 Neb. 842; 69 N. W. 135; Modern Woodmen Acc. Ass'n v. Shryock, 54 Neb. 250; 74 N. W. 607; 39 L. R. A. 826; Royal Neighbors of America v. Wallace, 64 Neb. 330; 89 N. W. 758; 66 Neb. 543; 92 N. W. 897; Bankers' Union of the World v. Mixon, 74 Neb. 36; 103 N. W. 1049; Modern Woodmen of America v. Wilson, 76 Neb. 344; 107 N. W. 568; Reppond v. National L. Ins. Co., 100 Tex. 519; 15 Ann. Cas. 618; 101 S. W. 786; 11 L. R. A. N. S. 981, and note.

ments expressing his understanding of what will be the effect of the insurance are statements not of fact, but of law, and cannot control the legal construction of the policy afterwards issued and accepted.[215]

In the case of Mathews v. Modern Woodmen,[216] the Court said: "Reading the questions, answers and statements of the application together with the by-laws into the policy (as its terms require should be done), it appears that some of the by-laws provide for forfeiture in case the member becomes a bartender. But those by-laws must be construed in connection with the third written question propounded in the application, viz.: 'Do you understand and agree that this order does not indemnify against death from suicide or death resulting from occupations prohibited to its members by its laws?' It seems to us there is great significance coiled up in that question. When it was propounded to Mr. Mathews his answer was 'yes.' Presumably the application was the sober and careful handiwork of defendant. It had an obvious purpose. Thereby defendant talked to Mathews and gave voice to its own view of the scope and character of its own indemnity contract. By necessary implication, does not that question mean that the insurance defendant offers, the indemnity, does not extend to death 'resulting' from prohibited occupations? Does it not thereby say to Mathews, if you do not go into a prohibited occupation the indemnity is general, but if you go into a prohibited occupation and death results from such occupation, I will pay nothing to your wife? Speaking of warranties (whether affirmative or promissory) and representations (whether affirmative or executory), the question spontaneously obtrudes itself, viz.: Is it alone the applicant who can make them or be impaled by them? May not defendant also impale itself on such hook? Did not this defendant, by asking that question of Mathews and in saying to him, 'Do you understand and agree' to that effect by the same token, also 'agree' by way of a promissory warranty or an

---

215 Accident Ins. Co. v. Crandall, 120 U. S. 533. See also as to effect of a question which calls for the opinion of the applicant, Louis v. Conn. Mut. L. Ins. Co., 58 App. Div. 137; 68 N. Y. Supp. 683; affd. 172 N. Y. 659; 65 N. E. 1119. See also *supra*, § 254.

216 236 Mo. 326; 139 S. W. 151; Ann. Cas. 1912-D 483.

executory representation (it taking two to make a bargain), that
the indemnity of the policy was not forfeited by a prohibited occupation unless death 'results' therefrom? Is not that question,
is not that answer and is not that agreement, *ex vi termini*, read
into the policy and writ large there? We think so. Therefore,
we are no more at liberty to cause that provision of the policy
to perish by construction, than we are at liberty to cause the provisions relied on by defendant to so perish. Our duty is to give
effect to them all by harmonizing them if that can be·done. To
that task we address ourselves. Counsel suggest the seeming policy
contradictions may be harmonized by construction, giving them
all due play and office by construing the contract to mean as if it
read this way: 'It is agreed between the parties hereto as follows: In consideration of the payment of Robert J. Mathews of
the initiation fee (now received) and the prompt payment of
all dues and assessments hereafter levied, the Modern Woodmen
of America (a corporation) does hereby insure the life of the said
Robert J. Mathews in the sum of two thousand dollars for the
benefit of Ida Mathews, his wife, subject to the by-law of this
corporation which provides that should any member engage in
any of the occupations by said by-law prohibited his certificate
shall become forfeited, and no indemnity shall be paid to his
widow, provided death results from his engaging in such prohibited occupation; and it is further agreed that no warranty
made by the said Robert J. Mathews in obtaining or securing this
insurance shall be deemed material or render this insurance void
unless the matter unwarranted against shall have actually contributed to the death of the said.Robert J. Mathews.' Allowing
for ambiguities and solving them in favor of the insured, allowing
for seeming contradictions and smoothing them away by construction so that all substantive provisions may be given some life, and
all substantive limitations assigned some office, we are of opinion
that the foregoing view of the contract is in substance the common sense of it and results in no injustice. Thereby the widow
is dealt tenderly with, all doubts are solved in her favor, and
peradventure the basic principles of fraternity and brotherhood
are in no wise wounded or subverted.''

490

§ 267. Answers to Questions in Applications for Membership in Benefit Societies Are Generally Warranties.—As a general thing the answers in a medical examination or an application for membership in a benefit society were formerly not warranties but representations. This statement is true as to the early forms of applications, but learning by experience, the applications now in general use are so worded as to make all statements contained therein express warranties. Whenever this is done the rules as to warranties apply.[217] In a case in the Federal Court of New York, where the form of the agreement, however, was not given,[218] the Court says: "The question of law is whether, under Semm's application to Humboldt Lodge for membership therein and the certificate which he received from said lodge, he warranted the truth of the answer which he gave to the question, 'Have you been rejected by the medical examiner of any lodge or society?' In my opinion, he was required, under the contract, to answer the question according to his knowledge or reasonable means of belief, and not to misrepresent or suppress known facts, but that he did not warrant the absolute truth of his answers." In a case in Indiana the Supreme Court held as follows:[219] "Statements made by the insured in his application for insurance are not deemed warranties unless they are incorporated in the policy, or, in some appropriate method, referred to in that instrument. The statements by the insured in his application are not set forth in the policy, nor in any way is reference made to them, and they cannot be considered warranties." The question was more squarely presented in a case in Illinois,[220] where the application concluded: "It is hereby declared, that the above are fair and true answers to the foregoing questions, in which there is no misrepresentation

[217] Knudson v. Grand Council N. W. L. of H., 7 S. D. 214; 63 N. W. 911; Foley v. Supreme Council R. A., 78 Hun. 222; 28 N. Y. Supp. 952; Home Friendly Soc. v. Berry, 94 Ga. 606; 21 S. E. 583; Levell v. Royal Arcanum, 9 Misc. 257; 30 N. Y. Supp. 205; Marcoux v. Soc., etc., 91 Me. 250; 39 Atl. 1027; Callies v. Modern Woodmen, 98 Mo. App. 521; 72 S. W. 713. As to fraud in application for reinstatement see Sieverts v. National Ben. Ass'n, 95 Ia. 710; 64 N. W. 671.
[218] Semm v. Supreme Lodge, etc., 29 Fed. 895.
[219] Presbyterian Mut. Ass. Fund v. Allen, 106 Ind. 593.
[220] Illinois Masons, etc., v. Winthrop, 85 Ill. 537.

or suppression of known facts; and I acknowledge and agree that the above statement shall form the basis of the agreement with the society." In an action on the*policy the defense was that false answers had been made in the application which voided the policy. The Supreme Court, in passing upon the matter, said: "The answers, of course, enter into the application, because, if for no other reason, assured expressly agreed they should be the basis of the agreement with the society, but the effect that shall be given to the representations is the principal question in dispute between the parties. Appellant claims they were intended to be, and should be, held to constitute a warranty of their truth, and if any or either of them are shown to be untrue, whether their falsity was known, or whether intentionally or unintentionally the truth was concealed, or it was only from the want of memory, or by inadvertence, there can be no recovery. On the other hand, it is contended that the answers are not warranties but simply representations; and that, if made in good faith, although some one or more of them may be untrue, if the misstatement was not intentional, but was made in good faith and under the belief that the statements were true, the misstatement did not operate to avoid the policy. The clause stating that the assured agreed 'that the statement shall form the basis of the agreement with the society,' is different from the agreements usually contained in life policies. In such instruments it is usually agreed, that the statement is a warranty and that if any part of it should prove to be untrue, the policy should be void. With persons of ordinary intelligence, the language used in this application would not be so understood. Nor do we suppose that the promoters of the enterprise, when they adopted this form, intended that it should operate as a warranty, such as is usually inserted in life policies. Nor can we suppose for a moment that they would adopt a form of words that would be understood one way by the applicant and would be construed another by the courts, and thus cheat, wrong or defraud a brother. Such a supposition cannot be for a moment entertained. If the language employed was intended to operate as the usual warranty, we apprehend it has not been so understood by those, or any portion of them, who had applied for membership before the death of Price. If intended as an absolute warranty.

that the statement and every part of it was true, why limit the previous part of the statement to 'no misrepresentation or suppression of known facts?' This the company required of each applicant, and when they made that requirement, they, by implication; absolved him from any injurious consequences from misrepresentation or failure to disclose unknown facts. If a warranty was required of the answers to some of these questions, it would be useless for persons to become members of the society. Each applicant is required to answer the question, whether he is able to earn a livelihood for himself and family. Now, with the great majority of men, this is problematical. That power depends upon so large a number of circumstances that a prudent man might well hesitate to answer it in the affirmative. The solution of this question depends, with most men, so decidedly on such a variety of contingencies, that almost any man, whatever his mental or physical endowments, would be regarded as extremely rash to warrant that he could. If able at the time, what guaranty that he could do so for any definite period? Does this statement require that he should remain so during life or for a shorter period? And if so, for what period?, It is manifest that all that can be required of the applicant is, that he should give to this question an answer based on an honest, fair and intelligent belief. The applicant is also asked if his ancestors generally reached old age. Now, who are his ancestors, referred to in this interrogatory? How many generations back is it intended to extend? And, suppose the applicant, on slight or unreliable information, answers in the affirmative, do the directors suppose they can show the misinformation and defeat a recovery? If such a construction is to be given to this application, then members, if not wronged, cheated, or defrauded, are, we have no doubt, generally deceived unintentionally. Suppose, to the question whether the applicant is, at the time, in good health, the answer is in the affirmative, is every slight obstruction to the performance of their proper functions by the various organs of the system to be held as a breach of warranty, and to avoid the policy? Such, we presume, was never intended to be the construction given to the answer, as all know that but a small percentage of the human family are entirely free from some infirmity, slight or serious. There is the question

493

whether the applicant has ever had any serious illness or personal injury. Suppose the applicant answers in the negative, may the society show that the applicant, in his early infancy, and so far back that it is beyond memory's reach, had serious illness, and defeat a recovery, although he had never been informed of the fact? That would be a fact that would, in all probability, be wholly unknown to him, and neither party intended that a negative answer should be a warranty that it did not so occur, and a misrepresentation or suppression of such an unknown fact was intended to be included in the exception in the statement. It was only known facts that were not to be misrepresented or suppressed. . . . From what has been said, we are unable to hold that the statement was made or intended as a warranty of the absolute truth of the answers, but the statement was only designed to insure honesty and good faith in making them. Otherwise the statement would not have contained the limitation that they were true and fair answers, 'in which there is no misrepresentation or suppression of known facts.' ''[221] If the applicant is a foreigner, with an imperfect knowledge of the language, this circumstance must be considered in determining the meaning of the words he has used.[222]

§ 268. **The Same Subject Continued.**—In construing the effect of false answers in applications for membership in benefit societies the courts have given effect to the provisions of the contract in regard to warranty of the truth of answers contained in such applications, but the decisions in regard to misrepresentation do not always harmonize. Thus the Court of Appeals of Maryland has held,[223] where an applicant represented a woman,

[221] Morrison v. Odd-Fellows, etc., Ins. Co., 59 Wis. 165; Clapp v. Mass. Ben. Ass'n, 146 Mass. 519; 16 N. E. 433; Swett v. Relief Soc., 78 Me. 541; Mut. Ben. Ins. Co. v. Miller, 39 Ind. 475; Grossmann v. Supreme Lodge, etc., Sup. Ct. N. Y., 13 N. Y. St. 592; Northwestern Benev., etc., Ass'n v. Cain, 21 Ill. App. Ct. 471; Sup. Council Royal Arcanum v. Lund, 25 Ill. App. 492.

[222] Knickerbocker L. Ins. Co. v. Trefz, 104 U. S. 197.

[223] Supreme Council American Legion of Honor v. Green, 71 Md. 263; 17 Atl. 1048. To the same effect is Gray v. Sovereign Camp W. of W., 47 Tex. Civ. App. 609; 106 S. W. 176, where the beneficiary was falsely

not related to him, to be his niece, that the statement was a warranty and avoided the contract, the Court saying: "In order to recover the insured knew that the appellee must be bound to meet the description of some one of the classes designated in the act, and in order to meet that requirement she was named by the insured in his application as his niece, which declared her a relative, and, therefore, a qualified beneficiary, whether a dependent or not. Now the utmost good faith is required in such cases, and the applicant so knew; for he agreed in his application that any untruthful statement, or any fraudulent statement, or any concealment of facts, should forfeit all rights under the insurance he was effecting. The association was entitled to know the facts, that they might agree or refuse to have the applicant a member and an associate in the society or not, and to allow the beneficiary named to be the recipient of its provisions for aid, as it might decide. It is contended that improper relations existed between the insured and the beneficiary named, to-wit, the appellee, and that the designation of her as applicant's 'niece' was a cover to conceal the true relation. The jury seem to have found that immoral relations did not exist and of course that question is not before us. Whatever may have been the motive of the deceased for stating the plaintiff, the beneficiary, to be his niece when she was not is wholly immaterial to the question for decision. A relationship was stated to exist which on its face placed the beneficiary named within one of the classes provided for by the corporation and allowed by the statutes of Massachusetts; and the corporation was called on to look no further, but might rely on the warranty of its truth and the agreement to forfeit if falsely stated. It is not pretended there was any kinship in fact between the parties. It is conceded that there was not. The plaintiff testifies there was not any relationship by blood but says she called him 'Uncle' and he treated her as a niece by mutual understanding. It is very clear that their agreement to act towards each other as uncle and niece could not have the effect to make them such and bring her within the class named in the statute as 'rela-

represented to be a cousin. So where the beneficiary was falsely stated to be a dependent. Caldwell v. Grand Lodge, etc., 148 Cal. 195; 82 Pac. 781.

495

tives,' so as to make her a qualified beneficiary to take under the statute as a relative. The question of dependency, we are not now considering. She is not named in the application or in the policy (or certificate) as a dependent, but as a 'niece' and it was as 'niece' she was intended to take: otherwise she would not have been so described. The relation of the parties to each other was certainly very peculiar and on the theory of entire purity the deceased was marvelously generous, but whether she could be regarded as a dependent within the meaning of the society's constitution and the statute of Massachusetts, would admit, at least, of serious doubts, if the case turned on that point. We think the false statement of the insured that the appellee was his 'niece' so manifestly material, as it declared her a relative and qualified beneficiary, in view of the warranty of its truth, and agreement to forfeit rights, that if false, it should defeat this action.'' In New Jersey and elsewhere the misrepresentation was held not to avoid the contract, but the designation, and that a resulting trust followed for the benefit of the next of kin. The leading case is Britton v. Supreme Council R. A.,[224] where a creditor of the member was falsely represented to be his cousin. The Court says: ''The question whether Brennan possessed the qualifications necessary to enable him to become Britton's beneficiary or not was so entirely aside from the question whether Britton should be admitted to membership or not, that it is almost certain that during the time the last question was under consideration the first never suggested itself to the mind of Britton, nor to the minds of the officers with whom he dealt. Whether the person designated by a member on his admission, as his beneficiary, is qualified or not, is a question which is wholly unimportant and immaterial to the defendant. The designation then made will only continue in force so long as the member chooses to let it stand. He has a right to change his beneficiary as often as his will changes. The only limitation upon his power in that regard is that he cannot make a designation that will divert that part of the fund payable on his death from its appointed channel. And whether he designates a qualified or incompetent person can have no effect whatever, in either increasing or diminishing the defendant's liability. The

[224] 46 N. J. E. 102; 18 Atl. 675.

sum which it must pay on the death of a member is fixed by its contract, as well as the person or persons to whom it must be paid. In no case can the defendant be required to pay until the certificate issued by it has been surrendered or declared invalid. Britton undoubtedly told a falsehood when he said Brennan was his cousin, but his falsehood did the defendant no harm. A falsehood or fraud that does not result in legal injury can neither be made the foundation of an action nor the ground of a defense.'' Other cases support this view.[225] And in Indiana is was held,[226] that an application directing payment to a person described as the wife of the applicant, was not a warranty that she was his wife. These cases were all those where the misrepresentation was as to the relationship of the beneficiary. While it is generally true that in applications for membership in beneficiary societies the statements are representations and not warranties,[227] these representations may be the basis of the contract, though not referred to in the certificate, and being false will avoid the contract whether regarded as representations or warranties. As was said in one case:[228] ''In this case it is not important whether the statement made by the insured is regarded as a warranty or a representation; for being the basis of the contract, and false in a material respect, it defeats the action whether more properly called by the one name or the other. It is therefore unnecessary to decide under which head it falls. The statement was material to the risk, and one about which the insured could not have been mistaken. The evidence shows that the plaintiff called five times for medical treatment at the German Polyclinic, to-wit, on October 12, 21, November 4, 9 and 15, 1886. She was also attended by Dr. Guden in July, 1886, and by Dr. Schmidt in the early part of October, 1886. If she had answered that she had been professionally attended at these several times the medical examiner of

[225] Vivar v. Supreme Lodge K. of P,. 42 N. J. L., 455; 20 Atl. 36; Mace v. Provident L. Ass'n, 101 N. C. 122; 7 S. E. 674.

[226] Supreme Lodge A. O. U. W. v. Hutchinson, 6 Ind. App. 399; 33 N. E. 816.

[227] Perine v. Grand Lodge A. O. U. W., 51 Minn. 224; 53 N. W. 367; ante, § 267.

[228] Numrich v. Supreme Lodge K. & L. of H., 3 N. Y. Supp. 552.

the defendant might and probably would have made a more searching medical examination or consulted these gentlemen, or without
going to further trouble, might have declined the risk entirely.
Her answers are supposed to have influenced his judgment more
or less; as they were favorable so was the impression they naturally created. The evidence proves that the answers were untrue and their falsity furnished the defendant with a complete
defense. As the amount insured is small, the defendant as a
benevolent organization, might (if it had chosen to do so)' have
thrown the broad mantle of charity over its deceased member
by adjusting the loss without litigation, but as truth and charity
seem to be concomitant requirements of the order, 'the defendant had the legal right to resist the demand made and interpose
the breach of the one obligation as a bar to the enforcement of
the other. The liability to pay is founded solely on the contract
obligation, which must be enforced (if at all) by the general
principles applicable to life insurance. The defendant agreed to
pay a specified sum on certain contingencies, and cannot be forced
to pay unless they occur in the manner agreed; and while it may
voluntarily bestow charity, it cannot be compelled to do so against
its will. In contracts for life insurance, the prevailing maxim
is *uberrima fides* and the best of faith must be observed by each
of the contracting parties, for the foundation stone of the obligations is truth.'' And the Supreme Court of New Jersey in a
similar case remarked:[229] ''In this class of cases warranties
should be regarded as the creatures of plain expression and not
of implication or construction. The certificate sued on contains
the contract, and the whole of the contract between the parties
to it, and neither the interrogatories nor the replies to them are
mentioned, or even in the most distant way alluded to. They
are therefore mere representations not warranted to be true, not
part of the agreement. But being intentionally false, with respect
to material matters, and having misled the society into the making of this obligation, such obligation is void by force of ordinary
legal principles.'' In another case where the occupation was misrepresented,[230] the Court says: ''In his application the deceased

229 McVey v. Grand Lodge A. O. U. W., 53 N. J. L. 17; 20 Atl. 873.
230 Holland v. Supreme Council O. C. F., 54 N. J. L. 490; 25 Atl. 367.

represented that his occupation was that of a printer, and that his business was pressman; that he was employed by P. Lorillard in Jersey City and had been so employed for nine years. In his statement to the medical examiner he answered in the negative the question: 'Are you engaged in the sale or manufacture of wine, beer or distilled liquors?' The proof at the trial was that the deceased was employed in the printing department of the works of P. Lorillard for a period of time down to December, 1881; that in July, 1883, he was employed in another department of the same works and left that employment in June, 1884; and that he had not been in Lorillard's employ after that date. It was also proved that after December, 1884, down to his last illness, and within a few days of his death, his employment was that of a bartender. He was so employed in December, 1889, when he made application for his membership in the society. The statement made by the deceased in his application and in his answers to the questions in the statement to the medical examiner with respect to his occupation was false, and if he had truly represented his occupation, he would by force of the relief fund laws, have been excluded from beneficial membership. Whether the statement in the application and the answers to the questions proposed by the medical examiner be regarded as a warranty or simply as representations, they were in a material respect willfully false and fraudulent and in either event they avoided the contract."[231] A misrepresentation of age will avoid the contract also.[232] It has been held,[233] that the statutes of Missouri, making false representation no defense unless they contributed to the death, do not apply to beneficiary orders or assessment concerns, they being expressly excepted by a subsequent statute, though probably unintentionally.

§ 269. **Concealment.**—According to the law of insurance concealment is the designed and intentional withholding of any fact, material to the risk, which the assured in honesty and good faith ought to communicate; and any fact is material, the

[231] McVey v. Grand Lodge A. O. U. W., 53 N. J. L. 17; 20 Atl. 873.
[232] Mut. Relief Soc. v. Webster, 25 Can. L. J. (N. S.) 206. *Post*, § 278.
[233] Whitmore v. Supreme Lodge K. & L. of H., 100 Mo. 36; Hanford v. Mass. Ben. Ass'n, 122 Mo. 50; 26 S. W. 680.

knowledge or ignorance of which would naturally influence an insurer in making the contract at all, or in estimating the degree and character of the risk, or in fixing the rate of insurance. All representations which enter into the essence of the contract, and which go to·lay the foundation of it, whatever would cause the company to accept or reject the application, should be truly stated.[234] The generally accepted definition of concealment is that given in the leading case of Daniels v. Hudson River, etc., Co.,[235] and is as follows: "Concealment is the designed and intentional withholding of any fact material to the risk, which the assured, in honesty and good faith, ought to communicate to the underwriter; mere silence on the part of the assured, especially as to some matter of fact which he does not consider it important for the underwriter to know is not to be considered as such concealment.' *Aliud est celare. aliud tacere.* And every such fact, untruly asserted or wrongfully suppressed, must be regarded as material, the knowledge or ignorance of which would naturally influence the judgment of the underwriter in making the contract at all or in estimating the degree and character of the risk or in fixing the rate of the premium.

§ 270. **Concealment of Material Fact Will Avoid the Contract.**—The English cases,[236] hold to the principle that an appli-

---

[234] Clark v. Union M. F. Ins. Co., 40 N. H. 333; 77 Am. Dec. 721; Locke v. North America F. Ins. Co., 13 Mass. 61; Kimball v. Aetna Ins: Co., 9 Allen 540.

[235] 12 Cush. 416.

[236] The English courts have been very strict in declaring life insurance policies invalid by reason of fraudulent practices in procuring them. The general rule obtains in England that failure to make known a material fact affecting the risk whether inquired into by the application or not, vitiates the policy. The authorities have thus been summarized in Encyclopaedia of the Laws of England, Vol. 7, page 438, as follows: "The answers in the declaration, however, may not cover all the facts material to be known; and if such facts are concealed the policy may be vitiated. Thus the non-disclosure of a serious illness of the person to be insured, though not specifically inquired about, may vitiate a policy (Morrison v. Muspratt, 1827, 4 Bing. 60; British Equitable Co. v. Musgrove, 1887, 3 T. L. R. 630). Among the facts which insurance companies and courts consider to be most material are whether or not the life has been accepted or refused by other companies, and the

cant is bound to disclose a fact material to the risk, even though no specific inquiry is made on that subject. The American cases, however, are not in entire accord, although the weight of authority seems to be in favor of the English rule. In a case in

name of the medical attendant who can give information as to the health of the life proposed. Thus where a man stated that he was insured by two other offices, but omitted to mention that several others had refused the risk, his policy was declared to be void (Wainwright v. Bland, 1836, 1 Mee & W. 33; London Assur. Co. v. Mansel, 1879, 11 Ch. D. 367). So also a reference to a medical practitioner who could give no information of any value, instead of to the one who had really attended, was held to be illusory (Huckman v. Fernie, 1838, 3 Mee. & W. 505). The person who acts as the usual medical attendant, even if unqualified, is the one whose name should be given (Everett v. Desborough, 1829, 5 Bing. 503; 30 R. R. 709.)" It was said in Lindenau v. Desborough, 8 B. & C. 586 (1828), by Littledale, J.: "It is the duty of the assured in all cases to disclose all material facts within their knowledge. In cases of life insurance certain specific questions are proposed as to points affecting in general all mankind. But there may be also circumstances affecting particular individuals which are not likely to be known to the insurers and which, had they been, would no doubt have been made the subject of specific inquiries." See also Life Ass. of Scotland v. Foster, 11 Ct. of Sess. Cas. 3rd series, 351; s. c. 4 Big. Life & Acc. Ins. Cas. 520, where the rule is thus well stated: "Concealment or non-disclosure of material facts by a person entering into a contract is, generally speaking, either fraudulent or innocent, and in the case of such contracts where parties are dealing at arm's-length, that which is not fraudulent is innocent. But contracts of insurance are in this, among other particulars, exceptional, that they require on both sides *uberrima fides*. Hence without any fraudulent intent, and even in *bona fides*, the insured may fail in the duty of disclosure. His duty is carefully and diligently to review all the facts, known to himself and bearing on the risk proposed to the insurers, and to state every circumstance which any reasonable man might suppose could in any way influence the insurers in concealing and deciding whether they will enter into the contract. Any negligence or want of fair consideration for the interests of the insurers on the part of the insured leading to the non-disclosure of material facts, though there be no dishonesty, may therefore constitute a failure in the duty of disclosure which will lead to the voidance of the contract. The facts undisclosed may not have appeared to the insured at the time to be material, and yet it turns out to be material, and in the opinion of a jury was a fact that a reasonable and cautious man proposing insurance would think material and proper to be disclosed, its non-disclosure will constitute such negligence on the insured as to void the contract." See note in last section.

501

Tennessee,[237] the Court said: "If the insured when he makes the application, knows or has any reason or ground to believe that he has any disease, even though it may be latent and undeveloped he is in duty bound to make it known, whether specially questioned or not and if he fail to do so, it will amount to a misstatement or concealment, as the case may be, that will avoid his policy." Judge Sharswood, in a charge to the jury in a case involving this question,[238] said: "There was at the time of the proposals a concealment by Daniel Lefavour of a fact material to the risk, which avoids the contract of insurance. There is no doubt that this is the law in life policies as well as in policies of marine insurance. Good faith is required on the part of the insured. He knows, and the underwriter is not presumed to know whatever is material, and he is not confined to the warranties contained in the policy." A leading case is Penn Mutual Life Ins. Co. v. Mechanics' Savings Bank, etc.,[239] in which the Court held that even if Schardt, the insured, who was a bank teller was not required by any specific question to disclose the fact of his embezzlements, of which it was claimed he was guilty, the policy would still be avoided if it were material to the risk, and he intentionally concealed it from the company. Judge Taft, in delivering the opinion of the court, said: "But even if Schardt was not required by any specific question to disclose the fact of his embezzlements, the policy would still be avoided, if it were material to the risk, and he intentionally concealed it from the company. This is not controverted. The issue of law between the parties is whether the policy would not be avoided even if his failure to disclose it were due, not to fraudulent intent, but to mere inadvertence, or a belief that it was not material. It is insisted for the plaintiff in error that the motive or cause of the non-disclosure is unimportant, if the fact be found material to the risk, and was known to the insured when he obtained the insurance. The trial court took the other view and instructed

[237] Knights of Pythias v. Rosenfeld, 92 Tenn. (8 Pickle), 508; 22 S. W. 204.

[238] Lefavour v. Ins. Co., 1 Phila. 558.

[239] 72 Fed. 413; 37 U. S. App. 692; 43 U. S. App. 75; 19 C. C. A. 286; 38 L. R. A. 33.

the jury accordingly. If this were a case of marine insurance, the contention for the plaintiff in error must certainly be sustained. The great and leading case on the subject is that of Carter v. Boehm,[240] where Lord Mansfield explained the effect of concealment of material facts in insurance to avoid the policy. He said: 'Insurance is a contract upon speculation. The special facts, upon which the contingent chance is to be computed,· lie most commonly in the knowledge of the insured only. The underwriter trusts to his representation, and proceeds upon confidence that he does not keep back any circumstances in his knowledge to mislead the underwriter into a belief that the circumstances do not exist, and to induce him to estimate the risk as if it did not exist. The keeping back such circumstances is a fraud, and therefore the policy is void. Although the suppression should happen through mistake, without any fraudulent intention, yet still the underwriter is deceived, and the policy is void, because the risk run is really different from the risk understood and intended to be run, at the time of the agreement.' . . . With respect to a contract thus made, it is clearly just to require that nothing but a fraudulent non-disclosure shall avoid the policy. Nor does this rule result in practical hardship to the insurer, for in every case where the undisclosed fact is palpably material to the risk the mere non-disclosure is itself a strong evidence of a fraudulent intent. Thus if a man ·about to fight a duel should obtain life insurance without disclosing his intention, it would seem that no argument or additional evidence would be needed to show the fraudulent character of the non-disclosure. On the other hand where men may reasonably differ as to the materiality of a fact concerning which the insurer might have elicited full information, and did not do so, the insurer occupies no such position of disadvantage in judging the risk as to make it unjust to require that before the policy is avoided it shall appear not only that the undisclosed fact was material, but also that it was withheld in bad faith. To hold that good faith is immaterial in such case is to apply the harsh and rigorous rule of marine insurance to a class of insurance contracts differing so materially from marine policies in the circumstances under which

[240] 3 Burr. 1905.

the contracting parties agree that the reason for the rule ceases.''
The Court also says: ''In every case where the undisclosed fact
is palpably material to the risk the mere non-disclosure is itself
strong evidence of a fraudulent intent, thus if a man about to
fight a duel should obtain life insurance without disclosing his
intention, it would seem that no argument or additional evidence
would be needed to show the fraudulent character of the non-
disclosure.'' There are a number of cases, however, where it has
been held that, if a company desires information, it should make
specific inquiries. These cases are well summarized in the case
above referred to as follows:[241] ''With respect to a contract
thus made, it is clearly just to require that nothing but a fraudulent non-disclosure shall avoid the policy. Nor does this rule result in practical hardship to the insurer, for in every case where
the undisclosed fact is palpably material to the risk the mere non-
disclosure is itself strong evidence of a fraudulent intent. Thus,
if a man about to fight a duel should obtain life insurance without disclosing his intention, it would seem that no argument or
additional evidence would be needed to show the fraudulent character of the non-disclosure. On the other hand, where men may
reasonably differ as to the materiality of a fact concerning which
the insurer might have elicited full information, and did not
do so, the insurer occupies no such position of disadvantage in
judging of the risk as to make it unjust to require that before the
policy is avoided it shall appear not only that the undisclosed
fact was material, but also that it was withheld in bad faith. To
hold that good faith is immaterial in such a case is to apply the
harsh and rigorous rule of marine insurance to a class of insurance contracts differing so materially from marine policies in the
circumstances under which the contracting parties agree that the
reason for the rule ceases.'' As a general thing, concealment in
most of the cases seems to have been a partial disclosure, omitting matters of importance, which if disclosed would make the
answer full and complete, but which if disclosed would have led
to the rejection of the risk. Such a case was one where a dan-

[241] Penn. Mut. L. Ins. Co. v. Mechanics' Savings Bank & Trust Co., *supra*.

gerous illness was concealed.[242]   Another, where the fact that
the applicant had had consumption was concealed, was held to
vitiate the policy.[243]   To the same effect are other cases.[244]   Another class of cases are those where delivery of the policy was
obtained by a fraudulent concealment of the fact that the applicant was at the time dangerously ill which illness soon resulted
in death.[245]   The concealment of a material fact, if inquiry is
made upon such point, will avoid the policy, although the assured did not suppose the fact to be material.[246]   ''The concealment which vitiates the policy must be such as misleads, or de-
ceives; such as a partial disclosure, omitting matters of importance, which, if disclosed, would make the answer full; as if
the answer about former sickness detail a slight illness, concealing a much more serious and recent sickness; as if the question
be whether the applicant had ever been seriously hurt by an
accident, and the answer be that an arm was broken ten years,
when the truth was that a serious internal injury was received
by a fall from a carriage. . . . If, in answer to the fifteenth
question, Dillard had said he had 'made an application to the
Continental company, which he had withdrawn,' when the truth
was, he had also made application to two other companies, which
had been rejected, it would be a case of concealment which
would avoid the policy, because the answer suggests that there
was no objection to the risk, whereas two companies had declined to take it.   The answer to this question is valuable to the

[242] Equitable L. Ass'n v. McElroy, 83 Fed. 631; 28 C. C. A. 365; 49 U. S.
App. 548.
[243] March v. National L. Ins. Co., 186 Pa. St. 629; 40 Atl. 1100.
[244] Drakeford v. Supreme Conclave, etc., 61 S. C. 338; 39 S. E. 523; Callies v. Modern Woodmen, 98 M. A. 521; 72 S. W. 713.
[245] Equitable Life Ins. Soc. v. McElroy, 83 Fed. 631; 28 C. C. A. 365; 49
U. S. App. 548; Piedmont, etc., Ins. Co. v. Ewing, 92 U. S. 377; Union Life
Ins. Co. v. Riggs, 123 Fed. 312; U. S. Life Ins. Co. v. Cable, 98 Fed. 761; 39
C. C. A. 264; 49 C. C. A. 216; 111 Fed. 19; 191 U. S. 288; Mut. Life Ins. Co.
v. Pearson, 114 Fed. 395.
[246] Vose v. Eagle, etc., Ins. Co., 6 Cush. 42; Curry v. Commonwealth Ins.
Co., 10 Pick. 535; Burritt v. Saratoga Co., etc., Ins. Co., 5 Hilt. 188; Conn.
Mut. L. Ins. Co. v. Young, 77 Ill. App. 440.   But a mere failure to state a
material fact, if not fraudulent, will not avoid. German Am. M. L. Ass'n
v. Farley, 102 Ga. 720; 29 S. E. 615.

insurer, as it opens the avenue to further inquiry, if the company desires to pursue the investigation.''[247]

§ 271. **The Same Subject—Further Illustrations.**—In holding that where an applicant willfully conceals from the insurer the fact of a previous illness, such concealment will avoid the policy if the disease was of such a character as to enhance the risk. The Court of Appeals of Georgia has said:[248] ''The insured stated unequivocally that he was in sound health. If this was untrue, and if he in fact was suffering from a serious disorder, which made him an undesirable risk, the policy would be void.[249] We do not mean to say that if an applicant for insurance acts in the utmost good faith, and fairly discloses to the company all of the information in his possession which would throw any light upon the condition of his health and the desirability of the risk, the policy would be void, even though it developed that he suffered from a disorder as to which he had no knowledge, and the existence of which was not ascertained by the examining physicians. But fraud voids all contracts, and there is nothing in the law relating to insurance contracts which laters this universal principle. Indeed, as if to emphasize the doctrine, Section 2479 of the Code provides that every application for insurance must be made in the 'utmost good faith' and any variation which changes the nature, the extent, or the character of the risk will void the policy. The question of the materiality of a representation or of a fact concealed is primarily one for the jury.'' And a man who as agent for his wife signs an application for insurance on her life in his own favor, binds her by his knowledge of her physical condition, as, for example, her having cancer, so as to render the policy void in case her answers to questions as to such condition are untrue,[250] and where insured after applying for life insurance in one company but before receiving the policy was told by another examining physician that he had Bright's

[247] American Ins. Co. v. Mahone, 56 Miss. 192; London Assurance v. Mansel, 11 Ch. Div. 363; Story v. Williamsburgh M., etc., Ass'n, 95 N. Y. 474.

[248] Aetna Life Ins. Co. v. Conway, 11 Ga. App. 557; 75 S. E. 915.

[249] Southern Life Ins. Co. v. Hill, 8 Ga. App. 857, 70 S. E. 186.

[250] Gamble v. Metropolitan Life Ins. Co., 92 S. C. 451; 75 S. E. 788; 41 L. R. A. (N. S.) 1199.

disease and he told the physician to make a microscopic examination which confirmed the diagnosis and then he arranged for
treatment, his failure to disclose his condition to the first insurer was an intentional concealment of a material fact which
avoided the policy.[251]

Whether or not an insurer is entitled to be informed of the
discovery by an applicant for life insurance of any change material to the risk occurring between the time of the application
and the final consummation of the contract is uncertain. The
Supreme Court of Nebraska has held that:[252] "When an application is made and approved there is no duty on the holder of
the certificate issued on such application to notify the company
of any subsequently discovered evidence of pregnancy, nor
would the fact if subsequently discovered prevent her from cer-
tifying that she was in sound bodily health, if such certificate is
otherwise true." The Supreme Court of Tennessee, however,
has held:[253] that where "plaintiff, before applying for insurance
to be issued by defendant, had suffered from one or more attacks
of renal colic, but in the application answered 'No' to questions
as to whether he had ever been afflicted with renal colic, but
between the date of the application and the delivery of the
policy was seized with a severe attack of renal colic, which persisted through several days, during which time he was informed
by his physician as to the nature of the disease, that it was his
duty to disclose such illness to defendant prior to the delivery
of the policy, and his failure to do so constituted such fraud as
avoids the policy. The English cases are in accord with this
view.[254] In the case last cited, it was said: "If there has been
a material change there ought to be an alteration of the repre-

251 United States Annuity & Life Ins. Co. v. Peak (Ark.) 182 S. W. 565.

252 Merriman v. Grand Lodge Degree of Honor, 77 Neb. 544; 110 N. W.
302; 8 L. R. A. (N. S.) 983; 15 Ann. Cas. 126. See also Carleton v.
Patrons', etc., Ins. Co., 109 Me. 79; 82 Atl. 649; 39 L. R. A. (N. S.) 951.

253 Harris v. Security Mut. Life Ins. Co., 130 Tenn. 325; 170 S. W. 474;
Ann. Cas. 1916 B 380.

254 Trail v. Baring, 4 De. G. J. & S. 318; 10 L. T. N. S. 215; British Eq.
Ins. Co. v. Great Western R. Co., 38 L. J. Ch. 314; Canning v. Farquhar, 16
Q. B. D. 727.

sentation and the ground for entering into the contract is altered."

In the case of Security Life Ins. Co. v. Booms,[255] the Court refers with approval to the statement in Thompson v. Travelers' Ins. Co.:[256] "It is well settled that the obligation rests upon an applicant for life insurance to disclose such changes in his physical condition as occur pending the negotiation, as would influence the judgment of the company as to the advisability of accepting the risk." In this case[257] the facts were that on or about October 12, 1910, the insured made application for the policy, payment of the first premium was made and policy delivered November 18th, 1910. On or about the 3rd day of November, 1910, the insured became ill with typhoid fever. The disease ran its course in ten or twelve days and she was substantially recovered therefrom on November 18th. After proof of death had been made the company commenced its action to cancel the policy, basing its demand upon the allegation that at the time the application for insurance was accepted and also at the time when the premium was paid and the policy delivered, the insured was not in good health. The Court held that the representations contained in the application must be deemed to refer to the time when the premium was paid and the policy delivered, and it concludes: "It follows that the assured at that time represented that she had not had any of the diseases to which she returned a negative answer and had not had any illness, or disease, other than as specifically stated by her. To say that these representations may be ignored in the instance of a person who receives a life insurance policy immediately following upon an atatck of typhoid fever, would be to deny one of the most important rights of the contracting party. The inherent probability that the plaintiff would have hesitated to issue a policy upon the life of Mrs. Young at that particular time raises to very substantial importance its right to have been informed of the facts."

[255] (Cal. App.), 159 Pac. 1000.
[256] 13 N. D. 444; 101 N. W. 900.
[257] Security Life Ins. Co. v. Brooms, *supra*.

§ 272. **Questions of Knowledge, Intent and Materiality Are for Jury.**—The question of knowledge concerning a fact and the intent of the party in withholding it and the question of materiality are for the jury.[258] On this point the Supreme Court of Massachusetts says:[259] ''The question whether the facts, if misrepresented, were known to the applicants, was a question of fact, to be left to the jury upon the evidence. The considerations referred to, as founding a legal conclusion of knowledge, are all fit and proper to be submitted to a jury; such as, that the assured and applicant is himself the owner of the property, and may be presumed to be acquainted with its condition; that the matter relates to things open and visible, things capable of distinct knowledge and not depending upon estimate, opinion, or mere probability; things in respect to which an owner is bound in honesty and good faith to know, takes upon himself to know, and usually does know; these and all other pertinent evidence bearing on the question are to be left to the jury, with directions that if they are satisfied from all the evidence, and can reasonably infer, that the assured did know the fact as it really existed, in regard to which misrepresentation is imputed, they are to find that he did know it; otherwise not.''

§ 273. **No Concealment When Facts Are Unknown to Applicant: Difference Between Representation and Concealment.**— Logically speaking there can be no concealment of a fact not known to the applicant, for one cannot conceal that of which he is ignorant. The subjects of representation and concealment are so closely allied that it is hard to tell where the dividing line is. Representation seems to be the active and positive statements of the party, while concealment is the want or omission

[258] Burritt v. Saratoga, etc., Ins. Co., 5 Hill. 188; Mut. Ben. Ins. Co. v. Wise, 34 Md. 582; Gates v. Madison, etc., Ins. Co., 2 N. Y. 43; Mallory v. Travelers' Ins. Co., 47 N. Y. 52; Monroe, etc,. Ins. Co. v. Robinson, 5 W. N. C. (Pa.) 389; Virginia, etc., Ins. Co. v. Kloeber, 31 Gratt. (Va.) 749; O'Hara v. United Brethren Aid Soc., 134 Pa. St. 417; 19 Atl. 683; Doty v. N. Y. State, etc., Ass'n, 9 N. Y. Supp. 42. See also Collins v. Catholic Order Foresters, 43 Ind. App. 549; 88 N. E. 87.

[259] Houghton v. Manufacturers', etc., Ins. Co., 8 Met. 121; 41 Am. Rep. 489.

of a statement. The Supreme Court of the United States has held,[260] that the suppression of a material fact which a man is bound in good faith to disclose is equivalent to a false representation. The connection and nature of these subjects will be clearer after discussion of the numerous decisions construing specific words and questions generally found in applications, which will close the present chapter.

§ 274. **Error or Fraud of Agent in Preparing Application.**— It is often the case that an applicant for insurance answers correctly the questions propounded, but the agent of the company, in writing down the replies, either from accident or design, changes the statements or omits it altogether, or fills in the answer from information obtained from another source. The question then arises whether the company is bound by the acts of its agent, so as to be estopped from insisting upon the forfeiture of the policy for a breach of the warranty of the truth of the statements in the application, or because of the false representations of the assured. The determination of this matter depends largely upon the fact whether the agent of the company is to be considered the agent of the assured in filling out the application. In some of the cases decided there was an express stipulation in the policy making the agent of the company the agent of the insured in preparing the application. The earlier decisions were favorable to the company upon this question, but the modern authorities are practically unanimous in holding that where the agents make out the applications incorrectly, notwithstanding the applicant has stated all the facts correctly, the errors will be chargeable to the insurer and not to the insured. The reason of this conclusion is that the insurance companies clothe the agents whom they send out to solicit business with an apparent authority, so that those dealing with them have a perfect right to regard them as the full and complete representatives of the companies by which they are employed, in all that is said and done in regard to the application.[261] This doctrine was followed

---

[260] Tyler v. Savage, 143 U. S. 79; 12 S. Ct. R. 340; citing Stewart v. Wyoming Ranch Co., 128 U. S. 383; 9 S. Ct. R. 101.

[261] Rowley v. Ins. Co., 36 N. Y. 550; 3 Keys 557; McCall v. Phœnix Mut. Ins. Co., 9 W. Va. 237; 27 Am. Rep. 558; Simmons v. Ins. Co., 8

although the companies, in order to avoid its application, had inserted in a policy a stipulation generally as follows: "It is a part of this contract that any person other than the assured who may have procured this insurance to be taken by this company shall be deemed to be the agent of the assured named in the policy, and not of this company, under any circumstances whatever, or in any transaction relating to this insurance." But the courts said that no man can serve two masters and no stipulation can successfully attempt such a logical and legal impossibility and have the same person guard two antagonistic interests at the same time. That if the agent was the agent of the company in the matter of making out and receiving the application he cannot be converted into the agent of the insured by merely calling him such in the policy subsequently issued. No mere form of words could wipe out the fact that the insured truthfully informed the insurer, through its agent, of all mat-

W. Va. 474; Grattan v. Metropolitan L. Ins. Co., 80 N. Y. 281; 36 Am. Rep. 617; Boos v. Ins. Co., 64 N. Y. 236; Baker v. Ins. Co., 64 N. Y. 648; Columbia Ins. Co. v. Cooper, 50 Pa. St. 331; Merserau v. Ins. Co., 66 N. Y. 274; Miner v. Phœnix Ins. Co., 27 Wis. 693; 9 Am. Rep. 479. In the following later cases the subject is considered and the authorities are reviewed: Wells v. Metropolitan L. Ins. Co., 163 N. Y. 572; 57 N. E. 1128; affg. 19 App. Div. 18; 46 N. Y. Supp. 80; O'Rourke v. John Hancock M. L. Ins. Co., 30 N. Y. Supp. 215; Mut. Ben. L. Ins. Co. v. Robinson, 7 C C. A. 444; 58 Fed. 723; 22 L. R. A. 325; affg. 54 Fed. 580; Howe v. Provident Sav. F. L. A. Soc., 7 Ind. App. 586; 34 N. E. 830; Whitney v. National Mas. Ac. Ass., 57 Minn. 472; 59 N. W. 943; Leonard v. State Mut. Ins. Co., 24 R. I. 7; 51 Atl. 1049; Mut. L. Ins. Co. v. Blodgett, 8 Tex. C. A. 45; 27 S. W. 286; Standard L. & A. Ins. Co. v. Davis, 59 Kan. 521; 53 Pac. 856; O'Farrell v. Metropolitan L. Ins. Co., 22 App. Div. 495; 48 N. Y. Supp. 199; Jacob v. N. W. Life Ins. Corp., 30 App. Div. 285; 51 N. Y. Supp. 967; 164 N. Y. 582; 58 N. E. 1088; Order Columbus v. Fuqua (Tex. Civ. A.), 60 S. W. 1020; Mullen v. Union Cent. L. Ins. Co., 182 Pa. St. 150; 37 Atl. 988; Boylan v. Prudential Ins. Co., 10 Misc. 444; 42 N. Y. Supp. 52; Quinn v. Metropolitan Life Ins. Co., 10 App. Div. 483; 41 N. Y. Supp. 1060; Bernard v. U. S. Life Ins. Co., 11 App. Div. 142; 42 N. Y. Supp. 527; Wells v. Metropolitan L. Ins. Co., 19 App. Div. 18; 46 N. Y. Supp. 80; Hamilton v. Fidelity M. L. Ins. Co., 27 App. Div. 480; 59 N. Y. Supp. 526; New York L. Ins. Co. v. Russell, 23 C. C. A. 43; 77 Fed. 94; Pfiester v. Mo. State L. Ins. Co., 85 Kan. 97; 116 Pac. 245; Continental L. Ins. Co. v. Ford, 140 Ky. 406; 131 S. W. 189.

ters pertaining to the application at the time it was made. "There is no magic power," said the Supreme Court of Illinois,[262] "residing in the words of that stipulation to transmute the real into the unreal. A device of mere words cannot, in a case like this, be imposed upon the view of a court of justice in the place of an actuality of fact." The Supreme Court of Minnesota added:[263] "If corporations are astute in contriving such provisions, courts will take care that they shall not be used as instruments of fraud or injustice."[264] The fraud, however, of the agent and assured will vitiate the policy,[265] although, if the agent, without the knowledge of the applicant, inserts false answers in the application, the contract will not be avoided.[266] The company can show that the policy was obtained by a conspiracy of the insured and the agent.[267]

[262] Commercial Ins. Co. v. Ives, 56 Ill. 402. See also Huestess v. South Atlantic, 88 S. C. 31; 70 S. E. 403; Metropolitan L. Ins. Co. v. Johnson, 49 Ind. App. 233; 94 N. E. 785.

[253] Kausal v. Minnesota, etc., Ins. Co., 31 Minn. 17; 47 Am. Rep. 776. In Whitney v. National Masonic Acc. Ass'n, 57 Minn. 472; 59 N. W. 943; the Supreme Court of Minnesota held that the rule applied in the preceding case applied to Mutual Benefit Societies. See also post, §§ 595, 603.

[264] Insurance Co. v. Wilkenson, 13 Wall. 222; Insurance Co. v. Mahone, 21 Wall. 152; Flynn v. Equitable L. Ins. Co., 78 N. Y. 568; 34 Am. Rep. 561; Planters' Ins. Co. v. Myers, 55 Miss. 479; 30 Am. Rep. 521; Campbell v. Merchants', etc., Ins. Co., 37 N. H. 35; 72 Am. Dec. 324; Gans v. Ben. L. Ins. Co., 31 Ia. 216; 7 Am. Rep. 122; Campbell v. New England Mut. L. Ins. Co., 98 Mass. 389; Plumb v. Ins. Co., 18 N. Y. 392. See ante, § 178.

[265] Centennial, etc., Ass'n v. Parham, 80 Tex. 518; 16 S. W. 316.

[266] Sawyer v. Equitable Acc. Ins. Co., 42 Fed. 30; Germania L. Ins. Co. v. Lunkenheimer, 127 Ind. 536; 26 N. E. 1082; Mut. Ben. L. Ins. Co. v. Robison, 7 C. C. A. 444; 58 Fed. 723; affg. 54 Fed. 580; Keystone v. M. B. Ass'n v. Jones, 72 Md. 363; 20 Atl. 195; Kan. Prot. U. v. Gardner, 41 Kan. 397; 21 Pac. 233; O'Brien v. Home Ben. Soc., 117 N. Y. 310; 22 N. E. 954; Pudridsky v. Supreme Lodge K. of H., 76 Mich. 428; 43 N. W. 373; Globe, etc., Co. v. Duffy, 76 Md. 293; 25 Atl. 227; Brewster v. National L. Ins. Co., 8 Times L. R. 648; Bowden v. London, etc., Ins. Co. (Ct. App.), 8 Times L. R. 566; Johnson v. Royal Neighbors, etc., 159 Ill. App. 269; affd. 253 Ill. 570; 97 N. E. 1084.

[267] Southern States Mut. L. Ins. Co. v. Herlihy, 138 Ky. 359; 128 S. W. 91; Mallen v. National Life Ass'n, 168 Mo. App. 503; 153 S. W. 1065.

§ 275. When Authority of Agent Is Known to Applicant.—

In spite of the great array of authority, however, in support of the foregoing propositions, much depends upon the special circumstances of each case. In a case which afterwards went to the Supreme Court of the United States in the Eastern District of Missouri,[268] the rule was applied on the trial below where the facts were these: The deceased was solicited by the agent of the company to take out the insurance and he, finally, consenting to do so, was told that it was necessary, as a mere form, to answer certain questions. The agent read to him these questions and as he answered the agent pretended to take down and write in the blank the substance of the answers, not reading them over to the assured nor telling him what he had written. When the applicant was asked whether he had any disease of the kidneys he said that his condition was well known to the agent, who was aware that he had been sick and under treatment for diabetes, that the doctor's office was opposite, and he could go there and find out everything. The applicant signed the paper without reading it. The answer in regard to disease of the kidneys was written in the application "No." The policy when issued had attached to it a copy of the application and a memorandum calling the attention of the insured to it and requesting that any errors in the application be reported to the company for correction. The assured died of diabetes and the false answer of the applicant was set up in defense to the action on the policy. The Court instructed the jury that if the assured answered the questions correctly and the false answers were written in by the agent, without the knowledge of the assured, and if the assured did not know of the misstatement until after the policy was issued, then such action of the agent was a fraud upon the assured, and the policy was not avoided. Upon the appeal of this case to the Supreme Court of the United States,[269] it was reversed, the Court, after stating that the company had a right to limit the authority of its agents if knowledge of such limitations was brought home to those having dealings with such agents, continues thus: "The present case is very

[268] Fletcher v. New York L. Ins. Co., 14 Fed. 846. See also Dimick v. Metropolitan L. Ins. Co., 69 N. J. L. 384; 55 Atl. 291.
[269] New York Life Ins. Co. v. Fletcher, 117 U. S. 531.

different from Insurance Co. v. Wilkenson,[270] and from Insurance Co. v. Mahone.[271] In neither of these cases was any limitation upon the power of the agent brought to the notice of the assured. Reference was made to the interested and officious zeal of insurance agents to procure contracts, and to the fact that parties who were induced to take out policies rarely knew anything concerning the company or its officers, but relied upon the agent who had persuaded them to effect insurance 'as the full and complete representative of the company in all that is said or done in making the contract;' and the court held that the powers of the agent are *prima facie* coextensive with the business intrusted to his care, and would not be narrowed by limitations not communicated to the person with whom he dealt. Where such agents, not limited in their authority, undertake to prepare applications and take down answers they will be deemed as acting for the companies. In such cases it may well be held that the description of the risk though nominally proceeding from the assured, should be re-.garded as the act of the company. Nothing in these views has any bearing upon the present case. Here the power of the agent was limited, and notice of such limitation given by being embodied in the application, which the assured was required to make and sign, and which, as we have stated, he must be presumed to have read. He is, therefore, bound by its statements. . . . The instruction given to the jury in the case before us, is, in effect, that the assured was bound by his application if it was not avoided for fraud, and that it was so avoided by reason of the false statements contained in it, and that, therefore, the plaintiff, as his representative, could recover. But if the application was avoided, it would seem to be a necessary consequence that the policy itself was also avoided, and his right limited to recovering the premiums paid. But such was not the conclusion of the court. It directed the jury that if the application was avoided for fraud, he could recover. It does not seem to have occurred to the court that had the answers been truthfully reported, and the fact of the assured having had diabetes within a recent period been thus disclosed, the insurance would in all probability have been refused. If the

[270] 13 Wall. 222.
[271] 21 Wall. 152.

policy can stand with the application avoided, it must stand upon parol statements not communicated to the company. This, of course, cannot be seriously maintained in the face of its notice that only statements in writing forwarded to its officers would be considered. A curious result is the outcome of the instruction. If the agents committed no fraud the plaintiff cannot recover, for the answers reported are not true; but if they did commit the imputed fraud he may recover, although upon the answers actually given, if truly reported, no policy would have issued. Such anomalous conclusions cannot be maintained. There is another view of this case equally fatal to a recovery. Assuming that the answers of the assured were falsified, as alleged, the fact would be at once disclosed by the copy of the application, annexed to the policy to which his attention was called. He would have discovered by inspection that a fraud had been perpetrated, not only upon himself, but upon the company, and it would have been his duty to make the fact known to the company. He could not hold the policy without approving the action of the agents and thus becoming a participant in the fraud committed. The retention of the policy was an approval of the application and of its statements. The consequences of that approval cannot, after his death, be avoided.''[272] This view, however, does not seem to prevail in every instance, as is shown by a recent case in Indiana,[273] where the Supreme Court of that State reviews the law and applies the principles in a way somewhat different. In that case the State agent wrote ''no,'' in place of ''yes,'' as answered by the applicant, and the court held the company estopped, although a copy of the application was attached to the policy, saying: ''It is claimed, however, by the appellant, that, inasmuch as a correct copy of the application was attached to and made part of the policy of insurance, the assured by accepting the policy

[272] Ryan v. World Mut. L. Co., 41 Conn. 568; 19 Am. Rep. 490; Lewis v. Phœnix Mut. Life Ins. Co., 39 Conn. 100; Franklin F. Ins. Co. v. Martin, 40 N. J. L. 568; American Ins. Co. v. Neiberger, 74 Mo. 167; Richardson v. Maine Ins. Co., 46 Me. 394. See also Schwartz v. Royal Neighbors of Am., 12 Cal. App. 595; 108 Pac. 51, and Bonewell v. North Am. Acc. Ins. Co., 167 Mich. 274; 132 N. W. 1067; affg. 160 Mich. 137; 125 N. W. 59; Sovereign Camp W. O. W. v. Lillard, Tex. Civ. App., 174 S. W. 619.

[273] Michigan Mut. L. Ins. Co. v. Leon, 138 Ind. 636; 37 N. E. 584.

was bound to know its contents, and became bound by the representations upon which it was issued. Whatever may be the rule as to the applications prepared by special agents, where the assured has knowledge of the limitations upon his authority, we are of the opinion that the rule contended-for the appellant should not be applied to a case like this, where the application is prepared by a general agent having no superior in the State. As we have seen, if the answers found in the application are untrue the wrong is with the appellant. As the appellant, through its duly authorized agent, was in possession of all the facts affecting the risk, we think the assured might well assume that the policy was properly prepared, and was based upon such facts, and that he was under no obligation to make a diligent reading of the policy with a view to ascertaining whether the appellant's own agent had perpetrated a fraud upon it. To permit the appellant now, since a loss has occurred, to void its policy on the ground that it was deceived by its own agent, without the fault of the assured, is to permit it to violate one of the best known principles of the law, namely, to take advantage of its own wrong. It is equivalent to permitting it to say, 'It is true I issued to the assured the policy upon which the suit is based, but I will not pay it because I, through my duly authorized agent, was guilty of the wrong of falsely recording the answers made by the assured to the questions asked him.' The case of Donnelly v. Insurance Co., [274] and the case of Boetcher v. Insurance Co., [275] are, we think, much in point here. In the latter case cited it was said by the court: 'We can readily see that the assured may be bound to take notice of the conditions and covenants in the policy that affects his rights, or that apply to matters in existence at the time the policy is delivered, or that may occur in the future, but we know of no principle of law which requires him to diligently examine the policy for the purpose of ascertaining whether it contains false statements of facts as to a past transaction, which he might well suppose closed.' Though the appellant in this case, through its agent, had full notice of the matters of which it now complains, it took no steps to avoid this

[274] 70 Ia. 693; 28 N. W. 607.
[275] 47 Ia. 253.

APPLICATION. • § 275

APPLICATION. • § 275

APPLICATION. • § 275

policy until the assured had been fatally injured in a railroad accident, and until it was too late to secure insurance elsewhere. Under such circumstances, in order to avoid the policy, we think it should be shown that the assured was guilty of some positive wrong. No wrong is attributed to him unless it be said that he was guilty of a wrong in neglecting to read the copy of the application attached to the policy issued to him by the appellant. We do not think this was such a wrong as would relieve. the appellant from liability on its policy under the circumstances surrounding this case." And in the recent case of Mc-Master v. New York Life Ins. Co., [276] the Supreme Court of the United States held that the omission of the insured to read a life insurance policy when delivered to him and payment of premiums made, and when in answer to his inquiry the insurance agent told him that the policy conformed to their agreement, does not constitute such negligence as to estop the insured from denying that by accepting the policy he agreed to a provision therein contained, but of which he was ignorant, and to which he had not agreed, to the effect that the annual premium should be paid in subsequent years on a date earlier than that on which the policy was issued. In a case where the application was signed by the applicant and taken away by the agent and filled out incorrectly by him, it was held by the Supreme Court of Michigan[277] that the beneficiary in an action on the policy "had the right to show by her testimony that the answers made by her daughter at the house were incorrectly written in by the agent after he went to his office, or that he filled in answers at such office that were not made at the house by Victoria (the assured). As such answers, if made by the agent, and not by Victoria, or without her knowledge or consent, could not bind her, the fact that they were so made could be established by parol. If the application had not been signed until filled out, a different rule might prevail."[278] Where the agent fills out the application and presents it to the applicant for signature, without acquainting him with its contents, the representations therein made are con-

[276] 183 U. S. 25; reversing 40 C. C. A. 19; 99 Fed. 856.
[277] Brown v. Metropolitan L. Ins. Co., 65 Mich. 306; 32 N. W. 610.
[278] *Ante*, § 172, *et seq.*

clusive against the company,[279] so where by advice of the agent certain statements are omitted from the application.[280] If the proposal for insurance be prepared by the agent and he incorrectly report the answers of the applicant, and if there be no fraud or collusion between the agent and the insured, the contract may be reformed in equity, and made to conform to the true facts stated to the agent..[281]

§ 276.   Answers to Referee: To Medical Examiner: Position of Latter.—If the policy so refers to the answers of a mutual friend, or referee, or to the answers of the applicant to the medical examiner as to warrant their truth and make them a part of the contract, they are warranties, otherwise they are representations which must be substantially true.[282]   The medical examiner has a wide latitude in his examination and the answers of the applicant must be substantially true.   The object of a physical examination of a person proposing to insure his life in an insurance company, by a competent physician, is to ascertain whether he is laboring under, or is subject to any disease or defects which may have a tendency to shorten life.   "It is impos-

[279] Dunbar v. Phoenix Ins. Co., 72 Wis. 492; 40 N. W. 386; Temminck v. Metropolitan L. Ins. Co., 72 Mich. 388; 40 N. W. 469; Mich. Mut. L. Ins. Co. v. Leon, 138 Ind. 636; 37 N. E. 584.

[280] Kansas Protective Union v. Gardner, 41 Kan. 397; 21 Pac. 233; Equitable L. Ass'n Soc. v. Hazelwood, 75 Tex. 338; 12 S. W. 621; O'Brien v. Home Ben. Ass'n, 117 N. Y. 310; 22 N. E. 954; Fidelity Mut. L. Ass'n v. Ficklin, 74 Md. 172; 21 Atl. 680; Mut. L. Ins. Co. v. Blodgett, 8 Tex. Civ. App. 45; 27 S. W. 286.

[281] Franklin F. Ins. Co. v. Martin, 40 N. J. L. 568; Collett v. Morrison, 9 Hare 162; In re Universal Non-Tariff F. Ins. Co., L. R. 19 Eq. 385; Malleable Iron Works v. Phœnix Ins. Co., 25 Conn. 465; Woodbury Savings Bank v. Charter Oak Ins. Co., 31 Conn. 517; Maher v. Hibernia Ins. Co., 67 N. Y. 283.   The effect of fault or fraud of agent will be further considered when we come to speak of estoppel.   See post, Ch. XV.   Also ante, § 172, et seq.

[282] Miller v. Mut. Ben. Life Ins. Co., 31 Ia. 235; United Brethren, etc., Soc. v. Kintner, 12 W. N. C. (Pa.) 76.   Provident Savings L. Ass. Soc. v. Reutlinger, 58 Ark. 528; 25 S. W. 835; Ins. Co. v. McMurdy, 89 Pa. St. 363; Equitable L. Ass. Soc. v. Hazlewood, 75 Tex. 348; 12 S. W. 621; Continental L. Ins. Co. v. Chamberlain, 132 U. S. 304; 10 Sup. Ct. Rep. 87; McCollum v. N. Y. Ins. Co., 8 N. Y. Supp. 249.

sible," says the New York Court of Appeals,[283] "to affix limits to the subjects, into which it is not only proper but necessary for an examining surgeon to inquire in order to arrive at a conclusion upon which he can safely advise the acceptance or rejection of a risk. Whether I am right or wrong in these views, I entertain no doubt that in many cases a knowledge of the pecuniary circumstances of a person desiring to be insured is material to the risk, as affecting in some degree the life and they are a legitimate subject of inquiry for the examining physician or surgeon." Where the medical examiner writes down false answers, when true information is given, there can be no misrepresentation. In a case in New York the facts were that the medical examiner was required by his instructions from the company to write the answers to the questions in his own handwriting and not to allow any person to dictate any portion of them. In answer to a question calling for the family history of the applicant he stated correctly the cause of the death of a sister. At the time the insured signed his name to the certificate, the answer had not been written in by the examiner; he subsequently filled in the cause of death as "not known to applicant." Under the facts the Court held:[284] "He (the examiner) was the agent of the defendant for the purpose of reporting the answers to the questions referred to and was so held out to Terence Grattan. He was, as medical examiner, charged with certain duties by the defendant, and was acting in concert with the soliciting agent of the company. On the part of the life insured was entire good faith and truthfulness, and there is no reason to suspect any intentional unfairness on the part of the examiner. The omission was inadvertent. Is the company thereby released from its obligation? Many decisions in this court show •

[283] Valton v. Loan Fund, etc., Soc., 1 Keys 21.

[284] Grattan v. Metropolitan Life Ins. Co., 80 N. Y. 293; 36 Am. Rep. 617. See also Ames v. Manhattan Life Ins. Co., 167 N. Y. 584; 60 N. E. 1106; affg. 40 App. Div. 465; 58 N. Y. Supp. 244; Robinson v. Metropolitan L. Ins. Co., 157 N. Y. 711; 53 N. E. 1131; Mass. Ben. L. Ass'n v. Robinson, 104 Ga. 256; 30 S. E. 918; 42 L. R. A. 261; Hackett v. Supreme Council, etc., 168 N. Y. 588; 60 N. E. 1112; Dimick v. Metropolitan L. Ins. Co., 69 N. J. L. 384; 55 Atl. 291.

that it is not.[285] Within the principle therein recognized as well established, the erroneous answer must be taken as the declaration of the defendant, and any controversy depending upon it must, as between the parties, be taken as true. In this case the physician was not the agent to solicit insurance, but he had an act to perform in regard to it as the agent of the company. His written instructions were to write out the answers. In this instance he failed to do it correctly. The principle upon which it has been held that the company and not the insured, is responsible for the error of the soliciting agent, is equally applicable here. This question has been repeatedly considered by this court, and in the recent case of Flynn v. The Equitable Life Ins. Co.[286] was again before us. The point presented was similar to the one under review. The decision was in conformity with the views above expressed, and the doctrine referred to must be deemed settled. Nor was it incompetent to prove by parol the actual transaction between the insured and the medical examiner. It was proper to do this in reply to the defendant's case, without reforming the contract or asking for equitable relief. Fraud and breach of warranty in regard to his sister's death, is averred in the answer, and the matter given in evidence was proper in reply thereto. If sufficient as the foundation for equitable relief or ground for reforming the contract, it was not improper to receive in this action evidence which would defeat the defendant's claim, or which would be competent in any action in a court of equity. This advantage is secured to the litigant by the union of legal and equitable remedies in one system.''[287] This opinion was adhered to in a subsequent case in the same court, and reason supports the view that the medical examiner is the agent of the company upon whom the burden rests if he incorrectly reports the answers of the applicant.[288] It has been

285 Mowry v. Rosendale; 74 N. Y. 360 and cases cited.

286 78 N. Y. 568; 34 Am. Rep. 561.

287 Emery v. Peace, 20 N. Y. 62; N. Y. Ice Co. v. N. Y. Ins. Co., 23 N. Y. 357; Arthur v. Homestead F. Ins. Co., 78 N. Y. 462.

288 Grattan v. Metropolitan Life Ins. Co., 92 N. Y. 285; Co-operative Life Ass'n v. Leflore, 53 Miss. 20; United Breth., etc., Soc. v. Kintner, 12 W. N. C. (Pa.) 76; Mut. Ben. L. Ins. Co. v. Wise, 34 Md. 582; Higbie v. Guardian Mut. L. Ins. Co., 53 N. Y. 603. To the same effect are Arnholst

held in New York,[289] that an agreement in an application that a medical examiner, employed and paid by the insurer, should not be its agent but solely that of the insured is invalid as being against public policy. So, also, where a printed application to a life insurance company was referred to in the policy and made a part thereof. The application was headed, "Questions to be asked by the medical examiner, who will fully explain the questions and witness the answers and signature of the person examined." At the time of an examination the medical examiner made certain verbal explanations of the meaning of these printed questions. The Court held[290] that the applicant for insurance might properly infer, from what was stated in the caption to the questions, that in answering them he should do so with reference to the construction and explanation given at the time, and if the questions were explained and answered in good faith, according to the interpretation put upon them at the time by the representative of the company, there could be no objection to proving the facts and submitting them to the jury, notwithstanding the insured warranted the truth of his answers to the questions. The Court approved the instruction to the jury of the Judge below that "if in good faith the insured answered these questions in view of the interpretation that was presented to him by the agent, then, gentlemen, there is no fraud; and if such you find to be the case, you must read in these interrogatories the explanation made by the agent at the time, and then read his answers to the interrogatories in the light of such explanations." So where the applicant truthfully stated to the medical examiner that she had

v. National Union, 179 Ill. 486; 53 N. E. 988; reversing 74 Ill. App. 482; Mutual Reserve F. L. Ass'n v. Ogletree, 77 Miss. 7; 25 Sou. 869; Endowment Rank v. Cogbill, 99 Tenn. 28; 41 S. W. 340; Mass. Ben. L. Ass'n v. Robinson, 104 Ga. 256; 30 S. E. 918; 42 L. R. A. 261; Alger v. Metropolitan L. Ins. Co., 32 N. Y. Supp. 323; 84 Hun. 271; Leonard v. State Mut. L. Ass. Co., 24 R. I. 7; 51 Atl. 1049. See also Supreme Lodge, etc., v. Jones, Tex. Civ. App., 143 S. W. 247; Sargent v. Modern Brotherhood of Am., 148 Ia. 600; 127 N. W. 52; Thomas v. Modern Brotherhood, 25 S. D. 632; 127 N. W. 572; Whigham v. Supreme Court I. O. F., 51 Ore. 489; 94 Pac. 968.

[289] Sternaman v. Metropolitan L. Ins. Co., 170 N. Y. 13; 62 N. E. 763; 57 L. R. A. 318; reversing 63 N. Y. Supp. 674.

[290] Connecticut General L. Ins. Co. v. McMurdy, 89 Pa. St. 363.

had "La Grippe" but by his advice the question was answered
no, it was held[291] that the company was estopped to deny the
truth of the answer.[292]   Rejection by the medical examiner of a
company renders false the answer of the applicant that he has
not been rejected by any other company.[293]   But a negative answer
to the question whether application has been made to any other
company for insurance, is true although an application had in
fact been made to another company which had not been passed
on.[294]   Where the medical examiner or agent upon a statement
of the facts, suggests the answer, the company afterwards will
not be heard to say that it is untrue.[295]   Still, in spite of this array
of authority, if the limitations on the power of the medical examiner are embodied in the contract it has been held that his
knowledge will not bind the company.[296]   Where an organizer
takes the applicant, who is the regular physician of the association, to another physician who signs a certificate without making
an examination, facts known by the latter will not bind the association.[297]

§ 277. **Rules of Construction in Particular Cases.**—A clearer
idea of the nature of warranties and representations and of the
rules of construction of answers of the applicant in his application will be gained from an examination of particular cases where
a direct ruling of the court has been had upon specific matters
contained in the application. We shall proceed therefore to refer
to some of these cases relating to such matters as age, condition,
occupation, habits, health, and residence of applicant, serious injury, sickness, other insurance, and questions relating to intemperance.

§ 278. **Age.**—Where it is provided that if any of the
statements made by the applicant as the basis of the contract

[291] Mutual L. Ins. Co. v. Blodgett, 8 Tex. Civ. App. 45; 27 S. W. 286.
[292] See also *ante*, § 276.
[293] Edington v. Aetna L. Ins. Co., 100 N. Y. 536.
[294] Langdon v. Union Mut. L. Ins. Co,. 14 Fed. 27.
[295] Higgins v. Phœnix, etc,. Ins. Co., 74 N. Y. 6. See also *post*, § 594.
This subject of answers to referee or medical examiner is also discussed
in the remaining sections of this chapter.
[296] John Hancock M. L. Ins. Co. v. Houpt, 113 Fed. 572.
[297] National Fraternity v. Karnes, 24 Tex. Civ. A. 607; 60 S. W. 576.

shall be found .in any respect untrue, then the policy shall be void, a misrepresentation as to age will avoid the policy. The question of age is so material that a false statement in regard to it will be fatal whether regarded as a representation or a warranty.[298] Where an applicant for admission to a voluntary association for mutual relief, the rules of which did not admit members over sixty years of age, stated his age, in his application, to be fifty-nine years, when in fact he was sixty-four years of age, it was held by the Supreme Court of Maine[299] that the misrepresentation avoided the contract of insurance issued thereon. In this case the Court says: "The age of the applicant was a material fact. If more than sixty he could not become a member. His representation of the fact was a warranty of its truth, and if not true, the contract was invalid. This rule is so uniformly held by the courts that no authorities need be cited.[300] Where the charter of a beneficial association limits the age of the applicants to fifty-one, a certificate issued to one older is void.[301] But where the agent of a life insurance company filled in the answers in the application, and the applicant, an old man who spoke English imperfectly, stated to the agent that he did not know his age, and the agent wrote in a certain age, which turned out to be incorrect, and upon the trial of an action upon the policy

[298] Hunt v. Supreme Council Chosen Friends, 64 Mich. 671; 31 N. W. 576; United Brethren, etc., Soc. v. White, 100 Pa. St. 12; Aetna Life Ins. Co. v. France, 91 U. S. 510; Alabama Gold Life Ins. Co. v. Mobile Mut. Ins. Co., 81 Ala. 329; 1 Sou. 561; Hartigan v. International, etc., Soc., 8 Low. Can. Jur. 203; Linz v. Mass. Mut. L. Ins. Co., 8 Mo. App. 363; Dina v. Supreme Council Cath. M. B. Ass'n, 201 Pa. St. 363; 50 Atl. 999; Dolan v. Mut. Reserve L. Ass'n, 173 Mass. 197; 53 N. E. 398; Marcoux v. Society of Beneficence, etc., 91 Me. 250; 39 Atl. 1027. See also Elliott v. Knights of Modern Maccabees, 46 Wash. 320; 88 Pac. 929; Logia, etc., v. Deaguirre, 14 Ariz. 390; 129 Pac. 503; Johnson v. American Nat'l Life Ins. Co., 134 Ga. 800; 68 S. E. 731; Maddox v. Southern Mut. L. Ins. Ass'n, 6 Ga. App. 681; 65 S. E. 789; Central Acc. Ins. Co. v. Spence, 126 Ill. App. 32.

[299] Swett v. Citizens' Mut. Rel. Soc., 78 Me. 541; 7 Atl. 394.

[300] See also McCoy v. Roman Catholic Ins. Co., 132 Mass. 272; 25 N. E. 289; Mutual R. Soc. v. Webster, 25 Can. L. J. (N. S.) 206.

[301] Steele v. Fraternal Tribune, 215 Ill. 190; 74 N. E. 121; affg. 114 Ill. App. 194; Taylor v. Grand Lodge, etc., 196 Minn. 441; 105 N. W. 408; 3 L. R. A. (N. S.) 114; Pirrung v. Supreme Council, 93 N. Y. Supp. 575; 104 App. Div. 571.

issued upon such application, the agent testified that on the applicant's failure to state his age, he expostulated with him and then
obtained some data from him which he (the agent) did not then
recollect, and from them he computed the age, and inserted it
in the application, the Court of Appeals of New York held that
an estoppel *en pais* was fairly established and the company was
precluded from setting up the falsity of the statement with reference to age in avoidance of the policy.[301a] So, where the agent
in writing in the age made a miscalculation[302] and where the
applicant was an ignorant man the agent computed it and
stated it falsely.[303] Where, however, the agent and the applicant
conspired to falsely state the age the contract was held void on
account of fraud.[304] A provision in the policy that "in case the
age of the insured shall have been understated by mistake, the
sum insured will be reduced to the amount the premium would
pay for at the true age," precludes the insurance company from
asserting the understatement as a breach of warranty, and its
remedy is to ask that the sum insured be reduced accordingly.[305]
The question of age is one of fact for the jury.[306] The insured
is bound by the statement of his father as to age, he having referred to his father for an answer, being unable to give it himself,[307] and misrepresentations by a member as to his age and
occupation bar a recovery.[308] It has been held[309] that a misrepresentation as to age defeats the policy only in part and in-

---

[301a] Miller v. Phœnix Mut. Life Ins. Co,. 107 N. Y. 292; 14 N. E. 271.

[302] Brink v. Guaranty Mut. Acc. Ass'n, 7 N. Y. Supp. 847.

[303] Keystone M. B. Ass'n v. Jones, 72 Md. 363; 20 Atl. 195.

[304] Hanf. v. N. W. Masonic Aid Soc., 76 Wis. 450; 45 N. W. 315.

[305] Singleton v. Prudential Ins. Co., 11 App. Div. 403; 42 N. Y. Supp.
446. See also Floyd v. Prudential L. Ins. Co., 72 Mo. App. 455.

[306] Deutscher, etc., v. Berger, 35 Ill. App. 112; Corbett v. Metropolitan
L. Ins. Co., 37 App. Div. 152; 55 N. Y. Supp. 775; Meehan v. Supreme
Council Cath. Benev. L. (App. Div.), 88 N. Y. Supp. 821. For discussion
of law of evidence as to age, see *post,* § 646.

[307] Mutual Reserve Life Ins. Co. v. Jay (Tex. Civ. App.), 101 S. W. 545.

[308] Hartmann v. National Council K. & L. of S., 190 Mo. App. 92; 175
S. W. 212; Daffron v. Modern Woodmen of America, 190 Mo. App. 303;
176 S. W. 498; Kribs v. United Order of Foresters, 191 Mo. App. 524;
177 S. W. 766.

[309] Germania Life Ins. Co. v. Klein, 25 Colo. App. 326; 137 Pac. 73.

surer is liable for the amount which the premium would have purchased at the true age. Under the law of Mississippi a misstatement of age only entitles the company to a readjustment of the policy.[310] Under the law of Missouri a condition in the policy for readjustment of its amount in case of false statement as to age is void.[311] Where a readjustment is made on account of misstatement of age a reinsuring corporation cannot take advantage of the false answer in the original application,[312] nor can a company claim a forfeiture because of misstatement of age inadvertently inserted in the policy by its agent.[313]

§ 279. **Whether Applicant is Married or Single.**—If the question is asked whether the applicant is married or single the answer must be true; for by asking the question the insurer has shown that an answer was considered material. The question arose in Jeffries v. Life Insurance Company, in the Supreme Court of the United States,[314] where it was argued that it was immaterial because, in this case, the insured having answered that he was single, when in fact he was married, and being married made the risk better, the company was not injured. The Court says: "This stipulation is not expressed to be made as to important or material statements only, or to those supposed to be material, but as to all statements. The statements need not come up to the degree of warranties. They need not be representations even, if this term conveys an idea of an affirmation having any technical character. Statements and declarations is the expression; what the applicant states and what the applicant declares. Nothing can be more simple. If he makes any statement in the application it must be true, if he makes any declaration in the application it must be true. A faithful performance of this agree-

[310] Coplin v. Woodmen of the World, 105 Miss. 115; 62 Sou. 7.

[311] Metropolitan Life Ins. Co. v. Stiewing, 173 Mo. App. 108; 155 S. W. 900; Burns v. Metropolitan Life Ins. Co., 141 Mo. App. 212; 124 S. W. 539.

[312] Lowenstein v. Old Colony Life Ins. Co., 179 Mo. App. 364; 166 S. W. 889.

[313] Fidelity & Casualty Co. v. Meyer, 106 Ark. 91; 152 S. W. 995.

[314] 22 Wall. 47. See also Makel v. John Hancock M. L. Ins. Co., 88 N. Y. Supp. 757; Travelers' Ins. Co. v. Lampkin, 5 Colo. App. 177; 38 Pac. 335.

ment is made an express condition to the existence of a liability
on the part of the company. There is no place for the argument
either that the false statement was not material to the risk, or
that it was a positive advantage to the company to be deceived
by it. It is the distinct agreement of the parties, that the company shall not be deceived to its injury or to its benefit. The
right of an individual or corporation to make an unwise bargain
is as complete as that to make a wise•bargain. The right to make
contracts carries with it the right to determine what is prudent
and wise, what is unwise and imprudent, and upon that point
the judgment of the individual is subject to that of no other tribunal. The case in hand affords a good illustration of this principle. The company deems it wise and prudent that the applicant
should inform them truly whether he has made any other applica-
tion·to have his life insured. So material does it deem this information, that it stipulates that its liability shall depend upon
the truth of the answer. The same is true of its inquiry whether
the party is married or single. The company fixes this estimate
of its importance. The applicant agrees that it is thus important
by accepting this test. It would be a violation of the legal rights
of the company to take from it its acknowledged power, thus to
make its opinion the standard of what is material and to leave
that point to the determination of a jury.''[315] This is true where
in an application for membership in a benefit society, the beneficiaries of which were limited to wife and children, a person is
represented to be the applicant's wife when she was not.[316] And
a false statement that the beneficiary is the wife if warranted
to be true avoids the policy.[317]

§ 280. **Residence.**—When the residence of the Applicant is
asked the meaning is that the ordinary place of abode of the
person should be given. "The term residence," says the Supreme Court of Alabama,[318] ''as employed in the questions pro-

315 United Brethren Mut. Aid Soc. v. White, 100 Pa. St. 12.

316 Smith v. Baltimore & Ohio R. Co., 81 Md. 412; 32 Atl. 181. But see
post, §§ 283, 333.

317 Gaines v. Fidelity and Casualty Co., 188 N. Y. 411; 81 N. E. 169;
affg. 97 N. Y. Supp. 836; 11 App. Div. 386.

318 Mobile Life Ins. Co. v. Walker, 58 Ala. 290.

pounded to the assured, was intended to signify the place of permanent, rather than mere temporary abode, in the sense of domicile, rather than of mere inhabitancy. It is undisputed that the domicile of the assured was truly stated, and that his sojourn in Kentucky was merely temporary. The domicile, and the place of temporary residence, are each within the territorial limits, in which, according to the stipulation of the policy, the assured had the right to visit or reside. The policy and the application must be construed together. Residence, as employed in the one, must have the same signification it bears in the other, there being no indication of an intention to employ them in a different signification. The word visit is manifestly employed in contradistinction to the word reside. The one conferring the right to travel and sojourn, and the other the right to acquire domicile by residence with the intention of remaining."[319] A false statement as to residence, when the answers are warranted to be true will avoid the policy.[320]

§ 281. **Occupation.**—Occupation is a term of broad signicance and includes the acts by which one makes a living. One having an occupation continues to have it until he abandons it either by quitting work without intending to resume it or by engaging in some other occupation not of a mere temporary nature.[321] The occupation of the applicant, which is required to be disclosed, means the business in which he is engaged at the time of making the application. "If it meant the trade he had learned in his youth and which he had followed years before, it would indeed be immaterial whether he told the truth or a falsehood, and it would have been mere folly in the insurers to ask him the question."[322] So, where the applicant stated that he was

[319] Southern Life Ins. Co. v. Booker, 9 Heisk. 606; 24 Am. Rep. 344; Perrins v. Marine, etc., Ins. Soc., 2 El. & El. 317; 29 L. J. Q. B. 242; 6 Jur. (N. S.) 627; 8 W. R. 563.

[320] Hutchinson v. Hartford L. & A. Ins. Co. (Tex. Civ. A.), 39 S. W. 325; Kansas City Life Ins. Co. v. Blackstone, Tex. Civ. App., 143 S. W. 702.

[321] Supreme Lodge K. & L. of H. v. Baker, 163 Ala. 518; 50 Sou. 958; Eversen v. General, etc., Assur. Corp., 202 Mass. 169; 88 N. E. 658; Taylor v. Ill. Commercial Men's Ass'n, 84 Neb. 799, 122 N. W. 41.

[322] Hartman v. Keystone Ins. Co,. 21 Pa. St. 478. In this case the occupation was stated as "farmer" when in fact he was a slave-taker.

a "laborer," and it appeared that, as a matter of fact, he had suspended labor for several years prior to making the application,
either on account of old age or other continuous disability, it was
held by the Supreme Court of Pennsylvania,[323] that the answer
was misleading and the policy thereby avoided. "It is indeed
true," says the Court, "that the rule would not embrace a merely
temporary suspension of the alleged occupation, but it does embrace a suspension extending through several years, or resulting
from old age or other continuous disability." So where the applicant stated his occupation to be "lockmaker," when in fact,
he was doing odd jobs in a livery stable, the policy was avoided.[324]
So where a cattle dealer stated his occupation to be "ice dealer
and proprietor transportation company."[325] So where a person
who stated his application as a pumpmaker was killed by dyna-
mite while blowing out a well."[326] Under a construction of the
language of the application a statement as to occupation may
apply to a time after the delivery of the policy.[327] The New York
Court of Appeals[328] has held where, in the application for the
policy, in answer to the question as to the occupation of the deceased, the answer was "soda-water maker," and the medical examiner's certificate, required to be signed by the applicant, stated
in answer to an inquiry as to the occupation of the applicant,
that "he is out of doors most of the time selling soda-water,"
and it appeared that the deceased both made and sold soda-water,
that the answers were to be taken together and stated the facts
correctly. And, where the applicant stated his occupation to be
"manufacturing," and it was shown that during the month the
application was made insured kept a billiard saloon, and that for
years previous he had been engaged in manufacturing soda-water,
and was about to resume this business, the Court held[329] that the

323 Mutual Aid Society v. White, 100 Pa. St. 12.
324 Fell v. Hancock M. L. I. Co., 76 Conn. 494; 57 Atl. 175.
325 Standard L. & A. Ins. Co. v. Ward, 65 Ark. 295; 45 S. W. 1065.
326 Mortensen v. Central Life Ass'n, 124 Ia. 277; 99 N. W. 1059.
327 McGurk v. Metropolitan L. Ins. Co., 56 Conn. 525; 16 Atl. 263.
328 Grattan v. Metropolitan Life Ins. Co., 80 N. Y. 281; 36 Am. Rep. 617.
329 Mowry v. World Mutual Life Ins. Co., 7 Daly 321. See also High
Court I. O. O. F., 70 Ill. App. 139; Perrin v. Prudential Ins. Co., 29 Misc.
597; 61 N. Y. Supp. 249; affd. 62 N. Y. Supp. 720; Hadley v. Provident
Savings L. A. Soc., 90 Fed. 390. But see Malicki v. Chicago Guaranty,
etc., Soc., 119 Mich. 151; 77 N. W. 690.

question might have been understood as calling for the usual rather than the temporary occupatio̎n, and there was nó breach of warranty. A statement that insured is a miller ie not false although insured operated a circular saw for cutting logs attached to his mill,[330] and that insured was part owner of a steam engine used in operating a saw-mill and met his death by its explosion, is not engaging in or using explosives within the meaning of a life policy.[331] Employment as a fireman on a yard switching engine is service in switching cars within the provision of a life policy,[332] but a man is not a railroad switchman although he was killed while operating a dead engine.[333] One employed about a restaurant who occasionally tends bar although not employed, or paid, for that purpose, is not a bartender or engaged in the sale of liquors,[334] and driving a beer wagon and taking orders from dealers and delivering orders does not constitute the sale of intoxicating liquors as a beverage within the meaning of a by-law,[335] and a representation that applicant had never been engaged in, or connected with, the manufacture of liquors is not false although when a boy he had worked about his father's still.[336] However, insured is a saloon keeper although his wife owned the saloon and he never served drinks, where she had nothing to do with its control.[337] A representation in an application for accident insurance that a professional gambler is a capitalist is material and if false avoids the policy, and the same may be said of a statement by the applicant that he was of good habits when he was living with a woman who was not his wife.[338] A director of

[330] Denoyer v. First National Accident Co,. 145 Wis. 450; 130 N. W. 475.

[331] Anchor Life Ins. Co. v. Meyer (Ind. App), 111 N. E. 436.

[332] Diseker v. Equitable Life Assur. Soc., 87 S. C. 187; 69 S. E. 153.

[333] Batten v. Modern Woodmen of America, 131 Mo. App. 381; 111 S. W. 513.

[334] Stevens v. Modern Woodmen of America, 127 Wis. 606; 107 N. W. 8; Supreme Council R. A. v. Urban, 137 Ill. App. 292; Graves v. Knights of the Maccabees, 112 N. Y. Supp. 948; 128 App. Div. 660.

[335] Supreme Tribe of Ben Hur v. Lennert, 178 Ind. 122; 98 N. E. 115; overruling 94 N. E. 889, which on rehearing affirmed 93 N. E. 869.

[336] Blackstone v. Kansas City Life Ins. Co. (Tex.), 174 S. W. 821; reversing 143 S. W. 702.

[337] Solomon v. American Guild, 151 Ala. 297; 44 Sou. 387.

[338] Eliott v. Frankfort, etc., Co. (Cal.), 156 Pac. 481.

a corporation, engaged in manufacturing and selling liquor, is not engaged as "principal, agent or servant" in the manufacture or sale of malt liquors.[339] In England it was held that a representation that the applicant was an "esquire" was sufficient, if true, although he was at the time engaged in business as an ironmonger. This was on the ground that the statement was not untrue, but imperfect.[340] When the applicant stated that he was a wholesale liquor dealer and importer and had a government license and sold liquor only at wholesale, it was held that the answer was true although he sold liquor by the pint or quart in bottles.[341] The fact that, where the occupation stated is that of "country merchant," liquor is carried in stock does not make false the answer that applicant is not engaged in the business of selling intoxicating liquor.[342] Nor is one engaged in the sale of liquor though as servant in a hotel he is occasionally called on to serve liquor to guests.[343] Where the applicant represented his occupation to be that of printer when in fact he was tending bar the contract was held void.[344] A fair disclosure is required and if that is made it is sufficient.[345] The company may be estopped if the agent incorrectly states the occupation, the applicant making no misrepresentation, as where a saloon keeper was described as a general merchant,[346] or where a railroad yardman was described as a "laborer,"[347] or where the agent knew that

339 People v. Supreme Tent, etc., 35 Misc. 424; 71 N. Y. Supp. 960.

340 Perrins v. Marine & Gen. Tr. Ins. Co., 2 El. & El. 317; 29 L. J. Q. B. 242; 6 Jur. (N. S.) 627; 8 W. R. 563. See also Southern Life Ins. Co. v. Booker, 9 Heisk. 606.

341 Kenyon v. Knights Templar, etc., Ass'n, 122 N. Y. 247; 25 N. E. 299; affg. 48 Hun. 278.

342 Fidelity Mut. L. Ass'n v. Ficklin, 74 Md. 172; 21 Atl. 680.

343 Guiltman v. Metropolitan L. Ins. Co., 69 Vt. 469; 38 Atl. 315; but to the contrary Malicki v. Chicago Guaranty, etc., Soc., 119 Mich. 151; 77 N. W. 690.

344 Holland v. Supreme Council O. C. F., 54 N. J. L. 490; 25 Atl. 367; See also Standard L. & A. Ins. Co. v. Fraser, 22 C. C. A. 499; 44 U. S. App. 694; 76 Fed. 705.

345 Brink v. Guaranty Mut. Acc. Ass'n, 7 N. Y. Supp. 847.

346 Continental L. Ins. Co. v. Thoena, 26 Ill. App. 495.

347 Wright's Admr. v. N. W. Mut. Life Ins. Co., 91 Ky. 208; 15 S. W. 242.

a country merchant carried liquor.[348]   No recovery can be had
upon a policy providing that it only extended to assured as ''yard-
master,'' where assured at the time was a yard conductor.[349]
To visit a mine is not prospecting or mining.[350]   One having
charge of a gang of laborers is properly called an ''inspector.''[351]
If the statement of present occupation is true a subsequent change
will not avoid the policy, unless it is so stipulated in the contract.[352]   But the stipulation must be clear.[353]

§ 282. **The Dwight Case.**—One of the most interesting cases
relating to life insurance questions, discusses this matter of occupation, and also the principles of construction of life insurance
contracts, and deserves somewhat full extracts. It is the famous
case of Dwight v. Germania Life Insurance Co.[354]   In this case,
by the terms of the contract, the assured warranted the truth
of his answers to questions in his application, and compliance
with the terms of the warranty was held to be a condition of the
contract, so that any substantial deviation from the truth in an
answer must be assumed to be material to the risk so as to forfeit the policy. The Court proceeded as follows: ''Among the
facts which the defendant deemed it important to know before
entering into a contract of insurance with the deceased, was his
previous business and occupation. The materiality of truthful
information in relation thereto was impressed upon the applicant
by specific inquiries and the requirement that truthful answers
thereto should be made the condition of a valid contract. With
the view of eliciting the information desired, a series of questions
was proposed to the deceased embracing not only an inquiry as
to his general business and occupation, but special inquiries as
to certain particular trades and employments. Among those which
we deem it important to refer to in this case were the following:
'A. For the party whose life is proposed to be assured, state the
business, carefully specified? Ans. Real estate and grain dealer.

[348] Fidelity Mut. L. Ass'n v. Ficklin, *supra.*
[349] Moore v. Citizens' Mut. L. Ins. Co., 26 N. Y. Supp. 1014.
[350] Butler v. Supreme Court I. O. F., 60 Wash. 171; 110 Pac. 1007.
[351] Smith v. Prudential Ins. Co., 41 N. Y. Supp. 925; 10 App. Div. 148.
[352] Provident Life Ins. Co. v. Fennell, 49 Ill. 180.
[353] Hobbs v. Ia. Mut. Ben. Ass'n, 82 Ia. 107; 47 N. W. 983.
[354] 103 N. Y. 341; 8 N. E. 654.

B. Is this business his own or does he work for other persons, and in what capacity? Ans. His own. C. In what occupation has he been engaged during the last ten years? A. Real estate and grain dealer. D. Is he now, or has he been engaged in or connected with the manufacture or sale of any beer, wine or other intoxicating liquors? Ans. No.' . . . Upon the trial it appeared that Dwight was engaged in the business of keeping hotel at Binghampton, from May, 1874, until March, 1877, and that during that period he regularly and systematically sold wines and liquors, in bottles of various sizes, bearing the name of his hotel blown in the glass, to such of his guests as desired them. He kept a wine or liquor room in which was stored a large supply of wines and liquors, and each year while so engaged he applied, paid for and received, from the representatives of both the State and National Governments, licenses and permits, authorizing him to carry on the business of selling beer, wine and liquors at retail, to be drank upon his premises. It also appeared that he kept no bar and did not sell to persons who were not his guests. These facts were undisputed. Their absolute truth was assumed by the trial judge in charging the jury, and by the general term in passing upon the appeal to that court. That the answer given by Dwight to the questions (relating to the sale of liquor) was incorrect was admitted by both tribunals. That Dwight did not misconceive the meaning and intent of the question conclusively appeared from repeated answers made by him to other companies within three weeks prior to this time to similar questions in applications for other insurance in which he stated that he had kept a hotel for three years in which liquor was sold in packages. Upon denying the motion for a non-suit, the trial court refused to pass upon the question as to whether the facts constituted a breach of warranty or not, but left it to the jury to say whether the sales of liquor, proved to have been made, were sales at all, within the intent and meaning of the contract. In this we think that the Court erred, no question arising upon the evidence which authorized its reference to the jury. If there was any room for doubt in respect to the true meaning and intent of the inquiry answered by the deceased, it presented a question of law for the Court to determine, and not one for the jury.[355] But we are of

[355] Lomer v. Merker, 25 N. Y. 361; Glacius v. Black, 67 N. Y. 563.

the opinion that no such doubt existed in the case. The contract was in writing, subscribed by the parties, and they expressed their agreement in clear, unambiguous and intelligible language. Its import and meaning was not obscured by any reference to the situation and circumstances, surrounding the transaction, or by the consideration of other parts of the same instrument. On the contrary, an examination of the context and associated questions make more certain and definite its object and intent. The assured had been previously interrogated as to his general business and employment, and it is to be assumed had given such answers in respect thereto, as satisfied the object of the inquirer. He was then specially requested to state whether he was then, or had been, engaged in, or connected with, the manufacture or sale of any beer, wine, or other intoxicating liquors. The information called for was made material, not only by the express agreement of the parties, but also by the object for which it was required, . plainly apparent from the nature of the transaction. The question called for no opinion, and was capable of a precise, definite and categorical answer. It was intentionally framed in broad and comprehensive terms, apparently to avoid any evasion of its object; but was, nevertheless, expressed in clear and unambiguous language. If an intention to inquire concerning the conduct of the regular or principal business of the assured could be implied from the use of the word 'engaged,' an idea that such was the only meaning of the question was negatived by the further words, 'or connected with the manufacture or sale of any beer,' etc., which pointed unmistakably to every transaction of the kind described, however limited its character, or remote his connection with it, might have been. The motive prompting the question was reasonable, natural and proper, and apparent even to the most careless reader. The inquiry could not have referred to the general business employment of the insured, because inquiries on that subject had previously been exhausted, and the question had no office to perform in that respect. It carried upon its face the object which the insurer had in making it, and required an answer as to whether the applicant was, or had been engaged in, or connected with, the manufacture or sale of liquors, etc., not in a limited or restricted capacity or employment, but in any and every way in which such acts could have been performed. The

533

question itself assumes that persons engaged in or connected with the manufacture or sale of liquors in any manner were more hazardous subjects for insurance than those occupied in more reputable employments, and that the insurer would regard such employment as an objection to the proposed contract. The extent to which the employment affected the character of the applicant, or his value as a risk, was a question solely for the insurer. The defendant had a right to a full and frank disclosure of any and all facts bearing upon the subject, and this confessedly it did not obtain. It was misinformed as to the precise fact which had been agreed upon as a fact material for it to know, in determining the propriety of entering into the proposed contract, and by the parties who had assented to the proposition, that such information should invalidate any contract made. If the fair import of the language used, indicates that the interrogatory intended to include within its scope and meaning single transactions or incidental occupations, neither courts nor juries have authority to say that such transactions may properly be disregarded in the answer made. The defendant must be deemed to have meant what is said, and its express language embraces all transactions, and its express contract has made every transaction of the kind referred to, material to the risk. . . . We are also of the opinion that the answers of the assured to the questions relating to his business and occupation, were evasive and untrue, and, upon the whole evidence, required the dismissal of the complaint. There was not only an absence of satisfactory evidence in the case that he had ever been engaged in the business of a real estate or grain dealer, for himself in the ordinary acceptation of those terms, but such an acceptation was negatived by his repeated sworn declarations to the contrary, and the proof of circumstances of the most convincing character. The evidence upon these questions is substantially all to the same effect, and presents a case so preponderating in character, that a verdict against it could not be allowed to stand. The case, therefore, presented a question of law as to whether the business engaged in by the deceased, constituted him a dealer in real estate and grain, within the ordinary meaning of those terms.''

534

§ 283. **Answers in Regard to Parents, Relatives, etc.**—The age of the parents of the applicant at the time of their death, the diseases of which they died, and facts relating to the relatives and family of the applicant, are all material and must be truly stated. The insured will be presumed to have known about his family history in answering questions relating thereto, including being treated by a physician.[356] Where the statements of the application are warranted to be true the stipulation is for absolute truth and not for the truth according to the belief of the applicant and if such applicant answers falsely that his brother never had insanity, the contract is void.[357] Answers to these questions assume knowledge, as in a case, where the assured in his application answered "no" to the question whether either of his parents, brothers or sisters had ever had pulmonary, scrofulous or other constitutional or hereditary diseases, in which it was held that the answer assumed his knowledge of the fact and, in an action on the policy, the beneficiary was precluded from alleging the want of knowledge on the part of the insured as an excuse for not answering correctly.[358] A statement that a sister died of kidney disease, when in fact she died of chronic pneumonia, has been held not to be *prima facie* a material misrepresentation.[359] Where in an application for membership in a benefit society, designating a beneficiary a person was falsely represented to be a niece the contract was held void.[360] So as to cousin.[361] So as to wife.[362] But the better rule is that in such case the contract is only avoided as to the person wrongfully designated as beneficiary and inures to the benefit of the next of kin as in case of no designa-

356 Kedder v. Supreme Commandery, etc., 192 Mass. 326; 78 N. E. 469; Hoagland v. Supreme Council R. A., 70 N. J. Eq. 607; 61 Atl. 982.

357 Johnson v. Maine, etc., Ins. Co., 83 Me. 182; 22 Atl. 107.

358 Hartford L. & A. Ins. Co. v. Gray, 91 Ill. 159. See also Jerrett v. John Hancock M. L. Ins. Co., 18 R. I. 754; 30 Atl. 793; McGowan v. Supreme Court I. O. O. F., 107 Wis. 462; 83 N. W. 775; Kansas Mut. L. Ins. Co. v. Pinson (Tex. C. A.), 64 S. W. 818.

359 New Era Ass'n v. McTavish, 133 Mich. 68; 94 N. W. 599.

360 Supreme Counc. A. L. H. v. Green, 71 Md. 263; 17 Atl. 1048.

361 Mace v. Provident L. Ins. Ass'n, 101 N. C. 122; 7 S. E. 674; Gray v. Sovereign Camp W. of W., 47 Tex. Civ. App. 609; 109 S. W. 176.

362 Travelers' Ins. Co. v. Lampkin, 5 Colo. App. 177; 38 Pac. 335. But see Bogart v. Thompson, 24 Misc. 581; 53 N. Y. Supp. 622.

tion.[363] As half-brothers are not generally regarded as brothers it will be left to the jury to say whether a failure to mention them is a concealment of a material fact.[364] A representation that the applicant had no brother dead, in the absence of fraud, has been held not to avoid the policy.[365] And a statement that the applicant's father enjoyed good health means only reasonably good health.[366] And the word, wife, in an application after the name of the payee is not a warranty but a mere description of the person.[367] But it has been held to the contrary.[368] A false statement that the beneficiary is a grandson, if made in good faith, will not avoid the policy.[369] So that the beneficiary was an uncle was not intended to be a warranty.[370] But-a false representation that insured had but two brothers and one sister where both had died of consumption and nine others had died in infancy avoids the policy whether made innocently or not.[371] The omission to mention the name of a brother who died before the applicant was born and of whom he had no knowledge is not a breach of warranty.[372] And it has been held that a question, as to whether certain relatives have died of consumption, so far as known, calls only for the applicant's knowledge and a false answer is not a breach of warranty unless he knew it was false.[373]

[363] Britton v. Supreme Counc. R. A., 46 N. J. Eq. 102; 18 Atl. 675; Vivar v. Supreme Lodge K. of P., 42 N. J. L. 455; 20 Atl. 36; Supreme Lodge A. O. U. W. v. Hutchinson, 6 Ind. App. 399; 33 N. E. 816; Mace v. Provident L. I. Ass'n, 101 N. C. 122; 7 S. E. 674.

[364] Spitz v. Mut. Ben. L. Ass'n, 25 N. Y. Supp. 469; Blackstone v. Kan. City L. Ins. Co. (Tex.), 174 S. W. 821; reversing 143 S. W. 702; Schmidt v. Supreme Court United Order of Foresters, 228 Mo. 675; 129 S. W. 653; reversing 124 Mo. App. 165; 101 S. W. 625.

[365] Globe Mut. L. Ins. Ass'n v. Wagner, 188 Ill. 133; 58 N. E. 970; 52 L. R. A. 649.

[366] Provident Savings L. A. Soc. v. Beyer, 23 Ky. L. 2460; 67 S. W. 827.

[367] Lampkin v. Travelers' Ins. Co., 11 Colo. App. 249; 52 Pac. 1040.

[368] Continental Casualty Co. v. Lindsay, 111 Va. 389; 69 S. E. 344.

[369] Afro-American L. Ins. Co. v. Adams (Ala.), 70 Sou. 119.

[370] Baltimore L. Ins. Co. v. Floyd (Del.), 94 Atl. 515.

[371] Kasprzwk v. Metropolitan L. Ins. Co., 140 N. Y. Supp. 211; 79 Misc. 268.

[372] Mutual L. Ins. Co. v. Baker, 10 Tex. Civ. A. 515; 31 S. W. 1072.

[373] Davis v. Supreme Lodge K. of H., 35 App. Div. 354; 54 N. Y. Supp. 1023.

§ 284. **Family Physician—Medical Attendant—Consulting a Physician.**—Where questions are asked as to the family physician, or medical attendant, of the applicant, they must be answered truthfully and in good faith or the policy will be avoided.[374] Whether this has been done or not is generally a question for the jury.[375] The question is material to the risk.[376] As the object of the question is to obtain the name of a medical attendant who can give information as to the quality of the life proposed, the failure to give full information may amount to a concealment, as where the applicant gave the name of a casual medical attendant but did not give the name of a physician who had recently attended him for delirium tremens, it was held that the duty of the applicant was to have made a full disclosure.[377] So, where the applicant was asked to state the physician usually employed by him, and if he had none, to name any other doctor who could be applied to for information as to the state of his health, and he answered "none," and it was shown that he had occasionally applied to a physician for serious ailments and had been examined for insurance and rejected by another physician, it was held that the failure to state the names of the two phy-

[374] In addition to authorities cited in this section may be added: Boland v. Industrial Ben. Ass'n, 26 N. Y. Supp. 433; Wilkins v. Mut. Reserve Fund L. Ass'n, 7 N. Y. Supp. 589; Cobb v. Covenant M. B. Ass'n, 153 Mass. 176; 26 N. E. 230; Philips v. N. Y. Life Ins. Co., 9 N. Y. Supp. 836; Sullivan v. Metropolitan L. Ins. Co., 12 N. Y. Supp. 923; Fidelity Mut. L. Ass'n v. Ficklin, 74 Md. 172; 21 Atl. 680; Provident, etc., Ass'n v. Reutlinger, 58 Ark. 528; 25 S. W. 835; Griffith v. Metropolitan L. Ins. Co., 36 App. D. C. 8; Mutual L. Ins. Co. v. Allen, 174 Ala. 511; 56 Sou. 568.

[375] Gibson v. American Mut. Life Ins. Co., 37 N. Y. 580; Maynard v. Rhodes, 1 C. & P. 360; 5 D. & R. 266; Scoles v. Universal Life Ins. Co., 42 Cal. 523; Cushman v. United States Ins. Co., 70 N. Y. 72; Edington v. Mutual, etc., Ins. Co., 67 N. Y. 185; Smith v. Metropolitan L. Ins. Co., 183 Pa. St. 504; 38 Atl. 103.

[376] Fidelity M. L. Ass'n v. McDaniel, 25 Md. App. 608; 57 N. E. 645; Modern Woodmen of Am. v. Lawson, 110 Va. 81, 65 S. E. 509; Schas v. Equitable Life Ass. Soc., 166 N. C. 55; 81 S. E. 1014; National Union v. Kelly, 42 Okla. 98; 140 Pac. 1157.

[377] Hutton v. Waterloo, etc., Soc., 1 F. & F. 735.

sicians was a fraudulent concealment and avoided the policy.[378] The applicant is answering the question calling for names of ailments he has had and the names of the physicians who have treated him, is not required to give the name of every trifling ailment.[379] Asking physician about a headache and receiving medicine is neither consulting a physician nor being treated by him,[380] nor is consulting a doctor for eczema, which had disappeared,[381] nor does the removal of wax from the ear make false the answer that applicant had not been attended by a physician.[382] The words "attended by a physician" are not the same as "consulting a physician,"[383] and the fact that the mother of the insured consulted a physician in his behalf does not constitute a breach of warranty.[384] Under the Missouri statute which provides that misrepresentation shall be no defense unless it contributes to the death, a false statement by insured that he had not been treated by a physician and was in sound health does not avoid the policy unless the disease for which the consultation and treatment was had occasioned his death.[385] Where the applicant is asked whether he has "consulted a physician, been prescribed for, or professionally treated," he must answer truthfully and it is immaterial whether he was prescribed for on account of disease or only temporary or trivial ailment;[386] this has been held to include medical

[378] Horn v. Amicable, etc., Ins. Co,. 64 Barb. 81; Huckman v. Fernie, 3 M. & W. 505; 1 H. & H. 149; 2 Jur. 444. See also Brady v. United L. Ins. Co., 9 C. C. A. 252; 20 U. S. App. 337; 60 Fed. 727; Caruthers v. Kansas Mut. L. Ins. Co., 108 Fed. 487.

[379] Modern Woodmen v. West, 76 Neb. 344; 107 N. W. 563.

[380] Modern Woodmen of America v. Miles, 105 Ind. 178; 97 N. E. 1009.

[381] Delbaux v. Metropolitan Life Ins. Co., 172 Ill. App. 537.

[382] Harris v. Knights & Ladies of Honor, 129 Mo. App. 163; 108 S. W. 130.

[383] Prudential Ins. Co. v. Lear, 31 App. D. C. 184.

[384] Valentina v. Metropolitan Life Ins. Co., 94 N. Y. Supp. 758; 106 App. Div. 487.

[385] Lynch v. Prudential Ins. Co., 150 Mo. App. 461; 131 S. W. 145.

[386] Cobb v. Covenant M. B. Ass'n, 153 Mass. 176; 26 N. E. 230; Insurance Co. v. McTeague, 49 N. J. L. 587; 9 Atl. 766; Provident Sav., etc., Soc. v. Reutlinger, 58 Ark. 528; 25 S. W. 835; Hubbard v. Mutual R. F. L. Ass'n, 40 C. C. A. 663; 100 Fed. 719; Metropolitan L. Ins. Co. v. Larsen, 85 Ill. App. 143; Flippen v. State L. Ins. Co., 30 Tex Civ. A. 362; 70 S. W. 787; Sladden v. N. Y. L. Ins. Co., 29 C. C. A. 596; 86 Fed. 102; Brock v. United

treatment two years previous.[387] In the case last cited the Court says: "If he (the assured) had consulted any physician in a professional character, or received any treatment or advice at the hands of one, it was his bounden duty to disclose the fact in answer to the inquiries, for his warranty fully covers such matters. The stipulation was a competent one for the appellee to make, and, so far as the evidence is concerned, was justified; and, in our opinion it clearly shows a breach of the warranty of the truth of the answers quoted. If there is any doubt of this, we add that the uncontradicted evidence unquestionably shows that the deceased was attended and treated by another physician, Dr. Cook, upon other occasions during the year 1888 or 1889, when he had indulged in protracted sprees and become sick. The appellant had a perfect right to make the questions and answers in the application a part of the contract, and we have no right to make any other or different contract for the parties. Such answers were material to the policy. They were made so by its terms, and no rule of construction will be suffered to destroy the effect of plain language. We hold that the statements by the deceased in the application for the insurance about a physician were warranted to be true, and that the stipulation and the evidence show a clear breach of such warranty. The policy is voided.[388] It makes no difference whether the deceased knew them to be untrue or not. It is a good defense to show that, as a matter of fact, they were untrue, without showing that he knew or believed them to be untrue.[389] Counsel for appellee directs our attention to the case of Moulor v. Insurance Co.,[390] and thinks

Moderns, 36 Tex. Civ. A. 12; 81 S. W. 340; McDermott v. Modern Woodmen, 97 N. W. App. 636; 71 S. W. 833; Roche v. Supreme Lodge K. of H., 21 App. Div. 599; 47 N. Y. Supp. 774; Wall v. Royal Society, etc., 179 Pa. St. 355; 36 Atl. 748; Fidelity, etc., Ass'n v. Harris (Tex. Civ. A.), 57 S. W. 635; Aloe v. Mutual Res. F. L. A., 147 Mo. 561; 49 S. W. 553.

[387] Mut. L. Ins. Co. v. Arhelger, 4 Ariz. 271; 36 Pac. 895. See also Bryant v. Metropolitan L. Ins. Co., 147 N. C. 181; 60 S. E. 983.

[388] Dwight v. Germania L. Ins. Co., 103 N. Y. 341; 8 N. E. 654; McCullum v. Ins. Co. (Sup.), 8 N. Y. Supp. 249; Boland v. Association (Sup.), 26 N. Y. Supp. 433. See also Dwyer v. Mut. L. Ins. Co., 72 N. H. 572; 58 Atl. 502.

[389] Provident L. Ass'n Soc. v. Llewellyn, 58 Fed. 940; 7 C. C. A. 579.

[390] 111 U. S. 335; 4 Sup. Ct. R. 466.

that case should govern this. The cases are clearly distinguishable.[391] In Moulor v. Insurance Co. it was held, in effect, that
there was doubt of the meaning of the contract, and it was therefore proper to consider the statements of the applicant as 'representations' and warranties only to the extent that they were made
in good faith, and were true as far as the insured knew. The
statements of the applicant were referred to in the body of the
policy as being representations, and this expression was made to
govern. But there is no doubt of the meaning of this contract.
Read it as you will, it remains a strict warranty. The words used
are plain, and are comprehended as soon as read. In such a
case there is no room for construction, for the very good reason
that there is no need for it.[392] The term 'rule of construction'
is confined by general usage to rules for the interpretation of
written documents in matters on which, in the absence of a rule
to aid, there might be a doubt.''[393] Still it has been held[394] that
the fact that the insured had twice been prescribed for for in-
digestion is not enough to show bad faith. Nor is an occasional
call on a physician, who found no serious ailment.[395] If the question be ambiguous, as for example, "How long since you have
consulted a physician," and the answer admits of two constructions, the one most favorable to the insured will be adopted.[396]
The question must have a reasonable interpretation, and casually
meeting a physician on the street and receiving a prescription
for a trivial ailment will not vitiate,[397] and consulting a physician
for drunkenness does not mean consulting him for disease.[398] But
calling at a physician's office, submitting to an examination and

[391] Provident L. A. Soc. v. Llewellyn, *supra.*
[392] 2 Pars. Cont. 500.
[393] Pol. Cont. 456.
[394] Fidelity M. L. Ass'n v. Ficklin, 74 Md. 172; 21 Atl. 680.
[395] Mut. Reserve L. Ins. Co. v. Dobler, 70 C. C. A. 134, 137 Fed. 550.
[396] Stewart v. Equitable Mut. L. Ass'n, 110 Ia. 528; 81 N. W. 782.
[397] Mut. Reserve F. L. Ass'n v. Ogletree, 77 Miss. 7; 25 Sou. 869; Blum-
enthal v. Berkshire L. Ins. Co., 134 Mich. 216; 96 N. W. 17; Plumb v. Penn.
M. L. Ins. Co., 108 Mich. 94; 65 N. W. 611; Woodward v. Iowa Life Ins. Co.,
104 Tenn. 49; 56 S. W. 1020; Mut. Life Ins. Co. v. Mullen, 107 Md. 457; 69
Atl. 385.
[398] Supreme Lodge K. P. v. Taylor (Ala.), 24 Sou. 247.

receiving a prescription is being attended by such physician.[399] And so is the fact that a physician paid eight visits to the insured while suffering from rheumatism.[400] A false answer to a question whether a physician had ever given an unfavorable opinion on the applicant's life will avoid the policy.[401] The Supreme Court of Minnesota[402] defines the term "family physician" as follows: "The phrase 'family physician' is in common use, and has not, so far as we are aware, any technical signification. As used in this instance, and for the purposes of the testimony appearing in this case, the Chief Justice and myself are of opinion that it may be sufficiently defined as signifying the physician who usually attends and is consulted by the members of the family in the capacity of physician. We employ the word usually, both because we do not deem it necessary to constitute a person a family physician that he should invariably attend, and be consulted by the members of a family in the capacity of a physician, and because we do not deem it necessary that he should attend and be consulted as such physician, by each and all of the members of a family. For instance, the testimony in this case shows that at the time when the application for insurance was made, the family of Richard Price consisted of himself, his wife and two or three children. We think that a person who usually attended and was consulted by the wife and children of Richard Price as a physician, would be the family physician of Richard Price in the meaning of the interrogatory, although he did not usually attend on, and was not usually consulted as a physician by Richard Price himself." A dissenting opinion was filed in this case, the judge reasoning that as the object of the question is to obtain the name of a person who can give information as to the risk, it obviously requires the name of the physician who ordinarily attends the party to be given. The opinion concludes: "I think the phrase, as used in this instance, means the physician who usually attends and is consulted by all or most of the members of the family of

[399] White v. Provident Sav. Life Ass. Soc., 163 Mass. 108; 39 N. E. 771; 27 L. R. A. 398.

[400] Fish v. Metropolitan L. Ins. Co., 73 N. J. L. 619; 64 Atl. 109; Peterson v. Independent Order of Foresters, 162 Wis. 162; 156 N. W. 951.

[401] Ferris v. Home L. Ass. Co., 118 Mich. 485; 76 N. W. 1041.

[402] Price v. Phoenix L. Ins. Co., 17 Minn. 497; 10 Am. Rep. 166.

the person whose life is assured, and that the person thus assured, if he has medical attendance, must be one of the members attended by such physician." The phrase, "family physician" is said by the Supreme Court of Missouri[403] to be one that is in common use and has no particular, definite or technical significance. It signifies one who usually attends and is consulted by the members of a family in the capacity of a physician; it means one who is accustomed to attend, and not one who occasionally attended. The mere calling at a doctor's office for some medicine to remove a temporary indisposition, not serious in its nature, cannot be considered an attendance by a physician, nor would the calling at the home by the doctor for the same purpose be so regarded. Attendance of a physician, in the meaning of the question generally employed in applications for life insurance, must be an attendance upon the assured for some disease or ailment of importance and not for an indisposition of a day or two, trivial in its nature, and such as all persons are liable to and yet who are considered to be in sound health generally.[404]

§ 285. Habits: Use of Intoxicants: Liquor, Opium, etc.— A false representation as to the use of liquor will avoid the policy,[405] and a warranty by the insured of total abstinence avoids the certificate when it is shown that the applicant has been intoxicated.[406] In the case of Provident Savings Life Assur. Society v. Dees,[407] the Court said: "The habits of the assured as to drinking intoxicants are a material matter of the insurer. In Mutual Life Insurance Company v. Thomson,[408] the question related to the former habits of the assured. But in that case the Court said: 'It is of vital importance for an insurance company

---

[403] Reid v. Piedmont & Arlington L. Ins. Co., 58 Mo. 421.

[404] Brown v. Metropolitan L. Ins. Co., 65 Mich. 306; 32 N. W. 610; Mut. Life Ins. Co. v. Owen, 111 Ark. 554; 164 S. W. 720; Cole v. Mut. L. Ins. Co., 129 La. 704; 56 Sou. 645; Yonda v. Royal Neighbors of Am., 96 Neb. 730; 148 N. W. 926; Sargent v. Modern Brotherhood of Am. 148 Ia. 600; 127 N. W. 52; Bryant v. Modern Woodmen of Am. 86 Neb. 372; 125 N. W. 621; 27 L. R. A. (N. S.) 326.

[405] Farwood v. Prudential Ins. Co,. 117 Md. 254; 83 Atl. 169.

[406] Collver v. Modern Woodmen of America, 154 Ia. 615; 135 N. W. 67.

[407] 120 Ky. 285; 86 S. W. 522.

[408] 94 Ky. 253; 22 S. W. 87.

to know, before issuing a life policy, whether the applicant is thus temperate in his habits, for obviously he would not be a fit subject for insurance, nor could a company prudently issue to him a life policy, if he was not then temperate in his habits of drinking intoxicating liquor; and, consequently, if he had made a false statement in that particular, it would be no answer to say the habits were not such as to impair his health, because insurers have a right to protect themselves by guarding against the risk of pernicious habits.' The questions here related to his habits at the time the insurance was taken, and, if the answers contained a material misrepresentation there can be no recovery." Applications for life insurance generally contain questions bearing upon the habits of the applicant, especially in regard to the use of intoxicants, tobacco and opium. In whatever language these questions are couched the words are to be taken in their plain, ordinary meaning. As where the inquiry was whether the applicant was "sober and temperate," the Court said :[409] "The words, sober and temperate, are to be taken in their ordinary sense. The language does not imply total abstinence from intoxicating liquors. The moderate, temperate use of intoxicating liquors is consistent with sobriety. But if a man use spirituous liquors to such an extent as to produce frequent intoxication, he is not sober and temperate within the meaning of this contract of insurance."[410] "The questions as to health and habits in respect to intoxicating drinks will be taken to mean what the words employed by those questions usually and commonly mean. They are not words of art, but words of every-day meaning; and this is a contract not between professional men or lawyers, but a contract that these companies profess to make with the world, and when they ask a man if his health is good there is no mystery in the question."[411] The words, "intemperate use" are equivalent to habitual intemperance, but the word "use" means the means by which death was caused

[409] Brockway v. Mut. Ben. Life Ins. Co., 9 Fed. 253. See also Knights of Pythias v. Bridges, 15 Tex. Civ. A. 196; 39 S. W. 333; Chambers v. N. W. Mut. L. Ins. Co., 64 Minn. 495; 67 N. W. 367.

[410] John Hancock Mut. Life Ins. Co. v. Daly, 65 Ind. 10; Holtum v. Germania Life Ins. Co., 139 Cal. 645; 73 Pac. 591. See also Schou v. Modern Woodmen of Am., 51 Wash. 482; 99 Pac. 25; Fludd v. Equitable L. Assur. Soc., 75 S. C. 315; 55 S. E. 762.

[411] Swick v. Home Life Ins. Co., 2 Dill C. C. 160.

if the provision is that if death should be caused by intemperate use of liquor the society would not be liable.[412] In a case involving similar questions, decided by the Supreme Court of the United States,[413] afterwards approved by the same court,[414] the question was, "Is the party of temperate habits? Has he always been so?" and it was said: "When we speak of the habits of a person, we refer to his customary conduct, to pursue which he has acquired a tendency, from frequent repetitions of the same acts. It would be incorrect to say that a man has a habit of anything from a single act. A habit of early rising, for example, could not be affirmed of one because he was once seen on the streets in the morning before the sun had risen; nor could intemperate habits be imputed to him because his appearance and actions on that occasion might indicate a night of excessive indulgence. The Court did not, therefore, err in instructing the jury that if the habits of the insured 'in the usual, ordinary, and every-day routine of his life were temperate,' the representations made are not untrue, within the meaning of the policy, although he may have had an attack of delirium tremens from an exceptional over-indulgence. It could not have been contemplated from the language used in the policy that it should become void for an occasional excess by the insured, but only when such excess had by frequent repetitions become a habit." "An occasional excess in the use of intoxicating liquor," says the Supreme Court of Ohio,[415] "does not, it is true, constitute a habit, or make a man intemperate, within the meaning of this policy; but if the habit has been formed and is indulged in, of drinking to excess and becoming intoxicated, whether daily and continuously, or periodically, with sober intervals of greater or less length, the person addicted to

[412] Ury v. Modern Woodmen of Am., 149 Ia. 706; 127 N. W. 665.

[413] Insurance Co. v. Foley, 105. U. S. 350.

[414] Northwestern Life Ins. Co. v. Muskegon Bank, 122 U. S. 501.

[415] Union Mut. Life Ins. Co. v. Reif, 36 Ohio St. 599; 38 Am. Rep. 613. And to the same effect is Grand Lodge A. O. U. W. v. Belcham, 145 Ill. 308; 33 N. E. 886; where it was held not sufficient to negative the answer that the appellant did not use liquor to show a single indulgence. See also Provident Savings, etc., Ass'n v. Exchange Bank, 126 Fed. 360; Equitable L. Ass. Soc. v. Liddell, 32 Tex. Civ. A. 252; 74 S. W. 87; Malicki v. Chicago Guaranty F. L. Soc., 119 Mich. 151; 77 N. W. 690; Bacon v. New England Order, etc., 123 Fed. 152.

such a habit cannot be said to be of temperate habits, within the meaning of the policy. . . : The habit of using intoxicating liquors to excess is the result of indulging a natural or acquired habit, by continued use, until it becomes a customary practice. This habit may manifest itself in practice by daily or periodical intoxication or drunkenness. Within the purview of these questions it must have existed at some previous time, or at the date of the application, but it is not essential to its existence that it should be continuously practiced, or that the insured should be daily and habitually under the influence of liquor. Where the general habits of a man are either abstemious or temperate, an occasional indulgence to excess does not make him a man of intemperate habits. But if the habit is formed of drinking to excess, and the appetite for liquor is indulged to intoxication,' either constantly or periodically, no one will claim that his habits are temperate, though he may be duly sober for longer or shorter periods in the intervals between the times of his debauches.'' The word ''addicted'' as applied to the use of liquor, means habitual or customary use and not occasional use.[416] An occasional use of liquor will not be construed as falsifying an answer that the applicant does not use liquor ''at all.''[417] In Van Valkenburgh v. American Popular Life Ins. Co.,[418] the question was: ''Does the insured use any intoxicating liquors or substances?'' And the Court held that this question did not direct the mind to a single or incidental use, but to a customary or habitual use.[419] In a

[416] Des Moines L. Ins. Co. v. Clay, 89 Ark. 230; 116 S. W. 232; Knights of Maccabees v. Anderson, 104 Ark. 417; 148 S. W. 1016; Metropolitan L. Ins. Co. v. Shane, 98 Ark. 132; 135 S. W. 836.

[417] Mut. L. Ins. Co. v. Simpson (Tex. Civ. A.), 28 S. W. 837; Supreme Lodge K. of P. v. Foster, 26 Ind. App. 333; 59 N. E. 877; Brignac v. Pacific Mut. L. Ins. Co., 112 La. 574; 36 Sou. 595; 66 L. R. A. 322; Arris v. Mut. L. Ins. Co., 54 Wash. 269-295; 103 Pac. 50, 53; Mut. Reserve F. L. Ass'n v. Cotter, 81 Ark. 205; 99 S. W. 67. But see Union Cent. L. Ins. Co. v. Lee, 20 Ky. L. 839; 47 S. W. 614; Sovereign Camp, etc., v. Burgess, 80 Miss. 546; 31 S. W. 809.

[418] 70 N. Y. 605; 9 Hun. 583.

[419] Tatum v. State, 63 Ala. 147; Mowry v. Home Life Ins. Co., 9 R. I. 346; National Fraternity v. Karnes, 24 Tex. Civ. A. 607; 60 S. W. 576. See also Columbian L. Ins. Co. v. Tousey, 152 Ky. 447; 153 S. W. 767.

case in Illinois[420] it was held that even a moderate use of tobacco implies a fixed habit, but the reverse is true as to liquor. False representations made by the insured concerning his habits as to temperance avoid the policy even though they were made in good faith without intent to deceive.[421] And there may be such a gross misstatement as to require a judgment for the company as a matter of law.[422] The use of intoxicating liquors and drunkenness are pernicious habits tending to shorten life.[423] Where deceased in his application was asked to what extent he used any liquor, and kind, and average quantity, etc., to which he answered "don't use them," and also answered yes to the question whether he had always been temperate, the purpose of such questions was held to be to ascertain not whether he used intoxicating liquor at all, but the extent to which he used them, and the answers were not false.[424] It is for the jury to weight all the circumstances and to determine, in view of them all, whether the applicant was habitually intemperate, or used liquors to excess, or otherwise answered the questions falsely.[425] Habits of intemperance acquired subsequent to the insurance, even though the cause of death, will not avoid the policy, unless expressly so

[420] Grand Lodge A. O. U. W. v. Belcham, 48 Ill. App. 346. See also Continental L. Ins. Co. v. Thoena, 26 Ill. App. 495.

[421] Hartwell v. Alabama Gold L. Ins. Co., 33 La. Ann. 1353.

[422] Mengel v. N. W. Mut. L. Ins. Co., 176 Pa. St. 280; 35 Atl. 197; Shea v. Great Camp, etc., 52 N. Y. Supp. 333.

[423] Schultz v. Mut. Life Ins. Co., 6 Fed. 672; Knecht v. Mutual Life Ins. Co., 90 Pa. St. 118.

[424] Endowment Rank K. P. v. Townsend, 36 Tex. Civ. App. 651; 83 S. W. 220. See also Hann v. Supreme Lodge, etc., 140 N. Y. Supp. 666; 155 App. Div. 665; Royal Union Mut. Life Ins. Co. v. Wynn, 177 Fed. 289. For construction of application for accident insurance as to habits, see Maloney v. Maryland Cas. Co., 113 Ark. 174; 167 S. W. 845.

[425] N. W. Ins. Co. v. Muskegon Bank, 122 U. S. 501. The Supreme Court of the United States has also discussed this subject at length in the two cases, Aetna L. Ins. Co. v. Davey, 123 U. S. 739; 8 S. C. 333, reversing 20 Fed. 482, and 494, and, on a subsequent appeal, Aetna L. Ins. Co. v. Ward, 140 U. S. 76; 11 S. C. 720; affg. 38 Fed. 650, and 40 Fed. 911. The question of use of narcotics or tobacco is considered in Continental L. Ins. Co. v. Thoena, 26 Ill. App. 495, and as to morphinism see note in 39 L. R. A. 262.

stipulated.[426] There may be an estoppel also where the habits were known to the agent.[427]

§ 286. **Good Health**—The expressions "good health," or "sound health," must be regarded as practically synonymous, and the question whether one is in good or sound health is generally one of fact for the jury.[428] Thus, it was left to the jury to say if the habit of taking opium was a breach of the warranty of perfect health.[429] Insanity is not a "diseased condition."[430] Nor will it be held as a matter of law to be an unsound condition of health.[431] In one of the earliest cases relating to life insurance,[432] Lord Mansfield said that a warranty of good health meant simply that the applicant was in a reasonably good state of health, and was such a life as ought to be insured on common terms. That it did not mean that he was free from every infirmity, and, in fact, though he had one, the life might be a good one, and the fact that the insured had several years before received a wound in the loins, which so affected him that he could not retain his urine or fæces, though not mentioned, was not inconsistent with a good insurable life. Afterwards the same eminent jurist said,[433] in a case where it appeared that the insured was at times troubled with spasms from violent fits of the gout, though at the time of insurance in his usual state of health: "The imperfection of language is such that we have not words for every different idea, and the real intention of the parties must be found out by the subject-matter. By the present policy the life is war-

[426] Reichard v. Manhattan Life Ins. Co., 31 Mo. 518; Horton v. Equitable Life A. Soc. (C. C. P. N. Y.), 2 Big. Life & Acc. Ins. Cas. 108.
[427] Newman v. Covenant Mut. Ben. Ass'n, 76 Ia. 56; 40 N. W. 87. See as to false answer as to Appendicitis, Aetna Life Ins. Co., Howell, 32 Ky. L. 935; 107 S. W. 294.
[428] Life Ins. Clearing Co. v. Altschuler, 55 Neb. 341; 75 N. W. 862; Keatley v. Travelers' Ins. Co., 187 Pa. St. 197; 40 Atl. 808. See also Modern Brotherhood v. Beshara, 42 Okla. 684; 142 Pac. 1014 and on second appeal, 158 Pac. 613.
[429] Forbes v. Edinburg, etc., Co., 10 Scotch Sessions Cas. 1st series, 451.
[430] Jackson v. National L. Ass'n, 24 N. Y. Supp. 746.
[431] Jacklin v. National L. Ass'n, 75 Hun. 595; 24 N. Y. Supp. 746; 27 N. Y. Supp. 1112.
[432] Ross v. Bradshaw, 1 W. Bl. 312, A. D. 1760.
[433] Willis v. Poole, 2 Parke on Ins. 650.

ranted in health; to others in good health. And yet there is no in good health, that does not necessarily nor ordinarily mean that a man has not in him the seeds of some disorder. We are all born with the seeds of mortality in us. A man subject to the gout is a life capable of being insured, if he has no sickness at the time to make it an unequal contract."[435] Sound health means reasonably sound health.[436] "The word 'health' as ordinarily used," says the New York Court of Appeals.[437] "is a relative term. It has reference to the condition of the body. Thus, it is frequently characterized. as perfect, as good, as indifferent, and as bad. The epithet 'good' is comparative. It does not require absolute perfection. When, therefore, one is described as being in good health, that does not necessarily nor ordinarily mean that he is absolutely free from all and every ill 'which flesh is heir to.' If the phrase should be so interpreted as to require entire exemption from physical ills, the number to which it would be strictly applicable would be very inconsiderable."[438] Another authority[439] states: "The term, good health, as here used, is to be considered in its ordinary sense, and means that 'the applicant was free from any apparent sensible disease, or symptoms of disease, and that he was unconscious of any derangement of the functions by which health could be tested.'[440] Slight, unfrequent, transient disturbances, not usually ending in serious consequences, may be consistent with the possession of good health as that term was here employed."[441] When a third person is asked if the applicant is

435 Watson v. Mainwaring, 4 Taunt. 763.

436 Clover v. Modern Woodmen of America, 142 Ill. App. 276.

437 Peacock v. New York Life Ins. Co., 20 N. Y. 296; affg. 1 Bosw. 338.

438 Morrison v. Odd Fellows' Mut. L. Ins. Co., 59 Wis. 170.

439 Goucher v. Northwestern Traveling Men's Ass'n, 20 Fed. 598 and note.

440 Conver v. Phoenix Ins. Co., 3 Dill. 226. See also Manhattan L. Ins. Co. v. Carder, 27 C. C. A. 344; 82 Fed. 986; Tooker v. Security Trust Co., 26 App. Div. 372; 49 N. Y. Supp. 814; Mass. Ben. L. Ass'n v. Robinson, 104 Ga. 256; 30 S. E. 918; 42 L. R. A. 261; Metropolitan L. Ins. Co. v. Howlie, 62 Ohio St. 204; 56 N. E. 908; Mulligan v. Prudential Ins. Co., 76 Conn. 676; 58 Atl. 230; Maryland Casualty Co. v. Gehrmann, 96 Md. 634; 54 Atl. 678; Packard v. Metropolitan L. Ins. Co., 72 N. H. 1; 54 Atl. 287.

441 Brown v. Metropolitan Life Ins. Co., 65 Mich. 306; 32 N. W. 610; French v. Mut. R. F. L. Ass'n, 111 N. C. 391; 16 S. E. 427; Hann v. Na-

now in good health, it does not mean whether he is actually free
from illness or disease, but simply that he has indicated in his
actions and appearance no symptoms or traces of disease, and to
the ordinary observation of a friend or relative is in truth well.[442]
A representation that the applicant had a florid appearance, when,
in fact, he was pale and emaciated, will not, of itself, avoid a life
policy of insurance, such appearance being no certain indication
of disease or feebleness, and would not necessarily cause the insurer
to refuse the risk.[443] But equivocation in the answers touching
health or anything which amounts to concealment is fatal.[444] As
the Supreme Court of Maine has said:[445] "The good faith of
the answers should be perfect. The presence of it goes very far
to protect a policy, while a want of it would be an element of
great power to the defense. There is obviously a close line between incipient disease, disease in its first stages, and merely a
bodily condition which is susceptible to the contraction of disease." In that case it was held that the insured had misrepresented her condition and had consumption at the time she stated
herself to be in good health. A person is not in good health who
has had asthma for three years.[446] An anaemic murmur of the
heart is not a bodily or mental infirmity.[447] An "inmate" of a
hospital is one who is there for any kind of treatment;[448] but one
was not "under treatment at a hospital" who went there simply
to have a foreign substance taken from her eye.[449]

tional Union, 97 Mich. 513; 56 N. W. 834; Brink v. Guaranty Mut. Ass'n,
7 N. Y. Supp. 847; Provident L. Ass'n v. Reutlinger, 58 Ark. 528; 25 S. W.
835; Metropolitan L. Ins. Co. v. Rutherford, 95 Va. 773; 30 S. E. 383.

[442] Grattan v. Metropolitan Life Ins. Co., 92 N. Y. 274.

[443] Illinois Masons' Benev. Soc. v. Winthrop, 85 Ill. 537.

[444] Smith v. Aetna Life Ins. Co., 49 N. Y. 211; Goucher v. N. W.
Traveling Men's Ass'n, 20 Fed. 598; Northwestern Mut. Life Ins. Co. v.
Heimann, 93 Ind. 24; Nelson v. Nederland L. Ins. Co., 110 Ia. 600; 81 N.
W. 807; ante, § 250.

[445] Maine Ben. Ass'n v. Parks, 81 Me. 79; 16 Atl. 339. Also see Metropolitan L. Ins. Co. v. Dempsey, 72 Md. 288; 19 Atl. 642.

[446] Volker v. Metropolitan L. Ins. Co,. 21 N. Y. Supp. 456.

[447] Manufacturers Acc. Ind. Co. v. Dorgan, 7 C. C. A. 581; 58 Fed. 945;
160 U. S. App. 290; 22 L. R. A. 620.

[448] Farrell v. Security Mut. L. Ins. Co., 60 C. C. A. 374; 125 Fed. 684.

[449] Chinnery v. U. S. Industrial Co., 15 App. Div. 515; 44 N. Y. Supp.
581.

§ 287. **The Same Subject Continued—Examples of Construction.**—In the case of Murphy v. Metropolitan Life Ins. Co.,[450] it
was said that the term ''sound health'' does not mean perfect
health, but an absence of any disease that has a direct tendency
to shorten life, and it has also been said[451] that the statement
that insured is in sound condition mentally and physically only
requires an honest belief in the truthfulness of the answer. Illness when applied to warranty must be of such character as to
affect the general soundness of the system and not a mere temporary indisposition.[452] There will be a liberal construction of
a warranty as to the physical condition of the applicant,[453] but
an untrue statement of the applicant as to her health warranted
to be true, vitiates the policy.[454] And where the applicant knew
that he had a fatal disease, his statement that he was in good
health avoids the policy.[455] Whether the insured, who was in
bed with a cold and afterwards died of pneumonia, was in good
health at the time of the delivery of the policy, was held a question for the jury.[456] Under the Missouri statute that the matter
misrepresented must contribute to the death, the policy is not
avoided even though the insured was not in good health when

[450] 106 Minn. 112; 118 N. W. 355.

[451] Mayes v. New Amsterdam Casualty Co., 40 App. D. C. 249; 46 L. R.
A. (N. S.) 1108; Ranta v. Supreme Tent, etc., 97 Minn. 454; 107 N. W. 156.

[452] Scofield v. Metropolitan Life Ins. Co., 79 Vt. 161; 64 Atl. 1107; Mut.
Life Ins. Co. v. Morgan, 39 Okla. 205; 135 Pac. 279; Prudential Ins. Co.
v. Sellers, 54 Ind. App. 326; 102 N. E. 894; Rupert v. Supreme Court,
etc., 94 Minn. 293; 102 N. W. 715; American Order of Protection v.
Stanley, 5 Neb. (unofficial) 132; 97 N. W. 467.

[453] Chicago Guaranty Fund Life Soc. v. Ford, 104 Tenn. 533; 58 S.
W. 239.

[454] Satterlee v. Modern Brotherhood, 15 N. D. 92; 106 N. W. 561. As
to what is a breach of a representation as to her health by a married
woman. Meriman v. Grand Lodge Degree of Honor, 77 Neb. 544; 110
N. W. 302.

[455] Royal Neighbors v. Wallace, 73 Neb. 409; 102 N. W. 1020; Aetna
Life Ins. Co. v. Crabtree, 146 Ky. 368; 142 S. W. 690.

[456] Barnes v. Fidelity Mut. Life Ass'n, 191 Pa. St. 618; 43 Atl. 341;
45 L. R. A. 264. See also Carmichael v. John Hancock Mut. Life Ins.
Co., 101 N. Y. Supp. 602; 116 App. Div. 291; Metropolitan Life Ins. Co.
v. Betz (Tex. Civ. App.), 99 S. W. 1140.

the policy was delivered, unless such ill health caused, or contributed, to the death.[457]

§ 288. **Latent Diseases Unknown to Applicant.**—If a representation of the applicant is that he is of sound body, and it be untrue; if it is made in good faith, without suspicion that he was of unsound body, though it afterwards be shown that he had then a fatal internal disease which caused his death, the policy will not be avoided.[458] But, where the applicant was asked if he had disease of the heart and he answered no, it was held, the answers being warranties, that the policy was void if the assured died of heart disease soon afterwards, although he could not have known that he had the disease.[459] In a case in Indiana,[460] the court below instructed the jury, the answers in the application of the insured being warranties, that if the assured had, at the time of making his application, some affection or ailment, of some one or more of the organs inquired about in the application, which ailment was of a character so well defined and marked as materially to derange, for a time, the functions of such organ, such ailment, whether known to the assured or not, would avoid the policy, and that "this would be so with reference to Bright's disease of the kidneys, if it was such a dis-

[457] Salts v. Prudential Ins. Co., 140 Mo. App. 142; 120 S. W. 714.

[458] Schwarzbach v. Ohio Valley P. Union, 25 W. Va. 622; Moulor v. Am. Life Ins. Co., 111 U. S. 335; Life Ass'n, etc., etc., v. Foster, 11 Sc. Sess. Cas. (3rd series) 351; Thompson v. Weems, L. R. 9 App. Cas. 671; Haun v. National Union, 97 Mich. 513; 56 N. W. 834; Endowment Rank K. of P. v. Rosenfield, 92 Tenn. 508; 22 S. W. 204; Ames v. Manhattan L. Ins. Co., 40 App. Div. 465; 58 N. Y. Supp. 244; Fidelity Mut. L. Ass'n v. Jeffords, 107 Fed. 402; 46 C. C. A. 377; 53 L. R. A. 193 and note. See also *ante*, § 265.

[459] Powers v. Northeastern Mut. L. Ass'n, 50 Vt. 630; Baumgart v. Modern Woodmen, etc., 85 Wis. 546; 55 N. W. 743; but the contrary was held in Hutchinson v. National Loan Co., 7 Scott. Session Cas., 2nd series, 467. See also Ross v. Bradshaw, 1 Wm. Bl. 312; Holloman v. Life Ins. Co., 1 Woods, 674; Breeze v. Metropolitan L. Ins. Co., 24 App. Div. 377; 48 N. Y. Supp. 753.

[460] Continental L. Ins. Co. v. Young, 113 Ind. 159; 15 N. E. 220. See also Boyle v. N. W. Mut. Relief Ass'n, 95 Wis. 312; 70 N. W. 351.

ease as I have just mentioned.''[461]   This view seems to be reasonable as well as consistent with authority. The rule, therefore, is that, where the answers to questions in the application are representations, the death of the applicant from a latent disease, which existed at the time of the application, but unknown to the applicant, he answering all questions in good faith, will not avoid the policy. But, where the answers are warranties, then the death of the applicant from a latent disease,. which existed at the time when he warranted himself to be free from it, will avoid the policy. It is a question for the jury to say how long the disease had existed and whether the insured was afflicted with it at the time the insurance was taken out.[462]   It has, however, been held,[463] that a warranty of good health is not broken though applicant suffering from disease of the heart without knowing it, and it has also been held,[464] that the failure of an applicant to disclose the existence of a latent defect concerning which he could have had no exact information, will not avoid the policy. In such case the warranty is only of the good faith opinion of the applicant.[465]   So it was held where the applicant answered that he was free from constitutional, or organic, disease, the answer was not false, although the insured was in the incipient stage of nephritis, of which condition he had no knowledge.[466]

§ 289. **Sickness or Disease.**—Where the answers to questions as to sickness or disease warranted to be true, or even represented to be true, are false and are material, they will avoid the policy. The insured will be deemed to have concealed matters material to be known.[467] Before any temporary ailment can be called a disease, it must be such as to indicate a vice in the constitution, or be so serious as to have some bearing upon general health and

461 Conn. Mut. L. Ins. Co. v. Union Trust Co., 112 U. S. 250; Cushman v. U. S. Ins. Co., 70 N. Y. 72.
462 Tucker v. United Life and A. Ins. Co., 133 N. Y. 548; 30 N. E. 723.
463 Greenwood v. Royal Neighbors of America, 118 Va. 329; 87 S. E. 581.
464 Suravitz v. Prudential Ins. Co., 244 Pa. 582; 91 Atl. 495.
465 Owen v. Metropolitan Life Ins. Co., 74 N. J. L. 770; 67 Atl. 25.
466 Blackman v. U. S. Casualty Co., 117 Tenn. 578; 103 S. W. 784.
467 Talley v. Metropolitan L. Ins. Co., 111 Va. 778; 69 S. E. 936; United Benev. Ass'n v. Baker, (Tex. Civ. A.) 141 S. W. 541.

the continuance of life, or such as, according to common under-standing, would be called a disease, and such has been the uni-form opinion of textwriters and courts.[468] So, a cold is not a disease,[469] though accompanied with more or less congestion of the lungs, and though most, if not all persons, will have at times congestion of the liver, causing slight functional derangement and temporary illness, yet in the contemplation of parties entering into contracts of life insurance, and having regard to general health and the continuance of life, it may be safely said that there is in such cases no disease of the liver.[470] Insanity is not a diseased condition[471] nor a disease,[472] nor is nearsightedness a bodily infirmity.[473] A severe sickness or disease noes not include the ordinary diseases of the country, which yield readily to medical treatment and when ended leave no permanent injury to the physical system, but refers to those severe attacks which often leave a permanent injury and tends to shorten life[474] The answer may be considered as a mere expression of opinion.[475] When the applicant says that he has never had any "serious illness" the courts will

[468] Cushman v. U. S. Life Ins. Co., 70 N. Y. 72; N. W. Mut. L. Ins. Co. v. Heimann, 93 Ind. 24; 2 Park on Ins. 933-935; Chattock v. Shawe, 1 M. & R. 498; Fowkes v. The M. & L. Life Ins. Co., 3 Fost. & F. 440; Barteau v. Phoenix Mut. Life Ins. Co., 67 N. Y. 595; 1 Hun. 430; 67 Barb. 354; 3 T. & C. 576; Peacock v. N. Y. Life Ins. Co., 20 N. Y. 293; Higbie v. Guardian Mut. L. Ins. Co., 53 N. Y. 603; Fitch v. Am. Popular L. Ins. Co., 59 N. Y. 557; 17 Am. Rep. 372; Woodmen, etc., v. Locklin, 28 Tex. Civ. A. 486; 67 S. W. 331; Rand v. Provident, etc., Soc., 97 Tenn. 291; 37 S. W. 7; Life Ins. Clearing Co. v. Bullock, 91 Fed. 487; 33 C. C. A. 365; 62 U. S. App. 625; Billings v. Metropolitan L. Ins. Co., 70 Vt. 477; 41 Atl. 516; Woodward v. Iowa Life, etc., 104 Tenn. 49; 56 S. W. 1020; Caruthers v. Kansas Mut. L. Ins. Co., 108 Fed. 487.

[469] Metropolitan Life Ins. Co. v. McTague, 49 N. J. L. 587; 9 Atl. 766; Cessua v. U. S. Life Endowment Co., 152 Ill. App. 653.

[470] Cushman v. U. S. Life Ins. Co., 70 N. Y. 72; Goucher v. Northwest Traveling Men's Ass., 20 Fed. 600; N. W. Mut. Life Ins. Co. v. Heimann, 93 Ind. 24.

[471] Jackson v. National Life Ass'n, 24 N. Y. Supp. 746.

[472] Accident Ins. Co. v. Crandall, 120 U. S. 533; 7 S. C. 685.

[473] Cotten v. Fidelity, etc., 41 Fed. 507.

[474] Holloman v. The life Ins. Co., 1 Woods C. C. 674; Goff v. Mut. L. Ins. Co., 131 La. 98; 59 Sou. 28.

[475] Supreme Ruling, etc., v. Crawford, 32 Tex. Civ. A. 603; 75 S. W. 844; Smith v. Prudential Ins. Co., 83 N. J. L. 719; 85 Atl. 190.

construe the meaning to be that he has never been so seriously ill as to permanently impair his constitution and render the risk unusually hazardous.[476] Clearly the term "severe" or "serious" illness does not mean slight, temporary physical disturbances or ailments, speedily and entirely recovered from, not interfering materially with the pursuit of one's avocation, producing no permanent effect on the constitution and not rendering the insurance risk more than usually hazardous.[477] If necessary the Court will admit evidence to explain what is meant by the term used, as, for instance, to show that the medical term, "spitting blood," means spitting of blood from the lungs exclusively,[478] or that gastritis and chronic gastritis are not the same, or that subacute rheumatism is not the disease of rheumatism.[479] Where the applicant had suffered one abortion her answer no to the question whether she had had "abortions" was not false.[480] The Court will not hold as a matter of law that either pneumonia or sunstroke is a severe sickness or disease, but will leave the question to the jury,[481] nor will it say that the omission to mention a temporary injury to the eye, by sand having·been thrown into it, which had produced an inflammation six years before the policy was applied for, and which was then cured, is conclusive evidence of fraud or a breach of the war-

[476] Ill. Masons' Benev. Soc. v. Winthrop, 85 Ill. 542; Dreier v. Continental L. Ins. Co., 24 Fed. 670.

[477] Goucher v. N. W. Traveling Men's Ass'n, 20 Fed. 600; Connecticut Mut. L. Ins. Co. v. Union Trust Co., 112 U. S. 250; Chattock v. Shaw, 1 M. & Rob. 498; Fowkes v. Manchester & L., etc., Ins. Co., 3 F. & F. 440; Watson v. Mainwaring, 4 Taunt. 763; Union Cent. Life Ins. Co. v. Cheever, 11 Ins. L. J. 264; affd. 36 Ohio St. 201.

[478] Singleton v. St. Louis Ins. Co., 66 Mo. 63; 27 Am. Rep. 321. See as to spitting blood: Smith v. N. W. Mut. L. Ins. Co., 196 Pa. St. 314; 46 Atl. 426; Eminent Household Columbian Woodmen v. Procter, 24 Okla. 214; 103 Pac. 558. Spitting blood includes hemorrhage. March v. Metropolitan L. Ins. Co., 186 Pa. St. 629; 40 Atl. 1100; Murphy v. Prudential Ins. Co., 205 Pa. St. 444; 55 Atl. 19; Peterson v. Des Moines L. Ass'n, 115 Ia. 668; 87 N. W. 397.

[479] Price v. Phoenix Mut. L. Ins. Co., 17 Minn. 518; 10 Am. Rep. 166.

[480] Mut. L. Ins. Co. v. Crenshaw (Tex. Civ. A.), 116 S. W. 375.

[481] Boos v. World Mut. Life Ins. Co., 64 N. Y. 236; Knickerbocker L. Ins. Co. v. Trefz, 104 U. S. 197.

ranty.[482] Nor that "chronic pharyngitis" is a "sickness" in contemplation of the parties putting the question. [483] An attempt at suicide is not a mental or nervous disease.[484] Nor is typhoid a serious illness.[485] Childbirth is not a personal ailment.[486] Nor is cancer a disease peculiar to women.[487] Chronic rheumatism is not a personal ailment.[488] A serious illness is one that permanently impairs the health of the applicant.[489] A representation that the only illness applicant had was one of typhoid pneumonia, is not substantially true where the applicant had a serious accident disabling him for four months.[490] An answer by the applicant that he had had an attack of insomnia and nervousness requiring the attendance of a physician and confinement in a sanitarium, is notice to the company of the symptoms and consequences usually resulting from such attack.[491] The words "Bodily infirmity," as used in an accident policy only include an ailment of somewhat established or settled character and not merely a temporary disorder.[492] A false answer as to inflammatory rheumatism will vitiate the contract.[493] So a statement by insured that he did not have fits when in fact he was an epileptic is material,[494] and answers to questions as to association with a person who has had tuberculosis are material,[495] and deafness constitutes a breach of warranty that insured did not suffer from any disease, or sick-

[482] Fitch v. American Popular Life Ins. Co., 59 N. Y. 557; 17 Am. Rep. 372.

[483] Mut. Ben. L. Ins. Co. v. Wise, 34 Md. 599.

[484] Mut. R. F. L. Ass'n v. Farmer, 65 Ark. 581; 47 S. W. 850.

[485] Myers v. Woodmen, etc., 193 Pa. St. 470; 44 Atl. 563.

[486] Rasicot v. Royal Neighbors of Am., 18 Idaho 85; 108 Pac. 1048.

[487] Shuler v. American Ben. Ass'n, 132 Mo. App. 123; 111 S. W. 618.

[488] National American v. Ritch (Ark.), 180 S. W. 488.

[489] Drakeferd v. Supreme Conclave K. of D., 61 S. C. 338; 39 S. E. 523.

[490] McEwen v. New York Life Ins. Co., 23 Cal. App. 694; 131 Pac. 242.

[491] Fidelity Mut. Life Ins. Co. v. Miazza, 93 Miss. 422; 48 Sou. 1017.

[492] French v. Fidelity & Casualty Co., 135 Wis. 259; 115 N. W. 869.

[493] Loehr v. Supreme Assembly Equitable Fraternal Union, 132 Wis. 436; 112 N. W. 441; Knights of the Maccabees v. Hunter, 103 Tex. 612; 132 S. W. 116; reversing 57 Tex. Civ. App. 115; 143 S. W. 359.

[494] Westphall v. Metropolitan Life Ins. Co., 27 Cal. App. 734; 151 Pac. 159.

[495] National Protective League v. Allphin, 141 Ky. 777; 133 S. W. 788.

ness, of any character.[496]   The words "this year" in a question, "Has your weight changed this year?" means one year past and not the preceding months of the then calendar year.[497]   In the question, "Have you suffered from chronic dyspepsia, or any other malady?" the latter words must be understood to refer to maladies of the same nature and gravity as chronic dyspepsia.[498]   Where an applicant falsely represents that he has not been intimately associated with anyone suffering from any transmissible disease within the past year, such representation is material and vitiates the policy unless the insurer waives the same with full knowledge of the facts.   In a case of this kind,[499] the Court said: "In life insurance, it is important for the company to know the individual history and characteristics of the applicant, his idiosyncrasies, or the peculiarities of his mental and physical constitution or temperament, and his environment at the time of his application.   In no other way could risk or hazard be well determined, or the premium fixed.   Is he weak in body or in mind, and if so, to what extent and in what particular way, and what are his inherited traits or the mental and physical characteristics of his progenitors?   The inquiry must be not only individual, but ancestral, and the investigation searching as to his past life and future intentions, as experience has shown, in order to make anything like a reliable estimate of the risk to be incurred.   And his habits and surroundings are also to be known, considered, and weighed.   Has he been exposed to any contagious, infectious, or transmissible disease, is a perfectly legitimate inquiry.   Does he propose to change his residence, so that his exposure to climatic or other diseases will be greater and the hazard correspondingly increased?   These and many other questions of like kind any prudent man engaged in the business of life insurance would be more than likely to ask, and the answers to them would surely tend to shape the judgment of the underwriter and influence his decision in regard to the risk. Any insurance company that would issue a policy or contract for

[496] Colaneri v. General Accident Assur. Corp., 110 N. Y. Supp. 678; 126 App. Div. 591.

[497] Sweeney v. Life Ass'n of America, 152 Ill. App. 173.

[498] Independent Order of Foresters v. Turmelle, 19 Que. K. B. 261.

[499] Gardner v. North State Mut. Life Ins. Co., 163 N. C. 367; 79 S. E. 806.

556

insurance upon any other basis and without proper inquiry would be so reckless as to forfeit the confidence of the public. However it may be generally, in our case it appears that the applicant had been intimately associated with his wife, who was afflicted with typhoid fever, requiring seventeen medical visits for treatment. He nursed his wife and a child in the same house afflicted with the same disease, throughout their illness, and shortly afterwards was himself attacked by it and died. There was ample evidence to show that typhoid fever is transmissible from one person to another in various ways—by flies and other insects, drinking water, milk and other substances of a like kind, when infected by flies, which carry the fatal germs from the stools or excreta of the typhoid patient. It was testified that when there is typhoid fever in a house or on the premises, it presents a very dangerous situation for those who occupy them or who visit there, as they are thereby brought in close contact with the germ-laden substances and are more exposed to infection. A person physically able to resist or throw off the disease may escape, or he may be so fortunate as not to become the victim of the germ bearers, but he is nevertheless in dangerous surroundings, where the chances of infection are greater than if he were more remote from the premises of the patient. There was also evidence that the application for insurance would have been rejected had the question been correctly answered. John B. Gardner knew, or rather must have known, at the time he answered the question, that he had very recently been intimately associated with his sick wife as her nurse during her severe illness, and the company, if ignorant of the fact, was misled by his answer as to the truth of the matter. Under the charge of the Court, which is sustained by our decisions, and was in accordance with the established doctrine, the jury found that the representation was false and was also material, and there was evidence to support the finding.'' By all the foregoing cases the doctrine is established that it will be left, ordinarily, to the jury to say whether the applicant has answered the questions correctly. In a leading case[500] the Court says: ''It was for the jury to decide whether 'chronic bronchitis' or 'bronchial difficulty,' or any other bodily affection or

[500] Campbell v. New England Mut. Life Ins. Co., 98 Mass. 381; 1 Big. I. & A. Ins. Cas. 229. See also as to spitting of blood, Eminent Household etc., v. Prater, 24 Okla. 214; 103 Pac. 558; 20 Ann. Cas. 287.

condition to which the assured was found by them to be subject,
amounted to bronchitis, consumption, disease of the lungs, or some
other of the infirmities stated in the application, and relied on by
the defendants; and whether the spitting of blood by him, if proved
to have taken place, was under such circumstances as to indicate
disease in his throat, lungs, air passages or other internal organs."[1]
In England it has been held that the applicant is bound to state
to the company a single instance of spitting of blood, although the
same Court said that the expression "has not had any spitting of
blood" does not mean that he had never spit blood, but never from
unascertained causes or disease tending to shorten life.[501]

[501] Geach v. Ingall, 14 M. & W. 95; 15 L. J. Ex. 37; 9 Jur. 691. But see
Smith v. N. W. Mut. L., 196 Pa. St. 314; 46 Atl. 426. The following list of
particular cases where special diseases or ailments were in question
is given: Appendicitis, Aetna L. Ins. Co. v. Howell, 32 Ky. L. 935; 107
S. W. 294; "Dyspepsia," Jeffrey v. United Order, etc., 97 Me. 176; 53
Atl. 1102; "Consumption" or "phthisis," Metropolitan L. Ins. Co. v.
Dempsey, 72 Md. 228; 19 Atl. 642; Tucker v. United L. & Acc. Ass'n,
133 N. Y. 548; 30 N. E. 723; affg. 16 N. Y. Supp. 953; Modern Woodmen
v. Van Wald, 6 Kan. App. 231; 49 Pac. 782; Doll v. Equitable Life Assur.
Soc., 71 C. C. A. 121; 138 Fed. 705; Maine Ben. Ass'n v. Parks, 81 Me.
79; 16 Atl. 642; "headache," Mut. L. Ins. Co. v. Simpson (Tex. Civ. A.),
28 S. W. 837; "hemorrhage," Brady v. Industrial Ben. Ass'n, 29 N. Y.
Supp. 768; "liver disease," Cushman v. U. S. L. Ins. Co., 70 N. Y.
72; Conn. Mut. L. Ins. Co. v. Trust Co., 112 U. S. 250; "brain disease,"
Knickerbocker L. Ins. Co. v. Trefz, 104 U. S. 197; "renal colic," Harris
v. Security Mut. L. Ins. Co., 130 Tenn. 325; 170 S. W. 474; "chronic
cough," Bertrand v. Franklin Life Ins. Co., 119 La. 423; 44 Sou. 186;
'Diabetes," Metropolitan L. Ins. Co. v. Schmidt, 29 Ky. L. 255; 93 S. W.
1055; "nephritis," Hoffman v. Metropolitan L. Ins. Co., 126 N. Y. Supp.
436; "heart disease," Metropolitan L. Ins. Co. v. Moravec, 214 Ill. 186;
73 N. E. 415; Haape v. Metropolitan L. Ins. Co., 150 Mich. 467; 114 N.
W. 380; "kidney disease," Alexander v. Metropolitan L. Ins. Co., 150 N.
C. 536; 63 S. E. 432; "local disease," Scoles v. Universal L. Ins. Co., 42
Cal. 523; "hereditary disease," Gridley v. N. W. Mut. L. Ins. Co., 14
Blatchf. 109; "serious disease," Holloman v. Life Ins. Co., 1 Woods, 674;
Life Ins. Co. v. Francisco, 17 Wall. 672; "throat disease," Eisner v. Guar-
dian L. Ins. Co., 3 Cent. L. J. 302; "piles," Baumgart v. Modern Wood-
men, 85 Wis. 546; 55 N. W. 713; U. S. Health & Acc. Co. v. Bennett, 32
Ky. L. 433; 105 S. W. 433; "vertigo," Mut. Ben. L. Ins. Co. v. Davies, 87
Ky. 541; 9 S. W. 812; "pimple on tongue developing into cancer," Story
v. United L. & Acc. Ass'n, 4 N. Y. Supp. 373; "asthma," Volker v. Metropolitan L. Ins. Co., 21 N. Y. Supp. 456; "gastritis," Mut. Ben., etc., Co. v.

§ 290. **Accident or Serious Injury or Sickness.**—In a case arising in Iowa the defense was that the applicant had not correctly answered the question whether the party had ever met with any accidental or serious injury,'' and the answers being warranted true, but in fact false, the policy was thereby avoided. The opinion of the Supreme Court of the State says:[502] ''The defendant claims that if the insured ever met with any . . . accidental injury,'' that will bar a recovery because the application is a warranty that she never did. In this construction we do not concur. The language of the question is to have a reasonable construction, in view of the purposes for which the question was asked. It must have reference to such an accidental injury as probably would or might possibly have influenced the subsequent health or longevity of the insured. It could not refer, and could not be understood by any person reading the question for a personal answer to refer,

Wise, 34 Md. 582; "open sores," Corbett v. Metropolitan L. Ins. Co., 37 App. Div. 152; 55 N. Y. Supp. 775; "tonsilitis," McCollum v. Mut. etc., Co., 55 Hun. 103; "Bright's disease," Continental L. Ins. Co. v. Young, 113 Ind. 159; "syphilis," Fitzrandolph v. Mut. Relief Soc,. 21 Nova Scotia R. 274; "La Grippe," Mut. L. Ins. Co. v. Blodgett, 8 Tex. Civ. App. 45; 27 S. W. 286; Davis v. Supreme Lodge, etc., 35 App. Div. 354; 54 N. Y. Supp. 1023; "priapism," Hubbard v. Mut. Res. F. L. Ass'n, 40 C. C. A. 665; 100 Fed. 719; "sprain," Tyler v. Ideal, etc., Ass'n, 172 Mass. 536; 52 N. E. 1083; "pneumonia," Henn v. Metropolitan L. Ins. Co., 67 N. J. 310; 51 Atl. 689; Carson v. Metropolitan Life Ins. Co., 1 Pa. Sup. Ct. 572; Iowa Life Ins. Co. v. Zehr, 91 Ill. App. 93; "sore throat," Penn. M. L. Ins. Co. v. Mechanics, etc., Co., 19 C. C. A. 286; 72 Fed. 413; 38 L. R. A. 33; "kidney trouble," Hogan v. Metropolitan L. Ins. Co., 104 Mass. 448; 41 N. E. 663; "gall stone," Weintrant v. Metropolitan L. Ins. Co., 27 Misc. 540; 58 N. Y. Supp. 295; "catarrh," Lippencott v. Royal Soc., etc., 64 N. J. L. 309; 45 Atl. 774; Endowment Rank v. Cogbill, 99 Tenn. 28; 41 S. W. 340; "hernia," Levie v. Metropolitan L. Ins. Co., 163 Mass. 117; 39 N. E. 792; Hilts v. U. S. Casualty Co., 176 Mo. App. 635; 159 S. W. 771; "bronchitis," Billings v. Metropolitan L. Ins. Co., 70 Vt. 477; 41 Atl. 516; French v. Fidelity & Cas. Co., 135 Wis. 259; 115 N. W. 869; "cancer," McClain v. Provident Sav. L. A. Soc., 49 C. C. A. 31; 110 Fed. 80; Brison v. Metropolitan L. Ins. Co. (Ky.), 115 S. W. 785; Peck v. Washington L. Ins. Co,, 91 App. Div. 597; 87 N. Y. Supp. 210; affd. 187 N. Y. 585; 74 N. E. 1122; "smallpox," Sovereign Camp, etc., v. Gray, 26 Tex. Civ. A. 457; 64 S. W. 801. General answers, Bancroft v. Home Ben. Ass'n, 12 N. Y. Supp. 718.

502 Wilkenson v. Conn. Mut. Life Ins. Co., 30 Ia. 127.

to a simple burn upon the hand or arm, in infancy; to a cut upon the thumb or finger, in youth; to a stumble and falling, or the sprain of a joint, in a more advanced age. The idea is that such a construction is to be put by the courts upon the language as an ordinary person of common understanding would put upon it when addressed to him for answer. The strict construction or hyper-criticism of the language, which would make the word 'any' an indefinite term, so as to include all injuries, even the most trifling, would bring a just reproach upon the courts, the law, the defendant itself and its business.'' Upon the same subject the Supreme Court of the United States says:[503] ''It is insisted by counsel for the defendant that if the injury was considered serious at the time, it is one which must be mentioned in reply to the interrogatory, and that whether any further inquiry is expedient on the subject of its permanent influence on the health, is for the insurer to determine before making insurance. But there are grave and obvious difficulties in this construction. The accidents resulting in personal injuries, which at the moment are considered by the parties serious, are so very numerous that it would almost be impossible for a person engaged in active life to recall them at the age of forty or fifty years, and if the failure to mention all such injuries must invalidate the policy, very few would be sustained where thorough inquiry is made into the history of the party whose life is the subject of insurance. There is, besides, the question of what is to be considered a serious injury at the time. If the party gets over the injury completely, without leaving any ill consequence, in a few days, it is clear that the serious aspect of the case was a mistake. Is it necessary to state the injury and explain the mistake to meet the requirements of the policy? On the other hand, when the question arises, as in this case, on a trial, the jury, and not the insurer, must decide whether the injury was serious or not. In deciding this are they to reject the evidence of the ultimate effect of the injury on the party's health, longevity, strength and other similar considerations? This would be to leave out of view the

[503] Ins. Co. v. Wilkenson, 13 Wall. 222. This case was approved in Confederation L. Ass'n v. Miller, 14 Can. Sup. Ct. 330; affg. 14 Ont. App. 218. For further consideration of the subject, see Coop. L. Ass'n v. Leflore, 53 Miss. 1; Fitch v. American Popular L. Ins. Co., 59 N. Y. 557; 17 Am. Rep. 372; Snyder v. Mut. L. Ins. Co., 3 Ins. L. J. 579.

essential purpose of the inquiry, and the very matters which would throw most light on the nature of the inquiry with reference to its influence on the insurable character of the life proposed. Looking, then, to the purpose for which the information is sought by the question and to the difficulty of answering whether an injury was serious, in any other manner than by reference to its permanent or temporary influence on the health, strength and longevity of the party, we are of opinion that the Court did not err in the criterion by which it directed the jury to decide the interrogatory propounded to them." A fracture of the skull, whether it affected the health or not, is such a serious and unusual an injury, that it must be disclosed.[504] So, where a blow on the throat had caused an abrasion of the windpipe and the raising of a little blood and a confinement to the bed for three days and the attendance of a physician, it was held[505] that the evidence was not sufficient to sustain a finding that the party had received a wound, hurt or serious bodily injury. In a case in Pennsylvania,[506] where the questions and answers were these: "4· Have you been subject to or had any of the following disorders or diseases. . . . Open sores, lumps, or swelling of any kind? Ans. Nothing of that kind to my knowledge. 9. Have you ever had any malformation, illness or injury, or undergone any surgical operation? Ans. No." The Court said: "These questions, it must be admitted, are in the most general terms, and if they are to be so read and understood, they are not only unreasonable but absurd. A slight cutting of the finger, with a penknife, may for a time produce both an open sore and a swelling; the mere indisposition arising from cold is an illness; the stubbing of a toe is an injury; and the most trivial operations with hand or knife may be said to be surgical. It would be impossible for a person of mature years to remember, and absurd for the association to inquire as to the common and trivial ailments or injuries he may have suffered from his earliest childhood, and it is unreasonable to suppose that these were in contemplation of the

504 Moore v. Conn. Mut. L. Ins. Co., 41 Up. Can. Q. B. 497; on appeal 3 Ont. App. 230; the court were equally divided.
505 Bancroft v. Home Ben. Ass'n, 120 N. Y. 14; 23 N. E. 997; reversing 54 N. Y. Superior Ct. 332, and 8 N. Y. St. 129; cited in first edition.
506 Home, etc., Life Ass'n v. Gillespie, 110 Pa. St. 88; 1 Atl. 340. See also National Fraternity v. Karnes, 24 Tex. Civ. A. 607; 60 S. W. 576.

parties. The form of the fourth question indicates, however, that
the open sore or swelling intended, is such as results from 'disease
or disorder,' that is to say, such as result by defective action, from
some functional derangement, and not from wounds or accidental
injuries, and the Court was right, we think, in saying that they
were to some extent permanent or continuous, connected or recur-
rent. So, the illness or injury referred to, must be of such nature and importance as would reasonably fall within the line of
inquiry proper to be pursued in such cases. We do not say that
the illness or injury must be such as would be material to the
risk, but such as in the judgment of the jury was reasonably in
contemplation of the parties, in view of the nature of the matter
under consideration. If the line of distinction is obscure, and
difficult to draw, the fault is with the association for making it
so. We do not believe that the assured was expected or required
to remember and to recite in his application all of the trivial ailments of his life.''

The word, ''injuries,'' refers only to serious wounds or injuries[507] Being born without fingers on his right hand is a bodily
deformity avoiding the policy the warranty being that he had no
bodily deformity.[508]   Answer to a question as to surgical operation in any hospital is not made false by proof of an operation at
the home of the insured.[509]

§ 291. .Serious Illness.—The Court of Appeals of Kentucky
has considered the subject of what is a serious disease, or complaint.[510]   The Court says: ''We find ourselves unprepared to
give any exact definition of a 'serious disease.' The record presents no testimony from any physician to show how serious might
be the effect of, or how lasting might be the consequences of, the
illnesses for which she had been treated shortly before the issual of
the policy. The Century Dictionary defines a serious illness as
'one attended by danger, giving rise to apprehensions.' In Brown

[507] Trenton v. North American Acc. Ins. Co. (Tex. Civ. A.), 89 S.
W. 276.
[508] Lynch v. Travelers' Ins. Co., 118 C. C. A. 379; 200 Fed. 193.
[509] Ladies of the Maccabees v. Kendrick (Tex. Civ. A.), 165 S. W. 110.
[510] Metropolitan Life Ins. Co. v. Little, 149 Ky. 77; 149 S. W. 988.

v. Metropolitan Life Ins. Co.,[511] a serious illness is said to be 'a grave, important, weighty trouble.' In Drakeford v. Supreme Conclave K. D. [512] it is said that a sickness may be very bad and very sad and yet not serious; that any permanent or material impairment of health is a serious illness. Certainly the idea is not to be tolerated in that mere temporary disorders or functional disturbances, having no effect upon the general health or duration of life, should, within even the strict terms of the contract, be considered serious illnesses. Upon the other hand, there are certain diseases, such as consumption, that the ordinary mind, untrained in medicine, knows beyond question to be serious. Between these extremes there is a broad line of ills of varying natures, the seriousness of which can only be told with any degree of exactitude by those who are trained in the study of the human body and of the effect of the various diseases and illnesses upon it. We incline to agree with the South Carolina court's view that a serious illness in insurance terminology must be one entailing some permanent or material impairment of health; and there is no testimony in the record before us of any one qualified to speak upon the subject, showing that any of the illnesses named were of such character, or that they might reasonably be expected to result in a permanent impairment of the health of the insured. In the light of the record, therefore, we cannot say that the diseases about which there is no contradiction in the testimony were such diseases as to fall within the category named as avoiding the policy.''

It has also been said that a serious illness means such as permanently impairs the health of the applicant. Spitting and coughing of blood used in a question by medical examiner means the disorder, so-called, whether the blood comes from the lungs or the stomach.[513] A serious illness means something more than an illness temporary in duration,[514] but a temporary ear trouble is not a violation of the representation as to health, but when the trouble was serious and there was an infection resulting in a

[511] 65 Mich. 306; 32 N. W. 61; 8 Am. St. Rep. 894.

[512] 61 S. C. 338; 39 S. E. 523.

[513] Eminent Household of Columbian Woodmen v. Prater, 24 Okla. 214; 105 Pac. 558; 20 Am. Cas. 287. See also Gruber v. German Catholic Aid Ass'n, 113 Minn. 340; 129 N. W. 581.

[514] Schas v. Equitable Life Assur. Soc., 170 N. C. 420; 87 S. E. 222.

disease the answer was both false and material.[515]   Where the insured five years before his application had fallen violently ill so that for a time his life was despaired of, and where he suffered from acute pains and was for sometime in a state of collapse and was attended by two physicians and a trained nurse, and recovered after five or six weeks, and the sickness followed a chronic stomach trouble, it was held material.[516]

§ 292.   **Other Insurance**—If the answers to the questions in the application are warranted to be true, a false answer to the inquiry concerning other insurance or application to other companies vitiates the policy.[517]   The suppression by the insured of the fact of the existence of other insurance on his life in violation of the condition of the policy is such concealment as will make void the policy.[518] And the question as to other insurance is material.[519] The answer is not false if no other insurance has been obtained by the applicant himself.[520]   And if the applicant states that "to the best of his belief" no company has refused to issue a policy on his life, the

[515] Aetna Life Ins. Co. v. Millar, 113 Md. 686; 78 Atl. 483.

[516] Equitable Life Assur. Soc. v. Keiper, 91 C. C. A. 433; 165 Fed. 595; reversing 159 Fed. 206. As to this subject, see also cases cited in previous section.

[517] Clemans v. Supreme Assembly Royal Soc. of Goodfellows, 131 N. Y. 485; 30 N. E. 496; 16 L. R. A. 33; reversing 16 N. Y. Supp. 378; Webb v. Bankers' L. Ins. Co., 19 Colo. App. 456; 76 Pac. 738; Webb v. Security Mut. L. Ins. Co., 61 C. C. A. 383; 126 Fed. 635; Dimmick v. Metropolitan L. I. Co., 69 N. J. L. 384; 55 Atl. 291; Home L. Ins. Co. v. Meyers, 50 C. C. A. 544; 112 Fed. 846; Security Mut. L. Ins. Co. v. Webb, 45 C. C. A. 648; 106 Fed. 648; National Life Ass'n v. Hopkins, 97 Va. 167; 33 S. E. 539; Williams v. St. Louis L. Ins. Co., 97 Mo. App. 449; 71 S. W. 376. See also Williams v. St. Louis Ins. Co., 189 Mo. 70; 87 S. W. 499; reversing 97 Mo. App. 449; 71 S. W. 376; Hardy v. Phoenix Mut. L. Ins. Co., 167 N. C. 22; 83 S. E. 569; Mut. L. Ins. Co. v. Hilton-Green, 211 Fed. 31; Prudential Ins. Co. v. Moore, 231 U. S. 560; Bonewell v. North Am. Acc. Ins. Co., 160 Mich. 137; 125 N. W. 59; Wyss Thalman v. Maryland Cas. Co., 113 C. C. A. 383; 193 Fed. 55.

[518] Studwell v. Mut. Ben. L. Ass'n, 19 N. Y. Supp. 709.

[519] March v. Metropolitan L. Ins. Co., 186 Pa. St. 629; 40 Atl. 1100; Am. Union L. Ins. Co. v. Judge, 191 Pa. St. 484; 43 Atl. 374. See also cases, *supra*.

[520] Aufderheider v. German Mut. L. Ins. Co., 66 Mo. App. 285.

fact that a policy has in fact been refused is a good defense.[521] Whether or not beneficiary societies are embraced in the question as to other insurance is not entirely settled, but it has been held that the act of the agent in stating to the applicant that certificates in beneficiary societies are not regarded as life insurance, is binding upon the company.[522]

The term "insurance" in its broader meaning includes fraternal associations but in a restricted and literal sense it does not.[523] The question as to other insurance does not include accident insurance.[524] Where the applicant stated that no company had ever declined to grant insurance on his life an application made by him to another company, indorsed "declined" by the medical director of such company, is admissible in evidence, it being shown that such action was a rejection of the application.[525] The medical examination not being a part of the application, a statement that no prior application for life insurance has been rejected is untrue if it appears that an application was in fact received by the agent and forwarded to the company although there was no medical examination, the medical examiner having pronounced

[521] Kemp v. Good Templars Mut. Ben. Ass'n, 64 Hun. 637; 19 N. Y. Supp. 435. See also Clapp v. Ass'n, 146 Mass. 519; 16 N. E. 433, in regard to answers to "best of the belief" of applicant. Also ante, § 254.

[522] Continental Life Ins. Co. v. Chamberlain, 132 U. S. 304; 10 S. C. 87; Equitable Life Assur. Soc. v. Hazelwood, 75 Tex. 338; 12 S. W. 622. See, however, McCollum v. New York Mut. L. Ins. Co., 55 Hun. 103; 8 N. Y. Supp. 249. A valuable note as to whether beneficiary societies are included in the term, other insurance, is appended in 38 L. R. A. 33 to Penn. M. L. Ins. Co. v. Mechanics, etc., Co,. 43 U. S. App. 75; 73 Fed. 653; 72 Fed. 413. In Bruce v. Conn. M. L. Ins. Co., 74 Minn. 310; 77 N. W. 210; Meyer-Bruno v. Pennsylvania Mut. L. Ins. Co., 189 Pa. St. 579; 42 Atl. 297; Alden v. Supreme Tent, etc., 178 N. Y. 535; 71 N. E. 104; a fraternal society was held to be embraced in the question. To the contrary are Newton v. S. W. Mut. L. Ass'n, 116 Ia. 311; 90 N. W. 73, and Fidelity Mut. v. Miller, 34 C. C. A. 211; 92 Fed. 63. It depends largely upon the form of the question as to whether there is a misrepresentation.

[523] Petersen v. Manhattan L. Ins. Co., 244 Ill. 329; 91 N. E. 466; 18 Am. & Eng. Ann. Cas. 96; reversing 115 Ill. App. 42; Mut. L. Ins. Co. v. Ford (Tex. Civ. A.), 130 S. W. 769; Lyon v. United Moderns, 148 Cal. 470; 83 Pac. 804; 4 L. R. A. (U. S.), 247.

[524] Mut. Reserve L. Ins. Co. v. Dobler, 70 C. C. A. 134; 137 Fed. 550.

[525] Elliot v. Mut. Ben. L. Ass'n, 27 N. Y. Supp. 696,

the applicant unfit without an examination.[526] A negative answer to the question whether any application had been made·to the agent for which a policy was not issued is not falsified by proof of an application that had not been finally passed upon by the company.[527] Where the medical examiner reported unfavorably on an application for additional insurance whereupon it was declined, it was held to be a refusal to insure within the meaning of the question, "Has any proposal to insure, etc., ever been declined."[528] Where the answers are warranted to be true there·will be a strict construction so that the policy will be saved if·possible."[529]

§ 293. **Rejection by Other Company.**—A false answer as to rejection by another company is material and avoids the policy.[530] In the case of Aetna Life Ins. Co. v. Moore,[531] the Court says: "'It is contended by respondent that this testimony shows that Salgue's application to the Penn Mutual was not rejected but was withdrawn; and, besides, whether it was rejected or withdrawn was a question for the jury. We are unable to concur with either contention. The question was a very broad one. It was whether any proposal or application had been made for which insurance had not been granted, and particulars were asked for, 'and the names of all such companies, associations, or agents.' Regarding the sense of the question—indeed, if not its letter—the answer

526 Edington v. Aetna L. Ins. Co., 77 N. Y. 564; 100 N. Y. 536.

527 Langdon v. Union Mut. L. Ins. Co., 14 Fed. 272. Other cases involving the truth of statements concerning other insurance are: N. Y. Life Ins. Co. v. Flack, 3 Md. 341; Mut. Ben. L. Ins. Co. v. Wise, 34 Md. 582; American L. Ins. Co. v. Mahone, 56 Miss. 280; Fowkes v. Manchester & London L. Ins. Co., 3 Foster & F. 440; London L. Ins. Co. v. Mansel, 11 L. R. Ch. D. 363; In matter Gen. Provincial L. Ins. Co., 18 W. R. 396.

528 Stuart v. Mut. Reserve F. L. Ins. Co., 28 N. Y. Supp. 944.

529 Robinson v. Supreme Commandery, etc., 38 Misc. 97; 77 N. Y. Supp. 111; 79 App. Div. 215; 79 N. Y. Supp. 13; Security Trust Co. v. Tarpey, 182 Ill. 52; 54 N. E. 1041; Kansas Mut. L. Ins. Co. v. Coalson, 22 Tex. Civ. App. 64; 54 S. W. 383; Commercial Mut. Acc. Ass'n v. Bates, 176 Ill. 194; 52 N. E. 49.

530 Mut. Life Ins. Co. v. Hilton-Green, 211 Fed. 31; Hardy v. Phoenix Mut. Life Ins. Co., 167 N. C. 22; 83 S. E. 5, and cases cited.

531 231 U. S. 541; 58 L. Ed. 356, where valuable note is appended.

was untruthful. The question certainly called for something more than an absolute negative. Its purpose was to ascertain the conduct of Salgue with reference to life insurance in order to judge of him as a risk. If it had been answered according to the fact, the company would have received information of circumstances certainly material for it to consider."[532] An indorsement upon an application "Declined by Ex." signed with the initials of the authorized medical examiner is competent evidence of the action of the insurance company in declining the application.[533] A false answer as to rejection vitiates the contract and it is immaterial whether the answer is regarded as a warranty, or a representation, or whether the representation is made in good faith or not,[534] but where false answers as to rejection is a defense, the company defending on that ground must show that the rejection was made known to the insured as he could not know that he was rejected until informed to that effect.[535] Where a fraternal beneficiary association had notice at the time of the issuance of the benefit certificate that the applicant had previously been rejected by it, it could not set up the falsity of the statement in the applicant that she had not been rejected.[536] Under the Oklahoma Statute a false answer as to previous application for insurance does not avoid the policy.[537]

§ 294. **Limitation of Time Within Which Defense Can be Made.**—It has become the custom among life insurance companies to insert in the policy a provision that such policy shall be incontestable after the lapse of a certain time, and one company at least makes its policies incontestable from date of issue. Upon principle it would seem that the defense of fraud could be made

[532] To the same effect, Security Mut. Life Ins. Co. v. Webb. 45 C. C. A. 648; 106 Fed. 808; 55 L. R. A. 132.

[533] Elliott v. Mut. Ben. Life Ass'n, 76 Hun. 378; 27 N. Y. Supp. 696.

[534] Masonic Life Ass'n v. Robinson, 149 Ky. 80; 147 S. W. 882.

[535] Metropolitan Life Ins. Co. v. Ford, 126 Ky. 49; 102 S. W. 876.

[536] Cundiff v. Royal Neighbors of America, 162 Mo. App. 117; 144 S. W. 128. See also Haughton v. Aetna Life Ins. Co., 42 Ind. App. 527; 85 N. E. 125, 1050; Dineen v. General Accident Ins. Co., 110 N. Y. Supp. 344; 126 App. Div. 167; Wright v. Fraternities Health & Accident Ass'n, 107 Me. 418; 78 Atl. 475.

[537] Shawnee Life Ins. Co. v. Watkins, Okla. 156 Pac. 181.

notwithstanding a general provision of incontestability from date of issue for fraud cuts under everything.[538]   But where the stipulation is that the policy shall be incontestable after a certain period the rule is that such an agreement is like a short statute of limitations, after the expiration of which even the defense of fraud is excluded.[539]   We shall consider the subject further in another place.[540]

[538] Welch v. Union Cent. L. Ins. Co., 108 Ia. 224; 78 N. W. 853; 50 L. R. A. 774.

[539] Wright v. Mut. Ben. L. Ass'n, 118 N. Y. 237; 23 N. E. 186; 6 L. R. A. 731; affg. 43 Hun. 61; Mass. Ben. L. Ass'n v. Robinson, 104 Ga. 256; 30 S. E. 918; 42 L. R. A. 261; Murray v. State Mut. L. A. Co., 22 R. I. 524; 48 Atl. 800; 53 L. R. A. 742; Clement v. N. Y. Life Ins. Co., 101 Tenn. 22; 46 S. W. 561; 42 L. R. A. 247; where valuable note is appended.

[540] *Post*, § 447.

CHAPTER VII.

§ 295. Insurable Interest.—A contract of life insurance is peculiar in that it is not every person who can become a party to it. The law forbids, from considerations of public policy, any person to insure the life of another unless he has some interest in the life of such person, and this fact makes it necessary to here discuss what is called the law of insurable interest. The difficulty courts have experienced is not so much in defining the rule, but in its application. It is in respect, to the beneficiary, or person for whose benefit the insurance is effected, that the greatest differences are found between the form of insurance furnished by benefit societies and that given by regular life insurance corporations. The latter are free to contract with whom they choose and in the manner they prefer, subject only to the restraints imposed by public policy; the beneficiaries of the societies, however, are generally limited to specified classes, either relatives or dependents, and out of these they cannot go. The subject of insurable interest is a most important one in the law of life insurance, for it has often been considered by the courts in the reported cases and has been discussed with great earnestness and vigorous reasoning. Though the contract of life insurance is not strictly one of indemnity, the policy of the law does not permit any one to insure the life of another in which he has not at the time what is called an insurable interest, because such contract would be in the nature of a wager or speculation in human life. The Supreme Court of the United States, in passing upon the point whether a divorced woman could recover upon a policy of insurance on the life of a former husband,[1] reviews the law of insurable interest as follows: "It is generally agreed that mere wager policies, that is, policies in which the assured party has no interest whatever in the matter insured, but only an interest in its loss or destruction, are void as against public policy. . . . But precisely what interest is necessary in order to take a policy out of the category of mere wager has been the subject of much discussion. In marine and fire insurance the difficulty is not so great because there insurance is construed as strictly an indemnity. But in life insurance the loss can seldom be measured by pecuniary values. Still an interest of some sort in the insured life must exist. A man cannot take out insurance on the life of a total stranger, nor on that of one who is not so connected with him as to make the continuance of the life a matter of some real interest to him. It is well settled that a man has an insurable interest in his own life and in that of his wife and children; a woman in the life of her husband; and the creditor in the life of his debtor. Indeed it may be said generally that any reasonable expectation of pecuniary benefit or advantage from the continued life of another creates an insurable interest in such life. And there is no doubt that a man may effect an insurance on his own life for the benefit of a relative or friend; or two or more persons on their joint lives for the benefit of the survivor or survivors. The old tontines were based substantially on this principle and their validity has never been called in question. The essential thing is that the policy shall be obtained in good faith, and not for the purpose of speculating upon the hazard of a life in which the insured has no interest. On this point the remarks of Chief Justice Shaw in a. case which arose in Connecticut (in

[1] Connecticut M. Life Ins. Co. v. Schaefer, 94 U. S. 457. To the same effect are: American, etc., Co. v. Barr, 16 C. C. A. 51; 32 U. S. App. 444; 68 Fed. 873; Prudential Ins. Co. v. Leyden, 20 Ky. L. 881; 47 S. W. 767; Prudential Ins. Co. v. Hunn, 21 Ind. App. 525; 52 N. E. 772; Albert v. Mutual L. Ins. Co., 122 N. C. 92; 30 S. E. 327; Cisna v. Sheibley, 88 Ill. App. 385; Crosswell v. Conn. Ind. Ass'n, 51 S. C. 103; 28 S. E. 200; Foster v. Preferred Acc. I. Co., 125 Fed. 536; Heinlein v. Imperial L. Ins. Co., 101 Mich. 250; 59 N. W. 615; 25 L. R. A. 627 and note.

which State the present policy originated), seems to us characterized by great good sense. He says:[2] 'In discussing the question in this commonwealth (Massachusetts) we are to consider it solely as a question of common law, unaffected by the statute of 14 Geo. III. passed about the time of the commencement of the revolution and never adopted in this State. All, therefore, which it seems necessary to show, in order to take the case out of the objection of being a wager policy, is that the insured has some interest in the *cestui que vie;* that his temporal affairs, his just hopes and well-grounded expectations of support, of patronage and advantage in life, will be impaired; so that the real purpose is not a wager, but to secure such advantages, supposed to depend on the life of another; such, we suppose, would be sufficient to prevent it from being regarded as a mere wager. Whatever may be the nature of such interest, and whatever the amount insured, it can work no injury to the insurers, because the premium is proportioned to the amount; and whether the insurance be a large or small amount the premium is computed to be a precise equivalent for the risk taken. We cannot doubt,' he continues, 'that a parent has an interest in the life of a child and *vice versa,* a child in the life of a parent; not merely on the ground of a provision of law that parents and grandparents are bound to support their lineal kindred when they may stand in need of relief, but upon considerations of strong morals, and the force of natural affection between near kindred, operating often more efficaciously than those of positive law.' We concur in these views. . . . We do not hesitate to say, however, that a policy taken out in good faith and valid at its inception, is not avoided by the cessation of the insurable interest, unless such be the necessary effect of the provisions of the policy itself.[3] Of course, a colorable or merely temporary interest would present circumstances from which want of good faith and intent to evade the rule might be inferred. And in cases where the insurance is effected merely by way of indemnity, as where a creditor insures the life of his debtor, for the purpose of securing his debt, the amount of insurable interest is the amount of the debt.'' The rule prevails in England under judicial construction of the statute of 14 Geo.

[2] Loomis v. Ins. Co., 6 Gray 399.

[3] See Tyler v. Odd Fellows, etc., 145 Mass. 134; 13 N. E. 360.

572

III.[4] that there must be an interest at the time of effecting the insurance, but that it need not continue until death.[5] The same rule applies to accident insurance policies.[6] If the policy is payable to the insured himself it is immaterial that one pays the premiums who has no interest in the life insured.[7]

§ 296. **The Same Subject—Later Cases.**—The courts are practically unanimous in holding that the insured has an unlimited insurable interest in his own life and can make the policy payable at will and can insure his own life for the benefit of another having no insurable interest, where he makes the contract and pays the premium himself.[8] And the rule applies to an accident policy.[9] The insurance of one's life for the benefit of another having no insurable interest therein is not contrary to public policy.[10] In the case of Thomas v. National Benefit Ass'n,[11] the Court of Errors and Appeals of New Jersey said: "Although, as was said by Field, J., in Warnock v. Davis,[12] it is not easy to define with precision what will constitute such an interest, it may be stated generally to exist whenever the relations between the in-

[4] Dalby v. Ins. Co., 15 C. B. 365; Overruling Godsall v. Boldero, 9 East 72; Law v. Lond. I. P. Co., 3 Eq. R. 338; 1 Kay & J. 223; 124 L. J. Ch. 196; 1 Jur. (N. S.), 178.

[5] Manhattan L. Ins. Co. v. Hennessy, 39 C. C. A. 625; 99 Fed. 64.

[6] U. S. Mut. Acc. Ass'n v. Hodgkin, 4 App. D. C. 516; Robinson v. U. S. Mut. Acc. Ass'n, 68 Fed. 825; Foster v. Preferred, etc., Co., 125 Fed. 536.

[7] Prudential Ins. Co. v. Cummings, 19 Ky. L. 1770; 44 S. W. 431; Merchants L. Ass'n v. Yoakum, 37 C. C. A. 56; 98 Fed. 251; Monast v. Manhattan L. Ins. Co., 32 R. I. 557; 79 Atl. 932.

[8] Pacific Mut. Life Ins. Co. v. O'Neil, 36 Okla. 792; 130 Pac. 270; Afro-American Life Ins. Co. v. Adams (Ala.), 70 Sou. 119; American National Ins. Co. v. Moore, (Ala. App); 70 Sou. 190; Western Life Indemnity Co. v. Rupp, 147 Ky. 489; 144; S. W. 743; Brogi v. Brogi, 211 Mass. 512; 98 N. E. 573; Western & Southern Life Ins. Co. v. Grimes, 130 Ky. 338; 128 S. W. 65; Deal v. Hainley, 35 Mo. App. 507; Pollock v. Household of Ruth, 150 N. C. 211; 63 N. E. 940; Hess v. Segenfelter, 127 Ky. 348; 105 S. W. 476; Reed v. Provident Savings Life Assur. Soc., 190 N. Y. 111; 82 N. E. 734.

[9] Allen's Admr. v. Pacific Mut. Life Ins. Co. (Ky.), 179 S. W. 589.

[10] New York Life Ins. Co. v. Murtagh, 137 La. 760; 69 Sou. 165; Locher v. Kueckenmiester, 120 Mo. App. 701; 98 S. W. 92; New York Life Ins. Co. v. Greenlee, 42 Ind. App. 82; 84 N. E. 1101.

[11] 84 N. J. L. 281; 86 Atl. 375; affg. 81 N. J. Law 349; 79 Atl. 1042.

[12] 104 U. S. 775; 26 L. Ed. 924.

sured and the beneficiary are such as to justify a reasonable expectation that the continuance of the life of the former will result
in advantage or benefit to the latter. It is not necessary, in order
to create such an interest, that the insured shall be under any
legal obligation, either financial or otherwise, to the beneficiary.
It is not even necessary that kinship shall exist between the parties. If the insured is under a moral obligation to render care
and assistance to the beneficiary in the time of the latter's need,
then the latter has an insurable interest, other than a mere pecuniary one, in the life of the former.'"[13] In the case of Kope-
tovske v. Mut. Life Ins. Co.,[13a] the Court held that a moral,
as distinguished from a legal, obligation resting on insurer
to render a pecuniary benefit or advantage to an assignee of certain life policies was sufficient to confer on such assignee an insurable interest, and the Court held that whether there was such
an obligation was a question for the jury. The Court said: "If,
from the facts in evidence, fair-minded men might honestly draw
different conclusions as to whether or not Berger's temporal affairs, his just hopes and well-grounded expectations of support,
of advantage in life, would be impaired by Rosenthal's death,
and as to whether or not the real purpose of the assignment of
the policies was not a wager, but to secure advantages supposed
to depend on Rosenthal's life, the questions are not of law, but
of fact, and are to be settled by the jury, under proper instructions.[14] We are of the opinion that men of that character might
thus differently conclude and that a court, taking that view of
the evidence most favorable to Berger and the bank, may not,
from such evidence and the inferences reasonably and justifiably
to be drawn therefrom, say that a verdict might not have been
found for them.[15] There was sufficient evidence to send the case

[13] Opitz v. Karel, 118 Wis. 527; 95 N. W. 948; 62 L. R. A. 982; 99 Am.
St. Rep. 1004; Chisholm v. Ins. Co., 52 Mo. 213; 14 Am. St. Rep. 414;
Cronin v. Ins. Co., 20 R. I. 570; 40 Atl. 497.

[13a] 111 C. C. A. 265; 187 Fed. 499.

[14] Mason & O. R. Co. v. Yockey, 103 Fed. 265, 267; 43 C. C. A. 228.

[15] Mason & O. R. Co. v. Yockey; Mt. Adams, etc., Ry. Co. v. Lowery,
74 Fed. 463; 20 C. C. A. 596; Milwaukee Mechanics' Ins. Co. v. Rhea,
123 Fed. 9; 60 C. C. A. 103; Rochford v. Penn. Co., 174 Fed. 81; 98 C.
C. A. 105; Erie R. Co. v. Rooney, 108 C. C. A. 118; 186 Fed. 16.

to the jury, and it was incumbent on the defendant to show that the assignment of the policies was but a gambling speculation on human life."[16] The Court of Appeals of Virginia has held[17] that an insurable interest is one which arises from the relations of the parties to such an extent as will justify a reasonable expectation of advantage, or benefit, from the continuance of the insured's life, though it is not necessary that such advantage be capable of pecuniary estimation, and in the same case it was held that good faith alone is not sufficient to sustain a policy taken upon the life of another by one without insurable interest. It is against public policy and contrary to law to permit anyone to obtain insurance upon the life of a human being by assignment, or otherwise, where such person has no insurable interest in the life of the insured.[18] The question of insurable interest most frequently arises where a policy has been assigned and the question of the validity of an assignment of a life insurance policy to one without insurable interest will be considered later.[19]

§ 297. **The Same Subject: Opposing Views.**—The doctrine that there must be an insurable interest to support a policy taken out on the life of another has been vigorously attacked by some writers[20] on the grounds not only that it is absurd to hold that human life is so sacred that public policy forbids one not interested in the continuance of the life of a person to obtain an insurance on it, but also that insurance policies should be like any other chose in action, or merchandise. We apprehend that the law of insurable interest is now too well established to look for any change, and moreover, the reasons upon which it rests are too substantial to allow any retrogression. Wagers may have been, and probably were, valid at common law, but modern law makers have decided that public policy requires wagering to be discountenanced because of its demoralizing tendencies. Insurance on

16 See also Northwestern Masonic Aid Ass'n v. Jones, 154 Pa. St. 99; 26 Atl. 253.

17 Chrisman v. Jones (Va.), 83 S. E. 1045.

18 Metropolitan Life Ins. Co. v. Elison, 72 Kan. 199; 83 Pac. 410; 3 L. R. A. (N. S.) 935 and note. Rylander v. Allen, 125 Ga. 206; 53 S. E. 1032; 6 L. R. A. (N. S.), 128.

19 *Post*, § 393.

20 Cooke on Life Ins., § 58, *et seq.;* Biddle on Ins., § 183.

life by persons having no interest in the continuance of such life, might not lead to an increase of murder, as insurance against fire by persons not interested in the property insured would stimulate arson, but it would certainly encourage fraud.   Whenever it becomes unnecessary for a policyholder to have any interest in the life of the insured we may expect to hear of numerous frauds on the insurers, for it is not difficult to concoct schemes against insurance companies and often make them succeed.[21]   In spite of the vast array of authorities in favor of the principle that an insurable interest must exist in order to make valid a policy of insurance upon life, the Supreme Court of the United States in a recent case,[22] says: ''On the other hand, life insurance has become in our days one of the best recognized forms of investment and self-compelled saving.   So far as reasonable safety permits, it is desirable to give to life policies the ordinary characteristics of property.   This is recognized by the bankruptcy law,[23] which provides that unless the cash surrender value of a policy like the one before us is secured to the trustee within thirty days after it has been stated, the policy shall pass to the trustee as assets. Of course, the trustee may have no interest in the bankrupt's life.   To deny the right to sell except to persons having such an interest is to diminish appreciably the value of the contract in the owner's hands.   The collateral difficulty that arose from regarding life insurance as a contract of indemnity only[24] long has disappeared.[25]   And cases in which a person having an interest lends himself to one without any, as a cloak to what is, in its inception, a wager, have no similarity to those where an honest contract is sold in good faith.''

[21] Mr. Cooke in a note cites the following authorities to sustain his view: Shannon v. Nugent, Hayes (Irish), 536; Schweiger v. Magee, Cooke & Alc. (Irish), 182; Trenton Mut. L. Ins. Co. v. Johnson, 4 Zab. (N. J.) 576; DeRouge v. Elliott, 23 N. J. Eq. 486; Vivar v. Supreme L. K. of P., 42 N. J. L. 455; 20 Atl. 36; Chisholm v. National Capital L. Ins. Co., 52 Mo. 213; Packard v. Conn. Mut. L. Ins. Co., 9 M. A. 469. As to lack of insurable interest being an incentive to crime; Ritter v. Smith, 70 Md. 261; 16 Atl. 187.

[22] Grigsby v. Russell, 222 U. S. 149; 56 L. Ed. 133; 36 L. R. A. (N. S.) 642.

[23] § 70.

[24] Godsall v. Boldero, 9 East 72.

[25] Phoenix Mut. L. Ins. Co. v. Bailey, 13 Wall. 616; 20 L. Ed. 501.

§ 298. **The Same Subject: Wagering Policies.**—As said in the previous sections, the right of a man to insure his own life and make the policy payable to whomsoever he chooses, irrespective of the question of insurable interest, has never been doubted,[26] but the transaction must not be a cover for a speculation and wager contravening the general policy of the law.[27] It is difficult, if not impossible, to state any general rule for determining when a policy is a wagering transaction; of necessity the facts in each particular case determine the question and courts like individuals may have different opinions on facts practically similar. In the case of Burbage v. Windley,[28] the Court said: "It thus clearly appears that the purpose of Windley, with the knowledge, consent and co-operation of Hammond, was to insure the latter's life in which he had no insurable interest, for his own benefit. He simply promised to pay the *feme* plaintiff of the money he might realize after the death of her husband $500, expecting to realize $9,500 for himself, less such premiums as he might pay. As the assured had no insurable interest in the life of the *cestui que vie*, the contract of insurance was simply a wager; it was not founded on any just of lawful consideration; it was a mere gambling speculation." The mere fact that the premium is paid by a third party who is payee of the policy, however, does not

[26] Connecticut Mut. Life Ins. Co. v. Schaefer, *supra;* Aetna Life Ins. Co. v. France, 94 U. S. 561; Goodrich v. Treat, 3 Colo. 408; Lemon v. Phoenix M. L. Ins. Co., 38 Conn. 294; Fairchild v. N. E. M. L. Ass'n, 51 Vt. 613; North Am. L. Ins. Co. v. Craigen, 6 Russ. & G. (Nova Scotia) 440; Elkhart, etc., v. Houghton, 103 Ind. 286; 2 N. E. 763; Bloomington M. L. B. Ass'n v. Blue, 120 Ill. 121; 11 N. E. 331; Heinlein v. Imperial' L. Ins. Co., 101 Mich. 250; 59 N. W. 615; 25 L. R. A. 627. See also cases cited in preceding sections.

[27] Mut. Ben. Ass'n v. Hoyt, 46 Mich. 473; Stevens v. Warren, 101 Mass. 564; Keystone M. B. Ass'n v. Norris, 115 Pa. St. 446; 8 Atl. 638; Ruth v. Katterman, 112 Pa. St. 251; Gilbert v. Moose, 104 Pa. St. 74. In this case the Court says: "If we admit that one man may insure his life for the benefit of another, who is neither a relative nor a creditor, our whole doctrine concerning wagering policies goes by the board." Ins. Co. v. Hogan, 80 Ill. 35; 22 Am. Rep. 180; Cammack v. Lewis, 15 Wall. 643; Exchange Bank v. Loh, 104 Ga. 446; 31 S. E. 459; 44 L. R. A. 372; Prudential Ins. Co. v. Hunn, 21 Ind App. 525; 52 N. E. 772.

[28] 108 N. C. 357; 12 S. E. 839; 12 L. R. A. 409.

make the contract a wagering one.[29]   Nor the taking out by a stranger of a policy on the life of another payable to one not having an insurable interest.[30]   In a recent case in Pennsylvania,[31] a State where the subject of insurable interest and wagering policies has been much discussed, the Supreme Court gives an intimation as to what should be a rule in determining insurable interest and what makes the policy a wagering one.   In this case the action was brought by the adminstrators of Grant to recover the amount of a policy taken out by Kline on Grant's life, less the debt of Grant to Kline.   The policy had been made payable to Kline and was for the sum of $3,000, while the debt of Grant was only $743, as Kline claimed, or $214 as claimed by the administrators.   The Court said: ''It was not disputed at the trial below that there was a *bona fide* indebtedness of Grant to Kline at the time the policy was taken out, of something over $300.   It was also in evidence that one or more policies had been taken out on Grant's life for Kline's benefit prior to the policy in question.   These policies had been abandoned because of the insolvency of the companies, or for other sufficient reason.   Kline had paid in premiums thereon several hundred dollars.   While the money thus fruitlessly paid in premiums may not have amounted to an insurable interest in the life of Grant, for the reason that such payments did not make him a creditor for their amount, we think they show good faith in the transaction.   This case is to be determined upon the facts as they existed at the time the last policy was taken out; and if both Grant and Kline saw proper to treat the premiums paid as an insurable interest, Grant's administrators have no standing to say they were not. The company could have defended upon this ground, but it did not.   It paid the money over to Kline without question.   This brings us to the main question, was the amount of insurance so disproportioned to Kline's interest in the life of Grant as to make this a wagering policy?   We approach this question with

[29] Mut. L. Ins. Go. v. Blodgett, 8 Tex. Civ. App. 45; 27 S. W. 286.   See *ante*, § 295.

[30] McCann. v. Metropolitan L. Ins. Co., 177 Mass. 280; 58 N. E. 1026; Union Cent. L. Ins. Co. v. Hilliard, 63 Ohio St. 478; 59 N. E. 230; 53 L. R. A. 462.

[31] Grant v. Kline; 115 Pa. St. 618; 9 Atl. 150.

caution, the more so that this court has not yet laid down a rule upon this subject. That we shall be compelled some day to do so is possible. We have said that the sum insured must not be disproportioned to the interest the holder of the policy has in the life insured. To take out a policy of $5,000 to secure a debt of five dollars would be such a palpable wager that no court would hesitate to declare it so as a matter of law. Care must be taken, also, that a debt shall not be collusively contracted for the mere purpose of creating an insurable interest. Mr. Dickens, in his inimitable 'Pickwick Papers,' has shown how a debt may be created for the purpose of lodging the debtor in prison by collusion with the creditor. Speaking for myself, it may be that a policy taken out by a creditor on the life of his debtor ought to be limited to the amount of the debt, with interest, and the amount of premiums, with interest thereon, during the expectancy of life as shown by the Carlisle tables. This view, however, has never yet been adopted by this court in any adjudicated case; nor do we feel compelled to define the disproportion now in view of the particular facts of the case in hand. We do not regard it as either immoral or wagering for Kline to attempt to secure the sums he had already fruitlessly paid in premiums on Grant's life; and if Grant had no objection thereto, and assisted him therein, I do not see that anyone could object to this but the company. Again, we have the declarations of Grant that he owed Kline a considerable sum of money—the precise amount not stated; that Kline had aided him in various ways; had never refused him a favor, etc. In view of this connection by marriage, and of their admitted relations, it is at least probable that Kline had aided him at many times and in various ways pecuniarily that are not represented by any evidences of debt. And, if the sum insured was regarded by Grant as a reasonable amount to indemnify Kline, with what grace can Grant's administrators come in and allege that it was not? They have no possible equity. Grant never paid one dollar of the premiums; and if they are allowed now to recover, it is not by virtue of any equity, but by force of an inexorable rule of public policy which treats it as a wagering policy, and declares the policyholder a trustee for the person insured as to the entire proceeds, save only the money actually loaned with the premiums paid. Assuming, then, that

Kline might, with Grant's consent and as against his administrators, lawfully seek to indemnify himself for the premiums paid
and lost, we have the sum of $743.56 as the amount which Kline
was out of pocket. We do not know what Grant's expectation
of life was when the policy was taken out, and there is nothing
before us upon which we could base any reliable opinion. But
it appears he was sixty-five years of age and was an unusually
good risk. While we do not know what the amount of the annual
premium was, we do know that it must have been a considerable
sum on $3,000 for a man of sixty-five years; and, with the annual
interest, it would roll up rapidly. That Grant died within a year
is not to the purpose, he might have lived long enough for the
debt and premiums at compound interest to have exceeded the
amount of the policy. Surely, in such case, we cannot say, as a
matter of law, that the disproportion was so great as to make it
a wagering policy.'' In another case in the same court,[32] where
A, an old woman, was living with her daughter, and B, the
father of her son-in-law, with whom the latter lived, had A's
life insured, his only interest being, as stated in the application,
that he had "kept her a certain length of time and promises to
keep her as long as she lives.'' Upon the death of A, B collected
the amount of the policies and was sued by A's executors for
the money so collected; it was held that as a matter of law, the
insurance could not be held to be speculative.[33] An agreement
of the beneficiary to pay the funeral expenses of the insured creates an insurable interest under certain circumstances.[34] And one
who has advanced money to pay premiums has an insurable interest.[35] The rule recently reasserted by the Supreme Court of
Pennsylvania is that a creditor may lawfully take out insurance
on the life of his debtor to an amount to cover the debt and cost
of the insurance, together with interest on such amounts during
the expectancy of the life of the assured according to the Carlisle
tables; and the fact that the debtor dies before the expiration
of his expectancy will not affect the validity of the policy or the

[32] Batdorff Exr. v. Fehler, 9 Atl. 468.
[33] Fitzgerald v. Hartford L. & A. Ins. Co., 56 Conn. 116; 13 Atl. 673.
[34] Burke v. Prudential Ins. Co., 155 Pa. St. 295; 26 Atl. 445.
[35] Reed v. Provident Savings L. A. Soc., 36 App. Div. 250; 55 N. Y.
Supp. 292.

right to recover the whole amount.[36] A promise on the part of a person not having an insurable interest to pay to the wife of the assured a specified amount after his death in consideration of permission to the promisor to insure his life is against public policy as being a gambling transaction and cannot be enforced.[37] Where a debtor at the solicitation of his creditor, to whom he owed $600, effected an insurance of $2,000 on his life for the benefit of his creditor, the latter being designated in the policy as the beneficiary; and agreeing to pay the expense of effecting the insurance and keeping it up, with a condition that the debtor might at any time pay the debt and reimburse the creditor, and thereby become entitled to an assignment of the policy; it was held[38] after the death of the assured and payment of the amount named in the policy to the beneficiary, that the administrator of the deceased could not maintain an action against the beneficiary to recover the excess over the debt and amount of premiums paid.

§ 299. **The Same Subject: Meritorious Object.**—An interesting case was recently decided by the Supreme Court of North Carolina, where a policy of life insurance was procured by a religious society, supported largely by voluntary contributions, on the life of one of its members. The Court, is holding the policy void as a wagering contract, said:[39] ''Except in cases where there are ties of blood or marriage, the expectation of advantage from the continuance of the life insured, in order to be reasonable,

[36] Ulrich v. Reinoehl, 143 Pa. St. 238; 22 Atl. 862; where the insurance was on a man of 42 for $3,000 to cover a debt of $100; Shaffer v. Spangler, 144 Pa. St. 223; 22 Atl. 865; Ritter v. Smith, 70 Md. 261; 16 Atl. 890, where certificates to the amount of $6,500, yielding, however, only $2,124.82, were taken out to secure a debt of $1,000. An insurance of $15,000 for a debt of $1,200 has been held not speculative. Equitable L. Ass'n Soc. v. Hazelwood, 75 Tex. 338; 12 S. W. 621. Nor $2,000 for a debt of $700. McHale v. McDonnell, 175 Pa. St. 632; 34 Atl. 966. Nor $5,000 for a debt of $2,001. Givens v. Veeder, 9 N. M. 256; 50 Pac. 316. Nor $2,000 for a debt of $300, it not being shown what the expectancy was. Nye v. Grand Lodge A. O. U. W., 9 Ind. App. 131; 36 N. E. 429. For an example of an unconscionable transaction, see United Security, etc., Co. v. Ritchey, 187 Pa. St. 173; 40 Atl. 978.

[37] Burbage v. Windley's Exrs., 108 N. C. 357; 12 N. E. 839.

[38] Amick v. Butler, 111 Ind. 578; 12 N. E. 518.

[39] Trinity College v. Travelers' Ins. Co., 113 N. C. 244; 18 S. E. 175.

as the law counts reasonableness, must be founded in the existence of some contract between the person whose life is insured and the beneficiary, the fulfillment of which the death will prevent; it must appear that by the death there may come damage which can be estimated under some rule of law, for which loss or damage the insurance company has undertaken to indemnify the beneficiary under its policy. When the contractual relation does not exist, and there are no ties of blood or marriage, an insurance policy becomes what the law denominates a "wagering contract," and under its rules, made and enforced in the interest of the best public policy, all such contracts must be declared illegal and void, no matter what good object the parties may really have in view. The end will not, in the eye of the law, justify the means." A building association has no insurable interest in the life of a stockholder.[40]

§ 300. **The Same Subject: Relatives.**—Although positive in its denunciation of wager policies, the Supreme Court of the United States has been liberal in its views concerning the insurable interest of relatives. In a leading case[41] it said: "The natural affection in cases of this kind is considered as more powerful—as operating more efficaciously—to protect the life of the assured than any other consideration. But in all cases there must be a reasonable ground, founded upon the relations of the parties to each other, either pecuniary, or of blood or affinity, to expect some benefit or advantage from the continuance of the life of the assured. Otherwise the contract is a mere wager, by which the party taking the policy is directly interested in the early death of the assured." The same Court has held[42] that a sister has an insurable interest in the life of her brother from the mere relationship. The same principle was also determined by the Supreme Court of Massachusetts in an early case.[43] The Supreme Court of Pennsylvania, *In re* Phillips Estate, cited *supra*, held that

40 Tate v. Commercial Bldg. Ass'n., 97 Va. 74; 33 S. E. 382; 45 L. R. A. 243.

41 Warnock v. Davis, 104 U. S. 779.

42 Aetna L. Ins. Co. v. France, 94 U. S. 561. See also *In re* Phillips' Est., 238 Pa. St. 423; 86 Atl. 289; Ann. Cas. 1914C, 282.

43 Lord v. Dall, 12 Mass. 115; 7 Am. Dec. 38. See also Hosmer v. Welch, 107 Mich. 470; 67 N. W. 504.

where the insured was childless and in good faith took out a policy in favor of his sister from a desire to make provision for her, the relationship between them created in her an insurable interest in his life. The Court of Appeals of Kentucky,[44] has said: "Where the relationship, as in the case of husband and wife, parent and child, sister and brother, is so close as to preclude the probability that mercenary motives would induce the sacrifice of life to gain the insurance, the element of pecuniary consideration is not deemed essential to sustain the validity of the policy."[45] Still it has been held by other courts that the mere relationship of brother or sister gives no insurable interest.[46] All these cases must be read with the qualification that if the insured takes out the policy and pays the premium he can make it payable to whomsoever he pleases, or if the relative is a creditor, the debt creates an insurable interest. Husband and wife each has an insurable interest in the life of the other,[47] and the relationship between parent and child is itself, it is said, sufficient to give either an insurable interest in the life of the other.[48] It has been held, however, that the mere relation of father and son is not sufficient to give an adult son an insurable interest in the father's life.[49] An illegitimate daughter has an insurable interest in the life of her father.[50] A brother has, however, been held to have no insurable interest in the life of a brother;[51] but under all circumstances a

[44] Hess v. Segenfelter, 127 Ky. 348; 105 S. W. 476; 14 L. R. A. (N. S.) 1172.

[45] See also Hahn v. Supreme Lodge of the Pathfinder, 136 Ky. 823; 125 S. W. 250; Barnes v. London, etc., L. I. Co., 1 Q. B. (Eng.) 864; Hosmer v. Welch, 107 Mich. 470; 65 N. W. 280; 67 N. W. 504.

[46] Lewis v. Phoenix Mut. Life Ins. Co., 39 Conn. 100; Masonic Beneficial Ass'n v. Bunch, 109 Mo. 560; 19 S. W. 23.

[47] Marquet v. Aetna Life Ins. Co., 128 Tenn. 213; 159 S. W. 733.

[48] Woods v. Woods, 130 Ky. 162; 113 S. W. 79.

[49] Life Ins. Clearing Co. v. O'Neill, 45 C. C. A. 641; 106 Fed. 800; 34 L. R. A. 225; Chicago Guaranty Fund, etc., Soc. v. Dyer, 79 Ill. App. 100; New York L. Ins. Co. v. Greenlee, 42 Ind. App. 82; 84 N. E. 1101.

[50] Maxey v. Franklin L. Ins. Co., (Tex. Civ. A.) 164 S. W. 438; Overton v. Colored K. of P. (Tex. Civ. A.) 173 S. W. 472.

[51] Lewis v. Phoenix Mut. Life Ins. Co., 39 Conn. 100; Fidelity Mut. L. Ass'n v. Jeffords, 46 C. C. A. 377; 107 Fed. 402; 53 L. R. A. 193. See also Reynolds v. Prudential Ins. Co., 88 Mo. App. 679.

wife' has an insurable interest in the life of her husband;[52] though it has been said that to support the interest she must be his law-'ful wife;[53] and divorce subsequent to the policy does not vitiate such policy,[54] and it has even been held that a woman, living with a man as his wife,'though not legally married to him, has an insurable interest in his life.[55] This is especially true if the insured paid the premiums.[56] If a woman is the wife of the insured the fact that she is named in the policy'by another name does not affect her rights.[57] The fact that a decree of divorce requires the husband to pay his wife alimony gives her an insurable interest in his life.[58] In a mutual benefit society the description of the beneficiary as the "wife" of the member, when she was not so in fact, has been held not to invalidate the designation.[59] A woman engaged to be married to a man has an insurable interest in his life;[60] but in Massachusetts an engaged woman has been held not to be a "dependent" upon her betrothed within the meaning of the statute authorizing members of benefit societies

[52] Conn. Mut. Life Ins. Co. v. Schaefer, 94 U. S. 457; Aetna Life Ins. Co. v. France, 94 U. S. 561; Warnock v. Davis, 104 U. S. 779; Baker v. Union Mut. Life Ins. Co., 43 N. Y. 283; Gambs v. Covenant Mut. Life Ins. Co., 50 Mo. 44; Ellison v. Straw, 116 Wis. 207; 92 N. W. 1094.

[53] Holabird v. Atlantic Ins. Co., 2 Dill. 166; 2 Ins. L. J. 588; Keeper v. Grand Lodge A. O. U. W., 38 M. A. 543; Filley v. Illinois L. Ins. Co., 93 Kan. 193; 144 Pac. 257, affg. 91 Kan. 220; 137 Pac. 793.

[54] Conn. Mut. Life Ins. Co. v. Schaefer, supra; McKee v. Phoenix Mut. Life Ins. Co., 28 Mo. 383; 75 Am. Dec. 129. But see Tyler v. Odd Fellows, etc., Soc., 145 Mass. 134; 13 N. E. 360. And as to divorce in Kentucky terminating interest, Sea v. Conrad, 155 Ky. 51; 159 S. W. 622. See also post, § 353.

[55] Equitable Ass. Soc. v. Patterson, 41 Ga. 338. See also Scott v. Scott, 25 (Part II) Ky. L. 1356; 77 S. W. 1122; Lampkin v. Travelers' Ins. Co., 11 Colo. App. 249; 52 Pac. 1040; Ruoff v. John Hancock M. L. I. Co., 86 App. Div. 447; 83 N. Y. Supp. 758.

[56] Mut. Ben. L. Ins. Co. v. Cummings, 66 Ore. 272; 133 Pac. 1169.

[57] Watson v. Centennial Mut. Life Ass'n, 21 Fed. 698.

[58] Begley v. Muller, 137 Ill. App. 278.

[59] Durian v. Central Verein, etc., 7 Daly 168.

[60] Chisholm v. National C. Life Ins. Co., 52 Mo. 213; 18 Am. Rep. 414. See also Bogart v. Thompson, 24 Misc. 581; 53 N. Y. Supp. 662; Opitz v. Karel, 118 Wis. 527; 95 N. W. 948; Taylor v. Travelers' Ins. Co., 15 Tex. Civ. App. 254; 39 S. W. 185.

to designate "dependents" as their beneficiaries;[61] and in one society at least a member is expressly allowed by the charter to designate his betrothed as his beneficiary.[62] Unless it appears that the wife was insane, or an invalid, the presumption is that she is a helpmate to her husband and he has an insurable interest in her life.[63] The mere relationship of a father and son has been held not to give the latter an insurable interest in the life of the former;[64] although other courts have decided that a son has an insurable interest in the life of a father·whom he may be compelled by law to support,[65] and a grandson in the life of his grandfather who resided with him.[66] And a granddaughter in the life of her grandfather;[67] and a daughter in the life of her father;[68] and a widow in the life of her brother;[69] and an orphan in life of uncle who had brought her up;[70] and an aunt in life of niece who lives with her.[71] In a number of cases, however, the rule has been declared that from the very relationship of the parties the parent has an insurable interest in the life of the

[61] Am. Legion of Honor v. Perry, 140 Mass. 580. But the same court has held that a betrothed woman may in fact be a dependent. McCarthy v. New England, etc., 153 Mass. 314; 26 N. E. 866. The rule of· Am. Legion of Honor v. Perry, was affirmed in Palmer v. Welch, 132 Ill. 141; 23 N. E. 412; affg. 33 Ill. App. 186. See *post*, § 336.

[62] Knights of Pythias.

[63] Currier v. Continental Life Ins. Co., 57 Vt. 496.

[64] Guardian Mut. Life Ins. Co. v. Hogan, 80 Ill. 35; 22 Am. Rep. 180; Life Ins. Clearing Co. v. O'Neill, 45 C. C. A. 641; 106 Fed. 800; 54 L. R. A. 225, where valuable note is appended. And a mother as such has no insurable interest in the life of her son. Prudential Ins. Co. v. Hunn, 21 Ind. App. 525; 52 N. E. 772. But see Wakeman v. Metropolitan Life Ins. Co., 30 Ont. 705.

[65] Reserve Mut. Life Ins. Co. v. Kane, 81 Pa. St. 154; 22 Am. Rep. 741.

[66] Elkhart Mut., etc., Ass'n v. Houghton, 103 Ind. 286. But see Burton v. Conn. Mut. L. Ins. Co., cited later in this section.

[67] Corbett v. Metropolitan L. Ins. Co., 37 App. Div. 152; 55 N. Y. Supp. 775.

[68] Farmers, etc., Ass'n v. Johnson, 118 Ia. 282; 91 N. W. 1074; Geoffrey v. Gilbert, 5 App. Div. 98; 38 N. Y. Supp. 643; Standard L. & A. Ass'n v. Catlin, 106 Mich. 138; 63 N. W. 897. But *contra*, Metropolitan L. I. Co. v. Blesch, 22 Ky. L. 530; 58 S. W. 436.

[69] Sternberg v. Levi, 159 Mo. 617; 60 S. W. 1114; 53 L. R. A. 438.

[70] McGraw v. Metropolitan L. I. Co., 41 W. N. C. 62; 5 Pa. Sup. Ct. 488.

[71] Cronin v. Vermont L. Ins. Co., 20 R. I. 570; 40 Atl. 497.

child, except possibly when the child is of age,[72] and the child in the life of the parent.[73] A mother has an insurable interest in the life of her son.[74] But a mother not residing with a son has been held not to be a "dependent" upon him within the meaning of the statutes of Massachusetts.[75] When a person assumed the position of father to one not related to him the latter has an insurable interest in the life of such person,[76] and a sister has an insurable interest in the life of her half-sister whom she has promised to support.[77] It has been said that a daughter by the mere virtue of relationship has no interest in her mother's life,[78] nor son in life of mother.[79] In Missouri the rule has been laid down that the insurable interest in the life of another person must be a direct and pecuniary interest, and that a person has not such an interest in the life of his wife or child simply in the character of a husband or parent.[80] In the same State it has been held that an uncle has no insurable interest in the life of a nephew;[81] nor niece in the life of her uncle;[82] nor a man in the

[72] Mitchell v. Union Life Ins. Co., 45 Me. 104; Worthington v. Curtis, L. R. 1 Ch. D. 419; 45 L. J. Ch. D. 259; 33 L. T. (N. S.) 828; 24 W. R. 221.

[73] Loomis v. Eagle Life Ins. Co., 6 Gray 396; Valley Mut. Life Ass'n v. Teewalt, 79 Va. 421; Mitchell v. Union Life Ins. Co., 45 Me. 104; 71 Am. Dec. 529; Reserve Mut. Life Ins. Co. v. Kane, 81 Pa. St. 154; Grattan v. National Life Ins. Co., 15 Hun. 74; Corson's Appeal, 113 Pa. St. 438; 6 Atl. 213; Forbes v. Am. Mut. Life Ins. Co., 15 Gray 249. Children named in a policy need not show an insurable interest. Vorheis v. People, etc., 91 Mich. 469; 51 N. W. 1109.

[74] Reif v. Union Life Ins. Co., 17 Ins. Chron. 3; 18 C. L. J. 347; Neal v. Shirley, 137 Ky. 818; 127 S. W. 471; O'Rourke v. Jno. Hancock M. L. I. Co., 10 Misc. 405; 31 N. Y. Supp. 130. But see Prudential Ins. Co. v. Hunn, 21 Ind. App. 525; 52 N. E. 772.

[75] Elsey v. Odd Fellows' Mut. Relief Ass'n, 142 Mass. 224.

[76] Carpenter v. U. S. Ins. Co., 161 Pa. St. 9; 28 Atl. 943.

[77] Barnes v. London, etc., L. Ins. Co., 8 Times L. R. 143; 1 Q. B. 864.

[78] Continental Life Ins. Co. v. Volger, 89 Ind. 572.

[79] Peoples, etc., Ass'n v. Templeton, 16 Ind. App. 126; 44 N. E. 809. But see Crosswell v. Com. Ind. Co., 51 S. C. 103; 28 S. E. 200.

[80] Charter Oak Life Ins. Co. v. Brant, 47 Mo. 419; Gambs v. Covenant Mut. Life Ins. Co., 50 Mo. 44.

[81] Singleton v. St. Louis, etc., Life Ins. Co., 66 Mo. 63; 27 Am. Rep. 321; nor a niece, Prudential Ins. Co. v. Jenkins, 15 Ind. App. 297; 43 N. E. 1056. To the same effect that the relationship of uncle and niece gives no insurable interest are Metropolitan L. Ins. Co. v. Elesin, 72

life of his half-uncle other than as a creditor;[83] and the Supreme Court of Pennsylvania has said[84] that a nephew has no insurable interest in the life of his aunt. The relationship of cousins does not create an insurable interest.[85] A brother has an insurable interest in the life of a brother.[86] A stepson has no insurable interest in his stepfather's father;[87] nor a stepson in the life of his stepfather,[88] nor a grandchild in life of grandfather,[89] but a son can insure his life for the benefit of his father;[90] nor has a son-in-law in the life of his mother-in-law;[91] nor his father-in-law;[92] nor one in the life of his brother-in-law.[93] The Supreme Court of Connecticut has held that the providing by a relative of a home and proper care for life is sufficient consideration for the assignment by a laboring woman, living apart from her husband and childless, of her life insurance policy if the transaction was in good faith and not a wager.[94] A friend as such has no insurable interest in life of a friend.[95] It has been said[96] that the insurable interest

Kan. 199; 83 Pac. 410; 3 L. R. A. (N. S.) 934; McRae v. Wamack, 98 Ark. 52; 135 S. W. 807; Equitable Life Ass. Soc. v. O'Connor, 162 Ky. 262; 172 S. W. 496; Hull v. Grand Lodge, etc., 32 Ky. L. 212; 105 S. W. 479; Doody Co. v. Green, 131 Ga. 568; 62 S. E. 984; Hardy v. Aetna L. Ins. Co., 152 N. C. 286; 67 S. W. 471.

[82] Wilton v. New York L. Ins. Co., 34 Tex. Civ. A. 156; 78 S. W. 403.

[83] Deal v. Hainley, 135 Mo. App. 507; 116 S. W. 1.

[84] Appeal of Corson, 113 Pa. St. 438; 6 Atl. 213.

[85] Ryan v. Metropolitan L. Ins. Co., 117 Mo. App. 347; Hess v. Segenfelter, 32 Ky. 225; 105 S. W. 476.

[86] Hahn v. Supreme Lodge of the Pathfinder, 136 Ky. 823; 125 S. W. 259. But see to the contrary, Locher v. Kueckenmiester, 120 Mo. App. 701; 98 S. W. 92.

[87] Gilbert v. Moose's Admr., 104 Pa. St. 74.

[88] United Brethren Aid Soc. v. McDonald, 122 Pa. St. 324; 15 Atl. 439.

[89] Burton v. Conn. M. L. Ins. Co., 119 Ind. 207; 21 N. E. 746.

[90] Tucker v. Mut. Ben. L. Ins. Co., 4 N. Y. Supp. 505.

[91] Rombach v. Piedmont, etc., Ins. Co., 35 La. Ann. 233; Stoner v. Line 16 W. N. C. 187. Nor mother-in-law in life of son-in-law. Adams v. Reed, 18 Ky. L. 858; 36 S. W. 568.

[92] Ramsey v. Myers, 6 Pa. Distr. 468.

[93] Chandler v. Mut. Life, etc., Ass'n, 131 Ga. 82; 61 S. E. 1036.

[94] Fitzgerald v. Hartford L. & A. Ins. Co., 56 Conn. 116; 13 Atl. 673.

[95] Condell v. Woodward, 16 Ky. L. 142; 29 S. W. 614; Glassey v. Metropolitan L. Ins. Co., 84 Hun. 350; 32 N. Y. Supp. 335.

[96] McFarlane v. Robertson, 137 Ga. 132; 73 S. E. 490. See also Hardy v. Aetna Life Ins. Co., 154 N. C. 430; 170 S. E. 828.

587

of a niece in the life of an uncle depends upon the existence of such facts as will create a reasonable expectation on her part of benefit from the continuance of his life, but where the only expectation of a pecuniary benefit is only an occasional gift, there is no insurable interest on the part of the niece in the life of the uncle.[97] Where plaintiff had loaned money to his wife's brother he had an insurable interest in the brother's life.[98] And the wife of a man taking a seventeen-year-old nephew into his family has an insurable interest in the nephew's life,[99] and one to whom assured assigns a life policy with the intention that she shall become on his death custodian of his minor children, has an insurable interest.[100] An agreement between the father and son that the son should insure the life of his mother and support his father for life out of the proceeds, does not vest in him the insurable interest in her life which his father had.[101]

§ 301. **The Same Subject: Creditors.**—A creditor has an insurable interest in the life of his debtor;[102] and can insure the life of a debtor without his consent;[103] but such interest is limited to the amount of the debt.[104] This rule applies to fraternal bene-

[97] Wilton v. New York Life Ins. Co., 34 Tex. Civ. App. 156; 78 S. W. 403.

[98] Dewey v. Fleischer, 129 Wis. 591; 109 N. W. 525.

[99] Mohr v. Prudential Ins. Co., 32 R. I. 177; 78 Atl. 554.

[100] Matlock v. Bledsoe, 77 Ark. 60; 90 S. W. 848.

[101] Schwerdt v. Schwerdt, 235 Ill. 386; 85 N. E. 613.

[102] Rawls v. American Ins. Co., 27 N. Y. 282; Mowry v. Ins. Co., 9 R. I. 346; Cunningham v. Smith's Exrs., 70 Pa. St. 450; Conn. Mut. L. Ins. Co. v. Schaefer, 94 U. S. 457; Cammack v. Lewis, 15 Wall. 643. But not in the life of his debtor's wife. Wheeland v. Atwood, 42 W. N. C. 178; 7 Pa. Super Ct. 86; Cameron v. Barcus, 31 Tex. Civ. App. 46; 71 S. W. 423; Lake v. N. Y. Life Ins. Co., 120 La. 971; 45 Sou. 959; Peoria L. Ass'n v. Hines, 132 Ill. App. 642.

[103] Suc. of Hearing, 26 La. Ann. 326.

[104] Cammack v. Lewis, *supra;* Warnock v. Davis, 104 U. S. 779; Drysdale v. Piggott, etc., 22 Beav. 238; Von Lindeman v. Desborough, 3 Car. & P. 353; 8 Barn. & C. 586; Ruth v. Katterman, 112 Pa. St. 251; Appeal of Corson, 113 Pa. St. 438; 6 Atl. 213; Siegrist Admr. v. Schmoltz, 113 Pa. St. 326; 6 Atl. 47; Exchange Bank v. Loh, 104 Ga. 446; 31 S. E. 459; 44 L. R. A. 372; Strode v. Meyer Bros., etc., 101 Mo. App. 627; 74 S. W. 379; Belknap v. Johnson, 114 Ia. 265; 86 N. W. 267; *ante,* § 295; *post,* § 558.

ficiary societies in the absence of some controlling prohibition.[105] The debt to give an insurable interest must be valid. The holder of a note. given for money won at play has no insurable interest in the debtor's life;[106] nor does a mere moral claim confer insurable interest;[107] but the fact that a debt is barred by the statute of limitations does not deprive a creditor of insurable interest;[108] nor that the debtor is insolvent without prospects of becoming solvent.[109] nor does the fact that the debtor is an infant.[110] It has been said[111] that to give a creditor an insurable interest in the life of the debtor he must have a valid existing debt and on the death of insured only retain the amount of the debt, premiums paid and interest. A partner has an insurable interest in the life of a partner;[112] but it ceases when such partner holding the insurance retires from the firm indebted to it.[113] Where the premiums are paid out of partnership funds, the partners have an insurable interest in the life of each other and if one dies the other can collect and retain the amount of the policy.[114] Where partners take out life policies on their several lives, payable to the firm, the amount of a policy of a partner dying after the dissolution of the firm must be paid to his representative and not to the surviving partner.[115] It has been said that the insurable interest of a partner where a policy was assigned to him is ex-

---

[105] Chambers v. Great State Council, etc., (W. Va.) 86 S. E. 467.

[106] Dwyder v. Edie, Ang. on Ins., § 296; 2 Parke Ins. (7th Ed.) 639.

[107] Guardian M. L. Ins. Co. v. Hogan, 80 Ill. 35.

[108] Rawls v. American L. Ins. Co., 27 N. Y. 282; Chicago Title and Trust Co. v. Haxtan, 120 Ill. App. 626.

[109] Morrow v. National L. Ass'n, 184 Mo. App. 308; 168 S. W. 881.

[110] Rivers v. Gregg, 5 Rich. Eq. 274.

[111] Taussig v. United Security L. & S. Co., 231 Pa. 16; 79 Atl. 810.

[112] Morrell v. Trenton, etc., L. Ins. Co., 10 Cush. 282; 57 Am. Dec. 92 and note; Valton v. National F. Ins. Co., 22 Barb. 9; 20 N. Y. 32; Conn. M. L. Ins. Co. v. Luchs, 108 U. S. 498; Hoyt v. N. Y. L. Ins. Co., 3 Bosw. 440; Bevin v. Conn. M. L. Ins. Co., 23 Conn. 244; *post*, §§ 393 and 559. But *contra*, see Powell v. Mut. Ben. L. Ins. Co., 123 N. C. 103; 31 S. E. 381.

[113] Cheeves v. Anders (Tex. Civ. App.), 25 S. W. 324.

[114] Rush v. Hawkins, 135 Ga. 128; 68 S. E. 1035. See also Rahders, etc., v. People's Bank, 113 Minn. 496; 130 N. W. 16.

[115] Ruth v. Flynn, 126 Colo. App. 171; 142 Pac. 194.

empt from the indebtedness of the insured.[116] A judgment creditor has an insurable interest in the life of the debtor,[117] and an agreement for further advances for which the policy was to stand as security gives an additional insurable interest.[118] A bondsman has an insurable interest in the life of the person on whose bond he is a surety;[119] and joint obligors in a bond in each other's lives;[120] and a surety on a note in the life of the principal;[121] a corporation in the life of its manager;[122] and a tenant has an insurable interest in the landlord's life when the latter is himself only a tenant for life, because the term depends upon the continuance of the life.[123] Where a member of a mining association employs a substitute to represent him and work in his stead in the mines, he has an insurable interest in the life of his substitute.[124] A master has an insurable interest in the life of his servant,[125] and a servant in the life of his master.[126] A general assignment by the debtor does not destroy the insurable interest of the creditor.[127] It has been held[128] that a creditor who insures the life of the debtor in his own name is entitled to the proceeds of the entire policy. Generally he can only retain the amount of the debt, premiums and interest.[129] The purchaser of a policy of insurance on a life in which he has no insurable interest except as a creditor, holds the proceeds of the policy above his debt

[116] Smith v. Hessey (Tex. Civ. App.), 134 S. W. 256.
[117] Walker v. Larkin, 127 Ind. 100; 26 N. E. 684.
[118] Curtiss v. Aetna L. Ins. Co., 90 Cal. 245; 27 Pac. 211.
[119] Scott v. Dickson, 108 Pa. St. 6.
[120] Brandon v. Saunders, 25 W. R. 650.
[121] Lea v. Hinton, 5 De G., M. & G. 823; Embry v. Haris, 107 Ky. 61; 52 S. W. 958.
[122] Mechanics' Nat. Bk. v. Comins, 72 N. H. 12; 55 Atl. 191. See also next section.
[123] Sides v. Knickerbocker L. Ins. Co., 16 Fed. 650.
[124] Trenton, etc., Ins. Co. v. Johnson, 24 N. J. L. 576.
[125] Miller v. Eagle Ins. Co., 2 E. D. Smith, 268; Summers v. U. S., etc., Trust Co., 13 La. Ann. 504; Woodfin v. Asheville, etc., Ins. Co., 6 Jones L. 558.
[126] Hebden v. West, 3 Best & Sm. 579; 32 L. J. Q. B. 85; 9 Jur. (N. S.) 747; 7 L. T. 854; 11 W. R. 422.
[127] Manhattan L. Ins. Co. v. Hennessy, 39 C. C. A. 624; 99 Fed. 64.
[128] Fitzgerald v. Rawlings Imp. Co., 114 Md. 470; 79 Atl. 915.
[129] Deal v. Hainley, 135 Mo. App. 507; 116 S. W. 1. See post, § 558.

in trust for the beneficiaries.[130] In this connection it is well to consider the effect of the bankrupt law upon the question to what extent a life insurance policy is a mere chosen action.[131] The official undertakers of an association whose business was to insure to each of its members a sum to defray his funeral expenses, deriving profits through sale of supplies, have no insurable interest in the lives of the member.[132] Where there are no ties of blood there must be an insurable interest under some contract, fulfillment of which would be prevented by death.[133]

§ 302. **Right of Corporation to Insure Life of Officer.**—In the case of Keckley v. Coshocton Glass Co.[134] the Court said: "In the first place, it is a misconception of the law to insist that a life insurance policy is a contract of indemnity merely. The later and better considered view is that a contract of life insurance is not a contract of indemnity, but is a contract to pay to the beneficiary a certain sum of money in the event of death.[135] So that, if the policy was valid in its inception and remained valid until its maturity, the beneficiary is entitled to the whole of the stipulated sum. Again, it does not appear that the purpose of the insurance was limited in indemnifying the company against loss by the death of Gainor while connected with the company. In the absence of any showing to the contrary, it may have been, and probably was in part, intended to secure the company against loss of his services at any time and in any way; and the courts below expressly find that Gainor represented that these policies belonged to, and were assets of, the company, and that he thereby obtained credit from banks and creditors and induced other persons to purchase stock in the company. From all this it may justly be inferred that such was the principal purpose to be effected by the insurance; and Gainor and his legal representatives would be estopped from claiming the contrary. And further, it thus

[130] Irons v. U. S. Life Ins. Co., 128 Ky. 640; 108 S. W. 904; Bendet v. Ellis, 120 Tenn. 277; 111 S. W. 795.

[131] See *post*, § 392.

[132] State v. Willett, 171 Ind. 296; 86 N. E. 68.

[133] Hinton v. Mut. Reserve Fund Life Ass'n, 135 N. C. 314; 47 S. E. 474; 65 L. R. A. 161.

[134] 86 Ohio St. 213; 99 N. E. 299; Ann. Cas. 1913-B.

[135] 1 Joyce on Ins., § 26.

591

distinctly appearing that the company had a direct pecuniary interest in the life and personal services of Gainor, the insurance for the benefit of the company was based on an insurable interest and was valid; and whether such insurable interest continued until the maturity of the policies or ceased before the maturity of the policy in the one case or ceased before the written assignment in the other case, is not material; for it has been held that the want of insurable interest is available only to the insurer,[136] and if that is too broad a statement of the law, there is abundant authority for holding that when the insurer has recognized the validity of the policy by paying the amount of the policy to the beneficiary, or into court, other parties claiming an interest in the fund cannot object on the ground that the beneficiary named in the policy had no insurable interest.[137] In the case of Mutual Life Ins. Co. v. Armstrong & Co.[138] the Court says: 'In the case of Mechanics' National Bank v. Comins,[139] it was held that any reasonable expectation of pecuniary benefit or advantage, either directly or indirectly, from the continued life of another creates an insurable interest in such life, though there may be no claim upon the person whose life is insured that can be recognized in law or in equity. The opinion says in part: 'It is hardly necessary to say that the success of a corporate enterprise may be so interwoven with the personality of its manager that its stock is taken, and money is loaned to carry it on, as much in reliance upon that personality as upon the intrinsic merit of the enterprise; and no good reason appears why a stockholder or creditor, the value of whose investment may be reasonably said to depend

[136] Chicago Title, etc., Co. v. Haxtun, 129 Ill. App. 626; Langford v. Freeman, 60 Ind. 55.

[137] Langford v. Freeman, 60 Ind. 46, *supra;* Standard L., etc., Ins. Co. v. Catlin, 106 Mich. 138; 63 N. W. 897; Mechanics' Nat. Bank v. Comins, 72 N. H. 12; 55 Atl. 191; 101 Am. St. Rep. 650; Hosmer v. Welch, 107 Mich. 470; 65 N. W. 280; 67 N. W. 504; Diffenbach v. New York Life Ins. Co., 61 Md. 370; Groff v. Mut. L. Ins. Co., 92 Ill. App. 207; Johnson v. Van Epps, 110 Ill. 551; Grigsby v. Russell, 222 U. S. 149; Ann. Cas. 1913-B 863; 32 S. Ct. 58, 56 U. S.(L. Ed.) 133; 36 L. R. A. (N. S.) 642, per Holmes, J., p. 155. And see also Lewis v. Phoenix Mut. L. Ins. Co., 39 Conn. 100; Hurd v. Doty, 86 Wis. 1; 56 N. W. 371; 21 L. R. A. 746.

[138] 115 Va. 836; 80 S. E. 565.

[139] 72 N. H. 12; 55 Atl. 191; 101 Am. St. Rep. 650.

upon the life or health of the man at the helm, should not have an insurable interest in his life, the same as one who invests money in a partnership, relying upon the skill or experience of his co-partner, has an insurable interest in the life of the latter, or one who equips a mining expedition has an insurable interest in the life of him to whom its management is committed. The creditor or stockholder, under such circumstances, would seem to have that 'reasonable expectation of pecuniary benefit or profit from the continuance of another's life' which is held sufficient to constitute an insurable interest. In such case 'the essential thing . . . that the policy should be obtained in good faith, and not for the purpose of speculating upon the hazards of life,' would appear to be present. In this view we are not prepared to say, as matter of law, . . . that the plaintiffs, who were furnishing the funds to carry on the business of the George T. Comins Company, had no insurable interest in the life of George T. Comins, the manager, and apparently the originating and directing personality in the enterprise.''

§ 303. **Want of Insurable Interest Makes Policy Void, But Payee May Be a Trustee.**—It is not settled whether or not a life insurance policy issued to one without an insurable interest is absolutely void, or whether a trust relation exists, where the payee will be held to be a trustee for the estate of the deceased. In the case of McRae, Admr., v. Warmack,[140] it was said: ''The principle upon which life insurance is based is that one who has a reasonable expectation of benefits and advantage growing out of the continuance of the life of the assured has such an interest in his life that he may insure the same; but where one is not thus interested in the life of the assured, but by insuring such life is rather interested in his early death, the contract of insurance is a mere wager, and against a sound public policy. Such contracts, it has been thought, would, if upheld, result in a mere traffic in human life, and would lend a great incentive to one thus disinterested in the life, but interested in the death, of the assured, to shorten that life. It is therefore well settled that the issue of a policy to one who has no insurable interest in the life

140 98 Ark. 52; 135 S. W. 807; 33 L. R. A. (N. S.) 949. See also Little v. Arkansas National Bank, 105 Ark. 281; 152 S. W. 281.

of the insured, but who pays the premiums for the chance of collecting the policy, is invalid because it is a wagering contract, and against a sound public policy." The Appellate Court of Indiana says, in relation to the same subject:[141] "It is clear that, unless the policy was void from its inception, appellee cannot recover in this action. Meeting this proposition, the only facts pleaded, and common to both paragraphs of the complaint, show that appellee applied to appellant, an Indiana corporation doing a general life insurance business on the assessment plan, for a policy of insurance on the life of Mrs. Hammond, his mother-in-law; that a policy on her life on such application was issued to him by appellant; that appellee paid the membership fee and all assessments or premiums as they became due on account of said policy. In our judgment these facts affirmatively show appellee's lack of a monetary interest in the life insured, and are *prima facie* sufficient to show that the policy was void *ab initio*. This conclusion is affirmed by the well-settled rule that an insurable interest in the life of another is founded upon a pecuniary interest, not satisfied by the relationship shown to exist between Mrs. Hammond and appellee.[142] It is not averred in either paragraph that Mrs. Hammond had any knowledge of the issuing of said policy; and, in the absence of such an averment, it may be presumed that she had none. This presumption, considered in connection with our conclusion on the facts stated, brings the transaction within the statute declaring such policies invalid.[143] In the case last cited it is said: 'All assessments were to be paid by him, and the policy was issued to him, without her knowledge or consent. The contract of insurance, therefore, was void, both as against public policy and by force of the statute'—citing authorities. For the reason given, we must act upon the theory that no contract ever existed

[141] American Mut. Life Ins. Co. v. Mead, 39 Ind. App. 215; 79 N. E. 526.

[142] Continental Life Ins. Co. v. Volger, 89 Ind. 572, 575; 46 Am. Rep. 185, and cases there cited. Prudential Life Ins. Co. v. Hunn, 21 Ind. App. 525; 52 N. E. 772; 69 Am. St. Rep. 380; Davis v. Brown, 159 Ind. 644; 65 N. E. 908; Ruse v. Mut., etc., Ins. Co., 23 N. Y. 516, 523; May on Ins., §§ 76, 103a; Lewis v. Phoenix Mut. Life Ins. Co., 39 Conn. 100, 104.

[143] § 4902, Burns' Ann. St. 1901; American, etc., Ins. Co. v. Bertram, 163 Ind. 51, 56; 70 N. E. 258; 64 L. R. A. 935.

between the parties to this action.[144] Appellee relies to some extent on the allegation found in the second paragraph 'that plaintiff had no insurable interest in the life insured.' This is not the averment of a fact, but a conclusion of law, and does not aid the pleading.[145] In our opinion, from the facts and the authorities above referred to, appellant's contention in this particular is not well taken. Having determined that the policy was void, it necessarily follows that appellant thereby incurred no risk or liability by reason thereof, and without some risk or liability any assessments paid by appellee were without consideration, and must be returned, provided the parties to the contract were not in *pari delicto*.[146] If the parties to the contract were equally guilty, neither would have any standing in court to enforce an affirmative against the other; the policy of the law being to leave them in the position regarding their rights under such illegal act precisely as they leave themselves.[147] But this general rule has its exceptions 'in cases where some statute provides a remedy, or perhaps in cases of oppression, or peculiar hardship, or those where public policy clearly necessitates the court's interference' and cases where from the facts disclosed the parties are not in *pari delicto*." In the case of Hinton v. Mutual Reserve Fund Life Ass'n,[148] it was said: "The testimony proposed in this case was that the agreement was made before or at the time of the application, and that the plaintiff was to pay the entrance fee and all further assessments; he not then having, or expecting to have, any insurable interest in the life of the insured. This is a very different case from one where the insured has taken out a valid policy, paying the premium thereon, and, either as a gift to some

[144] City of Indianapolis v. Wann, 144 Ind. 175, 187; 42 N. E. 901; 31 L. R. A. 743; Winchester Elec. Light Co. v. Veal, 145 Ind. 506; 41 N. E. 334; 44 N. E. 353.

[145] Franklin Life Ins. Co. v. Sefton, 53 Ind. 380, 384.

[146] Metropolitan Life Ins. Co. v. Bowser, *supra;* Metropolitan Life Ins. Co. v. McCormick, *supra;* Waller v. Northern Assur. Co., 64 Iowa, 101; 19 N. W. 865; Joyce on Ins., § 1390.

[147] Hutchins v. Weldin, 114 Ind. 80; 15 N. E. 804; Budd v. Rutherford, 4 Ind. App. 386, 392; 30 N. E. 1111; Woodford v. Hamilton, 139 Ind. 481; 39 N. E. 47; American, etc., Ins. Co. v. Bertram, *supra;* Blattenberger v. Holman, 103 Pa. 555, 558; Ruse v. Mut., etc., Ins. Co., *supra*.

[148] 135 N. C. 314; 47 S. E. 474; 65 L. R. A. 161.

friend, or as collateral security to a debt, assigns the policy with
the knowledge of the company. The plaintiff was to be paid his
debt from the proceeds of the policy, he paying all of the premiums and awaiting her death to reap the profits of his bargain.
In Ruse v. Mutual Ben. L. Ins. Co.[149] Selden, J., says: 'A policy
obtained by a party who has no interest in the subject of insurance is a mere wager policy. Wagers in general (that is, innocent wagers) are at common law valid, but wagers involving any
immorality or crime, or in conflict with any principle of public
policy, are void. To which of these classes, then, does a wagering
policy of insurance belong? . . . Such policies, if valid, not only
afford facilities for a demoralizing system of gaming, but furnish
strong temptation to the party interested to bring about, if possible, the event insured against.' The learned justice traces the
history of the law and its development in England, resulting in
the passage of the act of Parliament declaring all such policies
void, saying: 'My conclusion, therefore, is that the statute of
14 George III., avoiding wager policies upon lives, was simply
declaratory of the common law, and that all such policies would
have been void independently of that act.'[150] While there are
conflicting decisions in this country, a careful examination of them
brings us to the conclusion that the foregoing is the sound view
of the subject. 'Of all wagering contracts, those concerning the
lives of human beings should receive the strongest, the most em-
phatic, and the most persistent condemnation.' " In the case of
Griffin's Admr. v. Equitable Life-Assur. Soc.[151] it was said: "If,
as seemed to be admitted by counsel for both appellant and appellee, the persons named as beneficiaries in these policies were
not in fact creditors of Griffin, yet they and he fraudulently procured the policies by falsely representing them to be creditors.
The transaction as to each policy was clearly a speculation upon
the hazard of human life, and consequently a gambling scheme,
pure and simple, which rendered the policies void, because against
public policy; and, if void, no cause of action against appellee
exists in favor of Griffin's administrator for the recovery of their

proceeds.[152] Upon the other hand, if the policies were taken upon the life of Griffin without his knowledge or consent, they were also void, but anyone who in good faith paid premiums upon them would be entitled to recover the premiums so paid.''[153] If the person effecting the insurance has no insurable interest in the life of the insured he cannot recover more than the amount of premiums paid with interest, but if he collects the whole amount of the insurance he must pay over to the personal representatives of the insured the excess over the amount of the premiums and interest.[154] This is true as a general proposition, but there is authority to the contrary.[154a] And where the beneficiary has no insurable interest the heirs of the insured can, in an action brought by such beneficiary, to recover on the policy, intervene and recover in his place.[155] In a recent case[156] the Court of Civil Appeals of Texas thus states the rule: ''The fact that the premium was paid by the beneficiary does not give to the contract the character of a wagering contract; nor does the fact that the beneficiary has no insurable interest in the life of the assured render the policy void as against public policy. The courts will treat the person named as beneficiary, having no insurable interest, as a trustee appointed to collect the policy for the benefit of those legally entitled, thereby indorsing the contract by which the company has solemnly bound itself, and at the same time conserving public policy, by preventing the stranger

[152] Basye v. Adams, 81 Ky. 368; Warnock v. Davis, 104 U. S. 779; 26 L. Ed. 924; Keystone Mut. Ben. Ass'n v. Norris, 115 Pa. 446; 8 Atl. 638; 2 Am. St. Rep. 572.

[153] Metropolitan Life Ins. Co. v. Monohan, 42 S. W. 924; 19 Ky. L. 992; Same v. Blesck, 58 S. W. 436; 22 Ky. L. 530; Same v. Smith, 59 S. W. 24; 22 Ky. L. 868; 53 L. R. A. 817. See also American Mut. Life Ins. Co. v. Bertram, 163 Ind. 51; 70 N. E. 258; 64 L. R. A. 435; also Marquet v. Aetna Life Ins. Co., 128 Tenn. 213; 159 S. W. 733.

[154] Warnock v. Davis, 104 U. S. 775; Gilbert v. Moose, 104 Pa. St. 74; Ruth v. Katterman, 112 Pa. St. 251; Siegrist's Admr. v. Schmoltz, 113 Pa. St. 326; Downey v. Hoffer, 110 Pa. St. 109; 20 Atl. 655; Sanonette v. Laplante, 67 N. H. 118; 36 Atl. 981; post, § 558.

[154a] See last three sections.

[155] Mayher v. Manhattan L. Ins. Co., 87 Tex. 169; 27 S. W. 124. An interesting case under the law of Louisiana is New York Life Ins. Co. v. Neal, 114 La. 652; 38 Sou. 485.

[156] Mut. L. Ins. Co. v. Blodgett, 8 Tex. Civ. App. 45; 27 S. W. 286.

from gambling in the life of his fellow or profiting by his death.''
No action can be maintained on a policy of life insurance, issued
to one not having an insurable interest in the life insured, against
the company issuing it, by the personal representatives of the
person whose life was insured, for there is no privity of contract
between them; nor is the company bound by a notice from such
personal representatives forbidding it to pay over the amount of
such insurance to the payee named in the policy.[157] It is no de.
fense to an action on a policy by an administrator that the policy
was delivered to and the premiums paid by one who had no in.
surable interest in the life insured.[158] Yet, where the money due
on a policy void for want of insurable interest has been voluntarily
paid to the beneficiary, it has been held that the heirs of the in.
sured have no claim to it.[159] In the case cited the Court says:
''The complainants are not parties to the contract, neither have
they been injured by it. It could not have been enforced between
the parties in courts of justice, and the fact that one of the parties
has seen fit to pay over to the other the wage does not afford a
basis in equity for outside parties to lay claim to the reward of
iniquity.'' In the case of Sage v. Finney,[160] the Court seemed to
clearly state the present rule. It said: ''While one may insure
his own life, paying premium thereon himself, in favor of another who has no insurable interest therein, as was said in Locher
v. Kuechenmiester,[161] it is true the law looks with disfavor upon
such transactions as this, where the insurance is procured with
the consent of the insured but in favor of one with no insurable
interest, who undertakes to pay the premiums therefor, and de-
nounces them as wagering contracts. Though such contracts are
obnoxious to public policy, because they tend to encourage one
to hasten the event upon which the insurance depends, they are
not unlawful in the sense that they are immoral nor as is a contract

[157] Bomberger v. United Brethren, etc., Soc. (Pa.), 18 W. N. C. 459; 6 Atl. 41.

[158] Brennan v. Prudential L. Ins. Co., 148 Pa. St. 199; 23 Atl. 901.

[159] Smith v. Pinch, 80 Mich. 332; 45 N. W. 183. See also Meyers v. Schumann, 54 N. J. E. 414; 34 Atl. 1066. To the same effect is Smith's Admr. v. Hatke, 115 Va. 230; 78 S. E. 584.

[160] 156 Mo. App. 30; 135 S. W. 996.

[161] 120 Mo. App. 701, 720; 98 S. W. 92.

which stipulates for the doing of something prohibited by a positive statute. In this view, the courts accept such contracts as sufficient to give rise to equities between the parties which they will consider and apply, to the end of compensating one who has invested his means in good faith for the purpose of keeping the insurance in force. Indeed, the rule of decision with respect to such contracts seems to be that they are void only in so far as they purport to confer a right upon one who has no insurable interest in the life of another, to the insurance over and above the amount of the indebtedness of the insured person to the beneficiary and such premiums and interest thereon as may have been paid on the policy by the beneficiary. It is said, although such contracts are invalid in so far as they attempt to transfer all or any precise amount of the insurance above the indebtedness of the insured to the beneficiary and beyond such premiums and interest as the beneficiary may invest therein, they are not of that fraudulent kind with respect of which the courts regard the parties equally culpable and refuse to interfere with the result of their action. In other words, such contracts, though considered and treated as invalid because obnoxious to public policy in so far as they purport to give the beneficiary any precise or definite amount of the insurance without regard to the amount of the indebtedness which the insured may owe to the beneficiary or the premiums and interest thereon which the beneficiary may have invested therein, are always treated with as sufficiently efficacious to afford the beneficiary an equitable right to the insurance money vouchsafed in the policy to the extent of compensating the indebtedness, if any, existing in his favor against the insured together with such premiums and interest as he has expended in keeping the insurance in force.''

§ 304. **General Rule.**—It is seen from the preceding citations that the authorities are not altogether in harmony and it would be difficult, if not impossible, to lay down a general rule that would apply to all cases. It can with safety be said, however, that in all cases of insurance by one person upon the life of another some pecuniary interest or advantage, to be derived or received from the continuance of the life insured by the person procuring or effecting such insurance, must exist in order to re-

599

lieve the contract from the stigma of being a wager policy and against public policy. A careful examination of the cases will show that wherever the point has been raised the courts have considered whether or not the person procuring the policy was interested pecuniarily to an appreciable extent in the life insured. Perhaps a slighter interest will support a policy on the life of a relative than in other cases, but the interest must exist in some form. Where a wife insures the life of a husband or the husband that of the wife, it is clear that there is a pecuniary interest of a decided character, and so where a parent insures the life of a child, for there is the expectation of support when age shall impair the abilities of the former. "The interest required," says a leading case,[162] "need not be such as to constitute the basis of any direct claim in favor of the plaintiff upon the party whose life is insured; it is sufficient if an indirect advantage may result to the plaintiff from its life." The general rule has thus been stated by another authority:[163] "Except in cases where there are ties of blood or marriage the expectation of advantage from the continuance of the life of the insured in order to be reasonable, as the law counts reasonableness, must be founded on the existence of some contract between the person whose life is insured and the beneficiary, the fulfillment of which the death will prevent; it must appear that by the death there will come some damage which can be estimated by some rule of law, for which loss or damage the insurance company has undertaken to indemnify the beneficiary under its policy. When this contractual relation does not exist, and there are no ties of blood or marriage, an insurance policy becomes what the law denominates a wagering contract." Where it appeared that the beneficiary in a life insurance policy took the insured when seventeen years old from an orphan asylum, and gave her a home, and supported her until she became able to maintain herself, and on her death took charge of the funeral and paid the expenses, and though the beneficiary, who was not related to insured, was not appointed guardian, the insured looked on the beneficiary as such even after attaining full age, it was held that the beneficiary had an insurable interest in the life of the

[162] Trenton, etc., Ins. Co. v. Johnson, 24 N. J. L. 586.

[163] Hinton v. Mut. Reserve L. I. Co., 135 N. C. 314; 47 S. E. 174; 65 L. R. A. 161; 102 Am. Rep. 545.

insured, "more than a pecuniary interest," under the rule that it is not necessary, in order to create such an interest, that the insured shall be under any legal obligation to the/ beneficiary, nor that kinship shall exist between the parties.[164] Where the want of insurable interest was known to the company at the time of the insurance of the policy the company may be estopped.[165]

§ 305. **Benefit of Beneficiary Association Is Paid to a Person Designated By the Member, or By the Laws of the Society.**—In regular life insurance the choice of a beneficiary is unrestricted, except as limited by the law of insurable interest, which has been considered. Material differences, however, exist between the contracts of the ordinary life companies and those of benefit societies with their members which will more fully appear as we proceed. Such differences especially appear in the principles governing the selection of a beneficiary by the members of these societies, and of these we are now to treat. Nearly all benefit societies have for their principal object the payment of a stated sum of money upon the death of a member to his properly designated beneficiary, or, in default of such designation, then to his widow, children or heirs, as provided in the charter or by-laws of the society. Beneficiary in industrial insurance means the person who is to receive the proceeds of the policy according to the established course of the company.[166] Under some circumstances, if no designation is made as required by the fundamental law of the organization, the benefit may revert to the society. The authorities agree that the contract entered into by a benefit society with its members is executory in its nature and is contained in the certificate, if any be issued, taken in connection with the application, if any, the charter, or constitution and by-laws of the organization, and the statutes of the State under which it is formed. To the terms of this contract the member is conclusively presumed to have assented when he became such.[167]

[164] Thomas v. National Ben. Ass'n, 84 N. J. L. 281; 86 Atl. 375; Ann. Cas. 1914-D 1121.

[165] Mut. L. Ins. Co. v. Blodgett, 8 Tex. Civ. App. 45; 27 S. W. 286; Barnes v. London, etc., Ins. Co., 8 Times L. R. 1 Q. B. 864.

[166] Metropolitan L. Ins. Co. v. Hoopel, 76 N. J. Eq. 94; 74 Atl. 467.

[167] Hellenberg v. District No. 1, etc., 94 N. Y. 580; Maryland Mut. B. Ass'n v. Clendinen, 44 Md. 429; Arthur et al. v. Odd Felows' Ben. Ass'n,

§ 306. **Member Has No Property in Benefit, But Only Power to Designate Beneficiary.**—The contract of a benefit society is with the member, he alone is interested in it and the beneficiary has no rights which cannot be lost by the act of the member, and none that can be asserted while the member is living.[168] The member of the society as such has, under this contract, no interest nor property in this benefit, but simply the power to appoint some one-to receive it.[169] By the definition usually given a power is technically "an authority by which one person enables the other to do some act for him."[170] That a member of a benefit society has only this power, and nothing else, was decided in an early case in which the right was fully discussed.[171] In that case a power was defined to be "a liberty or authority reserved by, or limited to, a party to dispose of real or personal property for his own benefit, or for the benefit of others, and operating upon an estate or interest, vested either in himself or in some other person; the liberty or authority, however, not being derived out of such estate or interest, but overreaching or superseding it either wholly or partially."[172] It has been said: "That a person having a power over property has not in strictness any interest in, or right or title to, the property to which the power relates, appears

29 Ohio St. 557; Relief Ass'n v. McAuley, 2 Mackey, 70; Barton v. Provident Relief Ass'n, 63 N. H. 535; Richmond v. Johnson, 28 Minn. 447; Greeno v. Greeno, 23 Hun. 478; Masonic Mut. Ben. Soc. v. Burkhart, 110 Ind. 189; 10 N. E. 79; Van Bibber's Admr. v. Van Bibber, 82 Ky. 347; Worley v. Northwestern Masonic, etc., 10 Fed. 227; Kentucky Masonic, etc., Ins. Co. v. Miller, 13 Bush 489; Hammerstein v. Parsons, 29 Mo. App. 509; Boasberg v. Cronin, 9 N. Y. Supp. 664.

168 Pollak v. Supreme Council R. A., 40 Misc. 274; 81 N. Y. Supp. 942; Montour v. Grand Lodge A. O. U. W., 38 Ore. 47; 62 Pac. 524; Hofman v. Grand Lodge B. L. F., 73 Mo. App. 47; Deacon v. Clarke, 112 Tenn. 289; 79 S. W. 382; Hunter v. National Union, 197 Ill. 478; 64 N. E. 356; affg. 99 Ill. App. 146. To the same effect are practically all the cases relative to change of beneficiary.

169 Smith's Admr. v. Hatke, 115 Va. 230; 78 S. E. 584; Abeles v. Ackley, 133 Mo. App. 594; 113 S. W. 698; Slaughter v. Grand Lodge, etc., (Ala.), 683 Sou. 367; Coleman v. Anderson, 98 Tex. 570; 86 S. W. 1057. To the same effect are all the cases cited in this section.

170 Bouv. Law Dic. tit., Power; 2 Lilly Abr. 339.

171 Maryland Mut. Ben. Soc. v. Clendinen, 44 Md. 433.

172 Butl. Note 1, Co. Litt. 342b.

in early authority."[173]   This definition is not strictly accurate when applied to the powers possessed by members of benefit societies, yet probably is sufficiently so for all practical purposes. This right of designation is a naked power because it is a right or authority disconnected from any interest of the donee in the subject-matter, and is governed generally by the rules applicable to that class of powers.[174]   In the very first cases relating to benefit societies this principle was clearly recognized.   In 1876 the Supreme Court of Ohio[175] construed the rights of the member in the benefit to be a power to appoint a beneficiary, and a similar case had been decided in the same way the year before by the Supreme Court of Maryland.[176]   In this case the residuary legatees under the will of a deceased member, who left no wife nor children, sued to recover the benefit.   This benefit was not specifically mentioned in the will.   The charter of the defendant provided that the fund should be paid upon the death of a member "to the widow, child, children, or such person or persons to whom the deceased may have disposed of the same by will or assignment."   If there were none of these parties, and no disposition by will or assignment, then, after payment of funeral expenses, the balance was to revert to the society.   The Court said: "The interest acquired by a member of this association is not one payable to himself, or for his own benefit, further than his funeral expenses.   It is not a *'debitum in præsenti, solvendum in futuro;'* if the deceased had only a power, and not an interest or property in the sum or fund, it was not assets.   In 2 Chance on Powers,[177] it is said: "That an ordinary power is not in itself assets, is clear from all the cases.   This cannot be classed among the assets to be returned by an administrator in his inventory; it is not a chose in action or any species of personal property.   We know of no case in which the *jus disponendi* authorized by charter, under provisions like the present, has been declared a mere power: but powers arise at common law, under bonds to convey estates as an-

173 Albany's Case, 1 Rep. 110b; Lampet's Case, 10 Rep. 48b; Co. Litt. 265b.
174 Bloomer v. Waldron, 3 Hill 365.
175 Arthur *et al.* v. Odd Fellows' Ben. Ass'n, 29 Ohio St. 557.
176 Maryland Mut. Ben. Soc. v. Clendinen, 44 Md. 429; 22 Am. Rep. 52.
177 § 1820.

other shall appoint, or pay sums of money as another shall appoint, either generally, or among children, or under covenants for like purposes.[178] We cannot see why an authority or privilege acquired under a charter, to be exercised for the benefit of another, should not be governed by the same rules.'' And the benefit reverted to the society as there was no disposition by will or assignment according to the terms of the contract. A similar case afterwards arose in New York. In this case the charter provided that the fund should be ''paid to the wife of the deceased, if living, and if dead to his children, and, if there are none, then to such person as he may formally have designated to his lodge prior to his decease.'' The deceased had no wife nor children and so formally designated his mother, who died before him. He afterwards, and before his mother's death, made a will in which the benefit was given to his mother, or in case of her prior decease, then to his brother. The suit was brought by the executor under this will against the society and, in affirming the judgment of the lower court for the defendant, the Court of Appeals said:[179] ''The charter and by-laws of the defendant corporation constituted the terms of an executory contract to which the testator assented when he accepted admission into the order. The testator agreed on his part to pay certain dues and assessments as specified and the corporation agreed upon the death of the testator to pay $1,000 to his wife, if living; if dead, to his children; and if there should be neither wife nor children then to 'such person or persons as he may have formally designated to his lodge prior to his decease;' such sum to be collected for that purpose by assessments. The corporation contracted to pay to no one else, and were not bound to pay at all except 'to the person or persons' described in the agreement, and out of such collected assessments. Lowenstein, the plaintiff's testator, did so designate to his lodge prior to his decease, his mother, Rika Lowenstein. He had neither wife nor children, and so was at liberty to select and name the beneficiary. The designation which he thus made describes the payment directed as 'the $1,000 my heirs are to receive' of the corporation. This language was purely matter of description, intended to iden-

---

[178] 3 Atk. 656; 1 Vesey Sr. 86; Cro. Car. 219; 376, and other cases cited in 1 Chance on Powers.

[179] Hellenberg v. Dist. No. 1, I. O. B. B., 94 N. Y. 580.

tify the fund, and will not at all bear the interpretation sought to be put upon it of a designation of his 'heirs' as the recipients. On the contrary, the paper itself excluded any such interpretation, for its very purpose was to name and designate the particular recipient, irrespective of the question whether she should prove to be one of his heirs or not. If his mother had been living at his death she would have been entitled to the endowment because specifically named, and not by virtue of any relationship to the testator. The mother thus named had no interest in or title to the money to be paid while she was living. The testator could at any time have gone to his lodge and designated upon the books some other recipient, thus revoking his previous designation. The mother could not become entitled to the endowment at all unless she survived the testator, and her designation remained unrevoked. Nor did the testator have any interest in the future fund. He had simply a power of appointment, authority to designate the ultimate beneficiary, and that power and authority died with him, because it could only be exercised by him, and prior to his decease. If he did not so exercise it, nobody surviving or representing him could, and upon his death he could have nothing which would descend or upon which a will could operate. His contract effected that result. He agreed that the endowment to be collected should be paid not to his next of kin, not to the legatee named in his will, but to the person designated to his lodge, or in default of such person so named then to nobody.'' All of the authorities agree that the rights of the members of benefit societies in the sums agreed to be paid at death is simply the power to appoint the beneficiary and that the constitution, or charter, and the by-laws are the foundation and source of such power.[180]

[180] Greeno v. Greeno, 23 Hun. 479; Barton v. Provident Mut. Relief Ass'n, 63 N. H. 535; Eastman v. Provident Mut. R. Ass'n, 62 N. H. 555; 20 C. L. J. 266; Worley v. N. W. Mass. Aid Ass'n, 10 Fed. 227; Gentry v. Sup. Lodge K. of H., 23 Fed. 718; Swift v. Ry. Cond. Mut. Ass'n, 96 Ill. 309; Masonic Mut. R. Ass'n v. McAuley, 2 Mackey, 70; Presb. Ass'n Fund v. Allen, 106 Ind. 593; Masonic Mut. Ben. Soc. v. Burkhart, 110 Ind. 189; 10 N. E. 79; Richmond v. Johnson, 28 Minn. 447; Ky. Masonic Mut. Life Ins. Co. v. Miller, 13 Bush, 486; Van Bibber's Admr. v. Van Bibber, 82 Ky. 347; Sup. Counc. Catholic M. B. A. v. Priest et al., 46

The beneficiary has a mere revocable expectation not amounting to a property right.[181]   The cases must not, however, be under-stood to hold that the member of a benefit society has not a prop-erty right in the contract of membership, under which he has the power to designate a recipient of the benefit to be paid, because of such membership and under the contract.   The contract is one-of life insurance.[182]   The right of the member in this contract is a valuable one, which the courts will at all times recognize and protect, although strictly speaking, such member has no property interest in the benefit paid, or subject of the power.   The member-ship, which includes the right to pay the agreed consideration and to appoint a person to take the benefit, must be regarded as a species of property and is to be distinguished from the benefit, or sum to be paid, itself, in which the member has no property. This principle has been clearly recognized in later cases.[183]

§ 307. **This Power May Be General or Special.**—The power of a member to appoint a beneficiary may be general, if by the contract he is at liberty to appoint to whom he pleases, or special if he is restricted to an appointment to or among particular classes only.[184]   And we shall see as we proceed farther, the power, in nearly every instance, is special, because the appointment is limited to persons of a specified class.

§ 308. **Execution of Power Must Be in Compliance With Terms of Instrument Creating It.**—It follows, from the preced-ing citations, and also from general principles,[185] that the execu-

Mich. 429; Durion v. Central Verein, 7 Daly 168; Tennessee Lodge v. Ladd, 5 Lea, 716; Arthur v. Odd Fellows' B. Ass., 29 Ohio St. 557; Duvall v. Goodson, 79 Ky. 224; Masonic Ben. Ass'n v. Bunch, 109 Mo. 560; 19 S. W. 25; Keener v. Grand Lodge, etc., 38 Mo. App. 543.

181 Order of Scottish Clans v. Reich (Conn.), 97 Atl. 863.

182 Soehner v. Grand Lodge, etc., 74 Neb. 399; 104 N. W. 871; Cos-mopolitan L. Ins. Ass'n v. Koegel, 104 Va. 619; 52 S. E. 166.

183 Wist v. Grand Lodge A. O. U. W., 22 Ore. 271; 29 Pac. 610; Hogan v. Pacific Endowment League, 99 Cal. 248; 33 Pac. 924; Hysinger v. Su-preme Lodge K. & L. of H., 42 Mo. App. 627; Froelich v. Musicians' Mut. Ben. Ass'n, 93 Mo. App. 383; Lysaght v. Stonemasons', etc., Ass'n, 55 Mo. App. 538.

184 Washb. on Real Prop. 307.

185 2 Washb. on Real Prop. 317; 1 Sugden on Powers, 250.

tion of the power, to be valid, must be in precise compliance with the terms of the contract creating such power.[186] As Sugden[187] says: "Where forms are imposed on the execution of a power it is either to protect the remainder-man from a charge in any other mode, or to preserve the person to whom it is given from a hasty and unadvised execution of the power. In each case the circumstances must be strictly complied with; in the first it would be in direct opposition to the agreement to consider the estate charged when the mode pointed out is not adhered to; in the second, to dispense with the solemnities and forms required to attend the execution of the power, is to deprive a man of the bridle which he has thought proper to impose on his weakness or frailty of mind, in order effectually to guard himself against fraud or imposition. Besides, the circumstances required to the execu-tion of a power are perfectly arbitrary, and (except only as they are in fact required) unessential in point of effect to the validity of any instrument by which the power may be exercised." Consequently, a power to designate by deed, or written instrument in the nature of a deed, cannot be executed by will, or *vice versa*.[188] In executing this power, the instrument or will, if such disposition be allowed, should refer to it so as to show that the donee had in view the subject of the power at the time. The law itself prescribes no particular ceremonies to be observed in the execution of a power except those required for the execution of the instrument executing the power, as of a deed or will, in which case the requisite formalities of execution or attestation must be complied with. The contract creating the power governs in all respects its execution.[189] It has sometimes been a question whether the act of the member was an original designation or a change of beneficiary. The courts will, if possible, construe the act so as to

[186] Elliott v. Whedbee, 94 N. C. 115; Sup. L. K. & L. of H. v. Grace, 60 Tex. 571.

[187] 1 Sugden on Powers, 250.

[188] 2 Washb. on Real Prop. 317; 1 Sugden on Powers, 255; Worley v. N. W. Masonic Aid Ass., 10 Fed. 227; Daniels v. Pratt, 143 Mass. 216; 10 N. E. 166.

[189] Sugden on Powers, 250, 255; 2 Washb. on Real Prop. 317; Presbyterian Ass. Fund v. Allen, 106 Ind. 593; 7 N. E. 317; Am. Legion of Honor v. Perry, 140 Mass. 580; 5 N. E. 634.

carry out the intent of the member.[190]   The benefit will not pass
under the residuary clause of a will, nor by general disposition
of all of the testator's property,[191] unless some authority providing
otherwise is found in the laws of the organization.[192]   The beneficiary may be designated by will if that is the plan of the society.[192a]   Where the charter of a mutual benefit society provided
a certain time and manner of designating the beneficiary of an
insured, and where such formality did not go to the substance
of the contract of membership, nor affect the express object of
the association, it was a directory provision merely and strict
compliance with it was not necessary to make a valid designation.
Where such directory provisions, with relation to designating a
beneficiary, were never lived up to by the association nor required
of members, a strict compliance with them on the part of a member
was waived.[193]   It is now settled that defects or irregularities in
the designation or change of beneficiary may be waived by the
lodge,[194] although it has been held that the required formalities
in the laws of the society relative to designation of beneficiary
are part of the contract and must be strictly complied with.[195]

[190] Hanson v. Scandinavian, etc., Ass'n, 59 Minn. 123; 60 N. W. 1091;
Shryock v. Shryock, 50 Neb. 886; 70 N. W. 515; Allison v. Stevenson,
51 App. Div. 626; 64 N. Y. Supp. 481; Grand Lodge, etc., v. Ohnstein, 85
Ill. App. 355; Loewenthal v. District Grand Lodge, etc., 19 Ind. App.
377; 49 N. E. 610.

[191] Arthur v. Odd Fellows' Ass'n, 29 Ohio St. 557; Maryland Mut. Ben.
Ass'n v. Clendinen, 44 Md. 429; 22 Am. Rep. 52; Hellenberg v. Dist. No.
1, I. O. B. B., 94 N. Y. 580; Morey v. Michael, 18 Md. 241; Highland v.
Highland, 109 Ill. 366; Greeno v. Greeno, 23 Hun. 478; Eastman v. Provident R. Soc., 62 N. H. 555; 20 Cent. L. J. 267; contra., St. John's Mite
Soc. v. Buckley (D. C.), 5 Mackey, 406; Bown v. Catholic M. Ben. Ass'n,
33 Hun. 263; Kepler v. Sup. L. Knights of Honor, 45 Hun. 274.

[192] Weil v. Trafford, 3 Tenn. Ch. 108.   In Aveling v. N. W. Masonic
Aid Ass'n, 71 Mich. 681; 40 N. W. 28, it was held that a certificate payable to "the devisees, or if no will, to the heirs" passed under a will
though not specifically mentioned.   And in High Court Cath. Order,
etc., v. Malloy, 169 Ill. 58; 48 N. E. 392; a devise was given effect because of the evident intent of the testator.

[192a] Armstrong v. Walton, 105 Miss. 337; 62 S. W. 173.

[193] St. Louis Police Relief Ass'n v. Tierney, 116 Mo. App. 447; 91 S.
W. 968.

[194] Kepler v. Supreme L. of H., 45 Hun. 274, and see post, § 406.

[195] See post, § 404.

§ 309. **Equity Sometimes Aids Defective Execution.**—Equity will sometimes interfere to remedy a defective execution of a power, but the case must be very clear, and no opposing equity must exist.[196] It has been held[197] that a certificate in a benefit society may be reformed after the death of a member by inserting the name of the beneficiary when it appears that the secretary of the society and -the member both understood that the name should be entered on the record without further direction. The Supreme Court of Michigan has said upon this subject:[198] "It is possible—and we need not consider under what circumstances—that when a member has executed and delivered to the reporter (secretary) his attested surrender in favor of a competent beneficiary, his death before a new certificate is issued, may leave his power of designation so far executed as to enable a court of equity to relieve against the accident."

§ 310. **Consequences of Failure to Execute Power.**—The member of a benefit association having no interest nor property in the fund stipulated to be paid on his death to his appointee, but simply the power of appointment, failure to so appoint leaves the fund to be disposed of as provided for in the contract creating the power, and if no disposition is so provided for, then there is a total lapse of the power and the fund will revert to the society. In no case is this fund assets, and if collected by the executor or administrator it is to be regarded as a trust fund held for the benefit of the person entitled to it and the creditors cannot share in it. However, the disposition of the benefit is determined by the charter and by-laws of the society and is to be ordered accordingly.[199] In a case,[200] which was an action brought by plaintiff

---

[196] 1 Story Eq. Jur. 181, 182, *et seq.*

[197] Scott v. Provident Mut. R. Ass'n, 63 N. H. 556; and see also Eastman v. Provident Mut. R. Ass'n, 65 N. H. 176; 18 Atl. 745, where reformation was decreed. The question was touched on in Newman v. Covenant Mut. Ben. Ass'n, 76 Ia. 56; 40 N. W. 87.

[198] Knights of Honor v. Nairn, 60 Mich. 44; 26 N. W. 826.

[199] Eastman v. Prov. Relief, etc., Soc., 62 N. H. 555; 20 C. L. J. 266; Worley v. N. W. Mas. Aid, etc., 10 Fed. 227; Daniels v. Pratt, 143 Mass. 216; 10 N. E. 166; Hellenberg v. Dist. No. 1 I,. O. B. B., 94 N. Y. 580; Maryland, etc., v. Clendinen, 44 Md. 429; Greeno v. Greeno, 23 Hun. 478; Gould v. Emerson, 99 Mass. 154; Van Bibber's Admr. v. Van Bibber,

as the administrator of one Gigar, to recover the benefit stipulated to be paid by the defendant society, the society was organized for the object of securing "to dependent and loved ones assistance and relief at the death of a member," and by the by-laws, the benefit was payable "to such person or persons as he might by entry on the record book of the association or on the face of his certificate, direct the sum to be paid." No person was designated by the deceased on the record book or the face of the certificate. The defendant society offered to show by parol testimony that the deceased intended that the benefit should go to his affianced, and had often so declared. The Supreme Court of New Hampshire, in affirming judgment for the defendants, said: "The certificate was neither payable to the deceased, nor to his administrator, assigns, heirs, estate, or legal representatives. The defendant promised to pay the benefit to no one, save such person or persons as Gigar should direct by entry upon the certificate or record book of the association. By the contract he had the mere power of appointing the person who should receive the benefit. He was bound by the rules of the association, and could not change the beneficiary in a way not in conformity with them. We cannot know why he did not exercise his power of directing to whom the benefit should be paid. He may not have decided in his mind who should receive it. He may have intended that his associate members should not be called upon to contribute the sums required to fulfill his contract with the association. The only presumption is that he intended not to do what he omitted to do.[201] He had no personal interest in his membership and his personal representative, as such, can take no interest in it after his death. The benefit is not assets, for if the administrator can collect the money it must go primarily to Gigar's creditors. The

82 Ky. 347; Duvall v. Goodson, 79 Ky. 224; Masonic Rel. Ass'n v. Mc-Auley, 2 Mackey 70; McClure v. Johnson, 56 Ia. 620; Ballou v. Gile Admr., 50 Wis. 614; American Legion of Honor v. Perry, 140 Mass. 580; 5 N. E. 634; Sup. Counc., etc., v. Priest, 46 Mich. 429; 9 N. W. 481; Whitehurst, Admr. v. Whitehurst, 83 Va. 153; 1 S. E. 801; Covenant Mut. Ben. Ass'n v. Sears, et al., 114 Ill. 108; Swift v. San Francisco S. & E. Board, 67 Cal. 567; Fenn v. Lewis, 10 Mo. App. 478; West v. Grand Lodge A. O. U. W., 14 Tex. Civ. App. 471; 37 S. W. 966.

200 Eastman v. Provident Mut. Rel. Ass'n, 20 C. L. J. 266; 62 N. H. 555.
201 Worley v. N. W. Mass. Aid Ass'n, 10 Fed. 227; 11 Ins. L. J. 141.

charter, by-laws and certificate, all show that neither party had any such understanding. If Gigar had exercised the power of appointment, it is plain that the administrator could not maintain a suit to recover the money. How does Gigar's neglect to exercise it give him the power? There being no contract to pay to Gigar or to this legal representative, there is no breach. The plaintiff fails. In Worley v. N. W. Masonic Aid, etc.,[202] the facts are similar to those in this case and it was held that the plaintiff, who was administrator of the assured, could not recover. McClure, Exr. v. Johnson,[203] decides that where a life policy, by its terms, is payable to a person other than the assured or his representatives, the payee cannot by will make a different disposition of the fund from that directed by the policy. Our conclusion is that the plaintiff cannot recover. The evidence offered as to Gigar's intention as to whom the money should be made payable, was inadmissible to vary the construction of the certificate, and was insufficient to constitute a trust.''[204] And where a member never designated any beneficiary it was held that the fund reverted to the society even though he left a widow.[205] Where a competent beneficiary has been designated by the member the wife has no claim.[206] The Court of Appeals of Kentucky, in passing upon a case involving the disposition of a benefit,[207] says: "A life policy for the benefit of the family of the person procuring, though not a testament, is in the nautre of a testament, and in construing it the courts should treat it, as far as possible, as a will, as in so doing they will more nearly approximate the intention of the persons the destination of whose bounty is involved in such cases. As said in a former case, it is not to be supposed that a father, in procuring insurance on his own life for the benefit of his family, or in keeping such a policy alive, intends to benefit himself or his estate, and especially is that true when, by the terms of the charter of the company in which he insures, with which

[202] *Supra.*
[203] 56 Ia. 620.
[204] Wason v. Colburn, 99 Mass. 342.
[205] Grand Lodge A. O. U. W. v. Cleghorn (Tex. Civ. A.), 42 S. W. 1043; West v. Grand Lodge, etc., 14 Tex. Civ. A. 471; 37 S. W. 966.
[206] Sheehan v. Journeymen Butchers', etc., Ass'n, 142 Cal. 489; 76 Pac. 238.
[207] Duvall, etc., v. Goodson, 79 Ky. 224.

he must be supposed to be familiar, he cannot take insurance for the benefit of anyone except his wife or children, if he have either, and cannot dispose of the insurance if he leave either wife or child surviving. We, therefore, conclude that the charter gave the member a mere power of appointment in case he has neither wife nor child, and that he has no interest whatever in the fund, and, therefore, it did not pass under a will merely disposing of all his estate, but in which no mention is made of the fund to arise from his membership.''[208] In a case decided by the Supreme Court of Illinois,[209] where the charter of defendant declared the objects of the association to be ''to afford financial aid and assistance to the widows, orphans, heirs or devisees of deceased members,'' and the certificate was payable to the member's, ''devisees, as provided in last will and testament, or in event of their prior death, to the legal heirs or devisees of the certificate holder,'' the member died intestate and the complainants, his only heirs, brought a bill to recover the benefit money. The Court held that the clear intent was that the devisees, or the heirs—one or either of them should take. That if there were no devisee then to the heir.[210]

§ 311. **The Same Subject—A Leading Case.**—In the case of Supreme Colony United Order of Pilgrim Fathers v. Towne,[211] the Supreme Court of Connecticut says: ''Under the laws of the society and the law of its incorporation, the member had the power to designate to whom the death benefit should be paid, and also the power to substitute a new beneficiary. He had, under his contract, no other control over the benefit, and as a consequence no property interest in it. 'An appointment so made is revocable, because it is a mere unilateral act, not amounting to a transfer, and creating no vested interest.'[212] A mere power of appointment is not an asset in the donee of the power and conveys no title to or interest in the property conveyed,[213] and, unexercised by the donee prior to his death, becomes wholly inoperative. The in-

---

[208] See *ante,* § 306.

[209] Covenant Mut. Ben. Ass'n v. Sears, 114 Ill. 108.

[210] See also Smith v. Covenant, etc., Ass'n, 24 Fed. 685; and Newman v. Covenant Mut. Ben. Ass'n, 76 Ia. 56; 40 N. W. 87; see also Jewell v. Grand Lodge A. O. U. W., 41 Minn. 405; 48 N. W. 88.

[211] 87 Conn. 644; 89 Atl. 264; Ann. Cas. 1916 B 181.

[212] Colburn's Appeal, 74 Conn. 463, 468; 51 Atl. 139; 92 Am. St. R. 231.

[213] Co. Lit. 235b.

sured member can neither assign, transfer, pledge, nor will the benefit. Nor does it descend to his heirs. The estate of the assured is not among the classes of beneficiaries which may be named; hence the insured could not designate his estate as a beneficiary. What he could not dispose of in life neither the laws of the society nor the law of its incorporation attempt to give upon his decease. Not infrequently the laws of a fraternal benefit society provide for the disposition of a death benefit where the member has failed to exercise his right of designation, sometimes giving the benefit to certain classes of the beneficiaries open to designation, and occasionally to the estate of the insured member. In such instances the right to the benefits comes through the laws of the society or the law of its incorporation and not through any property interest of the insured member in the benefit. A classification of the estate of the insured among the beneficiaries open to designation would violate the theory of fraternal benefits, since such a provision would conform its contract in one important respect to the ordinary feature of life insurance, making the insurance a part of the assets of the insured and available for his debts. The authorities, with little dissent, agree that neither the insured member nor his estate has any property interest in the fraternal benefit, in the absence of provision in the laws of the society, or the law of its incorporation, or in the contract made, giving such interest.[214] For the reason that the disposition of the benefit is unprovided for by the contract made, and neither the beneficiary named, nor the insured member, ever acquired any property interest in the benefit, and hence no one under the contract is legally entitled to the benefit, a number of the courts have held that the legal position of the benefit is that it reverts to the society.[215] In a few of the States the courts have disposed

[214] Cook v. Improved Order Heptasophs, 202 Mass. 85, 88 N. E. 584; Eastman v. Ass'n, 62 N. H. 554, 556; Hellenberg Ex'r v. District No. 1, 94 N. Y. 580; Warner v. Modern Woodmen of Am., 67 Neb. 232, 237; 93 N. W. 397; 61 L. R. A. 603; 108 Am. St. Rep. 634; 2 Ann. Cas. 660; Pilcher v. Puckett, 77 Kan. 284, 288; 94 Pac. 132.

[215] Eastman v. Ass'n, 62 N. H. 554, 556; Hellenberg Ex'r v. District No. 1; 94 N. Y. 580; Warner v. Modern Woodmen of Am,, supra; Golden Star Fraternity v. Martin, 59 N. J. L. 207; 35 Atl. 908; Pilcher v. Puckett, 77 Kan. 284; 94 Pac. 132; Bishop Bros. v. Curphey, 60 Miss. 22; 29 Cyc. 157, 159.

of the fund in case of the decease or failure to designate the beneficiary upon the theory that a resulting trust arises either in favor
of the classes from whom the beneficiary might have been named
or in favor of the estate of the insured member. In the late case
of Cook v. Order Heptasophs,[216] the Court says: 'But to say
that, when there is a failure to make a valid appointment, the
fund shall go to the member as a resulting trust is to announce
a result totally inconsistent for the purpose for which the fund
was created. There can be no resulting trust which is inconsistent
with the trust created by statute.' The reference is to the statute
designating the classes of beneficiaries who may be named. We
have no occasion to determine whether, in the absence of designation of a beneficiary, a resulting trust exists in favor of the beneficiaries named in the statute, or whether the fund reverts to the
society. In Supreme Lodge N. E. O. P. v. Hine,[217] no question
was raised as to the right of the society to the fund, or as to the
legal right of the claimants to the fund. The fund was in court
to be disposed of among the claimants upon equitable considerations.''

§ 312. **Designation of Beneficiary Is Not Condition Precedent to Liability of Society.**—It has been questioned whether
the designation of beneficiary was not a condition precedent to the
liability of the society. The New York Court of Appeals has held
that the defect of designation may be supplied by construction
of the charter and by-laws.[218] The Court says: "By the act of
incorporation, the object of the defendant was to aid and support
members and their families in case of want, sickness or death;
and the act further provided that the corporation might create a
beneficiary fund for relief of members and their families, subject
to such conditions and regulations as might be adopted by the
defendant. This fund was to be set apart to be paid over to the

---

[216] 202 Mass. 85, 88 N. E. 584.

[217] 82 Conn. 315, 319; 73 Atl. 791.

[218] Bishop v. Gr. Lodge Empire Order Mut. Aid, 112 N. Y. 627; 20 N. E.
562, reversing 43 Hun. 472, which in the first edition of this work was
cited in support of a contrary doctrine to that now laid down. The same
rule was applied in Pfeifer v. Supreme Lodge Bohemian, etc., Soc. 173
N. Y. 418; 66 N. E. 108; reversing 77 N. Y. Supp. 1138; 74 App. Div. 630.
See also Munroe v. Providence, etc., Ass'n, 19 R. I. 491; 34 Atl. 997.

families, heirs or legal representatives of deceased or disabled
members or to such person or persons as the deceased might, while
living, have directed. Following out such general purpose, the
seventh section of the constitution of the defendant in order to
promote benevolence and charity, provided for the establishment
of this beneficiary fund, from which, on satisfactory evidence of
the death of a member of the order who had complied with all
its legal requirements, a sum not exceeding $2,000 was to be paid
to his family as he might direct. Stopping here, it is plain that
the parties who were to receive the $2,000 were, by the very terms
of the act of incorporation and of the constitution of the defendant, to be the families, heirs, or legal representatives of deceased
or disabled members, or such other person as the deceased member
might, while living, have directed; and we think that in case no
such direction was given, such payment was intended to be made
to the family, heirs or legal representatives of a deceased member.
It is true, the act and the constitution fail to state which it shall
be in case no direction is given, whether it shall be the family,
the heirs or legal representatives; but we think this expression
should be construed with reference to the general purpose of the
corporation and, having such purpose in view, we think it really
was meant, and that it should be held, to include those who would
take such property as in cases of intestacy. It is true that by the
twenty-fourth section of the laws of the defendant it is provided
that each member of the order shall be entitled to a certificate
setting forth the name and good standing of the member and the
amount of the benefit to be paid at death, and to whom payable.
But we do not think the issuing of such certificate is a condition
precedent to the right of such legal representatives to receive the
fund in question. The amount of the fund is provided in the
by-laws, and it is there stated to be $2,000. We think the certifi-
cate is only necessary in cases where the money is to be paid, as directed by the member, to some person or body other than the family, heirs or legal representatives of the deceased member. We cannot think that it was the intention of the defendant, in making up
its constitution, its general laws and its by-laws, to make the
issuing of such certificate a condition precedent to its liability to
pay this amount to the families, etc., of deceased members who
at the time of their decease were in good standing, and who had

615

paid all the assessments, and fully complied with all the rules and regulations of the defendant up to that time. The neglect of the company might thus result in a forfeiture of the fund.'' And where the certificate was executed, but withheld and never delivered on account of the alleged fraud of the member, it was held[219] that the society was liable, no proof of the alleged fraud having been offered. But if the membership is not complete, as, for example, because the applicant has not been initiated, the society will not be bound.[220] And a certificate payable to whom might be designated by will is valid.[221]

§ 313. **When Designation of Beneficiary Lapses.**—In event of the death of the party designated in the lifetime of a member of the society, then there is also a failure of the exercise of the power, and, unless the contract provides otherwise, or there is another designation of a person entitled to take, the power lapses and the society takes by reversion. This rule has always been applied, one of the first precedents being the early case of Oke v. Heath,[222] where Lord Hardwicke held, the case being one where an appointee, by a will, died in the lifetime of the testator, who had power only to appoint by will, that by such death the appointment became void. The quaint language used will apply to the exercise of powers by members of benefit societies which are as a rule revocable, for he says: ''Then she, executing her power by will, it must be construed to all intents like a will; the conditions of which are, that it is ambulatory, revocable and incomplete till her death; nor can anyone dying in the testator's life, take under it.'' Other old cases are to the same effect.[223] Modern authority follows the older precedents.[224] It has been

---

[219] Lorscher v. Supreme Lodge K. of H., 72 Mich. 316; 40 N. W. 545.

[220] Matkin v. Supreme Lodge K. of H., 82 Tex. 301; 18 S. W. 306.

[221] Ledebuhr v. Wisconsin Trust Co., 112 Wis. 657; 88 N. W. 607.

[222] 1 Ves. Sr. 139.

[223] Marlborough v. Godolphin, 2 Ves. Sr. 60; Burges v. Mawbey, 10 Ves. Jr. 319.

[224] Masonic Mut. Relief Ass'n v. McAuley, 2 Mackey 70; Gutterson v. Gutterson, 50 Minn. 278; 52 N. W. 530; Van Bibber's Admr. v. Van Bibber, 82 Ky. 347; Ballou v. Gile, 50 Wis. 614; Given v. Wisconsin Odd Fellows' Mut. L. Ins. Co., 71 Wis. 547; 37 N. W. 817; Duvall v. Goodson, 79 Ky. 224; Hellenberg v. Dist. No. 1, I. O. B. B., 94 N. Y. 580; American

held[225] that if the laws of the order do not provide what shall become of the benefit if the beneficiary die in the lifetime of the member the fund reverts to the society. It is but fair, however, to state that in a majority of these late authorities the reason of the decision has been, not the lapse of the designation, because it was ambulatory and liable to be revoked by the death of the appointee before that of the member, but a construction of the supposed intention of such member. One of the principal cases arose in the District of Columbia.[226] A member of the association designated his wife as the beneficiary of the fund; she died and he married again, but soon afterwards died, without changing his first appointment. The by-laws provided that on the death of a member the fund accruing because of the membership should be paid to "his widow, orphan, heir, assignee or legatee;" the right of the member to designate the beneficiary was recognized and this designation could be changed with the consent of the board of directors. If the member died "without legal representatives" the fund went to the association. Upon the death of the member the fund was claimed by the administrators of the deceased wife by the administrators of the husband and by the widow. The Court in deciding the question said: "It will be sufficient to remark that in this case the question at issue is controlled by the particular language of the designation made by the husband. He had the power to designate the beneficiary, and he had a right to do so either absolutely or conditionally, and the direction given by him was that, in event of his death, all benefits arising from his connection with the association should be paid to his wife, Ann Reed. Now, it is obvious that this direction cannot be literally gratified unless the wife survive the husband, and the whole language of the husband on this point is that of contingency or condition. He was looking forward to this provision for the benefit of his wife in case she should survive him—that is, in that contingency. His own death was not, of course, contingent; it was an

Legion of Honor v. Perry, 140 Mass. 580; 5 N. E. 634; Adams Policy Trusts, 23 Ch. Div. 525; 52 L. J. Ch. 642; 48 L. T. 727; 31 W. R. 810; Supreme Council A. L. H. v. Gehrenbeck, 124 Cal. 43; 56 Pac. 640; Screwmen's Benev. Ass'n v. Whitridge, 95 Tex. 539; 68 S. W. 501.

225 Home Circle Soc. v. Hanley, 38 Tex. Civ. App. 547; 86 S. W. 641.
226 Masonic Mut. Relief Ass'n v. McAuley, 2 Mackey 70.

event certain to occur; but it might be regarded as contingent with reference to some other event—the death of his wife for instance —and we think the fair interpretation of the language of the husband is that, in case of his dying before his wife, the benefits aris-` ing under this transaction were to inure to her, but not otherwise. To construe it otherwise would be to hold that the design of the husband in making this provision was that its benefits should go first, to the wife, if she survived, but otherwise to her relations; and it is not to be supposed that this association was organized and sustained by its members for the purpose of benefiting the relations of their widows. We think, therefore, the meaning of the language used by the husband in designating the beneficiary was that the benefits of this provision were to go to his wife only in case she survived him; and as she did not survive her husband, the provision falls to the ground so far as she is concerned, and the claims of her representatives are out of the question. The controversy remains then between the personal representatives or administrators of the husband and the surviving widow. In behalf of the former, the same general ground already stated is taken, namely, that this is virtually an insurance on the husband's life, and as such would pass to his estate. In some respects it is like a life insurance and in other respects it is different. It was not designed to provide for creditors of the husband or for those generally interested in his estate; but for his widow, orphans or immediate heirs; and therefore the charter provides for 'the immediate payment to the widow, orphans, heir, assignee or legatee of a deceased member, of as many dollars as there are members in good standing on the books of the corporation.' The charter and the by-laws control the destination of this fund, and they explicitly provide that in the condition of affairs which this case presents, the widow, orphans, heir, assignee or legatee shall be entitled to receive it. An argument is based on the language of article V, section 5 (of the charter) which provides that where the deceased member has no legal representative, the money shall become the property of the association. From this provision it is argued that if there are legal representatives of the deceased, they must be entitled to the fund. This argument, if it proved anything, would prove too much. It would prove that in a case where there were no legal representatives, notwithstanding the existence

618

of a widow, or an orphan, or heir, the money must go back into the general fund of the association to the direct frustration of the whole scheme and object of the association and in disregard of the express language of its charter and by-laws. We think, therefore, that the term, 'legal representatives,' here means those who are the legal representatives in the contemplation of this charter and by-laws, namely the very people who are there enumerated, 'the widow, orphans, heir, or legatee.' The fund is to go to some one of these parties. They are mentioned disjunctively: 'the money is to be paid to the widow, or the orphans,. or the heir, or the assignee or legatee. Now, that means one of two things, either that it shall go to some one of these to be selected by some authority, or else that they are to have precedence in the order in which they are named. But there is no authority provided for or indicated in either the charter or the by-laws by whom any one of these beneficiaries shall be selected; and, therefore, our conclusion is, that the order in which they are named is the order in which they are to benefit by this fund; first, the widow; if there is no widow, then the orphans; if there is no orphan, then the heir, etc. In this case the question is between the widow and the personal representatives. The latter are excluded entirely by our construction of the by-laws, and, therefore, the decree will be that the widow shall take the fund.'' It has been held that where, by the laws of the society and the State, the payment of benefits is confined to the heirs of the member, or members of his family, and the member designated his wife, and she afterwards became divorced from him, that the appointment was thereby revoked.[227] This view, however, has not always prevailed and there is authority to the contrary.[228] But divorce *a mensa et thoro* does not affect

[227] Tyler v. Odd Fellows' Mut. R. Ass'n, 145 Mass. 134; 13 N. E. 360. To the same effect are Saenger v. Rothschild, 123 N. Y. 577; 26 N. E. 3; affg. 2 N. Y. Supp. 794; Courtois v. Grand Lodge, etc., 135 Cal. 552; 67 Pac. 970; Order Railway Conductors v. Koster, 55 Mo. App. 186. See also Farra v. Braman, 171 Ind. 529; 86 N. E. 843; 84 N. E. 155; 82 N. E. 926.

[228] White v. Brotherhood, etc., 124 Ia. 293; 99 N. W. 1071; Overhiser v. Overhiser, 14 Colo. App. 1; 59 Pac. 75; Brown v. Grand Lodge, etc., 208 Pa. St. 101; 57 Atl. 176; Grego v. Grego, 78 Miss. 443; 28 Sou. 817. See also *post*, § 326.

the designation.[229]   The Supreme Court of Massachusetts has also
held that where the member designated his mother, and she was
a person whom he could lawfully so designate, as his beneficiary,
this appointment was not revoked by his subsequent marriage.[230]
Although in the cases just cited the courts have been controlled
by the supposed intent of the member, the same conclusions would
have been reached had the rules generally governing the execution of powers been followed. As the death of the appointee,
under a power executed by will, during the life of the testator,
causes the appointment to fall, so where a member of a benefit
society designates a benefiicary who dies during the lifetime of the
member, the designation is revoked, or lapses, and it has been
held that if the designated beneficiary dies after the designation
but before the issuance of a certificate and in the lifetime of the
member the designation fails.[231]   A provision in the laws of a
fraternal benefit society that benefits will be paid to the beneficiary designated by the insured or to his legal representatives
does not require payment to the legal representatives of a beneficiary who died in the lifetime of the insured.[232]   Where the member died without leaving wife or children and making no designation of beneficiary it was held that the sisters could not recover.[233]   The proceeds of a benefit certificate are no part of the
estate of the beneficiary who died before the member.[234]

§ 314. **The Same Subject Continued—Resulting Trust.**—
Conceding the rule to be that, if the person designated as beneficiary die in the lifetime of the member, a lapse of the designation results, it has been held that, under the rules of the society,
the benefit generally will not revert to the society but a resulting
trust accrues for the benefit of either those designated by the
laws of the organization to receive in case of failure of designa-

[229] Supreme Council A. L. H. v. Smith, 45 N. J. E. 466; 17 Atl. 770.
[230] Catholic Order of Foresters v. Callahan, 146 Mass. 391; 16 N. E.
14. See also Grand Lodge, etc., v. Child, 70 Mich. 163; 38 N. W. 1.
[231] Order Mut. Companions v. Griest, 76 Cal. 494; 18 Pac. 652; In re
Eaton, 23 Ontario R. (Ch. D.) 593.
[232] Order of Scottish Clans v. Reich (Conn.), 97 Atl. 863.
[233] Hepner v. Grand Lodge, 123 N. Y. Supp. 819; 68 Misc. 340.
[234] Sykes v. Armstrong (Miss), 71 Sou. 262.

tion, or for those entitled to take as heirs of the member under the statutes of distribution.[235] Thus where the certificate contained no provision that it was to accrue to the representatives of the wife, it was held that a resulting trust was created in favor of such member and the proceeds became part of his estate.[236] The same result follows where the designation is illegal. As was said by the Supreme Court of Massachusetts:[237] "The designation of beneficiaries in the policy or certificate of membership is invalid, as the statutes under which the defendant corporation was organized did not authorize it to grant insurance for the benefit of friends.[238] But an invalid designation of beneficiary does not render the whole contract invalid. The contract in terms recognizes that there may be a change or substitution of beneficiaries, and there is a provision that, if the member shall survive all original or substituted beneficiaries, then his membership shall be for the benefit of his legal heirs. This provision is within the authority of St. 1882,[239] heirs being included under the head of relatives, and if there is no other legal designation, this may take effect."· The Court of Chancery of New Jersey has also considered the subject and thus reasons: "The claim is that the right of a beneficiary to take depends on the fact that the power of appointment vested in a member has been exercised in his favor, and that if he cannot show such an appointment he is without right. But this view manifestly overlooks another very material part of the contract. One of the defendant's by-laws, it will be remembered,

235 Wolf v. District No. 1, etc., 102 Mich. 23; 60 N. W. 445; Carson v. Vicksburg Bank, 75 Miss. 167; 22 Sou. 1; 37 L. R. A. 559; Chicago, etc., v. Wheeler, 79 Ill. App. 241; Simon v. O'Brien, 87 Hun. 160; 33 N. Y. Supp. 815; Finn v. Eminent Household, etc., 163 Ky. 187; 773 S. W. 349; Beresh v. Supreme Lodge K. of H., 255 Ill. 122; 99 N. E. 349; affg. 166 Ill App. 571; Starke v. Plattdeutsche, etc., 166 Ill. App. 146; In re Viles, 155 N. Y. Supp. 401; Supreme Council A. L. H. v. Adams, 68 N. H. 236; 44 Atl. 380. See also cases cited, post, § 317.
236 Haskins v. Kendall, 158 Mass. 224; 33 N. E. 495; Walsh v. Walsh, 20 N. Y. Supp. 933; In re Eaton, 23 Ontario R. (Ch. D.) 593.
237 Rindge v. New England M. A. Soc., 146 Mass. 286; 15 N. E. 628; Supreme Lodge New England Order, etc., v. Hine, 82 Conn. 315; 73 Atl. 791; Murphy v. Nowak, 223 Ill. 301; 79 N. E. 112; 7 L. R. A. (N. S.), 393.
238 Daniels v. Pratt, 143 Mass. 221; 10 N. E. 166.
239 C. 195, § 1.

ordains in substance that if the beneficiary appointed by a member dies in the lifetime of the member, and the member shall subsequently make no other or further disposition of the part of the benefit fund payable on his death, it shall on his death be paid to his legal heirs dependent on him; and that if there be no person entitled to receive it, according to the laws of the order, it shall revert to the widows and orphans' benefit fund. If we look then at the whole contract and construe it in the light of all of its provisions, it would seem to be clear that there can be no lapse or reverter, except a member dies without leaving an heir dependent on him. This is the construction which similar contracts have already received. In the case of Legion of Honor v. Perry,[240] the Supreme Court of Massachusetts said,[241] 'The statute under which the plaintiff (corporation) is organized (the defendant in this case is organized under the same statute) gives it authority to provide for the widows, orphans or other dependents upon deceased members, and provides that such fund shall not be liable to attachment. The classes of persons to be benefited are designated and the corporation has no authority to create a fund for other persons than of the classes named. The corporation has power to raise a fund payable to one of the classes named in the statute, to set it apart to await the death of the member, and then to pay it over to the person or persons of the class named in the statute, selected and appointed by the member during his life and if no one is so selected it is still payable to one of the classes named.' The Appellate Court of the first district of Illinois in enforcing a contract made by the defendant in this case, containing substantially the same terms found in the contract now in suit, said, after adopting the view which has just been quoted from the opinion in Legion of Honor v. Perry, that where the beneficiaries are prescribed by law, it is an invasion of its policy and a violation of its letter to say that where a member has named a person not within the class to be benefited, and the corporation has issued the certificate to such person such acts shall deprive

[240] Supra.
[241] 140 Mass. 589; 5 N. E. 636. See also Clarke v. Schwartzenberg, 162 Mass. 98; 38 N. E. 17; Sargent v. Knights of Honor, 158 Mass. 557; 33 N. E. 650.

the proper person or class of persons of all right to or interest in the fund.[242] These decisions settle the construction which should be given to that part of the contract, which is put in contest in this case, and they settle it in strict accord with the purpose which the legislature had in view in authorizing the formation of such corporations as the defendant. The legislative purpose is clear. It was to provide a way by which men of small means might combine together to accumulate a fund for the benefit of those who should, as each dropped out by death, be dependent on him for food, raiment and shelter and from which his dependents should on his death, receive a certain fixed sum. So it would seem to be entirely clear that the complainant's case falls directly within both the terms of the contract on which her action is founded and the purpose of the statute from which the defendant derives its corporate life and power. She is one of the next of kin of a deceased member of the defendant corporation. She is also his heir by force of our statute regulating descents, but not according to the canons of the common law,[243] but the phrase 'legal heirs' as used in the defendant's by-laws, directing that in case a member shall have made no disposition of the benefit payable on his death his benefit shall, on his death, be paid to his legal heirs dependent on him, is obviously used as the equivalent of 'next of kin,' or perhaps in a still broader sense, meaning 'dependents' as well as 'next of kin.' That it is used in a sense broader than that which its words, understood in a technical sense, import, is placed beyond doubt when it is remembered that the fund from which the benefit is payable was established for the benefit of the widows and orphans of deceased members and persons dependent on deceased members. If in this case the deceased member had left no person who would have been entitled to succeed to his land as heir, but had left a widow, I do not think it would have been successfully contended that that part of the benefit fund payable on his death had lapsed because his widow was not his heir, and could not, therefore, take it. It would be impossible for any court so to adjudge without first declaring as a matter of law,

[242] Palmer v. Welch, 132 Ill. 141; 23 N. E. 412; affg. Parke v. Welch, 33 Ill. App. 188.
[243] Taylor v. Bray, 32 N. J. L. 182; on error, 36 N. J. L. 415.

that it was within the power of a corporation, organized to establish a fund for the benefit of widows of its deceased members, so to frame its by-laws as to cut off the rights of the very class of persons for whose benefit it was organized and thus defeat the fundamental object of its organization. The complainant was not only one of the next of kin of a deceased member but his dependent. She was the only person who was dependent on him at the time of his death. He left neither widow nor child and the only dependent on him at the time of his death, or to whose support he contributed during his life, was the complainant. The proofs on this part of the case are full and free from dispute. The complainant's right, therefore, to the fund for which she sues, is, in my judgment, clear.''[244] If the laws of the society provide that in case of the death of the beneficiary in lifetime of member it shall go to certain persons, such stipulation will govern and they will take.[245] The charter provision as to disposal of benefit if beneficiary dies in the lifetime of the member controls.[246] It has been held, under a construction of such laws, that, where the benefit was payable to the wife and she died and the member married again, it was on his death payable to the second wife, on the ground that such was the intent of the laws of the society.[247]

§ 315. **Death in Common Calamity.**—Where father, mother and children all perish in a common calamity, there is no presumption of survivorship, or priority of death, by reason of age

[244] See also Shea v. Mass. Ben. Ass'n, 160 Mass. 289; 35 N. E. 855; N. W. Masonic Aid Ass'n v. Jones, 154 Pa. St. 99; 26 Atl. 253; Keener v. Grand Lodge A. O. U. W., 38 M. A. 543; Sargent v. Supreme Lodge K. of H., 158 Mass. 557; 33 N. E. 650. But see also Supreme Council A. L. of H. v. Green, 71 Md. 263; 17 Atl. 1048, to the contrary. If one of several designated beneficiaries is incompetent the others take. Beard v. Sharp, 100 Ky. 606; 38 S. W. 1057.

[245] Britton v. Sup. Counc. R. A. and Keener v. Grand Lodge, *supra;* and see *post,* § 317.

[246] Runyan v. Runyan, 101 Ark. 353; 142 S. W. 519.

[247] Riley v. Riley, 75 Wis. 464; 44 N. W. 112; *In re* Griest's Estate, 76 Cal. 497; 18 Pac. 658; Given v. Ins. Co., 71 Wis. 547.

or sex, nor is it presumed that they all died at the same time.[248] But if two or more persons are lost in the same catastrophe and the ownership of property is afterwards drawn into litigation by contesting parties, each claiming to derive his right from one of the deceased persons as being the actual owner of the property when he died, and the question, of which of those deceased persons owned it at his death, turns on which survived longest, and there is no proof on this subject, the right to the property will be adjudged as it would be if it were known that both died at the same instant.[249] If the beneficiary and the member die simultaneously there is a lapse of designation and the benefit will go to the heirs of the husband, as in case of failure to designate under the laws of the society. In one case,[250] the Court says: "The court below finds that the wife, the beneficiary named by the husband, did not die before her husband, but died at the same instant. The result of this finding is that the beneficiary named at the time the policy was earned by the death of the husband did not survive him, and was incapable of taking the proceeds of the policy. The purpose of the contract of insurance entered into by the husband and the association was to provide a fund for his wife, payable at his death; and in the event she was incapable of taking, by reason of her death, then those heirs of the husband dependent upon him should take. These are plain provisions of the rules and by-laws of the association, that enter into and form part of the contract of insurance. The use of the words: 'die before' in the contract of insurance, was, evidently, intended to mean that the beneficiary named must be dead, and incapable of taking, at the time the policy was earned, by reason of the death of the husband. The instantaneous death of both the husband

[248] Cowman v. Rogers, 73 Md. 403; 21 Atl. 64; 10 L. R. A. 550. See also Johnson v. Merrithew, 80 Me. 111; 13 Atl. 132.

[249] Supreme Council R. A. v. Kacer, 96 Mo. App. 93; 69 S. W. 671. See also U. S. Casualty Co. v. Kacer, 169 Mo. 301; 69 S. W. 370; 58 L. R. A. 436; Balder v. Middeke, 92 Ill. App. 227; affd. 198 Ill. 590; 59 L. R. A. 653; In re Willbor, 20 R. I. 126; 51 L. R. A. 863, and notes. Coulter v. Linzee, 135 Mass. 468. An instructive case is Screwmen's Ben. Ass'n v. Whitridge, 68 S. W. 501; 95 Tex. 539.

[250] Paden v. Briscoe, 81 Tex. 563; 17 S. W. 42. And see cases cited last, supra.

and wife successfully accomplished the inability of the wife to take as if she had died before.''[250a]

§ 316. **Revocation of Designation.**—If the laws of the society either expressly or impliedly allow a revocation and change of designation the member may exercise that power. Such power is implied from the very nature of the contract.[251] The member may revoke the designation without exercising the right of appointment of a new beneficiary, in which case there will generally be no lapse of designation, but the benefit will go as provided by the laws of the society in case of failure to designate, or in event of the death of the beneficiaries in the lifetime of the member, or, if the laws make no such provision, a resulting trust will arise for the benefit of the heirs as shown in the section preceding. In a case of this kind,[252] the Court said, in awarding the fund to the widow: ''The intention is, to our minds, quite apparent; and it is that, in the event of the death of the beneficiaries, named in the certificate before the decease of the member, and if no other disposition be made thereof, or in a case where no direction has been made by the member in such certificate, the benefit should be paid to the beneficiaries of the deceased member first in the order named in section 10, which is, first to the widow, if there be one; if not, to the children, if any survive; if not, to the dependents, etc. It is true the plaintiff first designated Mrs. Rochford as the beneficiary in the certificate, but he subsequently revoked such designation, and thereafter the certificate remained without any designation. Mrs. Rochford would not be entitled, because her designation had been revoked. The fund would not revert to the supreme tent, because the constitution provides that it shall only so revert back in case the member does not leave a widow, children, etc. We think, therefore, that the certificate must be treated as if no designation had been made, and that, under our interpretation of the provisions of the sections quoted, the plaintiff becomes

250a See *post*, § 649, for further discussion.

251 Masonic Mut. Ass. v. Bunch, 409 Mo. 560; 19 S. W. 25. But see *post*, § 400, *et seq.*, where the subject is considered.

252 Cullin v. Supreme Tent K. O. T. M. (N. Y. Sup. Ct.), 28 N. Y. Supp. 276.

entitled to the fund."[253] Where a new certificate was issued without designating a beneficiary it was held that the designation in the first certificate governed.[254] Where a society amended its laws and provided that, "where marriage is contracted after the issuance of the policy and said policy becomes payable through death, it shall be paid to the widow, or, in event of her death, to their joint issue, if any, unless otherwise ordered," it was held[255] that such law did not operate so as to require a new designation, and where a member, before the adoption of the law, had designated his mother and afterwards married again the mother would take, the first designation being considered within the condition "unless otherwise ordered." The subsequent marriage of the member does not revoke his designation of beneficiary.[256] In some jurisdictions it has been held that divorce of the wife if she is designated as beneficiary operates as a revocation of designation, but in other cases the rule applies that a designation valid in its inception remains so.[257]

§ 317. **If Designated Beneficiary Die in the Lifetime of a Member, Benefit Will Be Disposed of in Accordance With Laws of Society.**—Although probably it sufficiently appears from the three preceding sections that, if there is a lapse of designation, there is a resulting trust in favor of those designated by the laws of the organization to receive in such event, or for those entitled to take as heirs of the member, it may be well to emphasize this principle by a few quotations from leading cases. The Supreme Court of Pennsylvania has said:[258] "There is a material and fundamental distinction between philanthropic or beneficial associations, which issue benefit certificates to their members, and life insurance companies, which is pointed out in Commonwealth v.

[253] See also Bishop v. Empire Order Mut. Aid, 112 N. Y. 627; 20 N. E. 562; Jewell v. Grand Lodge A. O. U. W., 41 Minn. 405; 43 N. W. 88.

[254] Derrington v. Conrad, 3 Kan. App. 725; 45 Pac. 458.

[255] Benton v. Brotherhood R. R. Brakemen, 146 Ill. 570; 34 N. E. 939; reversing 45 Ill. App. 112. See also *post*, Ch. IX, § 412.

[256] Green v. Grand United Order, etc. (Tex. Civ. A.), 163 S. W. 1068; Vanasek v. Western Bohemian, etc., Ass'n, 122 Minn. 273; 142 N. W. 333; Ladies' Auxiliary, etc., v. Flanigan (Mich.), 157 N. W. 355.

[257] See *post*, § 326.

[258] Fischer v. Am. Legion of Honor, 168 Pa. St. 279-285; 31 Atl. 1089.

Equitable B. Ass'n,[259] and has since been recognized in Dickenson v. A. O. U. W.,[260] and Lithgow v. Supreme Tent, etc.[261] It appears from the charter and by-laws that the association was organized for social, moral and intellectual purposes and for the relief of sick and distressed members. Insurance is not its only and primary object. It limits the persons or classes of persons who may be named as beneficiaries to 'the family, orphans or dependents' and provides that in the event of the failure of all such persons the sum due shall revert to the order. . . . Where the beneficiary has died the member may name another. These provisions are in entire harmony with the object of the order as a fraternal and beneficial organization, and they are entirely incompatible with the vesting of an interest in the fund before the death of the member. Such a construction would, in many cases, by giving the fund to the legal representatives of the beneficiary, divert it entirely from the purpose intended by the member and for which the organization was formed. It was the right of Charles F. Fischer, after the death of his first wife to name a new beneficiary within the limits as to persons and 'classes prescribed. Upon his failure to do so the law of the association fixed the persons to be benefited. Of this law he presumably had knowledge and his acquiescence in the selection made by it had all the effect of a new appointment by him.'' In another case[262] the Court said: ''The certificate was issued in 1888, the beneficiary died in 1895 and the member died in November, 1897. In 1897, prior to his death, Section 5 of By-law X was amended. He was bound by this change, and so far as that by-law is material it must be taken as it stood at the time of his decease. The beneficiary, having died before the member and no other or further designation of a beneficiary having been made upon which a certificate issued the case falls within the terms of Sec. 5, Art. X, as amended. . . . Ceiley was a member and a permanent officer of the organization, and it must be assumed that he knew and understood this by-law. He knew that it provided that unless he took out a new certificate,

259 137 Pa. 412.
260 159 Pa. 258.
261 165 Pa. 292.
262 Pease v. Royal Soc., etc., 176 Mass. 506; 57 N. E. 1003.

his next of kin would be considered as his beneficiaries, and that the money would be paid to them as such. It is not to be supposed that he intended to dispute the validity of this by-law, but rather that it should be operative, and that the fund should go in accordance therewith. Under these circumstances, his failure to take out a new certificate was in effect a designation of his next of kin as the real beneficiaries, and it was not any less a direction than it would have been if he had taken out a new certificate.'' This doctrine has generally been upheld.[263] It has, however, been held to the contrary in Maryland.[264] Where several beneficiaries are named and none of them dies in the lifetime of the member the surviving beneficiaries will take the whole, especially if the contract so provides.[265] But the contrary view has sometimes been taken.[266] In the case of Warner v. Modern Woodmen,[267] it was held that a member of a fraternal beneficiary society has no such interest or property in the proceeds of a certificate therein as will impress such proceeds with a trust in favor of his estate or his creditors; and where, by the statute, payment is limited to the family, heirs, relatives or dependents of the member, the death of such member without the existence of anyone who is entitled to be made a beneficiary creates no interest in his estate in the fund mentioned in the certificate, and his administrator cannot recover against the association on such certificate. The Court in that case says: ''There being no one competent to become beneficiary, and the deceased having failed to execute the

[263] Supreme Council A. L. of H. v. Adams, 68 N. H. 236; 48 Atl. 381; Moss v. Littleton, 6 App. D. C. 201; Given v. Odd Fellows', etc., Ass'n, 71 Wis. 547; 37 N. W. 817; Supreme Council R. A. v. Bevis, 106 Mo. App 429; 80 S. W. 739; Golden Star, etc., Frat. v. Martin, 59 N. J. L. 207; 35 Atl. 908; Supreme Council R. A. v. Kacer, 96 Mo. App. 93; 69 S. W. 671; Grand Lodge A. O. U. W. v. Connolly, 58 N. J. Eq. 180; 43 Atl. 286.

[264] Thomas v. Cochran, 89 Md. 390; 43 Atl. 792; 46 L. R. A. 160; Expressmen's Mut. Ben. Ass'n v. Hurlock, 91 Md. 585; 46 Atl. 957; and see In re Copeland's Estate, 75 N. Y. Supp. 1042.

[265] See post, § 341.

[266] Supreme Council Cath., etc., v. Densford, 21 Ky. L. 1574; 56 S. W. 172; 49 L. R. A. 776; Gault v. Gault, 25 (Part II), Ky. L. 2308; 80 S. W. 493.

[267] 93 N. W. 397; 67 Neb. 233; 61 L. R. A. 603. See also Gould v. Union Traction, etc., Ass'n, 26 R. I. 142; 58 Atl. 624.

power of designation, there is a total lapse of the power. The certificate in this case was neither payable to the deceased, nor to anyone, except as named by him. He had named his legal heirs as beneficiaries. It is not alleged in the petition that no persons were in existence who could have become Richardson's legal heirs at the time he made his designation and the certificate was issued. The allegation is that at the time of his death no such heirs could be found. It is not claimed that he named any other beneficiary, and why he did not do so, it is unnecessary to inquire. He may have intended that his associate members should not be called upon to contribute the sum required to fulfill the contract. As we have before stated, it could not go to the administrator, nor be subject to the payment of the· debts of the member. Where there is a failure to designate a beneficiary, or there is a void designation, or the death of the beneficiary occurs before that of the insured, and no new beneficiary is named, the association is not liable; and, if no disposition of the fund is provided for in the contract with the association, it reverts to the society.''

§ 318. **The Same Subject—Examples of Construction.**—Where the by-laws of the society forming part of the contract provide for the disposal of the benefit in case of the death of the beneficiary during the lifetime of the member, such provisions determine the right to the benefit.[268] However, the Court of Appeals of Kentucky has held[269] that if the beneficiary dies before the insured the benefit is payable to the administrator of the beneficiary, and the same rule seems to prevail in Tennessee.[270] Where the first wife designated as beneficiary is dead the second wife

---

[268] Polhill v. Battle, 124 Ga. 111; 52 S. E. 87; Davis v. McGraw, 206 Mass. 294; 92 N. E. 232; Hines v. Modern Woodmen of America, 41 Okla. 135; 137 Pac. 675; Schneider v. Modern Woodmen of America, 96 Neb. 545; 148 N. W. 334.

[269] Buckler v. Supreme Council Catholic Knights, 143 Ky. 618; 136 S. W. 1006. See also Vaughan v. Modern Brotherhood of America, 149 Ky. 587; 149 S. W. 937.

[270] Simms v. Randall, 117 Tenn. 543; 96 S. W. 971, and in New Jersey. Anderson v. Supreme Council, etc., 70 N. J. Eq. 810; 67 Atl. 1103; affg. 69 N. J. Eq. 176; 60 Atl. 759. .

was held entitled under the by-laws to the benefit.[271] And where the member while unmarried designated his father and afterwards married and died without having changed the designation, the widow was held to be entitled to the benefit.[272] This conclusion was reached by the court from a construction of a law and rule of the order, which provided that if a member in good standing dies without having designated a beneficiary, or if the designation of the beneficiary is contrary to the provisions of the charter, the Board of Directors shall determine to whom the money shall be paid, and further provided that in all cases the beneficiaries should not be in conflict with the provisions of the charter of the Knights of Columbus. In a case where the wife died before the member and thereafter the member married again and was divorced and subsequently married a third time, of which marriage there was a child, the third wife and all the children were held to be entitled to the benefit. The Court held that where the beneficiary is not in existence at the time of the member's death, and there are persons in existence who are eligible as beneficiaries, the fund is held in trust for those of the eligibles who stand first in order and where such eligible class consists of more than one, all within that class take the fund share and share alike and the order of eligibility must be as named in the statute.[273] And the wife has been held entitled to the benefit as against a child of the first marriage.[274] Where a benefit certificate was "payable as designated by will," and the will of the member named his executor as beneficiary, the Court held that the designation was void and under the by-laws the certificate became payable to the heirs of the member and that the executor might recover the amount due as trustee for the heirs.[275] However, it has been held[276] that where the beneficiary dies before the insured and

[271] Harris v. Thomas (Tex. Civ. App.), 97 S. W. 504; Speegle v. Sovereign Camp Woodmen of the World, 77 S. C. 517; 58 S. E. 435.

[272] Larkin v. Knights of Columbus, 188 Mass. 22; 73 N. E. 850. See also Knights of Columbus v. Rowe, 70 Conn. 545; 40 Atl. 451.

[273] Kaemmerer v. Kaemmerer, 231 Ill. 154; 83 N. E. 133.

[274] Cooper v. Order of Railway Conductors, 156 Iowa 481; 137 N. W. 472.

[275] Supreme Lodge K. of H. v. Bieler, 105 N. E. 244.

[276] Devaney v. Ancient Order of Hibernians, 122 Minn. 221; 142 N. W. 316.

no new beneficiary was designated the right to the benefit passed to the next of kin and payment of the money to the administrator of the insured constituted no defense in an action by such next of kin against the order. The general rule remains unimpaired that if the by-laws provide how the benefit should be disposed of in case the beneficiary dies in the lifetime of the member, such laws will control and the court will, where the money is paid into court, dispose of the fund in accordance with such by-laws.[277]

If the certificate be payable to the wife of the member, her heirs, etc., and she died leaving no children, the heirs of the husband will take and not those of the wife.[278] Where the benefit was payable according to will and the member died intestate it was held that under the laws of the society the benefit went to the father, the son leaving no widow.[279] There is no resulting trust where a policy of insurance on the life of a wife was payable to her children and she dies childless.[280] But there is in favor of the executors of the assured where the policy was payable to the wife who had poisoned him.[281] And this rule has been applied to a beneficiary association.[282]

§ 319. **Limitations Upon Power: Restricting the Designation to Certain Classes.**—In nearly all benefit societies limitations are placed by the charter and by-laws, or by statute, upon the power of the members to designate the beneficiaries of the money to be paid under the contract. Where the power is special it must be exercised within the restrictions imposed by the terms of its creation, which, in the case of the associations under consideration, are contained in the charter and by-laws as modified

[277] Supreme Colony United Order of Pilgrim Fathers v. Towne, 87 Conn. 644; 89 Atl. 264; Grand Lodge A. O. U. W. v. Edwards, 111 Me. 359; 89 Atl. 147; Supreme Council v. McKnight, 238 Ill. 349; 87 N. E. 299; Haberley v. Haberley, 27 Cal. App. 139; 149 Pac. 53; Supreme Lodge Knights of Honor v. Bieler, 58 Ind. App. 550; 105 N. E. 244.

[278] Lyon v. Rolf (Michigan Mut. Ben. Ass'n v. Rolf), 76 Mich. 146; 42 N. W. 1094.

[279] Jewell v. Grand Lodge A. O. U. W., 41 Minn. 405; 43 N. W. 88.

[280] McElwee v. New York Life Ins. Co., 47 Fed. 798.

[281] Cleaver v. Mut. Reserve Fund Life Ass'n, 1 Q. B. 147.

[282] Schmidt v. Northern Life Ass'n, 112 Ga. 41; 83 N. W. 800; 51 L. R. A. 141.

by statute. A case was decided in Kentucky where the society was organized under special charter, which provided among other things for the creation of a fund by assessments upon the members; this fund was declared to be "for the benefit of the widows and children of the deceased members, and the balance to defray the expenses of the company," and further: "The fund created for the benefit of the widow and children of the deceased member, shall be paid to them by said company. . . . Or if he should leave no widow or child, then to be appropriated according to his will; or if he makes no will, and leaves no widow and child, it shall vest and remain in the company." The certificate issued to Miller, the member, obligated the company to pay to "his heirs or as he may direct in his will." Miller died intestate leaving no child but a widow, whose committee in lunacy sued for the money. The fund was also claimed by Miller's administrator. The Court of Appeals, in passing on the case,[283] says: "We need not stop to inquire what may be the extent of the power of the company to make contracts, nor whether a covenant with the ancestor to pay to the heir after his death will pass to the personal representative of the ancestor, or to the heir for whose benefit the covenant was made, because we are of the opinion that whatever might be the answers to those inquiries, they could have no influence on the decision of this case. The charter prescribes who may become members of the society, and their obligations, and who shall be the beneficiaries of the membership after the death of the member, and it is not in the power of the company or of the member, or of both, to alter the rights of those who by the charter are declared to be the beneficiaries, except in the mode and to the extent therein indicated. The company and Miller could

[283] Kentucky Masonic Mut. Ins. Co. v. Miller's Admr., 13 Bush 489. In accord with this case it was said in the case of Ferbrache v. Grand Lodge, etc., 81 Mo. App. at page 270: "Incorporated associations or societies of the class to which the defendant order belongs are creations of the statute, incapable of exercising any power which is not therein either expressed or clearly implied. And so it has been held that if they attempt to provide for the relief of persons not named in the statutes or shall recognize as beneficiaries such as are not named in their organic law, their acts are *ultra vires*. Keener v. Grand Lodge, 38 Mo. App. 543; Wagner v. Ben. Soc., 70 Mo. App. 161; Masonic Ben. Ass'n v. Bunch, 109 Mo. 560." See also following section.

decide the question whether he should become a member, and having done so, from that moment the rights of the beneficiaries attached, subject to be defeated by his failure to comply with the terms of his membership, but subject to no other contingency whatever. If, therefore, the stipulation to pay to Miller's heirs should be construed to have been intended to secure the fund, payable on account of his membership, to his administrator, or his creditors, such stipulation could not prevail over the unequivocal provisions of the charter, that it shall be paid to his widow and children." In Massachusetts, Missouri, Ohio, and other States, statutes have been enacted limiting the beneficiaries of members of benefit associations to certain classes of persons. It is not necessary at this place to refer more particularly to the statutes, but they generally provide that benevolent and charitable associations may become incorporated and in their laws provide for benefits, to be paid upon the death of a member to his family, widow, relatives, orphans or other dependents. In American Legion of Honor v. Perry,[284] the Supreme Court of Massachusetts said: "The statute under which the plaintiff corporation is organized gives it authority to provide for the widow, orphans or other dependents upon deceased members, and provides that such fund shall not be liable to attachment. The class of persons to be benefited is designated and the corporation has no authority to create a fund for other persons than the class named. The corporation has power to raise a fund payable to one of the classes named in the statute, to set it apart to await the death of the member, and then to pay it over to the person or persons of the class in the statute, selected and appointed by the member during his life, and, if no one is so selected, it is still payable to one of the classes named." In a later case in the same court[285] the deceased was a member of a benefit association organized under the law of Massachusetts just referred to, authorizing such organizations to provide for a benefit for the family, widow, relations, orphans or other dependents of deceased members. He had designated as his beneficiary "my estate." The Court says: "The designation by Dewey that his money should go to his estate, was invalid.

[284] 140 Mass. 580; 5 N. E. 634.
[285] Daniels v. Pratt, 143 Mass. 221; 10 N. E. 166.

If it were a part of his estate, it would be assets for the payment of debts and expenses of administration, and would be subject to an unrestricted disposition by will. But this is inconsistent with the statute, and so beyond the powers of the parties.'' In this case the money had been paid to the executors, but the Court held that he held it in trust to pay it over to the person entitled thereto. The executor may be the proper party to sue to recover a benefit in case of the death in the lifetime of the member of the beneficiary, but in such case the fund is not assets as held in the preceding case, but is a trust fund for the persons for whose benefit the society was formed.[286] In Ohio, under a somewhat similar statute, the Supreme Court, in passing upon a case, where a member of a benefit society attempted to dispose of the benefit by will and to a creditor, not related to him, held:[287] ''That the plaintiff in error had no power to issue certificates of membership payable upon the death of an insured member to a person not an heir, or of the family of a deceased member, and that such a certificate is void, is too well established to admit of controversy. If the assured may designate the beneficiary of the insurance by testamentary appointment (a question the determination of which is not necessary in the case before us), it is very clear that such beneficiary must be either a member of his family, or one who, upon his death, may be his heir.'' In a case in Michigan,[288] the Supreme Court of that State said: ''It appears that under a Kentucky charter, and under the constitution as it stood prior to 1884, the benefits could be made payable to his family, or as the member should direct. This, apparently, would have made Nairn a competent beneficiary, if we can regard these constitutions as controlling the contract. But this benefit is payable by a corporation of the State of Missouri, and the laws of that State very clearly and expressly forbid–corporations of this sort from paying benefits to any but the member's family or dependents. This prohibition is further strengthened by some further provisions making it unlawful to issue policies of life insurance,

[286] Bishop v. Grand Lodge Empire Order M. A,. 112 N. Y. 627; 20 N. E. 562; and see *post*, § 562.
[287] National Mut. Aid Ass'n v. Gonser, 43 Ohio St. 1; 1 N. E. 11.
[288] Knights of Honor v. Nairn, 60 Mich. 44; 26 N. W. 826.

or for the benefit of the members themselves in any shape. The restrictions imposed by the laws of Missouri cannot be abrogated or changed by the corporation, and it cannot subject itself·to any outside control, which will override the laws of its organization as a corporate body. The intent of the prohibition is clearly to shut out all persons who are not actual relatives, or standing in the place of relatives in some permanent way, or in some actual dependence on the member." But the provisions of a State statute limiting the beneficiaries to certain classes, does not apply to foreign associations unless expressly so stated.[289] The numerous cases which have arisen throughout the country, as a rule, support the principles as above stated.[290] Under the statute of Massachusetts defining a contract of insurance upon the assessment plan to be one "whereby a benefit is to accrue to a party or parties named therein upon the death or physical disability of a person, which benefit is in any degree or manner conditioned upon per-

---

[289] Hoffmeyer v. Muench, 59 Mo. App. 20; Supreme Commandery, etc., v. Merrick, 165 Mass. 421; 43 N. E. 127. But see Courtney v. Ass'n, 120 Mo. App. 110.

[290] American Legion of Honor v. Perry, 140 Mass. 580; 5 N. E. 634; Elsey v. Odd Fellows', etc., 142 Mass. 224; 7 N. E. 844; Daniels v. Pratt, 143 Mass. 216; 10 N. E. 166; National Mut. Aid, etc., v. Gonser, 43 Ohio St. 1; 1 N. E. 11; State v. People's Mut. Ben. Ass'n, 42 Ohio St. 579; State v. Moore, 38 Ohio St. 7; State v. Standard Life Ass'n, 38 Ohio St. 281; Knights of Honor v. Nairn, 60 Mich. 44; 26 N. W. 826; Ky. Masonic Mut. Life Ins. Co. v. Miller's Admr., 13 Bush 489; Van Bibber's Admr. v. Van Bibber, 82 Ky. 347; Duvall v. Goodson, 79 Ky. 224; Masonic Mut. Relief Ass'n v. McAuley, 2 Mackey 70; Worley v. N. W. Masonic Aid Ass'n, 10 Fed. 227; Expressmen's, etc., v. Lewis, 9 Mo. App. 412; Ballou v. Gile, etc., 50 Wis. 614; Presb. Ass. Fund v. Allen, 106 Ind. 593; 7 N. E. 317; Dietrich et al. v. Madison Rel. Ass'n, 45 Wis. 79; Highland v. Highland, 109 Ill. 366; Addison v. N. E. Com. Travelers' Ass'n, 144 Mass. 591; 12 N. E. 407; Skillings v. Mass. Ben. Ass'n, 146 Mass. 217; 15 N. E. 566; Rice v. N. Eng. M. A. Soc., 146 Mass. 248; 15 N. E. 624; Condell v. Woodward, 16 Ky. L. 742; 29 S. W. 614; Gibson v. Imperial Council, etc., 168 Mass. 391; 47 N. E. 101; Groth v. Central Verein, etc., 95 Wis. 140; 70 N. W. 80; Grand Lodge Sons, etc., v. Iselt (Tex. Civ. A.), 37 S. W. 377; Fodell v. Miller, 193 Pa. St. 570; 44 Atl. 919; Journeymen Butchers' etc., v. Bristol, 17 Cal. App. 576; 120 Pac. 787; Farra v. Braman, 171 Ind. 529; 84 N. E. 155; 82 N. E. 926; Umbarger v. Modern Brotherhood of Am., 162 Mo. App. 141; 144 S. W. 893; Modern Woodmen v. Puckett (Kan.), 94 Pac. 132.

sons holding similar contracts'' an applicant may make the benefit payable to himself, in which case it must be administered as part of his estate.[291] Where by the statute the persons for whose benefit are declared to be the "widows, orphans, heirs or devisees" of deceased members, an executor is not of the class named and cannot take.[292] One not included in the classes of beneficiaries mentioned in the statute cannot indirectly become a beneficiary by agreement between the member and one lawfully entitled to become a beneficiary whereby the latter agreed to act as trustee for such excluded person.[293] The wife and children will be entitled to the benefit though another be designated.[294] It has been held that a subordinate lodge of an order can be a beneficiary, though unincorporated, no statutory requirement being violated.[295] But an old people's home is not a competent beneficiary.[296] A statute limiting the classes of beneficiaries does not apply to certificates issued before its enactment, but such statute will be given a prospective operation only.[297]

§ 320. **The Same Subject Continued.**—It has been held that a statute extending the powers of an association as to beneficiaries is effective although the society has not adopted rules extending such classes of beneficiaries,[298] although other authorities hold that a society cannot avail itself of the provisions of the statute enlarging the classes of beneficiaries without amending its charter

[291] Harding v. Littledale, 150 Mass. 100; 22 N. E. 703. See also Eastman v. Provident M. R. Ass'n, 65 N. H. 176; 18 Atl. 745.

[292] Northwestern Mass. Aid Soc. v. Jones, 154 Pa. St. 99; 26 Atl. 253.

[293] Gillam v. Dale, 69 Kan. 362; 76 Pac. 861.

[294] Knights of Columbus v. McInery, 163 Mich. 574; 117 N. W. 116. See also *supra*, § 314, *et seq.*

[295] Finch v. Grand Grove, 60 Minn. 308; 62 N. W. 384.

[296] Norwegian, etc., Soc. v. Willson, 176 Ill. 94; 52 N. E. 41.

[297] Moore v. Chicago Guaranty Fund L. Soc., 178 Ill. 202; 52 N. E. 882; affg. 76 Ill. App. 433; Grimme v. Grimme, 198 Ill. 265; 64 N. E. 1088; Roberts v. Grand Lodge A. O. U. W., 173 N. Y. 580; 65 N. E. 1122; affg. 60 App. Div. 259; 70 N. Y. Supp. 57; Voight v. Kersten, 164 Ill. 314; 45 N. E. 543; Baldwin v. Bagley, 185 Ill. 180; 56 N. E. 1065; Love v. Clune, 24 Colo. 237; 50 Pac. 34.

[298] Morey v. Monk, 145 Ala. 301; 40 Sou. 411.

to conform to the statute.[299] A society may limit the death benefits to fewer classes than those named in the statute;[300] it is not bound to accept the provisions of a statute enlarging the classes of beneficiaries.[301] The society cannot by a by-law enlarge, or diminish, the classes of beneficiaries mentioned in the statute,[302] nor can a fraternal benefit society waive the restriction as to beneficiaries which are imposed by statute.[303] The insertion of a name of a person not belonging to the classes entitled to be beneficiaries confers no right and the acceptance of assessments cannot help it.[304] The designation of a beneficiary not within the classes prescribed by the statute is absolutely void.[305] The limitation by a subsequently enacted by-law applies and the rights of the beneficiary are determined by the law in force at the time of death,[306] and it has been held[307] that a statutory amendment which restricts the classes of beneficiaries necessarily amends the charter of the society and thereafter its contracts must conform to the statute irrespective of the previous provisions of the charter. A

[299] Grimme v. Grimme, 198 Ill. 265; 64 N. E. 1088; affg. 101 Ill. App. 389; National Union v. Keefe, 263 Ill. 453; 105 N. E. 315.

[300] State ex rel Kane v. Knights of Father Mathew, 164 Mo. App. 361; Pettus v. Hendricks, 113 Va. 326; 74 S. E. 191; National Union v. Keefe, 263 Ill. 453; 105 N. E. 319; Ann. Cas. 1915-C 271; reversing 172 Ill. App. 101.

[301] Mathewson v. Supreme Council R. A., 146 Mich. 671; 116 N. W. 69.

[302] Wallace v. Maden, 168 Ill. 356; 48 N. E. 181; affg. 67 Ill. App. 524; Supreme Council L. of H. v. Niedlet, 81 Mo. App. 598; Di Messiah v. Gern, 36 N. Y. Supp. 824; 10 Misc. 3.

[303] Bush v. Modern Woodmen of America (Iowa), 152 N. W. 31.

[304] Modern Woodmen of America v. Comeaux, 79 Kan. 493; 101 Pac. 1; contra, Tolson v. National Provident Union, 114 N. Y. Supp. 1149; 130 App. Div. 884.

[305] Dolan v. Supreme Council, 152 Mich. 266; 116 N. W. 383; 113 N. W. 10; 15 L. R. A. (N. S.), 424, overruling 116 N. W. 583. For construction of Texas statute as to beneficiary, Green v. Grand United Order, etc. (Tex. Civ. App.), 163 S. W. 1068. As to foreign societies. Lloyd v. Modern Woodmen, 113 Mo. App. 19; Pauley v. Modern Woodmen, 113 Mo. App. 473; 87 S. W. 990; Dennis v. Modern Brotherhood of America, 119 Mo. App. 210. As to Colorado statute. Head Camp Pac. Juris., etc., v. Sloss, 49 Colo. 177; 112 Pac. 49.

[306] Supreme Council R. A. v. McKnight, 238 Ill. 349; 87 N. E. 299.

[307] Finnell v. Franklin, 55 Colo. 156; 134 Pac. 122.

member cannot make a bequest of the benefits to one not within the classes authorized by statute.[308] A declaration in the by-law as to the objects of the association does not restrict the rights of the member in the naming of a beneficiary,[309] and restrictions limiting the classes who may be designated must be expressed in specific and positive terms and cannot be inferred from general statements contained in either constitution or by-laws.[310] A fraternal beneficiary association under the laws of Kansas, regardless of by-laws, cannot discharge its obligations to a member seventy-five years of age except by paying the amount of the certificate on the member's death.[311] Where only one of two designated beneficiaries in a reissued certificate is eligible he is entitled to the entire fund, the original benefit certificate having been canceled.[312]

§ 321. **The Same Subject: Examples of Construction—Creditors.**—It sufficiently appears from the cases cited in the preceding section that creditors, not being of the classes for the benefit of whom fraternal beneficiary organizations were intended cannot be named as beneficiaries, nor acquire any rights in the benefit to be paid.[313] Cases have arisen where a member of a society has attempted to sell his benefit certificate or make it payable to some creditor. As this question is likely to arise still more frequently, we give, as bearing on the subject in its different phases, extracts from the opinions in several recent cases. In that of Boasberg v. Cronin,[314] the Superior Court of Buffalo passed upon the question whether a certificate could be made payable to a trustee for the benefit of the creditors of the member. Answering this in the negative, the Court said: "The Empire Order of Mutual Aid

[308] Hawkins v. Suberry (Miss.), 57 Sou. 919.
[309] Pleasants v. Locomotive Engineers', etc., Ass'n, 70 W. Va. 389; 73 N. E. 976; Ann. Cas. 1913-E 490.
[310] Christensen v. Madson, 127 Minn. 225; 149 N. W. 288; Ann. Cas. 1916-C 584.
[311] State v. Grand Lodge A. O. U. W., 97 Kan. 585; 155 Pac. 785.
[312] White v. White (Miss.), 77 Sou. 322.
[313] See also Clarke v. Schwartzenberg, 164 Mass. 347; 41 N. E. 655; National Exchange Bank v. Bright, 18 Ky. L. 588; 36 S. W. 10; and post, § 415.
[314] 9 N. Y. Supp. 664.

is a corporation created under and by virtue of chapter 189, laws 1879. Section 2 of said act provides that the objects of incorporation are to improve the moral, mental and social condition of the members, to prevent strikes, and to aid, assist and support members or their families in case of want, sickness or death. Section 3 authorizes the creation, management and disbursement of a beneficiary fund. Section 4 provides: 'Such beneficiary fund as may be ordained suitable by said grand lodge of the State of New York may be provided and set apart to be paid over to the families, heirs or legal representatives of deceased or disabled member or to such person or persons as such deceased member may, while living, have directed. .   .. And such beneficiary fund, so provided and paid, shall be exempt from execution and shall not be liable to be seized, taken or appropriated by any legal or equitable process, to pay any debt or liability of said deceased member.' The proof upon the trial tended to establish, and the court found, that the defendant was duly designated by deceased, in his lifetime, as beneficiary in the sum of $1,000; that said defendant, in consideration of said sum, agreed to pay the creditors of deceased the amounts due them, pay his funeral expenses and erect a monument over his grave; that plaintiff was a creditor and became entitled to judgment for the amount of his approved claim. The finding of the Court in language is 'that defendant in consideration of the sum of $1,000 agreed to pay creditors,' etc. If such finding be construed literally, it would, if warranted by the evidence, support the judgment rendered, but it is to be construed in connection with the other findings and the proof, and when so construed it appears that its true interpretation is that the thousand dollars received by defendant is such sum as he received by virtue of his designation as beneficiary in the certificate issued by the corporation, and alone furnishes the consideration to support the judgment; otherwise there would be a failure of evidence to support the finding. It is the duty of the Court to construe and harmonize findings, so as to give them effect, when possible.[315] It is clear from the provisions of the act of incorporation, that the fund authorized to be created has for its fundamental object, so far as the same relates to the payment

[315] Green v. Roworth, 113 N. Y. 467, 468; 21 N. E. 165.

of the fund after death, the providing a sum of money for the benefit of the families, heirs, or legal representatives of deceased persons, solely applicable to such purpose, freed from any liability of seizure for debt. The contract of insurance is executory in its character, and, under the provisions of this act, the agreement of the association was to pay to certain persons named in the statute, or to such person or persons as the insured should designate in his lifetime. There is nothing in the act or in the by-laws of the corporation which enlarges in this regard the rights of the parties with respect to the fund. There is no property vested in the insured, or property right in any sense, and it does not form any part of his estate.[316] As it forms no part of his estate it does not pass to his executor or administrator, and a will is ineffectual for the purpose of making it subject to the payment of debts.[317] In the event of failure of persons to take under the statute as therein named, and in the absence of a designation by the insured, there is no person to take, and the corporation is under no obligation to pay.[318] The right, therefore, of the insured, in and to the fund created, is not a property right, but a right to provide a fund to be disposed of by the statute, or by the naked power of designation; beyond this he cannot go in the control of the fund or its disposition.[319] The beneficiary named takes no vested right in the certificate of insurance until the contingent event of death happens.[320] If, therefore, the fund provided is not the property of the assured, and he has no property rights therein, he cannot deal with it as property and impress it with a trust for the payment of debts, as the impress of a trust upon the disposition of property necessarily presupposes a property right and interest upon which the trust may fasten; where that fails the whole is nugatory. Creditors dealing with the deceased can in no view be said to have so dealt upon the strength

[316] Bishop v. Grand Lodge, etc., 112 N. Y. 627; 20 N. E. 562; Greeno v. Greeno, 23 Hun. 478; Hellenberg v. District No. 1, etc., 94 N. Y. 580.

[317] Brown v. Ass'n, 33 Hun. 263.

[318] Hellenberg v. District No. 1, etc., *supra*.

[319] Sabin v. Grand Lodge, etc., 6 N. Y. St. 151; Soc. v. Clendinen, 44 Md. 429.

[320] Sabin v. Grand Lodge, etc., 8 N. Y. Supp. 185; Luhrs v. Lodge, etc., 7 N. Y. Supp. 487.

of the interest of the assured, as the act in terms gives notice of the exemption from debt, and the limitation upon the power of disposition is equally clear, so no equities can exist in that regard. It is said that, but for the agreement upon the part of defendant to distribute the fund, he would not have been named as beneficiary. and consequently that, having so received it, equity will lay hold upon the fund, impress it with the trust, and distribute it accordingly. If we assume this to be true, it does not aid plaintiff, for the reason that the trust provided for was in violation of law, and beyond the power of deceased to create; and if defendant by fraud procured himself to be designated and the designation should be held void for that reason, equity might lay hold so far as to fasten upon him a trust *ex maleficio*, and compel distribution of the fund among those empowered to take; but this would only include the other persons named in the statute, who would then be by law empowered to take, and would not embrace plaintiff or the other creditors.'"[321] A creditor cannot take by being designated as dependent friend.[322] Nor by assignment.[323] Where, by the by-laws of a benefit association, a foreigner could not be designated as beneficiary it was held[324] that he could take as beneficiary under a provision that if the designation first made should fail for any cause payment should be made to specified parties. The fund is not liable for funeral expenses of a member.[325] It has been held that the association is not obliged to formally accept the provisions of an enlarging statute which applies to certificates issued before the act was enacted.[326] And a reinstatement of a suspended member after the enactment of a statute restricting the beneficiaries to certain classes does not bring the case of a member so reinstated within the restrictions of such a statute.[327] It was held[328] where a certificate recognized

[321] *In re* O'Hara's Will, 95 N. Y. 403.
[322] Fodell v. Royal Arcanum, 44 W. N. C. 498.
[323] Rose v. Wilkins, 78 Miss. 401; 29 Sou. 397.
[324] Supreme Council R. A. v. Kacer, 96 Mo. App. 93; 69 S. W. 671.
[325] Voelker v. Brotherhood, etc., 103 Mo. App. 637; 77 S. W. 999.
[326] Marsh v. Supreme Council A. L. of H., 149 Mass. 512; 21 N. E. 1070.
[327] Lindsey v. Western M. A. Soc., 84 Iowa 734; 50 N. W. 29.
[328] Sargent v. Supreme Lodge K. of H., 158 Mass. 557; 33 N. E. 650.
See also Grand Lodge A. O. U. W. v. McKinstry, 67 Mo. App. 82.

the right of the superior body to change the laws of the order, by which changes the member would be bound, and afterwards the laws were so amended that payment of the benefit fund was limited to the members of the family of a member and persons dependent upon him, and afterwards such member being notified of the changes in the laws made affidavit that the person designated was a dependent, who was not in fact a dependent, such designation became illegal, notwithstanding the fact that when the certificate was issued to such person the laws of the society permitted the certificate to be made payable to anyone. We, have already considered the question as to the effect of an illegal designation of beneficiary, and the cases there referred to may be considered as also bearing on this subject.[329]   It has been held[330] that where a society in an interpleader proceeding pays the money into court the limitations in its charter cannot aid the widow's claim. But the better view is undoubtedly that in cases of this kind a court will be governed by the laws of the association. The Missouri Court of Appeals, in passing on this question, says:[331]   "It is insisted that the association is the only party which can take advantage of these objections, and as it is making no objection to the payment the judgment must be in favor of the interpleader. But this would be permitting the association to do indirectly what the law has forbidden it to do directly. The corporation, as an association, has its existence from the law, and it has no power to raise funds, or to pay them over to any other than those contemplated by the law.[332]   If we permit the mere acquiescence of the corporation to cause an illegal diversion of the fund. we enable it to thwart the object and evade the command of the law, its creator. Interpleader is in a court of equity asking that she be paid a fund which has been raised for others and which does not belong to her. The association does not confess it to be hers by right, but by paying the money into court and asking the court to adjudicate the matter it, in effect, says, the money may not

---

[329] *Ante*, § 314.

[330] Johnson v. Sup. Lodge K. of H., 53 Ark. 255; 13 S. W. 794; Knights of Honor v. Watson, 64 N. H. 517; 15 Atl. 125.

[331] Grand Lodge, etc., v. Keener, 38 Mo. App. 543.

[332] Bacon on Ben. Soc., §§ 244, 252, and authorities, *supra*.

belong to her. The fact of its fear that she is not the rightful party, is the cause of the association taking the course it has. In speaking of a matter of this nature the Supreme Court of Wisconsin says: 'The fact that the association has paid the money into court instead of paying it directly to the widow, to avoid litigation with other claimants, can make no difference as to the rights of the persons claiming the same. If the appellant could not have recovered this money in a direct action against the association, he cannot recover it in this action. The association not having, for prudential reasons, paid the money to the party entitled thereto, the court must see that it is paid out as directed and required by the rules and regulations of the society . . . The money having been paid into court, the court must now determine who is the proper person to receive it. . . . '[333] We have been cited to two cases as holding views contrary to the above. One of Story v. The Williamsburg M. M. B. A.,[334] is not in conflict. The case concedes that the by-law of the association may have contemplated only the lawful widow as the beneficiary, but that such was not a limitation on the power of the company recognizing as a beneficiary one whom the deceased had designated as holding to him the relation of wife, the plaintiff, in that case, having lived with the deceased for sixteen years, believing herself to be his lawful wife, and having children by him, dependent upon them for support. The opinion holds such a case to be one which the law aimed to protect. The other case cited is from New Hampshire,[335] and is contrary to the views we have expressed. But the reasons we have advanced appear not to have been suggested in that case, and we are so fully persuaded that the decision is unsound, that we are not inclined to follow it.''

§ 322. **The Same Subject: A More Liberal View.**—A seemingly contradictory case has been decided by the Supreme Court

[333]Ballou v. Gile, 50 Wis. 614.

[334] 95 N. Y. 474.

[335] Knights of Honor v. Watson, 64 N. H. 517; 15 Atl. 125.

[336] Maneeley v. Knights of Birmingham, 115 Pa. St. 305; 9 Atl. 41. Also Wolfert v. Grand Lodge K. of B., 39 W. N. C. 264. See, however, Northwestern Masonic Aid Soc. v. Jones, 154 Pa. St. 99; 26 Atl. 253.

in Pennsylvania.[336] The action was brought by a creditor of the deceased member to whom the certificate had been made payable. The defense was that the society had no power to issue certificates payable to any other than the families of its members, the language of the charter being:[1] "The purposes of this corporation shall be the maintenance of a society for the purpose of benefiting and aiding the widows and orphans of deceased members." The lower court sustained the defense and held that the charter prohibited such a contract. In reversing this decision the language of the Court was as follows: "We think this is too narrow and strained a view to take of this section of the charter. While it is true that the general purpose of the corporation is there stated to be, the maintenance of a society for benefiting and aiding widows and orphans of deceased members, it must be observed that this is only the statement of a general purpose. It is only the recital of an object sought to be accomplished, and which doubtless is accomplished in the great majority of cases, even though in exceptional cases the benefits may, by special contract, be paid to other persons than the widow or orphans. There is no prohibitory or restrictive language excluding from the powers of the corporation the right to contract specially with the member for the payment of benefits to other persons than his widow or orphans. Nor is such a contract to be held void by reason of any necessary implication from the language of the charter for the widow and orphans may be much benefited, and in many ways, by a contract designating another beneficiary; as, for instance, if the member in his lifetime, desiring to establish a home for his wife and children, which they might hold after his death, borrowed money for that purpose and so used it and to secure the loan designated the lender as the beneficiary of his membership. Certainly his widow and orphans would be most materially benefited by such an arrangement or, if having a home, he met with disaster, and was about to lose it by a judicial sale, and should save it by a similar provision, his widow and orphans would be thereby benefited. Or, if having property and also debts, but not to the point of insolvency, he could borrow money by means of a membership with such an association, and he should become a member for that very purpose, the creditor possibly also paying the dues, and he could to that extent diminish his indebtedness during his life and thus leave that much more of his property to his widow and orphans, undoubtedly they would be thereby benefited. Or, he might borrow the money, and give it directly to his wife or children during his life, pledging his membership to the lender as above, and then also they would receive the full advantage of the transaction without waiting until his death. Many more illustrations of a similar character might easily be suggested, but is unnecessary. They all prove the same proposition, to-wit: That it is entirely possible to benefit the widow or orphan by means of such a membership, although neither of them is the designated beneficiary.'' It must be noted, however, as to this case, that by the language of the charter, the object of the corporation was not to pay to the widows and orphans, etc., but for the purpose of benefiting and aiding the widows and orphans, etc. Other cases 'tend to support this liberal view, though none go so far.[337] In a Missouri case[338] a member of an order incorporated in Kentucky and subsequently in Missouri made his certificate payable to the trustees of his subordinate lodge for the purpose of erecting a tombstone and improving his burial lot. In upholding the validity of this designation the Court said: ''The words in the charter, 'or as he or she may have directed' gave to Levin absolute power to makes any disposition of the fund due under the certificate; provided such disposition was not repugnant to the declared purposes of the corporation [339] One of the objects of the defendant corporation is, 'to promote benevolence and charity,' and to this end a relief fund was provided for. We cannot agree with the defendant that the object of Levin, in providing the means to defray his own burial expenses and to improve the lot where he was to be buried, was not a benevolent or charitable one. It was a very natural impulse for him, if he was without property, or kindred, to provide against the contingency of being buried at

[337] Folmer's Appeal, 87 Pa. St. 135; Lamont v. Grand Lodge Ia. Leg. Honor, 31 Fed. 177; Sup. Lodge K. of H. v. Martin, et al. (Pa.), 12 Ins. L. J. 628.

[338] Hysinger v. Supreme Lodge K. & L. of H., 42 M. A. 628.

[339] Gentry v. Supreme Lodge Knights of Honor, 23 Fed. 718; Duvall v. Goodson, 79 Ky. 224; Lamont v. Grand Lodge, 31 Fed. 177; Highland v. Highland, 109 Ill. 366.

the expense of the public in an unmarked grave. This might very well be regarded as an act of charity. To say the least, the matter is debatable, and as the defendant accepted Levin's money, and permitted him to live and die under the belief that his body would be decently taken care of after his death, we are of the opinion that the corporation is in no position to split hairs in the discussion of the question. We, therefore, hold that the contract was authorized by the defendant's Kentucky charter. But, if the contract with Levin is to be governed by the Missouri statute, then it must certainly be held to be *ultra vires*. When the law or charter of such an institution confines the beneficiaries to a particular class the corporation can only accumulate a fund for the benefit of such persons who may fall within the class and are named as beneficiaries. Under our statute the choice of beneficiaries, when the corporation is organized in this State, is confined to some member of the family of the assured, or to some person or persons dependent upon him. It is quite clear, therefore, that the direction made by Levin in his certificate, would, under the Missouri statute, subject the contract to the charge of being *ultra vires.*" And in Minnesota in a somewhat similar case it was held[340] that where the benefit was payable to an unincorporated voluntary association the father of the member could not question the legal existence of the lodge or its capacity to take. The Supreme Court of Illinois has held[341] that, if a member under the charter could devise the benefits of his policy to a stranger, he might in the first instance take out the policy payable to a stranger, and that, having received the premiums and the contract being executed by the death of the member, the company was estopped to invoke the doctrine of *ultra vires* to defeat an action brought by the beneficiary.[342] The question is one of construction of particular words in the statutes and in the charters of these societies and necessarily no more general rule can be laid down than that if, by statute or charter, the beneficiaries of members are confined to certain classes, the designation of anyone not of such class

[340] Bacon v. Brotherhood R. R. Brakemen, 46 Min. 303; 48 N. W. 1127.
[341] Bloomington Mut. L. Ben. Ass'n v. Blue, 120 Ill. 121; 11 N. E. 331.
[342] See also Lamont v. Hotel Men's B. Ass'n, 30 Fed. 817; Lamont v. Grand Lodge Ia. Leg. Honor, 31 Fed. 177.

is void. The cases cited in the preceding and subsequent sections of this chapter sufficiently illustrate this doctrine.

§ 323. **Unless Contract or Statute Forbid, Choice of Beneficiary Is Unlimited.**—In all cases the member may have as broad a range of choice in selecting his beneficiary as the organic law of his society gives him. If there is nothing in the charter or by-laws of the organization, or in the statutes of the State, restricting the appointment, the member may designate whomsoever he pleases and no one can question the right.[343] Consequently the designation of a stranger as beneficiary will be valid, no statute or by-law preventing,[344] or one having no insurable interest.[345]

§ 324. **Liberal Construction of Charter and By-Laws: Lex Loci.**—In determining whether the designated beneficiary comes within the class specified or not, the charter and by-laws of the society will be construed liberally so as to carry out the benevolent purposes of its organization, and yet not so as to violate the statute law of the State or contravene public policy.[346] In deciding the

[343] Bayse v. Adams, 81 Ky. 368; Gentry v. Supreme Lodge, 23 Fed. 718; Massey v. Mut. Relief Soc., 102 N. Y. 523; 7 N. E. 619; Mitchell v. Grand Lodge, 70 Ia. 360; 30 N. W. 865; Freeman v. Nat. Ben. Soc,. 42 Hun. 252; Swift v. Ry. Conductor's Ass'n, 96 Ill. 309; Knights of Honor v. Nairn, 60 Mich. 44; 26 N. W. 826; Supreme Lodge, etc., v. Martin, 12 Ins. L. J. 628; 13 W. N. C. 160; Martin v. Stubbings, 126 Ill. 387; 18 N. E. 657; Brown v. Brown, 27 N. Y. Supp. 129; Eckert v. Mut. Ben. Soc., 2 N. Y. St. 612; Walter v. Odd Fellows', etc., Soc., 42 Minn. 204; 44 N. W. 57; Union Fraternal League v. Walton, 109 Ga. 1; 34 S. E. 317; 46 L. R. A. 424; Independent Order, etc., v. Allen, 76 Miss. 326; 24 Sou. 702; Delaney v. Delaney 175 Ill. 187; 51 N. E. 961; affg. 70 Ill. App. 130; Berkeley v. Harper, 3 App. D. C. 308; Derrington v. Conrad, 3 Kan. App. 725; 45 Pac. 458; Supreme Council, etc., v. Adams, 107 Fed. 335; Nelson v. Gibson, 92 Ill. App. 595; Strike v. Wisconsin, etc., Co., 95 Wis. 583; 70 N. W. 819; Supreme Council C. K. A. v. Fitzpatrick, 28 R. I. 486; 68 Atl. 367; Fair v. Thompson, 220 Pa. 241; 69 Atl. 758.

[344] Supreme Council C. K. A. v. Fitzpatrick, 28 R. I. 486; 68 Atl. 367.

[345] Dolan v. Supreme Council C. M. B. Ass'n, 152 Mich. 266; 116 N. W. 383.

[346] Supreme Lodge K. of P. v. Schmidt, 98 Ind. 374; Ballou v. Gile, 50 Wis. 614; Am. Legion of Honor v. Perry, 140 Mass. 580; Maneeley v. Knights of Birmingham, 115 Pa. St. 305; 9 Atl. 41; Elsey v. Odd Fellows, etc., 142 Mass. 224.

rights of the member in respect to the designation of beneficiary, the law of the place of the contract under which the power is given will govern, for a contract, good at the place where made, is good everywhere, unless the statutes òr public policy of the State where the contract is sought to be enforced forbid;[347] and the law of the *situs* of the subject of the power controls the execution of such power.[348]   A contract of a corporation will often be enforced by comity when made in conformity with its charter, although it would, if made by a domestic corporation, have been against the statutes of the State where the action is brought.''[349]

As an example of liberal construction it was held by the Supreme Court of Wisconsin,[350] where the constitution of a firemen's relief association organized pursuant to laws of Wisconsin[351] and acts amendatory thereof, prôviding for the organization of such associations, and designating that they may be organized for the purpose of giving relief to persons dependent upon the deceased members, but no others, stated the object of such association to be to give relief to families of deceased members, and provided that an insured could designate his mother or certain others as his beneficiary, that a designation by an insured of his stepmother as beneficiary was valid, where he was a single man living with her as a member of the same family at the time of his death, the term "mother" in this connection not being limited in meaning merely to a mother by blood, though used with such meaning in a subsequent provision of the association's constitution which specified the heirs to whom relief money should be paid in case no beneficiary be designated by the insured.   The Court said: "We think that a mother who can be named includes a mother by affinity who is a member of the family.   Without going

---

[347] Am. Legion of Honor v. Perry, 140 Mass. 580; Knights of Honor v. Nairn, 60 Mich. 44; Daniels v. Pratt, 143 Mass. 216; Bishop on Contr., §§ 1383-1389 inc.   See also *ante*, § 198.

[348] Bingham's Appeal, 64 Pa. St. 345.

[349] Hysinger v. Supreme Lodge K. & L. of H., 42 M. A. 627; Martinez v. Supreme Lodge, etc., 81 Mo. App. 590.

[350] Jones v. Mangan, 151 Wis. 215; 138 N. W. 618; Ann. Cas. 1914-B 59.   See also Faxon v. Grand Lodge Brotherhood Locomotive Firemen, 87 Ill. App. 262.

[351] 1885, c. 176 (St. 1898, §§ 1987, 1988).

into any extended discussion of the reason of the rule, it is obvious that in many cases the stepmother may have strong claims upon the child whom she cares for during minority, and no reason appears to us why such child should not have the right, under the articles of association in this case, to make the stepmother the object of his bounty.[352] Nor do we think that the word 'mother' must necessarily have the same meaning in the first and second classes named in art. IX. In the first class there is no restriction, either express or implied, but on the contrary, in view of the construction which should be given the articles of association to carry out the manifest corporate purpose of the defendant association, a mother by affinity, who is a member of the family may be named. In the second class the right to take the benefit seems by words to be limited to heirs. But it is only in case of failure to name a beneficiary that this classification providing that the fund shall go to the heirs is operative. There is no restriction where the member names a beneficiary, only that he keep within the class specified. True, as argued by counsel, the word 'mother' is used in each classification, but we cannot think that the proper rule of construction requires that the word 'mother' in the first class must necessarily mean mother by blood, capable of taking under the statute of distribution of this State. Appellants place reliance upon Koertz v. Grand Lodge Order of Hermann's Sons,[353] which holds that the same meaning must be given the same word in different sections. There the question was as to the meaning of the word 'survivors' when used to designate the 'survivors' of a member in a benefit society, and of course the meaning of the word was necessarily the same when used in the same connection in various sections. But there is no rule of construction requiring the same meaning to be given to the same word in different connections.''

§ 325. **The Doctrine of Insurable Interest Applied to Contracts of Benefit Societies.**—Many of the cases involving the

---

[352] The following authorities bear upon the question: Renner v. Supreme Lodge of Bohemian Slavonian Ben. Soc., 89 Wis. 401; 62 N. W. 80; Simcoke v. Grand Lodge A. O. U. W., 84 Ia. 383; 51 N. W. 8; 15 L. R. A. 114.

[353] 119 Wis. 520; 97 N. W. 163.

question of insurable interest, cited in the preceding sections, are those in which benefit societies were parties. As a rule, however, it is only when the right of designation of beneficiary is unrestricted, can the question of insurable interest be raised. Even then as the member must be *prima facie* considered as the party effecting the insurance and free to choose whom he pleases as the recipient of his bounty, he can designate whomsoever he likes.[354] Clearly, however, the contract must not be, in fact, a cover for a wagering transaction and if the creditor, or a person having no insurable interest, should himself pay the entrance fee and assessments and be the mover in the matter, the certificate would be void and the beneficiary could not recover.[355] Where, by a by-law of a beneficiary society, no person could be named as beneficiary, unless he should have an insurable interest in the life of the member, the designation of one not having such an interest is invalid and confers no rights on the one so designated.[356] If the beneficiaries are, by the charter, limited to certain classes, as family, relatives, etc., and the member designate someone not of such classes, the designation is void, and, if the money be paid to such beneficiary, he holds it as trustee for the persons entitled to receive, under the laws of the society, in default of a designation.[357]

§ 326. **Policy or Designation of Beneficiary Valid in Its Inception Remains So.**—The general rule undoubtedly is that a

[354] Masonic Ben. Ass'n v. Bunch, 109 Mo. 560; 19 S. W. 25; Sabin v. Phinney, 134 N. Y. 423; 31 N. E. 1087; affg. 8 N. Y. Supp. 185; Overbeck v. Overbeck, 155 Pa. St. 5; 25 Atl. 646; Ingersoll v. Knights of the Golden Rule, 47 Fed. 272; Knights of Honor v. Watson, 64 N. H. 517; 15 Atl. 125; Manning v. United Workmen, 86 Ky. 136; 5 S. W. 385; Titsworth v. Titsworth, 40 Kan. 571; 20 Pac. 213; Milner v. Bowman, 119 Ind. 448; 21 N. E. 1094; Byrne v. Casey, 70 Tex. 247; 8 S. W. 38; Schillinger v. Boes, 85 Ky. 357; 3 S. W. 427; Ancient Order United Workmen v. Brown, 112 Ga. 545; 37 S. E. 890; Lane v. Lane, 99 Tenn. 639; 42 S. W. 1058.

[355] Metropolitan L. Ins. Co. v. O'Brien, 92 Mich. 584; 52 N. W. 1012; Lyon v. Rolfe, 76 Mich. 151; 42 N. W. 1094; Mut. Ben. Ass'n v. Hoyt, 46 Mich. 473; 9 N. W. 497.

[357] Union Fraternal League v. Walton, 112 Ga. 315; 37 S. E. 389.

[357] Am. Legion of Honor v. Perry, 140 Mass. 580; Daniels v. Pratt, 143 Mass. 216; *ante*, § 319.

policy of life insurance, or a designation of beneficiary, valid in its inception, remains so, although the insurable interest, or relationship of the beneficiary, has ceased, unless it is otherwise stipulated in the contract.[358]   Where, however, the beneficiaries of members of benefit societies were, by statute, restricted to the family, or dependents, or relatives of their members, and a member of one of such societies designated his wife, from whom he afterwards was divorced, it was held[359] that she lost her rights under the designation in consequence of such divorce.   This case might seem to be apparently against authority, but the reason given is, that under the statute, the relationship or status must exist at the time of the maturity of the contract. Especially is this true if the regulating statute specifies certain classes to which payment of benefits shall be made.   If designation of beneficiary is analogous to making a will, as we shall see,[360] and, like a will, speaks from the death of the member, it might be well said that if the status does not exist at the time the designation is to take effect the

[358] Connecticut Mut. L. Ins. Co. v. Schaefer, 94 U. S. 457; McKee v. Phoenix M. L. Ins. Co., 28 Mo. 383; 75 Am. Dec. 129; Clark v. Allen, 11 R. I. 439; Dalby v. India & London Ass. Co., 15 C. B. 365; Campbell v. N. Eng. Mut. L. Ins. Co., 98 Mass. 381; Provident L. Ins. Co. v. Baum, 29 Ind. 236; Wist v. Gr. Lodge A. O. U. W., 22 Ore. 271; 29 Pac. 610; Overhiser's Adm'x. v. Overhiser, 63 Ohio St. 77; 57 N. E. 965; 50 L. R. A. 552; Caldwell v. Grand Lodge, A. O. U. W., 148 Cal. 195; 82 Pac. 781; State v. State, 228 Ill. 630; 81 N. E. 1146; Wallace v. Mut. Ben. L. Ins. Co., 97 Minn. 27; 106 N. W. 84; 3 L. R. A. (N. S.) 478; Schmidt v. Hauer, 139 Ia. 531; 111 N. W. 966; Langford v. National L. & A. Ins. Co., 116 Ark. 527; 173 S. W. 414; Coghlan v. Supreme Conclave I. O. H., 86 N. J. L. 41; 91 Atl. 132; In re Williams, 14 Ont. L. Rep. 482; Humphrey v. Mut. L. Ins. Co., 86 Wash. 672; 151 Pac. 100. See post, § 556.

[359] Tyler v. Odd Fellows' Mut. Relief Ass'n, 145 Mass. 134; 13 N. E. 360. To the same effect are Order Ry. Conductors v. Koster, 55 Mo. App. 186; Saenger v. Rothschild, 123 N. Y. 577; 26 N. E. 3; affg. 2 N. Y. St. 794. See also Green v. Green, 147 Ky. 608; 147 S. W. 1073; 39 L. R. A. (N. S.), 370; Ann. Cas. 1913-D 683; Green v. K. & L. of S., 147 Ky. 614; 144 S. W. 1076; Dahlin v. Knights of Modern Maccabees, 154 Mich. 644; 115 N. W. 975; Larkin v. Knights of Columbus, 188 Mass. 22; 73 N. E. 850; Knights of Columbus v. Rowe, 70 Conn. 545; 40 Atl. 451; Davin v. Davin, 99 N. Y. Supp. 1052; 114 App. Div. 396; Griffin v. Grand Lodge A. O. U. W., 99 Neb. 589; 157 N. W. 113; L. R. A. 1916-D 1168.

[360] Post, § 328.

benefit shall go as the laws of the society provide. There is eminent authority, however, for a doctrine contrary to that just stated. The Supreme Court of Iowa has said:[361] "The statute provides only for the relationship that shall exist when the certificate is issued, and does not in words, or by fair implication, limit payment to those only who occupy such relation at the time of death. It was the evident intent of the legislature to prohibit anything in the nature of gambling contracts, and to so limit the beneficiaries as to accomplish such a result. Under the statute, and under the laws of the order, the member's legatee may be his beneficiary, and this without reference to who the legatee may be. A person may will his property as he pleases, and it is therefore evident that the statute was not intended to limit beneficiaries to those for whom the law would provide in the absence of a last will and testament. When the certificate was issued, the beneficiary being one of the class named by the statute and by the laws of the order, it created a valid contract with the member, agreeing to pay the sum therein named to the named beneficiary. True, the member had the right to change his beneficiary, but he did not do so, nor attempt to do so, and we see no reason why we should change the contract and deprive the appellant of the provision which was thus made for her. It is a well recognized rule that a policy of life insurance or a designation of a beneficiary, valid in its inception, remains so although the insurable interest or relationship of the beneficiary has ceased, unless it is otherwise stipulated in the contract." It has been held[362] that an Illinois decree of divorce did not affect rights of the wife to the proceeds of a policy payable to her, it not appearing that it was the duty of the Illinois Court to restore the property obtained by one spouse through the other. The Missouri Court of Appeals

[361] White v. Brotherhood of American Yeomen, 124 Ia. 294; 99 N. W. 1071. And to the same effect are Brown v. Grand Lodge A. O. U. W., 208 Pa. St. 101; 57 Atl. 176; Overhiser v. Overhiser, 14 Colo. App. 1; 59 Pac. 75. See also Leaf v. Leaf, 92 Ky. 166; 17 S. W. 354; Farra v. Braman, 171 Ind. 529; 86 N. E. 843; Snyder v. Supreme Ruling Fraternal Mystic Circle, 122 Tenn. 248; 122 S. W. 981; Royal League v. Casey, 144 Ill. App. 1; Marquet v. Aetna Life Ins. Co., 128 Tenn. 213; 159 S. W. 733; Ann. Cas. 1915-B 677.

[362] Guthrie v. Guthrie, 155 Ky. 146; 159 S. W. 710.

has held[363] that while the designation of a beneficiary, if valid in its inception, remains so, still a subsequent incorporation subjects the society to the limitations of the statute and such designation may become invalid.

§ 327. **Lawfulness of Designation of Beneficiary a Question of Construction.**—From the preceding sections it appears that the question, who is entitled to be the beneficiary of a member of a benefit society, is one of construction of the laws of such society, and the terms used in them. Hardly any two of such societies, as far as the cases show, use precisely the same language, yet in all certain generic terms are used. The benefits are variously required to be made payable to: "the widow and children of deceased member;"[364] "widow, orphan, heir, assignee or legatee;"[365] "families or assigns;"[366] "family or dependents,"[367] "widow, orphan children and other persons dependent on him;"[368] "person or persons last named by deceased and entered by his order, on the will-book of the company;"[369] "widows, orphans, heirs or devisees;"[370] "legal representatives;"[371] "widows, orphans, heirs and devisees;"[372] "to his family or as he may direct;"[373] "families and heirs;"[374] "to his family or those dependent on him;"[375] "to family, orphans or dependents;"[376] "families or relatives;"[377]

363 Gibbs v. K. of P., 173 Mo. App. 34; 156 S. W. 11.

364 Duvall v. Goodson, 79 Ky. 224; Dietrich v. Madison Relief Ass'n, 45 Wis. 79; Kentucky Masonic M. L. I. Co. v. Miller's Admr., 13 Bush 489.

365 Masonic Mut. R. Ass'n v. McAuley, 2 Mackey 70.

366 Massey v. Mut. R. A., 102 N. Y. 523.

367 Knights of Honor v. Nairn, 60 Mich. 44; 26 N. W. 826.

368 Addison v. N. E. C. Travelers' Ass'n, 144 Mass. 591; 12 N. E. 407.

369 Sup. Counc. Catholic Ben. Ass'n v. Priest, 46 Mich. 429.

370 Covenant M. Ben. Ass'n v. Sears, 114 Ill. 108.

371 Expressmen's Aid Soc. v. Lewis, 9 Mo. App. 412.

372 Worley v. N. W. Masonic Aid Ass'n, 10 Fed. 227.

373 Gentry v. Sup. Lodge, etc., 23 Fed. 718; Mitchell v. Grand Lodge, etc., 70 Ia. 360; 30 N. W. 865.

374 National Mut., etc., Ass'n v. Gonser, 43 Ohio St. 1.

375 Ballou v. Gile, etc., 50 Wis. 614.

376 Am. Legion of Honor v. Perry, 140 Mass. 580.

377 Presbyterian Assur. Fund v. Allen, 106 Ind. 593; Van Bibber's Admr. v. Van Bibber, 82 Ky. 347.

"families of deceased members or their heirs."[378] By the statutory provisions of many of the States payment of benefits by a fraternal beneficiary society is restricted to certain classes, usually: "Families, heirs, blood relatives, affianced husband or affianced wife of, or to, persons dependent upon the member."[379] In many charters or by-laws, other generic terms are used, such as "orphans," "devisees or legatees," and "legal representatives," and sometimes there is an ambiguous designation, such as "estate." It becomes important, then, to know who are included in these generic terms, "families," "orphans," "widow," "affianced husband or affianced wife," "children," "heirs," "legatees," "relatives," "legal representatives," "devisees," and "dependents."

§ 328. **Rules of Construction in Cases of Designation of Beneficiary.**—The principles governing the construction of the charters, laws and certificates of benefit societies, as well as of the various statutes relating to them, are of a manifold nature and analogous to the general rules of construction of statutes, contracts and wills, for the subject-matter partakes of the characteristics of all. The first essential of the designation of beneficiary is that it conform to the requirements of the statute under which the society exists, or at least violate no provisions of any statute; the designation must also be in conformity with the terms of the contract of the membership. If the meaning of the member is not clear, then the inquiry is to ascertain it. The same general rules of construction apply to the designation of beneficiaries that apply to all written documents, but the interpretation of some generic terms must be separately discussed. The primary rule is that the intent of the legislature, parties to a contract or designator must be first ascertained and then carried into effect,[380] and his intention must be judged of exclusively by the words of the instrument, if unambiguous, as applied to the subject-matter and the surrounding circumstances.[381] The whole of the statute law, or designatory writing, must be looked at and considered and

[378] Elsey v. Odd Fellows', etc., 142 Mass. 224.
[379] Revised Stats. Mo. 1899, § 1408.
[380] Bishop on Con., § 380; 2 Pars. on Con., p. *494; 1 Redf. on Wills, p. *433 and Vol. 2, p. *20.
[381] Redf. on Wills, p. *433; Bishop on Con., § 381.

words are supposed, unless the contrary be shown, to have been used in their ordinary every-day sense and with the meaning a long line of judicial decisions has given them.[382]   It is not necessary to here refer in detail to the other numerous rules of construction that have been laid down by a long series of judicial decisions, collected and digested by learned and accurate commentators; the textbooks upon contracts, statutes, wills and kindred subjects must be consulted by those who wish to search deeper into the law governing particular cases.   The courts substantially agree that the rules and regulations of benefit societies are to be construed liberally in order to effect the benevolent objects of their organization.[383]   And the court will, if possible, so construe the designation to bring it within the power given by the statutes and sustain its legality.[384]   We can have a wider range of authority in searching for precedents for construing the meaning of the language used in designations of beneficiary, as well as in the laws of these societies and statutes relating to them, because of the analogies that have been found between such designations and laws, so far as disposition of property is concerned, and wills.   The Supreme Court of Michigan, for example, has said:[385]   ''The same rules of construction should be applied to dispositions of property created by those mutual benefit associations as are applied to bequests by will.''   And Chief Justice Cofer, of the Kentucky Court

---

[382] Bishop on Con., § 377; 1 Redf. on Wills, pp. *434 and 438, and Vol. 2, p *19.

[383] Supreme Lodge K. of P. v. Schmidt, 98 Ind. 381; Ballou v. Gile, 50 Wis. 614; Erdmann v. Mut. Ins. Co., 44 Wis. 376; Maneely v. Knights of Birmingham, 115 Pa. St. 306; 9 Atl. 41; Sup. Lodge K. of H. v. Martin (Pa.), 12 Ins. L. J. 628; 13 W. N. C. 160; American Legion of Honor v. Perry, 140 Mass. 580; Gundlach v. Germania, etc., 4 Hun. 339; Expressman's Mut. Aid Ass'n v. Lewis, 9 Mo. App. 412; Dietrich et al. v. Madison Relief, etc., 45 Wis. 79; Massey et al. v. Mut. Relief Ass'n, 102 N. Y. 523; Van Bibber's Admr. v. Van Bibber, 82 Ky. 347; Duvall v. Goodson, 79 Ky. 224; Masonic Mut. Relief Ass'n v. McAuley, 2 Mackey 70; Whitehurst Admr. v. Whitehurst, 83 Va. 153; 1 S. E. 801.

[384] Elsey v. Odd. Fellows' Mut. Relief Ass'n, 142 Mass. 224; Am. Legion of Honor v. Perry, 140 Mass. 580; 2 Pars. on Con. p. *505.

[385] Union Mut. Aid Ass'n v. Montgomery, 70 Mich. 587; 38 N. W. 588. To the same effect is Kottmann v. Gazett, 66 Minn. 88; 68 N. W. 732.

of Appeals, has said:[386] "A life policy for the benefit of the family of the person procuring, though not a testament, is in the nature of a testament, and in construing it the courts should treat it as far as possible as a will, as in so doing they will more nearly approximate the intention of the persons, the destination of whose bounty is involved in such cases." In other cases this analogy has been mentioned.[387] It is a settled principle in wills that they take effect upon the death of the testator, and are treated as speaking from that time.[388] Following the analogies above noticed, it follows that the designation of beneficiaries by the members of mutual benefit societies takes effect only upon the death of such members and the benefit certificate confers upon the beneficiary only an inchoate, contingent expectancy, liable to be diverted either by the death of the beneficiary before that of the member, or by a revocation of the appointment and a naming of another beneficiary. Upon the death of the member then the benefit certificate takes effect, so far as to vest in the beneficiary an absolute right to the benefit money.[389] In a case in Illinois,[390] the Court said: "A benefit certificate in a society of this character differs from an ordinary policy of life insurance in that it speaks with reference to the conditions existing at the time of the death of the member whose life has been insured by it. A beneficiary named in a certificate of a fraternal benefit society organized under the statutes of the State of Illinois, or like statutes of other States, has no vested interest in such certificate or the fund provided for its payment, until the decease of the member whose death matures the

386 Duvall v. Goodson, 79 Ky. 224.

387 Continental L. Ins. Co. v. Palmer, 42 Conn. 65; Thomas v. Leake, 67 Tex. 469; 3 S. W. 703; National American Ass'n v. Kirgin, 28 Mo. App. 80; Chartrand v. Brace, 16 Colo. 19; 26 Pac. 152; Felix v. Grand Lodge, etc., 31 Kan. 81; Masonic Benev. Ass'n v. Bunch, 109 Mo. 560; 19 S. W. 25; Knights Templars', etc., Ass'n v. Greene, 79 Fed. 457.

388 Redf. on Wills, 10-12; 2 Jarm. on Wills, 406; Shotts v. Poe, 47 Md. 513; Davidson v. Dallas, 14 Ves. 576.

389 Thomas v. Leake, 67 Tex. 469; 3 S. W. 703; Union M. Aid Ass'n v. Montgomery, 70 Mich. 587; 38 N. W. 588; Chartrand v. Brace, 16 Colo. 19.

390 Kirkpatrick v. Modern Woodmen, 103 Ill. App. 468-473, citing Order Railway Conductors v. Koster, 55 Mo. App. 186. See also Supreme Lodge O. M. P. V. Dewey, 142 Mich. 666; 106 N. W. 140.

certificate. The constitution and by-laws of the society and the statutes of the State must be construed not only to the terms of the certificate but to the status of the parties existing at the time of the death.''[391] In De Grote v. De Grote,[392] it was held that a woman, to whom the member was bigamously married but to whom he was afterwards legally married, became a competent beneficiary because of the subsequent marriage.

§ 329. Family.—In the specification of the persons who may be designated as beneficiaries, the term which most frequently occurs in the charters of benefit societies, and also in the statutes authorizing their existence and doing of certain acts, is "family." The word has been frequently the subject of judicial discussion in two classes of cases, those involving homestead rights and those relating to the construction of wills. Very different results follow as the one or the other class of decisions is followed, for in homestead laws the intent of the legislature is evidently to protect a person who has others, who are dependent upon his labors, abiding with him under the same roof. On the other hand, in construing wills, the object is to ascertain the intention of the testator. The latter body of cases favor a more liberal construction than the former. The definition given by Bouvier is comprehensive[393] and is this: "Father, mother and children. All the individuals who live under the authority of another, including the servants of the family. All the relations who descend from a common ancestor, or who spring from a common root." We cannot understand that those persons who are hired to assist in household work are included among those termed servants in this definition. In discussing this word as affecting rights of homestead, and after the review of the authorities, a learned writer says:[394] "The family relation is obviously a relation of *status,* and not of *contract* merely. An assemblage of persons held together by a mere contract, other than the marriage contract, although such a contract may raise a duty of support on the part of one member, and create a state of depend-

[391] Delaney v. Delaney, 175 Ill. 187; Lister v. Lister, 73 Mo. App. 99.
[392] 175 Pa. St. 50; 34 Atl. 312.
[393] Law Dic., tit. Family.
[394] Thompson on Homesteads, § 47.

ence on the part of the others, is not a family. Of such a nature are the ordinary contracts of service now in vogue in the United States. And, hence, the relation of master and servant, or more properly speaking, of employer and employe, as it ordinarily exists in this country, does not constitute a *family*. 'There is absent that peculiar feature, which can be better understood than described, which distinguishes the family even from those who may dwell within the limits of the same curtilage.' And, therefore, a single man, who has no other persons living with him than servants and employes, is not the head of a family within the means of the statutes creating homestead exemptions.'' In questions involving both the construction of wills and homestead rights the courts are inclined to adopt liberal views. In testing the right of a debtor to be considered the "head of a family" certain tests are applied which are easily understood. The first of these is whether the law imposed upon the head of the associated persons the duty of supporting them, which would be a simple and uniform test, but this test would not apply to all cases, consequently there is the further inquiry whether a moral duty to support existed. There is the test of condition of dependence and also those of common residence and good faith. In applying these tests and in construing who are included in the family of any person, the courts will be liberal.[395] Accordingly it has been held that indigent mother and sisters who live with a man and are supported by him are members of his family;[396] and a widowed daughter and her minor child residing with a father who was a widower are members of his family;[397] also dependent mother and dependent minor brothers and sisters residing with an unmarried man are members of his family;[398] so also minor brothers and sisters residing with an unmarried man;[399] also a widowed sister supported by a brother, whether she has or has not dependent children.[400] Children of a wife by a

[395] Thompson on Homesteads, § 4.

[396] Marsh v. Lazenby, 41 Ga. 153.

[397] Blackwell v. Broughton, 56 Ga., 390; Cox v. Stafford, 14 How. Pr. 521.

[398] Connaughton v. Sands, 32 Wis. 387.

[399] Greenwood v. Maddox, 27 Ark. 658.

[400] Wade v. Jones, 20 Mo. 75; Bailey v. Cummings, cited Thompson on Homesteads, § 59.

former husband are members of the husband's family[401] and adopted children.[402]   The Supreme Court of Massachusetts has held[403] that under the statute of that State, limiting beneficiaries to the widow, orphans or dependents of deceased members, the mother, who was living with her husband away from a son was not a "dependent" upon him, nor strictly speaking a member of the son's family in the sense of being dependent. In a Michigan case[404] the Supreme Court of that State said: ":Now this word 'family' contained in the statute, is an expression of great flexibility. It is applied in many ways. It may mean the husband and wife having no children and living alone together, or it may mean children, or wife and children, or blood relatives, or any group constituting a distinct domestic or social body." The Court therefore held, where the insured was an old man and his beneficiary a young woman, who was not related to him, but who had lived for many years with him in the same household and was treated by him as a daughter, the term, family, as used in the statute covered the case and included her. A woman living with a man as his mistress is not a member of his family within the meaning of the statute.[405]   In construing wills the word family is very comprehensive, and, in its ordinary sense, comprises the same persons as "kindred" or "relations."[406]   In some of the older cases bequests to one's family have been held void for uncertainty.[407]   It was said by Romilly, M. R.,[408] that the primary meaning of family is children, and that there must be some circumstances arising on the will itself, or from the situation of the parties, to prevent that construction.[409]   Jessel, M. R., also said[410] that the primary meaning was children. And so in this country;[411] though ordinarily it in-

[401] Allen v. Manasse, 4 Ala. 554; Sallee v. Waters, 17 Ala. 488.
[402] Thompson on Homesteads, § 48.
[403] Elsey v. Odd Fellows' Mut. R. Ass., 142 Mass. 224.
[404] Carmichael v. N. W. Mut. Ben. Ass'n, 51 Mich. 494.
[405] Keener v. Grand Lodge A. O. U. W., 38 M. A. 543.
[406] 2 Williams on Exrs. 1213.
[407] 2 Jar. on Wills, Ch. 29.
[408] In re Terry's Will, 19 Beav. 580.
[409] Snow v. Teed, 9 Eq. Cas. 622.
[410] Pigg v. Clarke, 3 Ch. D. 674.
[411] Spencer v. Spencer, 11 Paige, 159.

cludes the wife.[412] An adult son is a member of his father's family although he does not live under the same roof.[413] Where the designation was "family" and it consisted of wife and daughter, they are the beneficiaries, and if the daughter die before the father the mother takes the whole.[414] In the English cases collected in the last edition of Jarman on Wills,[415] various meanings have been given to the word according to the supposed intent of the testator, as heir or children, relations, descendants, or wife. As said by Vice-Chancellor Kindersley in Green v. Marsden,[416] "family" is not a technical word, but is of flexible meaning. It has been held even to mean ancestors, and not infrequently next of kin, but often the parents have been excluded.[417] Judge Redfield, in his work on wills, says:[418] "There has been considerable controversy in the English courts in regard to the proper construction of bequests to the family of the testator, or of others. The state of things is so different in England, as it regards families, from what it is here, that the ordinary import of the word can scarcely be regarded the same. And the fact that so many cases, where the meaning of this term came in question, have arisen in the English courts upon the construction of wills, and so comparatively few in this country, leads us to the conjecture, that the word, family, will but seldom occur in a will, in this country, where there will not be something, either in other portions of the will or in the surrounding circumstances, which may lead to a reasonable ground of inferring, with probable certainty, the sense in which it was used by the testator." When used in the statutes in connection with other words, as where it says, "the families, widows, orphans, or other dependents of the deceased members,"[419] it may include those not embraced in any of the other classes[420] and, therefore, was probably used in the larger sense of kindred or relations. Later cases

---

[412] Bowditch v. Andrew, 8 Allen 339; Bradlee v. Andrews, 137 Mass. 50.
[413] Klotz v. Klotz, 15 Ky. L. 183; 22 S. W. 551.
[414] Brooklyn Mas. R. Ass'n v. Hanson, 6 N. Y. Supp. 161.
[415] Vol. 2, p. 622, *et seq.*
[416] 1 Drew 651.
[417] 2 Redf. on Wills *73.
[418] 2 Redf. on Wills *71.
[419] Rev. Stat. of Mo. 1889, § 2823.
[420] Grand Lodge v. Elsner, 26 Mo. App. 116.

seem to incline to the definition of family approved by the cases relating to homestead rights. For example, it has been said :[421] "We are not of the opinion that the words 'or their families,' as used in section 47, *supra*, of the constitution of the order, should be construed to embrace all kindred of the same degree, but that the family therein intended to be benefited, where one exists, is the family as understood in its usual and ordinary sense, that is to such persons as habitually reside under one roof and form one domestic circle, or to such as are dependent upon each other for support, or among whom there is a legal or equitable obligation to furnish support." Under this definition immediate relatives often cannot be included in the term and a mother has, under this construction, been excluded.[422] Under some circumstances a father would be included ;[423] and a child by the member's prior marriage ;[424] and an aunt ;[425] and a mother ;[426] and a sister ;[427] and an orphan child taken into the family when an infant ;[428] and a grandchild of a sister of the insured.[429] The only child of a deceased member, his wife being divorced, was awarded the fund in preference to the member's brother who lived in the member's family, the term used in the charter being "immediate family."[430] But the term "immediate family" does not include a married daughter not living with her father.[431] Nor does the term "family" include a son who has come to maturity and has left his father's home permanently.[432]

[421] Hofman v. Grand Lodge B. L. F., 73 Mo. App. 47. See also Lister v. Lister, 73 Mo. App. 99.

[422] Lister v. Lister, 73 Mo. App. 99; Knights of Columbus v. Rowe, 70 Conn. 545; 40 Atl. 541.

[423] Ferbrache v. Grand Lodge A. O. U. W., 81 Mo. App. 268.

[424] Hutson v. Jenson, 110 Wis. 26; 85 N. W. 689.

[425] Knights of Columbus v. Rowe, *supra*.

[426] Manley v. Manley, 107 Tenn. 191; 64 S. W. 8.

[427] Supreme Assembly Royal Soc., etc., v. Adams, 107 Fed. 335; Hosmer v. Welch, 107 Mich. 470; 67 N. W. 504; Supreme Council L. of H. v. Nidelet, 81 Mo. App. 599.

[428] Grand Lodge A. O. U. W. v. McKinstry, 67 Mo. App. 82.

[429] Grand Lodge A. O. U. W. v. Fisk, 126 Mich. 356; 85 N. W. 875.

[430] Norwegian Old People's, etc., Ass'n v. Wilson, 176 Ill. 94; 52 N. E. 41.

[431] Danielson v. Wilson, 73 Ill. App. 287.

[432] Brower v. Supreme Lodge N. R. A., 87 Mo. App. 614.

§ 330. **The Same Subject—Examples of Construction.**—In the case of Starnes v. Atlanta Police Relief Association,[433] a minority of the Court, while agreeing with the majority opinion that the word "family" should be given a broad construction, said: "However, we think that the word 'family' should be given an even broader meaning than he has given it. Upon the theory, well recognized by the courts in dealing with insurance and similar beneficial contracts, that a death benefit bought and paid for by a person in life should not fail upon his death for lack of a beneficiary competent to take, no hesitancy has been shown, in the construction of such contracts, in giving great elasticity to the meaning of words, where necessary to do so in order to find a beneficiary. Such a rule of construction is desirable from the standpoints both of the insurer and of the insured. One of the chief objections hitherto made against fraternal insurance is that it does not offer freedom in the designation of beneficiaries, and that the member is liable to pay for insurance which can never be collected, by reason of some strict and technical construction of the limitations imposed as to who shall be a beneficiary. The result of a course of judicial construction which liberally construes such contracts, so as to make it more certain that the benefits bought will reach some person or persons whom the member would really wish such benefits to reach, is, therefore, to give popularity to this form of insurance. In such contracts the word 'family' has been most liberally extended, wherever necessary to effectuate the beneficial purpose. It is a word which must vary in meaning according to the conditions surrounding the member at the date of his death. From a review of the decisions we deduce the following order of precedence which should ordinarily be observed in determining who are entitled to take under the words 'family of the member' or similar designations: ·(1) Wife and unmarried children, minor or adult; or, if no unmarried children (2) wife alone; or, if no wife, (3) unmarried children alone; or, if no wife, and no unmarried children, (4) persons related by consanguinity or affinity, living with the member in the same household; or, if none of these, (5) any person related by consanguinity or affinity upon whom the member is dependent; or (6) any person related by con-

[433] 2 Ga. App. 237; 58 S. E. 481. See also Jackson v. Brothers & Sisters, etc., 2 Ga. App. 761; 59 S. E. 11.

sanguinity or affinity, dependent on and supported by the member;
or, if none of these, (7) married children, irrespective of dependency; or, if none of these, (8) father, mother, brothers and sis-'
ters, irrespective of active household connection and irrespective of
the question of dependence; and in some instances an even further extension may be made, if ncessary, in order to find a beneficiary. The existence 'of the benefit connotes a contemplated
beneficiary, and the law will find one, if possible.'' The family
may include step-children who reside with the member and are
supported by him. The term ''adopted child'' may include a step-
daughter in the same family,[434] and a step-mother is the member
of the family of a single man who is living with her.[435] So is a
woman who had taken the member into her family and supported
him without charge, though not dependent upon him.[436] Though
a daughter of a member of a beneficial association more than twenty-one had left his home intending to make a living for herself,
she had not necessarily ceased to be a member of his immediate
family.[437] But the mother of a member is not a member of his
family when living apart from her son, nor is she a dependent,[438]
nor is a step-father a member of a step-daughter's family at the
time of her death although he had been previously a member
of the family,[439] nor was the defendant a member of the family
of the insured where the husband and wife had separated, the
defendant remaining with the wife,[440] nor is the wife of a person
in whose home the member lived a member of his family.[441] Where
the marriage of insured's father was null under the laws of Wisconsin, where marriage is a contract, the father was entitled to
be designated a beneficiary.[442]

[434] Anderson v. Royal League, 130 Minn. 416.
[435] Jones v. Firemen's Relief Ass'n (Wis.), 138 N. W. 618.
[436] Peterson v. National Council K. & L. of S., 189 Mo. App. 662; 175
S. W. 284.
[437] Dalton v. Knights of Columbus, 80 Conn. 212; 67 Atl. 510; Norwegian Old People's Home Soc. v. Wilson, 176 Ill. 94; 52 N. E. 41.
[438] Western Commercial Travelers' Ins. Co. v. Tennent, 128 Mo. App.
541; 106 S. W. 1073.
[439] Supreme Lodge O. M. P. v. Dewey, 142 Mich. 660; 106 N. W. 140;
3 L. R. A. (N. S.), 334.
[440] Grand Lodge A. O. U. W. v. McKay, 149 Mich. 90; 112 N. W. 730.
[441] Supreme Commandery v. Donahgey, 75 N. H. 197; 72 Atl. 419.
[442] Mund v. Rehaume, 51 Colo. 129; 117 Pac. 159.

§ 331. **Children.**—Where the word "children" as well as all other descriptive names of classes or relations, is used it must always, when that can be done, be understood in its primary and ordinary signification,[443] and where the word has received a larger and more extended construction it has been based upon a supposed intention of a testator, grantor, or law-making power to so extend it.[444] Life insurance policies payable to the children of insured include those subsequently born.[445] When there are those answering to the description, only legitimate children are included under the term,[446] but the authorities seem to agree that the question is one of intent, and if the term "children" is used by a testator who leaves one legitimate and one illegitimate child, both will generally take;[447] so, if an unmarried man leaves children who have been recognized by him, they will take.[448] If supported by him they can take as dependents.[449] It has also been held that the term "child" will not include an illegitimate child.[450] An assignment of a policy of life insurance by a man to the mother of his illegitimate child to secure its support has been upheld.[451] Step-children will take if such can be supposed to have been intended.[452] Also children by different marriages,[453] and posthumous children,[454] and adopted children,[455] but the right of the latter depends upon whether the child was legally adopted and whether there was an intent that it

[443] 2 Redf. on Wills, *15; Bedford's Appeal, 40 Pa. St. 18.

[444] 2 Redf. on Wills, *16 and note; Wigram on Extrinsic Evidence, 42.

[445] Roquemore v. Dent, 135 Ala. 292; 33 Sou. 178; Scull v. Aetna L. Ins. Co., 132 N. C. 30; 43 S. E. 504; 60 L. R. A. 615.

[446] Van Voorhis v. Brintnall, 23 Hun. 260.

[447] 2 Redf. on Wills, *24 and cases cited in note.

[448] 2 Redf. on Wills, *25.

[449] Hanley v. Supreme Tent, etc., 38 Misc. 161; 77 N. Y. Supp. 246.

[450] Savigne v. Ligue des Patriotes, 178 Mass. 25; 59 N. E. 674; 54 L. R. A. 814.

[451] Brown v. Mansur, 64 N. H. 39; 5 Atl. 768.

[452] Tepper v. Supreme Council R. A., 61 N. J. Eq. 638; 47 Atl. 460.

[453] Redf. on Wills, *29; Jackman v. Nelson, 147 Mass. 300; 17 N. E. 529; State L. Ins. Co. v. Redman, 91 Mo. App. 49.

[454] Kent Comm. 412; 2 Washb. on Real Prop. 654; 2 Redf. on Wills, *10.

[455] Barnes v. Allen, 25 Ind. 222; Virgin v. Marwick, 97 Me. 578; 55 Atl. 520.

should take. The motive for the adoption is immaterial.[456] In a case where a policy of life insurance on the life of a husband was payable "to my wife M. and children," the Court held that a child of the insured by a former wife was included;[457] and it has been held that "children" means children of the assured by several wives, but not children of a wife by another husband.[458] And where the policy on the life of a man was payable to his wife his child by a subsequent marriage takes nothing.[459] Where the benefit was payable to certain children by name a child subsequently born is not included;[460] but where the applicant designated his wife and children and the agent informed him that afterborn children would be included it was held,[461] that the company was estopped to claim the contrary. An adult son can be properly designated although he does not live with his father and the latter leave a widow.[462] Ordinarily, the word "child" does not include a grandchild,[463] but the general rule is, that whether grandchildren will take under the term children, depends entirely upon the construction of the intent of the party using the word. A leading English case[464] says: "Children may mean grandchildren when there can be no other construction, but not otherwise." The late American cases are apparently conflicting, but seem to agree that the question is one of intent, depending upon the special circumstances of each case.[465] The Court of Appeals of Kentucky has held,[466] that under the circumstances of that case any other construction

[456] Kemp v. N. Y. Produce Ex. 34; 34 App. Div. 175; 54 N. Y. Supp. 678.

[457] McDermott v. Centennial M. L. Ins. Ass'n, 24 Mo. App. 73. See also Jackman v. Nelson, *supra.*

[458] Koehler v. Centennial M. L. Ins. Co., 66 Ia. 325.

[459] Aetna Mut. L. Ins. Co. v. Clough, 68 N. H. 298; 44 Atl. 520.

[460] Spry v. Williams, 82 Ia. 61; 47 N. W. 890; 10 L. R. A. 863.

[461] Saurbier v. Union Central L. Ins. Co., 39 Ill. App. 620.

[462] Klotz v. Klotz, 15 Ky. L. 183; 22 S. W. 551.

[463] Churchill v. Churchill, 2 Metc. (Ky.), 469; Hughes v. Hughes, 12 B. Mon. 121; Carson v. Carson, 1 Phill. Esq. 57; Robinson v. Hardcastle, 2 Br. Ch. C. 344; In re Cashman, 3 Demarest (N. Y.), 242; Succession of Roder, 121 La. 692; 46 Sou. 697; Martin v. Modern Woodmen, 253 Ill. 400; 97 N. E. 693, affg. 163 Ill. App. 548.

[464] Reeves v. Brymer, 4 Ves. 692-698.

[465] Castner's Appeal, 88 Pa. St. 478.

[466] Duvall v. Goodson, 79 Ky. 224.

would defeat the intention of the maker of the instrument, and that, there at least, the words, child and grandchild, were synonymous. In a Rhode Island case,[467] the Supreme Court held the opposite. In a case where the policy was payable to the wife of the assured, if she survived him, and if not, then to his "children," it was held,[468] that grandchildren were not included. In another case,[469] where the policy was payable to the wife of assured "and children," the same court held that parol evidence was not admissible to show that a grandchild was intended to be included. The word, in a statute, has been construed to embrace grandchildren.[470] Obviously, rather than admit a construction that would result in intestacy, children would be held to mean descendants;[471] but there must be special and satisfactory reasons to justify a departure from the primary import of the word;[472] the rule, however, is not general.[473] Often, in order to carry out a supposed intention, children may mean issue generally.[474] An illegitimate daughter may be a beneficiary.[475] Where the laws of a mutual benefit society provided that the beneficiaries of a member might be his "adopted children," such term will include a foster mother of the insured whom he legally adopted, though an adult, as his heir.[476]   All the persons who come within the designation and are in existence at the time the bequest or designation takes effect, will take unless

[467] Winsor v. Odd Fellows' Ass'n, 13 R. I. 149.

[468] Continental L. Ins. Co. v. Webb, 54 Ala. 688.

[469] Russell v. Russell, 64 Ala. 500.

[470] Cutting v. Cutting, 6 Sawy. C. C. 396; Walton v. Cotton, 19 How. 355.

[471] Royle v. Hamilton, 4 Ves. 437; Radcliffe v. Buckley, 10 Ves. 195; Beebe v. Estabrook, 79 N. Y. 246.

[472] Jackson v. Staats, 11 Johns. 337; Hallowell v. Phipps, 2 Whart. 376; Feit v. Vanata, 21 N. J. Eq. 84; Scott v. Guernsey, 48 N. Y. 106.

[473] Thompson v. Ludington, 104 Mass. 193.

[474] 2 Redf. on Wills, *22, 23; Prowitt v. Rodman, 37 N. Y. 42; Churchill v. Churchill, 2 Metc. (Ky.), 466; Bond's Appeal, 31 Conn. 183; Collins v. Hoxie, 9 Paige 81; Hone v. Van Schaick, 3 N. Y. 538; Dickenson v. Lee, 4 Watts 82. But see Hopson v. Commonwealth, 7 Bush 644.

[475] Stahl v. Grand Lodge A. O. U. W. (Tex. Civ. A.), 98 S. W. 643; Shelton v. Minnis, 107 Miss. 133; 65 Sou. 114. Or a step-daughter. O'Brien v. Grand Lodge A. O. U. W., (Mass.), 111 N. E. 955.

[476] Mellville v. Wickham (Tex. Civ. A.), 169 S. W. 1123.

the language used clearly conveys a different import.[477] A benefit certificate takes effect, so far as to vest in the beneficiaries an absolute right to the benefit money, at the death of the party to whom it is issued, and hence the same rules should hold to them which prevail as to wills and policies of life insurance. Where the certificate was issued payable to the "children" of the applicant without naming them, the term does not mean certain named children then in existence, but those together with such as may thereafter be born to the member.[478] The words "their children" mean those common to the husband and wife.[479] They will take an equal share *per capita*, but if there are not words indicating a purpose to have the bequest or benefit go in shares, it will be so construed and the several classes will take *per stirpes*.[480] Generally, where the fund is payable to "wife and children" they are tenants in common,[481] and the statutes of distribution govern.[482] Under the Illinois statute abolishing distinctions between the kindred of the whole and the half blood, the Supreme Court of that State has held,[483] children of the same mother by different fathers are as much brothers and sisters as children of the same father by different mothers. Where a policy was made payable to the children

[477] 2 Redf. on Wills, § 2, Ch. 1, Part II; Chesmar v. Bucken, 37 N. J. Eq. 415; Campbell v. Rawdon, 18 N. Y. 412; Felix v. Grand Lodge, etc., 31 Kan. 81.

[478] Thomas v. Leake, 67 Tex. 469; 3 S. W. 703; Union Mut. Aid Ass'n v. Montgomery, 70 Mich. 587; 38 N. W. 588. To the contrary is Conn. Mut. L. Ins. Co. v. Baldwin, 15 R. I. 106; 23 Atl. 105. See also *post*, § 389.

[479] Evans v. Opperman, 76 Tex. 293; 13 S. W. 312.

[480] Hallan v. Gardner, 5 Ky. L. 857; Covenant Mut. Ben. Ass'n v. Hoffman, 110 Ill. 603; Malone v. Majors, 8 Humph. 577; 2 Redf. on Wills, *34; Harris' Estate, 74 Pa. St. 452; Kean v. Roe, 2 Harr. (Del.), 103; Morgan v. Pettitt, 3 Demarest (N. Y.), 61; Campbell v. Wiggins, Rice (S. C.), Ch. 10; Lemacks v. Glover, 1 Rich. Eq. 150.

[481] Seyton v. Satterthwaite, 34 Ch. D. 511; Milburn v. Milburn, 83 Ind. 55.

[482] McLin v. Calvert, 78 Ky. 472; Taylor v. Hill, 86 Wis. 99; 56 N. W. 738; Kelley v. Ball, 14 Ky. S. 132; 19 S. W. 581; Grand Lodge A. O. U. W. v. Sater, 44 M. A. 445.

[483] Oglesby Coal Co. v. Pasco, 79 Ill. 164. For further discussion, see *post*, § 341.

of the insured and she died before any were born it was held[484] that her executor could not maintain an action for the amount of the insurance. The Court (Thayer, J.) says: ''The policy was obviously intended as a provision for such children as might be born of the marriage between Mr. and Mrs. Vail, and for no one else. The promise was to pay to the children, they were the beneficiaries. If Mrs. Vail had contemplated the possibility of death before she had given birth to any children, some provision would probably have been inserted in the policy touching the disposition of the insurance money in that event. What such provision· would have been it is impossible to say and it is useless to indulge in speculation on that subject, as the Court is powerless to make a contract for the parties covering that contingency. It can only enforce such a contract as the parties have themselves made. Some stress is laid on the fact that, according to the rule which prevails in some States, Mrs. Vail retained the power, so long as she held the policy, to change the beneficiaries with the consent of the insurer.[485] It is claimed that because she retained such power her administrator may recover on the policy. I am unable to assent to that proposition. Even if she had a right to change the beneficiary it was a mere power, to be exercised with the company's consent, and, as the agreed case shows, she never exercised it, or attempted to do so. The existence of such power, even if its existence be conceded, is not sufficient to make the policy a part of her estate, or authorize her administrator to sue thereon. Furthermore, it is said by taking out the policy for the benefit of her children, Mrs. Vail constituted the defendant company a trustee, for her children, and, the trust having failed because she died childless, that the fund in the trustee's hands inures to the benefit of her estate in the same manner that a fund left in trust for a given purpose will inure to the benefit of the donor or his heirs, if for any reason the trust cannot be executed. It is sufficient to say of this contention that, if the principle invoked has any application to the case at bar it is only applicable to the premiums actually paid up to the time of Mrs. Vail's death and the interest accumu-

[484] McElwee v. N. Y. Life Ins. Co., 47 Fed. 798. See also Vanormer v. Hornberger, 142 Pa. St. 575; 21 Atl. 887.
[485] Kerman v. Howard, 23 Wis. 108; Gambs v. Ins. Co., 50 Mo. 47.

669

lated thereon; and the remedy is in equity. Mrs. Vail did not place $5,000 in the hands of the defendant company to be held for the benefit of or in trust for her children. She contracted to pay $39.60 quarterly, and up to the time of her death had paid only two quarterly installments. The contract was entered into with the expectation that Mrs. Vail would live many years and that the premiums paid in the meantime, with accumulated interest, would equal the face of the policy at the end of her expectancy. Under the circumstances, it cannot be maintained, even on the trust theory above outlined, that the defendant is liable to the plaintiff in the sum of $5,000, or in any other sum in a strictly legal proceeding.''

§ 332. **Orphans.**—In the statutes of Massachusetts, Missouri and other States relative to benefit associations, and in the charters of many societies, the benefits are expressed to be, among other classes, for ''orphans'' of deceased members. An orphan is defined to be a minor, or infant child, who has lost both of his or her parents. Sometimes the term is applied to a person who has lost only one of his or her parents.[486] Webster's dictionary defines the noun orphan substantially as Bouvier, but the adjective as ''bereaved of parents.'' The English authorities usually cited[487] and at least one American case,[488] substantially support this definition. In a Pennsylvania case involving the construction of the word in Girard's will[489] the subject received exhaustive discussion, the conclusion being that a fatherless child was an orphan, as well as a child who had lost both parents. The most reasonable view of the subject is that in the use of the word in connection with benefit societies, the orphans of a member are his children for, although a member's children cannot be orphans so long as he lives, his orphans must certainly be his children, and the word ''orphans'' has been held to be synonymous with ''children.''[490] But in a Missouri case[491] it was held, from consideration of the rules of the association, that

[486] Bouvier's Law Dic., tit. ''Orphan.''

[487] 2 Salk. 426; 2 Bl. Com. 519; 4 Burns Ecc. Law, 443-444; 7 Vin. Abr. 213; 1 McPherson on Inf. 54.

[488] Heiss, Exr., etc., v. Murphey et al., 40 Wis. 276.

[489] Soohan v. City of Philadelphia et al., 33 Pa. St. 9.

[490] Jackman v. Nelson, 147 Mass. 300; 17 N. E. 529.

[491] Hammerstein v. Parsons, 29 Mo. App. 509.

in that case, the true construction demanded that the term "orphan children" be taken as intended to mean minor children and not fatherless adults.

§ 333. **Widow.**—By "widow" we are undoubtedly to under: stand an unmarried woman whose husband is dead,[492] and that the word is used in its ordinary popular sense. An interesting case was recently decided by the Supreme Court of Maine[493] where the facts were as follows: Bolton insured his life in two societies to a considerable amount, payable to his widow; he then living with a woman who for many years had passed as his wife. Upon his death the money passed to this supposed widow, but afterwards the true widow appeared and sued the pretender for this insurance money. The Court decided in the claimant's favor, holding' that there could be but one widow of a man. Under this rule a divorced woman whose husband is dead is not his widow.[494] In a New York case it was held[495] that the term wife after the name of a woman who was not the wife of the member will not invalidate the designation of her as his beneficiary. The word wife may be a mere description of the person and not a warranty.[496] Nor does adultery affect the widow's right[497] If a man designate as his beneficiary a woman with whom he is living as his wife the designation will be held good, although he may not in fact have been legally married to the woman, because if there be no violation of the laws of the society in the designation, the society by the issue of the certificate assents to such designation.[498] And where a man lives with a woman as his wife in good faith and has chil-

[492] Bouvier's Law D., tit. Widow.

[493] Bolton v. Bolton, 73 Me. 299.

[494] Schonfield v. Turner, 75 Tex. 324; 12 S. W. 626; Deahlin v. Knights of Modern Maccabees, 151 Mich. 644, 115 N. W. 975. See as to industrial policy; Breeden v. Western & Sou. L. Ins. Co., 148 Ky. 488, 146 S. W. 1104.

[495] Durian v. Central Verein, 7 Daly 168; Vivar v. Supreme Lodge, etc., 42 N. J. L. 455; 20 Atl. 36. But under the limitations of the charter a woman not a lawful wife may be precluded from taking the benefit. Keener v. Grand Lodge A. O. U. W,. 38 M. A. 543.

[496] Slaughter v. Slaughter, 186 Ala. 302; 65 Sou. 348.

[497] Shamrock Ben. Soc. v. Durm, 1 Mo. App. 320.

[498] Story v. Williamsburg Masonic, etc., Ass'n, 95 N. Y. 474; Standard L. & A. Ass'n v. Martin, 133 Ind. 376; 33 N. E. 105.

dren by her she is a dependent and can take.[499]   If the woman knew that her marriage was bigamous she cannot be named beneficiary as wife.[500]   But where the by-laws of the society designate the widow of a deceased member as the party to whom the benefit is to be paid, it has been held[501] that in the absence of qualifying circumstances the lawful wife of the member is intended, although it is legally possible for such member to designate as his beneficiary a person living with him as his wife, though not legally married to him, and if such designation is assented to and becomes a part of the contract, the person so designated may, on the member's death, recover on the contract, though the burden of proof is on her clearly to establish such designation.   But in such a case the proof must be clear, for courts will not encourage concubinage, and no right of a lawful wife or child will be permitted to be taken away except upon clear proof.   Where insured was forced into marriage and never lived with his wife she is not his widow.[502]   In a case in Missouri[503] where the laws of the order designated the widow of the member as his beneficiary, the deceased had abandoned his wife in a foreign country and had lived in Missouri many years with a woman who was held out to be his wife and by whom he had reared a large family.   The Court held, on a contest between the lawful and the alleged widow, that the former was entitled to the benefit and the intention of the member in effecting the insurance and the good faith of the putative wife in considering herself his wife were immaterial facts.   A woman living with a man on separation from his wife who survived him is not entitled to benefits though designated as wife.[504]   A divorced wife has no equities over the widow of a man who subsequently married,[505] and a woman separated from her husband and who remarried is estopped from claiming the benefits as the widow of

[499] Supreme Lodge A. O. U. W. v. Hutchinson, 6 Ind. App. 399; 33 N. E. 816. See post, § 336.

[500] Miller v. Prelle, 121 Ill. App. 380; Appelbaum v. Order United Commercial Travelers (N. C.), 88 S. E. 722.

[501] Schnook v. Independent Order, etc., 21 Jones & Sp. 181.

[502] Grand Lodge K. P. v. Smith, 89 Miss. 718; 42 Sou. 89.

[503] Grand Lodge v. Elsner, 26 Mo. App. 108.

[504] Meinhardt v. Meinhardt, 117 Md. 426; 85 Atl. 715.

[505] Farra v. Braman, 171 Ind. 529; 84 N. E. 155; 86 N. E. 843.

the member against the member's second wife.[506]   But a woman named in a policy of life insurance as wife but not so in fact may recover.[507]

§ 334.   **Heirs.**—In construing the meaning of the word heirs the intent will also be considered and regarded, if possible;[508] and if there is a plain demonstration that the word was used in any other than a strict legal sense a liberal interpretation will be given it.[509]   Accordingly, it has been held to have been used in the sense of family,[510] and in the sense of children.[511]   Legal heirs means those who take under intestate laws.[512]   The general current of authority is to the effect that when applied to the succession of personal estate the words mean next of kin and a husband or widow are excluded.[513]   Applied to benefit societies the word will not be given a technical meaning.   There are numerous cases which hold that by heirs those are meant who would take personal property under the statutes of distribution.[514]   And a widow is in-

[506] Woodson v. Colored Gr. Lodge K. of H., 97 Miss. 210; 52 Sou. 457.

[507] Prudential Ins. Co. v. Norris (N. J.), 70 Atl. 924.

[508] Tillman v. Davis et al., 95 N. Y. 17; s. c. 47 Am. Rep. 1; Criswell v. Grumbling, 107 Pa. St. 408; Bradlee v. Andrews, 137 Mass. 50; Greenwood v. Murray, 28 Minn. 120; Addison v. N. E. Travelers' Ass'n, 144 Mass. 591; 12 N. E. 407; Sweet v. Dutton, 109 Mass. 591; De Beauvoir v. Beauvoir, 3 H. L. Cas. 524; In re. Rootes, 1 Drew & Sm. 228.

[509] Rivard v. Gisenhof, 35 Hun. 247; Addison v. N. E. C. Trav. Ass'n, 144 Mass. 591; 12 N. E. 407.

[510] Bradlee v. Andrews, 137 Mass. 50; Rivard v. Gisenhof, 35 Hun. 247; Criswell v. Grumbling, 107 Pa. St. 408; Brown v. Harmon, 73 Ind. 412.

[511] Morton v. Barrett, 22 Me. 257; Mace v. Cushman, 45 Me. 250.

[512] Burke v. Modern Woodmen of Am., 2 Cal. App. 611; 84 Pac. 275.

[513] Hodge's Appeal, 8 W. N. C. (Pa.) 209; Hascall v. Cox, 49 Mich. 435; Irwin's Appeal, 106 Pa. St. 176; 51 Am. Rep. 516; Tillman v. Davis, et al., 95 N. Y. 17; s. c. 47 Am. Rep. 1; Wright v. Trustees, Hoff. Ch. 202; Ketaltas v. Ketaltas, 72 N. Y. 312; Luce v. Dunham, 69 N. Y 36; Dodge's Appeal, 106 Pa. St. 216; s. c. 51 Am. Rep. 519; Blackman v. Wadsworth, 65 Ia. 80; Wilkins v. Ordway, 59 N. H. 378; s. c. 47 Am. Rep. 215; Gordon v. Small, 53 Md. 550; Phillips v. Carpenter, 79 Ia. 600; 44 N. W. 898; Knights Templars, etc., Ass'n v. Greene, 79 Fed. 461.

[514] Withy v. Mangles, 10 Clark & Fin. 215; Evans v. Salt, 6 Beav. 266; Jacobs v. Jacobs, 16 Beav. 557; Low v. Smith, 2 Jur. Pt. 1344; Doody v. Higgins, 2 Kay & J. 729; Elmsley v. Young, 2 Myl. & K. 82; In re Porter's Will, 6 W. R. 187; Gittings v. McDermott, 2 Myl. & K. 69; Eby's Appeal;

cluded[515]   The son of a deceased wife and not his widow is his
heir.[516] In an Illinois case the Supreme Court of that State[517] held
that the designation "legal heirs" in a benefit certificate gave
the money to the next of kin and excluded the widow.   However,
where under the laws of the State a widow is a distributee of her
husband's personal estate she is entitled to share in the proceeds
of insurance on his life payable to "his heirs at law."[518]   Under
the statute of Iowa a wife is included in the class of legal heirs.[519]
In a case in Missouri[520] "heirs or representatives" was held to
mean next of kin, if the intent of the assured could be shown to
be that the money was not to go to his executors or administrators
to be administered as ordinary assets.   The Supreme Court of
Massachusetts has held[521] that the word "heirs" was used in the
by-laws of a benefit society "in its limited sense, to designate such
persons as would be the legal heirs or distributees of the member
at the time of his application or designation. This view is strengthened by the fact that, in the fourth clause of the same section, the

84 Pa. St. 241; Sweet v. Dutton, 109 Mass. 591; Welsh v. Carter, 32 N. J.
Eq. 177; Freeman v. Knight, 2 Ired. Eq. 72; Alexander v. Wallace, 8 Lea
569; Houghton v. Kendall, 7 Allen 72; Johnson v. Supreme Lodge K. of
H., 53 Ark. 242; 13 S. W. 794; Lawwill v. Lawwill, 29 Ill. App. 643; Walsh
v. Walsh, 20 N. Y. Supp. 933; N. W. Masonic, etc., Ass'n v. Jones (Appeal
of Chance), 154 Pa. St. 99; 26 Atl. 253; Anderson v. Groesbeck, 26 Colo.
3; 55 Pac. 1086; Pleimann v. Harbung, 84 Mo. App. 283; Burns v. Burns,
190 N. Y. 211; 82 N. E. 1107.

[515] Leavitt v. Dunn, 56 N. J. L. 309; 28 Atl. 590; Lyons v. Yerex, 100
Mich. 214; 58 N. W. 1112; Hanson v. Scandinavian, etc., Ass'n, 59 Minn.
128; 60 N. W. 1091; Burns v. Burns, 190 N. Y. 211; 82 N. E. 1107; affg.
95 N. Y. Supp. 797; 109 App. Div. 98. See also Wharton v. Drewry, 138
Ga. 587; 69 S. E. 1117.

[516] Royal League v. Kolne, 169 Ill. App. 646.

[517] Gauch v. St. Louis M. L. I. Co., 88 Ill. 251. See also Mearns v. Ancient Order United Workmen, 22 Ont. R. 34, and Fraternal Ass'n v.
Teutsch, 170 Ill. App. 47.

[518] Lyons v. Yerex, 100 Mich. 214; 58 N. W. 1112, where all the cases
bearing on the subject are reviewed.

[519] Thompson v. Northwestern M. L. Ins. Co., 161 Ia. 446, 143 N. W. 518.

[520] Loos v. John Hancock L. Ins. Co., 41 Mo. 538. To the same effect are
Britton v. Supreme Counc. R. A., 46 N. J. E. 102; 18 Atl. 675; Leavitt v.
Dunn, 56 N. J. L. 309; 28 Atl. 590; Hannigan v. Ingraham, 8 N. Y. Supp.
232.

[521] Elsey v. Odd Fellows, etc., 142 Mass. 224.

same words are used in this sense, it being provided that, 'if the designator leave no widow, or children, or assignee, then it shall be payable to his heirs.' In the case at bar, W., in his application for membership, designated his wife as the person to whom the benefit was to be paid upon his death. At a later day he attempted to change the designation from his wife to his mother. It is agreed that his mother was not living with him, but was living with her husband in' another town and county. It was not suggested that she was dependent upon him. She was not one of those who would be his heirs, and she was not one of the 'members of the decedent's family,' within the meaning of the by-law.'' In another case, however,[522] the mother of deceased, under the special facts in the case, was held to be a dependent. In another case, heirs was held to mean widow,[523] and the term has been construed to mean wife and children.[524] The widow of a member of a mutual benefit association is the beneficiary under a certificate issued by it which is payable to "his heirs," he having brothers and sisters but no children.[525] The Supreme Court of Ohio has held that it is not within the power of a member of a benefit society to try to make one who is not related to him his beneficiary and heir within the statute limiting beneficiaries to the families of heirs of members,[526] and a divorced wife has no share in the benefit[527] unless equities exist in her favor and the fund is in court.[528] In a Michigan case[529] it was held that, where a benefit was payable to the wife of the member, "her heirs, executors, etc.," and she died before her husband, leaving a will bequeathing the benefit to such husband, his heirs who were collateral kindred were within the statute providing for the

[522] Am. Legion of Honor v. Perry, 140 Mass. 580.

[523] Addison v. N. E. C. Travelers' Ass'n, 144 Mass. 591; 12 N. E. 407; Kaiser v. Kaiser, 13 Daly 522; Lawwill v. Lawwill, 29 Ill. App. 643.

[524] Janda v. Bohemian, etc., Union, 71 App. Div. 150; 75 N. Y. Supp. 654; affd. 173 N. Y. 617; 66 N. E. 1110; Taylor v. Hill, 86 Wis. 99; 56 N. W. 738.

[525] Alexander v. N. W. Masonic Aid Ass'n, 126 Ill. 558; 18 N. E. 556; Jamieson v. Knights Templar, etc., Ass'n, 12 Cin. L. Bul. 272 (Superior Ct. Cin.)

[526] National Aid Ass'n v. Gonser, 43 Ohio St. 1.

[527] Schonfield v. Turner, 75 Tex. 324; 12 S. W. 626.

[528] Leaf v. Leaf, 92 Ky. 166; 17 S. W. 354.

[529] Silvers v. Mich. Mut. Ben. Ass'n, 94 Mich. 39; 53 N. W. 935.

· payment to "heirs, etc." Under the general rules and the statutes, in most States governing such cases of legacies to a class, heirs would take *per stirpes.*[530] Where the benefit was payable to a woman designated as wife but not legally married to him. the parents were held to be entitled to the benefit as legal heirs.[531]

§ 335. **Relatives.**—In the Massachusetts statute and in charters of some benefit societies the word "relatives" is used. This term undoubtedly is synonymous with relations or kindred,[532] and is to be construed accordingly. It has long been settled that the word "relatives," when used in a will or statute, includes those persons who are next of kin under the statutes of distribution, unless from the nature of the bequest or from the testator having authorized a power of selection, a different construction is allowed.[533] In the construction of a statute it has been held not to include a step-son[534] nor a wife.[535] A son-in-law of the member is not a relative,[536] nor a brother-in-law,[537] nor a niece of deceased member's father's first wife, deceased being a son of the second wife.[538] In this latter case the Court said: "There seems to be no authority for holding that the word relation, in its strict legal and technical sense, includes husband or wife. On the contrary, authorities are found very direct and explicit to the point that they are not relations. Thus in 2 Williams on Executors,[539] it is

[530] Redf. on Wills, *34; Burgin v. Patton, 5 Jones Eq. (N. C.), 425; Gosling v. Caldwell, 1 Lea (Tenn.), 454; Conigland v. Smith, 79 N. C. 303; Bell v. Kinneer, 101 Ky. 271; 40 S. W. 686.

[531] Severs v. National Slavonic Soc., 138 Wis. 144; 119 N. W. 814.

[532] Bouvier Law Dic., tit. "Relative;" Sheehan v. Journeymen's, etc., Ass'n, 142 Cal. 489; 76 Pac. 238; Donithan v. Independent Order, etc., 209 Pa. St. 170; 58 Atl. 142.

[533] Drew v. Wakefield, 54 Me. 291; 2 Jarm. on Wills, 661; Bouvier's Law Dic., tit., "Relative."

[534] Kimball v. Story, 108 Mass. 382; Morey v. Monk, 145 Ala. 301; 40 Sou. 411. To the contrary, Simcoke v. Grand Lodge A. O. U. W., 84 Ia. 383; 51 N. W. 8.

[535] Esty Admr. v. Clark, *et al.*, 101 Mass. 36.

[536] Supreme Lodge New England Order, etc., v. Hine, 82 Conn. 315; 73 Atl. 791.

[537] Sanders v. Grand Lodge, etc., 153 Ill. App. 7.

[538] Smith v. Supreme Tent K. O. -T. M., 127 Ia. 115; 102 N. W. 830; 69 L. R. A. 174.

[539] P. 1004.

laid down that 'no person can regularly answer the description of relations but those who are akin to the testator by blood. A wife, therefore, cannot claim under a bequest to her husband's relations nor a husband as a relation to his wife.' " The Supreme Court of Pennsylvania[540] has decided that in a will the terms, "my nearest relations or connections," do not include the testator's wife. The decision says: "A wife is no more a relation of her husband than he is of himself." The English rule is the same.[541] The word "relations" includes only relations by blood and not connections by marriage, even a husband or wife.[542] This, however, is not always true, for a more liberal construction has been adopted and, in construing statutes relative to benefit societies, the wife of a nephew has been held to be a relative of the uncle. In a case of this kind the Court says:[543] "In our modern dictionaries we find that a 'relation' or 'relative' is defined as a person connected by blood or affinity. When used in a contract, as in this case, I do not find that it has such a fixed and definite meaning that we must thwart the purpose of this decedent, who supposed that, by the terms of the article giving him control of his benefit in the relief fund he could bestow it on any one of those popularly called 'relatives' whom he might select. It seems also that a liberal rather than a restricted meaning given to the word 'relative,' used in this article of the association, would better comport with its benevolent purpose. The construction contended for against this certificate would exclude a member's wife unless she came within the other part of the phrase by being dependent on him for her support. The ties of affinity are often stronger than those between collateral or even lineal, kinsmen by blood; and there is nothing unreasonable in saying that this certificate was made payable to one whom the holder supposed was properly classed among his relatives and that the council so intended. Where there is no fixed legal or technical meaning which the Court must follow in

540 Storer v. Wheatley, 1 Pa. St. 506.

541 Garrick v. Lord Camden, 14 Ves. 372.

542 Paine v. Prentiss, 5 Met. 396; Esty v. Clark, 101 Mass. 36; Dickinson v. Purvis, 8 S. & R. 71; Kimball v. Story, 108 Mass. 582. To the contrary is Tepper v. Supreme Council R. A., 61 N. J. Eq. 638; 47 Atl. 460; reversing 45 Atl. 114.

543 Bennett v. Van Ripper, 47 N. J. E. 563; 22 Atl. 1055; reversing Supreme Council, etc., v. Bennett, 47 N. J. E. 39; 19 Atl. 785.

the construction of a contract, then 'the best construction,' says Chief Justice Gibson, 'is that which is made by viewing the subject of the contract as the mass of mankind would view it; for it may be safely assumed that such was the aspect in which the parties themselves viewed it. A result thus obtained is exactly what is obtained from the cardinal rule of intention.'[544] It seems that the objects of this association will be best attained by the adoption of a common, though it may be arf inexact, interpretation of the words 'related to' as used in the article above referred to, rather than by a restricted meaning that may not have been known, and is certain to defeat the purpose of this deceased member; and that no rule of legal construction will be violated by giving it such a meaning." So the term relative has been held to be broad enough to include one who married a sister of the wife of the member.[545] A step-son is a relative of the step-father. As the Supreme Court of Iowa says:[546] "It is urged that the certificate is void because plaintiff is not a 'relative' within the meaning of the statute. By particular specification the statute comprehends many classes of relatives, and then supplements their use by the term 'relative' without words of limitation. Nothing seems to indicate that the word is used in a restricted sense. A step-father is a relative by affinity and the relationship continues after the death of the wife on whom the relationship depends. In Spear v. Robinson[547] it is said: 'By the marriage one party thereto holds by affinity the same relation to the kindred of the other that the latter holds by consanguinity, and no rule is known to us under which the relation by affinity is lost on a dissolution of the marriage, more than that by blood is lost by the death of those through whom it is derived. The dissolution of a marriage, once lawful, by death or divorce, has no effect upon the issue; and it is apprehended, it can have no greater operation to annul the relation of affinity which it produced. There is nothing in the spirit or purpose of the law that indicates to us that relatives by affinity are not within

544 Navigation Co. v. Moore, 2 Whart. 491.

545 Tolson v. National Provident Union, 114 N. Y. Supp. 1149; 130 App. Div. 884; 113 N. Y. Supp. 334.

546 Simcoke v. Grand Lodge A. O. U. W., 84 Ia. 383; 51 N. W. 8.

547 29 Me. 531.

the legislative intent,' ''[548] and a step-daughter is included.[549]   A sister also is a relative within the meannig of the term used in a statute.[550]   Nephews and nieces are relatives.[551]   Where the laws of the order permitted the "survivors" of the member to be named as beneficiaries, one who is not a relative of the member is not a survivor.[552]

§ 336. **Dependents.**—The statutes of the various States and a majority of the charters of the leading benefit associations, restrict the payment of benefits, among other classes, to the "dependents" of the member, or "those dependent upon him." Webster's Dictionary defines the word primarily to mean, "One who depends; one who is sustained by another, or who relies on another for suport or favor; a retainer; as a numerous train of *dependents.*" In cases arising under the homestead and exemption laws, the courts have, with scarcely an exception, held that hired servants are not members of a family within the meaning of those laws.[553] Following the analogy of these precedents we must conclude that "retainers" or servants are not to be classed among dependents, nor is any person whose relation to the testator is fixed by contract and not by *situs*, except of course, husband and wife, who undoubtedly are dependents each upon the other. A servant therefore is not a dependent.[554] Nor a woman with whom the member boarded.[555] But a woman is a dependent who in good faith lives with him in the belief that she is his wife although there is no legal marriage.[556] In the case first cited the Court, reviewing a number

548 Anthony v. Mass. Ben. Ass'n, 158 Mass. 322; 33 N. E. 577.

549 Renner v. Supreme Lodge, etc., 89 Wis. 401; 62 N. W. 80.

550 Anthony v. Mass. Ben. Ass'n, 158 Mass. 322; 33 N. E. 577.

551 Wright v. Grand Lodge, etc. (Tex. Civ. A.), 173 S. W. 270; Supreme Tribe Ben Hur v. Gailey, 117 Ark. 145; 173 S. W. 838.

552 Grand Lodge, etc., v. Lemke, 124 Wis. 483; 102 N. W. 911.

553 Thompson on Homesteads, §§ 45-47.

554 Grand Lodge A. O. U. W. v. Gandy, 63 N. J. Eq. 692; 53 Atl. 142.

555 Faxon v. Locomotive, etc., Ass'n, 87 Ill. 262.

556 Supreme Lodge A. O. U. W. v. Hutchinson, 6 Ind. App. 399; 33 N. E. 816. To the same effect are: Crosby v. Ball, 4 Ont. L. R. 496; Supreme Tent, etc., v. McAllister, 132 Mich. 69; 92 N. W. 770; Senge v. Senge, 106 Ill. App. 140; James v. Supreme Counc. R. A., 130 Fed. 1014; Wojanski v. Wojanski, 136 Ill. App. 614. The ripening of an illicit connection into a lawful marriage makes the woman a wife. Busch v. Busch, 81 Mo. App. 562.

of cases bearing on the subject, which are also cited again in the text, says: "Margretta Hutchinson sustained to the deceased the actual, but not the legal relation of wife. She was not his wife and could not take as such. She was, however, in her relations with him, entirely innocent of any wrong intent, and being inno-cent, no principle of public policy can intervene to prevent the courts giving to her that to which she is otherwise entitled. This certificate is no more tainted with évil in her hands than in the hands of the lawful wife. While Margretta was not the wife, she was a dependent upon the deceased and she had at least a moral right to look to him for support. She and her children were in fact dependent upon him. He owed to her and to them a duty which was in part performed by taking out this certificate payable to her. While it was not lawful for him to live with Margretta, it was eminently lawful and proper that he should provide for the support of herself and children after he had wronged her so grievously. We think the true meaning of the word 'dependent' in this connection means some person or persons dependent for support in some way upon the deceased.[557] The beneficiary must be dependent upon the member in a material degree for support or maintenance or assistance, and the obligation on the part of the member to furnish it must rest upon some moral or legal or equi-table grounds.[558] In Keener v. Grand Lodge, etc.,[559] this language is used: 'I would not restrict dependency to those whom one may be legally bound to support, nor yet to those to whom he may be morally bound, but the term should be restricted to those whom it is lawful for him to support. It is not lawful to suport a woman knowingly occupying the illicit relationship in which interpleader places herself.' The case of Story v. Association,[560] meets every feature of the case in hand except that relating to the warranty. In that case the member was married, but lived with another woman as his wife, joined the association, and received a certifi-cate payable to 'Mary Story, his wife,' although she was not his wife. The Court says: 'The nondisclosure by Story of the prior marriage was not a fraud upon the society. Its obligation was not

557 Ballou v. Gile, 50 Wis. 614; 7 N. W. 561.
558 McCarthy v. Order of Protection, 153 Mass. 314; 26 N. E. 866.
559 36 Mo. App. 543.
560 95 N. Y. 474.

in any way enlarged by making the plaintiff the beneficiary. Nor did the appropriation of the fund for her benefit contravene the ,policy or objects of the association. The plaintiff for sixteen years lived with Story, believing herself to be his lawful wife. They had children dependent upon them for support. ' It was a case where it was the duty of Story to provide for them, and the provision he made through this insurance was in entire accord with the objects of defendant's organization.' And upon this ground expressly the judgment in favor of the plaintiff was affirmed.'' A mistress, however, is not a dependent in any sense.[561] We must logically exclude also those whose dependence upon the member is for favor, which may or may not take a pecuniary form, and which may be cast off at pleasure. Evidently, to bring a person within the circle of dependents, there must be some more substantial and open reliance, and yet we can easily conceive of cases where a state of dependency may be actual, although no legal nor moral duty rests upon the member to give aid or support to the dependent. Under the definition, three classes are left and even these have no well-defined limits, or bounds of separation; so that all persons can be segregated into one or the other division. ''One who depends''—what is included in this definition? We are all more or less dependent on each other, and so are dependents, yet none can affirm that all the world is included in the class named in the charters or statutes. ''One who is sustained by another, or who relies on another for support.'' Taking this definition as a whole, we are forced to the conclusion that they limit the term dependents to those who reasonably rely upon another for subsistence, nourishment and support. In a Wisconsin case[562] the Supreme Court defined dependent as follows: ''We think the true meaning of the word 'dependent,' in this connection, means some person or persons dependent for support in some way upon the deceased.'' This definition has been cited and seemingly approved by the Supreme Court of Massachusetts,[563] which held, under the special facts in the case, that the betrothed of the member was not

---

[561] Keener v. Grand Lodge, *supra;* West v. Grand Lodge A. O. U. W., 14 Tex. Civ. App. 471; 37 S. W. 966; Grand Lodge, etc., v. Riebling, 81 Mo. App. 545.

[562] Ballou v. Gile, 50 Wis. 614.

[563] American Legion of Honor v. Perry, 140 Mass. 580.

a dependent upon him, nor was his sister, nor a sister of his deceased wife. Although an affianced wife is generally not a dependent,[564] yet she in fact may be a dependent and it has so been held.[565] In another Massachusetts case[566] a mother was held not to be a dependent, and a brother is sometimes not a dependent.[567] Nor a father.[568] A child living with its parents and supported by them is not a dependent of a man who occasionally made her presents.[569] The question has also arisen in Missouri, where the statute[570] authorizes certain benevolent corporations to provide by assessments on their members certain benefits for "the relief and aid of the families, widows, orphans or other dependents" of the deceased members. In construing this section the St. Louis Court of Appeals says:[571] "Counsel for the appellant argues that section 972 contains a limitation of power, and, as the provision is for 'relief and aid,' the beneficiary must not only be a member of the family, or a widow, or orphan of the deceased member, but also must have lived dependent upon him for support. There is no warrant for this construction. The words 'other dependents' are inserted to include persons who, not being either members of the family of the deceased, nor his widow or orphans, are yet dependent upon him in some manner. Any other construction would require the Court in each case to enter into an investigation of the fact how far the widow or orphan, or any other member of the family, was self-supporting; which, in itself, instead of furthering the objects of these associations, would soon encompass their complete destruction. This is in accord with the construction placed upon the statute by the Supreme Court of Michigan in Supreme Lodge v.

564 Palmer v. Welch, 132 Ill. 141; 23 N. E. 412; affg. Parke v. Welch, 33 Ill. App. 186; Alexander v. Parker, 144 Ill. 355; 33 N. E. 183; reversing 42 Ill. App. 455; and Am. Legion of Honor v. Perry, *supra.*

565 In McCarthy v. New England Order, etc., 153 Mass. 314; 26 N. E. 866; Alexander v. Parker, *supra.* See also Kinney v. Dodd, 41 Ill. App. 49.

566 Elsey v. Odd Fellows, etc., 142 Mass. 224.

567 Supreme Counc. Am. L. of H. v. Smith, 45 N. J. E 466; 17 Atl. 770.

568 Brower v. Supreme Lodge, etc., 87 Mo. App. 614; Wagner v. St. Francis Ben. Soc., 70 Mo. App. 161.

569 Offill v. Supreme Lodge K. of H. (Tenn.), 46 S. W. 758.

570 § 972, Rev. Stat. 1879.

571 Grand Lodge v. Elsner, 26 Mo. App. 116.

Nairn,[572] where it is held: 'The laws of that State (Missouri) expressly forbid corporations of this sort from paying benefits to any but the member's family or dependents. The intent of the prohibition is clearly to shut out all persons who are not actual relatives *or* standing in place of relatives in some permanent way, *or* in some actual dependence on the member.' " From the definition and cases cited it seems that whether or not a person is included among the dependents of a member of a benefit society is a question of fact, and that each case must be decided upon its own merits.[573] In accordance with the liberal view of the Supreme Court of Michigan,[574] in defining who are included in the term family, we should say that if any person, relative of the member or not was supported by him, directly or indirectly, or wholly or in part, at his home or abroad, because of a legal or moral obligation, or merely from affection, such person might be called a dependent and be designated as the beneficiary of such member. But in all cases it would appear essential to apply the test of good faith, for mere capricious liking or temporary liberality in the way of gifts would not make the recipient a dependent.[575] A person whose only relation to the deceased member is that of a creditor, is not a person dependent upon him, within the meaning of the statutes authorizing the organization of societies to pay benefits to the families, *dependents,* etc., of deceased members, and a promise by the association to pay such a creditor is void. It has been said :[576] "Such a promise is beyond the powers of the association, and contravenes the intention of the statutes under which the association was organized. The plaintiff cannot, therefore, maintain an action on this promise either for his own use, or for that of any other person."[577]

[572] 60 Mich. 44.

[573] Alexander v. Parker, 144 Ill. 355; 33 N. E. 183; reversing 42 Ill. App. 455, and indeed all the cases cited in this section. See also Grand Lodge A. O. U. W. v. Bollman, 22 Tex. Civ. A. 106; 53 S. W. 829.

[574] Carmichael v. N. W. Mut. Ben. Ass'n, 51 Mich. 494. See also Carpenter v. U. S. Life Ins. Co., 161 Pa. St. 9; 28 Atl. 943.

[575] Thompson on Homesteads, § 50; Seaton v. Marshall, 6 Bush 429; Marsh v. Lazenby, 41 Ga. 153.

[576] Skillings v. Mass. Ben. Ass'n, 146 Mass. 217; 15 N. E. 566.

[577] Rice v. New England M. A. Soc., 146 Mass. 248; 15 N. E. 624; Briggs v. Earl, 139 Mass. 473; 1 N. E. 847; Am. Legion of Honor v. Perry, 140 Mass. 580; 5 N. E. 634.

§ 337. **Same Subject—Later Cases.**—In the case of Modern Woodmen of America v. Comeaux,[578] the Court said: "The word 'dependent' is here used in such relation to the preceding words as to indicate that the character of dependence intended should, in a general sense, be similar to the dependence which usually exists between parent and child, husband and wife, or such as obtains generally in the family relation. It has been held that, where there is no blood relationship, the member to whom the benefit certificate is issued must be under some recognized obligation to support the beneficiary and the beneficiary must be dependent upon such member for such maintenance." This definition was cited and approved in the case of Sovereign Camp Woodmen of the World v. Noel,[579] where the Court says: "It is evident, therefore, that, in order to bring a person within the meaning of the term 'dependent,' it is not necessary that they be a member of the family, an heir, or a blood relation. Hence, in all cases where the beneficiary claims as a dependent, the right of recovery must depend on the finding of fact as to whether the claimant is or is not a dependent. It is impracticable for a Court to define just what degree of dependence is necessary to a recovery. The amount of support or number of dollars contributed in one case might be sufficient to warrant a recovery, while in another, as in cases where the alleged dependent had ample means of suport in their own right, or by their own efforts, or where the contributions were more in the nature of gifts or presents, it would not be sufficient. The test in any case should be the question of good faith, purity of purpose a material dependence and material support on the part of the dependent and on the part of the person contributing to their support. There is nothing in this record which warrants the contention of bad faith." A mother has been held not to be a legal dependent of her son.[580] And a member who dies leaving no children, or relatives, other than brothers and sisters, nephews and nieces, not living with him, leaves no legal dependents.[581] A

---

[578] 79 Kan. 493; 25 L. R. A. (N. S.), 814; 101 Pac. 1; 17 Ann. Cas. 865.
[579] 34 Okla. 596; 126 Pac. 787; 41 L. R. A. (N. S.), 648.
[580] Vaughan v. National Council J. O. U. A. M., 136 Mo. App. 362; 117 S. W. 115.
[581] Little v. Colwell, 158 N. C. 351; 74 S. E. 10.

divorced wife may be a dependent,[582] and a housekeeper for the member may be a dependent,[583] and a woman working in the house of the deceased under the circumstances may be a dependent,[584] but a woman simply working for wages is not a dependent.[585] A child taken from an orphan asylum when three years old by the husband and wife and raised by them as their daughter was a dependent.[586] A hotelkeeper with whom an unmarried man lived is not a dependent;[587] nor is a creditor;[588] nor is a woman assisted by the member;[589] nor is a woman contracting a bigamous marriage with a member.[590]

§ '338. **Affianced Husband and Affianced Wife.**—Upon principle the words "affianced husband or affianced wife," used in the statute are to be construed in the ordinary and usual acceptation of the term, one to whom the member is affianced in good faith and not for the mere purpose of making such person a competent beneficiary. The question, ordinarily, would be one of fact. An affianced wife may be in fact a dependent,[591] although it has been held to the contrary.[592] Classes of beneficiaries mentioned in the statute relating to fraternal beneficiary associations cannot be restricted or enlarged by the by-laws of the society, and so where the statute provided that payment of benefits should be made, among other classes, to "the affianced husband or affianced wife" of the member, an affianced wife will take, even though the by-laws of the society contain no provision for such a class and the issue of the benefit certificate payable to such affianced wife had been re-

582 Johnson v. Grand Lodge A. O. U. W., 91 Kan. 314; 137 Pac. 1190.

583 Goff v. Supreme Lodge Royal Achates, 90 Neb. 578; 134 N. W. 239.

584 Wilbur v. Supreme Lodge, etc., 192 Mass. 477; 78 N. E. 445.

585 Caldwell v. Grand Lodge, etc., 148 Cal. 195; 82 Pac. 781.

586 Murphy v. Nowak, 233 Ill. 301; 79 N. E. 112; 7 L. R. A. (N. S.), 393.

587 Modern Woodmen of America v. Comeaux, *supra*.

588 Finch v. Bond, 158 Ky. 389; 165 S. W. 400.

589 Royal League v. Shield, 251 Ill. 250; 96 N. E. 45.

590 Deunser v. Supreme Council R. A., 262 Ill. 475; 104 N. E. 801; reversing 178 Ill. App. 645.

591 McCarthy v. New England Order, etc., 153 Mass. 314; 26 N. E. 866; Kinney v. Dodd, 41 Ill. App. 49; Farrenkopf v. Hohn, 237 Ill. 94; 86 N.; E. 702.

592 Palmer v. Welch, 132 Ill. 141; 23 N. E. 412; Alexander v. Parker, 144 Ill. 355; 33 N. E. 183.

fused by the society.[593] In a case in California a member of a fraternal society obtained a benefit certificate payable to a woman described as his "fiancee." On his death both she and his deserted wife claimed the benefit. In awarding the fund to the former the Court said:[594] "If any fraud or deception had been used in procuring the issuance of said certificate in reference to the designation of Mary E. Buzzard as fiancee, or otherwise, such certificate might have been declared void, and the sum specified therein forfeited, at the instance of the plaintiff company; but, as found by the Court, and as appears by the record, the company makes no complaint, and disclaims any right to the fund. The term employed may be considered as merely *descriptio personæ*: 'It may be stated that, where a policy of life insurance expressly designates a person as entitled to receive the insurance money, such designation is conclusive, in the absence of some question as to the rights of the creditors. The receipt of the person designated will discharge the insurer, and he may sue and recover the amount due at maturity of the policy. In such cases the legal representative of the insured has no claim upon the money, and cannot maintain an action therefor. It forms no part of the assets of the estate of the insured.'[595] And in that case it was suggested that the policy might lapse for want of a beneficiary, and the Court replies: 'Such a contingency cannot arise in any event here, for the defendant admits its liability, has paid the money into court, and only asks that the question as to the right of the two claimants may be determined so as to absolve it from liability.' It has also been held: 'Where a person makes an insurance on his life, he may make any one he pleases the beneficiary, and the latter is not obliged to show an interest in his life, in order to recover.'"[596] Although an affianced wife is named in the benefit certificate as cousin, she is entitled to the benefit, although the by-laws required the exact relationship of the beneficiary to be made known in writing.[597]

[593] Wallace v. Madden, 168 Ill. 356; 48 N. E. 181; affg. 67 Ill. App. 524. See also Supreme Council L. of H. v. Niedelet, 81 Mo. App. 598.

[594] Woodmen of the World v. Rutledge, 133 Cal. 640; 65 Pac. 1105. See also Mendelson v. Gausman, 142 N. Y. Supp. 293; 157 App. Div. 370; affg. 139 N. Y. Supp. 947.

[595] Winterhalter v. Ass'n, 75 Cal. 248; 17 Pac. 1.

[596] Lawson, Rights, Rem. & Prac., p. 3636.

[597] Farrenkopf v. Hohn, 237 Ill. 94; 86 N. E. 702; affg. 142 Ill. App. 330.

§ 339. **Legal Representatives: Devisee: Legatee.**—We may group under one heading the remaining terms most commonly used in describing the classes among whom the designation of beneficiaries must be made. "Legal representatives" is perhaps the most important of these. In construing the meaning of this word, as employed in a statute forbidding the use in business by any person of the name of any one formerly connected with him in partnership without the consent of such person so formerly connected, or his legal representatives, the Supreme Court of Massachusetts held[598] as follows: "There can be no doubt that the ordinary meaning of the term 'legal representatives' is executors and administrators,[599] and it has been so held in Missouri.[600] In wills, the term may mean whatever the testator intended; but, if the meaning is not controlled by the context, it means executors or administrators.[601] In the construction of statutes, technical words and phrases, and such others as have acquired a peculiar and appropriate meaning in the law, are to be construed and understood according to such peculiar and appropriate meaning, unless such construction would be inconsistent with the manifest intent of the legislature, or repugnant to the context of the same statute. Accordingly, in a particular statute, this term was held to include heirs.[602] Looking at the legislation now before us for construction, nothing is found to change the ordinary meaning of the term." And the Supreme Court of Minnesota has said:[603] "This word 'representative' means one who represents, or stands in the place of another. It has, however, many applications. An executor or administrator is called the representative of a deceased person, because he stands in his place as to personalty: while an heir is sometimes called his representative because he stands in his place as to realty. While the word may mean almost anything, especially in wills, which the context evidencing the intention of the party demands, yet, primarily, and in the absence of some reason

598 Lodge v. Weld, 129 Mass. 499.

599 Cox v. Curwen, 118 Mass. 198; Price v. Strange, 6 Madd. 159.

600 Ordelheide v. Modern Brotherhood of Am., 158 Mo. 677; 139 S. W. 269.

601 2 Williams on Ex., 1216-1220.

602 Johnson v. Ames, 11 Pick. 173, 180.

603 Walter v. Odd Fellows' Mut. Ben. Ass'n, 42 Minn. 204; 44 N. W. 57. See also Pittel v. Fidelity M. L. Ass'n, 86 Fed. 255; 30 C. C. A. 21.

for putting some other meaning upon it to be found in the context, it ordinarily means the executor or administrator.'' In the case of Hall v. Ayer's Guardian,[604] the Court held that a policy of assessment life insurance designating the wife and children of the assured as beneficiaries, is testamentary in character and must be construed according to the statute as well as the provisions of the policy, constitution and by-laws of the association, and the words "legal representatives" mean heirs and distributees, and the word "representatives" means the personal representatives of the insured. Legal representatives has been held to mean the executor,[605] or administrator.[606] Under the Tennessee statute, where a life insurance is made payable to the legal representatives of the insured and he dies without making disposition of the policy, the claim on the proceeds by the widow and next of kin will prevail over the claim of the general creditors, whether the estate is solvent or not and although the policy was issued before his marriage.[607] The words "legal representatives" in the contracts of beneficiary societies generally mean heirs, or next of kin, and are not given a technical meaning.[608] It may mean a widow or children who are legal representatives in the contemplation of the charter and by-laws,[609] or family,[610] or any of the persons entitled under the laws of the society to be beneficiaries,[611] or the widow.[612] "Devisee" is one to whom a devise, i. e., a gift of realty, is given by a will, and "legatee" is one to whom a legacy, i. e., a gift of personalty, is given by a will,[613] but in construing these terms the courts are

[604] 32 Ky. L. 288; 105 S. W. 911.

[605] Walker v. Peters, 139 Mo. App. 681; 124 S. W. 35.

[606] Hunt v. Remsberg, 83 Kan. 665; 112 Pac. 590; Ordelheide v. Modern Brotherhood of America (Mo.), 187 S. W. 1193; affg. 139 S. W. 269.

[607] Nashville, etc., v. First National Bank, 123 Tenn. 617; 134 S. W. 311.

[608] Schultz v. Citizens' Mut. L. Ins. Co., 59 Minn. 308; 61 N. W. 331.

[609] Masonic Mut. Relief A. v. McAuley, 2 Mackey 70; Griswold v. Sawyer, 125 N. Y. 411; 26 N. E. 464; reversing 8 N. Y. Supp. 517; Murray v. Strang, 28 Ill. App. 508.

[610] Sulz v. Mut. R. F. L. Ins. Ass'n, 28 N. Y. Supp. 263. See also Ins. Co. v. Flack, 3 Md. 341.

[611] Tucker v. Knights of Pythias, 135 Ga. 56; 68 S. E. 796.

[612] House v. Northwestern M. L. As. Co., 200 Pa. St. 178; 49 Atl. 987. But see Ordelheide v. Modern Brotherhood, supra.

[613] Bouvier's Law Dict. tit. "Devisee," "Legatee."

inclined to search for the intent of the instrument maker.[614]   A woman to whom the member was not married cannot be considered as a devisee, the laws of the order providing that benefits should be paid to the widow or other heirs.[615]   In one case[616] the designation was "to his devisees, as provided in last will and testament, or, in event of their prior death, to the legal heir or devisees of certificate holder," and the member died intestate.   In proceedings brought in equity to recover, the Court held these words to be equivalent to a promise to pay to the devisees, if there should be any, and if not, then to his heirs.[617]   The term "devisee" is capable of including anybody who may be designated as beneficiary in a benefit certificate if the charter is broad enough to include such persons, and so an affianced wife under these circumstances is eligible as a beneficiary.[618]

§ 340. **Ambiguous Designation:** "**Estate.**"—If the name of the person, for whose benefit the insurance is obtained, does not appear upon the face of the certificate or policy, or if the designations used are applicable to several persons, or if the description of the assured is imperfect or ambiguous, so that it cannot be understood without explanation, extrinsic evidence may be resorted to, to ascertain the meaning of the contract; and when thus ascertained it will be held to apply to the interests intended to be covered by it, and they will be deemed to be comprehended within it who were in the mind of the parties when the contract was made.[619]   So, where the agent was told that the insurance was desired for the benefit of the widow and heirs of Daniel Ross and the policy was made payable to "the estate of Daniel Ross," the Court of Appeals of New York[620] held that the rule above given

---

[614] Lodge v. Weld, 139 Mass. 499.

[615] Tutt v. Jackson, 87 Miss. 207; 39 Sou. 420.

[616] Covenant Mut. Ben. Ass'n v. Sears, 114 Ill. 108.

[617] Smith v. Covenant Mut. Ben. Ass'n, 24 Fed. 685; Newman v. Covenant M. B. Ass'n, 76 Ia. 56; 40 N. W. 87. See also People v. Petrie, 191 Ill. 497; 61 N. E. 469; affg. 94 Ill. App. 652.

[618] Dunbar v. Royal League, 184 Ill. App. 1.

[619] 1 Phil. on Ins. 163; Colpoys v. Colpoys, Jacob, 451; Burrows v. Turner, 24 Wend. 277; Davis v. Boardman, 12 Mass. 80; Newson's Admrs. v. Douglass, 7 Harr. & J. 417; Myers v. John Hancock Ins. Co, 41 Mo. 538; Globe Ins. Co. v. Boyle, 21 Ohio St. 119.

had direct application, as it is not essential that the person or persons assured should be named in the policy nor is that essential to the contract of insurance. In this case the Court said: "It is insisted, however, that the words 'estate of Daniel Ross' have a definite legal signification, meaning his administratrix, and that the policy is to be construed in the same manner as though she was named as the person assured thereby. This position has some support in the remark of Denio, C.· J., in Herkimer v. Rice,[621] to the effect that in common parlance and in legal language, when the estate of a deceased person is spoken of, the reference is to his effects in the hands of his executor or administrator. In that case the question was as to the right of the administrator and the creditors of the intestate on the one side, and the heirs upon the other, to certain money recovered upon policies of insurance upon the buildings on the land of the intestate, issued directly to the administratrix or renewed upon her application. The renewal receipts stated the premium to have been received of the estate of the intestate. In fact, the policies were renewed upon the application of and for the benefit of the administratrix and the creditors, and the Court gave effect to the contract according to the intention of the parties." The word "estate" in an industrial life policy naming the estate of the insured as a beneficiary and containing the usual facility of payment clause is ambiguous and parol evidence is admissible that the agent of the insurer at the time he procured the application for the policy informed the insured that her only child would be paid the policy, and the child in possession of the policy at the time of insured's death can compel payment.[622] In that case the Court said: "We think it obvious from this class of contracts, and they have been, as before said, many times before our courts, and on consideration of the fact that the provision is for the immediate happenings upon the death of the insured, and of the small amount provided for, that it cannot be said, with any propriety or with any proper consideration of this form of insurance, that they are intended to provide a fund for the benefit of creditors, unless that is distinctly set out in the policy itself,

620 Clinton v. Hope Ins. Co., 45 N. Y. 461.

621 27 N. Y. 163.

622 Renfro v. Metropolitan Life Ins. Co., 148 Mo. App. 258; 129 S. W. 444.

as has been done in several cases where a special provision, by pledge or otherwise has been made for a creditor. In general, to place a policy of this small amount and apparently consisting of the whole estate left by the decedent into the hands of an appointed administrator would be to tie up the whole fund, obviously intended to meet burial and other immediate expenses attendant upon death, to pervert it from its real object, and to cause it to be eaten into seriously by court expenses, and administrative and other allowances of various kinds. We consider these industrial policies highly benevolent, and that they are to be so treated. Looking into the facts in this case and considering, under the adjudications of the courts on these matters, that payment to this plaintiff absolves the defendant from any payment to any other possible claimant, we think that the judgment of the learned trial judge should have been for the plaintiff." In a case decided by the Supreme Court of Florida,[623] the contract of life insurance described the beneficiary thereunder as "for the benefit of the estate of the insured," and it was held that under the circumstances of the case the terms referred to and meant for the benefit of an only minor child less than five years of age at the date of the contract, and not to the administrator or distributee of the estate. The Court in its opinion said: "The term estate here in its strict legal signification embraces neither the administrator, the heir nor the creditor of the assured. It means the effects, personal and real, left by the decedent when given a signification with reference to a period subsequent to his death, and that is the date when the benefit was to accrue. Such literal legal signification would be absurd. The word benefit in a policy of insurance must be interpreted with reference to persons, not things. An insurance may be for the benefit of the person owning a house, not for the house. To benefit stocks and stores was not the intention of the parties. Without entering into any elaborate discussion of the subject we will simply state that the cases having a bearing upon the subject[624] show that these and similar terms, under the circumstances of this case, are so interpreted as to benefit the surviving members of the family rather than for the benefit of the

[623] Pace v. Pace, 19 Fla. 438.

[624] Myers v. John Hancock Ins. Co., 41 Mo. 538; Clinton v. Hope Ins. Co., 45 N. Y. 454; Globe Ins. Co. v. Boyle, 21 Ohio St. 119.

creditor or administrator, and that in this instance the beneficiary intended was the infant child. In the interpretation of contracts of this character the courts go a great way in this direction. This, we think, would have been the construction of this policy, independent of the policy of the statute, which, as a matter of course, should have some effect in controlling our action in the matter.[625] The term used in benefit certificates usually will be construed to mean wife and children.[626] The designation of "estate" in a benefit certificate is not valid and the benefit does not become part of the estate of the deceased member, but passes to the person who would take under the charter.[627] In a Massachusetts case,[628] the Supreme Court held that a designation by a member of a benefit society of "my estate" as the beneficiary, was illegal under the statutes of that State regulating benefit societies. And where the benefit was payable "subject to will" creditors were held to have no rights in it.[629] In a Kentucky case,[630] the controversy was over a benefit promised to be paid by the National Mutual Benefit Association on the death of one Throckmorton. By the charter the benefits could be paid to the "legal heirs or beneficiary" of the member. Throckmorton designated "my estate" as the beneficiary, but afterwards assigned the certificate to Basye, his creditor, for the sum of $500, the benefit being $4,000. The court awarded the amount, less what Bayse had paid, to the heirs on the ground that though the assignment was void because a wagering transaction, yet, as Basye's claim was the only one against the estate, it allowed it to be paid. The Court said: "He (Throckmorton) designated his estate as his beneficiary, by which he clearly meant that the amount payable at his death should become assets of his estate, to be paid over to his personal

---

625 See also Eppinger v. Canepa, 20 Fla. 262. Under the Florida act a life policy payable to the executrix, etc., is payable to the surviving widow and children, and is not a part of the estate of the deceased for the purpose of paying debts. Bradford v. Watson, 65 Fla. 461; 62 Sou. 484.

626 Dale v. Brumley, 96 Ind. 674; Hutson v. Jenson, 110 Wis. 26; 85 N. W. 689.

627 *In re* Smith's estate, 87 N. Y. Supp. 735; 42 Misc. 639.

628 Daniels v. Pratt, 143 Mass. 216.

629 Beeckman v. Imperial Counc., etc., 11 N. Y. Supp. 321.

630 Bayse v. Adams, 81 Ky. 368.

representative, according to the laws providing for the distribution of estates of deceased persons, and payment of debts against them.'' A benefit certificate payable to estate is payable to the legal representatives within the by-laws of the association.[631] The term ''survivors'' as used in a benefit certificate cannot include one not included in the classes mentioned in the charter.[632] ''Trustee and children'' means trustee for children.[633] ''To his will'' is a valid designation.[634] The word will is held to be the equivalent of wish, desire or direction when used in a benefit certificate.[635]

§ 341. **Several Beneficiaries, Construction.**—If a policy or certificate be payable to several beneficiaries, as for example to ''wife and children,'' all share equally and the wife will not take a moiety,[636] although it has been held that the statutes of distribution govern the designation of wife and children and the parties named do not take per capita,[637] and where a policy names as beneficiaries the wife and children they all take as tenants in common and the wife does not take a life estate.[638] Where there are several beneficiaries named in a policy it has been held, as to insurance policies proper, that if one or more of them die before the assured, the benefit of the policy inures to the survivors, and so long as any of the beneficiaries are living the as-

---

[631] Vaughan v. Modern Brotherhood of America, 149 Ky. 587; 149 S. W. 937.

[632] Koertz v. Grand 'Lodge, etc., 119 Wis. 520; 97 N. W. 163. See also Grand Lodge v. Lemke, 124 Wis. 483; 102 N. W. 911.

[633] Atkins v. Atkins, 70 Vt. 565; 41 Atl. 503. See also Reed v. Provident Savings L. Ass. Soc., 190 N. Y. 111; 82 N. E. 734, modifying 98 N. Y. Supp. 1111; 112 App. Div. 922.

[634] Hoffmeyer v. Muench, 59 Mo. App. 20.

[635] Prokes v. Bohemian, etc., Union, 165 Ill. App. 105.

[636] Taylor v. Hill, 86 Wis. 99; 56 N. W. 738; Felix v. Grand Lodge A. O. U. W., 31 Kan. 81; 1 Pac. 281; Jackman v. Nelson, 147 Mass. 300; 17 N. E. 529; Gould v. Emerson, 99 Mass. 154; Grand Lodge v. Sater, 44 M. A. 445; Bell v. Kinneer, 101 Ky. 271; 40 S. W. 686.

[637] Kelly v. Ball, 14 Ky. L. 132; 19 S. W. 581; following McLin v. Calvert, 78 Ky. 472.

[638] Seyton v. Satterthwaite, 34 Ch. D. 511; Milburn v. Milburn, 83 Ind. 55. See also Brown v. Iowa L. of H., 107 Ia. 439; 78 N. W. 73.

sured has no interest in the policy and cannot assign it.[639] Generally it may be said that the law of survivorship applies to designations of beneficiary and the last survivor takes the whole.[640] The laws of most benefit societies, however, cover this point and provide that in case of the death of one or more beneficiaries during the lifetime of the member the survivors shall take.[641] And where a benefit certificate was payable to "Mrs. M. H. Case or lawful heirs," and it appeared that at the time the certificate was issued to the member he had a wife Amelia, named in the designation as Mrs. M. H. Case, who afterwards died leaving a daughter, Inez, and the member subsequently married and died leaving a widow Emma, it was held that when the wife, Amelia, died, the designation lapsed as to her and as Inez was the' only heir of the member the benefit went to her.[642] Under a certificate of a mutual aid society naming two beneficiaries, and providing that "in case of the death of either, full amount to go to the survivor—if living; if not living then to the heirs of said member," —upon the death of the member, the beneficiaries both living, the shares of such beneficiaries vest in them, and if one dies before the payment of the benefit, his share goes to his executor, not to the survivor. In a case where the member had directed that the benefit be paid to a son and daughter, or the survivor of them, the money was payable ninety days after receipt of proofs of the death of the member and the son died after his father, but within the ninety days. The daughter claimed the entire fund on the ground that the period of survivorship related to the time of payment of the money, not to the time of death of the member.

[639] Robinson v. Duvall, 79 Ky. 83. See also Small v. Jose, 86 Me. 120; 29 Atl. 976.

[640] Farr v. Trustees Gr. L. A. O. U. W., 83 Wis. 446; 53 N. W. 738; Walsh v. Mut. L. Ins. Co., 133 N. Y. 408; 31 N. E. 228; reversing 15 N. Y. Supp. 697; U. S. Trust Co. v. Mut. Ben. L. Ins. Co., 115 N. Y. 152; 21 N. E. 1025; Brooklyn Mas. R. Ass'n v. Hanson, 5 N. Y. Supp. 161; Murray v. McDonald, 22 Ont. (Q. B.), 557. See also Hemenway v. Draper, 91 Minn. 235; 97 N. W. 874; Dennis v. Modern Brotherhood of Am., 119 Mo. App. 210; 95 S. W. 967.

[641] But to the contrary, see Supreme Counc. Cath., etc., v. Densford, 21 Ky. L. 1574; 56 S. W. 172; 49 L. R. A. 776; Gault v. Gault, 25; (Part II), Ky. L. 2308; 80 S. W. 493.

[642] Day v. Case, 43 Hun. 179.

694

In awarding the son's share of the fund to his executor the Court said :[643] ''The scheme of the corporation is to raise a fund which shall pass to designated beneficiaries at the death of the member. The right, which before was inchoate and contingent, becomes upon the death of the member fixed and certain in the beneficiary. He may compel the corporation to levy the assessment, if it refuses, after the time limited for payment. The provision relating to survivorship applies to the one of the two who shall survive the donor. If neither survive him, the fund goes to the heirs of the member. The time of payment provided for, namely ninety days after the death of the member, has no reference to who shall take as survivor. The time of payment is defined simply to enable the corporation to raise the fund by assessment upon the members. If the son, N. Lyon Franklin, had died before his father, Edward C., the whole sum would have been payable to the daughter, Charlotte A., and, if she had also died before her father, the fund would have been payable to his heirs. The words 'if living,' and 'if not living' refer to living at the time of Edward C. Franklin's death.''[644] Where a father insured his life for the benefit of his children and some die in his lifetime he can, with the consent of the insurer, substitute other beneficiaries for the deceased parties, but if he does not the share he inherits from the deceased beneficiaries goes to his personal representatives.[645] If the constitution and by-laws of a benefit society provide that in default of a designation of a beneficiary by the member that the sum shall be paid to certain persons; as, for example, to the widow, orphans, heirs, etc., the word ''or'' will be understood between the names of these different classes and the fund in such case would go first to the widow, if there was one, if there was no

[643] Union Mut. Aid Ass'n v. Montgomery, 70 Mich. 587; 38 N. W. 588.
[644] See Thomas v. Leake, 67 Tex. 469; 3 S. W. 703; Chartrand v. Brace, 16 Colo. 19; 26 Pac. 152.
[645] Shields v. Sharp, 35 Mo. App. 178. This is on the theory of the vested rights of the payees named in life insurance policies, the right being fixed by the issue of the policy but beneficiaries under conrtacts with benefit societies, take as legatees, the designation speaking from the death of the member, and only those living at the time of the death can take.

695

widow, then to the orphans, or if there were no orphans or widow then to the heirs, and so on.[646]

§ 342. **Incorporated and Unincorporated Benefit Societies: Ultra Vires.**—Whether a benefit society is incorporated or a mere voluntary association, it is believed that the laws governing the designation of beneficiary are the same. It is a question of construction of the contract, modified by statute, and the effect of non-compliance with the laws of the society or statute is to generally vitiate the designation. Whether or not an incorporated benefit society can invoke the doctrine of *ultra vires* to avoid a contract must depend upon the general rules of law applicable to corporations, which we have already discussed. There are authorities which hold that it is always lawful to set up such a defense, but of late years the courts seem to frown upon this action, especially when the contract has been executed as by the death of the person insured and the later rule is that, in an action upon a benefit certificate, the society will not be allowed to assert in defense that the designation of the beneficiary in the certificate was one of a class of persons not included in the enumeration, in the charter, of those for whom benefits were to be provided. This is especially the case when the society has been receiving the assessments on the policy with knowledge.[647] It has been held, however, that members of a beneficiary society are all in equality

[646] Relief Ass'n v. McAuley, 2 Mackey 70; Kentucky Masonic Aid, etc., v. Miller's Admr., 13 Bush 489; Addison v. N. E. C. Travelers' Ass'n, 144 Mass. 491; 12 N. E. 407; Ballou v. Gile, 50 Wis. 614; Covenant M. B. A. v. Sears, 114 Ill. 108.

[647] Matt. v. Roman Catholic Mut. Pro. Soc., 70 Ia. 455; 30 N. W. 799; Lamont v. Hotel Men's Mut. Ben. Ass'n, 30 Fed. 817; Bloomington Ben. Mut. Ass'n v. Blue, 120 Ill. 121; Lamont v. Grand Lodge Ia. Leg. of Honor, 31 Fed. 177; Folmer's Appeal, 87 Pa. St. 135. But see Elsey v. Odd Fellows, 142 Mass. 224; Am. Legion of Honor v. Perry, 140 Mass. 580; Mut. Ben. Ass'n v. Hoyt, 46 Mich. 473; Knights of Honor v. Nairn, 60 Mich. 44; Rice v. N. Eng. M. A. Soc., 15 N. E. 624. The Supreme Court of Massachusetts is firm in holding these contracts *ultra vires* and void, although with the limitations as to resulting trust as stated in the text. The Court of Appeals of Maryland holds that a misrepresentation as to relationship of the beneficiary vitiates the contract. Supreme Counc. A. L. H. v. Smith, 45 N. J. E. 466; 17 Atl. 770. See also Ferbrache v. Grand Lodge A. O. U. W., 81 Mo. App. 268.

696

and are bound by the restrictions imposed by statute and that the doctrine of *ultra vires* does not apply to such societies because public policy forbids. Otherwise the beneficiary of an illegal contract might receive its benefits because it had been executed on the side of the member.[648] The reason does not, however, apply where there are no statutory restrictions, but only a by-law of the association.[649] But under the rule of later cases, that the designation of a person not entitled to take under the laws of the society, or its charter, does not invalidate the contract but only the designation, so that the benefit will go, either as the laws of the society provide in case of the death of all the beneficiaries, or to the next of kin, the difficulties in the way of application of the doctrine of *ultra vires* are not so great.[650] The contracts of a benefit society may be *ultra vires* only in part.[651] After a contract is executed the society cannot claim that it had no power to make a reinsurance contract.[652]

[648] Montgomery v. Whitbeck, 12 N. D. 385; 96 N. W. 327; Dennis v. Modern Brotherhood of Am., 119 Mo. App. 210; 95 S. W. 967; Tuite v. Supreme Forest Woodmen Circle, 193 Mo. App. 619; 187 S. W. 137.

[649] Gruber v. Grand Lodge, etc., 79 Minn. 59; 81 N. W. 743.

[650] Britton v. Supreme Council R. A., 46 N. J. E. 102; 18 Atl. 675; Sargent v. Supreme L. K. of H., 158 Mass. 557; 33 N. E. 650; Shea v. Mass. Ben. Ass'n, 160 Mass. 289; 35 N. E. 855; Ky. Grangers, etc,. Soc. v. McGregor, 7 Ky. L. B. 550; see *ante*, § 216.

[651] Rockhold v. Canton Masonic, etc., Ass'n, 129 Ill. 440; 21 N. E. 794; 19 N. E. 710; Grand Lodge, etc., v. Waddill, 36 Ala. 313. As to comity in enforcing contract made in another State, see Hysinger v. Supreme L. K. & L. of H., 42 Mo. App. 628.

[652] Campbell v. Order of Washington, 53 Wash. 398; 102 Pac. 410; Cooley v. Gilliam, 80 Kan. 278; 102 Pac. 1091.

CHAPTER VIII.

Consummation of Contract—Incomplete Contracts—Jurisdiction of Equity to Reform or Cancel.

698

§ 343. **To Complete Contract of Insurance Negotiations Must Be Concluded.**—We have seen[1] that the contract of insurance is the result of negotiations which are generally conducted through the medium of agents. On the one side is the proposal, or application, of the insured, on the other is the acceptance of such offer by the insurer before there can be a complete contract. Various important and interesting questions arise as to when the contract is complete and at what point in the negotiations it becomes binding upon one side or the other. The business of life insurance companies, as now conducted in this country, is done in this way: an agent solicits the application, which, accompanied with the certificates of medical examination and of the agent, is sent to the company, whose immediate officers accept or reject it. If accepted a policy is forwarded to the agent, who countersigns it, if that is required, and delivers it on payment of the premium. The customs of the various companies are somewhat' different, but their methods of doing business are substantially the same. Benefit societies pursue a somewhat similar course. In applying for membership, and the insurance incident thereto, the applicant sends his application to the officers of the local lodge, accompanied with the prescribed fee: he is examined by the lodge physician, and the papers are sent to the grand medical examiner, who approves or rejects. If approved and the investigating committee reports favorably, the applicant is voted on by the lodge, and, if received, is initiated into membership, after which the Grand or Supreme Lodge issues the certificate, which is countersigned by the officers of the local lodge and delivered. In different societies these processes are not always the same, nor are 'they always in the order stated, for often the member is not initiated until the Grand Lodge approves of the examination and issues the certificate. Generally, the course pursued is as first indicated. There is this difference between the methods of conducting the business of benefit societies and ·that of life insurance companies: the

[1] *Ante,* § 235, *et seq.*

lodges have greater powers than the insurance agents. The lodge is the sole judge of the moral and social qualifications of the applicant, as the Grand or Supreme Lodge is the judge of his physical qualifications. The powers of insurance agents are limited: subordinate lodges, like agents of life insurance companies, seldom have the authority to absolutely conclude a contract. Their powers are ordinarily confined to the procuring of applications for insurance without any right to make a•binding agreement. In some cases, 'as when an agent represents a foreign company, the agents may have a qualified authority to make their contracts temporarily binding during the period necessary to transmit the application to the company, or the Grand or Supreme Lodge officers, and receive a reply. But the usage that lodges, or agents, cannot conclude a contract, is so general that if an exception is alleged there must be evidence of actual authority, or of the repeated exercise of the authority with the knowledge of the company. In the case of benefit societies the constitution and by-laws is the source of authority and in applying for membership the applicant will be presumed to have acquainted himself with their requirements and limitations of the authority of lodges.[2] Before the company, or society, can be held liable for the insurance applied for, the negotiations must have reached such a point that nothing remains for either party to do except to comply with the terms of the contract.[3]

§ 344. **Application Must Be Accepted to Make a Contract.**— The application for insurance is a mere proposal on the part of the applicant.[4] When the insurer signifies his acceptance of it to the proposer, and not before, the minds of the parties meet and the contract is made. This acceptance must be signified by some act, a simple mental acceptance, a mere thought unexpressed,

[2] Supreme Lodge, etc., v. Grace, 60 Tex. 569.

[3] Connecticut Mut. L. Ins. Co. v. Rudolph, 45 Tex. 454; Todd v. Piedmont & Arlington L. Ins. Co., 34 La. Ann. 63. As applied to revival of lapsed policy: Diboll & Aetna L. Ins. Co,. 32 La. Ann. 179.

[4] McCully v. Phoenix M. L. Ins. Co., 18 W. Va. 782; Heiman v. Phoenix M. L. Ins. Co., 17 Minn. 157. See also Kilcullen v. Metropolitan L. Ins. Co, 108 .Mo. App. 61; 82 S. W. 966; Travis v. Nederland L. Ins. Co., 43 C. C. A. 653; 104 Fed. 486.

amounting to nothing.[5] This application must be in due form and signed by the applicant if the rules so require. As where the rules of a society required that the medical examination of an applicant and his application for a benefit certificate, which contained an agreement and warranty of the truth of the answers, be signed by him, which was not done, and no certificate was issued o● that account, it was held that no liability resulted.[6] In this case the Court said: "The minds of the respective parties never met. There was no such mutual agreement and understanding of the matter between them as is essential in order to create the contract and give it binding force on both parties, under the rules and regulations by which the relations of the deceased to the appellant were governed." Where application was made to a benefit society in due form, and the agent received the papers and the applicant was examined by the medical examiner and gave his note for the first payment, but was killed before the note was paid or the application forwarded, it was held[7] that until the application was approved by the company there was no contract. The Court said: "The application in such cases is a mere proposal, and, until it is accepted, there can be no contract, for until that time the minds of the parties have not met. There is simply an offer on one side, which may be accepted or rejected by the other. There must be a meeting of the minds of the parties, in all cases, as to the whole subject and the substantial conditions of the whole 'contract, or there is obviously no contract." And the payment of the premiums at the time of signing the application does not make a binding contract unless the agent is authorized to accept the application.[8] Sometimes what is termed a binding

[5] Ala. Gold Life Ins. Co. v. Mayes, 61 Ala. 163; Heiman v. Phoenix Mut. L. Ins. Co., 17 Minn. 157; Tayloe v. Merch. F. Ins. Co., 9 How. 390; Armstrong v. Provident, etc., Soc., 3 Ont. L. 771; New York L. Ins. Co. v. Levy's Admr., 122 Ky. 457; 92 S. W. 325; 5 L. R. A. (N. S.), 739; Provident Savings L. Ins. Co. v. Elliot's Admr., 29 Ky. L. 552; 93 S. W. 659; New York L. Ins. Co. v. McIntosh, 86 Miss. 236; 38 Sou. 775; Ross v. N. Y. Life Ins. Co., 124 N. C. 395; 32 S. E. 733; Supreme Lodge K. of P. v. Graham (Ind. App.), 97 S. E. 806; Fitzgerald v. Metropolitan L. Ins. Co., etc., 98 Atl. 498.

[6] Supreme Lodge, etc., v. Grace, 60 Tex. 570.

[7] Covenant M. B. Ass'n v. Conway, 10 Bradw. 348.

[8] Allen v. Mass. Mut. Acc. Ass'n, 167 Mass. 18; 44 N. E. 1053; Pace v. Provident Savings L. A. Soc., 51 C. C. A. 32; 113 Fed. 13; Rossiter

slip is given when the application is made and the first premium paid. This is a mere written memorandum of the most important terms of the contract of insurance and only protects the applicant in case the application is accepted and the policy delivered.[9] Where payment of the first premium was made on a receipt stating that in event of acceptance of the application the policy shall be in force from the date of its acceptance and the company accepted the application, the policy was in force from the date it left the home office.[10] The company may accept the application conditionally, that is, the policy shall not be binding until a certain thing is done by the applicant.[11] In a case in Missouri the printed receipt issued to the deceased by the defendant's agent for the first premium on a policy of life insurance provided that he was to be insured from the date of the receipt, if accepted by the company as an insurable risk under its rules and regulations, and stated that he was otherwise acceptable on the plan and for the amount applied for. Upon its receipt by the defendant, the word "approved" was indorsed upon the application of the deceased and a policy was issued the same in every respect as that applied for, except that the amount of premium was increased, but acknowledging and treating the first premium as paid in full. The deceased committed suicide before receiving or accepting the conditional policy. It was held, as a matter of law, that by placing the printed form of receipt in his hands, the company authorized its agent to bind it in accordance with its terms, and the company having by its action on the application approved and accepted it without such condition as amounted to a new proposition, there was a contract of temporary insurance completed in Missouri from the date of the receipt until the conditional policy issued was presented to the deceased for acceptance.[12]

v. Aetna L. Ins. Co., 91 Wis. 121; 64 N. W. 876. See also Northwestern Mut. L. Ins. Co, v. Neafus, 145 Ky. 563; 140 S. W. 1026; 36 L. R. A. (N. S.), 1241.

[9] Gardner v. North St. Mut. L. Ins. Co., 103 N. C. 367; 79 S. E. 806.

[10] Harrington v. Home Life Ins. Co., 128 Cal. 531; 38 Pac. 180.

[11] Aetna Life Ins. Co. v. Hocker, 39 Tex. Civ. App. 330; 89 S. W. 26.

[12] Kempf v. Equitable Life Assur. Soc. (Mo. App.), 184 S. W. 133. A writ of *certiorari* was, however, granted by the Supreme Court in this case which has not yet been determined. It would seem under the rule that if the policy is different from that applied for it is not binding

§ 345. **Proposal May Be Withdrawn At Any Time Before Acceptance.**—It follows that the applicant can, at any time before the application is accepted, withdraw it, and if he does so, is not bound to accept the policy.[13] The principle is that laid down in relation to all contracts,[14] that "the party making the promise is bound to do nothing unless the promisee, within a reasonable time, engages to do, or else does or begins to do, the thing which is the condition of the first promise. Until such engagement or doing, the promisor may withdraw his promise, because there is no mutuality, and, therefore, no consideration for it."[15] An interesting case on this subject is that of Travis v. Nederland Life Ins. Co.,[16] in which Judge Sanborn said: "Propositions, negotiations, correspondence, conversations do not make a contract unless the minds of the parties meet upon the same stipulations and they con-

upon the company until accepted by the applicant (*post*, § 347). The change in the amount of the premium was a material change, making the policy issued different from that applied for and hence not binding upon the company until accepted by the applicant. The receipt in this case was as follows: "Received of Joseph E. Kempf, one hundred and eleven and 25/100 dollars, the first semi-annual premium on proposed insurance for $5,000 on the life of self for which the above mentioned application is this day made to the Equitable Life Assurance Society of the United States. Insurance subject to the terms and conditions of the policy contract shall take effect as of the date of this receipt, provided the applicant is on this date, in the opinion of the society's authorized officers in New York; an insurable risk under its rules and the application is otherwise acceptable on the plan and for the amount applied for; otherwise the payment evidenced by this receipt shall be returned on demand and the surrender of this receipt. M. A. Nelson Agent. Dated as Springfield, Mo., 6/12/13." The company after inspection of the risk added five years to the age of the insured, making the semi-annual premium $137.55 instead of $111.25, and issued the policy so reciting, sending it to its agent for delivery on payment of the increased premium, but the policy was never delivered in consequence of the death of the applicant.

13 Globe Mut. L. Ins. Co. v. Snell, 19 Hun. 561. See also Newcomb v. Provident Fund Soc., 5 Colo. App. 140; 38 Pac. 61; Coker v. Atlas M. Acc. Ins. Co. (Tex. Civ. A.), 31 S. W. 703. See also Hartford F. Ins. Co. v. Whitman, 75 Ohio St. 342; 9 Ann. Cas. 218 and exhaustive note.

14 1 Pars. on Con. 550.

15 Real Estate M. F. Ins. Co. v. Roessle, 1 Gray 336.

16 43 C. C. A. 653; 104 Fed. 486.

sent to comply with them. Until this has been done, either party
has the right to withdraw or to modify his proposition, to make
new conditions or proposals, or to retire absolutely from the negotiations. The addition of a new term or condition to an earlier
proposal before the latter has been accepted is the withdrawal of
the earlier proposition, and the submission of a new proposal of
which the new condition or term is a part. From the time the
new condition is submitted the earlier proposition is withdrawn,
and it is no longer open to acceptance or rejection by the party to
whom it was presented. An application for life insurance is not
a contract. It is only a proposal to contract on certain terms
which the company to which it is presented is at perfect liberty to
accept or to reject. It does not in any way bind the company
to accept the risk proposed, to make the contract requested, or to
issue a policy. Nor does it in any way bind the applicant to take
the policy, to make the contract he proposed, or to pay the premium until his proposal has been accepted by the company and
its policy has been issued. Until the meeting of the minds of
the parties upon the terms of the same agreement is effected by
an acceptance of the proposition contained in the application
or of some other proposition, each party is entirely free from
contractual obligations. The applicant may withdraw his application and refuse to take insurance on any terms. He may modify
his proposal, may affix additional conditions or terms to it, or
may make an entirely new proposition, while the company may
refuse to entertain any proposition or may reject that presented
and submit a substitute. Nor is the freedom of the parties to
retire from the negotiations or to modify their proposals, at any
time before some proposition has been agreed upon by both, ever
lost or affected by the fact that the applicant accompanies his
proposal or application with a promise to pay the premium in
the form of promissory notes, or even by actual payment thereof.
Until his application is accepted, such a promise or payment is
conditional upon the acceptance, and his application is still no
more than a proposition to take and to pay for the insurance if
the company accepts his terms. The payment of the premium
when the application is signed does not bind the company to accept his terms nor does it estop the applicant from recovering
the money he pays if the company rejects his proposal. These

704

are fundamental rules of the law of contracts, which are constantly applied in this and other courts, and which are decisive of the case before us."[17] An agreement in the application to accept the policy is only an agreement not to withdraw the offer before the policy is delivered, and by a refusal to accept the policy it was held that the applicant withdrew his offer and was not liable on his premium note, the agreement not being supported by any consideration.[18]

§ 346. **Death of Applicant Before Delivery of the Policy Is Withdrawal of Proposition.**—The death of the applicant before the delivery of the policy operates as a withdrawal of the proposal.[19] in this case[20] the Court says: "The death of Kendall on June 3, 1890, before the application had reached defendant's home office, revoked his offer to become insured by the defendant company, which was contained in his application and rendered the making of the proposed contract of insurance impossible. An offer is revoked by the death of the proposer, or by the death of the party to whom the offer is made before acceptance. The continuance of an offer is in the nature of its constant repetition, which necessarily requires some one capable of making a repetition. Obviously, this can no more be done by a dead man than

---

[17] Paine v. Ins. Co., 51 Fed. 689, 691; 2 C. C. A. 459, 461; 10 U. S. App. 256, 263, 264; Soc. v. McElroy, 83 Fed. 631, 640; 28 C. C. A. 365, 374; 49 U. S. App. 548, 564; McMaster v. Ins. Co., 40 C. C. A. 119; 99 Fed. 856, 866; Giddings v. Ins. Co,. 102 U. S. 108, 112; 26 L. Ed. 92; Griffith v. Ins. Co., 101 Cal. 627; 36 Pac. 113, 115; Ins. Co. v. Young's Admr., 23 Wall. 85, 107; 23 L. Ed. 152; Ins. Co. v. Ewing, 92 U. S. 377, 381; 23 L. Ed. 610; Harnickell v. Ins. Co., 111 N. Y. 390, 399; 18 N. E. 632; 2 L. R. A. 150; Whiting v. Ins. Co., 128 Mass. 240; Markey v. Ins. Co., 118 Mass. 178; Id., 126 Mass. 158; Rogers v. Ins. Co., 41 Conn. 97, 106; Ins. Co. v. Collerd, 38 N. J. Law, 480, 483; Heiman v. Ins. Co., 17 Minn. 153, 157 (Gil. 127); Hogben v. Ins. Co., 69 Conn. 503; 38 Atl. 214-216.

[18] See Citizens' National Life Ins. Co. v. Murphy, 154 Ky. 88; 156 S. W. 1069. See also Wheelock v. Clark, 21 Wyo. 300; 131 Pac. 35; Ann. Cas. 1916-A 956.

[19] Paine v. Pacific Mut. L. Ins. Co., 2 C. C. A. 459; 51 Fed. 689; Mut. L. Ins. Co. v. Jordan, 111 Ark. 324; 163 S. W. 799; Ann. Cas. 1916-B 674 and note. Starr v. Mut. Life Ins. Co., 41 Wash. 228; 83 Pac. 116.

[20] Paine v. Pacific M. L. Ins. Co., *supra*.

a contract can in the first instance be made by a dead man.[21] Conceding that the defendant could and did determine to accept the application on June 7, 1890, one day after its receipt, and four days after the death of Kendall, still such acceptance and the contract, if so made, were void, because the life that was the subject-matter of the contract was not then in existence. The first party to this proposed contract was Kendall; the second the defendant; the subject-matter of the contract, Kendall's life. The contract was not made, in any event, before June 7, when defendant's medical director approved the application and at that time the first party to it was dead, and its subject-matter did not exist. Neither party would have knowingly made an insurance contract regarding a life that was not in being. Parties make no contract where the thing which they supposed to exist, and the existence of which was indispensable to the making of their contract, had no existence.[22] Conceding that the action of the medical director in approving the application on June 7th, in ignorance of the applicant's death was a determination to accept the application by the defendant, still there was no contract because no notice of the acceptance of the application was in any way communicated to the applicant or his representatives. The acceptance of an offer not communicated to the proposer does not make a contract.[23] Conceding that the application was accepted on June 7th, 1890, by the defendant, it expressly provided that the contract of insurance should take effect and be in force only upon compliance with three conditions precedent, viz.: that a policy should be delivered, that it should be delivered during the life and good health of the applicant, and that the premium should be paid when the policy was delivered. These conditions were

[21] Pratt v. Trustees, 93 Ill. 475, 479; Dickenson v. Dodds, L. R. 2 Ch. Div. 463, 475; Phipps v. Jones, 20 Pa. St. 260, 264; Wallace v. Townsend, 43 Ohio St. 537; 3 N. E. 601.

[22] Franklin v. Long, 7 Gill. & J. 407, 419; Gibson v. Pelkie, 37 Mich. 380; Stickland v. Turner, 7 Exch. 208, 219; Couturier v. Hastie, 5 H. L. Cas. 673, 682; Clifford v. Watts, L. R. 5 C. P. 577; Hazard v. Ins. Co., 1 Sum. 218, 226; Ins. Co. v. Ewing, 92 U. S. 381.

[23] Jenness v. Iron Co., 53 Me. 20, 23; McCulloch v. Ins. Co., 1 Pick. 278; Thayer v. Ins. Co., 10 Pick. 325, 331; Borland v. Guffey, 1 Grant Cas. 394; Beckwith v. Cheever, 21 N. H. 41, 44; Duncan v. Heller, 13 S. C. 94, 96; White v. Corlies, 46 N. Y. 467.

706

never complied with. The vital indispensable condition was that the policy should be delivered and take effect during the life and good health of the applicant; but that life had ended, that applicant was no more, and that condition could never be complied with, and therefore the contract could never take effect.''[24] But where the secretary of an organization was authorized to accept applications, his notice that the application is accepted will bind the company though given by mistake, if the applicant dies before the notice is recalled.[25] And where the application provides that there shall be no liability until it is approved and accepted and the applicant dies pending its consideration the company is not liable.[26] Where the applicant died before his medical examination reached the medical officer, its subsequent approval by him in ignorance of the death of the applicant created no liability.[27] And so where the applicant made application and paid a part of the premium but died before the acceptance of the application and payment of the additional premium there was no contract.[28]

§ 347. If the Policy Be Different From That Applied for, It Is Not Binding Upon the Company Until Accepted By the Applicant.—The law is that a party to whom an offer is made is at liberty to accept wholly or reject wholly, but one of these things he must do. A proposition to accept on terms different from those offered is a rejection of the offer and a substitution in its place of a counter proposition. It puts an end to the negotiations so far as the original offer is concerned.[29] It follows that if the policy, issued by a company, is in any particular, different from that applied for, it is not binding upon

[24] Eliason v. Henshaw, 4 Wheat. 227, 229; Carr v. Duval, 14 Pet. 77, 81.

[25] Moulton v. Masonic Mut. Ben. Soc., 64 Kan. 56; 67 Pac. 533.

[26] Jacobs v. New York Life Ins. Co., 71 Miss. 656; 15 Sou. 639; Miller v. Northwestern Mut. L. Ins. Co., 49 C. C. A. 330; 111 Fed. 465.

[27] Erickson v. Brotherhood Locomotive Firemen, etc., 129 Minn. 264; 152 N. W. 537.

[28] McNicol v. N. Y. Life Ins. Co., 79 C. C. A. 14; 140 Fed. 141. See also Mut. Life Ins. Co. v. Jordan, 111 Ark. 324; 163 S. W. 799; Ann. Cas. 1916-B 674.

[29] Lewis v. Johnson, 123 Minn. 409; 143 S. W. 1127.

the company until it is accepted by the applicant.[30] An interesting and important case determining this point was decided by the Supreme Court of the United States,[31] where the facts were these: The applicant, in due form, applied for a policy of life insurance, the premiums on which were to be paid quarterly, and gave his note for the amount of the first payment; the company accepted the risk, but changed the amount of the premium and antedated the policy. The agent received the policy and six days afterwards sent a communication of that fact to the assured, and asked him what he should do with it. It did not appear whether this communication was received by the assured or not, and he died a few days after it had been sent. Suit was brought on the policy, judgment rendered against the company in the Federal Court and an appeal was taken to the Supreme Court of the United States, which reversed the case, holding that, owing to the change in the terms of the policy from those contemplated by the applicant, the acceptance of the company was a qualified acceptance, which the applicant was not bound to accept, and that, in the absence of evidence of such acceptance, the company was not held by the policy. In its opinion, the Court said: "The mutual assent, the meeting of the minds of both parties, is wanting. Such assent is vital to the existence of a contract. Without it there is none, and there can be none. In this case it is not established by any direct proof and there is none from which it can be inferred. .... . If he had received notice of the proposition made through the policy, it would have been at his option to give or refuse his assent. He was certainly in no wise bound until such assent was given. Until then there could be no contract on his part, and if there was none on his part, there could be none on the part of the company. The obligation in such cases is correlative. If there is none on one side, there is none on the other. The requisite assent must be the work of the parties themselves.

[30] Home L. Ins. Co. v. Myers, 50 C. C. A. 544; 112 Fed. 846; Leigh v. Brown, 99 Ga. 258; 25 S. E. 621; Mut. L. Ins. Co. v. Summers, 12 Wyo. 389; 120 Pac. 185; 66 L. R. A. 812; Mohrstadt v. Mut. Life Ins. Co., 52 C. C. A. 675; 115 Fed. 27.

[31] Ins. Co. v. Young, 23 Wall. 85. See also Smith v. Provident Savings F. Soc., 31 U. S. App. 163; 13 C. C. A. 284; 65 Fed. 765, where it is held that whether there is an acceptance or not, where the policy is different from that applied for, may be a question for the jury.

708

The law cannot supply it for them. That is a function wholly beyond the sphere of judicial authority. As the applicant was never bound, the company was never bound.''[32] Of course, the applicant is not bound to accept a policy different from that applied for, and where the application contained no hint of a limited risk the applicant is not bound to accept a policy excepting death by smallpox.[33] The applicant is bound to examine his policy when he receives it and, if it differs from that applied for, rescind within a reasonable time or he will be bound as by an acceptance.[34] And where the plaintiff contracted to take out a policy for a premium less than the regular premium, he could refuse to accept a policy where the premium was greater than that originally contracted for.[35] In the case of Blunt v. Fidelity & Casualty Co.,[36] the Court said: ''In contracts of insurance, as in other contracts, the rights of the parties are determined from the terms of the contract, so far as it is lawful. The contract here in question consisted of the application for insurance made and delivered by the assured to the defendant, and the policy of insurance made and delivered by the defendant to the assured. It cannot be conceded that the company was not at liberty to insert conditions in the policy which were not mentioned in the application. The application contained the affirmative stipulations and warranties made by the assured, and the policy contained the stipulations and limitations made by the insurer. The two together constitute the contract. If the policy of the company, which was issued by the company upon receipt and approval of the application, had contained any clause to which the assured did not agree, he, of course, would have been at liberty to reject it, and either demand a rescission and return of the premium paid, or insist upon a policy without the clause to which he did not assent. But when he received the policy and accepted it without objection, and especially when, as the record here shows, with the policy in his possession, he twice re-

[32] Byrne v. Casey, 70 Tex. 247; 8 S. W. 38.

[33] Mut. L. Ins. Co .of Ky. v. Gorman, 19 Ky. L. 295; 40 S. W. 571.

[34] Bostwick v. Mut. L. Ins. Co., 116 Wis. 392; 92 N. W. 246. See also McMaster v. N. Y. L. Ins. Co., 183 U. S. 25; reversing 40 C. C. A. 119; 99 Fed. 856.

[35] Robinson v. Security Life & Annuity Co., 163 N. C. 415; 79 S. E. 681.

[36] 145 Cal. 268; 78 Pac. 729; 67 L. R. A. 793.

newed it for an additional year, neither· he nor the beneficiary·
can with good reason claim that there is anything contained in
it to which he did not fully consent and agree.''

In the case of Hartwig v. Aetna Life Ins. Co.,[37] the Court
said: ''While it is true that in making an insurance contract,
the same as any other, it is essential that there shall be a meeting
of minds; that does not mean that there must be an express agreement upon all details. The·acceptance by an insurance company
of an application for one of its policies and an unconditional
deposit· in the post office of such a policy, properly addressed, involves all requisites of a meeting of minds. That applies particularly to the rate of insurance. Under such circumstances, the
minds of the parties are presumed to have met that the policy shall ...
be as usual, and the rate the usual one, or a reasonable rate, or
the same as before where the applicant has previously had a similar policy.''

§ 348. **Where the Policy Or Certificate Differs As to Payee
Or Otherwise, From Application.**—The Supreme Court of North
Carolina has held[38] that where the application designated as beneficiaries the wife ''and children'' of applicant and the policy,
which was received without objection, was payable to the wife
and ''her personal representatives and assigns,'' the application,
as modified by the policy, will be deemed to be the contract and
the persons named in the policy are the beneficiaries, and says
that this is so plain that no citation of authority is necessary. The
Supreme Court of Michigan, however, had held[39] that where the
application was made a part of the contract and named his wife,
or, in case of her death, his son as beneficiaries,· and the certificate
only contained the name of the wife, the application governed,
and the fact that the member retained the certificate without objection would not imply his assent to the designation of the wife
as beneficiary. The Court says: ''It is insisted that Mr. Eckler,
by accepting and keeping the certificate without objection, assented to the designation, and that his representatives are there-

---

[37] (Wis.), 158 N. W. 280.

[38] Hunter v. Scott, 108 N. C. 213; 12 S. E. 1027. See also Grand Lodge
v. Sater, 44 M. A. 445.

[39] Eckler v. Terry, 95 Mich. 123; 54 N. W. 704.

fore bound by it. If this were so, then it would follow that if both beneficiaries designated in the application had been omitted from the certificate, and others named therein, the certificate would have been equally controlling and binding. This would ignore the rule of construction that the entire contract must be considered in determining the intention of the parties." It has been said[40] that in case of conflict between the provisions of the policy and the statements of the application the former will govern.

§ 349. **Delay in Acting Upon An Application Will Not Amount to Acceptance: Company Not Bound to Accept.**—The company is not obliged to act at once upon the application. The fact that an application has been made for insurance, and a long time has elapsed, and the rejection of the risk has not been signified, does not warrant a presumption of its acceptance. An unreasonable 'delay is not acceptance.[41] There must be an actual acceptance, or there is no contract.[42] In a case where it was claimed that the delay of the company in acting upon the application was to be deemed a consent[43] the Court said: "We are not aware of any authority for the proposition that mere delay—mere inaction, can amount to an acceptance of a proposal to enter into a contract. The opposite is the true doctrine, that if no answer is given to a proposition for a contract, within a reasonable time, the proposition is regarded as withdrawn. The principle is stated in Hallock v. Commercial Ins. Co.[44] that a contract arises when an overt act is done, intended to signify an acceptance of a proposition, whether such overt act comes to the knowledge of the proposer or not, and unless a proposition is withdrawn, it is considered as pending until accepted or rejected, provided the answer is given in

[40] Goodwin v. Provident Sav. L. Ass. Soc., 97 Ia. 226; 66 N. W. 157; 32 L. R. A. 473.

[41] Brink v. Merchants' etc., Ass'n, 17 S. D. 235; 95 N. W. 929; Misselhorn v. Life Ass'n, 30 Fed. 545; Heimann v. Ins. Co., 17 Minn. 153; 10 Am. Rep. 154; Modern Woodmen of Am. v. Owens (Tex. Civ. A.), 130 S. W. 888; Richmond v. Travelers' Ins. Co., 123 Tenn. 307; 130 S. W. 790.

[42] Haskin v. Agricultural F. Ins. Co., 78 Va. 707; Markey v. Mut. Ben. Ins. Co., 103 Mass. 92; Haden v. Farmer's & M. F. Ins. Co., 80 Va. 683; Winnesheik Ins. Co. v. Holzgrafe, 53 Ill. 523.

[43] Alabama Gold L. Ins. Co. v. Mayes, 61 Ala. 163.

[44] 26 N. J. L. 263; 27 N. J. L. 645; 72 Am. Dec. 379.

a reasonable time. If the applicant was dilatory in acting on
the proposal, the deceased could have quickened its diligence by
demanding prompt action; or, if not assenting to the delay, he
could have retracted his proposal, and reclaimed the money he
had advanced and his note. He had no right, without an inquiry
as to the cause, without any action on his part, to rely on the
supineness of the appellant, no greater than his own, as an ec-
ceptance of the proposal.''[45] The company is not bound to accept if no good cause for rejection exists.[46] If a mutual organization, the directors may be actuated by other considerations than
the quality of the risk.[47] The company can reject the application,
although part of the premium or all of it has been paid.[48] This
doctrine applies to mutual companies.[49] Where the application
and premium were duly forwarded by mail, but the company
never received them or heard of them, so that neither policy was
issued nor money returned to the applicant as was provided in
the receipt given by the agent, it was held that no contract existed.[50] In this case[51] the Court says: "Counsel for plaintiff
contend that, although Baylor was unauthorized to execute contracts of insurance, yet that the transaction became a contract as
soon as the company could have an opportunity to accept the risk,
and failed to do so or return the premium. If the defendant had
received the application and premium, and retained the same, and
remained silent, it may be that it should be held to have approved
the application, but this question is not in the case. The company had no knowledge that any application had been made and
premium paid, and no contract can therefore be implied from
any neglect to issue the policy founded upon the knowledge of the

[45] Ins. Co. v. Johnson, 23 Pa. St. 72; Bentley v. Columbia Ins. Co., 17
N. Y. 421; Flanders on Ins. 108.

[46] Ins. Co. v. Young, 23 Wall. 85; Ala. Gold Life Ins. Co. v. Mayes,
61 Ala. 163. But see Oliver v. Am. Legion of Honor, 17 Am. L. Rev. 301, and
post, § 354.

[47] Harp v. Granger's Mut., etc., Ins. Co., 49 Md. 309.

[48] Otterbein v. Ia. State Ins. Co., 57 Ia. 274; Todd v. Piedmont & Arlington L. Ins. Co., 34 La. Ann. 63; Supreme Lodge v. Grace, 60 Tex. 569.

[49] Walker v. Farmers' Ins. Co., 51 Ia. 679; 2 N. W. 583; Armstrong
v. State Ins. Co., 61 Ia. 212; 16 N. W. 94.

[50] Atkinson v. Hawkeye Ins. Co., 71 Ia. 340; 32 N. W. 371.

[51] Atkinson v. Hawkeye Ins. Co., supra.

defendant that such an application had been made. The case is very much like Walker v. Farmers' Ins. Co.,[52] where it was held that the giving of an application for insurance to an agent of the company authorized to receive applications only, and the execution of a premium note, do not constitute a contract for insurance. In that case the agent of the defendant neglected to forward the application and premium note, and the company had no knowledge of their existence until after the property was destroyed by fire. In this case the agent was not negligent. We think the case is controlled by that above cited, which was followed and approved in Armstrong v. State Ins. Co.''[53]

§ 350. **The Same Subject—Company May Be Liable for Damages for Negligence in Not Acting Upon the Application.**—It has been held that an insurance company obtaining an application and receiving payment of premium, must accept, or reject, the application within a reasonable time and is liable for damages resulting from its failure to do so.[54] In that case the Court said: ''The association was responsible for the conduct of Rogers when acting within the scope of his agency, and it is admitted that he allowed the application to lie on the physician's desk a month lacking a day, though it was his duty to forward it promptly to the association. But he was not alone at fault, for the association was aware as early as June 12, 1911, that the application had been taken, and yet did nothing in the matter during the 27 days intervening his death. In the case of another application taken at about the same time and in the same vicinity there was a delay of but 19 days in issuing the certificate. We think whether defendant in the exercise of ordinary diligence should have passed on the application prior to Duffie's death was fairly put in issue. The association was bound by the acts of its agents and chargeable with any consequences that resulted from the failure of Rogers to promptly forward the

[52] 51 Ia. 679; 2 N. W. 583.
[53] 61 Ia. 212; 16 N. W. 94.
[54] Duffie v. Bankers' Life Ass'n, 160 Ia. 19; 139 N. W. 1087; 46 L. R. A. (N. S.), 25. See also Carter v. Manhattan L. Ins. Co., 11 Hawaii 11; cited in Ann. Cas. 1916-B, p. 678, where long extract from the opinion is given.

application and physician's report. In other words, if the association was under a duty to promptly act on the application and notify Duffie, as we think it was, it cannot shield itself from the responsibility by the fact that the application and medical report had not been received by it and therefore it could not act.[55] The possession of these by its agents had the same effect as if they were in the possession of the association at its home office. Assuming, then, that the applic███n ·and medical report had been promptly forwarded by the agent, and that the application was not accepted or rejected within the time. intervening prior to his death, it seems manifest that whether this was an unreasonable delay was for the jury to determine, and we so hold. But it is argued that it was as much the duty of the applicant to inquire as it was that of the insurer to give the information, and this or similar expressions will be found in several decisions holding that mere silence on the part of the insurer is not as strong evidence of acceptance as of rejection.. Whether this were so or not, as bearing on whether an acceptance should have been inferred, it cannot be said that the duties of the parties were reciprocal. The applicant had done all he could or was required to do in the· matter. He had the right to assume that the application would be forwarded immediately after the· medical examination and was so assured. This, with the suggestion that the certificate would be in effect after passing the physical examination, was well calculated to lull him into supposed security. Moreover, about all he ·could have done was to withdraw his application and apply to another insurer for a policy, and this, one who has applied to a company of his choice would quite naturally hesitate to do. Under the circumstances, it cannot be said, as a matter of law, that the deceased was at fault in not stirring defendant to action by inquiry as to the cause of delay or in not withdrawing his application. At the most, this also was an issue appropriate for the determination of the jury. Assuming, then, that the defendant was negligent and Duffie without fault, as the jury might have ·concluded, can it be said that but for such negligence a certificate of insurance would have been issued? We think the jury might have found that, in all

[55] See Northwestern Mut. Life Ins. Co. v. Neafus, 145 Ky. 563; 140 S. W. 1026; 36 L. R. A. (N. S.), 1211.

reasonable probability, had the association passed upon the application, it would have been accepted. Duffie was a young man of 32 years, his medical examination was satisfactory, and the physician had recommended him; his employment as a farmer was not hazardous, and his character all that could be desired. The association was actively soliciting members, and it seems to us that the record leaves little if 'any doubt but that, had the association ever passed on the risk, it would have been accepted and the certificate issued. As observed in Continental Ins. Co. v. Haynes,[56] 'It is to be assumed that the company will accept the risk if advantageous to it, which it must be, if fairly and honestly contracted for, because that is the business in which it is engaged, and that is the object for which its agent acted; and therefore to allow it, under the reservation of the right to approve, to reject simply because a loss has occurred, would destroy the mutuality of the contract and inflict upon the party the misfortune he had provided against. Contingencies might have arisen, as suggested by counsel for appellee, which would have led to a different conclusion, as, upon inquiry, it might have been ascertained that applicant was so venturesome or reckless in his conduct as to render him an undesirable risk. It is enough to say that the record contains no intimation that such was the fact, and it ought not to be inferred that other than the truth would have been elicited by any inquiries which the insurer might have prosecuted. If the applicant was of such disposition or temperament that the association would not, if it had acted, have accepted the application and issued the certificate, then no injury can be said to have resulted from the delay. Whether or not in all reasonable probability the certificate would have been issued had the association acted on the application, can only be determined from the record as presented to the court. But it is said that a certificate or policy of insurance is simply a·contract like any other, as between individuals, and that there is no such thing as negligence of a party in the matter of delay in entering into a contract. This view overlooks the fact that the defendant holds and is acting under a franchise from the State. The legislative policy, in granting this, proceeds on the theory that chartering such association

[56] 10 Ky. Law, 276.

is in the interest of the public to the end that indemnity on specific contingencies shall be provided those who are eligible and desire it, and for their protection the State regulates, inspects and supervises their business. Having solicited applications for insurance, and having so obtained them and received payment of the fees or premiums exacted, they are bound either to furnish the indemnity the State has authorized them to furnish or· decline so to do within such reasonable time as will enable them to act intelligently and advisedly thereon or suffer the consequences flowing from their neglect so to do. Otherwise the applicant is unduly delayed in obtaining the insurance· he desires, and for which the law afforded the opportunity, and which the insurer impliedly has promised, if conditions are satisfactory. Moreover, policies or certificates of insurance ordinarily are dated as of the day the application is signed, and, aside from other considerations, the insurer should not be permitted to unduly prolong the period for which it is exacting the payment of premium without incurring risk. What was said in Northwestern Mutual Life Ins. Co. v. Neafus[57] is pertinent: 'If in this case there was evidence that the company was induced to reject the application for the sole reason that Neafus died before it acted upon it, or to show that his application, except for the fact of his death, would have been approved, we would have a very different question. We think there is a sound and well-defined distinction between a case in which the application under no circumstances would have been accepted, and a case in which it would have been accepted except for the fact that the applicant died before it was acted upon, and after the company had a reasonable time in which to act. While the application and receipt are to be treated merely as a proposal for insurance that it is with the company at its election to accept or reject, it may well be said that the company must act honestly and fairly on the application submitted to it, and which it impliedly at least agreed to accept, if satisfactory to it; and that if an application is satisfactory, and the company, if it had acted in a reasonable time, would have accepted the risk, it should not be allowed after holding the application for an unreasonable time to reject it, solely because of the death of the applicant. But, treat-

[57] 145 Ky. 563; 140 S. W. 1026; 36 L. R. A. (N. S.), 1211.

716

ing the case as we find it in the record, the delay, however unreasonable it may have been, cannot be construed into an acceptance of an application that no well-managed company, in the ordinary course of its business, would have accepted.'

In Boyer v. State Farmers' Mutual Hail Ins. Ass'n,[58] recovery for the amount of insurance applied for was awarded because of negligent delay in not issuing the policy until after the loss, and in a note to the case as reported,[59] the annotator says that: 'Whatever may be the decision of the jury on this question (delay), it cannot be doubted that the proposition that an insurer should be held liable for a loss sustained by an applicant for insurance because of the negligence of the insurer's agent in failing to forward the application within a reasonable time is sound.' In Walker v. Farmers' Ins. Co.,[60] the trial court instructed the jury that, if the agent had only the power 'to receive and forward applications to the company for their approval or rejection, then, as such, he would be held to the use of ordinary diligence, and the defendant would be liable for his negligence in the performance of such duty; and if you find that said agent neglected to forward such application for rejection or approval within a reasonable time, considering all the circumstances, then the defendant must be held liable for any loss occasioned by such neglect.' Of this, the Court said: 'It may be, but the point we do not decide, that defendant is liable for the neglect of its agent as contemplated in this instruction, but in order to recover for such negligence the action must be based thereon and the petition must so declare.' And the instruction was held to be erroneous for that no such issue was raised on the pleadings. We are inclined to the opinion that the principle announced in this instruction is sound and that the facts of the case were such as to require its application. The application named plaintiff as his beneficiary, and, had the certificate issued, likely she would have been named therein as such. But there was no contract, and the negligence, if any, was that of failing to discharge a duty owing the deceased. Had the certificate issued, whether plaintiff or some one else were

[58] 86 Kan. 442; 121 Pac. 329; 40 L. R. A. (N. S.), 164.
[59] 40 L. R. A. (N. S.), 164.
[60] 51 Iowa 679; 2 N. W. 583.

beneficiary would have been optional with the insured, and as the injury, if any, was to him, his representative alone can maintain the action for resulting damages.''[61]

§ 351. Company May Be Bound Though Application Has Been Rejected Or Not Acted On.—But it is possible under some circumstances for the officers of a company to bind it, although in fact the application has been declined; as where the secretary and director of a mutual company took the applicant's application, premium note and note for cash premium and promised to notify him if the application was rejected and in that case to return the notes. The application was rejected. Seven months afterwards the applicant's premises were burned, but he had received no notice of the rejection of his application. In an action on the contract the plaintiff recovered and this judgment was affirmed by a divided court.[62] So, where on the organization of a company a large number of applications with premium notes were received, and, before the approval of one of them, but the next day after the formal organization, a loss occurred, it was held that the company was liable.[63]

§352. When Contract of Insurance Becomes Complete.—A contract of insurance never becomes complete until the last act necessary to be done by either party has in fact been done, although one side or the other may conditionally bind itself by a proposition which, when unconditionally accepted, ripens the negotiation into a contract. In the case of fire insurance contracts there is often a contract before the policy is issued or before it is delivered to the insured, but this is seldom so with life insurance agreements, because there is usually, in the applications as well as the policies, a stipulation that the policy shall not be binding until delivery to the assured while in good health, and payment of the premium by him. Such conditions are valid and binding and will be enforced. The rule may be briefly expressed as follows: A con-

[61] See also Schmidt v. Ass'n, 112 Iowa 41; 83 N. W. 800; 51 L. R. A. 141; 84 Am. St. Rep. 323.

[62] Somerset Co. F. Ins. Co. v. May, 2 W. N. C. (Pa.), 43.

[63] Van Slyke v. Trempealeau, etc., Ins. Co., 48 Wis. 683; Chamberlain v. Prudential Ins. Co., 109 Wis. 4; 85 N. W. 128.

tract of life insurance is not complete until the last act necessary to be done by the insured under the conditions of the contract after acceptance of the application, has been done. The cases are not always in accord and much depends upon the facts, because special conditions may have been waived, or the law of estoppel may apply.[64] Life policies never delivered are not binding.[65] Delivery of a policy may have been obtained by fraud and, if so, it is considered never to have been in effect.[66] If so stipulated the contract is not complete until the premium has been actually paid.[67] Payment of premium by worthless check does not make the policy effective,[68] nor unauthorized acceptance a note for the premium.[69] But unless it is so stipulated delivery may be on credit.[70] This point was also considered and so held in a case where the meaning was not clear.[71] In a recent case[72]

[64] Busher v. New York L. Ins. Co., 72 N. H. 551; 58 Atl. 41; Stringham v. Mut. L. Ins. Co,. 44 Ore. 447; 75 Pac. 822; Allen v. Mass. Mut. Acc. Ass'n, 167 Mass. 18; 44 N. E. 1053; Gallant v. Metropolitan L. Ins. Co., 167 Mass. 79; 44 N. E. 1073; Langstaff v. Metropolitan L. Ins. Co., 69 N. J. L. 54; 54 Atl. 518; Russell v. Prudential Ins. Co., 176 N. Y. 178; 68 N. E. 252; reversing 76 N. Y. Supp. 1029; Ray v. Security Trust, etc., Co., 126 N. C. 166; 35 S. E. 246; Hawley v. Mich. Mut. L. Ins. Co., 92 Ia. 593; 61 N. W. 201; Maloney v. N. W. Masonic Aid Ass'n, 8 App. Div. 574; 40 N. Y. Supp. 918; Steinle v. N. Y. Life Ins. Co., 81 Fed. 489; 26 C. C. A. 491; Hewitt v. American Union L. I. Co., 66 App. Div. 80; 73 N. Y. Supp. 105, reversing 70 N. Y. Supp. 1012; Oliver v. Mut. L. Ins. Co., 97 Va. 134; 33 S. E. 536.

[65] John Hancock Mut. Life Ins. Co. v. McClure, 134 C. C. A. 355; 218 Fed. 597; Cunningham v. Royal Neighbors of Am., 24 S. D. 489; 124 N. W. 434.

[66] Fitzgerald v. Metropolitan Life Ins. Co. (Vt.), 98 Atl. 498.

[67] Armond v. Fidelity L. Ass'n, 96 N. C. 158; 1 S. E. 796; Ben. Ass'n v. Conway, 10 Ill. App. 348; McClave v. Mut. Reserve, etc., Ass'n, 55 N. J. L. 187; 26 Atl. 78; Quinby v. N. Y. L. Ins. Co., 24 N. Y. Supp. 593; Mut. Reserve F. S. Ass'n v. Summons, 46 C. C. A. 393; 107 Fed. 418.

[68] Brady v. N. W. Masonic A. Ass'n, 190 Pa. St. 595; 42 Atl. 962.

[69] Mut. L. Ins. Co. v. Logan, 87 Fed. 637; 31 C. C. A. 172; 57 U. S. App. 18.

[70] Jones v. New York L. Ins. Co., 168 Mass. 245; 47 N. E. 92.'

[71] Bushaw v. Women's, etc., Co., 8 N. Y. Supp. 423. And a decoy policy may be valid without payment of premium. Union L. Ins. Co. v. Haman, 54 Neb. 599; 74 N. W. 1090.

[72] Union Central L. Ins. Co. v. Pauley, 8 Ind. App. 85; 35 N. E. 190.

the Supreme Court of Indiana thus reviews the law on the subject: ''It is undoubtedly true that while, as a general rule, the delivery of the policy and payment of the premium, either in money or by note, both occur when the contract is consummated, still it is also true that there may be a valid and enforceable contract of insurance without payment, or without a manual delivery of the policy.[73] Such contract may also exist without either payment of premium or delivery of policy.[74] Yet such cases are recognized as exceptional, and, in order to sustain them, the proof, whether direct or circumstantial, should be of such a character as to reasonably support the assertion. . . . In Cronkhite v. Insurance Co.,[75] Brewer, C. J., says: 'The company should not be called on to pay where it has in fact received nothing, unless there is some clear and positive reason upon which the demand rests.' Keeping in mind the well-established rule of our court that, where there is a conflict of evidence, we will not undertake to weigh it, we are still unable to find in the evidence of this case any fact from which it may be reasonably and legitimately inferred that there was here a binding, completed contract of insurance. All of the evidence is consistent with the idea that there were simply negotiations looking towards an insurance. There is no indication of any purpose to contract other than by a policy to be made and delivered upon payment of at least half of the premium.[76] There is here an entire want of proof that the agent in any manner waived payment, or gave any credit except as to one-half the premium. Counsel for the appellee rely largely upon the postal card for proof that there was a constructive delivery of the policy, and a consummation of the contract. It is urged that by the language 'your policy,' used in this card, the idea is conveyed that

[73] Hamilton v. Ins. Co., 5 Pa. St. 339; Cronkhite v. Ins. Co., 35 Fed. 26; Carpenter v. Ins. Co., 4 Sandf. Ch. 408; Tayloe v. Ins. Co., 9 How. 390; Fried v. Ins. Co., 50 N. Y. 243; Ins. Co. v. Jenks, 5 Ind. 96.

[74] Bragdon v. Ins. Co., 42 Me. 259; Collins v. Insurance Co., 7 Phila. 201; Kohne v. Ins. Co., 1 Wash. C. C. 93; Sheldon v. Ins. Co., 25 Conn. 207; Hallock v. Ins. Co., 26 N. J. L. 268; 27 N. J. L. 645; Xenos v. Wickham, L. R. 2 H. L. 296; Ins. Co. v. Robinson, 25 Ind. 537.

[75] 35 Fed. 26.

[76] Heiman v. Ins. Co., 17 Minn. 173 (Gil. 127); Markey v. Ins. Co., 103 Mass. 78.

the policy then actually belonged to Pauley, and that the agent simply held it, as a trustee for him. When all the surrounding circumstances, as to which there is no dispute, are regarded, such a construction seems to us untenable. Such an inference cannot fairly and legitimately follow simply from the language of the card, which, when considered in the light of attendant circumstances, can mean only that the policy written for Pauley had come. Counsel for the appellee supports his proposition that the 'contract was executed, there was nothing further to be done,' when the postal card was written, by the cases of Cooper v. Insurance Co.,[77] and Tayloe v. Insurance Co.[78] In the former of these cases $50 was paid when the application was made, which was, according to the company's regulations, to be applied on the first year's premium, provided the company should conclude to make the insurance. The company did so conclude, entered its conclusion on its books, and forwarded the policy to the agent, and the money paid thereby became the money of the company, and the beneficiary became entitled to a policy upon complying with the other terms of the contract, which she offered to do in strict accordance therewith, although her husband had taken sick and died after the acceptance of the application, and before the delivery of the policy to her. In the Tayloe case, Tayloe applied for insurance. The company wrote the agent it would take it at a certain rate. The agent so notified Tayloe, telling him if he desired to effect insurance, to send him a check, and the 'matter is concluded.' On the day after receiving this letter, Tayloe sent a check by mail, with directions to leave the policy at a bank. The insurance was held to take effect from the mailing of the check, the matter being then 'concluded' so far as effecting a completed contract was concerned. These cases present very different features from the one at bar, where there is neither payment nor waiver, nor anything shown to have been accepted as a compliance with the contract. In the cases of Insurance Co. v. Jenks,[79] and Insurance Co. v. Robinson,[80] there were clear and distinct contracts for insurance, the terms of which were fully complied with

[77] 7 Nev. 116.
[78] 9 How. 390.
[79] 5 Ind. 96.
[80] 25 Ind. 536.

721

by the insured. If the minds of the parties ever met, and an agreement for an insurance was made, it must have been upon the 6th of October, which was the last time that Daily saw Pauley. Whatever the arrangement then made was, whether for $1,000 or $5,000, there is not a scintilla of evidence that there was any waiver of payment more than half the premium. Pauley then understood he was to pay half cash at least. Word was left with his son on the 14th that the policy had come; yet he made no move towards payment or consummation of the contract until December 6. The agent certainly acted with diligence. He wrote him a card about the 10th, and went out in person on the 14th, but no response came from Pauley. We are unable to see that it was incumbent upon the agent to specially urge payment upon Pauley as a condition to his policy becoming effectual; nor can we hold, as urged by counsel, that his failure to do so is to be deemed a waiver of payment. Presumptively, the payment of the premium and the delivery and effectiveness of the policy would go hand in hand.[81] Pauley had no right to expect anything else unless by special agreement. There was, as we construe it, nothing in Daily's postal card which could have tended to raise in Pauley's mind the belief that his policy was in force, although not paid for.'' Under some circumstances there may be a waiver of this condition by a delivery of the policy, but this question is more properly one of waiver. With benefit societies all these questions may arise, although their habits and course of business are more simple, for necessarily there is the same kind of an application or proposal which is to be accepted, either conditionally or unconditionally, by the directors of the society.[82] Unless provided otherwise in the contract, the acceptance of the proposal to insure for the premium offered, is the completion of the negotiation, and after the policy or certificate has been forwarded to the agent of the company for delivery the contract cannot be rescinded without the consent of the party insured.[83] It is, of course, different if any act remains to be done by the in-

---

[81] Heiman v. Ins. Co., 17 Minn. 153 (Gil. 127).

[82] See *post*, § 355.

[83] Hallock v. Ins. Co., 26 N. J. 278; Ala. Gold. L. Ins. Co. v. Herron, 56 Miss. 643; Shattuck v. Mut. L. Ins. Co., 4 Cliff. 598. See also Porter v. Mut. L. Ins. Co., 70 Vt. 504; 41 Atl. 970.

sured, as payment of premium,[84] or if it be stipulated that it shall not be binding until delivered by the agent. Thus, where the defendant made an application for insurance to the agent of the company in New Jersey and paid the premium, the policy to be issued and delivered to him if his application was accepted. The application was sent to the company in Pennsylvania and there approved and the policy issued and mailed to the applicant. It was held by the Supreme Court of New Jersey[85] that the contract was made in Pennsylvania and was complete as soon as the application was accepted and the policy deposited in the mail. Other authorities support this view.[86] And where it was agreed between the agent and the assured that the first premium should be paid by note, and accordingly, the application was forwarded, accepted by the company and returned to the agent, who refused to deliver it as the assured was sick, it was held[87] that the policy became binding upon the company when it was placed in the mail at the office of the company, if not, then certainly when it reached the hands of the local agent. So, when an application for insurance received by the agent was sent by him to the home office of the company, and the company accepted it and sent the policy to the agent, it was held by the Supreme Court of Minnesota[88] that it was the duty of the agent to deliver the policy upon tender of the premium, even though the person whose life was insured had become dangerously ill, unless it was otherwise agreed between the parties, or he was otherwise instructed by the company.[89] But delivery of the policy under circumstances which amount to fraud on the part of the assured will not change the relations of the parties. Thus, where negotiations were still pending between an agent of the company and the applicant concerning the precise terms of the contract and the mode of payment, a friend of the applicant

[84] Girard v. Metropolitan L. Ins. Co., Rep. Ind. Queb. 20 C. S. 532.

[85] Northampton, etc., Ins. Co. v. Tuttle, 40 N. J. L. 103; 29 N. J. L. 486. To the same effect are: Mut. Res. F. L. Ins. Ass'n v. Farmer, 65 Ark. 581; 47 S. W. 850; Triple Link, etc., Ass'n v. Williams, 121 Ala. 138; 26 Sou. 19.

[86] Adams v. Lindsell, 1 B. & Ald. 681; Mactier v. Frith, 6 Wend. 103; Tayloe v. Merchants' F. Ins. Co., 9 How. 390; 2 Kent's Com. 477.

[87] Yonge v. Equitable L. Ass. Soc., 30 Fed. 902.

[88] Schwartz v. Germania Life Ins. Co., 21 Minn. 215.

[89] Schwartz v. Germania Life Ins. Co., 18 Minn. 449.

paid the premium, concealing the fact that the assured was sick, and the latter in fact died a few hours later, and the agent, in ignorance of the facts, delivered the policy, the Supreme Court of the United States held[90] that there was no contract. So where delivery of the policy was held up because of sickness of the applicant but he died, without the policy being delivered, it was held that there was no contract.[91] But payment of premium shortly before death of the insured is not of itself fraudulent.[92] If the application provided that the policy shall not be in force until it is delivered to the applicant, the contract of insurance will not become binding upon the company until delivered.[93] If the policy is not accepted by insured there is no delivery.[94] Under a statute of Wisconsin it was held that the general agent of a company can contract for immediate insurance, although the application declares to the contrary.[95] The condition that the insured must be in good health at the time of the delivery of the policy is valid and violation of this condition relieves the insurer.[96] The question whether there has been delivery is sometimes one of fact for the jury.[97]

[90] Piedmont, etc,. Ins. Co. v. Ewing, 92 U. S. 377.

[91] Rushons v. Manhattan L. Ins. Co., 139 C. C. A. 520; 224 Fed. 74.

[92] Kendrick v. Mut. Ben. L. Ins. Co., 124 N. C. 315; 32 S. E. 728.

[93] Kohen v. Mut. Reserve Fund L. Ass'n, 28 Fed. 705; Misselhorn v. Same, 30 Fed. 545; Misselhorn v. Same, 30 M. A. 589; Weinfeld v. Same, 53 Fed. 208. See also Reese v. Fidelity, etc., Ass'n, 111 Ga. 482; 36 S. E. 637.

[94] Hoghen v. Metropolitan L. Ins. Co., 69 Conn. 103; 38 Atl. 503; Dickerson v. Prudential Savings L. A. Soc., 21 Ky. L. 611; 52 S. W. 825.

[95] Mathers v. Union Mut. Acc. Ass'n, 78 Wis. 588; 47 N. W. 1130.

[96] Gordon v. Prudential Ins. Co., 231 Pa. 404; 80 Atl. 882; Massachusetts Mut. L. Ins. Co. v. Crenshaw, 186 Ala. 460; 65 Sou. 65; Metropolitan L. Ins. Co. v. Willis, 37 Ind. App. 48; 76 N. E. 560; Gallop v. Royal Neighbors of Am., 167 Mo. App. 85; 150 S. W. 1118; Mohr v. Prudential Ins. Co., 32 R. I. 177; 78 Atl. 554. As to what is good health, see Austin v. Mut. Reserve F. L. A. 132 Fed. 555; affd. Mut. Reserve F. L. A. v. Austin, 73 C. C. A. 498; 142 Fed. 398; 6 L. R. A. (N. S.), 1064. Also ante, § 286.

[97] Prudential Ins. Co. v. Sullivan, 27 Ind. App. 30; 59 N. E. 873; Smith v. Provident Sav. L. A. Soc., 13 C. C. A. 284; 65 Fed. 765; Krause v. Equitable L. Ass. Soc., 105 Mich. 329; 63 N. W. 440; Union Cent. L. Ins. Co. v. Hallowell, 14 Ind. App. 611; 43 N. E. 277. When a life insurance policy is found in the possession of the insured there is a pre-

§ 353. **The Same Subject — Illustrations.** — Actual or constructive delivery of the policy is issential to its validity,[98] and without delivery of the policy there can be no liability if the policy so provides, but actual delivery can be waived.[99] Under the custom of the company delivery to the agent may be delivery to the insured.[100] Whether a policy delivered to the agent for delivery to the insured is binding while in the possession of the agent, depends upon the nature of the agent's authority and where the agent has simply the duty of transferring it, it is binding upon delivery to the agent.[101] But there is no delivery where the policy was mailed by the insurer to an agent but insured declined to receive it unless it passed through the hands of another agent.[102] Mailing the policy for unconditional delivery makes the policy binding.[103] If the policy so provides the good health of the insured is a condition precedent to the delivery of the policy, and an unauthorized delivery of the policy by the agent does not make the company liable, but where the insurer received and retained the proceeds of a check given in payment of the premium it was estopped to deny the liability.[104] The stipulation in the policy that

sumption of delivery. Mass. Ben. Ass'n v. Sibley, 158 Ill. 411; 42 N. E. 137. Writing that, "your policy has arrived," is not delivery. Union Cent. L. Ins. Co. v. Pauley, 8 Ind. App. 85; 35 N. E. 190.

[98] American Home Life Ins. Co. v. Melton (Tex. Civ. Ap), 144 S. W. 362; Powell v. Missouri State L. Ins. Co., 153 N. C. 124, 69 S. E. 12; Michigan Mut. Life Ins. Co. v. Thompson, 44 Ind. App. 180; 86 N. E. 503; Kirk v. Sovereign Camp Woodmen of the World, 169 Mo. App. 448; 155 S. W. 39.

[99] Yount v. Prudential Ins. Co. (Mo. App.), 179 S. W. 749; Clark v. Mut. Life Ins. Co., 129 Ga. 571; 59 S. E. 283; Rogers v. American Nat. Ins. Co. (Ga.), 89 S. E. 700.

[100] Payne v. Mut. Life Ins. Co., 77 C. C. A. 487; 141 Fed. 399; Shields v. Equitable Life Assur. Soc., 121 Mich. 690; 80 N. W. 793; Kilborne v. Prudential Ins. Co., 99 Mich. 176; 108 N. W. 801; Rayburn v. Pa. Cas. Co., 138 N. C. 379; 50 S. E. 762; Brown v. Mut. Ben. L. Ins. Co., 131 Ga. 38; 61 S. E. 1123.

[101] New York Life Ins. Co. v. Greenlee, 42 Ind. App. 82; 84 N. E. 1101; Francis v. Mut. Assessment Ins. Co., 55 Ore. 280; 106 Pac. 323; Thompson v. Michigan Mut. Life Ins. Co., 56 Ind. App. 502; 105 N. E. 700; Amarillo Nat. Ins. Co. v. Brown (Tex. Civ. App.), 166 S. W. 658.

[102] Nat. Life Ass'n v. Speer, 111 Ark. 173; 163 S. W. 1188.

[103] Du Preist v. American Central Life Ins. Co., 97 Ark. 229; 133 S. W. 826; Williams v. Philadelphia Life Ins. Co. (S. C.), 89 S. E. 675.

[104] American Bankers' Ins. Co. v. Thomas (Okla.), 154 Pac. 44.

it shall not be in force until payment of the first premium during the good health of the insured, refers only to the health of the insured between acceptance of the risk and the time when the first premium is paid.[105] Insanity occurring between the application and delivery of the policy relieves the insurer.[106] Payment of the first premium is not a condition precedent to make the contract complete unless the policy so provides.[107] Under a provision that the policy shall not be effective until delivered to and accepted by the insured while in good health, the reception of the policy and deposit in a safe by the agent with the consent of the insured is sufficient acceptance.[108] Under the facts shown it was held that the policy not being delivered until after the death of the insured was void.[109] Where the insured does not reject the life policy within a reasonable time after its delivery he is deemed to have accepted and is liable for the premium.[110] Failure of the insured to examine the policies has been deemed to be an acceptance.[111] Where the life insurance policy was found among other papers of insured after his death the question of delivery of the policy was held to be for the jury.[112]

105 Webster v. Columbian Nat'l Life Ins. Co., 196 N. Y. 523; 89 N. E. 1114; affg. 116 N. Y. Supp. 404; 131 App. Div. 837; Modern Woodmen of America v. Atkinson, 153 Ky. 526; 156 S. W. 1135; Gallop v. Royal Neighbors of America, 167 Mo. App. 85; 150 S. W. 1118.

106 Metropolitan L. Ins. Co. v. Orvillio, 37 Ind. App. 48; 76 N. E. 560.

107 New York Life Ins. Co. v. Greenlee (Ind. App.), 84 N. E. 1101; Clark v. Home Fund Life Ins. Co., 79 S. C. 494; 61 S. E. 80; McLean v. Tobin, 109 N. Y. Supp. 926; 58 Misc. 528.

108 Bell v. Mo. State Life Ins. Co., 166 Mo. App. 390; 149 S. W. 33. See also Connecticut Life Ins. Co. v. Mullen, 118 C. C. A. 345; 197 Fed. 299.

109 Reserve Loan Life Ins. Co. v. Hockett, 35 Ind. App. 842; 73 N. E. 842; Rusher v. New York Life Ins. Co., 72 N. H. 551; 58 Atl. 41. See also Snedeker v. Metropolitan L. Ins. Co., 160 Ky. 119; 169 S. W. 570, where though part of the premium was paid and the agent retained the policy there was no contract.

110 Gray v. Stone, 102 Ark. 146; 143 S. W. 114; Franklin Life Ins. Co. v. Boykin, 10 Ga. App. 345; 73 S. E. 545.

111 Robertson v. Covenant Mut. B. Ins. Co., 123 Mo. App. 238; 100 S. W. 686; Floors v. Aetna Life Ins. Co., 144 N. C. 332; 56 S. E. 915; 11 L. R. A. (N. S.) 357.

112 Metropolitan Life Ins. Co. v. Williamson, 98 C. C. A. 90; 174 Fed. 116.

Where a life policy provided that it should not go into effect until payment of the first premium, the fact that the agent delivered it and personally paid the amount of the premium, less his commissions, pursuant to his agreement with the insurer, did not operate as the payment of the first premium making the policy effective.[113] Where the insured receives a life policy different from the one applied for, he must reject it within a reasonable time after delivery, and retention without objection beyond such reasonable time is proof of acceptance. Where the insured received a policy in August and did not at that time return a receipt attached to the policy, which directed that the receipt should be signed and returned when the policy was delivered, insured cannot in December by writing across the face of the policy accepted and signing his name put the policy into effect as of that date, thus delaying time for payment of subsequent premiums, although the policy provided that it should not go into effect until the premium is paid.[114]

Delivery of a policy on the life of an infant to the father constitutes an acceptance.[115] Where a life insurance policy provided that no obligation is assumed prior to its date, nor unless on said date the insurer is alive and in good health, the company is not bound by the report of its examining physician made several days before the date of the policy.[116] A stipulation that insured must be in good health on the delivery of the policy is valid,[117] but such unsoundness so mentioned refers to unsoundness arising after the application.[118] The return of the policies to the company to have the beneficiary changed and new policies issued is a waiver of the provision that the policy shall not become effective until delivery.[119] Where insurance is applied for and a policy is issued and delivered, it is based on the status of the insured at the time of the application unless otherwise provided in the contract.[120]

---

[113] Lyke v. American National Assur. Co., 187 S. W. 265. See also Whiting v. Insurance Co., 129 Mass. 240.

[114] Lyke v. American National Assur. Co., *supra*.

[115] Ferguson v. Phoenix Mut. Life Ins. Co., 84 Vt. 350; 79 Atl. 997.

[116] Gallant v. Metropolitan Life Ins. Co., 167 Mass. 79; 44 N. E. 1073.

[117] Metropolitan Life Ins. Co. v. Willis, 37 Ind. App. 48; 76 N. E. 560.

[118] Metropolitan Life Ins. Co. v. Moore, 117 Ky. 654; 79 S. W. 249.

[119] Pierce v. New York Life Ins. Co., 174 Mo. App. 383; 160 S. W. 40.

[120] Rayburn v. Pa. Cas. Co., 138 N. C. 379; 50 S. E. 762.

§ 354. **The Same Subject: Contract May Be Complete Without Delivery of the Policy.**—A contract of insurance, however, may be complete without delivery of the policy, as where it has been made and executed and notice given to the assured,[121] or where the premium had been paid,[122] or if the applicant is notified that his application has been accepted;[123] and there need not be manual delivery of the policy.[124] The acceptance of the application, if nothing is left to be done*by the insured, makes a completed contract, though the assured die before delivery of the policy.[125] Actual delivery is not necessary to complete the contract if acceptance of the risk is indicated in any other manner.[126] And mailing the policy to the agent in accordance with instruction in the application is acceptance of the applicant and makes the contract binding without delivery of the policy.[127] But where, independent of the policy, there is nothing to show any acceptance of the application, or any agreement to insure, the presumption is that while there were negotiations there was no contract, and no purpose to contract otherwise than by a policy made and delivered upon simultaneous payment of premium. Where there has been no transfer of the legal manual possession of the policy to the insured, or to any person for him, so as to constitute a delivery in fact, the policy is *prima facie* incomplete as a

121 Sheldon v. Conn. Mut. L. Ins. Co., 25 Conn. 207; 65 Am. Dec. 565; Union Cent. L. Ins. Co. v. Phillips, 41 C. C. A. 263; 102 Fed. 19; revsg. 101 Fed. 33.

122 Mut. L. Ins. Co. v. Thompson, 94 Ky. 253; 22 S. W. 87.

123 Ala. Gold Life Ins. Co. v. Herron, 56 Miss. 643.

124 Insurance Co. v. Colt, 20 Wall. 560.

125 Lee v. Union Cent. L. Ins. Co., 19 Ky. L. 608; 41 S. W. 319. See also Dailey v. Preferred Masonic, etc., Ass'n, 102 Mich. 289; 57 N. W. 184; 26 L. R. A. 171; New York L. Ins. Co. v. Babcock, 104 Ga. 67; 30 S. E. 273; 42 L. R. A. 88; Carter v. Bankers' Life Ins. Co., 83 Neb. 810; 120 N. W. 455; Rose v. Mut. Life Ins. Co., 240 Ill. 45; 88 N. E. 204; Perry v. Security Life & A. Co., 150 N. C. 143; 63 S. E. 679.

126 Crohn v. Order United Commercial Travelers, 170 Mo. App. 273; 156 S. W. 472; Devine v. Federal Life Ins. Co., 250 Ill. 203; 95 N. E. 174; Tuttle v. Iowa State Traveling Men's Ass'n, 132 Ia. 652; 104 N. W. 1131; 7 L. R. A. (N. S.) 223; McCracken v. Travelers' Ins. Co. (Okla.), 156 Pac. 640.

127 Bowman v. Northern Acc. Co., 124 Mo. App. 477, 101 S. W. 691; Starr v. Mut. L. Ins. Co., 41 Wash. 228; 83 Pac. 116.

contract, and it devolves upon the alleged insured to show that the real intention was to pass the legal title and possession of the policy without or before payment of premium, and without delivery in fact, and that though retained by the company's agent, the policy was constructively delivered.[128] It is usually a question of fact, depending upon the special, circumstances of the case, whether anything remained to be done to complete the agreement, or if there was, whether doing it was waived.[129] The proof must be strong to establish such an agreement and mere urging the insured to call and get his policy is enough,[130] but the contract may be complete when the proof is sufficient. For example, in a case in Nevada, the facts shown were that an application was made to the agents of defendant for a policy of insurance on the life of plaintiff's husband; at the time the application was made fifty dollars was paid, according to the regulations of the company, which was to be applied on the first year's premium, provided the defendant should conclude to make the insurance. The application thus made was forwarded to the proper office of the company and a policy made out and sent on to the agent for delivery; but the insured having died before it was delivered, the agent refused to deliver it, although demanded and the balance of the premium tendered. The Court held that this proof justified a conclusion that a contract for a policy was completed. It said:[131] "The application for a policy by the assured, with the payment of a portion of the premium, and acceptance of the risk by the defendant, left nothing to be done but the delivery of the policy and the payment by the plaintiff of the balance of the premium, which, it appears, was not required by the rules of the company until the completion of the transaction. These facts show a valid contract for a policy between the parties. The moment the company concluded to make the insurance, the fifty dollars paid to its agent became its property, without any further action on its part.

128 Heiman v. Phoenix Mut. Life Ins. Co, 17 Minn. 153.

129 Gay v. Farmers', etc., Ins. Co., 51 Mich. 245; Kelly v. St. Louis M. L. Ins. Co., 3 Mo. App. 554; Diboll v. Aetna Life Ins. Co., 32 La. Ann. 179; Fried v. Royal Ins. Co., 50 N. Y. 243; 47 Barb. 127; Cooper v. Ins. Co., 7 Nev. 116; Banker, etc., Ass'n v. Stapp, 77 Tex. 517; 14 S. W. 168.

130 Union Cent. L. Ins. Co. v. Pauley, 8 Ind. App. 85; 35 N. E. 190. See extract, ante, § 352.

131 Cooper v. Pacific Mut. Life Ins. Co., 7 Nev. 122.

It was paid upon the condition that if the company concluded to make the insurance, it should be applied in payment of the premium; when, therefore, the risk was taken, it became the property of the defendant, and at the same time the assured became entitled to the policy. Thus, there was the acceptance of the application by the company, and the payment of a portion of the premium, as a consideration therefor, by the plaintiff, which is all that was necessary to make a valid contract between the parties. Such contracts are as available to sustain an action for the amount of the insurance as if the policy had been issued.[132] Under the terms of a ''binding receipt'' there may be a liability of the company until the application is declined.[133] The insurer is liable on a policy though never actually received by the insured where the premium had been paid, the application accepted and the policy mailed to the agent for delivery. Before the date of the sickness from which the insured died.[134] And so where notes were received for the first premium, the policy was in force, though not actually delivered.[135] Where the application and receipt for the first premium form the only evidence of a contract for a life insurance policy, the Kentucky statute requiring a copy of the application to be attached to the policy does not apply.[136]

§ 355. **The Same Subject: When Contract of Benefit Society is Complete.**—The same principles govern in construing the contracts of benefit societies as in the case of life insurance companies so far as applicable to the special circumstances of the case. In nearly all benefit societies the laws provide for a ceremony of induction into membership and in that case the contract is not complete without initiation.[137] Nor even though there

[132] Kohne v. Insurance Co., etc., 6 Binn. 219; 1 Wash. C. C. 93. See also Shields v. Equitable Mut. L. Ass. Soc., 121 Mich. 690; 80 N. W. 793; Lawrence v. Penn. Mut. L. Ins. Co., 113 La. Ann. 87; 36 Sou. 898.

[133] Halle v. New York Life Ins. Co., 22 Ky. L. R. 740; 58 S. W. 822. But see Mohrstadt v. Mutual Life Ins. Co., 115 Fed. 81; 52 C. C. A. 675.

[134] Unterharscheidt v. Missouri State Life Ins. Co., 160 Ia. 223; 138 N. W. 459.

[135] New York Life Ins. Co. v. Pike, 51 Colo. 238; 117 Pac. 899; Manhattan Life Ins. Co. v. Hereford, 172 Ala. 434, 55 Sou. 497.

[136] Commonwealth L. Ins. Co. v. Davis, 136 Ky. 339; 124 S. W. 345.

[137] Matkin v. Supreme Lodge K. of H., 82 Tex. 301; 18 S. W. 306. See *ante*, § 83.

has been an initiation, if the benefit certificate has not been delivered.[138] The relation between a society and its members is a contractual one and a certificate is not "issued" until it has been delivered to and accepted by the member if the by-laws so require.[139] But delivery may be to an officer of the society for the member.[140] And where partial payment of dues had been accepted it was held there that there was a waiver.[141] Under the by-laws the contract may be complete though no certificate has been issued,[142] or if duly signed not delivered.[143] Where, in order to become fully admitted to membership, it was necessary that two degrees be conferred and the applicant had received one degree, but was too ill to receive the other at the time appointed for him to receive it, and soon afterwards died, never having received it, it was held[144] that the contract was incomplete and that none of the conditions on which beneficiary certificates were issued had been waived. In a case in California[145] it was held that mutual benefit societies which undertake to pay money upon the death of the members are in law insurance companies and subject to the same rules. That whenever two constructions equally fair can be given that which gives the greater indemnity shall prevail. That a contract of insurance

[138] McLendon v. Woodmen of the World, 106 Tenn. 695; 64 S. W. 36; 52 L. R. A. 444; Roblee v. Masonic L. Ass'n, 38 Misc. 481; 77 N. Y. Supp. 1098; National Aid Ass'n v. Bratcher, 65 Neb. 378; 91 N. W. 379; 93 N. W. 1122. In this last case it was held that replevin of the certificate in justice court does not make a delivery. An unauthorized delivery of the certificate is no waiver. Driscoll v. Modern Brotherhood of Am., 77 Neb. 282; 109 N. W. 158.

[139] Logsdon v. Supreme Lodge Frat. Union, 34 Wash. 666; 76 Pac. 292; Wilcox v. Sovereign Camp, etc., 76 Mo. App. 573.

[140] Supreme Court Order Patricians v. Davis, 129 Mich. 318; 88 N. W. 874; Tracy v. Supreme Court of Honor, 4 Neb. unof. 195; 93 N. W. 702. To the contrary Lathrop v. Modern Woodmen of A., 56 Ore. 440; 106 Pac. 328; 109 Pac. 81. But see same case, 126 Pac. 1002.

[141] Home Forum Order v. Jones, 20 Tex. Civ. A. 68; 48 S. W. 219; National Union v. Armstrong, 74 Ill. App. 482; Taylor v. Supreme Lodge Columb. K,. 135 Mich. 231; 97 N. W. 680.

[142] Bishop v. Empire Order M. A., 112 N. Y. 627; 28 N. E. 562; reversing 43 Hun. 472.

[143] Lorscher v. Supreme Lodge K. of H., 72 Mich. 316; 40 N. W. 545.

[144] Taylor v. Grand Lodge A. O. U. W., 29 N. Y. Supp. 773.

[145] Oliver v. Am. Legion of Honor, Sup. Ct., San Francisco, Pac. Coast, L. J., Dec. 9, 1882; 17 Am. L. Rev. 301.

is complete when the terms offered are accepted, and the contract need not be in writing unless required by statute. That the contract may be made through the mail and the terms offered are accepted upon posting a letter to that effect. In mutual benefit societies the benefit certificate is merely evidence of the contract. That the medical examiner cannot reject applications arbitrarily, if made in good faith, after compliance with the requirements of the order and where the medical examiner ought to have approved an application, but the applicant dies before he does so, the application will be deemed approved. It is exceedingly doubtful if this be a true exposition of the law, for it is wrong on principle for the courts to force a construction against the common sense meaning of the language of the contract. In determining whether or not the contract with a benefit society is complete without issue of a certificate, the laws of the association must be alone regarded. The question is one of construction and the courts will save the contract whenever possible, even though a certificate be not issued.[146] It may be a question for the jury whether a certificate has been delivered, the evidence as to delivery being conflicting.[147]

While ordinarily no recovery can be had on a certificate never delivered,[148] or until the certificate is countersigned by the officers of the local lodge and delivered[149] a certificate of membership is not indispensable to the completion of a contract of a fraternal society, but the by-laws may be resorted to to determine the liability.[150] The society has been held liable on a certificate not delivered, the issue being a mere ministerial act,[151] and where the certificate had been missent by the Supreme body[152] and a parol contract by a beneficiary society is valid when the contract has been

---

[146] See also *ante*, § 312, for consideration of this subject.

[147] Wagner v. Supreme Lodge K. & L. of H., 128 Mich. 660; 87 N. W. 903. And parol evidence is admissible when uncertainty as to the time when the contract should become operative exists. Modern Woodmen Acc. Ass'n v. Kline, 50 Neb. 345; 69 N. W. 943.

[148] Alexander v. Woodmen of the World, 161 Ala. 561; 49 Sou. 883.

[149] Sterling v. Head Camp, etc., 28 Utah 505-526; 80 Pac. 375, 1110.

[150] Social Ben. Soc. v. Holms, 1127 Ga. 586; 56 S. E. 775.

[151] Rancipher v. Women of Woodcraft, 50 Wash. 68; 96 Pac. 829.

[152] Sovereign Camp Woodmen of the World v. Dees, 48 Tex. Civ. App. 318; 100 S. W. 366.

completed except as to the issue of the certificate.[153]   The approval
by the Supreme Medical Director of an application for membership is a condition precedent to membership.[154]   The words "in
person" used in the by-laws directing that there shall be no liability until the certificate is delivered to the member in person is not
synonymous with manual possession, but merely intended to require a delivery to the insured himself and not to another for him.
When the member had been initiated and had paid the dues and
the clerk held the certificate, it was a sufficient delivery.[155]

§ 356.   Fraudulent Delivery of Policy.—As has been intimated,
there may be a delivery of the policy to the assured under circumstances that amount to fraud by the latter.   As where the assured
was at the time of the payment of premium by a friend, dangerously
sick.[156]   The understanding is always, where a proposal is made,
that the state of facts therein represented to exist does in fact
exist at the time the proposition is accepted.   So, if after the application has been made, a material change in the health of the applicant takes place, and which would probably cause the rejection
of the risk by the insurer if known to it, will avoid the contract.[157]
Where the agent of a company wrongfully delivers a policy with
knowledge of a materially false representation therein on which
it was issued and that the insured is then suffering from his last
illness, he ceases in that transaction to represent the company, acts
in his individual capacity participating in the fraud of the insured, which vitiates the policy, and his knowledge will not be
imputed to the insurer.[155]   The reason of this rule is so obvious
that it need not be further considered.   When, however, a lapsed

[153] Knights of the Maccabees of the World v. Gordon, 83 Ark. 17; 102
S. W. 711.
[154] Patterson v. Supreme Commandery, etc., 104 Me. 355; 71 Atl. 1015.
[155] O'Neal v. Sovereign Camp Woodmen of the World, 130 Ky. 68; 113
S. W. 52.
[156] Piedmont Ins. Co. v. Ewing, 92 U. S. 377.
[157] Whitley v. Piedmont, etc., Ins. Co., 71 N. C. 480; Wemyss v. Med.
Ins., etc., Soc., 11 Ct. of Sess., 2 Ser. 345; Traill v. Baring, 4 DeGex, J. &
S. 318; Edwards v. Footner, 1 Camp. 530..
[158] Gardner v. North State Mut. Life Ins. Co., 163 N. C. 367, 79 S. E.
806; Ann. Cas. 1915-B 652. See also Sprinkle v. Knights Templar & Masons' L. Indemnity Co., 124 N. C. 405, 32 S. E. 734.

policy is to be reinstated no statement of intermediate changes need be disclosed unless asked for;[159] and so ~with~ changes between the date of the policy and the payment of the premium, unless otherwise stipulated, for the acceptance of the application and issue of the policy are upon the sole condition of payment of premium.[160] Policies delivered by mistake are not binding.[161]

§ 357. **After Contract is Complete Change in Risk Immaterial.** —The subsequent change in the habits of the insured after the delivery of the policy is immaterial, unless otherwise stipulated.[162] After the contract is complete, even though the policy has not been delivered or the premium paid, changes in the condition of the risk do not affect the agreement, as for example, where an application was made for life insurance and the premium tendered, which the agent refused to receive, saying that it made no difference. The policy was issued and received by the agent, who notified the applicant at the place of his residence, that he was insured and that he would bring the policy down the following week and get his money. The agent accordingly did go to the applicant's residence, but finding that he was sick, refused to deliver the policy unless the attending physician would certify that the assured was in no immediate danger. This certificate was given and the money again tendered, but was refused and the assured died two days later. Upon an action being brought on the policy the Supreme Court of Georgia held that the contract was complete upon the delivery of the policy to the agent, who could not subsequently impose additional terms, and the change in the health of the applicant was immaterial.[163] It has been held that where an insurance policy and the application therefor both provide that, if the application

159 Day v. Mut. Ben. L. Ins. Co., 1 McArthur 41.

160 Fourdrinier v. Hartford F. Ins. Co., 15 U. C. (C. P.) 403; Canning v. Farquhar, 16 Q. B. Div. 727.

161 Southern L. Ins. Co. v. Hill, 8 Ga. App. 857; 70 S. E. 186.

162 Life Ins. Co. of Va. v. Hairston, 108 Va. 832; 62 S. E. 1057; Western and Southern L. Ins. Co. v. Davis, 141 Ky. 358; 132 S. W. 710.

163 Southern Life Ins. Co. v. Kempton, 56 Ga. 339; Ellis v. Albany, etc., Ins. Co., 50 N. Y. 402; Schwartz v. Germania L. Ins. Co., 21 Minn. 215; Franklin F. Ins. Co. v. Colt, 20 Wall. 560; City of Davenport v. Peoria, etc., Ins. Co., 17 Ia. 276; Welsh v. Chicago Guaranty F. Soc., 81 Mo. App. 30.

is approved and the policy issued, it shall be in force from the date of the application that the contract shall not take effect until the first premium is paid, during the applicant's continuance in good health, is only a provisional agreement, authorizing the company to withhold delivery of the policy until such payment in good health; and after actual delivery it is estopped, in the absence of fraud, to assert that the policy is void either on account of non-payment of premium or ill health.[164] It has also been held that where an applicant for life insurance became fatally ill after his application for, but before delivery of, his policy, the fact that he reserved the right to inspect it before paying the first premium would not defeat recovery thereon, provided he waived the right and tendered payment, since the reservation was intended solely for his benefit.[165] If the policy does not provide that the insured should be in sound health at the time of its delivery, the company assumes the risk of a change in the health of insured between the time of the application and delivery.[166]

§ 358. **There May Be a Conditional Delivery of Policy.** — A policy of insurance may be conditionally delivered, it being held that, as policies usually are not under seal, the rule that a deed cannot be delivered conditionally to the grantee or his agent has no application.[167] As where policies were delivered to be returned by the insured if he did not realize a satisfactory amount upon the cancellation of certain other policies.[168] But where the policy is once delivered unconditionally, previous negotiations and stipulations are thereby merged and rendered of no effect.[169] The question is one of fact as to what was the intention of the parties and

[164] Grier v. Mut. Life Ins. Co., 132 N. C. 542; 44 S. E. 28. See also Metropolitan Life Ins. Co. v. Moore, 117 Ky. 651; 79 S. W. 219.

[165] Going v. Mut. Ben. Life Ins. Co., 58 S. C. 201; 36 S. E. 556.

[166] New York L. Ins. Co. v. Moats, 125 C. C. A. 143; 207 Fed. 481. See Nealy v. Metropolitan L. Ins. Co., 37 App. D. C. 240.

[167] Harnickell v. N. Y. Life Ins. Co., 40 Hun. 558; affd. 111 N. Y. 390; 18 N. E. 632; Benton v. Martin, 52 N. Y. 570.

[168] Harnickell v. N. Y. Life Ins. Co,. supra. See also Ray v. Equitable L. Ass. Soc., 76 App. Div. 194; 44 N. Y. Supp. 743; Westerfield v. N. Y. Life Ins. Co., 129 Cal. 68; 61 Pac. 667.

[169] Hodge v. Security Ins. Co,. 33 Hun. 583; Grace v. American Cent. Ins. Co., 109 U. S. 278.

of this the jury is the judge. The Supreme Court of Massachusetts has exhaustively discussed this subject in a case that was before it on four different appeals and where it was unable to find a delivery, although the assured had for a time had manual possession of the policy.[170] Of course, where the application stipulates that it shall be the basis of the contract, which shall be completed only by delivery of the policy, the latter must be actually and unconditionally delivered in order to make the insurer liable.[171] The subject of conditional delivery of the policy was discussed by the Supreme Court of Connecticut in Rogers v. The Charter Oak Life Ins. Co.[172] There the agent of the company meeting the applicant urged him to get his life insured and, after some objection from the latter, an application was made out and signed and the applicant examined by the physician. It was agreed that when the policy was made out by the company and received by the agent the latter should forward it to the assured's address in New York City, who, if it was found to be as agreed, was to send the premium or if not to return the policy. When the agent received the policy he mailed it, as agreed, but the letter was returned uncalled for. The agent then sent the policy to the place where he supposed the assured might be, but he had died two days before. The Court held that there was only an inchoate, not a complete, contract and that no liability attached under it. In one case it was held that there was no delivery of the policy, though the insured had possession of it for four months.[173] Delivery of the policy for inspection only is not sufficient to bind the company.[174]

§ 359. **Unconditional Delivery of Policy by Agent in Violation of Instructions.**—Where there has been an unconditional delivery of the policy in violation of the instructions of the company, the

[170] Hoyt v. Mut. Ben. L. Ins. Co., 98 Mass. 539; Markey v. Same, 103 Mass. 78; Same v. Same, 118 Mass. 178; Same v. Same, 126 Mass. 158.

[171] McCully v. Phoenix M. L. Ins. Co., 18 W. Va. 782; St. Louis Mut. Life Ins. Co. v. Kennedy, etc., 6 Bush. 450; Collins v. Ins. Co., 7 Phila. 201; Faunce v. State M. L. Ins. Co., 101 Mass. 279.

[172] 41 Conn. 97.

[173] Poste v. Am. Union L. Ins. Co., 52 N. Y. Supp. 910; 32 App. Div. 189; affd. 165 N. Y. 631; 59 N. E. 1129.

[174] Coffin v. New York L. Ins. Co., 62 C. C. A. 415; 127 Fed. 555; Amos-Ritchie v. Northwestern Mut. L. Ins. Co., 143 Mich. 684; 107 N. W. 707.

latter will generally be bound. For example, in a case in the Supreme Court of the United States the facts were these: A policy had been taken from agents who had only authority to take applications and submit them to the company, which issued the policies and sent them to the agents to deliver and collect the premium. The agents were instructed not to deliver the policies until the whole premium was paid, but were told if they did so the premium would stand charged to them until it was received by the company or the policies returned. It was the custom of the agents to deliver policies to persons whom they deemed responsible and call for the money when wanted. In this case the policy was sent to the assured by the agents, who wrote him that they would get the money of a third person. Upon the refusal of this third person to pay, the agents so informed the assured, who promised to soon send a draft. Payment being still neglected, and the agents having learned that the person assured was "quite sick" they informed him by letter that the policy was forfeited and returned the premium notes he had given. This letter did not reach the address of the assured until after his death. The Court held the company liable, saying:[175] "Where the policy is delivered without requiring payment, the presumption is, especially if it is a stock company, that a credit was intended, and the rule is well settled where a credit is intended, that the policy is valid, though the premium was not paid at the time the policy was delivered, as where credit is given by the general agent and the amount is charged to him by the company, the transaction is equivalent to payment."[176] In a somewhat similar case in Tennessee the facts were that the assured applied for a policy to one Smithurst, the agent of the company for Louisiana, who sent the application to the home office of the company in Memphis, where it was accepted and the policy issued.

[175] Miller v. Life Ins. Co., 12 Wall. 285. Other cases where the company has been held liable, either because of an implied authority of the agent to waiver, or because of the application of the doctrine of estoppel, are Home Forum v. Varnado (Tex. Civ. A.), 55 S. W. 364; Harrigan v. Home L. Ins. Co., 128 Cal. 531; 58 Pac. 180; National L. Ins. Co. v. Tweddell, 22 Ky. L. 881; 58 S. W. 699.

[176] The Court Cite Golt v. Ins. Co., 25 Barb. 189; Sheldon v. Atlantic F. & M. Ins. Co., 26 N. Y. 460; Wood v. Ins. Co., 32 N. Y. 619; Bragdon v. Ins. Co., 42 M. E. 259; Trustees v. Ins. Co., 18 Barb 69; 19 N. W. 305.

Part of the premium was to be paid by note, the remainder in cash, the agent being instructed to deliver the policy only upon the actual payment of the cash part of the premium. On its face the policy acknowledged receipt of the premium, but the application, shown to be a part of the contract, stipulated that the policy should not be binding upon the company "until the amount of the premium as stated therein shall have been received by said company, or some authorized agent thereof, during the lifetime of the person assured." Smithurst delivered the policy without the cash payment, accepting the note of the assured for the amount. Soon after, Smithurst was succeeded by Hatch & Smith as agents, and they found that the policy had been delivered without payment of the cash part of the premium. A draft was drawn for the amount, accepted by the assured, but was not paid and was afterwards surrendered and a note taken which was not paid, although payment was frequently demanded. Soon afterwards the assured died. The Court held[177] that the company was liable and that Smithurst was a general agent of the company and, "being a general agent, without special instructions limiting his power, he has the power to determine for himself what he is willing to accept as a payment of the cash premium—when the cash is actually paid to him, the company can only look to him for it—if he chooses to receive something else than cash, it is probable that as between him and his principal, the latter would have the right to treat it as a cash payment to him and hold him responsible accordingly—so that the company would have, if they choose to exercise it, the same right they had before, and the agent only would be the loser." In the case of mutual companies the rule might not apply if there was any by-law of the company to a different effect, for the applicant is supposed to acquaint himself with the laws of the concern. But the question is one of construction and of the intent of the parties.[178]

§ 360. **Commencement and Duration of Risk.**—Practically all the modern life insurance policies contain a stipulation in language much the same, to the effect that the contract shall only take ef-

[177] Southern Life Ins. Co. v. Booker, 9 Heisk. 606; 24 Am. Rep. 344.
[178] Mulrey v. Shawmut Mut., etc., Ins. Co., 4 Allen 116; Badger v. American Popular L. Ins. Co., 103 Mass. 244; Aetna F. Ins. Co. v. Webster, 6 Wall. 129.

fect upon delivery to the insured while in good health and upon payment of the first premium, whether annual, semi-annual, or quarterly. We have seen that this stipulation is valid and that the policy will not be in force until delivered in accordance with the stipulation of the parties, unless the condition has been waived, or under such circumstances as demand a different conclusion. Very often an interval elapses between the date of the policy and the delivery and the payment of the first premium. Sometimes, because the policy is dated the same as the application, there may be a greater or less period elapsing before the policy takes effect. In regard to the date when the policy takes effect, the intention of the parties will govern. In the absence of evidence to the contrary an insurance policy will be presumed to take effect from its date.[179] In the case of Noyes v. Phoenix Mutual Life Ins. Co.,[180] Judge Bakewell, speaking for the Court, says: "When the defendant accepted the risk they fixed the date from which it was to begin, in the written policy signed by them and mailed to their agent. That date is said to be the date on which the policy should be countersigned by the agent at St. Joseph. Their agreement said, as plainly as words could say it: We accept this risk, to commence at such date after the arrival of this policy at St. Joseph as shall be fixed by our agent, who shall evidence it by countersigning the policy, and by the same act give this contract life. There is no other date whatever mentioned in the policy for the commencement of the risk. . . . The most that can be said is that negotiations had gone thus far—that defendant had said that their agent, on the arrival of the policy, might make a contract with Noyes on the terms therein named. It is difficult to see what language more fitted to convey this idea could be employed. Not only does defendant expressly say that there is no contract until the policy has been countersigned after its arrival at St. Joseph, but it fixes the date of the commencement of the risk at a future, uncertain times, to be determined by this act."

Where an interval elapses between the date of the policy and the time when it becomes effective by delivery and payment of the

[179] Andersen v. Mut. L. Ins. Co., 164 Cal. 712; 130 Pac. 726; Ann. Cas. 1914-B 903.

[180] 1 Mo. App. 591.

first premium, it must be deemed the intention of the parties that
for the annual premium paid by the insured he should receive its
full equivalent. The litigation in the celebrated McMaster case is
an illustration in point. A suit in equity was brought by the administrator of the estate of McMaster against the insurance company claiming a reformation of certain policies on the ground that
the provision inserted therein making the second annual premium
payable on the 12th day of December, 1894, was not in accordance
with the agreement of the parties, it being intended by them that
the premiums should be payable later, because although the policies provided that the annual premium should be payable on December 12, the policies were dated December 18 and were not delivered until December 26, and inasmuch as the policies were not
to go into effect until delivery, the latter date was the actual date
for the payment of the second annual premium. The Court[181] entered a decree reforming the policy as prayed. Whereupon an
appeal was taken to the Circuit Court of Appeals where that decree was reversed, the Court, holding that the policies in the form
in which they were delivered must be held to represent a contract
of the parties and that no recovery could be had on the policies
either at law or in equity.[182] Plaintiff then brought an action at
law to recover on the policies and the trial judge rendered an elaborate opinion, wherein he argued[183] that the plaintiff ought to recover, but because of the opinion of the Circuit Court of Appeals
he felt bound to enter judgment for the defendant. An appeal was
taken by the plaintiff and the Appellate Court[184] affirmed the judgment of the lower court. Judge Caldwell, however, dissented and
argued that the insured was entitled to the full period of insurance for which the premium was paid and that when McMaster
received the policies dated December 18 and on December 26 paid
the premium, he was justified in assuming that if he died within
a year thereafter the policies would be paid. A writ of *certiorari*
was granted to the Supreme Court of the United States.[185] The
Court, in opinion rendered by Chief Justice Fuller, reversed the

[181] McMaster Admr. v. New York Life Ins. Co., 78 Fed. 33.
[182] New York Life Ins. Co. v. McMaster, 87 Fed. 63.
[183] 90 Fed. 40.
[184] 99 Fed. 856.
[185] McMaster v. New York Life Ins. Co., 183 U. S. 25.

judgment of the Circuit Court of Appeals. The Court said: "To hold the insurance forfeitable for non-payment of another premium within the year for which payment had already been fully made would be to contradict the legal effect under the application and policies of the first annual payment. Clearly, such a construction is uncalled for, if the words 'the 12th day of December in every year thereafter' could be assumed to mean in every year after the year for which the premiums had been paid. But if not, taking all the provisions together, and granting that the words included December 12, 1894, nevertheless, it would not follow that forfeiture cóuld be availed of to cut short the thirteen months' indemnity from December. 18, 1893, as the premiums had already been paid up to December 18, 1894. And the company could not be allowed, on this record, by making the second premiums payable within the period covered by the payment of the first premium, to defeat the right to the month of grace which had been proffered as the inducement to the applications, and had been relied on as secured by the payment. If death had occurred on December 18, 1894, or between the 12th and 18th, it is quite clear that recovery could have been had, and as the contracts were for life, and were not determinable (at least for twenty years) at a fixed date, but only by forfeiture, it appears to us that the applicable rules of construction forbid the denial of the month of grace in whole or in part.

It is worthy of remark that it was specifically provided that after the policies had been in force one full year they should become incontestable on any other ground than non-payment of premiums, and we suppose it will not be contended that if any other ground of contest had existed and death had occurred between December 12 and December 18, the company would have been cut off from making its defense, because the policies had been in force 'one full year' from December 12. And if not in force until December 18, the date of actual issue, how can it be said that liability to forfeiture accrued before the twelve months had elapsed?

The truth is, the policies were not in force until December 18, and as the premiums were to be paid annually, and were so paid in advance on delivery, the second payments were not demandable on December 12, 1894, as a condition of the continuance of the policies from the 12th to the 18th. And as the policies could not be forfeited for non-payment during that time, the month of grace could not be shortened by deducting the six days which belonged to McMaster of right. In our opinion the payment of the first year's premiums made the policies non-forfeitable for the period of thirteen months, and inasmuch as the death of McMaster took place within that period, the alleged forfeiture furnished no defense to the action.''

The same question arose in the case of Stinchcombe v. New York Life Ins. Co.[186] By the terms of the policy in that case the premium was payable on the 5th day of May in every year; the policy, however, was not delivered and the two years' premium paid until July 24, 1894. The insured died July 3, 1896. The Court held that the policy was in force at the time of the death and that any other interpretation would deprive the assured of a period of insurance that he had actually paid for. On much a similar state of facts the Supreme Court of Minnesota arrived at a similar conclusion,[187] and so did the Supreme Court of Missouri.[188] Other courts have held that the parties have a right to agree for conditions for forfeiture and that the policy being the contract of the parties, both are bound by its terms.[189] These cases distinguish the McMaster case on the ground that in that case the application was altered by the company so that the question of the decision of the Court was really bottomed on fraud. In the absence of an agreement as to time the policy shall take effect, it does not take effect until it is issued and the word issue is said to be used in the sense of preparing and signing the policy, but does not include delivery.[190] In the

---

[186] 46 Ore. 316; 80 Pac. 230.

[187] Stramback v. Fidelity Mut. L. Ins. Co., 94 Minn. 281; 102 N. W. 731.

[188] Halsey v. American Central Life Ins. Co., 258 Mo. 659; 167 S. W. 951. See also Stout v. Mo. Fidelity & Cas. Co. (Mo. App.), 179 S. W. 993, and Edington v. Michigan Mut. L. Ins. Co., 134 Tenn. 188; 183 S. W. 728.

[189] Jewett v. Northwestern Life Ins. Co., 149 Mich. 79; 112 N. W. 734; McConnell v. Provident Life Ins. Co., 92 Fed. 769; Tibbitts v. Mutual Life Ins. Co., 159 Ind. 671; Tigg v. Register L. & A. Ins. Co., 152 Ia. 720; 133 N. W. 322; Armstrong v. Provident, etc., Soc., 2nd Ont. Law R. 771; Mut. Life Ins. Co. v. Stegal, 1 Ga. App. 611; 58 S. E. 79; Johnson v. Mut. Ben. L. Ins. Co., 143 Fed. 950; Carrollton v. American, etc., Ins. Co., 115 Fed. 77; Wilkie v. New York L. Ins. Co., 146 N. C. 513; 60 S. E. 427; Rose v. Mut. Life Ins. Co., 240 Ill. 45.

[190] Dargan v. Equitable Life Assur. Soc., 71 S. C. 350; 51 S. E. 125.

case of Homestead Fire Ins. Co. v. Ison,[191] the Court says: "Issue as used in reference to the issuance of an insurance policy means when the policy is made and delivered and is in full effect and operation." In the case of Anderson v. Mutual Life Ins. Co.[192] the Court said: "It must, of course, be admitted, in accordance with the respondent's claims, that the expressions 'date of this policy' and 'issuance of this policy' are not, according to the ordinary acceptation of the terms, synonymous. The word 'issuance' as applied to a contract like a policy of insurance, would, if standing alone, probably be taken to mean, either the signing (without delivery) of the contract by the authorized officers of the insuring company,[193] or, perhaps, the act of delivery of a fully written and signed policy.[194] But in construing any writing, the usual definition of a single word is not a conclusive test of the meaning to be attributed to it in the connection in which it is found. We must endeavor to ascertain, from an examination of the entire instrument, read in the light of the circumstances surrounding its execution, the sense which the parties employed the particular phrase in question." So in the case of Stringham v. Mutual Ins. Co.[195] the Court said: "We will dispose first of the controversy relative to the meaning of the term 'issued' as employed in the application, it being insisted on the part of the plaintiff that it signifies simply the completion and signing up of the policy by the secretary and its execution at the office of the company, while upon the other hand, it is contended that it includes as well the delivery of the policy to the applicant. Among the many cases that have passed under our notice, the term seems to have been used interchangeably to denote either one or the other of these conditions, but we have been cited to no case that attempts to determine as a general rule when an insurance policy is deemed issued. We are impressed that the term has a double application, and its meaning is to be determined by the relation in which it is employed."

[191] 110 Va. 18, 65 S. E. 463.

[192] 164 Cal. 712; 130 Pac. 726; Ann. Cas. 1914-B 903.

[193] Kansas Mut. Life Ins. Co. v. Coalson, 22 Tex. Civ. App. 64; 54 S. W. 388; Stringham v. Mut. Ins. Co., 44 Ore. 447; 75 Pac. 822.

[194] Logsdon v. Supreme Lodge of Fraternal Union of America, 34 Wash. 666; 76 Pac. 292; Homestead Fire Ins. Co. v. Ison, 110 Va. 18; 65 S. E. 463; Sisk v. Citizens' Ins. Co., 16 Ind. App. 565; 45 N. E. 804.

[195] 44 Ore. 447; 75 Pac. 822.

§ 361. **Rescission.**—A life policy may as a matter of course be rescinded by mutual consent of the parties. They have the same power to rescind as they had to make the contract.[196] It is also an elemental principle in the law of contracts that one party can rescind upon tendering back the consideration received, whenever he has been induced to enter into the contract by the fraud of the other. Such fraud can be either by a fraudulent misrepresentation of a fact or a fraudulent concealment of something that in good faith ought to have been disclosed, and because of the non-disclosure of which the other party has been misled to his injury. This principle applies to its fullest extent to insurance contracts. Two classes of cases are found in the reports where the right of rescission has been considered. In one the company has claimed the right because of the fraud of the insured, generally a fraudulent misrepresentation or concealment. In the other, and the most numerous class of cases, the insured has claimed the right on account of the alleged fraud of the company, generally consisting of untrue representations of over-zealous, or knavish agents, or promises which were not realized. The rule is not one-sided, but should be applied impartially to right a wrong by whomsoever committed. In fire insurance contracts the company generally reserves the right to cancel the policy under certain conditions, or arbitrarily, and this right of rescission, or cancellation, in aid of which the powers of a court of equity are invoked, is a principle of importance also in life insurance law which will be further considered in another place.[197] In life insurance contracts, however, rescission on the part of the company may be attended with this important difference; it is not always possible for the company to put the insured in *statu quo* because his health may have become impaired so that he is not able to obtain insurance elsewhere.[198] The right of cancellation may, however, be reserved in a life insurance contract and if so reserved can be

---

[196] Equitable I. Assur. Soc. v. Stough, 45 Ind. App. 411; 89 N. E. 612; Akers v. Hite, 94 Pa. St. 394; German Ins. Co. v. Davis (Ark.), 12 S. W. 155.

[197] *Post*, § 372.

[198] Mut. Ben. L. Ins. Co. v. Robinson, 54 Fed. 580; Kellner v. Mut. Ins. Co., 43 Fed. 623.

asserted.[199] It is too late to rescind when the contract is ended by death.[200] The status of the beneficiary is fixed by the death of the insured and cannot be changed by an attempted rescission.[201] But in a case in California,[202] where the policy provided that the policy should not take effect unless at the time it was delivered the insured was in good health and at the time of delivery the insured was just recovering from an attack of typhoid fever, the Court held that in the absence of knowledge on the part of the company at the time of delivery of this fact the policy was properly rescinded. A cancellation is void where the secretary appropriated the money sent to pay dues to reimburse himself for dues previously advanced by him.[203] If the agent of a company, without knowledge of the assured, inserts in the application such misrepresentations as would, if made by the assured, avoid the policy, the assured may rescind the contract although the policy is binding upon the company.[204] So where the policy required all applications to be signed by the one proposed for insurance as a condition precedent to its validity, and the agent who solicited the plaintiff to insure her father's life for her benefit certified that he had seen and examined the father and recommended his acceptance when in fact the father's name was signed by the daughter on the agent's representation that she had authority to do so, it was held that the agent's knowledge as to the failure of the father to sign the application was the knowledge of the company, and, as the policy was void *ab initia,* the plaintiff was entitled to recover back the money paid by her for premiums. It was also held that since the policy was void, neither could revive

[199] Gerken v. Royal Ben. Soc., 18 App. Div. 38; 45 N. Y. Supp. 384; Travelers' Prot. Ass'n v. Dewey, 34 Tex. Civ. A. 419; 78 S. W. 1087.

[200] Porter v. Mut. L. Ins. Co., 70 Vt. 504; 41 Atl. 970; Metropolitan L. Ins. Co. v. Moore, 117 Ky. 651; 79 S. W. 219. See also Jones v. Commercial Travelers' Mut. Ass'n, 114 N. Y. Supp. 589; Pilgrims' Health, etc., v. Scott, 12 Ga. App. 749; 78 S. E. 469.

[201] Oplinger v. New York Life Ins. Co. (Pa.), 98 Atl. 568.

[202] Security Life Ins. Co. v. Booms (Cal. App.), 159 Pac. 1000.

[203] Cunningham v. Modern Brotherhood of Am., 96 Neb. 827; 148 N. W. 918.

[204] Michigan Mut. L. Ins. Co. v. Reed, 84 Mich. 524; 47 N. W. 1106. -

it without the consent of the other.[205] Generally where a life insurance company violates its contract the assured may   elect
whether to enforce the contract, or to treat it as rescinded and sue
to recover back the premiums paid with interest,[206] The same
rule applies when payment of premiums has been induced by
fraud.[207] Or where demand is made for larger premiums than
provided for by the contract.[208] Or by scaling down the amount
agreed to be paid.[209] If payment of excessive premiums has been
made under protest without fraud or duress the excess if wrongfully exacted can be recovered.[210] It has been held,[211] that one
who is the agent of an insurance company for the purpose of receiving applications for insurance has authority to agree, for the
company, that a life policy shall in its second year be reduced one-
half in amount, and if this agreement is repudiated by the company the assured can rescind and recover back the amount of the
first year's premium. If the association changes its system of doing business, so as to reduce the funds to which the member has
to look for the payment of the insurance contracted for, he can
rescind the contract of insurance and recover back the assessments paid thereon.[212] Or when a benefit society exceeds its

205 Fulton v. Metropolitan L. Ins. Co., 4 Misc. 76; 23 N. Y. Supp. 598;
affg. 21 N. Y. Supp. 470; Brewster v. National L. Ins. Co., 8 Times L. R.
648; Bawden v. London, etc., Co. (Ct. App.), 8 Times L. R. 566; Metropolitan L. Ins. Co. v. Asmus, 25 Ky. L. 1550; 78 S. W. 204.

206 Van Werden v. Equitable L. Ass. Soc., 99 Ia. 621; 68 N. W. 892; Mut.
L. Ins. Co. v. Elliot, 93 Tex. 144; 53 S. W. 1014; Key v. National L. Ins.
Co., 107 Ia. 446; 78 N. W. 68; McCarty v. N. Y. L. Ins. Co., 74 Minn. 530;
77 N. W. 426.

207 Hogben v. Metropolitan L. Ins. Co., 69 Conn. 503; 38 Atl. 214; God-
frey v. N. Y. L. Ins. Co., 70 Minn. 224; 73 N. W. 1.

208 Gwaltney v. Provident Sav. L. Ass. Soc., 130 N. C. 629; 41 S. E. 795.

209 Supreme Counc. v. Daix, 130 Fed. 101; Blach v. Supreme Counc.,
etc., 59 C. C. A. 414; 123 Fed. 650; Mowatt v. Prov. Sav. L. A. Soc., 27 Ont.
App. 675; Supreme Counc., etc., v. Batte, 34 Tex. C. A. 456; 70 S. W.
629; O'Neill v. Supreme Counc., etc., 70 N. J. L. 410; 57 Atl. 463; Lippencott v. Sup. Cl., etc., 130 Fed. 483.

210 Rosenfeld v. Boston Mut. L. Ins. Co., 222 Mass. 284; 110 N. E. 304.

211 Sengfelder v. Mut. L. Ins. Co. of N. Y., 5 Wash. 121; 31 Pac. 428.
For a case where it was held that the agent had no authority: Palmer v.
Metropolitan L. Ins. Co., 21 App. Div. 287; 47 N. Y. Supp. 347.

212 People Mut. Ins. Fund v. Bricken, 92 Ky. 297; 17 S. W. 625.

charter powers and engages in an unlawful business in unlawful ways the members can refuse to pay further assessments without forfeiting the payments already made and can have the fund accumulated distributed among the certificate holders.[213] But where the beneficiary named in a certificate has no insurable interest he cannot recover from the association dues and assessments paid by him for the insurance as for money paid on a consideration which has failed, if the association had no notice that the beneficiary, and not the assured, was paying such dues and assessments.[214] We append in a note reference to additional cases where the right of rescission on the part of the assured has been upheld and recovery allowed.[215] A policy of life insurance is not rescinded by the company merely by offering to return the premium to the assured if the assured himself does not accept such premium and surrender the policy.[216] If one has insured his life for the benefit of another he cannot rescind without tendering a release from the beneficiary of the policy.[217] In the case of Lewis v. New York Life Ins. Co.[218] it was said that the failure to perform does not afford ground for rescission unless it be such as to defeat the object of the contract and not simply go to a subsidiary part of it which can be fully compensated for in damages, and the refusal of a loan will not justify rescission.[219] The rule is otherwise where the

[213] Fogg et al. v. Sup. Lodge Golden Lion, 156 Mass. 431; 31 N. E. 289.

[214] Knights & Ladies of Honor v. Burke (Tex.), 15 S. W. 45. See also Nix v. Donovan, 18 N. Y. Supp. 435; Wheeler v. Mut. Res. F. L. Ass'n, 102 Ill. App. 48; Brokamp v. Metropolitan L. Ins. Co., 8 Ohio Dec. 116.

[215] McKay v. N. Y. Life Ins. Co., 124 Cal. 270; 56 Pac. 1112; Delouche v. Metropolitan Life Ins. Co., 69 N. H. 587; 45 Atl. 414; LaMarche v. Mut. L. Ins. Co., 126 Cal. 498; 58 Pac. 1053; Home Forum v. Varnado (Tex. Civ. App.), 55 S. W. 364; American Union L. Ins. Co. v. Wood (Tex. Civ. App), 57 S. W. 685; Metropolitan Life Ins. Co. v. Smith, 22 Ky. L. 868; 59 S. W. 24; McCann v. Metropolitan L. Ins. Co., 177 Mass. 280; 58 N. E. 1026; Stillwell v. Covenant Life Ins. Co., 83 Mo. App. 215; Bennett v. Mass. Mut. L. Ins. Co., 107 Tenn. 371; 64 S. W. 758. Recovery has been allowed though the applicant misrepresented his occupation. McDonald v. Metropolitan Life Ins. Co., 68 N. H. 4; 38 Atl. 500.

[216] McCollom v. N. Y. Mut. L. Ins. Co., 55 Hun. 103; 8 N. Y. Supp. 249.

[217] Jurgens v. N. Y. Life Ins. Co., 114 Cal. 161; 45 Pac. 1045.

[218] 104 C. C. A. 181; 181 Fed. 433; 30 L. R. A. (N. S.), 1202.

[219] See also New York Life Ins. Co. v. Pope, 24 Ky. L. 485; 68 S. W. 851.

agreement to make the loan was the inducement to the contract.[220]
The question whether the assured has acted with due diligence in
rescinding the contract is one for the jury.[221]

§ 362. **The Same Subject—Further Illustrations.**—The right
of an insurance company to rescind may be lost because of the
effect of the incontestable clause, or by failing to give prompt
notice of its election to rescind.[222] In order to defend a suit on an
insurance policy upon the grounds of false representations the
company must show that the contract has been rescinded and the
premiums tendered back, because such a contract is not void but
only voidable.[223] A company rescinding the policy must restore
the premium.[224] An insurer electing to avoid the policy for fraud
need only after death of the insured make such election known to
the beneficiary and it may pay or tender the premiums to the
beneficiary. It is not necessary to procure the appointment of an
administrator.[225] The father and mother of a minor as guardians
by nature cannot consent to a cancellation of a policy on the life
of a minor.[226] Where the only promise made by insurer was to
pay a sum of money on the death of the plaintiff, the fact that the
insurer wrongfully declared the contract void and denied that
plaintiff had any rights, did not constitute a breach of the contract
during the life of plaintiffs, nor justify a recovery of damages by

[220] Key v. National L. Ins. Co., 107 Ia. 446; 78 N. W. 68.

[221] Norton v. Gleason, 61 Vt. 474; 18 Atl. 45. In regard to the admissibility of evidence as to dealings with other policyholders and other
questions of evidence in cases of rescission, see Thompson v. N. Y. L. Ins.
Co., 21 Ore. 466; 28 Pac. 628. As to cancellation by the company of an accident policy, see *post*, § 545a.

[222] Mut. Life Ins. Co. v. Finkelsten (Ind. App.), 107 N. E. 557; American Central Life Ins. Co. v. Rosenstein, 46 Ind. App. 537; 92 N. E. 380;
affg. 88 N. E. 997; Supreme Tribe of Ben Hur v. Lennert, 172 Ind. 122; 98
N. E. 115; reversing 93 N. E. 869; 94 N. E. 889.

[223] State Life Ins. Co. v. Jones, 48 Ind. App. 186; 92 N. E. 879.

[224] Metropolitan Life Ins. Co. v. Johnson, 49 Ind. App. 233; 94 N. E. 785;
Catholic Order of Foresters v. Collins, 51 Ind. App. 285; 99 N. E. 745;
Metropolitan Life Ins. Co. v. Friedman, 159 Mich. 144; 123 N. W. 547.

[225] American Central Life Ins. Co. v. Rosenstein, 46 Ind. App. 537; 88
N. E. 97; 92 N. E. 380. If a premium note has been received it must be
tendered back. Iowa Life Ins. Co. v. Haughton, 46 Ind. App. 467; 85 N.
E. 127; 87 N. E. 702.

[226] Burke v. Prudential Ins. Co., 221 Mass. 253; 108 N. E. 1069.

him.[227] But, generally, a pérsòn induced by fraud to take out a life policy may rescind and recover back the consideration.[228] Insolvency of the company justifies a rescission of the contract and recovery of the consideration.[229] Where a certificate is void because of misrepresentation, the beneficiaries are entitled to recover the premiums paid thereon.[230] One whose name is stricken from the membership roll on discovery that he was over the age limit when admitted cannot recover the dues and assessments paid as for failure of consideration.[231] No recovery of premiums can be had in Florida on a policy of a mutual benefit association held to be *ultra vires* under the laws of Alabama, that being the home state of the corporation.[232] Insured under a life insurance contract is not entitled to rescind and to a return of the premiums paid because of the refusal of the company to make him a loan on the policy,[233] or because of the company's failure to pay him a commission on other business as agreed, where he had violated his agreement to assist in obtaining business.[234] Where the policy had run for about ten years and the company persuaded the insured to exchange it for a new form of policy which was a twenty-payment life policy, the old one being a level premium policy, in making the exchange ap-

[227] Kelley v. Mut. Life Ins. Co., 186 N. Y. 16; 78 N. E. 584; reversing 64 N. Y. Supp. 681.

[228] Glassner v. Johnston, 133 Wis. 485; 113 N. W. 977; Leirheimer v. Mut. Life Ins. Co., 122 Mo. App. 374; 99 S. W. 525; Mut. Life Ins. Co. v. Hargus (Tex. Civ. App.), 99 S. W. 880; Caldwell v. Life Ins. Co., 140 N. C. 100; 52 S. E. 252; Anderson v. New York Life Ins. Co., 34 Wash. 616; 70 Pac. 109; Urwan v. Northwestern Nat. Life Ins. Co., 125 Wis. 349; 103 N. W. 1102.

[229] Moore v. Mut. Reserve Fund Life Ass'n, 106 N. Y. Supp. 255; 121 App. Div. 335.

[230] Royal Neighbors of America v. Spore, 160 Ky. 572; 169 S. W. 984. But see Criscuolo v. Societa, etc., 89 Conn. 249; 93 Atl. 532.

[231] Currier v. Catholic Order of Foresters, 87 Vt. 83; 88 Atl. 525. See also Elliott v. Knights of the Modern Maccabees, 46 Wash. 320; 89 Pac. 929.

[232] Southern Mut. Aid Ass'n v. Cobb, 60 Fla. 198; 53 Sou. 505.

[233] Lewis v. New York Life Ins. Co., 104 C. C. A. 181; 181 Fed. 433; 30 L. R. A. (N. S.), 1202.

[234] Central Life Assur. Soc. v. Mulford, 45 Colo. 240; 100 Pac. 423. See as to other cases refusing the insured right to rescind. Smith v. Smith, 86 Ark. 284; 110 S. W. 1038; Clements v. Life Ins. Co. of Virginia, 155 N. C. 57; 70 S. E. 1076.

pellant's agent presented to the insured for his signature a note for the first year's premium, an application and a certificate of loan, the certificate of loan was an acknowledgment of an interest-bearing indebtedness amounting to $299.10, which was a lien on the policy which was for $1,000, and it carried itself without attention from the policyholder until his death, when so much of it as would not be absorbed by dividends would be deducted from the face of the policy. The insured was deceived by the appearance of the papers and the representations of the agent of the company and he executed the papers without knowing what the loan certificate was, and there was nothing on the face of the new policy to disclose the existence of a certificate of loan. Under these circumstances, it was held that the insured could rescind and recover the excess payment made under the new policy.[235] Where the insured after an increase in assessments tendered the former assessment, his action was an election to stand on the contract as still in force and was final and he could not afterwards maintain an action in disaffirmance of the contract on the ground that the increase of assessments was a breach of the contract.[236] If the beneficiary in a life policy has a vested interest the insured cannot surrender the policy for cancellation.[237] Otherwise, where the right to surrender is reserved in the policy,[238] and an endowment will be payable in spite of the wrongful surrender of the policy.[239]

§ 363. **The Same Subject—Measure of Damages.**—The authorities are far from agreeing what the measure of damages is for the wrongful cancellation of a policy. We apprehend that different rulings apply in regard to policies of regular life insurance and those of assessment, or beneficiary, insurance. In the one case a reserve is accumulated from the excess payments, while in the other the insurance is only carried from one payment to the next.

[235] Green v. Security Mut. Life Ins. Co., 159 Mo. App. 277; 140 S. W. 325.

[236] Blakeley v. Fidelity Mut. Life Ins. Co., 83 C. C. A. 155; 154 Fed. 43; affg. 143 Fed. 619.

[237] Mut. Life Ins. Co. v. Allen, 212 Ill. 134; 72 N. E. 200; Lawrence v. Penn. Mut. Life Ins. Co., 113 La. 87; 36 Sou. 898.

[238] Grice v. Illinois Ins. Co., 122 Ky. 572; 92 S. W. 560.

[239] Hopkins v. Northwestern National Life Ins. Co., 41 Wash. 592; 83 Pac. 1019.

In the case of Kelly v. Security Mutual Life Ins. Co.[240] it was said that the measure of damages is ascertained by discounting the amount of the policy for the number of years of insured's expectancy of life and deducting from that sum the discounted premiums for the same period. In the case of Merrick v. Northwestern Life Ins. Co.[241] the Court approved the rule laid down in Clemmitt v. New York Life Ins. Co.[242] and said :[243] "Where breach occurred and suit is brought during insured's life, and he dies before judgment, the value of the policy is the present value as at the date of the insurance company's repudiation of the sum assured, and payable at the death of the assured, to be diminished, however, at the same date, by the present value of the premiums previously subsequently accrued, and also by the amount of the premiums previously accrued (which are unpaid) and interest thereon? It was there strongly intimated that, even if the assured had been 'alive at the date of the judgment, with no decrease of health except from efflux of time' still she might have recovered such damages as she had actually sustained. It was there said that 'the rule to ascertain the value of a life policy is laid down in Universal Ins. Co. v. Binford.'[243] In that case the company was insolvent, and it was held that the policyholder was entitled to a sum of money which 'would purchase from a solvent company a policy of the same kind, for the same amount, and for the same rate of premium' and that such amount was ascertainable 'by treating the difference between the premiums paid the defendant company and the premiums to be paid to the new insuring company as an annuity for the assured's expectation of life, and calculating its cash value.' In the case at bar the company is solvent, and the assured is in poor health, and is not insurable. In Georgia it has been held that, where the company has breached the contract, the holder of the policy was entitled to 'recover any damages he may have sustained in consequence thereof.[244] It has been held in New

[240] 94 N. Y. Supp. 601; 106 App. 352; reversed on other grounds, 186 N. Y. 16; 78 N. E. 584.
[241] 124 Wis. 231; 102 N. W. 593.
[242] 76 Va. 355; 77 Va. 366.
[243] 76 Va. 103.
[243] 76 Va. 103.
[244] The A. G. I. Ins. Co. v. Garmany, 74 Ga. 51.

York that, where the policyholder is entitled to recover damages for the breach of the contract, the measure of his damages 'is the value of the policy destroyed; and in ascertaining this resort may properly be had to tables used in the business of life insurance, showing the average expectancy of life.'[245]   In a later case in New York it was held: 'That if, at the time of the refusal of the defendant to accept the premiums, the life of the plaintiff's father was still insurable, the measure of his damages was the difference between the then present value of the premiums he would have been compelled to pay during the life of his father under the policy issued by the defendant and the present value of the premiums which he would be compelled to pay under a policy which could then be obtained from another responsible company; that if at that time the life of his father was not insurable, his damages would be the actual value of the policy at the time of the breach, as being a valid and obligatory claim against an entirely responsible company.'[246]   In that State it is held that in case of such breach of the company the policyholder is entitled to recover as damages the value of the policy at the time of the breach.[247] The latest case in that State which has come to our attention, and applicable here, is Toplitz v. Bauer,[248] where it was said by the Court and held that 'The insurance company, having thus canceled its obligation, refused to reinstate it. The plaintiffs are entitled to complete indemnity for the loss thus sustained and the inquiry was, what was the loss in contemplation of law? . . . The reasonable and just rule of damages in such cases would seem to be the cost of replacing the policy on the same terms in a perfectly sound company at the time of the surrender, but the pledger had then ceased to be an insurable risk under any circumstances existing in the business of insurance; so that the real loss was the face of the policy less what it would cost to carry it by payment of another premium which fell due before the death of the insured.' " In the case of Mutual Reserve Fund Life Ass'n v.

[245] People v. Security Life Ins. & A. Co., 78 N. Y. 114, 125, 126; 34 Am. St. Rep. 522.

[246] Speer v. Phoenix M. L. Ins. Co., 36 Hun. 322.

[247] Farley v. U. M. L. Ins. Co., 41 Hun. 304; The People v. Empire M. L. Ins. Co., 92 N. Y. 105.

[248] 161 N. Y. 325, 336; 55 N. E. 1059, 1062.

Ferrenbaoh,[249] it was held that the measure of damages for a wrongful cancellation for alleged non-payment of premiums of an assessment insurance policy upon the life of the one, who at the time of cancellation is no longer an insurable risk, is the amount of the policy less the cost of carrying it to maturity had it remained in force, all amounts entering into the calculation and calculating upon the basis of the legal rate of interest as of the date of calculation. This rule does not apply in an action for conversion of a life policy where the measure of damages is the face value of the policy in the absence of any evidence that its collectable value is less.[250] In the case of Provident Savings L. Assur. Co. v. Statler,[251] it is said that the holder of a life policy induced by fraud may recover the premiums paid with interest without deducting for intervening insurance, and a complete repudiation of a policy of health insurance has been held to entitle plaintiff to rescind and recover the amount of premiums paid with interest, less any payments made to him while ill.[252] The Kentucky Court of Appeals has held[253] that the acceptance of a policy will not estop insured from maintaining an action to recover the premiums paid on the ground of false representations, but the insurer is entitled to credit for the actual cost of the insurance while the policy is in force. Many courts have held that where the insurer wrongfully renounces its contract, the insured can treat it as rescinded and sue to recover back what he has paid on the faith of it.[254] The Texas Court of Appeals in a comparatively recent case[255] reviews the authorities at length and the opinion is valuable, and from it we make the following extracts: "The reasoning of the court holding that the premiums paid with the interest thereon is the proper measure of damages, where an

[249] 75 C. C. A. 304; 144 Fed. 342; 7 L. R. A. (N. S.), 1163.

[250] Mut. Life Ins. Co. v. Allen, 212 Ill. 134; 72 N. E. 200; affg. 113 Ill. App. 89.

[251] 34 Ohio Cir. Ct. 391;, affd. 88 Ohio St. 549; 106 N. E. 1073.

[252] American National Life Ins. Co. v. Wilson (Tex. Civ. App.), 176 S. W. 623.

[253] Provident Savings Life Assur. Soc. v. Shearer, 151 Ky. 298; 151 S. W. 938. ·

[254] Supreme Council A. L. H. v. Black, 59 C. C. A. 414; 123 Fed. 650; affg. 120 Fed. 580.

[255] Supreme Lodge K. of P. v. Neeley (Tex. Civ. App.), 135 S. W. 1046.

insurance company has undertaken to repudiate its contract, is not at all satisfactory to our minds. We think much confusion on this subject would have been avoided, had the courts considered the fact that a suit upon such breach of contract is simply a suit for damages, and had they kept in mind the well-settled standard in all such cases. Punitory damages and penalties given by statute aside, there is no principle of law better settled than that the measure of damages is the •pecuniary loss sustained. Mr. Sedgwick announces this well-settled principle of law in the following language: 'In cases of civil injury and breach of contract, the declared object of awarding damages is to give compensation for pecuniary loss; that is, to put the plaintiff in the same position, as far as money can do it, as he would have been if the contract had been performed, or the tort not committed.'[256] All of the courts, we believe, except the North Carolina court, base their holding that the premiums paid, with interest on same, is the proper measure of damages upon the proposition that, inasmuch as the insured has not died, the company has been out nothing and the insured has received nothing. This assumed premise has been rejected by the majority of the courts, and is, to our minds, as baseless as that one has received no consideration for a premium paid for fire insurance, because his house has not burned. It is a well-established rule that, if a party sues for breach of an executory contract, he must account for the benefits, if any, which he has received under such contract.[257] In Speer v. Ins. Co. the Court said: 'The recovery of the premiums and interest could be sustained only on the ground of a total failure of consideration. When the policy was valid up to the time of its cancellation, there is no such failure.' If the policy was void *ab initio*, the premiums paid, with interest thereon, is the correct measure of damages, for the reason that in such cases no services have been rendered and no benefits have been received.[258] The North Caro-

[256] Sedgwick on the Measure of Damages, Vol. I, § 30; Am. & Eng. Ency. Law, Vol. 8, p. 632; Railway Co. v. Hill, 63 Tex. 385; 51 Am. Rep. 642; Smith v. Sherwood, 2 Tex. 460.

[257] Richards v. Allen, 17 Me. 296. In Speer v. Ins. Co., 36 Hun. (N. Y.), 323.

[258] Fisher v. Ins. Co., 162 Mass. 236; 38 N. E. 503; Ins. Co. v. McCormick, 19 Ind. App. 52; 49 N. E. 44; 65 Am. St. Rep. 392; Ellis v. Friendly Ass'n, 16 Pa. Super Ct. 607.

lina court[259] admits that the rule established by it, viz., recovery
of premiums with interest, falls short of theoretical justice, and
excuses itself for this rule on the ground that it is impracticable
to ascertain the value of the policy canceled. A knowledge of
the basic principles of life insurance leads, we think, to a different
conclusion. We are impressed with the statement of the Supreme
Court of Alabama on this subject. It says: 'The damages are
liquidated, being capable of the most accurate and certain mathe-
matic ascertainment. The legal measure of such damages is the
surrender, or equitable value, of the policy, calculated on the
basis of the American Table of Mortality, of which judicial notice
will be taken by the courts.[260] . . . We doubt if the cases holding
that the premiums paid, with interest on same, is the measure of
damages, where the contract has been wrongfully repudiated, is
satisfactory in those jurisdictions where the same has been held,
though the courts there may feel constrained to follow them. In
Smith v. Ins. Co.[261] the Supreme Court of Missouri said: 'It
will be seen that the petition in this case is not to enforce the contract of insurance, but to claim damages for its dissolution without justifiable cause,' and the damages claimed and awarded were
the value of this policy at the date of its dissolution by the company. The judgment rendered on this basis was affirmed. In the
case of Rumbold v. Ins. Co.,[262] the policy provided that the insured might surrender the same and receive in lieu thereof a
paid-up policy. The company refused to comply with this contract, and the insured brought suit for damages. The trial court
instructed that jury that plaintiff's measure of damages was the
premiums paid, with interest on same. The Appellate Court, in
its opinion reversing the judgment, said, among other things:
'The insurer bore the risk . . . It is clear that the measure of
damages here was the value of the new policy at the time of the
demand and refusal. . . . On such a policy the value was clearly
calculable.' The leading Missouri case in support of the proposition that the premiums, with interest, is the measure of dam-

259 Strauss v. Ins. Co., 126 N. C. 971; 36 S. E. 352; 54 L. R. A. 605; 83
Am. St. Rep. 699.
260 McDonnell v. Ins. Co., 85 Ala. 408; 5 Sou. 120.
261 64 Mo. 333.
262 7 Mo. App. 72, 73.

ages, is McKee v. Ins. Co.[263] In the Rumbold case the Court referred to the McKee case in the following language: 'Even if that case could, in view of later decisions, be considered as laying down a correct rule,' it is true, in the Rumbold case the Court bases its decision on the ground that it was the insured who voluntarily put an end to the policy by refusing to any longer pay the premiums thereon, but, inasmuch as it is the law that in every case where an insurance company wrongfully attempts to cancel a policy the insured may keep his policy alive by tendering the premiums according to the contract, it might, with equal reason, be said that in all such cases it is the insured who voluntarily puts an end to his policy. In either case the suit is upon breach of the contract, and we see no reason why there should be a different standard of damages. In the case of Ins. Co. v. Shultz,[264] where the facts were similar to the Rumbold case, *supra*, the Supreme Court of Pennsylvania attempted to draw a distinction between a case of rescission of contract and one of breach of contract. If the company has undertaken to wrongfully rescind or forfeit the policy, it is a breach of the contract, and the refusal to issue a paid-up policy, as provided in the contract, can be no more than this. To our minds it is a distinction without a difference, and indicates that the courts of those States are not satisfied with the rule on this subject which they have heretofore announced. . . . What is the present value of a life insurance policy? If the policy was paid up the answer would be obvious. It would be such a sum as, at a reasonable rate of compound interest, would equal the face of the policy at the end of the period of expectancy. If not paid up, its value can be computed with equal certainty. It would be a like sum, less the premiums which would become due during the period of its expectancy, with compound interest thereon. This, of course, presupposes that the party is still insurable. In line with the statement of the Supreme Court of Alabama, as hereinbefore quoted, and also with the decisions in other States, the Supreme Court of Kansas, in Barney v. Dudley,[265] said: 'The measure of damages is the difference between the rate of the premium paid for the old insurance and what

263 28 Mo. 383; 75 Am. Dec. 129.
264 82 Pa. 52.
265 42 Kan. 212; 21 Pac. 1079; 16 Am. St. Rep. 476.

another company of equal credit and standing would charge to issue a new policy on the same life, calculated on his expectancy.' In other cases it is said that the proper measure of damages is the difference between the premiums paid and the cost of carrying the insurance, with interest thereon. These are but methods of ascertaining the value of the policy at the time of its cancellation, and are equivalent to saying that the damage recoverable is what it would cost to carry the contract into effect, which, in all cases of breach of contract, is the true measure of damages. The North Carolina court adverted to the fact, that the insured may be in ill health or not insurable at all. If, in such a case, the measure of damages here proposed cannot be applied by reason of its uncertainty, this affords no excuse for not applying it in cases where such facts are not shown to exist. But in such supposed case, the value of the policy can be ascertained from the opinion of experts, with as much certainty, if not greater, as in the majority of cases where damages are allowed upon expert testimony. 'If the insured is in ill health or not insurable, this might be shown, and that a greater premium would be required than that shown by the tables of life insurance.' Dudley v. Ins. Co., *supra*. To the same effect is the opinion of the court in Ebert v. Ins. Co.[266] In such cases the amount of damages would be a fact to be determined by the jury, not arbitrarily, but upon the evidence of experts, as applied to the well-known principles of life insurance.'' While the reasoning in the foregoing case is persuasive, the Supreme Court of Texas seems to adhere to the rule that the measure of damages is the amount of assessments paid with interest.[267] In Blakeley v. Fidelity Mutual Life Ins. Co.[268] it was held that no interest could be allowed upon the recovery of assessments paid. In another case in the Federal Court[269] it was said that the measure of damages for the wrongful cancellation of a policy is the difference between carrying the insurance which he has and the cost of new insurance for the same amount together with all accumulations.

[266] 81 Minn. 16; 83 N. W. 506; 84 N. W. 457. See also Ins. Co. v. Fitzgerald, 1 White & W. Civ. Cas. Ct. App. (Tex.), § 1348.

[267] Ericson v. Supreme Ruling Fraternal Mystic Circle (Tex.), 146 S. W. 160; reversing 131 S. W. 92.

[268] 143 Fed. 619; affd. 154 Fed. 43; 83 C. C. A. 155.

[269] Krebs v. Security Trust L. Ins. Co., 156 Fed. 294.

§ 364. **Abandonment.**—Closely allied to the subject of rescission is that of abandonment. The question has been considered by the Supreme Court of the United States in a number of cases similar to each other in many respects, where that court held that an agreement to terminate a policy of life insurance made by the insured, who was also beneficiary, after a default in the payment of premiums, will end the contract; and an abandonment and rescission of a contract of life insurance by mautal agreement of the parties, after the insured is in default by the non-payment of premiums, will put an end to the contract, although a forfeiture could not have been declared by reason of failure on the part of the company to comply with certain requirements of law as to notice of premium.[270] And where the holder of a life insurance policy refused to pay a mortuary call on account of dissatisfaction with the rate, and announced that he had "quit," it was held that such action terminated the contract.[271] Where the policy on the life of the husband was payable to the wife it was held that it could not be terminated except as provided in the policy or in the statute except by consent of the wife and the fact of the husband taking out a second policy with intent to abandon the first was not an abandonment *per se*.[272] Where, however, the assured can change the beneficiary, and therefore is the only party in interest, his acts are binding on the beneficiary; because the member can sever his relations with the association at any time.[273]

So the insured has been held to abandon his policy by returning the renewal receipt for the premium although the company did not accept it,[274] and by surrender of a policy before maturity of the note given for the first premium[275] and by failure to pay eight

[270] Mut. Life Ins. Co. v. Phinney, 178 U. S. 327. Same Company v. Allen, 178 U. S. 351. Same v. Hill, 178 U. S. 347. Same v. Sears, 178 U. S. 345. See also Lone v. Mut. L. Ins. Co., 33 Wash. 577; 74 Pac. 689.

[271] Ryan v. Mut. Reserve Fund L. Ass'n, 96 Fed. 796; Haydel y. Mut. Reserve Fund L. Ass'n, 44 C. C. A. 169; 104 Fed. 718. See Roth v. Mut. Reserve L. Ins. Co., 89 C. C. A. 262; 162 Fed. 282. Also Robinson v. Mut. Reserve L. Ins. Co., 182 Fed. 850.

[272] Washington Life Ins. Co. v. Berwald, 97 Tex. 111; 76 S. W. 442; affg. (Tex. Civ. App.), 72 S. W. 436.

[273] See ante, § 137.

[274] Richmond v. Travelers' Ins. Co., 123 Tenn. 307; 130 S. W. 790.

[275] Pioneer Life Ins. Co. v. Cox, 112 Ark. 582; 166 S. W. 951.

assessments even though an unauthorized special assessment was made.[276] In the case of McGeehan v. Mutual Life Ins. Co.,[277] the Court said: "The further question therefore is presented whether that shows an abandonment of the contract on the part of the plaintiff regardless of non-action on the part of defendant concerning a right to declare a forfeiture. It must be conceded that so far as plaintiff's rights are concerned, he was at liberty to abandon and rescind the contract. He did not merely neglect a single payment of premium, nor several, but he abandoned all pretense of recognition of the contract for a long series of years. There is no law nor policy to prevent him, defendant consenting thereto, from giving up his contract. The statute of New York as to forfeitures while controlling or regulating defendant's rights, does not aid the plaintiff who has elected to abandon the contract." A member of a fraternal beneficiary association can abandon his membership at any time. In the case of Borgraefe v. Knights & Ladies of Honor,[278] Judge Seymour D. Thompson, speaking for the Court, said: "The order is a voluntary organization, the entering into it, the remaining in it and the performance of duties incumbent upon the member by reason of his membership are purely voluntary. Any member may absolutely terminate his connection with the order whenever he sees fit to do so." Later the same Court in the case of Lavin v. Grand Lodge A. O. U. W.,[279] held that if a suspended member, for whom it was claimed an assessment had been tendered and refused, did not either by way of protest or by tendering subsequent assessments, the laws requiring one assessment to be paid each month, object to his suspension he must be held to have abandoned his membership. So also where the beneficiary of an insane member did nothing by way of protest against suspension of her husband, or by tender of subsequent assessments, it was held that the contract was abandoned.[280] So a member failing to make application for reinstatement within a reasonable time after suspension

[276] Kray v. Mut. Reserve Life Ins. Co., 50 Tex. Civ. App. 555; 111 S. W. 421.
[277] 131 Mo. App. 417; 111 S. W. 604.
[278] 26 Mo. App. 226.
[279] 112 Mo. App. 1; 78 S. W. 325.
[280] Sheridan v. M. W. A., 44 Wash. 230; 87 Pac. 127.

must be taken to have acquiesced in his suspension,[281] but the mere statement of the member that he intended to give up his insurance does not justify a forfeiture of the policy in the absence of formal steps taken to forfeit it.[282]   The same rules are applied in determining whether an insurance contract has been abandoned as applied to other contracts. The question is generally one of fact, if the facts are disputed. If the facts are admitted the question becomes one of law. Abandonment of a contract of insurance is an affirmative defense which is waived if not pleaded, and in so holding the Court also said :[283] "We are not intimating that the assured may not abandon the contract, but no such question is before us, since abandonment is an affirmative defense which defendant waived by not pleading it in its answer, if pleaded it would have been unavailing in the absence of proof that Keeton failed to pay, or offered to pay, subsequent assessments which he was bound to pay to keep his insurance alive.[284]

§ 365. Court of Equity Can Correct Mistakes in Insurance Policies.—The same rules apply to actions to reform policies of insurance as to other equitable actions.[285] The reformation is subject to the same rules of law as applied to all other instruments in writing. It must be alleged and proven that the instrument sought to be corrected failed to express the real agreement or transaction because of mistake common to both parties, or because of mistake of one party and fraud or inequitable conduct of the other. A mere misunderstanding of facts is not sufficient ground for asking reformation. Where the mistake has been on one side only, reformation will not be decreed.[286] "It is

[281] Supreme Lodge Knights of Honor v. Hahn, 43 Ind. App. 75; 84 N. E. 837. See also Pfingston v. Grand Lodge, etc., 41 Ind. App. 9; 83 N. E. 254.

[282] Markgraf v. Fellowship of Solidarity, 201 N. Y. 587; 95 N. E. 1133; affg. 119 N. Y. Supp. 665; 134 App. Div. 984.

[283] Keeton v. National Union (Mo. App.), 182 S. W. 798.

[284] Purdy v. Bankers' Life Ass'n, 101 Mo. App. 91; 74 S. W. 486.

[285] Britton v. Metropolitan L. Ins. Co., 165 N. C. 149; 80 S. E. 1072; Ann. Cas. 1915-D 363.

[286] Britton v. Metropolitan Life Ins. Co., *supra*.

well settled," says Chancellor Walworth,[287] "that a court of equity has jurisdiction to correct mistakes in policies of insurance, as well as in all other written instruments.[288] But the evidence of such mistake, and that both parties understood the contract in the manner in which it is sought to be reformed, should be clear and satisfactory. In policies of insurance, the label or written memorandum from which the policy was filled up, is always considered of great importance in determining the nature of the risk and the intention of the parties." This is the case where the applicant trusts the agent to fill out the policy according to his wishes, although there is a mistake of law. Thus, where the plaintiff has been induced to act upon the superior knowledge of the defendant's agent; the fact being that an agreement had been made between the insured and the agent that certain insurance should be granted by the latter on the property of a firm of which the insured was a member. The agent, without fraud, induced the insured to have the policy made in his own name, assuring him that in that form it would protect the firm. The Supreme Court of the United States held[289] that the policy must be reformed to meet the intention of the parties, on the ground that the insured had trusted the agent concerning the proper mode of executing the policy. The case therefore was one of trust. So, where a mortgagee applied for insurance through an agent, intending to procure an insurance of his mortgage interest, and so stating to the agent, but the agent drew the application for an insurance on the property itself, in the name of the mortgagor and as his property, the amount to be payable in case of loss to the mortgagee, and so made the application and had the policy so made in the belief that such was the proper legal mode of effecting an insurance on the mortgage interest, it was held by the Supreme Court of Connecticut.[290] that the mistake

[287] Phoenix F. Ins. Co. v. Gurnee, 1 Paige Ch. 278. And see Frank v. Pacific Mut. L. Ins. Co., 44 Neb. 320; 62 N. W. 454. Unless fraud or mistake is clearly shown the Court will not interfere. McConnell v. Provident Savings L. A. Soc., 34 C. C. A. 663; 92 Fed. 769.

[288] Phil. on Ins. 14.

[289] Snell v. Ins. Co., 98 U. S. 85.

[290] Woodbury Savings Bank, etc., v. The Charter Oak, etc., Ins. Co., 31 Conn. 517.

could be corrected by a court of chancery, although it was one of law and not of fact. The principle has been generally adhered to,[291] and in general, equity will reform a policy which does not insure the interest upon which insurance was desired because of an error of law on the part of insurer's agent,[292] and this even after a loss.[293] In a recent case the Maryland Court of Appeals said:[294] "The law is well settled that where the general agent of a company is intrusted with the power to make and issue policies, and the insured fully and frankly discloses all facts material to the risk, and the agent in making out the policy, through fraud or mistake, fails to state such facts, such error or fraud on the part of the agent cannot be relied on by the company in avoidance of the policy, and a court of equity, upon application, will reform the policy so as to make it express the real contract between the parties."[295] The Court of Errors and Appeals of New Jersey goes farther and says.[296] "If the proposal for insurance be prepared by the agent of the company, and he misdecribe the premises, with full knowledge of their actual condition, and there be no fraud or collusion between the agent and the insured, the contract of insurance may be reformed in equity and made to conform to the condition of the premises as they were known to the agent."[297] So in a case where, after the issuing of

[291] Longhurst v. Star Ins. Co., 19 Iowa 364; Ben Franklin Ins. Co. v. Gillett, 54 Md. 212; Farmville Ins. Co. v. Butler, 55 Md. 233.

[292] Bailey v. American Cent. F. Ins. Co., 4 McCrary 221; 13 Fed. 250; Sias v. Roger Williams Ins. Co., 8 Fed. 183; Keith v. Globe Ins. Co., 52 Ill. 518; Oliver v. Ins. Co., 2 Curt. C. C. 277.

[293] Woodbury Saving Bank v. Charter Oak, etc., Ins. Co., 31 Conn. 517; Fink v. Queen Ins. Co., 24 Fed. 318; Hill v. Millville Mut. etc., Ins. Co., 39 N. J. Eq. 66.

[294] Ben Franklin Ins. Co. v. Gillett, 54 Md. 212.

[295] The court cites Ins. Co. v. Wilkinson, 13 Wall. 222; Ins. Co. v. Mahone, 21 Wall. 152; Saving Bank v. Charter Oak Ins. Co., 31 Conn. 517; Rowley v. Empire Ins. Co., 36 N. Y. 550; Columbia Ins. Co. v. Cooper, 50 Pa. 331; Masters v. Madison Ins. Co., 11 Barb. 624; Peck v. New London Ins. Co., 22 Conn. 575.

[296] Franklin F. Ins. Co. v. Martin, 40 N. J. Eq. 574.

[297] The court cites Collett v. Morrison, 9 Hare, 162; In re Universal, etc., F. Ins. Co., L. R. 19 Eq. 485; Malleable Iron Works v. Phoenix Ins. Co., 25 Conn. 465; Woodbury Savings Bank v. Charter Oak Ins. Co., 31 Conn. 517; Maher v. Hibernia Ins. Co., 67 N. Y. 283.

the policy to the plaintiff, he called the attention of the local agent to the erroneous description of the building insured, but was told that it made no difference, and afterwards the general agent and secretary of the defendant inspected the property, with a full knowledge of the description of the building, and pronounced the risk a good one, it was held[298] that the policy would be reformed. The Court said: "The plaintiff was not careless; was not thoughtlessly satisfied with the terms of the policy, but sought an emendation thereof, and was baulked of a successful pursuit thereof by the action and declaration of the defendants through their agents and officers." The Court continues: "It is enough to authorize the reformation of the contract, if it appear that, through the mistake of both parties to it, the intentions of neither have been expressed in it. Now, if a court of equity had a right to find from the evidence that both the insurer and the insured meant to insure the very building that was burned; and meant to put in the policy no expression as to the character or situation of it different from the facts; but, by a misconception as to the meaning and effect of language, have used terms which do express that which they did not intend to express, and which did fail to express that which they did intend to express; such evidence does make a case for a reformation of the policy so as to conform to the intentions and purposes of the parties."[299] Where there is a mistake or failure to express the intention of the parties, the jurisdiction of equity to reform is unquestioned and has been often exercised. This has been done where the language of the party who drew the contract failed to adequately or perfectly express the common intention of the parties. As where, in an action to reform a policy of insurance upon the plaintiff's life, which was expressed to be "for the sole and separate use and benefit of his wife, Lina Goldsmith, but in case of her previous death to revert to the insured," it appeared that the policy was drawn by the insurance agent upon general directions by the plaintiff as to its terms, and the plaintiff's intention then was,

[298] Maher v. Hibernia Ins. Co., 67 N. Y. 290.

[299] Many v. Beekman Iron Co., 9 Paige 188; Pitcher v. Hennessey, 48 N. Y. 415; McCall v. Ins. Co., 66 N. Y. 505; Grand Lodge A. O. U. W. v. Sater, 44 M. A. 445.

that the beneficiary named should have the insurance, if she was his wife at the time of his death, and that she had since been divorced for adultery. The Court held[300] that the policy should be reformed so as to run for her benefit so long as she remained a wife. Where in ignorance of the death of the insured the holder of the policy surrendered it for one paid up, equity will reinstate the first policy.[301] A policy payable to the wife if living, and if not living to the surviving children of insured, cannot after the wife's death in a suit by the daughter be reformed so as to provide that it should be payable to the daughter by name and such children of insured as might survive him.[302] An endowment policy may be reformed so as to provide for the payment of the endowment to the beneficiary in any event.[303] The fact that insured requested the agent to make a memorandum of the address of insured so that he might receive notices of premiums is no reason for reformation of the policy.[304]

§ 366. **When Equity Will Relieve If Agent Has Acted in Bad Faith.**—Where there is bad faith on the part of the agent, or where a policy is written materially differing from the prior agreement of the parties, equity will always interfere. Though the principle has been generally applied to fire insurance contracts, there seems to be no good reason why it should not be applied to cases of life insurance where the facts are analogous. For example, in a case in New York; the plaintiff having an insurance with the defendant of his interest as mortgagee, took another mortgage on the same premises and applied to defendant for a renewal of the first policy, with an increase of the insurance to the amount of both mortgages; this was agreed to, and a new policy was issued, which contained a clause, not in the first policy to the effect that, in case of loss, the assured should assign to the defendant all her rights to receive satisfaction from any other person, and that the loss should not be payable until after the enforcement of the original security and defendant should only

[300] Goldsmith v. Union Mut. L. Ins. Co., 18 Abb. N. C. 325.
[301] Reigel v. Am. Life Ins. Co., 140 Pa. St. 193; 21 Atl. 392.
[302] Equitable Life Assur. Soc. v. Sorter, 152 Ky. 787; 154 S. W. 32.
[303] Ulman v. Newman, 161 App. Div. 708; 146 N. Y. Supp. 696.
[304] Cowen v. Equitable L. Assur. Soc., 37 Tex. Civ. A. 430; 84 S. W. 404.

be liable for so much as could not be collected. The policy was renewed from time to time, and plaintiff did not discover the change until after a loss. Both mortgages contained the usual insurance clause, and it was agreed thereby that the mortgagors should pay the premiums and have the benefit of the policy in the payment of the debt. In an action to reform the policy and recover thereon as reformed the Court held:[305] that the plaintiff was entitled to relief and that it was bad faith on the part of the defendant to so change the terms without notice and to deliver the new as simply a renewal of the old policy. And further, that the negligence of plaintiff in not discovering the change and *laches* in not sooner seeking relief were only matters making the propriety of granting the relief discretionary. In this case the Court said: "It was bad faith on the part of the defendant to change so radically the terms of the policy and deliver it as a policy simply renewing the old one, without notice of the change. A party whose duty it is to prepare a written contract, in pursuance of a previous agreement, to prepare one materially changing the terms of such previous agreement, and deliver it as in accordance therewith, commits a fraud which entitles the other party to relief, according to the circumstances presented. Equity will reform a written instrument in cases of mutual mistake, and also in cases of fraud, and also where there is a mistake on one side and fraud on the other.[306] The negligence of the plaintiff in not discovering the change and *laches* in not sooner seeking relief, are questions which make the propriety of granting relief, in a given case, discretionary. The court below, upon the findings of fact, properly exercised its discretion in this case in granting relief. Policies of fire insurance are rarely examined by the insured. The same degree of vigilance and critical examination would not be expected or demanded as in the case of some other instruments." To the same effect is the recent case of Palmer v. Hartford F. Ins. Co.,[307] where the plaintiffs held a policy of insurance of the defendant and, on the policy expiring, applied to

[305] Hay v. Star F. Ins. Co., 77 N. Y. 235.

[306] Welles v. Yates, 44 N. Y. 525; Rider v. Powell, 28 N. Y. 310 and cases cited.

[307] 54 Conn. 488; 9 Atl. 248.

the defendants for a renewal policy, to be on the same terms with the expiring one, which the defendants promised to give. The defendants wrote and delivered the new policy and received the premium. The plaintiffs, supposing it to be on the same terms with the first, did not examine it until after the loss of the property by fire three months later, when, on reading it, they discovered an important variance from the former policy, materially affecting their right of recovery. If they had known of the change they would not have accepted the policy. In a suit for the reformation of the policy, and a recovery of what would become due under it, it was held that the plaintiffs could not be regarded as guilty of *laches* in not examining the policy and applying earlier for its correction, since they had a right to believe it to be in all essential respects like the former one. After a review of a number of authorities[308] the Court says: "It is a matter of common knowledge that a policy of insurance against fire, at the present day, is a lengthy contract, which, after specifying the main things, namely, the subject, its location, the owner, the amount, the time and the price, embodies very many stipulations and conditions for the protection of the underwriter. If a person desiring indemnity against loss applies to the underwriter and states the main things above enumerated, and says no more, he has knowledge that he has asked for and will receive a contract which, in addition to those, will contain many limiting conditions in behalf of the party executing it; and when he receives the policy he cannot avoid seeing and knowing that there are many more stipulations in it than were covered by his verbal request. It may well be that a due regard for the rights of others requires him to examine those stipulations, and express a timely dissent, or be held to an acceptance thereof. Nothing which has previously transpired between him and the underwriter furnishes justification for omission to read them. The underwriter has not invited his confidence by any promise as to what the writing shall

308 Andrews v. Essex Ins. Co., 3 Mason 10; 1 Story Eq. Jur., § 159; Oliver v. Mut. Com. Ins. Co., 2 Curtis 277; N. Amer. Ins. Co. v. Whipple, 2 Biss. 419; Phoenix F. Ins. Co. v. Gurnee, 1 Paige 278; Wood on F. Ins., § 484; Van Tuyl v. Westchester F. Ins. Co., 55 N. Y. 667; Nat. Trader's Bank v. Ocean Ins. Co., 62 Me. 519; Buckland v. Adams Exp. Co., 97 Mass. 124; Bidwell v. Astor Ins. Co., 16 N. Y. 263.

contain or omit. But if the underwriter solicits a person to purchase of him indemnity against loss by fire, and if they unite by making a written draft of all the terms, conditions and stipulations which are to become part of or in any way affect the contract, and if the underwriter promises to make and sign a copy thereof, and deliver it as the evidence of the terms of his undertaking, and if a material and variant condition is by mistake inserted, and the variant contract is delivered, and the stipulated premium is received and retained, the Court will not hear the claim that he is entitled to the benefit of the variant condition, where the other party had neither actual nor imputed knowledge of the change. In his promise to make and deliver an accurate copy, there is justification before the law for the omission of the other party to examine the paper delivered, and for his assumption that there is no designed variance. A man is not, for his pecuniary advantage, to impute it to another as gross negligence, that the other trusted to his fidelity to a promise of that character. The rule of law that no person shall be permitted to deliver himself from contract obligations by saying that he did not read what he signed or accepted, is subject to this limitation, namely, that it is not to be applied in behalf of any person who by word or act has induced the omission to read.'' The latter part of the foregoing remarks apply to applications as well as policies and is a statement of the same principle which has led the courts, in many cases, of which Insurance Co. v. Wilkinson[309] is one, to hold that when the agents of life insurance companies, in soliciting insurance, undertake to prepare the application of the insured, or make any representations to the insured or effect of the statements of the application, they will be regarded in doing so, as the agents of the insurance companies, and not of the insured, any stipulation in the policies to the contrary notwithstanding.

§ 367. **Or If the Policy Does Not Conform to the Application.** —Where the policy does not conform to the application it will be reformed and the taking away of the policy without having compared it with the application does not preclude the assured from

[309] 13 Wall. 222.

afterwards objecting to the mistake.[310] Oṅ the appeal to the court
in banc of the Nova Scotia case cited, which was one where the
policy did not conform to the application, it was affirmed, the
Court saying: "Admit the validity of the application, slip or
label, as variously called—and it is sought to be controverted
—admit the policy produced as that executed by defendants and
delivered to plaintiffs under the application—and neither party
denies it—and then a simpler, plainer case for the exercise of
the powers of an equity court, it would be difficult to conceive."
The judge adds: "Policies of insurance are a class of contracts
that require on the part of the assured the utmost good faith, but
it should be reciprocal."[311] The same rule has been applied by
the Supreme Court of the United States.[312]

§ 368. **Or If the Errors Are Manifest.**—Especially will equity
interpose to correct manifest errors, such as mistakes in dates or
time of beginning or expiration of the risk,[313] or as to name of
insured,[314] or as to the interest to be protected,[315] or in description
of premises,[316] or in the amount.[317] And that, too, whether the
member accepted the certificate with knowledge of the mistake
or not.[318]

§ 369. **Reasons for Refusal to Interfere.**—It is no reason for
not reforming a policy that the complainant might enforce payment of the loss in an action at law.[319] But delay in asking for

[310] Wylde v. Union Marine Ins. Co., 1 Nova Scotia Eq. 208; Motteaux
v. Gov. & Co. of London Ass., 1 Atk (545) 631; Bostwich v. Mut. L. Ins.
Co., 116 Wis. 392; 92 N. W. 246.

[311] Wylde v. Union Marine Ins. Co., 1 Russ. & Ch. (Nova Sc.), 205.

[312] Equitable Ins. Co. v. Hearne, 20 Wall. 494 (4 Cliff. 192).

[313] Mercantile Ins. Co. v. Jaynes, 87 Ill. 199; Knox v. Lycoming F. Ins.
Co., 50 Wis. 671; N. Am. Ins. Co. v. Whipple, 2 Biss. 419.

[314] Spare v. Home Mut. Ins. Co., 9 Sawy. 142; 17 Fed. 568.

[315] Williams v. North German Ins. Co., 24 Fed. 625; Fink v. Queen Ins.
Co., 24 Fed. 318; Banks v. Wilson, Nova Sc. Eq. 210. •

[316] Home Ins., etc,. Co. v. Lewis, 48 Tex. 622; Same v. Meyer, 93 Ill. 271.

[317] Gray v. Supreme Lodge K. of H., 118 Ind. 293; 20 N. E. 833.

[318] Gray v. Supreme Lodge, etc., *supra.* See also Eastman v. Provident
M. R. Ass'n, 65 N. H. 176; 18 Atl. 745; Wheeler v. Odd Fellows' Mut. R.
Ass'n, 44 Minn. 513; 47 N. W. 149.

[319] Delaware, etc., Ins. Co. v. Gillett, 54 Md. 219.

the relief may be considered to prevent the court acting,[320] and if an action at law has failed, the unsuccessful party cannot then apply to have the contract reformed;[321] nor if the error is so apparent that there is no necessity for reformation;[322] nor if the mistake resulted from the supine negligence of the party, who slept upon his rights, until other duties and responsibilities grew up;[323] nor if a new contract would be the result, imposing new liabilities on the defendant;[324] nor unless there was a mutual mistake;[325] nor if it appears that no action is maintainable on the policy because of lapse of time;[326] nor if the insurer was induced to issue the policy by the false representations of those who claim a benefit under it.[327] There must be either mutual mistake or fraud.[328] A policy of insurance cannot be reformed by parol evidence of mistake on the part of the insured alone, nor to the extent of altering a warranty. Courts will not lightly interfere and reform a contract. As was said by the New York Court of Appeals:[329] "The power[330] of courts of equity to reform written instruments is one in the exercise of which great caution should be observed. To justify the court in changing the language of the instrument sought to be reformed (except in the case of fraud), it must be established that both parties agreed to something different from what is expressed in the writing, and the proof upon this point should be so clear and convincing as to leave no room for doubt. Losing sight of these cardinal principles, in the administration of this peculiar remedy, would lead to the assumption of a power which no court possesses, of making

[320] Bishop v. Clay, etc., Ins. Co., 49 Conn. 167; Zallee v. Conn. Mut. L. Ins. Co., 12 Mo. App. 111; Union Cent. L. Ins. Co. v. Hook, 62 Ohio St. 256; 56 N. E. 906.

[321] Steinbach v. Relief F. Ins. Co., 77 N. Y. 498; 12 Hun. 641; Washburn v. Great Western Ins. Co., 114 Mass. 175.

[322] Amazon Ins. Co. v. Wall, 31 Ohio St. 628.

[323] Susquehanna, etc., Ins. Co. v. Swank, 102 Pa. St. 17.

[324] Sykora v. Forest City, etc., Ins. Co., 2 Cin. L. B. 223.

[325] Durham v. Fire & Marine Ins. Co., 10 Sawy. 526; 22 Fed. 468.

[326] Thompson v. Phoenix Ins. Co., 25 Fed. 296.

[327] Spare v. Home Mut. Ins. Co., 9 Sawy. 142; 17 Fed. 568.

[328] Doniol v. Commercial F. Ins. Co., 34 N. J. Eq. 30.

[329] Cooper v. Farmers' M. F. Ins. Co., 50. Pa. St. 299; 88 Am. Dec. 544.

[330] Mead v. Westchester F. Ins. Co., 64 N. Y. 455.

an agreement between parties to which they have not both assented.''[331]   The presumption is that the contract expresses the
will of the parties.[332]   The relation of a life insurance company
to a policy being that of contract and not that of a trustee and
cestui que trust equity cannot direct an accounting between the
parties concerning the funds arising from the plan.[333]

§ 370. **No Relief When Legal Effect of Plain Terms Was Misunderstood.**—There cannot be any relief if the party who procured the policy misunderstood the legal effect of plain and unambiguous words, no blame attaching to the other parties thereto.
As where a man took out a policy on his wife's life, payable in
four years to her, if living; and if not living to himself. He paid
the premiums, retained the policy, and received payments made
upon it. She was living at the maturity of the policy, but had
filed a petition for divorce. The husband and wife interpleaded
for the money. In deciding that the wife was entitled to the fund
the Court said:[334] ''Does the answer of said Volney show a case
of fraud or mistake? There is clearly no fraud alleged. We do
not think the answer shows a case for relief on the ground of
mistake. It does not allege that the policy differs in its terms
from what the parties intended. It simply alleges that said Volney
supposed it was payable to him, according to its terms, and not to
his wife, unless he died before it became payable. We do not
see how he could have possibly supposed so, for he does not allege
any ignorance of the terms; but if he did suppose so, he supposed
so because he misunderstood the legal effect of plain and unambiguous words. There is ordinarily no remedy for such a mistake,
if the other parties be not to blame, and here no circumstances
are alleged to take the case out of the ordinary rule.[335]

[331] Miaghan v. Hartford Fire Ins. Co., 12 Hun. 321; Bartholomew's v.
Mercantile, etc., Ins. Co., 34 Hun. 263.

[332] Harrison v. Hartford F. Ins. Co., 30 Fed. 862.

[333] Uhlman v. New York L. Ins. Co., 109 N. Y. 421; 17 N. E. 363.

[334] Aetna Life Ins. Co. v. Mason, 14 R. I. 583. See Avery v. Equitable L.
Ass'n, 117 N. Y. 451; 23 S. E. 3.

[335] Blackburn's case, 8 De G., M. & G. 177; Rashdall v. Ford, L. R. 2
Eq. Cas. 750; Farley v. Bryant, 32 Me. 483; Dill v. Shahan, 25 Ala. 694;
Lanning v. Carpenter, 48 N. Y. 408; Nelson v. Davis, 40 Ind. 366; Gerald
v. Elley, 45 Ia. 322; Story Eq. Jur., §§ 113, 116, 137; Kerr on Fraud and
M. 409, 428.

§ 371. Application of Foregoing Principles to Benefit Societies.—To what extent equity will aid the defective designation of beneficiary, or reform the certificate when issued, is uncertain. On general principles the same rules should apply to the contracts of benefit societies as to those of life insurance companies wherever the facts are similar. When equity is asked to aid the defective designation, or apparent failure to designate, it might be suggested that the case is one of non-execution of a power as distinguished from a trust, and again that there is no privity of contract between a benefit society and the beneficiary of its member, but neither of these objections would be insuperable. There is only one case where the subject was alluded to and there the case was one of evident mistake, for the secretary of the company was in fault. In this case,[336] the Supreme Court of New Hampshire said: "The defendant contracted to pay a sum not exceeding $2,000 as a benefit, upon due notice of the death of Gigar, the 'assured, and the surrender of his certificate of membership to such person or persons as he may, by entry on the record book of the association or on the face of this certificate, direct the same to be paid.' The bill alleges, and the demurrer admits, that, at the time he made application for membership, he stated to the association (which means to its proper officer or officers), that it was his intention that the benefit should be paid to the plaintiff, to whom he was then, and at the time of his decease, betrothed. The prayer of the bill is for a reformation of the contract by inserting in the membership certificate the name of the plaintiff as beneficiary, and that the benefit may be paid her. Section 3 of article 4 of the by-laws makes it the duty of the secretary to keep a record of the members of the association, and the persons to whom the relief is to be paid. If the fact is found at the trial term that the parties understood direction was given to enter the plaintiff's name upon the record-book as the beneficiary to whom the benefit was payable, and that Gigar understood that her name would be so entered without further direction from him, it was the duty of the secretary to enter it; and the accident or mistake was one which equity will remedy. The accident could not be said to have arisen from the negligence or fault of Gigar, so as

[336] Scott v. Provident Mut. Relief Ass'n, 63 N. H. 556; 4 Atl. 792. And see also Newman v. Covenant M. B. Ass'n, 76 Ia. 56; 40 N. W. 87.

to preclude relief,[337] nor would it be the case of non-execution of a power as distinguished from a trust, where equity does not afford relief.[338]   As equity interposes only as between the original parties and those claiming under them in privity[339] objection may be obviated by an amendment joining Gigar's administrator as co-plaintiff.   She may then prosecute this suit in his name, giving him indemnity, if he requires it, against costs and expenses.   The bill should also contain a prayer that the plaintiff's name may be inserted in the record-book as Gigar's beneficiary.''

§ 372. **Jurisdiction of Equity to Decree Cancellation.**—In policies of fire insurance, a clause is usually inserted providing for the cancellation and surrender of the contract at the option of either party.   Numerous cases have been decided in the courts in this country and of others involving questions relating to the manner of exercising this option and the time when it becomes effective.   It is not necessary to refer to these adjudications.   Similar stipulations in life policies are not so usual and instances of attempted rescission are comparatively rare.   The jurisdiction of equity to decree a cancellation upon proper showing has never been doubted, for insurance contracts, like other writings, may be reformed so as to express the intention of the parties, or, in cases of fraud, accident or mistake, be altogether avoided.   A broad distinction is made between applications made in the lifetime of the insured, and those that come after the contingency insured against has happened, in the latter event, as we shall see later, it has generally been held that equity will not interfere, because the reasons and facts, relied on for cancellation, would be equally available in defense to an action at law upon the contract.   As was said by Lord Bacon, ''chancery is ordained to supply the law, not to subvert the law.''[340]   In Fenn v. Craig[341] the general rule was laid down that a bill in equity would lie at the suit of a life insurance company to have a policy delivered up to be canceled on the ground of fraud in effecting the insurance, where the instrument is not void upon the face of it.   The Court seemed

[337] 1 Story Eq. Jur., § 105.
[338] Story Eq. Jur., §§ 169, 170.
[339] 1 Story Eq. Jur., §§ 105, 165.
[340] 4 Bac. Works, 488, cited Ins. Co. v. Stanchfield, 1 Dill. C. C. 431.
[341] 3 Young & Coll. 216.

772

to think, that the plaintiffs had a better equity if they brought their bill in the lifetime of the assured than if they waited until after his decease. The later case of London Assurance v. Mansel,[342] was one of concealment, and the Master of the Rolls did not seem to question the jurisdiction, but alone discussed the point whether there had in fact been a concealment, and whether it was material. The assured had equivocated about his application to other companies for insurance and rejection by them, and the Court held that the policy should be decreed to be delivered up, saying that it was a very plain and clear case. In Connecticut Mutual Life Insurance Company v. The Home Insurance Company,[343] in the United States Circuit Court of Connecticut, the suit was to cancel a policy that the company had already attempted to cancel upon the ground that the insured had become so far intemperate as to impair his health, the policy stipulating that it should be void if this contingency happened. The owner of the contract refused to agree to the cancellation, but continued to tender the premiums. The bill was filed to definitely determine the rights of the parties. A demurrer was interposed to the bill and overruled. Two reasons were alleged why the court should sustain the demurrer; the first was that while a court of equity has power to cancel instruments which are void by reason of fraud in their inception, it has no jurisdiction to cancel instruments which have ceased to be binding since their execution; second, that while, at the instance of the assured, a court of equity may compel an insurance company to reinstate a canceled contract, equity will not interfere to enforce a forfeiture. In passing upon the demurrer Judge Shipman said: "Upon the first proposition, it is true, that a court of equity has not, or will not, exercise jurisdiction to cancel a contract, merely because it has become void or inoperative by reason of some fact which has taken place since its execution. Such an exercise of power would give a court of equity concurrent jurisdiction with courts of law over all contracts which one contracting party may allege to have been broken by the other.[344] But, while relief from the consequences of fraud is peculiarly the province of a court of equity, it has not

.

---

[342] 11 Ch. Div. 363.

[343] 17 Blatchf. 142.

[344] Thornton v. Knight, 16 Sim. 508.

refused to cancel contracts which have been performed, or which have become inoperative, when the special circumstances of the case rendered it unjust or oppressive that the contract should be an outstanding claim against the plaintiff. The reasonable rule is, that a court of equity will exercise its power of setting aside contracts for defects not apparent on their face, although such defects arose after the execution of the contracts, in cases where the special circumstances render it inequitable or unjust, or a hardship, to compel the plaintiff to await a suit at law at the instance of the other party.[345] Chancellor Kent was inclined to think in Hamilton v. Cummings,[346] that a court of equity had jurisdiction to set aside a bond or other instrument whether the instrument was void for matter appearing on its face, or from the proofs, 'and that these assumed distinctions were not well founded.' He says: 'Perhaps all the cases may be reconciled on the general principle, that the exercise of this power is to be regulated by sound discretion, as the circumstances of the individual case may dictate, and that the resort to equity, to be sustained, must be expedient, either because the instrument is liable to abuse from its negotiable nature, or because the defense, not arising on its face, may be difficult, or uncertain at law, or from some other special circumstances peculiar to the case, and rendering a resort here highly proper, and clear of all suspicion of any design to promote expense and litigation. If, however, the defect appears on the bond itself, the interference of this court will depend on a question of expediency, and not on a question of jurisdiction.' Second, it is true, that courts of equity will not aid to enforce a forfeiture, or to divest an estate for breach of covenant or condition subsequent, unless, perhaps, under extraordinary circumstances.[347] When an estate has been forfeited, or when a pecuniary penalty has been incurred, by reason of the happening of a condition subsequent, or of the breach of a covenant, there is usually an immediate remedy at law to regain possession of the

---

[345] Hamilton v. Cummings, 1 Johns. Ch. 517; Hoare v. Brembridge, L. R. 8 Ch. App. 22; Hartford v. Chipman, 21 Conn. 488; Ferguson v. Fisk, 28 Conn. 501.

[346] 1 Johns. Ch. 517.

[347] Harsburg v. Baker, 1 Pet. 232; Livingston v. Tompkins, 4 Johns. Ch. 415; 2 Stor. Eq. Jur., § 1319.

estate or to recover the penalty. There being such a remedy equity will not interfere. 'The great principle is, that equity will not assist in the recovery of a penalty or forfeiture, when the plaintiff may proceed at law to recover it.'[348] In this case, there is no estate to be regained, there is no sum in damages to be recovered. The insured is still living, and a cancellation of the contract is the only result which is to be attained. The plaintiff has now no remedy at law and unless it can resort to a court of equity, it must wait and become a defendant at the future suit of the holder of the policy. When such suit will be commenced is a matter of uncertainty. The rule is not applicable to the cancellation of a policy of insurance upon the life of a living person.'' The Court then reasons that the relief should be given because of its expediency and in order to be just to the other policyholders. That the foundation of insurance is the law of averages and if the insured are permitted knowingly to indulge in practices that notoriously invite disease the investment of other insured persons is jeopardized. The Court quotes the language of Justice Bradley[349] that ''''the insured parties are associates in a great scheme. The associated relation exists whether the company be a mutual one or not. Each is interested in the engagements of all, for out of the co-existence of many risks arises the law of average, which underlies the whole business.'' The objection that the company has already exercised its option of declaring the forfeiture, is disposed of by the answer that it is important for the company to know before the death of the assured whether it has made an error in this action or not. That neither party should be left in doubt during a series of years as to his or its pecuniary rights in the policy. In a later case in the United States Circuit Court of North Carolina[350] it was sought to cancel a policy upon the same ground, the intemperance of the assured, the latter being still living. The Court, citing Insurance Co. v. Bailey,[351] held that á court of equity would not set aside a policy of life insurance during the life of the assured on the ground that it had been rendered void by something not appearing on the face of the policy,

[348] Livingston v. Tompkins, 4 Johns. Ch. 432.
[349] N. Y. Life Ins. Co. v. Stratham, 3 Otto (93 U. S.), 24.
[350] Connecticut Mut. L. Ins. Co. v. Bear, 26 Fed. 582.
[351] 13 Wall. 616.

and which could be proved by extrinsic evidence. That if such power existed it was not a case for the ordinary exercise of the discretionary power of a court of equity to order a cancellation, because the assured, who is now intemperate, may reform and live out the ordinary expectation of life. In Home Insurance Co. v. Stanchfield,[352] a case that was argued before Judges Miller and Dillon, in the United States Circuit Court in Minnesota, it was said, in the course of discussion, that before a loss occurred equity would cancel a policy obtained by false and fraudulent representations of the assured. This, however, would be simply an application of the general rule that whenever a contract is obtained by fraud or deception equity will decree its cancellation. And the rule undoubtedly now is that in a suit brought before loss a court of equity, on a proper showing, will cancel the policy and enforce rescission.[353] A contract obtained by fraud is void, and the fact that the assured took out a large amount of insurance at the same time is admissible as bearing on the question of fraud.[354] In an action to cancel a policy obtained by fraud the mere falsity of the statements and breach of warranty is not sufficient; it is essential that the applicant had knowledge of their falsity and acted in bad faith.''[355]

§ 373. **The Same Subject: Application to Benefit Societies.—** It might be an objection to this exercise of equity jurisdiction in the case of the contracts of benefit societies that the latter may expel the member for any fraud, or violation of the terms of the contract, that would justify the interference of a court of equity. The Kentucky Court of Appeals has held[356] that, where the by-laws of the company provide that if the assured misrepresent his

352 2 Abb. C. C. 1; 1 Dill. C. C. 424. And see also Maine Ben. Ass'n v. Parks, 81 Me. 79; 16 Atl. 339.

353 Security Trust Co. v. Tarpey, 66 Ill. App. 590; John Hancock M. L. Ins. Co. v. Houpt, 113 Fed. 572; Maine Ben. Ass'n v. Parks, 81 Me. 79; 16 Atl. 339; Am. Union L. Ins. Co. v. Judge, 191 Pa. St. 484; 43 Atl. 374; New York L. Ins. Co. v. Weaver, 24 Ky. L. 1086; 70 S. W. 628.

354 Whitmore v. Supreme L. K. & L. of H., 100 Mo. 36; 13 S. W. 495.

355 Pacific Mut. L. Ins. Co. v. Glaser, 245 Mo. 377; 150 S. W. 549. The opinion cites Schuermann v. Ins. Co., 165 Mo. 641; Kern v. Am. Legion of Honor, 167 Mo. 471; Keller v. Ins. Co., 198 Mo. 440; Modern Woodmen v. Angle, 127 Mo. 94.

356 Jones v. National Mut. Ben. Ass'n, 8 Ky. L. 599; 2 S. W. 447.

habits as temperate, the board of directors, upon hearing, may drop his name from membership, the action of the board upon the charge is conclusive and *res adjudicata* and it cannot be afterwards raised in a suit on the policy after the death of the assured. In Durantaye v. Societe St. Ignace[357] the court, in a mandamus proceeding, held that a member of a benevolent insurance society was rightfully expelled for suppression of the fact that he was laboring under a pulmonary complaint and falsely representing at the time of his admission that he was in good health.

§ 374. **The Same Subject: Cancellation After Loss.**—After a loss has occurred a court of equity will not interfere to order a cancellation of the contract unless some special circumstance exists establishing the necessity of a resort to equity to prevent an injury which may be irreparable and which equity alone is competent to avert. It is not sufficient that a defense exists, because it can be set up in an action at law on the policy,[358] nor that the evidence may be lost,[359] nor the inconvenience or risk of a reliance upon legal remedies.[360] In England it seems that a court of equity will order, upon a proper showing, a policy to be canceled even though the suit be brought after the death of the insured.[361] The same rule seems to prevail in Canada[362] and Michigan.[363] In the case last cited,[364] which was one where a bill

[357] 13 Low. Can. Jur. 1.
[358] Globe Mut. L. Ins. Co. v. Reals, 79 N. Y. 205.
[359] Town of, Venice v. Woodruff, 62 N. Y. 462.
[360] Fowler v. Palmer, 62 N. Y. 533.
[361] Whittingham v. Thornburg, Pre. Ch. 20; s. c. 2 Eq. Abr. 635; 2 Vern. 206; 24 Eng. Reprint 11; DeCosta v. Scandret, 2 Eq. Ca. Ab. 636; 2 P. Wms. 170; French v. Connolly, 2 Anstr. 454; British Eq. Ass. Co. v. Great Western Ry. Co., 20 L. T. R. (N. S.) 422; Fenn v. Craig, 3 Y. & Coll. 216; Lindeman v. Desborough, 8 B. & C. 592.
[362] North Am. L. Ass. Co. v. Brophy, 2 Ont. L. 559; affd. 32 Can. Sup. Ct. R. 261.
[363] John Hancock M. L. Ins. Co. v. Dick, 114 Mich. 337; 43 L. R. A. 566; 72 N. W. 179; Mactavish v. Kent, etc., 122 Mich. 242; 80 N. W. 1086. See also Mut. L. Ins. Co. v. Pearson, 114 Fed. 395, where the Court said: "But in cases like the present bill, where possession of the policy has been obtained by gross fraud, intentional or otherwise, and there are special circumstances showing that the remedy at law will not be 'as practical and efficient to the ends of justice and its prompt administration,' a court of

in chancery was filed to obtain the cancellation and surrender of
a receipt renewing a lapsed life insurance policy, which was obtained by fraud, the Court held that the bill might be maintained
although the fraud if proved would be a good defense to the
pending action at law on the policy. The Court said: ''There
is no doubt that the alleged fraud, if proved, should defeat the
claim of the plaintiff to any sum beyond the paid-up value of the
policy in a court of law. Such court could not, however, have
cancelled or compelled the surrender of the renewal receipt,.
though there is force in the suggestion that such cancellation
would be of little importance after an adjudication that it was
void. It is urged that the case falls within the general rule that
equity has no jurisdiction where there is an adequate remedy at
law, especially when the latter has been resorted to by the opposite party. Counsel for defendant cites two cases decided by the
Federal courts, which sustain his contention, under circumstances
closely resembling the situation in this case. These decisions are
based upon the 16th section of the Federal judiciary act, which
provides that 'suits in equity shall not be sustained in either of
the courts of the United States, in any case, where plain, adequate and complete remedy may be had at law.[365] We have no
similar statute, and we are cited to several similar cases which
sustain the jurisdiction of chancery, even after action at law is
commenced. These cases will be found collected in the com-
plaintiff's brief, and they seem to rest upon two grounds: 1. That
the jurisdiction is concurrent in cases of fraud. 2. That the
equity courts may grant more complete relief, where an instrument is fraudulently obtained, by compelling cancellation or surrender, and by rendering equitable relief.'' In Home Ins. Co. v.
Stanchfield,[366] which was heard before Judges Miller and Dillon
in the United States Circuit Court, a bill was filed by an insurance company against the assured to enjoin an action at law on

equity will entertain jurisdiction of the bill.'' The policy in this case
did not provide for the payment of a certain sum of money but for the
delivery of 240 bonds of $1,000 each, payable 35 years from their date
with interest coupons.

[364] John Hancock Mut. Life Ins. Co. v. Dick, *supra.*
[365] 1 U. S. Stat. at L. 82, Ch. 20, § 16.
[366] 2 Abb. C. C. 1; Dill. C. C. 424.

the policy, and to cancel the same because it had been procured by false and fraudulent representations, and the court held that it ought to be dismissed because founded solely upon matters which, if true, are a defense to the action at law, and no matters were shown making a resort to equity necessary or expedient. After a full review of the cases, Judge Dillon said: "The cases in the English books show that when bills are entertained, injunctions are refused or dissolved, thus leaving the real litigation to be had at law. If the verdict is for the policy, of course the bill is dismissed. If against it, then the bill may be brought to hearing, and the court will, in proper cases, order the policy to be surrendered, an order which, after such a verdict, is quite unnecessary and useless. The English cases referred to are not, as before observed, very satisfactorily reasoned, and are not free from conflict. The old cases are entitled to very little respect as authority, and the modern ones tend to show that equity will not oust the law jurisdiction, or interfere with the legal remedies where there is a full defense at law, and no obstacle in the way of making it. Insurance contracts should stand upon the same footing as other contracts with respect to equity interference, else we have an anomaly in law without any reason to justify it." The rule is now laid down in Cable v. U. S. Life Ins. Co.[367] which was followed by the U. S. Court of Appeals for the Eighth Circuit,[368] where the Court said: "Before the loss under an insurance policy occurs a company has no adequate remedy at law for the fraudulent representations or concealments which induce its issue, because an estoppel from denying its validity may arise in favor of third persons who advance their money in reliance upon it and because the time when an opportunity will be offered to establish the fraud as a defense to an action upon the policy is so remote and uncertain that indispensable witnesses and evidence may, and probably will, disappear before the opportunity will be offered. Hence a Federal Court sitting in equity has jurisdiction of a suit instituted before the loss under a policy occurs to compel

[367] 191 U. S. 288; reversing U. S. L. Ins. Co. v. Cable, 98 Fed. 761; 39 C. C. A. 264 and 111 Fed. 19; 49 C. C. A. 216.

[368] Riggs v. Union Life Ins. Co., 63 C. C. A. 365; 129 Fed. 207; reversing Union L. Ins. Co. v. Riggs, 123 Fed. 312. To the same effect is Griesa v. Mut. L. Ins. Co., 94 C. C. A. 635; 109 Fed. 509.

its cancellation and surrender on account of fraud or misrepresentation in its procurement and after the court has thus acquired jurisdiction by the commencement of the suit before loss it may proceed to a final decree, although the loss occurs during the pendency of the suit and before the final hearing.'' But after a loss has occurred no bill in equity to cancel can be maintained, because the company has an adequate remedy at law, and the plaintiff has the right to a trial by jury. This seems to be the better rule. To the same effect are other cases than those cited.[369] The Missouri statute as to misrepresentation has no application in a suit to avoid the policy during the life of the insured.[370] A condition of cancellation is the return of the premiums,[371] and tender into court of the initiation fee where the beneficiary refused to accept it is a sufficient offer to return the fee.[372]

§ 375. General Doctrine As to Interference of Equity Stated.

—The conclusion from the cases cited in the preceding sections is that in all cases arising upon insurance contracts, where the equitable jurisdiction is invoked to reform or cancel, or to give any other relief peculiar to courts of chancery, no distinction is to be made between such contracts and those relating to other matters; but, if relief is granted at all, it mus be because of the application to the facts of the broad and fundamental principles of equity. In other words, it is only when the complainant has no remedy at law, and, because of fraud, accident or mistake, injustice would result if the relief asked were not granted, that a court of equity will exercise its powers and by so doing prevent wrong from being successful.

[369] Kern v. American Leg. of Honor, 167 Mo. 471; 65 S. W. 723; Schuermann v. Union, etc., Ins. Co,. 165 Mo. 641; 65 S. W. 723; Imperial F. Ins. Co. v. Gunning, 81 Ill. 236; Des Monies L. Ins. Co. v. Seifert, 210 Ill. 157; 71 N. E. 349.

[370] Pacific Mut. L. Ins. Co. v. Glaser, 245 Mo. 377; 150 S. W. 549.

[371] National Council, etc., v. Garber, 131 Minn. 16; 154 N. W. 512.

[372] Porter v. Loyal Americans of the Republic, 180 Mo. App. 538; 167 S. W. 578.

CHAPTER IX.

781

§ 376. **The Subject of This Chapter.**—We propose in this chapter to consider the questions involving the interest of payees, or beneficiaries, in life insurance policies, the right of assignment and the subject of change of beneficiary by a member of a fraternal beneficiary society. In the case of Mutual Benefit Life Ins. Co. v. Swett,[1a] it is said: "The assignment of a policy and a change of beneficiary are not the same but different things. An assignment is the transfer by one of his right, or interest, in property to another. It rests upon contract and generally speaking the delivery of the thing assigned is necessary to its validity. The power to change the beneficiary is the power to appoint. The power of appointment must be exercised in the manner agreed upon in the contract of insurance." The distinctions between the contracts of beneficiary orders, or societies, and those of the regular life insurance companies under the earlier cases no where appeared more plainly than in the differences between the rights, or interests, of the respective beneficiaries. The earlier policies of life insurance generally conferred upon the beneficiary a vested interest and the insured was without power whether by deed, assignment, or will, or by surrender of the policy for a new one, or by any other act of his to transfer to any other person the interest of the person so named as beneficiary. In such a policy the beneficiary acquires

1a 137 C. C. A. 640; 222 Fed. 200.

the moment it is issued a vested right which cannot be affected by any act of the assured subsequent to the execution of the policy, except it be a breach of condition.[2a] Under the contract of a fraternal beneficiary society the member is the principal party to the contract and has the power of appointment of a beneficiary which he can revoke at his pleasure, thereby changing the beneficiary, and the beneficiary has no property in the benefit but a mere expectancy. It is now, however, customary in the policies of the regular life insurance companies for the right to change the beneficiary to be reserved thereby making the contracts of both classes of contracts very much the same in respect to the rights of the beneficiaries and also of the insured.

§ 377. **Vested Rights of Payees in Life Insurance Policies.**— When a policy of insurance is taken out payable to some other person than the insured, the beneficiary ordinarily has a vested right in the policy and its proceeds, consequently the assured cannot in any way control or dispose of the policy. This rule applies to a policy to which there are attached the incidents of loan value, cash surrender value and automatic extension by premiums paid so that when sufficient premiums have been paid to produce extended insurance beyond the time of the death of the insured, the surrender by him of the policy for its surrender value did not impair the rights of the wife beneficiary in the policy.[1] A leading writer on the subject says:[2] "We apprehend the general rule to be that a policy and the money to become due under it, belong the moment it is issued to the person or persons named in it as the beneficiary or beneficiaries, and that there is no power in the person procuring the insurance, by any act of his, by deed or by will, to transfer to any other person the interest of the person named. An irrevocable trust is created. . . . The legal representatives of the insured have no claim upon the money, and cannot maintain an action therefor, if it is expressed to be for the benefit of some one else." And this statement is

[2a] Mutual Benefit Life Ins. Co. v. Swett, *supra.*

[1] Mut. Ben. L. Ins. Co. v. Willoughby, 99 Miss. 98; 54 Sou. 834; Ann. Cas. 1913-D 836.

[2] Bliss on Life Ins., § 318.

cited and approved by the Supreme Court of Indiana.[3] In a case arising in Massachusetts, where, in pursuance of an understanding with the mother of the insured, he took out a policy payable to her, but, upon his subsequent marriage, surrendered it and received a new one payable to the wife, it was held that the mother's rights were not affected. In this case,[4] the Court said: "There appears to have been a full understanding between him (the assured) and his mother that the policy was to be taken out for her benefit, and afterwards that it had been so done. In point of fact, it was made payable to her, and this was done with the intention of giving to her the benefit of it. This constituted a valid settlement in her favor. Nothing remained to be done by him to complete it. He might, indeed, afterwards fail to pay the annual premiums. This, however, does not prevent it from being a good trust. An unrevoked trust is valid, even though there is an express power of revocation.[5] In this case the assured reserved to himself no power of revocation, or of changing the beneficiary. It is true that he entered into no obligation to continue to pay the premiums; but the omission to do this did not have the effect to give him an implied power of revocation. His mother might herself continue the payment of the premiums. Moreover, by the terms of the policy, after payment of two full annual premiums, it would not lapse, and certain valuable rights would still exist under it. Under these circumstances the assured could not legally surrender the policy without his mother's consent, and her rights are not affected by such surrender. This seems to us to be the true rule, and it is supported by the weight of authority."[6] So where a husband

[3] Harley v. Heist, 86 Ind. 196; 44 Am. Rep. 285; Holland v. Taylor, 111 Ind. 121. See also Irwin v. Travelers' Ins. Co., 16 Tex. C. App. 683; 39 S. W. 1097. Also Devin v. Connecticut Mut. L. Ins. Co. (Okla.), 158 Pac. 435.

[4] Pingrey v. National Life Ins. Co., 144 Mass. 381; 11 N. E. 502.

[5] Stone v. Hackett, 12 Gray 227.

[6] Chapin v. Fellowes, 36 Conn. 132; 4 Am. Rep. 49; Lemon v. Phoenix Ins. Co., 38 Conn. 294; Ferndon v. Canfield, 104 N. Y. 143; 10 N. E. 146; National Ins. Co. v. Haley, 78 Me. 268; Barry v. Brune, 71 N. Y. 261; Landrum v. Knowles, 22 N. J. Eq. 594; Manhattan Ins. Co. v. Smith, 44 O. St. 156; Ricker v. Charter Oak Ins. Co., 27 Minn. 193; 38 Am. Rep. 289; Weston v. Richardson, 47 L. T. (N. S.), 514; Kimball v. Gilman, 60

exchanges a policy payable to wife and children for one payable differently the new policy will be held to be a continuation of the first,[7] and so where policy is changed from the husband as trustee for his children to his wife;[8] nor can the wife's rights in a policy payable to her be affected by an unauthorized surrender.[9] Where the consent of the wife to a surrender was forged but the policy afterwards lapsed it was held that the wife's rights were lost, the company not being a party to the fraud.[10] The right ordinarily to assign is in the payee.[11]

The rights of a beneficiary upon the issuance of an ordinary life insurance policy become vested and can be defeated thereafter only as provided by the policy, and the provision that the insured can surrender the policy at the age of 64 does not impair

N. H. 54; City Savings Bank v. Whittle, 63 N. H. 587; Allis v. Ware, 28 Minn. 166; Olmstead v. Masonic Ben. Soc., 37 Kan. 93; 14 Pac. 449; Wilmaser v. Continental Life Ins. Co., 66 Ia. 417; Gould v. Emerson, 99 Mass. 154; Waldrom v. Waldrom, 76 Ala. 285; Drake v. Stone, 58 Ala. 133; Pilcher v. N. Y. Life Ins. Co., 33 La. Ann. 322; Packard v. Conn. Mut. Life Ins. Co., 9 Mo. App. 469; Southern Life Ins. Co. v. Booker, 9 Heisk. 606; Stillwell v. Mut. Life Ins. Co., 72 N. Y. 385; Block v. Valley M. Ins. Ass'n, 52 Ark. 201; 12 S. W. 477; U. S. Casualty Co. v. Kacer, 169 Mo. 301; 58 L. R. A. 436; 69 S. W. 370; Andrus v. Fidelity, etc., Ass'n, 168 Mo. 151; 67 S. W. 582; Laughlin v. Norcross, 97 Me. 33; 53 Atl. 834; Franklin L. Ins. Co. v. Galligan, 71 Ark. 295; 73 S. W. 102; Atkins v. Atkins, 70 Vt. 565; 41 Atl. 503; Bickel v. Bickel, 25 Ky. L. 1945; 79 S. W. 215; Union Cent. L. I. Co. v. Buxer, 62 O. St. 385; 57 N. E. 66; 49 L. R. A. 737 and note.

[7] Hooker v. Sugg, 102 N. C. 115; 8 S. E. 919; Mut. Ben. L. Ins. Co. v. Dunn, 106 Ky. 591; 51 S. W. 20.

[8] Garner v. Germania L. Ins. Co., 110 N. Y. 266; 18 N. E. 130.

[9] Putnam v. N. Y. Life Ins. Co., 42 La. An. 739; 7 Sou. 602; Duffy v. Metropolitan L. Ins. Co., 94 Me. 414; 47 Atl. 905; D'Arcy v. Conn. Mut. L. Ins. Co., 108 Tenn. 567; 69 S. W. 768; Sterrit v. Lee, 24 Misc. 324; 52 N. Y. Supp. 1132; affd. 58 N. Y. Supp. 1149; Brown v. Murray, 54 N. J. Eq. 594; 35 Atl. 748; Preston v. Conn. Mut. L. Ins. Co., 95 Md. 101; 51 Atl. 838; Lambert v. Penn. M. L. Ins. Co., 50 La. Ann. 1027; 24 Sou. 16; Jackson Bank v. Williams, 77 Miss. 398; 26 Sou. 965; Webster v. New Eng. Mut. L. Ins. Co., 21 D. C. 227.

[10] Schneider v. U. L. Life Ins. Co., 123 N. Y. 109; 25 N. E. 322; reversing 4 N. Y. Supp. 797; Miles v. Conn. M. L. Ins. Co., 147 U. S. 177; 13 S. C. 275.

[11] Irwin v. Travelers' Ins. Co., 16 Tex. Civ. A. 683; 39 S. W. 1097.

the beneficiary's vested interest.[12] A life insurance policy, application for which was signed in the wife's name by the husband and payable to her on his death, is a contract between her and the company and he has no power of disposition over the policy[13] and where the policy contains no power of revocation, no power of change of beneficiary, an irrevocable trust is created.[14] Although by decree of divorce the wife relinquished any claim to her husband's property, such an agreement does not divest the wife of a vested interest in a policy of life insurance not referred to.[15] The interest of the insured in a policy payable to her is vested and descends to her heirs, and where the husband is sole heir of his wife and he survives her, his executor is entitled to the proceeds of the policy,[16] and under a life insurance policy payable to the wife and children, a child who was living when the policy was delivered but who died before the insured, took a vested interest which passed by descent the same as other personal property.[17] A life policy vests ownership in the named beneficiary and it cannot be taken for debts of the insured without the consent of the beneficiaries, whether insured was solvent or insolvent when he paid the premium, although if the amount paid in premiums exceeded that allowed by law for the purpose, it is said the creditors will be entitled to a proportionate share of the insurance.[18] Under the Kentucky statute a life insurance policy payable to the wife is property settled upon her.[19] A policy taken out by a father on the life

[12] Filley v. Illinois Life Ins. Co., 93 Kan. 193; 144 Pac. 257; affg. 91 Kan. 220; 137 Pac. 793; L. R. A. 1915-D 130.

[13] Bradshaw v. Mut. Life Ins. Co., 205 N. Y. 467; 98 N. E. 851; modifying 125 N. Y. Supp. 1114; 140 App. Div. 917.

[14] Mut. Life Ins. Co. v. Cummings, 66 Ore. 272; 133 Pac. 1169.

[15] Wallace v. Mut. Life Ins. Co., 97 Minn. 27; 106 N. W. 84; Tillman v. John Hancock Mut. L. Ins. Co., 50 N. Y. Supp. 470; 27 App. Div. 392.

[16] Perry v. Tweedy, 128 Ga. 402; 57 S. E. 782.

[17] Woodworth v. Aetna Life Ins. Co. (Ala.), 45 Sou. 417; Mut. L. Ins. Co. v. Spohn (Ky.), 186 S. W. 633; Birge v. Franklin, 103 Minn. 482; 115 N. W. 278; Diehm v. Northwestern L. Ins. Co., 129 Mo. App. 256; 108 S. W. 139.

[18] Johnson v. Bacon, 92 Miss. 156; 45 Sou. 858. As to this last statement, see post, § 558, et seq.

[19] Troendle v. Highleyman (Ky.), 113 S. W. 812.

of his son payable to the executors, etc., of the son, confers a vested right on the son and he has the right to the policy.[20] Reserving to the insured the right to surrender a policy at the end of a specified time but not reserving a right to change the beneficiary creates a vested interest in the payees of the policy.[21] The fact that a policy is issued at fixed rates of premium and participates in the surplus does not place the contract on the footing of a benefit certificate so far as the rights of the beneficiary are concerned.[22] A life policy payable to wife and children designates the beneficiaries as a class and there is no devestiture unless all die before the insured.[23]

§ 378. **Opposing Authorities—When Beneficiary in Life Policies Can Be Changed.**—There is a class of cases which decide that after the death of a wife, to whom a policy of insurance upon the husband's life was made payable, he may surrender it and take a new one for the benefit of another person.[24] It has also been held that where the original beneficiaries of the policy die during the lifetime of the assured, who pays the premiums, such policy reverts to the insured and becomes part of his estate and goes to his administrator.[25] It has, however, also been held that if the husband does not surrender a policy payable to his wife, she dying before him, the presumption is that he wanted her representatives to take.[26] The reasons for these decisions are various, such as the supposed intention,[27] want of insurable interest in the personal representatives of the deceased wife,[28] and other reasons more or less cogent.[29] But in all these the prin-

[20] Burke v. Prudential Ins. Co., 221 Mass. 253; 108 N. E. 1069.

[21] Townsend v. Townsend, 32 Ky. L. 240, 263; 105 S. W. 937.

[22] Penn. Mut. L. Ins. Co. v. Norcross, 163 Ind. 379; 72 N. E. 132.

[23] Hartung v. Northwestern Mut. L. Ins. Co., 174 Mo. App. 289; 156 S. W. 980.

[24] Smith v. Metropolitan L. Ins. Co., 222 Pa. 226; 71 Atl. 11; Rankin v. Rankin, 83 N. J. L. 282; 84 Atl. 197.

[25] Ryan v. Rothweiler, 50 Ohio St. 595; 35 N. E. 679; Lamberton v. Bogart, 46 Minn. 409; 48 N. W. 230.

[26] Waldheim v. John Hancock L. Ins. Co., 13 N. Y. Supp. 577.

[27] Bickerton v. Jacques, 28 Hun. 119.

[28] Gambs v. Covenant Mut. L. Ins. Co., 50 Mo. 44.

[29] Foster v. Gile, 50 Wis. 603; Clark v. Durand, 12 Wis. 223; Roberts v. Roberts, 64 N. C. 695; Kerman v. Howard, 23 Wis. 108.

ciple of vested rights under a contract seems either to have been lost sight of, or some clause in the contract exempted it from the general rule, and they are, therefore, against the current of authority, except those cases where, from a construction of the policy, some power was reserved to the insured to change the beneficiary. A policy payable to the insured himself is assignable like any other chose in action,[30] or he may dispose of it by will to the exclusion of his wife,[31] and the insured may assign a policy payable to his legal representatives.[32] If the contract is made with the insured, and not the beneficiary, the policy can be assigned or the beneficiary changed by the assured,[33] and the right to change the payee may be reserved in the contract.[34]

While it is a general rule that unless the right to change the beneficiary is reserved the beneficiary named in the policy has a vested interest which cannot be divested except in the manner provided in the policy, it has been held otherwise. The Supreme Court of Wisconsin has said:[35] "In Wisconsin, however, there has existed from early times a principle of the law of life insurance which is unique and at variance with the law in most of the States. This principle is that a person who insures his own life for the benefit of another, and pays the premiums thereon, may . . . (except as limited by statute as to married women) dispose of the policy by will, or in other manner not inconsistent with the terms of the policy, to the exclusion of the beneficiary named therein.' Though the beneficiary in such a policy has a vested interest, he can do nothing to prevent the insured, as equitable owner, from revoking such beneficial interest, retain

[30] Stuart v. Sutcliff, 46 La. Ann. 240; 14 Sou. 912.

[31] Hamilton v. McQuillan, 82 Me. 204; 19 Atl. 167.

[32] Hurst v. Mut. Reserve F. L. Ins. Co., 78 Md. 59; 26 Atl. 956. See also Cyrenius v. Mut. L. Ins. Co., 26 N. Y. Supp. 248; where it was held that the term "assured" applied to the person whose life was assured and who paid the premiums although the policy was payable to the son.

[33] Denver L. Ins. Co. v. Crane, 19 Colo. App. 191; 73 Pac. 875; Robinson v. U. S. Mut. Acc. Ass'n, 68 Fed. 825.

[34] Bilbro v. Jones, 102 Ga. 161; 29 S. E. 118; John Hancock M. L. Ins. Co. v. White, 20 R. I. 457; 40 Atl. 5; Hopkins v. N. W. L. Ins. Co., 40 C. C. A. 1; 99 Fed. 199.

[35] Rawson v. Milwaukee Mut. Life Ins. Co., 115 Wis. 641; 92 N. W. 378.

it himself, or vest it elsewhere, when not prevented by the terms of the contract." And in that State this rule is adhered to.[36]

§ 379. **Reservation of Right to Change the Beneficiary Gives Payee Conditional Vested Interest.**—If the right to change the beneficiary is reserved in the policy the payee generally has no absolute vested interest, but a conditional vested interest. In the case of Mutual Benefit Life Ins. Co. v. Swett,[37] the Court said: "If, however, by the terms of the policy itself there is reserved to the insured the right, without the consent of the beneficiary, to change the appointee with the assent of the insurer, the beneficiary acquires only an expectancy and not a vested interest during the life of the insured.[38] The right so reserved rests upon the terms of the contract, and is the same as that conferred on the insured by the certificate, charter, or by-laws of a mutual or benefit association, when insurance is effected in such an organization. As the policy to Swett stipulated that he might, on his written request of the company for its appropriate indorsement on the policy, change the beneficiary, his wife did not acquire a permanent or vested interest in it. The existence of such an interest during her husband's lifetime was made impossible by the control over the contract of insurance given to him, independent of her will. Her right was inchoate, a mere expectancy during his lifetime, dependent on the will and pleasure of her husband as holder of the policy, and could not vest until his death happened with the policy unchanged. His control over the policy was, subject to its items, as complete as if he himself had been the beneficiary.[39] The wife had no vested interest which she could assign

[36] Opitz v. Karel, 118 Wis. 527; 95 N. W. 948; 62 L. R. A. 982; Meggett v. Northwestern Mut. Life Ins. Co., 138 Wis. 638; 120 N. W. 392; Slocum v. Northwestern National Life Ins. Co., 135 Wis. 288; 115 N. W. 796. See also *post*, § 389.

[37] 137 C. C. A. 640; 222 Fed. 200. See also Blinn v. Dame, 207 Mass. 159; 93 N. E. 601.

[38] Hopkins v. Northwestern Life Assur. Co., 99 Fed. 199; 40 C. C. A. 1 (C. C. A. 3); Hogan v. Fauerbach Brewing Co., 194 Fed. 846, 848; 114 C. C. A. 634 (C. C. A. 7); Lamb v. Mut. Reserve Fund Life Ass'n (C. C.) 106 Fed. 637; Robinson v. U. S. Mut. Acc. Ass'n (C. C.); 68 Fed. 825; Ins. Co. v. O'Brien, 92 Mich. 584; 52 N. W. 1012; Golden Star Fraternity v. Martin, 59 N. J. 207, 216; 35 Atl. 908.

[39] Denver Life Ins. Co. v. Crane, 19 Colo. App. 191, 200; 73 Pac. 875.

until the death of her husband—no assignable or transferable in-
terest.in the policy until some right of action on it accrued in her
favor.'' The California Court of Appeals in Waring v. Wilcox,[40]
has held that where a policy of life insurance reserves to the insured the right to change the beneficiary, upon written request
therefore, the interest of a designated beneficiary prior to the
death of the insured is that of a mere expectancy of an incompleted gift subject to revocation at the will of the insured. This
case was cited and approved in a later opinion of the same court.[41]
The Court said: ''Since the insured had the right to change the
beneficiary named in the policy, it must follow that plaintiff had
no vested interest therein. Until McEwen's death, he might have
named anyone, including his estate, as beneficiary in the policy,
and, this being true, the ownership of the policy must be deemed
to have been vested in him.''[42] Notwithstanding the principle stated
in the authorities cited it has also been held that where only the
right to change the beneficiary is reserved in the policy, the rights
of the beneficiary can only be divested in the way specified in the
contract and the control of the insured is not absolute but qualified. The Supreme Court of Indiana has said:[43] ''The contract
of insurance in this case was delivered and accepted on December 9, 1907, was in the possession of the appellee, the beneficiary,
and was not surrendered to the company. On November 30, 1908,
the appellant paid to the insured $140.45 in consideration of the
execution of a release. Appellee was not a party to such release,
and acquired no knowledge of it until December 8, 1908, when
appellant returned the check of the agent of the insured and
appellee, and notified appellee that such contract had been cancelled, and requested the surrender of the policy. It seems to us
that a pertinent inquiry here would be, who had the title to the
policy on November 30, 1908? Certainly some sort of a title
thereto was in the appellee, and, whatever that title was, she could
be divested of it only by a strict compliance with the conditions

40 8 Cal. App. 317; 96 Pac. 910.

41 McEwen v. New York Life Ins. Co., 23 Cal. App. 694; 139 Pac. 242.

42 Smith v. National Ben. Soc., 51 Hun. 575; 4 N. Y. Supp. 521.

43 Indiana National Life Ins. Co. v. McGinnis, 180 Ind. 9; 101 N. E.
289; 45 L. R. A. (N. S.), 192; reversing 99 N. E. 751; 101 N. E. 295,
which reversed 99 N. E. 756.

of the contract as therein provided, or by some act or proceeding to which appellee was a party so that she would be bound thereby. From the foregoing we conclude that the attempt to cancel the policy and terminate the liability of the appellant to this beneficiary was not in accord with the specific terms of the contract; that a change of beneficiary as provided therein contemplated the continuance of the contract, and did not contemplate annulment and determination thereof; that the beneficiary, upon the issuance, delivery and acceptance of the policy of insurance, took such a defeasible vested interest therein as under this contract was not to be divested by the agreement between the insurer and the insured canceling the policy; and that the trial court did err, therefore, in sustaining demurrers to the first, third, fourth and sixth paragraphs of appellant's answer to appellee's complaint.'' The Supreme Court of Georgia has said:[44] ''Any right to change the beneficiary is one of contract and it can be accomplished only, in the manner pointed out in the policy. There was no attempt by the insurer and insured in the instant case to change, or substitute, a different beneficiary. The insured reserved that right, in his policy, but did not act upon it. The insured and insurer attempted to surrender and cancel the policy, contending that as the insured reserved the right to change the beneficiary, he had the right to agree with the insurer upon the cancellation and surrender of the policy. The right to change the beneficiary in an ordinary life insurance policy does not include the power to surrender and cancel without the consent of the beneficiary. The right to change the beneficiary is quite different from the right to surrender the policy for the purpose of cancellation; as the former contemplates modification and continued existence of the policy, while the latter contemplates its complete destruction.''[45] In the case of Washington L. Ins. Co. v. Berwald,[46] the Court uses this language: ''The wife has an insurable interest in her husband's life, which she may insure, taking a policy payable to herself or to her children; therefore, it cannot be said that the insurance procured by the husband for the wife is a mere gratuity.

[44] Roberts v. Northwestern National Life Ins. Co., 143 Ga. 780; 85 S. E. 1043.
[45] Holder v. Prudential Ins. Co., 77 S. C. 299; 57 S. E. 853.
[46] 97 Tex. 111; 76 S. W. 442; 1 Ann. Cas. 682.

It is to protect an existing interest, as well as the performance of a duty to the wife. It is a contract about a matter of interest to the wife, and she can pay the premiums herself in case her husband fails to do so. . . . . If she has such interest in the contract that she might protect it against the wishes of her husband and the insurance company by making payments according to the terms of the contract, she is not a stranger to it, and surely her interest is of a character that she—cannot be deprived of it without her consent, except by her failure to see that the terms of the contract are complied with." The Supreme Court of Wisconsin in a case where the insured had attempted by will to dispose of a policy payable to his wife, who had been divorced, said:[47] "Since the wife took a vested interest in the policy at the time she was made a beneficiary, which interest could be divested only in the manner reserved in the policy contract, it becomes unnecessary to determine whether or not she sustained the status of wife for one year after the decree of divorce was granted. Conceding that she did not sustain such status, the policy would still belong to her, because her interest therein had not been effectually divested." The right of surrender of a policy payable to the insured wife, or, if she was dead, to his children, is personal and cannot be exercised by an assignee.[48] It has been held, however, that where the right to change the beneficiary has been reserved, the policy can be assigned by the insured to a creditor as security for a debt.[49] Where the right to change the beneficiary is reserved in the policy, it is not affected by the Missouri statute as to a policy payable to the wife.[50] The rights of a beneficiary become fixed at the death of the insured and are not affected by a contemplated change of beneficiary not perfected.[51]

[47] Christman v. Christman (Wis.), 157 N. W. 1099.

[48] Moser v. Connecticut Mut. Life Ins. Co., 134 Ky. 215; 119 S. W. 792.

[49] McNeill v. Chinn, 45 Tex. Civ. A. 551; 101 S. W. 465; Alba v. Provident Savings L. Ass. Soc., 116 La. 1021; 43 Sou. 663; Fuos v. Dietreich (Tex. Civ. A.), 101 S. W. 291; Cornell v. Mut. L. Ins. Co., 179 Mo. App. 420; 165 S. W. 858.

[50] Robinson v. New York L. Ins. Co., 168 Mo. App. 259; 153 S. W. 534. But see to the contrary, In re Orear, 111 C. C. A. 150; 189 Fed. 888.

[51] Freund v. Freund, 218 Ill. 189; 75 N. E. 925; reversing 1117 Ill. App. 565.

§ 380. **Subject to Certain Limitations, Life Insurance Policies Can Be Assigned Like Other Choses in Action.**—Life insurance policies can be ordinarily assigned subject to the limitations imposed by statute, and subject also to the condition that the assignee must have an insurable interest. Usually a policy contains a provision that no assignment thereof shall be binding on the company unless notice of such assignment has been given to it. Sometimes the policy prescribes modes of transfer which are reasonable provisions and generally will be enforced. The assignment must be made by the party having title to the policy. In the case of regular life insurance policies the payee has a vested right in the policy and is a necessary party to any assignment, unless the right to change the beneficiary is reserved in the contract. In this respect policies of life insurance are unlike benefit certificates issued by the fraternal beneficiary organizations where, as we have seen, the designated beneficiary has a conditional interest, or a mere expectancy, which does not ripen into property until the death of the member. An endowment policy payable to insured at maturity is assignable.[52] Contingent interests in life insurance policies may be assigned, such as the right to the cash surrender value payable after twenty years.[53] And where the policy is payable to insured's wife, if she survive him, otherwise to his executors, etc., he has a contingent interest which may be assigned by him.[54] The insured may borrow money on the policy although payable to the wife and children, if the right to change the beneficiary is reserved.[54a] An assignment procured by fraud will be set aside by proper proceedings brought for that purpose.[55] The Supreme Court of the United States has apparently modified its views in regard to the assignability of life insurance policies. In the case of Grigsby v. Russell.[56] it said: "Life insurance has become in our days one of the best recognized forms

[52] Eisenbach v. Mut. L. Ins. Co., 147 N. Y. Supp. 962; 162 App. Div. 395; affd. 212 N. Y. 593; 106 N. E. 1033.

[53] Cornell v. Mut. L. Ins. Co., 179 Mo. App. 420; 165 S. W. 858.

[54] Lanier v. Box, 112 Tenn. 393; 79 S. W. 1042; 64 L. R. A. 458.

[54a] Mut. L. Ins. Co. v. Twyman, 122 K. 513, 92 S. W. 335; Crice v. Ill. Life Ins. Co., 122 Ky. 572, 928 S. W. 560.

[55] McKeldin v. McKeldin, 104 Ky. 345; 47 S. W. 246; Plant v. Plant, 76 Miss. 560; 25 Sou. 151.

[56] 222 U. S. 149.

of investment and self-compelled saving. So far as reasonable safety. permits, it is desirable to give to life policies the ordinary characteristics of property. This is recognized by the bankruptcy law,[57] which provides that unless the cash surrender value of a policy like the one before us is secured to the trustee within thirty days after it has been stated, the policy shall pass to the trustee as assets. Of course, the trustee may have no interest in the bankrupt's life. To deny the right to sell except to persons having such an interest is to diminish appreciably the value of the contract in the owner's hands. The collateral difficulty that arose from regarding life insurance as a contract of indemnity only,[58] long has disappeared.[59] And cases in which a person having an interest lends himself to one without any, as a cloak to what is, in its inception, a wager, have no similarity to those where an honest contract is sold in good faith." And the tendency of the later decisions is to hold that a policy of life insurance is a mere chose in action and can be transferred the same as any other property. The Maryland Court of Appeals,[60] has said: "A policy of insurance like any other chose in action can be assigned.to a creditor absolutely, or in payment of his own debt."[61] The Supreme Court of Texas, however, has said:[62] "A policy of insurance is not a piece of property; it is the evidence of a contract, the contract being that a certain sum of money will be paid, upon the happening of a certain event, to a particular person named in the policy, or who may be the legal holder thereof."[63] We propose in the succeeding sections of this chapter to discuss the various principles governing the assignment of life insurance policies. The decisions of the courts are not always in harmony, although the law is reasonably well settled.[64]

[57] § 70.

[58] Godsall v. Boldero, 9 East 72.

[59] Phoenix Mut. L. Ins. Co. v. Bailey, 13 Wall. 616; 20 L. Ed. 501.

[60] Fitzgerald v. Rawlings, 114 Md. 470; 79 Atl. 915; Ann. Cas. 1912-A 650.

[61] Scudder v. Home Friendly Soc., 72 Md. 511; 20 Atl. 137.

[62] Martin v. McAllister, 94 Tex. 567; 63 S. W. 624; 56 L. R. A. 585.

[63] See for further discussion, *post*, § 393.

[64] The Lawyers' Reports Annotated and Annotated Cases have valuable notes appended to cases involving questions in relation to assignment of life insurance policies. Union Central Life Ins. Co. v. Buxer,

§ 381. **When the Policy Cannot Be Assigned or the Beneficiary Changed.**—If the policy provides expressly that no assignment thereof shall be made, the stipulation is binding upon the parties.[65] Where the laws of a benefit association provide that the benefit shall be paid to the person named in the application of the member, and no provision is made for a change of beneficiary, the rights of the latter are vested and cannot be affected by any act of the member.[66] In one of these cases[67] the Supreme Court of Indiana says: "We can see no way to avoid the conclusion that this charter provision requires the benefit to be paid to the person named in the application, or to those specified in the case of the death of those persons, or of some occurrence making it impossible to pay to them. Not only does the charter in direct terms declare that the benefit shall be paid to the persons thus named, but it also declares that if it becomes impossible to pay it to them, it shall go in the manner specified in the charter. The effect of these provisions is that the beneficiaries named must receive the money due on the policy, or it must be disposed of as provided by the charter creating the association. The provisions respecting the mode of disposing of the benefit deprives the insured and the insurer of any right to change the contract, as it leaves only two possible classes of beneficiaries, those named in the application and those specified in the charter, as entitled to take in case the designation in the

62 Ohio St. 385; 57 N. E. 66; 49 L. R. A. 737; McRae v. Warmack, 98 Ark. 52; 135 S. W. 807; 33 L. R. A. (N. S.) 949; Metropolitan Life Ins. Co. v. Elison, 72 Kan. 199; 83 Pac. 410; 3 L. R. A. (N. S.) 934; Rylander v. Allen, 125 Ga. 206; 53 S. E. 1032; 6 L. R. A. (N. S.) 128; Keckley v. Coshocton Glass Co., 86 Ohio St. 213; Ann. Cas. 1913-D 607; Fitzgerald v. Rawlings, 114 Md. 470; 79 Atl. 915; Ann. Cas. 1912-A 650; Rahders v. People's Bank of Minnesota, 113 Minn. 496; 130 N. W. 16; Ann. Cas. 1912-A 299.

65 Unity M. L. Ass. v. Dugan, 118 Mass. 219.

66 Kentucky Masonic M. L. Ins. Co. v. Miller, 13 Bush 489; Gibson v. Ky. Grangers, etc., Soc., 8 Ky. L. 520; Ky. Grangers, etc,. Soc. v. Howe, 9 Ky. L. 198; Olmstead v. Masonic Mut. B. Soc., 37 Kan. 93; 14 Pac. 449; Basye v. Adams, 81 Ky. 368; Presbyterian Ass. Fund v. Allen, 106 Ind. 593; Grand Lodge v. Elsner, 26 Mo. App. 108; Thomas v. Leake, 67 Tex. 469; 3 S. W. 703; Johnson v. Hall, 55 Ark. 210; 17 S. W. 874; Mingeaud v. Packer, 21 Ont. 267; affd. 19 Ont. App. 290.

67 Presbyterian Ass. Fund v. Allen, 106 Ind. 593; 7 N. E. 317.

application is 'changed by death,' or 'otherwise becomes impossible.' '' The general rule, however, in the case of benefit societies is that, as the beneficiary has no vested rights in the benefit until the death of the member, the latter can change the beneficiary at any time although the first beneficiary has possession of the certificate and has paid all the assessments.[68] If under an agreement with the member the beneficiary pays the assessments, the latter may acquire such a vested right which will prevent a change,[69] and an assignment may be conditioned on the assent of the original beneficiary.[70] When once the policy has matured the claim becomes a debt and is no longer subject to the restrictions of the policy.[71]

§ 382. **When the Policy Has Not Passed Out of Control of Party Effecting It.**—If the party who procures and pays for a policy of life insurance, which is by its terms payable to a third party, retains possession of the policy, he may generally surrender it, or revoke the designation of beneficiary and appoint a new person to receive the proceeds. In one case, one Peterson obtained a policy on his own life payable to himself, but afterwards surrendered it and had a new one issued payable to his betrothed, which he gave to her brother for her and so told her. Afterwards he obtained the policy, surrendered it and had a new one issued payable to a creditor, and then died. The Supreme Court of Connecticut, in holding the lady to whom the insured was betrothed entitled to the proceeds, said:[72] ''It is not claimed that the mere fact of making the policy payable to Miss Lemon, without more, vested in her a complete title. It is conceded that so long as Mr. Peterson retained it in his own possession, he might control it as his own. On the other hand it is not doubted that if Mr. Peterson delivered it to Miss Lemon as a gift to her, such delivery would vest in her a complete title.''

[68] Masonic Ben. Ass'n v. Bunch, 109 Mo. 560; 19 S. W. 25; *post,* § 401.

[69] Maynard v. Vanderwerker, 24 N. Y. Supp. 932.

[70] Helfrich v. John Hancock M. L. Ins. Co., 28 N. Y. Supp. 535.

[71] Briggs v. Earl, 139 Mass. 473; 1 N. E. 847; Mower v. Reverting Fund Ass'n, 1 Pa. Super. Ct. 170.

[72] Lemon v. Phoenix Mut. Life Ins. Co., 38 Conn. 301.

This view has obtained in other cases.[73] In a New York case[74] the constitution of a benefit society provided for a fund to be paid upon the decease of a member to his widow or minor children; afterwards this law was changed so as to allow the member to designate his beneficiary. The member under the new law, although he had belonged to the society from the first, and under the new constitution as well, designated a woman with whom he was living, describing her as his "wife." The claim was made by the society in defense to an action by the beneficiary, that the plaintiff was not the widow of the deceased and had not been designated as the beneficiary in accordance with the constitution of the society. In giving judgment for the plaintiff the Court said: "The case seems to me to be simply this: the title of Catherine Durian (the true wife) is not protected by the statutes of the State. If she be entitled to the insurance money, it must be because of a contract made between Philip Durian and the defendant, which it was out of their power afterwards to vary, because she had an interest in it which it would be unjust and unlawful to impair. What interest had Catherine in it? Why could it not be modified by the parties who made it? The counsel of the defendant has not shown. Conceding that Philip intended, at first, that she should receive the insurance money, he had a right to change the direction in which the money should go at any time before he had actually placed in her hands, or beyond his own control, the means of enforcing her claim to the money.[75] It was competent, in my opinion, for Philip and the Verein to modify their agreement in any manner satisfactory to both parties. It was competent for Philip, with the consent of the Verein, to name a beneficiary other than his wife, even though his wife were present. The amended constitution, to which he assented, formed a new contract between him and the Verein, under the terms of which he was at liberty to choose whom he pleased as an ap-

---

[73] Penn. Mut. Ins. Co. v. Watson, 3 W. N. C. 513; Weston v. Richardson, 47 L. T. 514; Garner v. Germania Life Ins. Co., 13 Daly 255; 17 Abb. N. C. 7; Johnson v. Van Epps, 14 Bradw. 201; 110 Ill. 551. But see Glanz v. Gloeckler, 10 Bradw. 484; 104 Ill. 573.

[74] Durian v. Central Verein, etc., 7 Daly 170.

[75] Lemon v. Phoenix Ins. Co., *supra*.

pointee. He named Barbara, the plaintiff.'' This was followed in a later case in the same State.[76] If the policy expressly covenants that upon the decease of the beneficiary the insured may substitute any other, this stipulation controls, but the option must be exercised within a reasonable time after the death of the first beneficiary. Such substitution cannot be made by will, nor after the payment of the next ensuing premium. The payment of each premium, so to speak, makes a new contract.[77]

Where a life insurance policy payable to executors, etc., of insured was delivered and shortly thereafter the insured procured from the agent a certificate, which was pinned to the policy, making his father the sole beneficiary, the certificate being as follows: "This is to certify that I, Yancey E. White, this day made my father, J. E. White, the sole beneficiary of the policy in the event of my death, by accident or otherwise. Witness my hand this the — day of October, 1902.'' It appeared that the insured never intended to assign the policy to his father, or to change the beneficiary herein except in such manner as would leave him the full control of the policy, such instrument being revocable at his pleasure and testamentary in character, and not executed with the formalities of a will, is void.[78] In that case the Court said: "It is manifest that White never intended to assign his policy to his father and it is equally manifest that he did not intend to change the beneficiary therein, except in such manner as would leave him in full control of the situation. In order to do this he executed an instrument revocable at his pleasure by which he directed what disposition should be made of the policy after his death. Such an instrument is testamentary in character and to be valid must be executed with all the formalities attending the execution of the will. This instrument not having been so executed is void."

§ 383. Life Insurance Policies, How Assigned.—At common law policies of fire or life insurance were not assignable, but the

76 Deady v. Bank Clerks', etc., Ass'n, 17 Jones & Sp. 246.

77 Eiseman v. Judah, 1 Flip. 627. See same case and note in 4 Cent. L. Jour. 345; Roberts v. Roberts, 64 N. C. 695; Robinson v. Duvall, 79 Ky. 84.

78 White v. Ratcliff, 99 Miss. 93; 54 Sou. 658.

assignee could sue in the name of his assignor.[79] The assignee, however, could sue in equity, but latterly it was considered that the remedy at law was adequate and complete.[80] Life insurance policies are said to be choses in action and may therefore be assigned by indorsement and delivery,[81] and a mere verbal assignment with delivery is sufficient,[82] and so very informal assignments have been held sufficient to vest in the assignee the equitable right to the proceeds.[83] The same rules generally govern as in other cases of personal property.[84] It is not always necessary that delivery be made; any act carrying out the intention of the insured and communicated to the insurer is enough in equity.[85] But generally to make a valid assignment there must be a delivery

[79] Jessel v. Williamsburg Ins. Co., 3 Hill 88; Palmer v. Merrill, 6 Cush. 282; 52 Am. Dec. 782; Hobbs v. Memphis Ins. Co., 1 Sneed 444; May on Ins., § 377.

[80] Carter v. United States Ins. Co., 1 Johns. Ch. 463.

[81] Bushnell v. Bushnell, 92 Ind. 503; Hutson v. Merrifield, 51 Ind. 24; 19 Am. Rep. 722; Harley v. Heist, 86 Ind. 196; 44 Am. Rep. 285.

[82] New York Life Ins. Co. v. Flack, 3 Md. 341; 56 Am. Dec. 742; Pierce v. Fire Ins. Co., 50 N. H. 297; Powels v. Innes, 11 Mees. & W. 10; Chapman v. McIlwrath, 77 Mo. 38; Manning v. Bowman, 3 Nova Scotia Dec. 42; Allen v. Hartford C. Ins. Co., 72 Conn. 693; 45 Atl. 955; Western Ass. Co. v. McCarthy, 18 Ind. App. 449; 48 N. E. 265; State v. Tomlinson, 16 Ind. App. 662; 45 N. E. 1116; Barnett v. Prudential Ins. Co., 86 N. Y. Supp. 482; Grogan v. U. S. L. Ins. Co., 90 Hun. 521; 36 N. Y. Supp. 687; Travelers' Ins. Co. v. Grant, 54 N. J. Eq. 308; 33 Atl. 1060; Hancock v. Fidelity, etc., Ass. (Tenn.), 53 S. W. 958; Embry v. Harris, 107 Ky. 61; 52 S. W. 958; Box v. Lainer, 112 Tenn. 393; 79 S. W. 1042; Opitz v. Karel, 118 Wis. 527; 95 N. W. 948. See cases cited in note 87 Am. St. R. 490. As to incomplete transfers see O'Brien v. Continental Cas. Co., 184 Mass. 584; 69 N. E. 308; Saling v. Bolander, 125 Fed. 701; Weaver v. Weaver, 182 Ill. 287; 55 N. E. 338; Smith v. Hawthorn, 22 Pa. Co. Ct. 519; Alvord v. Luckenbach, 196 Wis. 537; 82 N. W. 535; Lateer v. Prudential Ins. Co., 64 App. Div. 423; 72 N. Y. Supp. 235; Rahders v. People's Bank, 113 Minn. 496; 130 N. W. 16; Am. Cas. 1912-A 299; Nashville Trust Co. v. First Nat'l Bank, 123 Tenn. 617; 134 S. W. 311.

[83] Scott v. Dickson, 108 Pa. St. 6; 56 Am. St. R. 192; Green v. Republic Fire Ins. Co., 84 N. Y. 572; Richardson v. White, 167 Mass 58; 44 N. E. 1072.

[84] Potts v. Temperance, etc., Co., 23 Ont. R. 73.

[85] Marcus v. St. L. M. Ins. Co., 68 N. Y. 625; Fortesque v. Barnett, 3 Myl. & K. 36; In re Trough, 8 Phila. 214; Chowne v. Bayliss, 31 Beav. 351.

of the policy.[86] Delivery of the assignment to the company amounts to delivery.[87] Delivery of the assignment to the assignee's agent is sufficient.[88] An assignment is not such an instrument as requires acknowledgment and recording.[89] Under a general assignment of all property life insurance policies will pass.[90] Where an assignee of a life policy reassigned a part of it to the assured and delivered the policy to him with the assignment so negligently attached that it could easily be removed, it was held that he was guilty of such negligence as would prevent his recovery against the *bona fide* assignee of a paid-up policy issued on the surrender of the old.[91] The validity of the assignment is determined by the law of the place where it is made.[92] The objection that the assignment is irregular can be raised by anyone claiming an interest.[93] A partial assignment can be made.[94] Or a qualified assignment.[95]

§ 384. **The Same Subject—Further Illustrations.**—An assignment of a life insurance policy is a contract distinct and separate from that of insurance and is governed by the law of the place

[86] Ballou v. Gile, 50 Wis. 614; Dexter Savings Bank v. Copeland, 77 Me. 263; Falk v. Janes, 49 N. J. Eq. 484; 23 Atl. 813; Travelers' Ins. Co. v. Healey, 28 N. Y. Supp. 478; Spooner v. Hilbish, 92 Va. 333; 23 S. E. 751; Northwestern Mut. L. Ins. Co. v. Wright, 153 Wis. 252; 140 N. W. 1078; Ann. Cas. 1914-D 697, and note, where all the authorities are reviewed.

[87] McDonough v. Aetna Life Ins. Co., 38 Misc. 25; 78 N. Y. Supp. 217; Appeal Colburn, 74 Conn. 463; 51 Atl. 139; Hewins v. Baker, 161 Mass. 320; 37 N. E. 441; New York L. Ins. Co. v. Dunlevy, 130 C. C. A. 473; 214 Fed. 1; affg. 204 Fed. 670.

[88] Manhattan L. Ins. Co. v. Cohen (Tex. Civ. A.), 139 S. W. 51.

[89] Steeley v. Steeley, 23 Ky. L. 996; 64 S. W. 642; Mut. Res. F. L. Ass'n v. Cleveland, 27 C. C. A. 212; 82 Fed. 508; 54 U. S. App. 290.

[90] Hewlett v. Home, etc., Co., 74 Md. 350; 24 Atl. 324.

[91] Bridge v. Conn. Mut. L. Ins. Co., 152 Mass. 342; 25 N. E. 612.

[92] Union Cent. L. Ins. Co. v. Woods, 11 Ind. App. 335; 37 N. E. 180; Lee v. Abdy, 17 Q. B. D. 309; Miller v. Campbell, 140 N. Y. 457; 35 N. E. 651; Crouse v. Ins. Co., 56 Conn. 176; 14 Atl. 82. See also next section.

[93] Travelers' Ins. Co. v. Healy, 86 Hun. 524; 33 N. Y. Supp. 911.

[94] Stoll v. Mut. Ben. L. Ins. Co., 115 Wis. 558; 92 N. W. 277; Mut. L. Ins. Co. v. Houchins, 52 La. Ann. 1137; 27 Sou. 657.

[95] Burgess v N. Y. Life Ins. Co. (Tex. Civ. A.), 53 S. W. 602; Barrett v. N. W. Mut. L. Ins. Co., 99 Ia. 637; 38 N. W. 906.

where the assignment is made,[96] and the delivery of a duplicate copy of the assignment to the company is sufficient although the insured retained the policy.[97] An assignment of a life policy need not be attached to the policy itself,[98] and an assignment of a life insurance policy is valid between the parties even though not written upon, or attached to, the policy, and though no reference thereto was written or noted on the policy, and is valid without notice to the company.[99] An assignment of the policy may be required to conform to the laws of the State where the assignment is made, though the contract be executed in another State.[100] A writing signed and acknowledged by insured and beneficiary assigning the policy, is a contract with the beneficiary and an absolute assignment, though he was not named in the body of the instrument.[101] An alteration of the policy by insurer at insured's request is sufficient to transfer the interest, though unknown to the persons to whom the policy was transferred until after the death of the insured.[102] Entry in a pocket memorandum book of deceased reciting that defendant as surety held the policy by way of security, the policy not being described, is not an assignment of the policy,[103] but a letter written the assignee of an insurance policy as to the application of the proceeds passed by way of assignment, whatever value the policy possessed after satisfying the lien of a prior assignment and in determining the rights under the policy,[104] the assignee appointed can claim the money collected by him on the policy under the order. The designation of a trustee by the insured to administer the fund derived from the policy amounts to a change of beneficiary and not an assignment.[105] The alteration of a policy by inserting an additional

[96] Wilde v. Wilde, 209 Mass. 205; 95 N. E. 295; Manhattan Life Ins. Co. v. Cohen (Tex. Civ. App.), 139 S. W. 51.

[97] New York Life Ins. Co. v. Dunlevy, 130 C. C. A. 473; 214 Fed. 1; affg. 204 Fed. 674.

[98] Tower v. Stanley, 220 Mass. 429; 107 N. E. 1010.

[99] Herman v. Connecticut Mut. Life Ins. Co., 218 Mass. 181; 105 N. E. 450; Pierce v. New York Life Ins. Co., 174 Mo. App. 383; 160 S. W. 40.

[100] Northwestern Mut. L. Ins. Co. v. Adams, 155 Wis. 335; 144 N. W. 1108.

[101] Carson v. National Life Ins. Co., 161 N. C. 441; 77 S. E. 853.

[102] York v. Flaherty, 210 Mass. 35; 96 N. E. 53.

[103] Little v. Berry (Ky.), 113 S. W. 902.

[104] Mut. Ben. Life Ins. Co. v. Swett, 137 C. C. A. 640; 222 Fed. 200.

[105] Howe v. Fidelity Trust Co., 28 Ky. L. 485; 89 S. W. 521.

beneficiary does not affect the rights of the first beneficiary nor prevent her from showing the mutilation.[106]

§ 385. **Assent of Insurer to Assignment.**—It has been said that the reasons requiring the assent of the underwriter to make assignments of fire insurance policies valid do not apply to cases of insurance upon human lives.[107] Where the assent of the insurer to an assignment was required by the policy, but there was no provision that an assignment without the consent of the company should avoid it, a parol transfer with delivery was held valid.[108] Where the assent of the company to an assignment is expressly required, such a stipulation is valid and will be enforced and must be obeyed like any other condition. And where the contract so provides an assignment without the consent of the company, even by way of collateral security, confers no title.[109] This assent may be given by the secretary, or any other person who is held out to the public as having the requisite authority, and may be in any form.[110] This assent is a matter between the company and the person asserting the claim under the policy, and consequently an assignment may be good between the parties, although the assent of the company is required by the terms of the contract and has not been obtained.[111] If the assignment is good under the law of the place where made it is good everywhere,[112] and the consent once given cannot be withdrawn[113] unless given under a mistake or because of misrepresentation.[114] A general assignment

[106] Provident Savings Life Assur. Soc. v. Dees, 122 Ky. 285; 86 S. W. 522.

[107] New York Life Ins. Co. v. Flack, 3 Md. 341; 56 Am. Dec. 742; Carter v. Mut. Reserve F. L. Ins. Ass'n, 78 Md. 72; 26 Atl. 959.

[108] Marcus v. St. Louis Mut. L. Ins. Co., 68 N. Y. 625.

[109] Wallace v. Bankers' Life Ass'n, 81 Mo. App. 102; McQuillan v. Mut. Reserve F. L. Ass'n, 112 Wis. 665; 87 N. W. 1069; 88 N. W. 925; 56 L. R. A. 233; Urick v. Western Travelers' Acc. Ass'n, 81 Neb. 327; 116 N. W. 48.

[110] Hubbard v. Stapp, 32 Ill. App. 541; Linder v. Fidelity, etc., Ass'n, 52 Minn. 304; 54 N. W. 95; Tremblay v. Aetna L. Ins. Co,. 97 Me. 547; 55 Atl. 509.

[111] Marcus v. St. L. Mut. Life Ins. Co., 68 N. Y. 625; Lee v. Murrell, 9 Ky. L. (Ky. Sup. Ct.) 104; Richardson v. White, 167 Mass. 58; 44 N. E. 1072.

[112] Lee v. Abdy, 17 Q. B. Div. 309.

[113] Grant v. Ins. Co., 75 Me. 203.

[114] Eastman v. Carroll Co., etc., 45 Me. 307; Merrill v. Farmers', etc., Ins. Co., 48 Me. 285.

of all insurance policies, where the assignor has some which are assignable and some which are not will not carry those which are not assignable nor such as would be made void by assignment. The general words of an assignment are restrained by the particular words creating the subject of the assignment.[115] The provision that the policy cannot be assigned without the consent of the insurer does not apply to a pledge of the policy.[116] An assignment by way of pledge will not avoid the policy;[117] and consenting to an assignment estops the company from objecting to its validity,[118] but does not preclude the company from any defense it may have as against the assignor.[119] By paying the money into court the company assents to the assignment.[120]

§ 386. **Effect of Assignment.**—The effect of an assignment of a policy with the consent of the insurer is to place the assignee in the same condition and position with respect to all rights and liabilities under it, that the insured occupied before the transfer. It amounts only to the substitution for the assured of the assignee as a party to the policy; it is the same as a reissue of the policy to another party upon precisely the same terms and conditions as in the original.[121] An agreement between the company and the insured and beneficiary for a sealing down of the amount of the

[115] Armstrong v. Mut. Life Ins. Co., 11 Fed. 573; Lazarus v. Commonwealth Ins. Co., 19 Pick. 81.

[116] Dickey v. Pocomoke City Nat'l Bank, 89 Md. 280; 43 Atl. 33.

[117] Mahr v. Bartlett, 7 N. Y. Supp. 143; citing Griffey v. Ins. Co., 100 N. Y. 417; 3 N. E. 309; Dickey v. Pocomoke N. B., 89 Md. 280; 43 Atl. 33.

[118] Smith v. Old People's, etc., 19 N. Y. Supp. 432; Hewins v. Baker, 161 Mass. 320; 37 N. E. 441. But see Morrill v. Manhattan L. Ins. Co., 183 Ill. 260; 55 N. E. 656.

[119] N. W. Mut. L. Ins. Co. v. Montgomery, 116 Ga. 799; 43 S. E. 79; Mut. Ben. L. Ins. Co. v. First Nat. Bank, 115 Ky. 757; 74 S. W. 1066.

[120] Thornburg v. Aetna L. Ins. Co., 30 Ind. App. 682; 66 N. E. 922; Opitz v. Karel, 118 Wis. 527; 95 N. W. 948; McGlynn v. Curry, 82 App. Div. 431; 81 N. Y. Supp. 855. See also as to waiver of notice, Corcoran v. Mut. L. Ins. Co., 179 Pa. St. 132; 36 Atl. 203, and as to estoppel of company, John Hancock Mut. L. Ins. Co. v. White, 20 R. I. 457; 40 Atl. 5; Corcoran v. N. Y. Mut. L. Ins. Co., 183 Pa. St. 443; 39 Atl. 50; Mut. Life Ins. Co. v. Hagerman, 19 Colo. App. 33; 72 Pac. 889.

[121] Ins. Co. v. Garland, 108 Ill. 220; 9 Bradw. 571; Harley v. Heist, 86 Ind. 196; Bowen v. National L. Ass'n, 63 Conn. 460; 27 Atl. 1059; Atlantic Mut. L. Ins. Co. v. Gannon, 179 Mass. 291; 60 N. E. 933.

policy is binding on the assignee.[122]   The assignee can, upon notice
to assured, demand and receive a paid-up policy where the insured
had paid neither the debt nor premium.[123]   The assignee can only
take that which the assignment gives him,[124] nor can the transfer
be attacked when the company does not object.[125]   An assignment
obtained by fraud will be set aside in proper equitable proceedings for that purpose[126] and it has been held that an assignor of
insurance policies may maintain an action to recover the policies
or their value on the ground that he was incapacitated by drunkenness to make the assignments without first having the assignments set aside by a suit in equity.[127]   An assignment once made,
cannot be revoked if it is completed by delivery,[128] equity having
no jurisdiction in such cases; but it will be set aside if made in
fraud of creditors.[129]   An assignment to certain creditors who were
to pay the premiums and on the maturity of the policy to pay the
surplus above the debts to the heirs, is not in fraud of the other
creditors, and if the administrator of insured afterwards collects
the surplus the heirs can recover it from him.[130]   The rights of
creditors, however, in life insurance policies carried or assigned
by the debtor, depend largely upon the statutes of the place where
the assured resides.[131]   The exemption of life insurance from the
demands of creditors applies to policies issued by a foreign as
well as a domestic insurance company.[132]   Where a policy is
wrongfully surrendered the rights of the beneficiary attach to

[122] Leonard v. Charter Oak L. Ins. Co., 65 Conn. 529; 33 Atl. 511.

[123] Du Brutz v. Bank of Visalia, 4 Cal. App. 201; 87 Pac. 467; Bush v.
Block, 193 Mo. App. 704; 187 S. W. 153.

[124] Diffenbach v. Vogeler, 61 Md. 376.

[125] Diffenbach v. Vogeler,*supra*.

[126] Collins v. Hare, 2 Bligh (N. S.), 106.

[127] Bursinger v. Bank of Watertown, 67 Wis. 75; 30 N. W. 290.

[128] Crittenden v. Phoenix Mut. L. Ins. Co., 41 Mich. 442.

[129] Aetna Nat. Bk. v. Manhattan L. Ins. Co., 24 Fed. 769.   See also
Malburg v. Metropolitan L. Ins. Co., 127 Mich. 568; 86 N. W. 1026.

[130] Johnson v. Alexander, 125 Ind. 575; 25 N. E. 706.

[131] Pullis v. Robinson, 73 Mo. 202, as modified by First Nat. Bk. v.
Simpson, 152 Mo. 638; 54 S. W. 506, and Judson v. Walker, 155 Mo. 166;
55 S. W. 1083; Cole y. Marple, 98 Ill. 58; Thompson v. Cundiff, 11 Bush
567; Baron v. Brummer, 100 N. Y. 372; Stigler v. Stigler, 77 Va. 163;
Ex parte Dever, 18 Q. B. Div. 660.

[132] Cross v. Armstrong, 44 Ohio St. 613.

the substituted policy.[133]   Where all persons designated as beneficiaries in a life policy do not join in an assignment the interest of those not joining is not affected.[134]   An assignee of a life policy is not liable for allowing it to lapse, no agreement to pay the premiums being shown.[135]   Where the policy was payable to "the insured, his executors, administrators, or assigns," on a certain day, or if he should die before the day named then payment to be made to his two children, provided they should survive him, otherwise to his executors, etc., with power to the insured to assign the policy, or to surrender it at any time and receive the surrender value, it was held[136] that the rights of the children, whether regarded as contingent, or as vested subject to divesting contingencies, are subordinate in every respect to the rights given by the policy to the insured; and the rights of the children are therefore defeated where the insured assigns the policy and the assignee surrenders it. It was further held that every right given by the policy to the insured passes under a general assignment for the benefit of creditors, and further that the Massachusetts statute[137] providing that the beneficiary in a policy of life insurance shall be entitled to the proceeds of the policy as against the creditors and representatives of the insured, merely protects the rights of beneficiaries when ascertained and has no operation to increase or extend those rights. The Court said: "The right of his children was to receive the amount of the policy if he did not live until the appointed time and if they survived him and he had not in his lifetime surrendered the policy. If this right is regarded as contingent, it would not come into existence at all if the father should at any earlier time exercise his absolute right to surrender the policy; if their right was a vested one, it would be completely divested by their father's exercise of his right. Their right, in the opinion of

[133] Chaplin v. Fellowes, 36 Conn. 132; Lemon v. Phoenix Mut. L. Ins. Co., 38 Conn. 298; Singer v. Charter Oak Ins. Co., 22 Fed. 774; Union Mut. L. Ins. Co. v. Stevens, 19 Fed. 671; Stillwell v. Mut. L. Ins. Co., 72 N. Y. 385; Whitehead v. N. Y. Life Ins. Co., 102 N. Y 143; reversing 33 Hun. 425; Timayenis v. Union Mut. L. Ins. Co., 22 Blatchf. 405; 21 Fed. 223.
[134] Breard v. New York Life Ins. Co., 138 La. 774; 70 Sou. 799.
[135] Killoran v. Sweet, 25 N. Y. Supp. 295.
[136] Blinn v. Dame, 207 Mass. 159; 93 N. E. 601; 20 Ann. Cas. 1184.
[137] St. 1907, c. 576; § 73.

the majority of the Court, was strictly subordinate to the prior and superior right of their father. It was so made by the very language which created it. Either it was not to arise at all if the paramount right of their father should be exercised, or it would be completely divested by the exercise of his paramount right to surrender the policy. Whether their interest was vested or contingent, they could have no part of the proceeds of the policy if their father lived until its maturity, or if they did not survive him, or if he had at any earlier time surrendered the policy. Unless these three contingencies occurred in their favor, either their right never would vest, or it would be completely divested and cut off by the terms of the conditional limitations in their favor. We do not deem it material to determine whether their right was vested or contingent; for as we have seen, the result would be the same in either event. There is no question here of the attempted revocation of a trust. Such cases as Stone. v. Hackett[138] and Kelley v. Snow[139] and those cases in which an absolute interest was given to beneficiaries of life insurance policies, have no bearing. We are to construe the language of the policy and to determine what rights it gives to the children. The statute which has been referred to protects these rights when ascertained, but it has no operation to increase or extend them. Under this state of affairs, the elder Dame made his assignment to the predecessors of the plaintiffs in the first action, hereinafter called the plaintiffs. The language of that instrument is broad and sweeping. It passes all his 'estate, property and effects, real, personal and mixed, of whatever name and nature, legal and equitable, . . . also all claims, debts, choses in action, owing to him, whether now or hereafter payable, and all evidences thereof; also any and all other property, real or personal, of or belonging to him, of whatever description and wheresoever the same may be . . . except such property as is exempt from being taken on execution by law.' This exception does not cover property which could not be taken on a writ of execution at common law; it manifestly refers only to the statutory exemptions stated in R. L. c. 177, Sec. 34. The instrument, we are satisfied, was intended to convey, and does convey, to the assignees all the property and property rights of the assignor which the creditors

[138] 12 Gray (Mass.) 227.
[139] 185 Mass. 288; 70 N. E. 89.

could have reached for the satisfaction of their demands by any process, legal or equitable. We do not doubt that the right of the assignor under this policy to receive the amount thereof on July 10, 1918, if he shall then be living, and his right to have the same amount paid to his personal representative upon his earlier decease if his children shall not survive him, would have been available to his creditors and would have passed under the assignment.[140] It seems equally plain that he may not now, as against his assignees, surrender the policy and take the amount of the surrender value for his own benefit. As against the insurance company no doubt he has that right. But it is a right secured to him by his contract with the company, and is a valuable right of property available to his creditors.[141] It is a chose in action which was in existence at the time of the assignment and passed by its terms. What we have said is also, in our opinion, decisive upon the only remaining question in the case. His right of surrender was a valuable property right, vested in him by the language of the policy. It constituted an integral part of the value to him or his estate of the policy itself. That pecuniary value would be very much less either to himself or to any one to whom he might transfer his property rights if this unqualified and paramount right of surrender were not secured to him. There was here an agreement on the part of the company to pay the surrender value to him upon his surrender; this was a contract right given to him by the policy, which materially increased its value to him. This was not merely a right to surrender under the third article or the third clause of the eighth article of the provisions attached to the policy. Under the parenthetical clause contained in the promise of the company he had the right to surrender the policy at any time and to receive its surrender value. Moreover, this clause was made a part of the conditional limitation or appointment in favor of his children, apparently for the very purpose of saving to him the absolute ownership and control of the policy. The children's right was made subject to his unrestricted right of surrender. This was a valuable

140 Anthracite Ins. Co. v. Sears, 109 Mass. 383; Lord v. Harte, 118 Mass. 271; Brigham v. Home L. Ins. Co., 131 Mass. 319; Pierce v. Charter Oak L. Ins. Co., 138 Mass. 151; Haskell v. Equitable L. Assur. Soc., 181 Mass. 341; 63 N. E. 899; Alexander v. McPeck, 189 Mass. 34; 75 N. E. 88; Bigert v. Straub, 193 Mass. 77; 78 N. E. 770; 118 Am. St. Rep. 449.
141 See the cases last above cited.

property right incident to his general right under the policy, such as would pass with an assignment of the latter.   It now must be held, in the opinion of the majority of the court, that it did pass, with the policy itself, under the general language of the assignment.'' The rights of assignees of life insurance policies will be further considered under the subject, Maturity of Contract.[142]

§ 387. **Assignment After Loss.**—A provision in an insurance policy avoiding it in case of its assignment without the consent of the company, applies only to an assignment made before a loss,[143] and after death of the insured an assignment is not affected by the Iowa Code relative to assignment in certain cases.[144] Assignment after loss passes the legal title and invests the assignee with the exclusive right to sue upon it.   In his hands, however, it is subject to every defense which could have been set up against it in the hands of the previous owner before notice of the assignment was given to the company.   The fact that the assignment was made as a collateral security for a debt will not vary the rule.[145] Nor that the consideration was fictitious.[146] An assignment of an insurance policy made before loss, but not delivered until afterwards, does not take effect until delivery and then is the assignment of a

142 *Post*, § 556, *et seq.* The following cases also deal with questions as to effect of assignment: Crocker v. Hogan, 103 Ia. 243; 72 N. W. 411; Lamb v. Mut. Res. F. L. Ass'n, 106 Fed. 637; Towne v. Towne, 93 Ill. App. 159; First Nat. Bk. v. Terry Admr. Speece, 99 Va. 194; 37 S. E. 843; Hirsch v. Mayer, 165 N. Y. 236; 59 N. E. 89; affg. 54 N. Y. Supp. 1075; Terry v. Mut. L. Ins. Co., 116 Ala. 242; 22 Sou. 532; Brown v. Equitable L. A. Soc., 75 Minn. 412; 79 N. W. 968; Penn. M. L. Ins. Co. v. Union Trust Co., 83 Fed. 891; *In re* Hamilton, 102 Fed. 683; Clark v. Fast, 128 Cal. 422; 61 Pac. 72.   As to undue influence in procuring an assignment, Penn. Mut. L. Ins. Co. v. Union Tr. Co., *supra.*

143 Dogge v. Northwestern, etc., Ins. Co,. 49 Wis. 501; Roger Williams, etc., Ins. Co. v. Carrington, 43 Mich. 252; Combs v. Shrewsbury, etc., Ins. Co., 32 N. J. Eq. 515; Supreme Assembly, etc., v. Campbell, 17 R. I. 402; 22 Atl. 307; Commonwealth v. Order of Solon, 193 Pa. St. 240; 44 Atl. 327; Briggs v. Earl, 139 Mass. 473; 1 N. E. 847.

144 McCombs v. Travelers' Ins. Co., 159 Ia. 445; 141 N. W. 327.

145 East Texas F. Ins. Co. v. Coffee, 61 Tex. 287; Perry v. Ins. Co., 25 Ala. 360; Archer v. Ins. Co., 43 Mo. 434; Wetmore v. San Francisco, etc., 44 Cal. 294; Carter v. Ins. Co., 12 Ia. 292; N. Y. L. Ins. Co. v. Flack, 3 Md. 341.

146 Metropolitan L. Ins. Co. v. Fuller, 61 Conn. 252; 23 Atl. 193.

money demand against the insurers.[147] A provision in a policy of fire insurance that the same shall not be assigned after the money thereon becomes due is void, being inconsistent with the covenant of indemnity and contrary to public policy.[148]

§ 388. **Change of Beneficiary is Different from Assignment.**— The assignment of a policy and a change of beneficiary are not the same but different things. An assignment is the transfer by one of his right, or interest, in property to another. It rests upon contract, and generally speaking, the delivery of the thing assigned is necessary to its validity. The power to change the beneficiary is the power to appoint.[149] The requirements of the policy as to formalities to be observed in changing the beneficiary must be observed. So if the policy requires the change to be endorsed on the policy it is not complete until so endorsed.[150] Where, however, the policy was mailed to the insurer for the purpose of having an endorsement change of beneficiary made thereon, the death of the beneficiary before the policy was received by the company and the endorsement made, does not render the change ineffective.[151] Where insured requested a change of beneficiary before the policy became effective by delivery to her, the former beneficiaries had no vested interest therein and the change became effective though not endorsed on the policy as required by a clause thereof prior to the death of the insured.[152] The inadvertent omission of the insured to comply with the requirements of the policy for the change of beneficiary by forwarding it, does not make the change ineffectual.[153] But where the order directing the change of beneficiary and the surrender of the policy was not given to the company until after the death of the insured, it was held[154] that there was no privity of contract between

[147] Watertown Ins. Co. v. Grover, etc,. Co., 41 Mich. 131.

[148] Alkan v. N. H. Fire Ins. Co., 53 Wis. 136; Spare v. Home Mut. Ins. Co., 9 Sawy. 142; 17 Fed. 568; Goit v. Ins. Co., 25 Barb. 189; West Branch Ins. Co. v. Helfenstein, 40 Pa. St. 289.

[149] Mut. Ben. L. Ins. Co. v. Swett, 137 C. C. A. 640; 222 Fed. 200.

[150] Rumsey v. New York Life Ins. Co., 59 Colo. 71, 147 Pac. 337; French v. Provident Savings Life Assur. Soc., 205 Mass. 424; 91 N. E. 577; Freund v. Freund, 218 Ill. 189; 75 N. E. 925; reversing 117 Ill. App. 565.

[151] Mut. Life Ins. Co. v. Sowther, 122 Colo. App. 622; 126 Pac. 882.

[152] Pierce v. New York Life Ins. Co., 174 Mo. App. 383; 160 S. W. 40.

[153] Mut. Life Ins. Co. v. Clanton, 76 N. J. Eq. 4; 73 Atl. 1052.

[154] O'Brien v. Continental Cas. Co., 184 Mass. 584; 69 N. E. 308 .

the proposed beneficiary and the company so as to entitle her to recover on the policy. The remedy in such a case is to have an administrator appointed.

§ 389. **Wife's Policy.**—In pursuance of this doctrine of the vested rights of the beneficiary of a life insurance policy, it has been held that, when the wife is the beneficiary and the husband survives her, the property descends to her representative as other personalty. Thus, where the deceased insured his life in favor of • his wife, who died intestate in his lifetime, leaving an only child, and then the husband died intestate and insolvent, the child surviving, it was held that the proceeds of the policy were, under the intestate laws of Pennsylvania, to be distributed, share and share alike, between the child and the representatives of the husband.[155] In Olmstead v. Keys, et al.[156] the policy was payable to the trustee of a wife and after her death her husband married again and had the policy changed so as to be payable to his second wife. The husband afterwards died, leaving several children by his first and one by his second wife. The Court of Appeals of New York held that the widow was entitled to the proceeds and applied the common-law right of the husband surviving his wife to her choses in action which he might reduce to possession.[157] In another case the same court held that where the policy was payable to wife and children and some die in the lifetime of the insured, the proceeds go to the survivors, on the principle that the law of joint tenancy applies where a class is named.[158] But the better rule is that the beneficiaries are tenants in common and the interest of a deceased beneficiary descends to the next of kin, or if there is a widow and children, then to them.[159] An assignment to husband and wife creates a joint ownership and the survivor takes the whole.[160] Where

[155] Anderson's Estate, 85 Pa. St. 202; United Breth. Mut. Aid Ass'n v. Miller, 107 Pa. St. 162; Entwistle v. Travelers' Ins. Co., 202 Pa. St. 141; 51 Atl. 759.

[156] 85 N. Y. 593.

[157] See also Continental L. Ins. Co. v. Hamilton, 41 Ohio St. 274; Lee v. Murrell, 7 Ky. L. 598; Cole v. Knickerbocker L. Ins. Co., 63 How. Pr. 442.

[158] Walsh v. Mut. L. Ins. Co., 133 N. Y. 408; 31 N. E. 228; reversing 15 N. Y. Supp. 697; Lane v. DeMetz, 13 N. Y. Supp. 347.

[159] Voss v. Conn. L. Ins. Co,. 119 Mich. 161; 77 N. W. 697; 44 L. R. A. 689; Millard v. Drayton, 177 Mass. 533; 59 N. E. 436; 52 L. R. A. 117·

[160] Arn v. Arn, 81 Mo App. 133.

810

the policy was payable to wife if living, or if not to the children
then living, the death of the wife is the time which fixes the rights
of the children.[161] When the policy is payable to wife and children
after-born children are excluded,[162] and a child of a second
wife;[163] and in a case in Iowa[164] where the policy was payable to
the wife and her legal representatives or, if she were not living,
to her children, it was held that on her death the wife's rights
were extinguished. In the case of benefit societies, where the right
is reserved to the member to control and dispose of the benefit at
all times, if the certificate is made payable to the wife and she die
before her husband, her interest will be held to have terminated at
her death,[165] and under some conditions his representatives will
have the preference over hers, as where such appears to have been
the intent,[166] and where the certificate was payable to the wife "or
her legal representatives" and she died before the husband, it was
held by a divided Court[166a] that the trust was intended for the
wife alone and upon her death resulted to the husband, upon the
principle that where the object of the trust fails there is a resulting
trust to the grantor. If the wife die in the lifetime of the husband
a policy on his life payable to her may become his by being reduced
to possession as other personal property of the wife.[167] The words
"legal representatives" were held to have no signification different from that which is attributable to those words generally, viz.,
persons appointed either by will or by the law to administer upon

[161] U. S. Trust Co. v. Mut. Ben. L. Ins. Co., 115 N. Y. 152; 21 N. E. 1025;
reversing 4 N. Y. Supp. 543.

[162] Conn. Mut. L. Ins. Co. v. Baldwin, 15 R. I. 106; 23 Atl. 105. To the
contrary is Roquemore v. Dent, 135 Ala. 292; 33 Sou. 178. This on principle would not be so in the case of a benefit society.

[163] Aetna L. Ins. Co. v. Clough, 68 N. H. 298; 44 Atl. 520; Smith v. Aetna
Ins. Co., 68 N. H. 405; 44 Atl. 531.

[164] In re Conrad's Est., 89 Ia. 396; 56 N. W. 535. See also Waldheim v.
John Hancock L. Ins. Co., 28 N. Y. Supp. 766.

[165] Richmond v. Johnson, 28 Minn. 447; Tafel v. Knights of the Golden
Rule, 12 Cin. L. Bul. 35. But see Riley v. Riley, 75 Wis. 464; 44 N. W. 112;
Adler v. Stoffel (Breitung's Est.), 78 Wis. 33; 46 N. W. 891; 47 N. W. 17;
also § 244.

[166] Expressmen's, etc., Soc. v. Lewis, 9 Mo. App. 412.

[166a] Washington, etc., Ass'n v. Wood, 4 Mack. 19.

[167] Handwerker v. Durmeyer, 96 Tenn. 619; 36 S. W. 869; D'Arcy v.
Conn. Mut. L. Ins. Co., 108 Tenn. 567; 69 S. W. 768.

the estate of a deceased. Under special circumstances the proceeds
of a policy upon the husband's life payable to the wife who dies
before her husband will be divided between his estate and hers.[168]
The words "legal representatives" have also been held to include
assigns, as where a policy was payable to "legal representatives"
and the insured assigned it.[169] In an assignment to the wife, "if
living," the words mean if living at the maturity of the policy.[170]
A husband cannot assign a policy on his life payable to the wife,
if living at the time of his death, if not, to his estate.[171] Under
the Wisconsin statute the husband after divorce can change the
beneficiary from the divorced wife to his second wife.[172] The rule
in Texas is that divorce cancels the wife's interest in a policy of
life insurance.[173] In the case of a wife designated as beneficiary
in the certificate of a fraternal beneficiary society, where her interest is a mere expectancy it is held in many cases that divorce
operates as a revocation of designation.[174] Generally, the question
is one of construction of the policy and an application of the statutes governing descents, or governing the disposition of policies
payable to the wife.[175] Under some circumstances evidence of intent will be admissible and control the disposition, as where a policy of insurance was in the name of a wife on the life of her husband and the amount was payable to the wife, her executors, administrators or assigns, if she survived her husband; otherwise to
their children for their use or to their guardian if under age. The
wife did not survive her husband, and the only child was one by

168 Estate of Balz, 12 Phila. 29; National Life Ins. Co. v. Haley, 78 Me.
268.

169 Hurst v. Mut. Reserve F. L. Ins. Co., 78 Md. 59; 26 Atl. 956.

170 Burton v. Burton, 56 App. Div. 1; 67 N. Y. Supp. 338.

171 Union Cent. L. Ins. Co. v. Woods, 11 Ind. App. 335; 37 N. E. 180.

172 Ormond v. McKinley, 163 Wis. 205; 157 N. W. 786.

173 Northwestern Mut. Life Ins. Co. v. Whitselle (Tex. Civ. App.), 188
S. W. 22; citing Hatch v. Hatch, 35 Tex. Civ. App. 373; 80 S. W. 411. See
ante, § 378.

174 See ante, § 326.

175 Continental Life Ins. Co. v. Webb, 54 Ala. 688; Drake v. Stone, 58
Ala. 183; Fearn v. Ward, 65 Ala. 33; Fletcher v. Collier, 61 Ga. 653; Conn.
M. Life Ins. Co. v. Fish, 59 N. H. 126; Norris v. Massachusetts M. L. Ins.
Co., 131 Mass. 294; Troy v. Sargent, 132 Mass. 408; In re Adams Policy
Trusts, 28 Ch. Div. 525; In re Mellor's Policy Trusts, 6 Ch. Div. 127.

adoption who was of age. It was held[176] that the children were the sole beneficiaries and the policy was payable to them and that as the only child was one by adoption and the circumstances showed that the parties intended that he should be included in the benefits of the policy, he was entitled to all the proceeds of such policy. Generally, a policy payable to a married woman is her separate property and cannot be pledged for her husband's debts nor changed into separate property of the husband by surrender and issue of new policy,[177] but the assignee of a wife's policy may be entitled to a return of premiums paid by him.[178] A policy payable to the wife is usually subject to her debts,[179] but not when exempted by statute.[180] The contingent interest of a wife in a policy on the life of her husband, payable to her if living at the time of his death, and if not so living, to her children, does not constitute her separate property that can be charged under an assignment by her and her husband of the policy to secure the debt of the latter, even though she collected the policy, and the money so collected is not chargeable under such an assignment.[181] A husband cannot withdraw the accumulations of a policy payable to the wife, though she be ignorant of the existence of the policy.[182] A statute providing that a policy payable to a married woman shall inure to the benefit of her separate use and that of her children does not enlarge the rights of the children beyond what are secured to them by the contract.[183]

Under the Missouri law, which provides that in "the event of the death or divorcement of the wife before the decease of the husband" he may designate another beneficiary.[184] It has been

[176] Martin v. Aetna L. Ins. Co., 73 Me. 25.

[177] Putnam v. N. Y. Life Ins. Co., 42 La. Ann. 739; 7 Sou. 602.

[178] Conn. Mut. L. Ins. Co. v. Van Campen, 11 N. Y. Supp. 103.

[179] Amberg v. Manhattan L. Ins. Co., 171 N. Y. 314; 63 N. E. 111; reversing 67 N. Y. Supp. 872.

[180] Ellison v. Straw, 116 Wis. 207; 92 N. W. 1094.

[181] Stickton v. Schmidt, 64 Ohio St. 354; 60 N. E. 561. As to community property, Martin v. McAllister, 94 Tex. 567; 63 S. W. 624; 56 L. R. A. 585; reversing 61 S. W. 622.

[182] N. Y. Life Ins. Co. v. Ireland (Tex.), 17 S. W. 617; Weatherbee v. New York Life Ins. Co., 182 Mass. 342; 65 N. E. 383.

[183] Wirgman v. Miller, 98 Ky. 620; 33 S. W. 937.

[184] R. S. Mo. 1909, § 6944.

held[185] that the right is vouchsafed to the husband without regard as to who was adjudged to be at fault in the divorce proceedings and the statute violates no vested right of wife and is constitutional. It has also been held[186] that the ordinary meaning of the word divorcement is practically the same as divorce and simply means a legal dissolution of the marriage contract without any distinction as to who was in fault in bringing about the dissolution. A policy on the life of a husband payable to the wife is her property and her interest cannot be divested except by her own act or in accordance with the stipulations of the contract,[187] and making a policy payable to the wife and delivering it to her, she paying the premiums, is a settlement by the husband upon her, creating a separate estate.[188] Where the insured having a policy payable to his estate assigned it to his wife, the assignment providing that if the insured survive the tontine period of fifteen years, the assignment should be void, the insured having an option at the end of such period to withdraw the accumulated surplus, which option could be exercised by the insured without the consent of the beneficiary. After the insured had exercised such option the policy and original assignment remained in the custody of the husband. It was held that no formal reassignment of the policy to the wife was necessary and after the death of the husband she was entitled to the proceeds.[189] The Missouri statute providing that in case of the divorcement of the wife the husband may designate another beneficiary, has no application to a policy issued before the enactment of the statute which was payable to the wife, and she received a vested interest which was not affected by divorce.[190]

§ 390. **The Same Subject: Rights of Husband's Creditors.**— In nearly all the States it is provided by statute that a husband may insure his life for the benefit of wife and children and that the proceeds of such policies shall not be subjected to the payment

185 Orthwein v. Germania Life Ins. Co., 261 Mo. 650; 170 S. W. 885.

186 Haven v. Home Life Ins. Co., 149 Mo. App. 291; 130 S. W. 73.

187 American Central Life Ins. Co. v. Rosenstein, 46 Ind. App. 537; 88 N. E. 97; 92 N. E. 380.

188 Marquet v. Aetna Life Ins. Co., 128 Tenn. 213; 159 S. W. 733.

189 In re Sanson's Estate, 217 Pa. 203; 66 Atl. 334.

190 Blum v. New York Life Ins. Co., 197 Mo. 513; 95 S. W. 317; 8 L. R. A. (N. S.), 923.

of his debts. Where such a statute exists it is immaterial that the husband was insolvent at the time the insurance was effected,[191] nor is the amount of the insurance material.[192] But where the statute limits the amount that may be applied by the husband to the payment of premiums on policies for the wife's benefit the interest of the creditors in the excess of premiums so paid may be declared by a court of equity though the policies are not due.[193] To recover, the creditors must show not only that the husband was insolvent at the time but that the payments were made in fraud of existing creditors.[194] The protection of the statute does not apply to policies taken out by the debtor for his own benefit and assigned by him while insolvent to his wife and children.[195] The rights of creditors depend upon the statutes of the several States and it is not deemed necessary to examine them in detail. These statutes are to have a liberal construction.[196] It has been held that the endowment insurance is not within the act and creditors can have the same set set aside.[197] It is not clearly settled whether, when the assured has paid out for premiums an amount exceeding that fixed by the statute, creditors are limited to the excess of premiums paid or can share in the insurance proportionately as the

[191] Central Nat. Bank v. Hume, 128 U. S. 195; 9 S. C. 41; McCutcheon's Appeal, 99 Pa. St. 137; Johnson v. Bacon, 92 Miss. 156; 45 Sou. 858.

[192] Harvey v. Harrison, 89 Tenn. 470; 14 S. W. 1038; First Nat'l Bank v. Simpson, 152 Mo. 638; 54 S. W. 506.

[193] Stokes v. Amerman, 121 N. Y. 337; 24 N. E. 819; Ins. Co. v. Eckert, 6 Am. L. Rec. 482.

[194] Weber v. Paxton, 48 Ohio St. 266; 26 N. E. 1051; Central Nat. Bank v. Hume, *supra;* Wagner v. Koch, 4 Ill. App. 501; Jones v. Patty, 73 Miss. 179; 18 Sou. 794.

[195] Ionia Co. Sav. Bank v. McLean, 84 Mich. 625; 48 N. W. 159; Cross v. Armstrong, 44 Ohio St. 613; 10 N. E. 160; Elliot's App., 50 Pa. St. 75; see also Bank v. Ins. Co., 24 Fed. 770; Pence v. Makepeace, 65 Ind. 347; Succession of Hearing, 26 L. Ann. 326; Stigler's Exr. v. Stigler, 77 Va. 163; Thompson v. Cundiff, 11 Bush. 567; Barbour v. Conn. Mut. L. Ins. Co., 61 Conn. 240; Fearn v. Ward, 65 Ala. 33; 80 *Id.* 555.

[196] Felrath v. Schonfield, 76 Ala. 199; Cole v. Marple, 98 Ill. 58; Thompson v. Cundiff, 11 Bush. 567; Hathaway v. Sherman, 61 Me. 466; Elliott v. Bryan, 64 Md. 638; Earnshaw v. Stewart, *Id.* 513; Gale v. McLaurin, 66 Miss. 461.

[197] Talcott v. Field, 34 Neb. 611; 52 N. W. 400; Tompkins v. Levy, 87 Ala. 263; 6 Sou. 846. But see to the contrary Briggs v. McCullough, 36 Cal. 550.

excess is to the total amount; or in proportion as the premiums paid while insolvent bear to those paid when solvent.[198] In the case of Red River National Bank v. DeBerry,[199] the Court said: "We think these cases announce a just rule, provided the sum recoverable by appellants, if any, on account of premiums paid by Love while insolvent, be diminished by the amount which $300 would have purchased at the date of its investment, and provided there is nothing in the policies themselves to vary the rule. In other words, if Love was at all times solvent and not financially embarrassed, the statute does not limit his right of investment; if at all times insolvent or embarrassed, he could invest annually $300 in premiums, and the amount which that sum would buy would be the extent of the exemption in favor of his widow and children; if insolvent at the time of payments of some only of the premiums, then the sum recoverable should be diminished by the amount which $300 annually paid would have purchased for the year or years of such investments while insolvent or embarrassed, unless a different construction be necessary by reason of the terms and conditions of the policies, none of which is contained in the record, and we are not intending to state an invariable rule." The Supreme Court of Missouri has said:[200] "The rule above laid down in Pullis v. Robison[201] may be taken as the authoritative measure of the creditor's right of recovery under the statute as it stood when the rights in that case accrued. But in 1879 the statute as originally enacted had undergone the test of experience, and these questions having arisen the legislature, seemingly for the very purpose of putting them at rest, amended the act, by raising the amount permitted to be expended for this purpose by the insolvent husband, and specifying the measure of the creditor's recovery in case the insurance was obtained at a

---

[198] Supporting the latter proposition is Pullis v. Robinson, 73 Mo. 202; reversing 5 M. A. 548; also Charter Oak L. Ins. Co. v. Brant, 47 Mo. 419. As to proportion excess of premiums over statutory amount bears to all. In re Yeager, 5 Ins. L. J. 238. As to statutory limitations, Cole v. Marple, 98 Ill. 58; Ingler v. New Eng. L. Ins. Co., 15 Ins. L. J. 557; Brown v. Balfour, 46 Minn. 68; Cross v. Armstrong, 44 Ohio St. 613; Trough's Est., 8 Phil. 214. See also post, § 415.

[199] 47 Tex. Civ. A. 96; 105 S. W. 998.

[200] Judson v. Walker, 155 Mo. 166; 55 S. W. 1083.

[201] 73 Mo. 201.

greater cost out of the insolvent's estate. The proviso in the original act was in these words: 'But such exemption shall not apply when the amount of premiums annually paid shall exceed three hundred dollars.' That is what was before the court in Pullis v. Robison. But by the amendment in 1879 the proviso reads, 'but when the premiums paid in any year out of the funds or property of the husband shall exceed five hundred dollars, such exemption from such claims shall not apply to so much of said premiums so paid as shall be in excess of five hundred dollars, but such excess, with interest thereon, shall inure to the benefit of his creditors.'[202] So the law stood when the rights of the parties to these suits arose, and so it stands today. In the face of this plain expression of the lawmaking power of the State, what is the use of our searching to see what courts in other States have said on the common law of the subject or on statutes different from ours? The amount that the creditors are entitled to recover in this case is the amount Mr. Walker paid for this insurance at the time it was effected for the benefit of his wife and children, plus premiums thereafter paid, minus $500 which he is authorized to pay, and legal interest on the same. What did he pay? The trial court treated all the premiums paid from the incipiency of the policies at the cost of the insurance, amounting for the seven years to $7,874, and deducted the amount the statute allowed to be expended, $500 a year, total $3,500, leaving $4,374, the amount with interest for plaintiffs to recover. But the insurance obtained in January, 1894, for Mrs. Walker and her children did not cost $7,874. That was the sum of all the premiums that had been paid, and for so much of that sum as was paid before January, 1894, Walker, and through him his creditors, had received the benefit in the form of insurance carried, and to that extent the insurance companies had earned those premiums. But it was not all exhausted in carrying the insurance because at the end of that period, in January, 1894, the policies had a cash value, which could be realized, and which was utilized in this new insurance effected by Walker for his wife and children. If instead of changing the beneficiaries in the policies he had surrendered them and taken their values in cash from the companies and had afterwards applied for new policies in the same companies on the same plans,

202 Sec. 5978, R. S. 1879.

they would have cost him more than it cost him in 1888 to take out the same policies; his increased age would have increased the cost even if nothing else intervened. But by planting the new insurance on the old, he preserved not only the premium rate, but also other advantages which the evidence shows would accrue after a number of years on policies of that kind and did accrue on these policies. Those advantages gave the policies their cash value over and above the mere risk that had been carried, and it is that value that Walker utilized in the insurance taken for his family, and that they must account for. . . . Learned counsel say they look in vain in the policies in evidence in this case for any provision that entitled the insured to surrender his policy and receive the cash value therefor.' But their own proof showed that it was the fact, and it is as much a fact in the case as if it were so nominated in the bond, whether we call it a surrender value or a market value, the fact is there was a cash value which the holder could realize at his option. The evidence shows that the cash value of the two New York Life policies on January 20, 1894, was $1,820.33, to which is to be added $263 premiums paid on the $10,000 policy in December, 1894, making $2,083.33 less $500, leaving $1,583.33, which with interest at six per cent from January 20, 1894, is the amount of the recovery the defendants must suffer for these two policies, of which Mrs. Walker is to pay one-sixth and each of the children, after the four minors shall have been properly brought in, one-sixth. The cash value of the Equitable policy on January 26, 1894, was $204.85, to which add $375, the premium paid December 20, 1894, and six per cent interest on each amount from the respective dates above named, and the sum will be what Mrs. Walker is to pay on account of that policy.''
An administrator of an insolvent intestate by virtue of the powers conferred upon him by the statutes of Ohio, may maintain a suit in equity to recover personal property transferred by the decedent in fraud of his creditors, and for that reason can maintain an action to subject life insurance policy to the lien of the creditors.[203] In a late case[204] the Supreme Court of Missouri discusses the question as follows: ''Section 5853, Revised Statutes 1889,

[203] Mut. Life Ins. Co. v. Farmers, etc., Bank, 173 Fed. 390.
[204] Sternberg v. Levi, 159 Mo. 617; 50 S. W. 1114; 53 L. R. A. 438; reversing s. c. 76 Mo. App. 590.

gives a sister an insurable interest in her brother's life. Without this provision this policy of insurance would be void, and no matter how much premiums were paid neither the sister nor the brother's creditors would be able to collect a cent of the insurance after his death. So here, as in the Judson case, the proceeds of this insurance, 'are not the product of premiums alone, but of premiums united with the beneficiary's insurable interest.' For this reason alone it is clear that the rule laid down in the case of Pullis v. Robinson,[205] is not the true rule now, and was not the true rule even under the statute as it stood then. But if a man is entitled to his salary and certain exemptions as the head of a family which his creditors can not touch, and if he chooses to spend a part of his salary in premiums for life insurance for the benefit of his family after he is gone, his creditors are not thereby defrauded, for he has withdrawn no part of his property which his creditors could touch. Hence the provision added to the statute in 1879 did not change the right of a head of a family under the exemption laws. Under the law as it stood when the Pullis case was decided the head of a family could use his salary and his exempt property up to the value of $300, to pay the yearly premiums on insurance for his family, without defrauding his creditors. Such an use of his exempt property no more defrauded his creditors than if he had spent it in riotous and high living or than if he had paid necessary expenses or had given it away. The statute at that time was simply declarative of a right he had before. The amendment of 1879 raised the limit of exemptions, *pro hac vice,* from three hundred to five hundred dollars, but it did not change the principle involved. Afterwards, as before, it was a fraud for an insolvent to withdraw the excess of his property over his exemptions from the reach of his creditors and invest it in insurance for his family, and such excess, representing the extent of the fraud, with interest, the creditors can reach. But as the premiums did not alone produce the proceeds of the insurance and it required also an insurable interest to produce such proceeds, and as there is no legal formula for apportioning the proportion of such excess that should be credited to the payment of premiums and the portion that should be credited to insurable interest, the courts take the only practical course and do not at-

[205] 73 Mo. 201.

tempt to work out such formula or distribution, but award the creditor the known sum so fraudulently withdrawn from the reach of the creditors, the excess over the exemption, and restore it to the creditors with interest. Thus the creditor is placed in the same position that he would have been in if the fraud had not been perpetrated—he gets all the property of the debtor that he has a right to touch, and the interest allowed is the legal measure of his damages for not getting the money when he should have gotten it.'' Where life policies were issued to assured who afterwards made an assignment and the policies were treated as of no value he can surrender them and take out others payable to his wife instead of himself.[206] A statute authorizing a father to insure his life in favor of a minor child does not authorize him to assign to it a policy payable to himself, he being in debt at the time.[207]

§ 391. **Assignment By Wife of Policy on Husband's Life.**—In cases where a policy of life insurance on the husband's life has been made payable to the wife, her power to assign has often come in question. The decisions of the courts upon this subject have not been uniform, for in many States statutes exist regulating to a greater or less extent the rights of the wife, and the conclusions of the judges have been influenced largely by the provisions of those statutes and the supposed policy of the law. In the absence of statutory restrictions a wife can assign a policy on her husband's life just as any other chose in action and if her assignment has been obtained by fraud it will be set aside.[208] One of the leading cases on the subject is Eadie v. Slimmon,[209] where the Court of Appeals of New York held that a policy of life insurance, payable to the wife for her benefit, and that of her children in case of her death, could not be transferred so as to divest the interest of the wife or her children. This was under the supposed effect of the statute of the State which distinguished between a policy of life insurance payable to the wife and an ordinary chose in action. The Court said: ''The provision is special and peculiar, and looks

---

[206] Barbour v. Conn. Mut. Ins. Co., 61 Conn. 240; 23 Atl. 154.
[207] Friedman v. Fennell, 94 Ala. 570; 10 Sou. 649.
[208] Cockrell v. Cockrell, 79 Miss. 569; 31 Sou. 203.
[209] 26 N. Y. 9; see also Brick v. Campbell, 122 N. Y. 337.

to a provision for a state of widowhood, and for orphan children; and it would be a violation of the spirit of the provision to hold that a wife, insured under this act, culd sell or traffic with her policy as though it were realized personal property or an ordinary security for money.''[210]   But this reasoning was held not to apply to an endowment policy under a later statute authorizing a transfer of a life insurance policy by a married woman with the consent of her husband.[211]   Where the wife, under the New York statute, could not assign the policy, a subsequent removal of the disability will not validate a prior assignment,[212] and where the policy assigned was an endowment policy and the husband survived the endowment period it was held that an assignment made by the husband and wife during such period was valid as to the former, and made so as to the wife by her husband's survival, because by his survival the interest of the wife ceased, the policy being payable to her or to the husband if living at the end of the endowment period.[213]   Under the present law a beneficiary, though a wife, can assign a policy.[214]   If the written assent of the husband is by statute required an assignment without such consent is void.[215]   A mere pledge by husband and wife does not transfer the policy.[216]   If a statute provides that a policy on the husband's life shall be for the benefit of ''wife and children,'' even after the death of the husband the wife cannot dispose of the interest of the children and it is doubtful if she can

[210] Wilson v. Lawrence, 76 N. Y. 585; 13 Hun. 238; Barry v. Equitable Life Ass. Soc., 59 N. Y. 587.

[211] Brummer v. Cohn, 86 N. Y. 11; 9 Daly 36; 58 How. Pr. 239; 6 Abb. N. C. 409; 57 How. Pr. 386; DeJonge v. Goldsmith, 14 Jones & Sp. 131.

[212] Brick v. Campbell, 122 N. Y. 337; 25 N. E. 493. See also Miller v. Campbell, 140 N. Y. 457; 35 N. E. 651.

[213] Miller v. Campbell, 140 N. Y. 457; 35 N. E. 651; affg. 22 N. Y. Supp. 388.

[214] Spencer v. Myers, 26 N. Y. Supp. 371; 150 N. Y. 269; 44 N. E. 982; 34 L. R. A. 175; Travelers' Ins. Co. v. Healey, 19 Misc. 584; 44 N. Y. Supp. 1043. See also Morschauser v. Pierce, 64 App. Div. 558; 72 N. Y. Supp. 328.

[215] Danhauser v. Wallenstein, 52 App. Div. 312; 65 N. Y. Supp. 219; reversing 23 Misc. 690; 60 N. Y. Supp. 50.

[216] Travelers' Ins. Co. v. Healey, 164 N. Y. 607; 58 N. E. 1093; affg. 49 N. Y. Supp. 29.

assign at all.[217] The wrongful assignment of the policy is void-able at the wife's option;[218] and where the assignment by the wife was obtained by fraud the assignment will be held invalid, as where the wife was ignorant and the assignment was procured by the husband as security for his debt, she not knowing what the effect of the paper was that she signed.[219] The fact of an assign-ment must be fairly shown and a doubt will be solved in favor of the wife.[220] The fact that the assignment was made without the State does not affect it if the contract of insurance was made in the State.[221] The Supreme Court of Connecticut,[222] while in-clined to adopt the view of the New York court, seemed to believe that if the wife paid the premiums on the policy out of her own estate that would materially influence the case, for she ought under those circumstances to have the same rights to dispose of a life insurance policy as any other chose in action. And where the wife pays the premiums out of her own money the policy is ab-solutely hers regardless of its amount.[223] The assignment of a policy on the husband's life by the wife as a security for his debt has been held void under a statute forbidding the wife to become surety for her husband,[224] and the wife's assignments have often been avoided when made under duress or undue influence,[225] or obtained by fraud,[226] or if made have been released under prin-ciples of law applicable to sureties, as by extension of time of pay-

[217] Wanschaff v. Masonic, etc., Soc., 41 Mo. App. 206; Pratt v. Globe M. L. Ins. Co., 3 Tenn. (Shannon), 174; 17 S. W. 352; In Ellison v. Straw, 116 Wis. 207; 92 N. W. 1094, it was held that the wife had no power to assign.

[218] Frank v. Mut. Life Ins. Co., 102 N. Y. 266; modifyng 12 Daly, 267; Milhous v. Johnson, 4 N. Y. Supp. 199.

[219] Mut. Ben. L. Ins. Co. v. Wayne Savings Bank, 68 Mich. 163; 35 N. W. 853; Cockrell v. Cockrell, 79 Miss. 569; 31 Sou. 203.

[220] Weinecke v. Arbin, 88 Md. 182; 40 Atl. 709; 41 L. R. A. 142.

[221] Mut. L. Ins. Co. v. Terry, 62 How. Pr. 325; but see Bloomingdale v. Liberger, 24 Hun. 355.

[222] Connecticut Mut. L. Ins. Co. v. Burroughs, 34 Conn. 305.

[223] In re Goss' Est., 71 Hun. 120; 24 N. Y. Supp. 623.

[224] Stokell v. Kimball, 59 N. H. 13.

[225] Conn. Mut. Life Ins. Co. v. Westervelt, 52 Conn. 576; Whitridge v. Barry, 42 Md. 140; Barry v. Brune, 71 N. Y. 261; 8 Hun. 395; Barry v. Equitable Life Ass. Soc., 59 N. Y. 587.

[226] McCutcheon's Appeal, 99 Pa. St. 133. See also Miller v. Powers, 119 Ind. 79; 21 N. E. 455.

ment of the debt without her knowledge.[227] Under a statute of Georgia it has been held by the Supreme Court of that State that a wife cannot assign to a creditor of the husband a policy on the latter's life, nor without other consideration ratify the assignment after his death.[228] It has been held that the statutes of New York in force at the time of the assignment[229] did not apply to policies made payable to the wife "or her assigns."[230] A policy of insurance upon the life of the husband for the benefit of the wife, may be pledged as collateral security by her for the debt of the husband or assigned by her absolutely, unless prohibited by local statute, the policy being a writing obligatory for the payment of money and assignable at law as well as equity. "This," says the Supreme Court of Colorado,[231] "is, we think, settled by the great weight of authority."[232] The policy may be assigned by the wife by mere indorsement and delivery[233] and without the consent of the husband.[234] The assignment, however, must be in writing,[235] and need not, under a statute requiring recording of transfers between husband and wife, be recorded.[236] An assignment by the wife of a policy on her husband's life payable to her cannot be avoided by her creditors, either on the ground that it was not assignable, or because it was fraudulently assigned, the right to avoid can only be exercised by the wife or her personal representatives.[237] Upon the theory that a vested estate, even though

[227] Allis v. Ware, 28 Minn. 166.

[228] Smith v. Head, 75 Ga. 755.

[229] 1868.

[230] Robinson v. Mut. L. Ins. Co., 16 Blatchf. 194.

[231] Collins, et al. v. Dawley, 4 Colo. 140.

[232] DeRonge v. Elliot, 23 N. J. Eq. 486; Charter Oak Ins. Co. v. Brant, 47 Mo. 419; Chapin v. Fellowes, 36 Conn. 132; Merrill v. N. E. Mut. L. Ins. Co., 103 Mass. 245; Pomeroy v. Manhattan L. Ins. Co., 40 Ill. 398; Damron v. Penn. Mut. L. Ins. Co., 99 Ind. 478; Pence v. Makepeace, 65 Ind. 345; Scobey v. Waters, 10 Lea. 551; Mente v. Townsend, 68 Ark. 391; 59 S. W. 41; Rathborne v. Hatch, 90 App. Div. 161; 85 N. Y. Supp. 775.

[233] Conn. Mut. L. Ins. Co. v. Westervelt, 52 Conn. 586; Norwood v. Guerdon, 60 Ill. 253.

[234] Whitridge v. Barry, 42 Md. 140.

[235] Travelers' Ins. Co. v. Healey, 28 N. Y. Supp. 478.

[236] Morehead v. Mayfield, 109 Ky. 51; 58 S. W. 473. See also Miller v. Manhattan L. Ins. Co.., 110 La. Ann. 652; 34 Sou. 723..

[237] Smillie v. Quinn, 90 N. Y. 492; 25 Hun. 332.

liable to be defeated by a condition subsequent, is transmissible and devisable, it has been held that, where a wife insured the life of her husband, the amount payable to herself if living, if not, to their children, and she died before her husband, and one of the children died before him, leaving a child, a transmissible interest vested in the children upon the issuing of the policy, and that the child of the deceased child took by descent the interest of its parent and was entitled to the portion of the fund which its parent would have received if living.[238] In a prior case on a similar policy in the same court,[239] where the life of the husband was insured for the benefit of the wife, and in case of her death, to the children, and the wife assigned the policy to a creditor and died during the lifetime of the husband, it was held that the interests of the children were unaffected by the assignment. But if there had been no children then the assignment would have been good and the right of the wife's representatives would not have been affected by her divorce nor by the fact that the husband paid the premiums.[240] The interest of the husband in a policy payable to the wife is on her death purely equitable and his creditor cannot garnish;[241] but where the policy was payable to the "wife, her heirs and assigns" and she died before her husband, it was held that the proceeds were subject to his debts and did not go to her children;[242] so where the wife and children had assigned their interest to the husband the policy on his death is assets of his estate.[243] The title to a policy payable to the wife "or her representatives," or if not living to "their children" does not pass under a will by the wife to her husband of all her personal property;[244] it would pass, however, under such a will if she were child-

[238] Continental L. Ins. Co. v. Palmer, 42 Conn. 64. See also Cent. National Bank v. Hume. 128 U. S. 195; 9 S. C. R. 41; Stokes v. Amerman, 121 N. Y. 337; 24 N. E. 819; Harvey v. Harrison, 89 Tenn. 470; 14 S. W. 1083.

[239] Conn. Mut. L. Ins. Co. v. Burroughs, 34 Conn. 305; 19 Am. Rep. 530.

[240] Phoenix Mut. L. Ins. Co. v. Dunham, 46 Conn. 79; Brown's App., 125 Pa. St. 303; 17 Atl. 419.

[241] Nims v. Ferd, 159 Mass. 575; 35 N. E. 100.

[242] Tompkins v. Levy, 87 Ala. 263; 6 Sou. 346.

[243] Boyden v. Mass. M. L. Ins. Co., 153 Mass. 544; 27 N. E. 669.

[244] Evans v. Opperman, 76 Tex. 293; 13 S. W. 312.

less.[245] A father as guardian cannot assign a paid-up policy payable to his children.[246] And where an endowment policy was payable to the husband if living at its maturity and if not to his wife if living, otherwise to his estate or assigns, it was held that its delivery vested the title in the whole in both husband and wife and neither the husband or the wife could divest it by assignment because his act cannot divest her interest and her act under the Indiana statute is void.[247] The proceeds of a policy on the life of a husband in favor of his wife have been held to not be subject to the claims of her creditors,[248] upon the ground that the statute[249] was intended to secure something for the sustenance of the wife or children, and the object of the statute would be thwarted if creditors could take it from them. It has been held differently in New York.[250] Ordinarily a policy on the life of the husband payable to the wife can be assigned by the joint act of them both,[251] and it makes no difference that it is an endowment policy.[252] But if the policy on the life of the husband is payable to the wife, if living at the time of his death and if not to her children she has only a contingent interest and her death before that of her husband ends the interest of her assignee.[253] If the assignors have received the benefits of a void sale of the policy they may be estopped from setting up the illegality of the transaction, and the rule applies to married women.[254] The assignment by the wife of a policy payable to her children, if they survive her, which they did, is ineffectual against the children.[255] Where the policy was payable to the wife and she assigned her

[245] Harvey v. Van Cott, 25 N. Y. Supp. 25.

[246] Pratt v. Globe M. L. Ins. Co., 3 Tenn. (Shannon), 174; 17 S. W. 352.

[247] Union Cent. L. Ins. Co. v. Woods, 11 Ind. App. 335; 37 N. E. 180.

[248] Brosard v. Marsonin. 17 Low. Can. Jur. 270; Vilbon v. Same, 18 *Id.* 249.

[249] Queb., 33 Vic. c. 21.

[250] Crosby v. Stephan, 32 Hun. 478.

[251] Wirgman v. Miller, 98 Ky. 620; 33 S. W. 937.

[252] Lockwood v. Mich. Mut. L. Ins. Co., 108 Mich. 334; 66 N. W. 229.

[253] Mut. L. Ins. Co. v. Hagerman, 19 Colo. App. 33; 72 Pac. 889; Stevens v. Germania L. Ins. Co., 26 Tex. Civ. A. 156; 62 S W. 824.

[254] N. Y. Life Ins. Co. v. Rosenheim, 56 Mo. App. 27.

[255] Sullivan v. Maroney, 76 N. J. Eq. 104; 73 Atl. 842; Hargerman v. Mut. Life Ins. Co., 45 Colo. 459; 103 Pac. 276.

interest with the consent of her husband warranting its validity
and she died before her husband, her representatives are estopped
from disputing the validity of the assignment.[256] A policy payable to the wife, if living, if not living to the children, assigned
during the life of the husband by the wife to secure the debt
of the husband is valid if the wife survive.[257] Duress in inducing
the wife to join in the assignment of a policy does not affect the
validity of the assignment in the absence of knowledge on the
part of the company.[258] Though a policy payable to the wife
provides for change of beneficiary it is governed by the statute
of Wisconsin preventing divesting of the rights of a married
woman without her consent.[259]

§ 392. Effect of Bankruptcy.—The Bankruptcy Act of 1898[260]
provides, among other things, as follows: ''The trustee of the
estate of a bankrupt, upon his appointment and qualification, . . .
shall . . . be vested, by operation of law, with the title of the
bankrupt, as of the date he was adjudged a bankrupt, except in so
far as it relates to property which is exempt, to all property which,
prior to the filing of the petition, he could by any means have
transferred, or which might have been levied upon and sold under
judicial process against him; Provided, that, when any bankrupt
shall have any insurance policy which has a cash surrender value
payable to himself, his estate, or personal representatives, he may,
within thirty days after the cash surrender value has been ascertained and stated to the trustee, by the company issuing the
same, pay or secure to the trustee the sum so ascertained and
stated, and continue to hold, own, and carry such policy free from
the claims of the creditors participating in the distribution of his
estate under the bankruptcy proceedings, otherwise the policy shall
pass to the trustee as assets.'' Construing this statute the Supreme Court of the United States has held[261] that the words ''cash

256 Henry v. Thompson, 78 N. J. Eq. 142; 78 Atl. 14.

257 Herr v. Reimoehl, 209 Pa. 489; 58 Atl. 862.

. 258 Ely v. Hartford L. Ins. Co., 128 Ky. 799; 110 S. W. 265.

259 National L. Ins. Co. v. Brantigan, 163 Wis. 270; 154 N. W. 839.

260 § 70a, 30 Stat. at L. Ch. 541, 565; U. S. Comp. Stat. Supp. 1911,
p. 1511.

261 Hiscock v. Martens, 205 U. S. 202; 51 L. Ed. 771; 27 Sup. Ct. Rep.
488.

surrender value" embrace not only policies which by their terms had such value, but also those having a cash value under the practice or custom of the company issuing it. In the late case of Burlingham v. Crouse,[262] the Court held that the cash surrender value is to be ascertained as of the date of the filing of the petition, and that the bankrupt's right to secure to the trustee the cash surrender value and retain the policies is not extinguished by his death after the filing of the petition and before adjudication,[263] and that if he dies during that interval his executor takes the proceeds of the policy, less the cash surrender value, which passes to the trustee.[264]

Where by the terms of the policy itself there is reserved to the insured the right, without the consent of the beneficiary, to change the appointee, the beneficiary acquires only an expectancy and not a vested interest during the life of the insured, and it is generally held that any interest in a policy reserving the right to change the beneficiary which remains in the insured passes to his trustee.[265]   And on the bankruptcy of the holder of an endowment policy payable to the beneficiary, on the death of the bankrupt during the endowment period, the right therein of the bankrupt and beneficiary was held to be determined and the interest of the bankrupt sold unless redeemed.[266]   In the case of *In re* Shoemaker[267] it was held that under the law of Pennsylvania, where there has been merely a designation of a beneficiary, as, for example, the sister, to receive the moneys payable on the death of the assured, and this designation is open to recall and change by the insured, to whom also belongs the right to cancel, or surrender, the policies, the surrender value of the policy if the insured be bankrupt passes to his trustee, but where the wife,

[262] 228 U. S. 459; 57 L. Ed. 920.

[263] Andrews v. Partridge, 228 U. S. 479.

[264] Everett v. Judson, 228 U. S. 474; King v. Miles (Miss.), 67 Sou. 182; Morris v. Dodd, 110 Ga. 606; 50 L. R. A. 33 and note.

[265] Mut. Ben. Life Ins. Co. v. Swett, 137 C. C. 640; 222 Fed. 200; *In re* Jamison Bros. Co., 222 Fed. 92; *In re* Orear, 102 C. C. A. 78; 178 Fed. 632; *In re* Herr, 182 Fed. 716; 25 Am. Bankr. Rep. 142; *In re* Slinghuff, 69 C. C. A. 496; 106 Fed. 154; *In re* Welling, 51 C. C. A. 151; 113 Fed. 189; *In re* Coleman, 136 Fed. 818.

[266] *In re* Dreuil & Co., 221 Fed. 796.

[267] 225 Fed. 329.

children, or a dependent relative of the insured has been made
the owner of the policy by having it taken out for and in good
faith assigned to them, then nothing passes to the trustee.[268] If
the bankrupt's assignment to his wife of policies on his life was
void, the wife after his death may by payment of the surrender
value redeem them. The trustee is not entitled to the whole amount
of the insurance, but only the surrender value.[269] The Circuit
Court of Appeals for the second circuit has said:[270] "The policy
has no 'cash surrender value,' either provided for on its face, or
established by concession and practice of the company, as in Hiscock v. Mertens.[271] It is contended that it had a 'loan value';
that is, under its provisions the insured might now borrow of the
company about $2,000 on the sole security of the policy. This
loan, however, would be made only in the event that the beneficiary
consented to it and signed the note or agreement for repayment
of said loan. Life insurance is property, and would as such pass
to the trustee under the same conditions as other property, were
it not for the proviso to section 70a, which was construed by
this court In re Judson,[272] and by the Supreme Court in Burlingham v. Crouse,[273] where the Court says: 'True it is that life insurance policies are a species of property and might be held to
pass under the general terms of subdivision 5, section 70a, but a
proviso dealing with a class of this property was inserted and
must be given its due weight in construing the statute.' In the
case last cited the beneficiary was the estate of the insured and
the policy had a cash surrender; it was held that upon the payment of that sum to the trustee the policy should be undisturbed.
The question here presented is whether, under the ruling in the

[268] In re Jamison Bros., 222 Fed. 92. See also In re Dolan, 182 Fed.
949; Allen v. Trust Co., 143 Wis. 381; 127 N. W. 1003; In re Flanagan,
228 Fed. 399. A later law of Pennsylvania, Act May 5, 1915, P. L. 253,
broadens the exemption so as to provide that any policy taken out for
the benefit of or assigned to the wife or children, or any other relative
dependent upon the insured shall be exempt.

[269] In re Levy, 227 Fed. 1011.

[270] In re Hammel & Co., 137 C. C. A. 80; 221 Fed. 56.

[271] 205 U. S. 202; 27 Sup. Ct. 488; 51 L. Ed. 771.

[272] 192 Fed. 834; 113 C. C. A. 158.

[273] 228 U. S. 459; 33 Sup. Ct. 564; 57 L. Ed. 920; 46 L. R. A. (N. S.) 148.

Crouse case, the loan value of this policy is to be treated as a surrender value, and the sum which can be borrowed on it from the company is to be borrowed and turned over to the trustee. Not a dollar can be obtained on this policy from the company, unless the beneficiary consents and signs the loan agreement. That beneficiary is now Bertha Hofmann. The contention is that the insured should, under the power reserved in the contract with the insurance company, cancel the original designation of a beneficiary, and substitute himself or his estate, should then obtain the loan from the company and turn it over to the trustee—possibly the trustee, if the designation were changed to insured's estate, might himself obtain the amount of the loan from the company—that proposition need not be passed upon. Twelve years ago the bankrupt took out this policy for the benefit of his wife, so as to secure to her $3,000 in the event of his death. This was a laudable and proper thing to do; public policy encourages the making of such provisions for an uncertain future. The policy contains a clause authorizing the insured to change his beneficiary, a perfectly proper clause; she might predecease him, or desert him or become unfaithful. There is nothing to suggest any such reason for making a change. On the contrary, the presumption is that now, when he is a bankrupt, and his death in the near future would, except for this insurance, possibly leave her in poverty, he would not voluntarily cancel his designation of her as the beneficiary. It cannot be assumed that, of his own motion, he would take away from her the small sum which the beneficial system of life insurance and his own savings during twelve years have made it possible to secure to her as a last resource, should he die and leave nothing behind him. The proposition that he should be constrained against his will, by an order enforceable by imprisonment in the event of disobedience, to deprive his wife of her present interest in the policy, to make himself the beneficiary, to borrow two-thirds of the $3,000 from the company, and turn it over to his creditors, and then to make her again the beneficiary of the remaining third, seems contrary to public policy and to good morals. We are unwilling to give this effect to the statute, unless constrained to do so either by its language or by controlling

829

authority.''[274]   Where a policy was payable to the wife, if she
survived her husband, and in the event of her death in his lifetime then to him or his personal representatives, it was held that
subject to such contingent interest in the husband the policies and
the money which became due under them belonged to the wife and
it was beyond the power of the insured to transfer them to any
other person, or to surrender them.[275]   But it has also been held
to the contrary that where a wife's interest in the husband's
policy is contingent upon her surviving him, and in case of her
death in his lifetime it is payable to his estate, and which policy
he may surrender at any time and take a paid-up policy, or other
value, the policy is property and passes to his trustees in bankruptcy.[276]   In the case of Holden v. Stratton.[277] the Court held
that the purpose of the proviso was to confer a benefit upon the
insured bankrupt by limiting the character of the interest in a
non-exempt life insurance policy which should pass to the trustee
and not cause such a policy when exempt to become an asset of
the estate.   Where the policy is payable to the wife and under
the statutes of the State of the domicile it is exempt, the interest
in such a policy will not pass to the trustee of the bankrupt, notwithstanding the right to change the beneficiary is reserved.   In
the case of *In re* Orear[278] the Court said: ''The primary purpose
of such policies is still to insure against death and usually for the
benefit of those dependent upon the insured, and when a modern
policy is made, as in this case, payable upon the death of the insured to his wife by name as beneficiary, the fact that the insured
may have the right to change the beneficiary or enjoy certain
collateral rights in his lifetime does not make it any the less a
policy of insurance made by an insurance company expressed to be
for the benefit of the wife of the insured within the meaning of the

[274] See also *In re* Arkin (C. C. A), 231 Fed. 947.

[275] See also Luttgen v. Tiffany, 37 R. I. 416; 93 Atl. 182; *In re* Churchill,
126 C. C. A. 490; 209 Fed. 766; reversing 198 Fed. 711.

[276] *In re* White, 98 C. C. A. 205; 174 Fed. 333; 26 L. R. A. (N. S.), 481
and note; *In re* Draper, 211 Fed. 230; *In re* Holden, 51 C. C. A. 99; 113
Fed. 143; reversed on another point 198 U. S. 202.

[277] 198 U. S. 202.

[278] 111 C. C. A. 150; 189 Fed. Rep. 888. See also *In re* Cohen, 230 Fed.
733.

statute in question, and to hold otherwise would be to hold that the Legislature of Missouri enacted a statute with reference to a kind of policy no longer used. The second proposition of the trustee is equally without merit. Section 70a of the bankruptcy act expressly limits the property passing to the trustee to the property of the bankrupt as of the date he is adjudged a bankrupt 'except in so far as it is to property which is exempt.' This policy by the Missouri statute, if it belonged to the bankrupt in any sense, was declared to inure to the separate benefit of Myrtle L. Derr, independently of creditors of the husband and was not, therefore, of such a character as to pass to the trustee even if the act did not expressly exempt it and if the seventieth section did not expressly exclude all exempt property from the grant to the trustee. The trustee could take nothing save as of the date of the adjudication of bankruptcy, and he either took this property then or never. What the trustee took he obtained under section 70a, and the fact that nine months afterward Mrs. Derr obtained a divorce would not vest in the trustee property not covered by the grant to him. The Missouri statute, it is true, provides that upon the divorcement of the parties the husband may change the beneficiary; but this right was expressly reserved to him when he took the policy by its very terms. There is nothing to indicate that he has attempted up to this time to change the beneficiary either under this statute or the power reserved in the policy. The divorce itself did not operate to change the beneficiary.''[279] An insurance policy having no surrender value and providing that the insured may change the beneficiary without obtaining the consent of anyone is not assets of the estate as giving a power to be exercised by the bankrupt for the benefit of a third person, since the policy having no surrender value never becomes vested in the trustee. And where a husband and wife as co-partners and individuals went into bankruptcy such a policy payable to the wife is not assets of the estate vesting in the trustee on the death of the husband before the settlement of the estate, as her interest in

[279] Conn. Mut. Life Ins. Co. v. Schaefer, 94 U. S. 457; 24 L. Ed. 251. See also *In re* Booss (Pa.), 154 Fed. 594; *In re* Pfaffinger (Ky.), 164 Fed. 526; *In re* Whelpley (N. H.), 169 Fed. 1019; *In re* Johnson (Minn.), 176 Fed. 591; *In re* Carlon (S. D.), 189 Fed. 815; 27 Am. Bankr. Rep. 18.

the policy must be determined with reference to the filing of the petition and whatever interest she may have had at that time was subject to be defeated by action of the insured in changing the beneficiary, as permitted by the policy, which he had actually done before his death.[280] The opinion in the case cited refers with approval to what was said by the Court *In re* Judson:[281] "We think that the statute in question clearly indicates an intention upon the part of Congress to permit bankrupts to retain the advantages of existing life insurance policies, provided they will pay to their trustees all that could be obtained by surrendering such policies at the commencement of the proceedings. In the case of policies having a cash surrender value the proviso covers the case. In the case of policies having no cash surrender value the proviso does not apply expressly, but reading it in connection with the other provisions, we think that such policies are not 'property' within the meaning of the statute, but are in the nature of personal rights. True, they are 'property' within technical definitions of the term. But they represent nothing more than the right to pay future premiums at a fixed rate. Their value is altogether speculative, and in our opinion, it was not the intention of Congress that bankrupts should be deprived of their policies, to enable trustees of bankrupt estates to use their funds to speculate with."

§ 393. **The Question of Insurable Interest As Affecting the Validity of Assignments of Life Policies.**—In assignments of policies of life insurance the question of insurable interest again arises, and on this question there is more than the usual conflict of authorities; some holding that a policy is a mere chose in action, that may be passed from hand to hand like any other chattel, while others insist that a life insurance contract cannot be assigned to anyone who has not an insurable interest in the life insured.[282] The Supreme Court of Massachusetts thus reviews the

[280] Sanders, *et al.* v. Aetna Life Ins. Co. and French v. Aetna Life Ins. Co., 95 S. C. 36; 78 S. E. 532; Ann. Cas. 1915-B 1284.

[281] 192 Fed. 834; 113 C. C. A. 158.

[282] As to assignments to relatives, see Adams v. Reed, 18 Ky. L. 858; 38 S. W. 420; 35 L. R. A. 692; reversing 36 S. W. 568; Beard v. Sharp, 100 Ky. 606; 38 S. W. 1057; King v. Cram, 185 Mass. 103; 69 N. E. 1049.

authorities and deduces what is the most approved rule:[283] ''In England the question was raised whether the assignment of a life insurance without interest was prohibited by the statute of 14 Geo. III., c. 48, which forbids any insurance on the life of a person in which the person for whose benefit the insurance is made has no interest, or by way of gaming or wagering, and it was held that such an assignment was valid.[284] Shadwell, V. C., said: 'It appears to me that a purchaser for a valuable consideration is entitled to stand in the place of the original assignor, so as to bring an action in his name for the sum insured.' The same has been held in New York, where a similar statute exists.[285] It has been decided in New York that insurance on a life in which the assured has no interest is void at common law, and that the statute of 14 Geo. III., c. 48, so far as it prohibits such insurance, is a declaratory act.[286] In Rhode Island, in a well considered case, decided in 1877, a sale and assignment of a policy of life insurance to one who had no interest in the life, made, not as a contrivance to circumvent the law, but as an honest and *bona fide* transaction, was held valid.[287] In Cunningham v. Smith,[288] a person took out an insurance on his own life, and paid for it with the money of the defendants, intending to assign the policy to the defendants, and did so assign it. The assignment was sustained. The court say that the defendants may have had such an interest in the life insured as would have entitled them to insure his life in their own name, although this was doubtful; but that the assured had an interest in his own life, 'and if he was willing to insure himself with their money and then assign the policy to them, there is no principle of law which can prevent such a transaction.' This transaction is obviously more open to objection than the assignment of the interest in a valid subsisting policy. In Aetna Ins. Co. v. France,[289] a brother procured an insurance on his life for

[283] Mut. Life Ins. Co. v. Allen, 138 Mass. 31.
[284] Ashley v. Ashley, 3 Sim. 149.
[285] St. John v. American Ins. Co., 13 N. Y. (3 Kern), 31; Valton v. National Fund Ass. Co., 20 N. Y. 32.
[286] Ruse v. Mut. Ben. Ins. Co., 23 N. Y. 516.
[287] Clark v. Allen, 11 R. I. 439.
[288] 70 Pa. St. 450.
[289] 94 U. S. 561.

·the benefit of his married sister, who was in no way dependent upon him. It was held to be valid, and that it was immaterial what arrangement was made between them for the payment of the premium. In delivering the opinion of the court, Mr. Justice Bradley, referring to the case of Connecticut M. L. Ins. Co. v. Schaefer,[290] in which he delivered the opinion, said: "Any person has a right to procure an insurance on his life and to assign it to another, provided it be not done by way of cover for a wager policy; and where the relationship between the parties, as in this case, is such as to constitute a good and valid consideration in law for any gift or grant, the transaction is entirely free from any such imputation.' Several cases have been cited as deciding that any assignment of a life policy to one who has no interest in the life is void. We will notice them briefly. Cammack v. Lewis[291] and Warnock v. Davis[292] were both cases in which the policies were taken out, by the procurement of the assignees, in order that they might well be assigned to them, under such circumstances as that they might well be held to be in evasion of the law prohibiting gaming policies. The remark of Mr. Justice Field in the latter case that 'the assignment of a policy to a party not having an insurable interest is as objectionable as the taking out of a policy in his name,' was not necessary to the decision. In Franklin Ins. Co. v. Hazzard,[293] the assured had failed to pay the premiums, and had notified the insurers that he should not keep up the policy. He afterwards assigned it for $20, the insurer assenting and receiving the premiums. The assignment was held void, the Court saying that such policies are assignable, but not 'to one who buys them merely as matter of speculation without interest in the life of the assured.' Neither of these cases decides whatever *dicta* may have accompanied the decision, that all assignments without interest are illegal. The case last cited is affirmed in the case of Franklin Ins. Co. v. Sefton,[294] in which Chief Justice Worden, quoting from the opinion of the court in Hutson v.

290 94 U. S. 457.
291 15 Wall. 643.
292 104 U. S. 775.
293 41 Ind. 116.
294 53 Ind. 380.

Merrifield[295]—that 'the party holding and owning such a policy, whether on the life of another or on his own life, has a valuable interest in it which he may assign, either absolutely or by way of security, and it is assignable like any other chose in action,' —says that it is not stated that it is assignable to a person incapable of receiving an assignment; and adds, 'It may be added that where the policyholder dies before the death of the party whose life is insured, perhaps the administrator of the holder could, for the purpose of converting the assets into money and settling up the estate in due course of law, sell the policy to anyone who might choose to become the purchaser.' Missouri Valley Ins. Co. v. Sturges,[296] assumes and decides that the same objections lie to an assignment without interest as to an original insurance with no interest. The distinction between the two transactions is not considered. Basye v. Adams,[297] seems to decide, on the authority of Warnock v. Davis; Cammack v. Lewis; Franklin Ins. Co. v. Hazard, and Missourui Valley Ins. Co. v. Sturges, *ubi supra*, that an assignment without interest is void as against public policy. The case of Stevens v. Warren,[298] decided in 1869, has been supposed to hold that an assignment of the right of the assured in a life policy to one who has no interest in the life is void without regard to the circumstances and character of the particular transaction, and has been referred to in some of the cases just cited as an authority to that effect. We think that decision has been misunderstood, and that in connection with other decisions of this court, it shows that the law in this Commonwealth accords with that laid down in Clark v. Allen.'[299] The court then examines Campbell v. New England Ins. Co.,[300] Stevens v. Warren,[301] Palmer v. Merrill,[302] and Troy v. Sargent,[303] to show that assignments of life policies have been upheld when not covers for gambling transactions and concludes thus: ''The general rule

[295] 51 Ind. 24.
[296] 18 Kan. 93.
[297] 81 Ky. 368.
[298] 101 Mass. 564.
[299] 11 R. I. 439.
[300] 98 Mass. 381.
[301] 101 Mass. 564.
[302] 6 Cush. 282.
[303] 132 Mass. 408.

835

laid down in Stevens v. Warren, *supra,* 'that no one can have an insurance upon the life of another, unless he has an interest in the continuance of that life,' and from which the inference that an assignee of a party must have an insurable interest seems to have been drawn, we think, is not strictly accurate, or may be misleading. An insurable interest in the assured at the time the policy is taken out is necessary to the validity of the policy, but it is not necessary to the continuance of the insurance that the interest should continue; if the interest should cease, the policy would continue, and the insured would then- have an insurance without interest.[304] The value and permanency of the interest is material only as bearing on the question whether the policy is taken out in good faith, and not as a gambling transaction. If valid in its inception, it will not be avoided by a cessation of the interest. The mere fact that the assured himself has no interest in the life does not avoid or annul the policy.'' It is believed that this doctrine is supported by the weight of authority, although some cases bear to the extreme that policies of life insurance are mere choses in action and others insist that the assignee must have an insurable interest in the life insured. In one case,[305] it was held that wager policies were not prohibited by the laws of New Jersey. In Maryland life insurance policies are held to be mere choses in action and assignable as any other contract.[306] And so in other States.[307] Divorce has been held to end the interest of a woman in a policy assigned to her by her husband.[308] Pre-

[304] Dalby v. India & London Ass'n Co., 15 C. B. 365; Law v. London Policy Co., 1 Kay & J. 223; cited in Loomis v. Eagle Ins. Co., 6 Gray 396; Conn. Mut. Life Ins. Co. v. Schaefer, *supra;* Rawls v. American Ins. Co., 27 N. Y. 282; Provident Ins. Co. v. Baum, 29 Ind. 236.

[305] Trenton Mut. L. & F. Ins. Co. v. Johnson, 24 N. J. L. (4 Zab.) 576. ...

[306] Souder v. Home Friendly Soc., 72 Md. 511; 20 Atl. 137; Ins. Co. v. Flack, 3 Md. 341; Whitridge v. Barry, 42 Md. 150; Clogg v. McDaniel, 89 Md. 416; 43 Atl. 795; Fitzgerald v. Rawlings Imp. Co., 114 Md. 470; 79 Atl. 915.

[307] Croswell v. Conn. Ind. Ass'n, 51 S. C. 103; 28 S. E. 200; Allen v. Hartford L. Ins. Co., 72 Conn. 693; 45 Atl. 955; Brown v. Greenfield L. Ass'n, 172 Mass. 498; 53 N. E. 129; Strike v. Wisconsin, etc., Ass'n, 95 Wis. 583; 70 N. W. 819. See also next section.

[308] Hatch v. Hatch, 35 Tex. Civ. A. 373; 80 S. W. 411.

miums paid cannot be recovered on a void policy.[309]   And the incontestable clause in a policy does not apply to a. defense of want of insurable interest.[310]   An assignment may be subject to the right of insured to substitute another beneficiary.[311]   The second assignee stands in the shoes of the first.[312]   Where the certificate, or policy, is payable to the member or assured he may devise it to one not having an insurable interest, such party taking under the will and not as assignee.[313]   In Kansas the Supreme Court held that a policy of life insurance, assigned for a valuable consideration to one who' did not have an insurable interest, was worthless and void not only in the hands of the assignee but in the hands of the beneficiaries and their assignee.[314]   But though

[309] Am. Mut. L. Ins. Co. v. Bertram, 163 Ind. 51; 70 N. E. 258.

[310] Clement v. N. Y. L. Ins. Co., 101 Tenn. 22; 46 S. W. 561; 42 L. R. A. 247.

[311] Ogletree v. Ogletree, 127 Ga. 232; 55 S. E. 954.

[312] Brown v. Equitable L. Ass. Soc., 75 Minn. 412; 78 N. W. 103; Locke v. Bowman, 168 Mo. App. 121; 151 S. W. 468.

[313] Stoelker v. Thornton, 88 Ala. 241; 6 Sou. 680; Catholic Knights, etc., v. Kuhn, 91 Tenn. 241; 18 S. W. 385.

[314] Missouri Valley Life Ins. Co. v. McCrum, 36 Kan. 146; 12 Pac. 517, also to the same effect, Kessler v. Kuhns, 1 Ind. App. 511; 27 N. E. 980; Hoffman v. Hoke, 122 Pa. St. 377; 15 Atl. 437; Stambaugh v. Blake, 1 Pa. (Monaghan), 609; 15 Atl. 705. In the following cases the assignments of policies of life insurance have been sustained, although to one not having an insurable interest: Palmer v. Merrill, 6 Cush. 282; 52 Am. Dec. 782; St. John v. American, etc., Ins. Co., 2 Duer, 419; 13 N. Y. 31; Valton v. Nat. Fund L. Ins. Co., 20 N. Y. 32; Rawls v. American L. Ins. Co., 36 Barb. 357; 27 N. Y. 282; Olmstead v. Keys, 85 N. Y. 593; Hogle v. Guardian L. Ins. Co., 6 Robt. 567; Fairchild v. Northeast M. L. Ins. Co., 51 Vt. 613; Ashley v. Ashley, 3 Sim. 149; Lamont v. Hotel Men's, etc., Ass'n, 30 Fed. 817; Murphy v. Red, 64 Miss. 614; 1 Sou. 761; Bloomington M. L. Ass'n v. Blue, 120 Ill. 121; 11 N. E. 331; N. Am. Ins. Co. v. Craigen, 6 Russ. & G. (Nov. Sc.), 440; Eckel v. Renner, 41 Ohio St. 232; Mut. L. Ins. Co. v. Allen, 138 Mass. 24; Cannon v. N. W. Mut. L. Ins. Co., 29 Hun. 470; Conn. Mut. L. Ins. Co. v. Schaefer, 94 U. S. 457; N. Y. Mut. L. Ins. Co. v. Armstrong, 117 U. S. 591; Clark v. Allen, 11 R. I. 439; Bursinger v. Bank of Watertown, 67 Wis. 76; Chamberlain v. Butler, 61 Neb. 730; 86 N. W. 481; 54 L. R. A. 338; Metropolitan L. Ins. Co. v. Brown (Ind.), 65 N. E. 908; Steinback v. Diepenbrock, 158 N. Y. 24; 52 N. E. 662; 44 L. R. A. 417; affg. 1 App. Div. 417; 37 N. Y. Supp. 279; Mechanics' Nat. Bk. v. Comins, 72 N. H. 12; 55 Atl. 191; Dixon v. National L. Ins. Co., 168 Mass. 48; 46 N. E. 430; Prudential Ins. Co. v.

a second assignment by the first assignee may be void the latter may sue for the. proceeds.[315]

§ 394. **Same Subject—Later Cases.**—While it is still maintained by many authorities that an assignee of a policy of life insurance must have an insurable interest in the life of insured.[316] and other cases holding that the transfer of a policy to a creditor having no insurable interest operates only as a mortgage to secure the debt,[317] many other authorities hold that an assignee of a life policy valid in its inception need not have an insurable

Liersch, 122 Mich. 436; 81 N. W. 258; Fuller v. Kent, 13 App. Div. 529; 43 N. Y. Supp. 649. In Langdon v. Union Mut. L. Ins. Co., 14 Fed. 272, it was left to the jury to say whether the policy was a wagering one or not. In the following cases the want of insurable interest was held to vitiate the assignment: Franklin Life Ins. Co. v. Sefton, 53 Ind. 380; approving Franklin L. Ins. Co. v. Hazzard, 41 Ind. 116; Settle v. Hill, 5 Ky. L. 691; Keystone Mut. Ben. Ass'n v. Norris, 115 Pa. St. 446; 19 W. N. C. 248; 8 Atl. 638; Ala. Gold L. Ins. Co. v. Mobile Mut. Ins. Co., 81 Ala. 329; 1 Sou. 561; Price v. Knights of Honor, 68 Tex. 361; 4 S. W. 633; Downey v. Hoffer, 16 W. N. C. 184; Wegman v. Smith, *Id.* 186; Stoner v. Line, *Id.* 187; Meily v. Hershberger, 16 W. N. C. 186; Warnock v. Davis, 104 U. S. 775; Cammack v. Lewis, 15 Wall. 643; Missouri Vall. Ins. Co. v. Sturgis, 18 Kan. 93; N. Y. Life Ins. Co. v. Parent, 3 Queb. L. R. 163; Same v. Talbot, *Ib.* 168; Michaud v. British Med. Ass'n, Ramsey's App. Cas. (Low. Can.), 377; Basye v. Adams, 81 Ky. 368; Missouri Vall. L. Ins. Co. v. McCrum, 36 Kan. 146; 12 Pac. 517; Ruth v. Katterman, 112 Pa. St. 251; 3 Atl. 833; Gilbert v. Moose, 104 Pa. St. 74; McFarland v. Creath, 25 M. A. 113; Quinn v. Supreme Court, etc., 99 Tenn. 80; 41 S. W. 343; Schlamp v. Berner, 21 Ky. L. 324; 51 S. W. 312; Wilton v. N. Y. Life Ins. Co., 34 Tex. Civ. A. 156; 78 S. W. 403; Dugger v. Mut, L. Ins. Co. (Tex. Civ. A.), 81 S. W. 335; Thornburg v. Aetna L. Ins. Co., 30 Ind. App. 682; 66 N. E. 922; Moore v. Chicago G. Soc,. 178 Ill. 202; 52 N. E. 882.

315 Hoffman v. Hoke, *supra.*

316 Crismond v. Jones, 117 Va. 34; 83 S. E. 1045; Equitable Life Assur. Soc. v. O'Connor, 162 Ky. 262; 172 S. W. 496; Smith v. Agnew, 137 Ky. 83; 122 S. W. 231; Brawmley's Admr. v. Washington Life Ins. Co., 122 Ky. 402; 92 S. W. 17; 5 L. R. A. (N. S.) 747; Manhattan Life Ins. Co. v. Cohen (Tex. Civ. App.), 130 S. W. 51; Tripp v. Jordan, 177 Mo. App. 339; 164 S. W. 158; Jenkins v. Morrow, 131 Mo. App. 288; 109 S. W. 1051; Alexander v. Lane, 157 Fed. 276; McRae v. Warmack, 98 Ark. 52; 135 S. W. 807.

317 Harde v. Germania Life Ins. Co. (Tex. Civ. App.), 153 S. W. 666; Locke v. Bowman, 168 Mo. App. 121; 151 S. W. 468.

interest.[318]   In the case of Grigsby v. Russell,[319] the Supreme Court of the United States seems to have modified its previous holdings. The Court says: "The danger that might arise from a general license to all to insure whom they like does not exist. Obviously it is a very different thing from granting such a general license, to allow the holder of a valid insurance upon his own life to transfer it to one whom he, the party most concerned, is not afraid to trust. The law has no universal cynic fear of the temptation opened by a pecuniary benefit accruing upon a death. It shows no prejudice against remainders after life estates, even by the rule in Shelley's case. Indeed, the ground of the objection to life insurance without interest in the earlier English cases was not the temptation to murder, but the fact that such wagers came to be regarded as a mischievous kind of gaming.[320] On the other hand, life insurance has become in our days one of the best recognized forms of investment and self-compelled saving. So far as reasonable safety permits, it is desirable to give to life policies the ordinary characteristics of property. This is recognized by the bankruptcy law,[321] which provides that unless the cash surrender value of a policy like the one before us is secured to the trustee within thirty days after it has been stated, the policy shall pass to the trustee as assets. Of course, the trustee may have no interest in the bankrupt's life. To deny the right to sell except to persons having such an interest is to diminish appreciably the value of the contract in the owner's hands. The collateral difficulty that arose from regarding life insurance as a contract of indemnity only,[322] long has disappeared.[323] And cases in which a

[318] Dixon v. National Life Ins. Co., 168 Mass. 48; 46 N. E. 430; Foryciarz v. Prudential Ins. Co., 156 N. Y. Supp. 834; King v. Cram, 185 Mass. 103; 69 N. E. 1049; Harrison's Admr. v. Northwestern Mut. Life Ins. Co., 78 Vt. 473; 63 Atl. 321; Clark v. Equitable Life Ins. Soc., 143 Fed. 175; Volunteer State Life Ins. Co. v. Buchanan, 10 Ga. App. 255; 73 S. E. 602; Page v. Metropolitan L. Ins. Co., 98 Ark. 340; 135 S. W. 911; Johnson v. Mut. Ben. Life Ins. Co., 157 N. C. 106; 72 S. E. 847; Fitzgerald v. Rawlings Imp. Co., 114 Md. 470; 79 Atl. 915.

[319] 222 U. S. 149; 36 L. R. A. (N. S.), 642.

[320] Stat. 14 George III., Ch. 48.

[321] § 70.

[322] Godsall v. Boldero, 9 East 72.

[323] Phoenix Mut. L. Ins. Co. v. Bailey, 13 Wall. 616; 20 L. Ed. 501.

person having an interest lends himself to one without any, as a cloak to what is, in its inception, a wager, have no similarity to those where an honest contract is sold in good faith. Coming to the authorities in this court, it is true that there are intimations in favor of the result come to by the Circuit Court of Appeals. But the case in which the strongest of them occur was one of the type just referred to, the policy having been taken out for the purpose of allowing a stranger association to pay the premiums and receive the greater part of the benefit, and having been assigned to it at once.[324] On the other hand, it has been decided that a valid policy is not avoided by the cessation of the insurable interest, even as against the insurer, unless so provided by the policy itself.[325] And expressions more or less in favor of the doctrine that we adopt are to be found also in Aetna L. Ins. Co. v. France[326] and Mutual L. Ins. Co. v. Armstrong.[327] It is enough to say that while the court below might hesitate to decide against the language of Warnock v. Davis, there has been no decision that precludes us from exercising our own judgment upon this much debated point.'' In the case of Hardy v. Aetna Life Ins. Co.[328] it was said: "It is accepted doctrine here, and elsewhere, that in order to a valid policy of life insurance there must have existed, an insurable interest at the time the contract is entered into, and the question whether such a policy, valid at its inception, can be assigned to one who has no insurable interest has been very much discussed in the courts, and on this there is some conflict in the cases. We consider it, however, as established by the great weight of authority that where an insurant makes a contract with a company, taking out a policy on his own life for the benefit of himself, or his estate generally, or for the benefit of another, the policy being in good faith and valid at its inception, the same may, with the assent of the company, be assigned to one not having an insurable

[324] Warnock v. Davis, 104 U. S. 775; 26 L. Ed. 924.
[325] Connecticut Mut. L. Ins. Co. v. Schaefer, 94 U. S. 457; 24 L. Ed. 251.
[326] 94 U. S. 561; 24 L. Ed. 287.
[327] 117 U. S. 591; 29 L. Ed. 997; 6 Sup. Ct. 877.
[328] 152 N. C. 286; 67 S. E. 767. See also Matlock v. Bledsoe, 77 Ark. 60; 90 S. W. 848; Rylander v. Allen, 125 Ga. 208; 53 S. E. 1022; 6 L. R. A. (N. S.), 128; Manhattan Life Ins. Co. v. Hennessey, 39 C. C. A. 625; 99 Fed. 64.

interest in the life of the insured; provided this assignment is in good faith, and not a mere cloak or cover for a wagering transaction. Decided intimation in favor of this general principle was given by this court in the recent case of Pollock v. Household of Ruth,[329] and the position will be found sustained by a large number of authoritative and well-considered decisions and by textwriters of approved excellence. . . . In his learned and well-considered opinion in the case of Crosswell v. Insurance Co.,[330] the present chief justice of that State, speaking to the suggestion sometimes made in support of the view that these assignments are necessarily invalid, 'that the same reasons which condemn a policy procured by one without an insurable interest in the life of an insured, should also condemn an assignment to one without such interest' quotes with approval from May on Insurance as follows: 'On this point we quote from May on Ins.,[331] which is in brackets, showing that it is new matter. Indeed the doctrine that the assignment of a policy to one without interest in the life is as objectionable as the taking out of a policy without interest does not seem good sense. If this be so, it is difficult to understand how the designation of a beneficiary outside of those having an insurable interest in the life can be upheld. There seems to be a clear distinction between cases in which the policy is procured by the insured *bona fide* of his own motion and cases in which it is procured by another. It is a very different thing to allow a man to create voluntarily an interest in his termination, and to allow someone else to do so at their will. The true line is the activity and responsibility of the assured, and not the interest of the person entitled to the funds. It is well established that a man may take out a policy on his own life payable to any person he pleases, and it is drawing a distinction without a difference to hold that he cannot take out a policy and afterwards transfer its benefits. An assignment by the beneficiary, or by an assignee, unless with the consent of the 'life,' is, however, a very different matter, and involves what seems to be the real evil that the law is blunderingly seeking to exclude, viz., the obtaining by B of insurance on the life of A, in contradistinction to its obtainment

- [329] 150 N. C. 211; 63 S. E. 940.
  [330] 51 S. C. 103; 28 S. E. 200, *supra.*
  [331] Ed. 1891, § 398a.

by A for B's benefit.' " A pledgee of a policy may sell it to the highest bidder to realize money to pay the debt and the purchaser takes a good title, though he has no insurable interest.[332] In that case[333] the Court says: "The assignment by Gordon and his wife of the policy on his life to the bank as collateral security for the payment of his debt to it was a lawful pledge of the policy. One of the inherent and indispensable elements of a pledge is the right and the power to sell the subject of it to the highest bidder for cash, in order to realize the moneys to pay the debt. The restriction of this power to sell policies of life insurance to those purchasers who may have insurable interests in the lives insured thereby would greatly diminish, if it would not practically destroy, the value of such policies as security for loans or debts. They are now articles of commerce, the frequent subjects of purchase and of sale, and ready and valuable means of obtaining loans and securing obligations. The policy of the nation is to enlarge, not to restrict, commerce in choses in action. The conceded proposition that a pledge of a policy of life insurance to a creditor as security for a debt is lawful and valid carries with it the inevitable corollary that such a pledge vests in the pledgee the right and the power to sell and to assign the policy to the highest bidder to obtain money to satisfy the debt, whether that bidder has an insurable interest in the life secured by the policy or not. Our conclusion is that the lawful pledgee of a policy of life insurance has the right and the power to sell the policy to the highest bidder for the purpose of realizing money to satisfy the debt, and that the immediate and remote assignees under such a sale take good title to the policy and to its proceeds, although they may have no insurable interest in the life protected by the policy." In Kentucky, however, it has been held[334] that the rights of a purchaser at judicial sale consist only of a lien on the policy for the purchase price and interest. The bankrupt act evidently considers the possibility of sale of a life insurance policy, as we have seen.[335]

[332] Gordon v. Ware National Bank, 65 C. C. A. 580; 132 Fed. 444; 67 L. R. A. 550.
[333] Gordon v. Ware National Bank, *supra*.
[334] Irons v. U. S. Life Ins. Co., 128 Ky. 640; 108 S. W. 904.
[335] *Ante*, § 392.

§ 395. **Validity of Assignment, How Determined: Amount of Recovery By Creditor and Assignee.**—Love and affection is a sufficient consideration to constitute an assignment of a policy to the mother and sister of insured and the agreement in duplicate attached to the policy is valid, though the insured retained possession of the policy.[336] An assignee of a life policy who did not obtain possession of the policy, can maintain a bill in equity to have his rights established where the insured subsequently made an assignment of the same policy to another party.[337] The validity of the assignment is determined by the law of the domicile of the parties or the place where made.[338] A life insurance policy payable to the estate of the insured may be the subject of a gift without any assignment if there has been a delivery with intent to pass the title irrevocably, but the proof must be clear and convincing because the opportunity for fraud is great.[339] Proof that the assignee of a life insurance policy caused the death of the insured by felonious means is sufficient to defeat a recovery on the policy.[340] It has been held, under the principle that a policy valid in its inception remains so, that it is enough if the assignee has an insurable interest at the time of the assignment.[341] Unless there is a gross discrepancy between the amount of the policy and the debt, the assignee of the policy can recover the full amount of the latter.[342] If the debt is small and

[336] Northwestern Mut. L. Ins. Co. v. Wright, 153 Wis. 252; 140 N. W. 1078; Dunberry v. New York Life Ins. Co., 204 Fed. 670.

[337] Herman v. Connecticut Mut. L. Ins. Co., 218 Mass. 181; 105 N. E. 459; Ann. Cas. 1916-A 822.

[338] Mut. L. Ins. Co. v. Allen, 138 Mass. 24; Miller v. Manhattan L. Ins. Co., 110 La. 652; 34 Sou. 723; Miller v. Manhattan L. Ins. Co., 110 La. 652; 34 Sou. 723.

[339] Gledhill v. McCoombs, 110 Me. 341; 86 Atl. 247; Ann. Cas. 1914-D 294. See also Lord v. New York Life Ins. Co., 27 Tex. Civ. A. 139; 65 S. W. 699; Chapman v. McIlwrath, 77 Mo. 38; 46 Am. R. 1; Travelers' Ins. Co. v. Grant. 54 N. J. Eq. 208; 33 Atl. 1060; Knowles v. Knowles, 205 Mass. 290; 91 N. E. 213; Opitz v. Karel, 118 Wis. 527; 95 N. W. 948; 62 L. R. A. 982.

[340] New York Mut. L. Ins. Co. v. Armstrong, 117 U. S. 591. But only to the extent of the interest assigned to him. N. Y. Life Ins. Co. v. Davis, 96 Va. 737; 32 S. E. 475; 44 L. R. A. 305. See for further discussion of this subject, *post,* § 558, *et seq.*

[341] Manhattan L. Ins. Co. v. Hennessy, 39 C. C. A. 625; 99 Fed. 64.

the insurance large the insurance will be treated as security or indemnity only,[342] and the personal representatives may recover the excess over the debt.[344] Where a certificate for two thousand dollars was assigned for the consideration of three hundred dollars, the assignee agreeing to pay the assessments, it was held that the transaction would not be deemed a wager in the absence of proof of the expectancy of the life of the assured,[345] but a transfer of a certificate for $2,000 for a debt of $50 has been held void.[346] Where the creditor insured the debtor's life and afterwards made a general assignment but kept the policy which he afterwards assigned to a third party it was held that the administrator of the assured could not recover the proceeds from such transferee on the grounds that the creditor had no right to transfer it.[347] Where the creditor retains the policy after he has accepted fifty per cent of the debt secured

[342] Bevin v. Conn. Mut. L. Ins. Co., 23 Conn. 244; Trenton Ins. Co. v. Johnson, 24 N. J. L. 581; Amick v. Butler, 111 Ind. 578; 12 N. E. 518; Grant v. Kline, 115 Pa. St. 618; 9 Atl. 150; Hoyt v. N. Y. Life Ins. Co., 3 Bosw. 440; St. John v. Am. Mut. Ins. Co., 2 Duer 419; Miller v. Eagle Ins. Co., 2 E. D. Smith, 268; Grattan v. Nat. L. Ins. Co., 15 Hun. 74; Ferguson v. Mass. Mut. L. Ins. Co., 32 Hun 306; affd. 102 N. Y. 647.

[343] Cammack v. Lewis, 15 Wall. 643; Am., etc., Ins. Co. v. Robertshaw, 26 Pa. St. 189; Courtnay v. Wright, 2 Giff. 337. See Hebden v. West, 3 Best & S. 579; 9 Jur. (N. S.), 747; 32 L. J. Q. B. 85; 7 L. T. (N. S.), 854; where it is held that where two policies of life insurance are founded on the same insurable interest recovery on one bars recovery on the other.

[344] Siegrist v. Schmolz, 18 W. N. C. (Pa.), 321; 113 Pa. St. 326; 6 Atl. 47; Helmetag v. Miller, 76 Ala. 183; Tateum v. Ross, 150 Mass. 440; 23 N. E. 230. For examination of a special case where question was whether the firm or individual parties were entitled to the policy: Hurst v. Mut. Reserve F. L. Ins. Co., 78 Md. 59; 26 Atl. 956; Crotly v. Union L. Ins Co., 144 U. S. 621; 12 S. C. 749, where it was held that a recital in the policy of the fact is only an admission that the relation of debtor and creditor existed at the time the policy was issued and proof that the relation still exists must be made at the maturity of the policy. See also Cheeves v. Anders, 87 Tex. 287; 28 S. W. 274.

[345] Nye v. Grand Lodge A. O. U. W., 9 Ind. App. 131; 36 N. E. 429. And $5,000 for a debt of $1,900. Wheeland v. Atwood, 192 Pa. St. 237; 43 Atl. 946.

[346] Schonfield v. Turner, 75 Tex. 324; 12 S. W. 626.

[347] Shaak v. Meily, 136 Pa. St. 161; 20 Atl. 515. See as to questions of evidence, pleading and set-off in actions by the administrator: Brennan v. Franey, 142 Pa. St. 301; 21 Atl. 803; Shore v. Shore, 79 Wis. 497; 48 N. W. 647; Vanormer v. Hornberger, 142 Pa. St. 575; 21 Atl. 887.

thereby and continues without objection from the debtor to pay
the premiums, such policy is subject to the payment of the balance
of the indebtedness.[348] It has, however, been strongly insisted
that the rights of a creditor to a policy of life insurance on the
life of his debtor are always limited to the amount of the debt.[349]
In Armstrong v. Mutual Life Ins. Co.[350] it was said: "The assignment could not rise higher than the instrument assigned and
further the instrument itself limits the rights to be passed to
the assignees. Such right could not extend beyond an interest
in the life of the assured which could be proved. If the interest
was that of a creditor it would be limited by the amount of his
provable debt. As no debt is shown no interest is shown, and
nothing is shown to have passed to the assignee."[351] When the
debt is paid the debtor is entitled to a reassignment of the policy
although the policy has been reassigned to a third party,[352] and
an absolute assignment may be shown to have been a pledge.[353]
One claiming a paid-up policy under an assignment cannot hold
it under the theory that at the time of the execution of the assignment the assignor was indebted to him by virtue of a debt which
did not enter into the assignment.[354] An assignment may be to
secure future advances[355] which must be paid before the policy

[348] Shackleford v. Mitchell, 19 N. Y. Supp. 122.

[349] McDonald v. Birss, 99 Mich. 329; 58 N. W. 359; Riner v. Riner,
166 Pa. St. 617; 31 Atl. 347; Culver v. Guyer, 129 Ala. 602; 29 Sou. 779;
Widaman v. Hubbard, 88 Fed. 806.

[350] 11 Fed. 573.

[351] The court cites Cammack v. Lewis, 15 Wall. 643; Thatch v. Metro-
pole Ins. Co., 11 Fed. 29. This case cited in the text was afterwards reversed by the Supreme Court of the United States, N. Y. Mut. L. Ins.
Co. v. Armstrong, 117 U. S. 591, but chiefly on account of errors in admission of testimony. The Court said that life insurance policies are
assignable if not made to cover speculative risks, and payment thereof
may be enforced for the benefit of the assignee. See to the same effect
Lewy v. Gillard, 76 Tex. 400; 13 S. W. 304; Cawthon v. Perry, 76 Tex.
383; 13 S. W. 268; and also *post*, § 558, *et seq.*, for further discussion of
the subject.

[352] Bohleber v. Waldon, 23 N. Y. Supp. 391.

[353] McDonald v. Birss, 99 Mich. 329; 58 N. W. 359; Roller v. Moore,
86 Va. 512; 10 S. E. 241; Pratzman v. Joseph, 65 W. Va. 785; 65 S. E.
461; Crowell v. Northwestern Nat. L. Ins. Co., 140 Ia. 258; 118 N. W. 412.

[354] Bramblett v. Hargis, Ex'r. 123 Ky. 141; 94 S. W. 20.

[355] Curtiss v. Aetna L. Ins. Co., 90 Cal. 245; 27 Pac. 211.

can be demanded.[356]   If a policy be assigned to one without interest, or if, for any reason, the assignment is held void or imperfect, so that it does not pass the fund to the assignee, the latter has in equity a lien on the policy for the amount of premiums he has paid, with interest.[357]   But payments made by a stranger to the contract give him no lien or claim to the insurance money.[358] An assignment will hold against a levy of a judgment creditor though the company had no notice of such assignment.[359]   An assignment of a policy for $5,000 for $2,500 a few days before the death of the insured is unconscionable and void.[360]   An assignee of a policy as security for a note cannot hold it as security for a note taken for a subsequent loan,[361] but where a life policy was assigned as collateral security for a note several times renewed, additional assignments are not necessary to enable the creditor to recover upon the policy, the original debt remaining unpaid, and the creditor may surrender the policy and collect the cash value.[362] Where insurance policies are assigned to secure a particular indebtedness the assignee is bound to apply the insurance money on that indebtedness and can acquire no rights by his application thereof to a different indebtedness.[363]   Stopping payment of a check given in consideration of an assignment of a life policy precludes the assignee from thereafter asserting title to the policy.[364]   The assignee can collect the amount due from the insurer on a policy asisgned to him as collateral security.[365]

[356] Gilman v. Curtis, 66 Cal. 116.

[357] Conn. Mut. Life Ins. Co. v. Burroughs, 34 Conn. 305; Welsert v. Muehl, 81 Ky. 341; City Savings Bank v. Whittle, 63 N. H. 587; Unity Ass'n v. Dugan, 118 Mass. 219; Matlack v. Seventh Nat. Bk., 180 Pa. St. 360; 36 Atl. 1082.

[358] Lockwood v. Bishop, 51 How. Pr. 221; Burridge v. Rowe, 1 Y. & C. C. C. See ante, § 295, et seq.; post, §§ 457 and 560.

[359] Columbia Bank v. Equitable Life A. Soc., 61 App. Div. 594; 70 N. Y. Supp. 767.

[360] Prudential L. Ins. Co. v. LaChance, 113 Me. 550; 95 Atl. 223.

[361] Herman v. Connecticut Mut. L. Ins. Co., 218 Mass. 181; 105 N. E. 450.

[362] Mut. Ben. L. Ins. Co. v. First Nat. Bank, 160 Ky. 538; 169 S. W. 1028.

[363] Ward v. Ward, 154 Ky. 355; 157 S. W. 700.

[364] Prudential Ins. Co. v. Dugger, 163 Ill. 609.

[365] Morgan v. Mut. Ben. L. Ins. Co., 189 N. Y. 447; 82 N. E. 438; affg. 104 N. Y. Supp. 185.

§ 396. **Appointments Under Powers, When Revocable.**—
Ordinarily, appointments under powers are revocable. In Sugden
on Powers[366] it is said: "A power to appoint includes in itself
a power to revoke; and a power to do an act which can only be
effected by an appointment, authorizes an appointment and, therefore, a revocation." In regard to real property Washburn says:
"It should be understood that, when the donee of a power intends
to revoke the uses he appoints, he should expressly reserve this
right in the deed executing the power. If such reservation be not
made, the appointment cannot be revoked; and this is especially
true where the power has been executed upon receiving a valuable
consideration.[367] Wills are in their own nature always revocable
and, therefore, where the power is executed by a will, an express
power of revocation need not be inserted, but it may be revoked,
and the original power re-executed *toties quoties*.[368] "The result
of the authorities as to deeds (and the like observations apply to
other instruments *inter vivos*) executing instruments appears to
be: 1. That in a deed *executing* a power, a power of revocation
and new appointment may be reserved, although not expressly
authorized by the deed creating the power, and that such powers
may be reserved *toties quoties*. 2. That where an appointment
under a power is made by deed it cannot be revoked, unless an
express power be reserved in the deed by which the power is executed; a revocation will not be authorized by a general prospective
power in the deed creating the first power.[369] It follows as a necessary conclusion that to determine the power, and the manner of
its exercise, either by original designation or revocation, we must
look to the instrument creating the power; in the case of the certificates of beneficiary societies to their contracts or by-laws, in
the case of policies of regular life or accident insurance to the conditions of the policies themselves.

§ 397. **Designation of Beneficiary is an Act Testamentary in
Its Character.**—The designation of a beneficiary by a member of
a benefit society is an act testamentary in its character, and the

366 Vol. 1, p. 238 (Ed. 1856).
367 2 Washb. on Real Prop. 3&0.
368 Sugden on Powers, Vol. 1, p. 462.
369 Sugden on Powers, Vol. 1, p. 462.

same rules of construction apply as in the case of other testamentary writings.[370] In considering the validity of changes of beneficiary the courts have evidently been influenced by this fact. If, however, the certificate refer to the laws of the society, and these authorize the substitution or change of beneficiaries, it seems plain that the case is one where under the compact the right of revocation of the appointment is secured, and this right is again reserved in the instrument executing the power, so that no question should arise touching its validity.[371] An assignment of an interest in a policy to the son by his father a few days before his death is a testamentary act and is to be tested by the same rules regarding mental capacity.[372]

§ 398. **Beneficiaries Have No Property in Benefit But a Mere Expectancy.**—Under the contract entered into between a beneficiary society and the member, or wherever the right to change the beneficiary is reserved in the contract, the designated beneficiary has no property in the benefit to be paid, but a mere expectancy. The Supreme Court of California has thus stated the rule:[373] "The beneficiary named in the certificate has no interest or property therein that her heirs could succeed to. Her interest was a mere expectancy of an incompleted gift. It was revocable at the will of the insured and could not ripen into a right until his death.[374] Her right under the certificate was not unlike that of an heir apparent and that is not to be deemed an interest of

[370] Duvall v. Goodson, 79 Ky. 228; Washington Ben. Endowment Ass'n v. Wood, 4 Mackey 19; Continental Life Ins. Co. v. Palmer, 42 Conn. 64; 19 Am. Rep. 530; Union Mut. Aid Ass'n v. Montgomery, 70 Mich. 587; 38 N. W. 588; Thomas v. Leake, 67 Tex. 469; 3 S. W. 703; National American Ass'n v. Kirgin, 28 Mo. App. 80; Chartrand v. Brace, 16 Colo. 19; 26 Pac. 152; Masonic, etc., Ass'n v. Bunch, 109 Mo. 560; 19 S. W. 25; Aiken v. Mass. Ben. Ass'n, 13 N. Y. Supp. 579; Knights Templars, etc., Ass'n v. Greene, 179 Fed. 461.

[371] *Ante*, § 313, *et seq.*

[372] Borchers v. Barckers, 143 Mo. App. 72; 122 S. W. 357; Andrews v. Lavery, 159 Mich. 26; 123 N. W. 543.

[373] Supreme Court, etc., v. Gehrenbach, 124 Cal. 43; 56 Pac. 640.

[374] Hoeft v. Supreme Lodge, 113 Cal. 91; 45 Pac. 185; 33 L. R. A. 174; Jory v. Sup. Council, 105 Cal. 20; 38 Pac. 524; 26 L. R. A. 733; Hellenberg v. District No. 1, 94 N. Y. 580.

any kind." The same doctrine was fully set forth by the Court of Errors and Appeals of New Jersey,[375] where the Court said: "By the terms of such contracts (those of benefit societies) the beneficiary may be changed by the mere will of the member, and without the beneficiary's consent. In such case the right of the beneficiary is not property but a mere expectancy, dependent on the will of the member to whom the certificate is issued. For this reason the beneficiary's interest in the certificate and contract evidenced thereby differs totally from the interest of a beneficiary named in an ordinary life insurance policy, containing no provision for the designation of a new beneficiary. The cases, so far as I can discover, are agreed upon this doctrine." In the case of Modern Woodmen of America v. Headle[376] the Court said: "While the interest of the beneficiary designated in the original certificate is, during the lifetime of the insured member, a contingent interest —a mere expectancy—liable at any time to be defeated by the designation of a new beneficiary, it does not follow that such beneficiary has no interest in the certificate. He has an expectancy in the nature of an inchoate interest which, it is held in some jurisdictions, gives him the right to insist that a change of beneficiary be made, if attempted, in substantial conformity with the stipulations of the contract."[377] This principle is now so well settled that no further authorities need be cited.[378] While the beneficiary has no vested interest so as to prevent a change of beneficiary, she can maintain a suit for damages against a third person who fraudulently induces a change of beneficiary.[379] An assignment of a life insurance policy by the beneficiary before the death of the

[375] Golden Star Fraternity v. Martin, 59 N. J. L. 207; 35 Atl. 908.
[376] 88 Vt. 37; 90 Atl. 892.
[377] Holland v. Taylor, 111 Ind. 121; 12 N. E. 116; Farra v. Braman, 171 Ind. 529; 86 N. E. 843; Faubel v. Eckhart, 151 Wis. 155; 138 N. W. 615; note 5 L. R. A. 95. To the same effect are also Supreme Council A. L. of H. v. Adams, 68 N. H. 236; 44 Atl. 380; Attorney-General v. Supreme Council A. L. of H., 206 Mass. 158; 92 N. E. 140; Abels v. Ackley, 126 Mo. App. 84; 103 S. W. 974.

[378] Masonic Ben. Ass'n v. Bunch, 109 Mo. 560; 19 S. W. 25; Hofman v. Grand Lodge, 73 Mo. App. 47; Bernheim v. Martin, 45 Wash. 120; 88 Pac. 106. See also *ante*, § 309, *et seq.*

[379] Supreme Lodge Fraternal Brotherhood v. Price, 27 Cal. App. 607; 150 Pac. 803.

insured and without his consent is invalid under the New York law.[380]

While the beneficiary has no property in the benefit as above stated, still because of an agreement with the beneficiary a trust may be created, as where a brother was named as beneficiary and in consideration of the member not changing such beneficiary to his wife, the brother made an agreement that if the member would allow him to remain as beneficiary·so as to have the policy as security for a debt the member owed him, he, the brother, would upon the death of the insured collect the policy and after pàyment of the debt pay the balance to the insured's wife, it was held that this created a trust in the name of the beneficiary which the widow could enforcè against the brother. In this case the Court said:[381] "Conrad Alexander had the right to change the beneficiary at any time. By reason of the promise of plaintiff to pay the proceeds, over and above the debt, to Mrs. Alexander, he was allowed to remain as beneficiary therein. It was only by reason of this undertaking on the part of the plaintiff that he was allowed to retain his position as beneficiary in the policy. This created a trust for the benefit of Mrs. Alexander as to the part of the proceeds of the policy over and above the amount of the debt remaining unpaid at the time of Conrad's death. In Denithene v. Independent Order of Foresters,[382] an elder brother of insured, named as beneficiary in a benefit certificate, was held to be a trustee for the insured's widow under circumstances closely analogous, in many respects, to this case. While it is true the enforcement of such a trust is a matter of equitable jurisdiction, yet some courts have permitted a recovery at law, applying the general doctrine that a third person may sue upon a contract made for his benefit."[383]

§ 399. Distinctions Between Certificates of Beneficiary Societies and Policies of Life Insurance in Respect to Assignment or Change of Beneficiary.—It is well settled that the beneficiary in a benefit certificate issued by a fraternal beneficiary association

---

[380] Lesem v. Mut. L. Ins. Co., 149 N. Y. Supp. 559; 164 App. Div. 507.
[381] Alexander v. Woodmen of the World, 193 Mo. App. 411; 182 S. W. 2.
[382] 209 Pa. 170; 58 Atl. 142.
[383] Waterhoùse v. Waterhouse, 29 R. I. 485; Catland v. Hoyt, 78 Me. 355; Devries v. Hawkins, 70 Neb. 656; Ellis v. Harrison, 104 Mo. 270; Cowen v. Hurst, 83 N. W. 274; Katz v. Wott, 134 N. Y. Supp. 675.

has no vested interest in the lifetime of the member, in this respect benefit certificates being unlike the regular life insurance policies, where the right to change the beneficiary is not reserved, unless possibly where the by-laws do not authorize a change.[384] The Supreme Court of Indiana[385] points out the fundamental difference between a certificate of membership in a benefit association and an ordinary policy of life insurance so far as the change of beneficiary and assignment are concerned. As regards the former the designation is an appointment, subject generally to revocation; in the latter one party to a contract exercises his rights under such contract. In the above-mentioned case the Court says: "Whatever rights beneficiaries have in life policies, they have by virtue of the contract between the insurance company and the assured. In the case of an ordinary insurance policy, the right of the beneficiaries in the policy, and to the amount to be paid upon the death of the assured, is a vested right, vesting upon the taking effect of the policy. That right cannot be defeated by the separate or the combined, acts of the assured and insurance company without the consent of the beneficiary.[386] As in other cases, so here, whatever right of power Taylor, the assured, had to and over the certificate was by virtue of the terms of the certificate and the by-laws of the order, which together constituted the contract between him and the order. And whatever rights the beneficiary, Anna Laura, had, or now has, to the fund to be, and in this case paid, upon the death of the assured, her father, she had, and has, by virtue of the same contract. It should be observed that the Royal Arcanum is not a domestic corporation, and hence not affected by § 3848 R. R. 1881.[387] If then the Royal Arcanum were to be treated as an or-

[384] On the latter point see Hill v. Grosebeck, 29 Colo. 161; 67 Pac. 167. On the first proposition see Hoeft v. Supreme Council, etc., 113 Cal. 91; 45 Pac. 185; 33 L. R. A. 174; Fischer v. Am. Legion of Honor, 168 Pa. St. 279; 31 Atl. 1089; Kirkpatrick v. Modern Woodmen, 103 Ill. App. 468; Lahey v. Lahey, 174 N. Y. 146; 66 N. E. 670; 61 L. R. A. 791; Bunyan v. Reed, 34 Ind. App. 385; 70 N. E. 1002; Lamb v. Mut. Reserve F. L. Ass'n, 106 Fed. 637.

[385] Holland v. Taylor, 111 Ind. 195; 12 N. E. 116. See also Tate v. Commercial Bldg. Ass'n, 97 Va. 74, 32 S. E. 382; 45 L. R. A. 243.

[386] Harley v. Heist, 86 Ind. 196; 44 Am. St. R. 285; Damron v. Penn. M. L. Ins. Co., 99 Ind. 478.

[387] Presb. Mut. Ass. Fund v. Allen, 106 Ind. 593.

dinary life insurance company, and the certificate as an ordinary
life policy, it would be clear that Taylor, the assured, had no authority, by will or otherwise, to change the beneficiary, or in any
way affect her rights without her consent. For many, and indeed
for most purposes, mutual benefit associations are insurance companies, and the certificates issued by them are policies of life insurance governed by the rules of law applicable to such policies.
There are, however, some essential differences usually existing
between the contracts evidenced by such certificates and the ordinary contract of life insurance.[388] The most usual difference is
the power, on the part of the assured in mutual benefit associations, to change the beneficiary. But as in either case the rights
of the beneficiary are dependent upon and fixed by the contract
between the assured and the company or association, there seems
to be no reason why the assured should have any greater power
to change the beneficiary in one case than in the other, except as
that power may be inherent in the nature of the association, or is
reserved to him by the constitution, or by the laws of the association or by the terms of the certificate. In the case before us,
the right and power of the assured, Taylor, to change the beneficiary was reserved to him by the by-laws of the order, and recognized in the certificate. Because of that reservation, the beneficiary, Anna Laura, did not have a right in and to the certificate, and the amount to be paid upon the death of the assured
vested in such a sense that it could not be defeated. But it would
be saying too much to say that she had no rights. She was the
beneficiary named in the certificate. The executors, so far as
shown by the terms of the certificate, had no right at all either
in or to the certificate, or to the amount to be paid by the association. So far as shown by that certificate, they were mere
trustees to collect the amount for the use and benefit of the real
beneficiary, Anna Laura. So long as the contract remained as
executed, she had the right of a beneficiary, subject to be defeated
by a change of the beneficiary by the assured. So long as the
certificate remained as executed, the assured had reserved to him-

[388] Presb. Mut. Ass. Fund v. Allen, *supra;* Elkhart Mut. Aid. Ass'n v.
Houghton, 103 Ind. 286; 53 Am. Rep. 514; Bauer v. Sampson Lodge, etc.,
102 Ind. 262.

self the power to change the beneficiary, and that was the extent of his right in, or powr over, the certificate, or the amount agreed to be paid at his death. He had no interest in or to either the certificate or the amount agreed to be paid, that would have gone at his death to his personal representatives. By virtue of the by-laws and the certificate, which, as we have seen, constituted the contract between him and the Royal Arcanum, he had power to change the beneficiary." Where the right to change the beneficiary is reserved in a policy of regular life insurance there is no reason why the same rules should not apply.

§ 400. **Development of the Law Concerning Change of Beneficiary.**—In one of the earliest cases involving the right of a member of a benefit society to change his designation of a beneficiary,[389] the change was allowed for two reasons: one being that the laws of the organization permitted it and the second being the same given by the Supreme Court of Connecticut in sustaining an alteration and substitution of beneficiaries in a policy of life insurance,[390] viz.: that the evidence of the contract, the policy, had not been delivered to the beneficiary so as to become an executed settlement in favor of the latter.[391] The doctrine of executed settlement was the stumbling block in the way of holding from the first that a member of a benefit society might at pleasure change the beneficiary to another than the one first designated; but in a later case[392] it was avoided in the same way as in the New York case just cited, by holding that there was no valid executed transfer by delivery. In this case the Supreme Court of Tennessee said: "By the charter of the Knights of Honor, as we have seen, the benefit fund of a member 'shall be paid to his family, or as he may direct,' and by the constitution he may direct the payment 'by will, entry on the reporter's record book, or benefit certificate.' Of course, a direction by will may be changed at any time before the death of the party, and the constitution of the order expressly provides for a similar change in the case of an entry on

[389] 1877, Durian v. Central Verein, 7 Daly 168.
[390] Lemon v. Phoenix M. L. Ins. Co., 38 Conn. 301.
[391] See Deady v. Bank Clerks' M. B. A., 17 Jones & Sp. 246; Johnson v. Van Epps, 14 Bradw. 201; 110 Ill. 551.
[392] Tennessee Lodge v. Ladd, 5 Lea 716.

the record book. The benefit certificate only certifies the fact
that the member named is entitled to the benefit fund, and the
form in the lower left hand corner, when filled up, is only a direction to whom payment is to be made. There is no reason for supposing that such a direction in the certificate should have any
other effect than a direction on the record book, or a will. In
fact, the form is a will. 'It is my will' that the benefit shall be
made to the person named. Such an instrument, attested by two
witnesses, might be proved as a will of the fund under our law.[393]
No doubt the language was adopted for the express purpose of
obviating a difficulty which might arise upon a simple direction
as to whether it could have effect as an assignment without delivery. The execution of such an instrument, without more, would
not divest the member of his interest in the fund, nor vest the
fund in the person to whom it is directed to be paid. It would
still be the fund of the member and subject to his disposal. This
court has held that a husband who takes out a policy of insurance
on his own life in his own name, is entitled to treat it as his property and dispose of it by will.[394] If he take the policy in the name
of his wife, intending to give her the benefit of it, she would
thereby acquire a vested interest of which he could not afterwards deprive her.[395] The same rule would undoubtedly apply
where he voluntarily assigned to his wife, by an executed contract, a policy taken out payable to himself.[396] A benefit certificate, like the one before us, would be governed by the same rule,
and would remain the property of the husband, subject to disposition by will unless previously assigned for a valuable consideration, or voluntarily transferred by an executed contract.[397] In
this view, the 'will' of W. E. Ladd, in the direction on the face of
the last certificate, would carry the right to his daughter, unless
the evidence shows a valid executed transfer to the wife of the
first certificate. Her testimony fails, unfortunately, to establish
either the necessary intention or the requisite delivery." About

[393] McLean v. McLean, 6 Humph. 452.
[394] Rison v. Wilkerson, 3 Sneed 565; Williams v. Carson, 2 Tenn. Ch.
269; affd. on appeal.
[395] Goslin v. Caldwell, 1 Lea 454.
[396] Fortescue v. Barnett, 3 Myl. & K. 36.
[397] Weil v. Trafford, 3 Tenn. Ch. 103.

the same time the Supreme Court of Illinois came to a similar conclusion for a different reason. In this case the certificate and laws of the society provided that the benefit might be disposed of by will, if not so disposed of it should go first to the widow, or if he had no widow, then to his heirs. The member made his will leaving the benefit to his two daughters; afterwards, by a paper held to amount to an equitable assignment, he gave the benefit to his wife if she would pay certain assessments. In holding the assignment good the Court said:[397a] "It is strenuously insisted that this contract was of such a character that it could not be assigned, even equitably by Clark Swift. We think otherwise. Neither the wife nor children had any vested interest, conditional or otherwise, in this insurance money so long as Clark Swift lived and owned and controlled this contract. The contract was between the association and himself. The children paid nothing for their supposed interest. The certificate had not been delivered or sold to them. The delivery to White made him bailee for Swift. It was a contract which was capable of being rescinded by Clark Swift, with the assent of the association. It is not conceived that he had not complete control over it, to the same extent that he might have controlled a promissory note payable to him. The will, of course, was of no effect until he died. At the time of his death, he held no interest in that part of the money to arise from the contract relating to his death, which could pass to the executor by the will. That interest has been sold. It was assignable in equity, and had been assigned to and paid for by the wife." In 1881 the Supreme Court of Minnesota held that the beneficiary under a membership in a benefit society could be changed at the pleasure of the member because the contract permitted it, the reservation of such power being made in the laws of the society. In this case[398] the Court said: "Here is not an ordinary contract of insurance, made between an insurance company and another person, the rights of the parties to be determined exclusively by the policy. The rights of Charles H. Richmond, and of any one claiming through him, depended, not on the certificate alone, but rather

[397a] Swift v. Railway, etc., Ben. Ass'n, 96 Ill. 309.
[398] Richmond v. Johnston, 28 Minn. 449.

on his membership in the association; and such rights were defined and controlled by its constitution and by-laws.''

§ 401. **Present Doctrine.**—And the accepted doctrine, now generally approved by all the authorities, is that the beneficiary may be changed if the laws of the order so provide, or if, when such transfer is not prohibited by the laws of the society, or under some circumstances if the certificate or policy has not been delivered to the beneficiary.[399] The Supreme Court of New Hampshire goes further and[400] holds that from the nature of the power given members of benefit associations the right of its free exer-

---

[399] Cases, *supra;* Holland v. Taylor, 111 Ind. 121; Ireland v. Ireland, 42 Hun. 212; Supreme Lodge v. Martin, 13 W. N. C. 160; Splawn v. Chew, 60 Tex. 532; Highland v. Highland, 109 Ill. 366; Coleman v. Knights of Honor, 18 Mo. App. 189; Raub v. Mut. R. Ass'n, 3 Mackey 68; Lamont v. Hotel Men's Ass'n, 30 Fed. 817; Barton v. Provident Mut. R. Ass'n, 63 N. H. 535; Schillinger v. Boes, 9 Ky. L. 18; 3 S. W. 427; Masonic Mut. Ben. Ass'n v. Burkhardt, 110 Ind. 189; 11 N. E. 449; Sup. Council Catholic Mut. Ben. Ass'n v. Priest, 46 Mich. 429; Gentry v. Sup. Lodge, 23 Fed. 718; 20 Cent. L. J. 393; Supreme Council Am. Leg. of Honor v. Perry, 140 Mass. 580; Luhrs v. Luhrs, 123 N. Y. 367; 25 N. E. 388, reversing 7 N. Y. Supp. 487; Supreme Conclave, etc., v. Capella, 41 Fed. 1; Hopkins v. Hopkins, 92 Ky. 324; 17 S. W. 864; Metropolitan L. Ins. Co. v. O'Brien, 92 Mich. 584; 52 N. W. 1012; Beatty v. Supreme Commandery, etc., 154 Pa. St. 484; 25 Atl. 644; Appeal of Beatty, 122 Pa. St. 428; 15 Atl. 861; Fleeman v. Fleeman, 15 N. Y. Supp. 838; Sabin v. Grand Lodge, 8 N. Y. Supp. 185; Mulderich v. Grand Lodge A. O. U. W,. 155 Pa. St. 505; 6 Atl. 663; Schoneau v. Grand Lodge, etc., 85 Minn. 349; 88 N. W. 999; Carpenter v. Knapp, 101 Ia. 712; 70 N. W. 764; 38 L. R. A. 128; Sofge v. Supreme Lodge, etc., 98 Tenn. 446; 39 S. W. 853; Hamilton v. Royal Arcanum, 189 Pa. St. 273; 42 Atl. 186; Carpenter v. Knapp, 101 Ia. 712; 70 N. W. 764; 38 L. R. A. 128; Pollak v. Sup. Counc. R. A., 40 Misc. 274; 81 N. Y. Supp. 942; Hoffman v. Ins. Co., 56 Mo. App. 301; Masonic Ben. Soc. v. Tolles, 70 Conn. 537; 40 Atl. 448; Fischer v. Fischer, 99 Tenn. 629; 42 S. W. 448; Lane v. Lane, 99 Tenn. 639; 42 S. W. 1058; Tepper v. Sup. Council, etc., 59 N. J. Eq. 321; 45 Atl. 111; Supreme Council A. L. H. v. Adams, 68 N. H. 236; 44 Atl. 380; Belknap v. Johnston, 114 Ia. 265; 86 N. W. 267; Crocker v. Hogan, 103 Ia. 243; 72 N. W. 411; Voight v. Kersten, 164 Ill. 314; 45 N. E. 543.

[400] Barton v. Provident R. Ass'n, 63 N. H. 535; and see also Thomas v. Grand Lodge, etc., 12 Wash. 500; 41 Pac. 882. The Supreme Court of Arkansas has said that there can be no change of beneficiary unless one is provided in the laws of the society. Knights of Pythias v. Long, 117 Ark. 136; 174 S. W. 1197.

cise requires its continuance until death. The Court says: "The contract, though one of life insurance, must be interpreted according to its terms, in view of the laws of the defendant association and of the evident understanding of the parties. The by-laws provide that 'when a member dies the association shall pay within sixty days, to his direction as entered upon his certificate of membership, the sum of two thousand dollars,' if the death assessments amount to that sum. The certificate of membership provides that 'in accordance with the provisions and laws governing said association, a sum not exceeding $2,000 will be paid by the association as a benefit, upon due notice of his death and the surrender of the certificate, to such person or persons as he may by entry on the record-book of the association or on the face of this certificate, direct, said sum to be paid provided he is in good standing when he dies.' The power of direction as to the object of the benefit is given to the member both in the by-laws and in the certificate of membership, and there is nothing in either tending to show that the power is to be exercised at the time of becoming a member, or that, when exercised the power is exhausted and another beneficiary cannot be substituted. The power of selection is unlimited as to persons and is limited in time only by the death of the member. The certificate remains in the possession and control of the member until death, and the provision of paying the benefit to the person named in the certificate at the death of the member, as then appears, leaves the power to appoint the beneficiary continuous until that event. The power of appointment is the one thing in the contract which is given to the member, and over that power no other person has any control. The right of its free exercise requires its continuance until death. The appointment by Barton of the plaintiff, his wife, to the benefit at the time he became a member, was no bar to his right to appoint another or others by a subsequent change. She was no party to the contract, and acquired no vested right in the benefit. The contract was between Barton, her husband, and the defendant, which, on the performance of the conditions of membership, agreed to pay the benefit to any person whose name might appear by his entry on the record-book or the face of the certificate at his death. The power of appointment being free and continuous, no right to the benefit could vest in the plaintiff until it became certain that her name remained in the certificate as beneficiary, at her husband's death. If by the entry of her name as beneficiary, the plaintiff acquired any interest whatever in the benefit it was only a contingent interest, which her husband had the power to defeat, and which he has defeated by exercising the power of substitution in the appointment of other beneficiaries.'' The principle declared in the preceding case[401] is undoubtedly correct, and follows most closely the precedents relating to the execution of powers. If designating a beneficiary is like executing a will, a stronger argument in favor of the rule is found, for from its very nature a will, whether executing a power, or disposing of ordinary property, is ambulatory and liable to be revoked.[402] And in the best considered cases this characteristic of a benefit appurtenant to membership in a benefit society is recognized.[403] If the statute relating to beneficiary associations authorizes a change of beneficiary at the pleasure of the member a by-law of a society requiring the consent of the society to a change of beneficiary is void.[404] The beneficiary may be changed in accordance with a law adopted after the issue of the certificate where the law in force at the time of such issue required the assent of the first beneficiary.[405] The right to change the beneficiary is not affected by the fact that the first beneficiary paid the assessments of the member and the change was made without his consent,[405a] or that the beneficiary was a creditor.[406]

[401] Barton v. Provident R. Ass'n, *supra.*

[402] *In re* Davies, 13 Eq. Cas. 163; Oke v. Heath, 1 Ves. 135; Easum v. Appleford, 5 M. & C. 56; Lord Godolpnin's Case, 2 Ves. 78.

[403] Relief Ass'n v. McAuley, 2 Mackey 70; Masonic Mut. Ben. Soc. v. Burkhardt, 110 Ind. 189; *ante,* § 397.

[404] Garrett v. Garrett (Cal. App.), 159 Pac. 1050.

[405] Supreme Council Cath. Knights, etc., v. Morrison, 16 R. I. 468; 17 Atl. 57; Supreme Council, etc., v. Franke, 137 Ill. 118; 27 N. E. 86; affg. 34 Ill. App. 651; Catholic Knights, etc., v. Kuhn, 91 Tenn. 214; 18 S. W. 385.

[405a] Fisk v. Equitable Aid Union (Pa.), 11 Atl. 84. See also Masonic Mut. Ass'n v. Bunch, 109 Mo. 560; 19 S. W. 25; Grand Lodge, etc., v. Mc-Grath, 133 Mich. 626; 95 N. W. 739; Schiller-Bund, etc., v. Knack, 184 Mich. 95; 150 N. W. 337; Spengler v. Spengler, 65 N. J. Eq. 176; 55 Atl. 285; Heasley v. Heasley, 191 Pa. St. 539; 43 Atl. 364; Finch v. Grand

or that the affidavit of loss of the benefit certificate was false,[407] or that possession of the certificate was obtained by fraud.[408] The surrender of the old certificate is not essential.[409] Wherever a member could have avoided the change of beneficiary because of mental incapacity the beneficiary upon his death can do so.[410]

The children of a mother named as beneficiary who died before the member can question the change of beneficiary.[411]

§ 402. **Same Subject—Mental Capacity of Member.**—On principle the same rule should apply in determining the mental capacity of a member to make a change of beneficiary as is applied in the case of wills. It is said[412] that a member has mental capacity sufficient to enable him to change the beneficiary when he understands the business he is engaged in, the persons who are dependent upon him and how he wishes to dispose of the benefit. A member mentally incapacitated cannot make a change of beneficiary.[413] The validity of the revocation of the designation of beneficiary is not affected by making a false affidavit that the beneficiary was dead.[414] False representations as to the relationship between the parties made to the original beneficiary and her

Grove, etc., 60 Minn. 308; 62 N. W. 384; Grand Lodge, etc., v. Denzer, 129 Ky. 202; 110 S. W. 882; Supreme Council R. A. v. Heitzman, 140 Mo. App. 105; 120 S. W. 628; Royal Arcanum v. Riley, 143 Ga. 75; 84 S. E. 428; Lendry v. Sovereign Camp W. of W., 140 Mo. App. 45; 124 S. W. 530. The uniform fraternal beneficiary act provides that payment of assessments by a beneficiary shall not deprive the member of the right to change the beneficiary.

[406] Ptacek v. Pisa, 231 Ill. 522; 83 N. E. 221; affg. 134 Ill. App. 155.

[407] White v. White (Miss.), 71 Sou. 322.

[408] Brown v. Grand Lodge, etc., 80 Ia. 287; 45 N. W. 884; Hirschl v. Clark, 81 Ia. 200; 47 N. W. 78; Isgrigg v. Schooley, 125 Ind. 94; 25 N. E. 151.

[409] Delaney v. Delaney, 70 Ill. App. 136; affd. 175 Ill. 87; 51 N. E. 961.

[410] Wells v. Covenant M. B. Ass'n, 126 Mo. 630; 29 S. W. 607; Colby v. Life Ins. Co., 57 Minn. 510; 59 N. W. 539.

[411] Knights of Modern Maccabees v. Sharp, 163 Mich. 449; 128 N. W. 786. But see Stake v. Stake, 228 Ill. 630; 81 N. E. 1146; affg. 131 Ill. App. 634.

[412] Grand Lodge A. O. U. W. v. Brown, 160 Mich. 437; 125 N. W. 400.

[413] Sovereign Camp Woodmen of the World v. Wood, 114 Mo. App. 471; 89 S. W. 891.

[414] Crosby v. Mut. Ben. L. Ins. Co., 221 Mass. 461; 109 N. E. 365.

belief therein are of no consequence in determining the rights of
the substituted beneficiary, nor can any importance be attached to
a finding that the policy was delivered with the intent that it
should become the property of the original beneficiary, for it
contains a reserved right of substitution and vested no right other
than one to receive the benefit in event the insured did not elect
before his death to change the contract.[415]

§ 403. **Member May Be Estopped From Changing Beneficiary.**
—Although it is settled law that the beneficiary named by the
member of a fraternal organization has no property in the benefit agreed to be paid, nor vested right therein, so as to deprive
the member of the right to change the beneficiary at will, yet
there may be conditions under which it would be held that the
beneficiary has acquired equitable rights in the benefit, which will
be recognized and protected, and the member becomes estopped
from exercising his rights under the contract. In these cases it is
not held that, under the contract, the beneficiary has acquired a
vested right, but the member has parted with a right which he
otherwise might have exercised. A leading case is Jory v. Supreme Council,[416] in which the Court said: ''The principle here
under consideration is the most recent growth of mutual benefit
association law, a branch of the law which in itself is young in
years; and we know of nothing in the law which deprives a person
contemplating membership in a mutual benefit association from
so contracting with the proposed beneficiary as that, when such
certificate is issued, equities in favor of the beneficiary are born,
of such merit that the insured member has no power to defeat
them. The few authorities shedding light upon this question declare the rights of the beneficiary are such as to create a vested
interest in the proceeds of the certificate.[417] Possibly this is not
a correct declaration of the principle of law applicable to the conditions, for a second beneficiary might be substituted, wholly in-

---

[415] Waring v. Wilcox, 8 Cal. App. 317; 96 Pac. 910; citing Bowman v.
Moore, 87 Cal. 311; 25 Pac. 409.

[416] 105 Cal. 20; 26 L. R. A. 733; 38 Pac. 524.

[417] Smith v. Society, 123 N. Y. 85; 25 N. E. 197; 9 L. R. A. 616; Nix v.
Donovan (City Ct. N. Y.), 18 N. Y. Supp. 435; Maynard v. Vanderwerker
(Supp.), 24 N. Y. Supp. 932.

nocent of the contractual relations existing between the insured and the first beneficiary, and his substitution give rise to the creation of equities in his behalf all-controlling upon a judicial disposition of the rights of the parties concerned. If the original beneficiary's interest was vested, no subsequent conditions could possibly arise, which would defeat his right; and, for this reason, we think it can hardly be termed a vested interest. The whole matter seems to be rather a question of equities, and the stronger and better equity must prevail. The illustration we have used does not arise in the present case, for we here have no clash of equities. The second beneficiary possesses no equities. He is a volunteer pure and simple. His status during the life of the insured is well described in Smith v. Society, *supra,* where the Court said: 'The designation was in the nature of an inchoate or unexecuted gift, revocable at any moment by the donor, and wholly within his control.' We think a court of equity should declare the insured estopped from substituting a second beneficiary of the character there involved, whenever sound equities are extant in favor of the first beneficiary; and, such estoppel being in force against the insured, it is equally in force and may be successfully urged against the volunteer beneficiary. The respondent is a volunteer beneficiary, and it only remains for us to ascertain from the record what the appellant's equities are, as disclosed by the evidence. She claims by her answer that she and her mother entered into a mutual agreement whereby each should join a mutual benefit society and make the other a beneficiary under the certificates issued, and that said agreement was carried out. Appellant further alleges that she paid all initiation fees, dues, and assessments upon the benefit certificate taken out by her mother. If these moneys were paid out by appellant under and by virtue of a contract between the parties, and in pursuance of this agreement and scheme for mutual insurance, then she has equities which entitle her to recognition in a court of justice, for it would be gross imposition and fraud upon her to allow the insured to change her beneficiary under these circumstances. Though wrong and injustice form an unpleasant sight to a court of equity, yet that court will never close its eyes because the sight is an unpleasant one, but rather, with vision all the keener, will reach out its strong arm to protect the wronged and innocent party.'' In another case in Illinois,[418] the facts were, that the member had agreed with his wife that she should advance him a certain sum of money, and in consideration thereof he would make her his beneficiary. In pursuance of this agreement she paid her husband the money, and he turned over the certificate to her. Afterwards, he made affidavit that the certificate was lost and obtained a new one, payable to his daughters. The court held that the member was estopped from changing the beneficiary. The Court said: "If Tracy had entered into no contract with his wife, and received no money from her on a pledge of the benefit certificate, but merely designated her as his beneficiary in the certificate, we would not hesitate to hold that he had the right to surrender the certificate at any time he saw proper, and have the organization issue a new one with other beneficiaries. In such case the wife could have no vested interest in the certificate. This case, however, rests upon a different state of facts, and must be governed by a different principle. After Tracy, in consideration of a large sum of money to him paid, pledged the benefit certificate to his wife, she acquired equitable rights in it, which may be protected in a court of equity." In another case[419] it was held that, under the circumstances, the wife's equity was so strong that it could not be overcome, even if a new designation of beneficiary were properly made. There are cases other than those cited where, for various reasons, it has been held that the member could not change the beneficiary, and the person first designated had rights of which he could not be deprived.[420]

[418] Supreme Council R. A. v. Tracy, 169 Ill. 123; 48 N. E. 401.

[419] Supreme Council Cath. Benev. Leg. v. Murphy, 65 N. J. Eq. 60; 55 Atl. 497.

[420] Adams v. Grand Lodge, 105 Cal. 321; 38 Pac. 914; Anderson v. Groesbeck, 26 Col. 3; 55 Pac. 1086; Conselyou v. Supreme Council, 3 App. Div. 464; 38 N. Y. Supp. 248; McGrew v. McGrew, 190 Ill. 604; 60 N. E. 861; affg. 98 Ill. App. 76; Leftwich v. Wells, 101 Va. 255; 43 S. E. 364; Grimbley v. Harrold, 125 Cal. 24; 57 Pac. 558; Goodrich v. Bohan (Tenn.), 52 S. W. 1105; Kimball v. Lester, 167 N. Y. 570; 60 N. E. 1113; Benard v. Grand Lodge, etc., 13 S. Dak. 132; 82 N. W. 404. For cases militating against the doctrine, or where the member was held not to be estopped, see Clark v. Supreme Council, etc., 176 Mass. 468; 57 N. E. 787; Webster v. Welch, 57 App. Div. 558; 68 N. Y. Supp. 58; Cade v. Head Camp, etc., 27 Wash. 218; 67 Pac. 603.

By an agreement upon a sufficient consideration a beneficiary may acquire a vested interest,[421] and the promise of a member to keep a certificate in force for the benefit of a child is enforceable.[422] Where a member changed the beneficiary in a certificate in consideration of the promise of the new beneficiary to marry him and the marriage took place, the new beneficiary acquired a right to the benefit which could not be taken away from her without her consent.[423] A member who procures his certificate designating a certain person as the beneficiary pursuant to an agreement with her and upon a consideration moving from her, is precluded as against her from exercising the privilege ordinarily possessed by members of a society of changing the beneficiaries as often as desired.[424] A contract between the beneficiary and a third person by which the latter agreed to pay assessments, is an assignment,[425] and where the beneficiary is changed the former beneficiary may have a lien for the assessments paid by her,[426] but where the beneficiary was to have a vested interest upon paying assessements, ceases to pay assessments, change of beneficiary can be made.[427] A member of a fraternal association with the consent of the beneficiaries can contract with a third person so that the latter may obtain a vested interest in the fund.[428] This question of vested rights of beneficiaries in fraternal beneficiary societies and that of estoppel of a member from changing his bene-

[421] Savage v. M. W. A., 84 Kan. 63; 113 Pac. 802.

[422] Cooper v. Order of Railway Conductors, 156 Iowa 481; 137 N. W. 472.

[423] Supreme Lodge K. & L. of H. v. Ulanowsky, 246 Pa. 591; 92 Atl. 711. See also Kane v. Supreme Council M. A. Ass'n, 218 Pa. 553; 65 Atl. 1108; Ferrell v. Stanley, 83 Kan. 491; 112 Pac. 155.

[424] Strange v. Supreme Lodge K. P., 189 N. Y. 346; 82 N. E. 433; 12 L. R. A. (N. S.), 1206. See also Freitas v. Freitas (Cal. App.), 159 Pac. 610; Callahan v. Supreme Tent K. O. T. M., 121 N. Y. Supp. 354.

[425] Coleman v. Anderson, 98 Tex. 570; 86 S. W. 730; affg. 82 S. W. 1057.

[426] Grand Lodge A. O. U. W. v. O'Malley, 114 Mo. App. 191; 89 S. W. 68; Coleman v. Anderson, *supra*.

[427] Eastman v. Eastman (Tex. Civ. App.), 135 S. W. 165.

[428] Brett v. Warwick, 44 Ore. 511; 75 Pac. 1061; Brown v. Modern Woodmen of Am., 97 Kan. 665; 156 Pac. 767. But see Spengler v. Spengler, 65 N. J. Eq. 176; 55 Atl. 285. Also O'Brien v. Grand Lodge A. O. U. W. (Mass.), 111 N. E. 955.

ficiary, have become of little importance, because of the provision in the Uniform Fraternal Beneficiary Act adopted in many States, to the effect that "no contract between a member and his beneficiary that the beneficiary, or any person for him, shall pay such member's assessments and dues, or either of them, shall give the beneficiary a vested right in the benefit certificate, or in the benefit, or deprive the member of the right to change the name of the beneficiary, or revoke the certificate, if any, issued by the association." The language of the Act in the different States may vary, but in effect it reserves unqualifiedly to the member the right of change of beneficiary.[429] A change of beneficiary is void when forbidden by the constitution of the society and the laws of the State where it was organized, and such a society cannot waive a restriction as to beneficiaries imposed by the statutes of the State where it was organized.[430]

§ 404. **Change of Beneficiary Must Be in Way Prescribed by the Provisions of the Contract or Laws of the Society.**—While the courts were slow in recognizing the right of change of beneficiary and most of the cases considering the subject relate to the contracts of beneficiary societies, the right is now universally conceded. The regular life insurance companies yielding to the demand, began to insert in their policies a clause reserving to the insured the right to change the beneficiary and hence the manner of exercising this right is as important in the case of regular life as in fraternal insurance. Although the member of a benefit society, or insured under the regular life policy, is thus generally left free to revoke his designation of beneficiary and appoint a new one, he must do so in the way pointed out by the laws of the organization, or specified in the policy. It is but carrying out the rule laid down in regard to powers, that if a method of revocation of an appointment is created by the instrument conferring such power, this direction must be complied with. If the laws of the society prescribe certain formalities to be observed in the change of beneficiary, or if the assent of the society to a transfer is required, all the requirements must be obeyed. The

429 Laws of Mo. 1911, p. 299.

430 Gregory v. Sovereign Camp Woodmen of the World (S. C.), 89 S. E. 391.

Supreme Court of Indiana says[431] that the same contract that permits the change ''fixed the mode and manner in which that change might be made, and we think that, taking the by-laws and the certificate together, the mode and manner of changing the beneficiary was fixed as definitely, and was as binding upon the assured as was the right to make such change binding upon the association and the beneficiary. In other words, under the contract, the assured had a right to change the beneficiary, provided he made the change in the manner provided in the contract.'' So, the Supreme Court of Iowa says:[432] ''The contract between the association and Robert Stephenson was that the former should pay the insurance to the persons named in the certificate of membership, unless he should change the name of the beneficiaries; and the manner in which this should be done formed a part of the contract of insurance . . . Until the contemplated change was made on the books of the association, and a new certificate issued, the obligation to pay the beneficiary whose name appeared on the books of the association continued to exist. . . . Counsel for the plaintiffs insist that where a power is reserved, and no mode of executing it is provided, it may be executed by will. Possibly this is so, but whether so or not, it will be conceded for the purpose of this case. One difficulty in the application of such a rule to this case is, that a mode of executing the reserved power is provided in the contract, and it is conceded that such a mode was not adopted. It was perfectly competent for the parties to contract as they did, and the mode of executing the reserved power provided in the contract cannot be regarded as an idle ceremony, because substantially a new contract was made upon its being complied with, and thereby all doubt upon the part of the association as to who was the beneficiary was removed. Because such mode was not adopted in this case, creates the doubt we are called upon to solve. We, therefore, think the mode agreed upon in the contract, whereby the name of the beneficiary should be changed, was made a matter of substance, and should be complied with.'' In most of the cases where the method of change of beneficiary

[431] Holland v. Taylor, 111 Ind. 127.
[432] Stephenson v. Stephenson, 64 Ia. 534; 21 N. W. 19. See also Hainer v. Legion of Honor, 78 Ia. 245; 43 N. W. 185; Jinks v. Banner Lodge, 139 Pa. St. 414; 21 Atl. 4.

was drawn in question the member had attempted to either divert the benefit by will, or the assent of the society to the change was required and had not been obtained, and thereby the attempted change was abortive. The rule above laid down has been generally accepted.[433] So a mere delivery of the certificate is insufficient when the laws provide for certain formalities,[434] nor by writing the change on the certificate, the laws requiring it to be surrendered.[435] An agent can make the change under a provision that the change may be in writing filed with the association,[436] and the change is valid though the secretary of the lodge attested the

[433] National Mut. Aid Soc., v. Lupold, 101 Pa. St. 111; Gentry v. Knights of Honor, 23 Fed. 718; 20 C. L. J. 393; Ireland v. Ireland, 42 Hun. 212; Knights of Honor v. Nairn, 60 Mich. 44; 26 N. W. 826; Vollman's Appeal, 92 Pa. St. 50; Elliott v. Whedbee, 94 N. C. 115; Highland v. Highland, 109 Ill. 366; Greeno v. Greeno, 23 Hun. 478; Kentucky Masonic M. Ins. Co. v. Miller, 13 Bush 489; Manning v. Supreme Lodge A. O. U. W., 86 Ky. 136; 5 S. W. 385; 7 Ky. L. 751; Renk v. Herman Lodge, 2 Demar. 409; Olmstead v. Masonic Mut. Ben. Soc., 37 Kan. 93; 14 Pac. 449; Basye v. Adams, 81 Ky. 363; Daniels v. Pratt, 143 Mass. 216; Harman v. Lewis, 24 Fed. 97, 530; Eastman v. Provident Mut. Ass'n, 62 N. H. 552; 20 C. L. J. 266; Hotel Men's M. Ben. Ass'n v. Brown, 33 Fed. 11; Supreme Counc. A. L. H. v. Smith, 45 N. J. 466; 17 Atl. 770; Rollins v. McHattan, 16 Colo. 203; 27 Pac. 254; Masonic, etc., Ass'n v. Jones, 154 Pa. St. 107; 26 Atl. 255; McCarthy v. New England Order, etc., 153 Mass. 314; 26 N. E. 866; Gladding v. Gladding, 56 Hun. 639; 8 N. Y. Supp. 880; Charch v. Charch, 57 Ohio St. 561; 49 N. E. 408; Fink v. Fink, 171 N. Y. 616; 64 N. E. 506; reversing 68 N. Y. Supp. 80; Moore v. Chicago, etc., Soc., 76 Ill. App. 433; Conway v. Supreme Counc., etc., 131 Cal. 437; 63 Pac. 727; Modern Woodmen v. Little, 114 Ia. 109; 86 N. W. 216; Nat. Exchange Bk. v. Bright, 18 Ky. L. 588; 36 S. W. 10; Head v. Supreme Counc., etc., 64 Mo. App. 212; Shuman v. Ancient Order U. W., 110 Ia. 642; 82 N. W. 331; Clark v. Supreme Counc., etc., 176 Mass. 468; 57 N. E. 787; Schoneau v. Grand Lodge, etc., 85 Minn. 349; 88 N. W. 999; Bollman v. Supreme Lodge, etc. (Tex. Civ. A.), 53 S. W. 702; Smith v. Supreme Counc,. etc., 127 N. C. 138; 37 S. E. 159; Grand Lodge, etc., v. Fisk, 126 Mich. 356; 85 N. W. 875; Dean v. Dean, 162 Wis. 303; 156 N. W. 135.

[434] Rollins v. McHatton, 16 Colo. 203; 27 Pac. 254. But see Brown v. Mansus, 64 N. H. 39; 5 Atl. 768, where delivery was held good.

[435] Thomas v. Thomas, 131 N. Y. 205; 30 N. E. 61; affg. 15 N. Y. Supp. 16.

[436] Bowman v. Moore, 87 Cal. 306; 25 Pac. 409; Depee v. Grand Lodge, etc., 106 Ia. 747; 76 N. W. 798.

signature without seeing the member sign.[437]   The mention of one method of change has been held to impliedly or expressly exclude all others on the ground that, *"expressio unius est exclusio alterius."*[438]   And the first beneficiary has a right to object to the change because the requirements of the laws had not been complied with.[439]   Where a member of a benefit society becomes suspended for non-payment of assessments, he may, in his application for re-instatement, designate a new beneficiary, and the society in readmitting him acquiesces in the change.[440]   Inasmuch as the beneficiary has no vested rights in the certificate of a benefit society resulting from the assured's membership therein, not being a party to the contract, he cannot complain that a by-law, in existence at the time the certificate was issued, providing the member may surrender the certificate and receive a new one, with the consent of the beneficiary, was amended so as to allow such surrender and change without the consent of he beneficiary, the constitution of the society providing that its by-laws might be amended at any time.[441]   All the requirements must be complied with, and if one, for example, the payment of the fee, is omitted,

[437] Simcoke v. Grand Lodge A. O. U. W., 84 Ia. 383; 51 N. W. 8; Donnelly v. Burnham, 177 N. Y. 546; 69 N. E. 1122; affg. 86 App. Div. 226; 83 N. Y. Supp. 659.

[438] Coleman v. Knights of Honor, 18 Mo. App. 189; Olmstead v. Masonic Mut. Ben. Soc., 37 Kan. 93; Brown v. Grand Lodge A. O. U. W., 208 Pa. St. 101; 57 Atl. 176; McCarthy v. Supreme Lodge, etc., 153 Mass. 314; 26 N. E. 866; 11 L. R. A. 144; 25 Am. St. R. 637; Grand Lodge v. Ross, 89 Mo. App. 621; McLaughlin v. McLaughlin, 104 Cal. 171; 37 Pac. 865.

[439] Brown v. Grand Lodge, 208 Pa. St. 101; 57 Atl. 176; Grand Lodge, etc., v. Frank, 133 Mich. 232; 94 N. W. 731.

[440] Davidson v. Knights of Pythias, 22 Mo. App. 263.   But see Mason v. Mason, 160 Ind. 191; 65 N. E. 585.

[441] Byrne v. Casey, 70 Tex. 247; 8 S. W. 38; Supreme Council Cath. Knights v. Morrison, 16 R. I. 468; 17 Atl. 57; Supreme Council v. Franke, 137 Ill. 118; 27 N. E. 86; Cath. Knights v. Kuhn, 91 Tenn. 214; 18 S. W. 385. And a creditor who has been designated as beneficiary acquires no separate standing so as to exclude as against him the subsequent declarations of the assured, for the latter remains the contracting party. Smith v. National Ben. Soc., 123 N. Y. 85; 25 N. E. 197; Supreme Council A. L. H. v. Stewart, 36 M. A. 319; Bagley v. Grand Lodge A. O. U. W., 131 Ill. 498; 22 N. E. 487.

the change is incomplete.[442] A benefit certificate, subject by the laws of the order to change at will, on the compliance with certain formalities and the surrender of the old certificate, may be changed in the prescribed way, although it had been delivered to a third party who paid the assessments and was obtained from him without his consent.[443] A by-law requiring the member to give reasons for a change is reasonable and will be enforced.[444] The benefit is not part of the member's estate and cannot pass under a will[445] The mere fact that the member in an application for a change of beneficiary falsely stated that the benefit certificate was lost will not invalidate the change.[446]

§ 405. **The Same Subject—Later Authorities.**—Change of beneficiary must be in the manner prescribed by the laws of the society, and excludes all other methods, and the formalities for change of beneficiary must be substantially complied with.[447] But the failure of the order to record the change of beneficiary does not defeat the change.[448] It follows that a mere intention to

[442] Stonigham v. Dillon, 42 Ore. 63; 69 Pac. 1020; Independent Order Foresters v. Keliher, 30 Ore. 501; 59 Pac. 324-1109; Williams v. Fletcher, 26 Tex. Civ. A. 85; 62 S. W. 1082.

[443] Fisk v. Equitable Aid Union (Pa.), 11 Atl. 84.

[444] Murphy v. Metropolitan, etc., Ass'n, 25 Misc. 751; 55 N. Y. Supp. 620.

[445] Hutson v. Jenson, 110 Wis. 26; 85 N. W. 689; Grand Lodge v. Fisk, 126 Mich. 356; 85 N. W. 875; Stice v. Carter, 23 Ky. L. 915; 63 S. W. 770; Vance v. Park, 7 Ohio Dec. 564; Schardt v. Schardt, 100 Tenn. 276; 45 S. W. 340.

[446] Spengler v. Spengler, 65 N. J. Eq. 176; 55 Atl. 285.

[447] Grand Lodge A. O. U. W. v. O'Malley, 114 Mo. App. 191; 89 S. W. 68; affd. by Supreme Court, Grand Lodge v. McFadden, 213 Mo. 269; 111 S. W. 1172; Sullivan v. Maroney, 77 N. J. Eq. 565; 78 Atl. 150; affg. 73 Atl. 842; Pollock v. Household of Ruth, 150 N. C. 211; 63 S. E. 940; Abeles v. Ackley, 133 Mo. App. 594; 113 S. W. 698; Londry v. Sovereign Camp W. O. W., 140 Mo. App. 45; 124 S. W. 530; Modern Woodmen of America v. Haedle, 88 Vt. 37; 90 Atl. 893; Slaughter v. Slaughter, 186 Ala. 302; 65 Sou. 348; Knights of the Maccabees v. Sackett, 34 Mont. 357; 86 Pac. 423; Flowers v. Sovereign Camp, etc., 40 Tex. Civ. App. 593; 90 S. W. 526; Deal v. Deal, 87 S. C. 395; 69 S. E. 886; Finnell v. Franklin, 55 Colo. 156; 134 Pac. 122; Vanasek v. Western Fraternal Ass'n, 122 Minn. 273; 142 N. W. 333; Stemler v. Stemler, 31 S. D. 595; 141 N. W. 780; Modern Woodmen v. Puckett (Kan.), 94 Pac. 132.

[448] Modern Woodmen of America v. Terry (Okla.), 153 Pac. 1124.

change the beneficiary is not sufficient.[449] A letter expressing a desire that the son should have the benefit is not a sufficient change of beneficiary.[450] A will cannot dispose of the benefit payable to the beneficiary, nor amount to a change of beneficiary,[451] but where a right exists to change the beneficiary by will a designation of a person not within the classes named in the constitution, other than by will, is void.[452] The act of a member in appearing in open lodge and expressing desire for change of beneficiary is effective under the by-laws of the society.[453]

Where the by-laws provide that a change of beneficiary should not take effect until after the name of the new beneficiary has been furnished to the grand keeper of records and seals and inserted by him in the face of the policy, and the insured wrote a request for such change of beneficiary and directed it to be forwarded to the officer authorized to make the change but died before it was sent, the request being forwarded with proofs of his death, the right of the beneficiary named in the policy to its proceeds became vested and could not be defeated by the attempted change.[454] Where an administrator of the deceased member had prevented the change and afterwards collected the policy he is liable to the new beneficiary for the amount collected.[455]

§ 406. **The Society May Waive Requirements of Its Laws As to Change of Beneficiary.**—Although the rule is settled that change of beneficiary must be made in the manner prescribed by the laws of the society, with some exceptions[456] it is also now equally well settled that the society may waive compliance with

---

[449] Fraken v. Supreme Court I. O. F., 152 Mich. 502; 116 N. W. 188.

[450] Supreme Lodge A. O. U. W. v. Edwards, 111 Me. 359; 89 Atl. 147. See also Pettus v. Hendricks, 113 Va. 326; 74 S. E. 191.

[451] Arnold v. Equitable Life Assur. Soc., 228 Fed. 157; Burke v. M. W. A., 2 Cal. App. 611; 84 Pac. 275; Mineola Tribe v. Lizer, 117 Md. 136; 83 Atl. 149.

[452] Middlestadt v. Grand Lodge, etc., 107 Minn. 228; 120 N. W. 37.

[453] Robinson v. Robinson (Ark.), 181 S. W. 300.

[454] Wilkes v. Hicks (Ark.), 186 S. W. 830.

[455] O'Donnell v. Metropolitan Life Ins. Co. (Del.), 95 Atl. 239.

[456] *Post*, § 411.

the required formalities. In Splawn v. Chew,[457] which was a
controversy between the original beneficiary, named in the certificate, and the devisee of the same benefit in the will of the
member subsequently made, the Supreme Court of Texas said:
"The right to change the disposition of [the] money being established in the member, the next question is, how is it to be exercised? It is contended by appellees that it can be exercisd only
in the manner pointed out in the third section of the third by-
law, which reads as follows: 'Members may at any time, when
in good standing, surrender their certificate, and have a new one
issued, payable to such beneficiary or beneficiaries dependent upon
them as they may direct, upon payment of a certificate fee of
fifty cents.' This section is in further recognition of the right to
make the alteration, and it seems to be admitted that a surrender
of the old certificate and the issuance of a new one under this
section would effect a change in the beneficiaries of the policy.
But is this the only way in which such a change can be effected?
The right to make the change is given by a different section of
the by-laws, and exists in the insured so long as he remains a
member of the order. A method by which he may accomplish it
to the satisfaction of the order is pointed out in the section last
recited, but we do not consider this as exclusive of all other ways
of effecting the same object. The design of this section is to protect the interests of the corporation. The company are entitled
to know who are the parties entitled to the benefit money, and this
is an effectual and certain means of giving that information. But
like all such provisions in the by-laws of private corporations, it
may be waived at the option of the corporation, being for its benefit alone. This has been held in reference to such provisions when
prescribed in mandatory terms. If they can be waived in such
cases, much stronger would seem to be the reason why this can
be done when the course to be pursued is directed, as in this instance, in permissive language alone. . . . As a by-law of the
order this provision entered into the understanding between the
company and the member effecting the insurance, and the rights
of interested parties are not strengthened by the fact that the

[457] 60 Tex. 532. See also Supreme Lodge Fraternal Brotherhood v.
Price (Cal. App.), 150 Pac. 803.

same provision is found in the certificate. It is still a condition for the benefit of the company, to be insisted upon or waived according to their election.'' In a Kentucky case,[458] the laws of the order provided that a member might at any time change the beneficiary by revoking the first designation and designating a new beneficiary in a form given on the back of the certificate, having the same attested by the recorder of the subordinate lodge with its seal thereto attached, and paying a fee of fifty cents for a new certificate, which was thereupon to be issued by the supreme lodge upon receipt from the local lodge of this old certificate, the attested revocation and the fee. In this case the member had left the certificate in charge of the local lodge. Subsequently he married and wrote the lodge inclosing his dues and requesting the officer to send him the certificate made out to his wife. No fee was sent and the officer of the lodge wrote to him for it. Nothing was done until after the death of the member when the recorder of the lodge certified the letter to the supreme lodge, which issued the new certificate as requested and afterwards paid it. The suit was by the first beneficiary; judgment was given by the lower court for the defendant and in affirming this the Court of Appeals said: ''The appellant had but a contingent right to the benefit; not a vested and absolute one. It was subject to be defeated at the will of the assured. The law of the order, as above cited, provides how this shall be done. The regulation is a reasonable one; but the question arises whether it shall govern as between claimants to the benefit, the order has seen fit to waive it. We think not. Its object, beyond doubt, was to prevent the appellee from becoming involved in litigation with outside claimants. Upon this idea it was held in the case of Aid Society v. Lupold,[459] that where the certificate provided, 'This certificate may be assigned and transferred only by and with the consent of the association indorsed thereon,' and it was done without such approval, that it was a part of the contract, and that the society had a right to insist upon the protection which it was intended to afford. The direction by the insured to change the benefit was, in the case

[458] Manning v. Ancient Order of United Workmen, 86 Ky. 136; 5 S. W. 385.
[459] 101 Pa. St. 111.

now under consideration, given through the proper channel. The subordinate lodge referred it to the proper authority and it saw fit to waive the regulations intended for its benefit, and comply with the direction although made in an informal manner and without the payment of the fee. The intention of the insured was to change the benefit. He so directed in writing; and now, because he did not do so in the formal manner prescribed by the law for the benefit of the order, it is asked by a third party, whose interest in the insurance was liable to end at any time at the will of the assured, that his intention shall be defeated, although the party, for whose benefit the form was prescribed, has seen proper to waive it. Such a rule would sacrifice substantial justice to mere form; it would tend to defeat the benevolent aim and purpose of the organization, and the desire and intention of the insured. Members of the order may be remote from their lodge; they may not have their certificates with them, and therefore be unable to make the indorsement thereon as directed or to have it attested by the recorder of their lodge, or its seal attached thereto. If the appellee chooses to waive these formalities, it does not lie in the mouth of a third party to complain. The order is entitled to know who is entitled to the benefit fund, and the formal mode of changing its direction is for its benefit; while, upon the other hand, the right of the beneficiary rests in the mere will of the assured. . . . In our opinion, the letter of June 5, 1879, operated to change the direction of the benefit, inasmuch as 'the appellee saw fit to waive its informality; and, as the assured had therefore done all that was needed on his part, the fact that the appellee issued the new certificate after his death, does not affect the right of the parties. If the appellee were in court with the fund, asking that the conflicting rights of the claimants to it be determined, and was silent as to the informality of the direction to change the benefit, it seems to us that the widow ought to prevail.'' The facts of the above case, however, would seem to have justified the interference of equity to carry out the intention of the member, so clearly expressed, but imperfectly executed.[460] This doctrine is now well settled by a decided weight of authority.[461] In some

[460] *Post*, § 410.
[461] Titsworth v. Titsworth, 40 Kan. 571; 20 Pac. 213; Marsh v. Supreme

cases considered the change was held good not on the doctrine of waiver but because the contract authorized the change in the manner made.   In Raub v. Relief Association,[462] it was held that a by-law requiring the assent of the society to any change of beneficiary, was void because the charter gave the right to dispose of the benefit by will and without the assent of the lodge.   In Catholic Benefit Association v. Priest,[463] a disposition by will was sustained because the record did not show any law of the society taking away such right.   In a Georgia case,[464] a defective transfer to a wife was upheld on the ground of estoppel, for though the assent of the company was required to make an assignment valid, the agent of the company had agreed to attend to it. The officers of a subordinate lodge, however, have no power to waive.[465]   Nor can there be any waiver after the death of the member when the rights of the beneficiary have attached.[466]   It has been held that only the society can object to irregularities in the making of a change of beneficiary.[467]

Council A. L. of H., 144 Mass. 512; 21 N. E. 1070; South. Tier Masonic, etc., Assn. v. Laudenbach, 5 N. Y. Supp. 90; Martin v. Stubbings; 126 Ill. 387; 18 N. E. 657; Knights of Honor v. Watson, 64 N. H. 517; 15 Atl. 128; Anthony v. Mass. Ben. Ass'n, 158 Mass. 322; 33 N. E. 577; Adams v. Grand Lodge A. O. U. W., 105 Cal. 321; 38 Pac. 914; Schardt v. Schardt, 100 Tenn. 276; 45 S. W. 340; Fanning v. Supreme Counc., etc., 84 App. Div. 205; 82 N. Y. Supp. 733; Grand Lodge v. Reneau, 75 Mo. App. 402; Schoneau v. Grand Lodge, 85 Minn. 349; 88 N. W. 999; Kimball v. Lester, 43 App. Div. 27; 59 N. Y. Supp. 540; Allgemeiner Arbeiter Bund v. Adamson, 132 Mich. 86; 92 N. W. 786; Polish Nat'l Alliance v. Nagrabski, 71 N. J. Eq. 621; 64 Atl. 741; Bernheim v. Martin, 45 Wash. 120; 88 Pac. 106; Henderson v. Modern Woodmen of Am., 163 Mo. App. 186; 146 S. W. 102; Abels v. Ackley, 133 Mo. App. 594; 113 S. W. 698; Ladies of Modern Maccabees v. Daley, 166 Mich. 542; 131 N. W. 1127.

[462] 3 Mackey 68.

[463] 46 Mich. 429.

[464] Nally v. Nally, 74 Ga. 669.

[465] Grand Lodge A. O. U. W. v. Connolly, 58 N. J. Eq. 180; 43 Atl. 286.

[466] McLaughlin v. McLaughlin, 104 Cal. 171; 37 Pac. 865; Fink v. Fink, 171 N. Y. 616; 64 N. E. 506; reversing 68 N. Y. Supp. 80; Smith v. Herman, 28 Misc. 681; 59 N. Y. Supp. 1044; Ancient Order of Gleaners v. Bury, 165 Mich. 1; 130 N. W. 191.

[467] Knights of Pythias v. Long, 117 Ark. 136; 174 S. W. 1197; Longen v. Carter, 102 Ark. 72; 143 S. W. 575.

§ 407. **Where No Formalities Are Required Change Can Be Made in Any Way Indicating the Intention of the Member.**—If no formalities are required by the laws of the society for change of beneficiary it may be made in any manner indicating the intention of the member as by will.[468] In the leading case just cited the Court says:[469] "As we have already seen, neither constitution nor by-laws of plaintiff prescribed any formalities whatever for a change of beneficiary. In the absence of such, any clear, definite designation of a different beneficiary will suffice. So we think that the designation of a trustee by his last will formally executed and duly probated wrought an effectual change, particularly as he was authorized by the charter to give it to his devisees." It may also be made by a paper signed by the member, expressing the intention and mailed to the society and received after his death although the certificate is not surrendered but remains in the hands of the first beneficiary.[470] In this case[471] the Court says: "And it is to be observed that there is no requirement in the contract that the certificate shall be surrendered in order to effect a change of the beneficiary. It does not even provide that if is necessary to notify the association of the change at the time it is made. By the very terms of the contract the change of the beneficiary is a mere direction to the association which it is bound to obey. The disposal of the benefits may be made by the mere direction of the insured. This act does not require the assent of the association. It is not a new contract between the insurer and the insured. If the association received notice of the change in the beneficiary before it has been in any way prejudiced, it would seem that it would be bound to obey the direction. These views appear to us to be founded on sound reason. We look in vain for any law, rule or regulation enacted by the association with which Burrows failed to comply. It is true that the blank on the back of the certificate indicates that the

[468] Masonic Mut. Ass'n v. Bunch, 109 Mo. 560; 19 S. W. 25; Carruth v. Clawson, 97 Ark. 50; 133 S. W. 178; Brinsmaid v. Iowa St. Traveling Men's Ass'n, 152 Ia. 134; 132 N. W. 34; Order Columbian Knights v. Matzel, 184 Ill. App. 15.

[469] Masonic Mut. Ass'n v. Bunch, *supra*.

[470] Hirschl v. Clark, 81 Ia. 200; 47 N. W. 78; 9 L. R. A. 841.

[471] Hirschl v. Clark, *supra*.

manner of conducting the business of the association was to surrender the first certificate, and issue another to the new beneficiary, and the evidence shows that this was the practice of the company. But this was a mere regulation for the convenience of the company of which its members had no notice. It was no part of the constitution or by-laws of the association; and rules or regulations adopted by the officers of the company, in regard to the transaction of business, and which do not enter into the constitution of the company as provisions of its charter or by-laws are not embraced in the certificate. They are such rules as fix the rights of members of the company and are parts of the laws of the institution which are to be regarded as parts of the contract.[472] The case of Stephenson v. Stephenson,[473] is in no sense in conflict with the views we have expressed. In that case the by-laws which were made part of the contract, made that specific provision as to the manner of changing the beneficiary. It is there said that the manner in which this should be done formed a part of the contract of insurance. We have set out the facts attending the execution of the paper by Burrows and the time of its reaching the association with more particularity than may have been necessary. In our opinion the fact that Burrows died before the association received the instrument is not a material question. Under this contract Burrows could have changed the beneficiary by an assignment on the certificate, or by a separate paper, and it was complete, at least so far as Mary Burrows was concerned, when it was delivered to Clark, the trustee. Notice to the insurer of the assignment was not necessary unless required by the contract of insurance. Where a policy is assignable or where a benefit certificate authorizes change of beneficiaries, which is the same thing in effect as an assignment, notice of the assignment is not necessary to its validity, unless required by the contract of insurance. The execution of the instrument by Burrows, directing that the money be paid to his mother and brothers and sisters, operated as an equitable assignment. The consent of Mary Burrows was not necessary to effect the object. And she could not defeat it by refusing to deliver the certificate when it was demanded. She had no vested right in the paper nor in the insurance. If it had been

[472] Walsh v. Ins. Co., 30 Ia. 133; and the authorities there cited.
[473] 64 Ia. 534; 21 N. W. 19.

procured from her by fraud and a new certificate issued to another beneficiary she would have had no right to complain."[474] And a change of beneficiary in accordance with the custom of the association will be valid, the by-laws providing no method.[475]

§ 408. **When An Attempted Change of Beneficiary Becomes Complete.**—It often becomes important to know when an attempted change of beneficiary becomes complete. Much, however, depends upon the conditions expressed in the by-laws. It has been held[476] that the change of beneficiary under a policy cannot take effect at any other time than that agreed upon and the act to be done by the company is not a mere ministerial one. In general, the method is for the member to fill out a blank form on the back of the certificate, revoking his former and making a new direction of payment, and have the same attested by the secretary of the lodge, who farwards the same to the superior authorities, who thereupon cancel the old and issue a new certificate payable as requested. It is possible for the member to die before the various steps in the transaction have all been taken. The general rule is that if the member does all in his power, that is, does all things required of him under the contract to effectuate the change, it will be held complete although the new certificate has not in fact been issued.[477] In one case[478] the member requested a friend to

[474] Brown v. Grand Lodge, 80 Ia. 27; 48 N. W. 884.

[475] Schmidt v. New Braunfelser, etc., Verein, 32 Tex. Civ. A. 11; 73 S. W. 568; Waldum v. Homstadt, 119 Wis. 312; 96 N. W. 806.

[476] Sheppard v. Corlway, 61 Fla. 735; 55 Sou. 841.

[477] See, in addition to cases cited *infra* in this section, Heydorf v. Conrack, 7 Kan. App. 202; 52 Pac. 700; Berkley v. Harper, 3 App. D. C. 308; Waldum v. Homstadt, 119 Wis. 312; 96 N. W. 806; Collins v. Collins, 30 App. Div. 341; 51 N. Y. Supp. 932; Donnelly v. Burnham, 86 App. Div. 226; 83 N. Y. Supp. 659; Brierly v. Equitable Aid Union, 170 Mass. 218; 48 N. E. 1090; Coyne v. Coyne, 23 App. Div. 261; 48 N. Y. Supp. 937; Fink v. Delaware, etc., Ass'n, 57 App. Div. 507; 68 N. Y. Supp. 80; Supreme Lodge, etc., v. Terrell, 99 Fed. 330; McGowan v. Supreme Court I. O. F., 104 Wis. 173; 80 N. W. 603; Grand Lodge, etc., v. Kohler, 106 Mich. 121; 63 N. W. 897; Jory v. Supreme Council, etc., 105 Cal. 20; 38 Pac. 524; 26 L. R. A. 733; Berg v. Damkoehler, 112 Wis. 587; 88 N. W. 606; Hofman v. Grand Lodge, etc., 73 Mo. App. 47.   z

[478] Ireland v. Ireland, 42 Hun. 212. A case very much alike in its facts and conclusion is Knights of the Maccabees v. Sackett, 34 Mont. 357; 86 Pac. 423.

take his certificate to the secretary of the lodge and have him attest and complete the change; but before this was done and before the old certificate was delivered to the secretary, the member died. It was held that the change was incomplete and the old beneficiary recovered. In a Michigan case[479] the Supreme Court of that State, in declining to pass fully on the question, said: "By the express terms of that certificate, it is provided that Mrs. Richardson shall have the money unless the certificate is surrendered and canceled and a new one issued; and the form of surrender printed on the back conforms precisely to the clause also inserted in the constitution, requiring every surrender and new direction to be signed by the member, and attested by the reporter under the lodge seal, he being the officer into whose hands it must be placed for transmission to the home office for reissue. Under this arrangement, the purpose is evident that the corporation shall always be in written contract relations with a member who is alive and in good standing, which will show them the identity of the beneficiary to whom they are liable. It is possible—and we need not consider under what circumstances—that when a member has executed and delivered to the reporter his attested surrender, in favor of a competent beneficiary, his death before a new certificate is rendered, may leave his power to designation so far executed as to enable a court of equity to relieve against the accident. But in the present case the facts show conclusively that Traver did not mean to have any surrender made until after his death." In a case in Missouri,[480] a member of a benefit society was severely injured and desired a friend to take his certificate to the secretary of the lodge and have it changed. The friend did this, and the next day called at the central office and received the new certificate. At the time of issue of the latter the member was dead. The court held that, it not appearing that the officers who issued new certificates to members had any right to refuse, if the request was in form, but had merely ministerial duties in that respect, the transfer was good; for the member had done all that lay in his power to effect the change before he died. To the same effect is the case of Luehrs v. Luehrs,[481] where the Court of Appeals

479 Knights of Honor v. Nairn, 60 Mich. 44.
480 National Am. Ass'n v. Kirgin, 28 Mo. App. 80.
481 123 N. Y. 367; 25 N. E. 388; reversing 6 N. Y. Supp. 51.

said: "The deceased had expressed his desire in the premises as fully as it was possible for him to do. He had himself complied with all the requirements imposed by the supreme lodge as necessary for him to perform in order to obtain another certificate . . . The question is whether the valid and proper direction of the member shall be complied with when he has done everything that was required of him to do in order to effectuate his intention and all that remains to do is a purely formal piece of business, and one in doing of which there is not (upon the facts in this case) one particle of discretion remaining in the officers of the supreme body, or in any other body. . . We think these questions may fairly be answered in the affirmative." Where by collusion the seal of the lodge was not affixed but the society approved the change it was held effectual;[482] so also where the change was signed by the agent of the member, the latter dying before the new certificate was issued.[483] The Supreme Court of Pennsylvania has held,[484] that a new benefit certificate issued to change the beneficiary, upon application made in accordance with the by-laws of the association and signed by the proper officers of the supreme lodge and sealed with its seal, is not invalid because not signed and sealed by the officers of the subordinate lodge. Where a by-law provided that the change of beneficiary should not be complete until delivery of the new certificate, and the old certificate with the attempted change did not reach the office of the association until after the death of the member and the issue of the new certificate was then refused, it was held that there was no change.[485] And where the member was also secretary of his council and the certificate was found in his desk after his death, never having been forwarded to headquarters as required by the by-law, it was held that there was no change.[486] An arbitrary refusal of the directors to approve of a change will not invalidate it.[487]

[482] Marsh v. Supreme Counc. A. L. H, 144 Mass. 512; 21 N. E. 1070.

[483] Schmidt v. Ia. Knights of Pythias, 82 Ia. 304; 47 N. W. 1032.

[484] Fisk v. Equitable Aid Union, 11 Atl. 84; Mayer v. Equitable Reserve, etc., Ass'n, 2 N. Y. Supp. 79.

[485] Counsman v. Modern Woodmen, 69 Neb. 710; 96 N. W. 672.

[486] Hamilton v. Royal Arcanum, 189 Pa. St. 273; 42 Atl. 186.

[487] Sanborn v. Black, 67 N. H. 537; 35 Atl. 942.

§ 409. **The Same Subject—Later Cases.**—The later cases adhere to the general principle that if a member has done all that is required of him to effect a change of beneficiary, the change will take effect though all the details were not completed before the death of the member.[488] The courts will often consider comparatively slight acts sufficient to effectuate a change, as where the certificate was in the possession of the plaintiff who lived many miles away, and there was not sufficient time to go after it; the member was sick, and learning that he was about to die, signed a written request for the change, which was held sufficient under the circumstances.[489] And where the wife was fatally sick and her husband had deserted her; she sent for the agent of the society and gave him the certificate and directed a change from her husband to her father, mother and children, and paid the fee, the Court held that this amounted to a change of beneficiary.[490] However, where the constitution of the association authorized a change of beneficiary by a written declaration, signed and witnessed by two witnesses and acknowledged before a justice of the peace, and that a change in any other manner would not be legal, or binding on the order, it was held that an attempted change of beneficiary by a member which was witnessed only by the justice before whom the declaration was acknowledged, was insufficient.[491] It was held that where the constitution provided that in case of the loss of the certificate, the member desiring a

[488] Smither v. Locomotive Engineers, etc., Ass'n, 138 Ga. 717; 76 S. E. 44; Supreme Council R. A. v. Huckins, 166 Ill. App. 555; Hayden v. Modern Brotherhood of America, (Ia.), 155 N. W. 830; Wandell v. Mystic Toilers, 130 Ia. 639; 105 N. W. 448; Lockett v. Lockett, 26 Ky. L. 300; 80 S. W. 1152; Holden v. Modern Brotherhood of America, 151 Ia. 673; 132 N. W. 829; Supreme Tent K. O. T. M. v. Altmann, 134 Mo. App. 363; 114 S. W. 1107; Wood v. Brotherhood of American Yeoman, 148 Ia. 400; 126 N. W. 949; Supreme Court I. O. F. v. Frise, 183 Mich. 186; 150 N. W. 110; Garrett v. Garrett (Cal. App.), 159 Pac. 1050; Wintergest v. Court of Honor, 185 Mo. App. 373; 170 S. W. 346.

[489] Henderson v. Modern Woodmen of America, 163 Mo. App. 186; 146 S. W. 102.

[490] Jackson v. Brotherhood of American Yeomen, 167 Mo. App. 19; 150 S. W. 871. See also Walsh v. Trust Co., 148 Mo. App. 179; 127 S. W. 645; Supreme Lodge, etc., v. Philbin, 112 Mo. App. 260; 87 S. W. 58.

[491] Abbott v. Supreme Colony, etc., 190 Mass. 67; 76 N. E. 234.

change must actually furnish the sovereign clerk satisfactory proof under oath of such loss before the rights of the original beneficiary can be effected, it was held that where a member whose certificate was lost, mailed an application for change of beneficiary and died before the change was made, the rights of the original beneficiary were unaffected.[492] So where at the time of the death of the insured his application had not been received by the association through the mail, the fact that the application was actually mailed on the day of the insured's death did not affect the interest of the original beneficiary which attached instantly on insured's death.[493] It is immaterial that the member made a false affidavit of the loss of the benefit certificate in effecting a change of beneficiary.[494]

§ 410. **Jurisdiction of Equity in Aid of Imperfect Change of Beneficiary.**—The inquiry is suggested by the last section and the cases therein cited, to what extent equity will aid an imperfect change of beneficiary. Generally speaking equity will aid imperfect changing of beneficiary where the member attempts to make the change but it is prevented by the unlawful withholding of the benefit certificate.[495] In a recent case, the Supreme Court of Michigan considered the subject.[496] The facts of the case were as follows: By the laws of the order a member might at pleasure revoke his appointment of a beneficiary and designate a new one by signing a declaration to that effect on the back of the certificate; such declaration was to be attested by the recorder of the subordinate lodge and the lodge seal affixed; it was then to be sent by such recorder, with the prescribed fee, to the grand lodge officers, who canceled the old and issued a new certificate as re-

---

[492] Flowers v. Sovereign Camp Woodmen of the World, 40 Tex. Civ. App. 593, 90 S. W. 526.

[493] Knights of the Maccabees of the World v. Sackett, 34 Mont. 357; 86 Pac. 423; Sterling v. Head Camp, etc., 28 Utah, 505-526; 80 Pac. 375, 1110.

[494] Raschke v. Gegenseitige, etc., 130 Wis. 129; 119 N. W. 812.

[495] Modern Brotherhood of Am. v. Matkovitch, 56 Ind. App. 795; 104 N. E. 795; Hughes v. Modern Woodmen of Am., 124 Minn. 458; 145 N. W. 387.

[496] Grand Lodge A. O. U. W. v. Child, 70 Mich. 163; 38 N. W. 1. And also in Grand Lodge, etc., v. Noll, 90 Mich. 37; 51 N. W. 268; 15 L. R. A. 350 and note. See also Garrett v. Garrett (Cal. App.), 159 Pac. 1050.

quested. One Child became a member and designated his betrothed as beneficiary, he having a son then living. The certificate was exhibited to the beneficiary; but retained by the member and afterwards lost. Sixteen months after the issue of the certificate the lady designated as the beneficiary married another person than Child. The latter afterwards continued to pay his assessments and tried, by a written document, to change the designation and make his son the beneficiary, but the grand lodge refused to recognize the change, or issue a new certificate, unless the first one was surrendered; the subordinate lodge, however, advised the written document, expressing the intention of the member, and consented to it. After the death of the member the grand lodge filed a bill of interpleader against the first beneficiary and the son and paid the money into court. In awarding the fund to the son the Court said: "It clearly appears that the deceased, while living, never intended, after Miss Drury married O'Connor, that she should remain the beneficiary in the certificate. He continued to pay his dues and assessments until the time of his death, and within two years after she rejected his suit he undertook, and did all that he could, and all that he was required in equity to do, to change the donee in the certificate named to that of his son. The rules of the order allowed him to do this, and it was not in the discretion of the order to prevent it. It was a right, under the rules of the order, of which he could not be deprived, upon his complying with the conditions prescribed for such action, and which he performed so far as it was in his power to perform, and for these reasons it would be most unjust and inequitable for a court to disregard such action and such intention of the deceased, before he died, and award his property to the claimant who had forfeited all claim to his bounty and whom he had discarded. . . . All contracts are presumably made in view of the law governing their construction, and the rules of evidence applicable when the contract is sought to be established and applied. The law never requires impossibilities, and the rules of the order which required the certificate to be surrendered when a change of the beneficiary was made, that it might be indorsed upon the certificate, could only be construed as requiring that to be done when the certificate was in existence. The existence of the right to

share in the benefits of the order, and to direct who should receive the fund in case of the death of the member, was a right
vested in the member as soon as he became entitled thereto, and
the certificate was only evidence of the existence of that right,
and where that evidence was lost the right remained, and its existence could be established by any other competent evidence, and
the same is true of the existence of the change, directed by the
member of the beneficiary.   Mr. Child did all he could do in
making the change, and it should have been allowed and done
by the order. Equity will consider that done which ought to have
been done. For the purpose of determining the rights between
these defendants, the proceeding is governed by equitable principles. The fund is held in trust by the order for the person to
whom it belongs. And it is true in this, as in every other case,
equity follows the law as far as the law goes in securing the rights
of parties, and no further; and when the law stops short of securing the object, equity continues the remedy until complete justice
is done. In other words, equity is the perfection of the law, and
is always open to those who have just rights to enforce when the
law is inadequate. Any other conclusion would show our system
of jurisprudence not only a failure, but a delusion and a snare.
Justice alone can be considered in a court of chancery and technicalities never be tolerated, except to attain, and not to destroy
it; and the greater equity should always be allowed to prevail.
There can be, it seems to me, no doubt in this case, where it lies.''
In another case, a member before marriage agreed to substitute
his second wife as beneficiary, but died without doing so, it was
held[497] that equity would treat the change as having been made,
and the court awarded the fund to the wife. In that case the
Court said: "We then have the sister nominally the payee in the
certificate. The member, under the rules, had the right at any
time to name another in her stead. She was a mere volunteer,
having given no consideration, and, it must be presumed, had
full knowledge that her brother could at any time strike out her
name and substitute that of another, as he did when he struck
out his first wife's name and substituted hers. He promised to
substitute that of the second wife when she married him. She

---

[497] Pennsylvania Railway Co. v. Wolfe, 203 Pa. St. 269; 52 Atl. 247.

did marry him. He did not substitute, formally, her name. We have no reason to doubt this omission was from neglect, not because of willful wrong. But the moment the marriage contract was complete, the wife had an equitable claim to the certificate, or to the benefit it represented. It was not that sort of a mutual contract which could be very conveniently performed by each party at the same time. Marriage, the condition, must almost necessarily follow after the promise, and she had no right to substitution until after marriage. But when she married him, she had a vested right in the benefit—a right not dependent on his will or whim, but one no longer in his power, as between him and her, to confer or withhold. She could not take back the consideration she gave. He could not give it back to her. He could only formally transfer to her that which by the consummation of the contract was hers. He ought, in form, the day of the marriage, or immediately after, to have done that. Equity will now treat that as done which ought to have been done. To illustrate the application of the principle, suppose the intended wife had made the promise and the intended husband then had, regularly, under the rules of the association, appointed her the beneficiary, and then she had refused to marry him, and before he had time to create a new appointee he died; would equity, assuming the association did not interfere, have permitted her to receive the fruits of her fraud? There is no more reason why she should suffer the penalty of his neglect.'' In another case,[498] very informal acts on the part of the member were held to constitute a change, the Court saying: ''Seay having repeatedly declared his intention that his sister, Mrs. Emma Allen, should be the substituted beneficiary, and having actually done all he could in his condition to accomplish that purpose, and to accomplish it in the very mode prescribed by section 66, his acts being partly in writing and partly in parol, equity will treat that as done which ought to have been done, and decree as if the change had been made in conformity with said section. It will perfect his imperfect and incomplete, but partly accomplished, purpose and act, and deal with it as perfected, as between these claimants. The case falls strictly within the second and third exceptions to the general rule pointed out by Justice

[498] Hall v. Allen, 75 Miss. 175; 22 Sou. 4.

Brown, now of the United States Supreme Court, in Supreme Conclave v. Capella,[499] and in such case it is well settled that the death of the assured before the completion of the change in the beneficiary makes no difference." And the delivery of a certificate with verbal directions for a change has been held effectual.[500]

Equity will enforce a request for change of beneficiary sufficient in form although the change was not actually made until after the death of the member, but if the change was induced by fraud, the original beneficiary is entitled to the fund.[501] Equity also will protect the rights of an assignee where a sister relinquished her right in the policy to the wife although the wife's name was omitted from the relinquishment.[502] A request of the insured to amend the policy by making it payable to certain persons is a change of beneficiary and not an assignment.[503]

§ 411. **Summary of the Law Regarding Change of Beneficiary With Exceptions to General Rule.**—In a leading case,[504] Judge Henry B. Brown, then presiding in the Circuit Court of the United States for the Eastern District of Michigan, reviewed the law regarding change of beneficiary, and his statement of the principles involved will probably always be followed. The case is referred to with approval in nearly every case subsequently decided, involving the question of change of beneficiary. After referring to the right of the member to make a change of beneficiary the Court says: "In making such change of beneficiary, however, the insured is bound to do it in the manner pointed out by the policy and the by-laws of the association, and any material deviation from this course will invalidate the transfer. Thus, if the certificate provides that no assignment shall be valid unless approved by the secretary, an assignment without such approval will be invalid.[505] So, if it be provided that such change must be made on a prescribed form or blank the signa-

499 41 Fed. 1, cited in 1 Bac. Ben. Soc., § 310a.
500 Lockett v. Lockett, 26 Ky. L. 300; 80 S. W. 1152.
501 Daugherty v. Daugherty, 152 Ky. 732; 154 S. W. 9.
502 McCraw v. Vernon, 111 Va. 279; 68 S. E. 979.
503 In re Dolan, 182 Fed. 949.
504 Supreme Conclave Royal Adelphia v. Cappella, 41 Fed. 1.
505 Herman v. Lewis, 24 Fed. 97, 530.

ture to which shall be attested before a notary, and the change entered upon the books, an assignment to a creditor as collateral security not made upon the prescribed blank, and of which the association had no notice until after the death of the member, was held to be fatally defective.[506] So, where the certificate required every surrender to be in writing, attested by the reporter under the lodge seal, it was held that a conditional surrender of the same by the holder, not to take effect until after his death, and not made in the presence of, or attested by, such lodge reporter, was invalid.[507] So if the by-laws fix definitely the manner of changing the beneficiary by his action during his life, an attempt to divert the benefit by will has usually been held to be abortive.[508] There are, however, three exceptions to this general rule, requiring an exact conformity with the regulations of the association: 1. If the society has waived a strict compliance with its own rules, and in pursuance of a request of the insured to change his beneficiary has issued a new certificate to him, the original beneficiary will not be heard to complain that the course indicated by the regulations was not, pursued. This naturally follows from the fact that having no vested interest in the certificate during the life-time of the assured he has no right to require that the rules of the association, which are framed alone for its own protection and guidance, are not complied with.[509] The case of Wendt v. Legion of Honor,[510] appears upon its face to lay down a different rule, but, upon examination, it will be seen that the change was attempted to be made

[506] Ass'n v. Brown, 33 Fed. 11.

[507] Supreme Lodge v. Nairn, 60 Mich. 44; 26 N. W. 826. See also Wendt v. Legion of Honor, 72 Ia. 682; 34 N. W. 471; Elliott v. Whedbee, 94 N. C. 115; Mellows v. Mellows, 61 N. H. 137; Highland v. Highland, 109 Ill. 366.

[508] Holland v. Taylor, 111 Ind. 121; 12 N. E. 116; Stephenson v. Stephenson, 64 Ia. 534; 21 N. W. 19; Ins. Co. v. Miller, 13 Bush 487; Vollman's Appeal, 92 Pa. St. 50; Renk v. Herman Lodge, 2 Dem Sur. 409; Daniels v. Pratt, 143 Mass. 216; 19 N. E. 166.

[509] Martin v. Stubbings, 126 Ill. 387; 18 N. E. 657; Splawn v. Chew, 60 Tex. 532; Manning v. Ancient Order, 86 Ky. 136; 5 S. W. 385; Soc. v. Lupold, 101 Pa. St. 111; Brown v. Mansus, 64 N. H. 39; 5 Atl. 768; Knights of Honor v. Watson, 64 N. H. 517; 15 Atl. 125; Byrne v. Casey, 70 Tex. 247; 8 S. W. 38; Titsworth v. Titsworth, 40 Kan. 571; 20 Pac. 213.

[510] 72 Ia. 632; 34 N. W. 470.

by a paper which the insured called his last will, but which was no will in law, and the Court held that, the interest of the beneficiary having become vested by the death of the insured, they had acquired rights which could not be cut off, except in the manner prescribed in the contract. This case, evidently, has no application to a change made prior to the death of the insured. 2. If it be beyond the power of the insured to comply literally with the regulations a court of equity will treat the change as having been legally made. Thus in the case of Grand Lodge v. Child,[511] the insured made his betrothed the beneficiary and subsequently lost his certificate. His beneficiary having married another, he made a statement of the loss, and applied for a re-issue of the certificate, making his son the beneficiary. His application was refused. The rules of the organization required the change to be indorsed on the original certificate, but by the advice of the officers, he attempted to make the change of beneficiary by giving a power of attorney to another to collect the amount which should accrue under the certificate. It was held that such acts constituted an equitable change of beneficiary, and that the son was entitled to the fund. The Court held that the insured had done all that he could, and all that he was required in equity to do, to change the donee of the certificate. 'The rules of the order allowed him to do this, and it was not in the discretion of the order to prevent it. . . . The law never requires impossibilities and the rules of the order, which required the certificate to be surrendered when a change of beneficiary was made, that it might be indosed upon the certificate, could only be construed as requiring that to be done when the certificate was in existence. The existence of the right to share in the profits of the order, and to direct who shall receive the fund in case of the death of a member, was a right vested in the member as soon as he became entitled thereto, and the certificate was only evidence of the existence of that right, and when that evidence was lost, the right remained, and its existence could be established by any other competent evidence; and the same is true of the existence of the change directed by the manner of the beneficiary.' 3. If the insured has pursued the course

511 70 Mich. 163; 38 N. W. 1.

pointed out by the laws of the association and has done all in his power to change the beneficiary, but before the new certificate is actually issued, he dies, a court of equity will decree that to be done which ought to be done, and act as though the certificate had been issued. The case of Association v. Kirgin,[512] is an illustration of this exception. In this case, the insured having met with a fatal accident, called a friend and requested him to take his certificate to the association and surrender it, pay the fee of fifty cents, and request them to issue a new one, payable to his wife. This was done and a minute of the transaction was made on the records of the association for that day. On the following day the insured died. It was held that in doing this he had done all that the laws of the order required to be done on his part in order to have a new certificate; that his right to make the change was absolute, and that the association had no right to refuse his request; and further that the fact that the certificate was issued after his death was immaterial, since the certificate was not the right itself, but merely the evidence of the right.[513] The case of Ireland v. Ireland,[514] is distinguishable from these in the fact that the insured made no written request for a change, as required by the rules, but merely delivered the certificate to a friend, telling him he wanted it changed. This was manifestly insufficient.'' In accord with the principles laid down in the foregoing opinion are several other cases. For example, where the member complied with all the regulations of the society in making the change except that he did not surrender the certificate as required by the by-laws, being unable to do so because the certificate had been wrongfully taken from him, the change was held effectual.[515] So where the application for membership directed payment of the benefit to the applicant's wife, "subject to such further dis-

[512] 28 Mo. App. 80. And also see Luhrs. v. Luhrs, 123 N. Y. 367; 25 N. E. 388.

[513] See, to the same effect, Mayer v. Ass'n, 2 N. Y. Supp. 79; Supreme Lodge v. Nairn, 60 Mich. 44; 26 N. W. 826; Kepler v. Supreme Lodge, 45 Hun. 274; St. Louis Police, etc., Ass'n v. Strode, 103 Mo. App. 694; 77 - S. W. 1091.

[514] 42 Hun. 212.

[515] Isgrigg v. Schooley, 125 Ind. 94; 25 N. E. 151.

posal as he might thereafter direct,'' and the benefit certificate was made payable to the wife, naming her, and no mode of changing the beneficiary was specified by the laws of the association, or certificate, although the custom was to require a surrender of the old certificate, it was held that the paper signed by the member expressing his surrender of the certificate and directing payment to the new beneficiary and mailed to the officers of the association just before his death is a valid change, although the certificate remains in the hands of the wife who refused to deliver it up.[516] And so where a few hours before his death the member sent the certificate to the president of the lodge with the request that it should be transferred to the new beneficiary, it was held that an indorsement of the certificate made by the president of the lodge in accordance with the verbal message of the owner of the certificate was enough to effect the change.[517] In this case the Court says: "He (the member) showed his intent clearly by sending the certificate to Wing with verbal instructions to make the indorsement necessary to effect the change of beneficiary which he desired. His intention and the authority he gave having been ascertained, the acts of his agent in carrying them into effect should be enforced.'' But where the member, in a letter to the association, indicated a substitution of beneficiary which he desired to make, sending his certificate for that purpose, but the certificate was returned to him with directions to sign a formal revocation and reappointment of beneficiary indorsed on the certificate, which he did not do, but retained it without further action, it was held that the change was not effectual.[518] And so a delivery of the certificate to a third person for the benefit of the member's son is not a change of beneficiary.[519] And so where a power of attorney was given to a creditor to transfer a membership in the New York Cotton Exchange, which power was not exercised, it is not such a sale as will relieve the exchange from lia-

[516] Hirschl v. Clark, 81 Ia. 200; 47 N. E. 78.

[517] Schmidt v. Iowa K. of P., 82 Ia. 304; 47 N. W. 1032.

[518] Hall v. Northwestern Endowment, etc., Ass'n, 47 Minn. 35; 49 N. W. 524.

[519] Rollins v. McHatton, 16 Colo. 203; 27 Pac. 254. But see to the contrary, Brown v. Mansus, 64 N. H. 39.

bility.[520] And the designation of a substitute as a beneficiary, in a written order not witnessed, directing "the association," not naming any, to pay the benefit to the substitute who was a brother, which order was not brought to the attention of the association until after the holder's death, was held invalid.[521]

§ 412. **Interpleader and Questions Arising in Such Proceedings.**—Where the fund due from a beneficiary society on the death of a member, is claimed by two or more parties adversely to each other, it is usual for the association to absolve itself by interpleader proceedings in a court of equity, asking, as a mere stakeholder, to pay the money into court and be discharged, leaving the adverse claimants to litigate between themselves for the fund so paid into court. Interpleader proceedings are not to be regarded as actions *in rem*, and, therefore, to give the court jurisdiction, personal service must be had on each of the claimants, or anyone not served must voluntarily submit himself to the jurisdiction of the court. In holding that such proceedings are not actions *in rem* the Supreme Court of Iowa has said:[522] "If they were, the courts of a State may, by process of attachment against the property of a non-resident, or by the garnishment of a debt due to such person, appropriate the property, or debt, to the payment of the claim of the creditor, but in such case the judgment merely affects the property or thing seized. The action in chancery, relied upon in this case, was not in any sense a special proceeding in which it was sought to seize the property of a non-resident and apply it in payment of a debt; it was an attempt to adjudicate a mere personal right to a money demand claimed by the plaintiff herein." The foregoing statement cannot be regarded as stating the principle always to be followed. In the case of Morgan v. Mutual Ben. Life Ins. Co.,[523] the Court said: "To properly discuss the questions of law involved in this

[520] Dillingham v. N. Y. Cotton Exchange, 49 Fed. 719.

[521] Gladding v. Gladding, 56 Hun. 639; 8 N. Y. Supp. 880.

[522] Gary v. N. W. Masonic Aid Ass'n, 87 Ia. 25; 50 N. W. 27; 53 N. W. 1086.

[523] 16 Cal. App. 85; 116 Pac. 385. See also Ely v. Hartford Life Ins. Co., 33 Ky. L. 272; 110 S. W. 265; Bullows v. Provident, etc., Soc., 100 N. Y. Supp. 1058.

case, a somewhat extended statement of the facts will be necessary. They are as follows: On March 26, 1866, the appellant
insurance company, in the State of New York, issued to Elizabeth A. Morgan, mother of respondents, a policy of insurance
on the life of her husband, Orson A. Morgan, father of respondents. By the terms of said policy appellant agreed to pay $5,000
to Elizabeth A. Morgan, or assigns, or, in case she should die
before Orson A. Morgan, then to the children of said Orson A.
Morgan. Being unable to pay the premium due on March 26,
1871, Mr. and Mrs. Morgan, on or about that date, requested
one Dayton S. Morgan, since deceased, to pay the same, in order
to keep and preserve said policy in force. The said insurance
policy was thereupon assigned by said Elizabeth A. Morgan and
her husband to Dayton S. Morgan to secure the repayment of
that particular premium and also such other premiums as he
might thereafter pay, together with interest thereon, until such
advances should be repaid. Appellant insurance company assented to this assignment. Thereafter Dayton S. Morgan each
and every year until his death on April 9, 1890, paid the premium on said policy, and after his death the executors and
trustees of his estate continued to pay the same until the death
of Orson A. Morgan, the assured, which occurred in the year
✸1905. His wife predeceased him, having died in the year 1904.
At the time of the death of Orson A. Morgan the sums advanced
by Dayton S. Morgan and his personal representatives in payment of said premiums, together with interest thereon, largely
exceeded the face of said policy. When the policy of insurance
was executed and delivered, and at the time of the assignment
thereof, Elizabeth A. Morgan and Orson A. Morgan were residents of the State of New York. Dayton S. Morgan at all the
times mentioned herein resided in the said State of New York,
and the policy of insurance since its delivery has always been in
that State, in the possession of Dayton S. Morgan and his personal representatives. At the time of the death of the assured,
all his children before mentioned were and ever since have been
non-residents of said State. The appellant insurance company,
as to the State of New York, is a foreign corporation, having its
principal office and place of business in the State of New Jer-

sey, but since the year 1866 and prior thereto it has been doing business within the State of New York, having met the statutory requirements of that State. On October 6, 1905, proofs of the death of the assured having been furnished to the company, the personal representatives of Dayton S. Morgan commenced an action in the Supreme Court of New York against the insurance company and the heirs at law of said Orson A. Morgan, for the purpose of ascertaining the interest of the parties in said policy of insurance, and to establish an equitable lien in favor of the plaintiffs in that action upon said policy and the moneys due thereunder to the extent of the moneys paid by them and their testator upon said policy, and for the recovery of the amount of the policy from the company. The insurance company duly appeared. Thereafter, upon application of the plaintiffs therein (executors of Dayton S. Morgan), an order was granted directing the service of summons upon said heirs at law by publication, and service was made upon them pursuant to that order, but they did not appear in the action. Defendant insurance company answered the complaint, and admitted that it had issued said policy, and that the amount stated in said complaint was owing by it; but it alleged that in the month of November, 1905, the said heirs at law had commenced an action against it in the superior court of San Francisco, Cal., demanding judgment against it for the amount of said policy and interest. The insurance company, after some further references in its answer to the action pending in California, submitted its right to the judgment of said New York court. Thereafter said insurance company moved, upon the papers upon which the order of publication was granted, that said order of publication be set aside and canceled upon the ground that the court had no jurisdiction to direct publication of summons against the defendants, said non-resident heirs at law. The motion was denied, and an appeal was taken from such order to the Appellate Division of the Supreme Court, where, on May 1, 1907, the order was affirmed,[524] but leave was granted by that court to appeal to the Court of Appeals of New York. Accordingly the latter court was called upon to decide whether or not jurisdiction of the

[524] Morgan v. Mut., etc., Ins. Co., 119 App. Div. 645; 104 N. Y. Supp. 185.

said heirs at law could be acquired by the New York courts by publication of summons. The New York Court of Appeals, on November 1, 1907, answered the question certified to it by the Appellate Division of the Supreme Court in the affirmative.[525] Subsequent to this decision the case was tried in the Supreme Court upon its merits. The respondents, the said heirs at law, did not appear, and after trial judgment was, on September 16, 1908, duly given that the personal representatives of Dayton S. Morgan were entitled to all the money due under the policy, and that the said heirs at law were barred and foreclosed of all interest in said policy and its proceeds, and that plaintiffs in that action recover of the insurance company the sum of $5,-228.88 and costs. Thereafter, to-wit, on May 5th, 1909, the Appellate Division of the Supreme Court, to which court the insurance company appealed, affirmed this judgment.[526] The company then appealed to the New York Court of Appeals, which, on February 8, 1910, without an opinion, affirmed the judgment of said Appellate Division.[527] In November, 1905, as before noticed, the said heirs at law commenced this action. The defendant, in defense thereto, pleaded the judgment of the New York courts, and also set up the facts upon which said judgment was based. After a hearing said superior court rendered judgment against the defendant insurance company, and in favor of the said heirs at law. In due time the insurance company appealed to the Supreme Court, which court, by an order regularly made transferred the cause to this court for hearing and decision. The appellant contends that the New York judgment is conclusive on the respondents here; and, secondly, that even if that be not so, it is entitled to judgment on the facts of the case. The respondents, on the other hand, in support of the judgment of the superior court of the city and county of San Francisco, argue here (as was contended by the insurance company in the New York courts) that the courts of that State acquired no jurisdiction over them by the publication of summons, so that they are not concluded by the judgment rendered by

525 Morgan v. Mut., etc., Ins. Co., 189 N. Y. 451; 82 N. E. 438.
526 Morgan v. Mut., etc., Ins. Co., 132 App. Div. 455; 116 N. Y. Supp. 989.
527 Morgan v. Mut., etc., Ins. Co., 197 N. Y. 607; 91 N. E. 1117.

892

such courts; and furthermore that the assignment of the policy of insurance was void as to them; they being expressly named as beneficiaries of the policy and not having joined in the assignment. The question of whether the courts of New York acquired jurisdiction over the respondents by the publication of summons was considered by the Court of Appeals of that State.[528] And in adopting the conclusion there reached we quote quite extensively from the opinion. It is there said: 'The interest of the plaintiff's assignor, Elizabeth A. Morgan, in the policy of insurance was contingent upon her surviving her husband.[529] As she did not survive her husband the plaintiffs seek in this action to charge the policy and the proceeds thereof with the amount paid by them, and their intestate for premiums thereon.[530] The defendants other than the insurance company are proper and necessary parties to this action, citing cases. The defendant insurance company therefore had a standing in court to move to vacate the order of publication.[531] This is not disputed by the plaintiffs. Service of a summons upon non-residents of the State of New York may be made as provided by Section 438 of the Code of Civil Procedure. It is therein provided as follows: An order directing the service of a summons upon a defendant, without the State, or by publication, may be made in either of the following cases: . . . Where the complaint demands judgment, that the defendant be excluded from a vested or contingent interest in or lien upon, specific real or personal property within the State; or that such an interest or lien in favor of either party be enforced, regulated, defined, or limited; or otherwise affecting the title to such property. . . . The term 'personal property' is defined by statute. Section 4 of the statutory construction law,[532] provides as follows: The term 'per-

---

[528] Morgan v. Mut., etc., Ins. Co., 189 N. Y. 451; 82 N. E. 438.

[529] Bradshaw v. Mut. Life Ins. Co., 187 N. Y. 347; 80 N. E. 203.

[530] Pomeroy's Eq. Jur. Vol. 3, § 1243; 25 Cyc. 774, 775; Am. & Eng. Ency. of Law, Vol. 19, p. 90; Mandeville v. Kent, 88 Hun. 132; 34 N. Y. Supp. 622; Brick v. Campbell, 122 N. Y. 337; 25 N. E. 493; 10 L. R. A. 259; Conn. Mut. Life Ins. Co. v. Burroughs, 34 Conn. 305; 91 Am. Dec. 725; Lane v. N. Y. Life Ins. Co., 56 Hun. 92; 9 N. Y. Supp. 52.

[531] Brandow v. Vroman, 29 App. Div. 597; 51 N. Y. Supp. 943.

[532] Ch. 677, Laws 1892 (Consol. Laws 1909, c. 22, § 39).

sonal property' includes chattels, money, things in action, and all written instruments themselves as distinguished from the rights or interest to which they relate, by which any right, interest, lien or incumbrance in, to or upon property, or any debt or financial obligation is created, acknowledged, evidenced, transferred, discharged or defeated, wholly or in part, and everything except real property which may be the subject of ownership. The term 'chattels' includes goods and chattels.[533] It is not necessary to consider to what extent, if any, the Legislature simply by statutory definition or provision, can treat intangible personal property as within this State, and subject it to the jurisdiction of our courts as against persons not served with process within our territorial limits, because in this case not only are the plaintiffs as claimants residents of this State, but the debtor and the debt, as well as the written instrument by which the debt was created, acknowledged, and evidenced, are in contemplation of law within this State. A foreign insurance company is not allowed to do business in this State until it submits itself fully to the jurisdiction of our courts. It must obtain from our Superintendent of Insurance a certificate authorizing it to do business in this State. It is subject to examination by the insurance department of this State, and it is required to deposit with the Superintendent of Insurance of this State, or with the Auditor, Comptroller, or general fiscal officer of the State, by whose laws it is incorporated, stocks and bonds as provided by our statutes to the same amount as required by domestic insurance corporations, which stocks and bonds are held in trust for the benefit of all the policyholders of the corporation. A foreign insurance corporation is also required to appoint our Superintendent of Insurance its attorney in this State upon whom all lawful process in any action or proceeding against the corporation can be served. The authority of such foreign insurance corporation must be revoked in case it applies to remove into the United States Court any action brought against it in the courts of this State. Our statutes expressly provide that an action against a foreign corporation may be maintained

[533] Revised Stats. Pt. IV, tit. 7, c. 1, § 33; Code Proc. § 463; Code Civ. Proc. (1880), § 3343, subd. 7.

by a resident of the State or by a domestic corporation for any cause of action. Such an action may be maintained in this State by another foreign corporation or by a non-resident, when the action is brought to recover damages for the breach of a contract made within this State. The presence of the insurance company in this State is not temporary, but continuous. It is legally and actually here, not only because process has been served upon it and it has appeared in the action, but it is here pursuant to the provisions of our statutes, by authority of which it is doing business and maintaining offices in this State. The contract of insurance was made by it with a resident of this State through its agents so located and doing business here. Every transaction relating to the contract, its assignment, and the payment of premiums thereon has occurred here. The policy of insurance and the claim against the insurance company for the money payable on the policy of insurance are in the control of our court, and any judgment that may be rendered in the action can be enforced and made effectual in this State. As to such a claim, the insurance company should be treated as a domestic insurance corporation and as domiciled in this State. The *situs* of the debt would consequently be here, and the action is one to define and enforce any interest in specific personal property within the State within the meaning of the Code provision quoted. Whenever a question as to the *situs* of a similar claim against an insurance company doing business in a State pursuant to the statutes thereof has been directly involved in this court or in the federal courts, and it has been sought to uphold the *situs* of the claim in the State where the contract was made, it has been sustained. In Martine v. International Life Insurance Society,[534] an action was brought upon a policy of life insurance. The defendant was a foreign corporation. The Court says: 'The defendant sought and obtained the privilege of establishing and carrying on its business here under the regulations fixed by the statutes of this State. It established a permanent general agency and conducted its business here as a distinct organization, and was permitted by law to do this in the same manner as domestic institutions. . . . As to the business transacted here, the company

[534] 53 N. Y. 339; 13 Am. Rep. 529.

must be regarded as domiciled by the residence of its general
agent and its local organization. . . .' The Court then reviews
the cases of New England Mut. Life Ins. Co. v. Woodworth[535]
Sulz v. Mut. R. F. L. Ass'n,[536] and Matter of Gordon,[537] and cites
them in support of its conclusion. Other cases that may be cited
in support of the jurisdiction of the New York court are the
following.[538] It is next argued by respondents in support of
the judgment that the assignment of the policy of insurance was
as to them void; they being expressly named as beneficiaries
under the policy and not having joined in the assignment. The
answer of the appellant to this contention is that the assignee
of such a policy, who advances the premiums to keep the policy
in force, is entitled to a lien on such policy and its proceeds for
such advances, even though the assignment is void. This is the
question that was considered by the Appellate Division of the
Supreme Court of New York[539] and determined adversely to the
contention of respondents. That Court cites with approval and
follows the rule laid down in Pomeroy's Equity Jurisprudence[540]
as follows: 'Where a person, not being the owner of a policy
of life insurance, nor bound to pay the premium, but having
some claim or color of interest in it, voluntarily pays the premiums thereon, and thus keeps it alive for the benefit of a third
party, he may thereby acquire an equitable lien on the proceeds of the policy as security for the repayment of his advances.' This equitable rule was applied by our own Supreme
Court in the case of Stockwell v. Mut. Life Ins. Co.,[541] where,
even in the absence of an assignment of the policy, one of the
beneficiaries who had advanced premiums for the purpose of

[535] 111 U. S. 138; 4 Sup. Ct. 364; 28 L. Ed. 379.

[536] 145 N. Y. 653; 40 N. E. 242; 28 L. R. A. 379.

[537] 186 N. Y. 471; 79 N. E. 722; 10 L. R. A. (N. S.), 1089.

[538] Loaiza v. Sup. Ct. 85 Cal. 11; 24 Pac. 707; 9 L. R. A. 376; 20 Am. St.
Rep. 197; Murray v. Murray, 115 Cal. 266; 47 Pac. 37; 37 L. R. A. 626;
56 Am. St. Rep. 97; Chicago, etc., Co. v. Strum, 174 U. S. 710; 19 Sup. Ct.
797; 41 L. Ed. 1144; Jellenik v. Huron, etc., Co., 177 U. S. 1; 20 Sup. Ct.
559; 44 L. Ed. 647.

[539] Morgan v. Mut. Ben. Life Ins. Co., 132 App. Div. 455; 116 N. Y.
Supp. 989.

[540] Vol. 3, § 1243.

[541] 140 Cal. 198; 73 Pac. 833; 98 Am. St. Rep. 25.

keeping the policy alive, was allowed an equitablé lien upon the proceeds of the policy for the reimbursement of those advances, as against the claim of one of the other beneficiaries to receive her share of the policy free and without deduction from it of a pro rata of such advances.[542] Respondent finally makes the point in support of the judgment that the defendant insurance company cannot set up in its own defense equities alleged to exist in favor of other parties. But we think in the present case the matter set up by the defendant is much more than an equity in favor of other persons. It is a judgment against it, in an action in which the respondents were made parties, and which it is bound to pay.''

§ 412a.   **The Same Subject Continued.**—Conditions upon which a bill of interpleader may be filed have been stated as follows:[543] ''The same debt, fund, or thing must be claimed by hostile parties under adverse title derived from a common source. The interpleader must be a mere stakeholder, with no interest in the subject-matter; must have incurred no liability to either of the claimants personally; and must stand exposed to the risk of being vexed by two or more suits for the fund or other subject-matter in dispute. It is not, of course, necessary that he shall be liable to two judgments, for he cannot be unless he has assumed inconsistent obligations, and in that instance a bill of interpleader will not lie. The essential purpose of the bill is to protect an indifferent holder of a fund or bailee of an article from the annoyance and expense of seperate actions to recover what he is willing to pay. These views are taken from 3 Pomeroy, Eq. Jur.[544] and 2 Story, Eq. Jur.''[545] In another case,[546] it was said by the Court

[542] See also Unity, etc., Ass'n v. Dugan, 118 Mass. 219; Harley v. Heist, 86 Ind. 196; 45 Am. Rep. 285; Matlack v. Seventh Ave Bank, 180 Pa. 360; 36 Atl. 1082; Stevens v. Germania Life Ins. Co., 26 Tex. Civ. App. 156; 62 S. W. 824.

[543] Supreme Council L. of H. v. Palmer, 107 Mo. App. 157; 80 S. W. 699. See also Metropolitan L. Ins. Co. v. Hamilton, (N. J. Ch.), 70 Atl. 677.

[544] 2 Ed., § 1319, et seq.

[545] C. 20.

[546] Crane v. McDonald, 118 N. Y. 648; 23 N. E. 991. See also Woodmen of the World v. Wood, 100 Mo. App. 655; 75 S. W. 377.

of Appeals of New York: "It was not necessary for the plaintiff
to decide at his peril, either close questions of fact or nice questions of law, but it was sufficient if there was a reasonable doubt
as to which claimant the debt belonged. When a person, without
collusion, is subjected to a double demand to pay an acknowledged
debt, it is the object of a bill of interpleader to relieve him of
the risk of deciding who is entitled to the money. If the doubt
rests upon a question of fact that is at all serious, it is obvious
that the debtor cannot safely decide it for himself, because it
might be decided the other way upon an actual trial; while if it
rests upon a question of law, as was said in Dorn v. Fox,[547] 'so
long as a principle is still under discussion it would seem fair
to hold that there was sufficient doubt and hazard to justify the
protection which is afforded by the beneficent action of interpleader.' Although the claim of Mr. Goodrich has since been held
untenable by this court,[548] it does not follow that no doubt existed
when this action was commenced, because the Supreme Court, both
at special and general terms, held it was valid, and attempted to
enforce it. This conflict in the decisions of the courts shows that
the adverse claims of the defendants involved a difficult and doubtful question, and is a conclusive answer to the contention of the
appellant that the plaintiff did not need the aid of an action of
this character. Was it possible for him to safely decide a point
so intricate as to cause those learned in the law to differ so widely?"
It has also been said:[549] "The remedy by interpleader is so beneficial, has been resorted to so commonly in cases of this sort, and
the somewhat analogous, but not identical, jurisdiction under bills
for instruction by trustees, has been carried so far in this commonwealth, that we are disposed to resolve any doubts in favor
of plaintiff."[550] Under the well settled principles of equity jurisprudence if the bill is properly filed, and if the plaintiff has acted
in good faith, he is entitled to an allowance for his costs, out of
the fund in controversy, which costs, as between the defendants,

[547] 61 N. Y. 264.

[548] Goodrich v. McDonald, 112 N. Y. 157; 19 N. E. 649.

[549] Supreme Commandery v. Merrick, 163 Mass. 374; 40 N. E. 183.

[550] See also Sullivan v. Knights of Father Mathew, 73 Mo. App. 43;
Funk v. Avery, 84 Mo. App. 490.

ultimately must be paid by the unsuccessful party.[551]   Where a stakeholder pays money into court he cannot be held for subsequent accruing interest and costs.[552]   In most, if not all, of the cases cited in the last three preceding sections, the association had paid the money into court, which was called upon to dispose of the fund.   When the association pays the money into court it waives the right to question the validity of the assignment.[553]   It follows that the court, having possession of the fund, will dispose of it in accordance with the principles of equity, and the limitations imposed by the statutes of the forum.   If the designation of beneficiary is an act testamentary in its nature it would seem that equity requires that the intention of the member should be carried out if possible.[554]   It has been held that the limitations in the constitution of a society limiting the beneficiary cannot aid the claimant when the money is paid into court;[555] but opposed to this is the better reasoning of the Missouri Court of Appeals,[556] where the

[551] Pomeroy Eq. Jur., § 1328, and cases cited; Glaser v. Priest, 29 Mo. App. 1; 2 Daniel's Chan. Pl. & Pr., § 1569; Mut. L. Ins. Co. v. Farmers', etc., Bank, 173 Fed. 390. Also Franco-Am. Bldg. Ass'n v. Joy, 56 Mo. App. 433; Woodmen of the World v. Wood, *supra;* and Supreme Council L. of H. v. Palmer, *supra.* As to other questions, arising in interpleader cases, see Supreme Council, etc., v. Green, 71 Md. 263; 16 Atl. 1048; Britton v. Supreme Council, 46 N. J. E. 102; 18 Atl. 675; Davidson v. Hough, 165 Mo. 561; 65 S. W. 731; Smith v. Grand Lodge, etc., 124 Mo. App. 181; 101 S. W. 662; United Railways Co. v. O'Connor, 153 Mo. App. 128; 132 S. W. 262; Bacholzer v. Grand Lodge, etc., 119 Mo. App. 177; 95 S. W. 953; and, as to notice, Feldman v. Grand Lodge, etc., 19 N. Y. Supp. 73.

[552] Lambert v. Penn. Mut. L. Ins. Co., 50 La. Ann. 1027; 24 Sou. 16.

[553] K. of H. v. Watson, 64 N. H. 517; 15 Atl. 125, and also cases cited in last section.

[554] Hoffman v. Grand Lodge, etc., 73 Mo. App. 47.

[555] Johnson v. Supreme L. K. of H., 53 Ark. 255; 13 S. W. 794. And in support of this view are: Taylor v. Hair, 112 Fed. 913; Markey v. Supreme Council, etc., 70 App. Div. 4; 74 N. Y. Supp. 1069; Hall v. Allen, 75 Miss. 175; 22 Sou. 4; Tepper v. Supreme Council, etc., 61 N. J. Eq. 638; 47 Atl. 460; reversing 45 Atl. 111; Schoales v. Order, etc., 206 Pa. St. 11; 55 Atl. 766.

[556] Keener v. Grand Lodge A. O. U. W., 38 Mo. App. 543; Sofge v. Supreme Lodge K. of H., 98 Tenn. 446; 39 S. W. 853; Hoeft v. Grand Lodge,

court held that when the society brings the fund into court, it
does not thereby confess the right of either party to the money and
it is the duty of the court to see that the money is paid out as directed and required by the rules and regulations of the society
and to determine who is the proper person to receive it. In awarding the fund the court will often take into consideration the equities of the case without regarding the strict legal technicalities.
As where a certificate was payable to the wife of the member and
afterwards, on separation by divorce, the certificate was given
to her as her property and for two years or more she paid all
the assessments thereon. Thereafter, on making an affidavit that
the certificate was not in his possession, the member changed the
designation and obtained a new certificate payable to his sons by
a former marriage. The money being paid into court it was
held,[557] that the first beneficiary, the divorced wife, should take
the fund, although, if the society had paid the money to the second
beneficiary, such payment would have been upheld. The Court
said: "The wife had intercepted the fund before it reached the
children who are named as the beneficiaries and her equity is so
great that no chancellor should withhold a judgment in her favor."
The rights of a beneficiary under an ante-nuptial agreement where
the equitable interest of the sister had vested, will be determined,[558]
and the equities also of a beneficiary who has paid assessments
will be protected as against a mere volunteer.[559] Where the society
wrongfully files an interpleader suit, on notification by a claimant
not to pay to the assignee of the original beneficiary, the right
of the latter being clear, it will be adjudged liable for all costs.[560]
In determining the right to money paid into court the court may

etc., 113 Cal. 91; 45 Pac. 185; 33 L. R. A. 174. See also Grand Lodge,
etc., v. Ehlman, 246 Ill. 655; 92 N. E. 962; Knights of the Maccabees v.
Sackett, 34 Mont. 357; 86 Pac. 423; Faubel v. Eckhart, 151 Wis. 155; 138
N. W. 615.

[557] Leaf v. Leaf, 92 Ky. 166; 17 S. W. 354, also 854. See also Woodmen of the World v. Rutledge, 133 Cal. 640; 65 Pac. 1105.

[558] Ryan v. Boston Letter Carriers' etc., Ass'n, 222 Mass. 237; 110 N.
E. 281; L. R. A. (N. S.), 1916-C.

[559] McKeon v. Ehringer, 48 Ind. App. 226; 95 N. E. 604; Supreme
Council R. A. v. McKnight, 238 Ill. 349; 87 N. E. 299.

[560] In re Carroll's Policy, 29 L. R. Ir. 86.

900

make an equitable division of the fund between the claimants where it is impossible without injustice to give all to one.[561]

§ 413. **Effect of Illegal or Incomplete Change of Beneficiary on First Designation.**—The question occurs as to the effect on the ' rights of the beneficiaries first designated by an attempted change of beneficiary which is incomplete, or where the change, being effected by compliance with the required formalities and the issuance of a new certificate, is illegal because the second beneficiaries are not entitled to take. While it seems to be taken for granted in the cases cited in the preceding sections that if the attempted change of beneficiary is not complete the rights of the first beneficiaries are not affected, because the revocation is not made complete by the issuance of the new certificate, it is now settled that if for any reason the change of beneficiaries is invalid the rights of the first beneficiary remain in force.[562] It has been held[563] that a designation may be revoked without appointing a new beneficiary. Upon principle, where the designation of a new beneficiary is illegal, it would seem that the revocation should be held complete and that the benefit should be disposed of as in case of failure to designate.[564] The Supreme Court of Wisconsin in a case[565] where the facts were that the holder of a certificate in a beneficiary society applied for a change of beneficiary, stating that the former certificate was thereby returned and surrendered for the purpose of the change, and that the new certificate should be made payable to such persons as he might name in his will. The new certificate was accordingly issued but no beneficiaries were ever designated by

[561] Hagar v. Grand Lodge, etc., 96 Kan. 221; 150 Pac. 528.

[562] Elsey v. Odd Fellows' Mut. R. Ass'n, 142 Mass. 224; 7 N. E. 844; Smith v. Boston & Maine R. Ass'n, 168 Mass. 213; 46 N. E. 626; Offi.1 v. Supreme Lodge, etc. (Tenn.), 46 S. W. 758. See also Delaney v. Delaney, 175 Ill. 87; 51 N. E. 961; affg. 70 Ill. App. 130; Sturgis v. Sturgis (Ky.), 102 S. W. 884; Geyte v. National Council K. & L. of S., 178 Ill. App. 377; Royal League v. Shields, 251 Ill. 250; 96 N. E. 45; Sovereign Camp W. O. W. v. Israel, 117 Ark. 121; 173 S. W. 855.

[563] Cullen v. Supreme Tent K. O. T. N., 28 N. Y. Supp. 276.

[564] See ante, § 316, et seq, and also Carson v. Vicksburg Bank, 75 Miss. 167; 22 Sou. 1; 37 L. R. A. 559; Doherty v. Ancient Order, etc., 176 Mass. 285; 57 N. E. 463.

[565] Grace v. Northwestern Mut. Relief Ass'n, 87 Wis. 562; 58 N. W. 1041.

will or otherwise. In holding that no change of beneficiary took place, the Court said: "In Mr. Grace's 'application for change of beneficiary,' made on that day, it is stated in effect that the former certificate is thereby returned and surrendered 'for the purpose of securing a change of beneficiary;' and that the association in consideration thereof, would issue and forward to him a new certificate, payable to such person or persons as he should designate and name in his last will and testament. The certificate was issued accordingly, but no person was ever designated or named as such beneficiary by last will and testament or otherwise. The proposed change was never in fact effected by reason of such failure of Mr. Grace to so name or designate. Since the former certificate was so returned and surrendered for the sole purpose of securing such change, and since no such change was ever, in fact, effected by reason of such failure, the question recurs whether such return and surrender of such former certificate operated as a complete cancellation and extinguishment of the same, or whether such return and surrender remained inchoate, depending upon such change being made complete by such designation or naming of new beneficiaries or beneficiary. Upon careful examination we are constrained to hold that such return and surrender so remained inchoate and dependent. It is very much the same in principle as where attempts have been made to alter portions of a will by erasures without obliteration and by way of substituting new words by interlineation, which fail to go into effect for want of reattestation, and hence as there was no intent to revoke, except by way of such substitution which so failed, the courts have generally held that the attempted alteration is ineffectual.[566] So here we must hold that the attempted change of beneficiaries was left incomplete and hence, ineffectual; and that the contract of insurance must be regarded the same as though the former certificate had never been returned and surrendered." It is hard to see how the conclusions arrived at by the court in this case can be sustained by reason or authority, unless we consider that the arbitrary powers of a court of equity were exercised and, on the assumption

566 Will of Ladd, 60 Wis. 193, 194; 18 N. W. 734, and cases there cited. See also Short v. Smith, 4 East 419; Soar v. Dolman, 3 Curt. Ecc. 121; Brooke v. Kent, 3 Moore P. C. 334; *In re* Parr, 6 Jur. (N. S.), 56.

that the first beneficiaries were the most deserving and had a great moral claim to the consideration of the court, it awarded the fund to them on the same theory adopted by the Court of Appeals of Kentucky in a recent case.[567] By the execution of the revocation and the surrender of the certificate the designation was revoked and the new certificate was made payable according to will. No will being made, a lapse of designation resulted, and a resulting trust followed for the benefit of those entitled to take in such case under the laws of the society, or if the laws made no provision for such cases, for the next of kin.[568]

In a case where the benefit was made payable to one Curry, alleged affianced wife of the member, Barrett, and afterwards one Mackey, who was not eligible as beneficiary, persuaded the member to obtain another certificate from the Grand Lodge, payable to him, the Court said:[569] "Without entering into a discussion of the question, as to what effect on a designation of the beneficiary a breaking off of the engagement between Lelia Curry and Barrett, which some of the testimony tended to show occurred, may have had on the original certificate, we are of the opinion that a surrender of that certificate to the Grand Lodge by Barrett, and the acceptance thereof, and the issuance by the Grand Lodge of another certificate naming another beneficiary, had the effect of fully revoking the original certificate and destroying all rights that Lelia Curry had therein. This result would not be affected by the fact that appellee could not be legally designated as the beneficiary in the last certificate. Barrett undoubtedly had the right, with the assent of the Grand Lodge, to revoke his designation of Lelia Curry as the beneficiary in his life insurance, and that right was not contingent on the designation of another beneficiary, and his attempt to name a person as beneficiary who could not occupy that position under the laws of Texas did not affect the revocation of the former certificate.[570] In the case of Grace v. Northwestern Mut. Relief Association,[571] a contrary rule is announced; but it does not seem to be well considered, and is not

[567] Leaf v. Leaf, 92 Ky. 166; 17 S. W. 354, also 854.
[568] See *ante*, § 313.
[569] Grand Lodge, etc., v. Mackey (Tex. Civ. App.), 104 S. W. 907.
[570] Bacon Ben. Soc., §§ 243b, 310c.
[571] 87 Wis. 562; 58 N. W. 1041; 41 Am. St. Rep. 62.

supported, so far as we know, by any authority. The case may be differentiated, however, from this, to some extent, at least, by the fact that in the Wisconsin case no second beneficiary was named, and nothing was shown indicating that another would be substituted, unless it could be inferred from the bare fact of the surrender of the original policy. We think. the correct rule, so far as rights accruing by reason of a designation are concerned, is announced in Alfsen v. Crouch,[572] where it is said: 'The insured had a perfect right to surrender his policy on any ground and for any reason that he saw proper; and, when the first certificate was was canceled, complainant ceased to have any interest whatever in the insurance, and, so far as he was concerned, it was entirely immaterial whether the insurance company ever issued another policy, or to whom it made payment of such policy, or what became of the proceeds of the same.' The rule is supported by the following authorities[573] The Grand Lodge assented to the naming of a beneficiary who, under the laws of that body, had no insurable interest in the life of Barrett, and there is authority to the effect that such laws could be waived; but that doctrine could not prevail in a case where the designation is of a person not allowed by the statutes of the State to receive the benefits of such a policy.'' Where the association is estopped during the lifetime of the member to deny that a change of beneficiary was effected, it was held,[574] that the former beneficiary cannot raise objection. The second wife of a member can question the right of the divorced wife to the proceeds of a certificate,[575] and the original beneficiary may maintain a suit to cancel a new certificate secured by undue influence of the new beneficiary.[576] It has also been held[577] that

[572] 115 Tenn. 352; 89 S. W. 329.

[573] Hoeft v. Knights of Honor, 113 Cal. 91; 45 Pac. 185; 33 L. R. A. 174'; Brown v. Grand Lodge, 80 Ia. 287; 45 N. W. 884; 20 Am. St. Rep. 420; Byrne v. Casey, 70 Tex. 247; 8 S. W. 38.

[574] Wandell v. Mystic Toilers, 130 Ia. 639; 105 N. W. 448. See also Alfsen v. Crouch, 115 Tenn. 352; 89 S. W. 329.

[575] Knights of the Maccabees v. Brown (Mich.), 152 N. W. 1085.

[576] Wherry v. Latimer, 103 Miss. 524; 60 Sou. 563; Stemler v. Stemler, 31 S. D. 595; 141 N. W. 780.

[577] Supreme Lodge Fraternal Brotherhood v. Price, 27 Cal. App. 607. 150 Pac. 803. See also Mitchell v. Langley, 143 Ga. 827; 85 S. E. 1050; L. R. A. (N. S.), 1916-C 1134.

a beneficiary can maintain an action for damages against a third person who fraudulently induces a change of beneficiary.

§ 414. **Change of Designation Governed by Same Rules in Respect to Beneficiary as Original Appointment.**—If the charter of the society, or its by-laws, or the statutes of the State, limit the beneficiaries of members to certain classes of persons, so that at first the certificate can only be made payable to one of such classes, an assignment of the certificate cannot be made to one not of the prescribed classes, nor be changed so that one not of the class can become the beneficiary. If this could be done it would be possible to do indirectly what could not be done directly, and in that way the law of the State or society would be made of no effect.[578] If no restrictions are placed upon the designation of beneficiary the certificate may be changed at the will of the member and as often as he pleases and made payable to any one the member selects, unless, possibly, the law of insurable interest may be applied so as to exclude some.[579] It has been held, however, that the law of insurable interest does not apply to beneficiary societies where the contract is made with the member himself,[580] but this we apprehend must be taken with some modification, for if the transaction is one in which a speculator agrees in advance to pay

[578] Knights of Honor v. Nairn, 60 Mich. 44; American Legion of Honor v. Perry, 140 Mass. 580; Elsey v. Odd Fellows' Relief Ass'n, 142 Mass. 224; Daniels v. Pratt, 143 Mass. 216; Ky. Masonic Ins. Co. v. Miller, 13 Bush 489; Weisert v. Muehl, 81 Ky. 336; Bayse v. Adams, 81 Ky. 368; National Mut. Aid Ass'n v. Gonser, 43 Ohio St. 1; State v. Standard Life Ass'n, 38 Ohio St. 281; Folmer's Appeal, 87 Pa. St. 133; *In re* Phillips' Ins., 23 Ch. D. 235; 51 L. J. Ch. 441; 48 L. T. 81; 31 W. R. 511, C. A. See also Maneeley v. Knights of Birmingham, 115 Pa. St. 305; Price v. Supreme Lodge, etc., 68 Tex. 361; 4 S. W. 633; Schonfield v. Turner, 75 Tex. 324; 12 S. W. 626; Lyon v. Rolfe, 76 Mich. 146; 42 N. W. 1094; Kult v. Nelson, 24 Misc. 20; 53 N. Y. Supp. 95; Foss v. Patterson, 20 S. D. 93; 104 N. W. 915.

[579] Basye v. Adams, 81 Ky. 368; Sabin v. Grand Lodge, 6 N. Y. St. 151 Massey v. Mut. Rel. Ass'n, 102 N. Y. 523; 34 Hun. 254; Lamont v. Hotel Men's Mut. B. Ass'n, 30 Fed. 817; Lamont v. Iowa Legion of Honor, 31 Fed. 177; Bloomington Mut. Ass'n v. Blue, 120 Ill. 127.

[580] Ingersoll v. Knights of the Golden Rule, 47 Fed. 272; Sabin v. Phinney, 134 N. Y. 423; 31 N. E. 1087; affg. 8 N. Y. Supp. 185; Masonic Mut. Ass'n v. Bunch, 109 Mo. 560; 19 S. W. 25.

the assessments the rule ought to apply as in the case of regular life policies. In a suit by the assignee of a benefit certificate the burden is on him to show that he is of the class named in the charter.[581] One having no insurable interest to whom a certificate has been assigned cannot recover the assessments paid by him, the society having no notice of that fact.[582] If the statute has been amended after the issue of the certificate any change is governed, as to limitations as to beneficiaries, by the amended statute.[583]

§ 415. **Rights of Creditors in Benefit.**—It follows that where the beneficiaries are limited to the "family, widows, orphans or other dependents" of the members, or indeed to any class as heirs, legatees or devisees, creditors are excluded and they not only have no claims on the benefit but cannot obtain any. This is doubly the case where benefit societies are organized under statutes restricting the beneficiary to certain classes. As was said by the Supreme Court of Massachusetts:[584] "If the fund were subject to testamentary bequest, then, upon the decease of the member, it might go into the hands of his executor, or the administrator of his estate and become assets thereof, liable to be swallowed up by the creditors. If there were no creditors, the member by his will could divert it from the three classes named in the statute. In either case, this would defeat the purpose for which the fund was raised and held and would be in direct conflict with the object of the statute for which the association was formed, and would set aside the contract entered into between the member and the corporation;"[585] and the same court said in another case:[586] "A person whose only relation to the deceased member is that of a

581 Nye v. Grand Lodge A. O. U. W., 9 Ind. App. 131; 36 N. E. 429.

582 Knights and Ladies of Honor v. Burke (Tex.), 15 S. W. 45; Nix v. Donovan, 18 N. Y. Supp. 435.

583 Grand Lodge, etc., v. McKinstry, 67 Mo. App. 382; Briner v. Supreme Council, etc., Ass'n, 140 Mich. 220; 103 N. W. 603; Gibbs v. Knights of Pythias, 173 Mo. App. 34; 156 S. W. 66.

584 American Legion of Honor v. Perry, 140 Mass. 580.

585 Daniels v. Pratt, 143 Mass. 216. See also National M. Aid Ass'n v. Gonser, 43 Ohio St. 1.

586 Skillings v. Mass. Ben. Ass'n, 146 Mass. 217; 15 N. E. 566. See also Supreme Commandery v. Donaghey, 75 N. H. 197; 72 Atl. 419; O'Brien v. Catholic Order of Foresters, 220 Mass. 79; 107 N. E. 400.

creditor is not a person dependent upon him within the meaning of these statutes; and the promise to pay the plaintiff is void. Such a promise is beyond the powers of the association, and contravenes the intention of the statutes under which the association was organized. The plaintiff cannot, therefore, maintain an action on this promise, either for his own use or that of any other person.'' The general rule may be therefore laid down that a beneficiary fund payable on the death of a member of an association to persons named by him, is not to be treated as a part of his estate, subject to his debts, and does not go to the administrator, but should be paid directly to the beneficiaries who take directly from such association.[587] It is now expressly provided by statute that the benefit to be paid by a fraternal beneficiary association shall not be liable for the debt of either the member or beneficiary.[588] And an agreement by which a person paying the assessments, in consideration of having a share in the benefit, is void.[589] A creditor, who has advanced money to pay the assessments of the member, who has had the certificate renewed in his name to secure a loan and payments made by him and has paid subsequent assessments, has the right on the death of the member to be repaid his loan and the assessments paid, the surplus going to the member's representatives.[590] In the absence of a contract payments of assessments for another are gratuitous and give the person paying no lien.[591] Where there is no one in existence qualified to become a beneficiary

[587] Sup. Council Catholic Mut. Ben. Ass'n v. Priest, 46 Mich. 429; Sup. Council Catholic M. Ben. Ass'n v. Firnane, 50 Mich. 82; Knights of Honor v. Nairn, 60 Mich. 44; Felix v. Grand Lodge A. O. U. W., 31 Kan. 81; Briggs v. Earl, 139 Mass. 473; Swift v. San Francisco Stock & Exchange Board, 67 Cal. 567; Durian v. Central Verein, 7 Daly 168; Richmond v. Johnson, 28 Minn. 447; Brown v. Catholic Mut. Ben. Ass'n, 33 Hun. 263; Worley v. Northwestern Mas. Aid Ass'n, 3, McCrary, 53; 10 Fed. 227; Schmidt v. Grand Grove, 8 Mo. App. 601; Fenn v. Lewis, 81 Mo. 259; 10 Mo. App. 478.

[588] Revised Statutes of Mo. 1899, § 1418; Beall v. Graham, 125 Mo. App. 38; 102 S. W. 636.

[589] Spies v. Stikes, 112 Ala. 584; 20 Sou. 959.

[590] Levy v. Taylor, 66 Tex. 652; Schonfield v. Turner, 75 Tex. 324; 12 S. W. 626. See also Deal v. Hainley, 135 Mo. App. 507; 116 N. W. 1; Des Moines Savings Bank v. Kennedy, 142 Ia. 272; 120 N. W. 742; Kelly v. Searcy, 160 Tex. 566; 102 S. W. 100; reversing 98 S. W. 1080.

[591] Leftwich v. Wells, 101 Va. 255; 43 S. E. 364.

of a member of a fraternal beneficiary association no equitable rights accrue, either to the creditors or the estate of the member.[592] It has been held that where the member and beneficiary join in an assignment the latter is estopped from denying its sufficiency.[593] But the better rule is that no one who cannot directly become a beneficiary, because not within the statutory classes, can indirectly become a beneficiary.[594] Hence a contract to pay to a trustee for a creditor is invalid.[595] Where no limitations are placed upon the choice of beneficiary the member may have an unlimited range and then creditors may take,[596] and this by devise.[597] Life insurance is regarded by the courts in the nature of a provision for a man's family and they are reluctant to divert it from that destination. In most, if not all, of the States, statutes exist exempting policies of insurance upon the life of the husband or wife from the demands of creditors, and allowing every person to appropriate annually for the purpose of life insurance for the benefit of wife or children a sum not exceeding $500. Under a statute of this kind in Iowa, the Supreme Court of that State has held that even where the policy was payable to the assured, "his executors, administrators and asisgns," that the wife took the entire fund free from the demands of creditors,[598] and the fact of insolvency is immaterial.[599] In Illinois the Supreme Court has held[600] that it is incompetent for the parties to contract so as to exclude creditors, and the same doctrine has been laid down in California.[601] In Texas, in a case where the policy was payable to the "heirs or assigns" of the deceased and had not been assigned by him, it was held[602] that the proceeds did not form a part of the estate of the

[592] Warner v. Modern Woodmen (Neb.), 93 N. W. 397; 61 L. R. A. 603.

[593] Conway v. Supreme Council, etc., 131 Cal. 437; 63 Pac. 727.

[594] Gillam v. Dale, 69 Kan. 262; 76 Pac. 861.

[595] Bloodgood v. Mass. Ben. Ass'n, 19 Misc. 460; 44 N. Y. Supp. 563.

[596] Maneely v. Knights of Birmingham, 115 Pa. St. 305; Bloomington Mut. Ben. Ass'n v. Blue, 120 Ill. 127.

[597] Stoelker v. Thornton, 88 Ala. 241; 6 Sou. 680; Martin v. Stubbings, 126 Ill. 387; 18 N. E. 657.

[598] Rhode v. Bank, 52 Ia. 375.

[599] Masonic Mut. L. Ass'n v. Paisley, 111 Fed. 32.

[600] People, etc., v. Phelps, 78 Ill. 147.

[601] Swift v. San Francisco Stock & Exch. Board, 67 Cal. 567.

[602] Mullins v. Thompson, 51 Tex. 7.

deceased so as to be liable to the debts of the deceased, but went directly to the heirs. It is only upon the clearest proof of fraud, if at all, can the premiums paid by an insolvent upon a life policy for the benefit of his wife and children be recovered by creditors. And even then the recovery is limited to the amount of such premiums, or the excess over the sum allowed by the statute to be expended for life insurance for the debtor's family, where such statutes exist.[603] An assignment by the wife of a policy of insurance upon her husband's life for her benefit will not be decreed at the suit of creditors, nor its avails be appropriated in advance by operation of law.[604] These statutes do not affect the right of a solvent man to apply as much of his means as he likes to the payment of premiums upon policies of life insurance for his wife's benefit.[605] As between creditors seeking to have a common fund appropriated to the payment of their demands, he who files his bill first is entitled to priority.[606]

[603] Pence v. Makepeace, 65 Ind. 345; Stone v. Knickerbocker L. Ins. Co., 52 Ala. 589; Stigler v. Stigler, 77 Va. 173; Levy v. Taylor, 66 Tex. 652; Aetna Nat. Bk. v. U. S. Life Ins. Co., 24 Fed. 770; Central National Bank v. Hume, 3 Mackey 360; Pullis v. Robinson, 73 Mo. 202; 5 Mo. App. 548; Conn. M. L. Ins. Co. v. Ryan, 8 Mo. App. 535; Mut. L. Ins. Co. v. Sandfelder, 9 Mo. App. 285; Cole v. Marple, 98 Ill. 58; Filrath v. Schonfield, 76 Ala. 199; Thompson v. Cundiff, 11 Bush 567.

[604] Baron v. Brummer, 100 N. Y. 372.

[605] Pullis v. Robinson, 73 Mo. 202.

[606] Pullis v. Robinson, *supra;* George v. Williamson, 26 Mo. 190; U. S. Bank v. Burke, 4 Blackf. 141; Hills v. Sherwood, 48 Cal. 393. For further discussion, see *post,* § 560, *et seq.*